REPORT

OF THE

SECRETARY OF THE NAVY

IN RELATION TO

ARMORED VESSELS.

WASHINGTON:
GOVERNMENT PRINTING OFFICE.
1864.

LETTER

FROM

THE SECRETARY OF THE NAVY,

IN ANSWER TO

Resolutions of the House and Senate in relation to the operations of armored vessels employed in the service of the United States.

April 21, 1864.—*Resolved*, That there be printed, for the use of the Navy Department, two thousand copies of the report and documents of the Secretary of the Navy, relating to iron-clad vessels, &c., and three thousand for the use of the House.

Navy Department, *April* 11, 1864.

Sir: I have the honor to acknowledge the receipt of three several resolutions of the Senate and House of Representatives, respectively, in relation to armored vessels and to such information as may be in possession of this department concerning their efficiency, capability, and the service which may have been rendered by them, and especially as to operations in the harbor of Charleston. The resolutions are as follows:

In the Senate of the United States,
December 17, 1863.

Resolved, That the Secretary of the Navy be directed to communicate to the Senate all official reports and despatches and papers in the Navy Department relating to actions in which any of the armored vessels have been engaged, and especially the report of Captain Worden of the combat of the Monitor with the Merrimack, and the report of Captain John Rodgers of the attack on Fort Darling, together with the despatches of Rear-Admiral Goldsborough transmitting them; the reports of Captain Worden and Captain Drayton of the two attacks on Fort McAllister, on the Ogeechee, with the despatches of Rear-Admiral DuPont transmitting them to the department; the report of Rear-Admiral DuPont of the attack of April 7, 1863, on the defences of Charleston harbor, together with the reports of Captain Drayton of the Passaic, Commander Rhind of the Keokuk, Commander Downes of the Nahant, Captain John Rodgers of the Weehawken, Captain Worden of the Montauk, Commander Fairfax of the Nantucket, Commander George W. Rodgers of the Catskill, of Commodore Turner of the New Ironsides, and of Commander Ammen of the Patapsco, touching their several vessels during that attack; and also the reports of any investigations, after the action, into the condition of any of the armored vessels engaged in it, or respecting the repairs found necessary on any of those vessels after the action, made by those officers, or any of them, or any official statement respecting those vessels in connexion with the said action, or respecting experiments to test the value of rafts for the removal of obstructions made by those officers, or any of them, or by Engineers Lovering, Robie, or Stimers; and also the report of Captain John Rodgers of the action between the Weehawken and Atlanta, together with the despatch of Rear-Admiral DuPont transmitting it; and all other official correspondence with any of those officers in the Navy Department respecting or relating to those actions; and also the official report of the sinking of the Weehawken inside the bar off Charleston, and the official report of the springing a leak of the Sangamon at the Washington navy yard on the eve of departure on a cruise.

Attest: J. W. FORNEY, *Secretary.*

THIRTY-EIGHTH CONGRESS, FIRST SESSION.

CONGRESS OF THE UNITED STATES,
IN THE HOUSE OF REPRESENTATIVES,
January 13, 1864.

Mr. Spalding, from the Committee on Naval Affairs, submitted the following, which was adopted:

Whereas it seems probable that warfare on the ocean will in great measure depend in the future on armored vessels, whose form, structure, and armament must be determined by experience in action; and the attacks on Forts Darling and McAllister, the combats between the Monitor and Merrimack and the Weehawken and Atlanta, and the first great naval battle delivered by armored vessels in the harbor of Charleston, have at once illustrated the American name, and furnished the only information from experience in battle respecting the powers of resistance and aggression of armored vessels which exists to aid the deliberations of Congress in directing further constructions of such vessels; but the Secretary of the Navy, while conveying the gratifying intelligence that during the "vigorous assaults on Fort Sumter but comparatively slight injury was sustained by these vessels," though "no ships ever before sustained such a concentrated fire," has not communicated with his report the official and detailed despatches and reports of the officers in command of the armored vessels executing those attacks, from which alone exact and reliable information of the real capacity of those vessels for resistance, aggression, speed, manœuvring, and keeping the sea, as shown by experience, can be obtained, and without such information Congress must grope in the dark in ordering or refusing further construction of armored vessels: Therefore,

Resolved, That the Secretary of the Navy be directed to communicate to this house all official reports, despatches, and papers in the Navy Department relating to those actions: that is to say, the report of Captain Worden of the combat between the Monitor and the Merrimack; the report of Captain John Rodgers of the attack on Fort Darling, or the action near Drury's Bluff, on the James river; the reports of Captain Worden and Captain Drayton of the two attacks on Fort McAllister, on the Ogecchee, with the despatches of Rear-Admiral DuPont transmitting them to the department; the reports of Rear-Admiral DuPont of the attack of April 7, 1863, on the defences of Charleston harbor, together with the reports of Captain Drayton of the Passaic, Commander Rhind of the Keokuk, Commander Downes of the Nahant, Captain John Rodgers of the Weehawken, Captain Worden of the Montauk, Commander Fairfax of the Nantucket, Commander George W. Rodgers of the Catskill, Commodore Turner of the New Ironsides, Commander Ammen of the Patapsco, touching their several vessels during that attack; and also the reports of any investigation, after the action, into the condition of any of the armored vessels engaged in it, or respecting the repairs found to be necessary on any of these vessels after the action, made by those officers, or any of them, or any official statement respecting those vessels in connexion with the said action, or respecting experiments to test the value of rafts for the removal of obstructions made by those officers, or any of them, or by Engineers Lovering, Robie, or Stimers; and also the report of the action between the Weehawken and Atlanta, by Captain John Rodgers, together with the despatches of Rear-Admiral DuPont transmitting it; and all other official correspondence with any of those officers in the Navy Department respecting or relating to those actions; also the report of the sinking of the Weehawken within the bar off Charleston: *Provided*, That no call is hereby intended to be made for information already transmitted by the Secretary of the Navy to Congress.

Attest: EDWARD McPHERSON, *Clerk.*

THIRTY-EIGHTH CONGRESS, FIRST SESSION.

CONGRESS OF THE UNITED STATES,
IN THE HOUSE OF REPRESENTATIVES,
February 29, 1864.

On motion of Francis P. Blair, jr.,

Resolved, That the Secretary of the Navy be requested to communicate to this house the following information:

All his instructions relative to the attack upon Charleston, and all his correspondence with Rear-Admiral DuPont relative to that attack, previous to the 7th of April, 1863, and subsequent thereto, and all other information possessed by the department, or its bureaus, growing out of that memorable contest; and all the reports of officers and others relative to iron-clad vessels, and their adaptability for naval warfare; any order of the Navy Department relative to withdrawing the iron-clads to the Mississippi or elsewhere; also the telegraphic order of the President, dated 13th April, 1863, directing Rear-Admiral DuPont to remain inside of the bar at Charleston, and prevent the enemy from erecting batteries on Morris island, and whether this order was acknowledged and obeyed; also the telegraphic order of the President, dated April 14, 1863, directing Rear-Admiral DuPont and General Hunter to take the batteries on Morris and Sullivan islands, and whether said order was obeyed, or attempted to be obeyed; also the order of the Secretary of the Navy, dated June 6, 1863, directing Rear-Admiral DuPont to co-operate with General Gillmore, and whether said order was obeyed, and whether General Gillmore complained of a want of co-operation on the part of Rear-Admiral DuPont; also who devised the plan of attack attempted upon Fort Sumter by Rear-Admiral DuPont on April 7, 1863, and whether such plan was communicated to the department previous to its being made, and whether Rear-Admiral DuPont asked for more troops previous to April 7, 1863, or protested to the department against making said attack; and whether any order, previous to that date, was given to him to attack Fort Sumter, or in any manner act against his judgment in the operations before Charleston; or whether any suggestions or plans of that officer, or requisitions for more ships, were refused or declined by the Navy Department previous to his attack upon the defences of Charleston; and whether the port of Charleston is absolutely closed to blockade running since the monitors went inside of the bar.

Attest: EDWARD McPHERSON, *Clerk,*
By CLINTON LLOYD, *Chief Clerk.*

As the principal objects of inquiry in these several resolutions, though varying in detail, are essentially the same, the reply is made to embody in one document the official correspondence and records of the Department, commencing with the first recommendation of the Secretary of the Navy, on the 4th of July, 1861, and the legislation by Congress at the then special session consequent on that recommendation, together with the reports of the boards which have from time to time been constituted; also, the reports of naval officers, engineers, and others, with such general information deemed valuable as has been communicated to the Department from intelligent and reliable sources in regard to the qualities and services of the armored vessels.

In response to certain specific inquiries that are made in the resolution of the 20th of February, I have the honor to state that the order of the President dated April 13, 1863, "directing Rear-Admiral DuPont to remain inside the bar at Charleston, and prevent the enemy from erecting batteries on Morris island," was briefly acknowledged, but was not obeyed. The telegraphic order of the President, dated the 14th of April, "directing Rear-Admiral DuPont and General Hunter to take the batteries on Morris and Sullivan islands," was never, so far as this department is advised, obeyed or attempted to be obeyed by Rear-Admiral DuPont. The order of the Secretary of the Navy directing Rear-Admiral DuPont to co-operate with General Gillmore was not obeyed.

Major General Hunter, in a letter to the President, referring to the "attack by the iron-clads upon Charleston, an attack in which, from the nature of the plans of Admiral DuPont, the army had no active part," says, that on the morning after the attack the army was ready to proceed and take possession of Morris island, and "Fort Sumter would have been rendered untenable in two days' fire." General Hunter adds: "On the afternoon after the iron-clad attack on Fort Sumter, the troops on Folly island were not only ready to cross Light-house inlet, but were almost in the act, the final reconnoissance having been made, the boats ready, and the men under arms for crossing, when they were recalled, as I hoped merely temporarily, by the announcement of Admiral DuPont that he had resolved to retire, and that consequently we could expect no assistance from the navy.

"Immediately the admiral was waited upon by an officer of my staff, who represented the forwardness of our preparations for crossing, the evidently unprepared condition of the enemy to receive us, while any delay, now that our intentions were unmasked, would give the enemy time to erect upon the southern end of Morris island, commanding Light-house inlet, those works and batteries which he had heretofore neglected. To these considerations, earnestly and elaborately urged, the admiral's answer was that 'he would not fire another shot.'"

In answer to the inquiry "whether General Gillmore complained of a want of co-operation on the part of Rear-Admiral DuPont," it will be seen by the letter accompanying this communication that General Gillmore, on the 30th of June, said, "I can do nothing until Admiral DuPont's successor arrives and gets ready to work. The admiral has no instructions, and does not feel at liberty to put his vessels into action on the eve of relinquishing his command." Yet the department had written Rear-Admiral DuPont on the 6th of June, "General Gillmore has been ordered to take charge of the department of the south, and you will please afford him all the aid and assistance in your power in conducting his operations." The receipt of this order was acknowledged by Rear-Admiral DuPont on the 14th of June. It may be stated also that his original primary instructions in May, 1862, were to co-operate with the army, unless the movement should be purely naval, when the army would render him every assistance.

The department has no information as to "who devised the plan of attack on Fort Sumter by Rear-Admiral DuPont on April 7, 1863," but has never doubted that it originated and belonged exclusively to that officer. The plan was not "communicated to this department previous to its being made," nor did that officer ask the department for more troops, though he on one or two occasions incidentally mentioned that "more troops are necessary." On no occasion, anywhere nor at any time, did Rear-Admiral DuPont "protest to the department against making said attack." No "order previous to that date was given him to attack Fort Sumter, or in any manner act against his judgment in the operations before Charleston;" on the contrary, the department wrote him especially, on the 31st of January, 1863, that it did "not desire to urge an attack upon Charleston with inadequate means, and if after careful examination you deem the number of iron-clads insufficient to render the capture of that port reasonably certain, it must be abandoned." No "suggestions or plans of that officer or requisitions for more ships were refused or declined by the Navy Department previous to his attack upon the defences of Charleston." In his despatch of June 3, 1863, Rear-Admiral DuPont says he did not hesitate to "ask the department for all the iron-clads that could be spared, and I am happy to say that the department spared no pains to increase the force of these vessels." And finally, in answer to the inquiry "whether the port of Charleston is absolutely closed to blockade runners since the monitors went inside the bar," it gives me pleasure to state that the department has received no information that any vessel has reached the city of Charleston since the month of July.

In justice to the department it should be stated, that the averment in the preamble of the 13th of January, that the Secretary of the Navy "has not communicated with his report the official and detailed despatches and reports of the officers in command of the armored vessels executing those attacks," is a grave mistake—made inadvertently, I have no doubt, and without an examination of the annual reports and accompanying documents of this department for the years 1862 and 1863, for, included with them, were the "despatches and reports" referred to, which had been transmitted to Congress on the 1st of December, 1862, and on the 7th of December, 1863, respectively, and were severally printed with the reports of the Secretary of the Navy of those years.

I have the honor to be, sir, your obedient servant,

GIDEON WELLES,
Secretary of the Navy.

Hon. SCHUYLER COLFAX,
Speaker of the House of Representatives.

LIST OF PAPERS.

INTRODUCTORY.

Page.

From Report of Secretary of Navy, July 4, 1861 1
Act of Congress authorizing the construction of iron-clads 1
Copy of advertisement calling for plans and specifications 2
Order convening a board to examine plans for building iron-clads 2
Report of board to examine plans of iron-clads, under act of August 3, 1861 3
From the Report of the Secretary of the Navy, December 2, 1861 7
From the Report of the Secretary of the Navy, December 1, 1862 8
From the Report of the Secretary of the Navy, December 7, 1863 10
Ericsson's inception of Monitor vessels 12
Letter from Mr. Ericsson relative to contract for Monitor 14

NORTH ATLANTIC SQUADRON.

Arrival of the Monitor at Hampton Roads 14
Assistant Secretary Fox's telegram of the action at Hampton Roads 14
Assistant Secretary G. V. Fox's telegram to General McClellan relative to the fight at Hampton Roads 15
Major General Wool's telegram relative to condition of affairs in Hampton Roads 15
The President directs that the Monitor shall not go unattended to Norfolk 15
Captain John Marston's report of the attack of the Merrimack 16
Captain Van Brunt's account of the Minnesota's engagement with the Merrimack 17
Captain Purviance's report of the Merrimack's attack 19
Chief Engineer Stimers's report 20
Passage of the Monitor from New York to Hampton Roads 21
Flag-Officer Goldsborough reports sending three vessels up James river, and shelling Sewall's Point, May 8, 1862 21
Flag-Officer Goldsborough to the President of the United States 22
Flag-Officer Goldsborough reports destruction of the Merrimack 23
Flag-Officer Goldsborough encloses reports of engagement with fort on Drury's Bluff. 24
Lieutenant Commander Jeffers's report relative to the Monitor 27
Passage of the New Ironsides to Hampton Roads 30
Passage of the Passaic from Washington to Hampton Roads 31
Passage of the Passaic from Hampton Roads to Beaufort 32
Loss of the Monitor—
Report of Acting Rear-Admiral S. P. Lee 35
Additional report of Acting Rear-Admiral S. P. Lee 35
Report of Commander J. P. Bankhead 37
Report of Second Assistant Engineer Joseph Watters 40
The boilers and hull of the Galena 41
The Weehawken in a gale 42
Detailed report of the passage of the Weehawken to Hampton Roads 42
Extracts from private letters of John Rodgers relative to first trip of the Weehawken. 45
Passage of the Montauk to Beaufort 46
Preparations for passage of Montauk from Beaufort to Port Royal 48
Passage of the Nahant to Port Royal 49
Passage of the Roanoke to Hampton Roads 49
Report of Captain G. Gansevoort of a joint reconnoissance up James river 50

SOUTH ATLANTIC SQUADRON.

Page.

First instructions for the capture of Charleston 51
Rear-Admiral DuPont desires the Ironsides 52
Second instructions for the capture of Charleston 52
Transmits information relative to the harbor, &c., of Little river 53
Rear-Admiral DuPont's views upon the contemplated attack on Charleston 53
Department's letter advising Rear-Admiral DuPont to abandon the attack on Charleston if the number of iron-clads is insufficient 53
Department's letter relative to movements of iron-clads 54
The department informs Rear-Admiral DuPont that two more iron-clads will be added to his squadron 54
Rear-Admiral DuPont directed to send iron-clads to Mobile 55
First attack on Fort Sumter—
- Report of Rear-Admiral S. F. DuPont 55
- Report of casualties on the Keokuk 56
- Report of casualties on the Nahant 56
- Detailed report of Admiral S. F. DuPont 57
- Order of battle and plan of attack 60
- Report of Captain P. Drayton 61
- Report of Captain John Rodgers 63
- Report of Captain John L. Worden 64
- Report of Lieutenant Commander C. H. Cushman 65
- Report of Commander Daniel Ammen 66
- Report of Commander George W. Rodgers 67
- Report of Commander D. McN. Fairfax 68
- Report of Lieutenant Commander L. A. Beardslee 69
- Report of Senior Engineer George H. White 70
- Report of Commander John Downes 72
- Report of Commander A. C. Rhind 73
- Report of expenditure of ammunition, &c. 75
- Report of Captain T. Turner 76
- Letter to Rear-Admiral DuPont by the Secretary of the Navy 77
- Instructions of the President 77
- Further instructions of the President 78
- Letter from Rear-Admiral DuPont 78
- Chief Engineer Stimers's report of damages to the iron-clads 80

Telegrams of Assistant Secretary G. V. Fox relative to supposed preliminary attack upon Fort Sumter 82
Order to send Passaic to New York 82
Directing the Passaic to touch at Hampton Roads 83
Order for board of experts on damages to the Passaic 83
Report of board 83
Extract from a letter relative to the effect of the bombardment of Fort Sumter 85
Necessary for New Ironsides to remain at Charleston 85
Effect of shots upon Sumter 86
Statement of commanders of Monitors relative to first attack on Charleston 87
Rear-Admiral DuPont's reviews on the article in the Baltimore American 90
Letter of Secretary of the Navy to Rear-Admiral DuPont in reply to despatch of April 22, 1863 96
Rear-Admiral DuPont relative to failure to renew attack, being a reply to letter of the Secretary of Navy of May 15, 1863 97
Letter of Secretary of Navy to Rear-Admiral DuPont relative to first attack on Charleston 99
Reply of Rear-Admiral DuPont to department's letter of May 14, 1863 101
The Secretary of the Navy to Rear-Admiral DuPont 106
Inquiry relative to the guns of the Keokuk 107

Page.
Rear-Admiral DuPont relative to loss of the guns of the Keokuk 107
The Secretary of the Navy to Rear-Admiral DuPont relative to the guns of the Keokuk 107
Rear-Admiral DuPont relative to loss of guns of the Keokuk...................... 108
Opinion of Rear-Admiral DuPont relative to the qualities of the Monitors for blockading duty off Charleston 108
Opinions of commanding officers of the Monitors 109
Major General Hunter to the President relative to Rear-Admiral DuPont's refusal to co-operate.. 110
Letter relieving Rear-Admiral DuPont from the command of the South Atlantic Blockading Squadron 112
General Gillmore requesting the co-operation of Rear-Admiral DuPont 112
Rear-Admiral DuPont directed to co-operate with General Gillmore 113
General Gillmore states that operations are delayed for want of Rear-Admiral DuPont's co-operation.. 113
Congratulating Rear-Admiral DuPont upon his arrival home 113
Rear-Admiral Dahlgren to command the South Atlantic Squadron................... 114
Rear-Admiral DuPont prefers charges against Chief Engineer Stimers............. 114
Passage of the New Ironsides from Hampton Roads to Port Royal.................. 170
Passage of Passaic and Montauk to Port Royal.................................. 172
Attack upon rebel fort at Genesis Point, Great Ogeechee river—
Report of Rear-Admiral DuPont 174
Report of Commander John L. Worden.. 175
Attack on the battery on the Ogeechee river, &c.—
Report of Rear-Admiral DuPont 176
Report of Commander John L. Worden.. 176
Report of Captain P. Drayton.. 177
Arrival of the Weehawken at Port Royal.. 177
Report of survey, &c., on the Weehawken... 178
Passage of Patapsco to Port Royal... 180
Effects of shot on the Montauk.. 181
Passage of Nahant to Port Royal... 182
Relative to testing the Monitor vessels 183
Destruction of the privateer Nashville—
Report of Rear-Admiral DuPont... 184
Report of Commander John L. Worden 184
Attack on Fort McAllister—
Report of Rear-Admiral DuPont 185
Report of Captain P. Drayton.. 186
Report of Lieutenant Commander J. N. Miller 188
Report of Commander D. Ammen... 189
Report of Captain J. Downes 190
Arrival of the Catskill at Port Royal 191
Chief Engineer Stimers coming north to report................................... 191
Report of survey on the Montauk 192
Arrival of the Nantucket at Port Royal 193
Requesting commanding officers of iron-clads to make suggestions relative to their improvement.. 193
Passage of the Keokuk to Port Royal... 194
Calling attention to request for report upon improvement of iron-clads.......... 194
Injury to turret of the Nahant.. 195
Relative to forwarding suggestions of officers commanding iron-clads............ 195
Telegraphic report of the capture of the Atlanta 198
Capture of rebel iron-clad steamer Atlanta—
Report of Rear-Admiral DuPont... 198
Report of Captain John Rodgers.. 200

Page.

Capture of rebel iron-clad steamer Atlanta—*Continued.*
Sketch of the Atlanta .... 202-'3
Report of Commander John Downes 204
Report of survey on the hull, &c 204
Report of survey on the clothing, small stores, &c 208
Appraisal of equipments and inventory of ordnance, &c 210
Inventory of carpenter's, sailmaker's, boatswain's, and master's stores 212
Congratulatory letter to Captain John Rodgers 213
Congratulatory letter to Rear-Admiral DuPont 215
Report of survey on turret of Patapsco 215
Occupation of Morris island—operations of the iron-clads—
Report of Rear-Admiral J. A. Dahlgren 216
General Order of Rear-Admiral Dahlgren 218
Report of Commander Geo. W. Rodgers 219
Report of Lieutenant Commander F. M. Bunce 220
The Monitors inside the bar—attack on Fort Wagner delayed—
Report of Rear-Admiral Dahlgren 221
Combined attack on Fort Wagner—
Report of Rear-Admiral Dahlgren 221
Report of Commander Geo. W. Rodgers 223
Attack on Fort Wagner—
Report of Rear-Admiral Dahlgren 223
Additional reports of Rear-Admiral Dahlgren 224
Attack upon Forts Wagner and Sumter—
Report of Rear-Admiral Dahlgren 224
Letter, with notes of Flag-Lieutenant M. Forrest 226
Report of Lieutenant Commander C. C. Carpenter 227
Report of casualties on the Catskill 228
Report of Commander F. A. Parker 228
Report of Captain S. C. Rowan 228
Report of injuries sustained by the New Ironsides 229
Engagement with Fort Sumter—
Report of Rear-Admiral Dahlgren 229
Notes taken by Flag-Lieutenant M. Forrest 230
Engagement with Forts Moultrie and Sumter—
Report of Rear-Admiral Dahlgren 231
Evacuation of Fort Wagner and Battery Gregg—
Report of Rear-Admiral Dahlgren 233
Engagement with the forts in Charleston harbor—
Report of Rear-Admiral Dahlgren 233
Report of Commander E. R. Colhoun 234
Report of casualties on the Weehawken 235
Additional reports relative to the attack upon the forts on the 8th of September 236
Injuries to the Monitors 239
Services of the New Ironsides against the defences of Charleston—
Report of Rear-Admiral Dahlgren 239
Report of Captain S. C. Rowan 239
Report of casualties on the New Ironsides 240
Report of Executive Officer H. B. Robeson 241
Part taken by the Patapsco in the attack at Charleston 241
Reports from officers commanding Monitors in South Atlantic Blockading Squadron relative to their condition 243
Injuries, &c., received by the Weehawken 251
Operations of the Nantucket at Charleston 252
Report of injury to the turret of the Passaic 253
Repairs needed on the Nahant 254
Part taken by the Passaic in the attack at Charleston 254
Suggestions of Lieutenant Commander Simpson relative to the Monitors 256
Rear-Admiral DuPont's vindication of himself 260

Page.
Secretary of the Navy in reply to Rear-Admiral DuPont's letter........ 263
Journal of Surgeon Marius Duval........ 273
Operations of the Patapsco against Fort Sumter........ 279
Operations of the Lehigh against Fort Sumter........ 280
Rear-Admiral Dahlgren's report of operations against Fort Sumter........ 281
Trial of a torpedo........ 283
Repairs made on the Passaic........ 284
Ammunition expended by the Patapsco........ 286
Engagement of the Lehigh with the enemy while aground........ 286
Opinion of Acting Assistant Inspector Hughes on various points........ 289
Weekly report of the condition of the Monitors........ 290
Safety on southern coast depends upon the Ironsides and the Monitors........ 297
Sinking of the Weehawken........ 297

WESTERN GULF SQUADRON.

Engagements with the ram Arkansas—
Report of Flag-Officer Farragut........ 343
Report of Lieutenant Commanding Lowry........ 343
Destruction of the Arkansas........ 344
Report of Commander W. D. Porter........ 345
Additional reports of Flag-Officer Farragut........ 346
Attempt to blow up the Essex with a torpedo—
Report of Commander Caldwell........ 348
Report of Commander Townsend........ 349

MISSISSIPPI SQUADRON.

Report of Commander Walke of the part taken by the Mound City in the battle of Belmont, Kentucky........ 350
Telegram from Flag-Officer Foote........ 351
Letter from Flag-Officer Foote enclosing report of Commander W. D. Porter........ 352
Flag-Officer Foote's report of attack on Fort Henry, February 6, 1862........ 353
Report of part taken by the Carondelet in capture of Fort Henry........ 354
Report of Lieutenant Commanding S. L. Phelps of attack on Fort Henry........ 355
Letter from Flag-Officer Foote forwarding report of Lieutenant Commanding Phelps of operations on the Tennessee river........ 356
Flag-Officer Foote's report of attack on Fort Donelson, Feb. 14, with list of casualties 359
Report of part taken by the Carondelet in attack on Fort Donelson........ 360
Flag-Officer Foote leaves for Clarksville, &c.—
Report of Flag-Officer Foote........ 361
Report of Commander Walke........ 362
Report of Commander Dove........ 362
Flag-Officer Foot's contemplated reconnoissance to Columbus, &c........ 363
Result of the reconnoissance to Columbus........ 365
Lieutenant Commanding Bryant reports his arrival at Nashville........ 366
Flag-Officer Foote encloses reports of Lieutenants Commanding Gwin and Shirk of attack on Pittsburg, Tennessee........ 366
Flag-Officer Foote's report of the fall of Columbus........ 369
Flag-Officer Foote forwards report of Lieutenant Commanding Gwin communicating important information........ 371
Flag-Officer Foote's report of engagement with five rebel forts below Columbus, Kentucky........ 372
Lieutenant Commanding Gwin's report of reconnoissance to Chickasaw, Alabama... 373
Lieutenant Commanding Shirk's report of proceedings, March 15, 1862........ 374

Page.

Capture of Island No. 10—
- Reports of Flag-Officer Foote 375
- Report of casualties on the St. Louis.... 376
- Letter from General Halleck to Flag-Officer Foote.... 379
- Letter from General Strong to Flag-Officer Foote 379
- Letter from Flag-Officer Foote to General Halleck.... 380
- Letter from Flag-Officer Foote, enclosing report of Colonel Roberts.... 381
- Instructions to Commander Walke.... 383
- Letter from General Pope to Flag-Officer Foote.... 384
- Letter from Flag-Officer Foote to General Pope 385
- Report of passage of rebel batteries by the Carondelet 386

Engagement of the Carondelet and Pittsburg with the rebels near New Madrid—
- Report of Flag-Officer Foote.... 389
- Report of Commander Walke.... 390
- Report of Lieutenant Commanding Gwin.... 391
- Report of Lieutenant Commanding Shirk.... 392
- Thanks of the department to certain officers 933

Lieutenant Commanding William Gwin's report of the destruction of the trestle-work of the Memphis and Charleston railroad.... 394

Flag-Officer Foote reports his departure for New Madrid 394

Flag-Officer Foote's report of operations off Fort Pillow 395

Flag-Officer Davis's report of action near Fort Pillow 398

Flag-Officer Davis's report of action with rebel gunboats near Fort Pillow.... 398

Flag-Officer Davis's report of the surrender of Memphis 399

Flag-Officer Davis encloses report of action at St. Charles.... 402

Arrival of the rebel ram Arkansas under the guns of Vicksburg 406

Attack on the upper batteries at Vicksburg and the ram Arkansas—
- Report of Flag-Officer Davis.... 407
- Report of Commander W. D. Porter.... 408

Flag-Officer Davis reports his departure for Yazoo river.... 409

Captain Pennock's report of expedition up the Ohio river.... 410

Capture of the rebel transport Fairplay, &c 412

Lieutenant Commanding Phelps's report of the action at Bolivar, Mississippi 412

Loss of the Cairo—
- Report of Acting Rear-Admiral D. D. Porter 413
- Report of Captain Walke 413
- Report of Lieutenant Commander Selfridge.... 414
- Detailed report of Acting Rear-Admiral D. D Porter 416
- Instructions to Captain Walke.... 417

Engagement with Yazoo batteries—co-operation with General Sherman against Vicksburg—
- Report of Acting Rear-Admiral Porter.... 418
- Detailed report of Acting Rear-Admiral Porter 419
- Report of Acting Rear-Admiral Porter relative to General Sherman's assault.... 422

Position of affairs at Vicksburg—
- Report of Acting Rear-Admiral Porter.... 423
- Additional report of Acting Rear-Admiral Porter.... 424

Services of the ram fleet on the Yazoo river—
- Report of Acting Rear-Admiral Porter.... 424

Capture of Arkansas Post—
- Report of Acting Rear-Admiral Porter.... 425
- Detailed report of Acting Rear-Admiral Porter.... 425
- Casualties on the Louisville.... 427
- Report of Lieutenant Commander Shirk.... 428
- Report of Lieutenant Commander Walker 428
- Casualties on the Baron de Kalb.... 428
- Report of Lieutenant Commanding Bache.... 429
- List of rebel officers captured at Arkansas Post 429
- Acting Rear-Admiral Porter's report commendatory of the officers, &c.... 430
- Sketch of Fort Hindman.... 432-'3

Page

Evacuation of St. Charles, on the White river—
Report of Acting Rear-Admiral Porter.... 434
Report of Lieutenant Commander Walker.... 434

Burning of the steamers Jacob Mussbrain and Grampus—
Report of Acting Rear-Admiral Porter.... 435
Report of Lieutenant Commander Bishop.... 435

Expedition up the White river—
Reports of Acting Rear-Admiral Porter.... 436
Reports of Lieutenant Commander Walker.... 436

Expedition up the Cumberland river—
Report of Captain Pennock.... 438
Report of Lieutenant Commander Phelps.... 439
Telegram of Lieutenant Commander Le Roy Fitch.... 440

Passage of the Vicksburg batteries by the Queen of the West—
Report of Acting Rear-Admiral Porter.... 440
Orders to Colonel Ellet.... 441
Report of Colonel Ellet.... 441
Letter of Acting Rear-Admiral Porter.... 442
Additional report of Acting Rear-Admiral Porter.... 443
Instructions to Colonel Ellet.... 443
Additional report of Colonel Ellet.... 444

Approaches and defences of Vicksburg—
Report of Acting Rear-Admiral Porter.... 446

Attack on Dover, Tennessee—
Report of Captain Pennock.... 448
Map of Vicksburg and vicinity.... 449
Report of Lieutenant Commander Le Roy Fitch.... 450

Passage of the Vicksburg batteries by the Indianola—
Report of Acting Rear-Admiral Porter.... 451
Instructions to Lieutenant Commander George Brown.... 451
Report of Lieutenant Commander George Brown.... 452

Loss of the United States Steamer Glide—
Report of Acting Rear-Admiral Porter.... 454
Report of Captain Pennock.... 454
Report of Acting Volunteer Lieutenant Woodworth.... 454

Capture of the Queen of the West—
Report of Acting Rear-Admiral Porter.... 455
Additional report of Acting Rear-Admiral Porter.... 456
Report of Colonel Ellet.... 456
List of prisoners captured on the Queen of the West.... 459

Capture of the Indianola—
Report of Acting Rear-Admiral Porter.... 459
Report of Lieutenant Commander George Brown.... 460

Expedition through Steel's bayou and Deer creek—
Report of Acting Rear-Admiral Porter.... 462
Additional report of Acting Rear-Admiral Porter.... 466

Yazoo Pass expedition—
Report of Acting Rear-Admiral Porter.... 467
Report of Lieutenant Commander Watson Smith.... 468
Report of Lieutenant Commander J. P. Foster.... 469
Report of casualties on the Chillicothe.... 470
Report of casualties on the Rattler.... 471
Extract from report of Acting Rear-Admiral Porter.... 471
Additional report of Acting Rear-Admiral Porter.... 472
Additional report of Lieutenant Commander Foster.... 472
Map of the operations of the expedition.... 474
Map showing the route of the expedition, (facing 475.)
Report of Lieutenant Commander J. G. Walker.... 475

Sinking of the Lancaster and Switzerland—
Report of Acting Rear-Admiral Porter.... 475
Letter of Acting Rear-Admiral Porter to General A. W. Ellet.... 476

Page.

Sinking of the Lancaster and Switzerland—*Continued.*
Report of General A. W. Ellet 476
Letters from Rear-Admiral Farragut to Acting Rear-Admiral Porter 477
Extract from despatch of Rear-Admiral Porter 478

Selfridge's cut-off—
Report of Acting Rear-Admiral Porter 478
Report of Lieutenant Commanding T. O. Selfridge 479

Passage of the Vicksburg batteries by Acting Rear-Admiral Porter with his fleet—
Report of Acting Rear-Admiral Porter 480
Map of "Selfridge's cut-off." 481
Detailed report of Acting Rear-Admiral Porter 482
Instructions to commanders of vessels 483
Report of Captain Walke 484
Report of Acting Lieutenant Woodworth 485
Report of Lieutenant Commander J. A. Greer 485
Report of casualties on the Benton 486
Report of Lieutenant Commander E. K. Owen 486
Report of Lieutenant Commander Shirk 487
Report of Lieutenant Commander Wilson 488
Report of casualties on the Mound City 489
Report of Acting Volunteer Lieutenant Hoel 489
Report of Acting Lieutenant J. McLeod Murphy 489
Casualties in the squadron 490
Report of Lieutenant Commander K. R. Breese 490

Operations at Grand Gulf—
Report of Acting Rear-Admiral Porter 491

Capture of the batteries at Grand Gulf—
Report of Acting Rear-Admiral Porter 492
Report of Captain Walke 493
Reports of Lieutenant Commander J. A. Greer 494
Casualties on the Benton 496
Report of Lieutenant Commander E. K. Owen 496
Report of Lieutenant Commander Shirk 497
Casualties on the Tuscumbia 498
Report of Lieutenant Commander Wilson 499
Report of Acting Lieutenant J. McLeod Murphy 499
Report of Acting Volunteer Lieutenant Hoel 500
Casualties on the Pittsburg 501
Additional report of Acting Rear-Admiral Porter 501
Plan of the batteries at Grand Gulf, (facing 502.)

Capture of Forts De Russy, Red river, and Alexandria, Louisiana—
Report of Acting Rear-Admiral Porter 502
Destruction of Fort De Russy, &c 503
Plan of Fort De Russy 504

Feigned attack on Haines's Bluff—
Report of Acting Rear-Admiral Porter 505
Report of Lieutenant Commander K. R. Breese 506
Report of Lieutenant Commander J. G. Walker 507
Report of Lieutenant Commander F. M. Ramsay 508
Report of Lieutenant Commander J. M. Pritchett 509

Operations on the Tennessee and Cumberland rivers—
Reports of Lieutenant Commander Le Roy Fitch 509

Destruction of a water battery at Warrenton—
Report of Acting Rear-Admiral Porter 514

Destruction of the fortifications at Haines's Bluff—
Report of Acting Rear-Admiral Porter 514
Sketch of fortifications at Haines's Bluff, (facing 514.)

Attack on the Vicksburg batteries—
Report of Acting Rear-Admiral Porter 516
Letter of General Arthur to Acting Rear-Admiral Porter 517
Report of Lieutenant Commander J. A. Greer 518
Report of Lieutenant Commander B. Wilson, ... 519

Page.

Attack on the Vicksburg batteries—*Continued.*
- Report of Acting Ensign Coleman 519
- Casualties on the Mound City 520
- Report of Commander Woodworth 520
- Additional report of Lieutenant Commander Greer 521
- Additional report of Lieutenant Commander Wilson 521
- Report of Acting Lieutenant J. McLeod Murphy 522

Report of Acting Rear-Admiral Porter relative to the Tuscumbia 522

Expedition up the Yazoo river—
- Report of Acting Rear-Admiral Porter 523
- Report of Lieutenant Commander J. G. Walker 524

Lieutenant Commander Phelps's operations on the Tennessee river 525

Loss of the Cincinnati—
- Report of Acting Rear-Admiral Porter 526
- Letter of Major General Sherman 526
- Report of Lieutenant Commander G. M. Bache 527
- Additional report of Acting Rear-Admiral Porter 528
- Additional report of Lieutenant Commander Bache 528
- Letter from Major General Sherman 529
- Letter of thanks from Secretary of the Navy to Lieutenant Commander Bache 530

Expedition up the Yazoo river—
- Report of Acting Rear-Admiral Porter 530
- Report of Lieutenant Commander J. G. Walker 531

Siege of Vicksburg, and co-operation of the navy with the army—
- Reports of Acting Rear-Admiral Porter 532
- Report of Commander Woodworth 533
- Report of Lieutenant Commander Greer 534
- Report of Lieutenant Commander Wilson 534

Surrender of Vicksburg—
- Report of Acting Rear-Admiral Porter 535
- Detailed report of Acting Rear-Admiral Porter 537
- Letter from Major General Herron to Admiral Porter 540
- Letter from Major General Herron to Lieutenant Commander Greer 540
- Report of Lieutenant Commanding Selfridge 541
- Letter from Major General Sherman to Admiral Porter 541
- Congratulatory letter to Rear-Admiral Porter 542

Engagement at Milliken's Bend—
- Report of Acting Rear-Admiral Porter 543
- Report of Lieutenant Commander Ramsay 544

Movements of the gunboat fleet on the Tennessee river—
- Report of Lieutenant Commander S. L. Phelps 545

ngagement at Richmond, Louisiana—
- Report of Acting Rear-Admiral Porter 546
- Report of Brigadier General Ellet 546

Movements of the Marine Brigade from April 5 to May 29, 1863—
- Report of Acting Rear-Admiral Porter 547
- Report of Brigadier General Ellet 547

Action at Cerro Gorda—
- Report of Acting Ensign W. C. Hanford 549

Attack on black troops at Goodrich's Landing—
- Report of Acting Rear-Admiral Porter 550
- Report of Brigadier General Ellet 551

Rebel attack on Helena, Arkansas—
- Report of Acting Rear-Admiral Porter 553
- Report of Lieutenant Commander Pritchett 554
- Additional report of Acting Rear-Admiral Porter 554
- Report of Lieutenant Commander Phelps 554
- Letter from Major General Prentiss 555
- Congratulatory letter to Lieutenant Commander Pritchett 556

Expedition to Yazoo city—
- Report of Acting Rear-Admiral Porter 556

Page.

Expedition into Red river region—

Report of Acting Rear-Admiral Porter 557

Destruction of steam foundry in Vicksburg—

Report of Acting Rear-Admiral Porter 558

Report of Brigadier General Ellet 559

Report of Captain Groshon, of the Marine Brigade 559

Loss of the United States steamer Baron de Kalb—

Report of Acting Rear-Admiral Porter 560

Expedition to recover the Baron de Kalb 561

Engagement at Providence—

Report of Lieutenant Commander Wilson 562

Raising of the Cincinnati—

Report of Acting Rear-Admiral Porter 562

Morgan's raid into Indiana—

Report of Lieutenant Commander Le Roy Fitch 563

Complimentary letters from Generals Burnside and Cox 564

Congratulatory letter to Lieutenant Commander Le Roy Fitch 565

Expedition up the White river—

Report of Acting Rear-Admiral Porter 565

Report of Lieutenant Commander Bache 566

Report of Acting Volunteer Lieutenant Langthorne 567

Affairs on the Red river—

Report of Acting Rear-Admiral Porter 568

Expedition to Red river—

Report of Acting Rear-Admiral Porter 568

Report of Acting Chief Engineer Doughty 569

Attack upon General Dana at Morganzia—

Report of Lieutenant Commander J. P. Foster 570

MISCELLANEOUS REPORTS.

Rear-Admiral Goldsborough's opinion of iron-clads 571

Rear-Admiral Dahlgren's opinion of the Monitors 579

Rear-Admiral Porter's views upon iron-clads 588

Commander John Rodgers's opinion of iron-clads 592

Brigadier General Barnard's opinion of turreted vessels 594

Letter from Governor Morgan to the President, asking that an iron-clad be stationed in New York harbor 595

Memorial from Boston Board of Trade asking that the Nahant may remain at Boston .. 596

Letter of Governor Morgan relative to defence of New York harbor 597

Memorial from Boston Marine Society relative to the defenceless condition of Boston harbor 598

Telegram from Governor Morgan and Collector Barney 598

Mr. Ericsson on improvements in the Monitors 599

Rear-Admiral Gregory relative to gutta-percha life-rafts 599

Mr. Ericsson in reference to construction of Monitors 600

Trial of the Nantucket 602

Captain Ericsson upon speed and seaworthiness of the Monitors 603

Major General Wool anxious the Roanoke should remain in New York harbor 604

Mayor Opdyke desires the Roanoke to remain at New York 604

Governor Morgan requests that the sailing orders of the Roanoke be countermanded .. 604

General Wool urges retention of the Roanoke 604

Leak in the Sangamon 605

INTRODUCTORY.

From the report of the Secretary of the Navy, July 4, 1861.

IRON-CLAD STEAMERS OR FLOATING BATTERIES.

Much attention has been given within the last few years to the subject of floating batteries, or iron-clad steamers. Other governments, and particularly France and England, have made it a special object in connexion with naval improvements; and the ingenuity and inventive faculties of our own countrymen have also been stimulated by recent occurrences toward the construction of this class of vessels. The period is, perhaps, not one best adapted to heavy expenditures by way of experiment, and the time and attention of some of those who are most competent to investigate and form correct conclusions on this subject are otherwise employed. I would, however, recommend the appointment of a proper and competent board to inquire into and report in regard to a measure so important; and it is for Congress to decide whether, on a favorable report, they will order one or more iron-clad steamers, or floating batteries, to be constructed, with a view to perfect protection from the effects of present ordnance at short range, and make an appropriation for that purpose.

It is nearly twenty years since a gentleman of New Jersey, possessing wealth and talent, projected the construction of a floating battery, and the government aided the work by a liberal appropriation. The death of this gentleman a few years since interrupted the prosecution of this experiment, and application has been recently made by his surviving brother, the authorities of New Jersey, and others, for additional means to carry it forward to completion. The amount asked is of such magnitude as to require special investigation by a competent board, who shall report as to the expediency and practicability of the experiment before so large an expenditure should be authorized.

Act of Congress authorizing the construction of iron-clad vessels.

AN ACT to provide for the construction of one or more armored ships and floating batteries, and for other purposes.

Be it enacted by the Senate and House of Representatives of the United States of America in Congress assembled, That the Secretary of the Navy be, and he is hereby, authorized and directed to appoint a board of three skilful naval officers to investigate the plans and specifications that may be submitted for the construction or completing of iron or steel-clad steamships or steam batteries, and, on their report, should it be favorable, the Secretary of the Navy will cause one or more armored or iron or steel-clad steamships or floating steam batteries to be built; and there is hereby appropriated, out of any money in the treasury not otherwise appropriated, the sum of one million five hundred thousand dollars.

SEC. 2. *And be it further enacted,* That in case of a vacancy in the office of engineer-in-chief of the navy the appointment thereto shall be made from the list of chief engineers.

Approved August 3, 1861.

Copy of advertisement calling for plans and specifications

IRON-CLAD STEAM VESSELS.

The Navy Department will receive offers from parties who are able to execute work of this kind, and who are engaged in it, of which they will furnish evidence with their offer, for the construction of one or more iron-clad steam vessels of war, either of iron or of wood and iron combined, for sea or river service, to be of not less than ten nor over sixteen feet draught of water; to carry an armament of from eighty to one hundred and twenty tons weight, with provisions and stores for from one hundred and sixty-five to three hundred persons, according to armament, for sixty days, with coal for eight days. The smaller draught of water, compatible with other requisites, will be preferred. The vessel to be rigged with two masts, with wire-rope standing rigging, to navigate at sea.

A general description and drawings of the vessel, armor, and machinery, such as the work can be executed from, will be required.

The offer must state the cost and the time for completing the whole, exclusive of armament and stores of all kinds, the rate of speed proposed, and must be accompanied by a guarantee for the proper execution of the contract, if awarded.

Persons who intend to offer are requested to inform the department of their intention before the 15th August, instant, and to have their propositions presented within twenty-five days from this date.

August 7, 1861.

Order convening a board to examine plans for the construction of iron-clad vessels.

NAVY DEPARTMENT, *August* 8, 1861.

SIR: The provisions of the act of Congress approved August 3, 1861, directs "that the Secretary of the Navy be, and he is hereby, authorized and directed to appoint a board of three skilful naval officers to investigate the plans and specifications that may be submitted for the construction or completing of iron or steel-clad steamships, or steam batteries, and on their report, should it be favorable, the Secretary of the Navy will cause one or more armored, or iron or steel-clad steamships, or floating steam batteries, to be built; and there is hereby appropriated, out of any money in the treasury not otherwise appropriated, the sum of one million five hundred thousand dollars;" and the department hereby appoints you the senior officer of the board referred to in the foregoing enactment, with Commodore Hiram Paulding and Commander Charles H. Davis as your associates.

The board will convene at the Navy Department as early as practicable, and will make a written report of the result of its investigations of the subject embraced in the law before quoted.

I am, respectfully, your obedient servant,

GIDEON WELLES.

Commodore JOSEPH SMITH,
United States Navy, Washington, D. C.

Report of board to examine plans of iron-clad vessels, under act of August 3, 1861.

NAVY DEPARTMENT,
Bureau of Yards and Docks, September 16, 1861.

SIR: The undersigned, constituting a board appointed by your order of the 8th ultimo, proceeded to the duty assigned to them, in accordance with the first section of an act of Congress, approved 3d of August, 1861, directing the Secretary of the Navy "to appoint a board of three skilful naval officers to investigate the plans and specifications that may be submitted for the construction or completing of iron-clad steamships or steam batteries, and on their report, should it be favorable, the Secretary of the Navy will cause one or more armored or iron or steel-clad steamship or floating steam batteries to be built; and there is hereby appropriated, out of any money in the treasury not otherwise appropriated, the sum of one million five hundred thousand dollars."

Distrustful of our ability to discharge this duty, which the law requires should be performed by three skilful naval officers, we approach the subject with diffidence, having no experience and but scanty knowledge in this branch of naval architecture.

The plans submitted are so various, and in many respects so entirely dissimilar, that without a more thorough knowledge of this mode of construction and the resisting properties of iron than we possess, it is very likely that some of our conclusions may prove erroneous.

Application was made to the department for a naval constructor, to be placed under our orders, with whom we might consult; but it appears that they are all so employed on important service that none could be assigned to this duty.

The construction of iron-clad steamships of war is now zealously claiming the attention of foreign naval powers. France led off; England followed, and is now somewhat extensively engaged in the system; and other powers seem to emulate their example, though on a smaller scale.

Opinions differ amongst naval and scientific men as to the policy of adopting the iron armature for ships-of-war. For coast and harbor defence they are undoubtedly formidable adjuncts to fortifications on land. As cruising vessels, however, we are sceptical as to their advantages and ultimate adoption. But whilst other nations are endeavoring to perfect them, we must not remain idle.

The enormous load of iron, as so much additional weight to the vessel; the great breadth of beam necessary to give her stability; the short supply of coal she will be able to stow in bunkers; the greater power required to propel her; and the largely increased cost of construction, are objections to this class of vessels as cruisers which we believe it is difficult successfully to overcome. For river and harbor service we consider iron-clad vessels of light draught, or floating batteries thus shielded, as very important; and we feel at this moment the necessity of them on some of our rivers and inlets to enforce obedience to the laws. We, however, do not hesitate to express the opinion, notwithstanding all we have heard or seen written on the subject, that no ship or floating battery, however heavily she may be plated, can cope successfully with a properly constructed fortification of masonry. The one is fixed and immovable, and though constructed of a material which may be shattered by shot, can be covered, if need be, by the same or much heavier armor than a floating vessel can bear, whilst the other is subject to disturbances by winds and waves, and to the powerful effects of tides and currents.

Armored ships or batteries may be employed advantageously to pass fortifications on land for ulterior objects of attack, to run a blockade, or to reduce temporary batteries on the shores of rivers and the approaches to our harbors.

From what we know of the comparative advantages and disadvantages of ships constructed of wood over those of iron, we are clearly of opinion that no iron-clad vessel of equal displacement can be made to obtain the same speed as one not thus encumbered, because her form would be better adapted to speed. Her form and dimensions, the unyielding nature of the shield, detract materially in a heavy sea from the life, buoyancy, and spring which a ship built of wood possesses.

Wooden ships may be said to be but coffins for their crews when brought in conflict with iron-clad vessels; but the speed of the former, we take for granted, being greater than that of the latter, they can readily choose their position, and keep out of harm's way entirely.

Recent improvements in the form and preparation of projectiles, and their increased capacity for destruction, have elicited a large amount of ingenuity and skill to devise means for resisting them in their construction of ships-of-war. As yet we know of nothing superior to the large and heavy spherical shot in its destructive effects on vessels, whether plated or not.

Rifled guns have greater range, but the conical shot does not produce the *crushing* effect of spherical shot.

It is assumed that 4½-inch plates are the heaviest armor a sea-going vessel can safely carry. These plates should be of tough iron, and rolled in large, long pieces. This thickness of armor, it is believed, will resist all projectiles now in general use at a distance of 500 yards, especially if the ship's sides are angular.

Plates hammered in large masses are less fibrous and tough than when rolled. The question whether wooden backing, or any elastic substance behind the iron plating, will tend to relieve at all the frame of the ships from the crushing effect of a heavy projectile, is not yet decided. Major Barnard says, "to put an elastic material behind the iron is to insure its destruction." With all deference to such creditable authority, we may suggest that it is possible a backing of some elastic substance (soft wood, perhaps, is the best) might relieve the frame of the ship somewhat from the terrible shock of a heavy projectile, though the plate should not be fractured.

With respect to a comparison between ships of iron and those of wood, without plating, high authorities in England differ as to which is the best. The tops of ships built of iron, we are told, wear out three bottoms; whilst the bottoms of those built of wood will outwear three tops. In deciding upon the relative merits of iron and wooden-framed vessels, for each of which we have offers, the board is of opinion that it would be well to try a specimen of each, as both have distinguished advocates. One strong objection to iron vessels, which, so far as we know, has not yet been overcome, is the oxidation or rust in salt water, and their liability of becoming foul under water by the attachment of sea grass and animalcules to their bottoms. The best preventive we know of is a coating of pure zinc paint, which, so long as it lasts, is believed to be an antidote to this cause of evil.

After these brief remarks on the subject generally, we proceed to notice the plans and offers referred to us for the construction of plated vessels and floating batteries.

It has been suggested that the most ready mode of obtaining an iron-clad ship-of-war would be to contract with responsible parties in England for its complete construction; and we are assured that parties there are ready to engage in such an enterprise on terms more reasonable, perhaps, than such vessels could be built in this country, having much greater experience and facilities than we possess. Indeed, we are informed there are no mills and machinery in this country capable of rolling iron 4½ inches thick, though plates might be hammered to that thickness in many of our workshops. As before observed, rolled iron is considered much the best, and the difficulty of rolling it increases rapidly with the increase of thickness. It has, however, occurred to us that a difficulty might arise with the British government, in case we should undertake to construct ships-of-war in that country, which might complicate their delivery; and, moreover, we are of opinion that every people or nation who can maintain a navy should be capable of constructing it themselves.

Our immediate demands seem to require, first, so far as practicable, vessels invulnerable to shot, of light draught of water, to penetrate our shoal harbors, rivers, and bayous. We, therefore, favor the construction of this class of vessels before going into a more perfect system of large iron-clad sea-going vessels of war. We are here met with the difficulty of encumbering small vessels with armor, which, from their size, they are unable to bear. We, nevertheless, recommend that contracts be made with responsible parties for the construction of one or more iron-clad vessels or batteries of as light a draught of water as practicable consistent with their weight of armor. Meanwhile, availing of the experience thus obtained, and the improvements which we believe are yet to be made by other naval powers in building iron-clad ships, we would advise the construction, in our own dock-yards, of one or more of these vessels upon a large and more perfect scale, when Congress shall see fit to authorize it. The amount now appropriated is not sufficient to build both classes of vessels to any great extent.

We have made a synopsis of the propositions and specifications submitted, which we annex, and now proceed to state, in brief, the result of our decisions upon the offers presented to us.

J. Ericsson, New York, page 19.—This plan of a floating battery is novel, but seems to be based upon a plan which will render the battery shot and shell proof. We are somewhat apprehensive that her properties for sea are not such as a sea-going vessel should possess. But she may be moved from one place to another on the coast in smooth water. We recommend that an experiment be made with one battery of this description on the terms proposed, with a guarantee and forfeiture in case of failure in any of the properties and points of the vessel as proposed.

Price, $275,000; length of vessel, 172 feet; breadth of beam, 41 feet; depth of hold, 11½ feet; time, 100 days; draught of water, 10 feet; displacement, 1,255 tons; speed per hour, nine statute miles.

John W. Nystrom, Philadelphia, 1216 *Chestnut street, page* 1.—The plan of (quadruple) guns is not known, and cannot be considered. The dimensions would not float the vessel without the guards, which we are not satisfied would repel shot. We do not recommend the plan.

Price, about $175,000; length of vessel, 175 feet; breadth of beam, 27 feet; depth of hold, 13 feet; time, four months; draught of water, 10 feet; displacement, 875 tons; speed per hour, 12 knots.

William Perine, New York, 2777 *post office box,* presents three plans. The specifications and drawings are not full. The last proposal (No. 3, page 2) for the heavy plating is the only one we have considered; but there is neither drawing nor model, and the capacity of the vessel, we think, will not bear the armor and armament proposed.

Price, $621,000; length of vessel, 225 feet; breadth of beam, 45½ feet; depth of hold, 15½ feet; time, 9 months; draught of water, 13 feet; displacement, 2,454 tons; speed per hour, 10 knots.

John C. Le Ferre, Boston, page 9.—Description deficient. Not recommended. Sent a model, but neither price, time, nor dimensions stated.

E. S. Renwick, New York, 335 *Broadway,* presents drawings, specification, and model of an iron-clad vessel of large capacity and powerful engines, with great speed, capable of carrying a heavy battery, and stated to be shot-proof and a good sea-boat. The form and manner of construction and proportions of this vessel are novel, and will attract the attention of scientific and practical men. She is of very light draught of water, and on the question whether she will prove to be a safe and comfortable sea-boat we do not express a decided opinion. Vessels of somewhat similar form, in that part of vessel which is immersed, of light draught of water on our western lakes, have, we believe, proved entirely satisfactory in all weathers. To counteract the effect of the waves, when disturbed by the winds, by producing a jerk, or sudden rolling motion of flat, shoal vessels, it is proposed to carry a sufficient weight above the centre of gravity to counterpoise the heavy weight below, which is done in this ship by the immense iron armor. If, after a full discussion and examination by experts on this plan, it should be decided that she is a safe vessel for sea service, we would recommend the construction upon it of one ship at one of our dock-yards.

The estimate cost of this ship, $1,500,000, precludes action upon the plan until further appropriations shall be made by Congress for such objects.

Time not stated; length of vessel, 400 feet; breadth of beam, 60 feet; depth of hold, 33 feet; draught of water, 16 feet; displacement, 6,520 tons; speed per hour, at least 18 miles.

Whitney & Rowland, Brooklyn, Greenpoint, page 13, propose an iron gunboat, armor of bars of iron and thin plate over it. *No price* stated. Dimensions of vessel, we think, will not bear the weight and possess stability. Time, 5 months. Not recommended.

Length of vessel, 140 feet; breadth of beam, 28 feet; depth of hold, 13½ feet; draught of water, 8 feet.

Donald McKay, Boston, page 16.—Vessel, in general dimensions and armor, approved. The speed estimated slow. The cost precludes the consideration of construction by the board.

Price, $1,000,000; length of vessel, 227 feet; breadth of beam, 50 feet; depth of hold, 26½ feet; time, 9 to 10 months; draught of water, 14 feet; displacement, 3,100 tons; speed per hour, 6 to 7 knots.

William H. Wood, Jersey City, N. J., page 14.—Dimensions will not float the guns high enough. Not recommended.

Price, $255,000; length of vessel, 160 feet; breadth of beam, 34 feet; depth of hold, 22 feet; time, 4 months; draught of water, 13 feet; displacement, 1,215 tons; speed, not stated.

Merrick & Sons, Philadelphia, pages 7 *and* 8.—Vessel of wood and iron combined. This proposition we consider the most practicable one for heavy armor. We recommend that a contract be made with that party, under a guarantee, with forfeiture in case of failure to comply with the specifications; and that the contract require the plates to be 15 feet long and 36 inches wide, with a reservation of some modifications, which may occur as the work progresses, not to affect the cost.

Price, $780,000; length of vessel, 220 feet; breadth of beam, 60 feet; depth of hold, 23 feet; time, 9 months; draught of water, 13 feet; displacement, 3,296 tons; speed per hour, 9½ knots.

Benjamin Rathburn, ————, page 20.—We do not recommend the plan for adoption.

Price not stated; length of vessel not stated; breadth of beam, 80 feet; depth of hold, 74 feet; time not stated; draught of water, 25 feet; displacement, 15,000 tons; speed not stated. Specification incomplete.

Henry R. Dunham, New York, page 11.—Vessel too costly for the appropriation; no drawings or specifications; not recommended.

Price $1,200,000; length of vessel, 325 feet; breadth of beam, 60 feet; depth of hold not stated; time, 15 to 18 months; draught of water, 16 feet; displacement not stated; speed per hour, 12 miles.

C. S. Bushnell & Co., New Haven, Conn., page 121, propose a vessel to be iron-clad, on the rail and plate principle, and to obtain high speed. The objection to this vessel is the fear that she will not float her armor and load sufficiently high, and have stability enough for a sea vessel. With a guarantee that she shall do these, we recommend on that basis a contract.

Price, $235,250; length of vessel, 180 feet; breadth of beam, — feet; depth of hold, 12⅝ feet; time, 4 months; draught of water, 10 feet; displacement, —— tons; speed per hour, 12 knots.

John Westwood, Cincinnati, Ohio, page 17.—Vessel of wood, with iron armor; plan good enough, but the breadth not enough to bear the armor. No detailed specification; *no price or time* stated; only a general drawing. Not recommended.

Neafie & Levy, Philadelphia, page 5.—No plans or drawings; therefore not considered. Neither *price nor time* stated.

Length of vessel, 200 feet; breadth of beam, 40 feet; depth of hold, 15 feet; draught of water, 13 feet; displacement, 1,748 tons; speed per hour, 10 knots.

Wm. Norris, New York, 26 *Cedar street, page* 6.—Iron boat without armor. Too small, and not received.

Price, $32,000; length of vessel, 83 feet; breadth of beam, 25 feet; depth of hold, 14 feet; time, 60 to 75 days; draught of water, 3 feet; displacement, 90 tons; speed not stated.

Wm. Kingsley, Washington, D. C., page 10, proposes a *rubber-clad* vessel, which we cannot recommend. No price or dimension stated.

A. Beebe, New York, 82 *Broadway, page* 18.—Specification and sketch defective. Plan not approved.

Price, $50,000; length of vessel, 120 feet; breadth of beam, 55 feet; depth not stated; time, 100 days; draught of water, 6 feet; displacement, 1,000 tons; speed per hour, 8 knots.

These three propositions recommended, viz: Bushnell & Co., New Haven, Connecticut; Merrick & Sons, Philadelphia, and J. Ericsson, New York, will absorb $1,290,250 of the appropriation of $1,500,000, leaving $209,750 yet unexpended.

The board recommends that armor with heavy guns be placed on one of our river craft, or, if none will bear it, to construct a scow, which will answer to plate and shield the guns, for the river service on the Potomac, to be constructed or prepared by the government at the navy yard here for immediate use.

We would further recommend that the department ask of Congress, at its next session, an appropriation for experimenting on iron plates of different kinds, of $10,000.

All of which is respectfully submitted.

JOSEPH SMITH.
H. PAULDING.
C. H. DAVIS.

Hon. GIDEON WELLES,
Secretary of the Navy.

From the report of the Secretary of the Navy, December 2, 1861.

ARMORED SHIPS.

To carry into effect the provisions of the act approved August 3, 1861, providing for the construction of one or more armored ships and floating batteries, I appointed Commodores Joseph Smith and Hiram Paulding and Captain Charles H. Davis, skilful and experienced naval officers, to investigate the plans and specifications that might be submitted. The subject of iron armature for ships is one of great general interest, not only to the navy and country, but is engaging the attention of the maritime powers of the world. Under the appropriation made by Congress, the department, on the favorable report of the board, has contracted for the construction of three iron-clad ships of different models, the aggregate cost of which will be within the limits of the appropriation. The difficulty of combining the two qualities of light draught and iron armor, both of which are wanted for service on our coast, could not be entirely overcome; but the board, in this new branch of naval architecture, has, I think, displayed great practical wisdom, and I refer to their very full and able report, which is appended, for a more explicit and detailed exhibit of their inquiries and conclusions.

From the report of the Secretary of the Navy, December 1, 1862.

IRON-CLAD VESSELS.

The attention of this department was turned to the subject of iron-clad vessels immediately after the commencement of hostilities and the adoption of measures for the enlargement of the navy. It was a subject full of difficulty and doubt. Experiments upon a large scale of expense, both in England and France, if not resulting in absolute failure, had achieved but a limited and questionable success. Yet it was evident that a new and material element in maritime warfare was developing itself, and demanded immediate attention. In this view I recommended to Congress, at its extra session, on the 4th of July, 1861, the whole subject, and asked authority to organize a commission for investigation. Thirty days after this action on my part, Congress conferred the authority requested, and appropriated fifteen hundred thousand dollars for the construction of one or more iron-clad vessels upon such models as should receive the approval of the department. On the day after the law had been approved the commission was constituted, and the department advertised for proposals. Of the various plans and propositions submitted, three vessels of different models were recommended by the board, which received the approval of the department. Contracts were forthwith made for constructing the Monitor, the Galena, and the Ironsides. All of these vessels are now in the service. It was the intention and constant effort of the department and the contractors that the Monitor should be completed in the month of January, but there was delay in consequence of the difficulties incident to an undertaking of such novelty and magnitude, and there were also some slight defects which were, however, promptly remedied, and she left New York early in March, reaching Hampton Roads on the night of the eighth.

Her arrival, though not as soon as anticipated, was most opportune and important. For some time the department had heard with great solicitude of the progress which the insurgents had made in armoring and equipping the large war steamer Merrimack, which had fallen into their hands when Norfolk was abandoned. On the afternoon of the 8th of March this formidable vessel, heavily armored and armed, and fully prepared to operate both as a ram and a war steamer, came down the Elizabeth river, accompanied by several smaller steamers, two of them partially armored, to attack the vessels of the blockading squadron that were in and about Hampton Roads. When the Merrimack and her attendants made their appearance, the Congress and the Cumberland, two sailing vessels, were anchored off Newport News, and the remaining vessels were in the vicinity of Fortress Monroe, some six miles distant. The Minnesota, the Roanoke, and St. Lawrence got immediately under way and proceeded towards the scene of action.

The Congress, being nearest to the Merrimack, was the first to receive her fire, which was promptly returned by a full broadside, the shots falling apparently harmlessly off from the armored side of the assailant. Passing by the Congress, the Merrimack dashed upon the Cumberland, and was received by her with a heavy, well-directed and vigorous fire, which, like that of the Congress produced unfortunately but little effect. A contest so unequal could not be of long continuance, and it was closed when the Merrimack, availing herself of her power as a steam ram, ran furiously against the Cumberland, laying open her wooden hull, and causing her almost immediately to sink. As her guns approached the water's edge, her young commander, Lieutenant Morris, and the gallant crew stood firm at their posts, delivered a parting fire, and the good ship went down heroically, with her colors flying. Having thus destroyed the Cumberland, the Merrimack turned again upon the Congress, which had, in the mean time, been engaged with the smaller rebel steamers, and after a heavy loss, in order to guard against such a fate as that which had befallen the Cumberland, had been run aground. The Merrimack now selected a raking position astern of the Congress, while one of the smaller steamers poured in a constant fire on her starboard quarter. Two other steamers of the enemy also approached from James river, firing upon the unfortunate frigate with precision and severe effect. The guns of the Congress were almost entirely disabled, and her gallant commanding officer, Lieutenant Joseph B. Smith, had fallen at his post. Her decks were strewn with the dead and dying; the ship was on fire in several places, and not a gun could be brought to bear upon the assailants. In this state of things, and with no effectual relief at hand, the senior surviving officer, Lieutenant Pendergrast, felt it his duty to save further useless destruction of life by hauling down his colors. This was done about four o'clock p. m. The Congress continued to burn till about eight in the evening, and then blew up.

From the Congress the Merrimack turned her attention to the remaining vessels of the squadron. The Roanoke had grounded on her way to the scene of the conflict; and although she succeeded in getting off, her condition was such—her propeller being useless—that she took no part in the action. The St. Lawrence also grounded near the Minnesota, and had a short engagement with the Merrimack, but suffered no serious injury, and, on getting afloat, was ordered back to Fortress Monroe.

The Minnesota, which had also got aground in the shallow waters of the channel, became the special object of attack, and the Merrimack, with the Yorktown and Jamestown, bore down upon her. The Merrimack drew too much water to approach very near; her fire was not therefore particularly effective. The other steamers selected their position, fired with much accuracy, and caused considerable damage to the Minnesota. She soon, however, succeeded in getting a gun to bear on the two smaller steamers, and drove them away—one, apparently, in a crippled condition. About seven p. m. the Merrimack also hauled off, and the three stood towards Norfolk.

All efforts to get the Minnesota afloat during the night, and into a safe position, were totally unavailing. The morning was looked for with deep anxiety, as it would, in all probability, bring a renewed attack from the formidable assailant. At this critical and anxious moment the Monitor, one of the newly finished armored vessels, came into Hampton Roads, from New York, under the command of Lieutenant John L. Worden, and a little after midnight anchored alongside the Minnesota. At six o'clock the next morning the Merrimack, as anticipated, again made her appearance and opened her fire upon the Minnesota. Promptly obeying the signal to attack, the Monitor ran down past the Minnesota and laid herself close alongside the Merrimack, between that formidable vessel and the Minnesota. The fierce conflict between these two iron-clads lasted for several hours. It was, in appearance, an unequal conflict; for the Merrimack was a large and noble structure, and the Monitor was, in comparison, almost diminutive. But the Monitor was strong in her armor, in the ingenious novelty of her construction, in the large calibre of her two guns, and the valor and skill with which she was handled. After several hours' fighting the Merrimack found herself overmatched, and, leaving the Monitor, sought to renew the attack on the Minnesota; but the Monitor again placed herself between the two vessels, and re-opened her fire upon her adversary. At noon the Merrimack, seriously damaged, abandoned the contest, and, with her companions, retreated towards Norfolk.

Thus terminated the most remarkable naval combat of modern times, perhaps of any age. The fiercest and most formidable naval assault upon the power of the Union which has ever been made by the insurgents was heroically repelled, and a new era was opened in the history of maritime warfare.

Before the occurrence of these events, entertaining a conviction that at least one of the models of iron-clad vessels—that of the Monitor, an original invention of John Ericsson, of New York—would prove a successful experiment, and that it was particularly adapted to our harbor and coast defence, and service on the shallow waters of our seabord, I estimated, in my annual report, last December, for the immediate construction of twenty iron-clad steamers. The House of Representatives promptly responded to this recommendation, and passed a bill "authorizing and empowering the Secretary of the Navy to cause to be constructed, by contract or otherwise, as he shall deem best for the public interest, not exceeding twenty-one iron-clad steam gunboats." The Senate delayed action on this bill until February, when, foreseeing that the country would suffer from longer inaction, I addressed the chairman of the Naval Committee of the Senate on the subject, and the result was the immediate passage of the bill which had originated in the House in December.

At the earliest practicable moment after the enactment of this law the department commenced entering into contracts for the construction of armored vessels, most of them on the plan of the Monitor.

The Galena, a less formidable vessel, was for some time under fire from plunging shot at Drury's Bluff, on James river. As yet the Ironsides, recently completed, has not been tested in action, but it is believed she will prove a formidable fighting vessel. That we might be prepared for extraordinary emergencies, it was deemed advisable to put armature on one of our steam frigates, and the Roanoke was selected for that purpose.

Whatever success may attend the large and costly armored ships of the Warrior class, which are being constructed by some of the maritime powers of Europe cruising in deep waters, they can scarcely cause alarm here, for we have within the United States few harbors that are accessible to them, and for those few the government can always be prepared whenever a foreign war is imminent. It has been deemed advisable, however, that we should have a few large-sized armed cruisers, of great speed, for ocean service, as well as of the class of smaller vessels for coastwise and defensive operations.

In the construction of iron-clads of the Monitor class, the nautical qualities of the vessel have not been the governing object, for with light draught and heavy armament, high speed is not attainable. But they are adapted to the shallow waters of our coast and harbors, few of which are accessible to vessels of great magnitude. While the larger armored vessels, with their heavy armament, cannot nearly approach our shores, those of the Monitor class can penetrate even the inner waters, rivers, harbors, and bayous of our extended double coast.

From the report of the Secretary of the Navy, December 7, 1863.

In the responsible task of applying to naval vessels and naval armament the principles which modern invention and improvement have developed, the department has been compelled to pursue a path hitherto, to a great extent, unexplored. The Monitor class of armored ships, with revolving turrets and few guns of heavy calibre, has proved itself to be well adapted for harbor defence and coast service, and in some emergencies these vessels, from their great powers of endurance, have shown themselves to be efficient and serviceable in offensive operations. This form and description of vessel, which originated in the inventive genius of Captain John Ericsson, will perform not only all that should be expected of them to make our harbors secure, but, when of enlarged capacity, may supersede ships of higher pretensions. To maintain our rightful maritime position, and for predominance upon the ocean, vessels of greater size than any turreted vessel yet completed may be essential. Not only must they carry guns of a heavier calibre than have heretofore been used at sea, but in order to make long cruises, and to cope successfully with any force, these vessels must have all possible strength, endurance, and speed. Their structure must, therefore, afford space enough for full sailing power, and for the most powerful steam machinery, and the large supplies of fuel needful to keep it at work. Being, unlike the other great maritime nations, without distant colonies, where coal depots can be established on the shore of almost every sea, we must conform to the necessities of our condition, and build ships with capacity enough to take on board fuel sufficient for a long cruise. The space for other supplies, for munitions of war, and for the accommodation of officers and crews, should also be ample, and, in addition to this, each of these vessels must, in order to accomplish its work, present in its construction, armor, armament and propulsion, all the power that the resources of modern invention and mechanical science and art can furnish for attack, resistance, and pursuit. A vessel of this description must, of course, cost a large price. But then a wise statesmanship will not fail to perceive that the possession of even a very few such unconquerable ships must, while vastly augmenting the force and renown of our navy, afford us, at the same time, an inestimable guarantee of peace with foreign nations; nor, in counting the cost of such floating structures, can we forget that, large as that cost may be, it yet sinks into insignificance in contrast with the expenditures and sacrifices of a single year, or even a month of foreign war.

The strength and durability of wooden vessels are in some respects inferior to those made of iron, and consequently they are less capable of sustaining the heaviest armament, and when they are plated with iron the disparity is increased. Consequently large ships-of-war, by which maritime supremacy is to be achieved and maintained, will, in all probability, be ultimately constructed chiefly of iron. The comparative advantages and disadvantages of iron and wood as the material to be used in the construction of vessels are obvious and practical. Among the considerations in favor of iron-clad vessels with hulls of wood are the rapidity with which they can be built, the abundance of material on our whole coast, and the facility with which workmen can be procured. Such vessels, moreover, can be coppered, and thereby retain their speed for a longer period. They will be less affected by a solid shot below the armature or plating, and the fracture made by the shot can be more easily mended. The disadvantages of wooden vessels are want of strength, as compared with those of iron structure, and the more rapid decay of the material, particularly when covered with iron plating; the action of the immersed iron armor on the copper sheathing near it, causing the copper to become foul and the immersed armor plates to waste; the difficulty of keeping the vessels tight under the armor plates, and the probably greater damage to which they are exposed from shells. On the other hand, the greater strength of iron permits the construction of ships of greater size and finer lines; and having greater internal capacity, they can be at any time inspected in all their parts, are safe from fire, and are better protected from great leaks, as they can have water-tight compartments; their repairs can generally be more easily made, and, from their great durability, they are probably in the end not more costly. An iron vessel, moreover, can be taken from the water and placed on land for preservation, which cannot be done with wooden vessels. The disadvantages of iron vessels are the serious local weakness of the thin plates composing the bottom of an iron ship; the danger that would result from getting on rocks or submerged obstructions; their liability to rapidly become foul in salt water, whereby their speed becomes greatly impaired, thus requiring to be frequently docked for cleaning; the great danger from a shot striking below the armor plating as they roll; the injury caused by the splinters of iron when the plates are broken or smashed by shot; the corrosion inside from bilge-water; the difficulty in making temporary repairs of shot holes; and the limited number of artisans yet to be procured having skill in this description of employment. It should also be borne in mind that, while we have several navy yards for building wooden vessels, the government possesses not a single yard and establishment for constructing those of iron, nor even for making plates and shafting.

While the principal attention of the department has, in this crisis of our affairs, been necessarily given to present and more pressing necessities, it has, nevertheless, kept in view the important end of establishing our naval power on a permanent basis. Proposals were issued for an iron-clad ship of the largest class, (under the authority contained in the appropriation bills,) but the cost, as shown by the propositions received for a ship of the necessary magnitude, was so great that it was deemed advisable to enter into no contract involving so large an expenditure, except by the express sanction of Congress.

In order, however, that justice should, in some degree, be done to the naval branch of the public service, and that it might be able to sustain its rightful position upon the ocean in the event of a foreign war, the parties competing for the large steamers were invited to make proposals for one of about half the proposed tonnage. One offer made under this invitation, at the most reasonable rate that could be obtained, and which it was deemed the interest of the government not to exceed, was, with some modifications, accepted.

There are no parties in this country fully prepared to build iron vessels of the magnitude and description proposed, and the present high prices of material and labor unavoidably enhance the cost. The government itself is unprepared to execute any such work, having no suitable yard and establishment, and is consequently wholly in the hands of private parties, to demand what they think proper, and prescribe their own terms. On former and repeated occasions, and elsewhere in this report, the department has fully expressed its opinion of this policy and the necessity why the government should be prepared to build iron vessels, and the necessary machinery, of the largest class.

Ericsson's inception of Monitor vessels.

NEW YORK, *June* 28, 1862.

SIR: I have the honor to transmit herewith copies of plans and specifications of an impregnable battery and revolving cupola constructed by me and presented to his Majesty Emperor Napoleon III in the year 1854.

Several members of the English government and prominent members of Parliament have recently stated in Parliament that the revolving cupola is the invention of Captain Cowper Coles, Royal Navy. These gentlemen base on this supposed fact a claim that the principle upon which the United States gunboat Monitor is constructed emanates from an English officer.

Public documents show that in the year 1855 Captain Coles proposed to the admiralty a "raft," with a *stationary* shield for protecting the guns, and that shortly after Captain Coles obtained the assistance of persons in the office of the celebrated engineer, E. K. Brunel, to make plans of said raft. Published statements further show that Captain Coles, in 1859, proposed a *revolving* cupola. Blackwood's Magazine for December, 1860, contains an engraving of this revolving cupola, with the mechanism for turning it by hand.

I need not point out the groundlessness of the claim set up by the English government that Captain Coles is the inventor of the revolving cupola which forms so important a feature of the structure of the United States gunboat Monitor.

I respectfully suggest that you order the enclosed documents to be kept on record in your department as a reference in future.

I am, sir, respectfully, your obedient servant,

J. ERICSSON.

Hon. GIDEON WELLES,
Secretary of the Navy, Washington, D. C.

The following is an extract of a communication forwarded from the city of New York to Emperor Napoleon III at Paris by J. Ericsson, on the 26th of September, 1854. The receipt of said communication was at once acknowledged by his Majesty:

[Extract.]

"*New system of naval attack.*—The vessel to be composed entirely of iron. The midship section is triangular, with a broad, hollow keel, loaded to balance the heavy upper works. The ends of the vessel are moderately sharp. The deck, made of plate iron, is curved both longitudinally and transversely, with a spring of five feet; it is made to project eight feet over the rudder and propeller. The entire deck is covered with a lining of sheet iron three inches thick, with an opening in the centre sixteen feet diameter. This opening is covered by a semi-globular turret of plate iron, six inches thick, revolving on a column and pivot by means of steam power and appropriate gear work. The vessel is propelled by a powerful steam-engine and screw-propeller. Air for the combustion in the boilers and for ventilation within the vessel is supplied by a large self-acting centrifugal blower, the fresh air being drawn in through numerous small holes in the turret. The products of the combustion and impure air from the vessel is forced through conductors leading to the cluster of small holes in the deck and turret. Surrounding objects are viewed through small holes at appropriate places. Reflecting telescopes, capable of being protruded or withdrawn at pleasure, also afford a distinct view of surrounding objects. The rudder stock passes through a water-tight stuffing-box, so as to admit of the helm being worked within the vessel. Shot striking the deck are deflected, whilst shell exploding on it prove harmless. Shot (of cast iron) striking the globular turret will crumble to pieces or are deflected.

"This new system of naval attack will place an entire fleet of sailing ships during calms and light winds at the mercy of a single craft. 'Boarding,' as a means of defence, will be impracticable, since the turret guns, which turn like the spokes in a wheel, commanding every point of the compass at once, may keep off and destroy any number of boats by firing slugs and combustibles.

"A fleet at anchor might be fired and put in a sinking condition before enabled to get under way. Of what avail would be the 'steam guard-ships' if attacked on the new system? Alas! for the 'wooden walls' that formerly 'ruled the waves.' The long-range Lancaster gun would scarcely hit the revolving iron turret once in six hours, and then, six chances to one, its shot or shell would be deflected by the varying angles of the face of the impregnable globe. When ultimately struck at right angles, the globe, which weighs upwards of forty tons, will be less affected by the shot than a heavy anvil by the blow of a light hammer. Consequently the shot would crumble to pieces, whilst the shell would strew the arched deck with harmless fragments.

"During contest the revolving turret should be kept in motion, the port-holes being turned away from the opponent, except at the moment of discharge, which, however, should be made during full rotation, as the lateral aim in close quarters requires but little precision."

Letter from Mr. Ericsson relative to contract for Monitor.

NEW YORK, *April* 25, 1862.

SIR: In your remarks on the administration of the Navy Department in to-day's Herald you have inadvertently done the Secretary of the Navy great injustice relative to the construction of the Monitor. A more prompt and spirited action is probably not on record in a similar case than that of the Navy Department as regards the Monitor. The committee of naval commanders, appointed by the Secretary to decide on the plans of gunboats laid before the department, occupied me less than two hours in explaining my new system. In about two hours more the committee had come to a decision. After their favorable report had been to the Secretary, I was called into his office, where I was detained less than five minutes. In order not to lose any time, the Secretary ordered me to "go ahead at once." Consequently, while the clerks of the department were engaged in drawing up the formal contract, the iron which now forms the keel plate of the Monitor was drawn through the rolling mill.

I am, respectfully, your obedient servant,

J. ERICSSON.

JAMES GORDON BENNETT, Esq.

NORTH ATLANTIC SQUADRON.

Arrival of the Monitor at Hampton Roads.

UNITED STATES STEAMER MONITOR,
Hampton Roads, March 8, 1862.

SIR: I have the honor to report that I arrived at this anchorage at 9 o'clock this evening, and am ordered to proceed immediately to the assistance of the Minnesota, aground near Newport News.

Respectfully, your obedient servant,

JOHN L. WORDEN,
Lieutenant Commanding.

Hon. GIDEON WELLES,
Secretary of the Navy.

Assistant Secretary Fox's telegram of the action at Hampton Roads.

FORTRESS MONROE, *March* 9, 1862.

The Monitor arrived at 10 p. m. last night and went immediately to the protection of the Minnesota, lying aground just below Newport News. At 7 a. m. to-day the Merrimack, accompanied by two wooden steamers and several tugs, stood out towards the Minnesota and opened fire. The Monitor met them at once and opened her fire, when all the enemy's vessels retired excepting the Merrimack. These two iron-clads fought, part of the time touching each other, from 8 a. m. to noon, when the Merrimack retired. Whether she is injured or not it is impossible to say. Lieutenant J. L. Worden, who commanded the Monitor, handled her with great skill, and was assisted by Chief Engineer Stimers. Lieutenant Worden was injured by the cement from the pilot-house being driven into his eyes, but I trust not seriously. The Minnesota kept up a continuous fire and is herself somewhat injured. She was moved considerably to-day, and will probably be off to-night. The Monitor is uninjured, and ready at any moment to repel another attack.

G. V. FOX,
Assistant Secretary.

Hon. GIDEON WELLES,
Secretary of the Navy.

Assistant Secretary G. V. Fox's telegram to General McClellan relative to the fight in Hampton Roads.

FORT MONROE, VA., *March* 9, 1862.

Your telegram to Major General Wool received. The performance of the Monitor to-day against the Merrimack shows a slight superiority in favor of the Monitor, as the Merrimack was forced to retreat to Norfolk after a four hour's engagement, at times the vessels touching each other. The damage to the Merrimack cannot be ascertained. She retreated under steam without assistance. The Monitor is all ready for her to-morrow, but I think the Merrimack may be obliged to lay up for a few days. She is an ugly customer, and it is too good luck to believe we are yet clear of her. Our hopes are upon the Monitor, and this day's work shows that the Merrimack must attend to her alone. Have ordered the large frigates to leave.

G. V. FOX,
Assistant Secretary.

Major General McCLELLAN,
Washington, D. C.

Major General Wool's telegram relative to condition of affairs in Hampton Roads.

FORT MONROE, VA., *March* 8, 1862.

The Merrimack came down from Norfolk to-day, and about two o'clock attacked the Cumberland and Congress. She sunk the Cumberland, and the Congress surrendered. The Minnesota is aground and attacked by the Jamestown, Yorktown, and Merrimack. The St. Lawrence just arrived and is going to assist. The Minnesota is aground. Probably both will be taken; that is the opinion of Captain Marston and his officers. The Roanoke is under our guns. It is thought the Merrimack, Jamestown, and Yorktown will pass the fort to-night.

JOHN E. WOOL,
Major General.

Hon. E. M. STANTON,
Secretary of War.

The President directs that the Monitor shall not go unattended to Norfolk.

NAVY DEPARTMENT, *March* 10, 1862.

It is directed by the President that the Monitor be not too much exposed, and that in no event shall any attempt be made to proceed with her unattended to Norfolk. If vessels can be procured and loaded with stone and sunk in the channel, it is important that it should be done. The San Jacinto and Dakota have sailed from Boston to Hampton Roads, and the Sabine in tow of Baltic and a tug, from New York. Gunboats will be ordered forthwith. Would it not be well to detain the Minnesota until other vessels arrive?

GIDEON WELLES.

Captain G. V. Fox,
Assistant Secretary of the Navy, Fortress Monroe.

Captain John Marston's report of the Merrimack's attack and the arrival of the Monitor.

UNITED STATES STEAMER ROANOKE,
Hampton Roads, March 9, 1862.

SIR: I have the honor to inform you that yesterday at one o'clock one of the lookout vessels reported, by signals, that the enemy was coming out. I immediately ordered the Minnesota to get under way, and, as soon as the two tugs appointed to tow this ship came alongside, I slipped our cable. The Merrimack was soon discovered passing out by Sewall's Point, standing up towards Newport News, accompanied by several small gunboats. Every exertion was made by us to get all the speed on the Roanoke that the two tugs were capable of giving her; but, in consequence of our bad steerage, we did not get ahead as rapidly as we desired to. The Merrimack went up and immediately attacked the Congress and Cumberland, but particularly the latter ship, which was hid from us by the land. When about seven or eight miles from Fortress Monroe the Minnesota grounded. We continued to stand on, and when we came in sight of the Cumberland we saw that she had careened over, apparently full of water. The enemy, who had been joined by two or three steamers from the James river, now devoted themselves exclusively to the Congress, but she being aground could bring but five guns to bear on them, and at ten minutes before four o'clock we had the mortification of seeing her haul down her flag. I continued to stand on until we found ourselves in three and a half fathoms of water and were on the ground astern. Finding that we could go no further, I ordered one of the tugs to tow us round, and as soon as the Roanoke's head was pointed down the bay and I found she was afloat again, I directed the tugs to go to the assistance of the Minnesota, under the hope that, with the assistance of the two others which had accompanied her, they would be able to get her off, but up to the time that I now write they have not succeeded in doing so. At five o'clock the frigate St. Lawrence, in tow of the Cambridge, passed us, and not long after she also grounded, but by the aid of the Cambridge she was got afloat again, and being unable to render any assistance to the Minnesota, came down the harbor. In passing the batteries at Sewall's Point, both going and returning, the rebels opened fire on us, which was returned from our pivot guns, but the range was too great for them, while the enemy's shot fell far beyond us. One shot went through our foresails, cutting away two of our shrouds, and several shell burst over and near the ship, scattering their fragments on the deck. Between seven and eight o'clock we discovered that the rebels had set fire to the Congress, and she continued to burn till one o'clock, when she blew up. This was a melancholy satisfaction to me, for as she had fallen into the hands of the enemy, it was far better to have her destroyed than she should be employed against us at some future day. It was the impression of some of my officers that the rebels hoisted the French flag, but I could not make it out. At eight o'clock I heard that the Monitor had arrived, and soon after Lieutenant Commanding Worden came on board, and I immediately ordered him to go up to the Minnesota, hoping she would be able to keep off an attack on the Minnesota till we had got her afloat again. This morning the Merrimack renewed the attack on the Minnesota, but she found, no doubt greatly to her surprise, a new opponent in the Monitor. The contest has been going on during most of the day between these two armored vessels, and most beautifully has the little Monitor sustained herself, showing herself capable of great endurance. I have not received any official accounts of the loss of the Congress and Cumberland, but no doubt shall do so, when it will be transmitted to you.

I should do injustice to this military department did I not inform you that every assistance was freely tendered to us, sending five of their tugs to the relief of the Minnesota, and offering all the aid in their power. I would also beg leave to say that Captain Poor, of the ordnance department, kindly volunteered to do duty temporarily on board this ship, and from whom I have received much assistance. I did hope to get this off by this day's mail, but I have been so constantly employed that I fear I shall not do so.

I am, very respectfully, your obedient servant,

JOHN MARSTON,
Captain and Senior Officer.

Hon. GIDEON WELLES,
Secretary of the Navy.

Captain Van Brunt's account of the Minnesota's engagement with the Merrimack.

UNITED STATES STEAMER MINNESOTA,
March 10, 1862.

SIR: On Saturday, the 8th instant, at 12.45 p. m., three small steamers, in appearance, were discovered rounding Sewall's Point, and as soon as they came into full broadside view I was convinced that one was the iron-plated steam battery Merrimack, from the large size of her smoke-pipe. They were heading for Newport News, and I, in obedience to a signal from the senior officer present, Captain J. Marston, immediately called all hands, slipped my cables, and got under way for that point to engage her. While rapidly passing Sewall's Point, the rebels there opened fire upon us from a rifle battery, one shot from which going through and crippling my mainmast. I returned the fire with my broadside guns and forecastle pivot. We ran without further difficulty within about one and a half mile of Newport News, and there, unfortunately, grounded. The tide was running ebb, and although in the channel, there was not sufficient water for this ship, which draws 23 feet. I knew that the bottom was soft and lumpy, and endeavored to force the ship over, but I found it impossible to do so. At this time it was reported to me that the Merrimack had passed the frigate Congress and ran into the sloop-of-war Cumberland, and in fifteen minutes after I saw the latter going down by the head. The Merrimack then hauled off, taking a position, and about 2.30 p. m. engaged the Congress, throwing shot and shell into her with terrific effect, while the shot from the Congress glanced from her iron-plated sloping sides without doing any apparent damage. At 3.30 p. m the Congress was compelled to haul down her colors. Of the extent of her loss and injury you will be informed from the official report.

At four p. m. the Merrimack, Jamestown, and Patrick Henry bore down upon my vessel. Very fortunately, the iron battery drew too much water to come within a mile of us. She took a position on my starboard bow, but did not fire with accuracy, and only one shot passed through the ship's bow. The other two steamers took their position on my port bow and stern, and their fire did most damage in killing and wounding men, inasmuch as they fired with rifled guns; but with the heavy gun that I could bring to bear upon them I drove them off, one of them apparently in a crippled condition. I fired upon the Merrimack with my pivot 10-inch gun without apparent effect, and at seven p. m. she too hauled off, and all three vessels steamed toward Norfolk.

The tremendous firing of my broadside guns had crowded me further upon the mud bank, into which the ship seemed to have made for herself a cradle. From ten p. m., when the tide commenced to run flood, until four a. m. I had all hands at work with steam-tugs and hawsers, endeavoring to haul the ship off the bank, but without avail; and as the tide had then fallen considerably, I suspended further operations at that time. At two a. m. the iron battery Monitor, Commander John L. Worden, which had arrived the previous evening at Hampton Roads, came alongside and reported for duty, and then all on board felt that we had a friend that would stand by us in our hour of trial.

At six a. m. the enemy again appeared, coming down from Craney island, and I beat to quarters, but they ran past my ship and were heading for Fortress Monroe, and the retreat was beaten to allow my men to get something to eat. The Merrimack ran down near to the Rip-Raps, and then turned into the channel through which I had come. Again all hands were called to quarters, and when she approached within a mile of us I opened upon her with my stern guns, and made signal to the Monitor to attack the enemy. She immediately run down in my wake, right within range of the Merrimack, completely covering my ship as far as was possible with her diminutive dimensions, and, much to my astonishment, laid herself right alongside of the Merrimack, and the contrast was that of a pigmy to a giant. Gun after gun was fired by the Monitor, which was returned with whole broadsides from the rebels, with no more effect, apparently, than so many pebble stones thrown by a child. After a while they commenced manœuvring, and we could see the little battery point her bow for the rebels, with the intention, as I thought, of sending a shot through her bow port-hole; then she would shoot by her, and rake her through the stern. In the mean time the rebels were pouring in broadside after broadside, but almost all her shot flew over the little submerged propeller, and when they struck the bomb-proof tower, the shot glanced off without producing any effect, clearly establishing the fact that wooden vessels cannot contend with iron-clad ones; for never before was anything like it dreamed of by the greatest enthusiast in maritime warfare.

The Merrimack, finding that she could make nothing of the Monitor, turned her attention once more to me. In the morning she had put an 11-inch shot under my counter, near the water line; and now, on her second approach, I opened upon her with all my broadside guns and 10-inch pivot—a broadside which would have blown out of water any timber-built ship in the world. She returned my fire with her rifled bow gun, with a shell which passed through the chief engineer's state-room, through the engineers' mess-room, amidships, and burst in the boatswain's room, tearing four rooms all into one in its passage, and exploding two charges of powder, which set the ship on fire, but it was promptly extinguished by a party headed by my first lieutenant. Her second shell went through the boiler of the tug-boat Dragon, exploding it, and causing some consternation on board my ship for the moment, until the matter was explained. This time I had concentrated upon her an incessant fire from my gun deck, spar deck, and forecastle pivot guns, and was informed by my marine officer, who was stationed on the poop, that at least fifty solid shot struck her on her slanting side without producing any apparent effect. By the time she had fired her third shell the little Monitor had come down upon her, placing herself between us, and compelled her to change her position, in doing which she grounded; and again I poured into her all the guns which could be brought to bear upon her. As soon as she got off she stood down the bay, the little battery chasing her with all speed, when suddenly the Merrimack turned around and run full speed into her antagonist. For a moment I was anxious; but instantly I saw a shot plunge into the iron roof of the Merrimack, which surely must have damaged her. For some time after this the rebels concentrated their whole battery upon the tower and pilot-house of the Monitor, and soon after the latter stood down for Fortress Monroe, and we thought it probable she had exhausted her supply of ammunition, or sustained some injury. Soon after the Merrimack and the two other steamers headed for my ship, and I then felt to the fullest extent my condition. I was hard and immovably aground, and they could take position under my stern and rake me. I had expended most of my solid shot, my ship was badly crippled, and my officers and men were worn out with fatigue, but even in this extreme dilemma I determined never to give up the ship to the rebels, and, after consulting with my officers, I ordered every preparation to be made to destroy the ship after all hope was gone of saving her.

On ascending the poop deck, I observed that the enemy's vessels had changed their course and were heading for Craney island. I then determined to lighten the ship by throwing overboard my 8-inch guns, hoisting out provision, starting water, &c. At 2 p. m. I proceeded to make another attempt to save the ship by the use of a number of powerful tugs and the steamer S. R. Spaulding kindly sent to my assistance by Captain Talmadge, quartermaster at Fortress Monroe, and succeeded in dragging her half a mile distant, and then she was immovable, the tide having fallen. At 2 o'clock this morning I succeeded in getting the ship once more afloat, and am now at anchor opposite Fortress Monroe.

It gives me great pleasure to say that during the whole of these trying scenes the officers and men conducted themselves with great courage and coolness.

I have the honor to be your very obedient servant,

G. J. VAN BRUNT,
Captain U. S. Navy, Commanding Frigate Minnesota.

Hon. GIDEON WELLES,
Secretary of the Navy.

Captain Purviance's report of the Merrimack's attack.

UNITED STATES FRIGATE ST. LAWRENCE,
Hampton Roads, March 10, 1862.

SIR: I have the honor to report the arrival of this ship on the 6th instant, in Lynnhaven bay, from New York. After anchoring, a strong gale from the northwest commenced, and continued through the night and following day. On Saturday the wind abated, and, while waiting for wind and tide, the United States gunboat Cambridge came alongside and reported that the rebel steam-ram Merrimack, and some side-wheel steamers were engaging the frigate Congress and Cumberland at Newport News. At half-past 2 we got under way in tow of the Cambridge, and when abreast of the rebel battery at Sewall's Point, the battery opened fire, one of the shells exploding under the forepart of the St. Lawrence, doing, however, no material injury. The fire was returned, and, it is believed, with some effect. The Cumberland had, at this time, gone down, having been run into by the Merrimack, and the Congress had surrendered, after a terrible slaughter of her men, and when rendered perfectly powerless by the fire of the rebels. The Minnesota was aground, and was engaging the enemy, whose force consisted of the rebel steam-ram and four or five side-weel gunboats. When near the Minnesota, the St. Lawrence grounded, and at that time opened fire, but her shot did no execution, the armor of the Merrimack proving invulnerable to her comparatively feeble projectiles. Taking advantage of these portentous circumstances, the Merrimack directed her attention to firing several projectiles of formidable dimensions; one of which, an 80-pound shell, penetrated the starboard quarter about four inches above the water-line, passed through the pantry of the ward-room, and into the state-room of the assistant surgeon, on the port side, completely demolishing the bulkhead; then struck against a strong iron bar, which secured the bull's-eye of the port, and returned into the ward-room expended. It fortunately did not explode, and no person was injured. The damage done by this one shot proved the power of the projectiles which she employed, and readily explained the destruction of our wooden and antiquated frigates.

Our position at this time was one of some anxiety. Being aground, the tug Young America came alongside and got us off; after which a powerful broadside from the spar and gun decks of the St. Lawrence, then distant about half a mile, thrown into the Merrimack, induced her to withdraw; whether from nedessity or discretion is not known: certainly no serious damage could have been done. After which we proceeded slowly to the anchorage, which we reached about — p. m.

The Merrimack again appeared the following morning, and sustained, for several hours, the consolidated fire of the Minnesota and Monitor, abandoning the conflict finally, but apparently unharmed. The Minnesota remained aground during the night, was supplied with additional ammunition, and in the morning, when attacked by the Merrimack, fought her guns with an energy, skill, and indomitable perseverance worthy of the noble and patriotic cause she was defending. Unable to move, she was forced to present her full broadside to the enemy, who remained at long range, offering the smallest possible surface to her antagonist. The Monitor, whose performance more than equalled the highest expectations, contributed most powerfully to the withdrawal of the Merrimack; and her earlier arrival would have prevented the unfortunate loss of our two defenceless frigates. All the officers and crew zealously and efficiently performed their duties.

Very respectfully, your obedient servant,

H. Y. PURVIANCE, *Captain.*

Hon. GIDEON WELLES,
Secretary of the Navy.

Chief Engineer Stimer's report.

IRON-CLAD MONITOR,
Hampton Roads, March 9, 1862.

MY DEAR SIR: After a stormy passage, which proved us to be the finest sea boat I was ever in, we fought the Merrimack for more than three hours this forenoon, and sent her back to Norfolk in a sinking condition. Iron-clad against iron-clad. We manœuvred about the bay here and went at each other with mutual fierceness. I consider that both ships were well fought; we were struck twenty-two times—pilot-house twice, turret nine times, side-armor eight times, deck three times. The only vulnerable point was the pilot-house. One of your great logs (9 by 12 inches thick) is broken in two. The shot struck just outside of where the captain had his eye, and it has disabled him by destroying his left eye and temporarily blinding the other. The log is not quite in two, but is broken and pressed inwards one and a half inch. She tried to run us down and sink us, as she did the Cumberland yesterday, but she got the worst of it. Her bow passed over our deck and our sharp upper edged side cut through the light iron shoe upon her stem and well into her oak. She will not try that again. She gave us a tremendous thump, but did not injure us in the least. We are just able to find the point of contact.

The turret is a splendid structure. I do not think much of the shield, but the pendulums are fine things, though I cannot tell you how they would stand the shot, as they were not hit.

You are very correct in your estimate of the effect of shot upon the man on the inside of the turret when it was struck near him. Three men were knocked down, of whom I was one; the other two had to be carried below, but I was not disabled at all, and the others recovered before the battle was over. Captain Worden stationed himself at the pilot-house, Greene fired the guns, and I turned the turret until the captain was disabled and was relieved by Greene, when I managed the turret myself, Master Stodden having been one of the two stunned men.

Captain Ericsson, I congratulate you upon your great success. Thousands have this day blessed you. I have heard whole crews cheer you. Every man feels that you have saved this place to the nation by furnishing us with the means to whip an iron-clad frigate, that was, until our arrival, having it all her own way with our most powerful vessels.

I am, with much esteem, very truly yours,

ALBAN C. STIMERS,
Chief Engineer.

Captain J. Ericsson,
No. 95 *Franklin street, New York.*

Passage of the Monitor from New York to Hampton Roads.

United States Steamer Monitor,
Hampton Roads, March 27, 1862.

Sir: I received to-day your communication of the 25th instant. I do not consider this steamer a sea-going vessel. During her passage from New York her roll was very easy and slow, and not at all deep. She pitched very little and with no strain whatever. She is buoyant and not very lively. The inconveniences we experienced can be easily remedied. But she has not the steam power to go against a head wind or sea, and I think it very doubtful if she could go from here to Delaware bay by herself. As she would be unable to make headway against a sea she would not steer. Even in smooth water, and going slow, she does not mind her helm readily. At sea she would be unable to work her guns, as we are obliged to keep the ports closed and calked, they being but five feet above water. For smooth water operations, such as she was engaged in on the 9th instant, I think her a most desirable vessel. The opinion of experienced seamen on board is the same as my own.

I am, very respectfully, your obedient servant,

S. D. GREENE,
Lieutenant United States Navy.

Hon. Gideon Welles,
Secretary of the Navy, Washington, D. C.

Flag-Officer Goldsborough reports sending three vessels up James river and shelling Sewall's Point, May 8, 1862.

United States Flag-Ship Minnesota,
Hampton Roads, Va., May 9, 1862.

Sir: The Galena, Aroostook, and Port Royal (by direction of the President for me to detail the Galena and two gunboats for the purpose) went up James river early yesterday morning.

Also, by direction of the President, our vessels shelled Sewall's Point yesterday, mainly with the view of ascertaining the practicability of landing a body of troops thereabouts. The Merrimack came out, but was even more cautious than ever. The Monitor was kept well in advance, and so that the Merrimack could have engaged her without difficulty had she been so disposed, but she declined to do it, and soon returned and anchored under Sewall's Point. The Jamestown arrived here yesterday. Her condition is such that I shall have to despatch her to Philadelphia for repairs.

The Cayuga also arrived here yesterday from the Mississippi river with despatches, and left for New York in the evening. The St. Lawrence sailed this morning for Key West.

In all there are now seven of our vessels up the York river, and three of them up the James river. Could I have exercised my own judgment, I should have withdrawn some from the York river, and thus increased the number of those sent up the James.

Our vessels up the James river were no doubt engaged for several hours during yesterday, but whether with the enemy's vessels or with one of his forts on the south side of the river we have not yet ascertained. All the enemy's gunboats that were at Norfolk, eight in number, including the Jamestown and Yorktown, are up the James river, and our three vessels must be this side of them.

I am, very respectfully, your obedient servant,

L. M. GOLDSBOROUGH,
Flag-Officer, Commanding N. Atlantic Blockading Squadron.

Hon. GIDEON WELLES,
Secretary of the Navy, Washington, D. C.

[Telegram.]

Flag-Officer Goldsborough to the President of the United States.

UNITED STATES FLAG-SHIP MINNESOTA,
Hampton Roads, Va., May 9, 1862.

SIR: Agreeably to a communication just received from the Hon. Edwin M. Stanton, I have the honor to report the instructions I gave yesterday to the officers commanding the several vessels detailed to open fire upon Sewall's Point were: that the object of the move was to ascertain the practicability of landing a body of troops thereabouts, and to reduce the works if it could be done; that the wooden vessels should attack the principal works in enfilade, and that the Monitor, to be accompanied by the Stevens, should go up as far as the wreck, and there operate in front on the Merrimack's appearance outside of the wrecks.

The Monitor had orders to fall back into fair channel way and only to engage her seriously in such a position that this ship, together with the merchant vessels intended for the purpose, could run her down, if an opportunity presented itself. The other vessels were not to hesitate to run her down, and the Baltimore, an unarmed steamer of light draught, high speed, and with a curved bow, was kept in the direction of the Monitor expressly to throw herself across the Merrimack, either forward or aft of her plated house; but the Merrimack did not engage the Monitor, nor did she place herself where she could have been assailed by our ram vessels to any advantage, or where there was any prospect whatever of getting at her.

My instructions were necessarily verbal, and in giving them I supposed that I was carrying out your wishes in substance, if not to the letter. The demonstration resulted in establishing the fact that the number of guns at the principal work on Sewall's Point has been essentially reduced, and is not greater now than about seventeen, and that the number of men now stationed there is comparatively quite limited. The quarters connected with the work were set on fire by our shells, and no doubt seriously injured.

I am, very respectfully, your obedient servant,

L. M. GOLDSBOROUGH,
Com. Naval Blockading Squadron.

His Excellency the PRESIDENT *of the United States.*

Flag-Officer Goldsborough reports the destruction of the Merrimack, &c.

UNITED STATES FLAG-SHIP MINNESOTA,
Hampton Roads, Va., May 12, 1862.

SIR: In the surrender of Norfolk by its civil authorities, day before yesterday, to the forces of our army under General Wool, which landed at Willoughby's Point, nothing but the city itself was given up. Early yesterday morning I witnessed an awful explosion in the direction of Craney island, and inferred immediately that either the works on that island or the Merrimack had been blown up. A few minutes afterwards an officer from the guardship Dakota came on board and informed me that the Merrimack no longer existed, for from the Dakota they had seen her blown to pieces. Supposing from this that Craney island and all the rest of the exterior defences of Norfolk were about to be abandoned, or, if not, that they might be subdued, I immediately ordered the Monitor, Stevens, Susquehanna, Dakota, Seminole, San Jacinto, and Mount Vernon to get under way, and gave them such orders as I judged necessary in the premises. Before they could get off, however, I had despatched my aid, Lieutenant Selfridge, in a tug to proceed off Sewall's Point, and as far above as he could get with safety, in order to ascertain the real condition of things. He landed at Sewall's Point and hoisted our flag on the works, which he found had been abandoned, but the guns were not spiked. Commander Case, captain of the fleet, went on to Craney island in another tug, and there hauled down two rebel flags and hoisted our own in their places. Our ships proceeded on to Norfolk unmolested, and there the Susquehanna, Seminole, Dakota, and San Jacinto now lie, immediately off the town, and in close proximity with it.

The Monitor and Stevens have both gone up the James river, with orders from me to reduce all the works of the enemy as they go along, spike all their guns, blow up all their magazines, and then get up to Richmond, all with the least possible delay, and shell the city to a surrender.

With the above works reduced, I can keep our vessels supplied with coal, ordnance stores, provisions, &c., without difficulty.

I intended to have discharged to-day the Arago, Illinois, and Ericsson, but the President ordered me not to do it until I should be written to upon the subject from Washington, and gave me his orders why he wished those vessels to be longer detained.

I accompanied the President and Secretaries Chase and Stanton yesterday to Norfolk, on board of the Baltimore, but I did not return with the party.

In the afternoon I visited the navy yard and went all over it. It was still burning in very many places. Nearly everything is destroyed. Of the buildings the officers' quarters alone remained intact. There are a large number of iron tanks, however, apparently in perfect condition, a good deal of mast and other timber, a number of old and generally worthless guns, and considerable machinery of one kind or another. The dock gates are all destroyed, and the pier ends connected with the gates have been blown up to a partial degree, but otherwise the dock seems uninjured.

The President said to me verbally that he wished all the guns at the forts and dock-yards to be removed to Fortress Monroe, and unless he should think proper to communicate to you otherwise, I presume I am to have this work done.

On returning from Norfolk I left our naval forces there under the command of Captain Lardner, an officer in whose discretion and good sense I have great confidence. I gave him full directions as to intercourse, &c., with the shore; but I shall have to go there again to-day or to-morrow, and for several days afterwards, on matters of importance.

I am, very respectfully, your obedient servant,

L. M. GOLDSBOROUGH,

Flag-Officer, Commanding North Atlantic Blockading Squadron.

Hon. GIDEON WELLES,

Secretary of the Navy, Washington, D. C.

Flag-Officer Goldsborough encloses reports of engagement with fort on Ward's or Drury's Bluff, eight miles from Richmond.

UNITED STATES FLAG-SHIP SUSQUEHANNA,

James River, Virginia, May 18, 1862.

SIR: I have the honor to enclose herewith the reports of an engagement which took place on the 15th instant between our vessels up this river and a fort of the enemy on Ward's or Drury's Bluff, which fort is at the obstructions that have been placed in the river, and about eight miles from Richmond.

The Stevens went to Norfolk last night to carry seven of the wounded to the hospital; thence to return to Hampton Roads. The force now up this river consists of the Wachusett, Galena, Monitor, Maratanza, Aroostook, Port Royal, and the tug Dragon.

I am, very respectfully, &c.,

L. M. GOLDSBOROUGH,

Flag-Officer, Commd'g North Atlantic Blockading Squadron.

Hon. GIDEON WELLES,

Secretary of the Navy.

UNITED STATES STEAMER GALENA,

Off City Point, James River, May 16, 1862.

SIR: I have the honor to report that this vessel, the Aroostook, the Monitor, and Port Royal, with the Naugatuck, moved up the river yesterday, getting aground several times but meeting no artificial impediments until we arrived at Ward's Bluff, about eight miles from Richmond, where we encountered a heavy battery and two separate barriers, formed of piles and steamboats and sail vessels. The pilots both say that they saw the Jamestown and Yorktown among the number.

The banks of the river we found lined with rifle-pits, from which sharpshooters annoyed the men at the guns. These would hinder all removal of obstructions, unless driven away by a land force.

The Galena ran within almost six hundred yards of the battery, as near the piles as it was deemed proper to go, let go her anchor, and with a spring swung across the stream, not more than twice as wide as the ship is long. Then, at 7.45 a. m., opened fire upon the battery.

The wooden vessels, as directed, anchored about thirteen hundred yards below. The Monitor anchored near, and at 9 o'clock she passed just above the Galena, but found that her guns could not be elevated enough to reach the battery. She then dropped a little below us, and made her shots effective.

At five minutes after eleven o'clock the Galena had expended nearly all her ammunition, and I made signal to discontinue the action. We had but six Parrott charges, and not a single filled nine-inch shell. We had thirteen killed and eleven wounded.

The rifled one hundred-pound Parrot of the Naugatuck burst, half of the part abaft the trunnions going overboard. She is therefore disabled.

The Galena and Monitor can, with a supply of ammunition, silence the battery at Hardin's Bluff. The result of our experiment with the Galena I enclose. We demonstrated that she is not shot-proof. Balls came through, and many men were killed with fragments of her own iron. One fairly penetrated just above the water-line, and exploded in the steerage. The greater part of the balls, however, at the water-line, after breaking the iron, stuck in the wood. The port side is much injured—knees, planks, and timbers started. No shot penetrated the spar deck, but in three places are large holes—one of them a yard long and about eight inches wide, made by a shot which, in glancing, completely broke through the deck, killing several men with fragments of the deck plating. The Galena should be repaired before sending her to sea. I would suggest the Washington navy yard, since so many people there have an interest in iron plating, and she so well shows the effect of various shot. No gun is disabled, but we need ammunition.

On James river an army can be landed within ten miles of Richmond, on either bank. We command City Point, and are ready to co-operate with a land force in an advance upon Petersburg. In going up James river, above this point, it will be desirable to protect the crew from sharpshooters upon the river. They annoyed us. To command important points, and to prevent the reoccupation of old Fort Powhatan, at Hood's, more vessels are needed. Some should continually pass up and down the river, to prevent the erection of new batteries.

I cannot too highly commend the cool courage of the officers and crew. Lieutenant Newman, the executive officer, was conspicuous for his gallant and effective services. Mr. Washburne, acting master, behaved admirably. These are selected from among the number.

The Aroostook, Port Royal, and Naugatuck took the stations previously assigned them, and did everything that was possible. The Monitor could not have done better.

The barrier is such that vessels of the enemy, even if they had any, probably cannot pass out; ours cannot pass in.

I have the honor to be your obedient servant,

JOHN RODGERS,
Commander United States Navy.

Flag-Officer L. M. GOLDSBOROUGH,
Commanding North Atlantic Blockading Squadron.

UNITED STATES STEAMER GALENA,
Off City Point, James River, May 16, 1862.

SIR: In obedience to your order of this day, I have the honor to submit the following report of the condition of this ship's hull:

On the port side her bulwarks, between ports Nos. 5 and 6, are started in about an inch, and the timbers broken. Thirteen shot and shell have perforated her side, splintering considerably. Forward of No. 1 port the bulwarks are badly shattered. Several hanging knees are started off from side and spar deck beams; many seams are opened in the side, and the gun deck, beneath the guns, will require calking.

In forward room of wardroom the hanging knee is started about 2½ inches, and the side injured. In forward part of steerage a shell perforated the side and started the hanging knee about two inches. In after room a diagonal knee is slightly started, and the air port stove in. In the coal bunkers the side is also injured.

On spar deck several glancing shot have made indentations in the iron plates and broken deck planks; in two instances apertures, about 18 inches by 4 inches, have been made. The hammock netting is shattered; the wheel is injured, one boat davit gone, and several awning and rail stanchions. The armor is started from the stem, also at the junction of the bars on the stem, and on the starboard quarter, near port No. 8.

Respectfully, your obedient servant,

L. H. NEWMAN,
Executive Officer.

Commander JOHN RODGERS,
Commanding United States naval forces in James River.

UNITED STATES IRON-CLAD STEAMER MONITOR,
James River, Virginia, May 16, 1862.

SIR: I submit the following report of the movements of this vessel during the action of yesterday:

Shortly after weighing anchor from our position near Kingsland creek, a sharp fire of musketry was commenced from both banks on all the ships.

At half past seven I discovered an extensive fortification on an elevation of about two hundred feet, with several smaller batteries, all apparently mounting guns of the heaviest calibre; at the foot of the bluff in the river an obstruction, formed of sunken steamers and vessels, secured with chains, and the shallow water piled across the river.

The Galena, having anchored at about one thousand yards from the fort, and being warmly engaged, I endeavored to pass ahead of her to take off some of the fire, but found that my guns could not be elevated sufficiently to point at the fort. I then took position on the line with the Galena, and maintained a deliberate fire until the close of the action, when, in company with the other vessels, I dropped down to the anchorage of the morning.

The fire of the enemy was remarkably well directed, but vainly, towards this vessel. She was struck three times—one solid 8-inch shot square on the turret, two solid shot on the side armor forward of the pilot-house. Neither caused any damage beyond bending the plates. I am happy to report no casualties.

In conclusion, permit me to say that the action was most gallantly fought against great odds, and with the usual effect against earthworks. So long as our vessels kept up a rapid fire they rarely fired in return, but the moment our fire slackened they remanned their guns. It was impossible to reduce such works, except with the aid of a land force.

Very respectfully, your obedient servant,

WILLIAM N. JEFFERS,
Lieutenant Commanding.

Commander JOHN RODGERS,
Commanding James River Flotilla.

Lieutenant Commander Jeffers's report relative to the Monitor.

UNITED STATES IRON-CLAD STEAMER MONITOR,
James River, May 22, 1862.

SIR: I have hitherto refrained from making any official report relative to this vessel, as most of her prominent defects have been pointed out to or discovered by Chief Engineer Stimers, the government inspector, and provided for in the contract for the new ones; nor did I consider it expedient, in our then state of constant readiness for a naval battle, to supply information which, by some accident, becoming known to the enemy, might be used to our detriment. Other points have lately developed themselves.

Immediately on taking the command it struck me that the commander could have very little control of his guns if in the pilot-house, and that the revolution of the turret would not allow the officer pointing to see the object to be fired at, unless previously notified when this object was nearly in the line of fire.

The firing at Sewall's Point, on the 9th instant, clearly demonstrated this fact. It was impossible, from the smoke, to see from the pilot-house the effect of the shot, so as to correct the subsequent aim; and the process of turning the turret successively backward and forward, searching for the object through the small aperture of the ports, was so slow, that an active enemy with a large number of guns must inevitably fire into the ports during the operation.

After I took my station on top of the turret I roughly sighted by the lines of parallel plates, greatly increasing the rapidity and accuracy of fire; but to do this, independent of the exposure of so important a person as the commander, there was a constant danger of shells passing through the opening in which I stood, and, by exploding within the turret, producing the greatest danger and demoralization.

At the fight at Drew's Bluff, on the James river, this inconvenience became still more evident. The river being lined with riflemen on both banks, the barricade of hammocks which I had placed round my station became a target for them; I had no means of replying with musketry, nor could I elevate my guns to their position on a high bank, so that every time I stuck my head up to observe the fire, they had a deliberate fire at me. The pilot-house being placed forward, the guns cannot be fired nearer to the line of the keel than 30° with accuracy without deafening the persons in the pilot-house. I tried this experiment myself, and the pain and stupefaction caused by the blast of the guns satisfied me that half a dozen similar discharges would render me insensible. From this cause, either in approaching a ship or battery, she is exposed to fire a long time without the power of returning it, thereby diminishing her military force 5 per cent.; or if the enemy be a ship, and it is determined to allow her to close, this vessel, in order to return the fire, must allow her to approach nearly on the beam, thus giving her the opportunity to act as a ram with great effect. This would have been the difficulty had a second encounter taken place with the Merrimack. It was rumored, and generally believed, that she had been provided with a gun firing directly ahead, also with a ram, adjusted to pierce this vessel below the water. In either case of closing, this vessel would have been unable to return the fire without laying herself open to the ram.

If the power existed of fighting her "head-on," the side armor would be almost completely protected, and the turret would protect the most vulnerable parts of her deck. For these reasons, it is essential that the lookout and steering apparatus shall be placed on top of the turret.

Except in case of great necessity, such as being at anchor in a tideway, and boats or steamers should come up astern for the purpose of boarding, it would be highly imprudent to fire aft at a greater angle than 50°. The effect of firing over the boilers is very great, and several successive fires would undoubtedly set them leaking, if nothing worse happened.

The bomb-proof smokestack, at least as high as the guns, is absolutely necessary. Her military force is greatly diminished by inability to fire, or rather to run out, both guns at once. The time lost in raising the pendulum and in running out the second gun often loses the favorable position, besides giving the enemy better opportunities for getting shot into the ports.

The ports have not sufficient elevation to allow the guns to be pointed at a battery placed on an eminence without losing all the advantages of an iron-clad vessel; that is, proximity to the battery, in order certainly to hit and dismount the guns.

The preceding defects are most of them irremediable, as far as the vessel is concerned, until she shall undergo a general repair. But a new and most important defect has developed itself with the warm weather, which demands immediate attention. It is essential that some other mode of ventilation shall be provided, not derived from the air-passage through the fire-room. When the weather was cold it was quite warm below, but no inconvenience was felt other than the impurity of the air passing up through the turret; but, with the heat of the last ten days, the air stood at 140° in the turret when in action, which, when added to the gases of the gunpowder and smoke, gases from the fire-room, smoke and heat of the illuminating lamps, and emanations from the large number of persons stationed below, produced a most fetid atmosphere, causing an alarming degree of exhaustion and prostration of the crew. In the action at Drew's Bluff, I was obliged to discontinue the action for a quarter of an hour and take the men below to the forward part of the ship for purer air.

The vessel cannot go to sea until this defect is remedied. If the hatches were all closed (as they must be at sea) in this warm weather, the crew would be unable to live for forty-eight hours shut up. Quite one-third of the crew are now suffering from debility; there being no shelter on deck, they have to keep below to avoid sharpshooters.

Some modification of the galley must also be made. Several men have already literally wilted down by the intense heat of its position against the rear end of the boiler. Although not bearing on this vessel, yet I mention a fact of importance. I understand that in some of the new vessels it is proposed to take the air down through the turret. This would, I conceive, be a fatal mistake; when firing to windward, there is already a great deal of smoke in the turret—quite as much as can clear away by the time the next shot can be fired—and, if the draught were downward, such a body of smoke would fill the turret as to prevent the aim for several minutes.

There are several defective details about the engine, particularly the arrangement of the blowers, which can be readily altered at a machine shop. Either in action or at sea, the loss of the vessel might readily be caused by the *failure of a leather belt.* In fact, coming round from New York, some water getting down through the air pipes, and wetting the belts, caused the blowers to stop, and the gases from the furnace poured into the fire-room, driving the firemen and engineers out and nearly asphyxiating the chief engineer. If this had occurred in action the vessel must have been surrendered, every one having been driven on deck.

I have partially corrected the evil by putting a blast-pipe in the uptake, to continue the draught in case such an accident should occur in future. There are several other details of considerable importance which I do not enlarge upon, as they are provided for in vessels of this class hereafter to be constructed.

The opportune arrival of this vessel at Hampton Roads, and her success in staying the career of the Merrimack, principally by the moral effect of her commander's gallant interposition between that vessel and the Minnesota, caused an exaggerated confidence to be entertained by the public in the powers of the

Monitor, which it was not good policy to check. I, however, feel that I owe it to you, sir, as the commander of the fleet, and to the department, to put on record my deliberate opinion of her powers.

First. With her present guns, she cannot engage another iron-plated vessel of good construction with advantage. The ball has not sufficient velocity to penetrate, and must rely on its smashing effects only. It would not penetrate, though it might shatter, an inclined side of four (4) inches, well backed with wood, or our own vertical side.

Second. Although she manœuvres very quickly, her speed is not six knots at a maximum. She must, therefore, as against a vessel, await the enemy's pleasure to close, and is much trammelled, as herein before stated, by the limitation of the field of fire to 220° of the 360°.

Third. As against a fort: If she is permitted to approach a fort within a couple of hundred yards, and the fort is not above her reach, she has sufficient endurance to stand its fire until she can dismount its guns, one by one; or, if one of our masonry-casemated works, quarry a hole into the face of the wall until it tumbled down by the superincumbent weight. The reduction of forts by a vessel of this class, alone requires the concurrence of many favorable contingencies. She must be able to approach close to it, on nearly the same level; otherwise, the fire is not sufficient in either accuracy or rapidity to dismount guns or drive the gunners to their bomb-proof shelter. It is evident that the guns in embrasure or casemate can be loaded quite as quickly as in the turret, and with entire impunity, while the turret guns are turned away for loading. This gun can then be carefully aimed at position of the ports, and fired, when the turret revolves, so as to expose the port, giving, at least, equal chances of disabling the turret gun. After we deliver our fire, if we do not dismount the gun, they reload without risk for another trial. It is, of course, always to be presumed that the crew of an iron-clad vessel is composed of picked men, while all the forts cannot be provided with such gunners, nor with guns of heavy calibre.

Fourth. She can run by any fortification now in existence, being, in my opinion, invulnerable to shot of eight-inch and lower calibres. The chances of hitting, with monster calibres, are so small as scarcely to be taken into account.

Fifth. A solid shot, of ten-inch and higher calibres, fired with heavy charges, striking near the same spot half a dozen times at short ranges, would dislocate the turret plates, drive in fragments, and end by coming through.

Sixth. That she requires very considerable changes in the mode of ventilation, during action, to enable her to be fought in warm weather, and that it is impossible that she should go to sea until these changes have been made.

Notwithstanding the recent battle in Hampton Roads, and the exploits of the plated gunboats in the western rivers, I am of the opinion that protecting the guns and gunners does not, except in special cases, compensate for the greatly diminished quantity of artillery, slow speed, and inferior accuracy of fire, and that, for general purposes, wooden ships, shell guns, and forts, whether for offence or defence, have not yet been superseded.

I have the honor to be, very respectfully, your obedient servant,

WILLIAM N. JEFFERS,
Lieutenant, Commanding.

Flag-Officer L. M. GOLDSBOROUGH,
Commanding North Atlantic Blockading Squadron.

Passage of the New Ironsides to Hampton Roads.

UNITED STATES NEW IRONSIDES,
Hampton Roads, August 27, 1862.

SIR: I have the honor to inform you of my arrival here, after a passage of twenty-four hours from Delaware breakwater. Fortunately, I could not have selected a more favorable moment to come out, as the sea has been smooth and the wind very light.

As a matter of course, it could be hardly expected that a very favorable report could be made upon the first performance of so novel a vessel, despatched with such unprecedented haste as this was from Philadelphia.

I think, considering everything, there is much less to do, to alter and repair, than could have been anticipated, after the trial of such a vessel, constructed and equipped as the New Ironsides has been.

It is but just to the contractors to state that they have done all they could, under the circumstances, to make everything complete.

The ship has made an average, from the breakwater, of about five and a quarter knots. Any attempt to increase her speed beyond that (which was done several times, and easily done) rendered her unmanageable by the helm. The rudder must be altered, which can be easily done, and it is absolutely necessary, in my judgment, that her masts and spars be returned to her. Without them, nothing can be done with the ship in a gale of wind. She would be utterly unmanageable; she could not be kept head to sea, nor could I scud her—the consequence would be she would be constantly in the trough of the sea, and her decks would be swept, bulwarks, boats, and everything. I hope the honorable Secretary may be pleased to direct that her masts, spars, rigging, and sails may be sent from Philadelphia as soon as possible. Whilst that is being done, the contractors will make every alteration that is required without detaining her beyond that time. They have already ordered down mechanics, who are here to commence the work to be done.

There is nothing whatever to discourage me from entertaining the highest hopes of the perfect success of the New Ironsides. I anticipated great sluggishness in her movements when at sea, owing to the mass of solid weight upon her. On the contrary, I have been most agreeably disappointed; she is light, active, buoyant, in her rolling motion, and will, I think, prove a good sea-boat.

Quite a leak has been discovered on her starboard side, which will have to be stopped, and there are several small matters which will be remedied as soon as the workmen get on board.

The galley was made for 160 men, the complement of the ship originally intended. There are now four hundred on board—none too many; consequently, my crew are suffering in their meals, and are absolutely living upon raw beef and pork, in a measure, which has produced much diarrhœa on board. I think it may be necessary to send a galley from the Washington yard, for I doubt if these persons are in the habit of constructing galleys to accommodate so many persons.

I regret to be obliged to report that a vessel last night ran into me coming up the bay, and was considerably injured. The fault was all their own, trying to cross my bow.

I herewith enclose the report of the chief engineer of this ship.

I have the honor to be, very respectfully, your obedient servant,

T. TURNER, *Captain.*

Hon. GIDEON WELLES,
Secretary of the Navy.

UNITED STATES STEAMER NEW IRONSIDES,
Off Fortress Monroe, Virginia, August 27, 1862.

SIR: In obedience to the orders of G. J. Pendergrast, "to proceed in the New Ironsides as far as Fortress Monroe, to see to the working of the engines, and to report upon the performance of the machinery in all respects," I have the honor to make the following report:

The New Ironsides left the navy yard at Philadelphia on the afternoon of Thursday, 21st instant, drawing fifteen feet six inches forward and fifteen feet one inch aft; engines making from forty-eight to fifty-two revolutions—working well—and none of the journals heating. The ship was anchored off League island during the night of the 21st, and proceeded down the river on the 22d, the engines and all their appendages performing excellently well; the boilers steaming easily with natural draught, furnishing steam for fifty-two revolutions of the engines. The greatest speed logged was seven knots, with 48.2 revolutions.

On the 23d the ship proceeded down the river and bay to the breakwater, the engines performing well. The maximum vacuum (of the fresh water surface condenser) obtained was twenty-six inches.

The ship left her anchorage at the breakwater on the afternoon of the 25th, and proceeded to sea, making the run from Cape Henlopen to Cape Henry in twenty-four hours. During this run the engines were not worked up to the maximum development of their power in consequence of the effect on the steering, which was difficult, uneven, and tortuous. The patent log gave the distance of 5.7 knots from six p. m. of the 25th to four a. m. of the 26th, (ten hours,) or $5\frac{7}{10}$ knots per hour for ten hours.

The average consumption of coal per hour for 47.2 revolutions per minute was 3,123 pounds. The average consumption of coal per hour for 50 revolutions of engines per minute was about 3,200 pounds, or 34 tons 640 pounds per day for a speed of about six knots per hour, the ship drawing fifteen feet.

I deem it proper to state that a more favorable result will be produced after the firemen have had more experience in the management of the fires.

I also enclose herewith a copy of the steam log for reference, and also the indicator diagrams.

The draught of the ship is now, as near as can be ascertained, fifteen feet forward and aft.

I am, respectfully, your obedient servant,

WM. W. W. WOOD,
Chief Engineer, United States Navy.

Hon. GIDEON WELLES,
Secretary of the Navy, Washington, D. C.

Passage of the Passaic from Washington to Hampton Roads.

UNITED STATES IRON-CLAD PASSAIC,
Hampton Roads, December 26, 1862.

SIR: I have the honor to report the arrival of my vessel at this place to-day at 10 a. m. I was towed from Aquia creek by the steamer Mount Washington, which was sent from Hampton Roads by Rear-Admiral Lee for that purpose. The engine worked very well, but the foaming has only been corrected to a moderate extent, and prevented more than fifty revolutions to be made per minute. This gave a speed, while alone and in the rivers, of from four and a half to five and a half miles per hour, depending on the tide, and when *in tow*, making forty revolutions, with a perfectly smooth bay, only five and a half miles an hour could be made from Smith's point to Hampton Roads. As I doubt much our ever being able to get the full number of revolutions of which the engine is supposed to be capable, and, even supposing it could be done, am satisfied that it will not add more than a mile per hour to the speed, I think it will be a cause of disappointment if the vessels of this class are looked upon as more than steam-batteries, to be towed from point to point in fine weather, and, in my case at least, rendered much less seaworthy than would otherwise have been the case, owing to the great error in the calculation of draught, which, by bringing the deck almost to the water, not only takes away from buoyancy, but greatly increases the difficulty of getting coal or provisions, except in very exceptional circumstances.

I am, very respectfully, your obedient servant,

P. DRAYTON, *Captain.*

Hon. GIDEON WELLES,
Secretary of the Navy, Washington.

Passage of the Passaic from Hampton Roads to Beaufort.

UNITED STATES IRON-CLAD PASSAIC,
Beaufort, N. C., January 2, 1863.

SIR: I have the honor to report my arrival here yesterday at five p. m., having left Hampton Roads on the 29th ultimo in tow of the State of Georgia.

The weather continued fine until meridian of the 30th, Cape Hatteras lighthouse then bearing west, and having averaged up to that time five miles an hour, we carrying twenty-seven pounds of steam.

The wind now commenced freshening from the SW., causing the vessel to pitch and labor a good deal, and, in consequence, to make water rapidly through the lower part of the turret and in the bow where the armor bulkhead joins the main body of the vessel; and the limbers becoming choked under the boilers, where they could not be reached, made it necessary, for the purpose of throwing the water from the forward part into the engine-room, where it could be taken up by the steam-pumps, to depend on a hand force-pump and buckets. By this means the water was kept down to about twelve inches; but as early as four o'clock I had commenced a signal to the State of Georgia to stand to the northward, satisfied that there was no other way of checking the bow leak and general strain. There being, however, a sudden change in the weather, I determined to hold on. The change being, however, only temporary, at nine and a half p. m. I again signaled the State of Georgia to run for a lee under Hatteras, which she did.

The pumps now began to give out, owing to the rise of water washing so much dirt into the bilge as to choke them, and in consequence the engine-room would not be kept clear, and about three o'clock the water was within three inches of the fires, some of which, from the splashing, were actually being extinguished. Fortunately, when a little more delay would have been fatal, the engineers by great exertion managed to get all the pumps in order, and to once more clear the engine-room floor, which, however, was on several occasions afterwards covered to the depth of some inches, owing to the choking of the limbers and temporary derangement of the pumps.

At five a. m. of the 30th the wind came from the N. NW. As I was, however, now nearer Hampton Roads than Beaufort, and the pumps in a most unsatisfactory condition, and many repairs necessary, I determined to keep on to the former place; but about one o'clock, the sea again getting up, I found it necessary, to check the increasing leak in the bow, to again stand to the southward. The wind continued to blow hard all night, and the vessel to labor considerably and make a great deal of water; but at sunset of the first of January I was off Beaufort, and, fortunately, finding a pilot outside, went immediately in and anchored.

During the heaviest part of the southwest gale, and when it was evident that something must be done to relieve the thumping forward, I threw overboard about ten tons of scrap iron and thirty-two pounder shot, which was under my cabin, and this I should not consider it safe to put back so long as the vessel is liable to be again exposed to a gale of wind, which I do not think even then she would stand for any length of time, supposing the wind to be on shore, so that she could not run before it and thus avoid the enormous strain brought on the hull, in a heavy sea, by the guards which surround it. These, with the opening round the turret, will prevent these vessels from ever being safe at sea. The turret might, perhaps, be made comparatively tight could it be lowered and hoisted when necessary, but the means afforded are totally inadequate for this purpose, and all my exertions to get the key out at a time when the safety of the vessel depended on it to a certain extent failed, which it is not difficult to understand when it is considered that all the appliances of the Washington yard were necessary to force it in sufficiently to raise the turret a quarter of an inch, and this only after the work of half a day or more. Another great cause of trouble we found to be the very incomplete drainage, the only means of communicating with the well being through the keel, which is very easily stopped up, as is proved in our case, and when so in many places, as under the boilers, can only be reached by taking out the coal, the consequence of which was, that to free the forward part of the vessel we were obliged to depend on a hand-pump and bailing.

The chain supplied us is, I think, too small and of an inferior quality, as some of the studs have already broken out, and this, with the very great difficulty there would be to clear a foul anchor—an accident very liable to occur, and which in the case of the Monitor delayed her leaving Hampton Roads—will, I think, render these vessels very liable to loss if ever caught by bad weather in any except the best protected harbors. I herewith enclose the report of the engineer, from which it will be seen that some time will be required to repair damages and get things again in complete order. I shall, however, do all in my power to accomplish these objects. Owing in a great measure to a stormy weather cloth, which increased the height of the turret three feet, very little water came over it; but that caused us great inconvenience from wetting the bands of the blower engines, which were made so slack as at times not to be able to turn the blowers. Owing to the peculiar form of the vessel aft, the rudder has no power except through the water thrown on it by the propeller, and then only when it is going at full speed; when the engine is stowed down all means of direction seem to cease. This might become serious in a narrow channel, or one with sharp turns. Accompanying this is the report of the engineer.

I am, very respectfully, your obedient servant,

P. DRAYTON, *Captain.*

Hon. GIDEON WELLES,
Secretary of the Navy.

UNITED STATES IRON-CLAD STEAMER PASSAIC,
Off Beaufort, N. C., January 3, 1863.

SIR: When we left Fortress Monroe, the afternoon of the 29th December, the engines and boilers and all bilge connexions were working very well, and continued so until December 30, at 11.30 p. m. At that time the water began to gain in fire-room. The bilge injection, bilge pump of engines, and both steam pumps refused to work. We examined them, and found the strainer into which all the pipes lead, and all pipes, completely choked up with ashes and dirt. At the time the sea was very high and aft, and the ship was leaking badly through engineer's storeroom. The strainer being so low and having no cover, the water being above, the dirt was by motion of the ship carried over into the strainer.

We succeeded in cleaning bilge injection a little, so that it worked very irregularly and kept the water from gaining much, and at 3.30 the following morning we had everything clear, with the exception of one pump, and we found steam valve of that broken, and of course rendered unfit for service. The water now commenced going down, but it was at this time within three (3) inches of fires, and the rolling of the ship carried the water up to the fires and nearly quenched three (3) of them.

At five o'clock the water was down below fire-room floor, but it was necessary to keep men stationed at strainer and limber holes to clean them. The water did on several occasions afterwards get above fire-room floors, but only to the height of about four (4) inches. It was caused by the limber holes stopping. They are very poorly constructed and are not sufficiently large, and not enough of them, and there is no way of getting at those between boilers and turret to clear them without taking out the coal.

There is only one way for me to account for the water gaining so fast aft. The sea being direct aft, did most certainly loosen the projection astern, and I account for the leak being forward for the same reason.

Respectfully, your obedient servant,

G. S. BRIGHT, *Senior Engineer.*

Captain PERCIVAL DRAYTON,
Commanding Iron-clad Steamer Passaic.

Forwarded. P. DRAYTON, *Captain.*

UNITED STATES IRON-CLAD STEAMER PASSAIC,
Off Beaufort, N. C., January 2, 1863.

SIR: It will be necessary to examine the interior of cylinder air-pump and condenser, on account of using bilge injection constantly to free ship of water. A large amount of dirt and ashes having passed through the engines, I am afraid it has done considerable damage. There will have to be a larger and better strainer made for the bilge pumps and injection, as the one we have is perfectly worthless; it is easily stopped with ashes, &c. It was the cause of the pumps and injection refusing to work and the water gaining in the engine-room. After great exertions we did clear the strainer and pipes leading to it, and then the water was within three (3) inches of the grate bars.

All the engine and steam pumps require a thorough overhauling, and pipes leading to same need repairing. The engines require repacking and brasses need thorough overhauling. The fire-room plates should be firmly secured in their places to prevent dirt and ashes from going in the bilge. The blowing and vacuum engines need overhauling, as it was impossible to do anything to them on our passage here.

We require a more efficient arrangement for raising and lowering the turret. The one we have is too light. We also require for engine-room hatch a new dead-light plate, as the sea cracked the one we have and rendered it unfit for use. I would like to have steam off the boilers to examine them, and also to make some new joints on steam-pipes, as some of them leak very badly.

I have noticed that whilst at sea, a great quantity of water comes in aft through the engineer's storeroom, and also in coal bunkers. It seems to come from the projection of the sides—strained, no doubt.

Very respectfully, your obedient servant,

GEO. S. BRIGHT, *Senior Engineer.*

Captain PERCIVAL DRAYTON,
Commanding U. S. Iron-clad Steamer Passaic.

Forwarded.

PERCIVAL DRAYTON.

Loss of the Monitor.

Report of Acting Rear-Admiral S. P. Lee.

UNITED STATES FLAG-STEAMER PHILADELPHIA,
Hampton Roads, Va., January 3, 1863.

SIR: I have the painful duty to perform of reporting the loss of the Monitor at sea, south of Cape Hatteras, on Tuesday night, the 30th ultimo. I am informed by Commander Armstrong that two officers and twenty-eight men of the Monitor and Rhode Island were drowned. See his report enclosed.

The Passaic is at Beaufort, North Carolina. Both these vessels departed from the roads in good weather. I left it to the discretion of their commanders to choose the weather and time of their departure.

I have the honor to be, sir, very respectfully, yours,

S. P. LEE,
Acting Rear-Admiral, Commanding N. A. B. Squadron.

Hon. GIDEON WELLES,
Secretary of the Navy.

Second report of Acting Rear-Admiral S. P. Lee.

UNITED STATES FLAG-STEAMER PHILADELPHIA,
Hampton Roads, Va., January 4, 1863.

SIR: I submit the following report, based on the reports received by me from Commander Bankhead, of the Monitor, and Commander Trenchard, of the Rhode Island. * * * * * * *

Commander J. P. Bankhead, commanding the Monitor, reports to me that he left the roads Monday, 29th ultimo, at 2.30 p. m., with light southwest wind, clear, pleasant weather, and every prospect of its continuing so. At 6 p. m. he passed Cape Henry; water smooth, and everything working well. The same good weather continued during the night and until 5 a. m. on Tuesday, the 30th, when the Monitor felt a swell from the southward, and a slight increase of wind from southwest, the sea breaking over the pilot-house and striking the base of the tower; speed about five knots. Until 6 p. m. the weather was variable, with occasional squalls of wind and rain, with less swell in the afternoon. Bilge pumps were amply sufficient to keep her free. At 7 p. m. the wind hauled more to the southward, increased and caused sea to rise, the computed position being fifteen miles south of Cape Hatteras. At this time the Monitor was yawing and towing badly, the vessel working and making more water; the Worthington pumps were set to work and the centrifugal pumps got ready. At 8 p. m. the sea was rising rapidly, (the Monitor plunging heavily,) completely submerging pilot-house, and at times entering the turret and blower pipes. When she rose to the swell, the flat under surface of the projecting armor would come down with great force, causing considerable shock to the vessel. Stopping the Rhode Island, which was towing her, did not make the Monitor ride easier or cause her to make less water, as she would then fall off and roll heavily in the trough of the sea. The centrifugal pump was at length started, the others failing to keep the water down. With all the pumps working well, the water continued rising, and at 10 p. m., after a fair trial of the pumps, and the water still gaining rapidly, Commander Bankhead made signal of distress, cut the hawser, steamed close to and under the lee of the Rhode Island, received two boats from her and ordered the crew of the Monitor to leave her—a dangerous operation, as the sea was breaking heavily over the deck. The two vessels touched, and, owing to the sharp bow and sides of the Monitor, the Rhode Island was endangered and she steamed ahead a little. At 11.30 p. m. the water was gaining rapidly, though all the pumps were in full play, the engine working slowly, and the sea breaking badly over the vessel, making it dangerous to leave the turret. At this time several men were supposed to have been washed overboard. The engine and pumps soon ceased to work, the water having put the fire out. While waiting for return of boats, bailing was resorted to. As the Monitor was now laboring in the trough of the sea, Commander Bankhead let go the anchor, which brought her head to sea. The vessel filling rapidly, Commander Bankhead ordered the twenty-five or thirty men, then left on board, to leave in the boats then approaching cautiously, as the sea was breaking violently over the Monitor's submerged deck. In this perilous position, Commander Bankhead held a boat's painter until as many men could get in as the boat could carry. Some men left in the turret, terrified by the peril, declined to come down, and are supposed to have perished. Commander Bankhead did not leave his vessel so long as he could do anything towards saving his crew, in which efforts he was ably assisted by Commander Trenchard, the officers and crew of the Rhode Island.

When the crew of the Monitor was mustered on board the Rhode Island, four officers and twelve men were found missing, some of whom it is hoped were picked up or survived the gale in the Rhode Island's boat. A list of the Monitor's missing is enclosed in Commander Bankhead's report of the 3d instant, accompanying this report; Acting Assistant Surgeon Weeks suffered amputation of three fingers, his hand having been badly jammed.

Commander Bankhead speaks warmly of the good conduct of the officers and crew, with but few exceptions. He commends particularly Lieutenant Samuel D. Greene, his executive officer, and Acting Master L. N. Stodder, as worthy of all praise. He warmly praises the deportment of Acting Master's Mate Peter Williams, and Quartermaster Richard Anjier; the latter would not desert the ship until his commander left.

The officers and crew lost everything. They will, the latter at least, doubtless receive appropriate relief from the government.

Commander Trenchard, commanding the Rhode Island, with the Monitor in tow, left on Monday, December 29, at 2.30 p. m., with wind light from SW., sea smooth, and weather favorable that night, and next day, the 30th, the Monitor towing easily. At 1 p. m. on the 30th, Hatteras light bore W.SW., distant 14 miles; at sunset it bore NW., distant 17 miles, and the State of Georgia, with the Passaic in tow, to the northward and eastward; the wind was then light from SW., with indications of good weather. Between 8 and 9 p. m. the wind hauled more to the southward, and freshened with rainy and squally weather. At 11 p. m., when 20 miles S.SW. of Hatteras, the Monitor made signal of distress, at which Commander Trenchard sent his two largest boats to her assistance; one of them, the launch, was stove under the quarter of the Rhode Island by the Monitor. While the Monitor was in that position, ropes were thrown to her from the Rhode Island; but so reluctant was the crew of the Monitor to leave the vessel that they did not take advantage of the opportunity to save themselves. Acting Master's Mate D. R. Brown, of the Rhode Island, twice brought that vessel's first cutter full of men from the Monitor; he attempted a third trip, probably through a misunderstanding of orders, and did not return, though waited for that night, and searched for next day, the 31st. There is room to hope that this boat, with its crew, and probably with some of the missing Monitor's men, survived the gale. Commander Trenchard commends the skill and good conduct of Acting Master's Mates D. R. Brown and Stevens, of D. T. Compton, cockswain, and the missing crew of the cutter, a list of which is enclosed in Commander Trenchard's report of January 3, accompanying this.

I hope that the dependent families of the dead will receive the relief needed by their losses, and the faithful survivors the consideration deserved for their good conduct. * * * * * * * *

Herewith I forward—

(A.) Report of Commander J. C. Bankhead (late of the Monitor) to Acting Rear-Admiral Lee, dated January 3, and enclosing (1) his detailed report of January 1; (2) the report of his senior engineer; (3) list of missing.

(B.) Report of Commander Trenchard (commanding the Rhode Island) to Acting Rear-Admiral Lee, dated January 3, and enclosing (1) list of missing.

(C.) Report of Commander J. F. Armstrong (commanding the State of Georgia) to Acting Rear-Admiral Lee, dated January 3.

I have the honor to be, sir, very respectfully, yours,

S. P. LEE,
Acting Rear-Admiral, Commanding N. A. B. Squadron.

Hon. GIDEON WELLES,
Secretary of the Navy, Washington, D. C.

A.

Report of Commander J. P. Bankhead.

UNITED STATES STEAMER RHODE ISLAND,
Hampton Roads, January 3, 1863.

SIR: I regret to have to report to you that the United States iron-clad steamer Monitor foundered at sea at about 1 a. m. of the 31st day of December, 1862, with a loss of four officers and twelve men missing, some of whom may possibly have been saved. I enclose herewith a detailed account of the loss of the vessel, with the probable cause, the report of the senior engineer, and a list of the men and officers missing.

Respectfully, your obedient servant,

J. P. BANKHEAD,
Commander United States Steamer Monitor.

Acting Rear-Admiral S. P. LEE,
Commanding North Atlantic Blockading Squadron.

UNITED STATES STEAMER RHODE ISLAND,
January 1, 1863.

SIR: I have the honor to report to you that the Monitor left Hampton Roads, in tow of the United States steamer Rhode Island, on the 29th of December, 1862, at 2.30 p. m., wind light at SW., weather clear and pleasant, and every prospect of its continuation. Passed Cape Henry at 6 p. m.; water smooth, and everything working well.

During the night the weather continued the same until 5 a. m., when we began to experience a swell from the southward, with a slight increase of the wind from the SW., the sea breaking over the pilot-house forward and striking the base of the "tower," but not with sufficient force to break over it. Found that the packing of oakum under and around the base of the tower had loosened somewhat from the working of the tower, as the vessel pitched and rolled. Speed at this time about five knots; ascertained from the engineer of the watch that the bilge pumps kept her perfectly free, occasionally "sucking." Felt no apprehension at the time. The weather during the day, and until 6 p. m., was variable, with occasional squalls of wind and rain, and towards evening the swell somewhat decreased, the bilge pumps being found amply sufficient to keep her clear of the water that penetrated through the sight-hole of the pilot-house, hawser-hole, and base of tower, (all of which had been well calked previous to leaving.) At 7.30 the wind hauled more to the south, increasing in strength, and causing the sea to rise. Computed position at this time about 15 miles south of Cape Hatteras shoals. Found the vessel towed badly, yawing very much, and with the increased motion making somewhat more water around the base of the tower. Ordered engineer to put on the Worthington pump bilge injection, and get the centrifugal pump ready, and report to me immediately if he perceived any increase of the water. 8 p. m.: the sea about this time commenced to rise very rapidly, causing the vessel to plunge heavily, completely submerging the pilot-house, and washing over and into the turret, and at times into the blower pipes. Observed that when she rose to the swell, the flat under surface of the projecting armor would come down with great force, causing a considerable shock to the vessel and turret, thereby loosening still more the packing around its base. Signalized several times to the Rhode Island to stop, in order that I might ascertain if, by so doing, she would ride easier, or decrease the influx of water, but could perceive no difference, the vessel falling off immediately into the trough of the sea and rolling heavily. The engineer at this time reported that it would be necessary to start the centrifugal pump, as the others failed to keep the water under. Ordered him to do so immediately, and report to me the effect. Sea continued to rise, the vessel striking heavily forward. The engineer reported that the pumps were all working well, but produced no effect upon the water, which by this time had risen several inches above the level of the engine-room floor.

About 10.30 p. m., having given the pumps a fair trial, and finding the water gaining rapidly upon us, I determined to make the preconcerted signal of distress, which was immediately answered by the Rhode Island. I ranged up close to her and reported that the water was gaining rapidly upon us, and requested her commander to send boats to take off the crew. Finding that the heavy stream-cable used to tow the Monitor rendered the vessel unmanageable while hanging slack to her bow, and being under the absolute necessity of working the engines to keep the pumps going, I ordered it to be cut, and ran down close under the lee of the Rhode Island, at times almost touching her. Water continued to gain upon the pumps, and was now above the "ash-pits." Two boats reached us from the Rhode Island, when I ordered Lieutenant Green to put as many men into them as they could safely carry. While getting the men into the boats (a very dangerous operation, caused by the heavy sea breaking entirely over the deck) the vessels touched slightly, nearly crushing the boat, and endangering the Rhode Island herself, as our sharp bow and sides would undoubtedly have stove her near the water's edge had she struck upon us heavily. The Rhode Island steamed slightly ahead, and the vessels separated a short distance. At 11.30, my engines working slowly, and all the pumps in full play, but water gaining rapidly; sea very heavy, and breaking entirely over the vessel, rendering it extremly hazardous to leave the turret; in fact, several men were supposed to have been washed overboard at this time.

While waiting for the boats to return, the engineer reported that the engines had ceased to work, and shortly after all the pumps stopped also, the water putting out the fires, and leaving no pressure of steam. A bailing party had been previously organized, not so much with any hope of diminishing the water, but more as an occupation for the men. The engine being stopped, and no longer able to keep the vessel head to sea, she having fallen off into the trough and rolling so heavily as to render it impossible for boats to approach us, I ordered the anchor to be let go and all the chain given her, in hopes that it might bring her up. Fortunately it did so, and she once more swung round, head to wind. By this time, finding the vessel filling rapidly, and the deck on a level with the water, I ordered all the men left on board to leave the turret and endeavor to get into the two boats which were then approaching us. I think at that time there were about twenty-five or thirty men on board. The boats approached very cautiously, as the sea was breaking upon our now submerged deck with great violence, washing several men overboard, one of whom was afterwards picked up by the boats. I secured the painter of one of the boats, (which, by the use of its oars, was prevented from striking the side,) and made as many get into her as she would safely hold in the heavy sea that was running. There were several men still left upon and in the turret, who, either stupefied by fear, or fearful of being washed overboard in the attempt to reach the boats, would not come down, and are supposed to have gone down in the vessel. Feeling that I had done everything in my power to save the vessel and crew, I jumped into the already deeply-laden boat and left the Monitor, whose heavy, sluggish motion gave evidence that she could float but a short time longer. Shortly after we reached the Rhode Island she disappeared.

I must testify to the untiring efforts and zeal displayed by Captain Trenchard and his officers in their attempts to rescue the crew of the Monitor. It was an extremely hazardous undertaking, rendered particularly so by the heavy sea and the difficulty in approaching the Monitor.

While regretting those that were lost, it is still a matter of congratulation that so many were saved under the circumstances. There is some reason to hope that a boat, which is still missing, may have succeeded in saving those left on board, or may have reached the vicinity of the vessel in time to have picked up some of them as she went down. Upon mustering the officers and crew on board the Rhode Island, four officers and twelve men were found to be missing, a list of whom I herewith enclose, as well as the report of Second Assistant Engineer Watters, acting chief engineer.

I am firmly of the opinion that the Monitor must have sprung a leak somewhere in the forward part, where the hull joins on to the armor, and that it was caused by the heavy shocks received as she came down upon the sea.

The bilge pumps alone, up to 7 p. m., had easily kept her free, and when we find that all her pumps a short time after, with a minimum capacity of 2,000 gallons per minute, not only failed to diminish the water, but, on the contrary, made no perceptible change in its gradual increase, we must come to the conclusion that there are, at least, good grounds for my opinion.

Before closing my report I must testify to the coolness, prompt obedience, and absence of any approach to panic on the part of the officers, and with but few exceptions on that of the crew, many of whom were at sea for the first time, and (it must be admitted) under circumstances that were well calculated to appal the boldest heart. I would beg leave to call the attention of the admiral and of the department to the particular good conduct of Lieutenant Greene and Acting Master L. N. Stodder, who remained with me until the last, and by their example and bearing did much towards inspiring confidence and obedience on the part of others. I must also mention favorably Acting Master's Mate Peter Williams, and Richard Anjier, quartermaster, who both showed on that occasion the highest qualities of men and seamen. The latter remained at his post, at the wheel, when the vessel was sinking, and when told by me to get into the boat, replied, "No, sir, not till you go."

The officers and crew have lost everything but the clothes they wore at the time they were rescued.

There were no serious injuries received, with the exception of Acting Assistant Surgeon G. M. Weeks, who jammed his hand so badly as to require a partial amputation of several of his fingers.

Every attention and kindness has been shown to us by Captain Trenchard and his officers, to whom we all feel deeply grateful.

Very respectfully, your obedient servant,

J. P. BANKHEAD, *Commander.*

Acting Rear-Admiral S. P. LEE,
Commanding North Atlantic Blockading Squadron.

Report of Joseph Watters, second assistant engineer.

UNITED STATES STEAMER RHODE ISLAND,
At sea, January 1, 1863.

SIR: The following is a report of the condition of the engines and pumps connected with the engineer's department of the United States iron-clad Monitor on the night of the 30th of December, 1862. Between the hours of 8 and 9 p. m. of that evening I received orders from Captain Bankhead to examine and have ready for use all pumps connected with the engineer's department; an order which I promptly obeyed.

I immediately went in the engine-room, and found the bilge pump connected with the main engine in good condition and working well, as it had been during the day. I had the discharge-pipe of the centrifugal pump connected to its proper place, and all ready for use, and before leaving the engine-room I gave orders to Mr. Hands, the engineer then on duty, in case the water should in crease to let me know, and at the same time to start the Worthington pump, and use the bilge injection. I then left the engine-room, and reported to Captain Bankhead that all pumps were ready for use. In a few minutes I returned to the engine-room again, and found the water about one inch deep on the engine-room floor. The Worthington pump and bilge injection at that time were both in use. I remained in the engine-room, and finding that the water did not decrease, I had the centrifugal pump started. It worked well and constant, but still the water increased. I reported to Captain Bankhead that I would have to reduce the speed of the main engines in order to save steam for the use of the Worthington and centrifugal pumps. The ash-pits at that time were more than half full of water, allowing but very little air to reach the fires. At the same time the blowers, used for producing a current of air to the fires, were throwing a great amount of water. The speed of the main engines was reduced, but still the pressure of steam decreased, and the amount of water in the ship increased, until it reached the fires and gradually extinguished them. The pressure of steam in the boilers at that time was five pounds per square inch, and the main engine stopped; the Worthington and centrifugal pumps still working slowly, but finally stopped.

I reported the circumstances to Captain Bankhead. A few minutes later I received an order to leave the engine-room, and proceed to get in the boats. It was then between the hours of 12 p. m. and 1 a. m., and the fires nearly extinguished.

I am, sir, very respectfully, yours, &c.,

JOSEPH WATTERS,
Second Assistant Engineer, United States Steamer Monitor.

Commander BANKHEAD,
United States Steamer Monitor.

The boilers and hull of the Galena.

UNITED STATES FLAG-SHIP MINNESOTA,
Off Newport News, Va., January 14, 1863.

Previous to ordering a survey on the boilers of the Galena, as directed by the department under date of ———, I called on Lieutenant Commander Paulding for a report, and have the pleasure of informing the department that no survey is necessary.

The Galena's boiler and machinery are in good order, as will appear from the enclosed copy of reports, dated the 12th instant, (which were called for yesterday, and received last evening,) from Lieutenant Commander Paulding and the engineer of the Galena.

I regret having referred to Captain Turner's verbal report without having first made this investigation. In this connexion I beg to observe that, in desiring to have another iron-clad here, I wished to secure this position, and to leave myself at liberty to visit the outside blockade with this vessel.

I have the honor to be, sir, very respectfully, yours,

S. P. LEE,
Acting Rear-Admiral, Commanding N. A. B. Squadron.

Hon. GIDEON WELLES,
Secretary of the Navy, Washington, D. C.

UNITED STATES STEAMER GALENA,
Newport News, January 12, 1863.

SIR: I have the honor to enclose the report of Acting First Assistant Engineer James E. Young respecting the boilers and engine of this vessel.

It will be observed that the engines and boilers of this vessel are in almost perfect condition. Her battery is also perfect, and the only defect in the vessel is on the port side, which was seriously damaged in her engagements on the James river.

Very respectfully, your obedient servant,

LEONARD PAULDING,
Lieutenant Commander.

Acting Rear-Admiral S. P. LEE,
United States Steam Frigate Minnesota.

A true copy.

F. R. WEBB, *Acting Ensign.*

UNITED STATES STEAMER GALENA,
January 12, 1863.

SIR: In obedience to your order, I herewith report to you the condition of the engines and boilers of this ship.

The exhaust-pipe of the starboard engine, which is cast iron, is split about three feet of its length. We have banded it with six wrought-iron straps; it is now stronger than it was before the accident. The engines, in my opinion, are in as good working order as when the ship sailed from New York. In my report of the 24th December I stated that the shells of the boilers were leaking, and that serious injury would result on account of the salt accumulating on the iron below the leaks. We have repaired all the leaks that could be reached, and there are at present none remaining of any consequence. Four of the tubes (two in each boiler) have given out at the ends, which we have securely plugged up.

I consider the boilers in good order, and require no immediate repairs.

Very respectfully, your obedient servant,

JAMES G. YOUNG,
Acting 1st Assistant Engineer U. S. N.

Lieut. Commander LEONARD PAULDING,
Commanding United States Steamer Galena.

A true copy.

F. R. WEBB, *Acting Ensign.*

The Weehawken in a gale.

[Received at Washington, D. C., January 22, 1863.]

U. S. MILITARY TELEGRAPH,
Newport News, January 22, 1863.

The Weehawken anchored off the Horseshoe last night; weather foggy. She wants her centrifugal pump and some oakum calking around deck openings; all right otherwise. She encountered the heavy gale of Tuesday night off Chincoteague. Rodgers declined being towed during the worst of the gale, to which he and Case attribute the Weehawken's safety. No news of the Nahant; I suppose she is at the breakwater. The Iroquois wants repairs which will take five days here.

S. P. LEE,
Acting Rear-Admiral, Commanding Squadron.

Hon. GIDEON WELLES,
Secretary of the Navy.

Detailed report of the passage of the Weehawken to Hampton Roads.

U. S. IRON-CLAD WEEHAWKEN,
Norfolk Navy Yard, January 26, 1863.

SIR: I have the honor to report that on the 18th instant, while lying in New York harbor, the Boardman, side-wheel tug, came alongside to tow us to the Chesapeake, whereupon we immediately got under way for sea.

When just outside of the Hook, the wind suddenly chopped round to the northeast, and the pilots thought gave indications of a gale. These I could not perceive, but I knew the Boardman would founder in rough weather, and the Weekawken be left, in case of accident to her machinery, to drift upon a lee shore. I felt it my duty to anchor, and report the character of the tug to the admiral commanding the station.

It was found that no better vessel could be procured, and we sailed next morning, the 19th, towed by the Boardman, and under convoy of the Iroquois, Captain Case, which in the meanwhile had anchored near us at Sandy Hook.

We steamed down the coast, generally in sight of the land, and with the water smooth. On the 20th we were, at daylight, off the entrance to the Delaware.

At about eight o'clock it was reported to me that the Boardman, with us in tow, had turned, and was seeking shelter under the breakwater. The weather was no longer fine, but I did not think the appearance justified my seeking shelter, and the tug was ordered to stand on for the Chesapeake.

The weather grew continually worse, and the barometer fell regularly, but I did not anticipate more than I judged the Weehawken could easily weather.

The performance of the vessel in the sea was admirable. I remarked, however, that when the tow-line, from any cause, was slackened, the motion of the vessel was better than when it was stretched.

At about 2.30 p. m. the Boardman was no longer of use, and it seemed probable that we should find her an incumbrance. Made signal to her to leave us and look out for her own safety. We cut the tow-line, in order not to endanger our propeller; with the sea breaking over our decks, it would not have been safe to send men to gather it in had she cast it off. We were in sight of Fenwick's Island light. The Boardman ran to the northward, and was soon out of sight. I have since heard that she arrived safely inside the breakwater, but half full of water.

Upon seeing the Boardman leave us the Iroquois promptly ran down from her station to windward and offered to tow us; but I declined, thinking we should do better alone.

The vessel commenced leaking through the hawse-hole; put new parcelling and lashing on to restrain the leak, which gradually increased, notwithstanding our efforts. It was thought openings in the overhang admitted water from the deck. We commenced leaking badly from the after overhang. Here, too, the flow of water increased as the gale grew worse, but it was still thought that these leaks were from the deck.

The steam-pumps were continually choked, and much time was lost in clearing them. Our limbers which, when we received the vessel, it was reported, had been carefully cleaned, proved to be very foul. Cotton-waste lamps, oil-feeders, hammers, and chips obstructed the flow of water to the pumps, and interrupted their action. We cleared as much of them out as we could.

The water at last forced up the floor plates in the fire-room, and covered the ash-pits. The leaks still increasing, it was found that the fires had been neglected; that two furnaces were so far out as to need rekindling with wood; that the others were very low, and we had only ten pounds of steam. In this emergency, one of the passengers, Mr. John Farren, chief engineer in the navy, promptly took measures to re-establish the fires and procure the necessary pressure of steam. The sea was about thirty feet high, and was made irregular and trying, in consequence, probably, of the proximity of the land. Through all this the behavior of the vessel was easy, buoyant, and indicative of thorough safety. Her movements filled me with admiration. I saw in them everything to admire; nothing to improve. The waves rolled furiously across the deck. Instead of expending their force against the side, as in an ordinary vessel, they swept harmlessly by. A plate of flat iron two inches thick, and weighing some thirty-three hundred pounds, was broken from its lashing upon the deck, and transported about forty feet to some side stanchions, which arrested its course overboard, and to which it was secured.

The opinion formed then confirmed my anticipations, that a hull rising but little above the surface of the water, and having a central elevation, as in the Monitors, is the shape to form a good sea boat; and I am convinced that on this idea all successful iron-clads must be built. This form reduces the surface to be plated to a minimum, and puts the part having the necessary elevation above the sea for fighting guns, where it can be carried without inconvenience, and in the Weehawken is easily carried. With us, I think, safety is solely a question of strength.

I had relied upon former experience to correct any faulty motion which I might discover, in a sea way, by shifting or reducing weights. I abandoned, however, the idea of improvement; as I watched the action of the vessel it was perfect.

The sea exercised great power upon the upper hull, and our speed, while we could measure it, fell to two and a half knots, and she trembled through all her plating at some of the blows which she received. During the height of the gale the waves swept over us so violently that no one could go on the deck to heave either the log or lead.

The stanchions on the side were of the greatest service; without their aid, men whose feet were swept from under them would have been carried overboard. Life-lines at sea cannot be too much multiplied.

The pendulum or port-stopper of the 11-inch gun, during the gale, swung so as to knock out the port-buckler; a piece of matting, however, wedged between the side and pendulum, temporarily repaired the damage, and the pendulum secured by shipping and lashing its monkey tail.

Spray came over the turret, but no sea. The water ran copiously down along the base of the smoke-stack. This is now securely calked, I hope.

A gasket of plaited hemp packing, saturated with tallow, was put around the base of the turret, between it and the deck; the iron ring covering the joint was lifted for the gasket. I do not know that this precaution was necessary, but no water came in around the turret.

The hatches for entrance into the vessel were carefully calked with oakum, and paid with white lead. They leaked enough to show how much care is requisite with openings in the deck.

Now, with the deck free from water, I do not believe that the vessel leaks more than before she sailed. Careful scrutiny has failed to detect any injury to the iron in the after overhang, from which the greatest part of the water flowed. I think that removing the covers to the propeller and anchor-wells had a good effect.

When the vessel raised her immersed bow, the water which this lifted ran out through the well, and plunging, the sea rose through it high above the deck.

About a gallon of water a minute runs from the port side overhang into the after overhang. In New York this was attributed to a loose rivet, and I attach no importance to it.

On the night of the 20th and morning of the 21st the wind blew very hard; hardest from two to four a. m. We had been running all night on our course rather in the trough of the sea. At about eight o'clock the bad weather had passed away, and the sea was much smoother. I then made signals to the Iroquois for a tow line, which Captain Case promptly gave. There was still so much motion that we parted a couple of new 9-inch hawsers. I found that by bending my tow-line to his we did much better, on the principle of a long scope of cable in a sea-way. The length, and consequent elasticity, prevented any injurious jerk, and the line held.

At eleven a. m. we made "Cape Henry light-house." At about one p. m. the Iroquois made signal that she had disabled her machinery. We cast off her tow-line, and came in alone, anchored in the fog off the tail of the Horseshoe, and got under way next morning, the 22d, as soon as we could see the light-boat, and came up to Fortress Monroe, from which I telegraphed our arrival.

Both Captain Case and I remarked that the Weehawken did much better, as regards motion, without the tow-line.

I cannot withhold my expressions of thanks to Captain Case for the noble manner in which he kept by me during the night. His boats were fully prepared, provisioned, and watered for service, in a night too wild for any boat to live. He was always near us, and handled his vessel in a daring manner in giving us tow-lines, where a collision would inevitably have sunk him. I must also express my thanks to the engineer passengers for the purpose of observation: Messrs. John Farren, chief engineer of the navy, N. C. Davis, assistant to Mr. Farren, and William Alden, sent out by the contractors. Without their efficient and experienced aid in attending to the machinery, I dare not assert the result.

I have the honor to be your obedient servant,

JOHN RODGERS, *Captain.*

Hon. GIDEON WELLES,
Secretary of the Navy.

Extracts from private letters of Captain John Rodgers relative to first trip of the Weehawken

NEW YORK, *January* 11, 1863.

SIR: For the information of the Navy Department, and to place on its files, I have the honor to enclose herewith a copy of an extract of a letter from Captain John Rodgers, in reference to the great gale which the United States iron-clad Weehawken experienced on her first trip to Hampton Roads.

I am, sir, respectfully, your obedient servant,

J. ERICSSON.

Hon. GIDEON WELLES,
Secretary of the Navy, Washington.

Copy of a letter received by Captain Ericsson from Wm. L. Hodge, esq.

WASHINGTON, *January* 27, 1863.

DEAR SIR: I wrote you yesterday; to-day I have a letter from my son-in-law, Captain Rodgers, the following extract from which may interest many.

Very truly,

WM. L. HODGE.

"NORFOLK, *January* 24, 1863.

"The gale was very severe, but my vessel behaved admirably during the highest of the storm. I stood on the turret and watched her movements with great interest. They gave the impression of great safety; whilst water can be kept out of it, as safe as a raft or cake of ice. The vessel leaked dangerously—entirely, I think, through unguarded openings in her deck; she is now quite tight, which would not be the case had anything started. These openings will be well calked and paid with white lead before we start. The hawse-hole let in much water. We shall arrange that, and intend to put a pump in the anchor-room, and are now fitting a centrifugal pump that will throw out one thousand gallons per minute. We can with all our pumps keep out any quantity of water, less than a plate falling off.

"I cast off my tug, and sent her away, for she would have been lost in the weather I anticipated, and which we actually had, and refused a tow from the Iroquois, not only because I thought it would have been a hindrance, but in case the towing cable parted, it probably would have fouled the propeller, which would have been fatal, for no one could venture on deck to cut the tow cable loose. These iron-clads should only be towed in good weather; in bad weather they can do better alone. No boat from the Iroquois could have lived, for she was rolling her guns under; our fate, therefore, depended on the safety of our own vessel.

"The waves swept over the deck with great violence; an iron plate, two inches thick and eleven feet long, weighing three thousand pounds, was broken loose from its lashings and carried forty feet against the iron stanchions; and another plate, as much as two men could slide along the deck, was lifted and thrown upon some kedges. We could neither throw the log nor sound, as no one could live on the deck to do either.

"Whilst I watched the motion of the vessel in the hardest of the storm, I saw nothing to improve. I believed I could have corrected any wrong tendency by shifting or throwing overboard *weight*, but I gave up that idea as unnecessary. The sea had great force and hold upon the hull, so as to impede our way very much, but she had no drift, and goes where she looks.

"JOHN RODGERS."

Extract from a letter of Captain Rodgers, addressed to the Assistant Secretary of the Navy, dated on board the United States steamer "Weehawken," Norfolk, July 22, 1863.

"On Tuesday night, when off Chingoteague shoals, we had a very severe gale from E.NE., with a very heavy sea, made confused and dangerous by the proximity of the land. The waves I measured after the sea abated; I found them twenty-three feet high. They were certainly seven feet higher in the midst of the storm. During the heaviest of the gale I stood upon the turret, and admired the behavior of the vessel. She rose and fell to the waves, and I concluded that the Monitor form had great sea-going qualities. If leaks were prevented, no hurricane could injure her.

"I presume in two days we shall be ready for any service, as we need no repairs, and only some little fittings."

Passage of the Montauk to Beaufort.

UNITED STATES FLAG-SHIP MINNESOTA,
Newport News, Virginia, January 24, 1863.

SIR: I respectfully enclose copies of reports of the 5th and 9th instant, from Commander J. L. Worden, reporting the arrival of his vessel, the United States steamer Montauk, at Beaufort, her grounding at the entrance of the harbor, and concerning certain changes which he had been making to put her in good trim for sea-service.

I have the honor to be, sir, very respectfully, yours,

S. P. LEE,
Acting Rear-Admiral, Commanding N. A. B. Squadron.

Hon. GIDEON WELLES,
Secretary of the Navy, Washington, D. C.

UNITED STATES STEAMER MONTAUK,
Beaufort, North Carolina, January 5, 1863.

SIR: I respectfully report that this ship, under my command, arrived off this harbor at 7½ o'clock a. m. yesterday, and on entering grounded (on the beginning of the ebb tide) in 10½ feet of water, about a mile inside of the bar; two army tugs coming to our assistance, I carried out with one of them an anchor, and discharged into the other our projectiles and a quantity of ballast. At 5 o'clock p. m., with the assistance of the United States steamer Miami and one of the tugs, I succeeded in hauling her off, and reached this anchorage at about 6 o'clock p. m.

When aground, at low water, she had 8½ feet of water alongside; on floating, she showed no increase of water in the hold, and during the night at anchor made no more than usual. I therefore infer that she is not materially strained. I am now taking in our shot, shell and ballast, and shall break out the thwartship coal-bunker in order to satisfy myself that there is nothing under it likely to choke the limbers.

I shall adopt every means that my experience and judgment suggest, to avoid accidents, and to render the ship as efficient as possible for the service required of her.

On the passage from Hampton Roads the weather was unexceptionably fine and the water smooth, except off Cape Hatteras, where I encountered a heavy swell from the northward and eastward, which caused the ship to roll considerably, taking water in large quantities on her deck.

Respectfully, your obedient servant,

JOHN L. WORDEN, *Commander.*

Acting Rear-Admiral S. P. LEE,
Commanding N. A. B. Squadron.

A true copy.

F. R. WEBB, *Acting Ensign.*

UNITED STATES STEAMER MONTAUK,
Beaufort, North Carolina, January 9, 1863.

SIR: Your communication of the 7th instant, directing me to proceed to Port Royal, South Carolina, is just received.

Since my arrival here, I have been employed in breaking out the coal-bunkers and the shot ballast under the cabin and around the anchor well, in order to clean out the bilges under them thoroughly.

All the shot ballast from the forward "overhang" around the anchor well I have distributed in the body of the vessel, under the ward-room.

I shall also take a portion of the shot from under the cabin and put them further aft. These changes will put the vessel in good trim for sea-service, and will greatly tend to relieve her of much of the strain upon the "overhang" in a head sea, and they can easily be restored to their position when necessary to put her in fighting trim.

I have yet to take in coal and provisions, and shall be ready for sea in two or three days, when I will take advantage of the first favorable weather to make the passage to Port Royal.

I am, very respectfully, your obedient servant,

JOHN L. WORDEN, *Commander.*

Acting Rear-Admiral S. P. LEE,
Commanding N. A. B. Squadron, Hampton Roads, Virginia.

A true copy.

F. R. WEBB, *Acting Ensign.*

Preparations for passage of Montauk from Beaufort to Port Royal.

UNITED STATES FLAG-SHIP MINNESOTA,
Newport News, Virginia, January 29, 1863.

SIR: I beg to enclose a copy (January 14) of a report from Commander J. L. Worden, commanding United States iron-clad steamer Montauk, at Beaufort, North Carolina, on his preparations for his passage to Port Royal, South Carolina.

I have the honor to be, sir, very respectfully, yours,

S. P. LEE,
Acting Rear-Admiral, Commanding N. A. B. Squadron.

Hon. GIDEON WELLES.

UNITED STATES STEAMER MONTAUK,
Beaufort, North Carolina, January 14, 1863.

Your order of the 8th instant, directing me to order the paymaster of this vessel to take passage in the steamer towing her, with his books, accounts, funds, &c., and to make every professional arrangement I may judge best for the safety of the vessel, and of the officers and crew under my command, is received.

Since my communication of the 9th instant, I have completed the changes therein indicated; have taken in coal, provisions, &c., and was ready to go to sea on the 12th instant; but the weather looking unsettled, I did not deem it prudent to do so. It is now blowing from the southward and westward. I shall take advantage of the first favorable change to proceed to Port Royal, in obedience to your order of the 7th instant.

Other than the changes I have made in the vessel in relation to the rearrangement of the ballast, nothing more occurs to me to be done that will be likely to add to her safety at sea. I do not think it prudent to take any amount of weight from the hold on account of her great top weight. I have, however, only taken in ninety tons of coal, which amount will give her sufficient stability, and, of course, not bring her so deep, bodily, as would full bunkers, which hold about 130 tons. The vessel's trim now is, out of the water forward, 38 inches; out of the water aft, 30½ inches; out of the water amidships, 15¾ inches. These measurements make her draught forward 10 feet 9½ inches; aft 11 feet 5 inches, which I consider a good sea trim. A change of ballast can soon be made to put her in fighting trim. When in fighting trim (with full coal-bunkers) she would be deeper in the water, bodily, with a greater draught of water forward, but no material change in the draught aft.

Respectfully, your obedient servant,

JOHN L. WORDEN,
Commander.

Acting Rear-Admiral S. P. LEE,
Commanding N. A. B. Squadron, Hampton Roads.

A true copy.

F. R. WEBB,
Acting Ensign.

Passage of the Nahant to Port Royal.

UNITED STATES FLAG-SHIP MINNESOTA,
Newport News, Va., March 2, 1863.

SIR: Commander Armstrong, commanding United States steamer State of Georgia, reports to me from Port Royal, South Carolina, under date of February 23, that he left Hampton Roads on the 16th with the United States iron-clad Nahant in tow, in obedience to my orders; that he had rainy and disagreeable weather on the passage, but that the Nahant seemed buoyant, and made good weather, towing easily, his engine working to its full pressure to attain its greatest speed, and that he arrived safely at Port Royal on the 20th. He proposed to leave on the 23d ultimo to rejoin the blockade off Wilmington.

I have the honor to be, sir, very respectfully, yours,

S. P. LEE,
Acting Rear-Admiral, Comd'g N. A. B. Squadron.

Hon. GIDEON WELLES,
Secretary of the Navy, Washington, D. C.

Passage of the Roanoke to Hampton Roads.

UNITED STATES IRON-CLAD FRIGATE ROANOKE,
Hampton Roads, Va., July 11, 1863.

SIR: I have the honor to report my arrival in Hampton Roads with the United States iron-clad frigate Roanoke after her trial trip at sea.

Having been detained by fogs in the lower bay of New York, after the repairing of the pillow block of one of the turrets, I got to sea on Thursday, the 9th instant, passing the bar at New York at two o'clock p. m.

A heavy swell from the south had set in, sufficiently to test her buoyancy, which I found much greater than I had expected, from the immense quantity of iron she carries. Her rolling motion, however, is so great as to preclude the possibility of fighting her guns at sea, and I was obliged to secure them by bracing them with pieces of timber to prevent their "fetching away" in the rolling motion to which the ship is subjected, in even the swell we encountered. We made the trip in less than forty-eight hours, making a speed of from five to six knots an hour, with from thirty to thirty-five revolutions, with occasional heatings of the journals, for cooling which she had to be stopped, for the particulars of which I refer to the report of the engineers. The tug which accompanied us was not brought into requisition to tow or assist, we making the trip under our own steam and motive power alone. Her steering gear we found to be inconvenient, taking two men one minute and a half to put the helm hard down from amidships, and requiring nineteen (19) revolutions of the wheel in the operation. The steam steering apparatus of Mr. Sickles I considered much better, requiring but one man to handle the wheel, seven turns only of which were needed to heave it hard down, and to do this but twenty (20) seconds were required, and would, with a larger barrel to the wheel, require only the same number of turns as our ordinary steering wheels. I only regretted it was not fitted to the forward turret, where our best compass (Ritchie's) was fitted.

Though I do not consider the Roanoke adapted to fighting a battle at sea on account of her rolling, rendering her guns unserviceable, and exposing her to shot below her iron plating, yet she has proved herself capable of being safely and readily transported from harbor to harbor upon our coast for the defence of any part thereof.

I have the honor to be, very respectfully, your obedient servant,

B. F. SANDS,

Captain United States Navy, senior officer present.

Hon. GIDEON WELLES,

Secretary of the Navy.

Report of Captain G. Gansevoort of a joint reconnoissance up James river.

UNITED STATES IRON-CLAD ROANOKE,

Off Newport News, Va., August 8, 1863.

SIR: I have the honor to inform the department that, in accordance with the permission asked and granted, I accompanied Major General Foster in his recent reconnoissance up the James river. The force consisted of the Sangamon, Commander S. Nicholson; Commodore Barney, Acting Lieutenant Commander S. Huse; and Cohasset, Acting Master S. Cox; also the John Farron, an army boat. All these vessels were armed, except the latter, which had aboard a corps of sharpshooters.

The Sangamon, towed by the gunboat Barney and the tug Cohasset, left the anchorage off Newport News about 2 p. m., August 4. The John Farron, with Major General Foster and staff, Brigadier Generals Naglee and Potter, with myself, Surgeon Woodworth, and Acting Master Hargous, soon followed. At 8 p. m. the vessels under my command and the Farron anchored off Jamestown island in seven fathoms water. Got under way next morning at half-past four. At eight the flag-of-truce boat New York, with prisoners, passed us, bound to City Point. At half-past eight passed Fort Powhatan, which remained in a dismantled state. At eleven all the army and navy officers left the Farron and went on board the Sangamon. When off Tillman's wharf there was a slight discharge of musketry from the shore, which was responded to by the Sangamon with one eleven-inch shot. At half-past four p. m. the Sangamon anchored off Dutch Gap, owing to the low stage of water on the bar. General Foster and staff, myself, and Acting Master Hargous, then went aboard the Commodore Barney, and were followed by the Cohasset. When just beyond Coxe's two torpedoes exploded under the starboard bow of the Barney, producing a lively concussion, and washing the decks with the agitated water. Some twenty men were either swept or jumped overboard, two of whom are missing, and may have been drowned. The engine of the vessel was partly disabled by the cutting of the steam-pipe and the connexion of the steam-whistle. The Commodore Barney was then taken in tow by the Cohasset, and they came to anchor at Dutch Gap about half-past seven. At half-past eight o'clock the Cohasset went up the river on picket duty.

The next morning at early daylight the Sangamon got under way, towed by the Barney and Cohasset. Near Four Mile creek, about 5 a. m., the enemy opened fire with artillery and musketry. The Sangamon and Barney returned the fire. The Barney was disabled by a shot through the boiler, below the water-mark. The tug was sent to her assistance, and got her off, she having drifted ashore. The Sangamon anchored, the narrowness of the stream preventing her from turning and going to the aid of the Barney. At half-past seven a. m. the Sangamon again weighed, with the Barney in tow, and the Cohasset on the port side. About this time the army tug Jesup came up the river, and assisted in towing the disabled vessel. At 9.25 a. m., when near Turkey Island bend, the enemy opened with artillery and musketry, and repeatedly hit all the vessels, but did them no material damage, and injured no one. The fire was briskly returned by the Barney and Jesup. At 9.45 the firing ceased. For much of the time the vessels were exposed to a raking fire. More than thirty round shot penetrated the Barney. The Jesup and Cohasset were hit several times, and the Sangamon once in the port bow, making only a slight indentation. The marks of musketry on the different vessels were almost innumerable, the difficulty being rather to avoid than miss the targets. Below City Point the tug-boat John Farron, which was left behind on our passage up the river, came alongside, and assisted in towing. About 8 p. m. army boats cast off, and Sangamon anchored below Deep Water shoals. Shortly after, the Farron grounded, got off at daylight, and reached Newport News at 6 a. m. The other vessel arrived and anchored shortly afterwards.

The casualties were few. Acting Master Cox, of the Cohasset, was killed by a round shot, which perforated his body. Three men were slightly wounded from musketry, and two were supposed to be drowned at the time of the explosion of the torpedoes.

Officers and crew all behaved with that characteristic gallantry which has ever distinguished the navy.

The purpose of the reconnoissance was fully and satisfactorily accomplished.

Very respectfully, your obedient servant,

GUERT GANSEVOORT,
Captain and Senior Officer.

Hon. GIDEON WELLES,
Secretary of the Navy, Washington, D. C.

SOUTH ATLANTIC SQUADRON.

The capture of Charleston—first instructions.

[Confidential.]

NAVY DEPARTMENT, *May* 13, 1862.

SIR: This department has determined to capture Charleston as soon as Richmond falls, which will relieve the iron boats Galena and Monitor. These vessels, and such others as can be spared from Hampton Roads, will be sent to Bull's bay under convoy of the Susquehanna.

The glorious achievements of our navy, inaugurated by yourself, give every reason to hope for a successful issue at this point, where rebellion first lighted the flame of civil war.

The War Department send instructions to-day to General Hunter, with whom you will consult and with whom you will co-operate fully, unless the move should be purely naval, when he will render you every assistance.

Very respectfully, &c.,

GIDEON WELLES.

Flag-Officer S. F. DUPONT,
Commanding S. A. B. Squadron, Port Royal, S. C.

Rear-Admiral DuPont desires the Ironsides.

FLAG-SHIP WABASH,
Port Royal Harbor, S. C., September 5, 1862.

SIR: The iron-clads or rams built at Charleston have been described to me, by intelligent persons who have seen them, as well protected by their armor, but as not formidable for offensive operations against our ships, in consequence of their deficiency in steam power, it having been intended to place in them engines taken from old steamers belonging to South Carolina.

If it be true that English steam engines have been provided for them, as reported to me by the department, it becomes my duty to urge upon it the necessity of sending some iron-clad vessels of our own to render our position off Charleston tenable.

Vessels, even imperfectly covered with armor, emerging from the protection of forts, and always provided with a place of refuge, would be comparatively secure, while they might do great harm to wooden ships, especially of the light class, which form the chief material of this squadron. If by any possibility the blockading force off Charleston could be destroyed or compelled to retire, it would produce a moral impression to our disadvantage even more disastrous than the actual loss itself. If it be possible to send the Ironsides to take up a position off that harbor, the efforts of the enemy would be completely frustrated.

Very respectfully, &c.,

S. F. DUPONT,
Rear-Admiral, Com'dg S. A. B. Squadron.

Hon. GIDEON WELLES,
Secretary of the Navy.

Second instructions for the capture of Charleston.

[Confidential.]

NAVY DEPARTMENT, *January* 6, 1863.

SIR: The New Ironsides, Passaic, Montauk, Patapsco, and Weehawken, (iron-clads,) have been ordered to, and are now on the way to, join your command, to enable you to enter the harbor of Charleston and demand the surrender of all its defences, or suffer the consequences of a refusal.

General Hunter will be sent to Port Royal with about ten thousand men, to act as shall be deemed best, after consultation with yourself. The capture of this most important port, however, rests solely upon the success of the naval force, and it is committed to your hands to execute, with the confidence the department reposes in your eminent ability and energy. Successful at Charleston, the only remaining point within the limits of your command is Savannah. If this place can be captured by the iron-clads, attack it immediately under the panic which will be produced by the fall of Charleston. If part only of the iron-clads are required to make the attack at Savannah, (and I trust such may be the case,) send off the remainder under careful towage to Pensacola. If Savannah cannot be attacked with iron-clads, send immediately, upon the fall of Charleston, the New Ironsides and two of the others (convoyed) to Pensacola. Do not allow the New Ironsides to wait for her masts—she can be convoyed. The importance of striking a blow at once at Mobile, in the event of the fall of Charleston, will be apparent to your mind.

Very respectfully,

GIDEON WELLES,
Secretary of the Navy.

Rear-Admiral S. F. DUPONT,
Commanding S. A. B. Squadron, Port Royal, S. C.

Transmitting information concerning harbor and anchorage of Little river.

[Confidential.]

NAVY DEPARTMENT, *January* 15, 1863.

SIR: I transmit herewith, for your information, a copy of an intercepted letter signed "Maj. A. B. Magruder, Wilmington, N. C.," giving instructions relative to the harbor and anchorage of Little river, near the boundary line of North and South Carolina.

Very respectfully,

GIDEON WELLES,
Secretary of the Navy.

Rear-Admiral S. F. DUPONT,
Commanding S. A. B. Squadron, Port Royal, S. C.

Rear-Admiral DuPont's views upon the contemplated attack on Charleston.

[Despatch No. 36, 1863.—Confidential.]

FLAG-SHIP WABASH,
Port Royal, S. C., January 24, 1863.

SIR: I have the honor to acknowledge the receipt of the department's confidential despatch of the 15th instant.

The department has been informed, through private letters to the Assistant Secretary, of the general character and extent of the defences of Charleston.

I shall endeavor to execute its wishes with such force as it may deem necessary for this purpose.

The department is aware that I have never shrunk from assuming any responsibility which circumstances called for, nor desired to place any failure of mine on others. But the interests involved in the success or failure of this undertaking strike me as so momentous to the nation, at home and abroad, at this particular period, that I am confident it will require no urging from me to induce the department to put at my disposal every means in its power to insure success, especially by sending additional iron-clads, if possible, to those mentioned in your despatch.

The army is not ready, even for the limited co-operation it can give, though anxious to render every assistance.

Very respectfully, your obedient servant,

S. F. DUPONT,
Rear-Admiral, Com'dg S. A. B. Squadron.

Hon. GIDEON WELLES,
Secretary of the Navy.

Letter of the Secretary of the Navy advising Rear-Admiral DuPont to abandon the attack upon Charleston if he deems the number of iron-clads insufficient to render its capture certain.

[Confidential.]

NAVY DEPARTMENT, *January* 31, 1863.

SIR: Your confidential despatch No. 36, dated the 24th instant, has been received.

The department does not desire to urge an attack upon Charleston with inadequate means; and if, after careful examination, you deem the number of iron-clads insufficient to render the capture of that port reasonably certain, it must be abandoned. The department is not acquainted with the harbor obstructions constructed by the rebels, and therefore cannot advise with you in regard to those obstacles. If they are not considered sufficient to prevent your entrance, it is not believed possible for the rebels to prevent your success with all other means combined. The five iron-clads sent you are all that the department has completed on the Atlantic coast, with the exception of one retained at Newport News to watch the iron-clad Richmond. No others are likely to be finished and sent to sea within the next six weeks. A large number of our best wooden vessels, necessary for the blockade, but not for the attack, are unfortunately required in the West Indies to pursue the Florida and Alabama. This withdrawal of blockading vessels renders the capture of Charleston and Mobile imperative, and the department will share the responsibility imposed upon the commanders who make the attempt.

Enclosed is a copy of a memorandum furnished by the Secretary of War.

Very respectfully,

GIDEON WELLES,
Secretary of the Navy.

Rear-Admiral S. F. DuPont,
Commanding S. A. B. Squadron, Port Royal, S. C.

Secretary of the Navy to Rear-Admiral DuPont relative to movements of iron-clads.

[Confidential.]

Navy Department, *February* 18, 1863.

Sir: The department believes that, with great exertion, it will be able to get the Catskill, Commander George W. Rodgers, to Port Royal in the course of the next ten days.

After the attack upon Charleston, you will send one iron clad back to Hampton Roads for the attack upon Wilmington; the others to be sent as previously ordered.

Very respectfully,

GIDEON WELLES,
Secretary of the Navy.

Rear-Admiral S. F. DuPont,
Commanding S. A. B. Squadron, Port Royal, S. C.

The Secretary of the Navy advises Rear-Admiral DuPont that two more iron-clads are added to his squadron.

[Confidential.]

Navy Department, *March* 6, 1863.

Sir: The Nantucket and Keokuk are added to your squadron. The force of iron-clads, therefore, will be the Montauk, Weehawken, New Ironsides, Passaic, Nahant, Patapsco, Catskill, Nantucket, and Keokuk.

Assuming that these vessels escape from loss in contemplated movements, you will, immediately after your attack upon Charleston and Savannah is completed, send to Hampton Roads the Passaic, Montauk, and Keokuk.

Let all others proceed without delay to Pensacola. The condition of affairs in the gulf requires a force of iron-clads to be sent there without delay; but you may retain two of the Monitors destined for the gulf, unless the attack upon Savannah results in the destruction of the iron-clads in that port. Even in that event, the department leaves it to your judgment to send the six remaining iron-clads south, or only four; only impressing upon you that the exigencies of the public service are very great in Rear-Admiral Farragut's squadron.

Very respectfully,

GIDEON WELLES,
Secretary of the Navy.

Rear-Admiral S. F. DuPont,
Commanding S. A. B. Squadron, Port Royal, S. C.

To send iron-clads to Mobile.

[Confidential.]

Navy Department, *April* 2, 1862.

Sir: The exigencies of the public service are so pressing in the gulf that the department directs you to send all the iron-clads that are in a fit condition to move, after your present attack upon Charleston, directly to New Orleans, reserving to yourself only two.

Very respectfully,

GIDEON WELLES,
Secretary of the Navy.

Rear-Admiral S. F. DuPont,
Commanding S. A. B. Squadron, Port Royal, S. C.

First attack on Fort Sumter.

Flag-Ship New Ironsides,
Inside Charleston Bar, April 8, 1863.

Sir: I yesterday moved up with eight iron-clads and this ship and attacked Fort Sumter, intending to pass it and commence action on its northwest face, in accordance with my order of battle.

The heavy fire we received from it and Fort Moultrie, and the nature of the obstructions, compelled the attack from the outside. It was fierce and obstinate, and the gallantry of the officers and men of the vessels engaged was conspicuous.

This vessel could not be brought into such close action as I endeavored to get her; owing to the narrow channel and rapid current she became partly unmanageable, and was twice forced to anchor to prevent her going ashore, once owing to her having come into collision with two of the Monitors. She could not get nearer than one thousand yards.

Owing to the condition of the tide and unavoidable accident, I had been compelled to delay action until late in the afternoon, and toward evening, finding no impression made upon the fort, I made the signal to withdraw the ships, intending to renew the attack this morning.

But the commanders of the Monitors came on board and reported verbally the injuries to their vessels, when, without hesitation or consultation, (for I never hold councils of war,) I determined not to renew the attack, for in my judgment it would have converted a failure into a disaster; and I will only add that Charleston cannot be taken by a purely naval attack, and the army could give me no co-operation. Had I succeeded in entering the harbor I should have had twelve hundred men and thirty-two guns, but five of the eight iron-clads were wholly or partially disabled after a brief engagement.

The reports of the commanding officers will be forwarded with my detailed report, and I send Commander Rhind home with this despatch, whose vessel sank this morning from the effects of the bombardment yesterday, and who will give the department all the information it may desire.

I have alluded above only to Forts Sumter and Moultrie, but the vessels were also exposed to the fire of the batteries on Cummings's Point, Mount Pleasant, the Redan, and Fort Beauregard.

Very respectfully, your obedient servant,

S. F. DUPONT,
Rear-Admiral, Commanding S. A. B. Squadron.

P. S.—I forward herewith a list of the casualties, marked Nos. 1 and 2, on board the Keokuk and Nahant.

S. F. DUPONT.

List of casualties on board the Keokuk.

UNITED STATES FLAG-SHIP NEW IRONSIDES,
Charleston Harbor, April 8, 1863.

The following is a list of casualties on board the United States steam battery Keokuk in the action of April 7:

Wounded.—Alexander McIntosh, (acting ensign,) and Charles McLaughlin, (seaman,) dangerously; James Ryan and William McDonald, (seamen,) severely; Charles B. Mott, (landsman,) painfully; Commander A. C. Rhind, slightly; Richard Nicholson, (quartermaster,) David Chaplin, J. W. Abbott, George Watson, O. C. Clifford, J. O'Connell, J. E. O'Connor, Henry Swords, John Brown, 2d, (seamen,) and J. Cuddybuck, (ship's cook,) slightly.

Very respectfully, your obedient servant,

A. C. RHIND, *Commander.*

Rear-Admiral S. F. DUPONT.

Casualties on board the Nahant.

UNITED STATES IRON-CLAD NAHANT,
Off Charleston, April 7, 1863.

SIR: I have to report the following casualties in the action of to-day:

Commander John Downes, (Massachusetts,) slight contusion of foot from a piece of iron loosened from pilot-house. Pilot Isaac Sofield, (New Jersey,) severe contusion of neck and shoulder from flying bolt in pilot-house; is doing well. Quartermaster Edward Cobb, (Massachusetts,) compound communicated fracture of skull from flying bolt in pilot-house; has since died. John MacAlstine, seaman, (Canada,) concussion of brain from flying bolt in turret striking him on the head; is doing well. John Jackson, seaman, (Massachusetts,) Roland Martin, seaman, (Massachusetts,) James Murray, seaman, (Massachusetts,) were very slightly hurt by flying bolts in turret, not disabling any of them.

Very respectfully, your obedient servant,

C. EMERY STEDMAN,
Assistant Surgeon United States Navy.

Commander JOHN DOWNES, U. S. N.,
Commanding U. S. Steamer Nahant.

Forwarded:

JOHN DOWNES, *Commander.*

Detailed report of Rear-Admiral Samuel F. DuPont.

FLAG-SHIP WABASH,
Port Royal Harbor, S. C., April 15, 1863.

SIR: In my previous despatch of April 8 I gave a brief account of the attack on Fort Sumter on the afternoon of the 7th instant, and I have the honor to present to the department a more detailed report.

On the morning of the 2d instant I left Port Royal for North Edisto, hoisting my flag on the United States steamer James Adger, Commander Patterson, and crossed the bar the same day.

As there was some reason to believe that, on the departure of the iron-clads from Port Royal, there might be an attempt to commit a raid by the Atlanta and other rams at Savannah, and as the army was apprehensive of an attack on their positions at Hilton Head and Beaufort, I had ordered Captain Steedman to Port Royal with his vessel, the Paul Jones, having previously directed the Wabash, Commander Corbin, and Vermont, Commander Reynolds, to be hauled over to the Hilton Head shore to protect the vast amount of public property there. The Sebago was also stationed in Calibogue sound, the Marblehead in Savannah river, and the E. B. Hale in Broad river; whilst the Paul Jones, owing to her light draught, was also to make frequent reconnoissances up the latter stream and the Beaufort river.

On the 5th instant, having provided steamers to tow the iron-clads, I left North Edisto for Charleston with all the vessels intended to participate in the attack on that place, and arrived there in the afternoon.

In accordance with my previous arrangements, the Keokuk, Commander Rhind, aided by Captain Boutelle, of the United States Coast Survey, and Acting Master Platt, with Pilot Godfrey and others, proceeded at once to buoy the bar, and to report the depth of water which could be availed of in crossing the next morning with the New Ironsides.

The Patapsco, Commander Ammen, and the Catskill, Commander G. W. Rodgers, covered the Keokuk during this operation, and afterwards anchored inside the bar that same evening, in order to protect the buoys.

On the morning of the 6th instant I crossed the bar with the New Ironsides, Commodore T. Turner, and the rest of the iron-clads, viz., Passaic, Captain Drayton; Weehawken, Captain John Rodgers; Montauk, Captain J. S. Worden; Patapsco, Commander Ammen; Catskill, Commander G. W. Rodgers; Nantucket, Commander Fairfax; Nahant, Commander Downes, and the Keokuk, Commander Rhind, intending to proceed the same day to the attack of Fort Sumter, and thence to the city of Charleston; but after reaching an anchorage inside, the weather became so hazy, preventing our seeing the ranges, that the pilots declined to go further. I herewith enclose (marked No. 1) the order of battle and the plan of attack, in which the Weehawken, Captain John Rodgers, with a raft in front, was to be the leading vessel of the line, and the Keokuk, Commander Rhind, was to be the last, the New Ironsides being in the centre, from which signals could be better made to both ends of the line.

On the following day, April 7, at noon, this being the earliest hour at which, owing to the state of the tide, the pilots would consent to move, I made signal to the vessels to weigh anchor, having previously ordered them not to reply to the batteries on Morris island, but reserve their fire until they could pass Fort Sumter, in case there were no obstructions, and attack the northwest face. The chain of the Weehawken, the leading vessel, had, however, become entangled in the grapnels of the pioneer raft, and the vessels were delayed in moving until about fifteen minutes past one, when, everything being clear, the Weehawken moved on, followed by the Passaic and others in the regular order of battle.

On the way up the leading vessel passed a number of buoys strewed about in every direction, causing a suspicion of torpedoes, one of which burst near the Weehawken, without, however, producing any serious injury.

At ten minutes past two the Weehawken, the leading vessel, signalled obstructions in her vicinity, and soon after approached very close to them. They extended across the harbor from Fort Moultrie to Fort Sumter, and were marked by rows of casks very near together, and in several lines. Beyond these, again, piles were seen extending from James island to the middle ground.

At 2.50 the guns of Fort Moultrie opened upon the Weehawken, followed shortly after by all the batteries on Sullivan's island, Morris island, and Fort Sumter.

Not being able to pass the obstructions, the Weehawken, and, successively, the Passaic, Nahant, and others, were obliged to turn, which threw the line into some confusion as the other vessels approached. This was particularly the case with the flag-ship, which became, in a measure, entangled with the Monitors, and could not bring her battery to bear upon Fort Sumter without great risk of firing into them. She was obliged on her way up to anchor twice, to prevent her from going ashore, and on one of these occasions in consequence of having come into collision with two of the iron-clads.

The Monitors and the Keokuk were able to get within easy range of Fort Sumter at distances varying from 550 to 800 yards, in which positions they were subjected, successively, to a tremendous concentrated fire from all the batteries on Sullivan's island, Morris island, Sumter, and others of the most formidable kind, and from guns of the heaviest calibre.

Not being able to place the New Ironsides where I desired, though she was within a distance of 1,000 yards, and evening approaching, at 4.30 I made signal to withdraw from action, intending to resume the attack the next morning.

During the evening the commanding officers of the iron-clads came on board the flag-ship, and, to my regret, I soon became convinced of the utter impracticability of taking the city of Charleston by the force under my command.

No ship had been exposed to the severest fire of the enemy over forty (40) minutes, and yet in that brief period, as the department will perceive by the detailed reports of the commanding officers, five of the iron-clads were wholly or partially disabled; disabled, too, (as the obstructions could not be passed,) in that which was most essential to our success—I mean in their armament, or power of inflicting injury by their guns.

Commander Rhind, in the Keokuk, had only been able to fire three times during the short period he was exposed to the guns of the enemy, and was obliged to withdraw from action to prevent his vessel from sinking, which event occurred on the following morning.

The Nahant, Commander Downes, was most seriously damaged, her turret being so jammed as effectually to prevent its turning; many of the bolts of both turret and pilot-house were broken, and the latter became nearly untenable in consequence of the nuts and ends flying across it.

Captain P. Drayton, in the Passaic, after the fourth fire from her 11-inch gun, was unable to use it again during the action; and his turret also became jammed, though he was, after some delay, enabled to get it in motion again.

Commander Ammen, of the Patapsco, lost the use of his rifled gun after the fifth fire, owing to the carrying away of the forward cap square bolts. On the Nantucket, Commander Fairfax reports that after the third shot from the XV-inch gun, the port stopper became jammed, several shot striking very near the port and driving in the plates, preventing the further use of that gun during the action.

The other iron-clads, though struck many times severely, were still able to use their guns, but I am convinced that, in all probability, in another thirty minutes they would have been likewise disabled.

In the detailed reports herewith forwarded, from the commanding officers of all the vessels engaged, excepting that of the New Ironsides, not yet received, (respectively marked Nos. 2, 3, 4, 5, 6, 7, 8, 9,) the department will be fully informed of the character and extent of the injuries received by these vessels, and to which I have only partially referred.

I also forward herewith a statement in tabular form, (marked No. 10,) drawn up by the ordnance officer, Lieutenant Mackenzie, by which, among other things, it appears that only one hundred and thirty-nine shot and shell were fired by our vessels, though during the same period the enemy poured upon us an incessant storm of round shot and shell, rifled projectiles of all descriptions, and red-hot shot.

Any attempt to pass through the obstructions I have referred to would have entangled the vessels, and held them under the most severe fire of heavy ordnance that has ever been delivered; and while it is barely possible that some vessels might have forced their way through, it would only have been to be again impeded by fresh and more formidable obstructions and to encounter other powerful batteries, with which the whole harbor of Charleston has been lined.

I had hoped that the endurance of the iron-clads would have enabled them to have borne any weight of fire to which they might have been exposed; but when I found that so large a portion of them were wholly or one-half disabled by less than an hour's engagement, before attempting to remove (overcome) the obstructions, or testing the power of the torpedoes, I was convinced that persistence in the attack would only result in the loss of the greater portion of the iron-clad fleet, and in leaving many of them inside the harbor, to fall into the hands of the enemy.

The slowness of our fire, and our inability to occupy any battery that we might silence, or to prevent its being restored under cover of night, were difficulties of the gravest character, and until the outer forts should have been taken, the army could not enter the harbor or afford me any assistance.

The want of success, however, will not prevent me from bringing to the notice of the department the gallant officers and men who took part in the desperate conflict.

Commodore Turner of the New Ironsides, Captain Drayton of the Passaic, Captain John Rodgers of the Weehawken, Captain J. L. Worden of the Montauk, Commander Ammen of the Patapsco, Commander George W. Rodgers of the Catskill, Commander Fairfax of the Nantucket, Commander Downes of the Nahant, and Commander Rhind of the Keokuk, did everything that the utmost gallantry and skill could accomplish, in the management of their untried vessels. These commanding officers have long been known to me; many of them served in this squadron before, and were present at the capture of the Port Royal forts; they are men of the highest professional capacity and courage, and fully sustained their reputations, coming up to my requirements. I commend them and their reports, which speak of those under them, to the consideration of the department.

I took my personal staff with me to the New Ironsides. On this, as on all other occasions, I had invaluable assistance from the fleet captain, Commander C. R. P. Rodgers, who was with me in the pilot-house, directing the movements of the squadron. For now over eighteen months in this war this officer has been afloat with me, and, in my opinion, no language could over state his services to his country, to this fleet, and to myself as its commander-in-chief.

Lieutenant S. W. Preston, my flag lieutenant, who has also been with me for the same period, exhibited his usual vigilance and zeal, and, with that ability which is so far beyond his years, he arranged a special code of signals, which was used, and served on the gun-deck battery of the New Ironsides.

My aid, Ensign M. L. Johnson, full of spirit and energy, made the signals under difficult circumstances, and kept an accurate note of all that were made to and from the fleet.

Lieutenant A. S. Mackenzie, the ordnance officer of the squadron, had been preparing his department of the expedition with ceaseless labor, care, and intelligence. He served also on the gun deck of the New Ironsides.

The reserved squadron of wooden vessels referred to in my general order of battle, under Captain J. F. Green, of the Canandaigua, was always in readiness, but their services in the engagement were not called into action.

Very respectfully, your obedient servant,

S. F DUPONT,
Rear-Admiral, Commanding S. A. B. Squadron.

P. S.—Since the above was written, the report of Commodore Turner, of the New Ironsides, has been received, and is herewith enclosed, (marked No. 11.)

S. F. D. P.
Rear-Admiral, &c.

Order of battle aud plan of attack upon Charleston, South Carolina.

FLAG-SHIP JAMES ADGER,
North Edisto, S. C., April 4, 1863.

The bar will be buoyed by the Keokuk, Commander Rhind, assisted by C. O Boutelle, assistant United States Coast Survey, commanding the Bibb, by Acting Ensign Platt and the pilots of the squadron.

The commanding officers will, previous to crossing, make themselves acquainted with the value of the buoys.

The vessels will, on signal being made, form in the prescribed order ahead, at intervals of one cable's length.

The squadron will pass up the main ship channel without returning the fire of the batteries on Morris island, unless signal should be made to commence action.

The ships will open fire on Fort Sumter when within easy range, and will take up a position to the northward and westward of that fortification, engaging its left or northwest face at a distance of from six hundred to eight hundred yards, firing low and aiming at the centre embrasure.

The commanding officers will instruct their officers and men to carefully avoid wasting a shot, and will enjoin upon them the necessity of precision rather than rapidity of fire.

Each ship will be prepared to render every assistance possible to vessels that may require it.

The special code of signals prepared for the iron-clad vessels will be used in action.

After the reduction of Fort Sumter, it is probable that the next point of attack will be the batteries on Morris island.

The order of battle will be the line ahead in the following succession:

1. Weekawken
2. Passaic.
3. Montauk.
4. Patapsco.
5. New Ironsides.
6. Catskill.
7. Nantucket.
8. Nahant.
9. Keokuk.

A squadron of vessels, of which Captain J. F. Green will be the senior officer, will be formed outside the bar, and near the entrance buoy, consisting of the following vessels: Canandaigua, Housatonic, Huron, Unadilla, Wissahickon, and will be held in readiness to support the iron-clads when they attack the batteries on Morris island.

S. F. DUPONT,
Rear-Admiral, Commanding S. A. B. Squadron.

Report of Captain Percival Drayton, commanding United States iron-clad Passaic

UNITED STATES IRON-CLAD PASSAIC,
Off Morris Island, S. C., April 8, 1863.

In obedience to your signal, I yesterday at 12.30 got under way, prepared to follow the Weehawken, which vessel had on the bow a raft projection for catching torpedoes; this, however, pulling her anchor and causing some delay. I at 12.40 signalled for permission to go ahead. The Weehawken, however, having at length cleared her anchor, proceeded at 1.15 towards Charleston, followed by this vessel. On the way up a number of buoys of various descriptions were passed, strewed about in every direction, and causing suspicion of torpedoes, one of which machines we saw burst under the bow of the Weehawken. At 2.50 Fort Moultrie and the batteries on Sullivan's island opened, to which I replied with the XI-inch in passing, and pushed on for Sumter, whose guns began almost immediately to fire, and were at once answered by my two. When opposite the centre of the fort, we came pretty close to some obstructions, which seemed to extend the whole way from Fort Moultrie across; here I stopped, as the Weehawken had done just before. At the fourth shot from XI-inch gun, I was struck in quick succession in the lower part of the turret by two heavy shot, which bulged in its plates and beams, and forcing together the rails on which the XI-inch carriage worked, rendered it wholly useless for the remainder of the action, several hours being necessary to put it again in working order. Soon after it was discovered that there was something the matter with the turret itself, which could not be moved, and on examination it was found that a part of the brass ring underneath it had been broken off, and being forced in board, had jammed; on clearing this the turret could again be moved, but for some time irregularly.

A little after, a very heavy rifle shot struck the upper edge of the turret, broke all of its eleven plates, and then glancing upwards took the pilot-house, yet with such force as to make an indentation of two and a half inches, extending nearly the whole length of the shot. The blow was so severe as to considerably mash in the pilot-house, bend it over, open the plates and squeeze out the top, so that on one side it was lifted up three inches above the top on which it rested, exposing the inside of the pilot-house, and rendering it likely that the next shot would take off the top itself entirely.

At 4.10, being desirous of more carefully examining into the injuries to the gun carriage and turret, as the engineer thought one of the braces which supports the latter was broken, and also to see what was the external injury to the pilot-house, and whether it was possible to get the top into place, and not being able to do this in the crowd of vessels which were all around, and under so fierce a fire, I dropped a little below Fort Moultrie, and anchored, having signalled for your permission, which was not, I think, seen, however.

I soon satisfied myself that there was nothing to be done either to the pilot-house or XI-inch gun; and the injury to the turret not proving very serious, I was just about returning to the upper fort, when you made signal to follow your motions, and very soon after, at 4.30, to retire from action.

At 5 I got under way, and followed the Ironsides to my present anchorage.

The only really serious injuries were the ones mentioned above, although the vessel was struck thirty-five times, as follows: outside armor, fifteen times, which it has been too rough to examine; deck, five times, once very badly; turret, ten times; pilot-house, twice; smoke-pipe, once; flag-staff over turret shot away, and boat shattered.

There was a little motion, and in consequence some of the outside shots are low down. Several bolt-heads were knocked off, and thrown into the pilot-house and turret, and the former might have done serious injury to those inside, had they not been stopped by a sheet-iron lining which I had placed there while at Port Royal.

Owing to the delays caused by the various accidents ending in the entire disabling of one gun, I was only able to fire four times from the XI-inch, and nine from the XV-inch gun. There was some loss of time, also, from the necessity of using the sectional rammer, as the fire was all around, and required the ports to be kept closed.

On account of the dense smoke I was not able to see the effect of my own shots, but, except a few scars, I could not perceive either yesterday or this morning, when I had a very good view of its lower face, that the fort was in the least injured, and I am satisfied that our limited number of guns, with their slow fire, and liability to get out of order, were no match for the hundreds which were concentrated on them, at distances, perhaps, scarcely anywhere beyond a half mile, and nearly as well protected against injury from shot as were ours.

I could see several ranges of plies running nearly across the upper harbor, the first line having a narrow opening, just beyond which were the enemy's steamers, three of them apparently iron-clads.

I was more than usually incommoded by smoke during the action, owing, no doubt, to the difficulty of keeping the blower-bands in working order, with such an amount of water as has been for days pouring over them through the lower part of the turret—a most serious evil, and which I think calls for a remedy, if the turret is to be kept up in any but the smoothest water.

My experience at Fort McAllister satisfied me that the decks were not strong enough; and this of Fort Sumter, that the pilot-house is not capable of withstanding heavy shot for any length of time, and even throws a doubt on the turret itself or at least its machinery.

The fire to which we were subjected was as fierce, I suspect, as vessels are often exposed to; and one of my officers, who was below, tells me that at one time in a few seconds he counted fifteen shots which passed over his head just above the deck, and at times the whistling was so rapid he could not keep count at all.

This certainly shows how much battering our iron-clads escaped by being so low on the water. You probably observed yourself, in the Ironsides, the great difficulty of managing these vessels and keeping them clear of each other and the bottom, with the limited power of vision which the holes in the pilot-house afford; and when to this is added the smoke, I consider it a piece of great good luck that none of us got ashore, or received injury from collision.

In conclusion, I have to thank Lieutenant Commander Miller, and the other officers, and the crew generally, for the quiet and efficient manner in which all their duties were performed.

I am, very respectfully, your obedient servant,

P. DRAYTON, *Captain.*

Rear-Admiral S. F. DuPont,
Commanding S. A. B. Squadron, Flag-Ship Ironsides.

Report of Captain John Rodgers, commanding United States iron-clad Weehawken.

United States Steamer Weehawken,
Inside Charleston Bar, S. C., April 8, 1863

Sir: I have the honor to submit the following report:

Yesterday, April 7, one of the grapnels of the raft attached to us became so entangled in our chain that the Weehawken was detained about two hours in getting under way. In obedience to given signal we succeeded, however, in arriving under the fire of Fort Sumter at about 2.50 p. m.

The accuracy of the shooting on the part of the rebels was very great, having been obtained, no doubt, by practice at range targets, since I remarked that, as we passed a buoy, all the guns opened at once. The missiles were very formidable, being, I infer from their marks, bolts, balls, rifled shell, and steel-pointed shot. More than 100 guns, I think, fired upon us at once, with great rapidity, and mostly at short range. My counted shot-marks are fifty-three; some, I presume, have escaped attention

Two or three heavy shot struck the side armor near the same place. They have so broken the iron that it only remains in splintered fragments upon that spot; much of it can be picked off by hand, and the wood is exposed.

The deck was pierced so as to make a hole, through which water ran into the vessel; but it was not large. Thirty-six bolts were broken in the turret, and a good many in the pilot-house; but as these are concealed by an iron lining, I have no means of knowing how many.

At one time the turret revolved with difficulty in consequence of a shot upon its junction with the pilot-house, but it worked well again after a few turns had been made with higher steam. The guns and carriages performed well. At 5 o'clock, in obedience to signal, withdrew from the range of fire and anchored. From the nature of the attack the vessels were alternately under the hottest fire, and no one, I presume, may be said to have had it very severe for more than forty minutes.

We approached very close to the obstructions extending from Fort Sumter to Fort Moultrie—as near, indeed, as I could get without running upon them. They were marked by rows of casks very near together. To the eye they appeared almost to touch one another, and there was more than one line of them. To me they appeared thus:

The appearance was so formidable that, upon deliberate judgment, I thought it right not to entangle the vessel in obstructions which I did not think we could have passed through, and in which we should have been

caught. Beyond these, piles were seen between Castle Pinkney and the middle ground.

A torpedo exploded under us, or very near to us; it lifted the vessel a little, but I am unable to perceive that it has done us any damage. I have no accident to report.

The raft which we had attached to our bow did not much impede our steering, but while lying at anchor the waves converted it into a huge battering ram. In two days it had started the armor upon our bow. No vessel can carry it except in smooth water. Its motions did not correspond to the movements of the Weehawken. Sometimes, when she rose to the sea the raft fell, and the reverse. Thus we were threatened with having it on our decks or under the overhang. No prudent man would carry the torpedo attached to the raft in a fleet; an accidental collision would blow up his own friend, and he would be more dreaded than an enemy.

All the officers and men behaved so admirably, that I am unable to select one for especial commendation. I am much indebted to Mr. Robert Platt, of the United States Coast Survey steamer Bibb, for his cool and efficient pilotage of the vessel, which he continued to direct after a ball touching the pilot-house immediately over his head had given him a severe concussion.

The guns, machinery, and in a word all our appliances, were in excellent order, owing to the care and attention of the executive officer, Lieutenant Commander L. H. Newman, Acting First Assistant Engineer James G. Young, and of the other officers.

With your present means, I could not, if I were asked, recommend a renewal of the attack.

I have the honor to be your obedient servant,

JOHN RODGERS, *Captain.*

Rear-Admiral S. F. DuPont,
Commanding South Atlantic Blockading Squadron..

Report of Captain John L. Worden, commanding United States iron-clad Montauk.

United States Steamer Montauk,
Inside Charleston Bar, April 8, 1863.

Sir: I have the honor to report, that on yesterday, at thirty minutes past noon, this vessel got under way in accordance with signal from the flagship, taking the position assigned in line next astern of the Passaic, and proceeded up the channel. At fifty minutes past two o'clock p. m. Fort Moultrie opened fire at long range upon the advanced vessels, and soon after all the forts on Sullivan's island, and the two upon the upper end of Morris island, did the same. At ten minutes past three o'clock this vessel opened fire upon Fort Sumter at about eight hundred yards distance, and still advancing. A few minutes later, the leading vessels having stopped in position about six hundred yards from the fort, I also stopped in my assigned position near the Passaic, and at about the same distance from the fort as the other vessels, and delivered my fire deliberately.

Some minutes later, the flood tide having made, and setting the vessel close to some formidable looking obstructions, (which I deemed it highly important to avoid,) they turned their heads towards the flood, and I followed in their wake. As soon as I could get my vessel under control, which it was quite difficult to do in avoiding the other vessels, I turned towards the fort again, got within about seven hundred yards of it, and delivered my fire as long as I was able to hold that position; but the tide drifting us, and the other vessels being close around me, I again turned to avoid fouling them, still delivering my fire as opportunity occurred.

At about five o'clock I ceased firing and withdrew from action, in accordance with signal from flag-ship, and stood slowly down against the tide, and at 5.40 o'clock p. m. anchored in the channel about two and one-quarter miles below Fort Sumter.

For about fifty minutes only the vessels of the fleet were under a concentrated and terrific fire, and received their injuries during that time.

This vessel was hit fourteen times, but received no material damage. I enclose a report of the injuries she received, and another of the ammunition expended. I am happy to be able to report no casualties.

I desire to say that I experienced serious embarrassment in manœuvring my vessel in the narrow and uncertain channel, with the limited means of observation afforded from the pilot-house, under the rapid and concentrated fire from the forts, the vessels of the fleet close around me, and neither compass nor buoys to guide me.

After testing the weight of the enemy's fire, and observing the obstructions, I am led to believe that Charleston cannot be taken by the naval force now present, and that, had the attack been continued, it could not have failed to result in disaster.

To the officers and crew *en masse* I can proudly give unbounded praise for their coolness and efficiency and for their cheerful and ready support.

To the executive officer, Lieutenant Commander C. H. Cushman, I am much indebted for the very efficient organization of the crew, and for all the arrangements for battle. He has given me an earnest, intelligent, and efficient support on all occasions.

Acting Assistant Paymaster Samuel F. Brown, having volunteered to act as signal officer, and made himself familiar with the new code of signals adopted, was with me in the pilot-house, and, by his quickness of sight and of apprehension, was of material service to me, particularly in view of my much impaired eye sight.

Very respectfully, your obedient servant,

JOHN L. WORDEN,
Captain, Commanding Montauk.

Rear-Admiral S. F. DuPont,
Commanding South Atlantic Blockading Squadron,
United States Steamer New Ironsides, inside Charleston Bar.

Report of Lieutenant Commander C. H. Cushman, of injuries sustained by the Montauk.

The following is the report of the effect upon the United States steamer Montauk of the enemy's fire in the attack on Fort Sumter, April 7, 1863:

Hits on side armor, four. One of these is severe, detaching the entire after starboard section of plating about three-eighths of an inch from the backing. The section will require refastening. Three of these are not injuries.

Hits on turret, three; none injurious.

Hits on pilot-house, one. This hit is tolerably severe, loosening three bolts and starting in the plating somewhat. In addition, there are some light scars from grape or langrage.

Hits on the deck plating, three; none very severe. In addition, there are some grape marks also on deck, and one grape-shot lodged between bolts of forward warping chock.

Hits on upper smoke-stack, three; all unimportant. Second cutter was cut adrift and lost, and flags and staffs considerably riddled by grape-shot.

Respectfully, &c., &c.,

C. H. CUSHMAN,
Lieutenant Commanding and Executive Officer.

Captain JOHN L. WORDEN,
United States Steamer Montauk.

Report of Commander Daniel Ammen, commanding United States iron-clad Patapsco.

IRON-CLAD PATAPSCO,
Port Royal Harbor, S. C., April 14, 1863.

SIR: I have the honor to report, that on arriving off Charleston on the afternoon of the 5th, I proceeded, as directed, to cover the movements of the Keokuk when she sounded the bar, anchoring with the Catskill, as near as safety would permit. It was near sunset when the work was completed, and our pilot had received instructions. The Patapsco was immediately got under way, crossed the bar, and anchored near the inner buoy. After dark we were joined by the Catskill. At 11 p. m. a steamer was discovered approaching from the direction of Charleston. She left as soon as she found herself in our vicinity, and disappeared before I had an opportunity to fire on her. In obedience to your signal, at 12.15 p. m. of the 7th we got under way and took the position in line as assigned. Owing to unavoidable delays at the head of the line, the leading vessel reached an effective range for the heavy ordnance of the enemy at about 3 p. m., when she was opened upon from Fort Sumter, and shortly after from a sand battery above Fort Moultrie, with adjacent sand batteries, sand battery Beauregard, and the heavy guns on Cummings's Point.

The Patapsco was the fourth vessel in line, and at 3.10 opened with the 150-pounder rifle, when at a distance of 1,500 yards from Sumter. Following in position, we opened, when at about 1,200 yards, with the heavy gun. After the fifth discharge of the rifle that gun was rendered useless, from carrying away the forward cap square bolts, an injury which could not be repaired for two hours, notwithstanding the strenuous exertions of the executive officer and the senior engineer.

Shortly after our leading vessel, following the head of the line, turned seaward. At that time, or before, I discovered several rows of buoys above us; also one or two rows of piles or heavily moored wooden buoys above them, one row, to the left of Sumter, high out of the water. This last appeared to be some distance above. Endeavoring to turn, a ship's length short of the Montauk, we found the headway of the vessel cease, and that she no longer obeyed the helm. Backing, we got off, but had been sufficiently long on the enemy's obstruction to receive the concentrated fire of the batteries mentioned, consisting, as far as I can judge from the marks and pieces, of projectiles of 7 and 8-inch rifles and 10 and 11-inch columbiads. At this time we were probably within 600 yards from Fort Moultrie, and a little more than double the distance from Sumter.

We had passed several buoys for range of guns or other purposes on going up, and after getting off of the obstructions, passed down on the same side. Although I endeavored, I found it impossible at the time to make the signal that we were on an obstruction, and I have to regret that, observing the effect of our fire, the want of space or means of observation in the pilot-house, and manœuvring the vessel, prevented that close observation of the obstructions or the forces of the batteries of the enemy which would have been desirable, the seeing of all the signals made by you, or the accurate noting of the times.

After a few heavy blows on the turret, the quantity of steam before ample to turn it was insufficient, and this was also cause of annoyance, delay, and a decreased fire from the only gun available.

Obeying the signal to withdraw from action, I anchored on the port bow of the New Ironsides, ready to aid her if required, and afterwards, obeying instructions, anchored for the night in line.

Forty-seven projectiles of the enemy struck the vessel. No damage was done which disabled her, although injuries were received which multiplied would do so. Forty bolts of the smoke-stack were broken, and a chain around it will be necessary to its continued security.

The officers and crew acquitted themselves as usual. I am indebted to Acting Master Vaughan, transferred temporarily to this vessel, for valuable aid in avoiding collisions, as it is out of the question for one person to observe properly from the various light holes. I think a want of vision one of the most serious defects of this class, making it impossible to fight them advantageously, to avoid dangers, or to make a satisfactory reconnoissance.

Another question of great importance as relates to their efficient employment is the character of the battery. If it is proposed to batter down forts with a 15-inch gun, then it is quite plain that we have to come within distances at which heavy ordnance, if employed in heavy batteries against us, cannot fail in the end to injure or perhaps disable us. A comparatively light projectile, with the same charge of powder, might enable us to take such distance as would be effective, and yet be comparatively free from injury to us.

Owing to the early disabling of the rifle and the various discomfitures referred to, only five projectiles were fired from each gun. I saw several of them were effective.

I have the honor to be, very respectfully, your obedient servant,

DAN'L AMMEN,
Commander.

Rear-Admiral S. F. DuPont,
Commanding S. A. B. Squadron.

Report of Commander George W. Rodgers, commanding United States iron-clad Catskill.

UNITED STATES IRON-CLAD CATSKILL,
Inside Charleston Bar, April 8, 1863.

SIR: I have the honor to report, that immediately after the arrival of this ship off Charleston, on the 5th instant, I went close in to the bar, to cover the Keokuk while sounding out the channel. About sundown, the channel having been buoyed, I got under way, in obedience to your order, and went over the bar. It was too dark to see the buoys, but the Patapsco having gone over and being alone inside, I pushed on and anchored safely inside. During the night a steamer came in sight, apparently reconnoitring, but returned upon being discovered. The 6th, the weather was too thick to see the ranges for proceeding up the channel. The 7th, at 12.15 p. m., in obedience to signal, I got under way with the fleet. At 1.45, having formed in order of battle, line ahead, my position being next astern the flag-ship, started ahead. At 2.50, Forts Moultrie, Sumter, and Beauregard, with the batteries at Cummings's Point, Mount Pleasant, and the causeway or redan extending from Fort Moultrie, opened upon the head of the line; the flag-ship becoming unmanageable from shoal water and strong tide, I passed her. At 3.35, the first shot struck the Catskill, and at 3.39 I opened fire upon Fort Sumter, disregarding the others, the leading vessels having proceeded as far as the obstructions. I pushed on, and approaching within six hundred yards of Fort Sumter, near the Keokuk, continued my fire, which I could see take effect; one 15-inch shot apparently dismounted one of the barbette guns. At 5, in obedience to signal, I withdrew from action and anchored with the fleet inside the bar, out of range.

The cross fire from the forts and batteries was most severe. Several lines of buoys extended from Fort Sumter across the channel, and from the middle ground extended a row of piles, inside of which were several steamers. I was surprised to find, even with this severe fire, that these vessels could be so much injured in so short a time, two or three having passed me during the action to which some disaster had happened. This vessel was struck some twenty times, but without any serious injury except one shot upon the forward part of the deck, which broke both plates, the deck planking, and drove down the iron stanchion sustaining this beam about one inch, causing the deck to leak.

I am glad to say that no person was injured during the engagement. The officers and crew of this vessel all behaved with coolness and courage. Lieutenant Commander C. C. Carpenter, the executive officer, and Acting Master J. W. Simmons, directed the fire of the guns in the turret with energy and skill. To Senior Engineer George D. Emmons and Peter Trescott, quartermaster, who steered this ship, I am much indebted for the assistance rendered me.

I am, very respectfully, your obedient servant,

G. W. RODGERS, *Commander.*

Rear-Admiral S. F. DuPont,
Commanding S. A. B. Squadron.

Report of Commander D. McN. Fairfax, commanding United States iron-clad Nantucket.

UNITED STATES IRON-CLAD NANTUCKET,
Off Cummings's Point, April 8, 1863.

SIR: I have the honor to make the following report of the part taken by this vessel in the attack of yesterday upon the forts at the entrance to Charleston by the iron-clad fleet under your command.

At 1.15 p. m., in obedience to a general signal from the flag-ship, weighed anchor and took up a position the seventh vessel in order of battle, "the line ahead."

At 3.50 the batteries opened their fire upon our advanced line. About this time the New Ironsides seemed to have become unmanageable, falling off and out of line, with her head down stream. Her slow progress prevented the rearmost vessels from closing up with those already under fire. It was then the signal was thrown out to "disregard the motions of the commander-in-chief," and the rearmost vessels pushed on to gain a position within effective range of the forts.

At 3.20 the guns from Fort Beauregard opened upon this vessel at a distance of 750 yards. At 3.50, having arrived within 750 yards of Fort Sumter and 1,000 yards of Moultrie, and close up to the obstructions thrown across the channel, I directed the fire of the two guns to be opened upon Fort Sumter. We were then under the fire of three forts, and the most terrific was it for forty-five to fifty minutes. Our fire was very slow, necessarily, and not half so observable upon the walls of the forts as the rain of their rifle-shot and heavy shell was upon this vessel. After the third shot from the XV-inch gun the port stopper became jammed, several shot striking very near the port and driving in the plating; it was not used again. The XI-inch gun was fired during the entire time of one hour and fifteen minutes only twelve times.

At 5 o'clock the signal to cease firing was made. As the fleet withdrew the forts materially slackened their fire, evidently not wishing to expend their ammunition without some result. Certainly, their firing was excellent throughout; fortunately, it was directed to some half dozen iron-clads at a time. The effect of their fire upon the Keokuk, together with that of their heavy rifle-shot upon the Monitors, is sufficient proof that any one vessel could not long have withstood the concentrated fire of the enemy's batteries. The obstructions being placed at a concentrated point of fire from the three forts, shows, conclusively, that they must have been of no mean character. Our fire always drew down upon us four or five heavy rifle-shots, aimed at our ports. One rifle-shot struck within less than six inches of the XV-inch port; several struck very near. I am convinced that, although this class of vessels can stand a very heavy fire, yet the want of more guns will render them comparatively harmless before formidable earthworks and forts. I must say that I am disappointed beyond measure at this experiment of Monitors overcoming strong forts. It was a fair trial.

I am gratified to be able to say that the officers and crew behaved with becoming coolness and bravery. Lieutenant Commander L. A. Beardslee, the executive officer, and the senior engineer, Mr. George H. White, rendered me great assistance in the working of guns, turret, and even the vessel, as the bell-gear broke early in the fight and the orders had to be passed down to turret-chamber, and thence by a tube into the engine-room.

Herewith are the reports of executive officer and senior engineer. They will explain the condition of the vessel after the attack.

Very respectfully, your obedient servant,

D. McN. FAIRFAX,
Commander United States Navy.

Rear-Admiral S. F. DuPont,
Commanding South Atlantic Blockading Squadron.

Report of Lieutenant Commander L. A. Beardslee of injuries sustained by the Nantucket.

United States Iron-clad Nantucket,
Inside Charleston Bar, April 8, 1863.

Sir: In obedience to your order, I furnish you with a statement of the injuries received by this ship during the engagement yesterday.

We were struck fifty-one times, besides a number of dents by fragments of shells. The turret was struck eighteen times, principally by 10-inch solid and 6-inch rifle-shot. One rifle-shot struck on the lower corner of the XV-inch port, denting the outer plate about 1½ inch, and bulging the whole thickness, so much as to prevent the port stopper from swinging. This shot was received after the third fire of the XV-inch, and disabled the gun for the rest of the fight, we not being able to open the port. A 10-inch shot struck directly opposite, and near the top of the turret, starting a number of bolts, and breaking the clamp-ring inside. The others did no serious damage, further than breaking and loosening a number of bolts. There may be more damage, but we will not be able to ascertain without removing the "pilasters" covering the bolt-heads—a job that cannot be done without, for the time, disabling the turret. During the action the turret became jammed. Upon examination, we discovered six or seven bolt-heads and nuts that had fallen inside and into the recess around the bottom of the turret, rendering it necessary to key the turret higher in order to clear them. Upon attempting to revolve the turret again to-day, found that another had fallen since the first were removed. The pilot-house was struck once, a square hit, but doing no damage. The side armor was struck nine times—once below the water-line. A number of the side plates are started so much that another shot in their vicinity would, in my opinion, knock them off. One bolt was driven through the iron, and is buried in the oak. One of the deck plates is started from a blow on the side armor. The smoke-stack was riddled in the upper sections, and received five shots in the lower sections—one, a solid 10-inch, fell, after striking upon the deck, and was secured.

The steam-whistle was cut off. The deck plates were cut in twelve places. One shot cut through the iron, and about two inches into the beam, starting the plate, several bolts, and the planking for some feet below. This was directly over the Andrews pump, in the engine-room. The others are not serious. The first discharge of XV-inch gun blew off eight of the heads of the bolts securing the muzzle box. The discharge of the XI-inch gun, or else the blow of a shot on the turret, lifted one of the perforated plates on top. These plates are not properly secured. The outer turret plate, in the XV-inch port, is started about one-fourth of an inch—the next layer in a less degree. Two of the "guides" to the XI-inch carriage were carried away through the gun not being properly compressed. Some of the gear to the engine-room bell was disabled at the first fire, causing trouble and confusion in getting orders promptly conveyed from pilot-house to engine-room. Fortunately, we had had a speaking tube from the turret chamber to the engine-room put up at Port Royal. The ship is tight, and can, if necessary, go into another fight at once; but to do so would, in my opinion, greatly endanger the ship, unless considerable repairs are first given her, there being several places too much weakened to resist a second blow.

Very respectfully, your obedient servant,

L. A. BEARDSLEE,

Lieutenant Commanding and Executive Officer.

Commander D. McN. Fairfax, U. S. N.,

United States Iron-clad Nantucket.

Report of Senior Engineer George H. White of injuries sustained by the Nantucket.

United States Iron-clad Steamer Nantucket,

Inside Charleston Bar, S. C., April 8, 1863.

Sir: I would report the damage done this vessel during the engagement of the 7th instant as follows: Of the shots striking the deck, two have made large scores and cracked the top plate; another, on the starboard side, over the engine-room platform, and directly above the Andrews pump, has cut through the deck plates, and several inches into the deck, forcing one of the bolts through the beam, and the deck planks down on each side of it. The fastenings of both deck plates and planks are started for several feet. This should receive attention before the ship takes part in another fight. The other shots on deck have done no material damage. All the shots striking the side armor have started the bolts and plates. In one or two places the plates are cracked, but to no serious extent. Though some of these shots are on or near the water-line, there are no leaks from them, the vessel remaining as dry as before. The turret has been struck in a number of places, breaking off the heads of several bolts and a number of the nuts on the inside. Under the 15-inch port a shot has started all the plates, causing them for a time to jam the port closer. This difficulty was overcome this morning, None of the plates are broken. Directly opposite, but near the top of the turret, a shot has bent the plates badly, carried away the inner ring, and a number of nuts. The full extent of the injury cannot be seen, as it is covered by a pilaster, but I cannot think it serious. Two shots struck the ring at the bottom of the turret, bending it badly, and causing it to jam. It is of no use in its present condition.

The muzzle-box of the 15-inch gun was carried away from the turret on the forward side, breaking eight bolts, five on the side and three on the bottom. This part of the vessel is a bad fit, which, I think, accounts for all the trouble.

On the forward side of the 11-inch port the three outer courses of plates have started by the firing of this gun, the outer one being three-tenths of an inch beyond its proper position. The port-hole is cut near the edge of the plate, and there are no bolts to hold it in place. In revolving the turret it has pressed several times on the nuts, which have been carried away and fallen down ; for some reason, that as yet I have been unable to find out, the turret does not revolve as freely as before, but I hope to be able to remedy this trouble. The braces between the deck beams under the turret work slack, and should be provided with jam nuts. The effect of all the shot that have struck the turret nearly in a line with the axis seems to indicate that the bolts fit too loosely, and the iron of the bolts is of such a character as to break too easily. The violent recoil of the 11-inch gun on one occasion forced a hole through one of the pilasters, and backed one of the bolts some three inches out of the turret, at the same time carrying away the two after guides on the carriage ; the repairs required are being made, but in the mean time the gun is ready for duty. The perforated plate over this gun was raised out of its position, but has been replaced, and is being firmly secured. In order to learn how many bolts are broken, the shot-racks and plates in the turret will have to be taken up, in order to remove the pilasters, which would for a time disable the vessel, and I have not thought it advisable to recommend it at present.

The impregnable smoke-pipe was struck several times, breaking the heads of bolts, and carrying away a piece about three inches deep at the top where the temporary pipe was fastened. The temporary smoke-pipe is full of holes, but still answers every purpose. The whistle and whistle-pipe are both shot away, as the after awning stanchions. The pilot-house was struck once, but no damage was done. During the early part of the engagement the bell-pull gave way, rendering it necessary to pass the word from the pilot-house. This has been repaired.

The fact of nearly all the shot striking the turret and the after part of the vessel shows clearly that the object of the enemy was to either disable the guns or machinery. Fortunately, the attempt was unsuccessful ; the machinery and boilers are in good order, and as soon as the bolts promised have been sent on board, the guns will be as perfect as before the engagement.

I am, very respectfully, your obedient servant,

GEORGE H. WHITE,
Senior Engineer.

Commander D. McN. Fairfax, U. S. N.,
Commanding U. S. Iron-clad Steamer Nantucket.

Report of Commander John Downes, commanding United States Iron-clad Nahant.

UNITED STATES IRON-CLAD STEAMER NAHANT,
Port Royal, April 13, 1863.

SIR: I have the honor to submit the following account of the part taken by this vessel in the action of the 7th instant with the forts and batteries in Charleston harbor:

Weighing anchor, in compliance with signal, we occupied the position assigned us in the order of battle next to the rear of the line, entering into action at about 3 p. m.; and at 4 o'clock becoming hotly engaged with Forts Sumter and Moultrie, and the various other batteries which lined the northern shore of the harbor, and concentrated an intense fire upon us, while floating obstructions of a formidable nature, apparently, drawn between Moultrie and Sumter, barred the way to further progress up the harbor.

We soon began to suffer from the effects of the terrible, and I believe almost unprecedented, fire to which we were exposed; and at 4.30 the turret refused to turn, having become jammed from the effects of three blows from heavy shot, two of them on the composition ring about the base of the pilot-house, (one of these breaking off a piece of iron weighing seventy-eight pounds from the interior that assisted to keep the house square on its bearings, throwing it with such violence to the other side of the house, striking, bending, and disarranging steering-gear in its course, that it bounded from the inside curtain and fell back into the centre of the house,) and the other on the outside of turret, bulging it in and driving off the $1\frac{5}{8}$-inch apron bolted on to the inside to keep in place the gun-rails, and down the main trace of turret. The bolt-heads flying from the inside of pilot-house at the same time struck down pilot, Mr. Sofield, twice struck and senseless—and the quartermaster, Edward Cobb, helmsman, fatally injuring with fractured skull, leaving me alone in the pilot-house, the steering-gear becoming at the same time disarranged. We were within five hundred yards of Fort Sumter, unmanageable, and under the concentrated fire of, I think, one hundred guns at short range, and the obstructions close aboard. But fortunately we got the preventer steering-gear in working order in time to prevent disastrous result. And getting my vessel once more under command, I endeavored to renew the action, but after repeated futile efforts to turn the guns on the fort, I concluded to retire for a time from close action and endeavor to repair damages. At this time the squadron commenced retiring from action, in compliance with signal, and we permanently withdrew, having been about forty minutes in close action, during which we were struck thirty-six times heavily, had one man fatally, two severely, and four slightly injured, all by flying bolts and iron inside of turret and pilot-house; and we received the following injuries to the vessel and fittings, besides those already enumerated, the plates on side armor broken badly in several places, and in one, where struck by two shot in close proximity, partly stripped from the wood and the wood backing broken in, with edging of deck plates started up and rolled back in places. On port quarter side armor deeply indented, and started from side and extremity of stern. The deck is struck twice damagingly—one shot near the propeller well, quite shattering and tearing the plating in its passage, and starting up twenty-five bolts; another starting plate and twenty bolts; and slighter blows are numerous. In smoke-stack armor there are three shot-marks—one that pierced the armor, making a hole fifteen inches long and nine inches broad, displacing grating inside and breaking seven bolts. In the turret there are marks of nine shot; fifty-six of the bolts are broken perceptibly to us, the bolt-heads flying off inside of turret, and the bolts starting almost their length outside, some of them flying out completely, and being found at a considerable distance from the turret on the deck. Doubtless many others are broken that we cannot detect, as by trying them we find others loosened. One shot struck the upper part of the turret, breaking through every plate, parting some of them in two, three, and four places. In pilot-house there were marks of six shot, three of them 11-inch; twenty-one of the bolts were broken perceptibly, and others evidently started. The plates are also much started, and the pilot-house itself, I think, much damaged and wrecked; indeed, it is my opinion that four more such shot as it received would have demolished it. One shot at the base broke every plate through, and evidently nearly penetrated it. Both flagstaffs were struck, but were not entirely shot away, and the ensign remained flying throughout.

In making this minute detailed report of the damaging effects of shot upon this vessel, I have been influenced by a wish to point out wherein weak points are practically shown to exist; and I will add that this experience has proved in my mind, beyond a doubt, that to those above enumerated may be added all hatch plates, anchor well and propeller well plates, and the tops of the turret and pilot-house, as entirely inadequate to defend the place they cover from being entirely penetrated; and in the propeller well, wherein the propeller would probably be injured, and the pilot-house, wherein is contained the wheel for steering, and where exists the only lookout for the guidance of the vessel, and the top of the turret, from which the iron would be driven in upon the heads of those fighting the guns below, the effect, necessarily, would be damaging. During the action we fired four 15-inch shell, 3½ 7.10″ fuze, three 15-inch cored shot, four 11-inch shell, 10″ fuze, and four 11-inch solid shot.

The bearing of men and officers was most admirable. The guns were fought coolly, by Acting Ensign Clark, in command of division, and all the duties performed promptly and quietly in the turret, under the general supervision of Lieutenant Commander Harmony. Of the men struck by flying bolts, not one left his station at the gun voluntarily, and only one at all, and he remained until he fell senseless, and was carried below. Mr. J. Sofield, the pilot, performed his duties coolly and satisfactorily until he fell senseless while in the act of seizing the spokes of the wheel just dropped by the quartermaster, (Cobb,) though struck in the head by a bolt at the same time, but falling almost simultaneously with him from the effect of another blow.

In conclusion, I have to state that it was not until the following day, at 5 p. m., that the turret was cleared sufficiently to be turned, although a corps of workmen brought out from New York, and under skilful supervision, were present, and commenced work upon the damages early the following morning.

I am, very respectfully, your obedient servant,

JOHN DOWNES, *Commander.*

Rear-Admiral S. F. DuPont,
Commanding South Atlantic Blockading Squadron,
Flag-Ship Wabash, Port Royal.

Report of Commander A. C. Rhind, commanding United States iron-clad Keokuk.

United States Flag-Ship New Ironsides,
Off Cummings's Point, South Carolina, April 8, 1863.

Sir: I have the honor to report that I got the Keokuk under way at 12.30 p. m. yesterday, in obedience to the signal from the flag-ship, and took a position in the line prescribed in your order of advance and attack. At 3.20, the flag-ship having made signal to disregard her motions, I ran the Keokuk ahead of my leading vessel to avoid getting foul in the narrow channel and strong tideway. I was forced, in consequence, to take a position slightly in advance of the leading vessel of the line, and brought my vessel under a concentrated heavy fire from Forts Moultrie and Sumter, at a distance of about five hundred and fifty yards from the former. The position taken by the Keokuk was maintained for about thirty minutes, during which period she was struck ninety times in the hull and turrets. Nineteen shots pierced her through at and just below the water-line. The turrets were pierced in many places, one of the forward port shutters shot away; in short, the vessel was completely riddled.

Finding it impossible to keep her afloat many minutes more under such an extraordinary fire, during which rifled projectiles of every species and the largest calibre, as also hot shot, were poured into us, I reluctantly withdrew from action at 4.40 p. m., with the gun-carriage of the forward turret disabled, and so many of the crew of the after gun wounded as to prevent a possibility of remaining under fire. I succeeded in getting the Keokuk to an anchor out of range of fire, and kept her afloat during the night in the smooth water, though the water was pouring into her in many places.

At daylight this morning it became so rough that I saw the vessel must soon go down. Assistance being sent me, I endeavored to get the vessel round, and tow up, and in that effort, at about 7.30 a. m. she went down rapidly, and now lies completely submerged to the top of her smoke-stack. The officers and crew were all saved, the wounded having been put on board a tug a few minutes before the Keokuk went down. Owing to the loss of papers, and the separation of officers and crew, I am unable to furnish an officer's medical report, but give as nearly as possible the casualties in the action of yesterday.

Very respectfully, your obedient servant,

A. C. RHIND, *Commander*

Rear-Admiral S. F. DuPont,
Commanding South Atlantic Blockading Squadron.

Abstract of expenditure of ammunition, ranges, &c., during the engagement with the fortifications in Charleston harbor, April 7, 1863.

Vessels.	Class of guns.	Total number of fires.	No. of fires with— Shell.	Solid shot.	Cored shot.	Length of fuze.	Charges of powder.	Object aimed at.	Remarks.
							Pounds.		
New Ironsides	XI-inch, No. 1, port	1		1			20	Fort Moultrie	
Do	XI-inch, No. 3, port	1		1			20	do	
Do	XI-inch, No. 4, port	1		1			20	do	
Do	XI-inch, No. 5, port	1		1			20	do	
Do	XI-inch, No. 6, port	1		1			20	do	
Do	XI-inch, No. 7, port	1		1			20	do	
Do	XI-inch, No. 8, port	1		1			20	do	
Do	150-pdr., No. 2, starboard	1		1			16	Fort Wagner	
Montauk	XV-inch	10			10		35	Fort Sumter	
Do	XI-inch	17	1	16		5-second	4.20 13.15	do	
Passaic	XV-inch	9	9			7-second	35	1 XV-inch and 1 XI-inch shell at Fort Moultrie; the rest at Fort Sumter.	
Do	XI-inch	4	2	2		10-second	2.20 2.15		
Weehawken	XV-inch	11	11			10-second	35	Fort Sumter	After fourth fire XI-inch gun disabled by shot striking turret, causing the turret to act as a compressor.
Do	XI-inch	15	15			10-second	15	do	
Patapsco	XV-inch	5	5			10-second	35	do	
Do	150-pdr	5	5			Schenkle percussions	16	do	After 5th fire forward cap-square belt broke.
Catskill	XV-inch	10	10			10 and 15-second	35	do	After 3d fire the turret was bulged in by a shot, so that the port stopper could not be revolved.
Do	XI-inch	12	12			10 and 15-second	15	do	
Nantucket	XV-inch	3	3			5-second	35	do	
Do	XI-inch	12	12			5-second	15	9 Sumter, 2 Wagner, 1 Moultrie.	
Nahant	XV-inch	7	4		3	3 3½-second 1 7-second	35	1 7-second XII-inch shell and 1 10-second XI-inch shell at Moultrie; rest at Fort Sumter.	
Do	XI-inch	8	4	4		3 5-second 1 10-second	4.20 4.15		
Keokuk	XI-inch, in forward turret	3	3				20	Fort Sumter	At 3d fire, gun not being entirely run out, the after haster was sprung and the breeching stranded.

Vessels, 9; guns, 23; fires, 139; shell, 96; solid shot, 30; cored shot, 13. Range, from 550 to 2,100 yards.

Respectfully submitted:

A. S. MACKENZIE, *Lieut. and Ordnance Officer, South Atlantic Blockading Squadron.*

Rear-Admiral S. F. DuPont, *Commanding South Atlantic Blockading Squadron.*

Report of Captain T. Turner.

UNITED STATES SHIP NEW IRONSIDES,
Off Charleston, S. C., April 10, 1863.

ADMIRAL: Your presence on board of this ship during the severe engagement of the 7th of April against the forts Sumter, Moultrie, Beauregard, Cummings's Point, and the adjacent batteries, which concentrated their fire on your advancing fleet, relieves me from representing many details which your absence, under like circumstances, would have made incumbent.

You will, however, have observed how correct my representation was, that this ship could not be depended upon in a tide-way, and how unmanageable she became, compelling the pilot to order the anchor to be let go twice in order to avoid grounding, which would have involved the loss of the ship.

The unavoidable delay in commencing action was a severe test to my officers and crew, as they were all the time under a heavy fire of shell and shot, the effects of some of which you have personally examined

The steadiness and discipline, under an ordeal of this kind, without the relief of active engagement in battle, I need not state to you, was a very gratifying spectacle to myself, though what I had expected from my officers and men.

The iron turret of this ship being too small to contain more than yourself, the fleet captain, and the pilot, who were controlling the movements of this ship and the fleet, I took up my position at the batteries, commanding them in person, where there was, with port-shutters down and gratings on, scarce light enough to discern the face of the nearest person to me.

I obtained the soundings as best I could from time to time by tricing up a port-shutter and heaving the lead from the sill of the port, and I found the ship frequently within a foot of the bottom. I attribute to the extraordinary skill of the pilot, Acting Master Godfrey, the fact that she was kept clear of it.

Forcing her way up the channel, she received the fire of the enemy generally obliquely, excepting only when she fell off one way or the other. One of these shots striking the forward facing of the port-shutter, carried it away instantly. My impression is, had you been able to get this ship into close position, where her broadside would have been brought to bear, that not one port-shutter would have been left under the fire of such enormous projectiles as were thrown from the enemy's works, multiplied on every side of us. The damage done to this ship, with the exception of the loss of a port-shutter, is not material. The wood work at both ends, where struck, will be repaired at once.

I have supposed that the distance at which she received the severest fire of the enemy was about one thousand (1,000) yards, and I think she has clearly proved the invulnerability of her armor at that distance, for there was very little damage done.

So dense was the smoke in the channel that I could with difficulty at times see beyond fifty yards from the ship, and experienced great embarrassment in training my guns, even when she fell off so that I could use them.

I have briefly expressed in a foregoing passage my admiration of the deportment of my officers and men under these trying circumstances. I realized all I have expected from them, but I should fall short of my duty, sir, if I omitted to present to your especial notice the 1st lieutenant of this ship, Lieutenant Commander George E. Belknap. It was not in the hour of battle only that great demand was made upon him; there was a constant pressure upon the high qualities which distinguish him as an efficient officer to meet exigencies which through a week of toil and labor he had to provide for. He was equal to his work, gave me a perfect support at all times, and I desire here, and through you, to commend him to the favorable consideration of the government as an officer of the highest merit.

Very respectfully, your obedient servant,

T. TURNER, *Commodore.*

Rear-Admiral S. F. DuPont,
Commanding South Atlantic Blockading Squadron.

Letter to Rear-Admiral DuPont by the Secretary of the Navy.

Navy Department, *April* 11, 1863.

Sir: It has been suggested to the department by the President, in view of operations elsewhere, and especially by the army of the Potomac, that you should retain a strong force off Charleston, even should you find it impossible to carry the place. You will continue to menace the rebels, keeping them in apprehension of a renewed attack, in order that they may be occupied, and not come north or go west to the aid of the rebels, with whom our forces will soon be in conflict. Should you be successful, as we trust and believe you will be, it is expected that General Hunter will continue to keep the rebels employed and in constant apprehension, so that they shall not leave the vicinity of Charleston. This detention of the iron-clads, should it be necessary in consequence of a repulse, can be but for a few days.

I trust your success will be such that the iron-clads can be or will have been despatched to the gulf when this reaches you. There is intense anxiety in regard to your operations. This day is the anniversary of the assault on Sumter, and God grant that its recurrence may witness the destruction of that fortress by our naval forces under your command.

I am, very respectfully, your obedient servant,

GIDEON WELLES,
Secretary of the Navy.

Rear-Admiral S. F. DuPont,
Commanding S. A. B. Squadron, Port Royal, S. C.

Instructions of the President.

[Telegram.]

Executive Mansion,
Washington, April 13, 1863.

Hold your position inside the bar near Charleston; or if you shall have left it, return to it and hold it till further orders. Do not allow the enemy to erect new batteries or defences on Morris island. If he has begun it, drive him out. I do not herein order you to renew the general attack. That is to depend on your own discretion or a further order.

A. LINCOLN.

Admiral DuPont.

Further instructions of the President.

EXECUTIVE MANSION,
Washington, April 14, 1863.

This is intended to clear up an apparent inconsistency between the recent order to continue operations before Charleston, and the former one to remove to another point in a certain contingency. No censure upon you, or either of you, is intended; we still hope that, by cordial and judicious co-operation, you can take the batteries on Morris island and Sullivan's island, and Fort Sumter. But whether you can or not, we wish the demonstration kept up for a time, for a collateral and very important object; we wish the attempt to be a real one, (though not a desperate one,) if it affords any considerable chance of success. But if prosecuted as a *demonstration* only, this must not become public, or the whole effect will be lost. Once again before Charleston, do not leave till further orders from here; of course this is not intended to force you to leave unduly exposed Hilton Head, or other near points in your charge.

Yours truly,

A. LINCOLN.

General HUNTER and Admiral DUPONT.

P. S.—Whoever receives this first, please send a copy to the other immediately.

A. L.

Letter from Rear-Admiral DuPont.

FLAG-SHIP WABASH,
Port Royal Harbor, S. C., April 16, 1863.

SIR: I have the honor to acknowledge the receipt this morning, by the Freeborn, of your communication of the 11th instant, directing the maintaining of a large force off Charleston, to menace the rebels and keep them in apprehension of a renewed attack in the event of our repulse.

I have also to acknowledge the receipt of a copy of a telegraphic despatch of the 13th instant from the President of the United States, sent from Fortress Monroe.

The department will probably have known, on the 12th instant, the result of the attack. In my despatch of the 11th instant, dated off Charleston, the department was made aware of my withdrawal, with the iron-clads, from the very insecure anchorage inside the bar, and just in time to save the Monitors from an easterly gale, in which, in my opinion and that of their commanders, they would have been in great peril of being lost on Morris island beach. Their ground tackling has been found to be insufficient, and from time to time they have dragged even in close harbors.

I have since been doing all in my power to push forward their repairs in order to send them to the gulf, as directed, but I presume that your despatch of the 11th instant, and the telegraphic message from the President, revoke your previous order.

I shall spare no exertions in repairing, as soon as possible, the serious injuries sustained by the Monitors in the late attack, and shall get them inside Charleston bar with all despatch in accordance with the order of the President. I think it my duty, however, to state to the department that this will be attended with great risk to these vessels from the gales which prevail at this season and from the continuous fire of the enemy's batteries, which they can neither silence, nor prevent the erection of new ones.

The New Ironsides can only cross the bar with certainty at spring tides, which are twice a month. She is more vulnerable than the Monitors, and at the distance she must necessarily anchor could not elevate her guns sufficiently to reach any batteries of the enemy, while, at the same time, she would be liable to injury, particularly in her wooden ends, from a fire which she could not return. If this vessel is withdrawn from the blockade and placed inside, the blockade may be raised by the rebel rams coming out of Charleston harbor, at night, by Maffit's channel, in which case she could give no assistance to the fleet outside. But for the New Ironsides the raid of the 31st January would have been repeated with more serious effect.

The lower and greater part of Morris island exhibits a ridge or row of sand hills, affording to the enemy a natural parapet against the fire of shipping, and facilities for erecting batteries in very strong positions. The upper part of the island is crossed by Fort Wagner, a work of great strength, and covered by the guns of Fort Sumter. The island is in full communication with Charleston, and can, in spite of us, draw fresh re-enforcements as rapidly as they may be required. Shoals extend from the island which prevent the near approach of the Monitors, and our experience at Fort McAlister does not encourage me to expect that they will reduce well defended sand batteries where the damage inflicted by day is readily repaired by the unstinted labor of the night. The ships, therefore, can neither cover the landing nor afterwards protect the advance of the small force of the army available for operations in this quarter, which will meet fresh troops at every sand hill, and may look, also, for a reverse fire from the batteries on James island.

As it is considered necessary to menace Charleston by a demonstration of land and naval forces, North Edisto will afford a better point from which to threaten an advance, and a concentration of troops and ships in that quarter would accomplish the purpose of the government, mentioned in your despatch of the 11th instant, as it is a military point from which Charleston could be attacked now, James island being fully occupied by the enemy's batteries.

I have deemed it proper and due to myself to make these statements, but I trust I need not add that I will obey all orders with the utmost fidelity, even when my judgment is entirely at variance with them, such as the order to reoccupy the unsafe anchorage for the iron-clads off Morris island, and an intimation that a renewal of the attack on Charleston may be ordered, which, in my judgment, would be attended with disastrous results, involving the loss of this coast.

For eighteen months in these waters I have given whatever of professional knowledge, energy, and zeal I possess to the discharge of my duties and to the close study of our military and naval position in the tenure of the sea-coasts within the limits of my command, and I claim to know what best pertains to the disposition of my fleet in carrying out the instructions of the department.

I know not yet whether the confidence of the department, so often expressed to me, has been shaken by the want of success in a single measure which I never advised, though intensely desirous to carry out the department's orders, and justify expectations in which I could not share.

I am, however, painfully struck by the tenor and tone of the President's order, which seems to imply a censure, and I have to request that the department will not hesitate to relieve me by an officer who, in its opinion, is more able to execute that service in which I have had the misfortune to fail—the capture of Charleston. No consideration for an individual officer, whatever his loyalty and length of service, should weigh an instant if the cause of his country can be advanced by his removal.

Very respectfully, your obedient servant,

S. F. DUPONT,
Rear-Admiral Commanding S. A. B. Squadron.

Hon. GIDEON WELLES,
Secretary of the Navy, Washington.

Chief Engineer Stimer's report of damages to the iron-clad steamers.

GENERAL INSPECTOR'S OFFICE,
413 *Broadway, New York, April* 14, 1863.

SIR: I arrived in this city, having left the fleet off Charleston, South Carolina, on the 11th instant, and I beg leave to report to the department some of the detail facts connected with the naval attack upon Charleston essayed by Rear-Admiral DuPont with his fleet of iron-clad steamers, which came especially within my province as the general inspector of iron-clad steamers and harbor obstruction submarine shells.

Previous to the attack I recommended to the admiral that two of the Monitor vessels should have attached to their bows one, each, of the submarine shells which had been furnished by the department, and that these should precede the others and attack the obstructions, attaching to the rafts which carried the shells several grapnel hooks suspended by chains to explode any torpedoes over which the vessels were about to pass, with a view to exploding them before the vessels themselves should come into dangerous proximity to them. There appeared, however, to be a feeling of objection to these shells, arising from an expressed apprehension that they would either run into some of our own vessels and blow them up, or if fired as designed, against the obstructions, would recoil against the vessel carrying them and sink it.

I explained, to the best of my ability, the experiment I had tried with one of them in New York harbor, which proved how impossible it was that this latter event would happen, and urged their trial until I was informed I was wasting valuable time in pressing forward something which it had already been decided would not be used. It is with exceeding regret that I am thus compelled to report that this powerful weapon, for which we have every reason to suppose the enemy was entirely unprepared, should not have been used in an attack which could have few hopes of success without it.

One of the rafts which had been prepared to carry the shells was, however, attached to the bow of the Weehawken, with the prepared hooks attached, to protect the vessel against torpedoes. This she carried in and out again in safety, having proceeded as far as the line of obstructions stretching from Fort Sumter to Moultrie would permit.

Having been directed to remain outside of the bay during the fight, I witnessed the conflict from the deck of the Coast Survey steamer Bibb, at the mouth of the Swash channel. The firing on the part of the enemy was very terrific. He was not only able to keep up a very rapid fire from his numerous guns, but, I felt satisfied, was using reckless charges of powder, which it was clearly wisdom for him to do. I therefore expected to find, upon my visit to them, at least an approach to the destructive results which had been obtained by the chief of the Bureau of Ordnance in his experiments against iron targets in the ordnance yard at Washington. I was, however, agreeably disappointed to find, upon my inspection of the Monitor vessels the next morning, that there were no clear passages through the decks, and no penetrations through the sides of the vessels or the pilot-houses. The blunt-headed shots had proven much less effective than round shot, not only in confining their injury to the indentation made more distinctly than is the case with round shot, but the indentations themselves were less than those made by the spherical balls. On the other hand, I found casualties had occurred, which occasioned loss of life in one instance, and disabled guns in others, through faults of design which only such experience could point out, and which, I think, can be entirely removed in the new vessels now building.

In the case of the Keokuk, although I never believed her armature would withstand the shock of heavy ordnance at short ranges, (*vide* my reports dated June 30, July 14, and July 31, 1862,) I was rather surprised that it should have proven so easily penetrable. If the lesson which this should teach is properly received, the loss of the vessel will be a positive gain to the government in preventing the construction of armored ships of more than doubtful impenetrability to ordinarily heavy ordnance.

Although the Ironsides was not built under my inspection, it may not be considered improper for me to compare in this report the effect of shot upon her solid forged plates, of four and a half inches thickness, with the laminated plates, of five inches thickness, which protected the sides of the Monitors.

This vessel was twice as distant from fort Sumter as several of the Monitor vessels; the effects are not, therefore, strictly comparable; still the difference in the appearance of the two descriptions of armature is very instructive, and should not be passed lightly over by the engineer. When the laminated plates upon the side of the Monitors were struck severely, the indentations were deep, the bolts securing them to the wooden backing started loose, the entire plates bent and separated from each other to an extent which impressed the non-professional observer with the idea of great injury; but when the engineer examined them, with a view of judging how well they would withstand another blow of the same force upon precisely the same place, he perceived that the original power to resist shot has not been greatly reduced.

On the other hand, the solid plates of the Ironsides were not so deeply indented; there appeared to be no disturbance of the plates by bending, but few bolts were started, and few persons other than the critical engineer could look closely enough to see that the plate was entirely broken through in a manner which would inevitably permit the passage of the second shot striking the same place.

To the casual observer, therefore, the solid plates will have the appearance of having withstood the bombardment better than the laminated, but the unprejudiced engineer will perceive that the latter disposition of the metal is much the most effective in attaining the desired end.

In consideration of the vast importance to our country that that stronghold of rebellion should be reduced, I take the liberty to express to the department my firm opinion that the obstructions can be readily passed with the means already provided, and our entire fleet of iron-clads pass up successfully to the wharves of Charleston, and that the Monitor vessels still retain sufficient enduring powers to enable them to pass all the forts and batteries which may reasonably be expected.

I am, respectfully, your obedient servant,

ALBAN C. STIMERS,
Chief Engineer United States Navy.

Hon. GIDEON WELLES,
Secretary of the Navy, Washington, D. C.

Telegrams of Assistant Secretary G. V. Fox, relative to supposed preliminary attack upon Fort Sumter.

[Telegram.]

NAVY DEPARTMENT,
Washington, D. C., April 10, 1863.

The sum of all the telegraphs, *via* Richmond, up to 9 a. m. yesterday at Charleston, is this: Tuesday at 2 p. m. the iron-clads engaged Fort Sumter at nine hundred yards. At 4 p. m. they retired. The next day the Keokuk was observed ashore on Morris island beach. Up to yesterday morning the iron-clads were still inside the bar. I infer the attack was for the purpose of obtaining full information, otherwise it would have been made in the morning. They are now preparing for more serious work. Their depot of coal and ammunition inside the bar is a safe one, even in bad weather. If there are obstructions to prevent passing Sumter they now know them, and will reduce the fort. It is evident they can attack it every day, and at night retire to their anchorage inside the bar. The damage upon Sumter cannot be repaired. The only question is, can the iron-clads stand the work? I believe the Monitors can. The Keokuk was a small experimental vessel, and was probably injured so that they beached her. I see no reason whatever to be in the least discouraged; on the contrary, my faith in the vessels and the officers is strengthened by these rebel accounts.

G. V. FOX.

Hon. M. BLAIR,
Postmaster General, Astor House, New York.

No. 1. Send a copy of this telegram to Captain Ericsson, 93 Franklin street, New York.

[Telegram.]

NAVY DEPARTMENT,
Washington, D. C., April 10, 1863.

I have your telegraph of last evening and to-day. As to the signals, it seems too important to give out to our people; a knowledge of the fact will cause a change. The Keokuk is not a Monitor battery, and no doubt was injured so as to oblige them to beach her. Commencing the fight at two and withdrawing at four, looks as though it was not the main attack. The real attack would be made in the morning, so as to have all the day for the work. The next affair will decide the matter, and will be made after preparations found necessary from the experience of the four hours' work of Tuesday. The reported transports inside the bar are probably coal and ammunition vessels—are, in fact, his depot—and if the obstructions in the harbor render the reduction of Sumter necessary, the admiral may have to go back to his base several times before finishing that work.

G. V. FOX,
Assistant Secretary.

Major General DANIEL BUTTERFIELD,
Chief Staff, Headquarters.

Order to send the Passaic to New York.

NAVY DEPARTMENT, *April* 15, 1863.

SIR: Send the Passaic home, to New York.
I am, respectfully, &c.,

GIDEON WELLES,
Secretary of the Navy.

Rear-Admiral S. F. DUPONT,
Commanding S. A. B. Squadron, Port Royal, S. C.

Directing the Passaic to touch at Hampton Roads.

NAVY DEPARTMENT, *April* 16, 1863.

SIR: You were instructed a few days ago to send the Passaic to New York. Let her touch at Hampton Roads on the way up, and there await further orders from the department. It is designed to replace her either with the Sangamon or the Lehigh.

Very respectfully,

GIDEON WELLES,
Secretary of the Navy.

Rear-Admiral S. F. DUPONT,
Commanding S. A. B. Squadron, Port Royal, S. C.

Order for board of experts on damages to the Passaic.

NAVY DEPARTMENT, *May* 21, 1863.

SIR: You will request the following gentlemen, viz: C. W. Copeland, George W. Quintard, M. F. Merritt, and J. J. Comstock, to constitute a board for the examination of the United States iron-clad steamer Passaic, whilst she is on the ways, and report in writing the full extent of the damage done to that vessel by the fire of the batteries in the harbor of Charleston; also whether she has been strained or injured in any part by the gales she has encountered, or from any cause whatsoever.

Captain S. C. Rowan has been directed to report to you as a member of the board.

Very respectfully,

GIDEON WELLES,
Secretary of the Navy.

Rear-Admiral F. H. GREGORY, *U. S. Navy, New York.*

Report of Board.

NEW YORK, *June* 2, 1863.

SIR: I have now the honor to transmit the report called for by your order of the 21st ultimo of the condition in which the iron-clad Passaic returned to this port. Every facility was given to the board of examiners, and their researches were very thoroughly made, and I have not been able to find any fact omitted. Great care is now being taken to fit that vessel perfectly under the care of Captain Worden. The work is progressing rapidly as possible, and it is expected she will be taken off the ways in a week.

I have the honor to be, very respectfully, your most obedient servant,

F. H. GREGORY,
Rear-Admiral, Superintendent.

Hon. GIDEON WELLES,
Secretary of the Navy, Washington.

NEW YORK, *June* 2, 1863.

DEAR SIR: In compliance with a request contained in the copy of a communication from the Navy Department, dated May 21, to examine the United States iron-clad steamer Passaic while she is on the ways, and report in writing the full damage done to that vessel by the fire of the batteries in the harbor of Charleston; also, whether she has been strained or injured in any part by the gales she has encountered, or from any cause whatever, we have made the examination as requested, and beg leave to report:

1st. In regard to the damage by the fire of the batteries, but four shots have damaged any part of the structure to an extent to be worthy of any particular description. The first, marked A on the accompanying diagrams, struck the upper edge of the turret, glanced upward and striking the pilot-house as shown. The second, marked B, struck near the lower edge of the turret, broke the loose outside ring on the deck, and indenting the turret so as to break the lugs off the inside composition ring. The third, marked C, indented the turret about $1\frac{1}{4}$ inch, cracking slightly the inside plate. The fourth, marked D, struck the armor on the port side about forty-seven feet eight inches from the bow, and nine and a half inches below the deck, starting or bending the three outer plates, breaking or starting one-third of the fastening bolts, leaving the remainder undisturbed and all the plates still in position.

As to the effects of these shots, the 1st raised the pilot-house $\frac{1}{2}$ inch and started it over on one side, breaking two bolts in the pilot-house, but did not in any manner affect the working of the turret or the operations of the vessel.

The 2d shot, marked B, by the damage already mentioned, checked the operation of the turret, until the lugs of the composition rings, which got jammed under the turret, were removed, after which the turret could be operated as usual.

The 3d shot, marked C, apparently a 10-inch shot, so started or disturbed the turret as to damage the slides of the 11-inch gun, rendering it, for the time, unserviceable, by forcing the rails hard against the guide pieces on the carriage.

The 4th shot did not affect the efficiency of the armor, as, though a portion of bolts were broken, the whole of the plates still remained in their proper position.

The only damage affecting the fighting efficiency of the vessel was that by the 3d shot, disabling the working of the 11-inch gun, and the breaking of the lug, alluded to; and we would take the liberty of suggesting that this form of injury may hereafter be guarded by fastening a very heavy ring or band around the base of the turret, to prevent its distortion, and leaving sufficient freedom between the rails of the carriage and the turret, so that any slight distortion of the turret will not affect the gun carriages.

There were some seven or eight shots received upon the deck, though but three of them produced effect so serious as to require repairs, and these repairs had been made before her return to this port. All the shots received upon the turret are shown in diagram No. 1, which represents the whole exterior circumference of the turret, laid down as a plane. The indentations by the shots varied from $\frac{1}{4}$ to $1\frac{1}{4}$ inch in depth, none, however, damaging the turret further than described. Upon the pilot-house three other shots than that described, struck, making indentations from $\frac{1}{2}$ inch to $\frac{7}{8}$ inch depth, but doing no further damage.

Upon the armor of the vessel, besides the shots already described, there were marks of twelve other shots, making indentations varying from $\frac{1}{2}$ inch to $2\frac{1}{2}$ inches in depth, but inflicting no other serious damage.

The accompanying diagrams show the effects of the four worst shots already mentioned, and the diagram No. 1 shows all the shots received by the turret; No. 2 shows the effects of shot A upon the turret and pilot-house, and No. 3 shows the effect of shot D upon the armor, as already described.

On the whole, we are of the opinion that the only damage done by the batteries, affecting the fighting efficiencies of the vessel, was by the shot upon the turret, which disabled the 11-inch gun by deranging the gun-slides.

The ship, so far as the board could discover, is not strained or injured by the gales she has encountered. There has been a serious leak about the bow, which the board find difficulty in accounting for. It is probable that in dropping into the sea the water got under the deck plates around the top of the anchor well; this can be guarded against hereafter by a slight alteration in the construction. There is also evidence of some slight leaks in some of the rivets, which can be easily remedied.

All of which is respectfully submitted, by your obedient servants,

J. C. ROWAN, *Captain U. S. N.*
CHAS. W. COPELAND.
GEO. W. QUINTARD.
M. F. MERRITT.
JOS. J. COMSTOCK.

Admiral F. H. GREGORY,
U. S. Navy, New York.

Extract of a letter found on a blockade runner relative to effect of bombardment of Sumter.

FORT SUMTER, *April* 26, 1863.

* * * * * * * * *

It appears from the Yankee accounts that we injured their iron-clads more than we thought we did. Some of their accounts are mostly true, interspersed here and there with some awful lies. There was no breach made in the fort at all. Two of their shots, a 15-inch shell and a 11-inch shot, did come through, but they hit in weak places. The greatest penetration in good, sound masonry was three feet, but then everything around was cracked and started more or less. The most severe blow, I think, was about three or four feet below the crest of the parapet, where two or three balls struck and just loosened everything clear through for a space of about six feet in length. As for knocking two embrasures in one, all humbug; equally so about any of their boats getting entangled in the obstructions. They did not go within five hundred yards of them, or torpedoes exploding, &c. Mr. Langdons Cheves, who had charge of the torpedo, said that for ten minutes he could not have placed the Ironsides more directly over the torpedo, if he had been allowed to go, but the confounded thing, as is usual with them, would not go off when it was wanted—the isolation of the wire, I suppose, defective. I think one thing has been proved—that brick forts can't stand 15-inch shot, &c., for a very long time, but it has also proved that iron-clads are not as invulnerable as supposed.

I went down to the Keokuk the other day. She lies off Pumpkin Hill channel. She was actually riddled, 10-inch shot going right through her; but our inspection was rather short, for a miserable little gunboat came up and gave us shot and shell, and I expect we made the best time on record for Morris island and the sand hills.

* * * * * * * * *

Yours, sincerely,

F. H. THRALSTON.

Necessary for New Ironsides to remain at Charleston.

[Despatch No. 171, 1863.]

FLAG-SHIP NEW IRONSIDES,
Inside Charleston Bar, April 11, 1863.

SIR: I have the honor to acknowledge your despatch of the 2d instant, marked *confidential*, and shall make every effort to despatch immediately five (5) iron-clads to New Orleans.

The department has already been informed of the loss of the Keokuk. I will retain, in obedience to its orders, two, (2,) the Passaic and Montauk, these being the most injured and the weakest, and their 15-inch guns having been much more frequently fired than those of the others.

I did not understand that the department included the New Ironsides in its order, and our failure to take Charleston renders it, in my judgment, absolutely necessary that she should resume her station off Charleston as the great protective force of the blockading vessels against raids from the rebel rams, now increased, as I have reason to believe, to three; and I can assure the department, from my recent experience, that she would be wholly unmanageable in the rapid currents of the Mississippi.'

Very respectfully, your obedient servant,

S. F. DUPONT,
Rear-Admiral, Com'dg S. A. B. Squadron.

Hon. GIDEON WELLES,
Secretary of the Navy, Washington.

Effect of shots upon Sumter.

NEW YORK, *May* 13, 1863.

MY DEAR SIR: I telegraphed you this morning to the effect that out of eighty shots fired by us, forty struck the fort. A part of parapet was knocked off at the corner of an embrasure, and *one* breach was made in the middle of the wall, thus:

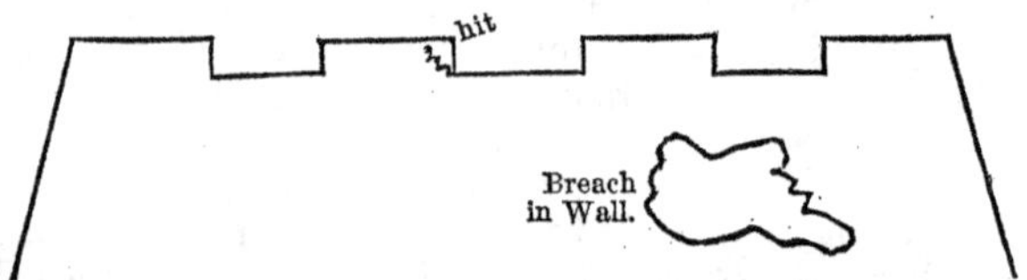

If they had continued to hit in this breach the wall above must have tumbled in; but the ebb-tide had turned, our fleet had only half the ebb, and had to stop when *it* did. By attacking at an earlier hour, so as to have the *whole* ebb, more could be accomplished.

The enemy had thirty-seven guns from one fort, and thirty-nine from another, bearing on our iron-clads; in all, seventy-six guns.

Two thousand shots were fired, and five hundred and twenty hit—say one-fourth; while one-half of our shots hit.

From Sumter, running north or northwest, is a line of obstructions.

This is the amount of information I could get this morning from the ——. * * *

I forgot to say that no guns burst in the fort.

* * * * * * * * *

Very truly yours,

P. S. FORBES.

Hon. G. V. FOX,
Assistant Secretary of the Navy, Washington, D. C.

NEW YORK, *June* 17, 1863.

MY DEAR SIR: I have only now been able to get the details about Sumter, and send them as I receive them.

The effect of the attack of the 7th of April was, more or less—

Shots striking.—No. 3. Shell; embrasure A, exterior (concrete) keystone and interior arch knocked out; masonry cracked.

No. 9. Three shots; one 15-inch; other two not known. Parapet wall cracked twenty-five feet in length; serious damage; perhaps by exploding shell.

No. 10. 15-inch; interior arch of embrasure B dislocated; masonry between piers and embrasure badly shaken, and projections.

No. 21. 15-inch; masonry around embrasure D badly cracked and projecting inside.

No. 25. 15-inch; destroyed embrasure F.

No. 38. 11-inch; exploding shell cracked parapet wall.

* * * * * * * * *

Yours truly,

P. S. FORBES.

Hon. G. V. FOX, *&c., &c.*

Statement of commanders of Monitors relative to first attack on Charleston.

NORTH EDISTO, S. C., *April* 24, 1863.

SIR: We have lately seen in different newspapers, particularly in the Baltimore American, detailed accounts of the recent attack on Fort Sumter, in which our opinions, the condition of the vessels, and the facts in general, are so perverted and falsified that, as it is not proper for us to correct them through the same medium, we beg leave to offer a statement to the department of what really did occur in connexion with the attack referred to, in hopes that it may perhaps permit it to be made public, both in the interest of truth and of our reputations.

It may appear uncalled for on our part to answer ill-natured and false statements coming from irresponsible parties through the public prints; but when it is considered that the opinion of those at home is almost entirely formed on just such statements, we think they may be considered of sufficient importance to notice, particularly when, as in the case of the American, they are uttered so immediately in the neighborhood of the seat of government; and this being the case, we shall more particularly criticise the remarks which, first appearing in that paper, have thence so widely circulated in others.

Although, as might be expected, there were differences of opinion as to the probabilities of taking Charleston, not one of us ever doubted that the attempt should be made, believing, as we did, that under the circumstances almost anything would be better than to give up, without a fair trial, what had so long been prepared for. But after the experience gained under the fire of the enemy, we were unanimously of opinion that a renewal of the attack would be unwise in the extreme, and for the following reason: Our vessels had been very much injured before passing the first of the three lines of defences which protect Charleston, and perhaps, considering the obstacles to be met with further up, not the strongest of the three. In receiving these injuries, they had not been able to do any to Fort Sumter, at least sufficient to slacken its fire; and even supposing this point passed, there still remained to go over more than three miles of water before reaching the city, part of which we could see was obstructed by piles, and all of which offered the utmost convenience for torpedoes, cables, and every other known means of stopping an advancing naval force, to say nothing of the guns. When, in addition to this, it had been proved that any heavy blow on the turret was very apt to disorder and stop it; that our side armor and decks were penetrable, and the pilot-house, where is the steering apparatus, and from which is the only lookout, could be made untenable, as two of them to a great extent had been, it is scarcely surprising that we should have arrived at the above conclusions.

It is said by the writer in the American that, had the torpedo been used on the front vessel, the obstructions at Fort Sumter might have been blown away, and the fleet could have proceeded then without difficulty to Charleston; overlooking entirely the fact that there would have still remained to destroy whatever the ingenuity of our enemies could have laid down for the remaining long distance.

These torpedo rafts had merely a theoretical reputation for removing obstacles, never having been tried at the north or elsewhere, except in blowing up water, and certainly being a source of great danger to our own vessels in fouling each other—a matter very likely to occur, taking into consideration the tide, the shoal water, and the imperfect steering qualities of the vessels, and which actually did occur on several occasions.

The result of the effort to use these torpedoes against the "Keokuk," after the action fully sustains the opinion formed of them.

It is said that these rafts, sent down to be attached to the bows of our vessels, were refused without trial and from mere naval prejudice or personal feeling; that is no truer than the other statements. Although plain to us, that vessels which, at the best, are very unmanageable from losing steerage way the very instant that the propeller stops, and from scarcely being able to go more than four knots, and some of them not even that, would be made more so by these great projections forward, which could never have been prepared for in the original plans of the iron-clads; still one of them was tried in our presence and under favorable circumstances for steering, as the torpedoes were not attached. We were soon, however, convinced that our unfavorable impressions with regard to them were correct, and that in the rapid currents and narrow channels of Charleston we would most likely get our vessels ashore, clogged with such a hindrance to their turning quickly. As regards the attempt to blow up the "Keokuk" with one of them, the failure was not owing to any difficulties thrown in the way of the experiment by any officers of the squadron, but was given up very much to the chagrin of the admiral, simply because the engineer who came down in charge of it was not able to put it in order for work and to make the attachment, although at the time the sea, for that anchorage, was unusually smooth. When, afterwards, Mr. Stimers said the firing attachment could be made, the heavy ring-bolts used to direct its safe action had drawn out. As it has also been stated that our vessels came out of the action almost unharmed, we will here mention some of the injuries received by them, which will, we think, go to show that such was not the case, and that it would have been out of the question to renew the action on the next day, if at all, when we consider that, although again liable to the same fire as at first, in their after condition, they would have been infinitely less able to endure it.

1st. Passaic. A large piece of brassing, under the turret, broken off, owing to which, and its being forced over, the turret could not be moved for some time, and has not worked well since. The gun carriage of the XI-inch gun disabled until the next afternoon, and the top of the pilot-house forced up, so as to expose the inside to shot, and not got into place until late the next day.

2d. Weehawken. Side armor broken through, exposing the wood. The flange supporting the gun-platform of XI-inch gun, broken ; smoke-stack very much injured, and both this and the turret greatly weakened from the loss of bolts. The latter also for a time stopped.

3d. Patapsco. Rifled gun disabled at fifth fire; smoke-stack penetrated in several places through the upper part of armor, out of which were forced forty bolts, rendering the whole structure very insecure until strengthened again; besides this, the turret had been stopped for a time.

4th. Nantucket. XV-inch gun lost at the third fire, owing to a blow on turret jamming the port stopper, which could not be moved afterwards. The turret stopped several times, besides severe injury to smoke-stack and deck. The concussion box, in this short time, lost eight bolts, and the turret was made to move with great difficulty.

5th. Nahant lost seventy-six bolts from the turret and pilot-house; the latter very much injured. The steering gear deranged and the plates started. The braces that hold down the inner gun-tracks and brace of turret knocked off, and turret rendered immovable and not cleared until 5 o'clock the following afternoon. Even at present, after long repairs, it can only be made to revolve very slowly, with thirty pounds of steam.

We have now met and, we think, refuted most of the falsehoods published in the American, and would merely beg to add, in further support of our views expressed against a renewal of the attack, that the liability of the guns to become disabled, on occasions which require steady use, has been shown, as well as that the turret almost invariably refuses to work after receiving heavy blows from shot, not only because the consequent bulging in injures the machinery, but from its being pushed from the perpendicular. In addition, the very slow fire possible from the XV-inch gun, and the fact that, to be effective against stone walls, it must be brought so near as to take away from the impenetrable character of the iron-clads, are considerations of great moment to all those who wish to see these vessels in the highest degree effective; nor have we, unfortunately, reason to believe that the batteries or turrets will, on any future occasion, when exposed to the fire of heavy guns, show more offensive power or endurance than was the case at Sumter.

Very respectfully, your obedient servants,

P. DRAYTON,
Captain, Passaic.
JOHN RODGERS,
Captain, Weehawken.
DANIEL AMMEN,
Commander, Patapsco.
GEORGE W. RODGERS,
Commander, Catskill.
D. M. FAIRFAX,
Commander, Nantucket.
JOHN DOWNES,
Commander, Nahant.

Hon. GIDEON WELLES,
Secretary of the Navy, Washington, D. C.

Forwarded.

S. F. DUPONT,
Rear-Admiral.

Rear-Admiral DuPont reviews an article in the Baltimore American.

[Despatch 208, 1863.]

FLAG-SHIP WABASH,
Port Royal Harbor, S. C., April 22, 1863.

SIR: I desire to call the attention of the department to an article published in the Baltimore American, of April 15, describing and commenting upon the attack by the iron-clads, under my command, upon the forts at Charleston, in terms injurious to myself, unjust to the officers whom I had the honor to lead, derogatory to the naval service, and utterly false in its most important particulars.

I should not consider it necessary or proper to bring this matter to the notice of the department, but for two reasons, which seem to demand it. These reasons are: Firstly, that the writer of the article in question well known to be Mr. C. C. Fulton, of the Baltimore American, came here in the steamer Ericsson, when that vessel, chartered by the Navy Department, brought to this port rafts and torpedoes, and came, as I understood, by the sanction and with the permission of the department.

With this understanding, I permitted Mr. Fulton to go to the Ogeechee, in the Coast Survey steamer Bibb, Captain Boutelle, placed under my direction by Professor Bache, Superintendent of the Coast Survey. As the time came near for the attack upon Charleston, Mr. Fulton was still on board the Ericsson, from which vessel he again went on board the Bibb, and took up his quarters with Captain Boutelle.

Secondly, I learned from Captain Boutelle, quite accidentally, that Mr. Fulton was under an obligation to send a duplicate of his correspondence to the Assistant Secretary of the Navy for his censorship, before it could be published. An editor and correspondent of an influential newspaper, domiciled, with the permission of the department, on board a steamer under its control, and submitting his letters to the inspection of one of its highest officials, is manifestly in a different position from ordinary correspondents of the press; and when a reporter thus situated writes of an action which he witnessed at a distance, and presumes to represent the sentiments of nine-tenths of the officers present, it becomes advisable to place upon the record of the department a refutation of his calumnies.

Although I cannot doubt, from the statements of Captain Boutelle, copies of whose letters on the subject I enclose, that Mr. Fulton had engaged to submit his correspondence to the revision of the Assistant Secretary of the Navy, I desire to state here, most explicitly, that I do not for a moment suppose he complied with the arrangement in this instance. The honor and the high standing of the naval service of the United States, as signally manifested in this war, as in other wars, must be as dear to the Assistant Secretary as to myself and to my brother officers, and it is simply impossible for me to believe that he should have been aware, before its publication, of the infamous statements contained in this letter, (marked No. 1.)

But as Mr. Fulton avowed to Captain Boutelle and to others this he bore this semi-official relation to the department, and as the department afforded him, if I have been correctly informed, the opportunity to be present, it seems but right that I should at least deny his statements in a communication which will find its place upon the records of the department.

Mr. Fulton assumes to express the feelings of nine-tenths of the officers, and of all the spectators of the action, as to the farcical nature of the assault, and its disgraceful abandonment. One of the spectators, whose opportunities for observation were certainly equal to those of Mr. Fulton, whose education as a soldier, and whose position as the general commanding the land forces then awaiting the result of the naval attack, should entitle his opinions to at least equal consideration, has expressed his impression of the assault in terms very different from those employed by the editor of the Baltimore American; and here I am content to rest the matter as far as spectators are concerned.

As to the opinions of nine-tenths of the officers in favor of the renewal of the attack, I have only to say that I am not aware of what the impressions of so large a proportion of the squadron may be, but, what is perhaps more german to the matter, the nine captains of the nine iron-clad vessels, and my fleet captain, were unanimous in their conviction that the attack should not be renewed; and as the evidence of experts on the spot is to be preferred, even to that of other experts remote from the scene of action, whose opportunities for observation are less favorable, I am at a loss to know how my own determination not to resume the offensive could be strengthened.

The writer for the press makes me hold a council of war after the attack. I did not hold a council of war either before or after the attack; nor have I ever held a council of war in all my life. I did not desire to throw upon the gallant officers who commanded the iron-clads, and who had so nobly conducted themselves in this novel mode of warfare, any of the responsibility which pertained to my own station, and I did not hear their opinion, as to the withdrawal of the fleet, until after I had announced my own determination in the matter.

My decision on the evening of the battle, after ascertaining the injuries received by the vessels, was entirely my own; and after further developments, upon a more complete examination than was then practicable, the correctness of that decision is fully confirmed.

It was, however, most gratifying to me to find my own determination receive the unanimous and cordial support of all the commanders of the iron-clads upon the day after it had been announced, when they called upon me and expressed in emphatic terms their conviction that a persistence in the naval attack upon Charleston, with the means at my disposal, could afford no hope of success, and could not fail to result in disaster.

The department selected these captains with care, and with a full knowledge of their high professional character; and I suppose that their opinions, thus coinciding with my own and with those of my well-tried chief of staff, will stand the test of impartial and intelligent criticism, even if adverse to those of the correspondent of the Baltimore American.

When I made the signal to withdraw from action, on the evening of the 7th, the Ironsides was but slightly injured, though she had been under a heavy fire. I did not then know the condition of the Monitors, and I recalled the ships only because it was too late to attempt further to force the obstructions that night. Subsequently, when I learned from the several captains the difficulties they had encountered, the extent of the damages they had sustained in their hulls and turrets, and the fact that five out of eight of their vessels were, for the time, either wholly or half disabled as to the use of their guns, it was made perfectly clear to my mind that, once entangled among the obstructions, should we attempt to pass them under a fire so crushing as that from the forts had been, even the extraordinary power of endurance pertaining to these Monitors could not sustain this fire again during another hour of attack.

This correspondent reports that on the morning of the 8th Mr. Stimers and his workmen had put all the Monitors in as good condition as they had been on the 7th, before the action; that the turret of the Nahant was freed from the difficulty which had prevented it from revolving, and that the workmen had all left at one o'clock, reporting every difficulty as to the working of turrets, guns, &c., fully remedied.

The turret of the Nahant did not begin to turn until 5 p. m., and it was late at night before she could have gone into action again.

Seventy-six bolts were driven out of her turret and pilot-house, which could not be replaced, and she would have been utterly disabled by a few more shot. The Weehawken thought her battery was in good condition, whereas it was discovered that her XI-inch was disabled; and it is not yet repaired. I will only add here that the side armor of the Weehawken, at the water's edge, was pierced through and the wood laid bare; one more blow there, and she would have gone down. I am having a careful drawing made of this fracture, to send to the department.

The repairs that it was practicable to make at the time were of course slight, and temporary in their character. I had hoped that those made on the Passaic, after the Ogeechee affair, would carry her through this fight; but she broke down in forty minutes in a worse manner than she did under her eight hours' fire from Fort McAllister. The Nahant and Patapsco, unhurt in that engagement, were almost immediately crippled in this one.

I visited the Monitors on the 18th instant, and upon examining into their condition myself, I found their captains had rather underrated the damage they had received, and so far from the seven vessels being in as good order by noon of the 8th as they had been at noon of the 7th, according to Mr. Fulton, three of them are now, at this date, in Station creek, undergoing important and much-needed repairs. I wish I could get them out in as good order as they were at noon of the 7th.

The writer states that the naval officers and myself have been haunted and oppressed by the dread of invisible torpedoes and of other obstructions in the channel; that the fear of these ghosts prevented the success of the attack; that the Navy Department had provided means for the removal of these torpedoes, and that the naval officers were afraid to use them.

Torpedoes are not placed so as to be visible. The Cairo was destroyed by an invisible torpedo in the western waters; the Montauk was damaged by an invisible torpedo at the Ogeechee; an invisible torpedo exploded under or near the Weehawken, from whose propeller shaft two hundred and fifty feet of rope, then furled around it, have just been removed; and the Patapsco was brought up by, and hung upon, an invisible obstruction for ten minutes, in the focus of the storm of shot. To have ventured further into that labyrinth would have been to anchor the vessels helplessly by their sterns, (those of them, at least, that escaped the invisible torpedoes,) and thus expose them to a fire which they could neither endure nor effectively return, and, finally, to have allowed them to fall into the possession of the enemy.

Imputations like these upon the judgment, the conduct, and the courage of officers of high character and of long standing in the service, who have been tried over and over again in this war, and who, in my judgment, have no superiors in the navy, coming from a person in a manner indorsed by the Navy Department, and in communication with it, have not been received with perfect composure. If Mr. Fulton is correct in this impeachment of these gentlemen, then the captains of the four leading Monitors, whose orders were to pass around to the northwest side of Sumter and to gain a position off its inner face, failed in their duty to me, to the service, and to their country. Either they were unworthy of the occasion, or Mr. C. C. Fulton is guilty of most inexcusable calumniation.

One more item, and I have done. Mr. Fulton avers that sufficient experiments were not made with the rafts and torpedoes, and states that they were condemned without an examination from a dislike to Ericsson and his naval innovations. I refer the department to the letter of Captain John Rodgers, upon the matter of the rafts and torpedoes, as satisfactorily disposing of the question of experiments, and of their use or disuse in the attack upon Charleston. (Enclosure, marked No. 2.)

As to the officers of the Monitors being afraid to blow up the Keokuk with their appliances, Mr. Fulton certainly had the means for obtaining accurate information upon this point from Chief Engineer Robie, who was likewise quartered on board the Ericsson. The Weehawken, Captain John Rodgers, was put at the disposal of Chief Engineer Robie for that purpose, and every facility given to them in my power to afford. This engineer, who was sent out by the department in charge of the raft and torpedoes, did not find it practicable to use the torpedo against the Keokuk, then lying hard aground, remote from other vessels, and undisturbed by any fire from the enemy.

It is possible to ask too much of men at certain times and under certain circumstances; and, in this instance, to have attached these rafts and torpedoes to the bows of the Monitors with the expectation that these vessels could be fought amid such a storm of shot and shell from the enemy, and at the same time carry on submarine mining operations, would perhaps have overtasked the faculties of most persons, and in all probability have "hoist the engineer with his own petard," or, if not him, his friend, instead of his enemy.

I now take leave of this the most odious subject I have ever had occasion to notice. Some other assertions of Mr. Fulton, which might be flatly contradicted, I have not discussed, nor have I thought it worth while to consider his opinions upon purely professional points. To undergo the fire of the enemy and the stabs of an assassin of character at one and the same time is too much for my philosophy, and for my further protection against assaults of the latter kind I look for and expect the countenance of the department.

I make this request to the department because up to the latest dates received here none of my official reports had been published, while the statements which I have made the subject of this communication have been spread unanswered throughout the country.

So far as I have seen, the tone of the press generally has been just, and in many instances generous. The exception is the Baltimore American, which seems to have had its own hostile proclivities heightened by an association with an officer of the service whose name appears frequently and prominently in its report in connexion with the repairs upon the iron-clads and in relation to the torpedoes and the rafts; I mean Mr. A. C. Stimers, a chief engineer in the naval service of the United States.

Very respectfully, your obedient servant,

S. F. DUPONT,

Rear-Admiral, Comd'g S. A. Blockading Squadron.

Hon. Gideon Welles,
Secretary of the Navy, Washington.

[Despatch No. 208, 1863.—Enclosure No. 1.]

Bibb, *April* 22, 1863.

My Dear Sir: In reply to your note of yesterday, I beg to say that I first saw Mr. Fulton on the 24th of February, when he came on board this vessel with Messrs. Stimers and Newton, naval engineers.

The latter officers were directed by you to take passage in the Bibb to Wassau and Ossabau for the purpose of inspecting the Passaic and Montauk, and I understood that Mr. Fulton accompanied them by your permission and authority.

We were two days at Wassau and one at Ossabau. At each place Mr. Fulton visited the "Monitors" with the inspecting engineers, and made such notes as he thought proper.

During our voyage a conversation took place in my cabin between Mr. Fulton, Mr. Bartlett, (paymaster of the Bibb,) and myself upon the responsibilities attaching to a newspaper correspondence from the centres of active operations in face of the enemy. Mr. Fulton said it was his practice to use a "manifold letter-writer" in writing his notes, making several copies. One was mailed to his brother at Baltimore, and another copy was sent by the mail to Mr. Fox, Assistant Secretary of the Navy. Mr. Fulton went on to say that his brother did not publish the letter until sufficient time had elapsed for Mr. Fox to receive and examine the manuscript and telegraph to Baltimore if he objected to any portion thereof. Anything written here, and objected to by Mr. Fox, was stricken out, and did not appear in the paper.

Mr. Fulton had with him document envelopes, with Mr. Fox's printed official address upon them, and, in at least one case, mailed his notes in one of these envelopes while on board my vessel.

As this arrangement gave Mr. F. a semi-official character, and as he was living on the Ericsson, chartered as a naval transport, I naturally inferred that you knew all about it, and on my return to Port Royal mentioned it incidentally in conversation with you as a matter with which you were familiar. It surprised me greatly to find that you were ignorant of it.

On reading the above to Mr. Bartlett, I find that his recollection of Mr. Fulton's statements perfectly accords with mine.

Yours, respectfully and truly,

CHARLES O. BOUTELLE,

Assistant C. S., Comd'g U. S. Steamer Bibb.

Rear-Admiral S. F. DuPont, U. S. N.,

Comd'g S. A. Blockading Squadron.

[Enclosure No. 2.—Despatch No. 208, 1863.]

United States Steamer Weehawken,

Port Royal, April 20, 1863.

Sir: In compliance with your order of this day, I have the honor to submit the following report in regard to the raft said to have been invented by Mr. Ericsson, for the purpose of carrying a torpedo to be used in blowing up obstructions:

Upon trial in this harbor I found that the vessel with the simple raft steered as well, I thought, as usual—certainly not so much worse as to render its use objectionable. Whether she would handle as well with the resistance of the torpedo 12 feet under water added on to the raft, I have not tried, and therefore can express no opinion.

There was another trial of the simple raft attached to this vessel in North Edisto harbor, with the captains of the iron-clads on board. They did not judge of it so favorably as to be willing to use it. I thought that it would not be wise to carry the torpedo into action, since, in evolutions, we might come into contact with some of our own vessels, and thus blow them up.

The event proves that the anticipation was not ill founded—two iron-clads actually came into collision with the Ironsides, and she had to stop to avoid the Weehawken.

Had those vessels which actually touched her been provided with formidable torpedoes to explode upon contact, the result might have been most disastrous. In plain words, that folly would rise into crime which should carry loaded torpedoes in a rapid tide-way in a somewhat narrow channel, without known buoys, under fire, and with the attention divided amongst a friendly fleet.

The proposition is so evident that it would lose by argument. I declined accordingly to attach the loaded torpedo to the Weehawken during the attack upon Fort Sumter, unless I should receive positive orders to do so. I stated, however, that I thought the raft might be useful, with grapnels hanging from it, to catch obstructions. This, accordingly, I carried into action, and this I brought out.

The raft was cut so as to fit the bow of the vessel, and secured by chains from ring-bolts in the raft, *a* and *c*, to ring-bolts on the bow of the Weehawken, and further secured by rope lashings to the same bolts, and also from the ring-bolts, *b* and *d*, I presume, as designed by the inventor.

In crossing Charleston bar the chains from *a* and *c* parted; all the lashings broke; this happened twice in the short period in crossing from the outside of the bar to the anchorage inside.

When inside, it was found that the sea converted the raft into a huge battering ram, which shook the vessel at every undulation.

It is obvious that with the pitching which always accompanies a swell, the two bodies would be brought into collision with a power proportionable to their weight. The raft, I think, displaces about 90 tons of water. Its motions did not at all correspond with the motions of the vessel. The raft rose while the vessel fell, and the reverse. It was a source of apprehension, lest it should get upon the deck or under the overhang.

The conclusion forced upon me was, that no vessel can carry it attached to the bow, except in smooth water. After it had started the 5-inch iron armor upon the bow I cut it adrift.

Afterwards I offered to use the one still in tow of the Ericsson, to blow up the Keokuk. It was brought in in weather when, confessedly, I could not carry it, and it was anchored. When the sea became smoother it was put upon the bow, with the torpedoes all ready to be raised and lowered into their place.

There was still some sea with a cross current, and Chief Engineer E. D. Robie, who, in conjunction with Chief Engineer Stimers, was sent out from New York in special charge of the rafts and torpedoes, found that the water was too rough, with too much spray for him to attach the lock and fit the instrument for use.

He said that the force of the waves which came over the bow of the raft would not permit the torpedo to be hoisted outside against their beating.

I went on board the Ironsides to report the fact to you. On board the Ironsides he made the same report. In the meanwhile Chief Engineer Stimers came on board the Weehawken, where I met him on my return. The sea had somewhat fallen, and he said that the torpedo could now be filled for firing; but I found that during my absence the heavy ring-bolts, *a* and *b*, had drawn out of the raft, and left it liable to swing round and bring the torpedo, when ready to explode, against the Weehawken's side. A chain, I was told, had been prepared to come up and under the raft from beneath the point E, and to be secured inside the anchor well. It was beneath the raft, and I did not see it. I had no faith that the chain would stand a strain which had drawn out from solid wood two ragged bolts 24 inches long and nearly five inches in circumference.

All sailors know, from experience, that chain is less reliable against surges than lashings.

The raft, in its battering tendencies, had become unbearable; in the sea and cross currents it drew the bolts intended to keep it pointed towards the object it was desired to use it upon, and it was ready to turn its destructive power against those who were to employ it.

It was decided not to make the first trial of it attached to the bow of a vessel under circumstances so adverse.

Very respectfully, your obedient servant,

JOHN RODGERS, *Captain.*

Rear-Admiral S. F. DuPont,
Commanding South Atlantic Blockading Squadron.

Letter of Secretary of the Navy to Rear-Admiral DuPont, in reply to despatch of April 22.

NAVY DEPARTMENT,
May 15, 1863.

SIR: Your communication of the 22d ultimo, controverting, commenting on, and refuting the criticism of the Baltimore American, which contained some strictures on yourself, was duly received, and your despatch and the accompanying papers are placed on file, although the criticism which called out your remarks is not, for the Baltimore American is not even among the papers which are received at the department.

The press of the country, as you seem to be aware, has been generally lenient and indulgent towards you, and the censures, under a great disappointment, have been comparatively few. That all should not have taken the same view of so important a movement and failure is not surprising, and that there should have been some harsh, and even unjust, criticism, was, perhaps, to have been expected. The injustice of your suspicions and conclusions as regards Mr. Fox will appear on the perusal of his letter, a copy of which I herewith enclose. I have no doubt that equal wrong is done Mr. Stimers, who has never expressed an unkind word or any complaint against you to the department.

While complaining of the criticism of the Baltimore paper, you express your disappointment that your official report is not published. What public benefit, let me ask, could be derived from its publicity? You had received, both from the President and myself, communications enjoining upon you to continue to menace Charleston in view of operations in other quarters. It must be obvious to you that a publication of your letters, stating that a purely naval attack on Charleston could not succeed, that you had never advised the measure, representing it as utterly hopeless, could be productive of no public benefit, and would involve yourself and, probably, others in a controversy that would be in every respect injurious.

In a period of such extraordinary activity as the present, our officers can be better employed than in explaining and repelling newspaper criticism. Their reputation, and that of all public men, may be safely left with the people, who will judge them by their acts, and not by undue commendation of friends, or undeserved censure of enemies. The country and its welfare, and not merely personal considerations, must govern in times like these.

I have not published your reports, because, in my judgment, duty to the country forbade it. They may justify the failure at Charleston, and excuse you for abandoning, after a single brief effort, a purpose that the nation had deeply at heart, and for which the department had, with your concurrence and supposed approval, made the most expensive and formidable preparations ever undertaken in this country, but such publications could have inspired no zeal among loyal men, and would have encouraged those in rebellion.

In abandoning the great object for which we have labored for so many months, and precipitately withdrawing from the harbor, your motives have not been questioned; but I have not deemed it expedient or wise to publish to the world your reports of your failure, and your hopelessness of success.

Newspaper animadversion and criticism, though often annoying and erroneous, cannot be prevented, nor do I know that it is desirable they should be, for the public crave information, and will comment on what so much concerns them. But while the press may comment within reasonable limits, it would be an error, to say the least, to make an official exposition of the weakness of our national armament and defences, and still more reprehensible to magnify and publish that weakness.

It has not appeared to me necessary to your justification that the powers of assault or resistance of our iron-clad vessels should be depreciated, and I regret that there should have been any labored effort for that purpose.

Very respectfully, &c.,

GIDEON WELLES,
Secretary of the Navy.

Rear-Admiral SAMUEL F. DUPONT,
Commanding S. A. B. Squadron, Port Royal, S. C.

NAVY DEPARTMENT, *May* 13, 1863.

SIR: Rear Admiral DuPont's despatch No. 208, dated April 22, 1863, from Port Royal, contains a statement that C. C. Fulton, esq., editor of the Baltimore *American*, went to Port Royal with the sanction of this department, and under an obligation that a duplicate of his despatches was to be sent to me for censorship before publication. Mr. Fulton, according to the admiral's statement, seems to have written an account of the late attack upon Fort Sumter, and published it in the Baltimore *American* of April 15, wherein he reflects injuriously upon the admiral.

The facts in regard to Mr. Fulton are these: In March he was appointed by the Postmaster General special post office agent at Port Royal, and, as such, received a permit from yourself to go to that port in any supply steamer of the navy.

He was not under any obligations to send me his despatches, nor have I seen the article to which the admiral refers, either in manuscript or in the Baltimore *American*, nor have I seen Mr. Fulton since the day he applied for the pass, nor have I held any correspondence with him, or received or seen a copy of his paper.

I have given Admiral DuPont my confidence and esteem to the fullest extent, and the extraordinary insinuations in his despatch above referred to are as unjust to me as they are unworthy of him.

Very respectfully,

G. V. FOX,
Assistant Secretary.

Hon. GIDEON WELLES,
Secretary of the Navy.

Letter of Rear-Admiral DuPont to Secretary of the Navy, relative to failure to renew attack.

No. 267.]

FLAG-SHIP WABASH,
Port Royal Harbor, S. C., May 27, 1863.

SIR: I have the honor to acknowledge the receipt of your letter of the 15th instant, enclosing one from the Assistant Secretary of the Navy, which, you are pleased to say, will show me the injustice of any suspicions and conclusions in regard to that gentleman.

I beg leave most respectfully to state, that in my communication to the department I expressed no such impressions or conclusions as are attributed to me. On the contrary, I explicitly declared my belief that Mr. Fox had never seen the scandalous account of the action at Charleston in the Baltimore *American*, or authorized its publication; but I did call the attention of the Navy Department to the fact that this account was published over the initials of the editor of the *American*, who was domiciled on board a naval transport, and had openly declared on this station that his letters to his paper were submitted to the censorship of the Assistant Secretary, and that he was authorized to suppress any portion of them to which he might object. Mr. Fox asserts precisely that in which I had already formally expressed my belief.

I have not troubled the department with other libellous attacks which have appeared in a few journals of the day, and I should not have called its attention to that in the Baltimore *American*, had not its editor assumed to speak with the concurrence of the department, by pretending to submit his letters to the revision of one of its highest officials.

Mr. Fox states that Mr. Fulton was under no obligation to send his letters from this squadron to him, and that he has never seen the letter of which I complained, either in print or in manuscript. It is therefore to be presumed that the letter was never sent to Mr. Fox, and that Mr. Fulton's statement was utterly untrue, and his ostentatious exhibition of envelopes with the printed address of the Assistant Secretary was only intended to give a false respectability to his correspondence. It was the falsely assumed connexion of Mr. Fulton with the Navy Department of which I complained; stripped of that, his libels are simply deserving of contempt.

I should deeply regret having done injustice to Mr. Fox, with whom I had always held the most cordial and friendly relations, and I therefore congratulate myself that, in calling the attention of the department to Mr. Fulton's pretensions, I held the following explicit language:

"Although I cannot doubt, from the statements of Captain Boutelle, copies of whose letters on the subject I enclose, that Mr. Fulton had engaged to submit his correspondence to the revision of the Assistant Secretary of the Navy, I desire to state here, most explicitly, that I do not for a moment suppose he complied with that arrangement in this instance. The honor and the high standing of the naval service of the United States, as signally manifested in this war as in other wars, must be as dear to the Assistant Secretary as to myself, and to my brother officers, and it is simply impossible for me to believe that he should have been aware, before its publication, of the nefarious statements contained in this letter."

You are also pleased to say that I seem aware that the press of the country has been generally lenient and indulgent to me. You must pardon me for taking exception to this statement. I admit that the public press has been generally just and generous towards me, but there can be no leniency where there has been no offence; and I claim to have done my whole duty to the country faithfully and skilfully in the attack which I made upon the defences of Charleston, and while I gratefully prize the generous spirit with which my countrymen have received this great disappointment, I ask for no leniency. The terms in which the department is pleased to comment upon the expression of my regret that the official reports of the attack upon Charleston had not been published, are not gratifying to me, but it is my duty to submit to your decision, and I shall offer no further comment upon the terms in which that decision is conveyed.

I desire to call the attention of the department to its statement that I precipitately withdrew from the harbor of Charleston, abandoning the great object for which we had labored so many months. This charge is a serious one, and highly derogatory to my professional character. When I withdrew the iron-clad vessels from action, on the evening of the 7th, I did so because I deemed it too late in the day to attempt to force a passage through the obstructions which we had encountered, and I fully intended to resume offensive operations the next day; but when I received the reports of the commanders of the iron-clads, as to the injuries those vessels had sustained, and their performance in action, I was fully convinced that a renewal of the attack could not result in the capture of Charleston, but would, in all probability, end in the destruction of a portion of the iron-clad fleet, and might leave several of them sunk within reach of the enemy, (which opinion, I afterwards learned, was fully shared by all their commanders.) I therefore determined not to renew the attack.

But had not my professional judgment, sustained by all my commanding officers engaged in the attack, decided against further operations, I would have felt compelled by the imperative order of the department, dated the 2d of April, and received on the 9th, to withdraw my vessels. The words of this despatch I beg leave to recall to the attention of the department:

"The exigencies of the public service are so pressing in the gulf that the department directs you to send all the iron-clads that are in a fit condition to move, after your present attack upon Charleston, directly to New Orleans, reserving to yourself only two."

Accompanying this despatch was an unofficial letter from the Assistant Secretary, giving the reasons for this order, and closing with the remark, "This plan has been agreed upon after mature consideration, and seems to be imperative."

These documents were received, as I have stated, on the 9th April, from the hands of Colonel Hay, the private secretary of the President, and three days later I crossed the bar and proceeded to Port Royal to put the iron-clads in condition for the new duty assigned them.

In conclusion, I respectfully submit that there has been no labored effort on my part to depreciate the iron-clad vessels under my command, unless to report their obvious defects, and place the department in possession of the result of the experience gained by their commanders and myself in battle, may be so construed.

To report their defects was not only my plain duty, but was also in compliance with an order from the department to the commanders of the iron-clad vessels. I cannot, therefore, but express my surprise that the department should have felt authorized to characterize the performance of this obvious duty as a labored effort to depreciate the powers of assault and resistance of the iron-clads.

Very respectfully, your obedient servant,

S. F. DUPONT,
Rear-Admiral, Commanding S. A. B. Squadron.

Letter of the Secretary of the Navy to Rear-Admiral DuPont relative to the first attack on Charleston.

NAVY DEPARTMENT, *May* 14, 1863.

SIR: Your several despatches, with the reports of yourself and the commanding officers who participated in the affair of the 7th of April, were duly received. If the results at Charleston were not all that are wished, there was much in them that was gratifying. Brief as was the conflict, the fire brought to bear on the Monitor vessels was such as could have been sustained by no *ordinary* boats, and demonstrates their power of resistance and their adaptation for harbor purposes. That the vessels in that engagement should have returned from the encounter with so few casualties and the loss of but one life is certainly remarkable, and in itself a subject of congratulation.

In view of operations elsewhere it was deemed essential that the military forces at Charleston and its vicinity should for a time at least be retained there, whatever might be the termination of the naval engagement. Hence my letter of the 11th, and also the telegram of the President which you received by the Freeborn, and which appear to be not only not in unison with your convictions, but have, I am sorry to perceive, inflicted pain when none was intended.

Nothing was further from the purpose of the President or of the department than any censure upon you in those communications. We had not sufficient data when they were written to form an opinion of the merits of the conflict. It would be wrong to say we have not been in some degree disappointed, but until the 8th of April the harbor and defences of Charleston were to us a sealed book. We knew little of them, but had hoped that you, during the blockade and months of preparation, had become possessed of their true character. I had, it is true, received no intimation from you that you were thus informed, nor had I, indeed, been advised of your opinions and views in regard to the feasibility and probable results of the demonstrations that were to be made, but which had been canvassed and fully understood when you visited Washington last autumn, and any subsequent movement had, I supposed, your concurrence. I had not pressed you to be communicative, for to you had been confided, as naval commander, the entire management of not only the attack on Charleston, but the whole operations of the naval forces of the South Atlantic squadron. I did suppose the attack on Charleston had your hearty approval, and hence for many months we have bent the earnest energies of the department and the service to answer your requisitions and afford you the necessary assistance, often by depriving other squadrons of that support that was actually necessary for their efficiency.

Had you at any time expressed an opinion against the expediency of an attack, or a belief that it would be disastrous, such was my confidence in you, and my respect for your intelligence and capability, that I should certainly have reviewed the subject, and not unlikely an entirely different arrangement of our forces would have been projected. I had supposed there was between us an entire concurrence of opinion, and the expression in your despatch of the 16th ultimo, that you did not advise the attack, is the first intimation to the department or the government that you, the admiral in command, entertained a doubt of either the propriety or expediency of the movement.

I regret that there should not have been entire frankness in this matter. It was certainly due not only to me, your friend, but to the country and the service, that you, who have, as you remark, had eighteen months' experience and close study of the military and naval position in the tenure of the sea-coast within the limits of your command, should have given to the department, that so implicitly trusted you, the benefits of your knowledge, observation and experience.

I can well suppose that you may have been reluctant to give an opinion adverse to an object that earnestly engaged the attention of the department and of the whole country; yet, such were and are the relations between us, that I had reason, personally as well as officially, to expect from you a free expression of your opinions, your views, and your judgment on a measure of such transcendent importance.

A young and inexperienced officer might have been excused for being sensitive in such a matter; but an officer of established reputation, of mature age, whose courage, sagacity, and experience had placed him at the head of his profession, and on whose knowledge and judgment the department, as you well knew, relied, should not have been backward in communicating his views and opinions on a question that so materially affected the character of the navy and the welfare of the country.

I have been disappointed in receiving from you no suggestion in regard to future movements since the conclusion you arrived at, that a purely naval attack on Charleston cannot be successful. Would you recommend a combined naval and army movement, and that promptly, or deliberately; or, would you advise an entire abandonment of operations against the place, and limit ourselves to a mere blockade of the harbor? Your information and experience ought not at such time to be withheld from, but should be communicated to, the department. There should be no reserve in this matter. We all have a duty to perform, and should give our undivided energies of body and mind, and whatever useful information we possess, to the country.

In a late communication elaborately refuting a newspaper criticism on your proceedings, you express some disappointment that the official reports of yourself and the officers in command of the iron-clad vessels have not been published. As no inconsiderable portions of these reports were devoted to a detail of the imperfections, or supposed imperfections, of a class of formidable vessels of our service, the effect of such a publication would have been to discourage our friends and to encourage the rebels. This I could not do, although the disparagement of those vessels might have furnished an ample justification, if one were necessary, for the failure to obtain complete success at Charleston.

I regretted there was not a report of the battle, which we might have published at once, and another and distinct report in regard to the turreted vessels which we are just bringing into service, and concerning which it would have been inexcusable to have informed our enemies. But as the whole subjects were blended in the reports, and the failure imputed not so much to the defences, obstructions, and other causes, as to the vessels which, if not in every respect all that was expected, certainly sustained a fire such as no vessels ever before encountered and escaped, the county is, I conceive, better served by omitting, for the present, their publication.

Very respectfully, &c.,

GIDEON WELLES,
Secretary of the Navy.

Rear-Admiral SAMUEL F. DUPONT,
Commanding S. A. B. Squadron, Port Royal, S. C.

Reply of Rear-Admiral DuPont to department's letter of May 14.

No. 285.]

FLAG-SHIP WABASH,
Port Royal Harbor, S. C., June 3, 1863.

SIR: I have the honor to acknowledge the receipt of the department's communication of the 14th ultimo, informing me of the receipt of my several despatches, accompanied by the reports of the commanding officers who participated in the attack upon the forts at Charleston on the 7th of April last.

The tone of this communication is so different from the one which immediately followed it, dated on the 15th ultimo, and to which I have already replied by the Arago, that I desire to answer it more at length, and to meet the statements of the department, as contained therein, as fully as may be in my power, and with every mark of consideration due to its distinguished head.

I am well aware, as the department observes, that the results at Charleston were not all that were wished for, and quite agree with the department that there was, nevertheless, much in them that was gratifying, particularly that the loss of life was so small, and that the capacity of the iron-clads for enduring the hot and heavy fire brought to bear upon them, which would have destroyed any vessels of wood heretofore used in warfare, was made so evident. But I must take leave to remind the department that ability to endure is not a sufficient element wherewith to gain victories; that endurance must be accompanied with a corresponding power to inflict injury upon the enemy; and I will improve the present occasion to repeat the expression of a conviction, which I have already conveyed to the department in former letters, that the weakness of the Monitor class of vessels in this latter important particular is fatal to their attempts against fortifications having outlying obstructions, as at the Ogeechee and at Charleston, or against other fortifications upon elevations, as at Fort Darling, or against any modern fortifications before which they must anchor or lie at rest, and receive much more than they can return. With even their diminished surface they are not invulnerable, and their various mechanical contrivances for working their turrets and guns are so liable to immediate derangement that, in the brief though fierce engagement at Charleston, five out of eight were disabled, and, as I mentioned in my detailed report to the department, a half an hour more fighting would, in my judgment, have placed them all "hors de combat."

The department refers to its order of the 11th of April, and to a telegram from the President, which directed the retention of the military forces of the United States near to Charleston, in view of operations elsewhere, and the department states its impression that these despatches were not in unison with my convictions, and expresses its regret that I should have been pained by their nature, when nothing was further from the intentions of the President or of the department than a design to censure me in those communications.

The letter of the department of the 11th of April was unexceptionable, but I certainly did consider the telegram of the President as implying a censure upon myself, and I desire most respectfully to submit, as some evidence that such a belief was not unreasonably entertained by me, that the President, with great kindness, in a second despatch, and before he could have known what impression his first had made, took occasion to state, much to my gratification, that he had not intended to censure me.

In regard to the subject-matter of the order of the department of the 11th of April, and to that of the accompanying telegram, I desire to state here that the order of the department of the 2d of April had been received by me on the 9th, and was so imperative, and so fully explanatory of the reasons for making it imperative, that I had, as mentioned in my despatch No. 267, proceeded on the 12th, as soon as was practicable, to Port Royal with the Monitors to put them under repairs before sending them to their new destination. The order of the 11th and the telegram found me here, in compliance with this previous order of April 2.

It was in replying to this telegram, which I then believed to imply a censure upon my action at Charleston, that I deemed it due to myself to state that I had never advised the attack on Charleston, and I perceive that the department has taken especial exception to this expression, and has dwelt upon it at considerable length in its letter to which I am now replying. A reference to my correspondence with the department, and more particularly to my letters to the Assistant Secretary of the Navy, will certainly show that I never advised the attack upon Charleston at all; but if made, it should be accompanied by a sufficient number of troops to insure success; and an inspection of this correspondence, which, with the Assistant Secretary, was constantly maintained, and which put him and, as I supposed, the department also in full possession of my views as to every matter connected with my command, will relieve me, I feel assured, from the imputation that I did not keep the department sufficiently advised of my opinions as to the operations contemplated on this coast; and I beg to refer to the same correspondence as containing all the information obtained by me from every source in regard to the defences of Charleston; and if, after such information, Charleston harbor continued to be a sealed book to the department, it was equally so to me.

The department, in continuing its remarks upon the want of such information from me as the admiral commanding, observes, nevertheless, "that the feasibility and the probable results of the demonstrations that were to be made had been canvassed and fully understood when I visited Washington last autumn."

The honorable Secretary will remember how very few words passed on the subject between him and myself. It was, however, more fully discussed with the Assistant Secretary, who proposed that I should return to my station by way of Hampton Roads, in order that we might further canvass the matter, and he accompanied me that far from Washington. But nothing was matured, and for the reason that all was still in the vague future. Not a new iron-clad except the New Ironsides was yet finished, and the original Monitor was on the dock in the Washington navy yard. The defects of the New Ironsides were glaring, particularly the contracted size of the pilot-house and its improper location behind the enormous smoke-stack, shutting out all view ahead, and most materially interfering with the management of the vessel in battle—defects painfully realized in the attack on Charleston.

I remember, however, that in our discussion the confidence of the Assistant Secretary in the Monitor class of vessels was so profound as to lead him to say that one Monitor alone would cause the immediate evacuation of Charleston; upon which occasion, not entertaining such unlimited faith in the powers of those vessels, nor disposed to underrate an enemy, I took the liberty of reminding him that one Monitor, aided by the Galena and Naugatuck, both iron-clads, with several wooden gunboats, had failed to take Fort Darling, notwithstanding the great gallantry displayed on that occasion.

The department will therefore perceive that when I left Washington there was really nothing matured, though I was firmly impressed with the fixed determination of the department that Charleston should be attacked; and that, with the iron-clads, that attack must necessarily be successful.

The powers and adaptability of these vessels were as much a sealed book to me as the defences of Charleston to the department; but under all the circumstances, to wit, the imperfect knowledge of those defences and of the powers of the iron-clads, in which the department had expressed unbounded confidence, no officer could hesitate to make the experiment, and I gave to it my whole heart and energy, not hesitating to ask the department for all the iron-clads that could be spared; and I am happy to say that the department spared no pains to increase the force of those vessels.

While preparations were making, and the completion of the Monitors was going on, the trials in the Ogeechee took place. As the department is aware, the results here were most discouraging. Two attacks successively made by one Monitor with gunboats and a mortar vessel, had no effect on a fort of seven (7) guns, protected with piling and torpedoes. This was followed by a bombardment of eight (8) hours, with three Monitors, with the gunboats, and three mortar vessels, and, as before, with a like result. The injuries to the Monitors were extensive, and their offensive powers found to be feeble in dealing with forts, particularly earthworks.

It may perhaps be said that it was my duty to have placed before the department, in more emphatic terms than were used by me, the deductions to be drawn from these preliminary trials; for if three Monitors, with gunboats and mortar vessels, following two previous trials on Fort McAllister with one Monitor and the wooden boats, had failed to reach or take a seven (7) gun battery, how were eight or nine iron-clads of all kinds to capture the defences of Charleston, consisting of continuous lines of works and forts extending for several miles, and mounting some hundreds of guns of improved make, and with a more complicated and more formidable system of obstructions? But as these were deductions patent on the perusal of my despatches, I did not deem it necessary to do more than lay all the facts of those trials before the department for its judgment and decision; and in my despatch No. 41, written as early as January 28, 1863, I expressed myself as follows: "My own previous impressions of these vessels frequently expressed to Assistant Secretary Fox have been confirmed, viz., that whatever degree of impenetrability they might have, there was no corresponding quality of aggression or destructiveness against forts."

* * * * * * *

"This experiment also convinces me of another impression, firmly held and often expressed, that in all such operations, to secure success, troops are necessary."

These facts, however, seemed not to have changed the views of the department; and in accordance with its previous orders and its well-known determination to effect the capture of Charleston, I determined to make the experiment, and to risk and possibly lose whatever of prestige pertained to a long and successful professional career, in order to meet the necessities of the war and the wishes of the government.

The experiment was made, and, in my opinion, sufficiently, thoroughly, and conclusively. That it did not succeed in capturing the forts and the city of Charleston is a matter of regret as keen, and of disappointment as great, to myself and to those who shared in it, as can be felt by the department or by the country. It was not, however, without important results, for it established anew the supremacy of artillery in forts as against floating batteries, and confirmed the truth of the opinion expressed by me in my previous despatches, that in all such operations, to secure success, troops are necessary.

Had the land forces on this occasion been at all adequate to the emergency, the result might have been all that the country desired. With the army in possession of the land approaches to Charleston, the attack from the sea could have been pushed to desperation, and the sacrifice of some of the iron-clad vessels could then have been properly made, as they would not have fallen into the hands of the enemy. But, unsupported by operations on shore, it would have been a most culpable waste of material upon an unjustifiable forlorn hope, to have carried the assault by sea to extremities, with the prospect of leaving a certain proportion of the iron-clads with the enemy, in condition perhaps to be raised and repaired by them, and afterwards used from their interior lines most effectively against the wooden blockaders.

The department expresses disappointment at not receiving from me suggestions in regard to future movements.

I stated to the department in my first report, on the 8th of April, that, in my judgment, to renew the attack would convert a failure into a disaster, and that Charleston could not be taken by a purely naval attack. In my detailed report of the 15th April, I repeated that it was wholly impracticable to take Charleston with the naval force under my command.

In making the above declarations without reserve, with a full knowledge of the responsibility involved, and under a high sense of duty, regardless of consequences to myself, I thought I would, at the same time, be relieving the department of all embarrassment in reference to any immediate movements, and that the department would appreciate my motives in so doing.

I did not, therefore, make any suggestions, but waited to hear from the department in acknowledgment of my reports; and I deeply regret to say that the long and unusual silence maintained by the department has been to me a cause of very sore disappointment.

Coming out of a battle of so novel a character as to attract the attention of the world, and being the most momentous event in the service of this squadron since its victory in this harbor, the admiral commanding feels that he had a right to look for ordinary official courtesy, if not for approval.

The department has declined to let my countrymen see my official reports, and to this I submit; but the reasons assigned for this course surely did not preclude me from being honored by an acknowledgment of the receipt of my despatches in the usual course of mail. For such acknowledgment, however, I waited in vain, until six weeks after the battle, and I had the mortification of reading European comments upon it before I received a line from the department.

The favorable opportunity for the capture of Charleston presented itself when the gunboats first took possession of Stono inlet, and the army landed, under their protection on James island, which at that time was not strongly fortified. The attack, however, failed, from causes which it is not necessary to mention here, and the opportunity was lost. James island has been thoroughly protected since that event, and the labor upon the harbor defences has not ceased since the fall of Sumter.

When I stated to the department that in my opinion Charleston could not be taken by a purely naval attack, I have wished to be understood in the ordinary acceptation of these terms as used in war, and as conveying the idea of measuring the importance of the operation with its cost. I do not doubt that there is material enough in the country to accomplish this result in time; but nevertheless, obstructions in the way may be made insuperable, and to take a place it must first be reached. By a siege, and with the aid of iron-clads armed differently from the present Monitors, whose turrets could be relied on to continue to turn, at least for a few hours consecutively, and sufficient in number to relieve the disabled ones, the forts can be gradually reduced so as to get at the obstructions, which cannot be removed at night or during daylight by the Monitors while under fire; but the department will remember how opposed it was to taking Charleston by siege, whether from Morris island or elsewhere.

The reason for such joint co-operation is now passing away, as, during the summer, James island is said to be too unhealthy for whites to remain upon it. This, though bad for the enemy, would be fatal to our troops. It is probable, taking into consideration the number and the strength of the forts upon James island, that military science would indicate Bull bay as the point from which the army should move; this bay was suggested as available for a base of operations against Charleston by the board convened by the department in 1861.

If a joint operation on a sufficient scale is not to be undertaken at this moment, I see nothing to recommend now, but to endeavor to enforce the blockade of Charleston, which, notwithstanding the presence here of a larger force than I have had before it previously, is still evaded.

The safety of the blockading force must also be looked to, and I respectfully and earnestly appeal to the department to contemplate the condition of the blockade of the whole coast from North Carolina to Florida. If, as seems probable, it should have to contend with sea-going iron-clads of the enemy, preparing in their own waters and abroad, it is to be greatly feared that the Monitors will not be equal to the occasion. They can protect the inside stations, but they are not adapted for ocean work, and iron-clad vessels that can cruise and keep the sea are now alsolutely needed. The want of such vessels will be more imperatively felt as the events of this war continue to develop themselves, and I feel myself greatly hampered at this moment, because the force under my command, so far as iron-clads are concerned, is composed of vessels whose necessities require them to be kept in smooth water.

But as I have already called the attention of the department to this subject in a special despatch, I need not dwell any further upon it at present.

Very respectfully, your obedient servant,

S. F. DUPONT,
Rear-Admiral, Commanding S. A. B. Squadron.

Hon. GIDEON WELLES,
Secretary of the Navy, Washington, D. C.

The Secretary of the Navy to Rear-Admiral DuPont.

NAVY DEPARTMENT, *June* 26, 1863.

SIR: Your despatch of the 3d instant (No. 285) was received. Some delay attended the acknowledgment of your official report of the demonstration of the 7th of April, in consequence of my daily expectation of hearing from you in relation to the order of the President. A prompt response on your part to that order would have prevented delay, although your report itself, it should be mentioned, was not received until the 20th April—a fortnight after the occurrence.

As regards the demonstration of the 7th April and the circumstances attending it, I do not propose to discuss them, nor would it be profitable now. I must repeat my regret that your views were not understood by the department before the event took place, for had they been known, matters would undoubtedly have been ordered differently.

When you were here last autumn, and Rear-Admiral Dahlgren solicited the opportunity of making the attack on Charleston, I was compelled to refuse him, because I supposed what he sought as a privilege, you claimed as a right. In the brief interviews that took place, our conversations respecting Charleston were general; but I never doubted they were frank, cordial, and sincere. The duty was confided to you, who had made the subject a study and had it in hand for more than a year.

With the Assistant Secretary, who has made Charleston a specialty and is familiar with all the points—having, as you are aware, not only visited that place at the commencement of the troubles, but commanded the expedition for the relief of Sumter in the spring of 1861—you went more fully into particulars, and he, like myself, supposed there was entire coincidence of views on the subject.

It is unfortunate, in every respect, that there was not a more explicit understanding at an earlier period. If, prior to the demonstration of the 7th April, you had not confidence in the Monitor vessels and their armament, as the department understands you have intimated to others, it is to be regretted that you did not make known your distrust of their capabilities to the department itself, before any demonstration was attempted.

Sincerely regretting that any portion of the correspondence which the department has felt compelled to make should have given dissatisfaction or caused you pain, I am, very respectfully, your obedient servant,

GIDEON WELLES,
Secretary of the Navy.

Rear-Admiral S. F. DUPONT,
Commanding S. A. B. Squadron, Port Royal, S. C.

Inquiry relative to guns of the Keokuk.

NAVY DEPARTMENT, *May* 22, 1863.

SIR: Enclosed is an article from the Charleston Mercury, in which it is stated that the guns of the Keokuk have been removed from the wreck and taken to Charleston. Have you any information upon this subject?

Very respectfully, &c.,

GIDEON WELLES,
Secretary of the Navy.

Rear-Admiral S. F. DUPONT,
Commanding S. A. B. Squadron, Port Royal, S. C.

Admiral DuPont relative to loss of guns of Keokuk.

No. 287.] FLAG-SHIP WABASH,
Port Royal Harbor, S. C., June 6, 1863.

SIR: I have the honor to acknowledge the department's despatch of May 22, 1863, enclosing an article from the Charleston Mercury, in which it is stated that the guns of the Keokuk have been removed from the wreck and taken to Charleston.

I have no information on the subject, other than is given in the enclosed slip, and which I have seen before.

I have very little doubt of its truth. The work, however, must have been done at night.

The department has already been informed in my despatch (No. 208) that I offered every facility to Chief Engineer Robie to blow up the Keokuk with Mr. Ericsson's raft, but that officer found it too dangerous to use.

Very respectfully, your obedient servant,

S. F. DUPONT,
Rear-Admiral, Commanding S. A. B. Squadron.

Hon. GIDEON WELLES,
Secretary of the Navy, Washington, D. C.

The Secretary of the Navy to Rear-Admiral DuPont relative to the guns of the Keokuk.

NAVY DEPARTMENT, *June* 27, 1863.

SIR: The department learns with regret, by your letter of the 6th instant, that the paragraph from the Charleston Mercury, forwarded to you, stating that the guns of the Keokuk have been removed from the wreck and taken to Charleston, is probably correct. You remark, however, that "the work must have been done in the night;" and add, that the "department has already been informed, in your despatch No. 208, that you offered every facility to Chief Engineer Robie to blow up the Keokuk with Mr. Ericsson's raft, but that officer found it too dangerous to use."

The duty of destroying the Keokuk, and preventing her guns from falling into the hands of the rebels, devolved upon the commander-in-chief rather than on Chief Engineer Robie. I do not understand that the operations were necessarily limited to Mr. Ericsson's raft, of which such apprehensions appear to have been entertained. The wreck and its important armament ought not to have been abandoned to the rebels, whose sleepless labors appear to have secured them a valuable prize.

Very respectfully, &c.,

GIDEON WELLES,
Secretary of the Navy.

Rear-Admiral S. F. DuPont,
Com'dg S. A. B. Squadron, Port Royal, S. C.

Rear-Admiral DuPont relative to loss of guns of the Keokuk.

No. 362.]

Flag-Ship Wabash,
Port Royal Harbor, S. C., July 5, 1863.

Sir: As I was preparing to hand over, at an early hour in the morning, the command of the South Atlantic Blockading Squadron to Rear-Admiral Dahlgren, in accordance with the orders of the department, I received from the latter its communication of the 27th June, the latest date which has reached me, referring to the guns of the Keokuk.

Having indulged the hope that my command, covering a period of twenty-one months afloat, had not been without results, I was not prepared for a continuance of that censure from the department which has characterized its letters to me since the Monitors failed to take Charleston.

I can only add now, that to an officer of my temperament, whose sole aim has been to do his whole duty, and who has passed through forty-seven years of service without a word of reproof, these censures of the Navy Department would be keenly felt if I did not know they were wholly undeserved.

Very respectfully, your obedient servant,

S. F. DUPONT,
Rear-Admiral, Com'dg S. A. B. Squadron.

Hon. Gideon Welles,
Secretary of the Navy, Washington.

Letter of Rear-Admiral DuPont on the qualities of the Monitor vessels for blockading duty off Charleston.

Flag-Ship Wabash,
Port Royal Harbor, S. C., June 3, 1863.

Sir: I had the honor in a previous despatch to report to the department the necessity of increasing the vessels in this squadron, in order to make the blockade more effective, particularly off Charleston.

I desire now to call the attention of the department to another important point in connexion with the blockade of this coast.

It has hitherto been maintained by wooden vessels, many of which are of the most vulnerable character, but the time is approaching when they will be liable at any moment to be driven off by iron-clads of the rebels from the harbors of Charleston and Savannah, and, if reports speak true, by iron-clads from abroad. To meet this serious difficulty I have only one vessel which can do outside blockading duty, and that is the New Ironsides, and her commander expresses doubts of her ability to remain off Charleston in the hurricane season. The other iron-clads, the Monitors, and particularly in the coming hot season, are totally unfit for this duty. They are not sea-going or sea-keeping vessels. In even a slight sea the hatches must be battened down, and the effect upon the crew, if continued for a brief period in hot weather, would be most deleterious; indeed, in such weather they are not habitable; but, in addition to this very serious objection, the speed of these vessels, owing to the foulness of their bottoms, is so slow that they are not only unfit to chase, but in a gale of wind could not keep themselves from going ashore. Even in a strong tide-way, owing to the deficiency or weakness of their ground tackling, they frequently get adrift. These vessels can maintain a blockade in inland waters, but the nearest point to Charleston where they can be placed is North Edisto.

I have on different occasions referred to the qualities of these iron-clads for keeping the sea, but I deem it my duty to call the attention of the department to them in an especial despatch.

In this connexion, I forward a copy of a letter from the commanding officers of the iron-clads, addressed to me when they understood it might be deemed necessary to order them on blockading duty off Charleston.

Very respectfully, your obedient servant,

S. F. DUPONT,
Rear-Admiral, Commanding, &c.

Hon. GIDEON WELLES,
Secretary of the Navy, Washington, D. C.

Opinion of commanding officers of Monitor vessels.

NORTH EDISTO, S. C., *May* 25, 1863.

SIR: Having understood that when it shall be necessary to withdraw the New Ironsides from the blockade of Charleston for purposes of repairs or refreshment that vessels of this class may be regarded as necessary and fit to take her place, we beg leave to express our opinion on that point.

The hatches would have to be battened down the whole time, and the vessels could not fail to be disabled from loss of health to the crew. The loss of speed from foulness of bottom, now amounting to one-half of what they had when put in commission, would put it out of their power to chase effectively, or to get off shore in a gale of wind, even with the assistance of an ordinary steamer. The extreme sluggishness of the compass would make it impossible to make any given course of a cloudy night. If clear, setting the course by a star and giving time for the compass to traverse, would make its use possible. The ground-tackle in a heavy sea-way would, in our opinion, be quite inadequate to hold her. In short, we think these vessels are entirely inadequate to maintain a blockade at sea.

Very respectfully, your obedient servants,

JOHN RODGERS, *Captain.*
DANIEL AMMEN, *Commander.*
GEO. W. RODGERS, *Commander.*
D. M. FAIRFAX, *Commander.*
JOHN DOWNES, *Commander.*

Rear-Admiral S. F. DUPONT,
Commanding South Atlantic Blockading Squadron,
Flag-Ship Wabash, Port Royal.

Major General Hunter to the President relative to Rear-Admiral DuPont's refusal to co-operate.

HEADQUARTERS DEPARTMENT OF THE SOUTH,
Hilton Head, Port Royal, South Carolina, May 22, 1863.

DEAR SIR: It is more than six weeks since the attack by the iron-clads upon Charleston—an attack in which, from the nature of the plans of Admiral DuPont, the army had no active part.

On the day of that attack the troops under my command held Folly island up to Light-house inlet. On the morning after the attack we were in complete readiness to cross Light-house inlet to Morris island, where, once established, the fall of Sumter would have been as certain as the demonstration of a problem in mathematics. Aided by a cross-fire from the navy, the enemy would soon have been driven from Cummings's Point; and with powerful batteries of one and two hundred-pounder rifled guns placed there, Fort Sumter would have been rendered untenable in two days' fire. Fort Pulaski was breached and taken from Goat's Point, on Tybee island, a precisely similar proposition, with 32-pounder Parrott guns, 42-pounder James's guns, and a few 10-inch columbiads; the 13-inch mortars used in that bombardment having proved utterly valueless. I mention these things to show how certain would have been the fall of Fort Sumter under the fire of the one and two hundred-pounders rifled now at my command.

On the afternoon after the iron-clad attack on Fort Sumter, the troops on Folly island were not only ready to cross Light-house inlet, but were almost in the act, the final reconnoissance having been made, the boats ready, and the men under arms for crossing, when they were recalled, as I hoped merely temporarily, by the announcement of Admiral DuPont that he had resolved to retire, and that, consequently, we could expect no assistance from the navy.

Immediately the admiral was waited upon by an officer of my staff, who represented the forwardness of our preparations for crossing, the evidently unprepared condition of the enemy to receive us, while any delay, now that our intentions were unmasked, would give the enemy time to erect upon the southern end of Morris island, commanding Light-house inlet, those works and batteries which he had heretofore neglected. To these considerations, earnestly and elaborately urged, the admiral's answer was that "he would not fire another shot."

A lodgment on Morris island was thus made impossible for us, the enemy having powerful works on the island, more especially at the northern end, out of which we could not hope to drive him unless aided by a cross-fire from the navy. I therefore determined to hold what we had got until the admiral should have had time to repair his vessels; and to this hour we hold every inch of ground on Folly and Cole's and Seabrook's islands that we held on the day of the expected crossing.

Since then I have exercised patience with the admiral, and have pushed forward my works and batteries on Folly island with unremitting diligence; the enemy meanwhile, thoroughly aroused to their danger, throwing up works that completely commanded Light-house inlet, on the southern end of Morris island; so that the crossing which could have been effected in a couple of hours and with little sacrifice six weeks ago, will now involve, whenever attempted, protracted operations and a very serious loss of life. And to what end should this sacrifice be made without the co-operation of the navy? Even when established on the southern end of Morris island, the northern end, with its powerful works and commanded by the fire of Forts Sumter and Johnson, would still remain to be possessed. The sacrifice would be of no avail without the aid of the navy; and I have been painfully but finally convinced that from the navy no such aid is to be expected. I fear Admiral DuPont distrusts the iron-clads so much that he has resolved to do nothing with them this summer; and therefore I most urgently beg of you to liberate me from those orders to "co-operate with the navy," which now tie me down to share the admiral's inactivity. Remaining in our present situation, we do not even detain one soldier of the enemy from service elsewhere. I am well satisfied that they have already sent away from Charleston and Savannah all the troops not absolutely needed to garrison the defences, and these will have to remain in the works whether an enemy be in sight or not.

Liberate me from this order to "co-operate with the navy in an attack on Charleston," and I will immediately place a column of ten thousand of the best drilled soldiers in the country (as unquestionably are the troops of this department) in the heart of Georgia, our landing and marching being made through counties in which, as shown by the census, the slave population is seventy-five per cent. of the inhabitants. Nothing is truer, sir, than that this rebellion has left the southern States a mere hollow shell. If we avoid their few strongholds, where they have prepared for and invited us to battle, we shall meet no opposition in a total devastation of their resources; thus compelling them to break up their large armies and garrisons at a few points into scores of small fractions of armies for the protection of every threatened or assailable point. I will guarantee, with the troops now fruitlessly though laboriously occupying Folly and Seabrook islands, and such other troops as can be spared from the remaining posts of this department, to penetrate into Georgia, produce a practical dissolution of the slave system there, destroy all railroad communication along the eastern portion of the State, and lay waste all stores which can possibly be used for the sustenance of the rebellion.

My troops are in splendid health and discipline, and, in my judgment, are more thoroughly in sympathy with the policy of the government than any other equal body of men in the service of the United States to-day. With the exception of one brigadier general and one colonel commanding a brigade, there is not an officer of any consequence in the command who is not heart and soul in favor of prosecuting this war by any and every means likely to insure success. Only once liberate me from enforced waiting on the action of those who, I fear, are not likely to do anything, and I promise you that I will give full employment to twice or thrice my number of the enemy; and that while Rosecrans threatens Bragg in front, I will interrupt his communications, threaten his rear, and spread a panic through the country.

In this connexion, I would ask, if possible, for a regiment of cavalry, and that the brigade sent by me to the relief of Major General Foster may be ordered back from North Carolina. If no cavalry can be spared, then that five hundred horses and a thousand saddles and equipments may be sent to me immediately. Also, that the pikes drawn for my chief of ordnance may be supplied immediately; these weapons being the simplest and most effective that can be placed in the hands of the slaves who are liberated in our march into the interior.

In conclusion, I would again call attention to my request to be endowed with the same powers intrusted to Adjutant General Thomas, for raising colored regiments and giving commissions to their officers. I think this of the utmost importance, as each commission promptly given to a deserving non-commissioned officer or private has the effect of conciliating the sentiment of the regiment from which the appointee is taken; and it is of the utmost importance that the experiment of colored soldiers should have the hearty acquiescence of the troops with whom they are to serve.

I deem this matter of so much importance, and am so weary of inactivity, that

I send this letter by special steamer to Fortress Monroe, and have instructed the captain of the vessel to wait for your reply.

I have the honor to be, sir, very respectfully, your most obedient servant,

D. HUNTER,
Major General, Commanding.

His Excellency A. LINCOLN,
President of the United States.

I send this letter by Captain Arthur M. Kinzie, one of my aides-de-camp, who will await your answer and return immediately by the steamer which bears this to Fortress Monroe.

D. HUNTER, *Major General.*

Letter relieving Rear-Admiral DuPont from command of South Atlantic Blockading Squadron.

NAVY DEPARTMENT, *June* 3, 1863.

SIR: Your despatch, No. 267, under date of May 27, is received.

I do not find in this nor in any communication received from you since the 7th of April any proposition for a renewed attack upon Charleston, or suggestions even for active operations against that place. No acknowledgment of the despatch which the President made jointly to yourself and General Hunter has been received at this department.

The government is unwilling to relinquish all further efforts upon a place that has been so conspicuous in this rebellion, and which continues to stimulate treason and resistance to the Union and the government, and whose reduction is so essential. I regret that you do not concur in these views, for your long experience upon the coast, the prestige of your name, with your intelligence, profound skill, and your past success, had induced me to hope that you would lead in this great measure, and that it might be the crowning achievement of a successful career.

From the tone of your letters it appears that your judgment is in opposition to a renewed attack on Charleston; and in view of this fact, with your prolonged continuance on the blockade, the department has concluded to relieve you of the command of the South Atlantic squadron, and to order Rear-Admiral Foote as your successor.

Very respectfully, your obedient servant,

GIDEON WELLES,
Secretary of the Navy.

Rear-Admiral S. F. DUPONT,
&c., &c., Port Royal, South Carolina.

General Gillmore requesting the co-operation of Rear-Admiral DuPont.

NEW YORK, *June* 4, 1863.

MY DEAR SIR: I learn by conference with Admiral Foote that fifteen or twenty days may possibly elapse before he can start south. As I expect to start by Monday next at furthest, and as it may be of vital importance for us to secure a lodgment on Morris island before its defences, now rapidly progressing, are completed, I respectfully request that Admiral DuPont be advised to co-operate in such preliminary operations as it may be necessary to inaugurate in order to secure that end.

Admirals Foote and Dahlgreen coincide with me in this view of the matter.

Very respectfully, your obedient servant,

Q. A. GILLMORE, *Brigadier General.*

Captain G. V. Fox,
Assistant Secretary of the Navy, Washington, D. C.

Rear-Admiral DuPont directed to co-operate with General Gillmore.

NAVY DEPARTMENT, *June* 6, 1863.

SIR: General Gillmore has been ordered to take charge of the Department of the South, and you will please afford him all the aid and assistance in your power in conducting his operations.

Very respectfully, &c.,

GIDEON WELLES,
Secretary of the Navy.

Rear-Admiral S. F. DUPONT,
Commanding S. A. B. Squadron, Port Royal, S. C.

NOTE.—The receipt of this despatch was acknowledged by Rear-Admiral DuPont under date of June 14, 1863.

General Gillmore states that operations are delayed for want of Rear-Admiral DuPont's co-operation.

HEADQUARTERS DEPARTMENT OF THE SOUTH,
Port Royal, S. C., June 30, 1863.

SIR: I have to report no important changes in the condition of things at Folly island. My preparations are nearly completed, but I can do nothing until Admiral DuPont's successor arrives and gets ready to work. The admiral has no instructions,* and does not feel at liberty to put his vessels into action on the eve of relinquishing his command. I believe we could get Morris island without the assistance of the navy; but so long as they lie outside the bar the enemy's iron-clads and other gunboats could annoy us so much that we could accomplish very little towards the erection of batteries.

Very respectfully, your obedient servant,

Q. A. GILLMORE, *Brig. Gen. Comm'g.*

Major General H. W. HALLECK,
General-in-Chief U. S. Army, Washington, D. C.

Congratulating Rear-Admiral DuPont upon his arrival home.

NAVY DEPARTMENT, *July* 15, 1863.

SIR: I received your letter of the 10th instant, announcing your arrival. In acknowledging the receipt of your letter, I avail myself of the occasion to congratulate you on your safe return to Delaware after the severe labors of your late arduous command.

* Receipt of instructions acknowledged by Rear-Admiral DuPont under date of June 14, 1863.

Elsewhere, and in public official communications, I have expressed my high appreciation of your services and of the ability that you have exhibited.

Wishing you health and happiness, I am, very respectfully,

GIDEON WELLES,
Secretary of the Navy.

Rear-Admiral S. F. DuPont,
U. S. Navy, Wilmington, Delaware.

Rear-Admiral Dahlgren to command the South Atlantic Squadron.

Navy Department, *June* 24, 1863.

Sir: Rear-Admiral Foote being unable from sickness to proceed to Port Royal, Rear-Admiral Dahlgren, who was appointed next in command, has been ordered to repair thither and relieve you of the command of the South Atlantic blockading squadron, and you will turn over to him all unexecuted orders.

Very respectfully, &c.,

GIDEON WELLES,
Secretary of the Navy.

Rear-Admiral S. F. DuPont,
Commanding S. A. B. Squadron, Port Royal, S. C.

Rear-Admiral DuPont prefers charges against Chief Engineer Stimers.

[Despatch No. 236—1863.]

Flag-Ship Wabash,
Port Royal Harbor, S. C., May 12, 1863.

Sir: I have the honor to enclose charges and specifications against Alban C. Stimers, a chief engineer in the navy of the United States, and to request the department to arrest this officer and send him to this station for trial, where most of the witnesses are.

In order to ascertain with more precision the extent of his unofficerlike conduct and disregard of truth, I was compelled to wait for the arrival of the "Arago" on her present trip.

Very respectfully, your obedient servant,

S. F. DUPONT,
Rear-Admiral, Commanding S. A. B. Squadron.

Hon. Gideon Welles,
Secretary of the Navy, Washington, D. C.

Charges and specifications of charges preferred by Rear-Admiral Samuel F. DuPont, commanding South Atlantic blockading squadron, against Chief Engineer Alban C. Stimers, United States navy.

Charge First: Falsehood.

Specification.—In this: that between the eleventh and fifteenth days of April, eighteen hundred and sixty-three, the said Alban C. Stimers, a chief engineer in the United States navy, being then on board the steamship Arago, by the authority and direction of Rear-Admiral Samuel F. DuPont, commanding the

South Atlantic blockading squadron—the said Arago being on her passage from Port Royal, South Carolina, to New York city, *via* Charleston bar—did, at the table of said steamer, in the presence of officers of said steamer and other persons, a number of whom were correspondents of the public press, and at divers other times during the passage of the said steamer, falsely assert, knowing the same to be untrue, that he was told by one or more of the commanders of the iron-clad vessels engaged in the attack upon the forts and batteries in Charleston harbor, on the seventh day of April, eighteen hundred and sixty-three, that the attack of that day ought to have been renewed; and that they did further state to him that the said iron-clad vessels were in fit condition to renew it; and the said Alban C. Stimers did further falsely assert, knowing the same to be untrue, that several of the commanders of the said iron-clad vessels had said to him in his presence and hearing that they, the said commanders, were, after the attack aforesaid, "hot for renewing the engagement," or words to that effect.

CHARGE SECOND: Conduct unbecoming an officer of the navy.

Specification.—In this: that between the eleventh and fifteenth days of April eighteen hundred and sixty-three, the said Alban C. Stimers, a chief engineer in the United States navy, being then on board the steamship Arago, by the authority and direction of Rear-Admiral S. F. DuPont, commanding South Atlantic blockading squadron—the said Arago being on her passage from Port Royal, South Carolina, to New York city, *via* Charleston bar—did, at the table of said steamer, in the presence of officers of the said steamer and other persons, a number of whom were correspondents of the public press, and at divers other times during the passage of the said steamer, with the intent to disparage and injure the professional reputation of his superior officer, Rear-Admiral S. F. DuPont, criticise and condemn, in terms unbecoming the circumstances and his position as an officer of the navy, the professional conduct of his superior officer, Rear-Admiral S. F. DuPont, in the attack upon the forts and batteries in Charleston harbor on the seventh day of April, eighteen hundred and sixty-three, and did, with the like intent, knowingly make false statements, using, among other improper and unfounded expressions, words in substance as follows: "That the Monitors were in as good condition on Wednesday, the eighth day of April, eighteen hundred and sixty-three, after they had undergone some slight repairs, to renew the attack, as they had been to commence it the day before; that they could go into Charleston in spite of guns, torpedoes, and obstructions, and that Rear-Admiral DuPont was too much prejudiced against the Monitors to give them a fair trial."

S. F. DUPONT,
Rear-Admiral, Commanding S. A. B. Squadron.

FLAG-SHIP WABASH,
Port Royal Harbor, S. C., May 12, 1863.

WITNESSES.

Brigadier General Geo. H. Gordon, U. S. A.; Henry A. Gadsden, captain of the Arago; Frederick Gratagean, purser of the Arago; Arthur Hughes, chief engineer of the Arago; —— Fernandez, doctor of the Arago; J. H. Baker, chief officer of the Arago; C. C. Fulton, editor and proprietor of the Baltimore American and Commercial Advertiser; —— Colwell, of New York, builder of one of the iron-clads, passenger in the Arago; —— Mars, coppersmith, of New York, passenger on the Arago; Commodore Thos. Turner, U. S. N.; Captain Percival Drayton, U. S. N.; Captain John Rodgers, U. S. N.; Captain John L. Worden, U. S. N.; Commander Daniel Ammen, U. S. N.; Commander Donald McN. Fairfax, U. S. N.; Commander John Downes, U. S. N.; Commander Alexander C. Rhind, U. S. N.; Assistant Surgeon George D. Slocum, U. S. N.; Acting Assistant Paymaster A. S. Poor, U. S. N.

Record of the proceedings of a naval court of inquiry, held at the United States marine barracks, Brooklyn, in the State of New York, on Friday, the fifth day of June, in the year of our Lord one thousand eight hundred and sixty-three, by virtue of a precept signed by the honorable the Secretary of the Navy, the original whereof is hereunto annexed, and which is in the words and figures following:

"To Rear-Admiral FRANCIS H. GREGORY, *United States Navy:*

"By virtue of the authority contained in the act for the better government of the navy of the United States, approved July 17, 1862, I hereby appoint Rear-Admiral Francis H. Gregory, president; Rear-Admiral Silas H. Stringham and Commodore William C. Nicholson, members; and Edwin M. Stoughton, esq., judge advocate, of a naval court of inquiry, which is ordered to convene at the marine barracks, Brooklyn, New York, on Monday, the first day of June, A. D. 1863, for the purpose of inquiring into the grounds of the charges hereunto annexed and made a part of this precept, preferred by Rear-Admiral Samuel F. DuPont against Chief Engineer Alvan C. Stimers, of the navy. The court will diligently and fully inquire into the matters embraced in the specifications of the said charges, and report to the department their opinion as to the necessity or propriety of further proceedings in the case.

"Given under my hand and the seal of the Navy Department of the United States, this 21st day of May, A. D. 1863.

[L. S.]

"GIDEON WELLES,
"*Secretary of the Navy.*"

And also, by virtue of the orders contained in the letters and communications of the honorable the Secretary of the Navy, which are hereunto appended, and are in the words and figures following:

"NAVY DEPARTMENT, *May* 21, 1863.

"SIR: Enclosed herewith is a precept for a court of inquiry, of which you are appointed president, and which will convene at the marine barracks at Brooklyn, New York, on Monday, the 1st day of June next, or as soon thereafter as practicable.

"I am, respectfully, your obedient servant,

"GIDEON WELLES,
"*Secretary of the Navy.*

"Rear-Admiral F. H. GREGORY,
"*United States Navy, New York.*"

"NAVY DEPARTMENT, *May* 30, 1863.

"SIR: E. M. Stoughton, esq., being unable to act as judge advocate of the naval court of inquiry ordered to convene at Brooklyn on the 1st proximo, Edward Pierrepont, esq., has been appointed judge advocate, in his stead.

"I am, respectfully, your obedient servant,

"GIDEON WELLES,
"*Secretary of the Navy.*

"Rear-Admiral F. H. GREGORY,
"*United States Navy, New York.*"

"JUNE 2, 1863.

"Judge Pierrepont having declined to act as judge advocate, the court are desired to select one.

"GIDEON WELLES,
"*Secretary of the Navy.*

"Rear-Admiral F. H. GREGORY,
"*United States Hotel.*"

And also by virtue of orders appointing Hiram L. Sleeper, esq., as judge advocate, which are hereunto appended, and in words and figures as follows:

"UNITED STATES MARINE BARRACKS,
"*Brooklyn, New York, June* 4, 1863.

"SIR: By order of a precept of the honorable the Secretary of the Navy, dated at the Navy Department of the United States the 21st day of May, 1863, appointing Rear-Admiral Francis H. Gregory president, Rear-Admiral Silas H. Stringham and Commodore Wm. C. Nicholson members, and Edwin M. Stoughton judge advocate of a naval court of inquiry, and by virtue of a communication directed to Rear-Admiral Francis H. Gregory, president of said court, by the Secretary of the Navy, dated June 2, 1863, you are hereby appointed judge advocate of the naval court of inquiry convened by virtue of said precept. Should you accept the appointment you will report without delay to the president of the court.

"Very respectfully, your obedient servant,

"F. H. GREGORY,
"*Rear-Admiral, President.*

"HIRAM L. SLEEPER, Esq., *New York.*"

"NAVY DEPARTMENT, *June* 4, 1863.

"SIR: You are hereby appointed judge advocate of a naval court of inquiry, which is now in session at the navy yard, Brooklyn, New York, and of which Rear-Admiral Francis H. Gregory is president.

"I am, respectfully, your obedient servant,

"GIDEON WELLES,
"*Secretary of the Navy.*

"HIRAM L. SLEEPER, Esq., *New York.*"

UNITED STATES MARINE BARRACKS,
Brooklyn, New York, Friday, June 5, 1863.

The court convened in pursuance of the foregoing precept and orders:

Present, Rear-Admiral Francis H. Gregory, president.

Members, Rear-Admiral Silas H. Stringham, Commodore Wm. C. Nicholson; Hiram Sleeper, judge advocate.

Present, also, Alban C. Stimers, a chief engineer in the navy of the United States, the accused.

The precept and orders hereinbefore set forth were produced and read by the judge advocate in the presence of Chief Engineer Stimers.

The judge advocate then asked Chief Engineer Stimers if he had any exception or cause of challenge to make against any member of the court named in the foregoing precept, to which he replied that he had not.

Thereupon the judge advocate administered to the members of the court, and each of them, in the presence of Chief Engineer Stimers, the oath required by the 25th article of the act of Congress, entitled "An act for the better government of the navy of the United States," approved July 17, 1862; and the president of the court administered to the judge advocate the oath prescribed by the statute aforesaid.

Chief Engineer Stimers here requested that the court would allow him the privilege of counsel, and named Edwin M. Stoughton and Charles H. Glover, esquires, as such counsel. The court thereupon granted the request, and Edwin M. Stoughton and Charles H. Glover, esquires, appeared as counsel for Chief Engineer Stimers.

The court now being organized, the judge advocate read the charges and specifications of charges in the presence of the accused, hereunto appended, of which the following is a copy:

Charges and specifications of charges preferred by Rear-Admiral Samuel F. DuPont, commanding South Atlantic blockading squadron, against Chief Engineer Alban C. Stimers, of the United States Navy.

CHARGE FIRST: Falsehood.

Specification.—In this: that between the eleventh and fifteenth days of April, eighteen hundred and sixty-three, the said Alban C. Stimers, a chief engineer in the United States navy, being then on board the steamship Arago, by the authority and direction of Rear-Admiral Samuel F. DuPont, commanding the South Atlantic blockading squadron—the said Arago being on her passage from Port Royal, South Carolina, to New York city, *via* Charleston bar—did, at the table of said steamer, in the presence of officers of said steamer and other persons, a number of whom were correspondents of the public press, and at divers other times during the passage of the said steamer, falsely assert, knowing the same to be untrue, that he was told by one or more of the commanders of the iron-clad vessels engaged in the attack upon the forts and batteries in Charleston harbor on the seventh day of April, eighteen hundred and sixty-three, that the attack of that day ought to have been renewed; and that they did further state to him that the said iron-clad vessels were in fit condition to renew it; and the said Alban C. Stimers did further falsely assert, knowing the same to be untrue, that several of the commanders of the said iron-clad vessels had said to him, or in his presence and hearing, that they, the said commanders, were, after the attack aforesaid, "hot for renewing the engagement," or words to that effect.

CHARGE SECOND: Conduct unbecoming an officer of the navy.

Specification.—In this: that between the eleventh and fifteenth days of April, eighteen hundred and sixty-three, the said Alban C. Stimers, a chief engineer in the United States navy, being then on board the steamship Arago, by the authority and direction of Rear-Admiral Samuel F. DuPont, commanding South Atlantic blockading squadron—the said Arago being on the passage from Port Royal, South Carolina, to New York city, *via* Charleston bar—did, at the table of said steamer, in the presence of officers of the said steamer and other persons, a number of whom were correspondents of the public press, and at divers other times during the passage of the said steamer with the intent to disparage and injure the professional reputation of his superior officer, Rear-Admiral Samuel F. DuPont, criticise and condemn, in terms unbecoming the circumstances and his position as an officer of the navy, the professional conduct of his superior officer, Rear-Admiral Samuel F. DuPont, in the attack upon the forts and batteries in Charleston harbor, on the 7th day of April, eighteen hundred and sixty-three, and did, with the like intent, knowingly make false statements, using, among other improper and unfounded expressions, words in substance as follows: "That the Monitors were in as good condition on Wednesday, the eighth day of April, eighteen hundred and sixty-three, after they had undergone some slight repairs, to renew the attack, as they had been to commence it the day before; that they could go into Charleston in spite of guns, torpedoes and obstructions, and that Rear-Admiral DuPont was too much prejudiced against the Monitors to be willing to give them a fair trial."

S. F. DUPONT,
Rear-Admiral, Commanding S. A. B. Squadron.

The judge advocate then asked Chief Engineer Stimers if he was ready to proceed, to which he replied he was.

The judge advocate then called as a witness on the behalf of the government, Captain Henry A. Gadsden, who being duly sworn, testified as follows:

Question. What is your name; and what is your profession or occupation?

Answer. My name is Henry A. Gadsden, and I am commander of the steamship Arago.

Question. Were you in command of the said steamship Arago the whole time between the eleventh and fifteenth days of April, 1863? If yea, where was the Arago during that time, and on what service engaged?

Answer. I was in command of the Arago during the whole time inquired of in the question, and she was then on her homeward passage from Port Royal to New York. She came by the way of Stono inlet and *via* Charleston bar and Fortress Monroe.

Question. Do you know Chief Engineer Alban C. Stimers, of the United States navy, now present? If yea, how long have you known him?

Answer. I do know Mr. Stimers, and have known him since about the 10th of April, 1863.

Question. Was or was not Chief Engineer Stimers a passenger on board the Arago during her voyage from Port Royal, South Carolina, in the month of April last, to New York? If yea, when and where did he join the Arago, and by whose orders and authority?

Answer. He was a passenger, and joined the ship off Charleston bar about the eleventh day of April last; by whose order or authority I do not know. He left the Arago at New York, about the 14th of April last.

Question. During the time Chief Engineer Stimers was a passenger on board the Arago, at the time you have referred to in your last answer, did you have any conversation with the said Stimers relative to the attack made by the United States naval forces on the forts and batteries of Charleston harbor, on the 7th day of April last? If yea, you will please state such conversation as nearly as you can recollect.

Answer. I saw but very little of Mr. Stimers on the passage, and only recollect one conversation of a few moments' duration that I had with him. I think that one was all; and it being so long ago, I cannot pretend to give the words of Mr. Stimers. I can only give the substance of the conversation, which was to the effect that the Monitors had not received any serious damage in their attack on the forts—none but what could be repaired in a very few hours, and that after these repairs were finished they would be in as good condition to engage the forts again as they were when they went into the engagement first on the 7th of April last; that he considered the trial they had had was not sufficient to condemn them, or that they should not be condemned for what they had failed to perform, or words to that effect.

Question. Did you have any conversation with Chief Engineer Stimers, at the time last referred to, respecting the conduct of Rear-Admiral S. F. DuPont, of the United States navy, during the attack aforesaid, or did Chief Engineer Stimers at any time during the passage on the Arago make any remarks to you or in your presence respecting Rear-Admiral S. F. DuPont, or the part he had taken in the said attack?

Answer. None that I am aware of. He only did in general terms; he did not individualize any officers. Of course I took it to be disparaging to Rear-Admiral DuPont when he said the Monitors had not had a fair trial, because I thought at the time that it was Rear-Admiral DuPont's duty to give them a fair trial.

Question. Did or did not Chief Engineer Stimers, in the course of his conversation, say to you, in substance, that the Monitors were in as good condition on Wednesday, the eighth day of April last, after they had undergone some slight repairs, to renew the attack, as they were to commence it the day before? If he did make such remark, what did you reply to it?

Answer. In substance he did make such remark, but as to my reply I cannot now say.

Question. Have you at any time had any conversation with Chief Engineer Stimers respecting the nature of the injuries sustained by the Monitors in the attack on the forts at Charleston, on the 7th day of April last? If yea, state what such conversation was, and when and where it occurred.

Answer. I only recollect that on the deck of the Arago I asked him if the Nahant had not received very serious damage, as I had been informed that the bolts were sticking out of the turret, so that a person could climb to the top of the turret on them. He replied that that was no injury to her, as she had been bolted too much, or had had too many bolts put into her, or words to that effect; that was in the same conversation that I have first referred to.

Question. Has or not Chief Engineer Stimers at any time remarked to you, or in your presence, that the Monitors could go into Charleston in spite of guns, torpedoes, and obstructions? If yea, when and where did he make such remark?

Answer. That remark was made by him, and in the same conversation; but I am not so positive but that he added, if the *devils* or *boot-jacks* were attached to them, or words to that effect.

Question. Has or not Chief Engineer Stimers at any time remarked to you, or in your presence, that Rear-Admiral DuPont was prejudiced against the Monitors too much to be willing to give them a fair trial, or words to that effect? If yea, when and where did he make such remark?

Answer. He only spoke of the officers of the navy in a general way, not individualizing any one, as being prejudiced against the Monitors. This occurred in the same conversation referred to previously.

Question. During the coversation to which you have referred, did Chief Engineer Stimers say anything about being identified with the Monitors? If yea, what did he say on that subject?

The counsel for Chief Engineer Stimers objected to the question, because it is not relevant to any matter contained in any of the charges or specifications before the court.

The court was thereupon cleared for deliberation and consultation, decided the question was proper, and the witness should be allowed to answer it.

Answer. I do not recollect any remark of his on that point.

Question. Has Chief Engineer Stimers at any time said to you that, after the attack on the forts at Charleston on the 7th of April last, the commanders of the iron-clads engaged in the attack were "hot for renewing the engagement," or that he had been told so by one or more of the said commanders, or words to that effect?

Answer. Not that I recollect. I recollect distinctly of that having been said, but whether by Mr. Stimers or not I cannot say.

Question. Have you related all that you can recall of the conversation which took place between yourself and Chief Engineer Stimers respecting the attack on the forts at Charleston harbor, on the 7th of April last, or all that he said in your hearing respecting the said attack, or respecting the conduct of Rear-Admiral DuPont? If nay, state anything further that you can recall, in regard to either of those matters.

Answer. I have stated all that I recollect.

The judge advocate said that he had no further questions to ask the witness.

Cross-examined by Chief Engineer Stimers.

Question by Chief Engineer Stimers. You have stated that I told you that the Monitors were as well able to renew the fight, after some slight repairs upon them, as they had been to commence it. Did I state that as an established, generally acknowledged fact, or as my individual opinion?

Answer. He did not state which, but I received it as his opinion. It gave me that impression. I think it was his individual opinion, for I think he coupled it with saying that he had examined them. I will not be positive as to that point.

Question by Chief Engineer Stimers. What was the tone and manner of Mr. Stimers in the conversation as to which you have testified?

Answer. It was that of a gentleman speaking of a public act in a very general way.

The counsel for Chief Engineer Stimers said he had no further question to ask the witness.

Question by the court. Did you understand or believe that Mr. Stimers intended purposely to cast any reflections or reproach upon the conduct and management of Rear-Admiral DuPont in the remarks occasionally made in conversation by him, while on board the Arago, relating to the attack on Charleston, or were they only incidental expressions of his opinions without any sinister design?

Answer. I did not discover any sinister design. I took them as his own individual opinions, whatever expressions he made use of. I did not take it as reflecting upon the conduct of Admiral DuPont.

The court had no further questions to ask the witness.

Direct examination resumed by the judge advocate.

Question. Did Chief Engineer Stimers say to you, or in your presence, why the Monitors did not renew the attack on the 8th of April last?

Answer. He did not say why.

Question. Did he not say that Admiral DuPont had given an order not to renew the attack?

Answer. I think he did—I will not be positive—for I had understood so from many.

Question. Did not Chief Engineer Stimers say that Rear-Admiral DuPont had given the order not to renew the attack without consultation, or that he had been told so by one of the commanders engaged in the attack, or words to that effect?

Answer. I cannot answer that; I was told that, but whether by Mr. Stimers or not I cannot recollect; I conversed with so many on the subject.

The judge advocate having no further questions to put to the witness, and neither the counsel for Chief Engineer Stimers nor the court having any further questions, the witness was discharged after his testimony had been read to him.

Frederick Greautegien was then called as a witness by the judge advocate, who, being sworn and examined, testified as follows:

Question. What is your name, and what is your occupation?

Answer. My name is Frederick Greautegien; and I am purser on board the steamer Arago.

Question. Were you attached to the steamer Arago during the whole time between the eleventh and fifteenth days of April last, and on board of her?

Answer. I was attached to her, and was on board of her.

Question. Do you know Chief Engineer Alban C. Stimers, of the United States navy, now present; if yea, how long have you known him?

Answer. I do know him; I became acquainted with him when he came on board the Arago as a passenger, shortly after the attack on the forts at Charleston?

Question. Did you have any conversation with Chief Engineer Stimers while he was a passenger on board the Arago, or did he in your presence make any remarks respecting the attack on the forts at Charleston on the 7th of April last? If yea, please state the substance of any conversation which you then had with him, or of any remarks that he made in your presence, and when and where such conversation occurred.

Answer. Mr. Stimers made some remarks at the dinner table, of which I have rather an indistinct recollection. He spoke of the affair at Charleston and the Monitors. The substance of the conversation was, that he regretted that the attack was not to be renewed, as, in his opinion, the Monitors, after some repairs, might again be efficient. Mr. Stimers thought there was some prejudice existing in the navy against the Monitors. He furthermore said that Admiral DuPont had at first intended to renew the attack, but after receiving the reports of the commanders of the different Monitors had concluded not to renew it. He spoke of Admiral DuPont only in admiring terms—spoke of him and the navy officers as being very brave, but rather prejudiced, as I said before, against the Monitors. I did not hear him say that he had been told by one or more of the commanders of the iron-clad vessels engaged in the attack that the attack ought to be renewed. There were three engineers at the table, and he spoke of the attack in a professional way, and my duties frequently calling me away from the dinner table I only heard fragments of the conversation. I have no distinct recollection of anything more.

Question. Did or not Chief Engineer Stimers, while on board the Arago, at any time say in your presence that the Monitors were in as good condition on Wednesday, the 8th day of April, 1863, after they had undergone some slight repairs, to renew the attack, as they had been to commence it the day before, or words to that effect?

Answer. I have not heard him say so. I have heard him say that the officers in the navy, generally, were prejudiced against the Monitors, but he did not include or exclude Rear-Admiral DuPont. I only heard him personally speak of Rear-Admiral DuPont in the highest terms. I really could not speak of anything clearly beyond what I have stated.

Question. Did Chief Engineer Stimers, while a passenger on board the Arago, speak of being identified with the Monitors; if yea, in what manner?

Answer. I heard Mr. Stimers say that being identified with the Monitors, and convinced of their efficiency, he would defend them whenever attacked; that he did not seek any newspaper publicity, but would defend himself if attacked.

Question. What, if anything, had been said by any person to call forth the remark of Mr. Stimers which you have related in your last answer?

Answer. I do not recollect; I was repeatedly called away from the table on business.

Question. Who was present at the table where this conversation of Mr. Stimers occurred?

Answer. Chief Engineer Hughes, Doctor Fernandez, and myself, all three officers of the Arago; Mr. Colwell, Mr. Ed. Moss, two gentlemen of the navy, one named Poor; the name of the other officer of the navy I forget. Mr. Stimers and Mrs. Stimers, and two ladies besides, I believe. The conversation was generally in an undertone, and confined to the three engineers and the officers of the ship. There were several other tables in the same room, all standing in two lines the whole length of the room.

The judge advocate said he had no further questions to ask the witness, and neither the counsel for Chief Engineer Stimers nor the court having any questions to ask, the witness was discharged after his testimony had been read to him.

The court thereupon adjourned to meet on Saturday, the 6th day of June instant, at 10 o'clock.

U. S. MARINE BARRACKS, BROOKLYN, NEW YORK,
Saturday, June 6, 1863.

The court met pursuant to the adjournment of yesterday. Present: All the members and the judge advocate; also present, Chief Engineer Stimers and his counsel.

The proceedings of yesterday were read and approved correct.

The court having waited in session until 11 o'clock a. m., and the witnesses who had been summoned not being in attendance, and there being no further business, the court adjourned to meet on Monday, the 8th instant, at 11 o'clock a.m.

U. S. MARINE BARRACKS, BROOKLYN, NEW YORK,
Monday, June 8, 1863.

The court met pursuant to the adjournment of Saturday. Present: All the members and the judge advocate. The judge advocate then read a letter from the accused, of which the following is a copy:

"GENERAL INSPECTOR'S OFFICE IRON-CLAD STEAMERS,
"256 *Canal Street, New York, June* 8, 1863.

"ADMIRAL: I would respectfully state to the court that I am too ill this morning to attend. I am perfectly willing, however, that it should proceed without me if my counsel is in attendance.

"I am, very respectfully, your obedient servant,

"ALBAN C. STIMERS,
"*Chief Engineer, United States Navy.*

"F. H. GREGORY, *Rear-Admiral U. S. Navy,*
"*President of Court of Inquiry, Marine Barracks, Brooklyn, N. Y.*"

The court then adjourned to meet on Tuesday, the 9th day of June instant, at 11 o'clock a. m.

U. S. MARINE BARRACKS, BROOKLYN, NEW YORK,
Tuesday, June 9, 1863.

The court met pursuant to the adjournment of yesterday. Present: All the members and the judge advocate; also present, the accused and his counsel.

The proceedings of yesterday were read by the judge advocate and approved.

The judge advocate then called as a witness Joseph Colwell, who, being sworn and examined, testified as follows:

Question by the judge advocate. What is your name, and what your profession or occupation?

Answer. My name is Joseph Colwell, and my present occupation an iron founder in New York city.

Question by the judge advocate. Were you or not a passenger on board the steamship Arago on her homeward passage from Port Royal, South Carolina, in the month of April last? If yea, when and where did you join the ship and where did you leave her?

Answer. I was a passenger on board of that ship during her homeward passage, and joined her at Port Royal on or about the eleventh day of April last, and touched at Fortress Monroe; I left the ship on her arrival at New York.

Question by the judge advocate. Do you know Alban C. Stimers, a chief engineer in the United States navy? If yea, how long have you known him, and was he a passenger on board the steamship Arago at the time you have last referred to?

Answer. I do know him, and have known him about one year. He was a passenger at the time referred to.

Question by the judge advocate. During the time Chief Engineer Stimers was a passenger on board the steamship Arago at the time to which you have referred, did you have any conversation with the said Stimers relative to the attack made by the United States naval forces on the forts and batteries at Charleston harbor on the seventh of April last? If yea, please state the substance of such conversation as nearly as you can.

Answer. We were all on board talking with Mr. Stimers and others in regard to the fight. I recollect asking him about the fight, and how the Monitors stood the fire of the batteries. His reply was, in substance, that they were in the fight, and were hit very often, and were but very little damaged; and that he sent his men aboard, and in five hours after his men had them in good condition; and that after the repairs they were ready for the fight again.

Question by the judge advocate. Did you at any time while Chief Engineer Stimers was a passenger on board the Arago, at the time hereinbefore referred to, hear him say anything in regard to the nature of the attack made on the forts at Charleston, or whether the iron-clads had had a fair trial in that fight?

Answer. I heard him remark that he supposed they were going in again the next day after they were repaired; and I think the purport of his words were, that there was no doubt of their being able to reduce the forts, if they had gone in after they had been repaired.

Question by the judge advocate. Did you, at any time, hear Mr. Stimers say what he had been told by one or more of the commanders of the iron-clads engaged in the attack of the 7th of April last at Charleston? If yea, state what he then said on that subject.

Answer. I cannot call to mind the words of Mr. Stimers on that subject, but I think he said something in regard to some of the captains of the iron-clad vessels; I think he said some of them were against the iron-clads.

Question by the judge advocate. Did you or not, during the passage aforesaid, hear Mr. Stimers say that he had been told by one or more of the iron-clad commanders that the attack of the 7th of April ought to have been renewed, or words to that effect?

Answer. I cannot say that I heard him say so; but I think he said they supposed they were going to renew the engagement; but I could not say that he said that any of the commanders told him so. I heard him say that he had supposed that certainly the iron-clads were going to renew the fight, until after the meeting or consultation of commanders after the engagement; but I cannot say that he said he had been told so by any one of the commanders.

Question by the judge advocate. Did or not Mr. Stimers say to you, or in your presence, that several of the commanders of the said iron-clads had said to him, or in his presence, anything respecting the said commanders being "hot for renewing the engagement"? If yea, please state what he then said on that point.

Answer. I do not think he ever made any remark to me in that way; but he may have said, and I think he did, that some of the captains expected to go into the fight the next day. I took it that he might have been talking with some of the commanders on that subject, but he did not say so.

Question by the judge advocate. During the passage aforesaid did Mr. Stimers relate to you anything that he had been told by any of the commanders of the iron-clad vessels relative to the attack on the forts at Charleston on the 7th of April last? If yea, state what he then told you.

Answer. I do not recollect that he told me anything that the commanders had told him. I do not recollect that he mentioned them.

Question by the judge advocate. Did Mr. Stimers, during the passage aforesaid, say anything to you relative to the condition of the Monitors to renew the attack? If yea, what did he say?

Answer. He talked on that subject. I asked him what the damages were, and then he commenced explaining. He said that one of the gun-slides was somewhat bent from a shot received on the outside of the turret; that the turret-ring had, from a shot, jammed up against the turret and wedged so tight as to prevent its turning. There was another ship—I think the Nahant—which he said had several of the bolt-heads broken off.

Question by the judge advocate. Did Mr. Stimers or not say that the Monitors were in as good condition on Wednesday, the 8th of April, 1863, after they had undergone some slight repairs, to renew the attack, as they had been to commence it the "day before," or words to that effect?

Answer. He did say so.

Question by the judge advocate. What, if anything, did Mr. Stimers say, during the passage aforesaid, respecting the ability of the Monitors to go into Charleston?

Answer. He said they were able to withstand the guns of the forts, or batter them down; or, in other words, that they were able to take the forts.

Question by the judge advocate. Did or not Mr. Stimers say why the Monitors did not take the forts at the time of the attack of the 7th of April last?

Answer. He did not tell me why, but said they were able to take them. I do not pretend to give the exact words of Mr. Stimers.

Question by the judge advocate. Did or not Mr. Stimers, during the passage aforesaid, say anything to you, or in your presence, respecting the trial the Monitors had had on the 7th day of April last? If yea, what did he say on that subject?

Answer. The substance of his remarks was, that he did not think the attack of the 7th of April was a fair test of the Monitors; that the injuries they had received did not warrant their withdrawal; if the attack had been renewed again, they would have had a better chance to show what they were.

Question by the judge advocate. Did or not Chief Engineer Stimers, during the passage aforesaid, say anything relative to Rear-Admiral DuPont being prejudiced against the Monitors? If yea, what did he say?

Answer. I think I heard him say that Rear-Admiral DuPont was prejudiced against the Monitors, or that he thought that he was. He did not say to what extent Rear-Admiral DuPont was prejudiced against the Monitors. It was a mere casual remark.

Question by the judge advocate. Did or not Chief Engineer Stimers, during the passage aforesaid, say to you, or in your presence, that Rear-Admiral DuPont was too much prejudiced against the Monitors to be willing to give them a fair trial, or words to that effect?

Answer. I did not hear him make a remark of that kind.

Question by the judge advocate. Did you hear Chief Engineer Stimers, during the passage aforesaid, say anything respecting the professional conduct of Rear-Admiral DuPont during the attack of the 7th of April last, or respecting the manner in which Rear-Admiral DuPont performed his duties during that engagement?

Answer. I did not. I recollect that I asked him on what vessel Rear-Admiral DuPont was during the engagement, and he replied on board the Ironsides.

Question by the judge advocate. Did or not Chief Engineer Stimers, during the passage aforesaid, in your presence, criticise or condemn the failure of Rear-Admiral DuPont to renew the attack of the 7th of April last? If yea, repeat his language as nearly as you can.

Answer. The whole purport of it was, that he was disappointed, as he expected that they would renew the fight again the next day. He was surprised that they did not renew it, and was surprised when he heard they had concluded to withdraw. He said to me, during the passage, that he had been called on board the vessel on which Admiral DuPont was—I presume the flag-ship—to hold a consultation with him. This was at the dinner table, and we were talking of the fight. We were all asking him questions respecting the fight, as we were all anxious to know, and of course he answered. He said that he had sent his men on board the various vessels to repair them very early on the morning after the fight, and then he went on board the admiral's ship, and reported to him that they were in good condition. Of course there was a good deal of talking, but I cannot now tell what was said.

Question by the judge advocate. Did you sit at the same table with Mr. Stimers at dinner at the time you have referred to in your last answer?

Answer. I did.

Question by the judge advocate. Was the failure to renew the attack of the 7th of April last the subject of frequent conversation on the part of Mr. Stimers during the passage aforesaid?

Answer. It was not. It was more for the first day or two. After that the matter cooled off; at least I did.

Question by the judge advocate. Have you at any time been engaged in making iron-clad vessels, or did you build any of the iron-clads which were engaged in the attack on the forts and batteries at Charleston harbor on the 7th of April last?

Answer. I have been engaged in building iron-clads, and one of them was in the attack at Charleston on the 7th of April last.

The judge advocate then said he had no further questions to ask the witness.

Cross-examined by the accused.

Question by Chief Engineer Stimers. Will you please state what was my general tone and manner when speaking of the attack upon Charleston, and especially when speaking of Rear-Admiral DuPont, while at the table in the cabin of the Arago, and at other times and places during the passage?

Answer. I have never seen anything but a respectful demeanor on the part of Mr. Stimers toward Admiral DuPont. I never saw anything that looked like slurring him in any way or form.

Question by Chief Engineer Stimers. Was I or not very reserved in making any remarks concerning the fight at Charleston, or of the condition of the vessels, and were or were not such remarks made, in each instance, as replies to questions put to me by various persons?

Answer. He was very reserved about it. In fact, I do not know as I got any remark from him unless in reply to some question.

Question by Chief Engineer Stimers. May you not be mistaken in your statement that you heard, or think you heard, me say that Rear-Admiral DuPont was prejudiced against the Monitors? And if you still think you heard me make any such statement, state where, in particular, such remark was made, and in whose presence.

Answer. I cannot say where it was made, and neither am I so certain the remark was made, but I think it was. We were all talking at the time. There was scarcely a man on board the Arago who was not discussing DuPont's management of the battle, and they universally condemned his action in not going into the fight again. From that fact I might have got the impression that Mr. Stimers said so, while we were all warm and were all talking against DuPont's management of the battle, and some one else might have said it, and I thought it was Mr. Stimers, when it was not; I am not positive.

The counsel for Chief Engineer Stimers had no further questions to ask the witness. The judge advocate said he had no further questions, and the court not having any to ask, the witness was discharged, after his testimony had been read to him

The court then adjourned to meet on Wednesday, the tenth day of June instant, at eleven o'clock of the forenoon of that day.

U. S. MARINE BARRACKS, BROOKLYN, NEW YORK,
Wednesday, June 10, 1863.

The court met pursuant to the adjournment of yesterday. Present: All the members and the judge advocate; also present, the accused and his counsel.

The judge advocate then read the proceedings of yesterday, which were approved.

The judge advocate then called as a witness Charles C. Fulton, who, being sworn and examined, testified as follows:

Question by the judge advocate. What is your name, and what your profession or occupation?

Answer. My name is Charles C. Fulton, and I am the editor and proprietor of the Baltimore *American.*

Question by the judge advocate. Were you or were you not a passenger on board the steamship Arago, on her homeward passage from Port Royal, South Carolina, during the month of April last? If yea, when and where did you join that ship, and where did you leave her?

Answer. I was a passenger on board the Arago on her homeward passage during the month of April last. I joined her at Charleston bar, and left her at Fortress Monroe; I joined her on the eleventh of April last.

Question by the judge advocate. Do you know Chief Engineer Stimers, of the United States navy? If yea, how long have you known him, and was he a passenger on board the Arago at the time you have referred to?

Answer. I do know him, and have known him since the fight of the Monitor with the Merrimack, in March, 1862; and he went on board the Arago as a passenger at the time I did, and I left him on board when I left the ship.

Question by the judge advocate. During the time you were a passenger on board the Arago, as you have said, did you have any conversation with Chief Engineer Stimers respecting the failure to renew the attack on the forts at Charleston, which had been made by the United States naval forces on the 7th day of April last? If yea, relate such conversation.

Answer. I had a great deal of conversation with Mr. Stimers, both during the passage and previously, having been with him nearly two months, and it is difficult for me to separate the conversations which were before we went on board the vessel and afterwards; they were all, however, strictly private conversations, and never in the presence of a third party. I heard Mr. Stimers say that he visited all the Monitors on the morning of the eighth of April last, at the request of Admiral DuPont, taking with him workmen to repair the damages, he having some thirty or forty mechanics under his charge for that purpose; that he visited all the vessels, having workmen on them wherever required, with the materials for repairing; that, having done so, at one o'clock on that day he proceeded to the flag-ship Ironsides, and reported to Admiral DuPont that the vessels were all in a condition for immediate service; that he was then told by the admiral that he had determined not to renew the attack; that on his leaving the various vessels they were all anticipating a signal to prepare to get under way at one o'clock of that day to renew the fight; that he heard nothing of an intention not to renew the fight until it was communicated to him by Admiral DuPont; that, though he had no direct conversation with the commanders of the Monitors, there was every indication of preparation on their part to renew the fight; that on his return from the Ironsides to the Ericsson, he communicated the fact to some of the vessels that the fight was not to be renewed, which created great surprise among the junior officers of those vessels. He made no mention of the opinion of any of the commanders further than that Commander Raymond Rogers had told him that the admiral had determined to renew the fight, but had been persuaded not to renew it by all the Monitor captains. I heard him say that one of the executive officers, but I do not remember the vessel or officer, told him that he felt personally disgraced by the failure to renew the fight, and he desired to be relieved from the squadron as soon as possible. I have heard him say that he believed Admiral DuPont would have renewed the fight if he had not been influenced by others. These conversations were strictly private, and have always been so regarded by me. These statements have never been published, so far as I know, at least from me.

Question by the judge advocate. During the time you were a passenger on board the Arago, at the time to which you have referred, did Chief Engineer Stimers say to you, or in your presence, that the Monitors were in as good condition on Wednesday, the 8th day of April, 1863, after they had undergone some slight repairs, to renew the fight, as they had been to commence it the day before, or words to that effect?

Answer. He told me he had reported them to the admiral before one o'clock on the 8th as ready for immediate service; that the damages had all been repaired. I do not remember that he said that they were in as good condition on the day after the fight as they were when the attack commenced. He, however, considered their general efficiency as unimpaired.

Question by the judge advocate. Did or not Chief Engineer Stimers say anything to you, or in your presence, during the passage aforesaid, respecting the ability of the Monitors to go into Charleston in spite of obstructions? If yea, what did he say on that subject?

Answer. I never have heard him say that he believed the Monitors could enter Charleston harbor, though he did say to me that the attack on Sumter was not an earnest one—I mean of the 7th of April last—and the Monitors were capable, in his opinion, of renewing the attack. He had in his charge the Ericsson rafts and torpedoes, which were intended to remove the obstructions in Charleston harbor, and had great faith in their ability to remove any obstructions inside of Fort Sumter. He frequently told me that, in his opinion, if the rafts had been used, the Monitors could have reached the city. He expressed disappointment and chagrin at the unwillingness of Admiral DuPont and the fleet authorities to examine the rafts and torpedoes, or to listen to him when he attempted to explain their use. He, however, never expressed confidence in the ability of the Monitors, without the aid of the rafts, to succeed in entering the harbor of Charleston.

Question by the judge advocate. Did or not Chief Engineer Stimers, at any time during the passage aforesaid, say anything to you, or in your presence, respecting Admiral DuPont being prejudiced against the Monitors? If yea, what did he say on that subject?

Answer. I do not think he ever said anything to me about Admiral DuPont being prejudiced; but he, however, intimated to me that there was prejudice existing on the part of some of the officers of the fleet. He frequently said he thought Admiral DuPont would have renewed the attack, if it had not been for the influence on him of those who were prejudiced.

Question by the judge advocate. Did or not Chief Engineer Stimers, at any time during the passage aforesaid, say to you, or in your presence, anything respecting the fairness of the trial which the Monitors had had in the attack of the 7th of April last? If yea, what did he say on that point?

Answer. All that he said to me, or in my presence, on that point, (and he never conversed with me except privately in relation to the attack,) was, that he had reported to the admiral that the defensive powers of the Monitors were but slightly impaired, and the offensive powers unimpaired.

Question by the judge advocate. Did Chief Engineer Stimers, at any time during the passage aforesaid, say to you why the attack of the 7th of April last was not renewed?

Answer. He told me that Commander Raymond Rogers informed him that the commanders of all the iron-clads visited the admiral on the night of the 7th of April last, at which time the admiral had determined to renew the attack at one o'clock the next day; that on hearing the reports of the commanders of the Monitors, he had retired, without expressing any change in his determination to renew the fight the next morning; that on rising on the morning of the 8th he announced his determination not to renew the fight.

Question by the judge advocate. Did Chief Engineer Stimers, at any time during the passage aforesaid, say to you, or in your presence, that he had been told, by one or more of the commanders of the iron-clad vessels engaged in the attack of the 7th of April last, that the said iron-clad vessels were in fit condition to renew it, and that the attack of that day ought to have been renewed, or words to that effect?

Answer. No, sir; he never said that the commanders, or any of them, expressed any opinion to him on the subject after the decision of the admiral was made known; that previous to that he visited all, or nearly all, the vessels, and heard no opposition to its renewal from any of the commanders. He said the men and petty officers were all anxious to renew the fight, so far as he observed. He said the commanders were silent on the subject to him.

Question by the judge advocate. Did Chief Engineer Stimers, at any time during the passage aforesaid, in your presence, criticise or condemn the conduct of Rear-Admiral DuPont in failing to renew the attack of the 7th of April last on the forts of Charleston? If yea, repeat what he then said.

Answer. I do not think on board the Arago we had had any further conversation which would have a bearing on the question further than that I have already given. It was his opinion the Monitors were capable of much heavier work than they had performed.

Question by the judge advocate. Did Chief Engineer Stimers, at any time during the passage aforesaid, say to you, or in your presence, that the attack of the 7th of April last ought to have been renewed, or words to that effect?

Answer. He said to me, if Admiral Gregory had been there, he thought the fight would not have stopped on the first day. He did not directly criticise the conduct of Admiral DuPont, but regarded others as influencing him against his own better judgment.

Question by the judge advocate. Were there any other correspondents of the public press who were passengers on board the Arago, at the time you have referred to, except yourself? If yea, please name such persons.

Answer. There were eight or ten members who were passengers on board the Arago, but none of them were present at the conversations between Mr. Stimers and myself. One was Mr. Coffin, of the Boston Journal; Mr. Winder, of the New York Times. I do not recollect the names of any others.

The judge advocate said he had no further questions to ask the witness.

Cross-examined by the accused.

Question by Chief Engineer Stimers. Was I or not reserved in my tone and manner when speaking of the attack upon Charleston, or of the conduct and character of Admiral DuPont, when conversing with you or with the other passengers on board the Arago; or was I talkative, pushing my views forward in a loud, obtrusive manner, such as you would infer from reading the second specification of the charges which have been made against me by Admiral DuPont?

Answer. His conversation with me was always alone and always in an undertone, and when any other persons were present he would always change the subject. He avoided all conversation with others, and told me he went into his state-room to avoid being questioned.

Chief Engineer Stimers said he had no further questions to ask the witness, and the judge advocate said he had no further questions to ask, and the court not having any, the witness was discharged after his testimony had been read to him.

The court then adjourned, to meet on Thursday, the 11th day of June instant, at 11 o'clock a. m.

UNITED STATES MARINE BARRACKS,
Brooklyn, New York, Thursday, June 11, 1863.

The court met pursuant to the adjournment of yesterday. Present, all the members and the judge advocate; also present, the accused and his counsel.

The proceedings of yesterday were read and approved.

The court was here cleared to consider a report of the proceedings of yesterday, and the evidence published in The New York Times and The Sun of to-day, contrary to the directions of the court, the court being informed that such report was furnished to the said papers from a copy of the testimony of the witness furnished by the accused. The court here called upon the accused to make a statement in relation to the matter. The accused stated that he furnished a copy of Mr. Fulton's testimony to Mr. Fulton; that he had asked of the president of the court liberty to publish the testimony of the witness, but had been refused; that at the time he furnished Mr. Fulton with a copy of his testimony, he said to him, if he published the same it must be on his own responsibility.

The court here directed the judge advocate to enter upon the records its disapproval of the conduct of Mr. Stimers in furnishing a copy of the evidence referred to to Mr. Fulton; and the court direct that the accused shall furnish no minutes to any one for publication, hereafter, until the testimony in the case be concluded.

Upon the above being read in open court, Mr. Stimers being present, that officer requested that it might be entered on the minutes that he regretted that anything in his conduct had met with the disapprobation of the court, for whom, as a body, and for each of whom, individually, he had the highest respect; and he begs leave to assure them that hereafter they shall have no cause for finding fault with him. The court ordered the foregoing to be entered on the record.

The judge advocate then called as a witness Captain John L. Worden, of the United States navy, who, being sworn and examined, testified as follows:

Question by the judge advocate. What is your name, and what is your rank in the navy?

Answer. My name is John L. Worden, and I am a captain in the navy.

Question by the judge advocate. Were you engaged in the attack made on the forts and batteries at Charleston, South Carolina, on the 7th day of April, 1863? If yea, to what vessel, if any, were you then attached?

Answer. I was engaged in the attack made on the forts at Charleston on the 7th of April, 1863, and I was in command of the United States iron-clad steamer Montauk.

Question by the judge advocate. Who at that time was the commander-in-chief of the South Atlantic blockading squadron, and who was then commander of the naval forces which made the said attack?

Answer. Rear-Admiral Samuel F. DuPont was the commander of the South

Atlantic blockading squadron, and he had command of the fleet which made the attack of the 7th of April last.

Question by the judge advocate. Do you know Chief Engineer Stimers, of the United States navy? If yea, how long have you known him?

Answer. I do know him, and have known him for about two years.

Question by the judge advocate. Did you, or not, ever state to Mr. Stimers that the iron-clad vessels engaged in making the attack on the forts at Charleston on the 7th of April last, 1863, were in fit condition to renew the attack, or words to that effect?

Answer. No, sir; I never said anything of the kind. I know that my vessel was in a condition to have renewed the attack, but I never made that statement to Mr. Stimers, that I recollect.

Question by the judge advocate. Did you ever say to Chief Engineer Alban C. Stimers, or in his presence, that the commanders of the said iron-clad vessels were, after the attack aforesaid, "hot for renewing the engagement," or words to that effect?

Answer. No, sir; never.

Question by the judge advocate. Were or not the Monitors, or iron-clad vessels, in as good condition on Wednesday, the 8th day of April, 1863, after they had undergone some slight repairs, to renew the attack, as they had been to commence it the day before?

Answer. I do not know anything of the condition of the other vessels from my own observation. It was reported by the commanders of some of them that their vessels were very considerably damaged, some of their guns disabled, and the impression left upon my mind was that they were not in a condition to renew the attack on the next day. I am convinced, however, that, with the battering they had received, they could not have been in as good condition after the repairs to resist shot as they were before they went into the engagement—that none of them were in as good condition. Every shot received by a vessel of that description must weaken it to a greater or less degree, and render it less capable of resisting shot. I will say that I went on board the Weehawken for a few moments, in a day or two after the fight. I did not examine her very critically. She had received a shot on the side armor on the upper works, which had penetrated and broken the five thicknesses of iron, leaving the wooden backing bare, and also a shot which had penetrated the armor of the deck, and broken through the wood partially; and the jacket of her smoke-stack had been penetrated by a shot. I mean by the jacket the impregnable part of the smoke-stack. That was all the injury that she had received; that I said she had received various other shots which had affected her armor, but nothing so decisive as those I have mentioned.

Question by the judge advocate. Had the injuries of the Weehawken, which you have enumerated, been repaired at the time you were on board of her?

Answer. No, sir; I think not.

Question by the judge advocate. Was or not the attack made on the forts and batteries at Charleston, on the 7th of April last, an earnest one?

Answer. Very decidedly, I should say.

Question by the judge advocate. Could or not, in your opinion, the Monitors have gone into Charleston in spite of guns, torpedoes, and obstructions, either on the 7th day of April last, or on the following day, had the attack been renewed?

Answer. I think not.

Question by the judge advocate. State, if you know, any reasons why the attack of the 7th of April, 1863, on the forts at Charleston should not have been renewed on the 8th of April, 1863.

Answer. I am and was of the opinion that a renewal of the attack on the 8th would have been likely to have resulted in a very serious disaster to the iron-clads. After feeling the weight of the enemy's fire on the 7th of April last, and after looking at the obstructions, which were of a very formidable character, I thought, if we had attempted to break through the obstructions and gotten the propellers of the ships involved in the network which we were well advised was there, and which we stood a good chance of doing, they would have become unmanageable, and, in all probability, so injured by the torpedoes that they would have sunken in the harbor, or have fallen into the enemy's hands; and I did not think that the risk of such a disaster was justifiable under the circumstances. The rebel iron-clads were lying behind the obstructions, and any vessel of our forces being disabled would have been exposed to them, and I have no doubt they were lying there for that purpose.

Question by the judge advocate. Was or not Rear-Admiral DuPont too much prejudiced against the Monitors to be willing to give them a fair trial on the 7th of April last; or did Rear-Admiral DuPont say or do anything which led you to think he was prejudiced against the Monitors? If yea, relate what he then said or did that led you to think him prejudiced against them.

The counsel for Chief Engineer Stimers objected to the question for the following reasons:

"First. That no witness has yet stated that Chief Engineer Stimers ever said that Rear-Admiral DuPont was too much prejudiced against the Monitors to be willing to give them a fair trial on the 7th of April last; and

"Second. That the question calls for information from the witness as to the state of Admiral DuPont's mind; that such an inquiry is not proper. The only proper way of proving whether Rear-Admiral DuPont was prejudiced or not being to prove what he said and did."

The court was then cleared for consultation, and the judge advocate withdrew the first part of his question, leaving the question as follows:

Question by the judge advocate. Has or not Rear-Admiral DuPont done or said anything which led you to think he was prejudiced against the Monitors, on the 7th of April last? If yea, relate what he then said or did which led you to think him prejudiced against them.

The court decided the question as it now stands should be answered by the witness, and the court was thereupon opened.

Answer. He has never said or done anything to lead me to think that he was prejudiced against them.

Question by the judge advocate. Were or not the various commanders of the iron-clad vessels engaged in the attack of the 7th of April last called together on board the Ironsides on the 8th of April last by Admiral DuPont, for any purpose? If yea, for what purpose?

Answer. They were not, to my knowledge.

The judge advocate said he had no further questions to ask the witness.

Cross-examined by Chief Engineer Stimers.

Question by Chief Engineer Stimers. You have stated that upon the armor of the Weehawken a shot had penetrated through all the five one-inch plates and torn them off, exposing the wooden backing. Will you please state whether you observed particularly whether more than one shot had struck so near this torn place as to have had an effect upon it, and will you explain how near the top of the vessel this shot or shots struck, and whether, in your opinion, another shot striking the same place would have penetrated the vessel?

Answer. I supposed it to be the effect of only one shot, without examining it critically. It struck near the top of the plating on the side armor near the deck. I do not think another shot striking the same place would have broken through into the vessel. It would probably have penetrated sufficiently to have torn off the deck plating to a considerable extent.

Question by Chief Engineer Stimers. Was there an informal meeting of the commanders of the iron-clad vessels in the admiral's cabin on board the Ironsides on the evening of the fight on the 7th of April last? If yea, did said commanders report verbally to the admiral the general condition of the several vessels?

Answer. There was no meeting of the commanders of the iron-clads in a body. I went on board the Ironsides myself to report the condition of my ship, and I think I met some of the other commanders of the iron-clads who were there for the same purpose. This was on the evening of the 7th of April, 1863. I reported to the admiral the general condition of my vessel. I do not know in regard to the other commanders.

The counsel for Chief Engineer Stimers having no further questions to ask the witness, and the judge advocate not having any further questions to ask, and the court not having any, the witness was discharged, after his evidence had been read to him.

The court having no further business, adjourned to meet on Friday, the 12th day of June instant, at eleven o'clock a. m.

U. S. MARINE BARRACKS, BROOKLYN, N. Y.,
Friday, June 12, 1863.

The court met pursuant to the adjournment of yesterday. Present, all the members and the judge advocate; also present, Chief Engineer Stimers, the accused, and his counsel.

The proceedings of yesterday were read and approved.

The judge advocate then produced as witness Edward Mars, who, being duly sworn and examined, testified as follows:

Question by the judge advocate. What is your name and what your occupation?

Answer. My name is Edward Mars, and I am a coppersmith; also an engineer.

Question by the judge advocate. Were you a passenger on board the steamer Arago on her homeward passage from Port Royal, South Carolina, in the month of April last? If yea, when and where did you join that ship, and where did you leave her?

Answer. I was a passenger on board the Arago. I joined her on her homeward passage at Hilton Head, and left her on her arrival at New York.

Question by the judge advocate. Do you know Alban C. Stimers, a chief engineer in the United States navy? If yea, how long have you known him; and was he a passenger on board the Arago at the time referred to?

Answer. I do know him, and have known him personally about two years. He was a passenger on board the Arago at the time referred to.

Question by the judge advocate. Did you, at any time during the passage aforesaid, have any conversation with Chief Engineer Stimers respecting the failure to renew the attack on the forts at Charleston harbor, made on the 7th of April, 1863? If yea, state any conversation that you may then have had with him on that subject.

Answer. I had a conversation with him in relation to the attack on the forts, and merely asked him his opinion, and he said that he did not know anything about it, but when they went into the action they were in good condition (the Monitors) for that service. I asked him, if they were in that condition, why they did not renew the attack the next day. He said that he did not know. That is about the amount of the conversation that I had with him. I asked him a few other questions in relation to the matter, and he appeared as if he did not wish to speak about it at all.

Question by the judge advocate. Were you, or not, seated at the same table with Chief Engineer Stimers when at dinner, while on board the Arago at the time aforesaid?

Answer. I sat at the same table, opposite to Mr. Stimers.

Question by the judge advocate. Did, or not, Chief Engineer Stimers, at any time during the passage aforesaid, say to you, or in your presence or hearing, that the Monitors were in as good condition on Wednesday, the 8th day of April, 1863, after they had undergone some slight repairs, to renew the attack, as they had been to commence it the day before, or words to that effect?

Answer. I did not hear him say so.

Question by the judge advocate. Did you hear Chief Engineer Stimers, during the passage aforesaid, say whether the Monitors could go into Charleston harbor?

Answer. I never heard him express that opinion.

Question by the judge advocate. Did you, at any time during the passage aforesaid, hear Chief Engineer Stimers say that the attack of the 7th of April last ought to have been renewed, or words to that effect?

Answer. No, sir.

Question by the judge advocate. During the passage aforesaid, did you, at any time, hear Chief Engineer Stimers make any remarks respecting the renewal of the attack of the 7th of April last, other than you have already stated; or did you hear him, during that passage, say anything respecting the condition of the Monitors, other than you have already stated?

Answer. I merely heard him say, in his opinion they could be put in as good order again in a few days as they were before they went into the action. That is about the whole that I heard him say. I spoke to him two or three times professionally about the Monitors, and he told me that he had great faith in them for attacking land batteries. In speaking of the machinery he said the machinery was put up in the most workmanlike manner.

Question by the judge advocate. Did you, during the passage aforesaid, hear Chief Engineer Stimers say anything respecting Rear-Admiral DuPont being prejudiced against the Monitors? If yea, what did he say?

Answer. He never did, in my hearing.

Question by the judge advocate. Did you hear Chief Engineer Stimers, during the passage aforesaid, say anything respecting Rear-Admiral DuPont? If yea, what did he say of him, or his failure to renew the attack?

Answer. I heard him say nothing.

Question by the judge advocate. Did you hear Chief Engineer Stimers, during the passage aforesaid, say that he had been told by one or more of the commanders of the iron-clad vessels engaged in the attack upon the forts and batteries at Charleston on the 7th of April, 1863, that the attack of that day ought to have been renewed?

Answer. I heard him say that he understood that it was to be renewed. That is all that I heard him say. I did not hear him say who told him it was to be renewed.

Question by the judge advocate. Did you, at any time during the passage aforesaid, hear Chief Engineer Stimers say that he had been told by any of the commanders of the said iron-clad vessels that they, the said commanders, after the attack aforesaid, were "hot for renewing the engagement," or words to that effect?

Answer. I did not.

Question by the judge advocate. Did you hear Chief Engineer Stimers, during the passage aforesaid, say why the attack of the 7th of April, 1863, on the forts at Charleston was not renewed? If yea, what did he say?

Answer. I did not hear him say. I asked him if he knew the reason, and he said he did not. He said nothing more to me about it at any time, nor anything that I heard.

Question by the judge advocate. Did you, during the passage aforesaid, have any further conversation with Chief Engineer Stimers, or did he say anything while in your presence, respecting any of the matters set forth in the specifications and charges of Rear-Admiral DuPont? If yea, state fully all he then said to you, or in your hearing.

Answer. I did not hear him say or express any opinion respecting any of the matters inquired of, except what I have already stated.

The judge advocate said he had no further questions to ask the witness; and neither Chief Engineer Stimers nor the court having any, the witness was discharged after his testimony had been read to him.

The court thereupon adjourned to meet on Saturday, the thirteenth day of June instant, at eleven o'clock a. m.

UNITED STATES MARINE BARRACKS,
Brooklyn, New York, Saturday, June 13, 1863.

The court met pursuant to the adjournment of yesterday.

Present, all the members and the judge advocate; also present, the accused and his counsel.

The proceedings of yesterday were read to the court and approved as correct.

The judge advocate then called as a witness Captain Percival Drayton, of the United States navy, who, being sworn and examined, testified as follows:

Question by the judge advocate. What is your name, and what is your rank in the navy?

Answer. My name is Percival Drayton, and I am a captain in the navy.

Question by the judge advocate. Were you present at the attack made by the United States naval forces on the forts and batteries at Charleston harbor, on the seventh of April last? If yea, to what ship or vessel were you then attached?

Answer. I was then present, and had the command of the iron-clad Passaic.

Question by the judge advocate. Do you know Alban C. Stimers, a chief engineer in the United States navy? If yea, how long have you known him?

Answer. I do know him, and have known him about six months.

Question by the judge advocate. Did you ever say to Chief Engineer Stimers that the attack on the forts and batteries at Charleston harbor, made on the 7th of April, 1863, ought to have been renewed, or words to that effect?

Answer. No.

Question by the judge advocate. Did you ever say to Chief Engineer Stimers that the iron-clad vessels engaged in making the attack aforesaid were in a fit condition to renew it, or words to that effect?

Answer. No.

Question by the judge advocate. Did you ever say to Chief Engineer Stimers, or in his presence and hearing, that the commanders of the said iron-clad vessels after the attack aforesaid were "hot for renewing the engagement," or words to that effect?

Answer. No.

Question by the judge advocate. Were or not the Monitors or iron-clad vessels in as good condition on Wednesday, the eighth day of April, 1863, after they had undergone some slight repairs, to renew the attack, as they had been to commence it the day before?

Answer. They were very far indeed from it.

Question by the judge advocate. Could the Monitors, either on the 7th day of April, 1863, have gone into Charleston in spite of guns, torpedoes, and obstructions, or on Wednesday, the 8th day of April, 1863, had the attack been renewed?

Answer. I think not; certainly not in my opinion.

Question by the judge advocate. Have you ever heard Rear-Admiral Samuel F. DuPont say, or has he to your knowledge ever done, anything to lead you to think that he was prejudiced against the Monitors on the 7th day of April, 1863?

Answer. No; nothing to show that he was prejudiced against them. I do not think he had a very high opinion of them. He could not have had a very high opinion after my reports to himself and to the Navy Department, as well as those of other captains, before the fight.

Question by the judge advocate. Was or not the attack made on the forts and batteries at Charleston on the 7th of April, 1863, an earnest one?

Answer. Thoroughly.

Question by the judge advocate. Did the iron-clad Passaic, of which you had command, receive any, and if so, what, injuries during the attack of the seventh of April, aforesaid?

Answer. She did receive many injuries. The three principal were the disabling of the XI-inch gun by a shot on the turret, which bulged in the turret and jammed the carriage in such a way that it took nearly twenty-four hours to get it in a condition to work; another shot broke off a piece of the ring under the turret which was caught in some of the machinery and stopped the turret for some time, and caused it to work badly for some time after; a third shot mashed in the pilot-house and forced up the cover some three inches, so as to lay open the inside to shot, and rendered the position of those who were managing the ship, one of considerable exposure, as they were to a certain extent uncovered. There were a number of other shots received on the turret, side armor, and other parts of the vessel, but these were the only three that were very serious.

Question by the judge advocate. Do you know why the attack of the 7th of April, 1863, on the forts at Charleston was not renewed?

Answer. I have understood because the vessels were not considered in a proper condition to renew it.

Question by the judge advocate. Did you at any time after the engagement of the 7th of April aforesaid make a report to Rear-Admiral DuPont of the condition of your vessel? If yea, when did you make such report?

Answer. I made a verbal one in his presence on the evening of the engagement, and a written one a day or two after.

Question by the judge advocate. Did you ever hear Admiral DuPont say anything, or have you observed him do anything, which led you to infer that he was unwilling to give the Monitors a fair trial in the attack upon Charleston?

Answer. Never; quite the contrary.

Question by the judge advocate. Do you know anything further respecting the specifications of charges made by Rear-Admiral DuPont against Chief Engineer Stimers? If yea, state the same as fully as though you had been particularly interrogated thereto.

Answer. I did not hear any of the remarks said to have been made by Mr. Stimers on board the Arago, and I think of nothing further to state.

Question by the judge advocate. Have you any reason to believe, from anything said or done by Rear-Admiral DuPont that the failure of Rear-Admiral DuPont to renew the attack of the 7th of April, 1863, on the forts at Charleston, was owing to any prejudice on his part against the Monitors?

Answer. No; I have not.

The judge advocate said he had no further questions to ask.

Cross-examined by the accused.

Question by Chief Engineer Stimers. From what direction would a shot have necessarily come to have entered the pilot-house of the Passaic after the cover had been raised three inches on one side, as you have described?

Answer. A shot nearly horizontal, I think, would have knocked the cover off, and I think it would have entered. It might have gone in pieces, and it might have entered whole. If the shot had struck from above it would have knocked it down. I mean nearly horizontal with the cover.

Chief Engineer Stimers said he had no further questions to ask, and the judge advocate said he had not any further questions to ask, and the court not having any, the witness was discharged, after his testimony had been read to him.

The judge advocate then read to the court a letter from the honorable the Secretary of the Navy, of which the following is a copy:

"NAVY DEPARTMENT, *June* 9, 1863.

"SIR: On and after the 15th instant the court of inquiry of which you are president will, unless its investigations be sooner concluded, sit in the room provided for courts-martial at the navy yard, New York.

"I am, respectfully, your obedient servant,

"GIDEON WELLES,
"*Secretary of the Navy.*

"Rear-Admiral F. H. GREGORY,
"*President Naval Court of Inquiry, Brooklyn, N. Y.*"

The court thereupon adjourned to meet at the Naval Lyceum, navy yard, New York, on Monday, the 15th day of June instant, at 10 o'clock a. m.

NAVAL LYCEUM, NAVY YARD, NEW YORK,
Monday, June 15, 1863.

The court met pursuant to adjournment of the 13th instant.

Present, all the members and the judge advocate; also present, Chief Engineer Stimers and his counsel.

The proceedings of Saturday, the 13th instant, were read and approved.

The judge advocate stated to the court that several of the witnesses named on his list were at this time, as he was informed, at a great distance from the court, to wit, on duty in the South Atlantic blockading squadron, and Chief Engineer Stimers stated to the court that he desired to have the testimony of certain witnesses taken also at a distance from the court, to wit, on duty in the South Atlantic blockading squadron. The court thereupon, by and with the consent of Chief Engineer Stimers and the judge advocate, directed that the testimony of those witnesses be taken on interrogatories and cross-interrogatories on the terms contained in a stipulation of which the following is a copy:

"It is, by and with the consent of the judge advocate and Chief Engineer Stimers, ordered by the court that the case of Chief Engineer Alban C. Stimers stand adjourned for a reasonable time, on the following terms, that is to say: that Rear-Admiral Samuel F. DuPont, Commodore Thomas Turner, Captain John Rodgers, Commodore Daniel Ammen, Commodore Donald McN. Fairfax, Commodore John Downes, Commodore Alexander A. S. Poor, all of the United States navy, and Brigadier General George H. Gordon, of the United States army, C. Rhind, assistant surgeon, George D. Slocum, acting assistant paymaster, may be examined on interrogatories to be propounded on the part of the judge advocate and transmitted by him, through the Navy Department, to their proper destination; a copy of such interrogatories to be served on E. M. Stoughton, esq, of counsel for Chief Engineer Stimers, within five days from the date hereof, with leave to the said counsel to propound cross-interrogatories—a copy of said cross-interrogatories to be served on the judge advocate within ten days from the date hereof—to each of said witnesses, if he desires to do so; which said cross-interrogatories shall accompany the direct interrogatories, on both of which, direct and cross-interrogatories, each of the witnesses shall be examined on oath or affirmation in writing. Also, that the said Alban C. Stimers shall have leave to examine on interrogatories—a copy of which interrogatories shall be furnished to the judge advocate within ten days from the date hereof—First Assistant Engineers B. B. H. Wharton and F. J. Lovering, Acting First Assistant Engineer J. F. Young, Second Assistant Engineers George L. Emmons and George H. White, all of the United States navy, with the right on the part of the judge advocate to propound cross-interrogatories to the witnesses last named and referred to, to accompany the direct interrogatories of Chief Engineer Stimers; on both of which, cross as well as direct interrogatories, the said witnesses shall be examined, in writing, on oath or affirmation. Also, that in all cases a copy of the cross-interrogatories shall be served, within ten days after the service of the direct interrogatories, on the said judge advocate and the said E. M. Stoughton, esq., respectively. Also, that the examination of the witnesses, as well on behalf of the government as of the said Chief Engineer Stimers, must be taken before some commissioned officer of the United States navy, or of the United States army, to be named by the Navy Department; it being expressly understood that a commissioned officer of the navy or the army, who has been or is to be himself examined as a witness in this case, is not to take the examination of any of the witnesses hereinbefore named or referred to.

"That the said judge advocate and the counsel for the said Chief Engineer Stimers, respectively, shall, notwithstanding anything herein contained, have the right to object, on the further hearing of this case, to any of the direct or cross-interrogatories that may be propounded by the other of them to any of the witnesses hereinbefore named, and also to any of the answers that may be made or given thereto by any of the witnesses who may be examined under this order. That the examination of each of the witnesses shall be diligently taken and returned, and that each party shall have the right to read the testimony of the other given by the said witnesses, or any of them, before the same shall be submitted to the court; and that each party shall have the right to put in evidence any testimony given by the witnesses of the other party, and to read to the court the interrogatories in answer to which any testimony may be given by the witness or the witnesses examined by either party. It is also ordered that a copy of this order be incorporated in the record of the proceedings in this case."

The court thereupon adjourned to meet on Tuesday, the seventh day of July, 1863, at 11 o'clock of the forenoon of that day.

NAVAL LYCEUM, NAVY YARD, NEW YORK,
Tuesday, July 7, 1863.

The court met pursuant to the adjournment of June 15, 1863.

Present, all the members and the judge advocate; also present, Chief Engineer Stimers and his counsel.

Chief Engineer Stimers stated to the court that he could not probably be in attendance at its next session, but that he was willing and consented that the proceedings should go on in his absence if his counsel, Charles H. Glover, esq., should be present.

The depositions of the witnesses for which the court adjourned on the 15th ultimo not having been returned, and there being no further business, the court adjourned to meet on Thursday, the 9th day of July, 1863, at 11 o'clock of the orenoon.

NAVAL LYCEUM, NAVY YARD, NEW YORK,
Thursday, July 9, 1863.

The court met pursuant to the adjournment of the 7th of July instant. Present, all the members and the judge advocate; also present, Charles H. Glover, esq., counsel for Chief Engineer Stimers.

The proceedings of the last session were read, and the judge advocate then called as a witness Luis Fernandez, who, being duly sworn, testified as follows:

Question by the judge advocate. What is your name, and what your profession or occupation?

Answer. My name is Luis Fernandez, and I am a surgeon on board the steamship Arago.

Question by the judge advocate. Do you know Chief Engineer Stimers, of the United States navy? If yea, how long have you known him?

Answer. I do know him; and I was first introduced to him in the month of April last, during the trip of the Arago home from Port Royal, South Carolina.

Question by the judge advocate. Were you a passenger on board the steamship Arago on her homeward passage from Port Royal, South Carolina, in the month of April last? If yea, when and where did you join that ship, and where did you leave her?

Answer. I was attached to that ship, and acting as surgeon on board of her during the passage referred to. I joined her more than a year ago, and am still attached to her. I was on board of the Arago during the whole of the passage referred to in the interrogatory.

Question by the judge advocate. Was or not Chief Engineer Stimers a passenger on board the Arago during the whole passage referred to in the last interrogatory?

Answer. He was, during the whole passage. He came on board at Charleston bar, and left the steamer at New York.

Question by the judge advocate. During the time Chief Engineer Stimers was a passenger on board the Arago, during her homeward passage from Port Royal, South Carolina, to New York city, in the month of April last, did you have any conversation with the said Stimers relative to the attack made by the United States naval forces on the forts and batteries at Charleston harbor on the 7th day of April, 1863? If yea, you will please relate such conversation.

Answer. I did not have any conversation with Mr. Stimers. The conversation referred to was in the presence of the officers of the Arago and two naval officers, one of whom was surgeon of the Keokuk. The conversation referred to was addressed directly to the two engineers, Mr. Mars and Mr. Colwell, sitting also at the table. I heard in that conversation the following statement: Mr. Stimers said that, in pursuance of orders from Admiral DuPont, he had visited each one of the Monitors after the firing had ceased, with instructions to examine their condition; that he had done so, and had reported to the admiral that, in his professional opinion as an engineer, each one of the Monitors was in a fit condition to renew the attack the next day; that the damages which each one had suffered were trivial. I heard him also say that he had advised the use of the torpedo-exploders on board the Ericsson. I do not mean to say that he used that expression, but I understood him to refer to torpedoes to blow up obstructions. In that conversation I did not hear him say that the commanders of the Monitors were willing to renew the engagement.

Question by the judge advocate. Did you at any time, during the passage aforesaid, hear Chief Engineer Stimers say that he was told by one or more of the commanders of the iron-clad vessels engaged in the attack upon the forts and batteries in Charleston harbor on the 7th April, 1863, "that the attack of that day ought to have been renewed," or words to that effect?

Answer. I did not.

Question by the judge advocate. Did you at any time, during the passage aforesaid, hear Chief Engineer Stimers say that he had been told by one or more of the commanders of the said iron-clad vessels that the said iron-clad vessels "were in a fit condition to renew the attack" above referred to, or words to that effect?

Answer. I did not.

Question by the judge advocate. Did you at any time, during the passage aforesaid, hear Chief Engineer Stimers say that several of the commanders of the said iron-clad vessels had said to him, or in his presence and hearing, that they, the said commanders, were "hot for renewing the engagement," or words to that effect?

Answer. No, sir; I did not.

Question by the judge advocate. What, if anything, did you hear Chief Engineer Stimers say, during the passage aforesaid, respecting the failure of Rear-Admiral DuPont to renew the attack of April 7, 1863, made upon the forts and batteries at Charleston harbor?

Answer. I did not hear him say anything in regard to it, not having had any conversation with him in reference to the attack on Charleston at any time.

Question by the judge advocate. Did you at any time, during the passage aforesaid, hear Chief Engineer Stimers say "that the Monitors were in as good condition on Wednesday, the 8th day of April, 1863, after they had undergone some slight repairs, to renew the attack, as they had been to commence it the day before," or words to that effect?

Answer. I did hear him make that statement.

Question by the judge advocate. Where on board the Arago did he make such statement as you have last referred to?

Answer. He made that statement at the table, while at dinner, in conversation with two other engineers, Mr. Mars and Mr. Colwell.

Question by the judge advocate. Did you at any time, during the passage aforesaid, hear Chief Engineer Stimers say anything respecting the Monitors being able to go into Charleston in spite of guns, torpedoes, and obstructions? If yea, what did he then say on that subject?

Answer. I did not hear him make any assertion to that effect.

Question by the judge advocate. Did you at any time, during the passage aforesaid, hear Chief Engineer Stimers say that Rear-Admiral DuPont was too much prejudiced against the Monitors to be willing to give them a fair trial, or words to that effect?

Answer. I did not; I did not hear him say anything about his being prejudiced.

Question by the judge advocate. Did you hear Chief Engineer Stimers, at any time during the passage aforesaid, say whether the Monitors had had a fair trial on the attack made upon the forts and batteries at Charleston harbor on the 7th day of April, 1863?

Answer. I heard him, in the conversation referred to, say that, in his opinion, the Monitors had not had a fair trial.

Question by the judge advocate. What, if anything, did you hear Chief Engineer Stimers, during the passage aforesaid, say respecting Rear-Admiral DuPont or his conduct during the attack aforesaid, or his failure to renew it? State all you heard him say respecting Rear-Admiral DuPont.

Answer. I never heard him make any allusion to Admiral DuPont, to his conduct during the attack on Charleston, or his failure to renew it; I did not hear him say anything in reference to Rear-Admiral DuPont.

Question by the judge advocate. Do you know any other fact, matter, or thing relating to the specifications of charges read to you herein? If yea, state all of the same as fully as if you were particularly interrogated thereto.

Answer. I do not know any other fact, matter, or thing, except what I have stated.

The judge advocate having no further questions, and neither the counsel for Chief Engineer Stimers nor the court having any, the testimony was read over to the witness, and approved as correct, and the witness discharged.

The judge advocate then called as a witness Arthur Hughes, who, being duly sworn, testified as follows:

Question by the judge advocate. What is your name, and what your profession or occupation?

Answer. My name is Arthur Hughes, and I am chief engineer on board the steamship Arago.

Question by the judge advocate. Do you know Chief Engineer Alban C. Stimers, of the United States navy? If yea, how long have you known him?

Answer. I do know him, and made his acquaintance on his passage home, in the Arago, from Port Royal, South Carolina, in the month of April last. He joined the ship at Charleston bar.

Question by the judge advocate. What, if anything, did you hear Chief Engineer Stimers, during the voyage aforesaid, say respecting the attack made on the forts and batteries at Charleston harbor on the 7th day of April last?

Answer. I do not recollect all that he said; and the conversation being general, I should prefer to be asked questions.

Question by the judge advocate. Did you hear Chief Engineer Stimers, during the passage aforesaid, say that he was told by one or more of the commanders of the iron-clad vessels engaged in the attack upon the forts and batteries in Charleston harbor on the 7th day of April, 1863, "that the attack of that day ought to have been renewed," or words to that effect?

Answer. I did not hear him say that one or more of the commanders had said so, to my best recollection; but I did hear him say that the attack was discontinued after the report of the commanders.

Question by the judge advocate. Did you hear Chief Engineer Stimers, at any time during the passage aforesaid, say that one or more of the commanders of said iron-clad vessels had stated to him "that the said iron-clad vessels were in a fit condition to renew the attack," or words to that effect?

Answer. I do not recollect that he stated so.

Question by the judge advocate. What, if anything, did Chief Engineer Stimers say that any of the commanders of the said iron-clad vessels had said to him, or in his presence and hearing, respecting their being "hot to renew the engagement" after the said attack?

Answer. I do not recollect that he fetched the commanders in personally at all in his discourse. What I wish to impress is, that Mr. Stimers, coming from the action, or seeing it, every one was anxious to question him; some of which questions he answered, and others he was reserved in.

Question by the judge advocate. What, if anything, did Chief Engineer Stimers, during the passage aforesaid, say respecting the condition of the Monitors to renew the attack on the 8th day of April, 1863, after they had undergone some slight repairs?

Answer. I think he said that after some slight repairs they would have been in a condition to commence the action again.

Question by the judge advocate. Did or not Chief Engineer Stimers, during the passage aforesaid, say that the Monitors were in as good condition on Wednesday, the 8th day of April, 1863, after they had undergone some slight repairs, to renew the attack, as they had been to commence it the day before, or words to that effect?

Answer. He might have used words to that effect, but not using the words "in as good condition," that I am aware of.

Question by the judge advocate. What, if anything, did Chief Engineer Stimers, during the passage aforesaid, say respecting the Monitors being able to go into Charleston in spite of guns, torpedoes, and obstructions?

Answer. I do not recollect that he said so, but said they refused to use the "devil," I believe, as it was called, to remove the obstructions. I mean the "devil," with everything attached to it.

Question by the judge advocate. Did you hear Chief Engineer Stimers say anything respecting Rear-Admiral DuPont's being prejudiced against the Monitors? If yea, what did he say?

Answer. I did not hear him say that Rear-Admiral DuPont was prejudiced against the Monitors; I did not hear him say anything about Rear-Admiral DuPont but what was very respectful.

Question by the judge advocate. Did you hear Chief Engineer Stimers, at any time during the passage aforesaid, say whether the Monitors had had a fair trial in the attack aforesaid?

Answer. I do not recollect that he said they had not had a fair trial, but the impression that he gave me from the tenor of his discourse was that he thought they might have stood a great deal more; in other words, he was disappointed in the attack; I mean in the length of the attack, or its not being continued or renewed.

Question by the judge advocate. What, if anything, did Chief Engineer Stimers, during the passage aforesaid, say respecting the failure to renew the attack aforesaid; or as to the reason why Rear-Admiral DuPont did not renew it?

Answer. The reason that he assigned was, that after the commanders had a consultation with the admiral it was postponed. That was all that he said that I know of in reference to the officers.

Question by the judge advocate. Did you, at any time during the passage aforesaid, hear Chief Engineer Stimers criticise or condemn the professional conduct of Rear-Admiral DuPont in the attack aforesaid? If yea, state what language he then made use of.

Answer. I did not.

Question by the judge advocate. Do you know of any other fact, matter, or thing in relation to the specifications of charges read to you herein? If yea, state the same particularly.

Answer. I do not remember anything further that is not embodied in my answers.

The judge advocate said he had no further questions, and neither the counsel for Chief Engineer Stimers nor the court having any, the testimony was then read to the witness and pronounced correct.

There being no further business, the court thereupon adjourned, to meet on Friday, the 10th instant, at 10 o'clock in the forenoon.

NAVAL LYCEUM, NAVY YARD, NEW YORK,
Friday, July 10, 1863.

The court met pursuant to the adjournment of yesterday. Present, all the members and the judge advocate; also present, Chief Engineer Stimers and his counsel.

The proceedings of yesterday were read in the presence of Chief Engineer Stimers, and approved as correct.

There being no further business, the court adjourned to meet on Monday, the 13th day of July, 1863, at 11 o'clock in the forenoon.

NAVAL LYCEUM, NAVY YARD, NEW YORK,
Monday, July 13, 1863.

The court met pursuant to the adjournment of July 10, 1863. Present, all the members and the judge advocate; also present, Chief Engineer Stimers and his counsel.

The proceedings of July 10 instant were read, and there being no further business, the court adjourned to meet on Wednesday, the 15th day of July, 1863, at 11 o'clock in the forenoon.

NAVAL LYCEUM, NAVY YARD, NEW YORK,
Wednesday, July 15, 1863.

The court met pursuant to the adjournment of July 13 instant. Present, all the members and the judge advocate; also present, Chief Engineer Stimers and his counsel.

The proceedings of the last session were read and approved.

The judge advocate then called as a witness Commander Daniel Ammen, of the United States navy, who, being duly sworn, testified as follows:

Question by the judge advocate. What is your name, and what your rank in the navy?

Answer. My name is Daniel Ammen, and I am a commander in the navy.

Question by the judge advocate. Do you know Chief Engineer Alban C. Stimers, of the United States navy? If yea, how long have you known him?

Answer. I have known Chief Engineer Stimers perhaps a year, more or less, on board the Merrimack. I have served with him also about six months on board the Roanoke.

Question by the judge advocate. Were you or not present at an attack made by the United States naval forces on the forts and batteries at Charleston harbor, South Carolina, in the month of April last? If yea, to what vessel or ship were you then attached, and in what capacity, and did the vessel to which you were attached take part in the said attack?

Answer. I was present, and commanded the iron-clad Patapsco, and the Patapsco took part in that engagement.

Question by the judge advocate. Did you ever say to Chief Engineer Alban C. Stimers that the attack upon the forts and batteries in Charleston harbor, made on the 7th day of April, 1863, ought to have been renewed, or words to that effect?

Answer. I did not; I saw him only a moment, near midnight, on the day of the attack, since that event.

Question by the judge advocate. Did you ever say to Chief Engineer Stimers that the iron-clad vessels engaged in the said attack were in a fit condition to renew it, or words to that effect?

Answer. I did not; I think no conversation passed between us except simply a salutation. I had reported at half past eight p. m., of the 7th of April, that the Patapsco was ready for work, although the smoke-stack was much damaged, and I feared the recurrence of disabilities such as we had had during the engagement.

Question by the judge advocate. Did you or not say to Chief Engineer Stimers, or in his presence and hearing, that the commanders of said iron-clad vessels were, after the attack aforesaid, "hot for renewing the engagement," or words to that effect?

Answer. I did not.

Question by the judge advocate. Were or not the Monitors in as good condition on Wednesday, the 8th day of April, 1863, after they had undergone some slight repairs, to renew the attack, as they had been to commence it the day before?

Answer. I can only answer in regard to the Patapsco, not having visited the others. As stated before, I reported her ready for action at half past eight in the evening of the 7th day of April last, although certainly not in as good condition, as the heavy part of the smoke-stack was very much damaged by five or six heavy shots from the enemy. I considered, however, placing chains around as capable of supplying the want of forty bolts more or less broken by the projectiles of the enemy.

Question by the judge advocate. Could, in your opinion, the Monitors have gone into Charleston harbor in spite of guns, torpedoes, and obstructions, either on the 7th day of April last, or on the 8th of said April, had the attack been renewed?

Answer. I thought so previous to the engagement; seeing, however, the disabilities of the vessels, more particularly the one under my command, the force of the fire of the enemy with extraordinary projectiles and increased charges of powder, I was, after our experience of the 7th of April, clearly of opinion that the force was entirely inadequate to the end. On the fifth discharge the rifle gun of the Patapsco was disabled by the carrying away of the forward cap square bolts, and the subsequent necessity of nearly doubling the steam to move the turret. At that time the Patapsco was on an obstruction nearly between the two forts, Sumter and Moultrie, and receiving a fire from them and other works, which could not but, in the end, have disabled her.

Question by the judge advocate. Did you, at any time prior to the 9th day of April, 1863, hear Rear-Admiral DuPont say anything, or did he do anything, to lead you to think that he was prejudiced against the Monitors, or that he was unwilling from prejudice to give them a fair trial?

Answer. Rear-Admiral DuPont has stated to me, or in my presence, that he feared the aggressive powers of the Monitors, owing to slowness of fire and other causes, such as sighting the guns in the turrets, would prove less formidable than supposed. He has stated nothing to me or before me which would lead me to suppose that he was what I would regard prejudiced in regard to the subject, although I differed with him, particularly before I had experienced the want of effect of our fire, and the effect of the fire from the heavy batteries, with, as I supposed, increased charges, delivered by the enemy. I think my answer covers the whole question.

Question by the judge advocate. What was the character of the aforesaid attack made on the forts and batteries at Charleston harbor? Was it an earnest one or otherwise?

Answer. The attack, as I considered it, was an attempt to get into position, and the effect of the enemy's fire and the disabilities of our batteries, with few guns, of such a nature that I would have regarded a serious attempt to reduce the works as likely to lead to a disaster and with little hope of success.

Question by the judge advocate. How frequently was the Patapsco struck by the enemy's shot or shell during the said attack of April 7, 1863?

Answer. I think fifty-one times, including the logs laid over her berth-deck for the purpose of protecting it from shells.

Question by the judge advocate. How was the Patapsco injured or disabled in said attack except as you have stated?

Answer. There was no injury that would not have to be considerably multiplied to lead to her disability except that already stated in the course of my evidence.

Question by the judge advocate. Do you know any other fact, matter, or thing, relating to the charges or specifications of charges made by Rear-Admiral DuPont against Chief Engineer Stimers? If yea, state the same as fully as if particularly interrogated thereto.

Answer. There is nothing further that I know of that has not been embodied in my testimony.

Question by Chief Engineer Stimers. Why was it necessary to nearly double the steam to turn the turret, as you have stated in your evidence?

Answer. I regarded it as the effect of the fire of the enemy, heavy projectiles having struck the turret about that time. The turret was struck twenty-one times; within the space of five minutes, perhaps, fifteen or more heavy shots struck the turret. I observed about this time that when I wished to turn the turret it was necessary to run up the steam to 30 pounds or more. I did not find any special shots which appeared to make the turning of the turret difficult or impossible.

Question by Chief Engineer Stimers. Did you observe, in your examination of the turret after the battle, that any of the deep indentations upon it were near the bottom—say within a foot of the bottom?

Answer. There was one about that distance; it may have been half a foot more from the bottom; I think nearly three inches in depth; but I regarded the general effect of the mass of metal thrown against the turret as the cause of requiring a greater amount of steam.

The judge advocate having no further questions, and neither the court nor Chief Engineer Stimers having any, the witness was discharged after his testimony had been read to him.

The judge advocate stated to the court that there were no other witnesses in the case in the vicinity of the court, and that the depositions of the witnesses to which interrogations had been forwarded in accordance with the order entered herein on the 15th day of June last, had not returned. Chief Engineer Stimers here stated that he consented that the court should adjourn to meet when the president of the court should call the same together again, and that notice of the time when the court shall next assemble shall be given to Chief Engineer Stimers. It being uncertain when the depositions in the case might return, the court adjourned to meet again when notified to that effect by the president of the court.

NAVAL LYCEUM, NAVY YARD, NEW YORK,
Thursday, October 1, 1863.

The court met, pursuant to the adjournment of the last meeting, at the call of the president. Present, all the members and the judge advocate; also Chief Engineer Stimers and his counsel.

The judge advocate then read to the court letters, of which the following are copies:

"NEW YORK, *August* 30, 1863.

"SIR: I have the honor to state that the court of inquiry on Chief Engineer A. C. Stimers, having examined all the witnesses present, adjourned on the 8th of July, forwarding to the department interrogatories for other witnesses at the south, to which no answers have been returned. I would now respectfully request instructions as to the course most proper to be taken by the court under these circumstances.

"I have the honor to be, very respectfully, your most obedient servant,

"F. H. GREGORY,
"*Rear-Admiral, President.*

"Hon. GIDEON WELLES,
"*Secretary of the Navy, Washington.*"

"NAVY DEPARTMENT,
"*Washington, September* 1, 1863.

"SIR: Your letter of the 30th ultimo has been received. The interrogatories to which you refer were transmitted by the department to Admiral Dahlgren on the 8th of July, and have not yet been returned.

"It will be for the court to decide, after communicating on the subject with the officer whose conduct is the subject of inquiry, whether it is actually necessary or not to await the answers to the interrogatories.

"I am, respectfully,

"G. V. FOX,
"*Acting Secretary of the Navy.*

"Rear-Admiral F. H. GREGORY, U. S. N.,
"*New York.*"

The president of the court then stated that the interrogatories and cross-interrogatories which had been forwarded to witnesses at the south had not been returned. The court thereupon decided, upon the request of the judge advocate, that, without waiting further for the return of said interrogatories, the judge advocate should summons any witnesses named in the list furnished by the government who may be now within reach of the court. The judge advocate then called as a witness Captain John Rodgers, of the United States navy, who being sworn, testified as follows:

Question by the judge advocate. What is your name and what your rank in the navy?

Answer. My name is John Rodgers, and I am a captain in the navy.

Question by the judge advocate. Do you know Alban C. Stimers, a chief engineer in the United States navy? If yea, how long have you known him?

Answer. I met him first, as far as I recollect, last winter, in New York, when the Weehawken was fitting out.

Question by the judge advocate. Were you or not present at an attack made by the United States naval forces on the forts and batteries at Charleston harbor, South Carolina, on the 7th of April last? If yea, to what vessel were you then attached, and in what capacity, and did the vessel to which you were attached take part in the said engagement?

Answer. I was present at said attack, and commanded the Monitor Weehawken, which took part in said engagement.

Question by the judge advocate. Did you ever say to Chief Engineer Stimers that the attack of the 7th of April, 1863, on the forts at Charleston, "ought to have been renewed," or words to that effect?

Answer. I never did.

Question by the judge advocate. Did you ever state to Chief Engineer Stimers that the iron-clad vessels engaged in making the aforesaid attack "were in a fit condition to renew the said attack," or words to that effect?

Answer. I never did. I may have said to Mr. Stimers that the Weehawken was ready, or in a fit condition, to renew the attack, which was my opinion when I came out of action. I do not recollect saying so to Mr. Stimers. I recollect expressing such an opinion, and Mr. Stimers may have heard it, or I may have said it directly to him. I afterwards changed my opinion.

Question by the judge advocate. Did you ever say to Chief Engineer Stimers, or in his presence and hearing, that the commanders of the said iron-clad vessels were, after the attack of the 7th of April last, "hot for renewing the engagement," or words to that effect?

Answer. I never did.

Question by the judge advocate. Did the Weehawken, during the said engagement of the 7th of April, 1863, receive any, and what, injuries from the rebel forts and batteries?

Answer. She did receive certain injuries. The side armor in one spot was beaten off, exposing the wood. It was where several shots had struck almost immediately in the same place. The turret had been stopped with twenty-five pounds of steam; upon raising the steam to thirty pounds it turned again, and seemed to work satisfactorily. Actually it did hang a little, but I would not have hesitated to go into action with it again. The material injury, leaving out minor ones, was that a shot, striking the base of the turret, had broken the ring on the inside of that base, upon which the gun-slide rested, leaving me in doubt whether the gun-slide would not give way in case of using the guns. I have left out minor things. There was a small hole through the deck in the coal-bunkers. This did not materially injure the ship for our purposes. A shot struck the base of the pilot-house, broke the brass ring, and interfered with the turning of the turret to some extent, but, as I have said before, after using a little more steam it started again.

Question by the judge advocate. Were or not the Monitors, on Wednesday, the 8th day of April, 1863, after they had undergone some slight repairs, in as good condition to renew the attack as they had been to commence it the day before? If nay, state why not.

Answer. I think not. In the Weehawken, of which I have personal knowledge, I have a very strong conviction the band on the inside of the turret, and which supported the gun-slide, and which was the material damage, was not repaired the next day. The side armor was not repaired, and the hole in the deck was not repaired. In regard to the other ships I have no personal knowledge.

Question by the judge advocate. In your opinion could the Monitors, or not, have gone into Charleston in spite of guns, torpedoes, and obstructions, either on the 7th day of April, 1863, or on the 8th of said April, had the attack been renewed?

Answer. My opinion is that they could not.

Question by the judge advocate. Did you, at any time prior to the 9th day of April, 1863, hear Rear-Admiral DuPont say anything, or did he do anything, to lead you to think that he was prejudiced against the Monitors, or that he was unwilling, from prejudice, to give them a fair trial?

Answer. No; neither the one nor the other. I think he did give them a fair trial.

Question by the judge advocate. What was the character of the aforesaid attack on the forts and batteries at Charleston harbor? Was it an earnest one, or otherwise?

Answer. It was an earnest attack.

Question by the judge advocate. Do you know of any other fact, matter, or thing relating to the grounds of the specifications of charges made by Rear-Admiral DuPont against Chief Engineer Stimers, which have been read to you? If yea, state all that you know in relation thereto.

Answer. I do not recollect anything else. Not being in the Arago, I could have no knowledge relating to that matter.

The judge advocate having no further questions, and neither the counsel for Chief Engineer Stimers nor the court having any, the witness was discharged after his testimony had been read to him.

There being no further business before the court, it thereupon adjourned, to meet on Wednesday, the 7th instant, at 11 o'clock a. m.

NAVAL LYCEUM, NAVY YARD, NEW YORK,
Wednesday, October 7, 1863.

The court met pursuant to the adjournment of October 1, 1863. Present, all the members of the court and the judge advocate; also present, Chief Engineer Stimers and his counsel.

The judge advocate read the proceedings of the last meeting, which were approved.

The judge advocate then called as a witness Commodore Thomas Turner, of the United States navy, who, being sworn, testified as follows:

Question by the judge advocate. What is your name, and what your rank in the navy?

Answer. My name is Thomas Turner, and I am a commodore in the navy.

Question by the judge advocate. Were you present, and did you take part in the engagement between the United States naval forces and the rebel forts and batteries at Charleston harbor, on the 7th of April, 1863? If yea, what vessel or ship did you then command?

Answer. I was present, and did take part in said engagement. I commanded the frigate New Ironsides, an iron-clad, but not a Monitor.

Question by the judge advocate. Did the vessel which you commanded in the aforesaid attack receive any injuries during said attack? If so, state what such injuries were.

Answer. Yes, sir; she received various injuries. She lost one port shutter, shot away. She had one of her plates cracked by a shot. She had a breeching bolt driven in. She received a shot on her beak, which twisted it a little, and cracked it. Whenever she was struck in her wooden work, she was damaged; I cannot tell how many times. There was nothing to impair her efficiency in the slightest degree, either in her iron or wood work. She was as ready to go into the fight ten minutes afterwards as she ever was.

Question by the judge advocate. Did you ever say to Chief Engineer Stimers, or in his presence, that the attack on the forts and batteries in Charleston harbor, made on the 7th day of April, 1863, ought to have been renewed, or words to that effect?

Answer. Never. I never had any conversation with Mr. Stimers about it, at all.

Question by the judge advocate. Did you ever say to Mr. Stimers, or in his presence and hearing, that the commanders of the aforesaid iron-clad vessels were, after the attack aforesaid, "hot for renewing the engagement," or words to that effect?

Answer. No; never.

Question by the judge advocate. Did you ever state to Chief Engineer Stimers, or in his presence, that the said iron-clad vessels were in a fit condition to renew the attack of the 7th of April, 1863, or words to that effect?

Answer. No; never.

Question by the judge advocate. Were, or not, to your knowledge, the Monitors in as good condition on Wednesday, the 8th day of April, 1863, after they had undergone some slight repairs, to renew the attack, as they had been to commence it the day before?

Answer. I have no knowledge whatever on the subject. I did not look at one of them after the fight.

Question by the judge advocate. Did you, at any time prior to the 9th day of April, 1863, hear Rear-Admiral DuPont say anything, or did he do anything, to lead you to think that he was prejudiced against the Monitors, or to lead you to think he was unwilling to give them a fair trial in the aforesaid attack?

Answer. Never; nothing.

Question by the judge advocate. Were you or not a passenger on board the Arago at the time referred to in the charges read to you herein?

Answer. No, sir.

Question by the judge advocate. Do you know of any other fact, matter, or thing relating to the charges, or specifications of charges, made by Rear-Admiral DuPont against Chief Engineer Stimers, which have been read to you? If yea, state all you know in relation thereto.

Answer. I heard Mr. Stimers say to the admiral that the Monitors would be in condition by five o'clock that afternoon, or the next day, to renew the fight. I think this conversation was the 8th of April, 1863. I did not hear him say anything about going into Charleston, or about torpedoes or obstructions.

Question by the judge advocate. Could or not, in your opinion, the Monitors have gone into Charleston, either on the 7th of April, 1863, or on the 8th of said April, had the attack been renewed, in spite of guns, torpedoes, and obstructions?

Answer. No; I have not the least idea that they could.

The judge advocate said that he had no further questions to ask the witness.

Question by Chief Engineer Stimers. Will you please state whether any shot or shell entered the Ironsides; if yea, please describe the effect both upon and within the ship; also the preparations which you had made for such casualties; also the inconveniences to those living on board of such preparations?

Answer. No shot or shell entered the iron-clad part of the Ironsides. Some came in through the wood work, but did not penetrate the sand bags. My impression is that, had it not been for the sand bags on the spar-deck, I should have lost many of my crew. The iron plating of the spar-deck is confined to the wooden deck above it by iron bolts, half-screw. There were about thirty of these bolts over each gun. Wherever shots struck where there were no sand bags the bolts would be driven down like bullets; one shot did strike where there were no sand bags, and the bolts underneath were driven out by the concussion. All the wood work, both forward and abaft the iron bulkhead, was barricaded by sand bags eight or nine feet in a horizontal direction nearly to the beams. Immediately before going into fight I turned the hose upon the sand bags both fore and aft, and saturated them thoroughly with water; water was several inches deep in my cabin. I put green rawhides on the spar-deck fore and aft, making a carpet of them from one end of the ship to the other; over those a layer of sand bags fore and aft, as far as each iron bulkhead; these were some five or six inches thick. After the fight was over it could be seen where the shot struck the sand bags, as they were ripped up and the sand driven in all directions. These preparations caused great inconvenience. The state-rooms were filled with sand, and my cabin, and the hides smelt very badly from the start.

Chief Engineer Stimers having no further questions, and neither the court nor the judge advocate having any, the witness was discharged, after his testimony had been read to him.

The judge advocate then called as a witness Commander D. McN. Fairfax, of the United States navy, who being sworn, testified as follows:

Question by the judge advocate. What is your name, and what your rank in the navy?

Answer. My name is D. McN. Fairfax, and I am a commander in the navy.

Question by the judge advocate. Were you, or not, present at an attack made by the United States naval forces on the forts and batteries at Charleston harbor on the 7th of April, 1863; if yea, what vessel did you then command, and was your vessel engaged in said attack?

Answer. I was present and commanded the Monitor Nantucket; she took part in said engagement.

Question by the judge advocate. What injuries, if any, did the Monitor Nantucket receive in the aforesaid attack?

Answer. She had eight bolts of her smoke-box carried away; the turret under the 15-inch port-hole was pressed in so as to jam the port-stopper, preventing the use of the 15-inch gun at the third round. It required some thirty-six hours to put the gun in serviceable order so as to be available; she had one severe cut over her engine-room, or over the Andrews pump; beyond the carrying away of some of the clamps to the 11-inch carriage the vessel received comparatively little damage, having been struck fifty-three times in her strongest parts.

Question by the judge advocate. Did you ever say to Chief Engineer Alban C. Stimers, of the United States navy, that the attack made on the forts and batteries in Charleston harbor, on the 7th day of April, 1863, "ought to have been renewed," or words to that effect?

Answer. No.

Question. Did you ever state to Chief Engineer Stimers that the iron-clad vessels engaged in making the aforesaid attack "were in a fit condition to renew the said attack," or words to that effect?

Answer. No.

Question by the judge advocate. Did you ever say to Chief Engineer Stimers, or in his presence and hearing, that the commanders of the said iron-clad vessels were, after the aforesaid attack, "hot for renewing the engagement," or words to that effect?

Answer. No.

Question by the judge advocate. Were or not the Monitors in as good condition on Wednesday, the 8th day of April, 1863, after they had undergone some slight repairs, to renew the attack, as they had been to commence it the day before?

Answer. I should say not; the repairs were not completed within twenty-four hours, at least on board my vessel.

Question by the judge advocate. Could or not the Monitors have gone into Charleston in spite of guns, torpedoes, and obstructions, either on the 7th or 8th day of April, 1863?

Answer. In my opinion they could not.

Question by the judge advocate. Did you at any time prior to the 9th day of April, 1863, hear Rear-Admiral DuPont say anything, or did he do anything, which led you to think that he was prejudiced against the Monitors, or that he was unwilling to give them a fair trial in the aforesaid attack?

Answer. No.

Question by the judge advocate. What was the character of the aforesaid attack made on the forts and batteries at Charleston harbor? Was it an earnest one or otherwise?

Answer. It was a very earnest attack.

Question by the judge advocate. Do you know any other fact, matter, or thing relating to the specifications of charges made by Rear-Admiral DuPont against Chief Engineer Stimers, which have been read to you? If yea, state all you know in relation thereto.

Answer. No.

Question by the judge advocate. Do you know why the aforesaid attack of the 7th of April, 1863, was not renewed on the 8th of April, 1863?

Answer. I cannot answer that question, not having any knowledge of the admiral's determinations in connexion with the renewal of the fight.

The judge advocate having no further questions to ask the witness, and neither Chief Engineer Stimers nor the court having any, the witness was discharged after his testimony had been read to him.

The court thereupon adjourned, to meet on Thursday, the 8th day of October, 1863, at 11 a. m.

NAVAL LYCEUM, NAVY YARD, NEW YORK,
Thursday, October 8, 1863.

The court met pursuant to the adjournment of yesterday. Present, all the members of the court and the judge advocate; also present, Chief Engineer Stimers and his counsel.

The proceedings of yesterday were read and approved.

The judge advocate then called as a witness Commander A. C. Rhind, of the United States navy, who being sworn, testified as follows:

Question by the judge advocate. What is your name, and what your rank in the navy?

Answer. My name is A. C. Rhind, and I am a commander in the navy.

Question by the judge advocate. Were you present, and did you take part in the attack made by the United States naval forces on the forts and batteries in Charleston harbor on the 7th day of April, 1863? If yea, what vessel did you then command?

Answer. I was present and took part in said engagement, and commanded the iron clad-Keokuk. She was not a Monitor.

Question by the judge advocate. Did the Keokuk receive any injuries in the aforesaid attack? If yea, state what those injuries were.

Answer. She received injuries to such an extent as to cause her sinking the following morning. She was penetrated in many places near the water-line, on her bows, sides, turret, quarter, and all parts of the ship.

Question by the judge advocate. Do you know Chief Engineer Alban C. Stimers, of the United States navy? If yea, how long have you known him?

Answer. I do know the gentleman, and have known him since some time last fall.

Question by the judge advocate. Did you say to Chief Engineer Stimers that the iron-clad vessels engaged in making the attack on the forts and batteries in Charleston harbor on the 7th of April last were in a fit condition to renew the said attack, or words to that effect?

Answer. No.

Question by the judge advocate. Did you ever state to Chief Engineer Stimers that the aforesaid attack of the 7th of April, 1863, "ought to have been renewed," or words to that effect?

Answer. No.

Question by the judge advocate. Did you ever state to Chief Engineer Stimers, or in his presence and hearing, that the commanders of the aforesaid iron-clad vessels were, after the said attack, "hot for renewing the engagement," or words to that effect?

Answer. No. I had no conversation with Mr. Stimers on the subject nor in his hearing, that I know of. I left the squadron the evening of the next day after the action.

Question by the judge advocate. Could or not the Monitors have gone into Charleston in spite of guns, torpedoes, and obstructions, either on the 7th of April, 1863, or on the 8th of said April?

Answer. In my opinion very few of them would have gone in or come out.

Question by the judge advocate. State the nature of the obstructions which prevented the Monitors from entering the harbor as far as Charleston.

Answer. I did not examine the obstructions sufficiently so as to say of my own knowledge what the nature of the obstructions was. I can only state what they were supposed to be. I saw what I supposed to be a cable stretched across in a line between Sumter and Moultrie. This cable was supported by buoys at short intervals. Further up the harbor, and, as nearly as I could judge, extending across the eastern channel, and partially over the western side, and also on the shoal between Sumter and Cummings's Point, rows of piles were seen. I had a better view of the row between Sumter and Cummings's Point. The other rows were at a distance of over a mile, I should judge, and could not be very distinctly seen. The means of observation were very limited on board all the vessels engaged in said attack, being from slits or sight-holes in the pilot-house. I had also an occasional view from the hatch overhead, which I left open for that purpose.

Question by the judge advocate. Were or not the Monitors in as good condition on Wednesday, the 8th day of April, 1863, after they had undergone some slight repairs, to renew the attack, as they had been to commence it the day before?

Answer. I did not go on board of any of the Monitors subsequent to the action; but on the evening of the action, on board the Ironsides, the flag-ship, I met most of the commanders of the Monitors, and from what was said by them I judged the Monitors were not fit to renew the attack immediately.

Question by the judge advocate. What was the character of the aforesaid attack? Was it an earnest one or otherwise?

Answer. It was as earnest as the means used could make it—as earnest as the character of the vessels employed could make it.

Question by the judge advocate. Did you ever hear Rear-Admiral DuPont say anything, or did he do anything, prior to the 9th day of April, 1863, to lead you to think he was prejudiced against the Monitors, or that he was unwilling to give them a fair trial in the aforesaid attack?

Answer. No; neither.

Question by the judge advocate. Do you know any other fact, matter, or thing relating to the specifications of charges made by Rear-Admiral DuPont against Chief Engineer Stimers, which have been read to you? If yea, state all you know in relation thereto.

Answer. I know nothing whatever in relation to the subject-matter of the charges which it is alleged occurred on board the Arago, where I was not.

The judge advocate having no further questions, and neither the court nor Chief Engineer Stimers having any, the witness was discharged, after his testimony had been read to him.

The judge advocate then called as a witness Commander John Downes, of the United States navy, who, being duly sworn, testified as follows:

Question by the judge advocate. What is your name, and what your rank in the navy?

Answer. My name is John Downes, and I am a commander in the United States navy.

Question by the judge advocate. Were you or not present at an attack made on the forts and batteries in Charleston harbor by the United States naval forces on the 7th day of April, 1863? If yea, what vessel or ship did you then command, and did such vessel take part in said attack?

Answer. I was present, and I commanded the Monitor Nahant, and she took part in said attack.

Question by the judge advocate. Did the Monitor Nahant receive any injuries in the aforesaid attack? If yea, state what such injuries were.

Answer. She did. She had her turret stopped by a couple of shot striking on the composition ring at the base of the pilot-house, and driving it down into the intersection between the pilot-house and the turret. She had a large iron plate driven off the inside of the pilot-house, placed there for the purpose of steadying the pilot-house in position, and injuring somewhat the steering gear. She had another large iron apron, which was placed over one of the iron braces of the turret for the purpose of keeping it down; this was knocked nearly off. She lost some eighty-three bolts out of her pilot-house and turret. A large piece was cut out of the armored part of the smoke-stack abaft, breaking the grating inside and dropping it below. The decks were cut through in two or three places. There was no other material injury that I can recollect at present.

Question by the judge advocate. Were the injuries referred to in your last answer repaired either on the 7th or 8th day of April, 1863? If so, to what extent?

Answer. They were not repaired either on the 7th or 8th day of April, 1863. They were partially repaired by the evening of the 8th; that is, we were enabled to turn the turret by 5 p. m. of the 8th. That was the extent of the repairs, as nearly as I can recollect, that the Nahant had received at that time. I will add, that it required a force of over thirty-three pounds of steam to turn it then.

Question by the judge advocate. Did you ever state to Chief Engineer Alban C. Stimers, of the United States navy, that the iron-clad vessels engaged in making the aforesaid attack upon the forts and batteries in Charleston harbor were in a fit condition to renew the attack, or words to that effect?

Answer. I did not.

Question by the judge advocate. Did you ever state to Chief Engineer Stimers that the said attack of the 7th of April, 1863, "ought to have been renewed," or words to that effect?

Answer. No; I never did.

Question by the judge advocate. Did you ever say to Chief Engineer Stimers, or in his presence and hearing, that the commanders of the aforesaid iron-clad vessels were, after the attack aforesaid, "hot for renewing the engagement," or words to that effect?

Answer. No; I never did.

Question by the judge advocate. Were, or not, the Monitors in as good condition on Wednesday, the 8th of April, 1863, after they had undergone some slight repairs, to renew the attack, as they had been to commence it the day before?

Answer. I can only answer for the Nahant, and she was not.

Question by the judge advocate. Could not the Monitors have gone into Charleston in spite of guns, torpedoes, and obstructions, either on the 7th or 8th days of April, 1863?

Answer. I think not.

Question by the judge advocate. State the nature of the obstructions in Charleston harbor, which prevented the Monitors from entering as far as Charleston.

Answer. I cannot name them. I do not know what they were. I saw what I took to be piles driven in two or three rows, across from Sumter towards battery Bee. I saw no others.

Question by the judge advocate. Did you, at any time prior to the 9th day of April, 1863, hear Rear-Admiral DuPont say anything, or did he do anything, which led you to think that he was prejudiced against the Monitors, or that he was unwilling to give them a fair trial in the aforesaid attack?

Answer. I never heard him say anything, nor did he do anything, to give me that impression.

Question by the judge advocate. What was the character of the aforesaid attack? Was it an earnest one, or otherwise?

Answer. It was decidedly an earnest one, I should say.

Question by the judge advocate. Do you know any other fact, matter, or thing, relating to the charges or specifications of charges made by Rear-Admiral DuPont against Chief Engineer Stimers, which have been read to you? If yea, state all you may know in relation thereto.

Answer. I know nothing more.

The judge advocate said he had no further questions to ask.

Cross-examined by Chief Engineer Stimers.

Question by Chief Engineer Stimers. You have stated that the deck of the Nahant was cut through in two or three places, in the attack of the 7th of April, last. Will you please describe, as exactly as you can, the nature, size, &c., of the holes thus cut through?

Answer. I cannot give you an idea of the size. I do not recollect it. The plating was cut through. I think the deck was crushed in underneath. The plating had to be renewed over the injured places. When I say the deck was crushed in, I mean the wood work was crushed beneath. The plating was cut through, but there was no hole through the wood work.

Question by Chief Engineer Stimers. You have stated that the only repair effected on board of your ship on the day after the fight was that of putting the turret in such condition that it could be turned by steam. Were the other injuries of a character which rendered your vessel unfit for action? If yea, state in what manner they thus unfitted her.

Answer. I have stated that, to the best of my recollection, such was the only repair. The injury to the turret was not sufficiently repaired to permit the vessel to go into action on the day following the fight, as it required a force of something over thirty-three pounds of steam to turn the turret at the time referred to in my evidence. Moreover, the pilasters covering the bolt-heads inside the turret, and the curtain which hung round the turret, were down. The apron referred to as keeping in place the brace of the turret had not been refastened in its place. It took a long time—I do not recollect how long—to turn the turret. It took some three minutes to make a complete revolution of the turret, after the repairs, as nearly as I can recollect. The injury to the apron which held the brace of the turret in place was, in my judgment, of such a nature as to unfit the vessel for action, because the same brace, I believe, kept in place one of the tracks of the 15-inch gun. Moreover, had it come off, I think the turret on that side would have settled on the gearing below. There was a decided uncertainty as to the turning of the turret, with any pressure which we applied.

Question by Chief Engineer Stimers. Were any of the injuries of such a character as unfitted your vessel for action, excepting that which prevented the turret from turning and the injury to the apron?

Answer. There was no other injury which, in my opinion, would have prevented her going into action on the night of the 8th of April, 1863, had the emergency called for it; her steering gear was bent, and, in my opinion, unreliable; the pilot-house was very much injured, partially unbolted; the plates out of place; the apron referred to in my evidence before, as steadying it in place, was still off; I think the bolt-heads were partially uncovered by the pilasters being down in the pilot house.

Chief Engineer Stimers having no further questions to ask, and neither the court nor the judge advocate having any, the witness was discharged after his testimony had been read to him.

Chief Engineer Stimers here stated to the court that he had important official duties to perform on Friday, the 9th instant, and thereupon the court adjourned, to meet on Saturday, the 10th day of October, 1863, at 11 o'clock a. m.

NAVAL LYCEUM, NAVY YARD, NEW YORK,
Saturday, October 10, 1863.

The court met pursuant to the adjournment of the 8th instant. Present, all the members and the judge advocate; also present, Chief Engineer Stimers and his counsel.

The judge advocate read the proceedings of the last meeting, which were approved.

The judge advocate then called as a witness Commander C. R. P. Rodgers, of the United States navy, who, being sworn, testified as follows:

Question by the judge advocate. What is your name, and what your rank in the navy?

Answer. My name is C. R. P. Rodgers, and I am a commander in the navy.

Question by the judge advocate. Were you present at an attack made by the United States naval forces on the forts and batteries in Charleston harbor, on the 7th of April, 1863? If yea, did you take part in said engagement, and in what capacity?

Answer. I was present. I did take part in said engagement, and acted in the capacity of fleet captain.

Question by the judge advocate. Do you know Chief Engineer Alban C. Stimers, of the United States navy? If yea, how long have you known him?

Answer. I do know him. I have known him since he came to the South Atlantic blockading squadron, some weeks prior to the attack of the 7th of April last.

Question by the judge advocate. State, if you know, by whose authority and direction Chief Engineer Stimers was a passenger on board the steamship Arago, during the passage of said steamer from Port Royal, South Carolina, to New York city, between the 11th and 15th days of April, 1863.

Answer. I understood it was by the authority of Admiral DuPont, to whom he applied to take passage in that vessel.

Question by the judge advocate. Did you have any opportunity of knowing the condition of the Monitors on the 8th day of April, 1863? If yea, state what their condition then was for renewing the attack.

Answer. I did not visit them on the 8th. I heard the statements of their commanders. I remember to have seen the bolts protruding from the turret of the Nahant, as she came out of action on the 7th of April, 1863. I heard, also, statements from Chief Engineer Stimers. Not having visited them, my knowledge is not so exact as those who commanded them.

Question by the judge advocate. Could, or not, the Monitors, in your opinion, have gone into Charleston either on the 7th or 8th day of April, 1863? If nay, state why not.

Answer. I think they could not have delivered any attack on Charleston on the 8th, with any reasonable hope of success. I formed this opinion from the fact that the channel was obstructed, and in endeavoring to force those obstructions the Monitors would have been exposed to a fire which they could not withstand without being disabled. During the time which they were under the heaviest fire, which was less than an hour, on the 7th of April, 1863, several of the Monitors were wholly or in part disabled in their guns and turrets, and a persistence in the attack on the following day would, in my opinion, have ended in disaster.

Question by the judge advocate. State, if you know, the nature of the obstructions which prevented the Monitors from entering the harbor as far as Charleston.

Answer. To the best of my belief they consisted of buoys, suspending a net-work, intended to foul the screws of the Monitors and hold them entangled under fire. We could only see the buoys. I was led to suppose that the net-work was attached to them from statements of deserters, and knowing that such a system of obstructions had been proposed by engineers. There was also a row of piling which we supposed to be across the middle ground; whether it crossed the deepest water or not I cannot say. We also had information that torpedoes, some of them of extraordinary size, had been laid down in the approaches; as to the truth of their being torpedoes, I had, of course, no knowledge at the time. Since the attack, I have seen a letter, captured in the Atlantic, from an officer who was in Fort Sumter at the time of the attack, who stated to his correspondent that Captain Cheves, the officer who had charge of placing the torpedoes, had informed him that had he himself placed the Ironsides, and, I think, some other vessels, he could not have put her more precisely over the largest torpedo. My impression is, that he conveyed the idea that she was over the torpedo for some time, but that he could not make it explode; there was some trouble with the wire.

Question by the judge advocate. To the fire of what forts and batteries would the Monitors have been exposed had they become entangled in the network to which you have referred?

Answer. To the guns of Fort Sumter, Fort Moultrie, Battery Bee, and, I think, to Fort Beauregard and the battery on Cummings's Point.

Question by the judge advocate. Had the enemy any vessels-of-war in Charleston harbor at the time of the aforesaid attack? If yea, state how many, and where in said harbor they were stationed.

Answer. They had the iron-clads Chicora and Palmetto State; what other vessels they had I do not know; they were understood to be near the piling of the middle ground.

Question by the judge advocate. What was the character of the attack made on the forts and batteries in Charleston harbor on the 7th of April, 1863? Was it an earnest one, or otherwise?

Answer. I thought it a very earnest one, and very gallantly delivered.

Question by the judge advocate. State, if you know, the reasons why the attack of the 7th of April last was not renewed on the following day.

Answer. The movement of the vessels on the 7th was ordered to take place at noon, the pilots refusing to move before that hour on account of the tide. The iron-clad fleet was detained for an hour and a half by the Weehawken fouling her anchor and being unable to move. In passing up the channel difficulty was found in steering the Ironsides, which fell off in consequence of the current, and we were obliged to drop an anchor in order to bring her head in the right direction. It was very quickly raised and the ship was pushed up stream, when the Weehawken, which had turned off from the obstruction, (she was the leading vessel,) came across the Ironsides's bow, and it was necessary to stop again. There was some confusion in the line—the Catskill and the Nantucket came in collision with the Ironsides; the Patapsco with difficulty avoided her. The Ironsides was in very shoal water, having less than a foot under her. Admiral DuPont asked me the time; it was nearly 5 o'clock. He said, "It is too late to force our way in to-night; haul off and we will renew the attack early to-morrow." I directed the flag-lieutenant to make the signal to withdraw from action. All the vessels had then been under a severe fire. I think the Keokuk, Passaic, and Nahant had been compelled to turn off temporarily in consequence of injuries received at that time. When we withdrew from the attack I had no thought that it was to be abandoned, and I am convinced of Admiral DuPont's thorough intention to renew it on the following day. The Ironsides anchored abreast of Fort Wagner, and, passing out of the pilot-house, I received the reports from the different commanders of the different vessels. Up to that time I did not know that the vessels had been seriously injured, the Ironsides having not been disabled or materially hurt. Captain Rhind, in the Keokuk, passed first, and hailed to say his vessel was disabled. I saw myself that she was completely riddled. Captain Downes, in the Nahant, next hailed to say that his turret was disabled and would not turn, and that his pilot-house was badly injured. The Passaic made a signal that her XI-inch gun was disabled; the Nantucket, that her 15-inch gun was disabled. The first vessels, as they passed us, were directed by me to pass out of range of the enemy's guns, and anchor. After they had passed, the Ironsides got under way and dropped out of range. The sun had then set, and after dark the captains of the different vessels came on board and reported the condition of the vessels. Admiral DuPont heard their reports; left the captains talking with me, and went to bed, expressing no opinion whatever, to the best of my recollection. I saw him no more that night. Early the next morning he informed me that, having considered the reports of the commanders and the circumstances of the engagement, he had come to a positive determination, which would not be reversed, that he had decided not to renew the attack; that the vessels could not endure the fire to which they would be exposed, and that a persistance would lead to disastrous results, and could not be successful. That was the substance of what I learned from him; he seemed desirous not to commit myself or any other commander to any responsibility in the matter, and therefore asked no opinion from me, and, to the best of my belief, from no one else. I, however, told him that although this was a great disappointment and sorrow to me, that nevertheless my views corresponded with his, and I afterwards heard every commanding officer who was engaged in the action express the opinion that the action could not have been successfully renewed. Chief Engineer Stimers was energetic, and active, and prompt in his efforts to repair the vessels, and expressed to me his opinion that the vessels could be made ready for the action during the 8th. I think he said by noon.

Question by the judge advocate. Did you at any time prior to the 9th day of April, 1863, hear Rear-Admiral DuPont say anything, or did he do anything, to lead you to think that he was prejudiced against the Monitors, or that from prejudice he was unwilling to give them a fair trial in the attack of the 7th of April last?

Answer. Messing with Admiral DuPont, and from my position as fleet captain, he conversed very freely with me in relation to subjects pertaining to the squadron and the expected attack. Prior to the engagement of the Monitors in the Ogeechee, I think he was very strongly prejudiced in their favor; the circumstances of that attack led him to doubt their aggressive power against batteries, made him conscious of the weakness of their decks, of the trouble arising from the method of fastening their turrets, and led him to believe that he had overrated their powers. I do not think he was prejudiced against them; he would have been glad to have had more of them, if it had been possible for the government to furnish them. So far as I could judge, certainly he was not unwilling to give them a fair trial, and in my opinion they were fairly tried.

Question by the judge advocate. Was any, and what, opportunity afforded during the attack of the 7th of April last to test the efficiency of certain submarine shells in forcing obstructions concealed in the harbor?

Answer. The sub-marine shells were not used at all. The admiral and the commanding officers generally believed that whatever might be the merits of these shells under other circumstances, it would not be judicious or justifiable to affix them to the bows of the Monitors intended to operate in squadron, in a narrow channel and rapid tide-way, where collisions were to be expected, and where those percussion shells might be as dangerous to friend as foe. Each of these shells contained several hundred pounds of powder, I believe.

Question by the judge advocate. Was any, and what, opportunity afforded for testing the efficiency of certain rafts to be used in forcing obstructions at or about the time of the aforesaid attack?

Answer. Those rafts were brought by the Ericsson to Port Royal. Shortly after their arrival Captain John Rodgers, of the Weekawken, was ordered to affix one of these rafts to the bow of his vessel and experiment with it. He tried it without the shell. After we reached Edisto, a few days before the attack, Admiral DuPont directed me to ask the iron-clad commanders to assemble on board the Weehawken and to have one of the rafts affixed to the bows of that vessel, to move her in a tide-way in order that these commanding officers might become acquainted with these rafts and the appliances. Chief Engineer Stimers was also on board the Weekawken. The vessel was got under way and the raft tried, but it was somewhat late and the channel somewhat crowded, and after moving a short distance it was deemed expedient to anchor. In the attack on the 7th of April, 1863, the commanding officers generally preferred to be without a raft. Captain John Rodgers, of the Weehawken, expressed his readiness to attach one with grapnel hanging from it to his vessel, without the shell, but declared to me explicitly that without a positive order to affix the shell, he would not attach it to the raft. Chief Engineer Stimers expressed, with great earnestness, his conviction that the shell might be attached with advantage and might render important service to us, and urged that they should be used. Without doubting his judgment as an engineer, we preferred to trust our nautical judgment as to the expediency of attaching such percussion shell to the bows of vessels destined to operate together in the narrow channels and rapid currents of which I have spoken.

Question by the judge advocate. Do you know any other fact, matter, or things pertaining to the grounds of the specifications of charges made by Rear-Admiral DuPont against Chief Engineer Stimers which have been read to you? If yea, state all you may know in relation thereto.

Answer. Nothing occurs to me.

The judge advocate said he had no further questions to ask the witness.

Cross-examined by the counsel of Chief Engineer Stimers.

Question by Chief Engineer Stimers. What precise position did you occupy on board the Ironsides during the conflict of the 7th of April, 1863, and did you leave that vessel during the day?

Answer. I was in the pilot-house during the whole engagement, and did not leave the vessel during the day.

Question by Chief Engineer Stimers. You have spoken of receiving reports from the commanders of the iron-clads as they passed the Ironsides whilst retiring from action. Did they all pass you whilst so retiring? If not, please state the exception or exceptions.

Answer. After the signal was made to withdraw from action, the Ironsides was gotten out of shoal water and anchored, as I have stated before. The enemy ceased to fire at her, and soon ceased to fire at the vessels which were above her. I think all the vessels passed her before she got under way to move down to her berth for the night. The Keokuk and Nahant only hailed; the Passaic, Patapsco, and Nantucket reported their guns disabled by signal. Any reports which were made to me were not in virtue of my own authority, but as fleet captain and the agent of my superior.

Question by Chief Engineer Stimers. About what length of time elapsed between the exhibition of your signal to retire from action and the time when the last of the iron-clads passed the Ironsides?

Answer. I have no memoranda. I have never thought to fix the time. I should say twenty minutes, possibly more. Those first in action were first out. I think each of the Monitors was about the same time under the heavy fire. The Keokuk was not of the Monitor class. She was the last vessel of the line, the closest engaged, and was soon placed in an almost sinking condition.

Question by Chief Engineer Stimers. How long prior to the 7th of April had you been aware of the existence of the buoys and piles forming, as you believed, obstructions to the entrance of the harbor?

Answer. Prior to the action my knowledge was not positive and was very indefinite. I had gathered from the deserters and others whom I had examined the belief as to the existence of the piles. The information as to the floating obstructions was conflicting and unsatisfactory. We did not know what to expect. I expected we would be able to make our way into the harbor so as to attack Fort Sumter on its northwest face.

Question by Chief Engineer Stimers. Did you have such information, prior to the 7th, as led you to believe that there were buoys with network such as you have described obstructing the harbor?

Answer. Our information was vague and indefinite; I thought we might find floating cordage intended to foul our propellers; I did not know how it would be arranged, nor that it actually existed.

Question by Chief Engineer Stimers. Did the engagement of the 7th disclose to you or Admiral DuPont the existence of obstructions from network, or from piles, with which you were previously unacquainted. And if you answer yea, state what in particular was disclosed, and by whom, and on what vessel discovered.

Answer. Before the action of the 7th we only knew vaguely that there was some arrangement of ropes to foul the screws of the vessels; during the engagement we discovered the close arrangement of buoys, which we supposed suspended this system of ropes, but the ropes themselves we could not see; our belief in their existence was simply conjectural; such a system has been matured and described for the defence of harbors. My impression is, that the buoys were seen by the vessels generally; my own knowledge of them was gained chiefly from Captain John Rodgers, who was very near them, and reported them minutely.

Question by Chief Engineer Stimers. Did his report of their existence confirm your previous belief on that subject?

Answer. The knowledge that I had prior to the attack was not sufficient to enable me to form a belief; I thought we might find buoys supporting floating ropes.

Question by Chief Engineer Stimers. Did Captain John Rodgers, in reporting any obstructions of this character, state that the action of his propeller was impeded or destroyed during the action, and when did he first make any such report?

Answer. I do not remember that Captain John Rodgers, at that time, reported that his propeller had been impeded; after returning to Port Royal he found some rope on his propeller, which was cut off by a diver; I do not know where that rope came from.

Question by Chief Engineer Stimers. When Admiral DuPont stated, as you have testified, "it is too late to force our way in to-night, haul off, and we will renew the attack early to-morrow," did you understand him to mean it is too late to force our way into the harbor and beyond the supposed obstructions? If not, what did you understand him to mean by the phrase "it is too late to force our way in?"

Answer. Our plan of battle required us to go in beyond the obstructions. I understood the admiral to mean that we could not accomplish our purpose that night; it was too late. The substance of his words I have given accurately; I am not sure that I have used his precise words. The leading vessel had not felt authorized to force herself through obstructions which her commander deemed so formidable; the plan of battle was necessarily somewhat deranged for the time.

Question by Chief Engineer Stimers. Was any discovery made during the action on the 7th of the existence of torpedoes not previously supposed to exist as obstructions? If yea, state who made any such discovery, and where, and by whom the same was first reported to Admiral DuPont.

Answer. We found no more than we expected.

Question by Chief Engineer Stimers. You have stated, in substance, in answer to the question "What was the nature of the obstructions which prevented the Monitors from entering the harbor?" that they consisted, to the best of your belief, of buoys suspending network; of piling across the middle ground, and of torpedoes. You have stated, also, that Admiral DuPont stated to you that it was too late to force your way in that night. Am I to understand, from your testimony in view of these statements, that Admiral DuPont determined on the following morning not to go in because of these obstructions which he supposed to exist on the day previous, or do you now think that determination was arrived at upon some other grounds?

Answer. When Admiral DuPont gave the order to haul off for the night, I think he fully intended to renew the engagement on the morrow. I think he changed that determination chiefly because he found the iron-clads so much damaged, and some of them so soon disabled, for the time which they had been exposed. I think, also, that he became satisfied that the obstructions between Fort Sumter and Fort Moultrie were sufficiently strong to hold the vessels too long under the heavy fire of the enemy's guns.

Question by Chief Engineer Stimers. What number of guns were brought to bear upon the Monitors at any one time; and how closely to the enemy's guns were they engaged; and what was the weight of artillery used against them?

Answer. I do not know how many guns were brought to bear upon the Monitors; they were exposed to a very heavy fire. Our information prior to the attack as to the number of guns was not accurate, and I have not since learned. The officers commanding the Monitors, who could best estimate, thought their vessels were within seven or eight hundred yards. Some of them thought, I believe, that they were as near as six hundred yards. My impression is, that 10-inch columbiads were probably the heaviest guns used. I form this opinion from indentations on the armor of the vessels. Some of the officers on board the Ironsides thought that a shell which entered her bow and exploded was from an 11-inch gun. I did not examine the fragments; the only projectile that I remember to have examined, which came from the rebels, was a rifle shot weighing between sixty and seventy pounds, which came through the wooden side of the Ironsides. I think, however, that much heavier rifle projectiles than that were fired.

Question by Chief Engineer Stimers. Were there, in your judgment, fifty to one hundred guns bearing upon the Monitors at any one time?

Answer. Yes; in my judgment, the fire was by far the heaviest that I ever saw, or that any one engaged had ever seen.

Question by Chief Engineer Stimers. Was more than one life lost on board the Monitors during that battle?

Answer. No.

Question by Chief Engineer Stimers. Did either of the Monitors, and if either, state particularly which, disclose an incapacity of armor to resist safely the enemy's shot?

Answer. The wood was laid bare on the Weehawken in one place. Many bolts were started from the turret of the Nahant, and the bolts became useless. I thought the armor showed great endurance, but I doubt if it would have endured for a long time a fire so heavy as that to which it was subjected; the test was an extraordinarily severe one.

Question by Chief Engineer Stimers. Name either of the Monitors so injured in its armor by the impact of shot as to make it probable that other shot following would have destroyed it.

Answer. I think another shot striking the Weehawken in the place I have named would have gone through. The impression left upon my mind was, that the pilot-houses of the Passaic and Nahant would have been dangerously injured by other shot striking the same places.

Question by Chief Engineer Stimers. When Chief Engineer Stimers urged the use of these sub-marine shell did you get an impression that he would not have been willing to have been upon the Monitors in action to which such shell were to be attached?

Answer. I had no such impression. Chief Engineer Stimers volunteered to go into action, and I advised him not to do it.

Question by Chief Engineer Stimers. Did Engineer Stimers, in conversation with you, express the opinion that the Monitors should attempt to pass those obstructions without the aid of those shell?

Answer. I do not remember that he did. I do not remember his speaking to me on the subject at all.

Question by Chief Engineer Stimers. Did you possess any such knowledge of the construction of these shells, and of the manner in which they were to be employed, as to be able to form an opinion that they would be dangerous to the vessels employing them? If yea, state their construction, and your reason for such an opinion.

Answer. They were long iron castings, filled with powder, to be fastened on the end of the raft to be attached to the bows of the Monitors, and to explode when they came in contact with any serious obstacles, such as piling or the sides of a vessel. Such was my understanding of them. As to the peculiar construction of the shell I was not versed, but as to the manner in which they were to be used I think I did understand generally—not, perhaps, in detail. I was convinced that they would be dangerous to the vessels of the fleet with which they might come in contact. I should have been willing to incur the risk to the vessel to which it should be attached.

Question by Chief Engineer Stimers. Then, what objection was there to attaching it to a Monitor which should lead the fleet and attempt to pass obstructions?

Answer. There would still have been danger of collision had there been any interruption in the order of battle.

The counsel for Chief Engineer Stimers said he had no further questions to ask; and neither the judge advocate nor the court having any, the witness was discharged after his testimony had been read to him.

The judge advocate stated to the court that he had no further evidence to offer in the case.

The court thereupon adjourned, to meet on Monday, the 12th day of October instant, at 11 o'clock a. m.

NAVAL LYCEUM, NAVY YARD, NEW YORK,
Monday, October 12, 1863.

The court met pursuant to the adjournment of the 10th instant. Present, all the members and the judge advocate; also present, Chief Engineer Stimers and his counsel.

The judge advocate read the proceedings of the last meeting, which were approved.

The judge advocate asked Chief Engineer Stimers if he had any testimony to offer, to which he replied that he had none to offer.

Chief Engineer Stimers asked of the court two weeks in which to prepare a written defence, stating as a reason that his counsel could not find time to prepare a defence sooner than that time, on account of other engagements.

The judge advocate asked to have the court cleared; whereupon the court was cleared for the purpose of considering the request of Chief Engineer Stimers.

The court decided to give Chief Engineer Stimers until Monday, the 19th instant, at 10 o'clock, in which to prepare his defence.

The court thereupon adjourned, to meet on Monday, the 19th day of October instant, at 10 o'clock of the forenoon of that day.

NAVAL LYCEUM, NAVY YARD, NEW YORK,
Monday, October 19, 1863.

The court met pursuant to the adjournment of the 12th instant. Present, all the members and the judge advocate; also present, Chief Engineer Stimers and his counsel.

The judge advocate read the proceedings of the last meeting, which were approved.

Chief Engineer Stimers then read to the court his defence in writing, which is hereunto annexed, marked ———.

The court was then cleared for deliberation, and the judge advocate read to the court a part of the testimony in the case. The court then adjourned, to meet on Tuesday, the 20th day of October, 1863, at 10 o'clock of the forenoon of that day.

NAVAL LYCEUM, NAVY YARD, NEW YORK,
Tuesday, October 20, 1863.

The court met pursuant to the adjournment of yesterday. Present, all the members and the judge advocate.

The court having diligently and fully inquired into the matters embraced in the specifications of charges in this case, hereby report that, in their opinion, there is no necessity or propriety of further proceedings in the case.

Dated October 20, 1863.

F. H. GREGORY,
Rear-Admiral, President.
HIRAM L. SLEEPER,
Judge Advocate.

May it please this honorable court:

The testimony introduced by the judge advocate to sustain the charges made against me by Rear-Admiral DuPont is now closed. Acting in view of the proof thus placed before the court, I deem it wholly unnecessary to offer evidence in reply. The very foundation on which these charges must rest is wanting, and hardly an attempt has been made to supply it. They were carelessly, if not recklessly, made by a high officer of the government, willing to give them the sanction of his name, apparently without inquiring whether they were capable of proof, or founded upon worthless rumor. Much time has been uselessly spent in apparent efforts to prove them; but any one attentively reading the evidence discovers that the real purpose has been not to establish the charges in question, but to justify their author in failing effectively to use the formidable means for destroying the defences of Charleston, which our government in its confidence and hope had lavished upon him. That I am not unjust or uncharitable in making this suggestion will be manifest from an examination of the charges and proof which I will now proceed to make.

1st. The first specification charges me with having, whilst on board the steamer Arago, on her voyage from Charleston to New York, at table, in presence of her officers and other persons, a number of whom were correspondents of the public press, falsely asserted, knowing the same to be untrue, that I was told by one or more of the commanders of the iron-clads engaged in the attack on Charleston that it ought to have been renewed; that the vessels were in a fit condition to renew it; and that several of the commanders had said to me that they were hot for renewing the engagement.

A person observant of Christian precepts, considerate of his duty towards a fellow-man, or actuated by self-respect, would, before deliberately framing a charge calculated to consign a brother officer to disgrace and infamy, have inquired carefully into its truth, and the means of establishing it. Indeed, he would hardly have been content to make it before conversing personally with those capable of proving it; and then a just man would have withheld the accusation, so painful for a gentleman to bear, until satisfied that his witnesses were entitled to full credit. The course which my accuser has seen fit to pursue presents a wide departure from the path thus indicated. The names of persons who were on board the Arago during the voyage were appended as witnesses to the charges made, and most of them have been examined. It appears that I sat at the public table of the steamer in the immediate neighborhood of several other persons, all no doubt accessible to my accuser, or to those seeking to support these charges. If, therefore, I, during the voyage, used the language imputed to me, it was susceptible of easy proof. Not a particle of testimony to that effect has, however, been furnished. No one pretends I ever said that any commander of the iron-clads had stated to me either that the attack on Charleston ought to have been renewed, or that the iron-clads were in a fit condition to do so, or that their commanders were hot for renewing the engagement. No language bearing the least resemblance to that charged is proven to have been uttered by me at any time; and I am bound to assume that neither of the witnesses named ever stated otherwise than they have here sworn. If not, then upon what information could the charges in question have been framed? Was it believed that they could be proven? And if not, were they wantonly made, so that upon pretence of sustaining them, the naval inactivity, painful to a whole nation, might be justified by proof quite irrelevant to the charges being tried, and therefore quite likely to pass uncontradicted by me?

2d. The second charge made against me is for conduct unbecoming an officer of the navy, and specifies, in substance, that at the table of said steamer, and elsewhere on board of her, during the passage, I criticised and condemned, in terms unbecoming the circumstances, the professional conduct of Rear-Admiral DuPont, by stating that the Monitors were in as good condition on the 8th day of April, 1863, after they had undergone some slight repairs, to renew the attack, as they had been to commence it the day before; that they could go into Charleston in spite of guns, torpedoes, and obstructions; but that Admiral DuPont was too much prejudiced against the Monitors to give them a fair trial.

Now if, under the circumstances, I had stated all that is charged, it would, in my judgment, have been no more than I was authorized to say. I had been charged by the government with the important duty of inspecting the construction and armament of these vessels whilst they were being made. They were new in the history of the world; but in the contest between the Monitor and Merrimack, although the latter on the day previous had defied a fleet of our largest frigates, carrying an armament fifty times greater than the Monitor, destroying some and threatening all with the same fate, yet the Monitor, working her two eleven-inch guns behind an invulnerable shield, tested her powers, offensive and defensive, by so terrible an ordeal, that intelligent and unprejudiced men here and in Europe from that hour saw that naval supremacy must be maintained, if at all, by abandoning wooden ships and adopting those which the genius, engineering skill, and ripe practical knowledge of their author had taught the world how to construct. My knowledge of this class of war vessels had been acquired not only by watching and inspecting their construction step by step, but under the orders of the government I had enjoyed the good fortune of participating in the contest to which I have referred, and which had developed the capacity of the Monitor system to sustain unharmed the fire of heavy guns at short range, and at the same time to inflict deadly injuries upon an adversary's ship of great power heavily sheathed in iron. With an experience thus gained I might, as I think, have justly claimed the right to express an opinion as to the value and capacities of the Monitors, even had this differed from the views entertained by Rear-Admiral DuPont, whose knowledge concerning them was probably derived from casual inspection and the reports of others. Moreover, I was charged by the government with the duty of proceeding to Charleston to watch and report the performance of these vessels in action, to assist in maintaining them in readiness for battle, and to afford to the officers having them in charge such information as might be needful.

In addition to all this, it may be here proper to say, that at great expense, shells had been devised by Captain Ericsson, the author of the Monitor system, which, in connexion with rafts to be attached to the bows of the vessels, were to be used for removing, by means of explosive force, obstructions within the harbor, and of firing torpedoes supposed to be sunk by the enemy in the track of our advancing fleet. The effectiveness of these shells had been so tested by me, before they were sent to Admiral DuPont, as to make it clear to my mind and to that of the government that they would be practically safe, and capable of clearing the track of battle. I strongly urged Admiral DuPont to use these shells, and requested permission to participate in the action of the 7th, on board a Monitor which should be thus armed. This privilege was denied to me, and although, in view of supposed obstructions, I had expressed to Admiral DuPont and to his officers the opinion that the Monitors could successfully pass them, my confidence in expressing it was greatly strengthened by, and somewhat founded upon, the assumption that these shells were to be employed, and this the admiral knew. He nevertheless declined to order their employment, and thus was lost to the government and nation a powerful means of penetrating to the cradle of this great rebellion.

Under these circumstances, and well aware that the government had expected much from the attack upon Charleston with the abundant means furnished to the rear-admiral commanding, I was greatly disappointed that the important instruments I have mentioned were not used by him, especially as I believed (and as an earnest of my conviction had offered to hazard life and limb) that with shells attached the Monitors could pass all obstructions and hold the city of Charleston at their mercy.

All this was certainly calculated to awaken in my mind criticism upon the conduct of Rear-Admiral DuPont, which, as the evidence shows, I refrained from expressing, maintaining a reserve not merely respectful to him, but calculated to defend him from the censures freely and openly cast upon him for failing to renew the attack of the 7th of April.

I will now briefly examine the proof introduced to maintain the second charge, the mere reading of which will show that even if I had said all that is charged against me, it was but the statement of views which, if honest, I had a right in common with all other persons to express. Entertaining the opinion, and officially reporting it as I did to Rear-Admiral DuPont, that the Monitors were on the 8th substantially, and for practical purposes, as fit to renew the attack as they had been to make it on the day previous, I was bound neither by courtesy nor by any rule of the service with which I am acquainted, to withhold or conceal it; and believing, as I certainly did, that the Monitors, with the rafts and shells attached, could have gone into Charleston in spite of guns, torpedoes, and obstructions, I was equally entitled to state, in respectful language, that opinion also; and, moreover, I think the disrespect, if there be any, in imputing to Rear-Admiral DuPont prejudice against the Monitors, was so slight that his self-respect can hardly have been increased by noticing it. Indeed, whilst there is no proof in the case that I ever charged him with entertaining this prejudice, and whilst by asserting that I did, he, by implication at least, denies the existence of the prejudice so imputed, the evidence introduced on his behalf very clearly establishes that he was prepossessed against them, for Captain Drayton in substance declares he *don't think Admiral DuPont had a high opinion of the Monitors, and that he could not have had after reading his (Drayton's) reports concerning them, made before the fight.*

What these reports were does not appear, but that the witness believed he had succeeded in instilling into the admiral's mind his own unfavorable opinion is quite clear.

The proof, however, fails to show that I made the statements charged against me. The evidence on this subject consists of the testimony of Captain Gadsden, of the Arago, and of several other persons who were on board of that steamer during her voyage from Charleston to New York. He says in substance that I stated that the Monitors had received no serious injury; that they could be repaired in a few hours; that the trial ought not to condemn them; that they had not had a fair trial; that with the shells attached to them they could go in. He further swore that I said the *officers* of the navy were prejudiced against the Monitors, but that I mentioned no one in particular, and did not reflect upon Admiral DuPont.

The purser of the Arago testified that I said that the officers of the navy were rather prejudiced against them, but that I spoke of Admiral DuPont personally in the highest terms. Mr. Colwell swore that those on board the Arago were much excited about the fight at Charleston, and condemned the admiral for his failure; but he did not intimate that I took part in any such conversation, stating only that I said the Monitors were very little injured, and were repaired in about five hours; that I was respectful in my remarks concerning Admiral DuPont; and although this witness at one time said he was under the impression that I had said the admiral was prejudiced against the Monitors, he afterwards stated that I might not have said so, but that as the passengers generally united in condemning him, the witness may have confounded their statements with mine.

Mr. Fulton, in his testimony, states that my conversations with him on the subject of the attack were private, and in an undertone, and that I said I had sometimes retired to my state-room to avoid being questioned; that I said the attack was not an earnest one, and expressed disappointment that the shells were not employed, but did not say the Monitors could have entered the harbor without them, nor that the admiral was prejudiced against the Monitors, but that I did say he would have renewed the attack but for the influence of some of those who were.

Mr. Mars, a passenger, testified that I appeared not to wish to speak on the subject of the attack, and that although he sat opposite to me at the table, he did not hear me say that the admiral was prejudiced.

Having thus failed to prove that I had uttered any of the language as charged, and it appearing upon the evidence that I had spoken of Rear-Admiral DuPont in high terms, studiously refraining from talking upon the subject of the attack, it appeared to me remarkable that the prosecution, instead of acknowledging the injustice of these charges, should persist in calling witnesses to prove that the Monitors were seriously injured in their attack upon the forts, and could not have renewed it without probable disaster.

Whilst this attempt has signally failed, it has nevertheless disclosed the real purpose of this prosecution to have been, not an inquiry into any language or conduct of mine, but, under that pretext, an effort to justify a failure by Rear-Admiral DuPont, which had attracted the observation of the world, by condemning as inadequate the instruments which a liberal government had placed in his hands.

His desire to justify himself was natural, but that he should have been willing to achieve even his own vindication by making and persisting in prosecuting unfounded charges against a brother officer, is extraordinary. How utterly he has failed to accomplish this a brief examination of the proofs will show.

It appears from these that before the attack was made it was supposed by Rear-Admiral DuPont that torpedoes had been placed in the channel along which his fleet must pass. That network had been suspended from buoys designed to entangle the propellers and thus prevent their action, and that for some purpose piles had been placed across the middle ground to obstruct the entrance of Monitors in that direction. It moreover appears, especially from a careful reading of the deposition of Commander C. R. P. Rodgers, the admiral's fleet captain, that no additional information upon either of these subjects was obtained by means of the attack. After that was over the existence of torpedoes of network and the purpose of the piles were shrouded in the same mystery as before. It was ascertained, however, that if torpedoes lurked in the channel, they were probably harmless, for none had been exploded; and that they were incapable of being fired is shown by the letter referred to by this witness, written by a rebel officer in Fort Sumter, stating that the effort to explode a torpedo whilst directly under the hull of the Ironsides had failed.

We must therefore accept it as established, that as no information was obtained during the conflict which could be used to strengthen the surmises before existing as to the character of these obstructions, their supposed existence could not have afforded ground for declining to renew the engagement which was not equally good as an objection against having made it at all; and this being so, we must look for some other reason for the failure of the admiral to offer battle on the 8th, in pursuance of his declared intention, when he gave the signal for the Monitors to haul off on the previous day.

It is true that some of this testimony conveys the impression that the fear of encountering these supposed obstructions was a controlling element in the admiral's mind in forming the determination not to renew the attack; but in this there is evident mistake, for a brave and intelligent commander would hardly be so fearful of obstructions which might or might not be real, as to abandon a great enterprise without practical effort to learn whether obstacles to its achievement existed or not. Against such a suspicion I feel disposed to defend Admiral DuPont, and hence am constrained to look elsewhere for some reason why he failed to renew an attack which, if persisted in, might have succeeded. His witnesses on this subject next point to the injuries sustained by the Monitors, and to their alleged inability to withstand a repetition of the terrible fire to which they were subjected on the 7th. A glance at the testimony will show how utterly unfounded is this effort at an excuse, whilst it will also establish to the satisfaction of intelligent and unprejudiced men, that the capacity of the Monitors to resist unharmed the most terrible fire from guns and rifles of the heaviest calibre, has never been overstated. It appears from the testimony of the fleet captain that the fire to which they were exposed was by far more terrific than that which he or any one connected with the fleet had ever before seen. From fifty to one hundred rebel guns, of heavier calibre than were ever before employed against ships-of-war, were brought to bear upon the Monitors at the same time, and probably many more. The Patapsco was struck by fifty-one shots, twenty-one of which hit the turret, and fifteen or more of these—all heavy balls—struck it within the period of five minutes, and yet at 8½ o'clock on the evening of the 7th she was in a fit condition to renew the engagement.

The Nantucket was struck fifty-three times; and although the mechanism which worked her XV-inch gun was disordered, this was repaired on the 8th. Captain Drayton states that the top of the pilot-house of the Passaic was raised up by a shot, but it is quite evident, from his account of it, that this in no manner disabled the vessel, whilst it hardly increased the chances of danger to those within. It sufficiently appears that the Weehawken was fit to have renewed the engagement on the following day, although she was struck several times on her side armor in nearly the same place.

Without following this subject further in detail, it is sufficient to state, what appears from the proof, that each and all of the Monitors were in fighting trim within twenty-four hours after they came out of battle, whilst the injuries received by them were so trifling, when the terrible means employed for inflicting them are considered, that they may be pronounced substantially invulnerable to the strongest artillery. But one life was lost on board of them during the conflict; and whilst one or two of the turrets were by the impact of shot partially prevented from turning until repaired, it should be remembered that, turning by their rudders, each could at all times present her guns to the enemy at pleasure. Indeed it was partly by this means that the guns of the Monitor were brought to bear on the Merrimack in that first engagement of iron-clads to which I have before referred. One of the witnesses has suggested that if other shots had struck in the same place as previous ones, the armor might have been endangered. Entertaining, as I do, the opposite opinion, I would suggest that even if the witness was correct, he anticipates a hazard too remote to be much apprehended; for it is well known that the chances that one shot will strike exactly where a previous one had hit, are very slight.

The Keokuk, an iron-clad vessel, but not built upon the plan of the Monitors, was almost immediately disabled, having fired but three guns at the enemy; and the Ironsides, a much stronger and better armed ship, although she escaped serious injury, no doubt owed this to the temporary means employed to strengthen her before going into action, and to the care exercised in keeping her at a great distance from the enemy's guns.

That this distance was maintained is apparent from the testimony of the fleet captain, who stated in substance, that when the order was signalled for the Monitors to retire from the conflict *they all passed the Ironsides in moving out.* This shows that they were inside of her and much closer to the enemy's batteries; and how much nearer may be inferred from his cross-examination, in which he states that twenty minutes may have elapsed before the last of the Monitors passed by. They engaged the batteries within six hundred yards, and it need hardly be suggested, that no ship not constructed upon their plan could have lived under the heavy fire to which at that distance they were subjected.

I here close what I have thought it well to say concerning this attempt by Rear-Admiral DuPont to justify his inaction and failure by attacking that system of war vessels which has already, in my opinion, given us a more effective fleet than is possessed by any other nation. A judicious use of these vessels might have transmitted his name with honor far into the future. An assault upon the system can but recoil upon the assailant. From me it needs no defence. Time and battle will but confirm the opinions I have expressed concerning it, whilst its adoption by the nations of the world will bear unfailing testimony to the great skill and foresight of its contriver.

With these remarks, I submit my case to the just consideration of this honorable court.

Very respectfully,

ALBAN C. STIMERS,
Chief Engineer, United States Navy.

NAVAL LYCEUM, *New York, October* 19, 1863.

To Rear-Admiral Francis H. Gregory, United States navy:

By virtue of the authority contained in the "Act for the better government of the navy of the United States," approved July 17, A. D. 1862, I hereby appoint Rear-Admiral Francis H. Gregory president, Rear-Admiral Silas H. Stringham and Commodore William C. Nicholson members, and Edwin M. Stoughton, esq., judge advocate, of a naval court of inquiry, which is ordered to convene at the marine barracks, Brooklyn, New York, on Monday, the first day of June, A. D. 1863, for the purpose of inquiring into the grounds of the charges hereto annexed, and made a part of this precept, preferred by Rear-Admiral S. F. DuPont against Chief Engineer Alban C. Stimers, of the navy. The court will diligently and fully inquire into the matters embraced in the specifications of the said charges, and report to the department their opinion as to the necessity or propriety of further proceedings in the case.

[SEAL.] Given under my hand and the seal of the Navy Department of the United States this 21st day of May, A. D. 1863.

GIDEON WELLES,
Secretary of the Navy.

NAVY DEPARTMENT, *May* 21, 1863.

SIR: Enclosed herewith is a precept for a court of inquiry, of which you are appointed president, and which will convene at the marine barracks at Brooklyn, New York, on Monday, the first day of June next, or as soon thereafter as practicable.

I am, respectfully, your obedient servant,

GIDEON WELLES,
Secretary of the Navy.

Rear-Admiral F. H. GREGORY,
United States Navy, New York.

NAVY DEPARTMENT, *May* 30, 1863.

SIR: E. M. Stoughton, esq., being unable to act as judge advocate of the naval court of inquiry ordered to convene at Brooklyn on the 1st proximo, Edward Pierrepont, esq., has been appointed judge advocate in his stead.

I am, respectfully, your obedient servant,

GIDEON WELLES,
Secretary of the Navy.

Rear-Admiral F. H. GREGORY,
United States Navy, New York.

Telegram dated Washington, June 2, 1863; *received at New York June* 2, 1863.

3.25 *p. m.*

Judge Pierrepont having declined to act as judge advocate, the court are desired to select one.

GIDEON WELLES,
Secretary of the Navy.

Rear-Admiral F. H. GREGORY,
United States Hotel.

Certified by F. H. GREGORY,
Rear-Admiral, &c.

UNITED STATES MARINE BARRACKS,
Brooklyn, New York, June 4, 1863.

SIR: By virtue of a precept of the honorable the Secretary of the Navy, dated at the Navy Department of the United States the 21st day of May, 1863, appointing Real-Admiral Francis H. Gregory president, Real-Admiral Silas H.

Stringham and Commodore William C. Nicholson members, and Edwin M. Stoughton judge advocate, of a naval court of inquiry, and by virtue of a communication directed to Rear-Admiral Francis H. Gregory, president of said court, by the Secretary of the Navy, dated June 2, 1863, you are hereby appointed judge advocate of the naval court of inquiry, convened by virtue of said precept. Should you accept the appointment, you will report without delay to the president of the court.

Very respectfully, your obedient servant,

F. H. GREGORY,
Rear-Admiral, President.

HIRAM L. SLEEPER, Esq., *New York.*

NAVY DEPARTMENT, *June* 4, 1863.

SIR: You are hereby appointed judge advocate of a naval court of inquiry, which is now in session at the navy yard, Brooklyn, New York, and of which Rear-Admiral Francis H. Gregory is president.

I am, respectfully, your obedient servant,

GIDEON WELLES,
Secretary of the Navy.

HIRAM L. SLEEPER, Esq., *New York.*

Charges and specifications of charges prepared by Real-Admiral Samuel F. DuPont, commanding South Atlantic blockading squadron, against Chief Engineer Alban C. Stimers, of the United States navy.

CHARGE FIRST.—Falsehood.

Specification.—In this: that between the eleventh and fifteenth days of April, eighteen hundred and sixty-three, the said Alban C. Stimers, a chief engineer in the United States navy, being then on board the steamship Arago, by the authority and direction of Real-Admiral Samuel F. DuPont, commanding the South Atlantic blockading squadron, the said Arago being on her passage from Port Royal, South Carolina, to New York city *via* Charleston bar, did, at the table of said steamer, in the presence of officers of said steamer and other persons, a number of whom were correspondents of the public press, and at divers times during the passage of the said steamer, falsely assert, knowing the same to be untrue, that he was told by one or more of the commanders of the iron-clad vessels engaged in the attack upon the forts and batteries in Charleston harbor on the seventh day of April, eighteen hundred and sixty-three, that the attack of that day ought to have been renewed, and that they did further state to him that the said iron-clad vessels were in fit condition to renew it; and the said Alban C. Stimers did further falsely assert, knowing the same to be untrue, that several of the commanders of the said iron-clad vessels had said to him, or in his presence and hearing, that they, the said commanders, were, after the attack aforesaid, "hot for renewing the engagement," or words to that effect.

CHARGE SECOND.—Conduct unbecoming an officer of the navy.

Specification.—In this: that between the eleventh and fifteenth days of April, eighteen hundred and sixty-three, the said Alban C. Stimers, a chief engineer in the United States navy, being then on board the steamship Arago, by the authority and direction of Rear-Admiral Samuel F. DuPont, commanding South Atlantic blockading squadron, the said Arago being on her passage from Port Royal, South Carolina, to New York city *via* Charleston bar, did, at the table of said steamer, in the presence of officers of said steamer and other persons, a number of whom were correspondents of the public press, and at divers other times during the passage of the said steamer, with the intent to disparage and injure the professional reputation of his superior officer, Rear-Admiral Samuel F. DuPont, criticise and condemn, in terms unbecoming the circumstances and his position as an officer of the navy, the professional conduct of his superior officer, Rear-Admiral Samuel F. DuPont, in the attack upon the forts and batteries in Charleston harbor on the seventh of April, eighteen hundred and sixty-three; and did, with the like intent, knowingly make false statements, using, among other improper and unfounded expressions, words in substance as follows: "That the Monitors were in as good condition on Wednesday, the eighth day of April, eighteen hundred and sixty-three, after they had undergone some slight repairs, to renew the attack as they had been to commence it the day before; that they could go into Charleston in spite of guns, torpedoes, and obstructions; and that Rear-Admiral DuPont was too much prejudiced against the Monitors to give them a fair trial."

S. F. DUPONT,
Rear-Admiral, Commanding S. A. B. Squadron.

WITNESSES.

Brigadier General George H. Gordon, United States army.
Henry A. Gadsden, captain of the Arago.
Frederick Tratagean, purser of the Arago.
Arthur Hughes, chief engineer of the Arago.
——— Fernandez, doctor of the Arago.
J. H. Baker, chief officer of the Arago.
C. C. Fulton, editor and proprietor of the Baltimore American and Commercial Advertiser.
——— Colwell, of New York, builder of one of the iron-clads, passenger on the Arago.
——— Mars, coppersmith, of New York, passenger on the Arago.
Commodore Thomas Turner, United States navy.
Captain Percival Drayton, United States navy.
Captain John Rodgers, United States navy.
Captain John L. Worden, United States navy.
Commander Daniel Ammen, United States navy.
Commander Donald McN. Fairfax, United States navy.
Commander John Downes, United States navy.
Commander Alexander C. Rhind, United States navy.
Assistant Surgeon George D. Slocum, United States navy.
Acting Assistant Paymaster A. S. Poor, United States navy.

Passage of the New Ironsides from Hampton Roads to Port Royal.

FLAG-SHIP WABASH,
Port Royal Harbor, South Carolina, January 20, 1863.

SIR: I have the honor to report to the department the arrival here, on the 18th instant, of the United States steamers New Ironsides and Augusta; also the arrival, on the 19th, of the United States steamers James Adger and Montauk.

Enclosed, marked No. 1, is the report of Captain T. Turner, reporting the passage of the New Ironsides from Hampton Roads to this port.

Very respectfully, your obedient servant,

S. F. DUPONT,
Rear-Admiral, Commanding S. A. B. Squadron.

Hon. GIDEON WELLES,
Secretary of the Navy, Washington, D. C.

UNITED STATES STEAM FRIGATE NEW IRONSIDES,
Port Royal, January 19, 1863.

ADMIRAL: On my arrival in Hampton Roads, after my second passage to that place from Philadelphia, the honorable Secretary addressed me a letter expressive of his surprise that I had not reported the behavior and performance of this ship on her passage around. He will doubtless expect a report from me on the subject in my passage to this place. I have the honor to make it to you.

I left Hampton Roads on the 11th instant with fine weather and a northwest wind, which I held until about fifty miles to the southward of Cape Hatteras, when the wind hauled to the southwest, increasing to a smart gale, with a very rough, short sea. I sent down lower and topsail yards, and steamed against it with very poor progress, the ship being able, under these circumstances, barely to hold her own.

I adhere to all the opinions I expressed, in regard to her capacity as a sea boat, in my communication to him of October 5, 1862.

Away from land, where I could use her fore and aft sails, assisted by the propeller, I consider her safe and seaworthy in any gale; but if it became necessary to carry directly off a leeshore against a heavy sea and high wind she is unable to do it with her present steam power, and nothing could save her but her anchors.

Instead of carrying sixteen days' coal, burning daily twenty-five tons, as was supposed, she burns nearly forty tons a day, and carries, all full, only ten days' coal; consequently I should consider it unsafe to send her to sea on any passage that would require more than four or five days to perform it, unless accompanied by a steamer that would be able to give her assistance in case she should need it, which would be the case if she were met by a succession of adverse gales.

After the gale from southwest, of which I have spoken, the wind hauled again to the northwest, and carrying courses and top-gallant sails, she progressed at the rate of about six and a half knots, never being able to exceed that with steam and sails combined.

I reached here and anchored inside the light-ship at 9 o'clock p. m. on the evening of the 17th, having then only seventy-nine tons of coal on hand, having made the passage in six days and five hours.

Had I again encountered a heavy adverse gale at this end of the passage, her situation, for want of coal, would have been very critical.

Her motions, rolling and pitching in a seaway, are as easy as any ship I ever sailed in; indeed, I may say that they are graceful and playful, so buoyant is she, and taking in as little water as any frigate in service.

Were her steam power greater, and her capacity to carry coal increased, I should consider her as safe a vessel at sea as I could desire to be on board of. I should have no fear of anything but a direct lee shore.

Her drift in a seaway, ahead or abeam, is necessarily, from the formation of her hull, very great.

My last passage verified all the favorable opinions I had expressed in relation to her steerage.

As I had no opportunity of scudding her, I can, as yet, express no opinion upon that subject.

When steaming against a head sea she comes down with great violence upon her counters, as the sea catches her there, whilst forward she is buoyant and rising.

Very respectfully, your obedient servant,

T. TURNER, *Captain.*

Rear-Admiral S. F. DuPont,
Commanding South Atlantic Blockading Squadron.

Passage of Passaic and Montauk to Port Royal.

[Despatch No. 32.]

Flag-Ship Wabash,
Port Royal Harbor, S. C., January 22, 1863.

Sir: I have the honor to report to the department the arrival here, on the 21st instant, of the United States steamers Rhode Island and Passaic.

I have also the honor to enclose the reports (marked Nos. 1 and 2) of Captain Drayton, of the Passaic, and Commander Worden, of the Montauk, of the passage of those vessels from Beaufort, N. C., to this port.

Very respectfully, your obedient servant,

S. F. DUPONT,
Rear-Admiral, Commanding S. A. B. Squadron.

Hon. Gideon Welles,
Secretary of the Navy, Washington, D. C.

[Enclosure No. 1.—Despatch No. 32, 1863.]

United States Iron-clad Passaic,
Port Royal, January 22, 1863.

Sir: I have the honor to report that I arrived here last evening from Beaufort, N. C., which I left at sunset on the 17th, in tow of the Rhode Island, and in company with the Montauk.

The wind had been blowing for several days from the southward, but, after a severe storm, cleared off with a northwester, giving thus every promise of a continuation of fine weather. This, however, did not last, but, shortly after our getting outside, changed to the northeast, and very thick.

At one p. m. of the 19th we made the light-vessel off here, but the commander of the Rhode Island not being willing to run in while the weather was so thick, and the sea then breaking over my vessel so heavily that, had I been so inclined, I could not have unshackled the hawsers, it was determined to try anchoring under Martin's Industry, the Passaic continuing to ride by her fasts, under the stern of the other vessel. On swinging head to sea, however, it became at once evident that the former could not long bear the terrific shock of the waves on her bow without something giving way. I consequently directed Commander Trenchard to at once raise his anchors and stand out again.

During the remainder of that day and all the following it blew so very hard that we could not make the light-vessel until late in the afternoon of the 21st, when, as stated above, I anchored here at 7 p. m.

As, while at Beaufort, I had cleared out the limbers and put the pumps in good working order, although the vessel made a great deal of water, there was no difficulty in keeping her free; although to do this, in the heaviest weather, in addition to the bilge-pump, it was necessary to use one of the donkeys for two hours out of every four. The leak in the bow has increased a great deal, and, although I took the precaution to remove much of the iron ballast from forward, particularly that which most inconsiderately had been placed inside of the false bow, I think that before doing so, while on my way down from Hampton Roads, this part of the vessel was so seriously strained that a little more heavy weather would render the full working of all the pumps necessary to keep the water down. When the sea is at all forward of the beam the blows on the bow projection are, I think, more violent than I have ever known in my experience.

Very little water entered through the lower part of the turret as before, having managed this time to get it down, which I now know to be absolutely necessary for safety before going outside. Over the top the sea would have regularly broken, with the wind as far forward as abeam, had it not been for the weather-cloth and curtains. As it was, the water found its way in, but not in large quantities. The windlass seemed to have so completely rusted together in the joints, from the quantity of water which had been pouring over it for five days, that I had great difficulty in getting it to work, and had I been in a narrow channel the vessel must have gone ashore. Notwithstanding the many alterations it has undergone, I do not now consider it as very reliable, and am afraid it will yet get me into some trouble. At no time was there a greater pressure on the boilers than twenty-five pounds. With this, and forty revolutions, there was no foaming of consequence, and everything worked well and smoothly.

I am, very respectfully, your obedient servant,

P. DRAYTON, *Captain.*

Rear-Admiral S. F. DuPont,
Commanding S. A. B. Squadron, Flag-Ship Wabash, Port Royal.

[Enclosure No. 2.—Despatch No. 32, 1863.]

United States Steamer Montauk,
Port Royal, S. C., January 20, 1863.

Sir: I have the honor to report that this ship left the bar of Beaufort, North Carolina, at 5.30 p. m., on the 17th instant, weather clear, wind northerly, and a little of the old southwest sea still rolling. Continued clear and moderate until sunrise of the 18th, when the wind hauled to the northward and eastward, with cloudy threatening weather; at times it breezed up quite strongly, with the sea rising until sunset, when it partially cleared, and the wind backed into north by west and so continued until midnight; sea rather increasing and confused.

Towards the morning of the 19th, the wind hauled again to the northeast, weather thickening and sea rising and more confused At 10 o'clock a. m., crossed the southeast channel bar of Port Royal entrance, and at 11.45 came to at this anchorage. Average speed down, about 6½ knots, ship's motion easy both ways. On one occasion the stern overhang struck quite heavily five or six times, as reported by the engineer of the watch, but no unusual shock was felt in the turret at the time. Soon after, the port overhang limber began to deliver a small stream, indicating either, first, that water had made its way more than usual around the rudder hatch packing; or, secondly, that water had made its way up through the rudder head packing; or, thirdly, that she had sprung a small leak in the overhang.

During the whole passage considerable water forced its way into the foreward overhang and thence through the joints of the overhang bulkhead into the windlass-room. She leaked a great deal about the decks, deadlights, and hatch-covers.

In rolling, the shock of the impact of side overhang was very perceptible all over the vessel.

The sea sometimes broke over the deck as much as two and a half or three feet deep. In a small slow sea she is quite buoyant and lively. To a quick heavy sea, the extent of experience thus far shows little disposition to give to or recover from. She steers well and steadily as long as she has good way on, especially in running before the wind. On the whole, she has behaved so far very well with the moderate test she has had, but gives positive indications that if forced end on into a sea will strain both overhangs greatly; and if she gets into the trough of the sea will wallow very heavily, to such an extent, indeed, as to render the breaking of a tolerably high sea over the turret almost certain.

Respectfully, your obedient servant,

JOHN L. WORDEN, *Commander.*

Hon. GIDEON WELLES,
Secretary of the Navy, Washington, D. C.

Attack upon rebel fort at Genesis Point, Great Ogeechee river.

FLAG-SHIP WABASH,
Port Royal Harbor, South Carolina, January 28, 1863.

SIR: Considering it desirable to test in every way the efficiency of the iron-clads that have arrived, and to avail myself of their presence until others come, I sent Commander Worden down to Ossabaw to operate up the Great Ogeechee river, and capture, if he could, the fort at Genesis Point, under cover of which the Nashville was lying, now fitted as a privateer and waiting to run the blockade, and in case of success the railroad was also accessible.

I enclose a copy (marked No. 1) of Commander Worden's report, received at midnight by the hands of Ensign Johnson, one of my aids, who, in one of our armed tugs, witnessed and participated in the attack. He informs me that the fort was a very formidable casemated earthwork with bomb-proofs, and mounting nine guns, the firing from which was excellent.

We have obtained valuable information in the success of the working of the 15-inch gun, and although the Montauk was struck thirteen (13) times, she received no injury.

My own previous impressions of these vessels, frequently expressed to Assistant Secretary Fox, have been confirmed, viz: that whatever degree of impenetrability they might have, there was no corresponding quality of aggression or destructiveness as againt forts; the slowness of fire, giving full time for the gunners in the fort to take shelter in the bomb-proofs.

This experience also convinces me of another impression, firmly held and often expressed, that in all such operations to secure success, troops are necessary.

The distance at which Commander Worden was compelled to engage, not far from his extreme range, may modify, to some extent, the above views. The department, however, will observe how difficult, if not impossible, it will be to remove sunken obstructions and piling, in shallow water, under fire—very different from rafts or booms, floating chains, &c.

The Fingal left Savannah and has got to the mouth of St. Augustine creek, whether to try Pulaski and run by it to sea, or to Wassaw on her way to Ossabaw to convoy the Nashville, I know not, but most probably the latter. I am waiting for the weather to moderate to get the Passaic towed to Wassaw, in order to intercept the Fingal and protect the blockading force there; but these Monitors are so unsafe at sea, and so helpless in themselves, that the weather must be narrowly watched.

I had the smoke-stack of the Ironsides taken down, and ordered a trial-trip to be made without it, but the result proved so unfavorable, in consequence of the escape of gas, particularly in the engine-room, that I had it replaced.

I then directed a board of officers to examine into the practicability of removing the turret forward where it should have originally been placed, but the board has reported that though in every way desirable, yet, on account of its great weight—eighteen tons—it is impracticable, with the means at our command, to move it. Where there are no means of feeling one's way with the *lead*, it is of the utmost importance that the view should be clear ahead. A greater blunder, in a matter of so much moment, I do not remember to have met with before, as the vessel may be ashore before she is half in action.

Very respectfully, your obedient servant,

S. F. DUPONT,
Rear-Admiral, Commanding S. A. B. Squadron.

Hon. GIDEON WELLES,
Secretary of the Navy, Washington, D. C.

Report of Commander John L. Worden, commanding United States steamship Montauk.

UNITED STATES STEAMSHIP MONTAUK,
Great Ogeechee River, January 27, 1863.

SIR: I have the honor to report that this vessel, in tow of the United States steamship James Adger, arrived off the bar, at Ossabaw sound, at 1.50 p. m. on Saturday, 24th instant. I reported immediately to Captain Green, and on returning to this vessel a thick fog set in. At 3.27 p. m. it lifted, so that I was enabled to proceed up the channel, under the pilotage of Mr. Godfrey. At 5.10 p. m. the fog compelled us to anchor. The fog remained with us all day Sunday, being so dense that we were unable to proceed.

On Monday the fog hung with us most of the morning, during which time I called the commanding officers of the Seneca, Wissahickon, Dawn, and C. P. Williams together, and arranged our plans of attack. At 1.30 p. m. I got under way, with Mr. Murphy as pilot, and stood up the river, anchoring just outside of the range of Fort McAllister. During the afternoon the Seneca, Wissahickon, the Dawn towing the C. P. Williams, came up and anchored in line astern. At 8 o'clock one boat from the Seneca and one from the Wissahickon, both in charge of Lieutenant Commander Davis, proceeded up the river to reconnoitre and destroy the ranges of the enemy's guns which were placed near Harvey's Cut. This service was performed well, and Lieutenant Commander Davis reported to me. Just before midnight he went within a short distance of the obstructions of piles, and from appearances came to the conclusion that the obstructions were protected by torpedoes.

At 7 o'clock this morning I got under way, followed by the vessels enumerated, taking up a position about one hundred and fifty yards below the obstructions, at a point designated by a flag placed there by Lieutenant Commander Davis last night. The other vessels anchored in line, about one and a quarter mile astern.

At 7.35 a. m. we opened fire on the fort. After firing our 11 and 15 inch guns once, the enemy opened a brisk fire upon us. In less than an hour we had obtained our ranges, the enemy's fire slackening. Their practice was very fine, striking us quite a number of times, doing us no damage. Most of their shot struck inside of fifteen feet from us. Our practice was good, the enemy replying only at intervals.

At 11.15 a. m. all our shells being expended, and finding our solid shot not seriously affecting the enemy, I ordered the firing to cease, and stood down the river. A rain-storm and thick weather setting in, the other vessels were withdrawn out of range. The enemy have a very strong position. I send the Daffodil with this report, and shall await your further orders. I have no casualties to report from any of the vessels.

Very respectfully, yours, &c.,

JOHN L. WORDEN, *Commander.*

Rear-Admiral S. F. DuPont,
Commanding S. A. B. Squadron.

Attack on the battery on the Ogeechee river, &c.

Flag-Ship Wabash,
Port Royal Harbor, S. C., February 3, 1863.

Sir: I have the honor to enclose (marked No. 1) a copy of Commander John L. Worden's report of his second attack on the battery on the Ogeechee river.

I do not feel justified to authorize another attempt, as the ammunition for the 15-inch guns is now very much reduced.

I enclose also a copy of Captain P. Drayton's report of his reconnoissance up the Wilmington river, (marked No. 2.)

Very respectfully, your obedient servant,

S. F. DUPONT,
Rear-Admiral, Commanding S. A. B. Squadron.

Hon. Gideon Welles,
Secretary of the Navy, Washington, D. C.

Report of Commander Worden.

United States Steamer Montauk,
Big Ogeechee River, February 1, 1863.

Sir: I have the honor to report that, this morning at 6.40, I weighed anchor and proceeded up the river, followed by the Seneca, Wissahickon, Dawn, and C. P. Williams.

At 7.27 I anchored about 600 yards from the fort, the gunboats lying in the same relative position as on Tuesday last, about one and three-quarters mile distant from the fort. At 7.45 we opened fire, the enemy replying briskly. At this time the weather was thick, and so perfectly calm that the smoke hung over the fort, and around us, so as to prevent our seeing the effect of our shells.

At 8.45 I sounded, obtaining fourteen feet of water under us; and knowing the tide would fall about five feet more, we tripped our anchor and dropped down to a position about 1,400 yards distant from the fort, and into deeper water.

A gentle air springing up, we were enabled again to open fire with accuracy. Our shells then did good execution, tearing up their parapets; but as they shifted their guns so often, it was almost impossible to disable them. We fired slowly, endeavoring to expend our ammunition with effect.

At 11.53, finding it useless to shell them any longer, I withdrew out of range, and recalled the gunboats.

This vessel was hit forty-six times, but no material damage was done to her.

I have no casualties to report from any of the vessels.

I send this by Captain McKenzie, of General Hunter's staff, who was present at the engagement, in the steamer George Washington, and shall await your further orders.

The C. P. Williams will immediately proceed to Port Royal, in obedience to your orders.

Very respectfully, your obedient servant,

JOHN L. WORDEN, *Commander.*

Rear-Admiral S. F. DuPont,
Com'dg S. A. B. Squadron, Port Royal.

Captain Drayton's report of a reconnoissance of Wilmington river.

United States Steamer Passaic,
Wassaw, February 1, 1863.

Sir: I beg leave to state that, with the Marblehead in company, I went to-day in this vessel up the Wilmington river, to within sight of Wassaw or Thunderbolt, and two miles and a quarter distant, when I was stopped by shallow water, which my pilot would not venture on except at high tide. The batteries were very extensive, and large bodies of troops were drawn up on the shore. I was not fired on, although quite within range; a battery, which is about a mile nearer than the ones I saw, was covered by the woods, and I was not high enough to open upon it. I saw two small steamers, but nothing that looked like the Fingal.

I am, very respectfully, your obedient servant,

P. DRAYTON, *Captain.*

Flag-Officer S. F. DuPont,
Comd'g S. A. B. Squadron, Flag-Ship Wabash, Port Royal.

Arrival of the Weehawken at Port Royal.

[Despatch No. 60.]

Flag-Ship Wabash,
Port Royal Harbor, S. C., February 6, 1863.

Sir: I have the honor to report the arrival here on the 5th instant of the United States Steamer Lodona, towing the United States iron-clad steamer Weehawken; the latter with a disabled engine, on which I am ordering a survey.

Very respectfully, your obedient servant,

S. F. DUPONT,
Rear-Admiral Com'dg S. A. B. Squadron.

Hon. Gideon Welles,
Secretary of the Navy, Washington, D. C.

Report of survey, &c., on the Weehawken.

[Despatch No. 71—1863.]

FLAG-SHIP WABASH,
Port Royal Harbor, S. C., February 9, 1863.

SIR: I have previously reported the arrival of the Weehawken in a disabled condition.

I desire to call the particular attention of the department to the enclosed survey, (marked No. 1,) in which are clearly stated the damage sustained, the causes thereof, and the remedies to be used.

I forward, also, (marked No. 2,) a copy of Captain John Rodgers's report. These two papers cover all the information I have on this matter.

Very respectfully, your obedient servant,

S. F. DUPONT,
Rear-Admiral Comd'g S. A. B. Squadron.

Hon. GIDEON WELLES,
Secretary of the Navy, Washington.

[Enclosure No. 1.—Despatch No. 71.]

UNITED STATES STEAMER NEW IRONSIDES,
Port Royal, February 8, 1863.

SIR: In obedience to your order of the 7th instant, we held a strict and careful survey on the engines of the United States steamer Weehawken, and have to report as follows, viz:

Their condition.—The starboard engine is in a condition that, with small repairs and adjustments, it can be soon got ready for service. The port engine is in such a condition as to be entirely useless.

The damages sustained.—The port cylinder is badly broken, having three cracks extending longitudinally the whole length, transversely nearly half way round, and diagonally about half the length of the cylinder. The trunk is broken off close to the piston, and the inner cylinder-head broken, with eight of the bolts for securing the head, out, and broken into small pieces.

The cause.—The cause of the accident was without a doubt the insecure and careless manner in which the bolts securing the inner cylinder-head were fitted at and put in; these bolts having been put in in this manner, the nuts soon worked off, and the bolts dropped to the bottom of the cylinder. The clearance being sufficient, no immediate disaster followed; but we suppose that several bolts getting together in a peculiar manner, the piston struck them, breaking the inner cylinder-head, two pieces of which falling out, presented so great an obstacle to the piston that it canted, and the momentum of the engine carrying it along, cracked the cylinder and broke off the trunk of the piston.

The repairs.—To put the starboard engine in a serviceable condition, it will be necessary to remove the piston, secure the inner cylinder-head, and band the crank pin. The time required to do these repairs will be about one week. The air-pump was driven by the engine that is now broken, and it will be necessary to work the starboard engine non-condensing or "high-pressure." This, with the peculiarity of their arrangements, prevents us from being *positively* certain that one engine will work, but we entertain great hopes that it will do so, and consider that the short time and light cost will warrant a trial. To repair the engines permanently, it will be necessary to send to some northern port for a new cylinder and piston. If the deck will have to remain in its present condition until the cylinder arrives from the north, it will require at least one month to take up the deck, take out the broken cylinder and fit and connect the new one.

In conclusion we will beg leave to add that, in our opinion, there can be no blame whatever attached to Acting First Assistant Engineer James G. Young, senior engineer of the vessel.

We are, respectfully, your obedient servants,

H. NEWELL, *Chief Engineer.*
R. W. McCLEERY, *Chief Engineer.*
N. B. LITTIG, 1*st Assistant Engineer.*
A. K. EDDOWES, *Acting* 1*st Assistant.*

Rear-Admiral S. F. DuPont, *U. S. N.*,
Com'dg S. A. B. Squadron.

[Enclosure No. 2.—Despatch No. 71.]

United States Steamer Weehawken,
Port Royal Harbor, South Carolina, February 7, 1863.

Sir: I have the honor to report our arrival direct from Newport News, which place we left on Sunday last, the first of February.

The weather at the time of leaving was good, but on Sunday night it commenced blowing hard, and on Monday we had a gale from the southwest. It abated towards night, and we passed Cape Hatteras with pleasant winds.

On Tuesday it blew a gale from the northeast, which went round the compass, making a very rough sea. The first blast from the northwest was very violent; it took up the heavy brass top of our compass and hurled it overboard. The maker had trusted to its weight for keeping it in place. After this we had to rely, in a great measure, upon following the Lodona.

Wednesday, the 4th, we had a gale from the northeast; it blew very hard all Wednesday night. I have heard, indeed, from several sources since I came into port, that this was the hardest storm of the whole winter. The waves were high and violent. The wind abating little of its strength, hauled to the southeast and made a cross sea. On Tuesday the observation was very poor, the Lodona and Weehawken differing nine miles in the latitude observed. On Wednesday and Thursday we did not see the sun. Thursday afternoon, however, we made the light-boat off this harbor and came into port.

In all these successive gales the vessel behaved admirably. The leak was easily kept under by the Worthington and bilge pump.

Everything I saw confirmed the opinion formerly expressed, to the effect that the vessel's strength is the limit of her sea-going ability.

I have not yet found any signs of strain or injury from the very bad weather we have encountered.

While so far the hull has stood triumphantly the tests to which it has been subjected, at the moment of entering Port Royal, while still outside, the trunk of the port engine broke off, the piston canted and cracked the cylinder longitudinally and transversely. It is a total break-down. As the two cylinders were cast in one piece, both must be replaced.

The cylinders of the Comanche, building in Jersey City by Secor & Co., are identical in design, made from the same drawings, and cast in the same patterns. They are finished, and can be sent here immediately. They can be at work ten days after they arrive.

The trunk shows signs of an old crack all around the bottom where it gave way, and the cylinder and waste-pipe contained fifty-five scraps of iron, two of them $\frac{3}{4}$-inch bolts two inches long, the rest smaller. The iron of the trunk is, as far I can judge, of poor quality.

I do not think that any skill or care on the part of the engineers could have avoided the break-down. The trunk previously cracked gave way while fairly at work and working well.

The cylinder had no water in it, and we were not making more than forty turns of the propeller at the time.

The cylinder head had not been off since the vessel left the contractor's hands. Indeed, the haste left no time for any examination of it.

It is not impossible that the first crack was received when the air-pump gear gave way at the dock in Jersey City.

I have hopes that one engine may be made to work through; without a counterbalance it will scarcely do satisfactory service.

I have the honor to be, your obedient servant,

JOHN RODGERS, *Captain.*

Rear-Admiral S. F. DuPont,
Com'dg S. A. B. Squadron.

Arrival of the Patapsco at Port Royal.

[Despatch No. 74—1863.]

Flag-Ship Wabash,
Port Royal Harbor, South Carolina, February 11, 1863.

Sir: I have the honor to report to the department the arrival here, on the morning of the 10th instant, of the United States steamer Pawnee, towing the United States iron-clad steamer Patapsco.

Very respectfully, your obedient servant,

S. F. DUPONT,
Rear-Admiral, Com'dg S. A. B. Squadron.

Hon. Gideon Welles,
Secretary of the Navy, Washington, D. C.

Passage of the Patapsco to Port Royal.

Iron-clad Patapsco,
Port Royal, South Carolina, February 16, 1863.

Sir: As directed by you, I have the honor to make the following report of the passage of the Patapsco from Hampton Roads to this point.

The discretionary orders from Acting Rear-Admiral Lee enabled me to choose the time of sailing, and to put in, if deemed advisable, and thus avoid possible injuries from stress of weather.

The cessation of a gale of some days' continuance gave a favorable opportunity to leave Hampton Roads on the evening of the 30th ultimo in tow of the Pawnee. Our engines during the passage were kept under a steam pressure of about twenty pounds, and making an average of from thirty-five to forty revolutions, and a velocity a little exceeding six knots.

At 2 p. m. of the 31st, Cape Hatteras light bore about northwest some four miles distant, water smooth. A special signal was made on board the Pawnee, indicating dangerous soundings, and both vessels were sheered to port, the vessel parting her hawser from its leading board on the bow, and striking lightly once or twice, so lightly that I asked if she had not struck, not feeling certain of the fact. Finding the vessel afloat, I let go the anchor, in order to secure our safety, and to enable us to sound out the channel with boats. In the mean time the Pawnee had sheered off, and laid in seven fathoms of water.

Our coast pilot came from her in one of the boats, with lead and line provided, which he did not use—an omission which I could not pardon, and which led to his discharge on our arrival at this port.

Following a boat, we sounded our way through, and proceeded on our way, under tow, without further difficulty. As the pilot went through that channel from choice, and as it is the usual one for coasters, I did not suppose it a risk—the more as, at the time of our going through, there were several other vessels in transit. At 8 p. m. a southwest breeze sprang up, and by eleven blew half a gale. It then gradually subsided until, at daylight, it was almost calm. The rapid variations of the barometer, as well as rise, and the general appearance, showing an unsettled appearance of weather, I determined to go into Beaufort, North Carolina, and arrived off the bar at 5 p. m. of the 1st of February; but, no pilot coming off until dark, we anchored, and entered the port at daylight of the 2d, when I reported our arrival to the honorable Secretary of the Navy, and stated that I hoped to leave that evening, and made report, as per general order, in relation to the vessel having struck.

We coaled without delay at 2 p. m. When on the point of leaving, the pleasant northwest breeze, though with a suspiciously high barometer, changed to an easterly gale, which blew with great violence until the 6th, when the sea was so heavy on the bar as to cause yet further delay.

On the morning of the 8th of February we left, again in tow of the Pawnee. The weather gradually becoming pleasant and the water smooth, at 3 a. m. of the 10th we anchored near the outer buoy of the southeast channel, and at 8 a. m. came into this port.

The steadiness of this class of vessel in a sea-way is remarkable—purchased, no doubt, by the disadvantage of a great strain on the upper works. Should the "sponsons," now being placed on some vessels of this class, not meet the expectations of the department, I will be pleased to present some ideas in relation to that subject.

I take pleasure in stating that the vessel and engines appear to be well built, and that I believe them to be in good condition.

Some ideas "in relation to a supposed advantageous mode of levelling and pointing guns in this class of vessels" I will be pleased to submit to you upon a personal inspection of the vessel.

I have the honor to be, very respectfully, your obedient servant,

DANIEL AMMEN, *Commander.*

Rear-Admiral SAMUEL F. DUPONT,
Com'dg S. A. B. Squadron.

Effects of shot on the Montauk.

FLAG-SHIP WABASH,
Port Royal Harbor, South Carolina, February 19, 1863.

SIR: The fleet captain, Commander C. R. P. Rodgers, returned this evening from Wassaw and Ossabaw, where I had sent him. At the latter place he saw Commander Worden, and examined the effects of the enemy's shot on the Montauk. One result referred to by him had previously been called to my attention, though I have not yet reported it to the department. I allude to the effect of shot on the pilot-house, causing, by concussion or percussion, the large *nuts* screwed on to the bolts inside, to fly off with great violence, wrenching off the end of the bolt itself; they cross the pilot-house and rebound from the opposite side. This renders the pilot-house most dangerous, and, indeed, if often struck, untenable; and such, in the engagement with the Ogeechee battery, was almost the case on the Montauk, nearly ten of these nuts having been wrenched from the bolts as above stated.

Our machine-shop has been at work making new bolts, and Commander Worden would like to have them *all* replaced; but they are large and heavy, and we shall not be able to do it. We are also preparing a screen of boiler iron to go around the pilot-houses.

It may be well to mention that the above effect was produced without the round head of the bolt outside being struck, but by the impact of a shot between the bolts, not weighing over a 32-pounder. No such effect, however, was produced on the turret.

Thinking the department would like to have these facts, I write them in haste to save the mail.

Very respectfully, your obedient servant,

S. F. DUPONT,
Rear-Admiral, Commanding S. A. B. Squadron.

Hon. GIDEON WELLES,
Secretary of the Navy.

Passage of the Nahant to Port Royal.

[Despatch No 92—1863.]

FLAG-SHIP WABASH,
Port Royal Harbor, South Carolina, February 24, 1863.

SIR: I have the honor to report the arrival here, on the 20th instant, of the United States steamer State of Georgia, having in tow the United States iron-clad steamer Nahant.

Enclosed (marked No. 1) is Commander Downes's report of the passage of the Nahant from Hampton Roads to this port.

The State of Georgia, in pursuance of the orders under which she arrived here, left this port yesterday to rejoin the blockading force off Wilmington, North Carolina.

Very respectfully, your obedient servant,

S. F. DUPONT,
Rear-Admiral, Commanding S. A. B. Squadron.

Hon. GIDEON WELLES,
Secretary of the Navy, Washington, D. C.

[Despatch No. 92, 1863.—Enclosure No. 1.]

No. 9.] UNITED STATES IRON-CLAD STEAMER NAHANT,
Port Royal, February 20, 1863.

SIR: I have the honor to inform you of the arrival of this vessel at Port Royal in good condition this day, at 10.40 a. m., after a passage of three days and fifteen and two-thirds hours from Cape Henry, experiencing during the first part of the passage, until we had passed Cape Fear, rough and boisterous weather, from which, however, we suffered no injury, though the overhang thumped forward heavily on the head seas off Hatteras, shaking the vessel very much. The decks leaked badly, and considerable water forced its way under the turret, wetting the belts of the blowers, causing the belts to stretch and break or tear out their lacings, putting everybody to serious inconvenience for want of air below, besides causing instant depression of steam by stopping draught of the furnaces by constantly necessitating the stoppage of the blowers to repair damages to the belting. To guard against future contingencies of the kind, I have thought it advisable to ask for a couple of sets of gutta percha belts, and recommend that all vessels of that class be supplied with them before proceeding to sea.

I did not communicate with the blockading squadron off Charleston, as your order of the 12th instant directed me to do, as Commander Armstrong, commanding the State of Georgia, upon consultation before leaving Hampton Roads, coincided with me in the opinion that your subsequent telegraphic order of the 15th instant, "not to stop on the way if it could possibly be avoided," forbade our losing any time to do so, which, as we passed Charleston in the night, must have been the case had we stopped to communicate.

I am, very respectfully, your obedient servant,

JOHN DOWNES,
Commander.

Hon. GIDEON WELLES,
Secretary of the Navy, Washington, D. C.

Forwarded.

S. F. DUPONT,
Rear-Admiral, &c.

Relative to testing the Monitor vessels.

[Despatch No. 101, 1863.—Confidential.]

FLAG-SHIP WABASH,
Port Royal Harbor, South Carolina, February 27, 1863.

SIR: After very mature deliberation, I have determined to test the three iron-clads, Patapsco, Passaic, and Nahant, on the Genesis Point battery, on the Ogeechee. We find much in them to be attended to; and on a trip which I made in the Patapsco up the Broad river, though only firing each gun twice, some important matter was developed.

This operation will not retard the great work, but yield us advantages in many ways. The Weehawken, I hope, will be ready to try her engine to-morrow. Great expedition has been made on her.

I hope the Catskill will be along soon. These iron-clads require so much to be done that I am anxious for their early arrival. The army is not ready, but doing its best.

Attempts to run the blockade everywhere are increasing, and from Fernandina I have news to-day which makes me wish that I had a better vessel there than the Mohawk.

Colonel Townsend will inform the department that we are preparing in every possible way, working day and night.

Very respectfully, your obedient servant,

S. F. DUPONT,
Rear-Admiral, Commanding S. A. B. Squadron.

Hon. GIDEON WELLES,
Secretary of the Navy.

Destruction of the privateer Nashville.

FLAG-SHIP WABASH,
Port Royal Harbor, S. C., March 2, 1863.

SIR: I have the satisfaction to inform the department of the destruction of the privateer Nashville while lying under the guns of Fort McAllister, on the Great Ogeechee, Georgia, by the Montauk, Commander J. L. Worden, whose enclosed report states succinctly the interesting particulars.

The department is aware that I have had this vessel blockaded for eight months, and I am indebted to the extreme vigilance and spirit of Lieutenant Commander J. L. Davis, of the Wissahickon, Acting Lieutenant Barnes, of the Dawn, and later of Lieutenant Commander Gibson, of the Seneca, that I have been able to keep her so long confined to the waters of the Ogeechee.

For several months the Nashville was loaded with cotton, but though constantly on the alert, she never ventured to run out. She then withdrew up the Ogeechee, and reappeared after a length of time thoroughly fitted as a privateer, and presenting a very fine appearance.

Fort McAllister was strengthened, the river staked, with a line of torpedoes in front to prevent its ascent by light vessels, to cut her out. She has been frequently seen close under the fort ready to make a dash if the opportunity offered, or was quietly waiting for an iron-clad to tow her to sea.

If I am not misinformed she had a heavy rifle gun, on a pivot, as a part of her armament, was proverbially fast, and would doubtless have rivalled the Alabama and Oreto in their depredations on our commerce. I have, therefore, never lost sight of the great importance of keeping her *in*, or of destroying her if I could. I have accomplished both through the zeal and vigilance of my gunboat captains mentioned above, and the quick perception and rapid execution of Commander Worden, who has thus added to his already brilliant services.

Very respectfully, your obedient servant,

S. F. DUPONT,
Rear-Admiral, Commanding S. A. B. Squadron.

HON. GIDEON WELLES,
Secretary of the Navy, Washington, D. C.

Report of Commander John L. Worden, of the Montauk.

UNITED STATES IRON-CLAD MONTAUK,
Ogeechee River, Georgia, February 28, 1863.

SIR: I have the honor to report that yesterday evening the enemy's steamer Nashville was observed by me in motion above the battery known as Fort McAllister. A reconnoissance immediately made proved that in moving up the river she had grounded in that portion of the river known as the Seven-mile reach.

Believing that I could, by approaching close to the battery, reach and destroy her with my battery, I moved up at daylight this morning, accompanied by the blockading fleet in these waters, consisting of the Seneca, Lieutenant Commander Gibson, the Wissahickon, Lieutenant Commander Davis, and the Dawn, Acting Lieutenant Commander Barnes.

By moving up close to the obstructions in the river, I was enabled, al though under a heavy fire from the battery, to approach the Nashville, stil aground, within the distance of twelve hundred yards. A few well-directed shells determined the range, and soon succeeded in striking her with 11-inch and 15-inch shells. The other gunboats maintained a fire from an enfilading position upon the battery and the Nashville at long range.

I soon had the satisfaction of observing that the Nashville had caught fire from the shells exploded in her in several places, and in less than 20 minutes she was caught in flames forward, aft, and amidships. At 9.20 a. m. a large pivot gun mounted abaft her foremast exploded from the heat. At 9.40 her smoke chimney went by the board, and at 9.55 her magazine exploded with terrific violence, shattering her in smoking ruins; nothing remains of her.

The battery kept up a continuous fire upon this vessel, but struck her but five times, doing no damage whatever. The fire upon the other gunboats was wild, and did them no damage whatever. After assuring myself of the complete destruction of the Nashville, I, preceded by the wooden vessels, dropped down beyond the range of the enemy's guns. In so doing a torpedo exploded under this vessel, inflicting, however, but little injury.

I beg leave, therefore, to congratulate you, sir, upon this final disposition of a vessel which has so long been in the minds of the public as a troublesome pest.

I am, very respectfully, your obedient servant,

JOHN L. WORDEN,
Commanding, Senior Officer present.

Rear-Admiral S. F. DuPont,
Com'dg S. A. B. Squadron, Port Royal, South Carolina.

Attack on Fort McAllister.

Flag-Ship Wabash,
Port Royal Harbor, S. C., March 6, 1863.

Sir: The department has already been informed of my desire, before entering upon more important operations, to subject the various mechanical appliances of the iron-clads to the full test of active service, and to give the advantage of target practice to the officers and men with their new ordnance. For this purpose I had ordered a concentration in the Ogeechee of such of these vessels as were ready to attack Fort McAllister, and secure or destroy the Nashville.

Before this concentration could take place the Nashville was destroyed by Commander Worden, in the Montauk, the particulars of which occurrence I reported to the department by the last mail.

The iron-clads having, however, arrived in Ossabaw, I directed Captain Drayton, of the Passaic, to go on with the attack on the fort, accompanied by the Patapsco and Nahant; the Montauk having been three times under fire of the fort, and sufficiently tested, was not to join in.

I received, last evening, Captain Drayton's detailed report of his *eight hours'* bombardment, with a statement of the damage done to his vessel, and also the reports of Commanders Ammen and Downes to him, all of which are enclosed, (marked Nos. 1, 2, 3,) and I think will be read with great interest by the department, for it will not fail to perceive that valuable information has been elicited and most important data obtained, and I feel thankful that this I have done without any loss of life. Except that the fort might possibly protect another blockade runner, its capture was of no special practical importance.

The injury to the Montauk from the torpedo is the most serious that has occurred, and will require some ten days to repair, but the department will remember the invaluable service she performed while receiving it.

I think it worthy of mentioning that this bombardment, so fruitful as giving us experience, was witnessed by Brigadier General Seymour, the chief of artillery, and Captain Duane, the chief engineer of this military department, and I shall be able to receive from these gentlemen the results of their observation, which, representing, as they do, special branches of the military service, will be interesting and important.

I cannot close this communication without speaking of Captain Drayton, who has been one of my commanding officers since October, 1861. He has performed this service with that ability, judgment, and calm courage, which have ever marked his execution of my orders.

Very respectfully, your obedient servant,

S. F. DUPONT,
Rear-Admiral, Commanding S. A. B. Squadron.

Hon. GIDEON WELLES,
Secretary of the Navy, Washington, D. C.

Report of Captain Percival Drayton.

UNITED STATES IRON-CLAD PASSAIC,
Ogeechee River, March 4, 1863.

SIR: I wrote a short report last evening, after my return from the attack on Fort McAllister, and will now make one more in detail. A list of the ammunition expended, of the injuries to the vessel, and an extract from the log, I enclose with this, from which latter you will perceive that my vessel was under fire just eight hours. I was directly in front of the fort, the guns being, as we looked at them, in the centre between high traverses of earth, which were on each side. These, however, as we were placed, had no effect in protecting either guns or men. The latter never exposed themselves to our fire, usually discharging their pieces either while we were loading, or just as our port came in line, and before the guns were quite ready, the turret being painted black, not deceiving them any more than a different color had done in the first attack of the Montauk. I was as close to the fort as the pilot (who is the best on the river, as was proved in this case, by my being the only one whose vessel was not aground when the tide fell) would take me, and as high as the Montauk had been, except on her second attack, but only for an hour, when being in twelve feet, as I understand, Captain Worden was obliged to drop down to a position below where I was yesterday—a rather risky operation, too, in so narrow a channel, where, had the vessel grounded, she must have been exposed below the side armor. This being the case, I am satisfied that twelve feet cannot be carried when a vessel is to anchor above where I was. The channel is close to the marsh, opposite to the fort, and as the piles were only about four hundred yards beyond where I was lying, I don't see how more than two hundred yards can be gained nearer to the fort by being against them, as the river can't be crossed, and is very wide. Certainly, after discussing the matter with the pilot on the spot, I doubt being able to get nearer than a thousand yards without going above the piles, where the channel crosses over. My distance I judged to be twelve hundred yards, from the following data: The XI-inch gun was very carefully elevated by a spirit level to a little less than six degrees—this is, by ordnance manual, fifteen hundred yards, axis of bore ten feet above the water; mine was not four—which requires a deduction of one hundred and thirty yards; then the parapet of the fort was at least twenty feet above the water, which, requiring about half a degree more, will bring the distance about what I have stated it; then shot were always less than five seconds in reaching me from the flash, generally four, which would, considering their greater initial velocity, about agree with my calculation. My five-second fuzes, however, usually burst just before reaching; the seven after striking. The pilot called the distance a thousand yards.

The fort is very solidly built, with high traverses between the guns, and raised at least twenty feet above the river, and contained seven guns and an eleven-inch mortar. One of these guns was, I think, destroyed; the others used until we were out of range. Immense holes were cut into the earth, the traverses and face much cut away, but still no injury done which I think a good night's work would not repair, and I do not believe that it can be made untenable by any number of iron-clads which the shallow water and narrow channel will permit to be brought in position against it. The guns are one ten inch, a shot from which lodged on the top of our turret; one heavy rifle, about a hundred-pounder; and the remainder, I should judge, thirty-twos, with a light gun throwing bolts, which would be aimed at any one showing themselves on the deck. These with the mortar were, however, nothing as a defence to the river comparable to the shallow water and piles, as was proved by my being exposed to their fire for eight hours without serious injury; but they answer the purpose, which is simply to prevent the channel being cleared of obstruction. Our three mortar schooners kept up a fire during the day from about four thousand yards distance, but, so far as I could observe, without the least effect, the shells generally falling short.

The firing from this vessel was quite good, and I think very few shots missed striking about the parapet after the first hour, as I had carefully corrected each one up to that time from outside of the turret on deck, where the effect could be well followed. Although the attack was an unsuccessful one, it was certainly not owing to any want of zeal and attention to duty on the part of either officers or men; and I am greatly indebted to Lieutenant Commander J. N. Miller, the executive officer, as well as to Acting Master S. Huse, who attended, under him, to the management and pointing of the guns, and whose energy and zeal was very marked on this occasion, as it has been on several others.

I feel very much, of course, the failure to a certain extent of the attack, which you had intrusted to my direction, but am satisfied that the natural obstacles are such as to render another just as little likely to succeed. The experience obtained is worth something in future operations. I only withdrew when all my shell with fuzes long enough to reach (or over five seconds) had been expended, and when the crew were almost beyond further work, having been occupied for eight hours at the guns without even an intermission to eat: and then I should have remained had I seen the least sign of faltering or slackness of fire on the part of the enemy, but, on the contrary, I think that it was, if anything, more rapid towards the last.

The gunboats Seneca, Lieutenant Commander Gibson, Wissahickon, Lieutenant Commander Davis, and Dawn, Lieutenant Barnes, were anchored near the mortar schooners in signal distance of us, and prepared to give us assistance had any been required.

Everything about the guns and carriages worked to my satisfaction, except that the box round the XV-inch gun, on examination, was found to be almost detached from the side, owing to the breaking of the bolts which secured it to the turret. From its appearance this morning, I should think that it could scarcely stand a dozen more shots. My deck, having been very badly injured, will require some repairs before I could, I think, safely go outside. The mortar shell which fell on deck over the bread-room would undoubtedly have gone through had it not struck on a beam. As it was, it has completely crushed in the planking at the side of the beam, opening quite a hole through, and had it been loaded with powder instead of sand, might have set the vessel on fire. I have measured a piece of it, and it does not seem to have been larger than ten-inch. This certainly does not say much for the strength of the deck, the injury to which has been so much more serious than to that of the Montauk, that I must attribute it to a worse class of iron, unless heavier guns have been mounted since the attack made by Commander Worden.

I have gone into greater length than, perhaps, would be required, were it not that ill success always needs much explanation, and that things which relate to the iron-clads possess, from their want of precedents, an interest not otherwise belonging to them.

On the night previous to the attack, Lieutenant Commander Gibson, with his boats, swept for torpedoes in the neighborhood of the one which exploded under the Montauk, but did not meet with any.

I have omitted to mention that my pilot was the same one who had charge of the Montauk in her various operations in this river; and I have to thank Commanders Ammen and Downes for the hearty support which they gave me.

I send also the reports of Commanders Ammen and Downes.

I am, very respectfully, your obedient servant,

P. DRAYTON,
Captain, Senior Officer present.

Rear-Admiral S. F. DuPont,
Com'g S. A. B. Squadron, Port Royal Harbor, Flag-Ship Wabash.

Report of Lieutenant Commander J. N. Miller of injuries to the Passaic.

United States Iron-clad Steamer Passaic,
Ogeechee River, Georgia, March 4, 1863.

Sir: I submit the following report of the injuries we received in the attack on Fort McAllister.

We were struck nine times on the port side armor. Three of these were about fifty feet from the bow, and within the distance of three feet from each other. They made indentations of two inches, carried away several bolts, and raised the adjoining deck plating one inch. The other shots in side armor made indentations of about one inch, without injuring the bolts.

On deck plating we received thirteen shots. One over ward-room storeroom raised the plating and carried away several of the bolts. One struck over the hammock-room, near the turret, crushing in the plating and deck planking, causing the deck to leak when covered with water. Two shots struck over the engine-room, breaking a number of bolts in the plating, which it also broke through and raised the ends. A 10-inch mortar shell, loaded with sand, struck over the bread-room, crushing in the deck plating and planking. It struck partly on a beam and the angle-iron which supports it, but, as far as we can see, these are not injured. The remaining shots on deck did not seriously injure the plating.

Five shots struck the turret, making indentations varying from one-half inch to one inch. One of these is six inches below the XV-inch port.

Two shots struck the pilot-house, carrying away three of the bolts and making indentations of about one inch.

One shot struck the roof of the turret and broke one of its beams of railroad iron. The lower part of the smoke-stack was struck once close to the deck, making an indentation of one and one-fourth inch, and carrying away one of the bolt heads.

The concussion of the XV-inch gun broke all of the bolts holding the side of the box to the turret, and I have no doubt, unless the bolts are replaced, that a few more fires would destroy the box, one side of which is much bulged out. The bolt holding one of the rollers of the sliding plate, in concussion box, parted during the action; but as we always fired at the same elevation, the plate was lashed so that we could run the gun in and out.

During the action we were struck thirty-four times, nine of which were on side armor, thirteen on deck, five on turret, two on pilot-house, one on roof of turret, one on smoke-stack; one carried away pennant staff on pilot-house, one carried away boat-spar aft, and one the out-rigger forward.

I am, respectfully, your obedient servant.

J. N. MILLER, *Executive Officer.*

—

Report of Commander Daniel Ammen, of the Patapsco.

IRON-CLAD PATAPSCO,
Ogeechee River, March 3, 1863.

SIR: I have the honor to report that, in obedience to signal at 8 a. m. of to-day, the Patapsco was got under way, preceded by the Passaic and followed by the Nahant, and at about 8.30 a. m. anchored below Fort McAllister.

The enemy immediately opened fire, and had established a target for range on a marsh near the spot where the three vessels anchored, as near each other as was possible to swing clear on a turn of tide. Seven guns were visible on the face of the work, protected by heavy traverses, and in an adjoining wood one or two mortars and a rifle were in position, and directed their fire against us.

The difficulty of approach through a narrow channel and the shoalness of the water evidently left you without a choice of position. We followed your movements, and after firing a few shells, found the distance from the battery greater than had been supposed.

We fired deliberately, and finding the XV-inch gun required more elevation than is desirable, confined ourselves for some time to the use of the rifle.

The time fuzes of the rifle, except those made by the Ordnance department, did not appear generally to explode the shells, and the percussion shells did not explode with the ordinary percussion musket cap. By filing the nipple so as to receive an ordinary cap, few failed even when striking in the sand.

Fourteen XV-inch and forty-six 150-pound rifle shell were expended by us against the enemy.

No injury was sustained by this vessel, and only one shot was known to have struck the deck. Much the greater part of the firing of the enemy was directed against the Passaic.

The works of the enemy appeared very much cut up. The parapet was breached in several places, and three of the traverses very much injured.

When the Passaic and the Nahant swung to flood, at about 3 p. m., we remained across the tide, and I saw at once that we were aground, owing to having anchored a few yards on the port quarter of the Passaic as she rode to the ebb. A rising tide and working the engine enabled us to swing about 3.40 p. m.

The signal by whistle to get under way was not understood by us, and the flag was not seen. After seeing the Nahant leave, and learning verbally the order, I got under way, as directed, and proceeded to this anchorage.

I am, very respectfully, your obedient servant,

DANIEL AMMEN, *Commander*.

Captain PERCIVAL DRAYTON,
Iron-clad Passaic.

Report of Commander John Downes, of the Nahant.

IRON-CLAD NAHANT,
Ossabaw Sound, March 4, 1863.

SIR: I have the honor to submit the following report of the participation of this vessel in the attack yesterday upon Fort McAllister.

Weighing anchor at 7.30 a. m., the commencement of ebb tide, in compliance with signal, we steamed up the river, preceded by the Passaic and Patapsco, and at 8.30 grounded in close vicinity to our subsequent anchorage, and after the two leading vessels had anchored; but by backing our engines fortunately got afloat again before the tide had receded sufficiently to make us a fixture until the next high water. At 8.50, whilst still aground, we commenced action about seventeen hundred yards from the fort, the enemy having opened fire about ten minutes previously, and continued it subsequently at the reduced distance of about fifteen hundred yards, until ordered by signal to "discontinue and drop out of action," at near 4 p. m.; during which time we fired thirty-two XV-inch shell and thirty-nine XI-inch shell. After firing ten charges of thirty-five pounds from the XV-inch, with all the elevation I could give the gun, the shell falling short of the parapet, and not being able to reduce my distance from the fort, I considered it necessary to increase my charge of powder to thirty-eight pounds, after which the practice from this vessel was very satisfactory, and the effect upon the earthwork opposed to us apparently very damaging, tearing away the parapet and traverses, and bursting the shells with great certainty inside the work, and very often in close vicinity of the guns.

I can find no trace of this vessel having been struck by shot during the action; indeed, the leading vessel, the Passaic, seemed to attract the attention of the battery almost exclusively, they giving us only an occasional shot, which generally passed over. A mortar planted under cover of the woods in the vicinity of the fort, and a small rifled piece or two, aimed apparently at persons exposing themselves upon the deck, paid us particular attention, but without effect.

At various times during the action the compressor arrangements of the XV-inch gun became disarranged, the gun twice revolving so far in that it was with great difficulty, and once only with the assistance of a jackscrew, that we forced it out again; and at the twentieth fire the rivets of the brass guides on the after part of the carriage broke, the guides falling down into the turret chamber below, without, however, disabling the gun.

At the thirty-ninth fire of the XI-inch gun the cast-iron yoke snapped at the outer edge of the port trunnion, thereby effectually disabling the gun until another yoke is supplied to us.

I estimated the armament of the fort on the water faces at seven guns—a large rifle, and the remainder VI-inch, VIII-inch, and X-inch guns—besides one or two smaller rifles, not apparent to us, except from their execution, and the one mortar previously mentioned.

The bearing of the officers and crew was everything I had expected of them, entirely satisfactory, and assuring to me that under any circumstances they will perform their duties thoroughly. * * * * *

I am, very respectfully, your obedient servant,

JOHN DOWNES, *Commander.*

Captain PERCIVAL DRAYTON,
Com'g Iron-clad Passaic, and Senior Officer present, Ogechee River.

Arrival of the Catskill at Port Royal.

[Despatch No. 117—1863.]

FLAG-SHIP WABASH,
Port Royal Harbor, South Carolina, March 7, 1863.

SIR: I have the honor to inform the department of the arrival here on the 5th instant of the United States steamer Bienville, having in tow the United States iron-clad steamer Catskill.

The Bienville will leave on Monday next for her destination.

Very respectfully, your obedient servant,

S. F. DUPONT,
Rear-Admiral, Com'dg S. A. B. Squadron.

Hon. GIDEON WELLES,
Secretary of the Navy, Washington.

Chief Engineer Stimers coming north to report.

[Despatch No. 114—1863.]

FLAG-SHIP WABASH,
Port Royal Harbor, South Carolina, March 7, 1863.

SIR: Chief Engineer A. C. Stimers returns north in the Ericsson, taking charge of my despatches. He was on board the Passaic during the last attack on Fort McAllister, and is anxious to report his experience to the department. Though his services are valuable to me in the repair of the Monitors, I have concluded to let him go.

Very respectfully, your obedient servant,

S. F. DUPONT,
Rear-Admiral, Com'dg S. A. B. Squadron.

Hon. GIDEON WELLES,
Secretary of the Navy, Washington.

Report of survey on the Montauk.

[Despatch No. 122—1863.]

FLAG-SHIP WABASH,
Port Royal Harbor, S. C., March 7, 1863.

SIR: I have the honor to enclose the report of the survey on the Montauk, injured by the explosion of a torpedo on the 28th ultimo, after the destruction of the Nashville. Drawings are also forwarded herewith.

Very respectfully, your obedient servant,

S. F. DUPONT,
Rear-Admiral, Com'dg S. A. B. Squadron.

Hon. GIDEON WELLES,
Secretary of the Navy, Washington.

FLAG-SHIP WABASH,
Port Royal Harbor, S. C., March 5, 1863.

GENTLEMEN: You will hold a strict and careful survey on the hull of the United States iron-clad Montauk, and report to me in triplicate what damages she has sustained from the explosion of the torpedo on the 28th ultimo, the best mode of repairing the same, and the time required for that purpose.

Respectfully, your obedient servant,

S. F. DUPONT,
Rear-Admiral, Com'dg S. A. B. Squadron.

Chief Engineer ALBAN C. STIMERS, Chief Engineer R. MCCLEERY, U. S. steamer Wabash, Mechanical Engineer EDWARD FARON.

[Despatch No. 122, 1863.—Enclosure.]

PORT ROYAL, SOUTH CAROLINA, *March* 5, 1863.

SIR: In obedience to your orders of this date, we have examined the bottom of the iron-clad Montauk with reference to the injury sustained by the explosion beneath it of a torpedo in the Ogeechee river, and we beg leave very respectfully to report.

The explosion took place beneath the back end of the port boiler, under a part where the ship's bottom is very flat.

We found the cast iron portion of the boiler—blow-off pipe—which in all iron ships it is considered necessary to place between the copper pipes and the wrought iron of the ship's bottom to prevent galvanic action, which would otherwise take place, broken off, the bottom permanently indented two and a half inches; the indentation extending five feet athwartship and three feet fore and aft. The greatest force of the explosion was directly under a twelve-inch floor, along beneath which the plating of the ship is cracked a distance of two feet four inches, (2′ 4″;) thence diagonally aft and toward the keel one foot ten inches (1′ 10″,) its direction being indicated by saying that it extends aft nine inches (9″,) and athwartships one foot eight inches (1′ 8″,) the diagonal portion of the crack being in the next streak to garboard. This twelve-inch (12″) floor, and the sixteen-inch (16″) one forward of it, are warped and torn somewhat from the frames.

We would respectfully recommend that the ship be beached, and a soft patch tap bolted to the inside of the cracked plate; that the floors be straightened and refastened to the frames, and that a wrought-iron pipe be put in place of the cast-iron one which broke.

In making this last recommendation, we are aware that we are departing from what is considered the best practice in iron ship-building where copper pipes are used, and that a torpedo may never again explode with that nice adjustment of locality and force which may break a cast-iron pipe and not break through entirely into the ship. Yet we prefer to assume that this may occur, and to suffer the certain inconvenience of the galvanic action, than to replace a broken part with material which will certainly be broken upon an exact repetition of the accident.

We estimate the time required as follows:

To make the necessary preparations	4 days.
To remain on the beach	2 "
To complete all that it is proposed to do	4 "
Total time from date	10 days.

We are, very respectfully, your obedient servants,

ALBAN C. STIMERS,
Chief Engineer U. S. Navy.
R. W. McCLEERY,
Chief Engineer U. S. Navy.
EDWARD FARON,
Mechanical Engineer.

Rear-Admiral S. F. DuPont,
Commanding South Atlantic Blockading Squadron.

Arrival of the Nantucket at Port Royal.

[Despatch No. 132—1863.]

Flag-Ship Wabash,
Port Royal Harbor, S. C., March 15, 1863.

Sir: I have the honor to inform the department of the safe arrival this morning of the iron-clad Nantucket in tow of the Florida.

Commander Bankhead, in obedience to his orders, will return immediately to Hampton Roads. She needs twelve hours to repair.

Very respectfully, your obedient servant,

S. F. DUPONT,
Rear-Admiral, Com'dg S. A. B. Squadron.

Hon. Gideon Welles,
Secretary of the Navy, Washington, D. C.

Requesting commanding officers of iron-clads to make suggestions relative to their improvement.

Navy Department, *March* 25, 1863.

Sir: The department desires the commanding officers of the iron-clads to report frequently with regard to the qualities of those vessels, and to make any suggestions which experience may dictate for their improvement.

I am, respectfully, your obedient servant,

GIDEON WELLES,
Secretary of the Navy.

Real-Admiral S. F. DuPont,
Commanding S. A. B. Squadron, Port Royal.

Passage of Keokuk to Port Royal.

[Despatch No. 156—1863.]

FLAG-SHIP WABASH,
Port Royal Harbor, S. C., March 27, 1863.

SIR: I have the honor to report to the department the arrival here yesterday afternoon, in good order, of the United States iron-clad steamer Keokuk, accompanied by the tug Governor.

Enclosed (marked No. 1) is a copy of Commander Rhind's report of the passage from Hampton Roads to this port. She will be ready for service in three days.

Very respectfully, your obedient servant,

S. F. DUPONT,
Rear-Admiral, Commanding S. A. B. Squadron.

Hon. GIDEON WELLES,
Secretary of the Navy, Washington, D. C.

[Enclosure No. 1.—Despatch No. 156, 1863.]

UNITED STATES STEAM BATTERY KEOKUK,
Port Royal, March 26, 1863.

SIR: I have the honor to report the arrival of this vessel. We left Hampton Roads on Sunday evening at 9 o'clock, after a detention of several hours by fog. On the passage down, in tow of steam-tug Governor, we had rough weather after passing Cape Lookout shoals.

In a heavy sea the vessel rolls deeply, but easily. I consider her a good and safe vessel at sea.

The convoy steamer E. B. Hale was lost sight of on Tuesday evening in a heavy squall. When the engines are worked more, and in good order, the Keokuk will be able to go without convoy, and I think will attain a speed of over nine knots in smooth water.

Very respectfully, your obedient servant,

A. C. RHIND, *Commander.*

Rear-Admiral S. F. DUPONT,
Commanding South Atlantic Blockading Squadron.

Calling attention to request for report upon improvement of iron-clads.

NAVY DEPARTMENT, *May* 1, 1863.

SIR: On the 25th March last, the department requested that the commanding officers of the iron-clads should report frequently with regard to the qualities of those vessels, and make any suggestions for their improvement which experience might dictate. No reports having been received, it is thought the subject may have been overlooked.

Very respectfully, &c.,

GIDEON WELLES,
Secretary of the Navy.

Rear-Admiral S. F. DUPONT,
Commanding S. A. B. Squadron, Port Royal, S. C.

Injury to turret of the Nahant.

[Despatch No. 211—1863.]

FLAG-SHIP WABASH,
Port Royal Harbor, S. C., May 3, 1863.

SIR: I herewith enclose copies (marked 1 and 2) of the reports of Commander Downes, of the Nahant, and of his first assistant engineer, F. J. Lovering, an experienced officer, respecting the turret of that vessel.

I also enclose (marked No. 3) a slip from the Baltimore American, written, there is every reason to believe, either by Mr. Fulton or Mr. Stimers, in which, among other things, it is stated "that the damage done to the Nahant, Passaic, and Weehawken, the only vessels of the fleet materially injured, was completely remedied before noon on Wednesday." The turret of the Nahant is represented "to have been wedged by a shot striking it at the lower edge where it comes in contact with the deck."

This was not the case, and it was restored to working condition early next morning by Mr. Farren, who found that the difficulty was in the socket of the turret at the very bottom of the vessel, which had been jammed out of its place by a heavy concussion in the upper edge of the turret. In two hours he had it revolving at the rate of one and a half minute to the current.

The department will perceive, by the reports of Commander Downes and Mr. Lovering, that the turret of the Nahant is not yet in working order; that as late as the 28th of April, with thirty pounds of steam it required two minutes and forty seconds to make one revolution, and that when the pressure was reduced to twenty-three pounds the turret stopped.

Very respectfully, your obedient servant,

S. F. DUPONT,
Rear-Admiral, Commanding S. A. B. Squadron.

Hon. GIDEON WELLES,
Secretary of the Navy, Washington.

—

[Enclosure No. 1.—Despatch No. 211, 1863.]

IRON-CLAD NAHANT,
North Edisto River, April 29, 1863.

SIR: I have the honor to forward herewith enclosed the report of the senior engineer, Mr. Lovering, upon the working condition of the turret of this vessel, and the apparent causes of its unsatisfactory performance, by which it will be perceived that for the space of a week we will be unfitted for service. At the expiration of that time, however, I hope and think the obstacles to the moving of our turret will have been removed, and this vessel ready for service.

I am, very respectfully, your obedient servant,

JOHN DOWNES, *Commander.*

Rear-Admiral S. F. DUPONT,
Commanding S. A. B. Squadron, Port Royal, S. C.

[Enclosure No. 2.—Despatch No. 211, 1863.]

IRON-CLAD NAHANT,
North Edisto River, April 28, 1863.

SIR: I have the honor to report that, this forenoon, having cut out the pieces of the pilot-house ring, where it bound the base of the house, I turned the turret, and with thirty pounds of steam it required two minutes and forty seconds to make one revolution; with twenty-six pounds of steam, three minutes and eight seconds; and where the pressure was reduced to twenty-three pounds, the turret stopped.

The difficulty, in my opinion, is caused by the teeth of the main pinion and wheel washing too deeply, and by the after or fifteen-inch gun side of the turret settling, so that the main turret beam strikes the pinion in its revolution. To remedy this, it will be necessary to remove the main pinion and reduce its thickness from one-half to three-quarters of an inch, dress the teeth of the pinion and cut three-quarters of an inch off the end of the main pinion shaft. With the facilities at hand this can be done in one week.

I am, sir, very respectfully, &c.,

F. J. LOVERING,
Senior Engineer.

Commander J. DOWNES.

[Enclusure No. 3.—Despatch No. 211, 1863.]

IMPREGNABILITY OF THE MONITORS.

[From the Baltimore American.]

There will be found in our columns this morning a letter from Mr. Ericsson with regard to the test of the strength of the fleet of Monitors under the walls of Sumter and Moultrie. Having witnessed that great conflict, and after the battle visited all the Monitors engaged in it, we have no hesitation in asserting that it was a matter of astonishment to all experienced observers to see how little they were really injured. They were scarred and bruised, and their smoke-stacks penetrated by the projectiles literally rained on them by the enemy; but even in this respect not one of them fared as badly as the original Monitor in her conflict with the Merrimack. No one doubted her entire ability to renew the fight next day, and our entire fleet of Monitors were as competent to return to the walls of Sumter as she was to meet the Merrimack.

The damage done to the Nahant, Passaic, and Weehawken, the only vessels of the fleet really injured, was completely remedied before noon on Wednesday. The turret of the Nahant is represented to have been wedged by a shot striking it at the lower edge, where it comes in contact with the deck; this was not the case, and it was restored to working condition early next morning by Mr. Farren, who found that the difficulty was in the socket of the turret, at the very bottom of the vessel, which had been jarred out of its place by a heavy concussion on the upper edge of the turret. In two hours he had it revolving at the rate of one and a half minute to the current. Some of the bolts of her pilot-house were broken, but there was no penetration either there or in the turret. Her deck was scarred, her smoke-pipe cut through, and the deepest indentation, (two and three-quarter inches) received by any of the vessels made in her turret, but she could have fought as effectually next day as any of the fleet.

The only trouble in the Passaic was the protrusion of a bolt-head in the turret, which prevented one of the slides of her port stopper from opening. A cold chisel and an hour's application of the hammer remedied that obstruction.

The Weehawken was more extensively scarred by the shot of the enemy than any other of the vessels, and her deck was, at one point, penetrated by a steel-pointed rifle shot of small calibre. This shot cut a groove in the deck about eighteen inches long and very smooth, and is supposed to have passed underneath and into one of the coal bunkers. The fracture, however, was very small, and the damage of no account, so far as her efficiency was concerned. The side armor of her hull was also severely tested, four balls having struck on the upper edge within a space of two feet. It presented, at this spot, a very ragged appearance. Her gallant commander, Captain John Rodgers, led the battle, and was the first in and the last out, and never ceased firing. For a renewal of the fight she had received no real injury. So also with the other four: the Patapsco, Catskill, and Nantucket, and Montauk, were beautified by the scars of war, but not injured in the slightest manner, so far as ability to renew the fight was concerned.

As to their steering qualities, they are unequalled by any vessels ever constructed. We have sailed side by side with them for hundreds of miles on the ocean, and have seen them in the strong tide-way of narrow and shallow channels, and never heard any complaint of their steering qualities, until we read accounts in the New York papers, in their attempts to excuse the unsatisfactory operations of the naval authorities before Charleston.

We contend that this first practical test of the power of endurance of the iron-clad Monitors was most satisfactory, and that there was no more reason for not renewing the conflict next day than there would have been for not commencing it on the previous day. It was regarded by most of those who witnessed it as a most satisfactory reconnoissance, showing the entire capacity of the Monitors to withstand such a concentrated fire, and the inability of the enemy with the most powerful of modern projectiles to penetrate their armor.

Relative to forwarding suggestions of officers commanding iron-clads.

[Despatch No. 130—1863.]

FLAG-SHIP WABASH,
Port Royal, South Carolina, May 11, 1863.

SIR: I have the honor to acknowledge the receipt of the department's despatch of May 1, referring to a previous despatch, in which the commanding officers of the iron-clads were directed to make suggestions as to their improvement.

A copy of the original despatch was immediately delivered to these officers, and an answer has been prepared, which I had expected to have forwarded by this mail.

It will be sent by the next steamer.

Very respectfully, your obedient servant,

S. F. DUPONT,
Rear-Admiral, Commanding S. A. B. Squadron.

Hon. GIDEON WELLES,
Secretary of the Navy, Washington, D. C.

Telegraphic report of the capture of the Atlanta.

[Telegram at Washington—June 22, 1863.]

NEWPORT NEWS, *June* 22, 1863.

Your telegram just received. Admiral DuPont sent Weehawken, John Rodgers, and Nahant down to Wassaw sound to look out for the Atlanta. June 17th, at 6 a. m., Atlanta came down, accompanied by two gunboats. The engagement was exclusively between the Weehawken and Atlanta. The latter mounted four of the Brooke rifles, two of seven-inch on bow and stern pivots, and two of six-inch, one on each side. She could fight two of the former, and one of the latter, on a side. Rodgers engaged at close quarters. The first fifteen-inch shot, fired by himself, took off the top of Atlanta's pilot-house, and wounded two of her three pilots. Another fifteen-inch shot struck half-way up her roof, iron-plated, four inches thick, killing one and wounding seventeen men. Eleven shots were fired in all—five by Weehawken, six by Atlanta. The latter, aground, surrendered. The fight was short; the victory signal. The Weehawken sustained no injury of any sort. Atlanta steers well, and made six knots, against a head sea, going to Port Royal. She was completely provided with instruments and stores for a regular cruise. She had a ram, a saw, and a torpedo on her bow. Ex-Lieutenant W. A. Webb commanded her. Her complement was one hundred and sixty-five souls. Her wounded were left at Port Royal. The Atlanta is said to have come down confident of capturing the Monitors easily, and her consorts, filled with spectators, were prepared to tow them to Savannah. She will soon be ready for service under the flag of the Union.

S. P. LEE,
Acting Rear-Admiral.

Hon. GIDEON WELLES,
Secretary of the Navy.

Capture of rebel iron-clad Atlanta.

FLAG-SHIP WABASH,
Port Royal Harbor, South Carolina, June 17, 1863.

SIR: Having reason to believe that the Atlanta and other rebel iron-clads at Savannah were about attempting to enter Warsaw sound, by Wilmington river, for the purpose of attacking the blockading vessels there and in the sounds further south, I despatched, some days ago, the Weehawken, Captain John Rodgers, from this port, and the Nahant, Commander J. Downes, from North Edisto, to Warsaw, where the Cimmerone, Commander Drake, was maintaining the inside blockade.

I have the satisfaction to report to the department that this morning the Atlanta came down, by Wilmington river, into Warsaw sound, and was captured. This information has just been received in a telegram from Fort Pulaski, sent by Captain John Rodgers.

Very respectfully, your obedient servant,

S. F. DUPONT,
Rear-Admiral, Commanding S. A. B. Squadron.

Hon. GIDEON WELLES,
Secretary of the Navy, Washington, D. C.

FLAG-SHIP WABASH,
Port Royal Harbor, South Carolina, June 17, 1863.

SIR: I have the honor to inform the department that since mailing my despatch (No. 316) I have received further details of the capture of the Atlanta, sent, through the kindness of Colonel Barton, by telegraph from Fort Pulaski.

The Atlanta, Captain William Webb, came down this morning, *via* Wilmington river, to attack our vessels in Warsaw, accompanied by two wooden steamers, filled, it is said, with persons as spectators. The Weehawken, Captain John Rodgers, at once engaged her, firing in all five shots, three of which took effect, penetrating her armor, and killing or wounding the crews of two guns. Two or three of the pilots were also badly wounded, and the pilot-house broken up whereupon the vessel grounded, and immediately after surrendered. The Weehawken was not hit. The armament of the Atlanta was two seven-inch and two six-inch guns. She is but slightly injured.

Very respectfully, your obedient servant,

S. F. DUPONT,
Rear-Admiral, Commanding S. A. B. Squadron.

Hon. GIDEON WELLES,
Secretary of the Navy, Washington, D. C.

P. S.—The officers and crew of the Atlanta numbered one hundred and sixty-five persons.

S. F. D.

FLAG-SHIP WABASH,
Port Royal, South Carolina, June 19, 1863.

SIR: I have the honor to forward herewith (marked No. 1) the interesting report of Captain John Rodgers, of the Weehawken, of the capture, on the 17th instant, of the confederate iron-clad steamer Atlanta, better known as the Fingal, as well as the report of Commodore Rodgers, and the report of Commander Downes, of the Nahant, who participated in the capture, marked No. 2.

The Fingal, in a dense fog, ran the blockade of Savannah a few days after the Port Royal forts were taken, in November, 1861. She has been closely watched ever since, and, as in the case of the Nashville, the long and ceaseless vigilance of my officers has been rewarded. The Atlanta is now in Port Royal under the American flag, having, unaided, steamed into this harbor from Warsaw.

The department will notice, in this event, how well Captain Rodgers has sustained his distinguished reputation, and added to the list of the brilliant services which he has rendered to his country during the rebellion. It will be my duty to recapitulate those services which have taken place during his connexion with my command in another communication.

Commander Downes, with his usual gallantry, moved as rapidly as possible towards the enemy, reserving his fire until he could get into close action, but lost the opportunity, from the brief nature of the engagement, of using his battery.

I have been told that the confederate government considered the Atlanta as the most efficient of their iron-clads.

The officers and crew of the Atlanta, with the exception of the wounded and one of the surgeons, have been transferred to the United States steamer James Adger to be conveyed to Fortress Monroe. A list is herewith enclosed, marked No. 3.

I cannot close this despatch without calling the attention of the department to the coolness and gallantry of Acting Master Benjamin W. Loring, especially recommended by Captain Rodgers. I trust that the department will consider his services as worthy of consideration.

I forward herewith (marked Nos. 4, 5, and 6) the list of the officers and crews of the Weehawken, Nahant and Cimmerone.

Very respectfully,

S. F. DUPONT.

Rear-Admiral, Commanding S. A. B. Squadron.

Hon. GIDEON WELLES,
Secretary of the Navy.

Report of Captain John Rodgers, commanding United States steamer Weehawken.

UNITED STATES STEAMER WEEHAWKEN,
Warsaw Sound, Georgia, June 17, 1863.

SIR: I have the honor to report that this morning at 4.10 an iron-clad vessel was discovered coming down at the mouth of Wilmington river; also two other steamers, one a side-wheel and the other a propeller.

Beat to quarters and commenced clearing the ship for action. At 4.20 slipped the cable and steamed slowly down towards the northeast end of Warsaw island. At 4.30 turned and stood up the sound, heading for the iron-clad, which at this time was discovered to have the rebel flag flying. The Nahant, having no pilot, followed in our wake. At 4.55 the enemy, being about one and a half mile distant, fired a rifle shot, which passed across our stern and struck near the Nahant. At this time the enemy was lying across the channel waiting our attack. At 5.15, being distant from him about 300 yards, we commenced firing.

At 5.30 the enemy hauled down his colors and hoisted the "white flag;" we having fired five shots, steamed near the iron-clad, and ordered a boat to be sent alongside. At 5.45 Lieutenant Alexander came on board to surrender the confederate iron-clad Atlanta. He reported the vessel aground on the sand spit that makes to the southeast from Cabbage island. Shortly afterwards Captain W. A. Webb came on board and delivered up his sword. Sent a prize crew to take charge of the vessel, under the command of Lieutenant Commander D. B. Harmony, of the Nahant; sent also Lieutenant Commander J. J. Cornwell, of this vessel, and Acting First Assistant Engineer J. G. Young, to take charge of the engine.

About this time the Nahant came in collision with this vessel, striking her eighteen inches from the end of forward overhang, starting apart the armor at the stern two inches on the top, tapering to three-quarters of an inch at water-line, extending down as far as can be seen, and detaching the armor from the sides three-quarters of an inch, a distance of six feet, tapering to nothing at seven feet from the stern. The deck plating on the forward end of overhang is curved up twenty-two inches in length, the wood beneath being somewhat crushed.

On examination it was found that the enemy had been struck four times—first on the inclined side by a 15-inch cored shot, which, although fired at an angle of 50 degrees with her keel, broke in the armor and wood backing, strewing the deck with splinters, prostrating about 40 men by the concussion, and wounding several by broken pieces of armor and splinters. One man has since died.

The second shot, 11-inch solid, struck the edge of overhang, (knuckle,) doing no damage, except breaking a plate or two.

The third shot, 15-inch cored, struck the top of the pilot-house, knocking it off, wounding two pilots, and stunning the men at the wheel. The fourth shot, supposed to be the 11-inch, struck a port stopper in the centre, breaking it in two, and shattering it very much, driving many fragments in through the port.

At 8.30 the engine of the Atlanta was reversed by Engineer J. G. Young, and the vessel backed off into deep water, where she was brought to an anchor.

The wounded, 16 in number, were removed to the steamer Island City, which had been kindly brought over from Fort Pulaski by Colonel Barton, United States army.

The officers of the vessel were sent to the tug Oleander, and a portion of the crew to the United States steamer Cimmerone for transportation to Port Royal.

The Atlanta was found to have mounted two 6-inch and two 7-inch rifles; the 6-inch in broadside, the 7-inch working on a pivot, either as broadside or bow and stern guns. There is a large supply of ammunition for these guns, and other stores said to be of great value by some of the officers of the vessel.

There were on board at the time of the capture, as per muster-roll, 21 officers and 124 men, including 28 marines.

The captured confederate officers told me that they thought we should find the speed of the Atlanta reach ten knots. They believe her the strongest iron-clad in the confederacy, and confidently anticipated taking both the Nahant and the Weehawken.

The behavior of the officers and crew was admirable.

Lieutenant Commander J. J. Cornwell did his duty zealously and efficiently. Acting Master Benj. W. Loring, whom I recommended for promotion for gallant behavior under the fire of Fort Darling, served the guns admirably, as the result shows. His energy and coolness were everything which could be wished. Executive officer, Lieutenant Commander J. J. Cornwell, informs me that on the berth deck the powder and shell divisions, under Acting Master C. C. Kingsbury, wore the aspect of exercise so completely that no one would have thought the vessel was in action.

The engine, under the direction of Acting First Assistant Engineer James G. Young, always in beautiful order, was well worked. Mr. Young has, I hope, by his participation in this action, won the promotion for which, on account of his skill and valuable services, I have already recommended him.

In a word, every man in the vessel did his duty.

I have the honor to be, your obedient servant,

JOHN RODGERS, *Captain.*

Rear-Admiral S. F. DuPont,
Commanding South Atlantic Blockading Squadron.

The following is a list of officers of the late confederate iron-clad steamer Atlanta:

*William A. Webb, commander; *J. W. Alexander, 1st lieutenant; *Alfonse Barbot, 2d lieutenant; G. H. Arleage, 3d lieutenant; P. L. Wrag, master; *A. L. Freeman, surgeon; L. L. Gibbs, assistant surgeon; J. Macon, paymaster; *G. H. Johnson, 1st assistant engineer; W. F. Worrell, 2d assistant engineer; L. G. King, 3d assistant engineer; J. S. West, midshipman; R. J. Peters, midshipman, Wm. McBlair, master's mate; T. B. Travers, gunner; R. J. Thurston, 1st lieutenant marines; G. W. Casey, paymaster's clerk.

*Late of the United States navy.

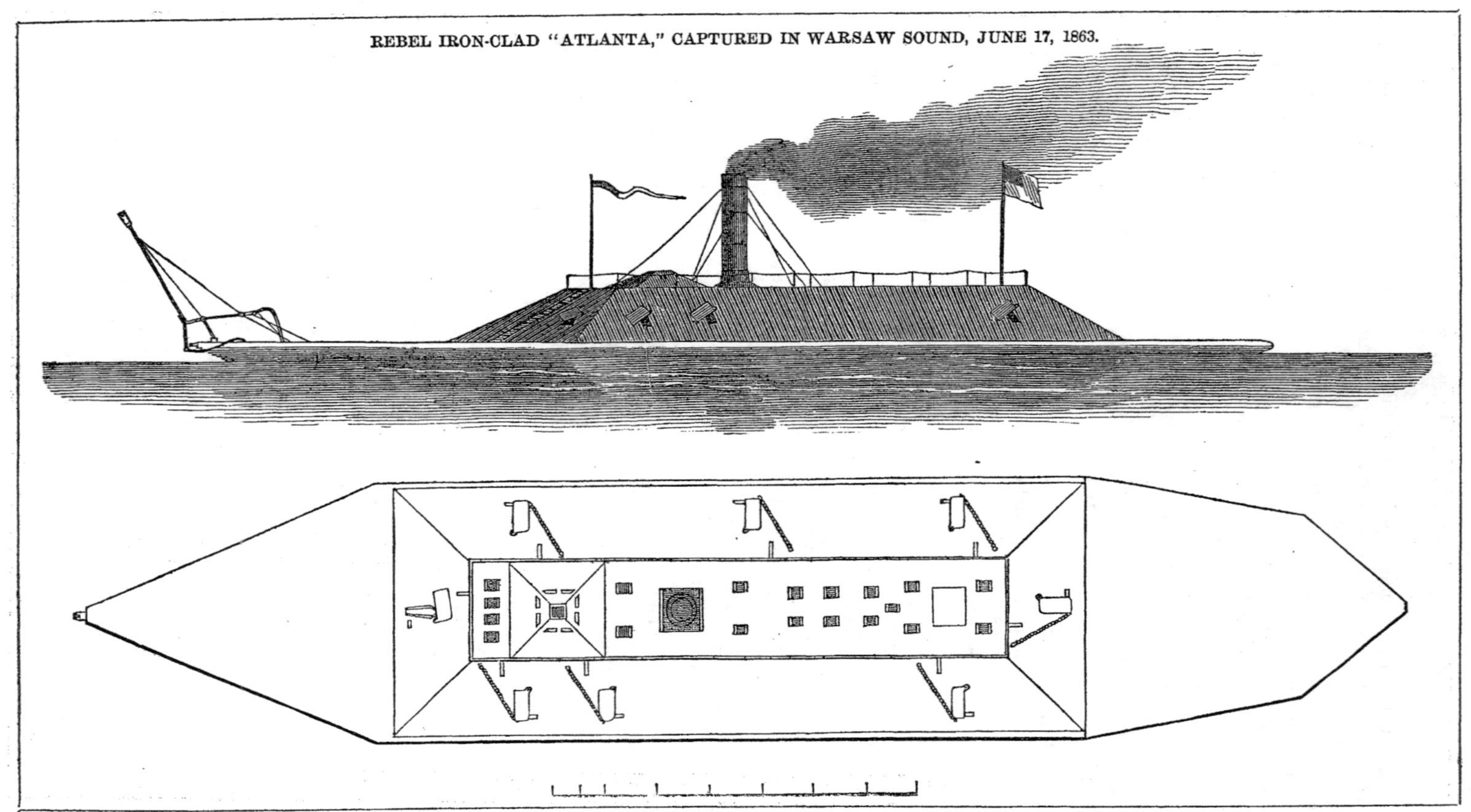

REBEL IRON-CLAD "ATLANTA," CAPTURED IN WARSAW SOUND, JUNE 17, 1863.

REBEL IRON-CLAD "ATLANTA," CAPTURED IN WARSAW SOUND, JUNE 17, 1863.

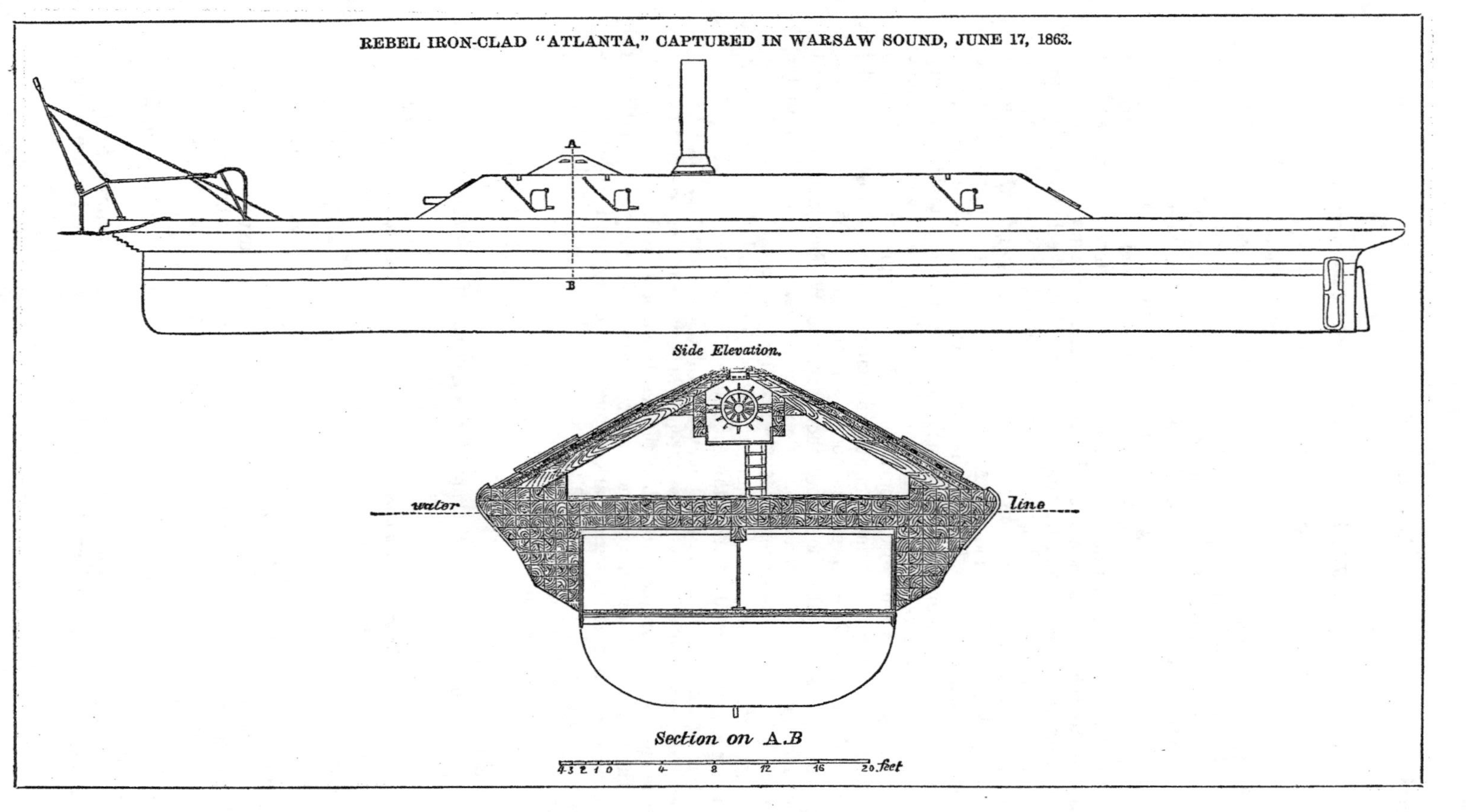

Report of Commander John Downes, commanding United States steamer Nahant.

UNITED STATES IRON-CLAD STEAMER NAHANT,
Warsaw Sound, June 18, 1863.

SIR: I have the honor to submit the following statement of the participation of this vessel in the capture of the rebel iron-clad steamer Atlanta, captured by the Weehawken and Nahant yesterday morning in these waters.

The Atlanta was first discovered at early dawn about three miles distant, standing towards us, coming out from the Wilmington river, and rapidly approaching. At first she was mistaken for our usual visitor, a steamer that had reconnoitred us daily about this hour, but a few moments sufficed to show us the true character of the vessel, and we instantly commenced weighing anchor and clearing ship for action. The Weehawken, slipping her cable, passed us, standing out seaward, at about 4.45 a. m. clearing ship for action, and in a few moments, our anchor being weighed, we followed in her wake. At this time the Atlanta fired the first shot, which passed close to our pilot-house. The Weehawken having at this time turned, was approaching the enemy, who continued, however, to direct his fire upon us, though without effect. At 5 a. m. the Weehawken closed with the enemy and opened fire on him with accuracy, this vessel approaching at the time with the intention of running him aboard before delivering fire; but at the fourth fire of the Weehawken the enemy struck and hoisted the white flag, the firing ceasing after one more shot from the Weehawken, this vessel not having had the satisfaction of expending one shot in reply to the enemy's fire, which had been directed exclusively at her.

Lieutenant Commander Harmony proceeded on board the prize at 5.30, taking possession and hoisting the American ensign.

During the action two of the enemy's armed steamers were in sight up the river, crowded with people, apparently observing the progress of events, who steamed off up the river when the result was attained.

The behavior of the officers and men, was, as usual, everything that could be desired. Acting Ensign Clark, though quite sick and under doctor's charge, proceeded to his station at the first call, and remained there until the affair was decided.

I am, respectfully, your obedient servant,

JOHN DOWNES, *Commander.*

Captain JOHN RODGERS,
Senior Officer present, United States Steamer Weehawken.

Report of survey upon the hull, armor, &c., of the Atlanta.

FLAG-SHIP WABASH,
Port Royal Harbor, S. C., June 25, 1863.

SIR: The department has been informed in previous despatches of the capture of the confederate iron-clad steamer Atlanta.

On the 20th instant I ordered a strict and careful survey to be made of her hull, armor, machinery, armament, &c., (enclosed, marked No. 1,) and I herewith submit the report made in pursuance thereof, (marked No. 2,) as well as a drawing made of the vessel by Second Assistant Engineer P. R. Voorhees, of this ship, and a pencil sketch by Mr. Xanthus Smith, Commander Corbin's clerk.

I also forward herewith a survey upon the paymaster's stores of the prize, (marked No. 3,) part of which, as the department will perceive, are reported as of good quality and fit for use in the storekeeper's department of the squadron; the rest of the stores are not considered suitable for that purpose, and it is recommended that they be sold. May I ask the department to give special directions whether they may be disposed of here, if practicable, or whether they should be sent north. I will forward, by the next mail, the report showing in detail the quantity and character of the ammunition found on board.

Very respectfully, your obedient servant,

S. F. DUPONT,
Rear-Admiral, Commanding S. A. B. Squadron.

Hon. GIDEON WELLES,
Secretary of the Navy, Washington, D. C.

—

FLAG-SHIP WABASH,
Port Royal Harbor, S. C., June 20, 1863.

GENTLEMEN: You will please make a strict and careful survey on the late confederate iron-clad steamer Atlanta, describing her hull, armor, machinery, armament, ammunition, the injuries to the vessel by the shot from the Weehawken, the repairs necessary to be made, and the general internal arrangement of the vessel for light and ventilation. You will report in duplicate.

Respectfully, your obedient servant,

S. F. DUPONT,
Rear-Admiral, Commanding S. A. B. Squadron.

Captain WM. R. TAYLOR, Commander C. R. P. RODGERS, Chief Engineer ROB'T DANBY, Lieutenant A. S. MACKENZIE.

—

UNITED STATES SHIP WABASH,
Port Royal Harbor, June 22, 1863.

SIR: In obedience to your order dated 20th instant, we have held a strict and careful survey on the late confederate iron-clad steamer Atlanta, and have the honor to submit the following report:

1st. We find that this vessel was originally an iron merchant steamer, called the Fingal. She has been cut down, so as to leave the deck about two feet above the water with her present draught. A casemate rises from this deck, sufficiently large to accommodate four guns, the sides and ends of which are inclined at an angle of about 29° with the horizon. The top is flat, and the roof of the pilot-house extends over it, pyramidally, to a height of about three feet. The deck overlaps the original iron hull six feet on each side, tapering towards the ends of the vessel, and projecting beyond them. The sides are protected by timber, running from a point several feet below the water-line to the edge of the deck, forming a heavy, solid overway of wood and armor.

The armor, four inches in thickness, is composed of two layers of 2-inch rolled iron plates, seven inches wide, the inner of which runs horizontally, and the outer vertically. They are secured to a backing of oak, three inches thick, and of pine fifteen inches thick, by bolts one inch and a quarter in diameter, countersunk on the outside of the armor, and drawn up on the inside of the vessel by nuts and washers. Wherever the bolts pass through, a space is left between the horizontal plates, which is filled in with oak plank, to avoid the expense and trouble of drilling through more than one layer, as we suppose.

The bow terminates in an iron beak or ram, which forms a part of the stem. A wooden pole connected with an iron lever, capable of being lowered below the water and raised again at pleasure, projects beyond the ram, and carries at its end a percussion torpedo.

There are three port-holes on each side, and one at each end. The bow and stern guns are pivoted so as to work at the end or at either of the nearest broadside port-holes. The broadside guns are not opposite to each other. Each port-hole is defended by an iron shutter made in the same manner as the armor of the vessel, except that the two layers of plates are strongly riveted together. The shutters are hung upon a pivot in one of the upper corners, and may be raised by a chain from one of the lower corners, passing through the side, and attached to a tackle on the inside of the vessel. When the tackle is let go, the shutter will fall into its place by its own weight, and close the port-hole.

The dimensions are as follows:

Extreme length, 204 feet; extreme breadth, 41 feet; draught of water, 15 feet 9 inches.

The battery deck is of great strength. It appears to be of solid timbers seventeen inches thick, resting on beams ten inches thick.

2. The machinery consists of two cylinders, thirty-nine inches in diameter and thirty inches stroke. The engines are vertical and direct acting, with a surface condenser. There is one "flue tubular boiler," having four furnaces—two at each end of the boiler. There are also one auxiliary boiler, three steam pumps, a blowing engine, and pans. The engines were built by James and George Thomas, of Glasgow, in 1861.

3. The armament is composed of two VII-inch and two VI$\frac{4}{10}$-inch rifled guns of the Brookes pattern, and they all bear the marks of the Tredegar foundry.

The rifling consists of seven grooves, each of which is formed by a curved cut, starting from the bore, running below it to a depth of about ten inches, and then returning to the bore upon an increased curve. The next groove commences where the last terminates.

The following are some of the principal dimensions:

		VII-inch.	VI$\frac{4}{10}$-inch.
Extreme length	inches..	147.00	142.00
Length to base ring to muzzle	inches..	124.25	121.00
Length from base ring to end of cascabel	inches..	22.75	21.00
Diameter of cylinder	inches..	31.30	24.65
at rimbases	inches..	31.40	24.75
at muzzle	inches..	14 15	10.79
Thickness of wrought-iron sleeve	inches..	2.00	2.00
Length of wrought-iron sleeve	inches..	30.25	30.00
Weight of wrought-iron sleeve	pounds.	15,300	9,200

The chambers of the guns are conical. The guns are not turned; their exteriors are in the same condition in which they left the mould. There is no chipping about the rimbases; but the metal runs from their faces, in a curve, to the proper diameter on the vertical plane between them.

The elevating screws are similar to those in use on board our own ships. The breech sights are described in the ordnance service as of the Brookes pattern. The bar slides through the boxes, with an angle in front; the graduation is in yards on one side, and in degrees on the other.

The locks correspond nearly with those in use on the modern navy guns.

The VII-inch guns are mounted on pivot carriages resembling our own very nearly. They traverse on iron circles.

The VI$\frac{4}{10}$-inch guns are mounted on Marsilly carriages, differing in some trifling particulars from our own standard. The port-holes are so small as to admit of very slight lateral training, and of an elevation not to exceed from 5° to 7°.

4. Owing to the extreme heat and foul air prevailing in the ship, but a slight examinatio n could be made of the ammunition. It will be necessar

to remove it before it can be safely overhauled. It is estimated, however, that the quantity will not vary far from 125 to 150 rounds.

The powder is stowed in wooden tanks, and consists of 8, 10, 12, 14, and 16 pound charges. There are two magazines—one forward and the other abaft.

We find on board various classes of projectiles for the guns: solid shot, shells with percussion and time fuzes, shells marked Robbins's fluid shells for VII-inch rifles, and a quantity of grape and canister for the VI$\frac{4}{10}$-inch rifles. The following are the weights and lengths of the shot and shell:

Kinds of projectiles.	VII-inch.		VI$\frac{4}{10}$-inch.	
	Length.	Weight.	Length.	Weight.
	Inches.	*Lbs.*	*Inches.*	*Lbs.*
Shells	16	100	13½	68
Wrought shot, long	15¼	133	12	94
Wrought shot, short	12	114	....	....
Cast shot	14	123	10½	76

The shot, shells, and small-arm ammunition are so scattered about the vessel, and some of those articles are in such insecure places, that no exact report, or even satisfactory examination of them, can be made until they are collected and classified.

The same remark applies equally to small-arms, locks, sights, gun-implements, &c., &c., which are scattered promiscuously about the vessel.

5. For the reason assigned in the preceding section of this report, we would respectfully recommend that the ship be thoroughly broken out, and all stores in every department be collected where they can be examined, and an accurate account be taken of them. At present any report upon them must, necessarily, be very imperfect and unsatisfactory.

6. The ship requires thorough cleansing; at present she is in great disorder. It is impossible that any one could remain below the battery deck for any length of time without serious inconvenience, if not danger, on account of the foul air prevailing there. The officers' apartments, as well as the berth deck, are very imperfectly ventilated, rendering them almost uninhabitable in hot weather; the heat upon the latter is almost insupportable, owing to the galley being placed there. Before employing this vessel in our own service, we would strongly recommend that measures be taken to provide light and air below.

7. The machinery, generally, is in good condition, and requires but slight repairs to fit it for service. There are marks of four shot upon the hull. One XV-inch struck the side of the casemate on a line with the port-holes; it broke the armor completely through, although its course was somewhat oblique. The wooden backing was much splintered, and several bolts were drawn from their places. It has left a large hole entirely through the armor and backing, though the shot itself did not pass through.

Another shot struck the midship port shutter on the starboard side, breaking both layers of plates, and indenting the armor beneath. The course of this shot was more oblique than that of the former.

A third shot struck the top of the pilot-house, broke the heavy iron casting that formed it, and displaced several plates below it, breaking and indenting them. A fourth shot struck the edge of the overway about amidships on the starboard side; it broke and displaced several plates, but did not penetrate them. The direction of this shot was very oblique.

The smoke-stack has a hole through it, caused by a splinter from the port shutter.

All necessary repairs to the hull can be made in a few days, with but trifling expense.

8. One feature in this vessel is particularly noticeable, and that is the roughness of all the work about her. No expense has been incurred for finish or ornament. The comfort of the crew, and its sanitary condition, appear to have been totally disregarded. Efficiency in battle seems to have been the sole point aimed at.

9. The armor appears to have been made of English railroad iron rolled into its present shape; in some of the fractures it has broken off almost as short as if it had been cast iron. The pine backing, it is probable, does not possess the best qualities for resistance, being very brittle, and, in consequence, dangerous to those inside of the casemates.

10. As chronometers and other nautical instruments were found on board, there is reason to suppose that this vessel was intended for sea purpose.

11. Drawings accompany this report, which will show the general appearance of the ship, and some of her arrangements.

We are, sir, very respectfully, your obedient servants,

WM. ROGERS TAYLOR, *Captain U. S. Navy.*
C. R. P. RODGERS, *Commander.*
ROBERT DANBY, *Fleet Engineer U. S. Navy.*
A. J. MACKENZIE, *Lieutenant U. S. Navy.*

Rear-Admiral S. F. DuPont,
Comd'g S. A. B. Squadron.

Note.—The backing of the armor is composed of three layers of wood. The outer one, of oak, runs vertically; the next, of pine, runs horizontally; and the third, also of pine, runs vertically.

Survey on clothing and small stores on board the Atlanta.

Flag-Ship Wabash,
Port Royal Harbor, S. C., June 19, 1863.

Gentlemen: You will please to hold a strict and careful survey on the provisions, clothing, and small stores on board the prize rebel iron-clad Atlanta, ascertain their quantity, appraise their value, and report the proper disposition to be made of them, reporting in triplicate.

Respectfully, your obedient servant,

S. F. DUPONT,
Rear-Admiral, Comd'g S. A. B. Squadron.

Paymaster Frank C. Cosby,
United States Steamer Vermont.
Paymaster R. J. Richardson,
United States Steamer Wabash.
Acting Assistant Paymaster J. S. Isaacs,
United States Steamer Vermont.

United States Ship Vermont,
Port Royal, South Carolina, June 23, 1863.

Sir: In obedience to your order of the 19th instant, hereunto appended, we have held a strict and careful survey upon the paymaster's stores of the prize rebel iron-clad steamer Atlanta, and beg leave to make the following report, viz:

PROVISIONS.

26 barrels bread, 2,217 pounds, at 4.68 cents	$103 76
1 barrel flour, 196 pounds	8 70
3 barrels rice, 586 pounds, at 8.56 cents	50 16
1 keg dried apples, 104 pounds, at 8 cents	8 32
Part keg dried apples, 10 pounds, at 8 cents	80
Part chest peas, 25 pounds, at 77 cents	19 25
2 barrels vinegar, about 50 gallons, at 12.19 cents	6 09
Part barrel vinegar, about 10 gallons, at 12.19 cents	1 22

Which we find to be of good quality, and recommend to be turned into the storekeeper's department of this squadron for issue. Also—

12 barrels pork, value $15	$180 00
14 barrels beef, value $14	196 00
1 barrel hams, 218 pounds, value 10 cents	21 80
3 barrels bacon, 515 pounds, value 7 cents	36 05
2 barrels flour, value $5	10 00
6 barrels peas, 147 gallons, value 12½ cents	18 37

Which are of medium quality, and are recommended to be sold for the benefit of the captors of the Atlanta.

CLOTHING.

28 blue cloth round jackets, value $3	$84 00
3 white duck overshirts, value 90 cents	2 70
154 white cotton undershirts, value 50 cents	77 00
147 pairs cotton drawers, value 50 cents	73 50
28 pairs mixed cotton trowsers, value 50 cents	14 00
10 white blankets, value $1 75	17 50
15 seamless woollen caps, value 90 cents	13 50

SMALL STORES.

7 jack-knives, value 10 cents	70
25 tin pots, value 3 cents	75
17 tin pans, value 4 cents	68

CONTINGENT.

8 boxes candles, 400 pounds, value 16 cents	64 00

All of which we recommend to be sold for the benefit of the captors, the articles not being of the kind or quality to issue in the navy.

Very respectfully, your obedient servants,

FRANK C. COSBY, *Paymaster.*
R. J. RICHARDSON, *Paymaster.*
JOHN S. ISAACS, *Acting Assistant Paymaster.*

Rear-Admiral S. F. DuPont,
United States Navy, Flag-Ship Wabash.

Appraisal of value of the Atlanta and her equipments, and inventory of ordnance and ordnance stores.

FLAG-SHIP WABASH,
Port Royal Harbor, South Carolina, July 2, 1863.

SIR: I forward herewith (marked No. 1) the report of a board of survey appointed to appraise the value of the hull, machinery, ordnance, ordnance stores, provisions and small stores, and equipments, of the prize iron-clad steamer Atlanta. The whole valuation amounts to three hundred and fifty thousand eight hundred and twenty-nine dollars and twenty-six cents, ($350,829 26.)

I also forward herewith an inventory of the ordnance and ordnance stores, (marked No. 2,) the survey on the provisions and small stores, (marked No. 3,) and the survey on equipments and stores in the master's, boatswain's, sailmaker's, and carpenter's departments, (marked No. 4.)

I have also forwarded by this mail, to the department, the flags of the Atlanta, the muster-roll of that vessel and the Georgia, and the log-book of the Atlanta.

Very respectfully, your obedient servant,

S. F. DUPONT,
Rear-Admiral, Commanding S. A. B. Squadron.

Hon. GIDEON WELLES,
Secretary of the Navy, Washington, D. C.

UNITED STATES SHIP HOUSATONIC,
Port Royal Harbor, July 1, 1863.

SIR: In obedience to your order of the 29th ultimo, we have made a "careful and accurate appraisement of the value of the captured confederate iron-clad steamer Atlanta, including therein her hull, machinery, ordnance, ordnance stores, provisions and small stores, and equipments," all of which we present below, under those heads, respectively:

Hull	$250, 000 00
Machinery	80, 000 00
Ordnance, ordnance stores, &c	14, 022 91
Medical stores	20 00
Provisions, clothing, and small stores	1, 012 85
Equipments and stores in the master's, boatswain's, sailmaker's, and carpenter's departments	5, 773 50
Total valuation	350, 829 26

We are, sir, very respectfully, your obedient servants,

WILLIAM ROGERS TAYLOR, *Captain.*
ROBERT DANBY, *Fleet Engineer.*
A. S. MACKENZIE, *Lieut. and Executive Officer.*
CHARLES BOARDMAN, *Carpenter U. S. N.*

Rear-Admiral S. F. DUPONT,
Commanding S. A. B. Squadron, Port Royal, S. C.

UNITED STATES SHIP HOUSATONIC,
Port Royal Harbor, *June* 30, 1863.

SIR: In obedience to your order of the 29th instant, we have made a careful and accurate inventory of the ordnance and ordnance stores on board the captured confederate iron-clad steamer Atlanta, and have the honor to submit the following report:

Two 7-inch pivot guns, weighing 15,305 and 15,162 pounds; two $6\frac{4}{10}$-inch broadside guns, weighing 9,110 pounds each

The above are rifled guns of the Brookes pattern.

Two pivot carriages and slides for 7-inch guns, complete, including ten slide and carriage levers; four pivot bolts; two elevating screws; four compressors; two Marsilly carriages for broadside guns, complete, including two elevating screws; sixty-nine 7-inch rifle shot, cast, Tennessee sabot; sixty-four 7-inch rifle shot, wrought, hollow bottom; fifty-three $6\frac{4}{10}$-inch rifle shot, cast, Tennessee sabot; twenty-five $6\frac{4}{10}$-inch rifle shot, wrought, hollow bottom; ninety 7-inch percussion shell, loaded and fuzed, Tennessee sabot; seventeen 7-inch percussion shell, loaded, not fuzed, Tennessee sabot; seventeen 7-inch Robbins's fluid shell, percussion, Tennessee sabot; nine $6\frac{4}{10}$-inch Robbins's fluid shell, 5″ time fuze, Tennessee sabot; ten $6\frac{4}{10}$-inch Robbins's fluid shell, 10″ time fuze, Tennessee sabot; three $6\frac{4}{10}$-inch Robbins's fluid shell, 15″ time fuze, Tennessee sabot; fifty-five $6\frac{4}{10}$-inch percussion shell, loaded and fuzed, Tennessee sabot; eighteen $6\frac{4}{10}$-inch shell, loaded, 5″ time fuze, lead sabot; eighteen $6\frac{4}{10}$-inch shell, loaded, 10″ time fuze, lead sabot; one 7-inch Robbins's fluid shell, 10″ time fuze, Tennessee sabot; three 7-inch shell, empty, Tennessee sabot.

The greater part of the above shells are in boxes.

Seventeen $6\frac{4}{10}$-inch grape-shot; seventeen $6\frac{4}{10}$-inch canister.

112 charges for	7-inch	guns,	12 pounds each	1,344	pounds.
77 "	"	"	14 "	1,078	"
54 "	"	"	16 "	864	"
87 "	$6\frac{4}{10}$	"	8 "	696	"
46 "	"	"	10 "	460	"
116 "	"	"	12 "	1,392	"
Loose cannon powder				150	"
Powder in good condition				5,984	"

Ten charges for 7-inch guns, 12 pounds each, (damaged,) 120 pounds; one hundred and twelve cartridge bags for 7-inch charges, 12 pounds; seventy-seven cartridge bags for 7-inch charges, 14 pounds; sixty-five cartridge bags for 7-inch charges, 16 pounds; eighty-seven cartridge bags for $6\frac{4}{10}$-inch charges, 8 pounds; forty-six cartridge bags for $6\frac{4}{10}$-inch charges, 10 pounds; one hundred and twenty-six cartridge bags for $6\frac{4}{10}$-inch charges, 12 pounds; forty-two wooden powder tanks, 200 pounds; two boring bits; six priming irons; five fuze wrenches; three vent punches; one tent drill; twenty gun tackles, (not serviceable;) two 7-inch truckings; three $6\frac{4}{10}$-inch truckings; six breeching pins; nine passing boxes, (only one serviceable;) one 7-inch ladle; one $6\frac{4}{10}$-inch ladle; two 7-inch gun scrapers; two $6\frac{4}{10}$-inch gun scrapers; one 7-inch worm, with guide rings; one $6\frac{4}{10}$-inch worm, with guide rings; three 7-inch rammers; three $6\frac{4}{10}$-inch rammers; three 7-inch woollen sponges, with Robinson's worm; three $6\frac{4}{10}$-inch woollen sponges, with Robinson's worm; three rubber handspikes; nine ordinary handspikes; twenty boarding pikes; two sponge caps; twenty-three Enfield rifles, calibre .58, (three broken;) eleven United States muskets, calibre .69; thirty Maynard's rifles, breech-loading; eleven sabre bayonets, Enfield; twenty-one sabre bayonets, Sharpe's pattern; twenty-eight sabre bayonet scabbards; thirty-six cap pouches; forty-nine cartridge boxes; twenty-nine waist belts; two arm chests; two cutlasses, old pattern; one cutlass, new pattern; nine cartridge-formers; twenty-six wipers for Maynard's rifles; twenty-nine bullet-moulds for revolvers; three bullet-moulds for muskets; twenty-five screwdrivers; nineteen screwdrivers and cone keys; five hundred revolver cartridges, (packages broken;) one bag of bullets; one box of bullets for Maynard's rifles, (two hundred;) five padlocks; two fuze wrenches; one hundred and thirty-five friction tubes; thirteen hundred cannon-primers; fifteen metal stock fuzes; seven cannon locks; four cannon locks, strings and toggles; four breech sights and screws, metal; five wooden truck sights; four reinforce sights and screws, metal; seven vent punches; five worms for sponges; two hundred and fifty-five musket cartridges; five torpedoes; six torpedo fuzes; four boxes rifle cartridges, (five hundred good;) twenty-one cartridge pouches; one pistol holster; one primer box; twenty-three rockets, (damaged;) one box blue-lights, (damaged.)

Except such articles as are specially noted in the foregoing inventory, these equipments and stores are in good condition, requiring but slight overhauling and repairs to fit them for immediate service.

We are, sir, very respectfully, your obedient servants,

WILLIAM ROGERS TAYLOR, *Captain.*
WILLIAM REYNOLDS, *Commander.*
A. S. MACKENZIE, *Lieutenant, Exec. Officer.*

Rear-Admiral S. F. DuPont,
Commanding S. A. B. Squadron, Port Royal, S. C.

Inventory of stores in carpenter's, sailmaker's, boatswain's, and master's departments.

FLAG-SHIP WABASH,
Port Royal Harbor, South Carolina, June 20, 1863.

GENTLEMEN: You will make a careful inventory of the stores in the carpenter's, sailmaker's, boatswain's, and master's departments of the prize iron-clad steamer Atlanta, and appraise the value of the same.

You will also superintend their transhipment to the storeship Valparaiso.

Respectfully, your obedient servant,

S. F. DUPONT,
Rear-Admiral, Commanding S. A. B. Squadron.

Acting Master A. S. GARDNER.
Acting Ensign JOHN BLITZ.
Sailmaker JOHN JOINS.

UNITED STATES SHIP VALPARAISO,
Port Royal Harbor, South Carolina, June 23, 1863.

SIR: In obedience to your orders of the 20th June, herewith annexed, we have made a careful inventory of the stores in the carpenter's, sailmaker's, boatswain's, and master's departments of the prize iron-clad steamer Atlanta, and respectfully report as follows:

SAILMAKER'S DEPARTMENT.

	Valuation.	
Eighty new hammocks	$100 00	
Four hundred yards old canvas	10 00	
Two old boat sails	3 00	
		$113 00

BOATSWAIN'S DEPARTMENT.

Fifty pounds spun yarn	5 00	
Forty oars	15 00	
Seven boat-hooks	3 00	
Seventy-five fathoms 1-inch manilla	5 00	
Fifty palmetto brooms	10 00	
		38 00

CARPENTER'S DEPARTMENT.

One tool-chest, with tools		10 00

MASTER'S DEPARTMENT.

Three gallons spirits turpentine	5 00	
One binnacle and compass	5 00	
One broken barometer	2 50	
		12 50
Total appraisal		173 50

Also, a quantity of old blocks, tackle, and rigging, and old iron, worthless

Very respectfully, your obedient servants,

A. S. GARDNER, *Acting Master.*
JOHN BLITZ, *Acting Ensign.*
JOHN JOINS, *Sailmaker.*

Rear-Admiral S. F. DuPont.

Congratulatory letter to Captain John Rodgers on the capture of the Atlantia.

NAVY DEPARTMENT, *June* 25, 1863.

SIR: Your despatch of the 17th instant, announcing the capture of the rebel iron-clad steamer Fingal, *alias* Atlanta, has been received.

Although gallantly sustained by Commander John Downes, of the Nahant, the victory, owing to the brevity of the contest, was yours, and it gives me unaffected pleasure to congratulate you upon the result.

Every contest in which the iron-clads have been engaged against iron-clads has been instructive, and affords food for reflection. The lessons to be drawn are momentous.

On the 8th of March, 1862, there were lying at anchor at Hampton Roads the first-class steam frigates Roanoke and Minnesota, the sailing frigates Congress and St. Lawrence, the razee Cumberland, and several gunboats. In the presence of this formidable force, representing the highest offensive power of the wooden navy, boldly appeared the rebel iron-clad steamer Merrimack; and, notwithstanding the broadsides poured into her by, and the heroic defence of, the Congress and the Cumberland, these two wooden vessels were easily destroyed, and the fate of the others was only reserved for the morrow. During the night, however, the Monitor, the first vessel of her class, arrived, and on the 9th of March, when the morning mists lifted and showed the Merrimack and her wooden consorts approaching to complete the work of destruction, our defence consisted not in the great ships that were still afloat and their numerous heavy guns, but in a single small iron-clad vessel armed with two guns. History has recorded the courage and skill of Commander John L. Worden, who, disappearing in the smoke of the advanced fleet, dispersed and put to flight their wooden steamers, turned at bay the Merrimack, grappled with that formidable monster, and drove her back into Norfolk, and kept her there until the evacuation of that place led the rebels to destroy their famous iron-clad, rather than encounter and risk her capture by her puny antagonist. The lessons of that contest taught us the inadequacy of wooden vessels and our existing ordnance to meet armored ships. For inland operations the Monitor turret was immediately adopted, and the fifteen-inch gun of Rodman, being the only gun of greater weight than the eleven-inch yet tested, was ordered to be placed in the turrets of the vessels that were constructing. The result of this policy is developed in the action through which you have just passed. In fifteen minutes, and with four shots, you overpowered and captured a formidable steamer, but slightly inferior to the Merrimack—a vessel that, the preceding year, had battled, with not very serious injury to herself, against four frigates, a razee, and for a time with one Monitor, armed with eleven-inch guns—thus demonstrating the offensive power of the new and improved Monitors armed with guns of fifteen-inch calibre.

Your early connexion with the Mississippi flotilla, and your participation in the projection and construction of the first iron-clads on the western waters—your heroic conduct in the attack on Drury's Bluff—the high moral courage that led you to put to sea in the Weehawken upon the approach of a violent storm, in order to test the sea-going qualities of these new craft, at the time when a safe anchorage was close under your lee—the brave and daring manner in which you, with your associates, pressed the iron-clads under the concentrated fire of the batteries in Charleston harbor, and there tested and proved the endurance and resisting power of these vessels, and your crowning, successful achievement in the capture of the Fingal, *alias* Atlanta, are all proofs of a skill, and courage, and devotion to the country and the cause of the Union, regardless of self, that cannot be permitted to pass unrewarded. To your heroic daring and persistent moral courage, beyond that of any other individual, is the country indebted for the development, under trying and varied circumstances on the ocean, under enormous batteries on land, and in successful rencontre with a formidable floating antagonist of the capabilities and qualities of attack and resistance of the Monitor class of vessels and their heavy armament. For these heroic and serviceable acts I have presented your name to the President, requesting him to recommend that Congress give you a vote of thanks in order that you may be advanced to the grade of commodore in the American navy.

GIDEON WELLES,
Secretary of the Navy.

Captain JOHN RODGERS, U. S. N.,
Commanding United States Steamer Weehawken,
South Atlantic Blockading Squadron, Port Royal, South Carolina.

Congratulatory letter to Rear-Admiral DuPont on the capture of the Atlanta.

NAVY DEPARTMENT, *June* 26, 1863.

SIR: The department has received your several despatches announcing the capture of the rebel iron-clad steamer Fingal, *alias* Atlanta, and enclosing the detailed reports of Captain John Rodgers and Commander John Downes of the affair.

I take occasion to express the department's appreciation of your prompt measures to prepare for the expected appearance of the rebel iron-clads by sending off Savannah two of our own, ably commanded, and congratulate you on the acquisition of so powerful a vessel, which promises to be of important service on the station.

To your ceaseless vigilance, and that of the officers under your command, were we indebted, some months since, for the destruction of the notorious steamer Nashville, which the enemy had armed and fruitlessly endeavored to send out to destroy our commerce; and now to your timely measures, and the efficient means provided, do we owe the capture of one of the most powerful iron-clads afloat—a vessel prepared after months of toil and great expenditure of money, and sent forth with confidence to disperse our blockading fleet and overcome our Monitors.

You may well regard this, and we may with pleasure look upon it, as a brilliant termination of a command gallantly commenced, and conducted for nearly two years with industry, energy, and ability.

The department desires you to recommend to it an officer of the South Atlantic blockading squadron to command the Atlanta.

Very respectfully,

GIDEON WELLES,
Secretary of the Navy.

S. F. DUPONT,
Commanding S. A. B. Squadron, Port Royal, S. C.

Report of survey on turret of Patapsco.

[Despatch No. 330—1863.]

FLAG-SHIP WABASH,
Port Royal Harbor, S. C., June 25, 1863.

SIR: I have the honor to forward herewith a copy of a report (marked No. 1) made by Lieutenant Commander Erben, of the Patapsco, stating that a tooth of the main pinion of the turret gearing of that vessel had given way a second time.

Commander George Rodgers, the senior officer in North Edisto, ordered a survey, the report of which is herewith enclosed, (marked No. 2.)

The board say that though it might be temporarily repaired at Port Royal, yet for efficient service in action a new pinion should be ordered from the north, where they have the pattern.

I desire, therefore, to call the particular attention of the department to this report.

Very respectfully, your obedient servant,

S. F. DUPONT,
Rear-Admiral, Commanding S. A. B. Squadron.

Hon. GIDEON WELLES,
Secretary of the Navy, Washington.

[Enclosure No. 1.—Despatch No. 330, 1863.]

UNITED STATES IRON-CLAD PATAPSCO,
North Edisto, S. C., June 19, 1863.

SIR: I have to report that to-day a tooth of the main pinion of the turret gearing gave way. On the 1st instant the same tooth gave way while turning the turret. The chief engineer repaired it by dovetailing a wrought-iron one in its place. The gearing was reported ready, and the turret turned three times.

To-day it gave way a second time, and the chief engineer reports his inability to repair the same here. The turret was used after the breaking of the tooth; but, with it gone, the whole pinion is liable to be broken.

Very respectfully, your obedient servant,

H. ERBEN, JR.,
Lieutenant Commander.

Rear-Admiral S. F. DUPONT,
Commanding S. A. B. Squadron, Port Royal, S. C.

[Enclosure No. 2.—Despatch No. 330, 1863.]

UNITED STATES IRON-CLAD STEAMER PATAPSCO,
North Edisto Inlet, S. C., June 20, 1863.

SIR: We have examined the condition of the main pinion of the turret gearing of this vessel, and are of the opinion that it would be impracticable to attempt to repair it here with the facilities at hand. It might be temporarily repaired at Port Royal, but a new pinion, for effective service in action, should be ordered from the north, where they have the pattern.

We are, very respectfully, your obedient servants,

B. B. H. WHARTON, 1*st Assistant Engineer.*
GEO. D. EMMONS, 2*d Assistant Engineer.*
GEO. H. WHITE, 2*d Assistant Engineer.*

Commander GEO. W. RODGERS, U. S. N.,
Commanding United States Iron-clad Catskill.

Occupation of Morris island.—Operations of the iron-clads.

STEAMER AUGUSTA DINSMORE,
Off Morris Island, July 12, 1863.

SIR: I have already informed you that an agreement existed between General Gillmore and myself to dispossess the enemy of Morris island. The first measure was taken on Friday, the 10th, when, conformably to said agreement, General Gillmore was to open his batteries on the north end of Folly island against the opposite batteries of the enemy placed on Morris island, and occupying the sandy eminences that form the southern portion of that island for about a mile north of Light-house inlet.

At 4 a. m. the four iron-clads, Catskill, Commander George W. Rodgers; Montauk, Commander D. McN. Fairfax; Nahant, Commander John Downes; and Weehawken, Commander E. R. Colhoun, passed the bar, my flag leading in the Catskill. About this time General Gillmore opened his guns with a rapid and well-sustained fire on the enemy. As soon as sufficiently near, the iron-clads began to fire with shell upon the enemy's batteries, which were replying to General Gillmore, and dispersed their men wherever seen to assemble. About 8 o'clock, being nearly abreast of the northern end of the ridge of sand hills, the batteries of General Gillmore ceased, and our troops were seen making their way upon Morris island. They advanced rapidly and in some force along the beach.

The iron-clads now moved parallel to the low flat ground that extends northward from the sand hills towards Fort Wagner, and as near to it as the depth of the water permitted, rolling shells in every direction over its surface to clear away any bodies of troops that might be gathered there.

Our troops pushed on, and about this time two or three buildings standing apart from each other were seen to be in flames, supposed to be the work of the enemy to unmask the guns of Fort Wagner looking down the beach.

The iron-clads were now laid abreast of Fort Wagner. This is an open sand work about two and three-quarter miles from the southern end of Morris island, lying about one and three-quarter miles north of the sand hills, and commanding the low intervening level.

The number of cannon mounted I am unable to state precisely. There may be ten or a dozen in all, looking seaward and landward.

It was about half past 9 o'clock when the first shot was fired at this work. My wish was to close to short grape range, but the chief pilot could not place the vessels nearer than twelve hundred yards. Our fire was met promptly and vigorously till noon, when the Monitors dropped down in order to allow the men an opportunity for dinner, after which our position was reoccupied, and the attack continued till 6 p. m., when I signalled the action to cease, for the men had now been at hard work for fourteen hours, and the weather excessively hot.

The four iron-clads fired five hundred and thirty-four shell and shrapnell during the day, and, so far as I could discern from the Catskill, and learn from others who had a better view from a distance, the practice was excellent.

I was most favorably impressed with the endurance of these iron-clads, and I had a good opportunity of judging, as the Catskill (according to report of Commander Rodgers, herewith enclosed) was struck sixty times, a large per-centage of the hits being very severe. The pilot-house, turret, side armor, and decks were all more or less damaged. Some of the shots were large ; one found on deck, where it fell after striking the turret, proved to be a 10-inch. When these heavy shot struck, the concussion was very great. An officer (Acting Master Simmons) touching the turret at such a time was knocked down senseless and much injured. The iron of the pilot-house was broken through entirely, and a nut from one of the bolts driven against the lining so as to break it through. The deck-plates are also cut through in many places, so as to make the entrance of water troublesome.

The test was most severe, as any one would admit who will look at the vessel. Yet after firing one hundred and twenty-eight rounds she came out of action in good working order, as was proven by her going into action next day.

The enemy seemed to have made a mark of the Catskill. The Nahant was hit six times, the Montauk twice; the Weehawken escaped untouched. The next morning I received a note in pencil from General Gillmore, stating that he had made an assault at early daybreak on Fort Wagner, and had been repulsed. He learned that re-enforcements were expected at 10 a. m., and asked for some action to prevent it. The four Monitors were again moved to position near Fort Wagner, and scoured the ground in that vicinity.

The acquisition of to-day may not convey an impression of importance, and yet the foothold on Morris island must lead to the fall of Sumter ; and the possession of the main ship channel cuts off the best of the three entrances, and, by that much, lessens the chances of passing the blockade.

It is proper for me to add that my staff, and the commanding and other officers and crews of the iron-clads, did their duties handsomely.

I have not yet heard from Commander Balch, who was directed to proceed up the Stono, in convoy of a column of troops, but believe that all went right. Lieutenant Mackenzie, of the Wabash, had charge of the boats that landed an assaulting column on Morris island, and did it well.

The Wabash is now here, and I shall endeavor to organize one or two battalions of marines and sailors for future operations.

May I ask to have the Passaic sent down, and a new pinion expedited for the Patapsco, which is almost useless without it. The tugs, such as Pusey, are exceedingly convenient for communication, and I would request three or four more of that class.

It would be advisable that General Gillmore, under whose direction the land operations have been so ably conducted, should be strengthened, for the enemy will make efforts to repossess himself of Morris island.

General Gillmore has been with me this morning, and we shall soon complete arrangements for pushing on. He does not consider it well to make another assault.

I forward enclosed (marked No. 1) a copy of my general order No. 1, issued this morning.

The department will please make allowance for the hasty character of this communication, as I only took command on Monday, was in action Friday and Saturday, and came here from the north so hastily that I have neither secretary nor experienced clerks.

I have the honor to be, very respectfully, your obedient servant,

JOHN A. DAHLGREN,
Rear-Admiral, Commanding S. A. B. Squadron.

Hon. Gideon Welles,
Secretary of the Navy.

General order of Rear-Admiral Dahlgren, thanking his officers.

General Orders No. 1.

My thanks are due to Commander George W. Rodgers, of the Catskill; Commander D. McN. Fairfax, of the Montauk; Commander John Downes, of the Nahant; and Commander E. R. Colhoun, of the Weehawken; to the executive and other officers, and to the crews of these iron-clads; and to the members of my personal staff, Fleet Captain William Rogers Taylor, Flag Lieutenant S. W. Preston, and Ensign LaRue P. Adams, (signal officer,) for the zealous and efficient manner in which they performed their duty during the attacks of the 10th and 11th instant upon Fort Wagner and other fortifications on Morris island. I have also to thank the ordnance officer, Lieutenant Commander O. C. Badger, for his systematic promptness in supplying the iron-clads with all requisite ordnance stores.

JOHN A. DAHLGREN,
Rear-Admiral, Commanding S. A. B. Squadron.

July 12, 1863.

Report of Commander George W. Rodgers, commanding iron-clad Catskill.

UNITED STATES IRON-CLAD CATSKILL,
Inside Charleston Bar, July 10, 1863.

SIR: I have the honor to report to you that upon your coming on board this ship at 4 this morning, I hoisted your flag forward and stood over the bar, crossing it at 5 o'clock, at which time our batteries on northern end of Folly island opened upon the enemy upon the south end of Morris island. We steamed up within range of the batteries upon the south end and middle of the island, and opened fire on them at about 6 o'clock. About 9 our troops crossed over and skirmished up the island; we got under way, and standing to the northward along the island, shelled the batteries in advance of the troops. About 10 arrived opposite and engaged Fort Wagner. At 1 hauled off to give the men their dinner. At 2.30 renewed the engagement, and at 6 hauled off and proceeded out of range to an anchorage inside the bar, and near the troops.

During the action Acting Master J. W. Simmons was stunned and severely bruised by the concussion of a shot upon the outside of the turret; First-class Boy James Meehan was wounded in the foot by a fragment of a shell which entered the port; Second Assistant Engineer Croline and Third Assistant Clark were prostrated by the intense heat in the engine-room, as were several of the firemen and crew. Ensign L. P. Adams, signal officer upon your staff, took Mr. Simmons's duties in the turret, and rendered excellent service.

I herewith enclose a requisition for ordnance stores and ammunition; a request for an assistant engineer to be temporarily detailed for this ship, and for some firemen to take the place of those broken down. I have fired fifty-seven 15-inch shell and seventy-two 11-inch at the batteries and Fort Wagner. The vessel was struck sixty times, as follows: hull, sixteen times; turret, seventeen; pilot-house, three; smoke-stack, seven; deck, seventeen. There are other marks upon the hull under water which could not be counted. Some of the effects of the shot are of a serious character; the deck has been entirely broken through in four places, two of these sufficiently large to admit large quantities of water, requiring shot plugs; the pilot-house was twice struck nearly in the same place by shot from a 10-inch columbiad, which broke off the nuts from the bolts, and forced one of them through the half-inch lining of the pilot-house. The hull was struck upon the port quarter, completely shattering all the plates; one 10-inch shell landed upon the deck after striking the turret, without fracture.

I have left twenty shell and shrapnell for 15-inch gun, and one 11-inch shrapnell. The smoke-box for the 15-inch gun, when we ceased firing at noon, was much damaged, three out of five bolts securing it to the turret having broken off. One of the bolts securing the single cross-pin under the turret was broken off. The whole fire of the fort was directed at this ship, and being at anchor at about 1,200 yards during the forenoon, we were very severely handled, their 10-inch smooth-bore doing us the most harm, the rifles generally glancing or striking sideways.

This report is very hastily written after a hard day's work.

I am, very respectfully, your obedient servant,

G. W. RODGERS, *Commander.*

Rear-Admiral J. A. DAHLGREN,
Commanding S. A. Blockading Squadron.

Report of Lieutenant Commander F. M. Bunce.

UNITED STATES STEAMER PAWNEE,
Stono River, July 15, 1863.

SIR: In obedience to your order, I, on the 9th instant, at 2 p. m., started from this vessel for the purpose of co-operating with the army in an attack on Morris island. Under my command were the launch of this vessel, armed with one rifled and one smooth-bore Dahlgren howitzer, Acting Master's Mate Bache; two launches of the Wabash, each with a smooth-bore 12-pounder Dahlgren howitzer, Ensign James Wallace and Acting Master's Mate Bonn; one army lighter, fitted up and armed with two 24-pounder Dahlgren smooth-bore howitzers furnished by the Commodore McDonough, Acting Ensign Knapp; two unarmed cutters of the Wabash, one of the New Ironsides, and one of the Flag, Lieutenant Robertson and Acting Master Frost. I proceeded up Folly river to General Gillmore, and, by his order, to General Strong. Lieutenant Mackenzie, in charge of transportation, not having arrived, I gave all the assistance in my power to General Strong, and by 1 a. m. of the 10th instant his brigade was in boats, ready to proceed to Light-house inlet.

Forming the boats in line ahead, Acting Ensign Knapp taking the lead, being well acquainted with the intricate channel, we proceeded up the creeks, and by daylight were, with the whole brigade, at or near the junction of the creeks with Light-house inlet.

Just after daylight the batteries on Folly island opened upon the enemy. Getting the armed launches in line abreast, I pulled into Light-house inlet, and at a distance of 1,800 yards opened fire upon the Morris island batteries with the rifled howitzer. Pulling down the inlet, slowly firing, till we got within good distance of the batteries, I opened with all the howitzers, using 4-second shrapnell. The enemy returned the fire briskly with three or four heavy guns, but without effect. After an hour's rapid firing the enemy's batteries ceased to answer, except with one gun.

General Strong determined to effect a landing with his brigade, and designated the point. I sent the two launches of the Wabash below, while I took up a position above this point, that with the heavier guns I might cover him and enfilade the enemy's rifle pits, should he attempt to occupy them to oppose the landing. The landing was successful, all the launches keeping up a rapid and effectual fire of shell and shrapnell over the heads of the troops, falling about a hundred yards in their front and between them. This fire did not cease till the assaulting forces had so far advanced as to render it unsafe to continue lest injury might result to our own forces. Although several of the transports were struck, and one sunk, none of the boats under my command were hit, we being in a measure protected by the banks, which, as the tide ran out, afforded some shelter. Every officer and man did his whole duty with alacrity.

Very respectfully, your obedient servant,

FRANCIS M. BUNCE,
Lieutenant Commander.

Commander GEORGE B. BALCH,
Commanding U. S. Steamer Pawnee, Senior Officer.

The Monitors inside the bar.—Attack on Fort Wagner delayed.

FLAG-STEAMER AUGUSTA DINSMORE,
Off Morris Island, July 17, 1863.

SIR: Under date of the 12th instant, I informed you that General Gillmore and myself were in occupation of the lower half of Morris island and the main ship channel.

Since that I have been occupied with measures for continuing the advance, and have the Ironsides, with five turret iron-clads, inside the bar.

The attack on Fort Wagner was to have taken place on the 16th, but was postponed to this day, as the shore batteries were not ready.

A very heavy rain through the night has, however, interfered with the progress ashore, and the general now says he will be ready to-morrow morning.

* * * * * * *

An attack was made on us yesterday at Stono, but repulsed. The Pawnee was hit forty-two times.

I have the honor to be, very respectfully, your obedient servant,

JNO. A. DAHLGREN,
Rear-Admiral, Commanding S. A. B. Squadron.

HON. GIDEON WELLES,
Secretary of the Navy, Washington, D. C.

Report of Rear-Admiral Dahlgren of combined attack by the army and naval forces on Fort Wagner.

FLAG-STEAMER AUGUSTA DINSMORE,
Off Morris Island, July 19, 1863.

SIR: On the 18th a combined attack was made on Fort Wagner by the troops under General Gillmore and the vessels of my command.

The 16th had been originally agreed on, but the shore batteries were not fully prepared before the 18th. At 11.30 a. m. I made signal to get under way from the anchorage near the bar, and led up, with my flag in the Montauk, followed by the Ironsides, Catskill, Nantucket, Weehawken, and Patapsco.

About 12.30 p. m. anchored the Montauk abreast of Fort Wagner, and fired the first gun, which was immediately followed by the other vessels. With an ebbing tide, the pilot did not deem it prudent to approach nearer than the inner edge of the channel, and the least distance at this time was about twelve hundred yards. Meanwhile the gunboats Paul Jones, Commander A. C. Rhind; Ottawa, Lieutenant Commander W. D. Whiting; Seneca, Lieutenant Commander Wm. Gibson; Chippewa, Lieutenant Commander T. C. Harris; and Wissahickon, Lieutenant Commander J. L. Davis, under charge of Commander Rhind, were using the pivot gun with effect at long range, and our batteries ashore were firing very deliberately and steadily.

About 4 p. m., the tide flowing, weighed anchor, and closed in with the fort to about three hundred yards, which silenced it so that, for this day, not a shot was fired afterwards at the vessels, nor was a man to be seen about it. It was nearly sunset when I received a note from General Gillmore, saying that he had ordered an assault, and we could see the battalions advancing along the beach. There might have been a thousand yards between our nearest shore batteries and Fort Wagner, and before our troops had reached the work it became too dark to discern them.

To this moment an incessant and accurate fire had been maintained by the vessels; but now it was impossible to distinguish whether it took effect on friend or foe, and, of necessity, was suspended.

Very soon afterwards, the rattle of musketry and the flashes of light artillery announced that our men were mounting to the attack. This continued, without intermission, till 9.30 p. m., gradually decreased, and then died away altogether.

The ill tidings of a repulse were not long in coming. After the lapse of an anxious hour, common report told me that the assault had been repulsed with some loss.

It now only remained to prosecute the work with patience and perseverance. At the same time, I cannot forbear repeating my opinion that the number of troops is inadequate. The officers and men are zealous, and labor hard.

The general plans are well conceived, but there is to my mind a manifest lack of force. This morning I sent a boat ashore, with Flag Lieutenant S. W. Preston and Surgeon Duvall, under flag of truce, to ascertain if our wounded had been cared for, and to offer to take charge of them. It was also impossible to renew our fire if any of them remained on the ground.

Lieutenant Preston reported that some of the dead and wounded were still lying about the work where they had fallen, and that the offer was declined; the answer being that the dead would be buried, and the wounded properly provided for. There being nothing more possible for the day, I caused the turret vessels to drop down out of range, so that the men might have some fresh air below, and the Ironsides also, inasmuch as she lay stern to the fort, without a gun bearing.

The conduct of officers and men is entitled to every commendation. Captain Rowan, of the Ironsides; Commander Rodgers, of the Catskill; Commander Fairfax, of the Montauk; Commander Beaumont, of the Nantucket; and Lieutenant Commander Badger, whom I assigned temporarily to the command of the Patapsco, did their duty well, and handled their vessels in the narrow channel and shoal water with great skill.

The spirit of the men was excellent; neither the incessant labor of action by day, or blockade by night, nor the privations of inhabiting turret vessels, checked their earnest determination, and they worked the cannon with great effect, as the silenced guns of the enemy makes manifest. The officers of my staff were, as usual, assiduous in the discharge of their duties. The vessels were well piloted by Acting Masters Godfrey and Haffords.

In conclusion, permit me to say that on this occasion the vessels did all that was intended or could be expected from them; they silenced the fort, and forced the garrison to keep under shelter. At the same time the loss sustained by our troops bears witness to the persevering gallantry with which they endeavored to storm the work, and which deserved the success that will, I trust, reward a renewed effort.

I have the honor to be, very respectfully, your obedient servant,

JOHN A. DAHLGREN,

Rear-Admiral, Commanding S. A. B. Squadron.

Hon. GIDEON WELLES,

Secretary of the Navy, Washington, D. C.

Report of Commander G. W. Rodgers.

UNITED STATES IRON-CLAD CATSKILL,
Off Morris Island, S. C., July 18, 1863.

SIR: I have the honor to inform you that in obedience to the signal from the flag-ship, I got under way at 11.52 this day, and followed the Montauk, bearing your flag, standing up the channel in the direction of Fort Wagner. Arriving within range, opened at 12.44 with my 11-inch gun upon Fort Wagner, and soon after anchoring in 13½ feet of water, some 800 yards from the fort, continued my fire until dusk, when the troops advancing to the assault, I fired rapidly into the fort, and then following in the motions of the Ironsides, ceased firing. Shortly after 8.15 p. m., in obedience to your order, got under way and proceeded out into the channel, anchoring near the Ironsides.

I have fired this day forty-seven 15-inch shell, sixty-three 11-inch shell, twelve 11-inch shrapnell, one 11-inch canister, one 11-inch grape, making 124 shots. My 11-inch shell and shrapnell being nearly expended, I reserved the remainder until just before the assault.

This vessel was not struck during the day, and I have no casualties to report.

I beg leave to call your attention to the zeal, energy, and tact shown by the executive officer of this vessel, Lieutenant Commander C. C. Carpenter, the good result of which is shown by the cheerfulness and alacrity of the officers and crew.

I am, very respectfully, your obedient servant,

G. W. RODGERS, *Commander.*

Rear-Admiral J. A. DAHLGREN,
Commanding S. A. B. Squadron.

Attack on Fort Wagner.

FLAG-STEAMER DINSMORE,
Off Morris Island, July 25, 1863.

SIR: Yesterday I went up with the iron-clads and opened a heavy fire on Fort Wagner, in order to prevent a sortie upon some new works which General Gilmore had pushed to within 600 yards of the fort.

The gunboats assisted at long range. The firing was good, and frequently excellent.

The firing of Fort Wagner was soon silenced, and the garrison driven to shelter, so that in the course of the morning a few new batteries were partially armed.

The fire was interrupted by a flag of truce, borne by a steamer having on board some of our wounded who had been taken prisoners at various times. General Gillmore tells me that his advance position is now secured. * * *

I have the honor to be, very respectfully, your obedient servant,

JOHN A. DAHLGREN,
Rear-Admiral, Commanding S. A. B. Squadron.

Hon. GIDEON WELLES,
Secretary of the Navy, Washington, D. C.

Additional reports of Rear-Admiral Dahlgren.

FLAG-STEAMER DINSMORE,
Off Morris Island, July 30, 1863.

SIR: The position of affairs is not materially changed since the date of my last despatch, (July 25,) except that our advanced batteries (600 yards from Wagner) are in operation, and will receive frequent additions to their armament. I have contributed four rifle cannon, with a detachment of seamen, (say 120,) under Captain Parker, and will land more when I have the men to spare.

Every day two or three of the iron-clads join in and sweep the ground between Wagner and Cummings's Point, or else fire directly into Wagner; the only objection to which is, that it is drawing largely on the endurance of our cannon. However, I have no doubt the Bureau of Ordnance will enable me to meet this difficulty.

The enemy also seek in every way to distract our attention. The night before last there was an alarm from Stono about a ram, and last night a deserter to the camp stated that the iron-clad at Savannah was to move. I had sent the Nahant to check this; but as the rumor added several gunboats, and the Unadilla alone was with the Nahant, it seemed better to make sure, so I sent down the Weehawken in tow of the Conemaugh.

The turrets receive a shot occasionally with the usual result, and the Ironsides has been struck repeatedly by 10-inch shot (1,200 to 1,400 yards) without material impression. A shot from Fort Sumter, in passing along the spar deck, glanced from the edge of it, and by the *concussion* damaged the beam below, with knees connecting.

If the depth of water would only permit her to approach, I would sweep the ground clean with her powerful broadside.

It is to be remembered that Wagner is the key to Sumter, wherefore the enemy will spare no effort for the defence, and will protract any result to the last.

I have the honor to be, very respectfully, your obedient servant,

JOHN A. DAHLGREN,
Rear-Admiral, Commanding S. A. B. Squadron.

Hon. GIDEON WELLES,
Secretary of the Navy, Washington, D. C.

Attack upon Forts Wagner and Sumter.

FLAG-STEAMER DINSMORE,
Off Morris Island, August 18, 1863.

SIR: Yesterday was begun another series of operations against the enemy's works.

Early in the morning General Gillmore opened all his batteries upon Fort Sumter, firing over Fort Wagner and the intermediate space.

About the same time I moved up with the entire available naval force, leading with my flag in the Weehawken, followed by the Catskill, Nahant, and Montauk; the Passaic and Patapsco in reserve for Sumter; the Ironsides in position opposite to Wagner; and the gunboats named in the margin at long range—Canandaigua, Captain J. F. Green; Mahaska, Commander J. B. Creighton; Cimarron, Commander A. K. Hughes; Ottawa, Lieutenant Commander W. D. Whiting; Wissahickon, Lieutenant Commander J. L. Davis; Dia Ching, Lieutenant Commander J. C. Chaplin; Lodona, Lieutenant Commander E. Brodhead.

As the tide rose the Weehawken was closed to about four hundred and fifty yards of Wagner; the other three Monitors followed, and the Ironsides as near as her great draught of water permitted. After a steady and well-directed fire, Wagner was silenced about 9.20 a. m., and that of our own vessels was slackened in consequence.

Meanwhile the fire of our shore batteries was working effectually upon the gorge of Sumter, which appeared to have been strengthened in every possible manner. At this time the flag was shifted to the Passaic, which, with the Patapsco, (both having rifle guns,) steamed up the channel until within two thousand yards of Fort Sumter, when fire was opened on the gorge angle and SE. front of the work. The Patapsco fired very well, and is believed to have struck the SE. front nine consecutive times.

To all this Sumter scarcely replied; Wagner was silenced, and Battery Gregg alone maintained a deliberate fire at the Passaic and Patapsco.

It was now noon. The men had been hard at work from daybreak, and needed rest, so I withdrew the vessels to give them dinner.

During the afternoon our shore batteries continued the fire at Sumter, with little or no reply from the enemy, and I contented myself with sending up the Passaic and Patapsco to prevent Wagner from repairing damages. The fort replied briskly, but in a brief time left off firing. I am not able to state with exactness the result of the day's work, but am well satisfied with what a distant view of Sumter allowed me. Our entire power is not yet developed, as it will be daily, while the enemy is damaged without being able to repair.

The officers and men of the vessels engaged have done their duty well, and will continue to do so.

All went well with us, save one sad exception: Captain Rodgers, my chief of staff, was killed, as well as Paymaster Woodbury, who was standing near him.

Captain Rodgers had more than once asked, on this occasion, if he should go with me as usual, or resume the command of his vessel, the Catskill, and he repeated the query twice in the morning, the last time on the deck of the Weehawken, just while preparing to move into action. In each instance I replied, "Do as you choose." He finally said, "Well, I will go in the Catskill, and the next time with you."

The Weehawken was lying about one thousand yards from Wagner, and the Catskill with my gallant friend just inside of me, the fire of the fort coming in steadily; observing the tide to have risen a little, I directed the Weehawken to be carried in closer, and the anchor was hardly weighed when I noticed that the Catskill was also under way, which I remarked to Captain Colhoun.

It occurred to me that Captain Rodgers detected the movement of the Weehawken, and was determined to be closer to the enemy if possible. My attention was called off immediately to a position for the Weehawken, and soon after it was reported that the Catskill was going out of action with signal flying that her captain was disabled; he had been killed instantly.

It is but natural that I should feel deeply the loss thus sustained, for the close and confidential relation which the duties of fleet-captain necessarily occasions, impressed me deeply with the loss of Captain Rodgers. Brave, intelligent, and highly capable, devoted to his duty and to the flag under which he passed his life, the country cannot afford to lose such men; of a kind and generous nature, he was always prompt to give relief when he could.

I have directed that all respect be paid to his remains, and the country will not, I am sure, omit honor to the memory of one who has not spared his life in her hour of trial.

I have the honor to be, very respectfully, your obedient servant,

JOHN A. DAHLGREN,
Rear-Admiral, Commanding S. A. B. Squadron.

Hon. GIDEON WELLES,
Secretary of the Navy, Washington, D. C.

Letter of Admiral Dahlgren, transmitting notes of the engagement taken by Flag-Lieutenant Moreau Forrest.

FLAG-STEAMER PHILADELPHIA,
Off Morris Island, August 19, 1863.

SIR: I enclose herewith, for your information, notes taken by Flag-Lieutenant Moreau Forrest during the engagement of the 17th instant, and also copies of reports showing the state of the marine battalion, and from commanding officer of the Catskill.

I have the honor to be, very respectfully, your obedient servant,

J. A. DAHLGREN,
Rear-Admiral, Commanding S. A. B. Squadron.

Hon. GIDEON WELLES,
Secretary of the Navy, Washington, D. C.

Notes of the engagement on Monday, August 17, 1863.

At 5.30 a. m. the admiral and his staff, Fleet Captain George W. Rodgers, Flag-Lieutenant Moreau Forrest, and Ensign Larue P. Adams, left the United States steamer Dinsmore, and at 5.40 flag was hoisted aboard the United States iron-clad Weehawken. Fleet Captain George W. Rodgers then left to take command of the United States iron-clad Catskill.

6.15.—Flag under way, and steaming up the channel to the buoy abreast Fort Wagner.

6.35.—All the Monitors under way, steaming up the channel.

6.40.—Flag anchored a little below and about seven hundred yards from Wagner.

6.45.—Flag opened with XI-inch shell at Wagner.

6.48.—First shot from Wagner at flag passed over.

6.49.—Weehawken opened with XV-inch shell.

6.52.—Ironsides opened fire a little high. At this time the shore batteries were delivering a telling fire on Sumter.

6.54.—Montauk opened a little astern of flag.

6.60.—Wagner firing grape and musketry at the Monitors.

7.03.—Wagner struck flag's deck.

7.05.—Wagner fired twice, one striking flag, the other passing through the smoke-stack of Ironsides.

7.12.—Ironsides apparently under way, as if to shift berth or insure swinging the right way.

7.16.—Nahant opened fire.

7.18.—Another shot through Weehawken's smoke-stack.

7.25.—Signalled to Ironsides—firing too high.

7.29.—Moultrie opened at Ironsides, making very good practice.

7.40.—Catskill anchored a little inshore of the flag.

7.42.—Catskill opened.

8.00.—Mahaska opened.

8.05.—All the wooden gunboats in action.

8.06.—Moultrie struck on top of Ironsides's deck.

8.08.—Passaic opened.

8.20.—Patapsco opened.

8.25.—Flag under way; and having shifted berth nearly to the battery, anchored.

8.35.—Catskill under way, moving a little further off.

8.50.—Catskill made signal "Captain is disabled," and went out of action.

9.20.—The firing from Wagner ceased.

9.30.—Flag ceased firing. The gunboats still firing slowly.

10.00.—Flag under way and moving towards Passaic, to which vessel the admiral shifted his flag, the enemy's sharpshooters keeping up a brisk fire.

10.05.—The flag being hoisted on the Passaic, the Passaic, accompanied by the Patapsco, headed up the channel and rounded to about eighteen hundred yards from Sumter.

10.30.—Passaic opened with rifle and struck the top of Sumter.

10.32.—Gregg opened on flag, shot passing over.

10 42.—Moultrie opened on flag and Patapsco.

10.44.—Patapsco opened on Sumter, making fine practice.

10.50.—Flag struck twice by Gregg.

11.05.—Catskill resumed position, firing slowly at Wagner and Gregg.

11.15.—Sumter opened.

12.00.—Montauk made signal that her small gun was disabled.

12.10.—Came down from action to go to dinner, and ordered the other vessels to do the same. As we passed the Catskill, learned that Fleet Captain George W. Rodgers and Assistant Paymaster Woodbury had been killed.

At 12.40 p. m. hoisted the flag aboard the Dinsmore.

Very respectfully,

MOREAU FORREST,
Flag-Lieutenant.

Rear-Admiral JOHN A. DAHLGREN, U. S. N.,
Commanding S. A. B. Squadron.

UNITED STATES IRON-CLAD CATSKILL,
Off Morris Island, August 17, 1863.

SIR: I have the honor to submit to you the following report of the action to-day:

About 7.30 steamed up abreast of Fort Wagner and anchored. Captain Rodgers, chief of staff, in charge, opened fire on the works, which was returned heavily.

About 8.30 a shot struck the top of the pilot-house, fracturing the outer plate and tearing off an irregular piece of the inside plate of about one square foot in area, and forcing out several of the bolts by which the two thicknesses are held together, pieces of which struck Captain George W. Rodgers and Acting Assistant Paymaster J. G. Woodbury, killing them instantly, also wounding the pilot, Mr. Penton, and Acting Master's Mate Trescott; after which I hove up the anchor, steamed down to the tug Dandelion, transferred them to her, and returned, taking position astern of the Weehawken; continued the fire until signal was made to withdraw.

We were struck, in all, thirteen times. The smoke-box of XV-inch gun is gradually becoming weaker, the angle iron around the bottom and eight or ten bolts having been broken off to-day, the other side being so badly sprung that the bolts cannot be replaced. The inside bearing of the after truck of XI-inch gun came off at the first discharge; was temporarily repaired, so as to use the gun, but found the axle to be broken; used it with a slide.

Enclosed I send the report of Dr. Abbott, of this vessel.

I am, very respectfully, your obedient servant,

CHARLES C. CARPENTER,
Lieutenant Commanding.

Rear-Admiral J. A. DAHLGREN,
Commanding S. A. B. Squadron.

UNITED STATES IRON-CLAD CATSKILL,
Off Morris Island, August 17, 1863.

SIR: I respectfully report the following casualties which occurred on board this vessel during the engagement this day with Fort Sumter and the Morris island batteries. These injuries were all caused by a single shot, which struck the top of the pilot-house and shattered the inner plating.

Killed.—Commander George W. Rodgers; Acting Assistant Paymaster Josiah G. Woodbury.

Wounded.—Pilot Abner C. Penton, wound of scalp, slight; Acting Master's Mate Peter Trescott, concussion, slight.

Very respectfully, your obedient servant,

SAMUEL W. ABBOTT,
Assistant Surgeon.

Lieutenant Commander C. C. CARPENTER,
Commanding United States Iron-clad Catskill.

UNITED STATES NAVAL BATTERY,
August 17, 1863.

SIR: I have the honor to inform you that I fired to-day from this battery one hundred and seventy shells and one hundred and twenty-five solid shot, the greater portion of which struck the face of Sumter or its parapet.

By making officers and men "cover" when shot or shell were passing over the battery, I avoided, through the mercy of a kind Providence, all casualties. The officers who were with me, Lieutenant Brower, Ensign Wallace, and Acting Ensign Owens, and the men, deserve great credit for their laborious exertions of fifteen hours under a burning sun.

Very respectfully,

FOXHALL A. PARKER, *Commander.*

Rear-Admiral J. A. DAHLGREN,
Commanding South Atlantic Blockading Squadron.

UNITED STATES STEAMER NEW IRONSIDES,
Off Morris Island, August 21, 1863.

SIR: I enclose herewith the report of Mr. Bishop, carpenter of this ship, showing the damage sustained by the fire of Forts Wagner and Gregg during the action of the 17th instant.

I also enclose the report of Lieutenant Robeson, ordnance officer, of the firing at Wagner, Gregg, and Sumter, on the 17th, 18th, 19th, and 20th instant.

I have the honor to be, very respectfully, your obedient servant,

S. C. ROWAN,
Captain Commanding.

Rear-Admiral DAHLGREN,
Commanding South Atlantic Blockading Squadron,
Flag-Ship Philadelphia, Off Morris Island.

UNITED STATES SHIP NEW IRONSIDES,
Off Morris Island, August 16, 1863.

SIR: I have the honor to make the following report respecting the injuries received by this ship in the action of to-day. I count, in all, thirty-one hits, though I think we were struck several times below the water-line. The plating received nineteen shots, eleven others struck the wood work, and eight passed through the smoke-stack. No material damage was done to the armor, though in four places the iron was so much crushed in as to crack it. The backing, except in one place where one width of the ceiling, just forward of No. 6 port on the starboard side, is driven in about three-fourths of an inch, shows no signs of having been started. The forward shutter of No. 3 port on the starboard side was shot off and lost overboard, having been struck on its upper edge near the pivot on which it swung. One shot came through the wood work on the starboard quarter into the cabin, and passed down into the wardroom, tearing out a large piece of the clamps in one of the cabin state-rooms, ripping up the coaming of the wardroom hatch, and splintering the beam underneath. One of the wheel ropes, which ran through the beam, barely escaped being cut away by this shot.

Another shot struck the deck, unprotected by sand bags, just abaft the parterners of the mizzenmast, going through the planking and glancing off as it met the iron underneath.

The iron, however, was crushed down to the depth of an inch and a half, and partially broken.

The deck pump on the starboard quarter was carried away, and the shot striking the sand bags, glanced forward and remained on deck, but the knee supporting the beam underneath the place where the sand bags lay was split, and one of the carlins broken.

All these hits were made by 10-inch solid shot, which seemed to have been fired with exceedingly heavy charges, some of them at a distance of not more than from nine hundred to one thousand yards.

Very respectfully,

T. H. BISHOP, *Carpenter.*

Captain S. C. ROWAN,
Commanding U. S. Steamer New Ironsides.

Engagement with Fort Sumter.

FLAG-STEAMER PHILADELPHIA,
Off Morris Island, August 23, 1863.

SIR: This morning, before daylight, I moved the five Monitors to about 800 yards from Sumter, and opened fire upon it. A fog arose, which prevented us from seeing the work a part of the time; nevertheless, much damage must have been done to its southeast and northeast faces.

Sumter only replied with six shots, but Moultrie, with its extended lines of earthworks, opened heavily, and struck the Monitors frequently with heavy shot. The Weehawken, in which was my flag, received two blows on the pilot-house, which were more forcible than any I have seen, owing, probably, to the diminished distance.

Notwithstanding the difficulties of manœuvring during the night in a channel edged with shoals, only one of the Monitors got aground, but extricated herself.

About 6 o'clock, the men being much exhausted by the labor of two successive days and nights, I drew off in full daylight under the steady fire of Fort Moultrie.

It is now blowing from the southeast, and when it subsides I propose passing Sumter into the harbor, if the obstructions are not of such a nature as to prevent it. The returns from all the vessels have not yet been received, so that I am unable to render a full statement in detail at this time.

The gorge of Sumter has been completely ruined by the severe fire of the shore batteries, which has also reached the other faces of the work, and must have dismounted most of their barbette guns, besides seriously injuring the walls themselves. In this the naval battery of four rifled cannon has participated, under Captain F. A. Parker.

I have the honor to be, very respectfully, your obedient servant,

J. A. DAHLGREN,
Rear-Admiral, Commanding S. A. B. Squadron.

Hon. GIDEON WELLES,
Secretary of the Navy, Washington, D. C.

P. S.—Fort Wagner is quite as strong as ever, perhaps more so. The trenches have, however, been pushed quite close to it, and an assault may again take place before long. Battery Gregg is also unimpaired.

Notes of the engagement, taken by Flag-Lieutenant Moreau Forrest.

FLAG-STEAMER PHILADELPHIA,
Off Morris Island, August 24, 1863.

SIR: I enclose herewith, for your information, notes taken by Flag-Lieutenant Forrest, of the engagement on the morning of the 23d instant.

I have the honor to be, very respectfully, your obedient servant,

J. A. DAHLGREN,
Rear-Admiral, Commanding S. A. B. Squadron.

Hon. GIDEON WELLES,
Secretary of the Navy, Washington, D. C.

Notes of the engagement with Fort Sumter on the night of the 22d of August, 1863.

11.05 p. m.—Admiral, accompanied by his staff, Flag-Lieutenant Forrest, Ensign Adams, and the pilot, left flag-steamer Philadelphia, and at 11.30 hoisted the flag on the Weehawken.

11.40.—Under way, and sent tug to other Monitors to tell them to get under way.

11.50.—Heading up the channel, accompanied by Montauk and Nahant.

12.—Shoved alongside Patapsco, and told him to proceed, whilst flag hailed Ironsides to show a red light as soon as the firing commenced.

12.30.—At the lower buoy.

1.—Hailed Passaic, and shortly afterwards Patapsco, to tell them that flag would take the extreme left.

1.15.—Anchored.

1.30.—Flag weighed anchor and headed for the upper buoy.

2.—Saw the lights flashed by Ensign Porter at upper buoy and headed for them.

2.30.—By the upper buoy. Ensign Porter came aboard.

2.45.—Anchored near Sumter, and sent Porter to tell the other Monitors to anchor on our right in a line extending towards Moultrie.

2.55.—All the Monitors anchored. The Passaic on our right, the Patapsco on our left, the Montauk on our extreme right, the Nahant just astern of flag, flag being about 900 yards from Sumter.

3.03.—Flag fired first shot at Sumter, XI″.

3.10.—Flag fired XV″.

3.15.—Montauk opened.

3.20.—Passaic opened.

3.30.—Patapsco opened and the firing became general. The practice was very good; the heavy thugs distinctly heard as the shot struck the fort.

3.20.—Sumter fired first gun at flag, just after sending up rocket; passed over.

3.45.—Gregg opened on flag.

4.10.—Heavy fog came over from Moultrie completely enveloping the fort. Flag fired in the direction, however, having taken its bearing under a star. Hailed the Patapsco and Passaic, giving them the bearing, and told them to do the same.

4.15.—Flag moved up, about 150 yards, towards Sumter.

4.20.—Fog having lifted, Moultrie opened with a heavy fire on the Monitors.

4.30.—Flag struck by Moultrie, and quartermaster wounded.

5.—Another fog-bank came over, accompanied by a breeze from the eastward that swung the ships, and we had to suspend operations again.

5.20.—Resumed firing again and fired until 6.10, at which time there being no signs of the fog lifting, and it being broad daylight, flag got under way and moved down towards the lower buoy. In passing, hailed the Monitors to follow flag down in line.

6.30.—Made signal "withdraw from action."

6.40.—At lower buoy. Monitors taking their positions for coming down under a heavy fire from Moultrie, Bee, and Beauregard, which batteries continued their fire until we had passed well down below the Ironsides. In looking at the fort it appeared to be very severely battered on the sea-coast wall.

7.—Admiral and staff took a tug, and at 7.20 hoisted the flag on board the Philadelphia.

I have the honor to be, very respectfully, &c., &c.

MOREAU FORREST,
Flag-Lieutenant.

Rear-Admiral J. A. DAHLGREN,
Commanding South Atlantic Blockading Squadron.

Engagement with Forts Sumter and Moultrie.

FLAG-STEAMER PHILADELPHIA,
Off Morris Island, September 2, 1863.

SIR: The present condition of affairs here, so far as my information extends, may be stated thus:

The siege batteries of General Gillmore opened on Sumter on the 17th and continued in operation through the week. The distance of the batteries from the object exceeded anything of the kind hitherto attempted in such operations.

By the expiration of the week the work was ruined. The gorge was completely cut down, and the guns on the other faces almost entirely disabled.

It was a new illustration of the engineering art, and will always be deemed a great triumph for General Gillmore. Without regard to further results, I think he has already handsomely earned his next step in rank.

Having thus rendered Sumter useless to the confederate system of defences here, it still remains to turn the acquisition fully to account. A glance at the map, and at the means at disposal, will show that the entire advantage cannot yet be realized to ourselves, because we cannot occupy the fort.

The army is unable to do it unless possession of Fort Wagner is had; nor the navy, without forcing the defences by water in the shape of obstructions protected by Fort Moultrie, and under its full range, even to Sumter.

General Gillmore is actively engaged on the one, and deems the naval aid indispensable to success. I have agreed to render all that I have. This necessarily compels me to forego an immediate move on the obstructions. I had already begun, however, and some progress had been made.

On the night of the 1st of September I moored the Ironsides and Monitors up the channel before midnight, just before the flood tide had ceased.

The first purpose was to make sure that Sumter had no guns to fire on us. It was believed that they had remounted a few on the NE. and NW. faces. At my request General Gillmore had resumed fire yesterday; and in the evening notified me that he knocked down some four or five pieces that were perceived on the more remote fronts.

The nearest approach was about 500 yards with the Monitors, my flag being in the Weehawken; but so great was the force of the tide, that it was half past eleven o'clock before the first shot was fired by the Weehawken.

We lay right off the angle of the NE. and SE. fronts. Being much occupied in the movements of the vessels, I did not perceive that Sumter fired; but Flag-Lieutenant Preston saw distinctly two shots fired from a gun on the eastern angle.

The firing was steadily maintained from all the Monitors, which were well handled.

The Ironsides was brought up to a good range, and joined in the action.

Meanwhile Moultrie opened a rapid and sustained fire from its extended line, which told with effect; the obscurity of the night, however, interfered with their accuracy of aim at objects so small as the turrets.

Our fire was also directed at the floating obstructions that had been reported from day to day.

I should have wished to remain after daylight, so as to have had a good view of the scene of operations, but the flood tide set in before daylight, which would have exposed the Monitors unnecessarily, so I withdrew, leaving it to another morning to prosecute the matter.

The vessels were engaged for five hours, and in that time fired two hundred and forty-five shots, and received in all seventy-one hits; of these, the Ironsides fired fifty, and received seven.

The enemy fired some shot of wedge shape, samples of which were picked up on the decks of the Lehigh—an absurd practice, originating in the brain of some wild inventor. A round shot struck the base of the Weehawken's (flag) turret, and drove in a fragment of iron, which struck Fleet Captain Badger on the leg and broke it short—so that I have lost three flag-captains in the short space of two months, which has embarrassed me beyond measure in the transaction of public business; Captain Taylor went home sick, Captain Rodgers was killed in action, and now Captain Badger is badly wounded.

I shall feel greatly the loss of Captain Badger's service at this time. He has been with me for more than eight years, and his sterling qualities have rendered him one of the very best ordnance officers in the navy. I hope his disability may be short.

The commanders of the iron-clads—Captain S. C. Rowan, Commander Thomas H. Stevens, Commander A. Bryson, Commander E. R. Colhoun, Lieutenant Commander E. Simpson, Lieutenant Commander J. L. Davis, and Lieutenant Commander J. J. Cornwell—handled their vessels with ability in the narrow channel and the obscurity of the night.

I should have resumed operations with a view of forcing a passage, but General Gillmore is now ready for another movement, and I propose to assist him first.

I have the honor to be, very respectfully, your obedient servant,

JNO. A. DAHLGREN,
Rear-Admiral, Commanding S. A. B. Squadron.

Hon. GIDEON WELLES,
Secretary of the Navy, Washington, D. C.

Evacuation of Fort Wagner and Battery Gregg.

UNITED STATES FLAG-SHIP PHILADELPHIA,
Off Morris Island, S. C., September 7, 1863.

SIR: The enemy evacuated Fort Wagner and Battery Gregg during the night. An assault was to have been made at nine (9) a. m. this morning, preparatory to which a steady cannonade was maintained all of yesterday from the trenches and the Ironsides. A deserter gave notice to General Gillmore of the evacuation. I have demanded Sumter to surrender, being no longer defensible, and am waiting an answer from Charleston. If in the negative, I shall move at once on it and the obstructions. A Monitor has already taken position.

I have the honor to be, very respectfully, your obedient servant,

J. A. DAHLGREN,
Rear-Admiral, Commanding S. A. B. Squadron.

Hon. GIDEON WELLES,
Secretary of the Navy.

Engagement with forts in Charleston harbor.

FLAG-STEAMER PHILADELPHIA,
Off Morris Island, September 8, 1863.

SIR: I have already informed you, by express despatch, that the enemy evacuated the whole of Morris island yesterday morning, just previous to an assault. I immediately designed to put in operation a plan to capture Fort Sumter, and, as a preliminary, ordered the Weehawken to pass in by a narrow channel, winding about Cummings's Point, so as to cut off all communication by that direction. In so doing the Weehawken grounded, and though at low water, did not succeed in floating at the next high tide.

Late in the day, at the proper time, I went on board the Ironsides, and moved up with the iron-clads to feel and, if possible, pass the obstructions north of Sumter. Moultrie and batteries Bee and Beauregard quickly opened on us, and soon experienced a severe fire from our vessels, which was continued until I deemed it best to give entire attention to the Weehawken. Steam-tugs and hawsers were provided amply, but at the high tide of this morning did not succeed in floating her. About 7 a. m. the enemy perceived her condition and began to fire from Moultrie, about two thousand yards distant. I ordered up the iron-clads to cover the Weehawken, which, meanwhile, gallantly replied, and, in less than an hour's firing, blew up one of the enemy's magazines, which was recognized by a cheer from the men of our vessels near me. Some movement in Sumter seemed to draw attention from the Weehawken, which, with a few well-directed shells, settled that business.

Captain Colhoun has, in my opinion, more than compensated for the misfortune of getting aground by the handsome manner in which he has retorted on the adversary and defended the glorious flag that floats above him. At 11½ a. m. I telegraphed to him: "Well done, Weehawken. Don't give up the ship." We may lose the services of this vessel—I hope not—but the honor of the flag will be maintained.

It is proper to say that the iron-clads have been navigated under the most disadvantageous circumstances. They really have not had pilots. Mr Godfrey has left us, and Mr. Haffords fell off the turret at night, being the only real pilots in this squadron. The Monitors have been aground several times in action, and it is surprising that some of them have not been lost.

I have the honor to be, very respectfully, your obedient servant,

J. A. DAHLGREN,

Rear-Admiral, Commanding S. A. B. Squadron.

Hon. GIDEON WELLES,
Secretary of the Navy, Washington, D. C.

P. S.—6 p. m. I am happy to say that at high water the Weehawken was gotten off. I commend Captain Colhoun, his officers and crew, to the notice of the department. The crews of the other vessels cheered spontaneously as he passed.

J. A. D.

Report of Commander E. R. Colhoun, commanding the Weehawken.

UNITED STATES IRON-CLAD WEEHAWKEN,
Off Fort Wagner, S. C., September 9, 1863.

SIR: On the 7th instant, in obedience to your order, I proceeded with the Weehawken to buoy out the channel inside the buoy off Fort Wagner, in the direction of Cummings's Point. After passing the buoy off Wagner about 200 yards, I dropped a buoy in seventeen feet water, and again, 400 yards further on, a second one in fifteen feet water, steering up nearly midway between Cummings's Point and Sumter. I anchored at 8.30 a. m., about 300 yards from the last buoy, it being then nearly low water. At 9.30 a. m. she swung to the flood tide, and the channel being narrow, she touched bottom very lightly in eleven feet water. When the tide had risen sufficiently to float her I got under way, in obedience to your order, to "return to my anchorage near the New Ironsides," but in consequence of the shoal water she steered very badly; taking a "rank sheer" to port, she brought up on the bank in eleven feet water. In the afternoon, at high water, I failed to get her off, as also on the following morning, though every effort was made by taking coal and shot out, with one tug to assist us.

At 8.30 a. m. Fort Moultrie opened on us, the lower part of the overhang on the port side being then nearly out of water. As we lay upon the bank Fort Moultrie was nearly on our port beam. She fired slowly and deliberately at first to get the range, aiming under the overhang, then with rapidity, followed by other batteries on Sullivan's island. This I had expected and was ready for. I had been on deck from early in the morning, and had given orders to let the men sleep after their hard work during the night. We opened in a few minutes on Moultrie. The second shell from the XV-inch gun exploded a magazine to the left of the flag-staff, and she, was silent for some time. When the Ironsides and Monitors engaged the batteries they ceased firing at us. I then sent the men to breakfast, and after they had finished, opened on Sumter. When the Ironsides and Monitors withdrew from action they let the Weehawken alone.

I then made my preparations to get afloat at high water in the afternoon, and succeeded, though under a heavy fire from Sullivan's island and Fort Simkins on James island. I had three men wounded by a shot from battery Bee, striking on top of the turret, breaking the plating and railroad iron—one, John O. Grady, ordinary seaman, severely in the left thigh. I enclose herewith Assistant Surgeon E. M. Stein's report. We were hit twenty-four times, doing no material damage. One shot struck the lower part of the overhang, passed under, made a hole about three inches in diameter, and fractured the iron from the angles. The leak was soon stopped. We fired at Moultrie and battery Bee 36 shell; at Sumter 46—total 82.

The officers and men under my command deserve the highest praise for their behavior. Such a measure of endurance, patriotism, and valor as I have seen exhibited since I have been in command assures me they cannot be excelled.

Very respectfully, your obedient servant,

EDWIN R. COLHOUN, *Commander.*

Rear-Admiral J. A. DAHLGREN,
Commanding S. A. B. Squadron.

Report of Assistant Surgeon Stein of casualties on the Weehawken.

UNITED STATES STEAMER IRON-CLAD WEEHAWKEN,
Off Charleston, S. C., September 9, 1863.

SIR: I have to report to you that whilst this vessel was lying ashore off Cummings's Point yesterday afternoon, a shot from battery Bee struck her on the top of the turret, breaking off several pieces of railroad iron, which wounded the following three men, who were standing inside the turret at the time:

John O. Grady, ordinary seaman, fracture of the left thigh and slight wound near right arm; Edward Christiansen, ordinary seaman, wounded slightly in the left foot; Bernard Cassidy, landsman, wounded slightly in the breast and right leg.

Very respectfully, your obedient servant,

EDWIN M. STEIN,
Assistant Surgeon United States Navy.

Commander E. R. COLHOUN,
Commanding United States Steamer Weehawken.

Additional reports relative to the attack upon the forts on the 8th of September.

[Despatch No. 77.]

FLAG-STEAMER HARVEST MOON,
Port Royal Harbor, S. C., February 26, 1864.

SIR: I herewith transmit, for the information of the department, reports of Captain C. W. Pickering, of the Canandaigua; Lieutenant Commander F. M. Bunce, of the Patapsco; Lieutenant F. J. Higginson, of the Housatonic; Acting Master Commanding Benjamin C. Dean, of the Dan Smith; and Acting Master Commanding J. P. Carr, of the Daffodil, of their respective participation in the assault upon Sumter on the night of the 8th of September last.

These reports were not received until some time subsequent to my despatch upon the subject, and I now forward them in justice to all the officers concerned.

I have the honor to be, very respectfully, your obedient servant,

J. A. DAHLGREN,
Rear-Admiral, Commanding S. A. B. Squadron.

Hon. GIDEON WELLES,
Secretary of the Navy, Washington, D. C.

UNITED STATES STEAMSHIP HOUSATONIC,
Off Charleston, S. C., October 3, 1863.

SIR: In forwarding the enclosed report from Ensign Craven, I would state, in reference to the Housatonic's second launch, alluded to as not having been brought into action, that I have interrogated the cockswain of that launch upon the subject, who states as follows:

The launch had been employed for several days previous in the creek. Half of her crew, being sick, were put on board the flag-ship Philadelphia, and six marines with a sergeant took their place. There was *no officer* in charge of the boat, and none of the crew knew anything of their destination further than the fact that an attack was to be made *somewhere.* The tug, in approaching Sumter with the boats in tow, swept around a buoy, fouled the boats and cast them off. In the confusion which ensued, the launch followed the lead of the Housatonic's first launch, which was manned with a crew from the Powhatan, with no officer in charge. These two launches, instead of going to Fort Sumter, went alongside the Philadelphia; and from thence were ordered to the fort. Upon getting within forty or fifty yards of the fort, the cockswain of the second launch states that the sergeant told them that they had better go back; that there was no one to tell them where to go, and that they would only get shot—that some of the boats were already retreating, &c.

Whereupon the second launch alluded to in the report pulled for the Ironsides, where she made fast until the next day.

I am, respectfully, your obedient servant,

C. W. PICKERING, *Captain.*

Rear-Admiral J. A. DAHLGREN,
Commanding S. A. B. Squadron.

UNITED STATES IRON-CLAD PATAPSCO,
Port Royal, September 23, 1863.

SIR: I have the honor to acknowledge the receipt of your communication of the 21st instant.

In obedience to its requirements, I would state that I left the flag-steamer at 11 p. m., and with the other boats, in tow of a tug, stood up towards Fort Sumter.

After communicating with the two Monitors on picket, we were towed to within about nine hundred yards of Fort Sumter. The boats were then formed in three columns; Lieutenant Higgenson with his column was ordered to move up the northwest face; the other two columns to close up and move up towards Sumter.

As we approached the fort many of the boats gave way strongly and landed. The order was then given to push for the fort, and all gave way.

The foremost boats were received by a heavy fire of musketry, hand grenades, &c., from the fort. Moultrie and some of the Sullivan's island batteries also opened, together with one of the rebel gunboats. We pushed in till the boat grounded, and it became perfectly apparent that there was no footing for the men, nor any means of scaling the high walls. The order was then given for all boats to withdraw, and after some little delay all, as I supposed, had shoved off. We then withdrew to the tug, where a large number of boats were already collected.

I have the honor to be, very respectfully, your obedient servant,

FRANCIS M. BUNCE,
Lieutenant Commander, United States Navy.

Rear-Admiral JOHN A. DAHLGREN,
Comd'g S. A. B. S., Flag-ship Philadelphia, off Charleston, S. C.

In forwarding this report, I have to state that Ensign C. H. Craven is too sick to make the report required of him.

C. W. PICKERING, *Captain.*

UNITED STATES STEAMER HOUSATONIC,
Off Charleston, S. C., September 21, 1863.

SIR: I have the honor to make the following report of the part taken by the boats under my command in the naval assault on Fort Sumter on the 8th of September, 1863.

After casting off from the tug, I pulled up to the northeast face of the fort, in obedience to my instructions. I succeeded in reaching the fort without being seen, and immediately attempted to land.

I found myself upon a narrow ledge of sharp rocks, in which no foothold could be obtained. My boats were in danger of getting stove, and after several ineffectual attempts I withdrew.

I then pulled around to the southeast face, and found the boats were in retreat. Picking up a boat in which there were but two men, I pulled out. As I was pulling up to the northeast face, I observed a steamer close to the fort on my right. Whether she was an iron-clad vessel or a river steamer, I am unable to state. My impression is that she was the latter. As I neared the fort she steamed quietly away towards Charleston.

Very respectfully, your obedient servant,

F. J. HIGGINSON, *Lieutenant.*

Rear-Admiral J. A. DAHLGREN,
Flag-Steamer Philadelphia, off Morris Island, S. C.

UNITED STATES SCHOONER DAN SMITH,
Off Morris Island, S. C., September 9, 1863.

SIR: I would most respectfully beg leave to transmit the following report: At 6 p. m. on the 8th instant I received an order from the fleet captain to send two of my boats with men armed with revolvers and cutlasses.

At 7.30 p. m. I sent Acting Master's Mate Jacob C. Van Deventer, in charge of first and second cutters, with twelve men, armed as per order, to report to fleet captain.

At 4.15 a. m. Acting Master's Mate J. C. Van Deventer, returned in first cutter, after having reported on board flag-ship, whose report you will please find enclosed.

I have also to report that the second cutter has not returned, and that the following named crew are missing, namely: William Dowden, boatswain's mate; Alexander Clark, carpenter's mate; Henry B. Middleton, master-at-arms; Richard Kaine, ordinary seaman; Francis Swift, landsman.

At 12.15 a. m. I sent gig and four men on board flag-ship, which returned at 7.30 a. m.

Hoping this may meet your approval, sir, I remain, very respectfully, your obedient servant,

BENJAMIN C. DEAN,
Acting Master, Commanding.

Rear-Admiral JOHN A. DAHLGREN, U. S. N.,
Commanding South Atlantic Blockading Squadron.

UNITED STATES STEAMER DAFFODIL,
Off Morris Island, S. C., September 10, 1863.

SIR: In obedience to your order, I have the honor to make the following report. At 9 o'clock and thirty minutes on the 8th instant, by order of Captain Stevens, I left the flag-ship, with twenty-five boats in tow. We stopped at the Montauk, and Captain Stevens went on board of her. In fifteen minutes he returned, and ordered me to proceed up to the Patapsco. He went on board of her. In twenty minutes he returned, and put his pilot on board, and ordered me to proceed to Fort Sumter. At eleven o'clock and thirty minutes was within a quarter of a mile of Fort Sumter, in eight feet of water, which I reported to Captain Stevens. He then said he wanted to go nearer. I told him I could not go any nearer, as we had already touched the bottom. He then ordered me to go up to the picket Monitor, which I did, and he went on board. In a short time he returned, and took his pilot into the boat. He then ordered me to go toward Fort Sumter again, which I did; and after getting within a quarter of a mile of the fort, and in eight feet of water, I reported it to him. He ordered the boats to cast off from the steamer, and told me to come to an anchor, and wait for the boats to tow them out. After coming a short distance I saw the Philadelphia, and told them they would be ashore if they went twice their length further. I was then near the small buoy off the point of the flats near Sumter. About 2 o'clock I came to anchor in two and three-quarters fathoms of water. About 3 o'clock Captain Stevens came alongside, and ordered me to leave with the boats in tow, and take them to the steamer Memphis and leave them, which I did.

I am, respectfully, your obedient servant,

JOHN P. CARR,
Acting Master, Commanding Daffodil.

Rear-Admiral J. A. DAHLGREN,
Commanding S. A. B. Squadron, off Morris Island, S. C.

Injuries to the Monitors.

[Despatch No. 130.]

FLAG-STEAMER PHILADELPHIA,
Off Morris Island, September 8, 1863.

SIR: Conformably to your directions, I will cause weekly reports to be made of the injuries sustained by the iron-clads.

The heavy shot fired which have struck have generally been 10-inch, and are well borne at 1,200 yards; but when the distance is less than 1,000 yards there is a marked difference.

The shot which struck the top of the Catskill's pilot-house on a glance, killing Captain Rodgers and Paymaster Woodbury, must have been a 10-inch. To prevent similar accidents, the plate should be strengthened and have an interior lining.

The shot which struck the turret of the Weehawken at the base came from Moultrie, and was probably a 10-inch. It detached a portion of the interior lining, which broke Captain Badger's leg.

The decks always suffer severely, and two or three of the Monitors are now in need of repairs from this cause.

The Catskill has been eighteen days at Port Royal under repairs; when she returns another will be sent.

Ensign Johnson was slightly hurt last night in the turret by a bolt.

I am, very respectfully, your obedient servant,

J. A. DAHLGREN,
Rear-Admiral Commanding S. A. B. Squadron.

Hon. GIDEON WELLES,
Secretary of the Navy, Washington, D. C.

Services of the New Ironsides against the defences of Charleston.

FLAG-STEAMER PHILADELPHIA,
Off Morris Island, September 15, 1863.

SIR: I enclose herewith the reports concerning the part taken by the Ironsides in some of the recent actions, and concur with Captain Rowan in the estimate he takes of the services of the ship and ship's company, in which I consider himself as most conspicuous.

The spar deck, not included in the armor, exhibits evidence of the severe fire to which the vessel has been exposed.

I have the honor to be, very respectfully, your obedient servant,

J. A. DAHLGREN,
Rear-Admiral, Commanding S. A. B. Squadron.

Hon. GIDEON WELLES,
Secretary of the Navy, Washington, D. C.

Report of Captain S. C. Rowan.

UNITED STATES STEAMER NEW IRONSIDES,
Off Fort Wagner, Morris Island, S. C., September 10, 1863.

SIR: The Weehawken being hard aground off the pass between Sumter and Cummings's Point, the batteries from Fort Moultrie opened upon her. In obedience to orders, I moved this ship up (casting off the Memphis, which was at the time supplying me with shell) and anchored off buoy No. 3, interposing my ship, and completely covering the Weehawken from the fire of the enemy. The moment we anchored and commenced swinging head on to Fort Moultrie, the enemy opened a concentrated fire upon us which was terrific. Fortunately, however, we succeeded in getting her port broadside to bear by the time he had gotten our range. We opened slowly at first to get range on Moultrie, when I directed a very spirited and concentrated fire on that fort, which compelled it to slacken. I soon discovered that we suffered severely from their other batteries of 10-inch guns, between Moultrie and Beauregard, when I directed two guns to be opened on each of them. One of the heaviest guns in their works was dismounted, and the fire of the others sensibly slackened. I then directed one gun to continue rapid fire on each of these forts, and directed the remaining fire to open on Moultrie. The fire of all the forts slackened down to an occasional gun, when I directed a slow fire to be kept up to economize shell. The moment the enemy discovered this, he jumped from behind his sand bags and opened rapidly. I renewed our rapid fire and silenced him again. Having but thirty shells left, I directed the anchor to be weighed, keeping up a well-directed fire from such guns as were not rendered unavailable in working the cables and anchors, and so withdrew from action (for want of ammunition) without further molestation, after one of the severest artillery duels ever sustained by a ship through a space of two hours and fifty-five minutes.

It affords me great pleasure to bear testimony to the fine bearing, zeal, and gallantry of the divisional officers—Lieutenant H. B. Robeson, Acting Master George W. Domett, Acting Master John M. Skillings, Acting Ensign Charles W. Howard, and Ensign Benjamin H. Porter.

The captains of guns and their spirited crews have my warmest thanks for the splendid manner in which they handled their guns. Paymaster Russell has my thanks for great zeal and ability in command of the powder and shell division. I particularly recommend to your notice, and that of the department, the services of Lieutenant Commander Belknap, to whose zeal and ability as executive officer I am so much indebted, for his untiring efforts to make the ship efficient in every department, and for his fine judgment and bearing in carrying out my orders as commander of the gun deck during the fourteen times this ship has been under the fire of the enemy's batteries.

The pilot, Mr. Benjamin Dorey, merits my thanks for the able manner in which he has handled this ship, particularly in working her up to Moultrie in the night without lights, bearings, or compass. * * * *

I am happy to say I have but few casualties. The surgeon's report of them is enclosed.

I have the honor to be, very respectfully, your obedient servant,

S. C. ROWAN,
Captain Commanding.

Rear-Admiral JOHN A. DAHLGREN,
Commanding S. A. B. Squadron.

Report of Surgeon M. Duvall of the casualties on the New Ironsides.

UNITED STATES SHIP NEW IRONSIDES,
Off Fort Wagner, South Carolina, September 11, 1863.

SIR: In obedience to your order, I have to report that, in the action recently with the forts on Sullivan's island, Acting Master G. W. Domett was wounded in the upper lip from a splinter overhead, which cut through the lip and struck the gum. This was a slight wound, which did not prevent Mr. Domett from directing his guns, nor has it interfered with his duty since.

George M. Knapp, seaman, attached to gun No. 5, was wounded in the glans penis and prepuce by a splinter of iron, which was either a fragment of a shot or of a shutter. This fragment came in between the shutters nearly closed. This is a slight wound, but it renders it necessary to keep the patient recumbent. William Connell, ordinary seaman, contusion of knee, from a lever in working No. 6 gun. Mild case; will be restored in short time.

Very respectfully,

MARIUS DUVALL, *Surgeon.*

Captain S. C. ROWAN,
Commanding New Ironsides.

Report of Executive Officer H. B. Robeson of the firing of the New Ironsides.

UNITED STATES NEW SHIP IRONSIDES,
Off Morris Island, South Carolina, September 8, 1863.

SIR: I have the honor to make the following report of the firing of this ship during the recent engagements with the rebel defences of Charleston:

Name of vessel.	Date.	Rounds fired.	Hits by enemy.	Distance.	Object.	Remarks.
				Yds.		
New Ironsides...	Sept. 6, 1863	38	....	1,300	Fort Wagner.	The report of Sept. 6 includes firing from meridian to sundown.
	Sept. 7, 1863	152	24	1,200	Fort Moultrie.	
	Sept. 8, 1863	183	70	1,200	....do........	

Very respectfully, your obedient servant,

H. B. ROBESON,
Lieutenant and Ordnance Officer.

Captain S. C. ROWAN,
Commanding New Ironsides.

Part taken by the Patapsco in attacks at Charleston.

UNITED STATES IRON-CLAD STEAMER PATAPSCO,
September 23, 1863.

SIR: In accordance with the orders of the Navy Department, I have to state that, during the time I have been in command of this vessel, she has been engaged with the batteries and defences of Charleston and its approaches six times.

On the 22d of August opened fire on Fort Wagner, and engaged, in company with the Monitor Weehawken, for about two hours without receiving any damage. On the 23d of August, in company with all the Monitors and the Ironsides, went up within 800 yards of Sumter, and engaged it for three and a half hours, under a strong fire from the enemy's defences, without receiving any material damage from their fire; and that, on the 31st of the same month, with the Monitor Weehawken, opened fire upon Fort Moultrie, at a distance of about 1,000 yards, for half an hour. Subsequently, being joined on the same day by the Passaic and Montauk, and occupying the same relative position, again attacked the batteries on Sullivan's island, without receiving any material injury, the Patapsco being hit seven times. This engagement lasted for about two hours, and was terminated by the signal order from the admiral to withdraw from action. Upon the night of the next day another demonstration, participated in by all the Monitors and Ironsides, was made upon Sumter, which lasted for about four hours, under a heavy cross-fire from the enemy's guns, when we were struck several times, without receiving any important injuries, except from one shot which penetrated the deck badly.

Upon the 7th of September, at 5.30 p. m., the iron-clads again got under way, with the exception of the Weehawken, aground, the intention being for this vessel to go as close to the obstructions as was prudent, for the purpose of inspecting them, while the other vessels engaged heavily the enemy. We succeeded in going within 150 yards of them, when we met with a terrific fire from Fort Moultrie and Battery Bee, with all the surrounding batteries, which we sustained for half an hour, when the Patapsco dropped down to where the Ironsides was anchored near Moultrie, and I went on board to report to the admiral.

During this engagement we were struck twenty-three times in as many minutes, the ship receiving some very considerable wounds. Two of the shot broke through the deck plank; one stove in the top of the pilot-house badly; while another, striking upon the edge of the turret, carried away two of the T-iron beams.

On the morning of the 8th of September all the iron-clads, with the Weehawken, then aground, excepted, moved up to attack the defences upon Sullivan's island. At 11 o'clock a. m. anchored nearly abreast of Fort Moultrie, and within 800 yards of it, and opened an enfilading fire upon Battery Bee, the batteries upon Sullivan's island replying briskly. At 1.30, just as the signal from the Ironsides was made to withdraw from action, the smoke-stack was nearly carried away and our engine disabled from the effect of one of our shot; hailed the Nahant and requested to be taken in tow, which was gallantly performed by Lieutenant Commander Cornwell, who towed us out of action, and we anchored near the Ironsides, which had dropped to seaward and out of range of the forts and fire of the enemy. We received three shots—one of which cut the shank and stock of the spare anchor, stowed abaft the turret in two, and carried the upper half overboard.

The health of the officers and crew of the Patapsco is excellent, and their performance in the several engagements we have had with the enemy all that could be desired.

While it must be admitted that the vessel is not so good as new, I think, when the repairs in progress are completed, she will be in a condition to do good service and give and take hard blows. The effect of the firing upon the men below has not been complained of.

Very respectfully, your obedient servant,

T. H. STEVENS, *Commander.*

Rear-Admiral J. A. DAHLGREN, U. S. N.,
Commanding South Atlantic Blockading Squadron.

Reports from officers commanding Monitors in South Atlantic blockading squadron relative to their condition.

[Despatch No. 159.]

FLAG-STEAMER PHILADELPHIA,
Off Morris Island, September 23, 1863.

SIR: This document should have gone on the 19th by the Fulton, if the commander of that vessel had been so polite as to wait five minutes longer. Enclosed are sundry documents furnishing more or less of the information called for by the department in relation to the condition of the Monitors, viz:

Report from Mr. Patrick Hughes, assistant inspector of iron-clads, Port Royal; Commander A. Bryson, Lehigh; Lieutenant Commander J. L. Davis, Montauk; Lieutenant Commander E. Simpson, Passaic; Lieutenant E. C. V. Blake, Catskill; Lieutenant Commander J. J. Cornwell, Nahant.

From which it will be seen that my movements are now stayed by the necessity of repairing the Monitors, otherwise I should be ready to resume operations as soon as the side-wheel steamer arrives here. The department no doubt understands that this operation must be more or less decisive in its character. If the obstructions between Sumter and Moultrie are passed, little or no pause ought to ensue before moving against the next set, which is protected by the guns of Forts Johnson, Moultrie, and Ripley, and by three iron-clads. On the other hand, I ought to retire only after sustaining considerable loss. If I were free to choose, I should say that ten Monitors are the least number to meet contingencies. But I have only *seven*, and do not know whether the department may be prepared to send me any more.

The progress to Charleston will embrace—

1st. The passage of the obstructions between Sumter and Moultrie.

2d. Endurance of the fire of Moultrie, Johnson, and Ripley.

3d. The passage of obstructions near Ripley and encounter with the three iron-clads.

4th. Attack of Ripley.

5th. Obstructions beyond, attack of Pinkney, and any works at Charleston.

A certain portion of our force may be properly risked to *attain* the purpose, but I presume the department would hardly permit me to go so far as *not* to attain the object, and perhaps expose the communications of the land forces on the island.

It seems proper to bring this subject to your attention, because it may be more or less connected with other plans, of which I am ignorant, and which the department may prefer to keep within its own control. Will the department please to inform me if this is the case, or whether I am at liberty to encounter such risks as may offer? The report of Commander Stevens has not yet reached me, but may be expected very soon, he being at Port Royal, where his vessel is under repair.

I have the honor to be, very respectfully, your obedient servant,

JOHN A. DAHLGREN,
Rear-Admiral, Commanding S. A. B. Squadron.

Hon. GIDEON WELLES,
Secretary of the Navy, Washington, D. C.

STEAMER RELIEF, PORT ROYAL, *September* 20, 1863.

SIR: I received a copy of an order from you, dated September 9, ordering me to report weekly the injuries received by the iron-clads while engaged with the enemy, and particularly with reference to the shot that struck the pilot-house of the Catskill, causing the death of Commander Rodgers and Paymaster Woodbury.

I have the honor to report as follows:

The pilot-house covers of the Monitors are made of two plates of one-inch iron riveted together in the form of an arch. A plunging shot struck the pilot-house cover of the Catskill, bending the outside thickness in, and breaking the inside thickness, some of the broken pieces being driven with such force as to cause the melancholy occurrence within mentioned. The extent of the break is about eight square inches. I had a new pilot-house cover made out of three of the extra plates that were sent here for strengthening the covers of the pilot-houses. The Catskill also received the following damages: Five shots on her pilot-house, which broke twelve bolts. I had those replaced by new ones. The turret received about twelve shots, breaking fifteen bolts, which were also replaced. The smoke (or concussion) box of the fifteen-inch gun was jarred from its seat, and the fastenings and angle iron broken, which had to be renewed. The deck was struck seven times; five of the shots broke the deck plank through, requiring to be repaired with fourteen half-inch deck plates, and also pieces of deck plank put in where broken. The armature received a number of very hard shots, starting the plating and bolts in some places; this we could do very little with. I had the bolts driven home again where we could get at them. I am happy to inform you that all the additions were put on this vessel.

The Weehawken has received the following injuries: Twelve shots in her deck, six of which broke the deck plank through, requiring fourteen deck plates to repair. The turret received a number of shots, breaking fifty bolts, which will have to be replaced, and also breaking the flange of the composition ring that the turret slides on while revolving. The wood work of gutter will have to be cut away to give this ring clearings. Two of the T-iron beams of roof, which are broken, will have to be replaced. The pilot-house has received six shots, breaking twelve bolts, which will have to be replaced. Armature received twenty-two shots above the water-line, which have started off the plating in a good many places, and some of these shots have penetrated the five thicknesses of plating. The plating in the bow is started off the wood work four inches. Two of these plates will have to be taken off and straightened and put on again. This vessel also received one shot under the overhang, which broke through her side. To do the repairs that are necessary to this vessel, it will require almost eight days, and eight days additional to complete the additions, making in all sixteen days from the time we commenced, which was on the 17th instant.

The Patapsco received three shots in deck, two of which broke the deck plank, requiring six half-inch deck plates to repair, and also deck plank to go in where broken. One side of concussion box of fifteen-inch gun was carried away and the angle iron broken, requiring one sheet of boiler iron and twenty feet of angle iron to repair, and sixteen 1¼-inch bolts and thirty-four seven-eighths bolts.

The smoke-pipe is almost carried away by a shot from her own fifteen-inch gun. I have required a new one from New York, but in case it does not get here in time I will have it repaired as well as I possibly can, but it is impossible to make a good job of it without having a new one.

Two of the T-iron beams are broken in roof of turret. This vessel received a shot on her pilot-house cover, same place as Catskill; as hard a shot apparently, with the exception that the iron of the inner thickness did not fly off.

To repair this cover, I will have the old one taken apart, and the outside thickness brought to its original shape, and two of the extra plates put on, viz: one above and one below the outside thickness of old cover, and all fastened together with 1¼-inch rivets. I will put those rivets around the outer edge of cover, so that there will be no danger of their flying off inside if struck by shot. The time required to repair that vessel will be about twelve days. I have not got any base ring for turret or pilot-house of this vessel, but I am expecting them every day, and if they come in time, it will take twelve additional days from the time we commenced the work on this vessel, which was on the 13th instant.

I might be a little longer, as I have only one-third of my men working this vessel, two-thirds being on the Weehawken.

Very respectfully,

PATRICK HUGHES,
Assistant Inspector of Iron-clads.

Rear-Admiral J. A. DAHLGREN,
Commanding South Atlantic Blockading Squadron.

UNITED STATES IRON-CLAD LEHIGH,
Off Morris Island, September 18, 1863.

SIR: I herewith send you the information required in your order of September 15.

Commander Jno. C. Howell reported for duty February 14, 1863, and was detached July 27, 1863. I was her next commander.

The guns of this vessel had not been fired before the 10th July; up to this date the 15-inch has been fired forty-one times, and the 8-inch rifle twenty-eight times. The vessel has been struck in side-armor thirteen times; turret, seventeen times; pilot-house, twice; deck, once; smoke-stack, three times; total, thirty-six times. The general condition of the vessel is good. Her most serious wounds are, one within eight inches of the bow, on the port side, which opened the stem from one to four inches, starting four bolts, warping the whole bow, and opening side-armor on both sides. One 11-inch shot nearly abreast cabin-hatch, on port side, which penetrated four plates of the side-armor, and drove the fifth into wood backing, raised two of the deck plates, starting all their bolts, and knocking out nine of them. The backing is penetrated about five inches, and badly splintered; this wound caused the deck over cabin to leak badly. Three hits abreast the turret, on side-armor, within a space of six feet, have started all the plates, and raised two deck plates and wood backing, causing the deck to leak. Near the stern, on port side, a heavy shot has opened the side-armor about an inch, and starting the deck plates. The most serious wound on the turret has bent in all the plates, cutting entirely through a portion of the outer plate and cracking the inner one.

Extra plating is required over magazine, boilers, and shell-room.

The only repairs required are those of the wounds on the side-armor already described.

Not knowing what the facilities are for making such repairs at Port Royal, it is impossible for me to state the length of time necessary to make them.

I am, respectfully, your obedient servant,

A. BRYSON, *Commander.*

Rear-Admiral JOHN A. DAHLGREN,
Commanding South Atlantic Blockading Squadron.

UNITED STATES IRON-CLAD MONTAUK,
Off Morris Island, South Carolina, September 18, 1863.

SIR: In obedience to your order of the 15th instant, I have the honor to report as follows:

Commander D. M. Fairfax commanded this vessel from July 10 to August

22, 1863. Lieutenant Commander O. C. Badger temporarily in command the night of the 22d August, in the attack on Fort Sumter.

By your order of the 23d August I assumed the command.

I have the honor to enclose the reports of the executive officer and senior engineer in regard to the condition of the vessel and engines.

The probable length of time necessary to make the repairs at Port Royal, requisite for effective service, it would be difficult to state, as they are extensive.

I have the honor to be, very respectfully, your obedient servant,

JOHN L. DAVIS,
Lieutenant Commander.

Rear-Admiral J. A. DAHLGREN, U. S. N.,
Commanding South Atlantic Blockading Squadron.

[Forwarded by John L. Davis, lieutenant commander, to Rear-Admiral J. A. Dahlgren, U. S. N., commanding South Atlantic blockading squadron.]

UNITED STATES STEAMER MONTAUK,
Off Morris Island, September 18, 1863.

SIR: I have the honor to submit the following report of firing from this, prior to the 10th of July and up to this date; also, the number of hits received from the enemey:

Statement of firing, hits, distance, object, &c.

Date.	Rounds fired.	Hit by enemy.	Distance.	Object.	Remarks.
Dec. 16, 1862	XV-inch, 7				Trial trip in New York harbor.
Jan. 27, 1863	XV-inch, 28; XI-inch, 35	17 hits	1,200 yards	Fort McAllister	
Feb. 1, 1863	XV-inch, 26; XI-inch, 32	48 hits	900 yards	Fort McAllister	
Feb. 28, 1863	XV-inch, 6; XI-inch, 8	4 hits	1,400 yards	Nashville	
April 7, 1863	XV-inch, 10; XI-inch, 17	10 hits	1,200 to 800 yards	Sumter	
July 10, 1863	XV-inch, 67; XI-inch, 106	Not hit	1,400 to 700 yards	Batteries on Morris island	
July 11, 1863	XV-inch, 50; XI-inch, 66	2 hits	1,500 yards	Wagner and Gregg	
July 18, 1863	XV-inch, 52; XI-inch, 108	4 hits	1,000 to 500 yards	Wagner	
July 20, 1863	XV-inch, 1; XI-inch, 23	5 hits	1,400 yards	Wagner	
July 23, 1863	XV-inch, 5; XI-inch, 30	Not hit	1,200 yards	Wagner	
July 24, 1863	XV-inch, 4; XI-inch, 55	Not hit	1,000 yards	Gregg and Wagner	
July 29, 1863	XV-inch, 5; XI-inch, 19	Not hit	900 yards	Wagner	
Aug. 1, 1863	XV-inch, —; XI-inch, 3	Not hit	800 yards	Wagner	
Aug. 4, 1863	XV-inch, 1; XI-inch, 15	4 hits	1,300 yards	Wagner	
Aug. 12, 1863	XV-inch, —; XI-inch, 1	(Shell jammed in gun.)			At Port Royal.
Aug. 17, 1863	XV-inch, 12; XI-inch, 50	2 hits	1,400 yards	Wagner	XI-inch disabled.
Aug. 22, 1863	XV-inch, 20; XI-inch, —	Not hit	1,200 yards	Wagner and Gregg	
Aug. 23, 1863	XV-inch, 6; XI-inch, —	8 hits	900 yards	Sumter	
Sept. 1, 1863	XV-inch, 23; XI-inch, —	5 hits	800 yards	Sumter	
Sept. 6, 1863	XV-inch, 7; XI-inch, 1	Not hit	700 yards	Gregg	
Sept. 7, 1863	XV-inch, 6; XI-inch, —	2 hits	600 yards	Moultrie	
Sept. 8, 1863	XV-inch, 35; XI-inch, —	43 hits	500 to 250 yards	Moultrie and batteries on Sullivan's island.	

Total rounds fired: XV-inch, 371; XI-inch, 570. Fired prior to the 10th July: of the XV-inch, 70 rounds; from the XI-inch, 92 rounds. Fired since 10th July, inclusive: from XV-inch, 301 rounds; from XI-inch, 478 rounds.

The damages received to side-armor are of a serious nature. The plates are badly broken in a number of places, rendering it necessary to replace a number of them; many others require refastening.

A large number of bolts in turret and pilot-house are supposed to be broken off. Deck plating badly cut up. XI-inch gun disabled.

Respectfully submitted.

P. GIRAUD,
Acting 1st Lieutenant and Executive Officer.

JOHN L. DAVIS,
Lieutenant Commander.

[Forwarded by John L. Davis, lieutenant commander, to Rear-Admiral J. A. Dahlgren, U. S. N., commanding South Atlantic blockading squadron.]

UNITED STATES IRON-CLAD MONTAUK,
Off Morris Island, September 17, 1863.

SIR: In obedience to your orders, I have the honor to report to you the condition of the engines and boilers of this ship.

The main engines require an overhauling. The boilers are in a leaky condition. The ash-pans of the port furnaces are nearly burned through. The door frames of Nos. 2, 3, 4, 5, and 6 are broken in several places. The blower engines require an overhauling; the beam on which they are attached is not sufficiently rigid. The turret engines require a slight overhauling.

The turret has been jammed several times; and in the fight of the 8th the composition ring was bulged in so as to render it impossible to revolve the turret until it was keyed up nearly to its full extent. The turret at present does not come down to its proper place, and in rough weather admits a great quantity of water. Also, as regards the fracture in the bottom, immediately under the port boiler, caused by the explosion under the ship of a torpedo while in the Ogeechee river, which was only partially repaired. Having no centrifugal pump makes it very unsafe, as the pumps which we have are totally incompetent to expel any large amount of water. The ship leaks badly from the combined effect of two shot, one of which was received on the 8th instant, which necessitates the use of one donkey pump nearly all the while to free the ship of water. The ship at present makes twelve inches of water in four hours.

Very respectfully,

CHARLES A. STUART, *Senior Engineer.*

JOHN L. DAVIS,
Lieutenant Commander.

UNITED STATES IRON-CLAD STEAMER PASSAIC,
Off Morris Island, South Carolina, September 17, 1863.

SIR: In obedience to your order of 15th instant, I have to report:

First. That I have commanded this vessel since the 10th of July, having been ordered to her on the 22d of June, 1863.

Second. I am not supplied with the history of the guns of this vessel previous to the 10th of July, but since the date of my assuming the command the 15-inch has been fired 119 times; the 150-pounder rifle fired 107 times.

Third. This vessel has been hit ninety times.

Fourth. The injuries consequent upon the shot of the enemy, combined with the derangement of my steering gear, and the fact that the turret shaft and pilot-house revolve with the turret, force me to state that the vessel is disabled.

Fifth. The repairs necessary to put the vessel in good condition might be completed at Port Royal in two weeks excepting the adjustment of the turret and pilot-house, which may require a much longer time, and more conveniences than are supplied at Port Royal.

Very respectfully,

E. SIMPSON,
Lieutenant Commander, Commanding.

Rear-Admiral J. A. DAHLGREN,
South Atlantic Blockading Squadron.

CATSKILL,
Off Morris Island, September 16, 1863.

Commanding officers since July 10: Commander, George W. Rodgers, Lieutenant Commander, C. C. Carpenter.

Length of time in command: Commander George W. Rodgers, from February 24 to July 20; Lieutenant Commander C. C. Carpenter, from July 20 to September 14.

Number of guns fired before July 10: 15-inch, twenty, (20;) 11-inch, twenty-nine, (29.)

Number of guns fired to this date: 15-inch, one hundred and fifty-eight, (158;) 11-inch, four hundred and fifty-four, (454.)

Number of times the vessel has been struck, eighty-six, (86.)

General condition of the vessel, good.

UNITED STATES IRON-CLAD NAHANT,
Off Charleston, September 17, 1863.

SIR: In obedience to your order of the 15th instant, I have the honor to submit the following statement, viz:

First. Since the 10th of July, (inclusive,) this vessel has been commanded by Commander John Downes, one month and eighteen days; and by Lieutenant Commander J. J. Cornwell nineteen days. The *entire* command of Commander Downes was just eight months.

Second. The 15-inch gun has been fired prior to the 10th of July, fifty times; July 10 to date inclusive, 170 times. Total rounds 15-inch, 220.

The 11-inch gun has been fired prior to July 10, 66 times; July 10 to date inclusive, 276. Total rounds 11-inch, 342.

Third. The number of hits received from the shot of the enemy is sixty-nine.

Fourth. The general condition of the vessel is good.

Fifth. The only repairs requisite to make this vessel completely efficient is the rebolting of the smoke box of the 15-inch gun, which would probably occupy four days at Port Royal, during which time a sleeve could be placed upon the pilot-house.

I am, very respectfully, your obedient servant,

J. J. CORNWELL,
Lieutenant Commander

Rear-Admiral J. A. DAHLGREN,
Commanding South Atlantic Blockading Squadron,
Flag-Steamer Philadelphia, off Charleston.

UNITED STATES IRON-CLAD PATAPSCO,
Port Royal, September 18, 1863.

SIR: In reply to your requisition, I have to state that this vessel has been hit ninety-six times; that previous to the 10th of July the 15-inch gun was fired thirty-one times, and the rifle gun seventy times.

The battery is in good condition, with the exception of the rifle gun, which has a split on both sides of the muzzle, but has been fired a number of times since the discovery of the injury, without any perceptible increase of the injury.

It will require three weeks to make essential repairs.

This vessel has been commanded since the 10th of July by Lieutenant Commanders Erben and Badger, and by Commander T. H. Stevens.

Very respectfully,

T. H. STEVENS,
Commander.

Captain G. F. EMMONS,
Fleet Captain, &c.

UNITED STATES IRON-CLAD NANTUCKET,
Warsaw Sound, Ga., September 21, 1863.

SIR: In compliance with your order of the 15th September, instant, I would respectfully inform you I have been in command of this vessel since the 10th of July last, having assumed command of her on the 7th of May last, and have now been in command four months and thirteen days.

The 15-inch gun has been fired before the 10th of July last seven times, and up to this date fifty-one times; the 11-inch gun has been fired before the 10th of July last eighteen times, and up to this date one hundred and seventy-three times. This vessel has been hit fifty-three times.

The general condition of the vessel is good, excepting the defects in the engine department, specified in the accompanying report of senior Engineer George H. White.

The bottom of this vessel is exceedingly foul; so much so that her speed has decreased to about *one-half* of what it was on her passage out from New York.

The additional plates have not yet been put upon the pilot-house, and I am unable to estimate the time necessary to accomplish it.

The probable time necessary to make the requisite repairs in the engine department, to render the ship effective, is estimated by the senior Engineer George H. White, of this vessel, at about four days.

I am, sir, very respectfully, your obedient servant,

J. C. BEAUMONT,
Commander.

Rear-Admiral J. A. DAHLGREN,
Commanding S. A. B. Squadron, Flag-Steamer Philadelphia, off Morris Island, S. C.

UNITED STATES IRON-CLAD STEAMER WEEHAWKEN,
Port Royal, S. C., September 19, 1863.

SIR: In reply to your letter of the 15th instant, I beg leave to state that Commander E. R. Colhoun has commanded the Weehawken since the 10th of July, 1863, having assumed command on the 7th of July, 1863. The 15-inch gun has been fired, previous to July 10, 1863, 20 times; since July 10, 1863, 264 times; up to September 15, 1863, 284 times. The 11-inch gun has been fired, previous to July 10, 1863, 20 times; since July 10, 1863, 633 times; up to September 15, 1863, 653 times. Hits by the enemy since July 10, 1863, 82 times; previous to July 10, 1863; in the action of April 7, 1863, 52 times; up to September 15, 1863, 134 times.

The general condition of the Weehawken is good; some seventy bolts in turret are broken, and twelve in pilot-house; twelve hits on the deck, six of which broke the deck plank through, and one hit under the overhang, causing quite a leak in the hull. To make the necessary repairs to the vessel, it will require about eight days, and eight more to complete additions, making in all sixteen days from the time the work was commenced, which was on the 17th instant.

I arrived at Port Royal Tuesday morning, (15th,) too late to get in the creek; went in next morning; it rained that day, and also on the next, (17th.)

I will keep you advised from time to time of the progress made in our repairs. I should have written sooner, but have been delayed getting the necessary information. I have just received Fleet-Captain George F. Emmons's order to furnish a detailed report of the firing, hits, injuries, and casualties of this vessel, and will make it as soon as possible.

Very respectfully, your obedient servant,

EDMUND R. COLHOUN,
Commander.

Rear-Admiral JOHN A. DAHLGREN,
Commanding South Atlantic Blockading Squadron,
United States Flag-ship Philadelphia, off Charleston, S. C.

Injuries, &c., received by the Weehawken.

UNITED STATES IRON-CLAD STEAMER WEEHAWKEN,
Port Royal, S. C., September 24, 1863.

SIR: I have received your order of the 17th instant, with a copy of a letter from the Navy Department dated September 11, 1863, and addressed to Rear-Admiral John A. Dahlgren. My reports dated July 28, September 9, and 19, 1863, are full with respect to the number of rounds fired by this vessel, and number of times we were struck by the enemy. The most severe injuries received were from a 15-inch solid shot, which struck the turret, the shot that passed under the overhang when we were aground, making a hole about five inches in diameter and four on the deck, breaking through the one-inch plating and deck plank. The first struck the turret just clear of the deck, breaking two pieces from the flange of the composition ring upon which the turret slides when revolving; one piece wounding severely in the right leg Acting Fleet Captain O. C. Badger, and slightly in the left fore-arm Stephen McDonald, landsman, causing the turret to revolve with difficulty. With a base ring that hit would have been harmless. The second, which made a hole in the hull, struck about three feet eight inches below the overhang—so near an angle iron, with its support of iron bulkhead, as to prevent the shot penetrating. That leak was stopped during the action by driving a pine plug, and then filling up with smaller ones. Respecting the injuries to the deck, the worst were from rifle shot. One struck near the engine-room hatch, breaking the iron, driving splinters through, cutting steam-pipe of donkey engine, forcing bolts partly through the beam, and breaking gong-bell. The second struck over coal bunker on port side near the battle plate, driving it through, together with a portion of the iron plating of the deck. A third struck over the bread room with like effect, driving a piece of the deck plating through. The fourth was over the ward-room on the starboard side, and forced some splinters through. One (a round shot) struck on the top of the turret, breaking two of the T-iron beams, bending another, and wounding three men. All the shot which struck the Weehawken, either on or above the deck, glanced off. When aground off the north end of Morris island, the overhang being out of water, a round shot penetrated the armor, and now lies imbedded in the wood of the overhang just inside the armor. Being now under the water, I cannot ascertain the size of the shot. I think it is eleven inches. Others which have struck the side, though breaking the armor, making in some cases deep indentations, have not penetrated. I find it necessary to fire clear of the boilers, as firing over them causes them to leak. The guns and carriages are in good order. The guide irons always break off after firing a few rounds, notwithstanding our care in compressing, though not apparently making any difference, as we have fired much without them. The effect of the firing on the men is not perceptible. Those stationed below suffer most from imperfect ventilation. It is very close and hot there during action. The vessel, though sluggish in her movements in consequence of the bottom being so foul, steers very well when not in too shoal water. In some of the actions we were under way, and I found no difficulty in her management. During the night attack on Sumter, August 23, a mortar shell struck the sand bags around the extra plating over the shell-room, and, exploding, tore them to pieces, causing a visible depression of the iron plating for several feet. In reference to the injuries to the deck from rifle shot, I would remark that similar shot striking the side of the turret were not so injurious as round shot fired from the same battery.

In order that this letter may contain the additional information called for by the department, I will embody the substance of former reports:

The 15-inch gun has been fired, previous to July 10, 1863, 20 times; since July 10, 1863, 264 times; up to September 15, 284 times. The 11-inch gun has been fired, previous to July 10, 1863, 20 times; since July 10, 1863, 633 times; up to September 15, 1863, 653 times. Hits by the enemy since July 10, 1863, 85 times; previous to July 10, 1863, 52 times; up to September 15, 137 times. My former reports give "hits by the enemy since July 10, 1863, 82," but we have since discovered three more. Those she received during the action of April 7, 1863, are marked thus: I; since July 10, 1863, thus: II.

Very respectfully, your obedient servant,

EDMUND R. COLHOUN,
Commander.

Rear-Admiral JOHN A. DAHLGREN,
Commanding South Atlantic Blockading Squadron,
United States Flag-Steamer Philadelphia, off Morris Island, S. C.

Operations of the Nantucket at Charleston.

UNITED STATES IRON-CLAD NANTUCKET,
Warsaw Sound, Georgia, September 29, 1863.

SIR: In compliance with a general order from the Navy Department of September 11, I respectfully submit the following report:

This vessel joined the fleet off Charleston on the 11th of July last, and on the 16th she fired twenty-three 11-inch and eleven 15-inch shell at Fort Wagner. On this occasion she was hit twice abaft the smoke-stack on the deck, one breaking entirely through, dashing the deck armor down upon and breaking the cast-iron floor of the fire-room; Artemas L. Grow and George Reily, firemen, were slightly wounded by splinters.

I forward herewith a sketch of the injury done by this shot. The other shot crushed the deck-armor and breaking over the starboard coal bunker, but did not, as in the former case, show daylight through. Both shots glanced off.

They were fired from the heavy gun on the northeast angle of the fort, supposed to be a 10-inch columbiad.

On the 18th July the Nantucket fired forty-eight 11-inch and thirty-three 15-inch shell. On that occasion the smoke-box of the 15-inch gun had all four of its angle irons broken, and the box itself torn from its fastening to the turret, rendering further firing of the gun dangerous.

On the 20th she fired twenty-five 11-inch shell and three 11-inch shrapnell. On the 22d she fired nine 10-second 11-inch shell, and on the 24th she fired fifty-four 7, 10, and 20 second shell at Forts Wagner and Gregg.

No unpleasant effects were experienced by the officers and crew from the firing of the guns.

The highest range of the thermometer on the berth deck while engaged was 128°, and in the engine-room 141°.

I am, sir, very respectfully, your obedient servant,

J. C. BEAUMONT,
Commander.

Rear-Admiral J. A. DAHLGREN.

Report of injury to turret of the Passaic.

[Despatch No. 174.]

FLAG-STEAMER PHILADELPHIA,
Off Morris Island, September 30, 1863.

SIR: It grieves me to be obliged to transmit the enclosed, for, if correct, I shall be deprived of the use of a Monitor in preparing for a service which would require the addition of two or three more.

I have no time to inquire into the matter, for the papers have just reached me by the Massachusetts, which will leave almost immediately.

I have the honor to be, very respectfully, your obedient servant,

J. A. DAHLGREN,
Rear-Admiral Commanding S. A. B. Squadron.

Hon. GIDEON WELLES,
Secretary of the Navy, Washington, D. C.

UNITED STATES IRON-CLAD PASSAIC,
Port Royal Harbor, September 28, 1863.

SIR: I have to report that it is now one week since my arrival in this harbor, during which time I have been employed with the assistant inspector of iron-clads (Mr. Hughes) in trying all means to make the turret of this vessel revolve. Our efforts have been without success, and the vessel is conceded to be entirely disabled, and that by the effect of the fire of the enemy.

The report of Mr. Hughes states that the pilot-house must be taken off and the spindle removed. The spindle is in two parts, and if, after removing the upper part of the spindle, it should be found that the difficulty lies in the lower part of the spindle, the guns must come out, and the floor of the turret must be removed before it can be taken out. This is, in fact, taking the whole turret to pieces.

There are no means at hand for lifting the weights required. The pilot-house weighs twenty-four tons, which, with the friction to be overcome in starting it from its seat, will increase the strain to be brought on the purchases to an enormous degree.

The main yard of the Vermont is the only derrick that can be used; and even if it can be so secured as to bear the strain, there are no purchases on board of that vessel which can lift the weight. The blocks cannot possibly arrive before the return of the Massachusetts, and will probably be delayed still longer, and until they arrive not a blow can be struck in the way of repairs. After they arrive the assistant inspector estimates that he can complete the work in thirty-five days. This supposes that no difficulty arises in the lifting of the weights.

Allowing a fair margin in the arrival of the purchases, the lifting of the weights, and the completion of the work, it will require three months to put the vessel in fighting order, if her repairs are carried on at this place.

After maturely considering the subject with all the light I have collected, I have no hesitation in saying that I believe the most expeditious manner in which to get this vessel ready for service is to send her immediately to a northern port, where every facility can at once be placed at the disposal of those charged with her repairs. Such being my convictions, I respectfully recommend that this course be pursued.

Very respectfully, your obedient servant,

E. SIMPSON,
Lieutenant Commander, Commanding.

Rear-Admiral J. A. DAHLGREN,
Commanding S. A. B. Squadron.

Repairs needed on the Nahant.

UNITED STATES IRON-CLAD NAHANT,
Off Morris Island, October 2, 1863.

SIR: In obedience to your order of September 30, I report that this vessel will require twenty-one through-bolts in the turret, six of which are near the 15-inch port, and must be riveted, which will require mechanics.

The fresh-water condenser has been worn out and entirely unfit for use more than a month. At present one of the heaters is used for the purpose; and as cold, damp weather may be expected shortly, I think it absolutely necessary to have a new one.

The pilot-house was partly prepared to receive the sleeve the last time the vessel was at Port Royal, and is, I think, weakened thereby, and should have it put on.

The chief engineer requests ten days, if possible, to overhaul the engines and boilers, which has never been done since the vessel left home.

Very respectfully, your obedient servant,

J. J. CORNWELL,
Lieutenant Commander.

Rear-Admiral J. A. DAHLGREN,
Comd'g S. A. B. Squadron, Flag-Steamer Philadelphia.

Part taken by the Passaic in attacks on Charleston.

UNITED STATES IRON-CLAD STEAMER PASSAIC,
Port Royal Harbor, October 9, 1863.

SIR: Conformably to the call of the Navy Department for reports from the commanders of the iron-clads, of the actions in which they have been engaged, I have the honor to submit the following:

On the 29th day of July, 1863, I went into action in this vessel with Fort Wagner, on Morris island, at the distance of 1, 200 yards. In this action I fired thirteen rounds from the 15-inch, and ten rounds from the 150-pounder rifle.

A cap square bolt was carried away on the carriage of the rifle. I received no hits from the enemy.

On the night of the 15th of August, while employed on the same duty of close picket, I discovered a steamer of the enemy communicating between Fort Sumter and Cummings's Point. I opened fire upon her, which had the effect of causing her to move rapidly up the harbor. Battery Gregg opened fire in return, but I received no hits.

On the 17th of August I joined the squadron in the attack of the forenoon on Fort Wagner, after which I was engaged with Fort Sumter at a distance of 2,000 yards. In the afternoon of the same day I again engaged Fort Wagner at a distance of 900 yards, in company with the Patapsco, and succeeded in silencing the fire of two guns that had been mounted subsequently to the withdrawal of the squadron in the forenoon. During the day the vessel was hit thirteen times. I fired thirty shells from the 15-inch gun, and 9 from the rifle, having been ordered to retain the fire of the rifle for service against the walls of Sumter.

On the 18th of August I was again engaged with Fort Wagner at a distance of 1,000 yards. During the action I fired eighteen shells from the 15-inch gun, and received five hits from the enemy, one of them causing the water to run freely through the deck into the bread room.

On the night of the 23d of August I was engaged, in company with the rest of the squadron of iron-clads, in an attack on Fort Sumter, at a distance of about 750 yards. The mist obscured the fort so much as to make it very difficult to distinguish the object. I fired nine rounds from the 15-inch gun, and ten from the rifle. I was hit five times by the enemy.

On the afternoon of the 31st of August I was engaged, in company with the Patapsco, Weehawken, and Nahant, with Fort Moultrie, at a distance of 875 yards. I fired one round from the 15-inch gun, and nine rounds from the rifle, and received nine hits from the enemy. Three of the hits penetrated the deck, forcing pieces of broken iron through on the berth deck; one hole measured twenty inches by nine inches.

On the night of the 1st of September I was engaged, in company with the rest of the iron-clad squadron, in an attack on Fort Sumter, at a distance varying from 1,200 to 700 yards. During this action I fired twenty rounds from the 15-inch gun, and twenty-six from the rifle, and received seven hits from the enemy.

On the morning of the 6th of September I was engaged, in company with the other vessels of the iron-clad squadron, in shelling the covered way from Fort Wagner to Battery Gregg. There was no reply from the enemy. I fired six rounds from the 15-inch gun, and nine rounds from the rifle.

On the night of the same day I was on picket, under orders to fire an occasional shot to prevent re-enforcements crossing from Sullivan's island to Morris island. After firing one round from each gun, while revolving the turret, it was discovered that the central shaft or spindle of the turret had taken up motion with the turret, carrying the pilot-house with it. The steering gear was of course deranged; in revolving the spindle back to its proper place, a casting indispensable for the steering gear was broken. Temporary steering gear was rigged on deck, and I returned to the lower anchorage. During the night, finding it impossible to detach the spindle from the turret, a starting bar was shipped in the shaft of the turret engine, in the turret chamber, and relieving tackles were hooked to the steering chains and brought to the barrel of a wheel, temporarily rigged in the turret chamber. The vessel was reported as ready to go into action on the morning of the 7th.

On the 8th of September I was engaged, in company with the rest of the iron-clad squadron, with the batteries on Sullivan's island, and having been ordered to go well up and engage battery Bee, I became a prominent mark for the fire of the enemy. The turret, spindle, and pilot-house, all revolved together. I received three new holes through the deck; the side-armor was badly injured in several places, and was sprung off the side abreast of the turret. Eleven hits took effect on the ring around the base of the turret; one of these hits caused so much friction on the plate below the ring as to require thirty-four pounds of steam to revolve the turret, until it was eased by melted tallow squirted in from the outside. Had it not been for the elastic character of the packing under the plate, the turret would inevitably have stopped.

The difficulty of steering the ship with relieving tackles, the quartermaster below not having even the benefit of a compass to know when the vessel is running "steady," and the copious leaks through seven holes in the deck, combined with my desire to adjust the turret and spindle, induced me, after this action, to represent to you the condition of the vessel, and on being informed by you of the probable suspension of active operation for a while, I applied for permission to come to this place for repairs. The concussion from the guns is not found to inconvenience any one on board. During the last action a shot struck one of the armor plates on the roof of the turret, driving it down into the turret. Fortunately no one was seriously injured; one man was cut, and slightly bruised.

The wounds inflicted on the deck are very rough and jagged; all signs of fibre disappear from the iron, and the projecting pieces are broken off with a sledge. The shot generally burrows along on the plate that it first strikes until it comes in contact with the edge of the next plate, when it breaks.

The armor on the sides does not successfully resist the impact of the shot from the guns of the heavy calibre of the enemy. There are several places on the side of this vessel where all five plates are broken through.

The turret of this vessel is much battered, but very few bolts or nuts have broken off. The strength of the turret has been most severely tried; at one place two round shot of very large calibre (estimated by some as 11-inch, by others as 15-inch,) have struck close together on the same plate, the impression of the second shot overlapping a portion of that made by the first. The mass of iron has been pressed in, so as to form an extensive bulging in on the inside, and the outer plate is broken; but no serious effect was produced.

In an official report of the actions in which this vessel has been engaged, I cannot refrain from making especial mention of Lieutenant Wm. Whitehead, the executive officer, whose earnest zeal, fine ability, and untiring energy, make him most valuable in his position, and have been of the greatest assistance to me.

I must also specify Mr. Henry Mason, (the senior engineer,) and 3d Assistant Engineer Wm. A. Dripps, whose valuable services as rendered on board of this vessel, from their interest in the cause, have on several occasions called forth my commendation. If Mr. Dripps remains in the service, he is destined to occupy a prominent place in his corps.

I have the honor to be, very respectfully,

E. SIMPSON,
Lieutenant Commander, Commanding.

Rear-Admiral J. A. Dahlgren,
Commanding South Atlantic Blockading Squadron.

Suggestions of Lieutenant Commander Simpson relative to the Monitors.

United States Iron-clad Steamer Passaic,
Port Royal Harbor, October 14, 1863.

Sir: Conformably to a call from the Navy Department, I have made a report to the commander-in-chief on this station, of the actions in which this vessel has been engaged; but as the letter from the department implies a desire for such experience as the commanders of the iron-clads may have acquired, I respectfully submit the following remarks:

DECKS.

In order to prevent dampness on the lower deck of an iron-clad Monitor, it should be covered with two or three coats of paint, with shellac over all. All the washing that is then required is simply wiping with a wet cloth or swab. The wood does not absorb the water, and the consequence is a dry atmosphere.

The spar decks of these vessels, as at present constructed, are not sufficiently protected to resist such projectiles as are now in use. The six inches of wood are sufficient backing, but the two ½-inch plates of iron are unequal to perform the work required of them. In this vessel there have been seven holes made through the deck, the shot driving the iron and wood on the berth deck. The holes made over the berth deck caused such a leak, when the deck was awash, as to deprive the crew of a large portion of their accommodation, which at best is too contracted. Two of these holes are caused by shot which struck the base ring of the turret, near the bottom; one of them just cleared the steam-pipe of a blower engine, which, if disabled, would have been a serious damage, as the blowers are literally the life of the ship. One hole over the awning-room caused the wetting of all awnings, hammocks, &c., and another over the bread-room injured a quantity of bread before it could be removed to another place.

It is impossible to plug these holes so as to stop all the leak; in this vessel they have been rammed full of oakum, with heavy bags of sand on top, while below, after chipping off the splinters to obtain a smooth surface, sheet-lead has been nailed up under the hole, but all without being able to stop the flow of water. The surface of the iron on deck is very rough and jagged, and nothing can be done in the way of repair until time is given to cut off all the injured part, and to replace it with a new plate.

I recommend that the strength of the decks of the Monitors now in service be increased by laying extra plates of 1-inch iron from over the forward part of the magazine and shell-room as far aft as the condenser, extending the plates only to two feet from the edge of the overhang on each side forward and abreast of the turret, contracting the surface abaft the turret so as to cover only two feet of the coal-bunkers on each side of the boilers and abaft the smoke-pipe, running one plate amidships as far as the high-pressure valve. The uneven space thus left on the deck can be covered with planking, which, forward and aft, will be found a great comfort to officers and men. The wooden deck laid on this vessel is found to be a great advantage in preventing rheumatism, and, in hot weather, in modifying the temperature. The additional weight thus placed on the deck will be about 50 tons.

ARMATURE.

The side-armor, as disposed on the overhang of these vessels, does not perfectly fulfil the requirements. A shot of any size never strikes it without producing more or less of serious effect, sometimes breaking through all the plates, generally driving the mass of iron before it into the backing, and sometimes causing leaks. The solid plates of hammered iron on the New Ironsides, though only 4 inches in thickness, resist the impact of shot much better than the 5 inches of laminated iron on the sides of the Monitors.

This difference in effect may be caused by the different manner in which the surfaces are presented to the shot, the sides of the Ironsides being inclined, while those of the Monitors are vertical. The manner in which this armor is arranged at the stem is very insecure. These vessels are useless as rams, except against wooden vessels.

The security is by means of very small bolts at the extremity, which allow the armor to open on a very slight provocation. The armor of this vessel at the stem is sprung apart six inches by contact with another Monitor while in the act of turning; the collision was one with very slight force. I recommend that all these vessels should be fitted with a shoe for the purpose of reinforcing the stems.

The laminated iron, when disposed in a plane perpendicular to the flight of the projectile, does not seem to answer all demands; but when disposed in the form of a turret, no objection can be raised to it. The turrets are as near impregnable as anything can be made, and eleven inches of iron seem to be enough for all purposes of defence.

The only objection to them is the "through bolts," which allow the nut inside to fly when the head of the bolt is struck. The new system of making turrets now adopted by the Navy Department obviates this difficulty.

ROOF OF TURRET.

The most vital and dangerous part of this construction of vessel is the roof of turret, which must be apparent to every one as weak. It never can be struck without causing damage. The number of the beams should be increased; they should have a better bearing in the wall of the turret, (at present they have but two inches.) The railroad iron should be discarded, and good square iron, of proper dimensions, substituted.

The roof of the "Weehawken" was struck at long range; the result was the fracturing of the thigh of one man, and lighter wounds to two others; and this or worse must be the result as long as the roof is left in its present state.

PRESENT PRINCIPLE OF TURRET.

I will, perhaps, be excused if I hazard an objection to the principle involved in the present arrangement of turret, pilot-house, and spindle.

The turret has two bearings on the spindle—one on a shoulder, under the centre of the floor-beams, and another (through diagonal braces) from the ends of these beams to another shoulder at the level of the roof. These bearings are provided with composition rings to prevent "cutting."

The pilot-house is supported on the end of the spindle. In order to secure the pilot-house from being knocked off by the effect of a blow, a composition ring is secured to the roof of the turret, which, at its top, has a horizontal flange which overlaps a projecting ring attached to the base of the pilot-house.

This is the best manner in which the object could be attained, and, as long as the form of all parts remains as they came from the foundry or machine-shop, it will work well. But the battering effect of heavy ordnance will knock anything out of shape, even an 11-inch turret or pilot-house, as in the case of this vessel, causing the turret to revolve eccentrically. The effect of this eccentric motion on board of this vessel was the derangement of the whole system by the jamming of a piece of $\frac{7}{8}$-inch bolt between the composition ring and the old pilot-house.

The piece of bolt entered freely at the place where it had stopped in, but the eccentric motion caused the surfaces of ring and pilot-house to approach each other when the turret was revolved, and the jam took place; thus uniting the turret, pilot-house, and spindle, so that the turret could not be made to revolve without carrying with it the other parts of the system.

Efforts were made to force them apart, with 35 pounds of steam, at the risk of destroying the gearing of the turret engine, and causing the beams of the ship to work several inches; but no effect was produced, and the object could not be attained until the ring was detached from the roof of the turret, when the cause of the difficulty was discovered.

This difficulty is most serious in its consequences; the steering gear is, of course, deranged, and the pilot-house becomes useless. It may occur again in this vessel; it may occur on board of any other vessel of this class.

It is also possible that the bearings of the turret on the spindle may "cut," although the fact of having two composition surfaces to work on makes the danger remote. Great delicacy is required in adjusting the diagonal braces, and any yielding on their part can at any time stop the turret from revolving; they occupy, besides, much room in the turret, interfering with the work about the guns.

I recommend that a system of turret should be devised by which it will have no connexion with the spindle, but have a bearing all around its base, running on such anti-friction rollers as the inexhaustible ingenuity of our mechanics can invent.

The weight will not then be concentrated on one point of the vessel, but will be spread over a greater surface, and the duty of the spindle will be simply to support the pilot-house, without the remotest chance of derangement. The diagonal braces will be thus removed from the turret.

I would also recommend that the base of the turret should be carried below the spar deck. The base ring as now attached to the turret prevents injury to the bottom of the turret itself; but the liability of stopping the revolution of the turret by forcing the iron down to the deck plates is just as great as ever. In a late action in this vessel, owing to this cause, it required at one time thirty-four pounds of steam to revolve the turret, until melted tallow was squirted in from the outside; and had it not been for the elastic character of the packing under the plate below the ring, the turret would have inevitably stopped. I have also had two shots that penetrated the deck directly under this ring. If the base of the turret were carried down below the spar deck, it might be so enclosed as to prevent the rush of water into the vessel through the opening between the turret and deck, as is the case at present. I consider that, if it be found practicable to make the system work as I propose, it will be a great improvement.

The composition ring under the turret does not perform the work required of it. After the turret has been struck several times at the base this ring ceases to act independently, and attaches itself to the turret, becoming a part of it, and rises or falls, or revolves with it. It is also found to be dangerous, as the flange inside the turret is broken by the force of the blows on the base, the pieces flying in over the berth-deck beams. The extra base ring around the turret does not prevent this effect, for in this vessel there are three pieces of the flange broken off, one or two of them as much as four feet in length.

COMPRESSION OF THE GUNS.

The system of compression of the guns in the turret of these vessels is too delicate. The perfect action of the compressor plates between the beams forming the bed or slide depends on the preservation of the parallelism of these beams. If this parallelism be destroyed the plates take angling, and it has been found at times very difficult to run the guns in and out from this cause. To preserve the parallelism of these beams their elasticity must be perfect; but it is found in practice that, after being subjected to a certain amount of compression, they require to be wedged apart in order to relieve the effort of running in and out. A simple method of compression is proposed by Lieutenant Wm. Whitehead, the executive officer of this vessel, which is new only in its application, but which, I think, could be substituted with advantage for the method now in use. I enclose his sketch.

TURRET CHAMBER.

I would recommend that the floor of the turret chamber be covered with sheet zinc, which will prevent much oil and dirt from going down on the skin. Two hatches, forward and abaft, should also be cut in the deck, in the wake of the heel of the spindle, which, if unshipped when keying up or lowering the turret, would prevent any hindrance to the "rams" that are used for these purposes.

PROTECTION OF ARMATURE.

In remarking the track of shot that have struck on the deck of this vessel, I have noticed that, when they strike the edge of a plate they break, and their effect ceases, leaving the edge of the plate much injured, but not affecting the deck beyond. There are now on the deck of this vessel several places where the shot have struck on a plate, pursued its course, burrowing along until the edge of the next plate has suddenly stopped its further progress.

I cannot help thinking that something can be devised to be placed on the outside of the armature of iron-clads which might have the effect of robbing the shot of a great portion of its power by causing it to break immediately on contact, in fact, before its whole force is developed on the main armor. The plan that seems to me most feasible is to place over the armature a system of steel-pointed cones, extending over the whole side, these to be so arranged as to bring the points close enough together to prevent a shot of ordinary calibre from striking between the points.

The length of the cones would have to be determined by experiment, but I should think one inch, or one inch and a half, would be all that could be required. The projection would, of course, be flattened down by the force of the blow, but I am inclined to believe that they would have their effect in accelerating the moment when the shot would break. If they would not break the shot, of course they would be of no use; but the uniform manner in which the shots break when coming in contact with the edge of the deck plates of this vessel induces me to suppose that experiments carried on in this direction may lead to valuable results.

The department will judge of the value of this report; my effort has simply been to state impressions that I have received while in command of this vessel. They are not theories, but deductions from practical effects which I have remarked during very active operations. I shall be glad if they can be made of any service.

Very respectfully, your obedient servant,

E. SIMPSON,
Lieutenant Commander, Commanding.

Hon. GIDEON WELLES,
Secretary of the Navy.

Rear-Admiral DuPont's vindication of himself.

NEAR WILMINGTON, DELAWARE,
October 22, 1863.

SIR: Your communication of the 26th June, in reply to my despatch of the 3d June, was received the day before I left Port Royal.

I had trusted that my communications of the 27th May and 3d June would convince the department of the injustice of its imputations in its despatches of the 14th and 15th May. I had confined myself to a detailed, accurate, and calm statement of facts known to the department, not less than to myself, but of which I supposed it had been betrayed into a momentary forgetfulness by the sensation of disappointment at the failure of the Monitors. I was silent respecting its harsh language and unjust reproaches, trusting with confidence that, when the facts were recalled to its recollection, the department would retract the wounding words it had written, but which it could never expunge from its records. In this I have been painfully disappointed. It is with profound regret I perceive in your despatch of the 26th June a reiteration of the charges and reproaches of previous despatches, and in your silence since, during a period of three months, a resolution not to recall them. My last hope of justice at the hands of the department is therefore extinguished.

If I have failed in my duty I am liable to trial, but insulting imputations in official despatches are grave wrongs, perpetuated on the public records to my permanent injury.

The remedy which the law would afford me against a superior officer indulging in the language of your despatches does not exist against the civil head of the department. It only remains, therefore, for me to place again on the records of the department my indignant refutation of its renewed charges.

I concur with the department in the observation that the further discussion of what it is pleased to term the demonstration of the 7th April would not be profitable. I regret that this has not been adhered to in your present despatch, in which also I perceive new suggestions which I cannot pass over in silence.

I share the regret which the department expresses that my views were not understood by it before the event took place, but I must be permitted to say that, though not understood by the department, they were formally and clearly expressed by me on its records before the event took place. My despatch of the 3d of June, from which the department now understands them, merely cited and repeated what was already on its records.

My reply to the order to attack; my despatches, with the reports of Captains Drayton and Worden, of the operations on the Ogeechee, and my letter to the Assistant Secretary, informing him that the only limit to my demand for iron-clads was the capability of the government to supply them, if consulted, could not be misunderstood. The department was under no necessity of seeking my opinion of the Monitors from intimations to others: a much more authentic source of information was its own records.

Among them it possessed the official expression of exactly what I thought of the capabilities of the Monitors as against forts, accompanied by the experiments in the battle on which they were founded, in my despatch of the 28th January, transmitting the detailed report of Captain Worden, and followed by the detailed report of Captain Drayton, which I forwarded with my own report of the 6th of March. Just such a detailed exposition of the condition of the Monitors after the attack on Charleston was characterized by the department as "a labored effort to depreciate our national iron-clads."

It is a just subject of regret that these reports should have been overlooked, or thought not worthy of consideration by the department.

I was aware of the visit of the Assistant Secretary to Charleston, but I learn with surprise from your despatch that, without a commission in the navy, he *commanded* the expedition which witnessed the bombardment of Sumter without relieving it. But I am at a loss to see how such an inspection of the port at that time can make him familiar with all the points of fortifications created since his visit, though it may well explain the interest which led him to make it a specialty.

But the department will pardon me for saying, with all proper respect for its head, that it is incomprehensible to me that the Assistant Secretary could ever have supposed there was entire coincidence of views on the subject between him and myself. He cannot have forgotten his opinion of the power and invulnerability of the Monitors, which I always controverted. Still less can he have failed to recollect his persistent resolution to make the expedition depend for success solely on the naval force, and his anxiety to exclude the co-operation of a land force, against my opinion that a purely naval attack could give no assurance of success, and that to secure it troops were necessary, often and as formally expressed before the 7th of April as it is now contained in my report of the attack.

The department has been further misled in supposing I went with the Assistant Secretary into particulars respecting the attack on Charleston during my visit last fall. The only detail that was arranged and promised by the Assistant Secretary was never executed—the removal of serious defects in the New Ironsides. She came three months afterwards to Port Royal unchanged in important particulars.

I am not sufficiently sure that I understand the allusion of the department to Rear-Admiral Dahlgren, then Captain Dahlgren, to make any comment upon it; I therefore pass it in silence.

It is gratifying to me to perceive that the department is sensible of the propriety of assigning a reason for its unusual delay in acknowledging my reports of so important an action as that of the 7th of April. But the department must permit me to remind it that I answered the President's order of the 13th April, which the letter of the 14th merely repeated, modified and softened, on the 16th of April, the day of its receipt, in a full despatch, which left Port Royal on the 17th, the day after the transmission of my detailed report of the action of the 7th, and must have reached the department within four or five days of its date; and if the department delayed its reply to my report for several weeks, in daily expectation of a despatch then in its possession, it is another illustration of the neglect with which it treats my despatches. And while the department informs me that my detailed report of the action of the 7th was received only on the 20th April, the department should not forget that my report of the 8th, containing every material fact necessary for the comprehension of the attack on the 7th, and the causes of its failure, was delivered to the Secretary on the 12th of April, only five days after the battle, by Commander Rhind, himself a distinguished actor in that event.

That despatch was entitled to the courtesy of an acknowledgment, even if the department had no word of thanks to the brave men and officers who so gallantly tried its experiment.

I have no desire to question the power of the department to relieve me at its discretion, but its order of the 3d June assigns causes which do not exist, and ascribes to me opinions which I had neither expressed nor entertained.

In my despatch of the 28th January I advised the department that troops were necessary to secure success; it persisted in ordering a purely naval attack; reiteration of my repeated advice the department could not expect unless on its request.

That request was for the first time expressed in your despatch of the 14th May, and before it could receive my reply giving a detailed plan of operation the department relieved me.

The department will search my letters in vain for any justification of its regrets that I did not concur in the reluctance of the government to relinquish all further efforts against Charleston.

Long before the government ordered any attack, I opened the way on the Stono and placed its troops within reach of Charleston, and since this failed, because not supported, my suggestions to the department have been confined to pointing out the way to secure success in other directions, always holding the Stono, however, without which the present operations could not have been attempted by the military forces.

The tenor of my letters nowhere justifies the suggestion that my judgment was in opposition to a renewed attack on Charleston with an adequate land force supporting the naval attack. They expressly confined my opposition to "a purely naval attack" with forces that had just proved insufficient. If I am not misinformed, the department has not ordered such an attack, nor found an officer willing to undertake it, and the recent operations before Charleston sufficiently vindicate my judgment.

I have the honor to be, sir, very respectfully, your obedient servant,

S. F. DUPONT,
Rear-Admiral United States Navy.

Hon. GIDEON WELLES,
Secretary of the Navy, Washington.

Secretary of the Navy in reply to Rear-Admiral DuPont's letter of October 22.

NAVY DEPARTMENT, *November* 4, 1863.

SIR: Your communication dated "near Wilmington, Delaware, 22d of October," was received at this department on the 27th ultimo. This communication purports to be an acknowledgment of a letter of the department of the 26th of last June, the receipt of which you had already acknowledged several months since.

I have neither the time nor the inclination to enter into a controversy or review of the transactions attending the demonstration of the 7th of April, nor can I neglect public duties to discuss your alleged, but, in my opinion, entirely imaginary personal grievances. Your prompt abandonment of the harbor of Charleston after a brief attack—your disinclination to occupy the harbor—your declarations that the Monitors could not remain there with safety—your doubts and misgivings in relation to those vessels—your opposition to a naval attack—your omission to suggest or advise any system of naval proceeding—your constant complaints—the distrust that painfully pervaded your correspondence—your distressing personal anxiety about yourself that seemed to overshadow public duty—your assaults upon editors instead of assaults upon rebel batteries—your neglect of any reconnoissance of the harbor obstructions, or if such was ever made, your neglect to inform the department of the fact—these, with the querulous and censorious charges which subsequently, during four months' leisure, have been garnered up and cherished, and which finally find expression in your communication received on the 27th ultimo, are, agreeably to your wish, all on the files of the department; and the failure of the 7th of April has become history. In the department also are the records of my despatches to which you have taken exception, in language which is, if not unbecoming an officer, at least so unusual that, though conned and prepared as necessary for your vindication, it requires special indulgence in order to be permitted to be received on the public files.

Those despatches are not of the character you represent. "Insulting imputations in official despatches," by whomsoever made, are no more excusable than obtrusive impertinence and diliberate insolence. Concurring, as you declare you do, with the department that the further discussion of the brief demonstration of the 7th of April, which you feared, and have often declared, would, if repeated, result in disaster, you nevertheless, in your leisure, "near Wilmington," once more bring forward your failure and your grievance, and declare you must "place *again* on the records of the department my (your) indignant refutation of its renewed charges."

Four months had passed away since I had written you, except the brief despatch of July 15, congratulating you on your arrival in Delaware—our correspondence had closed—yet late in October you forward an elaborate despatch, reopening the subject, and accusing me of "renewed charges." The "imputation" that I have ever made charges against you is as incorrect as that I had "renewed" them.

Your reluctance to assail Sumter and occupy the harbor of Charleston, and the anxiety manifested to hastily withdraw the fleet, were facts which I learned with regret; but, though I did not concur in your views, I carefully abstained from making either "charges" or "imputations" against you.

Differing with you, it was my duty to express my opinions, and I did it in language and terms which you do not presume to quote to sustain your assertions. I lamented what appeared to me an error or infirmity of judgment, and the development of views that were in direct conflict with what I had previously supposed was our united and joint opinion, and I frankly but mildly communicated my disappointment on learning that you disapproved, or claimed never to have advised, the assault on Sumter, or the attempt to penetrate Charleston harbor.

But while thus differing with you and compelled to state my opinions, I was not unmindful of your ability and attainments, your topographical and hydrographical knowledge of the coast, and your professional experience and service exhibited not only at Port Royal, but in the general management of the blockade from the North Carolina boundary to Cape Canaveral. Everywhere, and on all occasions, I awarded you full and cheerful credit for what you are, and what you had done; but because I was surprised and disappointed at your failure and your conclusions at Charleston, which it appears was not your specialty, and because I did not wholly conceal my opinions, you accuse me of making charges and renewing them. It was no less my duty to inform you wherein we disagreed, than wherein we concurred. I knew that in the autumn of 1862 our views coincided in regard to assailing Sumter and occupying Charleston harbor; that you then expected to make that assault; that both of us then anticipated its success, and that we mutually spoke of it as the crowning glory of a successful career. Until within a few weeks prior to the attack your letters were all unmistakably of that character, and were calling for assistance for that work. As the crisis approached, doubts and misgivings, the almost certain precursors of failure, began to manifest themselves. Such, however, was then my confidence in your ability and sagacity, that I trusted and believed you would, resolutely as well as skilfully, press forward to the accomplishment of the object intrusted to you.

I expected that you would proceed fearlessly and intelligently, and if not with as much preparatory labor and care as you have exhibited in the composition of your late letters, certainly with a due regard to the public service, and with the intention at least of a successful result. I did not suppose that during the eighteen months you had blockaded Charleston you were ignorant of the true character of the obstacles to be overcome, or that when the assault was commenced the whole fleet would be compelled to huddle together without order under the fire of the batteries, but it was assumed that you would have some plan of attack; that there had been some previous reconnoissance of the harbor, and a thorough knowledge obtained of the submerged obstructions.

I was disappointed when I learned the true state of the case, and that all the vessels except your own, which was not and unfortunately could not be got near the batteries, after a demonstration of less than two hours, during which the Monitors were subjected to a terrific fire with the loss of one man, your forces were withdrawn, and you, having taken a night's reflection, concluded to leave the harbor and abandon the attack. The principal reason assigned for this abandonment was the injury that had been done the Monitors, and your inability to renew the assault in consequence. These vessels, which you claim not to have disparaged, have since been under fire for about two months, and, but for the submerged obstructions which you treated lightly, but of which you appear to have never obtained authentic information, they could have gone to the wharves of Charleston and returned. No batteries could have prevented.

Nevertheless you imputed your failure to the Monitors; you reported them greatly injured; you apprehended they could not remain inside the bar and ride out the storm; you urged the renewal of the blockade off the harbor.

The results which have since followed; the fire which the Monitors have sustained for many weeks; the safety with which for months they have rode out gales inside the bar; the much more stringent efficiency of the blockade with the Ironsides and Monitors inside, than it ever was while the vessels were outside, have confirmed me in the belief that the Monitors were not solely nor even mainly responsible for the failure of the 7th of April.

You complain because I did not acknowledge your preliminary despatch of the 8th, sent forward by Commander Rhind in the Flambeau. In this you seem strangely oblivious of my despatch of the 11th of April, written and forwarded immediately on receiving intelligence of your failure through rebel sources, confirmed by telegram from Fortress Monroe, informing us of the arrival of the Flambeau at Hampton Roads with tidings of the demonstration of the 7th. You were in that despatch promptly advised of the views of the President and the department in relation to a "renewed attack" and continued operations, for the brief demonstration of the 7th was at first regarded by us as a mere reconnoissance or preliminary attack, to be followed up by more decisive action.

When Commander Rhind arrived in Washington on the 12th he brought little if any new intelligence, and I had nothing to say in addition to my despatch of the 11th, which had anticipated your formal communication. Nor am I aware that there were any means of immediate conveyance had I made a formal acknowledgment of your brief report, for there was no regular communication.

The despatch of the 11th, which you received on the 16th, put you in possession of the views of the government after the attack of the 7th was known, without delaying to communicate till notice was formally received and acknowledged.

I did not communicate with you further on the subject, for I was in daily and hourly expectation of hearing from you as to the prosecution of the attack. That you had wholly neglected to inform yourself of the submerged harbor obstructions I was unwilling to believe, and yet I had no assurance on that point. Waiting for developments and suggestions which your opportunities, official position, and long experience on the coast authorized you to make, and which were a part of your duty, days wasted, and no communication from you as to an attack or future operations was received. Your detailed report, when transmitted, was soon followed by another and more ponderous document, but, to my regret and surprise, neither of them brought any more information or any suggestion of any plan of naval operations looking to its accomplishment. Your report, consisting of eight pages, and its accompaniments, expatiated on alleged deficiencies of the iron-clads and their injuries. I regretted that the report was not such a plain narrative of the attack, unconnected with other topics, as to justify its publication, but the account was so interwoven with complaints of the feebleness and inefficiency of the vessels that its publication would have been impolitic and injurious. There was no necessity to have exposed the deficiency of the vessels to the rebels, even if as great as represented. Only one object was to be gained by such exposure or exaggeration, and that was to place the entire failure on the Monitors. The tone which pervaded your report and despatches was by no means encouraging, but the reverse. You had evidently no enthusiasm or zeal for operations in Charleston harbor, but advised a return to the outside blockade.

The most elaborate as well as the most extended of all your despatches, however, at that interesting and exciting period when the government and the whole country were intent upon your action, and sympathizing with you in your arduous labors and responsibilities, was the ponderous document of the 22d of April. Not having been encouraged by your report or previous despatches, I anticipated that this document would contain a well matured plan of operations, and turned to it with high expectation, but, to my amazement, I found it consisted of fourteen foolscap pages, which you had prepared in that excited period, complaining of and criticising a newspaper article which commented with some sharpness on what the writer considered the errors of the seventh of April and the mistake in hastily withdrawing the fleet.

That an officer with such important trusts confided to him—the whole country interested in the results of his labors, and skill and bravery—the world itself a spectator of his acts—should at such a period so waste his time as to write fourteen full pages of personal defence and justification against newspaper remarks—berating and censuring others—was as pitiable as it was astonishing. I confess that, while as ready as ever to award you abilities of a certain description, I from that moment became satisfied that you would never reduce Fort Sumter nor capture Charleston. Still, remembering the services you had rendered, acknowledging your abilities in the sphere where your usefulness had been proved, and disposed to kindly regard your failure as an unavoidable infirmity, I worded my despatches in language as mildly expressive of my disappointment as I could frame. This forbearance of the department you have strangely misconstrued, and, after four months' deliberation, you come forward and seek to reopen the closed correspondence in order to manifest your latent indignation by denouncing my mild expressions as "insulting imputations" and "grave wrongs." Undoubtedly more terse and explicit language might have been used, but to you, I apprehend, it would have been much less satisfactory. It has evidently never occurred to you that the delays and failures at Charleston were in any degree imputable to the infirmities of the commander-in-chief.

You disapproved of the occupancy of the harbor, yet I am not aware that you ever caused or attempted to have a reconnoissance of the obstructions or an examination of the harbor made before the attack, nor am I aware that you have ever offered an excuse for this omission. After the attack was made you were dissatisfied with the Ironsides—dissatisfied with the Monitors—dissatisfied with Chief Engineer Stimers, against whom you prepared charges and desired that he might be arrested and sent to you for trial, he having expressed his surprise that you should abandon the assault on so brief an effort—dissatisfied with Surgeon Kershner, whom you court-martialed for a similar offence—dissatisfied with Mr. Fulton, the special agent of the Post Office Department, for his criticisms on your movements and acts—dissatisfied with the President for his telegram, and dissatisfied with the department for not more promptly and formally acknowledging and publishing your reports.

If these complaints and reports, wherein the admiral of the squadron devoted so large a portion of his time to his personal matters and so little towards marshalling his force for the occupation of the harbor of Charleston and the capture of the city, were not received with the patience to which they were entitled, it was my misfortune. I do not deny that it would have been more acceptable to the department to have witnessed the zeal manifested in hunting down newspaper editors, engineers, and surgeons, directed against rebel enemies and to the destruction of their works.

It is not my object to review or criticise your acts and doings, nor to consider other points than those which you in this elaborate and studied document have again obtruded upon the department after four months' rumination. The expedition to Ogeechee and assault on Fort McAllister, which you again refer to, was not such an exhibition of tact and strategy as to have commended itself to my judgment; yet, you having deemed it expedient, I did not object to or even criticise it. That it gave you more confidence in the Monitors in some respect you admit; but it is obvious your doubts and prejudices were not removed. If they did not inspire you with confidence and reliance, you congratulate yourself with the information you acquired. Did it ever occur to you that the information which the rebels derived from that experience was infinitely more valuable to them than any that you obtained was to you? When they beheld the invulnerability of the Monitors, they were convinced that no batteries could prevent the ingress of those vessels to Charleston, and that the defence of the city must be the submerged obstructions. How much the obstructions may have been increased, and the defence of the place strengthened, in consequence of the information so obtained by them, no reconnoissance or exploration of yours has ever informed us. If there was not entire coincidence of views between you and the department until within a brief period preceding the attack, your views were greatly misapprehended, not only by myself, but by the Assistant Secretary, with whom you held free unofficial correspondence.

Not until after the 7th of April was I aware of your disinclination to enter or occupy the harbor and encounter Sumter. The batteries, the storms, the anchorage, the rebel iron-clads, the torpedoes, were your apprehension, but the submerged obstructions you treated lightly, although they gave disquiet to the department, which could obtain no certain information from you in regard to them. You may have exercised a cautious and wary reserve in withholding "advice" on the subject of the assault, but the tenor of your despatches left me in no doubt of your opinion, while your conversations and private correspondence were explicit.

That your failure disappointed me I did not conceal, but frankly stated, not, however, in "harsh language" or "unjust reproaches." Your anxiety to leave the harbor and abandon naval demonstrations in that direction disappointed me more than your failure. For a long period the department had exerted itself assiduously to strengthen your command, had given you its efficient vessels, sometimes at the expense of other squadrons. It was for the admiral to inspire all with his opinions and resolution, and to give direction to all. That direction was, however, to withdraw after a single, brief, confused attack, in which one man was killed.

The detailed report was a deplorable representation of injuries to the Monitors, followed by expressed dissatisfaction because the account which decried them was not promptly acknowledged and published to the world. There was a manifest determination to fasten whatever weakness existed on the vessels. Fortunately they have vindicated their own reputation from this hasty condemnation, by months of endurance through storm and fire which the commander-in-chief declared they could not sustain.

You do not scruple to charge upon the department harsh language and unjust reproaches, yet nowhere in the correspondence to which you refer are they to be found, nor am I conscious of ever having entertained an unkind thought towards you to provoke them, even when lamenting what appeared to me your errors. In the overwhelming pressure of great events, and measures of deep public concernment, my language may have been unstudied, but never intentionally offensive. Nor did any intimation of "wounding words" ever escape you in the day when these occurrences transpired. There were regrets, disappointments, and differences of opinions, that were sufficiently painful without the addition of "harsh language," "unjust reproaches," or "wounding words." I had given you my willing confidence, and supposed there was entire frankness and sincerity between us, nor was I undeceived until after the 7th day of April, when you informed me that demonstration was "a measure you never advised." Until that declaration I had never suspected any want of concert or candor. In the same communication you indicated a general non-concurrence in the views of the President and of the department; said that you had "withdrawn the iron-clads from the very insecure anchorage inside the bar;" spoke of the "great peril of their being lost on Morris island beach;" asserted that "their ground tackling has been found to be insufficient;" dwelt on "the serious injury sustained by the Monitors," but stated you would "get them inside Charleston bar with all despatch, in accordance with the order of the President;" thought it your "duty, however, to state to the department that this will be attended with great risk to these vessels from the gales which prevail at this season, and from the continuous fire of the enemy's batteries, which they can neither silence nor prevent the erection of new ones." These are but parts of that despatch, not to dwell on others equally censorious, indicating disagreement with the previous policy and understanding—distrust and discontent—and concluding with your "request that the department will not hesitate to relieve me by any officer who is more able to execute that service in which I have had the misfortune to fail."

This letter was written on the 16th of April, immediately after receiving my despatch of the 11th, directing renewed operations, and before there had been time for formal acknowledgment of your communication of the 8th, and in fact superseding its necessity. Thenceforward, until you were relieved, I was painfully impressed, with the want of earnest zeal and enthusiasm, the lack of vigor, the omission to make suggestions, and the absence of will and energy and resolute determination to carry forward the vast operations intrusted to you. Your request to be relieved was not an unmeaning or unimportant expression. Uttered as it was at a critical period in front of the enemy, and with active operations in progress, I was not at liberty to disregard it. Taken in connexion with the changed tone of your correspondence, and the declaration that you "never advised" the measure, with the consequences that might follow, a responsibility devolved upon the department and the government, from that request and your evident discontent, that could not be evaded.

The whole condition of affairs, with your changed opinions and feelings, was deliberately considered, and contributed to delay the acknowledgment and reply to your detailed report. I was anxious to know whether this request to be relieved could be considered a mere momentary impulse, and waited further developments on that point, as well as in regard to your views and plans for attacking Charleston. But instead of plans and suggestions for naval operations such as I looked for and had a right to expect from the admiral in command, there came the dissertation of fourteen pages complaining of a newspaper article, and exhibiting a sensitive tenderness of what concerned yourself personally. What action could I take or what course pursue, when the officer who had been selected for this important command was at this crisis engaged in a newspaper dispute, complaining of his friends and requesting to be relieved? Disappointed that you, at the period when the government had a right to rely upon you most, should seem so indifferent to the public necessities, so solicitous for yourself, the department was embarrassed, but yet retained a lingering hope that you would feel sufficient interest to suggest some plan for prosecuting naval operations. When, however, weeks passed, and nothing substantial was received, but the apathy or indifference continued, you were finally relieved in June. Alluding to these matters and your neglect or omission to suggest a plan of operations, and to the request that I made in my letter of the 14th of May, specially inviting you to communicate your views to the department, you say: "Before it could receive my reply, giving a detailed plan of operations, the department relieved me." That relief was not unsolicited; but had it been given without request of any kind from you—had you been earnest and diligent in carrying out the policy of the government, and had all the imaginary wrongs which you conceive yourself to have suffered been real, was it right for you, as an officer and a patriot, after being specially invited to submit your views, to withhold from your government and country any "detailed plan of operations" which your abilities and long experience had enabled you to form? There is a patriotism that leads to self-sacrifice, and causes one to forget personal wrongs in devotion to his country. If you really had in your mind a "detailed plan of operations," could any personal consideration or private griefs, real or imaginary, induce you to suppress and withhold it from that government which had so honored and trusted you, and to which you were under so many and great obligations? If so, I must say that you were not relieved one moment too soon. And here let me say, that the plan of operations to which you refer as already existing in your mind, being the results of observations derived from eighteen months' experience, and, as you intimate, ready to be communicated, is still withheld.

You not only disavow advising the operations on Charleston, but have taken special occasion to say there was non-concurrence of views between yourself and the Assistant Secretary. In saying this you profess not to understand the character of the mission of that gentleman for the relief of Sumter in 1861, and to be ignorant of his making more than one visit to Charleston. It is not necessary that I should go into an explanation of the confidential trust which the President instituted to succor the famishing garrison at that time. But the Assistant Secretary had made himself so familiar with the harbor and defences that you communicated and advised with him freely and unofficially in regard to operations. If, as you remark, his visit in 1861 did not "make him familiar with all the points of fortifications," he knew enough of them to entertain no apprehension of their preventing the passage of the Monitors. But while the batteries are powerless to those vessels, the submerged obstructions may be formidable and dangerous. These are really the present chief and almost only defences of Charleston against a purely naval attack, and yet you always treated those obstructions lightly and as of little account. If, from the want of accurate information, you underestimated them before the demonstration of the 7th of April, the subsequent omission to obtain the facts and report to the department exhibits a want of vigilance that was not to have been expected from the commanding officer, who had been eighteen months on the coast, commencing before there were any submerged obstructions to be overcome.

As you express your surprise at, and your inability to comprehend, the trust confided to the Assistant Secretary in 1861, I herewith transmit a copy of his letter to me, embodying his authority from the Secretary of War, and also from Lieutenant General Scott, when commissioned to convey supplies to the famishing garrison in Fort Sumter. Unfortunately the bombardment of Sumter had commenced before the supplies arrived, and he was compelled, as you are pleased to remind us, to witness the surrender of the fortress without being able to relieve the garrison. You will also find appended extracts from your private and unofficial letters to him, alluded to in your late communication, and also to Commander Wise, which may serve to refresh your memory as to the views and feelings which you actually entertained at the time they were written in regard to operations, if you did not officially "advise" them.

I must also call your attention to one or two official despatches, not supposing that there were differences between us in regard to the operations which, since your failure, you say you never "advised." I did not scan your despatches with a view of ascertaining how far and to what extent you were committed to the undertaking. On my part there were no reserves; and if there were any on yours, to them perhaps may be attributed much of your difficulty. My despatches were frank and explicit. On the 6th of January I wrote you that "the New Ironsides, Passaic, Montauk, Patapsco, and Weehawken, iron-clads, have been ordered to, and are now on the way, to join your command, to enable you to enter the harbor of Charleston and demand the surrender of its defences, or suffer the consequences of a refusal."

There certainly was no question as to the views of the department in this despatch; and if you did not advise the measure, the fact that you did not intimate a doubt or make an adverse suggestion, permitted me to draw no other inference than that you concurred. It was, indeed, in conformity with all our previous understanding and preparation.

You, yourself, wrote on the 24th of January that, "The department is aware that I have never shrunk from any responsibility which circumstances called for, nor desired to place any failure of mine on others. But the interests involved in the success or failure of the undertaking strike me as so momentous to the nation at home and abroad at this particular period, that I am confident it will require no urging from me to induce the department to put at my disposal every means in its power to insure success, especially by sending additional iron-clads, if possible, to those mentioned in your despatch. The army is not ready for even the limited co-operation it can give, though anxious to render any assistance."

If this was not advising the measure, it was in concert with it. True it is that four days later, on the 28th of January, you made some allusions of a precautionary character, and which may have been intended to intimate more than was expressed. But on the 31st of January you were advised that, "The department does not desire to urge an attack upon Charleston with inadequate means, and if, after careful examination, you deem the number of iron-clads insufficient to render the capture of that port reasonably certain, it must be abandoned." But it was not abandoned, nor was there any intimation it should be, and it was consequently taken for granted that you "advised" the measure.

You were further informed in the same despatch that, "The department is not acquainted with the harbor obstructions constructed by the rebels, and therefore cannot advise with you in regard to these obstacles. If they are not considered sufficient to prevent your entrance, it is not believed possible for the rebels to prevent your success with all other means combined." On this point the department has not changed its views. But, unfortunately, you failed to inform yourself in regard to the obstructions; or if you had accurate knowledge of them, it has been withheld from the department.

Although trespassing on time that I cannot well spare, I have, induced by your extraordinary letter, read over the correspondence to which you have taken these late exceptions, and I perceive therein nothing to justify the accusations and complaints, which, in closing the subject, I must be permitted to say, are as unworthy of you as they are unjust to the department.

Very respectfully,

GIDEON WELLES,
Secretary of the Navy.

RearA-dmiral S. F. DuPont,
Near Wilmington, Delaware.

—

[Enclosures to the foregoing letter.]

Navy Department, *November* 3, 1863.

Sir: Rear-Admiral DuPont's despatch, dated near Wilmington, October 22, alluded to the Assistant Secretary of the Navy and the correspondence had with him, which being private and unofficial, has no place on the record.

As it is the evident wish of the admiral that that portion which relates to the contemplated attack upon Charleston should be before you, I have the honor to furnish extracts bearing upon the subject, including one from a note of the admiral to Commander Wise.

So much surprise is expressed by the admiral at my having commanded an expedition which "witnessed" the bombardment of Sumter in April, 1861, that

I append herewith the order of honorable Simon Cameron, Secretary of War, under which I acted; also an order of Lieutenant General Winfield Scott.

Very respectfully,

G. V. FOX, *Assistant Secretary.*

Hon. GIDEON WELLES,
Secretary of the Navy.

Private letter dated September 12, 1862.

Several reports have reached us which interest me, that you contemplated some attack on Charleston. Please not *give orders* without previously hearing from me. This is too serious a matter, and too much involved in a failure, not to be maturely considered.

I feel too sure of ultimate success to hesitate to check premature action.

Extract from private letter, dated January 8, 1863.

* * * We have a good deal of information from Norris. No obstructions to speak of, but the two iron-clads are formidable, and *they say* 140 guns can be brought to bear on an approaching vessel, and have not the slightest apprehension. * * *

Extract from private letter dated January 10, 1863.

* * * Norris, whom we took, represents the Charleston iron-clads as very formidable in everything but motive power. * * *

Extract from private letter dated February 25, 1863.

* * * The ammunition is all received, and we are working steadily in reference to its proper and available distribution. The Ordnance Bureau has done wonders for us in this line. * * *

The *experiment*—for it is nothing else, (the trying of 200 guns with 20)—is too momentous to be trifled with. You must therefore be patient until we are ready. Better be successful in March than fail in February. I am surprised you believe for a moment that we could be humbugged into a *siege*. * * * There is another battery going up nearer Cummings's Point, so we shall have to knock this over, as well as Fort Wagner, to win our harbor and get our own base of operations. To keep up the supply of ammunition in these vessels requires great preparation and system. * * * We are up and doing. Nothing will be wanting on our part, if it pleases God to give us the day.

Extract from private letter dated March 2, 1863.

* * * While I thank you for your great efforts, I think it right to say that the limit of my wants in the way of iron-clads is the capacity of the department to supply them. * * * If you send me all you can, I can ask no more. * * * Morris island has been covered with batteries, where we have to win our harbor and establish our naval base. * * *

Excuse me, but I could not but smile at your grand plan of sailing in silently on our friends. There is no question about what the result would be, and be as you say it would; but, my friend, you have to *get there*. We will do it if it can be done. I think we shall have to batter and pound beyond any precedent in history. * * *

—

Memorandum dated March 7, 1863.

The conclusion to be drawn from the very valuable practice at Fort McAllister is, that none of the 15-inch guns can be worked for more than a day's fight without repairs. The attack on Charleston may take a week before any final result is reached. Four Monitors have attacked Fort McAllister. Of these two got aground, two had their concussion boxes injured, one had her 15-inch gun-carriage injured, one was injured by a torpedo, and one by a bombshell, without taking a seven-gun fort. Part only of those vessels which go into the fight at Charleston will be efficient at the end of it, and part, therefore, of the attacking force must take the city.

Then Dahlgren gives the life of his gun at 300. That will never answer, I think. We had better have 11-inch. * * *

—

Extract of a letter from Port Royal dated January 16, 1863.

* * * In reference to the former it would appear, if we can rely upon recent statements—what I cared as much for and more than forts, (obstructions)—we are in a measure relieved. The depth of water, a gale or two, and some spring tides, have removed the great mass of them, well constructed as they were—five fourteen-inch timbers, hooped with iron, with iron points or heel to sink them, then fastened together by a chain cable about ten feet apart, with a torpedo hung to the festoons.

They are still at work on the defences, however, and the number of forts and guns is simply fabulous. My comfort and hope is, that with our experience and study of eighteen months on the coast, we can apply whatever means are furnished for the end desired, about as well as most people. * * *

—

WAR DEPARTMENT,
Washington, April 4, 1861.

SIR: It having been determined to succor Fort Sumter, you have been selected for this important duty. Accordingly you will take charge of the transports provided in New York, having the troops and supplies on board, to the entrance of Charleston harbor, and endeavor, in the first instance, to deliver the subsistence. If you are opposed in this you are directed to report the fact to the senior naval officer off the harbor, who will be instructed by the Secretary of the Navy to use his entire force to open a passage, when you will, if possible, effect an entrance and place both the troops and supplies in Fort Sumter.

I am, sir, very respectfully, your obedient servant,

SIMON CAMERON,
Secretary of War.

Captain G. V. Fox, *Washington.*

—

HEADQUARTERS OF THE ARMY,
Washington, April 4, 1861.

SIR: This letter will be handed to you by Captain G. V. Fox, ex-officer of the navy, and a gentleman of high standing, as well as possessed of extraordinary nautical ability. He is charged by high authority here with the command of an expedition (under cover of certain ships-of-war) whose object is to re-enforce Fort Sumter.

To embark with Captain Fox, you will cause a detachment of recruits, say about two hundred, to be immediately organized at Fort Columbus, with a competent number of officers, army ammunition, and subsistence. A large surplus of the latter, indeed as great as the vessels of the expedition will take, with other necessaries, will be needed for the augmented garrison of Fort Sumter. The subsistence and other supplies should be assorted like those which were provided by you and Captain Ward, of the navy, for a former expedition.

Consult Captain Fox and Major Eaton on the subject, and give all necessary orders in my name to fit out the expedition, except that the hiring of the vessel will be left to others.

Some fuel must be shipped, oil, artillery implements, fuzes, cordage, slow-match, mechanical levers, and guns, &c., &c., should also be put on board.

Consult also, if necessary, (confidentially,) Colonel Tompkins and Major Thornton.

Respectfully, yours,

WINFIELD SCOTT.

Lieut. Col. R. L SCOTT,
Aide-de-Camp, &c., &c.

Journal of Surgeon Marius Duval.

U. S. SHIP NEW IRONSIDES, OFF CHARLESTON BAR.

April 24, 1863.—The attack on the forts at the entrance of Charleston harbor is still the subject for reflection and conversation, but the discussion upon it is not conducted with coolness. An angry partisan feeling has been started here. Mr. Stimers has been assailed; Captain —— will cowhide him if he says or does so and so. The Monitors are decried, wooden vessels are put in invidious comparison with them, and a thousand silly side issues are started; so the real matter is lost sight of. We are all bound, in duty, to examine the subject attentively and dispassionately; any convictions founded on facts, and plainly expressed, need not be considered as centred upon any one. The truth never can be distasteful to honest people.

The Monitors attacked Fort Sumter (nothing else) at the distance of 600 or 800 yards; we were all under the fire of Fort Morgan and Cummings's Point battery, (on Morris island,) Fort Sumter, and Battery Beauregard, Moultrie, and Battery Bee, (on Sullivan's island.) The Monitors generally were closer to Fort Sumter and Battery Bee than this ship; all under fire about one hour. During this time it is computed the Monitors fired on an average 20 shot each; all theirs (with the exception of possibly 10 shot from all of them) were sent at Fort Sumter—these exceptional 10 were fired at Wagner, &c. This ship fired eight shot in all—seven 11-inch at Moultrie, and one rifle 200-pounder at Wagner. This ship fired not a shot at Sumter; could not get her broadside to bear for tide, &c.; (there was no thought, I believe, of anchoring.*) In this hour (under fire I mean) several minutes were lost because this ship and two or three Monitors were foul of each other, and neither of them could fire. It was not intended to fire on Moultrie, but our guns bore on it, and we fired. Then the vessels were ordered to haul out of action. It was after 5 p. m. when the action ceased. All the commanders of the attacking vessels were ordered to come on board this

*NOTE.—Did not anchor to engage the batteries, I mean. During the action the ship was drifting about, and was near grounding, the lead showing 17 feet. To prevent her grounding (and consequently her inevitable loss) the anchor was dropped under foot twice.

ship, (being the flag-ship,) and reported. The Keokuk riddled; the Nahant damaged, (turret would not revolve;) Nantucket damaged, (could not open and shut the big gun shutter, I believe;) Patapsco damaged, and one other. Up to this report, it was the common opinion that the attack would be renewed. I have heard said commanders *then* declared that there was no prospect of success even if the attack were renewed. Mr. Stimers said the Monitors were not much injured, and they could be repaired in less than 20 hours. The commanders supposed no damage had been done to Sumter. One commander certainly was convinced the 15-inch gun was useless. He represented the shot from that gun as lazily running on the water, and feebly falling against the walls of Sumter. The next morning we examined (I, Quartermaster English, remarkable for the accuracy of his vision, and others) Fort Sumter, about 3½ miles distant, and we could count the dents and holes in its walls. They were very plain to us, so much so to me that I could not refrain from calling the attention of the admiral to them. He took the glass from my hand, and after several minutes' scrutiny, he remarked, "Yes, it is a good deal pock-marked." As this was the first occasion that heavy ordnance, smooth-bore and rifled, had been tried in actual warfare on the brick walls of a fort, it struck me with surprise that a Monitor was not sent as close as possible to inspect these walls.

The rebel papers (and I have read a file of Charleston ones, from 7th to 20th April inclusive) admit damage to Wagner and Moultrie slight, but still some. The same papers state Sumter was *not* damaged, although struck 34 times. I am satisfied that one more hour's firing at Fort Sumter would have destroyed this face of it.

To me our ability to reconnoitre was extremely interesting. I examined attentively Fort Wagner and the battery on Cummings's Point; then Fort Johnson; all earthworks. The guns of the two first-mentioned were visible, uncovered; those of Fort Johnson could not be seen. Wagner and Cummings's Point are easily assailable by this ship, the Monitors, and gunboats. Fort Moultrie, Batteries Bee and Beauregard are also uncovered works, and could be assailed by our iron and wooden fleets, after Wagner and Sumter were demolished. An impression had been received (and it was so stated as a fact after we recrossed the bar) that the reason the iron-clads were withdrawn from the inside of the bar was because the private secretary of the President had brought orders to the admiral to that effect. This statement was made by Captain Turner to the officers and crew at muster; but it was a singular error, the explanation of which I intend to ask from Captain Turner. Preparations for withdrawing from the inside had been made before the arrival of the President's secretary. We trust the attack will soon be repeated. One of our shutters was knocked off; the shot dropped from our sides like boys' brickbats from the roof of a house.

There were several officers who had the opinion, *before going into the fight*, that the Monitors could not do much; that the 15-inch gun did not throw its shot with velocity enough, &c. Does this account for the opinion expressed, *after the fight*, that no damage had been done to Sumter?

April 25.—Our iron-clads were anchored after the action with Sumter in main ship channel, three miles distant from said fort, which bore about N.NW. Wagner bore about NW., about 1½ mile distant. The Monitors can easily get within 1,000 yards of last-named work, and this ship within a mile of it. It is an open work of nine or ten guns, four of which are pointed south to resist land forces approaching in that direction; only five or six could be brought to bear on our attacking fleet, together with the four or five on Cummings's Point. The iron-clads can bring 32 guns to bear upon these ten uncovered ones. How long ought it to take to demolish them? This demolition accomplished, or the guns in the works kept silent by the wooden vessels, we begin the attack again on Sumter; the Monitors can go at it, and this ship steaming up to Moultrie and Beauregard, within 1,200 yards of them, can occupy their time, and in this way make a fine diversion for the Monitors. The strength of the rebel fortifications here are greatly overrated. There are 22 guns in Moultrie, 9 in Bee, and 5 in Beauregard—36 guns in all from Sullivan's island. Possibly 35 in casemate and "en barbette" in Sumter, together with those stated on Morris island, make up the sum total of all the guns which protect the entrance of the harbor against our fleet. I venture to state that if the Monitors could be so relieved, the sea-face of Sumter would be destroyed in two hours. In the recent attack this ship was of no more use than if she had been at the Philadelphia navy yard. As it is, the damage done to that work is manifestly very great. Yesterday and to-day are plainly seen two scaffoldings along the wall battered, and more will have to be adjusted to embrace all the scars upon it. These scaffoldings have been up for ten days at least—the work of repairs going on all the time. Attention must be called to the fact already noticed, that in the recent action several minutes were lost by this ship's fouling the two or three Monitors. How small must have been the actual fire upon Fort Sumter, yet observe its effect upon the walls. My prayer now is, that in the next attack the Monitors may go up as close as possible to Sumter and *anchor*, while we *anchor* off Moultrie, then there will be no fouling each other. The enemy are erecting a battery about the middle of Morris island, to command the channel by which this ship crossed the bar. I hope Admiral DuPont, as soon as he hears it, will send us and some Monitors inside to look after those fellows.

May 20.—To-day the scaffoldings about Fort Sumter were not seen, have been removed, the work of repairs having been completed. With a glass we can see the walls smooth again, the impressions of fresh brick and mortar are still visible, however. It was on the 14th of April that these scaffoldings were first seen; they remained until the 20th of May—36 days. Will any military man say that, working as the occupants of Sumter must have worked in these 36 days to repair damages, the enemy still in sight, those damages to the work were anything but serious?

June 7.—This morning at dawn two deserters came off to us from Fort Beauregard; they state that the east angle of Sumter (this is the exact point where the scaffoldings were seen the longest period) was almost knocked to pieces in our attack; that the walls at that point are still "shaky," and "are backed by ten feet of sand bags." We have this same statement from other sources. They also state that there are few troops in or about Charleston at this moment, all nearly having been sent to Virginia and Vicksburg. Some days since word was received from our naval officer commanding off Georgetown, South Carolina, that all the troops had gone from that region to parts unknown. Would it not be a convenient season to repeat our attack now? A steamer running out a few nights since was forced back and sunk off Fort Beauregard; these deserters think it is the Isaac Smith, converted into a blockade runner. There are a great number of such now inside, watching to run out; many will succeed, for our vessels being outside, are too heavy and too slow to prevent them. A stringent blockade will never be had until our iron-clads are anchored inside the bar. Assistant Surgeon Kershner is to be tried by a court-martial for having written to the Baltimore American, passing some strictures upon the admiral because he withdrew his iron-clads from before Charleston, instead of repeating the attack. It is against orders to give information to newspapers, &c., and for violating this order Dr. Kershner is to be tried. How strange! It is known to the whole fleet that, on the night after the attack, a national vessel, the Flambeau, with Admiral DuPont's despatches, was sent to Hampton Roads. The correspondents of the New York Times and the New York Tribune were permitted to go in her. Everybody on board her knew that these correspondents would hasten to represent the affair in a manner the most favorable possibly to Admiral DuPont, and that, too, before the admiral's despatches could reach the department. Was that proper in Admiral DuPont? Was it subordinate?

Should not the Navy Department be allowed to judge of the acts of its agents' before the leading journals of the country should take the matter in hand. What constitutes the difference, so far as military offence is concerned, between an officer sending his information and comments to a newspaper by mail, and one who sends it in the pockets of correspondents of newspapers? The answer just occurs to me. One is humble, the other is exalted. A spider's web catches a small fly; a big one breaks through it. Dr. Kershner did violate a rule of discipline; but in this case, and for this cause, said rule was more honored in the breach than in the observance,

July 9.—Admiral DuPont has been relieved, and Admiral Dahlgren has been appointed to succeed him. He is now here with the Monitors outside. He is going in across the bar to-morrow morning to flank the batteries on the south end of Morris island, while the army batteries, secretly planted on the north end of Folly island, attack in front. All are alive with expectation now. 10th.—Just before sunrise, the batteries on Folly island open on the enemy on Morris island. At this moment Admiral Dahlgren is seen with the Monitors crossing the bar, his flag flying from the Catskill. The army practice is superb; artillery could not be served more rapidly; the shell seem to fly over the whole island, even beyond Wagner and Cummings's Point, and almost up to Sumter. By this time the Monitors have position and open their batteries. The rebels are evidently taken by surprise, and answer feebly and timidly. In about two hours and a half they are in full flight towards Wagner, and our troops are seen pouring upon Morris island. The Monitors are moving up towards Wagner, shelling the flying rebels all the time. At 8 a. m. the admiral is abreast of Wagner, and opens upon it, one other Monitor with him; continues the assault until 12 m., and hauls off to rest and refresh the men; resumes his assault at 2 p. m., and continues it until sunset. The tenacity of the admiral excites the enthusiasm of everybody; one of the petty officers of this ship was heard to exclaim, "By God! this ship's company will cheer that man."* The confidence in the Monitors is restored by the example of Admiral Dahlgren, and a great public service rendered to the government thereby. The enemy make a target of the Catskill because the admiral's flag is there. At night it is ascertained that that Monitor in this day's work was hit oftener (and as heavily) than any one of these vessels in the attack of April 7.

July 29.—The army have advanced their batteries to 800 yards of Wagner, and 3,500 yards of Sumter. The guns from Wagner and Gregg (Cummings's Point) annoy the working parties continually; every day the admiral is requested to silence these guns of the enemy; he complies with alacrity; the ship, the Monitors, and gunboats are continually put in requisition for this purpose. The admiral goes into action sometimes, I presume, to examine, and set an example; whenever he does his flag is made a target. This ship has been already tested; our shutters have been struck squarely in the centre with 10-inch shot, and were not broken through.

November 4.—About ten days ago the army batteries on Morris island (on Cummings's Point) opened again on Sumter, some intelligence having been received that the rebels were busily at work in it. Two Monitors joined in the bombardment, and splendid work have they done; Stevens in the Patapsco, and Bryson in the Lehigh. They have rifle guns, besides the 15-inch. The army people seem to be convinced now that Fort Sumter was not entirely reduced by the first bombardment.

* This remark was made in allusion to the fact that the crew had refused to cheer Admiral DuPont as he was leaving the ship. I put it in the record, not to preserve that indecorous and mortifying omission on the part of our crew, but to show the effect on it of Admiral Dahlgren's tenacity. Every person on board was convinced that this ship was the most powerfully offensive war vessel afloat at that time, and to have her taken into action, and eight random shots fired from her broadsides, and then put out to blockade again, filled the men with indignation.

Judging from some of the newspapers at home, one would suppose that some are angry because Charleston is not taken. Admiral Dahlgren is harshly spoken of for this. In my humble opinion, the admiral is doing everything that a commander-in-chief here can do. Besides many attacks on Wagner and Gregg, Admiral Dahlgren has assailed Sumter twice with the Monitors—himself being in one of them. These vessels have been greatly battered in all these attacks. I am free to say that these vessels have been hammered six times as much since the 10th of July as they were in the attack of April 7, some requiring repairs continually. The admiral cannot command more than five sound ones at any one time for an attack. Would it not be foolhardy to enter the inner harbor with so small a force? One or two might be disabled before getting there, where they have to encounter the rebel iron-clads. Every man here knows that if the iron-clads were lost our land forces could not remain on Morris island. The blockade is now perfect, why jeopard everything by an attack with a small force? Admiral Dahlgren was the first to take this ship under the guns of Bee, Moultrie, and Beauregard, which he did at night, when the Weehawken was aground. Yet, from the tone of some of the papers at home, one might suppose he had never *carried* the iron-clads into action. We all on board here know that after the April attack on Sumter this ship was pronounced a failure, that she would not steer, &c. But for the tests to which she has been subjected by Admiral Dahlgren the government would not have known her efficiency. In this recent bombardment of Fort Sumter by the two Monitors, under the command of Captains Stevens and Bryson, there was some experience of the 15-inch guns. Those officers have seen the 15-inch shell strike the walls at the distance of 1,600 yards, and have declared that their explosion has brought down heavier masses of the masonry than half a dozen rifle shot. I have heard Lieutenant Commander Bunce, ex-officer of some of them, make the same statement. Surely the observation of these officers is more accurate than any made in the April attack, when these 15-inch shell or shot were supposed to have fallen so feebly against Sumter.

December 13.—The defensive power of Charleston now to what it was in April last is about five to one, notwithstanding Sumter is considered out of the question. But my impression is, that when we enter the inner harbor we shall find ten or twelve guns to play on us from that work; all the guns in lower tier of casemates on northwest and some on northeast faces are probably in good working order. We saw what the batteries on Sullivan's island were—three detached works; now those are strengthened, and all connected by fresh earthworks, containing several mortar batteries, in addition to many newly mounted guns. Moultrie has been converted into an earthwork of great strength. After running by the fire of these batteries and we reach the inner harbor, we have the fire of battery Simkins and Fort Johnson, on James's island, Fort Ripley and Castle Pinkney, and those from the point of the city.

We cannot take Charleston to hold it, but we can burn it; and, as a military measure, it would be justifiable to do so. Its factories at work and vessels on the stocks are seen every day. We would hold the garrison in Sumter uneasy by cutting off their supplies, &c., and the troops on Sullivan's island also.

It is a great mistake to suppose the iron-clads have been idle at any time since the 10th of July. Up to the time of the capture of Wagner and Gregg, the demands upon this ship and the Monitors to engage those works to enable the army to carry on its sapping operations were so frequently made as to almost exhaust the officers and crews, so that I proposed to Captain Rowan that I, in my professional capacity, should see the admiral and ask him to give the men longer intervals between the engagements if possible. Since then the picket duty performed by the Monitors is probably the most laborious ever performed by naval vessels, necessitating frequent repairs, for which they must be sent to Port Royal. Since the attack of the torpedo on this vessel, the officers and crew may be said to sleep upon their arms, which is wearing upon us all. But we are all compensated by the fact that the blockade is perfect. Not one vessel has passed in since the iron-clads anchored inside; one certainly, possibly two, have run out since that time.

January 1, 1864.—Another year has passed away. Surely it has given some instructive lessons to those who have watched the military and naval operations about this harbor. Up to the arrival of Admiral DuPont with the Monitors to make the attack, we all on board here were in high glee at the prospect. The blockaders had been coming out constantly and running in; as we saw them, in the morning after they "got in," they were going by Sumter with hundreds of banners flying. Soon after the admiral's suite came on board this ship our hopes were dampened sensibly. Want of confidence in the Monitors was openly expressed by some of them, based upon the experience of two of them which had attacked an *earthwork* on the Ogeechee river. It was remarked contemptuously of these two, that after bombarding the fort for several hours "they had succeeded in killing one cat;" that the 15-inch gun was devoid of power; that its projectile was cast with too small velocity to injure the brick walls of Sumter. I heard the epithet "machine" applied to this class of vessels, with the remark that it was useless to expect to take Charleston by machinery. One of them was confident the rebels had 15-inch guns on Sumter and Moultrie. Well, the attack was made, and the result is "before the world." After the attack the Monitors, disabled seriously as it was said, were scattered about; the most of them were deposited in Edisto, because, as I heard, the anchorage in Port Royal was insecure for them. This ship took up her old position outside the bar. Three months later, Admiral Dahlgren, then in command of the fleet here, took these same crippled vessels (I had been told that seventy-seven bolts from the turret of the Nahant had been sent by Admiral DuPont to the Navy Department, and that some persons had said that if that Monitor had continued the attack, April 7, one hour longer, her entire turret would have been knocked to pieces) and began operations on Morris island. Since that time these Monitors have been hit five times as often as they were on the 7th of April, yet they do good work still. It seems to me a matter of demonstration that the officers who reported them so seriously damaged in the April attack on Sumter were in error. Why, it may be speculated, should Mr. Stimers be harshly spoken to and of, by naval officers, because he gave his professional opinion that these vessels were not much injured then? And why should he be assailed as an interested (and, from his connexion with the government, as a dishonest one, of course) agent of the "iron interests of the country?" And why should it have been said that he was improperly sent down here by the Navy Department? The events since then enacted by these Monitors have, to my mind, demonstrated the accuracy of Mr. Stimers's observation.

When the Weehawken was aground, September 8, nine hundred yards from Sumter, and forty guns playing on her from Sullivan's island, she sent a 15-inch shell ricochetting into Moultrie, 1,200 or 1,400 yards distant, and exploded a magazine there. As soon as two Monitors afloat were interposed between her and Moultrie, her guns were turned upon Sumter, and I saw the 15-inch shell pitched into that work time and again. Afterwards, Captain Colhoun, the commanding officer, told me he threw on that occasion forty shell into Sumter—more, according to rebel accounts, than all the iron-clads did on the 7th of April. When at a later period the Lehigh was aground, all the Monitors, with Admiral Dahlgren in one of them, were within 1,600 yards of Moultrie. The 15-inch gun of the Passaic was principally used by her commanding officer, Captain Simpson, with beautiful effect upon Moultrie. I have been told that when General Gillmore saw the great havoc made upon the walls of Sumter when it was being bombarded by the Patapsco and Lehigh, he declared that more damage was done to these walls by one 15-inch shell than by a half dozen of any other calibre. These facts, to my mind, demonstrate that those gentlemen who held the opinion at the April attack that not much could be expected from the 15-inch gun because of the slow motion of its projectile, and the feebleness of its impact, were also in error.

On the 8th of September this ship was directed by the admiral to interpose between the Weehawken and the forts assailing her. Captain Rowan took the ship up and *anchored* under Moultrie, 1,200 yards (say) distant, on the flood-tide too, so that the vessel was exposed to the fire until she had "swung to the tide," then she opened on Moultrie principally, and in less than an hour had silenced it utterly. This fact was witnessed by ten thousand people. Does it do too much violence to "loyalty to Admiral DuPont"* now to say that had this ship been so managed in the attack of April 7, she would have greatly assisted the Monitors, instead of "fouling them." This fact must demonstrate to any one that those gentlemen who held the opinion that the New Ironsides was a failure were also in error.

We have received the "report of the Secretary of the Navy." In the despatch of April 16, 1863, contained therein, Admiral DuPont says that the New Ironsides, if she were to go inside the bar, could not elevate her guns to reach any of the enemy's batteries, so great is the distance at which she would be compelled to anchor. Since the 10th of July last this ship has engaged the enemy's batteries here fifteen times. In those engagements she has sent into Wagner 3,300 shell; into Gregg, 300; and into Moultrie, 400; she alone silencing these works whenever she engaged them. Our ordnance officer, Lieutenant Robeson, informs me that of these shell 2,000 were five-second fuzes (for distance of 1,000 yards,) 1,500 were seven-second fuzes (for distance of 1,200 yards,) and 500 were ten-second fuzes (for distance of 1,600 yards.) When, on the 10th of July, Admiral Dahlgren with the Monitors engaged the batteries on the south end of Morris island, the 15-inch shell (as well as the 11-inch) of those vessels were easily thrown into those batteries with decided effect, as stated by the rebels then captured. In their subsequent contests with the works on the north end of Morris island these vessels threw their shell into them with the greatest ease; the same with Sumter and Moultrie. These facts clearly demonstrate that Admiral DuPont was not acquainted with the "offensive power" of the iron-clads, and hence was mistaken in the opinion which he in that despatch expressed.

The Monitors have been at anchor inside here since July 10. No one thinks of their being lost on Morris island beach. This fact is the best answer to the opinion as to the "insecure anchorage" here.

Operations of the Patapsco against Fort Sumter.

United States Iron-clad Patapsco,
Off Charleston, November 2, 1863.

Sir: I have the honor to inform you that, according to your instructions, I have been engaged for the past week in co-operation with the batteries on Morris island, formerly called Forts Gregg and Wagner, and in company with the Monitor Lehigh, Commander Bryson, in bombarding Fort Sumter. Upon Monday last, owing to some unfinished work upon the Lehigh, she did not participate. The Patapsco upon that occasion proceeded within 1,800 yards of the fort and opened fire. As the tide was running flood when the order was given, I was compelled to fight the ship under way, and of course to some disadvantage. Notwithstanding, the fire was effective, almost every shell

---

*The words "loyalty to Admiral DuPont" were frequently heard about here—they represented a well-defined sentiment and principle. A prominent officer (staff) in my presence remarked that "the New Ironsides was the only 'disloyal ship' in the squadron." Upon asking him what he meant, it appeared his idea was, 'disloyal" to Admiral DuPont. I know nothing better than this to show the strange distemper under which the minds of certain officers were laboring.

bursting near upon or inside the fort. The next two days, the 27th and 28th, as soon as the tide served, both Monitors opened upon the northeast bastion, the fire being very destructive upon this part of the fort and the walls adjacent; so that when the army batteries were directed to this position, the walls being already greatly weakened by our fire, they soon crumbled.

Subsequent to this our fire has been mainly directed to the Charleston face and interior of the fort, with what effect the appearance of Sumter will clearly indicate. The explosion of the 15-inch shell fired with 15″ and 20″ fuzes in the inside of the fort, which gun was fired occasionally, produced an effect which is hardly describable, throwing the bricks and mortar, gun-carriages, and timber in every direction, and high into the air.

The flag upon Sumter was yesterday at two o'clock shot away for the third time, and has not since been hoisted. A man was seen making an attempt to get it up again, but just at the time three shells from the army and navy batteries exploded over him, doubtless with fatal effect.

The shells of the enemy have fallen around and about us without causing any casualties. It was not, however, until last Saturday, the 31st, their fire seemed to be directed to us, when Battery Beauregard and a battery upon James's island opened upon us, striking the Lehigh twice, but doing no damage of importance. Upon hauling off from Sumter, I stood over toward Beauregard and delivered five shots, four of which landed in the battery and produced great excitement, the people in the neighborhood flying from our shells. Upon this, Fort Moultrie fired one gun. Yesterday we were not molested on that side, although the James's island batteries still continued to fire.

We have been engaged at a distance varying from 1,600 to 2,000 yards.

I enclose herewith a tabular statement of the firing, from which it appears that out of 455 shots 315 have taken effect upon some portion of the fort.

The guns appear to stand the firing well. I have forwarded to the Ordnance office an impression of the vents of both guns, taken yesterday after the firing was over. The rams of the enemy appear to be anchored in four-fathom hole, and above Fort Johnson.

On Friday last, as we were steaming up from the lower anchorage toward Sumter, a boat with a considerable number of men around and in it, was seen upon the north shore of Sumter, but before we could get in range the boat and men had disappeared.

Very respectfully, your obedient servant,

T. H. STEVENS,

Commander, Commanding U. S. Steamer Patapsco.

Rear-Admiral J. A. DAHLGREN,

Commanding S. A. B. Squadron.

Operations of the Lehigh against Fort Sumter.

UNITED STATES IRON-CLAD LEHIGH,

Off Morris Island, South Carolina, November 4, 1863.

SIR: I have the honor to inform you that, in accordance with your order, I have been engaged for the last nine days, in company with the Patapsco and the shore batteries, in the bombardment of Fort Sumter; during which time I have fired from the 8-inch rifle 408 percussion shell, and from the 15-inch smooth-bore twenty-four shell; the distance varied from 1,600 to 1,800 yards. The effects of the lodgment of many of these shell were those of displacing large masses of masonry, and throwing high in the air pieces of heavy timber, knocking over-gun carriages, and opening casemates. During the greater part of the bombardment, my attention was given almost wholly to the inner face of the northwest wall, and the result of the firing can easily be seen by the naked eye. On the afternoon of the 31st of October the flag of Fort Sumter was shot away by the shore batteries; a short time after, two flags were raised, very near each other. The rifle was then directed to the flags, and at the third fire both flags were shot away. (Lieutenant Commander Phythian had this pleasure.) On the fourth of November, my attention was given to the north-east face of the fort. At the angle at which I was firing, I found that the shell glanced from the face, doing but little damage; after having fired a few shell at the fair face, and finding that they would not lodge, I then directed the fire to the angle of the same face, nearest Cummings's Point, which was already somewhat broken. At this point I found that the shell lodged; I then continued the fire at this point with very fine effect, knocking down tons of masonry and exposing the arch of a new casemate.

After I had made a lodgment for the shell at this part of the wall, I inclined the fire gradually to the right, and succeeded during the day in cutting into the wall for about thirty feet along its fair or northeast face. On the afternoon of October 31, battery Beauregard opened on this ship and the Patapsco, (firing six shots,) doing, however, little damage; one shot cutting away half of the pennant staff of the Lehigh, and a shell exploding on the after part of the deck

I enclose a tabular statement of the firing.

I am, respectfully, your obedient servant,

A. BRYSON, *Commander*.

Rear-Admiral JOHN A. DAHLGREN,
Commanding South Atlantic Blockading Squadron.

Summary of shots fired by the United States iron-clad Lehigh, at Fort Sumter.

RIFLE 8-INCH PARROT.					XV-INCH SMOOTH BORE.				
Date.	No. of hits.	No. of misses.	Premature explo'ns.	No. of shots.	Date.	No. of hits.	No. of misses.	Premature explo'ns.	No. of shots.
October 27...	15	13	1	29	October 28...	....	2	....	2
28...	19	15	2	36	November 2...	6	2	1	9
29...	19	10	1	30	3...	3	1	....	4
30...	31	16	4	51	4...	6	2	1	9
31...	42	13	4	59					
November 1...	51	13	5	69					
2...	35	4	3	42					
3...	36	10	3	49					
4...	38	4	1	43					
Total........	286	98	24	408	Total........	15	7	2	24

Rear-Admiral Dahlgren's report of operations against Fort Sumpter.

[Despatch No. 225.]

FLAG-STEAMER PHILADELPHIA,
Off Morris Island, South Carolina, November 4, 1863.

SIR: Since my last on the general course of operations here, our own part has still been restricted to the repair of the Monitors and the cleansing of their bottoms, which had become so foul by the adherence of grass and barnacles, as to reduce their speed from 6½ or 7 knots, to 3½ and 4. The divers have been engaged in removing these from two or three of the Monitors, it is believed with good effect; but in this respect the information is not yet complete, and it is probable that a surer means has been discovered through the agency of Mr. Griffin; that is, the vessels are beached at a suitable place, and the barnacles, &c., removed completely from the sides, leaving only the flat part of the bottom to be cleaned by the divers. It was necessary to replace the rifle gun of the Patapsco, and the 11-inch of the Montauk.

There are now two Monitors at Port Royal; the Montauk arrived here last evening, with clean bottom, a new gun, and in good condition.

Mr. Griffin is now engaged with the Ericsson torpedo, and I am in hopes he will be successful in getting it into operation. The rough weather which has prevailed lately has stopped his proceeding for a week or ten days, but he thinks one will be ready for trial soon.

I wish very much that some measures could be taken to form a kind of framework, projecting from the Monitors, so as to prevent contact with the torpedoes at the bows of the enemy's iron-clads, and also to apply their method to the Monitors. Here, I have neither the time nor the means for such undertakings.

The army having sufficiently advanced with the re-fortification of Morris island, opened fire on Fort Sumter 26th October; the object being to complete its reduction by driving out the garrison and occupying it. The firing has been prosecuted steadily since, and I have examined the progress daily by going up the channel, where a near view could be obtained of the works.

I directed the Patapsco and Lehigh, being armed with rifle guns, to take position also at effective range, but not exposed to that of Fort Moultrie and its adjacent batteries.

The line of fire from Putnam passed directly through the northwest and southeast angles of Sumter, therefore looked equally on the gorge and southeast front.

The fire from the Monitors was nearly perpendicular to the southeast front, and looked acutely on the northeast front. At first the fire ashore seemed aimed at the gorge, which had been originally faced for two-thirds of its height with sand bags. Upon these the fragments of the top of the wall had lodged and formed one mass of sand and crumbled brick, where the rifle shells entered to no great depth.

The fire of the Monitors was directed at the southeast face, and appeared to exhibit a more marked action there, because the débris had fallen down into deeper water, and not lodged to the same extent as on the gorge.

The fire of Putnam and Strong was soon after applied to the southeast front, which gradually gave way to the united fire, until it, too, was reduced to a slope of fragments, much lower, however, than that of the gorge.

By the end of the week the opposite walls of the fort were cut and jagged by the shells which passed over the main front; and the northeast face looked very dilapidated.

On Sunday I had a conversation with General Gillmore on the state of affairs, and on Monday went up with him and General Seymour to view Sumter from Fort Strong; after which we had a conversation in General Seymour's tent on the best probable course to be pursued. General Gillmore finally concluded for the present to continue the fire on Sumter.

The fire of the Monitors has been generally very good, and on many occasions most excellent.

Captain Stevens reports that of 455 shells, fired in seven days, 315 took effect on or in the fort.

I regret to say that on the 2d two men were killed in the Patapsco by the premature explosion of the rifle gun. Their names were William Colter and John Morris.

Captain Stevens states: "The explosion of the fifteen-inch shells, fired with 15″ and 20″ fuzes in the inside of the fort, which gun was fired occasionally, produces an effect which is hardly describable, throwing the bricks and mortar, gun-carriages, and timber in every direction, and high into the air."

I find that the effect of these shells is also noticed by the commanding general ashore.

Last evening I examined the appearance of the fort, (as I have done every day,) and could plainly observe the further effects of the firing. Still this mass of ruin is capable of harboring a number of the enemy, who may retain their hold until expelled by the bayonet; which, in the proper order of things, will devolve on our comrades ashore.

Last evening the schooner Ward came down from Morrill's inlet and reported the capture of an officer and nine men by a party of the enemy, who were, no doubt, annoyed by the presence of the schooner, and her endeavor to prevent some effort to run in or out. I shall despatch a gunboat to stop that game. This is another of the indications that the perfect blockade of Charleston is driving speculators to the smaller ports to get cotton out, and a return cargo in.

I have the honor to be, very respectfully, your obedient servant,

JOHN A. DAHLGREN,
Rear-Admiral, Com'dg S. A. B. Squadron.

Hon. GIDEON WELLES,
Secretary of the Navy, Washington, D. C.

P. S.—The speed of the Montauk was tried this morning, and found to be improved from 3½ to 6 knots, with the same amount of steam. The Ericsson raft will be tried to-day on a Monitor.

Trial of a torpedo.

FLAG-STEAMER PHILADELPHIA,
Off Morris Island, November 6, 1863.

SIR: The torpedo was tried to-day, and its action was complete. There was said to be six hundred (600) pounds of powder in it, but the shock was so slight as not to compare with the shock even of distant cannon. The column of water was large, but not what I should have expected. The raft very naturally retards the motion of the Monitors, whether direct or lateral, but in the perfect smooth water which we had, (a miracle here,) not inconveniently. The vessel performed quite well.

I enclose the reports of Commander Stevens and Mr. Griffin.

I have the honor to be, very respectfully, your obedient servant,

JOHN A. DAHLGREN,
Rear-Admiral, Com'dg S. A. B. Squadron.

Hon. GIDEON WELLES,
Secretary of the Navy, Washington, D. C.

UNITED STATES IRON-CLAD PATAPSCO,
Off Morris Island, November 7, 1863.

SIR: I have the honor to report that after two trials, one of which failed on account of the damaged condition of the powder, we succeeded yesterday in exploding the torpedo designed by Mr. Ericsson. For the special purpose of removing fixed obstructions, I think it like all that Mr. Ericsson undertakes—a complete success. The shock of the explosion was hardly perceptible upon the vessel.

While I give my unqualified approval, resulting from this practical test in favor of this invention of Mr. Ericsson, I am constrained to believe that, for operations against iron-clads, or a moving force, the arrangement and attachment are too cumbersome and complicated. In my opinion, we require something, in the way of a torpedo, which can be managed with facility, and will not interfere with the steaming and manœuvring of the iron-clads.

I am, sir, yours respectfully,

T. H. STEVENS, *Commander*.

Rear-Admiral J. A. DAHLGREN,
Commanding South Atlantic Blockading Squadron.

UNITED STATES MONITOR PATAPSCO,
Off Charleston, South Carolina, November 7, 1863.

SIR: I respectfully submit the following report of an experiment made yesterday of an obstruction remover, which was designed by Captain Ericsson. This obstruction remover consists of a cast-iron shell, or torpedo, about twenty-three feet long and ten inches in diameter, containing six hundred pounds of powder. This is discharged by a trigger-board placed directly in front, and extending the entire length of the shell, adjusted on the plan of a parallel ruler. This board, by being pushed in contact with obstructions, will spring two locks, placed equi-distant on the torpedo, causing an explosion of the shell. These torpedoes are suspended from rafts carried on the bows of Monitors, and held in position forward by two booms, which are firmly secured to the raft. There is also attached to the forward part of the torpedo a series of air vessels, so arranged as to cause the explosive power to be expended in that direction. As this trial was only made to show the effect of the explosion on the Monitor and how much it interfered with the manœuvring of the vessel, it was carried on in deep water. The Patapsco, the vessel on which the trial was made, had, on account of the foulness of her bottom, only a speed of about 3½ knots with the raft on. I should judge she was not to be driven more than three knots; and in making a circuit, with the helm hard down, it takes at least half as much more room.

In exploding the torpedo, which was suspended at a depth of thirteen feet, the shock was hardly perceptible on the Patapsco, while the body of water displaced and thrown upwards to a height of from forty to fifty feet was really fearful. This body of water was thrown forward, and but a slight quantity of water fell upon the deck of the vessel. The raft was raised about two feet at the forward end, but sustained no material injury. In reference to the effectiveness of this arrangement for removing and destroying obstructions, such as spiles, chains, net-work, and torpedoes, which it can be brought in contact with, I believe it will be completely successful. The three rafts which are now at hand can have all the attachments made, except launching the torpedo overboard, so as to be ready for use at short notice.

I am, very respectfully, your obedient servant,

THOMAS J. GRIFFIN,
Assistant Inspector of Iron-clads.

Rear-Admiral J. A. DAHLGREN, U. S. N.,
Commanding South Atlantic Blockading Squadron.

Repairs made on the Passaic, &c.

UNITED STATES IRON-CLAD PASSAIC,
Off Morris Island, S. C., November 8, 1863.

SIR: I have the honor to report the return of this vessel from Port Royal, where she has been undergoing repairs.

In addition to the injuries to the deck, &c., caused by the fire of the enemy, the turret of this vessel was so jammed that it could not revolve without carrying with it the spindle and pilot-house. Much time was expended, under the supervision of Mr. Hughes, assistant inspector of iron-clads, in endeavoring to overcome this difficulty; during which endeavors the turret engines were subjected to much strain. He did not succeed in overcoming the difficulty, but the opportune arrival of Mr. Griffin, assistant inspector of iron-clads, from the north, prevented the vessel from going north for repairs.

Mr. Griffin detected the difficulty as existing in the composition ring on the roof of the turret, which is used for the purpose of steadying the pilot-house. He cut the ring in two, and found a piece of broken bolt which had jammed between the ring and the pilot-house. The removal of this obstruction allowed the turret to revolve independently of the spindle, and the repairs on the vessel were forthwith commenced.

Much of the old wooden deck had to be removed. Wherever it was cut away, the wood was found to be of the best quality and well preserved. The manner in which the original deck of this vessel had been calked cannot be surpassed. Much of the comfort of the crew on board this class of vessel must depend upon the ability to keep the lower deck dry; thus too much attention cannot be paid to the calking of the deck when it is first laid.

The work of repairs was carried on in an expeditious manner, the workmen working faithfully at the different jobs; but the manner in which the work of repairing the deck was designed has proved faulty. In several places bolts have been driven through the wooden deck so that the ends project below, thus causing leaks, depriving the crew of a portion of their sleeping room, already quite contracted. I hope to be able to correct this difficulty in this vessel, but I consider it as a very necessary precaution, in all repairs of the decks of these vessels, that the work must be so designed as not to require the driving of a single bolt through the deck. Short bolts should be required to "take" in a beam.

The armor of the stern of this vessel was sprung apart about six inches by contact with another Monitor. Holes were drilled, and three two-inch bolts were inserted, by which the parts of the armor were made to approach each other. When they were as close as they could be drawn by this means, the bolts and nuts were removed, and rivets substituted. Although the contact is not perfect, I consider the stern stronger than it was before.

While undergoing repairs in Station creek, the "divers," employed by the Bureau of Construction, were occupied in cleaning the bottom. They reported that but few barnacles were attached to the bottom, but that the grass was very thick and long. They brought up baskets full of grass in proof of their assertion. On leaving the creek, in order to test the work of the divers, the vessel was beached, and her bottom subjected to as careful an examination as the state of the tides would allow, the approach of the neap tides not permitting us to see more than a foot below the overhang. There were no barnacles nor oysters to be seen—nothing but a quantity of grass, evidently lately formed, with here and there a patch of old grass left by the divers.

It would seem that the reason why the barnacles and oysters do not attach themselves to the bottom of this vessel is, that it is covered with zinc paint, instead of the red lead with which the other Monitors are painted. The bottoms of the Montauk and Weehawken (which came under my notice) were perfect oyster beds. I think that there can be no doubt that the use of the zinc paint will enable an iron vessel to retain her speed for a much longer time than if she were painted with red lead. The zinc paint seems to have a tendency, however, to scale off, which might leave the iron exposed. Perhaps a judicious mixture of the zinc and red lead might meet both objects, viz: to protect the iron, while preventing the barnacles and oysters from attaching to the bottom.

After beaching, I took on board ordnance stores and coal, and, in tow of the Admiral DuPont, proceeded to this place.

Difficulty has always been experienced in stowing the amount of ammunition that was considered desirable to be kept on board of vessels of this class during active operations.

In order to make more room, I have removed, from under rooms in the ward-room, ballast to the amount of twenty-five tons, and have taken on board that additional amount of ammunition. In order to find room for the storage of powder, I now use my shell-room as auxiliary powder magazine, and the shells are stowed all along under the ward-room and berth deck.

I have been fortunate in having as my senior engineer an officer of much experience and ability, which will account for the trifling repairs that were required for the engine and boilers.

In conclusion, I would state that this vessel feels the effect of the battering she has received. Water finds its way into her much more freely than it did formerly, and when loaded full of coal, steady streams of water poured into the fire-room from leaks apparently existing in the upper parts of the overhang. I cannot say that any of the parts of the deck which have been repaired have proved to be perfectly tight.

Very respectfully, your obedient servant,

E. SIMPSON,
Lieutenant Commander, Commanding.

Rear-Admiral J. A. DAHLGREN,
Commanding S. A. B. Squadron.

Ammunition expended by the Patapsco.

UNITED STATES IRON-CLAD PATAPSCO,
Off Morris Island, November 10, 1863.

SIR: Since my last report of the bombardment of Sumter, I have the honor to inform you we have fired from this vessel ninety-six rifle projectiles at the fort, of which three were defective, eighty-two struck the fort, and eleven missed.

From the XV-inch gun twenty-two twenty-second fuzed shell have been fired at the same object, of which sixteen struck the fort, and six missed.

During all the time we have been engaged, there have been five hundred and seventy-three shells (of which five hundred and fifteen were from the rifle gun) fired, of which number four hundred and thirteen struck the fort, twenty-seven were defective, and one hundred and thirty-three missed.

Very respectfully, your obedient servant,

T. H. STEVENS,
Commander.

Rear-Admiral J. A. DAHLGREN,
Commanding S. A. B. Squadron.

Engagement of the Lehigh with the enemy while aground; gallantry of certain officers and men.

[Despatch No. 254.]

FLAG-STEAMER PHILADELPHIA,
Off Morris Island, November 17, 1863.

SIR: I beg leave to call your attention to meritorious service *under a severe fire* of the enemy, by certain persons of this squadron.

Last evening the enemy unexpectedly opened a very heavy fire from Moultrie upon our works on Morris island. General Gillmore telegraphed me accordingly thus: "The enemy have opened a heavy fire on Cummings's Point. Will you have some of your vessels move up so as to prevent an attack by boats on the sea face of the point?"

It was now about 10 p. m., and I at once ordered the Monitors on picket to move up, so as to attend to this duty, and also to cause the tugs on patrol to keep a good look-out.

This morning early it was reported that the Lehigh had grounded, and the enemy had opened heavily on her from Moultrie and the adjacent batteries. I at once signalized to the iron-clads to get under way, and myself went up in the Passaic. On reaching the spot I perceived that the Nahant was very close to the Lehigh, so I passed to her, where I found Lieutenant Commander Cornwell preparing to assist his comrade.

With difficulty and much danger it was contrived to get three or four hawsers successively from the Nahant to the Lehigh; two were cut by chafing and one by the enemy's shot; the last one held, and at high water the Lehigh floated off.

With pleasure I bring to your notice the gallant behavior of Acting Ensign R. Burke, who was severely wounded, and also of the medical officer of the Lehigh, Dr. W. Longshaw; twice he passed in a small boat from the Lehigh to the Nahant, carrying a line bent on the hawser; the shot and shells from cannon and mortars were flying and breaking all around.

The third time, this service was performed by three seamen, Horatio Young, William Williams, and Frank S. Gile. These I advanced on the spot in their rates.

I have also given appointments as master's mates to the two petty officers who rowed Dr. Longshaw, George W. Leland and Thomas Irving.

It would also have been very gratifying to me if it had been in my power to advance Acting Ensign Burke and Dr. Longshaw under the fire, when they so well performed their duty, and by which the former had been severely hurt; for a recognition of this kind has always been more valued in military service than any other. I beg leave to recommend them to the notice of the department, with the observation that they risked their lives to save an invaluable vessel, which, I am glad to say, sustained no great damage.

It is proper for me to remark that the few officers were actively employed in other duties at the time.

The Passaic and Montauk fired with great precision, and I think with effect, for their shells seemed to me to strike the test of the parapet every time.

Commander Bryson and Lieutenant Commander Cornwell, with their officers, did their duty handsomely on the occasion.

I enclose the report of Commander Bryson.

I have the honor to be, very respectfully, your obedient servant,

JNO. A. DAHLGREN,

Rear-Admiral, Commanding S. A. B. Squadron.

Hon. GIDEON WELLES,

Secretary of the Navy, Washington, D. C.

NOVEMBER 18.

I may add in continuation of this letter, that in the afternoon of to-day it was reported to me that the Lehigh had suddenly sprung aleak, which let in nine inches of water the hour. When I went on board the water was coming in at the bow with some noise, apparently a foot below the overhang. It is impossible to speak with certainty of the extent of this leak or the cause that has produced it; the latter would naturally be attributed to the events of yesterday, and yet its locality renders it difficult to understand that it could have been caused by the shot of the enemy or by contact with the shoal.

When the vessel has been beached I shall be able to report with certainty. The accident is unlucky just at this time, when three Monitors are absent under repair.

The inflow of water has now been reduced to five inches per hour, and I am in hopes that the injury will prove immaterial.

J. A. D.

BUREAU OF MEDICINE AND SURGERY,
November 28, 1863.

I beg leave to recommend, as a recognition of the gallant conduct and efficient service, under a heavy fire of shot and shell from the enemy's cannon and mortars, of Assistant Surgeon William Longshaw, of the Monitor Lehigh, so amply set forth by Rear-Admiral Dahlgren in general orders of the 17th instant, that an order issue giving Assistant Surgeon Longshaw the privilege of examination as soon as his two years' sea service required by law shall be completed, and if successful, that he shall rank as passed assistant surgeon from the date of his examination, without reference to others of his date or class.

W. WHELAN, *Chief of Bureau.*

UNITED STATES IRON-CLAD LEHIGH,
Off Morris Island, S. C., November 17, 1863.

SIR: I have the honor to report that, in obedience to your order of the night of November 15, I moved up, whilst on picket service, to a position which would enable me to use my guns on any boats of the enemy which might be seen approaching Cummings's Point.

I anchored the ship in three-quarters fathom of water, on a half ebb tide, feeling that she was perfectly secure. On the making of the flood tide she swung, and in swinging it is my belief that she touched on a lump and there hung. The water was so smooth, and she went on so easily, that it is impossible for me to say at what time during the night she touched. After daylight I made the attempt to get under steam, and found, to my surprise, that the ship was on the bottom. Signal was then made to this effect, and that assistance might be rendered me. I was within range of the enemy's batteries on Sullivan's island, and as soon as they perceived that the ship was ashore they opened on me from nine different batteries, striking twenty-two times, nine of which are wounds on the deck plating; and these are the most serious of all the wounds she received.

The Nahant being the nearest ship to me, immediately came to my assistance, and anchored near us. Lines were procured from the Nahant on three occasions, the first two being shot away, and the third successfully made fast. The Nahant then steamed ahead, the Montauk being ahead of her, the Lehigh backing, and in the course of an hour the ship floated. No injury has been done the ship by grounding that can be perceived. I regret to inform you that, while under the fire of the enemy's batteries, there were wounded one officer and six men—two seriously, the others slightly.

It is a pleasure for me to say that all under these trying circumstances did their duty, there being no confusion and everything working well.

I would especially mention the valuable services voluntarily rendered by Assistant Surgeon Longshaw, and the promptness and alacrity with which George W. Leland (gunner's mate,) and Thomas Irving (cockswain,) manned the boat which was engaged in passing lines under a heavy fire.

Acting Ensign Richard Burke also commanded my admiration for the courageous manner in which he performed all his duties, the value of which I cannot speak too highly of.

I am, respectfully, your obedient servant,

A. BRYSON, *Commander.*

Rear-Admiral JOHN A. DAHLGREN,
Commanding S. A. B. Squadron.

Opinion of Assistant Inspector Hughes on various points.

STEAMER RELIEF,
Port Royal, S. C., December 4, 1863.

SIR: I received from Commander William Reynolds a copy of your order dated November 26, desiring a report from me on any of the following questions that come within my knowledge:

1. The effect of the shot on the turret, pilot-house, deck, side-armor, and working parts, &c.

2. Quantity of excrescence on the bottom, and its nature. Was the work of the divers efficient on the Passaic and Patapsco; could they remove the oyster-shells as well as the grass? Does the beaching allow of the cleaning of all parts of the bottom; if not, are the divers able to complete the parts that are not reached on the beach? Which, paint, zinc, or lead, is most preventive of fouling?

3. How, beached and shored, does the operation appear to strain the hull, or effect its form or fastenings in any way? Is any effect perceptible on the machinery of the engine or turret?

4. What is the condition of the boilers? Had the scaling been injurious? Were the boilers blown as frequently as they should have been? What means can be adopted to give opportunity in service for ascertaining the state of the scale, preventing its formation and removal?

SIR: In answer to the above questions I have the honor to make the following report:

1. *The effect of the shot on turret.*—The shot make an indentation on the iron, and break the bolts that fasten the plating together. The greatest indentations that have come to my knowledge were to the depth of 2½ and 2¾ inches. In my opinion, those indentations were made from 11 and 13-inch solid shot, most of them from 11-inch. A shot of this kind will generally break from one to five or six bolts. The Nahant received a shot that broke twelve bolts. I find that the shot broke more bolts in the Nahant's turret than in any of the others.

I think the reason of this is, the bolts are not so good a fit in the Nahant's turret as in the others. Some of the Monitors' turrets have received seventy and eighty shots. When the bolts break they can soon be replaced. I do not see that the turrets are injured practically.

The effect of shot on pilot-house.—The shots make an impression on pilot-house about the same as on turret; but since the extra thickness of three inches has been put on, the shots do no other injury.

The effect of shot on the deck.—If the shot strikes on a beam, it generally cuts away the iron plating and makes an indentation in the beam; and if it strikes between the beams, it generally breaks the deck plank through.

The effect of shot on the armature.—The armature has been penetrated to the depth of the five thicknesses of inch plating, and some of the shot have lodged where they struck. The shot also bends the plating and starts the fastenings. I have never known any shot or shell to do any injury to any of the machinery or working parts of the vessel.

You will please observe that the shots I have been referring to, I believe to have taken effect when the Monitors were fighting the enemy at the shortest range. The Monitors have received shots on all parts that were scarcely perceptible.

2. *Quantity of excrescence on the bottom.*—The bottom of the Monitors is covered with a thick coating of oyster-shells and grass. The grass grows to a considerable length; I have a sample here of what came off the bottom of the Catskill. It seems to be grass coralized; it resembles strong broom-corn, and is twelve inches long. In my opinion, the work of the divers was efficient on the Passaic

and Patapsco. They must have removed the oyster-shells off those vessels. The quantity of excrescence on the bottom of the above named vessels was very different from what was on the Catskill. The beaching does not admit of cleaning all parts of the bottom; there are about two feet or two feet six inches not reached. In my opinion the divers can clean the part that is not reached as well as they can the other parts of the bottom.

In my opinion, zinc paint is the best to prevent fouling. I do not think that any kind of paint we can put on the bottom of the Monitors, while on the beach, will do a great deal of good. The time being so short from the time the paint is put on, it is covered with water before it gets a sufficient time to dry.

3. *How beached and shored.*—The Monitors are put broadside on the beach, without any shoring. When the Monitors are properly beached there is no danger whatever of straining any part of the vessel, or having any injurious effect on machinery or turret.

The Catskill lay on the beach in a very bad position for one tide. She lay stern on, and there was a difference of eight feet of water between bow and stern.

While she lay in this position some parts of the machinery had to be unfastened, and there was a perceptible alteration in the fire-room floor plates. When she floated the parts went back to their places. The vessel does not appear to have sustained any injury.

The fourth question, regarding the boilers, comes under the fleet engineer.

Very respectfully,

PATRICK HUGHES,
Assistant Inspector.

J. A. DAHLGREN,
Rear-Admiral, S. A. B. Squadron.

Weekly report of the condition of the Monitors.

PORT ROYAL, S. C.,
Steamer Relief, September 26, 1863.

SIR: In obedience to your orders requiring me to hand in a weekly report of the condition of the iron-clad Monitors, I have the honor to report as follows:

WEEHAWKEN.

The work on this vessel is very nearly completed. The deck is repaired, and new packing put around the turret. The bolts broken in turret and pilot-house have all been replaced—the extra thickness put on the pilot-house cover.

The men are working on the pilot-house sleeve, which will take five days to finish. The patch on her side, under the overhang, is nearly finished.

This vessel will be finished, with all the additions, about Friday, October 2.

PATAPSCO.

The deck of this vessel has been repaired, and smoke-box very nearly finished; bolts replaced on pilot-house and turret; the holes drilled in turret for base ring; new cover made for pilot-house. I am afraid I cannot repair the standing part of the smoke-pipe to make it satisfactory. I hope this vessel will not be required until a new pipe comes from New York. To finish the repairs and put all the additions on this vessel, it will take fourteen days.

PASSAIC.

I have examined this vessel, and report her condition as follows:

The deck has received eleven shots, seven of which have broken through the wood work of deck, requiring twenty deck plates to repair, and seven pieces of deck timber. The turret was struck forty-eight times; some of these shots were very heavy, having injured the turret and base ring considerably. Armature was struck twenty-eight times, which has started the plating off the wood work in a number of places. The plating on her prow is started open almost four inches by coming into collision with the Montauk. The pilot-house received three shots. The bolts in the turret and pilot-house of this vessel have stood well, considering the heavy shots received. There are only a few broken.

The turret of this vessel is in a very bad condition; the spindle has got jammed in the beam, and I tried all means in my power to make it revolve, without success. I had new chucks fitted in to hold the spindle, and the wooden beams in turret chamber all shored to keep them from springing. Thirty-five pounds pressure of steam got on boilers, (all that captain would allow,) and started the turret engines at the great risk of smashing the gearing, but I could not succeed in revolving the turret. I have come to the conclusion that the spindle will have to be taken out of turret. To do this the pilot-house and turret beams will have to come out. The pilot-house, as it is at present, weighs about twenty-three or twenty-four tons. I cannot make it any lighter, as the shots received on pilot-house prevents me from taking the sleeve off. It will take a great deal of labor and time, with the means we have here, to do the repairs to this vessel. It will require thirty-five days to put this vessel to rights with the work I have on hand at present.

Very respectfully,

PATRICK HUGHES,
Assistant Inspector.

J. A. DAHLGREN,
Rear-Admiral, S. A. B. Squadron.

P. S.—I do not know if Captain Reynolds will undertake to lift twenty-four tons on the yard-arm of Vermont.

P. H.

STEAMER RELIEF,
Port Royal, October 3, 1863.

SIR: I have the honor to report the condition of the following Monitors, to wit: Weehawken, Patapsco, and Passaic.

The Weehawken will be finished on Sunday evening, October 4, with all the additions on her. I tried to take the plates off her prow, but found that I could not take the bolts out that are under water.

Patapsco.—The smoke-box is finished, and broken bolts replaced in turret and pilot-house, and new cover made for pilot-house. I am having the deck cut out around the turret, and repairing the smoke-pipe. This vessel will be finished, with all the additions, by the 11th instant.

Passaic.—I am awaiting orders on this vessel.

Very respectfully,

PATRICK HUGHES,
Assistant Inspector.

J. A. DAHLGREN,
Rear-Admiral, S. A. B. Squadron.

STEAMER RELIEF,
Port Royal, S. C., October 10, 1863.

SIR: I have the honor to report the condition of the following Monitors, to wit: Patapsco, Passaic, and Montauk.

The Patapsco will be finished, with all repairs and additions put on, on Tuesday, 13th instant. The divers are now working on her bottom.

Passaic.—I am happy to inform you that the turret of this vessel now revolves. Mr. Griffin very wisely concluded that the trouble was in the pilot-house base-ring, (that is, the ring for keeping the pilot-house in its place.) We cut it apart and found a bolt one inch in diameter and one inch long between pilot-house collar and base-ring. It seems very strange how it got there. I would almost say that it was impossible to get there by accident. We were compelled to cut the ring apart to remedy the difficulty, as the sleeve on pilot-house prevents the ring from being lifted off. I will have the decks repaired and bow fixed, and turret and pilot-house in good order, and the vessel ready for action by the 2d of November.

Montauk.—The turret, pilot-house, and deck of this vessel have not suffered much. She received four pretty hard shots in her armature, from the effect of which she leaks a little. I will have the additions on her, and the vessel ready for action same time as Passaic, to wit, 2d of November. The pilot-house cover of this vessel has received a very severe shot, almost as bad as Catskill or Patapsco. I have not yet any extra plates for strengthening the pilot-house covers, but I expect some from New York, every day, and I believe will be here before I have done the rest of the work.

PATRICK HUGHES,
Assistant Inspector.

J. A. Dahlgren, *Rear-Admiral.*

Steamer Relief,
Port Royal, S. C., October 17, 1863.

Sir: I have the honor to report the condition of the following Monitors, to wit: Passaic and Montauk.

The repairs to the Passaic are progressing very satisfactorily. The men are working on her deck, turret, and bow. I will have her ready to leave here on the 25th instant. This will be seven days less than I stated in my last report. The reason of this is, that I employed four new men. These men answer me very well. They had left Key West, and were going north in the steamship Union. I employed those men after I saw a copy of an order from you to have the men work as much time as they were able; and also to employ more, if necessary, in order to get the Monitors done as quick as possible.

As I stated to you in my last report, there is not a great deal of repairs to be done to the Montauk. The men are putting on the base-ring of turret and working on pilot-house sleeve, and I expect to have the additions on about the same time as the Passaic, to wit, 25th October. I am happy to inform you that a new pilot-house cover arrived here in the steamer Karnak. It was made for the Catskill. I will put it upon the Montauk. It came in good time. You are aware we made a new cover for the Catskill, out of three of the extra plates that were for strengthening the covers.

If you can spare the Nahant, I will have the remainder of her additions put on in six days after I get through with the two Monitors that are now here. If she arrives here by the 25th instant, I will have her ready by the 2d of November.

Very respectfully,

PATRICK HUGHES,
Assistant Inspector.

J. A. Dahlgren,
Rear-Admiral, S. A. B. Squadron.

STEAMER RELIEF,
Port Royal, S. C., October 24, 1863.

SIR: I have the honor to report the condition of the following Monitors, to wit: Passaic, Montauk, and Nahant.

The Passaic is nearly finished. We are still working on her deck and bow. We will be through with the repairs to-morrow. The nuts of top row of bolts in turret are not covered by the pilasters. I am going to take them out and put rivets in their places. I do this at the request of Captain Simpson. It will detain the vessel about one and a half day. I will be all through with this vessel on Tuesday, 27th instant.

The additions to the Montauk are nearly finished. I am going to put a new light iron part on smoke-pipe, and take the bolts out of top row of turret and put rivets in their places. I have one small patch to put on her armature, to stop a leak. I will have this vessel done by Tuesday morning, 27th instant. The pilot-house cover that came from New York was a very rough job. I will have to make some alterations on it.

The Nahant is in very good coudition. All the repairs to be done to her can be done by three men in about three days. I will have the pilot-house sleeve put on, and this vessel ready to leave here on the 2d of November. I have not any plates here for strengthening the pilot-house cover. I expect some from New York; but, in case they do not come in time, I will strengthen the cover of pilot-house by some of the old covers that I took from other vessels.

If you could send the Nantucket here after I am through with those vessels, I can have her additions put on in twelve days.

When I get the additions put on the Nantucket, I will be through with the work that I came here to do. If you have any work of importance for me to do, you will please send me an order to the effect, as I could not take the responsibility of keeping this vessel and so many workmen without an order from you.

The workmen under my charge are pretty well used up. They had to work very hard and long hours. They did not expect to be here so long. Their garments are about worn out. I would like to get them and this vessel to New York as soon as possible.

Very respectfully,

PATRICK HUGHES,
Assistant Inspector.

J. A. DALGHREN,
Rear-Admiral, S. A. B. Squadron.

STEAMER RELIEF,
Port Royal, S. C., November 1, 1863.

SIR: I have the honor to report the condition of the following Monitors, to wit: Passaic, Montauk, and Nahant.

The Passaic is finished. I was through with the repairs yesterday morning, October 31. I have been longer with this vessel than I expected. The cause of delay was for want of machinery from the machine shop. I could not get the use of the shears and drill when I required them, as there is so much work on hand.

The Montauk is finished. I was through with the repairs and additions on Wednesday morning, October 28.

The work on Nahant is progressing satisfactorily. The sleeve was put on the pilot-house yesterday. I will have to make use of the old pilot-house cover of Montauk, to strengthen the pilot-house cover of this vessel. The extra plates, for strengthening the covers, have not yet arrived from New York. I will be through with the repairs and additions of this vessel on Tuesday morning, 3d instant.

I received a letter from Commander Reynolds, senior officer, containing an extract from a letter of yours, dated October 29, ordering me to have a framework of wood or iron carried around the bow of the Monitors, like the guards of a side-wheel steamer, or even projecting beams of wood or rods of iron, to keep the enemy's vessels off for the length of pole on which the torpedo is placed.

If you would please order the Nantucket here to have the additions put on, we could, at the same time, put on this torpedo preventive. I am afraid it will take considerable time to have anything made satisfactorily, with the means we have at our command, to keep off the enemy's vessels.

Very respectfully,

PATRICK HUGHES,
Assistant Inspector.

J. A. DAHLGREN,
Rear-Admiral, S. A. B. Squadron.

STEAMER RELIEF,
Port Royal, South Carolina, November 7, 1863.

SIR: I have the honor to report the condition of the following Monitors, viz: Nahant and Weehawken.

The Nahant is finished. I made some alterations at the request of the captain, viz: cutting holes in bulkheads to let the water get running to the pump, and cut a dead-light hole in deck *to change one of the deck.* This extra work has detained me two days longer. I completed this vessel on Friday, 6th instant.

The Weehawken came here on Wednesday, 4th instant. The work to be done to her is as follows: The eleven-inch gun to be taken out and a new one put in; a new turret pinion put on; smoke-box repaired, and bow repaired. The repairing of the bow will be the longest job. I think I will be able to get through it about Sunday, 15th instant. Captain Colhoun requested me to change his galley, and run the galley-pipe into the smoke-pipe. I will be able to have this work completed by the time I get the bow repaired, which will be the 16th instant.

If you cannot spare the Nantucket here, permit me the use of one of those side-wheel tugs to carry the brass ring for turret to Warsaw. I would take this vessel and men there, and put all additions on, with the exception of pilot-house sleeve. I could arrange it so that the vessel could come here and get the sleeve put on, and would not be detained longer than thirty hours.

Very respectfully,

PATRICK HUGHES,
Assistant Inspector.

J. A. DAHLGREN,
Rear-Admiral, S. A. B. Squadron.

STEAMER RELIEF,
Port Royal, South Carolina, November 22, 1863.

SIR: I have the honor to report the condition of the following Monitors, viz: Catskill and Patapsco.

The Catskill got off the beach this morning. I expect the captain will be ready to leave here in a few days. I am sorry there is not any iron in the boiler shop here to make the galley pipe, as I had plenty of time to change the galley. The captain is very anxious to have it done. I have made all the necessary arrangements so as the galley can be changed in short time when the pipe can be made.

The Patapsco is on the beach cleaning. I will be through with all work I have to do to this vessel on the 24th instant. I have changed the upper row of turret bolts and nuts into rivets. I had this done at the request of the captain. I am having her bow repaired, and the composition ring for holding down the pilot-house parted, and the holes cut in the coal-bunker bulkheads, so as to be in readiness to change the galley when the pipe can be made. The galley pipes can be made and sent to these two vessels as soon as the iron arrives. I have left the dimensions of those pipes in the boiler shop.

Seeing an order from you for concussion-box bolts in the machine shop, I take this opportunity to send six dozen of spare turret bolts and four dozen of concussion-box bolts.

Very respectfully,

PATRICK HUGHES,
Assistant Inspector.

J. A. DAHLGREN,
Rear-Admiral, S. A. B. Squadron.

[Despatch No. 283.]

FLAG-STEAMER PHILADELPHIA,
Off Morris Island, December 1, 1863.

SIR: I enclose herewith the report of the superintendent of repairs on Monitors at Port Royal, which has just been received.

The department will perceive that the work on them is nearly completed, except the Nantucket.

Last evening came the first rumor of General Grant's success, but I have no authentic information.

The army to-day has been saluting, and I shall follow the example.

I have the honor to be, very respectfully, your obedient servant,

JOHN A. DAHLGREN,
Rear-Admiral, Commanding S. A. B. Squadron.

Hon. GIDEON WELLES,
Secretary of the Navy, Washington, D. C.

STEAMER RELIEF,
Port Royal, South Carolina, November 29, 1863.

SIR: I have the honor to report the condition of the following Monitors, viz: Catskill, Patapsco, and Lehigh.

In my report of the 22d instant I informed you that the Catskill came off the beach that morning, and I expected she would leave here in a few days. This vessel went on the beach again that same evening, and remained there until the morning of the 28th instant, getting off at 10 o'clock. In trying to get the vessel off on the morning of the 27th, they carried away the anchor gear, breaking one tooth in each of the pinion-wheels, and bending the shaft. It will take three days to repair. On the morning of the 28th instant one of the tow-boats struck the plating on the bow and started the fastenings, breaking some of the blunt bolt-heads off. To fasten this plating properly, it will take about three days. I will have all the damages to this vessel repaired by Thursday morning, December 3.

The Patapsco has not yet got off the beach. The captain expects to get her off this morning at high tide.

The Lehigh arrived here on Monday, 23d instant. She has not yet been beached. This vessel has received the following damages: Eleven shots on deck, six of which have broken the deck plank through; the remainder struck on the deck beams; sixteen shots on turret, seven of them pretty hard, making an indentation of about two inches deep, and breaking twenty-two bolts; one shot on turret-roof, cutting a piece off the composition ring, and breaking one of the plates, and bending two of the T-iron bars; two shots on pilot-house, making an indentation of about two inches, doing no injury; one side of the smoke-box carried away; armature has received fourteen shots, one of them injuring the bow very much, starting nearly all the fastenings and opening the plating four inches. The hull has received one shot about twelve inches from the overhang, bending the plating in and opening the seams so as to make considerable of a leak. The following will be the material required to repair this vessel: Deck: Two full plates and twenty-seven parts of plates; twelve pieces of deck plank. Turret: Twenty-two bolts and one new plate for roof; T-iron bars straightened; side of smoke-box straightened and refastened, and one new wrought-iron strap made. Armature: Four light iron patches where the shots have penetrated, the five thicknesses of plates; bow refastened and plating straightened, if possible. Hull: One patch of $\frac{5}{8}$ iron on the outside where the shot struck; anchor gear overhauled. I expect to have this vessel finished on the 8th of December.

The captain of the Lehigh wants extra plating of one inch thick over the boilers, engine-room, magazine, and shell-room. There are not any inch plates at this place. I expect if there were any extra plating to go on this vessel it would have been put on when at New York.

Very respectfully,

PATRICK HUGHES,
Assistant Inspector.

J. A. DAHLGREN,
Rear-Admiral, S. A. B. Squadron.

STEAMER RELIEF,
Port Royal, S. C., December 5, 1863.

SIR: I have the honor to report the condition of the following Monitors, viz: Catskill, Patapsco, and Lehigh.

The Catskill is lying in Station creek. The divers are going to clean the parts of the bottom that were not reached on the beach. I am all through with her. I expect she will leave here the first of the week.

The Patapsco is still on the beach. I am afraid she will have to stop on the beach for seven or eight days. The tides are very low at present.

The repairs to the Lehigh are progressing very satisfactorily. The deck is finished, and the smoke-box nearly finished. I have commenced to repair the bow and armature.

I omitted to mention in my report of the 29th that this vessel requires a new light iron part of smoke-pipe, the old one being nearly shot away. I expect this vessel will be finished by the 8th or 9th instant. This vessel is on the beach. Her bottom looks well. The excrescence can be removed with brooms.

There is nothing growing on the bottom, so far as I can see, but grass almost two inches long.

Very respectfully,

PATRICK HUGHES,
Assistant Inspector.

J. A. DAHLGREN,
Rear-Admiral, S. A. B. Squadron.

The safety of the southern coast depends upon the Ironsides and the Monitors.

FLAG-STEAMER PHILADELPHIA,
Off Morris Island, January 19, 1864.

SIR: The department's letter of the 4th of January has been received.

The irregularities in regard to complement of officers is rather the result of circumstances. The Ironsides, as well as all the Monitors, occupy positions entirely exceptional. Our entire safety on the southern coast depends on these vessels. Without them, the rebel iron-clads would quickly ruin the blockade and capture our land forces. They also have the most severe and never-ceasing duties to fulfil while on picket, particularly in keeping off the various submerged devices of the rebels. I can, from frequent inspection of them after dark, bear witness to this. For these reasons I keep them at the highest possible state of efficiency, and, as a general rule, give whatever they ask for. * * * *

I have the honor to be, very respectfully, your obedient servant,

J. A. DAHLGREN,
Rear-Admiral, Commanding S. A. B. Squadron.

Hon. GIDEON WELLES,
Secretary of the Navy, Washington, D. C.

Sinking of the Weehawken.

[Despatch No. 294.]

FLAG-STEAMER PHILADELPHIA,
Off Morris Island, December 6, 1863.

SIR: With feelings beyond my ability to express, I have to announce that the Monitor Weehawken sank at her anchorage to-day at half past two o'clock. It was blowing a moderate gale from east by north at the time, and I had been occasionally noticing the motions of the Montauk, which was anchored the highest up the harbor, and had been under way.

Mr. Hughes, the superintendent of repairs of the Monitors, was talking to me at the time—asking leave to go home—when the signal officer announced that the Weehawken had flying a signal "for assistance," and this was followed almost immediately by the entrance of the fleet captain, who reported that the Weekawken appeared to be sinking.

Directions were given at once to let her make for the beach, but before the least measure could be taken the Weehawken disappeared beneath the water, and nothing was seen above but the flag and the top of the smoke-stack.

Scarcely five minutes elapsed between the time that the signal "for assistance" was made and the sinking of the vessel.

I am entirely unable, from the imperfect information at hand, to satisfy myself of the real cause of the disaster. Some attribute it to the entrance of a heavy sea into the fore hatch, filling the anchor well; others say that there was an excess of water in the vessel three hours before she went down, which is also attributed to the hawse-pipe. Some talk of the water forcing in at the joint of the overhang; but it would appear that no apprehension of danger existed until ten or fifteen minutes before the signal was made.

The Weehawken lay about east of the beacon-house on Morris island, and nearest to her were a mortar schooner, a tug, and my own steamer. The Ironsides and other vessels lay lower down, except the Montauk, which was on picket.

Steam-tugs and boats were despatched at once to pick up the crew, but it is to be feared that some lives have been lost. These cannot yet be known with exactness, as the survivors are scattered among different vessels, and it blows too fresh to communicate with facility.

I shall send to Port Royal for the divers and other means to raise the Weehawken, and would ask that the department would also send here any assistance that is available.

I have the honor to be, very respectfully, your obedient servant,

JOHN A. DAHLGREN,
Rear-Admiral, Commanding S. A. B. Squadron.

Hon. GIDEON WELLES,
Secretary of the Navy, Washington, D. C.

Detailed report of the sinking of the Weehawken.

FLAG-STEAMER PHILADELPHIA,
Off Morris Island, December 8, 1863.

SIR: Another despatch informs you of the sad disaster that has befallen the Weehawken. I have ordered an inquiry, which will supply all the evidence that is attainable. Meanwhile there are differences of opinion among well-informed officers. Some attribute the cause to the water in the anchor well, the influx through the hawse-pipe, and the depression forward, so that the water would not flow to the pumps.

A written opinion (A) from Lieutenant Commander Simpson, who has the Monitor Passaic, states that the water did run aft, and that the rotatory pump was in full action. He thinks that weakness from injuries in service, with, perhaps, some strain in beaching, had loosened rivets of bottom plates, and did the rest.

Among the melancholy consequences are the loss of life. Four engineers and twenty men are missing, the names of whom are enclosed, (B.) Every effort was made to save the crew, and in a few moments the water was alive with boats. It is to be hoped that some may have escaped ashore, but the chances are very slight.

I have the honor to be, very respectfully, your obedient servant,

JOHN A. DAHLGREN,
Rear Admiral, Commanding S. A. B. Squadron.

Hon. GIDEON WELLES,
Secretary of the Navy, Washington, D. C.

A.

UNITED STATES IRON-CLAD PASSAIC,
Off Morris Island, S. C., December 6, 1863

SIR: I respectfully submit my opinion of the cause of the sinking of the Weehawken:

From the testimony that I have been able to collect, it appears that between 11 a. m. and meridian the windlass-room was full of water; the forward hatch was then closed, and no water could find its way in except through the hawse-hole. At this time the centrifugal pump did not work, as there was not enough water aft to make it "fetch." This indicates a want of free communication through the limbers. It seems that this difficulty was overcome, for some time afterwards the water rose to about four inches of the fire-room floor (which would make it twenty-six inches below the grate bars) when the centrifugal pump was in operation discharging steadily its 2,000 or 3,000 gallons of water per minute. No apprehension seems to have been felt at this time as to the danger of sinking, the vessel was not noticed to be settling, but the commanding officer desired the presence of the captain, and commenced to signalize to that effect. At this instant the water suddenly rose in the vessel, and she commenced to settle forward. The signal "in want of assistance" was made immediately, and she went down. My conclusion is, that the sinking of the vessel was not occasioned by the water that found its way into her through the hawse-hole, for it seems clearly proven that free communication was established (through the limbers) between the hawse-hole and centrifugal pump, and I conceive that the centrifugal pump is able to discharge all water that enters by the hawse-hole. I believe that the injuries that the vessel had received in service, particularly while aground under the fire of the Sullivan's Island batteries, (assisted perhaps by the straining produced by being beached at Port Royal,) had so strained her that the rivets were loose on some of her bottom plates, and the rough sea that was running at the time of the disaster must have been sufficient to open the plates and admit the water. From all that I can learn, it was no gradual accumulation of water that caused the vessel to sink, but it was almost instantaneous. This could alone be caused by such reason as I here assign.

I merely submit this hurried paper with a view to rendering some slight aid towards assigning a reason for the terrible disaster.

Very respectfully, your obedient servant,

E. SIMPSON,
Commanding.

J. A. DAHLGREN,
Rear-Admiral, Commanding S. A. B. Squadron.

B.

List of the Weehawken's officers supposed to be lost.

Henry W. Merian, third assistant engineer.
Augustus Mitchell, third assistant engineer.
George W. McGowan, acting third assistant engineer.
Charles Spongbergh, acting third assistant engineer.

Very respectfully,

FREDERICK R. STOW,
Acting Assistant Paymaster.

Commander J. M. DUNCAN.

List of men's names who are supposed to be lost from the Weehawken.

1. Thomas Piper.
2. James Scollan.
3. John Buckley.
4. John Kerrigan.
5. John Carpenter.
6. Joseph Grogan.
7. Charles F. Davis.
8. John Williams, 2d.
9. Charles H. Wilson.
10. William H. Williamson.
11. Christian Anderson.
12. John Rutlage.
13. Ralph Anderson.
14. Edward Gayhan.
15. Edward Mullen.
16. Michael Clines.
17. James Lennan.
18. Thomas Mec.
19. Robert Nugent.
20. Thomas Donovan.
21. William G. Pike.
22. George Leighton.
23. Henry Sumner.
24. Thomas Stocker.
25. Thomas Donlon.
26. Stephen C. Newman.
27. (Not ascertained.)

Very respectfully,

FREDERICK R. STOW,
Acting Assistant Paymaster.

Reports of officers of Weehawken.

A. Commander Duncan .... December 7.
B. Lieutenant M. S. Stuyvesant .... December 7.
C. Lieutenant M. S. Stuyvesant .... December 9.
D. Lieutenant M. S. Stuyvesant .... December 11.
E. Acting Master C. C. Kingsbury .... December 8.
F. Assistant Surgeon E. M. Stein .... December 9.
G. Assistant Surgeon E. M. Stein .... December 11.
H. Acting Paymaster F. R. Stow .... December 7.
I. Ensign I. H. Reed .... December 7.
K. Acting Second Assistant Engineer J. B Allen .... December 9.
L. Acting Ensign B. H. Chadwick .... December 7.
M. Acting Ensign F. H. Crandall .... December 7.
N. Master's Mate and Gunner William E. Bayne .... December 10.
O. Pilot Levi Jump .... December 7.

A.

UNITED STATES FLAG-SHIP PHILADELPHIA,
Off Charleston, S. C., December 7, 1863.

SIR: I have to report that on the evening of the 4th instant I received orders detaching me from gunboat Paul Jones, and ordering me here to take command of the iron-clad steamer Weehawken. On the morning of the 5th I arrived here, and in the evening took command of her and went up on the advanced picket, and remained there until 9.30 of the morning of the 6th; then came down; made fast to buoy No. 2; then came on board this vessel.

About 1.30 p. m. a signal was made that the Weehawken wanted assistance. I immediately got in a boat with the pilot of this vessel. Before we could reach her she went down. Boats from all the vessels around went to the assistance of the men that were overboard, and succeeded in saving all but four of the engineers and twenty-seven of the men. When I left the vessel everything appeared to be right; the anchor-hold was all dry; no water coming through the hawse-pipe. I enclose you statements of all the officers now on board. Not being on board myself at the time, I am not able to give any account of the sad accident.

Very respectfully, your obedient servant,

J. M. DUNCAN,
Commander.

Rear-Admiral J. A. DAHLGREN,
Com'dg S. A. B. Squadron, Flag-Ship Philadelphia.

B.

UNITED STATES FLAG-SHIP PHILADELPHIA,
Off Morris Island, December 7, 1863.

SIR: In obedience to your orders of to-day, I make the following report of circumstances attending the loss of the United States iron-clad steamer Weehawken:

At or near 12 o'clock yesterday the seas were washing over the bows of the vessel, and water was going down the forward hatch in small quantities, as has frequently been the case.

To prevent its splashing into the cabin the iron door leading into the anchor-room was closed; and in order to ease the ship, fifteen fathoms of chain were veered. We were at our usual moorings, made fast to buoy No. 2. The wind freshened, and the seas grew larger very rapidly, and while closing down the forward battle-plate several seas went over, almost filling up the anchor-room. Men were immediately sent down to keep the limbers clear. The berth-deck battle-plate was then let down, and at this time I observed that the vessel was not so much by the stern as usual. This I attributed to the large body of water forward. As the limbers were clear, I had no fears but that the water would run aft, and be pumped out. It was now reported to me that my room was flooded, and while on my way to examine it, the captain of the hold reported five (5) inches of water, which was evidence that the water was making its way aft.

The leak in my room was around the end of one of the beams where it joined the side, and seemed to be one that could be easily stopped.

In the cabin the water was pouring in in small streams by the upper edge of the forward bulkhead. The hatches were taken off the cabin-lockers to let the water into the bilge.

For many minutes the vessel did not settle any by the head. I saw nothing serious in the condition of the vessel, but thought that the commanding officer ought to be on board, and began to make signal for him. I should have mentioned that the commander, James M. Duncan, was on board the flag-ship, near at hand.

The centrifugal and other pumps were started as soon as the water was high enough for their suction to take effect, and all of them worked well apparently.

After some minutes had elapsed with the vessel in this condition—I cannot say how long—she suddenly began to settle forward and to cant to starboard. Signal was made for assistance immediately, and all hands ordered on deck, but she sunk so rapidly now that many were caught below. Assistance arrived promptly, and I believe that all who succeeded in reaching the upper deck were picked up by boats. The saving of many lives is attributable to the self-possession displayed by all those officers and men who fell under my observation.

I have since heard from officers of the vessel that there were leaks in all the wing-rooms, and, as she had been much strained from various causes, my impression is that these leaks became suddenly enlarged, filling the ship forward, and causing her to sink almost immediately.

I am, respectfully, your obedient servant.

M. S. STUYVESANT,
Lieutenant and Executive Officer.

Rear-Admiral JOHN A. DAHLGREN,
Com'dg S. A. B. Squadron, off Charleston, S. C.

C.

UNITED STATES STORESHIP SUPPLY,
Off Morris Island, December 9, 1863.

SIR: Agreeably to your orders, I have questioned the officers and crew from the late United States steamer Weehawken regarding the use of a jackass in her hawse-hole.

A temporary one made of coal bags was used on her passage from New York to Fortress Monroe, but nothing has been seen of it since. None others made, nor any one detailed for that duty on the ship.

It will gratify you, sir, to know that the Weehawken's officers and men are well cared for in their new quarters, and as comfortable as possible under the circumstances.

I am, respectfully, your obedient servant,

M. S. STUYVESANT,
Lieutenant United States Navy.

Rear-Admiral JOHN A. DAHLGREN,
Commanding South Atlantic Blockading Squadron.

D.

UNITED STATES STORESHIP SUPPLY,
Off Morris Island, December 11, 1863.

SIR: I enclose copies of the reports of J. B. Allen, acting second assistant and senior engineer, and E. M. Stein, assistant surgeon; also, a second report from W. E. Bayne, acting master's mate, in accordance with your orders of December 10.

I forwarded the reports of the first two officers on the 9th ultimo, and am sorry they failed to reach.

I am, respectfully, your obedient servant,

M. S. STUYVESANT,
Lieutenant United States Navy.

Lieut. Com. J. M. BRADFORD,
Fleet Captain, S. A. B. Squadron.

E.

FLAG-SHIP PHILADELPHIA,
Off Morris Island, December 8, 1863.

SIR: In obedience to your orders, I beg leave to submit the following statement of what came under my observation in relation to the sinking of the iron-clad Weehawken:

At about 1 o'clock p. m., being in my room, received an order from Mr. Stuyvesant, the executive officer, to come on deck, and, in obeying the order, heard some one say "the water is coming in the cabin through the door." When I got on deck I received an order from executive officer to veer away chain, the vessel being fast to her mooring buoy; and whilst obeying the order, observed the sea washing over her from three to five feet in depth. After having obeyed the order, having given her about forty-five fathoms of chain, received permission to go below, and, upon my doing so, found the water rushing into my room in large streams; raised the hatch in my room, and found the place full of water; looked into the cabin, and also saw the hold full; then went on deck and reported the same to executive officer, and the want of some one to haul the limber chains; was ordered by executive officer to take some men and to go down and see to the hauling of them myself, and whilst executing the order saw the hold under the berth deck was rapidly filling. Saw Mr. Allen, second assistant acting chief engineer, and spoke to him about the water not running aft; he made answer, "the pumps work well;" then went into the turret-room, and heard the order given for everybody to come off the berth deck; then used all my endeavors to get the men up as quickly as possible; got up myself, leaving one or two on the ladder to come up after me.

In my opinion, the cause of her sinking was the shattered condition of her side armor, and a large increase of weight in ammunition and coals, which, with a rough sea, and her forward compartment full of water, caused an opening between the overhang and hull, which made itself manifest by the rushing in of water in all the side rooms.

I have the honor to be, very respectfully, your obedient servant,

CHA'S C. KINGSBURY,
Acting Master U. S. N.

Rear-Admiral J. A. DAHLGREN,
Commanding S. A. B. Squadron, Flag-Ship Philadelphia.

F.

UNITED STATES STORESHIP SUPPLY,
Off Charleston, S. C., December 9, 1863.

SIR: I am of opinion that the sinking of the Weehawken was caused by the filling of the forecastle with water, which caused her to go down by the head, besides straining her to such a degree as to separate the overhang from the hull, thereby causing a general leakage throughout the forepart of the vessel. The over-cramming of the vessel with shot and shells increased the strain on her, and no doubt caused her to sink more rapidly than she otherwise would have done. These are the chief causes, as it appears to me, to which the loss of this vessel is attributable.

Very respectfully, your obedient servant,

ED. W. M. STEIN, *Ass't Surgeon.*

Rear-Admiral J. A. DAHLGREN,
Commanding S. A. B. Squadron, off Charleston, S. C.

G.

UNITED STATES STORESHIP SUPPLY,
Off Charleston, S. C., December 11, 1863.

SIR: In obedience to your order requiring the officers of the Weehawken to present you with a statement of the *facts*, as far as they know, connected with the loss of that vessel, I would respectfully say, that the filling of the forecastle with water, and "the going down by the head" of the vessel in consequence of the accumulation of water in the forepart thereof, are the facts which immediately caused the sinking of the Weehawken, *as it appears to me.* The excessive quantity of shot and shells stowed away in the vessel is another *fact* which, I take it, caused her to sink sooner than she otherwise would have done.

I have the honor to be, very respectfully, your obedient servant,

ED. W. M. STEIN, *Ass't Surgeon.*

Rear-Admiral JOHN A. DAHLGREN,
Commanding S. A. B. Squadron,
Flag-Ship Philadelphia, off Charleston, S. C.

H.

FLAG-SHIP PHILADELPHIA,
Off Charleston, S. C., December 7, 1863.

SIR: In compliance with your request, I have the following statement to make in regard to the sinking of the iron-clad steamer Weehawken on the 6th instant.

About 1 o'clock p. m. I observed the water making so fast in the anchor-room that it was necessary to close the bulkhead door. About thirty or forty minutes afterwards I noticed that the anchor-room was so full of water as to cause it to flow over the top of the door and flood the cabin floor. The water did not appear to flow aft but a very little, but accumulated rapidly forward, and fast coming up with the cabin and ward-room floors. I also observed the water leaking rapidly into the officers' rooms and into my own room, through the seams in the sides of the ship. This latter I had never known to occur since I had been on board. When I observed this, I became at once convinced that she was making water fast throughout the entire forward part. When I left the ward-room, which was about five minutes before she sank, the water was an inch upon the floors.

The quantity of ammunition stowed forward was larger than it ever was since I have been on board, which caused her to be more down by the head than I have ever known her to be. Taking the large stock of shells and the vast quantity or weight of water in the anchor-room together, I believe so strained her forward as to let water into scores of places aft the cabin. She fast settled forward and prevented the water flowing aft. In my opinion the ship would not have sunk if she had not opened in her side.

Very respectfully,

FREDERICK R. STOW,
Acting Assistant Paymaster.

Commander J. M. DUNCAN,
Flag-Ship Philadelphia.

I.

FLAG-SHIP PHILADELPHIA,
Off Morris Island, December 7, 1863.

SIR: In obedience to your order, I respectfully submit an account of the circumstances connected with the sinking of the Weehawken that came under my observation.

At about 9.30 a. m. we came down from the picket ground and shackled on to the buoy known as buoy No. 2. At that time, and until 12 meridian, when I gave up charge of the deck, the sea was breaking over the ship forward, but being nearly an every day occurrence, no notice was taken of it.

Between 1.15 and 1.30 p. m. a heavy sea broke over the ship and filled the anchor-well with water. The forward battle-plate and also the berth-deck battle-plate were immediately closed, and the iron door connecting the captain's cabin and anchor-well was also closed and secured by iron turn-buckles. When the door was first closed the water leaked from the top to the bottom of the door, but in a short time it leaked but a very little from the bottom. This, in my opinion, proves that the limbers were clear, and that the hawse-hole, which was not closed, had nothing to do with the sinking of the ship. At about the same time a large leak was observed in the executive officer's room. This leak was about half way from the berth to the main deck. I reported it to the executive officer, and went on top of the turret.

The sea was then breaking over the ship forward, but not more than I have seen it before. In fifteen or twenty minutes it became apparent that we were sinking a little by the head. The centrifugal pump was started and threw a large stream of water through the out-board delivery on deck; but she did not rise any, and the executive officer ordered all the officers and men on deck, and also ordered the signal "captain needed on board" to be made.

I had mastheaded the first number of the signal, when she commenced to sink very rapidly. I was ordered to discontinue the first signal and substitute "assistance needed." The crew were directed to go aft and save themselves, and in from five to ten minutes the sea was making a clean run over the deck.

It is my opinion, and I believe the opinion of most of the officers, that the leak in the executive officer's room enlarged suddenly and caused the ship to sink.

I have the honor to be, very respectfully, your obedient servant,

J. M. REED, *Ensign, United States Navy.*

Rear-Admiral J. A. DAHLGREN,
Commanding South Atlantic Blockading Squadron.

K.

UNITED STATES STORESHIP SUPPLY,
Off Charleston, S. C., Wednesday, December 9, 1863.

SIR: In accordance with your order requiring those officers who were saved from the ill-fated iron-clad steamer Weehawken to send in to you their report regarding the sinking of that vessel, I herewith transmit my views.

After having made my usual visit, at 9 a. m., around that part of the vessel belonging to the engineer department, and finding all the machinery in good order, I retired to my room, feeling somewhat unwell. Soon after (I cannot exactly name the hour) I heard a rush of water forward, and went into the cabin to find out the cause. I there found Ensign Chadwick engaged in closing the communicating door between the anchor-well and cabin. I assisted him in closing this door and securing it, (which is done by means of iron turn-buckles and bars,) and by this means the water was prevented for a time filling up the bilge. I then went into the engine-room, and ordered *one* Worthington pump started to pumping out the bilge, and then went to the executive officer, and requested that the limber-chains might be hauled. This was done, and I returned to the engine-room, and there found that the water was coming aft very fast. I ordered the remaining Worthington pump started and the centrifugal pump cleared and got ready for use. I then went back into the cabin, and saw the water forcing its way through all sides of the communicating door, and that the water under the cabin floor covered the shot and shell, and was nearly over the floor. I returned to the engine-room, and ordered the centrifugal pump started. This pump worked well, but drew the water from the bilge faster than it ran through the limbers, and therefore, for a time, it was sucking.

All that possibly *could* be done by the engineers was done, as is plainly seen by those four noble fellows dying at their posts.

The vessel (Weehawken) having been *twice* subjected to heavy straining, (first while ashore near Fort Sumter, and lastly while beached at Port Royal,) and having an unusual weight of ammunition forward, I respectfully submit as my reasons for the melancholy loss. As fast as she filled with water forward, so much more did it pull her down by the head, and prevent the water from running aft; and I believe that heavy weight of ammunition and water caused a large opening between the overhang and hull.

I am, very respectfully, your obedient servant,

J. B. A. ALLEN, U. S. N.,
Acting Second Assistant Engineer,
Late Senior Engineer United States Steamer Weehawken.

Rear-Admiral JOHN A. DAHLGREN, U. S. N.,
Com'g S. A. B. Squadron, Flag-Steamer Philadelphia, off Charleston, S. C.

L.

FLAG-STEAMER PHILADELPHIA,
Off Charleston, South Carolina, December 7, 1863.

SIR: I have the following to report in relation to the disaster on the iron-clad Weehawken, on the afternoon of the 6th instant, as came under my observation, viz:

About 1 p. m. I was seated in the ward-room, when my first apprehension of any unusual occurrence in regard to the safety or sinking of the Weehawken was occasioned by the pilot's calling my attention to the volume of water flowing in around the bulkhead iron door, between the captain's cabin and the anchor-room, which was closed and only latched; and from the flow of the water in at the sides of the door, should judge the water in the anchor-room at that time to be about eighteen inches deep. This water was flooding the cabin floor. I called for assistance. Mr. Allen, the chief engineer, came, and we put on and screwed up the cross-bars to the door, which nearly stopped the water coming through. The water rose gradually in the anchor-room, as indicated by the leak about the door, and in about thirty minutes it was on the top of the door.

I next saw a leak around the end of a beam in executive officer's room, on starboard side forward, and, on opening a hatch in the starboard forward room, the water came up over the floor.

The sinking of the Weehawken I attribute to the excessive weight of ammunition, keeping the vessel down by the head, causing the water to flood the anchor-room through the hawse-pipe; *then* the combined weight of water and ammunition caused the ship to strain and leak badly between the overhang and the hull forward when in a sea way; and, lastly, the water would not flow aft to the pumps, making it impossible to free her.

Most respectfully submitted.

BENJ. H. CHADWICK,
Acting Ensign, United States Navy.

Commander J. M. DUNCAN.

M.

FLAG-SHIP PHILADELPHIA,
Off Charleston, S. C., December 7, 1863.

SIR: In obedience to your order, I respectfully submit the following statement in relation to the sinking of the United States Monitor Weehawken on December 6.

I relieved the officer of the deck at 12 meridian, noticing that we were shackled on to a buoy, and not very far from several steam-tugs lying at anchor. The wind was quite fresh from northward and eastward, and a pretty heavy sea on, breaking over the decks forward, which, I suppose, is a common occurrence to the Monitors during rough weather. About 1 p. m. a heavy sea partly carried away the forward hatch. I immediately called all of the watch on deck.

About this time Lieutenant Stuyvesant, the executive officer, came on deck also. I went forward with the watch to replace and secure it, and found the battle-plate unshipped, and hanging by the tackle. This was placed and closed down as soon as possible. The room which had been closed up below was about half full of water before the battle-plate could be shipped. Acting Master Kingsbury came on deck about now, and received orders from the executive officer to veer away chain, which was done. After everything was secured, Mr. Stuyvesant told me to go below and change my clothing for a dry suit. Before arriving below, I observed the water coming over the door from the anchor-room into the cabin. Just as I started to come on deck the water came up through the hatch in my room.

When I arrived on top of the turret the order was sent down by Mr. Stuyvesant for everybody to come on deck. Soon after, the order to go aft and save themselves. Under the circumstances, officers and men behaved with great coolness.

In going down she canted over to starboard. I staid aboard until a heavy sea washed me off, when I made a spring and caught hold of the boat, and was hauled in. I then took charge, but found her completely unmanageable. Her row-locks were gone, and all we could do was to keep her head to sea. Finally we were picked up by a tug-boat.

As to the real cause of her filling with water, I am not able to state. I judge she must have parted the "overhang" from the main hull. The anchor-room is supposed to be a water-tight compartment, which, being filled with water, would not affect the vessel.

Very respectfully, your obedient servant,

F. N. CRANDALL,
Acting Ensign, U. S. Navy.

Rear-Admiral J. A. DAHLGREN,
Comd'g S. A. B. Squadron.

N.

UNITED STATES STORESHIP SUPPLY,
Off Morris Island, December 10, 1863.

SIR: In obedience to your order, I transmit an account of what I saw in reference to the sinking of the United States steam iron-clad battery Weehawken.

The first intimation that I had of anything being wrong was, upon looking through one of the turret ports, I saw that the forward battle-plate over the captain's hatch had been washed by a heavy sea out of its place, and I also saw Mr. Stuyvesant, in person, having it put in its place. When, about five or ten minutes afterwards, I went and found the water rushing over the door leading to the anchor-well, which was closed but not secured; finding which, I looked for and found the cross-bars, and helped to secure it. The pilot was in the cabin at the same time. I also had the hatches taken off the forward shot-lockers to let the water run aft quicker to the pumps. After seeing all secure, went to dinner, thinking that the water would soon run aft. In fifteen minutes afterwards heard that the water was running into the first lieutenant's room; went to see what could be done with it. I sent for padding and tallow, and stopped it as far as possible. Afterwards I went to look at the cabin again, thinking it might be all clear, but found it worse than ever, but did not think there was any danger, as all the pumps were working well; but found things still getting worse and the water still rushing into the ship. I also thought that the ship was sinking by the head, and upon going to the top of the turret found it to be so; when I got an order to fire a gun, but could not do so for the boats. Heard the executive officer give an order to leave the ship by any means in our power. He was busy at that time with signals. Left the top of the turret, and held the boats till they were full of men, and got washed overboard, but got into the boat again.

I remain, very respectfully, yours,

WM. E. BAYNE,
Master's Mate, Acting Gunner.

Rear-Admiral J. A. DAHLGREN,
Commanding S. A. B. Squadron.

O.

OFF MORRIS ISLAND,
December 7, 1863.

SIR: The sinking of the United States iron-clad steamer Weehawken, moored at buoy No. 2, on the 6th instant, in my opinion, was caused by leaving the battle-plate over the captain's hatch off too long, causing the forecastle to be filled with water, and that, coupled with extra weight of shell, caused her to sink by the head, preventing the water from going aft; and the pressure of water was so strong as, in my opinion, to burst the main hull from the overhang, as all the leaks started were fresh ones.

Sir, I remain, very respectfully, your obedient servant,

LEVI JUMP, *Pilot.*

J. M. DUNCAN,
Late Commander of U. S. Iron-clad Weehawken.

List of officers and men saved from the United States steamer Weehawken.

Officers.—J. M. Duncan, commander; M. S. Stuyvesant, lieutenant; C. C. Kingsbury, acting master; E. M. Stein, assistant surgeon; F. R. Stow, acting assistant paymaster; J. H. Reed, ensign; B. H. Chadwick, acting ensign; F. H. Crandall, acting ensign; J. B. A. Allen, acting second assistant engineer; William E. Bayne, acting master's mate; Levi Jump, pilot.—Total, 11.

Men.—John Smith, first class fireman; John Hurley, do.; John Connolly, do.; Edward Clarkson, do.; Edward Carr, do.; David H. Serburne, second class fireman; James Collins, do.; James Byers, do.; Patrick Reardon, do.; Henry Sumner, do.; Maurice Phelan, coal-heaver; Bernard Cassiday, do.; Thomas Hogan, do.; Thomas Doran, second master; C. B. Brunn, do.; William A. Munson, second gunner; George Crotts, do.; William Brown, seaman; Michael Rice, do.; John Williams, 1st, do.; William A. Davis, do.; Thomas Goggin, captain of hold; Carl Grandman, ordinary seaman; Edward Christenson, do.; John Walters, do.; Thomas Bailey, landsman; John Nee, do.; Stephen McDonald, do.; L. Johnson, second class boy; Charles Drage, landsman; John Russell, do.; William Batten, do.; Edward Lewis, do.; Patrick McGovern, do.; Matthew T. Jackson, do.; Michael Dunn, do.; John Anderson, do.; E. A. Redding, do.; Samuel E. Seaman, do.; James T. Brace, do.; Francis Gallagher, do.; William H. Dunbar, do.; William Orange, do.; James Kohlay, do.; Dan. O'Brien, do.; Henry Dobson, ward-room cook; Harry Read, paymaster's steward; Benjamin S. Birdsall, doctor's steward; James Hagan, boatswain's mate on board the Home; William R. Nongle.

Missing.—Thomas Piper, second master; John Scallen, landsman; —— Buckley, do.; John Kerrigan, do.; John Carpenter, do.; Joshua Crogan, second class boy; Charles F. Davis, first class fireman; John Williams, 2d, landsman; Charles Wilson, master-at-arms; William H. Williamson, captain's cook; Christian Anderson, ship's cook; John Rutledge, landsman; Ralph Anderson, do.; James Gayhan, first class fireman; Edward Mullen, second class fireman; Michael Clines, coal heaver; James Lenman, second class fireman; Thomas Mee, first class fireman; Robert Nugent, coal-heaver; George M. Leighton, first class fireman; Thomas Stothers, do.; Stephen C. Newman, second class fireman; Thomas Donaran, ordinary seaman; William G. Pike, do.; Thomas Dowlin, landsman; Thomas A. Mason, yeoman, (since dead.)

[Despatch No. 351.]

FLAG-STEAMER PHILADELPHIA,
Off Morris Island, December 29, 1863.

SIR: The order of the department directing me "to convene a court of inquiry for the purpose of ascertaining all the facts relating to the sinking of the Weehawken" has been received.

Immediately after the disaster such was ordered. The commanders of three Monitors were selected for the purpose, (Lieutenant Commanders Simpson, Davis, and Cornwell,) as better qualified to judge by their experience in this class of vessel.

A succession of stormy weather has interfered with their proceedings, and required their personal attention to their own vessels, but I hope it will be soon completed and forwarded for your information.

The final repair of the Monitors still lingers. The Patapsco and Lehigh are at Port Royal. When completed, one will relieve the Nantucket, and the other will come this way. When I look back at my own anticipations in regard to the readiness of these vessels, I confess I am almost in despair. All that I could do to hasten the repair I have done, and, it may be, all possible despatch has been done. However, one thing is certain: when the other Monitors are called on for service, no one of these shall be out of line.

The boilers now begin to be troublesome, and I have just called the Montauk down, to draw her fires and patch up, leaving only three Monitors above to do duty. The air-pump was also disabled this morning by the negligence of an engineer.

There is almost too much dependent on the Monitors now here. There is not the least allowance possible for accidents.

My notice has just been called to a passage in the correspondence of the Tribune of the 14th of December, dated "Headquarters Department of the South, December 6," which attributes the delay here "to instructions from Washington."

I have only to say, that no person has ever heard me say anything of the kind, nor even allude to the views of the department. The two special documents from the department have not left my own custody, nor have they been seen even by my secretary, nor by any one except the commanding officers whom I convened to obtain their opinions, as directed by the department, and by General Gillmore, to whom the department directed them to be shown, and I feel sure that nothing ever would transpire from them.

It is another evidence of the unscrupulous propensity with which some writers are possessed to make news, if they cannot collect it.

The infamous abuse which these gentlemen have lavished on me for some months past very naturally precludes the possibility of my having intercourse with them.

The quantities of obstructions which were washed down by the freshet proves to be very considerable. I saw yesterday a string of railroad bars (22 feet long each) being drawn from the water, linked together, the wood work gone, and have been told that 33 of them have been beached, which would have extended two hundred and fifty yards.

The rebels are busy at work on a new iron-clad, and it is reported to be nearly plated.

I have the honor to be, very respectfully, your obedient servant,

JNO. A. DAHLGREN,

Rear-Admiral, Commanding S. A. B. Squadron.

Hon. GIDEON WELLES,

Secretary of the Navy, Washington, D. C.

Proceedings of a court of inquiry convened on board the United States ship Supply, off Morris Island, South Carolina, by virtue of the following order, viz:

FLAG-STEAMER PHILADELPHIA,

Off Morris Island, December 7, 1863.

GENTLEMEN: It is important that a full inquiry should be made into the causes of the deplorable disaster that befell the Weehawken yesterday. You are therefore appointed a court of inquiry to ascertain the facts in the case, and give your opinion thereon. Acting Assistant Paymaster Benjamin F. Munroe is appointed the judge advocate of said court. You will endeavor to regulate the proceedings so as not to interfere with your duties as commanders of Monitors.

Very respectfully, your obedient servant,

J. A. DAHLGREN,
Rear-Admiral, Commanding S. A. B. Squadron.

Lieutenant Commander E. SIMPSON,
Lieutenant Commander JOHN L. DAVIS,
Lieutenant Commander J. J. CORNWELL.

---

10 O'CLOCK A. M., *December* 10, 1863.

The court met pursuant to the above order. Present: Lieutenant Commander E. Simpson, Lieutenant Commander John L. Davis, and Lieutenant Commander J. J. Cornwell; Acting Assistant Paymaster Benjamin F. Munroe, judge advocate.

The court was duly sworn by the judge advocate, and the judge advocate was duly sworn by the presiding officer of the court.

Commander James M. Duncan, late of the Weehawken, was called, but being absent on duty, could not attend. Lieutenant M. S. Stuyvesant, late executive officer of the Weekawken, was called, and being duly sworn, testified as follows:

Question by judge advocate. What is your name and rank in the service?

Answer. M. S. Stuyvesant; lieutenant, and late executive officer of the Weehawken.

Question by judge advocate. State what you know of the causes that led to the sinking of the Weehawken.

Answer. Ship came to her moorings between ten and eleven a. m. on Sunday, 6th of December, 1863; wind from northeast, fresh breeze; spray washing over the deck and fore-hatch into the windlass-room. The battle-plate being up, one end of the battle-plate resting on the rabbet of the hatch, the other end being triced up by a tackle led across the deck; the berth-deck battle-plate being up and secured in the same manner. We were made fast to our usual moorings (buoy number two) by a chain from our on deck to a shackle on the buoy, having five or six fathoms scope. After securing to the buoy, I gave orders to bank the fires as usual, being a standing order of the ship to keep up twenty-five pounds of steam. About this time the captain left the ship. On going below, I noticed the water slopping in under the forward cabin door, a temporary wooden door; ordered the iron door to be secured; this was a common occurrence. Shortly after twelve o'clock Ensign J. H. Reed came below and remarked there was no change in the weather, in answer to a question from me, and that she was riding easy. Some time after, from half to three-quarters of an hour, I heard the watch being called on deck, which being an unusual occurrence, and the officer of the watch, Acting Ensign F. H. Crandall, having reported for duty only a day or so before, I went up to ascertain what he wished of the watch, not wishing to have them roused out unnecessarily. I found the sea and wind increased considerably, and that the forward hatch coaming, which was shaped like a hopper, was broken by the sea, and the battle-plate knocked down and across the hatch, but not so as to prevent a large portion of a sea from going into the anchor-room. I gave orders to have the battle-plate put in its place, but this could not be done before two or three other seas coming over, nearly filled the anchor-room. I then veered about fifteen fathoms of the mooring chain. Then closed the berth-deck battle-plate; also ordered the limber chains to be hauled previous to closing the berth-deck battle-plate. I ordered the watch to go below. The bilge pumps and centrifugal pumps were all started at about this time, but there was not yet sufficient water aft to enable the suction of the centrifugal pump to work. While veering chain, it was reported to me that there was a leak in my room. While on my way to examine it, after seeing everything properly secured on deck, the captain of the hold reported six inches of water in the hold abreast the berth-deck hatch amidships, which I regarded as evidence that the water from the windlass-room was going aft, as this hold had heretofore been dry. The leak in my room, which was the after wing room, on the starboard side, was round the edges of one of the beams where it joined the side.

Acting Master's Mate William E. Bayne was engaged in calking it up, and said it could be easily stopped, and did not appear to me to be anything serious. Then I went forward into the cabin and found the water making its way in over the upper edges of the forward cabin iron bulkhead in small streams. Had the covers taken off the cabin shot-lockers, filled with fifteen-inch solid and cored shot, to let the water in the bilge. Then went on deck and ordered signal to be made that the captain was needed on board, he being on board the flag-ship, near at hand; also ordered Acting Master Kingsbury to keep the limbers clear. Some little time was lost in getting signals out, and the first number was just answered when I noticed the vessel settling by the head and at the same time canting to starboard. I ordered everybody on deck, sending messengers below for that purpose, and the senior engineer, Acting Second Assistant Engineer J. B. A. Allen, jr., to send all out of the fire-room. Ordered signals to be changed to one for assistance, which was answered. Up to the time signals were made for assistance I did not consider the ship in any danger. Thinking the captain would prefer to be on board under the circumstances, I had ordered signals to be made accordingly, and the canting to starboard was the first indication I had of her being in a sinking condition. We had two boats made fast to the stern. As fast as the men came up, I ordered them aft to the boats. Acting Ensign Chadwick I ordered below to get life-preservers, at his own suggestion. He returned, driven back by the water, the vessel sinking so rapidly. In my opinion not more than two minutes elapsed from the time she canted to starboard until she disappeared. Acting Master Kingsbury staid below until the last moment, driving the men on deck. No report had been made to me of leaks, other than the one in my own room. I had noticed as soon as the windlass-room filled with water that it appeared to bring the ship on an even keel; previously she trimmed two feet by the stern. She remained in this position about half an hour before canting to starboard.

Question by the court. How soon after you received the report from the captain of the hold that there were five inches of water in the hold did you receive the report that the centrifugal pump was throwing water?

Answer. I cannot say definitely. I should judge the centrifugal pump was working well twenty minutes before she sank.

Question by the court. Did you receive a second report of the depth of water in the hold?

Answer. None.

Question by the court. Had you any reason to suppose that the depth of water was increasing gradually in the hold, or do you of your own knowledge know that the water accumulated in the vessel previous to the moment when she filled and went down?

Answer. Had no knowledge.

Question by the court. When the battle-plate or fore hatch was put down, was it secured there from below or by any means on deck?

Answer. It was not secured from below. We could not get at it; neither was it secured on deck.

Question by the court. What do you understand to have been the depth of water in the vessel when the captain of the hold reported five inches in the hold?

Answer. Five inches above the flooring of the hold.

Question by the court. Was the berth-deck, battle-plate, and the one over the fire-room secured from the time the vessel was making water up to the time she went down?

Answer. They were closed, but not secured.

Question by the court. Was there any way for the people in the fire-room to get out of the ship, except through the passage leading to the berth deck?

Answer. None, unless they could raise the fire-room battle-plate from below.

Question by the court. Was there a jackass on the chain leading out of the hawse-pipe, and was there one always used in rough weather?

Answer. None to my knowledge.

Question by the court. Was the valve at the bottom of the forward cabin bulkhead open or shut?

Answer. Don't know. To the best of my belief it was open, as the water ran aft freely. Do not know that there was a valve; never saw or heard of it; had understood there was a water communication from the windlass-room to the pumps.

Question by the court. Was the water in the windlass-room, at the time the leak in your room was discovered, on a level with that leak?

Answer. To the best of my belief it was.

Question by the court. How long have you been attached to the Weehawken as executive officer?

Answer. Since the 18th of October, 1863.

The testimony of the witness was here read over to him; he pronounced it correct.

J. B. A. Allen, jr., acting second assistant engineer, late senior engineer of the Weehawken, being called and sworn, testified as follows:

Question by judge advocate. What is your name and rank in the service?

Answer. J. B. A. Allen, jr., acting second assistant engineer.

Question by judge advocate. Were you the senior engineer of the Weehawken?

Answer. I was.

Question by judge advocate. State what you know of the cause that led to the sinking of the Weekawken.

Answer. At 9 a. m. last Sunday I made my usual visit around that part of the vessel belonging to the engineer's department. Feeling indisposed, I retired to my room. Soon after I heard a rush of water forward. I jumped up and went into the captain's cabin to find out the cause, and there found Ensign Chadwick had closed the communicating iron door leading from the windlass-room to the cabin. I saw water running under the door. I assisted Mr. Chadwick in securing it by the cross-bars and turn-buckles. Heard some one remark that the water was caused by the battle-plate being off, and the sea washing over the hatch. Having seen the door secured, I went on deck and saw the battle-plate had been put on. Went down in the engine-room; the water there was not higher than usual in the bilge. I ordered one Worthington pump started to pump the bilge, then went on deck and requested the executive officer, Lieutenant M. S. Stuyvesant, to send men down to haul the limber chains. Men were sent. I went into the cabin, and while they were hauling them asked if they worked free; told me yes. I then went back to the engine-room; saw the water was running aft very freely, and that it increased in the bilge. Ordered the remaining Worthington pump started, pumping the bilge, and the centrifugal pump cleared and made ready for use. I returned to the cabin, and found the water forcing its way through all sides of the communicating door. I raised the hatches of the cabin floor, and endeavored to find a cock leading from the water-tight bulkhead to the bilge. I was unable to find the cock on account of the shot or shell. I then concluded it was best not to open this door and allow the water to run in the bilge, it being a water-tight compartment and the ship being then down by the head, caused by the water, shot, and shell. On looking down the shot-locker hatches, I found the water was over the shell, and nearly up on the cabin floor. I went aft; the water still increased in the bilge aft in the engine-room. I ordered the centrifugal pump started. This pump worked well, but drew the water from the bilge faster than it would run aft. I returned to the cabin; there found about four inches water on the cabin floor and ward-room floor. Returned aft to the engine-room; found the water much increased there; noticed the pumps were all working well, and then went up and reported to the executive officer that I was doing all I could in the engine-room. While in the act of replying, the ship heeled over to starboard very heavily. I again asked the executive officer what was to be done. At that time there were signals flying, which I understood to be signals for assistance. The executive officer asked me if the ship was ever in that position before. I was in the act of replying, when he informed me he had passed the word for all hands to come on deck. The forward part of the vessel was then some distance under water. Seeing that she was sinking very rapidly, I first thought of those in the engine-room; could not get down through turret on account of the crowd of men coming up the hatch. I jumped off the turret on to the deck, ran for the engine-room hatch, the battle-plate of which was on, and jumped on this hatch, in hopes that those below would raise it. About this time I presume the water had struck the fires, and the steam issuing therefrom suffocated those in the engine-room, the ship being then far gone. I ran aft and jumped overboard, and swam to a boat.

Question by the court. You have stated the water came through around the door leading from the windlass-room to the cabin. Did you see any water come over the forward cabin bulkhead?

Answer. I did not.

Question by the court. You have stated that at one period the water did not come aft sufficiently fast to supply the centrifugal pump. Do you consider that the centrifugal pump would have been able to keep the vessel clear if the only feed of water had been through the valve at the bottom of the forward cabin bulkhead?

Answer. The Worthington pumps would have been able to keep her clear, provided the water could have come aft.

Question by the court. To what, then, do you charge the increase of water in the engine-room when you made the last visit?

Answer. The water had increased to such a height forward as to run aft.

Question by the court. Is it your opinion that the increase of water forward was caused by the water running into the hold through the valve at the bottom of the cabin bulkhead, or that water ran in from other places? If the latter, state your reasons for such an opinion.

Answer. The water ran in from other places. I saw water running in from the cabin-communicating iron door; saw a leak in the executive officer's room, and also one in the room of the master of the ship.

Question by the court. Was the amount of water large that came in around the door in the iron bulkhead?

Answer. Yes, but not more than the pumps would have taken out.

Question by the court. How extensive were the leaks in the executive officer's and master's room?

Answer. I saw the water coming in at the rate of two to three gallons per minute in the executive officer's room, and about the same in the master's room.

Question by the court. Do you consider that all the water that caused the vessel to sink came into her through the windlass-room?

Answer. I do not.

Question by the court. In what other way could water have got into her?

Answer. From the fact of seeing water coming in through the executive officer's room and the master's room, I judge it was caused by an opening between the overhang and hull, for when I noticed the leak it appeared to me to be about where the overhang joined the hull.

Question by the court. How far below the deck was it that you noticed the leak?

Answer. A foot and a half, or two feet and a half.

Question by the court. Have you ever seen the vessel before when she had any large quantity of water in her?

Answer. I have not. Have seen the water wash over the fire-room plate on the passage from Fortress Monroe to Port Royal.

Question by the court. Do you know what was the depth of water in the forward part of the vessel at the time you refer to in your answer to the last question?

Answer. Have no idea.

Question by the court. How long was the interval between the time that you noticed the water coming through all sides of the door in the forward cabin bulkhead and that at which the vessel filled and went down?

Answer. Between fifteen and thirteen minutes.

Question by the court. At the time you jumped on the engine-room hatch was there water over it, and could it be opened by those in the engine-room?

Answer. The water was on the starboard side of the vessel, and it could have been opened had any one been alive or there to do it.

Question by the court. Was there any other way by which information could be conveyed to the engine-room?

Answer. None other but by passing down through the turret.

Question by the court. Do you know if the people in the engine-room were informed of the order for all hands to come on deck?

Answer. I believe not.

Question by the court. When you left the engine-room hatch did you consider all had been done to communicate with the people down there?

Answer. I did all that could possibly have been done.

Question by the court. How long have you been attached to the Weehawken, and how long as senior engineer?

Answer. Since the twenty-ninth of January, eighteen hundred and sixty-three, and about two months as senior engineer.

Question by the court. When the men were being sent up from the berth deck, could the word have been passed through the speaking-tube into the engine-room?

Answer. I believe not.

Question by the court. Was the speaking-tube ever used to convey orders to the engine-room, and was it in order on the occasion of the Weehawken sinking?

Answer. Yes, as far as I know, the tube was in order.

Question by the court. Why could not the tube have been used on this occasion?

Answer. Because from the excitement on the berth-deck and in the turret chamber at the time the word was passed for all hands to come on deck, and the noise created by the working of the pumps, I doubt if anything could have been heard by speaking through the tube.

Question by the court. Was there any other effort made for the preservation of the men in the engine-room?

Answer. One man volunteered to go down into the engine-room. I permitted him to go, and presume he went, as he has not been accounted for. His name was Robert Nugent, coal-heaver.

The testimony was here read over to the witness; he delared it to be correct.

The court adjourned until 10 o'clock a. m., Friday, December 11, 1863.

UNITED STATES SHIP SUPPLY,
December 15, 1863.

The court met pursuant to adjournment; gales of wind having prevented their meeting since December 11, 1863.

Present: Lieutenant Commander E Simpson, Lieutenant Commander J. L. Davis, Lieutenant Commander J. J. Cornwell; Acting Assistant Paymaster B. F. Munroe, judge advocate. The proceedings of December 11, 1863, were then read over and corrected by the court.

Acting Second Assistant Engineer J. B. A. Allen, jr., being recalled, testified as follows:

Question by the court. State any causes, that you know of, which have operated upon the Weehawken to produce a tendency to open in the manner that you think she did.

Answer. From the heavy straining the ship got while ashore near Fort Sumter and while beached at Port Royal, and the unusual weight of ammunition in the forward part of the vessel, and the shock produced by the sea striking under the overhang, I think had a tendency to weaken her in those parts where the overhang joined the hull.

Question by the court. How much was the unusual weight of ammunition stowed forward, and when was it stowed?

Answer. I cannot tell how much was in there; have never seen the vessel stowed so full before. It was stowed since our return from Port Royal.

Question by the court. When you first joined the Weehawken, how many inches of water did she leak per hour as a general rule?

Answer. Six to eight inches in four hours.

Question by the court. Was any increase in the general leak perceptible after the causes of weakness mentioned by you in answer to a previous question?

Answer. After coming off the beach near Sumter, I perceived no difference in the vessel making water. After coming from Port Royal, and while at sea on our way to Charleston, a leak was discovered in our after overhang, the water coming in on both sides adjoining the after water-tight bulkhead. When first discovered, the water had filled the overhang as high as the man-hole leading into the after overhang of the vessel, the water turning into the engineer store-room. One pump kept this water clear by only occasionally pumping it out. I endeavored to find out where the water came from; could not on account of this bulkhead. After arriving inside Charleston bar, and in smooth water, for some reason or other this leak stopped—troubled us no further. Ever since I had been attached to the vessel there had been a leak on the port side of the vessel, about even with the deck, in the engineer's room.

Question by the court. Have you ever seen the cock or valve leading through the forward cabin bulkhead, and was it the custom in the ship to keep it open or shut?

Answer. I never saw the cock; judging from the fact of there being one in the after water-tight bulkhead, thought, as a matter of course, there must have been one in the forward water-tight bulkhead.

The testimony of the witness was here read over to him; he pronounced it correct.

Acting Ensign F. H. Crandell, being called and duly sworn, testified as follows:

Question by judge advocate. State what you know of the cause that led to the sinking of the Weehawken.

Answer. I relieved the deck at about ten minutes after twelve o'clock, December 6, 1863. Noticed we were shackled to a buoy, not very far from several tug-boats; also, it was blowing quite fresh from the northeast, an occasional sea breaking over forward. About one o'clock a heavy sea partly carried away the forward hatch combing. I immediately called the watch on deck. About the time the watch came on deck, Lieutenant Stuyvesant came up also. I went forward with the men and found the battle plate was unshipped, hanging in the windlass-room by a tackle. Hauled up the battle-plate and shipped it in its proper place in the hatch as soon as possible. The windlass-room was half full of water, or half the depth of the windlass-room. About this time Acting Master Kingsbury came on deck. He was ordered by Lieutenant Stuyvesant to veer chain, which was done. I had the gig called away (by orders) and manned. Sent her alongside the flag-ship for Captain Duncan. After the battle-plate was placed down and the chain veered, Lieutenant Stuyvesant told me to go below and put on a dry suit of clothes. I went below. The water was just beginning to wash in over the windlass-room door. While I was changing my clothes I heard the water flowing in much more rapidly over the door; thought I heard the water rushing between the wood and the iron at the side of my room. I occupied the starboard forward room. After I had put on my dry clothing, Acting Ensign Chadwick came down and went in my room; he raised the hatch in the deck to get at the life-preservers. I noticed the water rushed up right away in the room. I then made my way up through the turret, and about the time I arrived on top of the turret, Lieutenant Stuyvesant sent word down for everybody to come on deck. I noticed, also, they were signalling. Soon after the order was given for everybody to come on deck, another order was passed by Lieutenant Stuyvesant to go aft and save themselves. The vessel went down very quick.

Question by the court. When was the main or berth deck hatch closed, and was it secured down?

Answer. I don't know; was below.

Question by the court. When the battle-plate was put on, you say the windlass-room was half full of water, but when you went below to change your clothes you noticed the water coming in over the door in the water-tight bulkhead. To what do you charge this increase of water in the windlass-room?

Answer. I know little of the construction of these vessels. The real cause I am not able to state; my supposition is, the overhanging parted from the main hull.

Question by the court. At the time the rush of water was heard by you, at the side of your room, what was its height from the deck in your room, and where did it come from?

Answer. I should judge between six and seven feet. I do not know where it came from.

Question by the court. As officer of the deck, did you, or any one to your knowledge, order the forward battle-plate secured below?

Answer. Not that I know of.

Question by the court. Was the turret keyed up, and did any water wash in the vessel under it; and if so, in what quantity?

Answer. Do not know.

Question by the court. How long have you been attached to the Weehawken, and in what capacity?

Answer. I was attached to her about two days, as acting ensign.

Question by the court. Have you ever seen the cock, or valve, communicating through the water-tight bulkhead forward?

Answer. No.

Question by the court. What was the interval of time that elapsed between the putting on the battle-plate forward and your going below to change your clothes?

Answer. About half an hour.

The testimony was here read over to the witness; he pronounced it correct.

Ensign J. H. Reed being called, and duly sworn, testified as follows:

Question by judge advocate. What is your name and rank in the service?

Answer. J. H. Reed, ensign, late of the Weehawken.

Question by judge advocate. State to the court what you know of the causes that led to the sinking of the Weehawken.

Answer. I gave up charge of the deck at about twenty minutes after 12 o'clock, December 6, 1863. I went below, shifted myself, and came out of my room at about fifteen minutes after one. I then saw the senior engineer and Acting Ensign Chadwick engaged in closing the iron door connecting the windlass-room and captain's cabin; the water was then leaking through around the cracks of the door, about half way up. I then sat down to my dinner, and got through about 2 o'clock, and then took another look into the captain's cabin; the water then was not leaking through so high up as when the door was first closed. I then looked into Lieutenant Stuyvesant's room; saw the water was then leaking through the inner planking of the ship, a little above half way between the two decks—a leak about four or five feet long, and three-eighths of an inch wide. I started to go on the turret; met Lieutenant Stuyvesant on the berth-deck; told him his room was adrift. Then went on top of the turret and sat down. About fifteen minutes after Lieutenant Stuyvesant directed me to make signals, "Captain needed on board." I bent on the first number, signifying "captain," and a few minutes after hoisted it. The ship then commenced to settle quickly by the head, and I was ordered to make signals for assistance. I immediately hoisted No. 82: "Assistance, I am in want of," having hardly time to have the signal hoisted before she canted on her starboard side, and commenced sinking very rapidly.

Question by the court. Have you any reason to suppose that the amount of water which caused the Weehawken to sink accumulated gradually in her hold, or that it came in suddenly?

Answer. It came in suddenly; because, if it had been gradually accumulating, I think she would have sunk down by the head, so the officers would have all noticed it.

Question by the court. From the time that the windlass-room was closed to the time of the sinking of the vessel, were there, to your knowledge, any observations made of the amount of water running into the hold?

Answer. None at all.

Question by the court. Have you ever seen the cock or valve opening through the water-tight bulkhead forward?

Answer. No.

Question by the court. Was water rushing down the forward hatch before or at the time you were relieved?

Answer. No water going down that I know of. The battle-plate being up, the water was washing over the b——, but not high enough to go over the false coaming.

Question by the court. When you saw the water the first time leaking around the windlass-room door, did or did you not apprehend a serious leak in the vessel?

Answer. Not a serious one.

Question by the court. Was the turret keyed up or not?

Answer. I don't know.

Question by the court. To what do you attribute the rapid filling and sinking the vessel?

Answer. I was on top of the turret when she commenced to sink, and as I had not noticed before that her bows were much down by the head, I think her rapid sinking was caused by the leak in Lieutenant Stuyvesant's room suddenly enlarging.

Question by the court. Do you know, of your own knowledge, if the hatches were secured down in their places?

Answer. I know they were down, but I never have seen them secured down.

Question by the court. How long had you been attached to the Weehawken?

Answer. I think about one month and one day.

Question by the court. What was done with the signal-book when the vessel sank?

Answer. Left on top of the turret.

The testimony was here read to the witness. He pronounced it correct.

The court then adjourned till ten o'clock, December 16, 1863.

U. S. SHIP SUPPLY, *December* 19, 1863.

The court met pursuant to adjournment, gales of wind having prevented their meeting since December 15, 1863. Present: Lieutenant Commander E. Simpson; Lieutenant Commander J. L. Davis; Lieutenant Commander J. J. Cornwell; Acting Assistant Paymaster B. F. Munroe, judge advocate.

The proceedings of December 15, 1863, were then read over, and corrected by the court.

Pilot Levi Jump being called and duly sworn, testified as follows:

Question by judge advocate. What is your name, and rank in the service?

Answer. Levi Jump, southern coast pilot, late of the Weehawken.

Question by judge advocate. State to the court what you know of the causes that led to the sinking of the Weehawken.

Answer. Between one and two o'clock I came on deck on Sunday, December 6, 1863, on top the turret; wind from northeast, blowing fresh, with some sea making over the bows of the vessel, and at that time the officer of the deck ordered a tarpaulin to be put over the hatch that leads into the windlass room, the battle-plate of the forward hatch that leads into the windlass-room being up. After a few minutes there were four seas shipped over the bows, that caused the battle-plate to be unshipped and fall down into the windlass-room, and hang by the tackle. That instant, the officer of the deck called the watch; with the assistance of Lieutenant Stuyvesant replaced the battle-plate, and a bucket of tallow was called for to place over the seams. The sea was so rough they could not get the tallow into the seams. A few minutes after, the ward-room boy reported to me that dinner was ready. At that time Lieutenant Stuyvesant ordered chain to be given, which was done by Acting Master Kingsbury, to make the ship ride easy. At that time I returned to the ward-room, but I went to the captain's cabin and found the windlass-room full of water, and running over the top of the iron door that leads into the captain's cabin. At that time Senior Engineer Allen was securing the turn-buckles of the iron door, to make it water-tight. He took up the hatches in the captain's cabin, to let the water into the bilge. At that time I did not think it serious, thinking the water would run aft to the pumps. I returned to my dinner. After being at my dinner a few minutes, the ward-room boy came from Lieutenant Stuyvesant's room and reported the water was running in. I went there and found the water running in over the top of the ceiling, about a foot below the deck. I then returned to the captain's cabin, and found the water still rushing in, and the men were working the limber chains. I found the vessel was settling by the head. I returned to the engine-room. I found all the pumps at work. The water was just awash over the fire-room floor. I returned then to the captain's cabin, and found the water fully three inches on the cabin floor, and running into the ward-room over the b—— on the deck. I then returned to the berth deck; found the water was coming over the deck, through the hatches. At that instant I heard Lieutenant Stuyvesant sing out for all hands to come on deck and save themselves, or words to that effect. The battle-plate of the berth deck was shut down about fifteen minutes after the one over the windlass-room. The battle-plate of the berth-deck hatch was not secured; the turn-buckles were not on. In obedience to orders, I immediately came on deck, and found the vessel sinking by the head, the top of the ventilator just out of water. I then jumped from the top of the turret aft, and ran for the boats.

Question by the court. Did you have any idea that the vessel was likely to fill and go down?

Answer. I did not until within five minutes before she went down.

Question by the court. Do you consider that anything could have been done during that five minutes that was not done, which might have saved the vessel, or any of the crew who were drowned?

Answer. Yes, the crew could have been got on deck if they had had warning.

Question by the court. As the pilot of the vessel, did you, or did you not, suggest to the commanding officer what, in your opinion, was necessary to be done, under the circumstances, to save the vessel from sinking in the depth of water she did?

Answer. I did not, as Captain Colhoun, lately in command of the Weehawken, and Lieutenant Stuyvesant, gave me orders to have nothing to say or do, only when called on; that I was pilot, to point out deep water.

Question by the court. Have you ever seen the cock or valve at the bottom of the water-tight bulkhead forward, and was it the custom to keep it open or shut?

Answer. I have never seen it. I don't know what the custom was.

Question by the court. Where, in your opinion, did the water come in that caused the sinking of the vessel?

Answer. Through the hawse-pipe, and through the forward hatch.

Question by the court. How much do you think the vessel's draught was changed by the ammunition lately taken in?

Answer. Customarily she has been a foot by the stern; after the ammunition was in, only eight inches, which I found out by the marks used for that purpose.

The testimony was here read over to the witness, and he pronounced it correct.

E. M. Stein, assistant surgeon, being called and duly sworn, testified as follows:

Question by judge advocate. What is your name, and rank in the service?

Answer. Edward M. Stein, assistant surgeon, late of the Weehawken.

Question by judge advocate. State to the court what you know of the causes that led to the sinking of the Weehawken.

Answer. The principal cause that I know was the filling of the windlass-room with water so suddenly as to cause the vessel to incline down by the head, and thus preventing the water from running aft to the pumps. This is the only direct cause I know. I suppose that, after the vessel's head was submerged, there was a continuous stream running through the hawse-hole, which caused a further accumulation of water in the forward part of the vessel—sufficient, in my opinion, to cause her to sink.

Question by the court. Do you know, of your own knowledge, that the water accumulated gradually in the hold of the vessel, or that the water that caused her to sink came in suddenly?

Answer. I infer the water came in gradually. I saw the water rise gradually on the cabin floor and ward-room floor.

Question by the court. How deep was the water on the deck in the ward-room when you left the ward-room?

Answer. It was deeper forward than aft; in the deepest part about two or three inches.

Question by the court. How soon did the vessel sink after you left the ward-room?

Answer. I should say about a quarter of an hour.

Question by the court. Did you remark any leaks in any of the rooms?

Answer. No; heard there was a leak in Mr. Kingsbury's room; also in Lieutenant Stuyvesant's room.

Question by the court. At the time all hands were ordered on deck, do you know if the sick were saved or lost?

Answer. I infer they were all on deck, as those I met were all tending towards the turret. There were only about five on the sick-list, and all able to go on deck.

The testimony was here read to the witness; he pronounced it correct.

Frederick R. Stow, acting assistant pay master, being called and duly sworn, testified as follows:

Question by judge advocate. What is your name, and rank in the service?

Answer. Frederick R. Stow; acting assistant paymaster, late of the Weehawken.

Question by judge advocate. State to the court what you know of the causes that led to the sinking of the Weehawken?

Answer. Sunday morning, December 6, 1863, I went on deck at twenty minutes of twelve; went up on the turret and conversed with the officer of the deck, Mr. Reed. I was up there till he was relieved, which was about twelve o'clock. The wind was blowing fresh, the deck so wet you could not walk about. By the time the officer of the deck was relieved, the wind and sea had increased considerably. I then went below; some of the officers asked me how the weather was. I told them the sea was running high; it was a fine sight, and they had better go up and look at it. I remained below until I went on deck for the last time. I made one attempt to go up, but I was stopped by so much water coming down the berth-deck hatch. In the vicinity of half-past one o'clock I noticed Mr. Chadwick, Mr. Allen, and one of the ward-room boys, putting the bars on the bulkhead door, between the cabin and windlass-room, and in a short time I noticed the water pouring over the top of the door, and through the sides of it. It was flooding the floor so, they took up the hatches to have the water run off from the floor to the bilge. I went into my room several times and heard the water rushing under the floor. I noticed it through the air register. I had never heard any water underneath before. I went to the doctor and asked him if he had ever heard it underneath before in that great gale they had coming out. He told me yes, he had seen as much water then. I think it was a little after two when I sat down to dinner; spent about twenty minutes at table. When I got up from the table I went to my room; noticed the depth of water had increased. The water was nearer the register than when I sat down to dinner. I noticed the water leaking through the side of the ship in my room, near the beam on the top, and in various places down the sides. I never knew a drop of water to come in my room before from that source. Went from my room to Acting Master Kingsbury's room; it was leaking in his room worse than in mine; and I went from there to Lieutenant Stuyvesant's room; the water was pouring in there tremendously. I went back into my room, and again asked Doctor Stein, "Now, Doctor, did you ever see anything in that great gale like this?" He said no. I stooped over the register; the water underneath dashed up in my face. I stepped back to wipe the water off my face. The water washed up again, raised the hatch, and raised my iron safe that was on it, and dropped it again heavily. It was then I noticed a very great inclination of the vessel by the head. I then immediately took my overcoat and went on deck. When I got on top of the turret Mr. Reed was just hauling down a signal, and immediately hoisted another. I looked at her bows; they were submerged; should think the water was about two feet deep at her forward flag-staff. Immediately after the last signal was hauled down, Lieutenant Stuyvesant gave orders for all hands to come on deck. About three or four minutes after that the order was passed for the men to go aft and get into the boats. I fell off the turret, and was picked up and passed into one of the boats by Quartermaster Brown. I noticed after I was in the boat the vessel careened to starboard and went down.

Question by the court. Do you consider that the whole amount of water that caused the vessel to sink came in through the windlass-room?

Answer. No; do not think it did, because I saw it run in freely from other places.

Question by the court. Did you save the accounts of the officers and men and the funds belonging to the government?

Answer. No, I did not.

Question by the court. What was the amount of money belonging to the government at the time the vessel sunk, and where was it?

Answer. About four hundred dollars, in the safe.

The testimony was here read over to the witness, and he pronounced it to be correct.

Acting Ensign Chadwick being called and duly sworn, testified as follows:

Question by judge advocate. What is your name, and rank in the service?

Answer. Benjamin H. Chadwick; acting ensign, late of the Weehawken.

Question by judge advocate. State to the court what you know of the causes that led to the sinking of the Weehawken.

Answer. On the sixth of the present month, about half-past one, the first knowledge I had of anything being unusual, the pilot, Levi Jump, came down and called my attention to the quantity of water in the windlass-room, coming through the bulkhead door around the edges, the door being closed and latched. The water indicated a depth of about eighteen inches in the windlass-room above the bottom of the communicating door. The bars lay there, but were not put on. I called for assistance to put them on. Mr. Allen, senior engineer, came and assisted me in putting on the bars. I took the hand screws belonging to the upper or third bar and laid them on the deck, while placing the upper bar, when the hatch was suddenly opened, and the water carried the screws down into the shot locker. We then tried to lift the shot up, but they were too heavy. I then tried to assist Mr. Allen in getting shot away to open a valve or plish. Two hatches were left off to let the water run off into the lower hold. I cock, to let the water from the windless-room run aft, which we failed to accom-watched the rise of the water in the windlass-room, by its coming in around the edge above the second bar. It was about thirty minutes before it came over the top from the second or middle bar. I next saw a leak in the after state-room on the starboard side around the end of one of the main beams; it seemed to have a greater or less force at intervals, caused by the working or straining of the vessel. I went on deck about ten minutes after two; found Lieutenant Stuyvesant in charge of the deck. He asked me to relieve him while he went down on the berth deck, which I accordingly did. He returned in a few moments in company with Ensign Reed, signal officer. The vessel was then with her bows two feet under, indicated by the flag-staff forward; made signals, and ordered me to go and get out life-preservers. I went with the captain of the hold, Thomas Gaggin, to the forward state-room on the starboard side, in the ward-room, occupied by Acting Ensign F. H. Crandall. Opened the hatch and the water boiled up, indicating there were about four inches over the state-room floor. Gaggin and myself were taking out life-preservers; nearly all were found to be rotten—would come to pieces, and the cork fall out; but few could be got on account of the place being flooded with water. I passed on deck; while passing I told the men on the berth deck the vessel was sinking, and to go on deck. I went to the top of the turret, and considered the vessel was going down. I left the turret and went aft, shortly followed by Ensign Reed. Saw the men go into the boats. Mr. Reed and myself took a hatch-coaming from the engineer's hatch on the port quarter, shoved it off, and jumped overboard. Lieutenant Stuyvesant had ordered us to look out for ourselves.

Question by the court. Did you notice that the water was rising in the hold when the cabin hatches were off?

Answer. Yes.

Question by the court. Did the water seem to rise rapidly in the hold at the time you noticed it?

Answer. Yes.

Question by the court. Do you think that the rapid rising of the water in the hold was caused only by the water that came through around the iron door and through the cock or valve at the bottom of the bulkhead?

Answer. No; unless this cock or valve was very large and was open.

Question by the court. Do you consider that the whole amount of water that caused the vessel to sink came through the windlass-room?

Answer. No. At the time there was considerable water coming in under the turret and in through under the overhang, which you could hear striking against the inner ceiling on the starboard side forward by the ward-room state-rooms.

Question by the court. How much water was in the hold of the vessel when you say the leak in Lieutenant Stuyvesant's room appeared to have greater and less force at intervals?

Answer. About a foot from the floor in the captain's cabin.

Question by the court. To what do you attribute the rapid filling and sinking of the vessel?

Answer. To the various leaks before mentioned, and the unusual quantity of ammunition forward. The vessel was six inches by the head more than I ever saw her before; also to the starting the centrifugal pump and pumping the water from aft, which made her tip by the head.

Question by the court. How long had the life-preservers been under Acting Ensign Crandall's room, and were they rotten when put down?

Answer. They must have been rotten, as they were placed there but two or three days previous, having been previously stored in the hold.

Question by the court. How long have you been attached to the Weehawken, and in what capacity?

Answer. About three months, as acting ensign.

Question by the court. How much was the unusual amount of ammunition on board?

Answer. I cannot say.

Question by the court. To what do you attribute the increase of water in the windlass-room after the battle-plate had been put on?

Answer. Coming in through the hawse-pipe.

Question by the court. Is it your opinion that the unusual amount of ammunition in the vessel, bringing her down by the head, was the chief cause of her loss?

Answer. Yes.

Question by the court. Did you make any report to the executive officer when you noticed the water rising under the cabin deck?

Answer. No; because I knew Acting Master's Mate Bayne had done so.

Question by the court. At what moment did you first entertain the idea that the vessel was in danger of sinking?

Answer. When I saw the leak on the starboard side forward, and saw the vessel was by the head.

Question by the court. Between the time specified in your last answer and the time of the sinking of the vessel, do you consider that anything could have been done that would have saved her?

Answer. It might have been possible by rolling shot aft.

Question by the court. Do you know if word was conveyed to the engine or fire-room for all hands to assemble on deck?

Answer. I don't know. I heard the order started by Lieutenant Stuyvesant to the senior engineer, Mr. Allen.

The testimony was here read to the witness; he pronounced it correct.

The court adjourned until 10 a. m. on Monday, the 21st.

UNITED STATES SHIP SUPPLY,
December 21, 1863.

The court met pursuant to adjournment. Present: Lieutenant Commander E. Simpson, Lieutenant Commander J. L. Davis, Lieutenant Commander J. J. Cornwall; Acting Assistant Paymaster B. F. Munroe, judge advocate.

The proceedings of December 19, 1863, were then read over.

Acting Master's Mate William E. Bayne, being called and duly sworn, testified as follows:

Question by judge advocate. What is your name, and rank in the service?

Answer. William E. Bayne; acting master's mate, late of the Weehawken.

Question by judge advocate. State to the court what you know of the causes that led to the sinking of the Weehawken.

Answer. The first I knew of it was by looking out of one of the turret ports on the day she went down, about half-past eleven o'clock. I saw a good many men busy at the forward battle-plate. Going forward, found the sea had struck it and washed it down the forward hatch. Saw, I should judge, about five feet of water had gone down the hatch into the windlass-room. Then went down below after the plate had been put on; found the door closed that leads from the captain's cabin to the windlass-room, but not secured. Found the cross-bars and helped secure the door. At that time the water was coming over the top of the door into the captain's cabin. Lifted shot-locker hatches in the captain's cabin to allow the water to run quicker aft. About half an hour after a ward-room boy reported water coming to the officers' state-rooms. I stopped the leak in Lieutenant Stuyvesant's room as well as I could; found the beam started in two inches, as shown by the paint-marks having separated that distance from the ceiling. On examining the other beams found them all on both sides started in the same way. Saw the water, as if coming from the upper deck from outside, running between the skin and the iron side down into the bilges. She was tipping at that time rapidly by the head. Came up on top of the turret; found Lieutenant Stuyvesant making signals. The only report I made to Lieutenant Stuyvesant was that the windlass-room was filled with water. I kept going around all the time, trying to stop all the leaks I could see. Did not think the ship was going down till about five minutes before she went down. At that time Lieutenant Stuyvesant passed the word for everybody to leave the vessel. I believe the forward end of her was on the bottom before any of the boats left.

Question by the court. When you stopped the leak in Lieutenant Stuyvesant's room, did you prevent the water from coming into the vessel?

Answer. No; the water continued to run into her between the side and the skin.

Question by the court. What amount of water was coming into the vessel through the leak that you saw from Lieutenant Stuyvesant's room?

Answer. It would fill a barrel in about ten minutes.

Question by the court. Did you remark leaks in other places, where you say the beams were started?

Answer. Yes; the whole length forward, from Lieutenant Stuyvesant's room on one side, and from Mr. Kingsbury's room on the other side. The amount of water at all the leaks was about the same as at Lieutenant Stuyvesant's room.

Question by the court. Describe the position of the rooms occupied by Lieutenant Stuyvesant and Mr. Kingsbury.

Answer. The after rooms in the ward-room, next the ship's side, and run fore and aft the side.

Question by the court. Did you notice the water rising in the vessel under the berth deck?

Answer. No.

Question by the court. Was there more ammunition than usual on board the Weehawken at the time she went down?

Answer. Yes; she used to carry, on an average, about seventy-five fifteen-inch shell, and one hundred and twenty eleven-inch shell. When she went down, she had one hundred and forty-five fifteen-inch shell and three hundred and twenty-three eleven-inch shell. The quantity of solid shot, grape, canister and shrapnell, were the same in both cases. There was powder also taken in for the additional shell. After all the weight was in, she was seven inches by the stern; found this by actual measurement from the top of the deck to the surface of the water at stem and stern.

Question by the court. The projectiles you speak of in your last answer, where were they stowed, and was weight removed to give place for them?

Answer. Stowed all in the forward part of the vessel, and in the captain's storeroom on the berth deck. There was no weight removed to give place for it.

Question by the court. At what time did you measure the vessel's draught, as you describe, and was the water smooth at the time?

Answer. About eight o'clock, on the night after the ammunition was taken in. The water was perfectly smooth.

Question by the court. After the ammunition had been taken in, was any of it fired away before the loss of the vessel?

Answer. No.

Question by the court. What was the draught of the vessel before the extra ammunition was taken on board?

Answer. I don't know.

Question by the court. Were you in charge of the gunner's department on board the Weehawken?

Answer. Yes.

The testimony was here read over to the witness; he pronounced it correct.

Acting Master Charles C. Kingsbury, being called and duly sworn, testified as follows:

Question by judge advocate. What is your name, and rank in the service?

Answer. Charles C. Kingsbury; acting master, late of the Weehawken.

Question by judge advocate. State to the court what you know of the causes that led to the sinking of the Weehawken.

Answer. Between one and two o'clock on Sunday, sixth of December, 1863, I received an order from Lieutenant Stuyvesant to come on deck. In passing through the ward-room, I heard some one say the water is rushing into the cabin. On getting on deck, I was ordered by Lieutenant Stuyvesant to veer away chain. The men at that time were engaged about the forward battle-plate. Calling them aft, I commenced giving her chain. After giving chain until Lieutenant Stuyvesant said that would do, I received permission to go below. On going into my room, saw the water streaming in close to the top, between the knees; took the hatch up underneath; found the place full of water, so that it washed up against the hatch. Went into the cabin; saw a hatch off there, and water nearly to the top of the shot. Went on deck and reported to Lieutenant Stuyvesant the water in the cabin, and the want of some one to haul the limber chains. Received an order from him to go down below, take some one with me, and see to hauling them myself. Went down below; took Quarter Gunner Munson, with two men; sent them into the cabin to haul the limber chains, then went about the berth deck, and fell down one of the shot lockers; found the water there nearly to the top of the shot. Looked for the men in the cabin, and found they were gone; found the quarter gunner; asked him where they were; he told me they were there. While looking for more, saw a commotion; heard some one say, "All hands on deck." Then turned my attention to getting the crew on deck as soon as possible. Lifted Clarkson, first-class fireman, up through a grating in the after part of the turret, abaft the fifteen-inch gun; told him to take off the other gratings, so the men could get up. He took hold of one grating, lifted it, and said, "I can't get it up;" then got up myself, moved the shell and took off all the gratings on that side; then went around the other side, took off the other gratings, and called to them on the top of the turret to haul back the slide. Finding no attention paid to that, a man, Williams, suggested to me the propriety of putting in the port stoppers; I told him this was no time to put in port stoppers, but to get on deck as soon as he could. Seeing one or two on the ladder leading to the top of the turret, and the vessel careening to starboard, I got on top the turret as soon as I could. Took hold of the stanchion; saw the bows of the vessel under water, and she was sinking. Looked behind me; saw the ship's cook, Christian Anderson, about half way up the hatch, and, while stooping down to pull him up, a sea struck me and knocked me from the stanchion, all save my leg, which I had turned around it; looked for the cook and saw him nowhere. Saw Lieutenant Stuyvesant and one man on the turret, and the doctor and one man on the pilot-house. Was hauled from the stanchion to the top of the pilot-house by the man Williams, with the bight of a lead line. Remained there until all had left, then let go myself and paddled to a boat; was picked up by the "Racer's" boat. The large increase of weight of ammunition, and the forward compartment being full of water, caused an opening between the hull and overhang, which made itself manifest by a rush of water through all the side rooms, and was, in my opinion, the cause of her sinking.

Question by the court. When you left your room at the call of the executive officer, was water leaking into the room?

Answer. It was not.

Question by the court. How long were you occupied in veering chain on deck?

Answer. As near as I can judge, from half to three-quarters of an hour. The chain was veered and secured two or three times. While doing it, the sea washed the men and slack chain away along the deck.

Question by the court. After veering the chain, did you go at once to your room?

Answer. I did.

Question by the court. What amount of water was leaking into your room between the knees?

Answer. About a barrel a minute.

Question by the court. When you went below to haul the limber chains, did you at any time inform Lieutenant Stuyvesant of the amount of water in the vessel?

Answer. I did not.

Question by the court. What was your object in hauling the limber chains when you knew that the water was nearly to the top of the shot, on the berth deck?

Answer. Whenever there was any water in the ship forward, it had been customary to haul the limber chains; had heard an order given previously for some one to haul the limber chains, and when I saw no one there, I reported the water, and the fact of no one being there, to Lieutenant Stuyvesant.

Question by the court. At the time you were in the turret-chamber, where the speaking-tube leading to the engine-room is situated, did you, or any one to your knowledge, speak through it, passing the order for all hands to come on deck?

Answer. I did not, and no one to my knowledge.

Question by the court. Was there one or more ladders leading from the turret-chamber into the turret, at the time the people were coming up?

Answer. One leading from the turret-chamber into the turret; have never seen but one ladder.

Question by the court. How long have you been attached to the Weehawken, and in what capacity?

Answer. Since the 23d of last February, as an acting master.

Question by the court. Was the eleven-inch gun run in at the time the vessel sunk?

Answer. When I left the turret, it was.

Question by the court. As the master of the vessel, did you save the log-book, or anything belonging to your department?

Answer. I did not.

Question by the court. When did you begin to think the vessel was in a dangerous condition, and liable to sink?

Answer. Whilst down below with the men to haul the limber chains, at the time I fell into the shot locker on account of the water there.

Question by the court. Was the cock or valve at the bottom of the forward water-tight bulkhead open or shut?

Answer. Do not know.

Question. Could anything have been done, in your opinion, which would have saved the vessel, after you knew she was in danger?

Answer. I think she could have been saved by running her ashore.

Question by the court. Do you think that there was sufficient time to have slipped the chain and run the vessel ashore, after you knew her to be in danger?

Answer. Being employed as I was, I have a very indefinite recollection of the time.

Question by the court. Do you know if steam was ready to work the engine?

Answer. No other way but by the word of the chief engineer, at that time expressed while I was at work on the berth deck.

Question by the court. How long would it have taken to slip the chain when you left the deck?

Answer. Five minutes.

Question by the court. How much chain did you veer, and how much chain was out altogether?

Answer. I veered away about thirty fathoms; should judge there were twelve or fifteen fathoms out when I commenced.

The testimony was here read over to the witness; he pronounced it correct.

William A. Munson, quarter gunner, being called and duly sworn, testified as follows:

Question by judge advocate. What is your name, and rank in the service?

Answer. William A. Munson; quarter gunner, late of the Weehawken.

Question by judge advocate. State to the court what you know of the causes that led to the sinking of the Weehawken.

Answer. The first I knew of there being so much water in her, was after one o'clock. Acting Master Kingsbury came into the turret; asked if there were any petty officers there. I spoke; said I was there, and George Crotts, quarter gunner, told me he wanted to see me below. I followed him down below into the ward-room, then into the cabin. Says he, I want you to get two men and stop by three limber chains. Previous to that there had been two men, but there were none there at that time. He wanted me to put on the bar to the bulkhead door. I went out, got two men, led the limber chains into the ward-room, as it was impossible to haul them there, the water came down from over the door so fast. We hauled the limber chains several times; found them perfectly clear. The hold at this time was full of water up to the berth deck. The windlass-room was full of water, the water running through the speaking-tube to the turret-chamber. The two men, William J. Pike and Lewis, did not stop more than three minutes before they ran away. Went off and found Mr. Kingsbury; told him I could not keep men there; he told me I must get two men, stay there, and keep them there. I went out; asked for volunteers; Lewis said he would stay as long as I did, and went back with me. Found the water rising very fast; about eight inches of water on the cabin floor. I thought she was going to sink at that time. I spoke up; said she was filling very fast, and that it was about time we got out of this; they all started and went on deck. About a minute after, I heard Mr. Kingsbury pass the word for all hands to go on deck; I went on deck. I noticed large quantities of water in the morning going down the forward hatch, from ten o'clock until the hatch was knocked down, and spoke of it to Quarter Gunner Crotts; wondered why it was not put on, as it was usual to put it on in rough weather. Saw the hatch coamings capsized, and the battle-plate knocked down below. At that time they called for men to get the hatch up; the hatch was got up out of the windlass-room, and put in its place. I think this occurred after dinner; we got our dinner late that day—I think a few minutes before one o'clock. When I went on deck she was going down fast, and everybody was looking out for themselves. A few days previous to this we had taken in about one hundred and fifty eleven-inch shell, forty or fifty fifteen-inch shell, and about two hundred charges of powder; some few were put in the shell-room, the rest under the ward-room hatches. Myself, other of the men, and Mr. Bayne were talking about it. Mr. Bayne said it would do her no good to put so much in her; that he understood Captain Cornwell had trouble with the Nahant. I don't think he had any more ammunition in than we have now. It was the opinion of the men; they spoke about it several times, while taking in the ammunition. Think the ship was not started in any place, and that she was in as good order as ever, as far as I know of, up to the morning she sunk. A large quantity of water came in around the turret that day—more than I ever saw before.

Question by the court. Did you see any water come in over the top of the iron bulkhead, between the cabin and windlass-room?

Answer. A large quantity of water was coming in overhead, but I cannot say positively that it came over the top of the bulkhead or not.

Question by the court. While you were below in the cabin, or ward-room, did you see any water coming in through the rooms, or over the beams; and if so, was it in large quantities?

Answer. When I first went in I did not see any; but when I came out the last time I saw water coming in along the beams.

Question by the court. Was the turret keyed up, or not; and did the water come in under it, and at what rate?

Answer. The turret was keyed up. When at Port Royal we had two troughs made—one on each side, inside the turret—to make the water pass off; but that day they would overflow and not carry off more than a quarter of the water at times. After we came from Port Royal we found the base ring take the deck when keyed up to the old mark. We had to key it up higher, which let more water in. We generally used to have a large hawser to stop the leak; this day there was no hawser. So much water came in as to make it difficult to keep the blowers going. I said at the time it will take two pretty good pumps to keep the water out that comes in there.

Question by the court. Were the guns in or out; and did any water come in through the ports?

Answer. The 15-inch gun was out, the 11-inch gun run in, the compressors down. Occasionally a heavy sea would come in the 11-inch port. The smoke-box prevented my seeing any water run in the 15-inch port.

The testimony was here read over to the witness. He pronounced it correct.

The court adjourned to meet at 10 o'clock a. m., Tuesday, December 22, 1863.

UNITED STATES SHIP SUPPLY,
December 22, 1863.

The court met pursuant to adjournment. Present: Lieutenant Commanders E. Simpson, J. L. Davis, and J. J. Cornwell; Acting Assistant Paymaster B. F. Munroe, judge advocate.

The proceedings of yesterday were read over and corrected by the court.

Commander J. M. Duncan, being called and duly sworn, testified as follows:

Question by judge advocate. What is your name and rank in the service?

Answer. J. M. Duncan, commander, late of the Weehawken.

Question by judge advocate. State to the court what you know of the causes that led to the sinking of the Weehawken.

Answer. I joined the Weehawken on the 5th of December, 1863, off Morris island, South Carolina; think it was about 4 o'clock in the afternoon; went up that evening on the advance picket; lay there until next morning; at about 9 o'clock got under way and came down to the mooring buoy known as buoy No. 2, and made fast to that, giving her about twelve or fifteen fathoms chain; it was blowing quite fresh at that time, but no water coming over forward. I left the vessel a little before 10, probably about 9.50 a. m., and went on board the flag-ship Philadelphia. At the time I left the windlass-room was perfectly dry; the only water I could see was coming over forward and abaft the turret, as I have frequently seen it when lying near the iron-clads. Between 2 and half-past 2 o'clock the fleet captain told me a signal had been made; the Weehawken wanted assistance. I immediately jumped to the gangway and told the cockswain of the Weehawken's gig to haul up to the gangway. He was some distance astern, so I jumped into one of the boats of the Ironsides, with the pilot of the Philadelphia, and started for the Weehawken as soon as possible, telling the cockswain of the Weehawken's gig to go to the Weekawken as soon as possible. Before we got half way there she had sunk. Should think the distance of the Weehawken from the Philadelphia was about five hundred yards. After I discovered she had sunk I pulled astern to pick up all I could that were in the water; succeeded in picking up three, and then pulled up to near the Weehawken. A great many boats and three or four tugs were there picking up the men that were in the water.

Question by the court. While you were on board the flag-ship did you notice that the wind had increased in force, and that the sea was higher than when you left the Weehawken?

Answer. I did not.

Question by the court. What was the depth of water alongside when you made fast to the buoy?

Answer. I think four fathoms at nearly low water.

Question by the court. Did you remark when in the boat, after the Weehawken went down, that the sea was much higher than when you left her in the forenoon?

Answer. I did not notice any particular motion in the seas.

Question by the court. When you left the vessel was the door leading from the cabin to the windlass-room open or shut?

Answer. It was open.

Question by the court. Have you had any previous knowledge or experience of the Monitor class of iron-clads before you took command of the Weehawken?

Answer. None whatever.

Question by the court. When you took command of the Weehawken, whom did you relieve in command, and did you relieve him in person?

Answer. When I took command, the commanding officer was Lieutenant Stuyvesant. Lieutenant Commander Bunce had had charge for twenty-four hours previous. The regular commander who preceded me was Commander E. R. Colhoun. I did not relieve Commander Colhoun in person.

Question by the court. When you assumed the command of the Weehawken, did you receive any instructions as to the management of that class of vessels, and were you informed of the condition, stowage, &c., of the Weehawken?

Answer. I received no instructions, and was not informed of the condition, stowage, &c.

Question by the court. Were you aware that the vessel had stowed forward an extra allowance of ammunition, and did it occur to you that she was in good or bad trim?

Answer. No, I was not. It appeared to me she was in good trim.

Question by the court. When you left the Weehawken, in the forenoon, did you anticipate bad weather; and if so, what orders did you leave with the executive officer?

Answer. I did not anticipate any worse weather than it was at the time, and only left orders to look out for the vessel, as I always do.

The testimony was here read over to the witness. He pronounced it correct.

Henry Sumner, being called and duly sworn, testified as follows:

Question by judge advocate. What is your name and rank in the service?

Answer. Henry Sumner; second-class fireman, late of the Weehawken.

Question by judge advocate. State to the court what you know of the causes that led to the sinking of the Weehawken.

Answer. On Sunday, 6th of December, it was my watch in the turret chamber from twelve to four in the afternoon. About half past two Mr. Allen came in and asked me how much water there was in the bilge. I picked up one of the floor boards; he looked down, and then it wanted about a foot of coming over the floor. Mr. Allen went on top of the turret then; came down to me again and asked the reason why the blowers did not work; told him the water was coming on the belt, and the belt was slipping on the pulley. He started out on the berth deck, and that was the last I saw of him. I noticed the water rising; it was about six inches in about half an hour. I went up in the turret then, and I saw the vessel down forward under water. I returned to the turret chamber. Went on to the berth deck; the shot-locker hatch was raised, and I saw that full of water. While I was standing, the cry was for all hands on deck. I ran into the turret chamber, stopped the blowers, and went on deck. When I got on top of the turret I found a great many up there. I jumped over the side of the turret and ran aft. I jumped into the sea, and climbed into a boat. Saw her listing over when I was in the boat.

Question by the court. Was the amount of water coming in under the turret greater than usual, and how much do you estimate the quantity that came in in a minute?

Answer. I don't consider the quantity unusual, until about five minutes before I left the turret chamber; the water then poured in in a steady stream all round. I can't estimate the quantity; have been stationed in the turret chamber about a week.

Question by the court. Did you, or any one, to your knowledge, speak through the tube leading to the engine-room, calling the people to leave there and come on deck, when the order was given for all hands to do so?

Answer. No, I did not, nor anybody to my knowledge.

Question by the court. Was it usual to use the speaking tube as a means of communicating between the engine-room and turret chamber?

Answer. Yes, it was.

Question by the court. What was your object in stopping the blower engines?

Answer. It was no use running them; the belt slipped on the pulley. I tried the fans with my hands, and there was not a breath of air, and I did not stop them until all hands were called to go on deck, and many had passed up before me.

The testimony was here read over to the witness; he pronounced it correct.

Thomas Gaggin, being called and duly sworn, testified as follows:

Question by judge advocate. What is your name and rank in the service?

Answer. Thomas Gaggin; captain of the hold, late of the Weehawken.

Question by judge advocate. State to the court what you know of the causes that led to the sinking of the Weehawken.

Answer. On Sunday, the day the Weehawken went down, I heard some water had come in forward. Between one and two I went down the hatch for a deck tackle; noticed about five inches of water over the skin. The next I noticed, about fifteen minutes after that, coming through the speaking tube that led to the windlass-room, the water was leaking through the tube on the berth deck. Five minutes after that from two to three tons of water came down the berth-deck hatch. Next I went to the ward-room; found the hatches full of water. I was trying to get up life-preservers from the ward-room. When I could not get the life-preservers, on account of the water in that hatch, I went to another hatch on the berth deck, where there were others stowed, and found that full of water too. The engineer came to me (Mr. Allen) and asked me how much water there was in the hold; told him all the holds were full, when he said he would have it out, as the big pump was going. While he was speaking they called all hands on deck. The water was coming in the bigness of both ports in the turret. I went into the turret chamber to see if they wanted ropes or anything from the hold. Went back to the berth deck, got a life-preserver, and went up on the turret. I saw her bows under water and heel to starboard. I was then washed off.

Question by the court. How long have you been captain of the hold on board of the Weehawken?

Answer. Since the sixth of July, 1863.

Question by the court. Have you ever known water to rise any height in the hold before? If so, when and where?

Answer. Yes; I have seen it inside the bar here at Charleston once; I think in July. It was then seven inches over the skin; it was during a heavy blow. The bilges were choked at the time under the turret, and it was four hours before they got it pumped out. Once, at sea, I have known the water in the windlass-room to be over the gratings. This water was drawn out into the bilge by lead pipes leading from the windlass-room into a hatch in the captain's cabin. At that time the valve at the bottom of the water-tight bulkhead was jammed in the slide, and could not be opened. After we got to Port Royal the valve was enlarged, and made to turn instead of a slide.

Question by the court. At the time of the sinking of the Weehawken, was the valve at the bottom of the water-tight bulkhead open or shut?

Answer. Cannot tell.

Question by the court. Was it the custom of the ship to keep this valve open or shut?

Answer. Generally the custom to keep it open.

Question by the court. To your knowledge, were there any orders issued in regard to keeping the valve open, and were there any orders about the time when it should be shut?

Answer. No.

Question by the court. Did you make any reports to the executive officer about the amount of water in the hold during the day on which the Weehawken went down?

Answer. Yes; I reported to him once, when the five inches water was in the hold, between one and two o'clock.

Question by the court. Did you make any subsequent report that the water was rising in the hold?

Answer. No, I did not.

Question by the court. When was the berth-deck battle-plate put on?

Answer. Immediately after the large quantity of water came down that I mentioned before.

The testimony was here read over to the witness; he pronounced it correct.

Lieutenant Commander J. J. Cornwell, being called and duly sworn, testified as follows:

Question by judge advocate. What is your name and rank in the service?

Answer. John J. Cornwell, lieutenant commander, commanding the iron-clad Nahant.

Question by the court. In the testimony before the court it is stated that the Nahant, under your command, at one time made water to an unusual amount. State all you know in relation to the occurrence, and the cause leading to it.

Answer. During November last, while at Port Royal for repairs, I took in twenty-eight tons of ammunition in addition to what she had usually carried, which was stowed under the ward-room. It was remarked by several, and mentioned to me, the vessel sat lower forward in the water than before. I found she was still by the stern by measurement, and considered it an advantage for the vessel to be low in the water to avoid injuries from the enemy's shot. On proceeding to sea, in tow of the Admiral DuPont, found the sea outside rough, setting from the northeast. Before sailing, a jackass had been placed in the hawse-hole, in the anchor-well, but the chain, surging, dislodged it, and it could not be again replaced on account of the high sea; water came through the hawse-pipe with great force. The diameter of the hawse-pipe was about seven inches. The vessel's progress and heavy sea kept the water above the level of the hawse-hole all the time, although when in smooth water, at an anchor, it was at least six or eight inches below the hawse-hole. Feeling anxious lest the vessel should take in water forward, which would not run to the pumps, I examined frequently. Before we had been in rough water an hour there was two feet of water in the hold from the cabin to the turret; none in the engine-room. Ordered the Admiral DuPont to stop. Found that the water did not increase, none coming in the hawse-pipe. Waited one hour and a half to see if I could pump the ship out. Finding the water did not run to the pumps but slowly, returned to Port Royal. While on our return to the harbor the water gradually found its way to the pumps in the engine-room, and was pumped out. After returning, took out all the pig-iron, about fifteen or twenty tons, from under the cabin deck, which changed her draught about six inches, bringing her that much more by the stern. The vessel at this time had about one hundred tons coal. Since that time I have found no difficulty with the water running aft, although the coal has since been reduced to twenty tons, nor has an unusual amount of water come through the hawse-hole since.

Question by the court. Was the whole amount of the ammunition additional weight when you took it in in Port Royal, or did you take out any ballast in order to make room?

Answer. I think we took out about five tons to make room for the ammunition.

Question by the court. Why did you take in additional ammunition in the Nahant at the time specified?

Answer. The Monitors had previously carried but about one day's supply for action, and I thought it advisable to have more, as it could be carried without any inconvenience or danger to the ammunition or vessel. Experience since has taught me that the vessel is in better trim than before the ammunition was put in and the ballast taken out, as the ballast was in the bow, and the ammunition more in the body of the vessel, which caused her to ride easier.

Question by the court. Did you receive any order on the subject of increasing the ammunition of the vessel you commanded, or had you any intimation that such was the desire of the commander-in-chief?

Answer. I had no order, at any time, about the quantity of ammunition I was to carry; but in answer to a letter I addressed to Lieutenant M. Forrest, ordnance officer, he told me the admiral thought it was a good idea to increase the ammunition if possible.

Question by the court. You state that the water was about two feet from forward aft to the turret, but little made its way to the pumps in the engine-room. To what do you attribute the water not making its way to the pumps freely?

Answer. I did attribute it to the vessel being tipped by the head in consequence of the quantity of water in the forward part of the vessel, and I know of no other cause now.

The testimony was here read over to the witness; he pronounced it correct.

The court adjourned until 10 o'clock a. m. Wednesday, 23d December, 1863.

UNITED STATES SHIP SUPPLY,
December 23, 1863.

The court met pursuant to adjournment. Present: Lieutenant Commanders E. Simpson, J. L. Davis, J. J. Cornwell, and Acting Assistant Paymaster B. F. Munroe, judge advocate.

The proceedings of yesterday were read over and corrected by the court.

J. B. A. Allen, jr., acting second assistant engineer, was recalled by the court.

Question by the court. What amount of coal was on board the Weehawken when she went down?

Answer. I think about one hundred tons.

Question by the court. Had you any conversation with Acting Master Kingsbury, on the berth deck, on the subject of an effort to prevent the vessel going down in deep water? If so, state what the conversation was.

Answer. No, I had not.

Question by the court. Do you remember conversing with Acting Master Kingsbury on the berth deck, and mentioning to him anything about the amount of steam you were carrying?

Answer. Yes, I do.

Question by the court. Were you then carrying steam enough to run the vessel with any speed and for any distance in such weather?

Answer. Yes; the fires were spread and rather heavy. I think I could have run her all day long if necessary.

Question by the court. Did not the water that came in under the turret interfere with the working of the blowers, so as to make it very difficult to keep up steam?

Answer. No more than it had done in a heavy sea before. Water always did come down there in a heavy sea.

Question by the court. What is your estimate of the time that elapsed between your conversation with Acting Master Kingsbury and the moment when the vessel went down?

Answer. I should think about half an hour.

Question by the court. What engineers were on duty in the engine-room, and where were the other assistants, and what were they doing? State when you last saw each of them.

Answer. Messrs. Merrian, third assistant, and McGowan, acting third assistant engineers. Mr. McGowan relieved Mr. Sponburg, acting third assistant, to dinner. The last time I saw Mr. Mitchell, third assistant engineer, was on the berth deck, and appeared to me to be walking towards the ward-room. I saw each of them just before I went on top of the turret for the last time, and reported to Lieutenant Stuyvesant the condition of things in the engine-room. I saw Mr. Sponburg on the berth deck going towards the passage leading to the engine-room.

Question by the court. Was the entire force stationed in the engine-room lost? If any were saved, state who they were.

Answer. Of the entire watch stationed in the engine-room, I think none were saved. The one stationed in the turret chamber was saved.

Question by the court. Do you remember the day Commander Colhoun left the Weehawken to return north?

Answer. I think on Friday, the 4th of December, 1863.

Question by the court. Why was Mr. Merrian in the engine-room, it not being his watch?

Answer. Mr. Merrian went down there of his own accord, to superintend the working of the pumps.

Question by the court. You say you were repeatedly in the engine-room; did you at any time give any orders to Mr. Merrian?

Answer. I did.

Question by the court. Then did you not consider he was there on duty, and acting under your orders?

Answer. I did

Question by the court. When you received the order from the executive officer to send the people out of the engine-room, and when you found you could not pass down into the turret on account of the crowd of men coming up, did you make any effort to have the word passed through the speaking tube?

Answer. I did not, through the speaking tube. I did not think of the speaking tube at the time, but, as I mentioned in the former part of my testimony, I went to the engine-room hatch and jumped on it.

The testimony was here read over to the witness; he pronounced it correct.

George Crotts, being called and duly sworn, testified as follows:

Question by judge advocate. What is your name and rank in the service?

Answer. George Crotts; quarter gunner, late of the Weehawken.

Question by judge advocate. State to the court what you know of the causes that led to the sinking of the Weehawken.

Answer. The vessel being down by the head, the water came in the forward hatches and underneath the turret. The water being forward staid forward, and did not come to the pumps. A great deal of water came in under the turret that day. There was no packing under it. I was in the turret most of the day. Saw everything forward pretty much washed off deck by looking through the turret port. About ten minutes before the ship went down I was ordered by

Acting Master Kingsbury to see that the men were in the after part of the engine-room hauling the limber chains. I went there; saw the men were not there. Went out on the berth deck for volunteers to haul the limber chains, and could not get them. Up to that time no order had been given to leave the ship. The word was then passed for all hands to come up on the turret; went up into the turret; received an order from Mr. Bayne to run out the eleven-inch gun and fire it. I threw the cover off the gun and shipped the crank for running her out. I asked some men to help run her out, and could get no one; they ran right up the turret. When I saw them all going I went myself; left the crank shipped, the gun compressed.

Question by the court. Did you know, any time before the vessel went down, that she was filling with water?

Answer. I did not know it until I went on the berth deck; saw the lockers full of water.

Question by the court. Was it evident to you that the men on the berth deck considered the ship in danger, and that they considered the engine-room the place of greatest danger?

Answer. I know some men on the berth deck knew that the ship was in danger, for as I passed from the turret chamber to the alley way I heard a man say, "things look dubious." I suppose as no one would volunteer to go to the engine-room, they thought the ship would sink.

Question by the court. State the names of the officers and men that you saw in the engine-room when you left it?

Answer. Mr. Merrian, George Laighton, Davis, the engineer's yeoman, and Gayhen, a fireman. There were other men on the other side, by the centrifugal pump.

Question by the court. When you went to the engine-room did you observe any unusual excitement there, and did the officers and men there show any anxiety by words or actions?

Answer. When I went into the engine-room I spoke to the engineer's yeoman. He did not appear to be excited, or ask any questions about the water in the ship. Saw the men have hold of the laniards of the safety-valve; that I never saw before. Did not hear any of them speak. There did not appear to be any excitement that I saw.

Question by the court. When you left the engine-room did you meet anybody going to the engine-room?

Answer. I met nobody in the passage until I passed Robert Nugent in the turret chamber, who appeared in a great hurry, and was going towards the engine-room.

Question by the court. How long after you passed Coal-heaver Robert Nugent did the vessel go down?

Answer. I suppose in three minutes' time.

Question by the court. Were you, to the best of your knowledge, the last man who escaped from the engine-room?

Answer. I think I was the last man.

Question by the court. How many people did you notice on the berth deck and in the turret chamber when you were on your way for the last time to go into the turret?

Answer. I think I saw eight or ten trying to get up. There was a rush at the ladder and I told the men to go on the other side, some of them, and get up on the turret, engine, and blowers. I heard Mr. Kingsbury, who was taking off gratings, tell them to come up that side.

Question by the court. Do you know if any men in the turret chamber trying to get up failed to do so, and were lost? If any, give their names.

Answer. I don't know.

Question by the court. Did any man make use of the eleven-inch port to get clear of the vessel?

Answer. I did not see any. When I came up the turret chamber some water was coming in the port.

The testimony was here read over to the witness; he pronounced it correct.

Mr. T. J. Griffin, being called and duly sworn, testified as follows:

Question by judge advocate. What is your name and rank in the service?

Answer. T. F. Griffin; assistant inspector of iron-clads.

Question by the court. Is the iron bulkhead between cabin and windlass-room in Monitors water-tight?

Answer. It was the intention of the contractor; it should be such.

Question by the court. What is the arrangement in Monitors by which water is carried aft in the bilge to the pumps?

Answer. By a water limber or hollow keel, four inches in depth by eighteen inches wide.

Question by the court. Are there any holes in the sixteen-inch cross-floors? If yes, at what height are they from the keel, and what is their diameter?

Answer. To the best of my belief, there are two three-inch holes through each sixteen-inch cross-floor, at about eight inches above the base line, the base line being a line running across the top of the keel.

Question by the court. What holes are there in the forty-eight-inch cross-floors, and at what height are they from the base line, and what is their diameter?

Answer. There are two eight-inch holes through each forty-eight-inch cross-floor. The bottom of the hold is thirty-two inches from the base line.

Question by the court. Describe valve at bottom of water-tight bulkhead.

Answer. A sheet-iron slide valve, four inches by six inches.

Question by the court. What weight of water will the windlass-room hold?

Answer. About twenty-nine tons of water, exclusive of windlass beams, joiner work, &c.

Question by the court. How much will the bow of a Monitor, trimmed as the Weehawken was, (seven inches by the stern,) be depressed by having the windlass-room full of water?

Answer. It is necessary, in answering this question, to have the centre of weight. I do not think it would bring her more than on an even keel, and think she would still be by the stern.

Question by the court. Will that depression bring the hawse-hole under water?

Answer. I cannot reply, not knowing her draught.

Question by the court. How much water would have run in through the limber-hole, eighteen inches by four inches, in an hour, supposing the windlass-room to have been full of water all the time?

Answer. I think the quantity run in would sink the vessel in less than an hour without pumping.

Question by the court. Supposing the water to have free passage to the pumps, and that no water was coming into the hold except through the valve in the water-tight bulkhead, are the pumps sufficient to keep the vessel clear?

Answer. Yes.

Question by the court. Describe the manner in which the overhang and armature is secured to the hull of a Monitor.

Answer. The overhang is secured by the best five-eighths flanged iron, and double riveted. The armature is secured first by an angled iron shelf extending around the hull of the ship; to that is attached an armor shelf of five-eighths plate iron. The width of it is forty-eight inches amidships, decreasing to twenty-two inches at the end of the vessel. This shelf is also secured and held in place by angle iron which is riveted vertically to the hull of the vessel, and extends at right angles across the shelf; securely riveted to the angle iron are gusset or knee pieces of about five-eighths iron, extending at their lower side twenty-two are inches; these placed at about every three feet around the vessel. The vertical armor timbers, of oak, are placed between these knee pieces, and held in place at top by one-inch bolt passing through the hull of the vessel, and at bottom by an angle iron step. These timbers are also held in place by one-inch blunt bolts, which are driven through the knee pieces fore and aft the ship. The other armor timbers are composed of twelve-inch longitudinal timbers, the upper ones being of oak. The armor plates are placed on these, five thicknesses of one-inch plates breaking joints, and securely fastened by 1¼-inch blunt bolts to the timbers.

Question by the court. Is any effort made to prevent the entrance of water into the armor timber?

Answer. No.

Question by the court. What means are adopted to prevent water circulating in the armor timber from entering the vessel over the hull?

Answer. It would have to pass between the plank-sheer and top of the angle iron. This plank-sheer has been neatly fitted; it overlaps the topping of the angle iron about half way, and is secured to the deck-beams by blunt bolts; and in case of all the vessels, I know it has been calked, or has felt between it. The plank-sheer is also bolted to the armor timbers.

Question by the court. Is there any direct connexion by means of bolts between the plank-sheer and the topping of angle iron in which the hull of the vessel terminates?

Answer. I believe not.

Question by the court. Suppose the angle iron step securing the lower end of the vertical armor timber to be carried away, would water have much difficulty in entering *the vessel over the hull?*

Answer. It would have no effect.

Question by the court. In your opinion could a strain under the overhang, such as being much down by head or stern, produce an opening under it, but not separating it from the lower hull sufficient to admit water in the vessel to any amount, and in what quantity?

Answer. No.

Question by the court. From what you know of the construction of Monitors, and from what you know of the condition of the Weehawken, do you think that the increased weight of ammunition in her, combined with the weight of water when the windlass-room was full, increased by that of a quantity of water in the hold of the vessel, could so affect her armature as to make her take in water rapidly under the spar deck?

Answer. No, it would not affect her armature. The cause of leaks shown on that day would be due to the depth that the vessel was submerged.

Question by the court. Did you ever notice the water-tight bulkhead between the cabin and windlass-room of the Weehawken? And if so, state when, and what was its condition.

Answer. It had the same general appearance as the rest of the vessels.

The testimony of the witness was read over; he pronounced it correct.

Court adjourned, to meet December 24, 1863.

UNITED STATES SHIP SUPPLY, *December* 29, 1863.

The court met pursuant to adjournment, gales of wind having prevented their meeting since the 23d.

Present: Lieutenant Commander E. Simpson, Lieutenant Commander J. L. Davis, Lieutenant Commander J. J. Cornwell; Acting Assistant Paymaster B. F. Munroe, judge advocate.

The proceedings of December 23 were read over and corrected by the court.

Mr. T. F. Griffin was recalled, and testified as follows:

Question by the court. Since your last appearance before the court have you any further information to communicate on the subject of the holes in the sixteen-inch cross-floors?

Answer. I have found that in some of the vessels they are perforated, but not all of them; they are not to be depended on as water limbers.

Question by the court. Do you think that it is likely to be very injurious to Monitors to lie for any time in water where worms abound?

Answer. Some of the Monitors have been shattered in the armor plating, exposing the wood to the action of the worms; it may have been affected thereby.

Question by the court. You have had some experience in Monitors during bad weather in their present anchorage off Morris island; do you think that they are likely to be seriously affected by exposure to such influence for one year?

Answer. From examination of these vessels out of water, after the heavy seas the Monitors have been exposed to on their passage from the north to this place, I can see no danger of their rupturing themselves under their overhang, which is considered the most liable to be affected.

Question by the court. It is stated in evidence before the court, that at one period it was observed that the beams of the Weehawken showed indications of having moved inboard; what cause could have produced such an effect?

Answer. I can see no cause of such an effect while the vessel was afloat. Forces which would create such an effect would have to be greater inside than that outside the vessel; pressure of the water outside has the tendency to keep the vessel together.

Question by the court. Suppose the vessel to be actually ruptured; might not such an appearance be produced?

Answer. I cannot see how the beams could come inboard.

Question by the court. What is considered as the floating capacity of a Monitor when loaded with coals, ammunition, &c.?

Answer. Not less than one hundred and fifty tons.

Question by the court. What weight of water will a Monitor hold if filled up to the forty-eight-inch floors forward of the turret, supposing the ammunition, &c., to be stowed?

Answer. I suppose not less than two hundred tons.

Question by the court. About how much weight would sink the vessel one inch?

Answer. I cannot answer positively.

The testimony was here read over to the witness, and pronounced correct.

The court adjourned till ten a. m., December 30, 1863.

UNITED STATES SHIP SUPPLY, *December* 30, 1863.

The court met pursuant to adjournment.

Present: Lieutenant Commander E. Simpson, Lieutenant Commander J. L. Davis, Lieutenant Commander J. J. Cornwell; Acting Assistant Paymaster B. F. Munroe, judge advocate.

The proceedings of December 29 were read over and corrected by the court.

The testimony of a diver being necessary to complete the case, and the diver not being prepared to testify, the court adjourned till ten a. m., December 31, 1863.

UNITED STATES SHIP SUPPLY, *January* 2, 1864.

The court met pursuant to adjournment, gales of wind having prevented their meeting since the 30th December, 1863.

Present: Lieutenant Commander E. Simpson, Lieutenant Commander J. L. Davis, Lieutenant Commander J. J. Cornwell; Acting Assistant Paymaster B. F. Munroe, judge advocate.

The proceedings of December 30, 1863, were read over by the court. The prevailing bad weather interfering much with the work of the divers at the wreck of the Weehawken, and it being desirable to close the record in the case, the court concluded to dispense with the testimony of a diver.

All the evidence in the case being thus in possession of the court, the court was cleared for deliberation, and having maturely considered the evidence adduced, submit the following statement of the facts in the case of the sinking of the Weehawken.

On the forenoon of Sunday, the sixth of December, 1863, the Weehawken, under the command of Commander J. M. Duncan, came down from an advanced position up the channel, where she had been doing picket duty during the previous night, and was moored at a buoy called Buoy No. 2, with a scope of chain of about ten fathoms, there being about four fathoms water at the buoy at low water. Commander Duncan had assumed the command of the vessel on the afternoon of the fifth of December, and consequently had only been in charge of her for about eighteen hours. After the vessel was made fast to her moorings, Commander Duncan at about ten a. m. left the vessel and proceeded on board the flag-steamer Philadelphia, where he remained until the time of the disaster which befel his command.

On leaving the Weehawken Commander Duncan saw no water dashing over the deck except near the turret. The forward part of the deck was dry, and the battle-plates were up, admitting air to the lower deck of the vessel. The communicating door between the windlass-room and cabin was also open. At this time the wind was fresh from the northeast, but there was not much sea on. The open hatches over the windlass-room and berth deck were protected by high wooden coamings shaped like a hopper, which shed the water that soon began to flow on the deck as the sea rose. Notwithstanding the coaming around the forward hatch, some water continually flowed down in the windlass-room and began to slop into the cabin, when a temporary wooden door in the water-tight bulkhead was closed so as to prevent the water entering the cabin, but not preventing it from collecting in the windlass-room or running from there through the limber, into the vessel. The battle-plates for the hatches forward of the turret were resting with one of their ends on the rabbet of the hatch, while the other ends were triced up by tackles leading to ring-bolts on the opposite side of the deck. The anchor was up and hanging in the anchor-well, no precaution having been taken to prevent water finding its way into the vessel through the hawse-hole. The turret was keyed up quite high, such having been found to be necessary in order to avoid a friction of the new base-ring against the deck, and much water was finding its way into the vessel through the opening under the turret, the composition-ring having ceased to perform the work for which it was designed, viz., "that of preventing a leak at this place." The water that entered the vessel at this place was much more on this day than had ever been before noticed, and before the sinking of the vessel, is described as rushing in in a steady stream. It had been usual to wrap around the base of the turret on occasions of this kind a piece of a hawser, serving the purpose of a packing under the turret; but on this day the hawser was not in use.

The usual trim of the vessel with ammunition and coals on board had been about a foot by the stern, but a short time before the disaster there had been taken on board twenty-five tons additional weight in the form of shells and powder, all of which had been stowed in the forward part of the vessel. Her trim was thus changed, so that she was about seven inches by the stern. Such being the condition of things on board, it was evident that as the sea rose quite a large quantity of water was finding its way slowly into the vessel, and this water, owing to the trim of the vessel, could find its way aft to the pumps but slowly.

The limber was clear. The 11-inch gun was run in in the turret, and the port being open, added in the day another opening through which water found its way into the vessel.

No notice was taken of the condition of things as here stated, nor were any measures adopted for keeping the vessel more dry until about one p. m., when a heavy sea rolling over the bow broke down the coaming around the forward hatch, and tripping the battle-plate from its position, precipitated it into the windlass-room, where it hung by the tackle which was fast to it.

A watch was called on deck to ship the battle-plate, but before this could be done three or four more seas rolled down the hatch, depositing a large amount of water in the windlass-room, where, with the exception of such quantity as escaped through the limber, it was retained by the iron door in the water-tight bulkhead, which had been closed a short time before.

While securing the iron door below with its turn-buckles, much water came in on the cabin floor; and in order for this water to find its way into the bilge, two of the hatches in the cabin floor were taken up, when it was discovered that much water was under the cabin floor, and that it rose rapidly. This was thought to be caused by the water running aft through the valve at the bottom of the water-tight bulkhead; and when subsequently five inches of water was reported in the hold, it was still looked upon as proof that the water was finding its way aft, and would soon reach the pumps.

This mistake was fatal to the vessel; for at this time, notwithstanding the depth of the water in the forward part of the vessel, there was very little water aft at the pumps, showing that the vessel had been tipped down forward by the weight of water in the windlass-room, and that all the water in the vessel was tending to the depressed point forward.

Much time was then occupied in veering chain (about forty fathoms) on deck, no observation being made, meantime, of the accumulation of water in the hold. About fifteen minutes after the forward battle-plate was shipped in its place, the berth-deck battle-plate was also shipped, but not before two or three tons of water had found its way into the vessel through this opening. Neither the forward nor berth-deck battle-plates were secured down. After the chain was veered, which occupied about three-quarters of an hour, leaks were discovered in the rooms of the ward-room, which could only be caused by water finding its way in under the plank-sheer, owing to the state of immersion in which the bow of the vessel was then held. The volume of water pouring in through each of these leaks is described as in quantity about a barrel a minute. At the time these leaks made their appearance under the plank-sheer, the water had risen to about one foot below the cabin floor. A short time afterwards the water was found to have risen to the level of the deck in the ward-room, and about three inches above the deck in the cabin; while the water in the windlass-room, from being twenty inches high when the iron door was closed, had risen to the top, as was shown by the water leaking through the speaking-tube which passes from the windlass-room to the turret-chamber along the beams on the berth deck.

The water had now reached such an elevation forward, and the body of water was so large, that it began to make its appearance in considerable quantities aft. The fire-room floor was awash, and all the pumps working up to their greatest capacity. The centrifugal pump was throwing water freely.

About an hour and a half had elapsed from the time that the water flooded the windlass-room, when it was found that the water had risen to the top of the forty-eight-inch cross-floors forward of the turret; in fact, that the forward part of the vessel was full of water up to the berth deck. The weight of such a body of water amounts to more than the floating capacity of the vessel when loaded. It was then that for the first time the full danger of the vessel was recognized by those on board.

Signal was made for assistance. By the time it was answered, and the word passed for all hands to come on deck, the Weehawken careened to starboard, settled by the head, and in about five minutes sunk to the bottom, where she righted, her smoke-stack showing itself about two feet above water.

At the time of her sinking, there were attached to her fifteen officers and seventy-six men. Of this number there were saved eleven officers and fifty men, making the sad record of four officers and twenty-six men lost. These are supposed to have gone down in the vessel. The watch in the fire-room did not receive the order to come on deck, and they, with some others of the engineer's force, must have perished in the fire-room when the water struck the fires.

Third Assistant Engineer Henry W. Merrian was not on watch at the time of the disaster, but is known to have been in the fire-room acting as a volunteer. A coalheaver, Robert Nugent, undertook to carry the order to the fire-room; but as he is among the missing, it must be concluded that he only reached the fire-room in time to share the fate of those to preserve whom he nobly hazarded and sacrificed his own life.

The speaking-tube, in common use for passing orders from the turret-chamber to the fire-room, was entirely neglected on this occasion.

The opinion of the court on the facts in the case, as here detailed, is, that the causes of the sinking of the Weehawken were:

1. The additional weight of ammunition that had been lately put on board of her, leaving her trim so little by the stern as not to allow sufficient inclination for water to get to the pumps freely.

2. The neglect to close the hawse-hole, and the delay in closing the hatch over the windlass-room, which permitted the rapid accumulation, at the forward extremity of the vessel, of sufficient water to bring her nearly on an even keel.

3. The large amount of water that was permitted to come into the vessel under the turret through the XI-inch port, and down the berth-deck hatch, which assisted to tip the bows of the vessel.

4. The amount of water which, owing to the immersion of the forward part of the vessel, came in under the plank-sheer.

5. The absence of all effort to relieve the forward part of the vessel from its depressed position by rolling shot aft, or moving any weight from the bow.

The court does not consider that it has any positive evidence that the hull of the Weehawken is ruptured. Extensive openings were apparent under the plank-sheer, but there is nothing in the testimony to indicate a rupture of the hull, except the evidence of one witness, who states that he found the beams started in two inches, as shown by the paint-marks having separated that distance from the ceiling. The court is unable to account for this appearance. All other points in the evidence, it thinks, are reconciled in the statement of the facts in the case, as already set forth.

It remains for the court to express its opinion on the merits of the case, and it recognizes the propriety of further military proceedings in the case.

E. SIMPSON,
Lieut. Commander, Presiding Officer of the Court of Inquiry.
B. F. MUNROE,
Judge Advocate of the Court of Inquiry.

[Memorandum.]

FLAG-STEAMER PHILADELPHIA,
Off Morris Island, January 6, 1864.

In transmitting the foregoing to the Navy Department I beg leave to append the following remarks:

1st. I am of the opinion that the sinking of the Weehawken was entirely due to the quantity of water that found its way into her.

2d. It cannot, of course, be absolutely decided that there was no leakage from strain or rupture until the vessel is fully examined; but, so far as the evidence goes, it must be accepted as almost conclusive that the water which sunk the Monitor entered by the hatches and other apartures belonging to the construction.

3d. By assigning the additional weight of ammunition as one cause of the disaster, and giving it the first place in order, may lead to the opinion that the court considered it as the most important cause of the sinking of the Weehawken.

With this I am unable to concur.

Mr. Griffin states the floating capacity of a Monitor like the Weehawken to be not less than one hundred and fifty tons.

The weight of additional ammunition appears to have been about twenty-five tons, which is one-sixth of the floating capacity. It is evident, therefore, that with no more additional weight than twenty-five tons, the Weehawken would have ridden out the gale as easily as the other Monitors.

4th. How far the locality of the stowage of the additional ammunition might have effected the flow of the water aft is of moment. The pilot states that it changed the trim of the Weehawken from twelve inches astern to eight.

It does not appear from evidence that eight inches by the stern would be insufficient for the flow of water aft to the pumps, and it is certainly reasonable to suppose that the inclination thus given would suffice, unless there were impediments in the way. But the court states that it did not flow by the limbers, and that the pumps did not draw until the water was so high as to come over the berth deck.

Now I find in the report made to me by the senior engineer immediately after the disaster that the water did come "aft very fast," and occupied two Worthington pumps; but as it continued to gain forward, the centrifugal pump was started. "This pump worked well, but drew the water from the bilge faster than it ran through the limbers, and, therefore, for a time it was sucking," says the engineer. Hence, it follows that the trim of the vessel did not interfere with the flow of the water to the pumps, but that the quantity was limited by some other cause.

The limber or gutter by which the water passes to the pumps is eighteen inches wide by four inches deep; but the communication to this gutter from the chain-locker, where the water deposited, is an aperture six inches by four inches; and this, therefore, is the measure of the quantity of water delivered to the limber, and which, from the statement of the engineer, was much less than the pumps were capable of throwing off.

I cannot perceive, therefore, that the effect of the additional ammunition on the buoyancy or trim of the hull can be considered as a prominent cause of the accident.

The mischief was really done by the entrance of too much water through the hatches, hawse-pipes, &c., before proper measures were taken. When this was done, it was too late, and the example will lose some of its efficacy if, by any course of reasoning or statement of the case, the attention of Monitor officers is directed from the influx of water as the real source of peril to this class of vessels.

The foregoing report of the court of inquiry concludes "that further military proceedings are necessary."

As the Navy Department has directed a court of inquiry to be held, this opinion of the court belongs to it to decide upon. I therefore respectfully submit the whole to the pleasure of the Navy Department, and have the honor to be, very respectfully, your obedient servant,

J. A. DAHLGREN,
Rear-Admiral, Com'dg S. A. B. Squadron.

WESTERN GULF SQUADRON.

Engagements with the Ram Arkansas, July 15, 1862.

UNITED STATES FLAG-SHIP HARTFORD,
Below Vicksburg, July 17, 1862.

SIR: It is with deep mortification that I announce to the department that, notwithstanding my prediction to the contrary, the iron-clad ram Arkansas has at length made her appearance, and taken us all by surprise. We had heard that she was up at Liverpool, in the Yazoo river, and Lieutenant Colonel Ellet informed me that the river was too narrow for our gunboats to turn, and was also shallow in places, but suggested that Flag-Officer Davis might send up some of his iron-clad boats, which draw only six or seven feet of water.

When this was proposed to Flag-Officer Davis he consented immediately, and General Williams offered to send up a few sharpshooters. The next morning they went off at daylight, and by six in the morning we heard firing up the river, but supposed it to be the gunboats firing at the flying artillery, said to be lining the river. In a short time, however, the gunboats appeared, and the ram in pursuit. Although we were all lying with low fires, none of us had steam, or could get it up, in time to pursue her; but she took the broadside of the whole fleet. It was a bold thing, and she was only saved by our feeling of security. She was very much injured, and was only able to drift or go at the slowest speed—say one knot, and with the current she got down to the forts of Vicksburg before any of us had steam up.

I had a consultation with Flag-Officer Davis, and we thought it best to take the evening, when he dropped down to take the fire of the upper battery, and my squadron passed down with the determination of destroying the ram, if possible; but, by delays of getting in position, &c., it was so dark by the time we reached the town that nothing could be seen except the flashes of the guns, so that, to my great mortification, I was obliged to go down and anchor, with the rest of my fleet, to protect the transports, mortar-boats, &c.

The ram is now repairing damages—for we put many holes through her—though we do not know the extent of damage done to her. Be assured, sir, however, that I shall leave no stone unturned to destroy her. I regret to report that the loss from this vessel was one officer and two men killed, and five men wounded. The total loss in the fleet was five killed and sixteen wounded. I enclose herewith the fleet surgeon's report of casualties.

Very respectfully, your obedient servant,

D. G. FARRAGUT,
Flag-Officer, Comd'g Western Gulf Blockading Squadron.

Hon. GIDEON WELLES,
Secretary of the Navy, Washington, D. C.

Report of Lieutenant Commanding Lowry.

UNITED STATES GUNBOAT SCIOTA,
Above Vicksburg, July 15, 1862.

SIR: This morning, about 6.10 o'clock, heavy firing was heard on board this vessel, apparently from the direction of the Yazoo river, the cause of which soon manifested itself in the appearance of the gunboat Tyler, Lieutenant Commanding Gwinn, running before, and closely followed by, an iron-clad ram—since ascertained to be the Arkansas—escaped out of the Yazoo river. This vessel—of a similar construction to the Louisiana and Mississippi, destroyed at New Orleans; that is, with a screw propeller and inclined iron sides, armed with nine guns—seemed, from her movements, to trust entirely to her invulnerability for a safe run to the cover of the Vicksburg batteries. The Tyler made a running fight until within our lines, when the vessels opened as their guns bore, the rebel's speed diminishing very visibly. This gunboat was anchored fourth in line from up river, without steam and engines under repairs; but as soon as I heard the firing I ordered fire started and steam to be raised with all despatch. My eleven-inch gun being loaded with a ten-second shell, which I had endeavored in vain to draw, as the rebel came within my train I fired, striking him fair, but the shell glanced off almost perpendicularly into the air and exploded. At the same time I opened a brisk fire with all my small arms against his ports, which, I am confident, prevented them from manning her port guns till after she had passed us. I observed one man in the act of sponging tumble out of the port, sponge and all, evidently shot by a rifle ball.

I found my officers and men ready, but such was the suddenness of the appearance and passing of this formidable vessel of the enemy that but little time was afforded for any continued attack upon her with the unwieldy gun carried by this vessel. After passing down stream out of my line of fire, which he did in from four to six minutes, I was unfortunately only a spectator of the final result of this event.

I am, very respectfully, your obedient servant,

R. B. LOWRY,
Lieutenant Commanding U. S. Gunboat Sciota.

Flag-Officer D. G. FARRAGUT,
Commanding Western Gulf Blockading Squadron.

Destruction of the ram Arkansas.

FLAG-SHIP HARTFORD,
Baton Rouge, August 7, 1862.

SIR: It is one of the happiest moments of my life that I am enabled to inform the department of the destruction of the ram Arkansas; not because I held the iron-clad in such terror, but because the community did.

On the 4th instant I sent the Tennessee up to Baton Rouge with provisions for Commander Porter and the gunboats stationed at that place. On the night of the 5th she returned with the information that the enemy had made a combined attack upon Baton Rouge by the ram and two gunboats, the Webb and Music, and calling for assistance. At daylight the Hartford was under way for this place, with orders for the other vessels to follow me as fast as ready.

I arrived here to-day at 12 m., in company with the Brooklyn, Westfield, Clifton, Jackson, and Sciota. I had sent the Cayuga up before me, agreeably to a request of General Butler, in consequence of the guerillas firing into some of his transports. On my arrival I was informed by Commander W. D. Porter that yesterday morning at 2 o'clock the enemy's forces, under General Breckinridge, attacked General Williams, drove in his pickets, &c. General Williams, having had ample warning, was all prepared for him. The fight was continued with great energy on both sides until 10 a. m , by which time the enemy had been driven back two or three miles; but, unfortunately, the gallant General Williams, while cheering on his men, received a Minie ball through his heart.

General Williams had informed Lieutenant Commanding Ransom the evening before of his plans, and requested him not to fire a gun until he notified him; and when he did so, our gunboats—the Kineo and Katahdin—opened with fine effect, throwing their shells directly in the midst of the enemy, producing great dismay and confusion among them. Lieutenant Ransom had an officer on the State-house, which overlooks the adjacent country, and could direct the fire of every shell.

As soon as the enemy was repulsed, Commander Porter, with the gunboats, went up stream after the ram Arkansas, which was lying about five miles above, apparently afraid to take her share in the conflict, according to the preconcerted plan. As he came within gunshot he opened on her, and probably soon disabled some of her machinery or steering apparatus, for she became unmanageable, continuing, however, to fire her guns at the Essex.

Commander Porter says he took advantage of her presenting a weak point towards him, and loaded with incendiary shells. After his first discharge of this projectile, a gush of fire came out of her side, and from that moment it was discovered that she was on fire, which he continued his exertions to prevent from being extinguished. They backed her ashore and made a line fast, which soon burnt, and she swung off into the river, where she continued to burn until she blew up with a tremendous explosion, thus ending the career of the last iron-clad ram of the Mississippi. There were many persons on the banks of the river witnessing the fight, in which they anticipated a triumph for Secessia; but on the return of the Essex not a soul was to be seen.

I will leave a sufficient force of gunboats here to support the army, and will return to-morrow to New Orleans, and depart immediately for Ship island, with a light heart that I have left no bugbear to torment the communities of the Mississippi in my absence.

Very respectfully, your obedient servant,

D. G. FARRAGUT,

Flag-Officer, Commanding Western Gulf Blockading Squadron.

Hon. Gideon Welles,

Secretary of the Navy, Washington, D. C.

On Gunboat Essex,

Off Baton Rouge, August 6, 1862.

Sir: This morning, at 8 o'clock, I steamed up the river, and at 10 o'clock attacked the rebel ram Arkansas, and blew her up. There is not now a fragment of her left.

Very respectfully, your obedient servant,

W. D. PORTER,

Com'ding Division of Flotilla in Western Waters.

Rear-Admiral D. G. Farragut.

Report of Commander W. D. Porter.

United States Gunboat Essex,

Off Baton Rouge, August 6, 1862.

Sir: On the evening of the 4th instant I was informed by General Williams that the rebels, in considerable force, under General Breckinridge, were moving on this place. The rebel ram Arkansas, with two gunboats, the Webb and Music, were also in the vicinity of the city to support the attack of the rebel army. I made such a disposition of the naval force under my command as I thought would give the most aid to our small force on shore.

On the morning of the 5th instant, at 1 o'clock, the enemy made an attack on our land forces and drove in the left wing of our army, killing General Williams. Our men retreating, I opened fire with shot and shell over them on the advancing enemy, and turned them back.

It was the intention of the enemy to make a simultaneous attack by land and water; but the fire from the Essex and the other gunboats driving the enemy back, evidently disconcerted their plans.

Though not making her appearance, I had information of the vicinity of the ram Arkansas; and this morning I determined to steam up the river and attack her, and, if possible, prevent her rendering further assistance to the land forces she was co-operating with. At 10 a. m. I came in sight of her, at about the distance of half a mile, and immediately opened fire. After an action of about twenty minutes I succeeded in setting fire to her, and at meridian she blew up with a tremendous explosion.

The Arkansas had a crew of 180, and mounted ten guns, (six 8-inch and four 50-pound rifles.) This vessel, the Essex, mounts seven guns, and had only forty men on duty at the time of going into action. My first master, R. K. Riley, was in sick hospital, and his place was supplied by Second Master David Porter Rosenmiller, who conducted himself to my entire satisfaction.

I have the honor to be, very respectfully, your obedient servant,

W. D. PORTER,

Commanding Division of Flotilla in Western Waters.

Hon. GIDEON WELLES,

Secretary of the Navy.

Flag-Officer Farragut gives rebel reports of the Arkansas.

FLAG-SHIP HARTFORD,

New Orleans, August 10, 1862.

SIR: Since forwarding the reports of Lieutenants Fairfax, Ransom, and Roe, we have picked up a number of prisoners from the ram Arkansas, all of whom I have catechised very closely. They agree very well respecting her exit from the Yazoo, and her passing the fleets; they also agree as to the number of killed and wounded on each of these occasions, making in all eighteen killed and a large number wounded. At Vicksburg they plated the deck with iron, and fortified her with cotton inside. She then came down in command of Lieutenant H. K. Stevens, (Brown having been taken sick at Vicksburg,) with the intention of making a combined attack with General Breckinridge upon Baton Rouge; but her port engine broke down. They repaired it in the course of the day, and went out to meet the Essex the next morning, when they saw her coming up; but the starboard engine gave way, and they ran her ashore, she being perfectly unmanageable.

They say that when the gunboats were seen coming up, and the Essex commenced firing, the captain set the ram on fire and told the crew to run ashore. They also state that the gunboats Webb and Music were sent for to tow her up the river, but they did not arrive, and neither of them had been seen. This is the statement, all of which is respectfully submitted by your obedient servant,

D. G. FARRAGUT,

Flag-Officer, Commanding Western Gulf Blockading Squadron.

Hon. GIDEON WELLES,

Secretary of the Navy, Washington, D. C.

Engagement between the ram Arkansas and the Essex and Colonel Ellet's ram, on the 15th July, 1862.

FLAG-SHIP HARTFORD,
New Orleans, July 29, 1862.

SIR: I am happy to inform the department that I arrived here yesterday about noon, with the ships Brooklyn, Richmond, and Hartford, and gunboats Pinola and Kennebec, the other gunboats, excepting the Katahdin and Kineo, left at Baton Rouge for the protection of the troops, having preceded me.

On the 20th instant I received the order of the department to drop the ships down the river, and not to risk them before the batteries more than possible. The river had fallen very much, and my anxiety was great that I should not be able to get the large ships down. Unfortunately the iron-clad ram Arkansas came down on the 15th, before I received your order, and her commander being satisfied by the reception we gave her that she was not shot-proof, kept her close in under the forts, which are mounted with 8 and 10-inch columbiads and 50-pounder rifles. Still, Flag Officer Davis was determined that as Commander W. D. Porter thought his vessel, the Essex, was shot-proof, he would make an attack on the ram and drive her down to us or destroy her. He had also determined to let the Sumter run at her, and to let Colonel Ellis also attack her with one of his rams. The ram lay between the two forts, at the upper bend of the river, about four miles above the fleet.

It was stipulated that I was not to pass up the river, but be ready to receive her if she attempted to come down. Unfortunately, the attack was a failure. The Essex ran at the ram, but being so clumsy, they let the bow of the ram swing off from the shore so that the Essex ran fast aground; but she delivered her three 9-inch guns into the ram at not more than ten or twelve feet, and those who saw the ram afterwards say she had a large hole knocked into her. Colonel Ellet's ram also ran at the iron-clad, but the fire from the forts and ram so damaged her that it was with difficulty she got back to her anchorage, and it was only remarkable that she was not destroyed. We do not know that she damaged the ram. The Sumter, from some misunderstanding, did not go in.

This was a daring act on the part of Colonel Ellet, and one from which both Flag-Officer Davis and myself tried to deter him.

The Essex, after she got afloat, ran down to our fleet through a storm of shot and shell; and strange to say, not a shot struck her after she left the upper forts. She was only penetrated by three projectiles from the ram and forts, viz: one 9-inch and one 50-pound rifle solid shot, and one 50-pound conical shell. The last went through the casemates about six feet from the forwar corner, and exploded inside, killing one man and wounding three, which was nearly all the damage done the crew. The 9-inch solid shot penetrated the forward casemate nearly amidship, passed through the iron, but did not go through the wood. The 50-pounder rifle passed through the port quarter and lodged in the ward-room, doing no harm; but, of course, each of these shots started the wood and iron considerably, the other shot in the vicinity would have done much damage.

I waited a day or two for General Williams to make his preparations for leaving, as he had determined to do so, not having well men enough to take care of the sick ones. When all was ready, I settled with Flag-Officer Davis that Commander W. D. Porter was to take charge of the lower part of the river, with the Essex and Sumter. I do not, however, consider this force sufficient, for there are two gunboats in the Red river and two in the Yazoo. I presume Flag-Officer Davis will destroy those in the Yazoo, and my gunboats chased the Music and Webb up the Red river, but drew too much water to go far.

Very respectfully, your obedient servant,

D. G. FARRAGUT,
Flag-Officer, Commanding Western Gulf Blockading Squadron.

Hon. GIDEON WELLES,
Secretary of the Navy, Washington, D. C.

Attempt to blow up the Essex with a torpedo.

UNITED STATES IRON-CLAD ESSEX,
Off Baton Rouge, June 19, 1863.

SIR: I have respectfully to report an attempt on the part of the rebels to blow up this vessel with a torpedo, and its failure.

On the 18th instant I went up the river with the Essex to Port Hudson on a reconnoissance. Arriving abreast the centre of Profit's island, and between two points, one making out from the island, the other from the opposite shore, I observed what appeared to be a buoy. On examining it with my glass I found it to be a large demijohn, anchored about 400 yards from the island. I immediately suspected the reason of its being placed there, and turned my glass to the island shore, and near it observed another demijohn buoy, and ten or twenty yards outside of it a barrel nearly submerged. I wished to stop the vessel immediately; but as we were almost in a line with the buoys, the wind blowing half a gale, and right aft, and the vessel at full speed, it would have been impossible to stop in time, and I was forced to pass between the buoys and over the apparatus. We experienced no trouble, however, and proceeded on, finishing our reconnoissance of Port Hudson. On my return I stopped the vessel below the infernal machine, with her head up stream, sent the men to quarters, and despatched two boats to take up or destroy the apparatus. From the inside buoys an iron wire (apparently telegraph wire) was discovered leading up the beach, then over a glass bottle, (attached to a tree as an insulator,) and from thence into the woods. About fifty fathoms of this wire was hauled down to the boats, and its connexion with the buoys severed. All the buoys were then raised, and found to be connected by wires, and a torpedo of cylindrical form, three feet long and a foot in diameter, made of boiler iron, and finished in a most workmanlike manner, was found attached to the barrel buoy, and hung thereto with about a dozen turns of wire rove through two eye-bolts riveted in one end of the machine; the other end had a plug fitted in, with a wire leading through and communicating with the interior. A number of wires appeared to connect with this end of the machine, but the connexion could not be understood, as the wires were all broken while raising it, or cut immediately after, to prevent accident.

We raised, in all, one machine, three buoys, and about one hundred fathoms of telegraph wire. Other portions of the apparatus were lost, together with a quantity of wire, owing to the latter breaking by the heavy strain on it, in attempting to weigh the lost portions.

This apparatus was skilfully made, and carefully laid—exactly in our track, and between the points already mentioned, which contracted the river to its narrowest bounds Near the opposite shore the current runs with great velocity. I was extremely anxious to examine the contents of this machine, but after making a few careful experiments I found it could not be opened without danger of moving the wire; I therefore had it taken on shore and secured in a hole in the levee, and a long line bent to the wire;

then a boat pulled out with the other end of the line, and when it became taut the machine burst with a tremendous explosion, tearing away a large piece of the levee, and throwing the pieces of iron in every direction. One piece, weighing about two pounds, fell on board the vessel, distant about 300 yards. It would seem that the machine was made to explode *both* by *friction* and *electricity*. I think there were others besides the one raised. I consider these machines too dangerous to handle, and hereafter shall destroy the buoys, and taking the in-shore end of the wire, drag the apparatus well into the river and sink it.

Very respectfully, your obedient servant,

C. H. B. CALDWELL, *Commander.*

Rear-Admiral D. G. FARRAGUT, U. S. N.,
Commander-in-Chief, Western Gulf Blockading Squadron.

Forwarded by your obedient servant,

JAMES ALDEN,
Commanding Naval Forces, Baton Rouge.

Report of Commander Robert Townsend, commanding United States steamer Essex.

UNITED STATES STEAMER ESSEX,
Grand View Reach, July 10, 1863.

SIR: I have the honor to report, that, in obedience to your orders, given before your departure this morning, I proceeded in the Essex to the relief of the New London, the Monongahela, on our starboard beam, towing us more rapidly against the current than we were able to steam down with the current last evening. We found the New London ashore, made fast to the bank below Whitehall Point, and out of range from the battery, a position where Lieutenant Commander Perkins, after much difficulty, had succeeded in placing her. The Monongahela got her off, took her in tow on the port side, and made fast to the port side of the Essex.

Thus sheltered, they made the downward trip almost unscathed. As the New London is completely disabled by shots through her boiler, I sent word to Lieutenant Commander Waters, of the Kineo, to take her in tow to New Orleans and report to you. Lieutenant Commander Perkins having fruitlessly sent messages to Donaldsonville for assistance, was finally, this morning, obliged to proceed thither himself. Lieutenant Day, who was left in charge, although wounded, was on the alert and preserved good order and discipline among the crew.

On our way up, the battery at the head of Grand View Reach did not open upon us; but it did so, spitefully, upon our return. The battery opposite College Point gave us a warm reception both going and returning. Whilst the Monongahela was getting the New London afloat, we proceeded up in the Essex, off Whitehall Point, and opened upon the Winchester Plantation battery, both at long and short range. They did not return our fire. We counted seven embrasures, but saw no guns in position there. A crowd of sharpshooters, lining the levee, disappeared soon after we opened fire. Last evening and to-day we were struck by shot and shell nine times. One penetrated the solid timber of the starboard forward guard; three glanced from our plating on the sides and quarter, doing no particular damage; the others passed, respectively, through both sides of the wheel-house, the awning rail and furled awning, the starboard smoke-stack, the galley funnel, and both ventilators.

I will not particularize the pattering showers of musket balls, as they did no material damage. We expended of 100-pounder rifle, 9-inch, and 32-pounder shell and shrapnell, 150 rounds.

Lieutenant Commander Dewey displayed coolness, skill, and judgment in managing the Monongahela and in getting off the New London. He was able to use his bow and stern guns and boat howitzers, and, whilst passing the batteries, he did so effectively. Acting Master Parker, executive officer of the Essex, worked the battery with cool discretion and ability, and made a number of excellent shots. Mr. Attenborough, our pilot, occupied a very exposed position, but it did not militate against the skill with which he habitually directs the course of the ship. I am much pleased that I can speak in the most commendable terms of the conduct of all the officers and men. It is also gratifying that I am able to report the execution of your orders without loss or injury to any engaged in the expedition.

I have the honor to remain, very respectfully, your obedient servant,

ROBERT TOWNSEND,
Commander, United States Navy.

Rear-Admiral D. G. Farragut,
Com'dg W. G. B. Squadron, U. S. Flag-Ship Tennessee, New Orleans.

MISSISSIPPI SQUADRON.

Report of Commander H. Walke of the part taken by the Mound City in the battle of Belmont, Kentucky.

United States Gunboat Taylor,
Mound City, November 9, 1861.

Sir: I have the honor to report that on the evening of the 6th instant I received instructions from General Grant to proceed down the river, in company with the Lexington, under Commander Stembel, for a reconnoissance and as convoy to some half dozen transport steamers. We proceeded opposite to Norfolk, near the Kentucky shore, where we rounded to, and anchored for the night. I then learned for the first time the extent of the reconnoissance.

At 3 o'clock the following morning, at the request of General Grant, the Taylor and Lexington started down the river for the purpose of engaging their batteries at Columbus, but, after proceeding a few miles, we were met by such a dense fog as to render any further progress hazardous; we therefore rounded to, and returned to the point from whence we started. At 6 o'clock we all got under way, our two gunboats taking the lead and convoying the steamers containing Generals Grant and McClernand and their aids, and some 3,000 troops, two companies of cavalry, and some artillery. We proceeded down the river to the extreme end of Lucas's bend, and just without, as I thought, the range of their guns on Iron banks. After the troops had disembarked and were under marching orders, (half past eight o'clock,) our two boats proceeded to engage their batteries on Iron Banks, expending each several rounds of shell, and returning to the transports. Their shot passed over us, though in some instances coming very close to us. At this time, with their long-range rifled cannon, they sent a large number of shot half a mile above the transports. I requested the captains of the transports to move up and out of the range of their shot, which they did. At ten o'clock, the engagement having commenced at Belmont, we again engaged the Iron bank batteries, expending still more shell, their shot flying around us but doing no harm, while our shell seemed to go where they could be effective. We returned, after an engagement of about twenty minutes, to the transports.

At about noon, hearing the battle of Belmont still going on, our two gunboats made a third attack upon their batteries, this time going nearly a quarter of a mile nearer to them. We opened a brisk fire of shell, and seemingly with good effect, while in this engagement one of their 24-pounders struck us on the starboard bulwarks, and, continuing obliquely through the spar deck, took off the head of Michael Adams, seaman, and broke the arm and otherwise seriously injured James Wolfe, seaman, and slightly wounding a third. Acting Surgeon Kearney, who was cool and assiduous in the discharge of his duties, immediately dressed Wolfe's wound, but considers him in a critical condition. We fired a few more shell and returned, keeping up the fire from our stern guns as long as we were within reach of them.

It is providential that we have escaped with so little damage. A fragment of one of their shells struck us in the stern, doing but trifling damage.

When nearly all our troops had re-embarked, or were about ready to start, a sudden attack was made upon the transport vessels by a large force coming in from above. Our gunboats being in good position, we opened a brisk fire of grape, canister, and 5″ shells, silencing the enemy with great slaughter. After the transports were under way we followed them, throwing a shell occasionally to repel the enemy's approach to the banks. When a few miles up the river, we met one of the transports (Chancellor) with Brigadier General McClernand aboard, who stated that some of their men were left behind, and asked that we might return with our gunboats and see if we could find them. We did so, the Lexington accompanying us, and between us succeeded in securing nearly all there were left behind, together with about forty prisoners, including some badly wounded.

We then proceeded up to Island No. 1, when the Rob Roy met us, with instructions from General Grant to turn over all the troops and prisoners, and to remain until Colonel Cook, who was down the Kentucky shore on a reconnoissance, should return. He returned at ten o'clock, and at eleven I weighed anchor and proceeded to Cairo, having sent the Lexington on before me.

It is but an act of justice to the officers and crew to state that they acted throughout all our engagements with perfect coolness, ability, and courage, the crew answering the calls to quarters with an alacrity becoming earnest co-operators for the government. I was astonished, with the apparently new material we have, to see with what zeal and efficiency they all performed their parts.

The Lexington, under Commander Stembel, as consort, supported me throughout the day with the most commendable energy and efficiency.

Very respectfully, your obedient servant,

H. WALKE,
Commander U. S. N.

Captain A. H. Foote, U. S. N.,
Commanding Naval Forces on Western Waters.

[Telegram.]

United States Gunboat Taylor,
Mississippi, below Cairo, January 11, 1862.

Sir: Yesterday, as reported to the department, I sent Captain Porter, with the Essex, and Lieutenant Commanding Paulding with the St. Louis, down the river to protect the advance brigade under General McClernand,

and, also, have sent two other gunboats up the Tennessee river. This morning three rebel gunboats came up from Columbus, and opened the attack on the Essex and St. Louis at long-range, and for twenty minutes the fire was very brisk between the five boats engaged, when the rebel boats retreated, but a running fire was continued for an hour, until the rebel boats were driven behind their batteries at Columbus. Captain Porter believes that one of the rebel boats was disabled.

A. H. FOOTE, *Flag-Officer.*

Hon. GIDEON WELLES,
Secretary of the Navy.

Letter from Flag-Officer Foote, enclosing report of Commander W. D. Porter, of the gunboat Essex.

CAIRO, *January* 13, 1862.

SIR: I forward a report from Commander Porter. The rebel gunboat shells all fell short of our boats, while our shells reached and ranged beyond their boats, showing the greater range of our guns, but the escape of the rebels showed the greater speed of their boats.

I have the honor to be, &c.,

A. H. FOOTE, *Flag-Officer.*

Hon. GIDEON WELLES,
Secretary of the Navy.

UNITED STATES GUNBOAT ESSEX,
Fort Jefferson, January 13, 1862.

SIR: On the morning of the 11th General McClernand sent on board this vessel and informed me that the enemy were moving up the river from Columbus with several vessels, towing up a battery. I immediately signalled Lieutenant Commanding Paulding, of the St. Louis, to get under way and prepare for action. A very thick fog coming on, we were compelled to steam slowly down the river, but about 10 o'clock, or a little after, it rose, and showed us a large steamer at the head of Lucas's bend. We heard her whistle the moment we were seen by them. Shortly after whistling she was joined by another large and a small steamer. We pursued our course steadily down the river, and when within long range the large steamer fired a heavy shell gun, which struck the sand bar between us and ricocheted within about two hundred yards of this vessel and burst. We at this time did not return the fire, but continued our course down in order to near the vessel. By this time the large steamer was joined by her consorts, and they opened a brisk fire upon us. I now hailed Lieutenant Commanding Paulding, and directed him to try one of his rifle cannon. He instantly fired, and sent his shot completely over the enemy. I then opened from my bow guns, and the action became brisk on both sides for about twenty minutes, the enemy firing by broadsides. At the end of this time the enemy hauled off and stood down the river, rounding to occasionally and giving us broadsides. This running fight continued until he reached the shelter of his batteries on the Iron bank, above Columbus. We continued the action, and drove him behind their batteries in a crippled condition, as we could distinctly see our shell explode on his decks. The action lasted over an hour, and terminated, as I think, in a complete defeat of the enemy's boats, superior in size and number of guns to the Essex and St. Louis. On the 12th

General McClernand requested me to make a reconnoissance towards the Iron banks. I did so, and offered the enemy battle by firing a round shot at their battery, but they did not respond, nor did I see anything of their boats. I have since been informed, through the general, that the boats of the enemy were completely disabled, and the panic became so great at the Iron banks that the gunners deserted their guns.

The fire of the St. Louis was precise, and the shot told well. The officers and men of this vessel behaved with firmness—Mr. Riley, our first master, carrying out all my orders strictly, while the officers of the gun divisions, Messrs. Laning and Ferry, paid particular attention to the pointing of their respective guns. Mr. Brittan, my aid, paid all attention to my orders, and conveyed them correctly and with alacrity. In fact, all the officers and men on board behaved like veterans.

I have the honor to be, &c.

W. D. PORTER, *Commander.*

Flag-Officer A. H. Foote.

Flag-Officer Foote's report of attack on Fort Henry, February 6, 1862.

Cairo, Ill., *February* 7, 1862.

Sir: I have the honor to report that on the 6th instant, at 12½ o'clock p. m., I made an attack on Fort Henry, on the Tennessee river, with the iron-clad gunboats Cincinnati, Commander Stembel; the flag-ship Essex, Commander Porter; the Carondelet, Commander Walke, and St. Louis, Lieutenant Commanding Paulding; also taking with me the three old gunboats Conestoga, Lieutenant Commanding Phelps; the Taylor, Lieutenant Commanding Gwinn, and the Lexington, Lieutenant Commanding Shirk, as a second division, in charge of Lieutenant Commanding Phelps, which took position astern and inshore of the armored boats, doing good execution there in the action, while the armored boats were placed in the first order of steaming, approaching the fort in a parallel line.

The fire was opened at seventeen hundred yards distance from the flag-ship, which was followed by the other gunboats, and responded to by the fort. As we approached the fort under slow steaming till we reached within six hundred yards of the rebel batteries, the fire, both from the gunboats and forts, increased in rapidity and accuracy of range. At twenty minutes before the rebel flag was struck, the Essex, unfortunately, received a shot in her boilers, which resulted in the wounding, by scalding, of twenty-nine officers and men, including Commander Porter, as will be seen in the enclosed list of casualties. The Essex then necessarily dropped out of line, astern, entirely disabled, and unable to continue the fight, in which she had so gallantly participated until the sad catastrophe. The firing continued with unabated rapidity and effect upon the three gunboats, as they continued still to approach the fort with their destructive fire until the rebel flag was hauled down, after a severe and closely-contested action of one hour and fifteen minutes.

A boat, containing the adjutant general and captain of engineers, came alongside after the flag was lowered, and reported that General Lloyd Tilghman, the commander of the fort, wished to communicate with the flag-officer, when I despatched Commander Stembel and Lieutenant Commanding Phelps, with orders to hoist the American flag where the secession ensign had been flying, and to inform General Tilghman that I would see him on board the flag-ship. He came on board soon after the Union had been substituted by Commander Stembel for the rebel flag on the fort, and possession taken.

I received the general, his staff, and some sixty or seventy men as prisoners, and a hospital ship containing sixty invalids, together with the fort and its effects, mounting twenty guns, mostly of heavy calibre, with barracks and tents capable of accommodating fifteen thousand men, and sundry articles, which, as I turned the fort and its effects over to General Grant, commanding the army, on his arrival in an hour after we had made the capture, he will be enabled to give the government a more correct statement of than I am enabled to communicate from the short time I had possession of the fort. The plan of the attack, so far as the army reaching the rear of the fort to make a demonstration simultaneously with the navy, was frustrated by the excessively muddy roads and high stage of water preventing the arrival of our troops until some time after I had taken possession of the fort.

On securing the prisoners and making necessary preliminary arrangements, I despatched Lieutenant Commanding Phelps, with his division, up the Tennessee river, as I had previously directed, and as will be seen in the enclosed orders to him to remove the rails, and so far render the bridge incapable of railroad transportation and communication between Bowling Green and Columbus, and afterwards to pursue the rebel gunboats, and secure their capture, if possible. This being accomplished, and the army in possession of the fort, and my services being indispensable at Cairo, I left Fort Henry in the evening of the same day, with the Cincinnati, Essex, and St. Louis, and arrived here this morning.

The armored gunboats resisted effectually the shot of the enemy when striking the casemate. The Cincinnati (flag-ship) received thirty-one shots; the Essex fifteen; the St. Louis seven, and the Carondelet six—killing one, and wounding nine in the Cincinnati, and killing one in the Essex; while the casualties in the latter from steam amounted to twenty-eight in number. The Carondelet and St. Louis met with no casualties.

The steamers were admirably handled by their commanders and officers, presenting only their bow guns to the enemy, to avoid exposure of the vulnerable parts of their vessels. Lieutenant Commanding Phelps, with his division, also executed my orders very effectually, and promptly proceeded up the river in their further execution, after the capture of the fort. In fact, all the officers and men gallantly performed their duty, and, considering the little experience they have had under fire, far more than realized my expectations.

Fort Henry was defended with the most determined gallantry by General Tilghman, worthy of a better cause, who, from his own account, went into action with eleven guns of heavy calibre bearing upon our boats, which he fought until seven of the number were dismounted or otherwise rendered useless.

I have the honor to be, &c.,

A. H. FOOTE, *Flag-Officer.*

Hon. Gideon Welles,
Secretary of the Navy.

Report of part taken by the Carondelet in the capture of Fort Henry.

United States Gunboat Carondelet,
Fort Henry, Tennessee River, February 8, 1862.

Sir: In compliance with your special order of the 2d instant, and in accordance to your signal number of the morning of the 6th, I respectfully report the incidents which occurred on board this vessel, connected with the victory you so nobly won, in the capture of Fort Henry on that day.

The Carondelet was kept in line as nearly as possible with the other boats, (first order of steaming,) with the exception of being interlocked with the St. Louis a considerable portion of the time, in consequence of being crowded, and, by mistake of our pilot in ringing the bell to back, instead of one to go ahead, according to my repeated orders, the boat lost one length astern of her position for the space of two or three minutes. The mistake being immediately corrected, she resumed her position in line, keeping up a continued, steady, and careful firing upon the enemy's batteries from the instant you fired your first gun until he struck. None killed or wounded on board.

The Carondelet was struck nine or ten times during the engagement by the enemy's shot, as follows: five times on plating of the bow, four of which were within eight inches of the ports; one upon the starboard bow, under water; one on the port broadside, cutting the timbers and planking some six feet; one taking away a section of the port hammock nettings; one taking away a portion of the port awning stanchion; and another cutting away the gig's fall.

It is with pleasure and pride that I have to state that during the action the officers and crew under my command performed their duties with perfect courage, coolness, and ability, so far as I could observe; and I have reason to believe, from what I have seen and heard on shore, that their aim was correct, their shot striking with terrible effect on Fort Henry.

With most sincere congratulations, I have the honor to be, sir, most respectfully, your obedient servant,

H. WALKE,
Commander, United States Navy.

Flag-Officer A. H. Foote,
Com'dg Naval Forces, Western Waters.

United States Gunboat Conestoga,
Fort Henry, Tennessee, February 6, 1862.

Sir: In conformity with your directions, the division of gunboats under my command, consisting of the Tyler, Lieutenant Commanding Gwin; Lexington, Lieutenant Commanding Shirk, and this vessel, in the attack of this morning on this work, took up a position upon the left bank of the river, and opened fire with shells immediately after your first gun was fired, and continued firing until the rebel flag was hauled down, having succeeded in throwing shells without firing over your flag-ship, or over the other iron-plated boats in close contact with the fort. There were fired from this vessel seventy-five 32-pounder shells, fourteen 12-pounder rifled shells, and two round shot. No injury was done to either of the vessels, and no casualties occurred, though we were at times exposed to the ricochet of the close fire upon your vessel, as well as to the direct fire of a 32-pounder rifled piece until it burst. The commanders of the Tyler and Lexington handled their vessels with excellent judgment. I enclose their reports. The officers and crew of this vessel displayed coolness and an admirable spirit in this action.

I am, respectfully, your obedient servant,

S. L. PHELPS,
Lieutenant Commanding, United States Navy.

Flag-Officer A. H. Foote, U. S. N.,
Com'dg Naval Forces, Western Waters.

Letter from Flag-Officer Foote, forwarding Lieutenant Commanding Phelps's report of operations on the Tennessee river.

UNITED STATES FLAG-STEAMER ST. LOUIS,
Paducah, February 12, 1862.

SIR: I have the honor and high gratification to forward to the department the official report of Lieutenant Commanding Phelps, by which it will be seen that he has, with consummate skill, courage, and judgment, performed a highly beneficial service to the government, which, I doubt not, will appreciate it. I cannot too highly commend the conduct of Lieutenant Commanding Phelps for this his signal service in his long cruise to the head of navigation on the Tennessee river.

I am now, with three iron-clad steamers, ascending the Cumberland river, to co-operate with General Grant in an attack on Fort Donelson. Lieutenant Commanding Phelps, with his division, accompanies me.

In great haste, I have the honor to be your obedient servant,

A. H. FOOTE, *Flag-Officer.*

Hon. GIDEON WELLES,
Secretary of the Navy.

Lieutenant Commanding Phelps's report of operations on the Tennessee river.

UNITED STATES GUNBOAT CONESTOGA,
Tennessee River, February 10, 1862.

SIR: Soon after the surrender of Fort Henry, on the 6th instant, I proceeded, in obedience to your order, up the Tennessee river, with the Tyler, Lieutenant Commanding Gwin; Lexington, Lieutenant Commanding Shirk, and this vessel, forming a division of the flotilla, and arrived after dark at the railroad crossing, twenty-five miles above the fort, having on the way destroyed a small amount of camp equipage abandoned by the flying rebels. The draw of the bridge was found closed, and the machinery for turning it disabled. About a mile and a half above were several rebel transport steamers escaping up stream.

A party was landed, and in one hour I had the satisfaction to see the draw open. The Tyler being the slowest of the gunboats, Lieutenant Commanding Gwin landed a force to destroy a portion of the railroad track and to secure such military stores as might be found, while I directed Lieutenant Commanding Shirk to follow me with all speed in chase of the fleeing boats. In five hours this boat succeeded in forcing the rebels to abandon and burn three of their boats loaded with military stores. The first one fired (Samuel Orr) had on board a quantity of submarine batteries, which very soon exploded. The second one was freighted with powder, cannon, shot, grape, balls, &c. Fearing an explosion from the fired boats—there were two together—I had stopped at a distance of one thousand yards; but even there our skylights were broken by the concussion, the light upper deck was raised bodily, doors were forced open and locks and fastenings everywhere broken.

The whole river, for half a mile round about, was completely "beaten up" by the falling fragments and the shower of shot, grape, balls, &c. The house of a reported Union man was blown to pieces, and it is suspected there was design in landing the boats in front of the doomed home. The Lexington having fallen astern, and being without a pilot on board, I concluded to wait for both of the boats to come up. Joined by them, we proceeded up the river. Lieutenant Commanding Gwin had destroyed some of the trestle-work at the end of the bridge, burning with them a lot of camp equipage. I. N. Brown, formerly, a lieutenant in the navy, now signing himself "Lieut. C. S. N.," had fled with such precipitation as to leave his papers behind. These Lieutenant Commanding Gwin brought away, and I send them to you, as they give an official history of the rebel floating preparations on the Mississippi, Cumberland, and Tennessee. Lieutenant Brown had charge of the construction of gunboats.

At night on the 7th we arrived at a landing in Hardin county, Tennessee, known as Cerro Gordo, where we found the steamer Eastport being converted into a gunboat. Armed boat crews were immediately sent on board, and search made for means of destruction that might have been devised. She had been scuttled and the suction-pipes broken. These leaks were soon stopped. A number of rifle shots were fired at our vessels, but a couple of shells dispersed the rebels. On examination I found that there were large quantities of timber and lumber prepared for fitting up the Eastport; that the vessel itself—some 280 feet long—was in excellent condition, and already half-finished; considerable of the plating designed for her was lying on the bank, and everything at hand to complete her. I therefore directed Lieutenant Commanding Gwin to remain with the Tyler to guard the prize and to load the lumber, &c., while the Lexington and Conestoga should proceed still higher up.

Soon after daylight on the 8th we passed Eastport, Mississippi; and at Chickasaw, further up, near the State line, seized two steamers, the Sallie Wood and Muscle—the former laid up, and the latter freighted with iron destined for Richmond and for rebel use. We then proceeded on up the river, entering the State of Alabama, and ascending the Florence at the foot of the Muscle Shoals. On coming in sight of the town three steamers were discovered, which were immediately set on fire by the rebels. Some shots were fired from the opposite side of the river below. A force was landed, and considerable quantities of supplies, marked "Fort Henry," were secured from the burning wrecks. Some had been landed and stored. These I seized, putting such as we could bring away on our vessels, and destroying the remainder. No flats or other craft could be found. I found, also, more of the iron and plating intended for the Eastport.

A deputation of citizens of Florence waited upon me, first desiring that they might be made able to quiet the fears of their wives and daughters with assurances from me that they would not be molested; and secondly, praying that I would not destroy their railroad bridge. As for the first, I told them we were neither ruffians nor savages, and that *we were there to protect from violence and to enforce the law;* and with reference to the second, that if the bridge were away we could ascend no higher, and that it could possess no military importance, so far as I saw, as it simply connected Florence itself with the railroad on the south bank of the river.

We had seized three of their steamers—one the half-finished gunboat—and had forced the rebels to burn six others loaded with supplies; and their loss, with that of the freight, is a heavy blow to the enemy. Two boats are still known to be on the Tennessee, and are doubtless hidden in some of the creeks, where we shall be able to find them when there is time for the search. We returned, on the night of the 8th, to where the Eastport lay. The crew of the Tyler had already gotten on board of the prize an immense amount of lumber, &c. The crews of the three boats set to work to finish the undertaking, and we have brought away probably 250,000 feet of the best quality of ship and building lumber, all the iron, machinery, spikes, plating, nails, &c., belonging to the rebel gunboats, and I caused the mill to be destroyed where the lumber had been sawed.

Lieutenant Commanding Gwin had, in our absence, enlisted some twenty-five Tennesseeans, who gave information of the encampment of Colonel Drew's rebel regiment at Savannah, Tennessee. A portion of the six or seven hundred men were known to be "pressed" men, and all were badly armed. After consultation with Lieutenant Commanding Gwin and Shirk, I determined to make a land attack upon the encampment. Lieutenant Commanding Shirk, with thirty riflemen, came on board the Conestoga, leaving his vessel to guard the Eastport, and, accompanied by the Tyler, we proceeded up to that place, prepared to land 130 riflemen and a twelve-pounder rifle howitzer. Lieutenant Commanding Gwin took command of this force when landed, but had the mortification to find the camp deserted.

The rebels had fled at 1 o'clock in the night, leaving considerable quantities of arms, clothing, shoes, camp utensils, provisions, implements, &c., all of which were secured or destroyed, and their winter quarters of log huts were burned. I seized, also, a large mail-bag, and send you the letters giving military information. The gunboats were then dropped down to a point where arms, gathered under the rebel "press-law," had been stored, and an armed party, under Second Master Goudy, of the Tyler, succeeded in seizing about seventy rifles and fowling-pieces. Returning to Cerro Gordo, we took the Eastport, Sallie Wood, and Muscle in tow, and came down the river to the railroad crossing. The Muscle sprang a leak, and all efforts failing to prevent her sinking, we were forced to abandon her, and with her a considerable quantity of fine lumber. We are having trouble in getting through the draw of the bridge here.

I now come to the, to me, the most interesting portion of this report—one which has already become lengthy; but I must trust you will find some excuse for this in the fact that it embraces a history of labor and movements, day and night, from the 6th to the 10th of the month, all of which details I deem it proper to give you. *We have met with the most gratifying proofs of loyalty everywhere across Tennessee and in the portions of Mississippi and Alabama we visited. Most affecting instances greeted us almost hourly. Men, women, and children several times gathered in crowds of hundreds, shouted their welcome, and hailed their national flag with an enthusiasm there was no mistaking; it was genuine and heartfelt.* These people braved everything to go to the river bank, where a sight of their flag might once more be enjoyed, and they have experienced, as they related, every possible form of persecution. Tears flowed freely down the cheeks of men as well as of women, and there were those who had fought under the stars and stripes at Moultrie, who, in this manner, testified to their joy.

This display of feeling and sense of gladness at our success, and the hopes it created in the breasts of so many people in the heart of the confederacy, astonished us not a little, and I assure you, sir, I would not have failed to witness it for any consideration. I trust it has given us all a higher sense of the sacred character of our present duties. I was assured at Savannah, that of the several hundred troops there, more than one-half, had we gone to the attack in time, would have hailed us as deliverers and gladly enlisted with the national force.

In Tennessee the people generally, in their enthusiasm, braved secessionists and spoke their views freely; but in Mississippi and Alabama what was said was guarded. "*If we dared to express ourselves freely, you would hear such a shout greeting your coming as you never heard.*" "We know there are many Unionists among us, but a reign of terror makes us afraid of our shadows." We were told, too, "bring us a small organized force, with arms and ammunition for us, and we can maintain our position and put down rebellion in our midst." There were, it is true, whole communities who, on our approach, fled to the woods; but these were where there was less of the loyal element, and where the fleeing steamers in advance had spread tales of our coming with firebrands, burning, destroying, ravishing, and plundering.

The crews of these vessels have had a very laborious time, but have evinced a spirit in the work highly creditable to them. Lieutenant Commanding Gwin and Shirk have been untiring, and I owe to them and to their officers many obligations for our entire success.

I am, respectfully, your obedient servant,

S L. PHELPS,
Lieutenant Commanding, United States Navy.

Flag-Officer A. H. Foote,
Commanding Naval Forces Western Waters.

Flag-Officer Foote's report of attack on Fort Donelson, February 14, *with list of casualties.*

Flag-Ship St. Louis,
Near Fort Donelson, Cumberland River, February 15, 1852.

Sir: I have the honor to report to the department that, at the urgent request of Major General Halleck and General Grant, who regarded the movement as a military necessity, although not, in my opinion, properly prepared, I made an attack on Fort Donelson yesterday, the 14th instant, at 3 o'clock p. m., with four iron-clad and two wooden gunboats, the St. Louis, Carondelet, Louisville, and Pittsburg, and the Tyler and Conestoga. After a severe fight of an hour and a half, being in the latter of the action less than four hundred yards from the fort, the wheel of this vessel, by a shot through her pilot-house, was carried away; the tiller-ropes of the Louisville were also disabled by a shot, which rendered the two boats wholly unmanageable, and they drifted down the river, the relieving tackles not being able to steer or control them in the rapid current. The two remaining boats, the Pittsburg and Carondelet, were also greatly damaged between wind and water, and soon followed us as the enemy rapidly renewed the fire as we drifted helplessly down the river. This vessel, the St. Louis, alone received fifty-nine shots, four of them between wind and water; one in the pilot-house, mortally wounding the pilot and others, requiring some time to put her in repair. There were fifty-four killed and wounded in this attack, which, notwithstanding our disadvantages, we have every reason to suppose would, in fifteen minutes more, could the action have been continued, have resulted in the capture of the two forts bearing upon us. The enemy's fire had materially slackened, and he was running from his batteries, when the two gunboats helplessly drifted down the river from disabled steering apparatus, as the relieving tackles could not control the helm in the strong current, when the fleeing enemy returned to their guns and again reopened fire upon us from the river batteries which we had silenced.

The enemy must have brought over twenty heavy guns to bear upon our boats from the water batteries and the main fort on the side of the hill, while we could only return the fire with twelve bow-guns from the four boats. One rifle gun aboard the Carondelet burst during the action.

The officers and men in this hotly-contested but unequal fight behaved with the greatest gallantry and determination, all deploring the accident which rendered two gunboats suddenly helpless in the narrow river and swift current.

On consultation with General Grant and my own officers, as my services, until we can repair damages by bringing up a competent force from Cairo to attack the fort, are much less required here than they are at Cairo, I shall proceed to that point with two of the disabled boats, leaving the two others here to protect the transports, and, with all despatch, prepare the mortar boats and the Benton, with other boats, to make an effectual attack upon Fort Donelson.

I have sent the Tyler to the Tennessee river to render impassable the bridge, so as to prevent the rebels at Columbus re-enforcing their army at Fort Donelson. I am informed that the rebel batteries were served with the best gunners from Columbus. I transmit herewith a list of casualties.

Very respectfully, your obedient servant,

A. H. FOOTE,

Flag-Officer, Com'dg U. S. Naval Forces, Western Waters.

Hon. GIDEON WELLES,

Secretary of the Navy, Washington, D. C.

CASUALTIES.

St. Louis.—Killed: Charles W. Baker, ship's cook; F. A. Riley, pilot. Wounded: Flag-Officer A. H. Foote; R. G. Baldwin, pilot; Charles Smith, boatswain's mate; R. H. Medill, carpenter; Antonio Calderio, Thomas Kirkham, W. S. Coon, and John Thompson, seamen.

Carondelet.—Killed: Albert Richardson, Joseph G. Laycock, Albert Markham, and William Duff, seamen. Wounded: William Hinton, pilot, (since dead;) Samuel Brooks, 2d assistant engineer; John Doherty, second master; Thomas Brown, captain of gun; Richard Mahoney, quartermaster; John McBride, ship's cook; Owen Canty, James Plant, James Brown, Patrick Laughlin, Edward Green, Owen Conly, Henry Smith, Patrick Sullivan, John Owen, William B. Roney, James McFadden, John Diamond, Amos Dutch, Richard O'Brien, William Johnson, Patrick O'Brien, William Thielman, Benjamin Edger, Henry Anderson, Daniel F. Charles, John Doughty, John Murphy, John McConnell, seamen.

Pittsburg.—Wounded: Charles Merwin and George Smith, seamen.

Louisville.—Killed: James Curtiss, E. W. Avilla, Charles Billips, and John Williams, seamen. Wounded: Michael Kelley, E. S. Collins, William Higgins John Paul, Charles Might.

Report of part taken by Carondelet in the attack on Fort Donelson.

UNITED STATES GUNBOAT CARONDELET,
Cumberland River, February 15, 1862.

SIR: I hereby report the part which the gunboat Carondelet took in the bombardment of Fort Donelson on the 14th instant. Agreeably to your instructions, we weighed anchor at 2 p. m., and steamed up the river, slowly approaching the fort, and keeping a little in advance of our position on your extreme left against the eastern bank of the river.

At 3 p. m. commenced firing at about a mile distant from the fort, continuing a deliberate and well-directed firing from the instant your vessel commenced, and kept up the same until about 5.30 p. m. and until all the fleet had dropped down the river out of the enemy's range.

During the engagement one of our rifled guns burst, about 5 p. m., our officers and men serving the remaining two guns faithfully as long as the enemy were within reach. We suffered most severely in the latter part of the action being disabled by a shot striking our wheel-house and jamming the wheel, and being the last out of the enemy's reach.

I am sorry to add that an 8-inch, apparently from our flotilla, burst astern of us, the fragments of which penetrated our casemate. We were struck with 35 of the enemy's shot, 128-pounders to 32-pounders solid. Four of our crew were killed and thirty-two wounded, some dangerously, one of whom is our pilot; in all, forty-six wounded since the battle and capture of Fort Henry. Our boats were so much cut up that I have but one fit for service. We leak badly forward and aft, and require extensive repairs above and below water-mark and in almost every department.

The officers and crew on duty conducted themselves with admirable coolness and fidelity during the engagement; but I must, in justice to J. R. Hall, gunner United States navy, and Edward E. Brenard, master's mate, state that their intrepid and efficient conduct, under all emergencies, deserves my highest commendation.

We are in want of coal, provisions and ammunition.

I have the honor to be, sir, most respectfully, your obedient servant,

H. WALKE,
Commander United States Navy.

Flag-Officer A. H. Foote,
Commanding United States Naval Forces, Western Waters.

P. S.—As we dropped out of the action the Pittsburg, as she turned, struck us on our starboard quarter, and broke off our starboard rudder iron.

Flag-Officer Foote reports leaving for Clarksville, &c.

Cairo, *February* 17, 1862.

Sir: I forwarded a despatch this morning, announcing the fall or capture of Fort Donelson by the army.

I leave immediately, with a view of proceeding to Clarksville with eight mortar boats and two iron-clad boats, with the Conestoga, (wooden boat,) as the river is falling rapidly. The other iron-clad boats are badly cut up, and require extensive repairs. I have sent one of the boats already since my return, and ordered a second to follow me, which with eight mortar boats I hope to carry Clarksville.

I have no further information than that communicated by telegram this morning. Enclosed are papers from Commanders Walke and Dove, referring to matters the day before and the day after an attack upon Fort Donelson, which fort we sadly disabled in the fight of the 14th.

My foot is much inflamed; but with care, the surgeon considers, will soon be better, as I have two days' rest on board the Conestoga before reaching Clarksville. I leave Fleet-Captain Pennock in charge, who is performing excellent service; but we are sadly in want of men. I have ordered 150 carpenters to repair damages.

The department will please excuse this hasty communication, as I must leave immediately, and every moment of my time is occupied.

I have the honor to be, very respectfully, your obedient servant,

A. H. FOOTE, *Flag-Captain.*

Hon. Gideon Welles,
Secretary of the Navy.

P. S.—I have ordered Lieutenant Sanford, on his return with the ammunition steamers, now at Cincinnati, to inform the ordnance department of the loss or disabling of one gun and gun-carriage. Please inform that department.

A. H. F.

Report of Commander Walke.

UNITED STATES GUNBOAT CARONDELET,
Near Fort Donelson, Cumberland River, February 15, 1862.

SIR: I arrived here (towed by the Alps) on the 12th instant, about 11.20 a. m., and seeing or hearing nothing of our army, I threw a few shell into Fort Donelson to announce my arrival to General Grant, as he had previously desired. I then dropped down the river a few miles and anchored for the night, awaiting General Grant's arrival. On the morning of the 13th instant I weighed anchor and came again to this place, when I received a despatch from General Grant, notifying me of his arrival the *day before*, "and succeeded in getting position almost entirely investing the enemy's works. Most of our batteries (he writes) are established, and the remainder soon will be. If you will advance with your gunboats at 10 o'clock a. m., we will be ready to take advantage of our division in our favor." I immediately complied with these instructions by throwing some 139 15″ and 10″ shell into the fort, receiving, in return, the enemy's fire from all their batteries, most of their shot passing over us, and but two striking us, one of which was a 128-pound solid. It passed through our port casemate forward; glancing over our barricade at the boilers, and again over the steam-drum, it struck, and bursting our steam-heater, fell into the engine-room without striking any person, although the splinters wounded slightly some half dozen of the crew. I then dropped down to this anchorage, but the sound of distant firing being heard, we again attacked the fort, throwing in some 45 shell and receiving but little damage.

I returned to this place to wait for further orders, when I received a second depatch from General Grant that you were expected in the following morning.

I am, sir, most respectfully, your obedient servant,

H. WALKE,
Commander, United States Navy.

Flag-Officer A. H. FOOTE,
Commanding U. S. Naval Forces, Western Waters, Cairo, Ill.

Report of Commander Dove.

UNITED STATES GUNBOAT LOUISVILLE,
Off Dover, February 16, 1862.

SIR: At 2½ p. m. yesterday, shortly after your departure, I received the enclosed despatch (No. 1) from General Grant.

It seemed of so much importance for us to keep up a show of force that I decided not to accompany the Pittsburg down the river. I immediately went on board the Carondelet and St. Louis, to see their condition and consult with their commanders.

The Carondelet could not well be moved, but I ordered up the St. Louis and followed up with this vessel. The St. Louis threw a few shells, and towards dark both vessels returned to their former anchorage.

At 8½ p. m. yesterday I received the despatch marked No. 2, and early this morning went on board the vessels to give instructions. The condition of the Carondelet's wounded would not allow them to be moved or the guns to be used. I sent my own and those of the St. Louis on board of one of the transports, and got under way; steaming up towards the batteries at Fort Donelson, both vessels cleared for action.

On approaching near enough, two white flags were seen flying from the upper one. I then stopped the gunboats and proceeded in the tug, with a white flag flying, and landed at the foot of the hill below the fort. I was met by a major, who offered me his sword, which I declined to receive, thinking it most proper to consult with General Grant. I took the major on board the tug and proceeded up to General Buckner's headquarters, where I found General Wallace and his aids. General Grant arrived about half an hour afterwards. The fort had surrendered, but what the conditions were I was not officially informed.

The transports are all up at Dover, to receive the prisoners. The Carondelet, being most disabled of the gunboats, will go down this afternoon.

I will remain here with this vessel and the St. Louis until further orders, or until the fall of the river compels me to go down. The St. Louis will make a short reconnoissance up the river, at General Grant's suggestion, this afternoon. This vessel will remain off the town.

The Graham arrived to-day with the mortar and gunboat ammunition.

Very respectfully, your obedient servant,

BENJ. M. DOVE, *Commander.*

Flag-Officer A. H. FOOTE,
Commanding Mississippi Flotilla.

Flag-Officer Foote's report of contemplated reconnoissance to Columbus, February 23, enclosing telegram and proclamation.

FLAG-STEAMER CONESTOGA, *February* 22, 1862.

SIR: After having telegraphed for several hours with General Cullum, the chief of General Halleck's staff here, and finding that nothing definite could be ascertained, I ran down here; and to-morrow morning, at 6 o'clock, I go down with General Cullum, and four gunboats and two mortar boats, on an armed reconnoissance to Columbus, to see the condition of things at that point. I am excessively hurried to get ready, and please excuse this letter. I send copy of my first telegram.

I have the honor to be, &c.,

A. H. FOOTE, *Flag-Officer.*

Hon. GIDEON WELLES,
Secretary of the Navy.

I enclose copy of a telegram sent you yesterday. A. H. F.

UNITED STATES FLAG-STEAMER CONESTOGA,
Clarksville, Tenn., February 20, 1862.

We have possession of Clarksville. The citizens being alarmed, two-thirds of them have fled, and, having expressed my views and intentions to the mayor and Hon. Cave Johnson, at their request I have issued a proclamation assuring all peaceably-disposed persons that they may with safety resume their business avocations, requiring only the military stores and equipments to be given up, and holding the authorities responsible that this shall be done without reservation.

I left Fort Donelson yesterday, with the Conestoga, Lieutenant Commanding Phelps, and the Cairo, Lieutenant Commanding Bryant, on an armed reconnoissance, bringing with me Colonel Webster, of the engineer corps, and chief of General Grant's staff, who, with Lieutenant Commanding Phelps, took possession of the principal fort and hoisted the Union flag. A Union sentiment manifested itself as we came up the river. The rebels have retreated to Nashville, having set fire, against the remonstrances of the citizens, to the splendid railroad bridge across the Cumberland river.

I return to Fort Donelson to-day for another gunboat and six or eight mortar boats, with which I propose to proceed up the Cumberland. The rebels all have a terror of the gunboats. One of them, a short distance above Fort Donelson, had previously fired an iron rolling mill belonging to Hon. John Bell, which had been used by the rebels.

A. H. FOOTE,
Flag-Officer, Commanding Naval Forces, Western Waters.

Hon. GIDEON WELLES,
Secretary of the Navy.

PROCLAMATION

To the inhabitants of Clarksville, Tennessee.

At the suggestion of the Hon. Cave Johnson, Judge Wisdom, and the mayor of the city, who called upon me yesterday, after our hoisting the Union flag and taking possession of the forts, to ascertain my views and intentions towards the citizens and private property, I hereby announce to all peaceably-disposed persons that neither in their persons nor in their property shall they suffer molestation by me or the naval force under my command, and that they may in safety resume their business avocations with the assurance of my protection.

At the same time I require that all military stores and army equipments shall be surrendered, no part of them being withheld or destroyed; and further, that no secession flag, or manifestation of secession feeling, shall be exhibited; and for the faithful observance of these conditions I shall hold the authorities of the city responsible.

ANDREW H. FOOTE,
Flag-Officer, Commanding Naval Forces, Western Waters.

U. S. FLAG-STEAMER CONESTOGA,
Clarksville, Tenn., February 20, 1862.

Flag-Officer Foote to General Cullum about moving on Nashville.

PADUCAH, *February* 21, 1862.

General Grant and myself consider this a good time to move on Nashville. Six mortar boats and two iron-clad steamers can precede the troops and shell the forts. We were about moving for this purpose, when General Grant, to my astonishment, received a telegram from General Halleck, "Not to let the gunboats go higher than Clarksville." No telegram was sent to me.

The Cumberland is in a good stage of water, and General Grant and I believe we can take Nashville. Please ask General Halleck if we shall do it. We will talk per telegraph, Captain Phelps representing me in the office, as I am still on crutches.

A. H. FOOTE, *Flag-Officer.*

General CULLUM, *Cairo.*

Flag-Officer Foote reports result of reconnoissance to Columbus, Ky., February 23, 1862.

UNITED STATES FLAG-STEAMER CINCINNATI,
Mississippi River, near Columbus, Ky., February 23, 1862.

SIR: I have the honor to report that, in company with General Cullum, chief of General Halleck's staff, with four iron-clad boats, two mortar boats, and three transports, containing one thousand men, I made this day a reconnoissance in force towards Columbus to ascertain its condition; and when near the batteries a flag of truce came out to communicate with us, the result of which will be seen in the enclosed papers. The object of the reconnoissance being attained, and finding that fire from the mortars would lead the enemy to plant guns where they could reach them with their batteries should we again open upon them with a larger number of mortars, I concluded to return to Cairo; and there we must remain until the gun and mortar boats are completed, as otherwise the flotilla will be demoralized for want of time and means to properly prepare for active service. The army will not move without gunboats, yet the gunboats are not in condition to act offensively at present. On this subject I will soon write more fully. A telegram will be sent the department on my arrival at Cairo, referring to the events of to-day.

I have the honor to be your obedient servant,

A. H. FOOTE, *Flag-Officer, &c.*

Hon. GIDEON WELLES,
Secretary of the Navy.

P. S.—Columbus evinces no signs of an evacuation or dismounting guns. The batteries seem to be intact, and we saw great numbers of tents and troops.

A. H. F.

HEADQUARTERS FIRST DIVISION WESTERN DEPARTMENT,
Columbus, Ky., February 22, 1862.

Presuming you will be willing to reciprocate the courtesy shown to the families of officers of the United States army, after the battle of Belmont, in allowing them to visit those officers who were prisoners within my lines, I take the liberty of sending up, under a flag of truce, the families of several of our officers who were captured at Donelson. These are the families of General Buckner, Colonels Hawson and Medeira. They are accompanied by Colonel Russell, Mr. Vance, and Stockdale, as escorts; also by Mr. Mass.

Hoping you may find it convenient to send these ladies forward to their husbands, I have the honor to remain, respectfully, your obedient servant,

L. POLK,
Major General, Commanding.

The COMMANDING OFFICER U. S. FORCES, *Cairo, Ill.*

UNITED STATES FLAG-STEAMER CICINCINNATI,
Mississippi River, near Columbus, Ky., February 23, 1862.

GENERAL: Your letter of the 22d instant, received to-day by the hands of Captain Blake under a flag of truce, *nearly within range of your guns, and in the presence of our armed forces*, at half-past twelve o'clock to-day, will be answered to-morrow by a flag of truce at the same point of the river at which this was received.

Very respectfully, your obedient servant,

ANDREW H. FOOTE,
Flag-Officer Commanding Naval Forces, Western Waters.

GEO. W. CULLUM, *Brig. Gen.*,
Chief of Staff and Engineers, Department of Missouri.

Major General L. POLK,
Commanding at Columbus, Ky.

Lieutenant Commanding Bryant to Flag-Officer Foote, reporting arrival at Nashville, February 25, 1862.

GUNBOAT CAIRO,
Nashville, Tenn., February 25, 1862.

SIR: Uncertain that my letter of the 23d reached you, I repeat that I departed from Clarksville for this point by the request of Brigadier General Smith, commanding at Clarksville, and arrived here this morning, preceding seven steamboats, conveying an army commanded by Brigadier General Nelson. The troops landed without opposition. The banks of the river are free from any hostile force. The railroad and suspension bridges here are destroyed.

Very respectfully, your obedient servant,

N. C. BRYANT,
Lieutenant Commanding.

Flag-Officer A. H. FOOTE,
Commanding Flotilla, &c.

Flag-Officer Foote encloses reports of Lieutenants Commanding Gwin and Shirk of attack on Pittsburg, Tennessee, March 1, 1862.

CAIRO, *March* 3, 1862.

SIR: I have the honor to forward reports made to me by Lieutenants Commanding Gwin and Shirk, of the gunboats Tyler and Lexington, a synopsis of which I telegraphed to you immediately on their receipt. I cannot too highly commend the cautious, judicious, and bold conduct of Lieutenant Commanding Gwin and his command in the service. I have assigned him on the Tennessee river. I regret it is not in my power to go up the Tennessee in person; but the more important attack upon Columbus to-morrow with five gunboats, four mortar boats, in charge of Lieutenant Commanding Phelps, and the regiments, renders my presence at that point absolutely necessary.

I have the honor to be, very respectfully, your obedient servant,

A. H. FOOTE, *Flag-Officer,*
Comd'g U. S. Naval Forces on the Western Waters.

Hon. GIDEON WELLES,
Secretary of the Navy, Washington, D. C.

Report of Lieutenant Commander Gwin.

UNITED STATES GUNBOAT TYLER,
Savannah, Tennessee, March 1, 1862.

SIR: Having learned that the rebels had occupied and were fortifying a place called Pittsburg, nine miles above, on the right bank of the river, (the best point in the river for that purpose,) I determined to attack them.

At 12 m. the Tyler, followed by the Lexington, Lieutenant Commanding Shirk, proceeded up the river. When within twelve hundred yards of Pittsburg we were opened upon by the rebel batteries, consisting, as well as we could determine, of six or eight field-pieces, some rifled. Getting within one thousand yards, the Tyler and Lexington opened a well-directed fire, and we had the satisfaction of silencing their batteries.

We then proceeded abreast of the place, and, under the cover of grape and canister, landed two armed boats from each vessel, containing, besides their crews, a portion of company "C," Captain Thaddeus Phillips, and company "K," First Lieutenant John T. Rider, of the 32d regiment Illinois volunteers, (sharpshooters.) Second Master Jason Goudy commanded the boats of the Tyler, and Second Master Martin Dunn commanded the boats of the Lexington. The landing was successfully accomplished; and this small force actually drove back the rebels and held them in check until they accomplished their difficult object, which was to discover their real strength and purpose, and to destroy a house in close proximity to where the batteries had been placed.

I found that, in addition to their artillery, they had a force of not less than two regiments of infantry and a regiment of cavalry. In conclusion, I have to state that the result was entirely satisfactory. Their batteries were silenced in a short time, the landing was effected, the house destroyed, and we discovered from their breastworks that they were preparing to fortify strongly this point.

Too much praise cannot be given to Lieutenant Commanding Shirk for the efficient manner in which his vessel was handled. My thanks are due to Captain Phillips, Lieutenant Rider, and their men, for the gallant manner in which, in the face of the enemy, they charged up the hill, drove back and held in check the rebels, until the boats' crews had effected the destruction of the house designated. The officers and men of this vessel behaved with the greatest spirit and enthusiasm. Much praise is due to First Master Edward Shaw and Third Master James Martin for the efficient manner in which the batteries were worked. I would particularly call your attention to the gallant conduct of Second Master Jason Goudy, in charge of the boats inshore, who succeeded in destroying the house under such heavy fire, and Gunner Hermann Peters, in charge of the howitzer, who displayed the greatest coolness and courage, although exposed to the whole fire of the enemy, all but one of his men having been wounded. My thanks are also due to Pilots Herier and Sebastian for their coolness under such a tremendous fire of musketry, our vessel being perfectly riddled with balls. My aid, Acting Paymaster William B. Coleman, rendered me valuable assistance during the action.

I have sent Lieutenant Commanding Shirk to Cairo with the transport Izetta, loaded with the balance of the wheat I left at Clifton. I shall remain about here, paying Pittsburg a daily visit, which I hope will prevent the rebels from accomplishing their object. Captain Shirk will lay before you the importance of keeping open this as well as all other points above here.

I have learned from reliable authority that the rebels have some 4,000 troops in Florence, 5,000 or 6,000 in and about Eastport and Iuka, (near

Bear Creek bridge,) and that they are fortifying in that vicinity. You will therefore see the necessity of my remaining here.

We expended ninety-five shells, thirty stand of grape, ten of canister, and sixty-seven rounds of shrapnell, grape, &c., from howitzer.

Enclosed is the report of casualties, by Acting Assistant Surgeon T. H. Kearney, to whom I am indebted for his unremitting attention to the wounded. I feel confident that we inflicted a severe loss on the enemy, as several bodies were seen on the ground, and many seen to fall. I also enclose Lieutenant Commanding Shirk's report.

Hoping that my course will meet your approbation, I have the honor to be, &c.,

WM. GWIN,
Lieut. Comd'g Division of Gunboats on Tennessee River.

Flag-Officer A. H. Foote,
Commanding Naval Forces in Western Waters.

List of casualties sustained in the action at Pittsburg, Tennessee, March 1, 1862.

On the gunboat Tyler: Pleasant Gilbert, seaman, gunshot wound of leg, necessitating amputation of the limb; Crawford T. Hill, seaman, gunshot wound of forearm; John Matthews, seaman, gunshot (flesh) wound of shoulder, slight; G. W. Shull, seaman, gunshot wound of back, slight; Robert Bell, seaman, gunshot wound of arm (flesh) and chest, not penetrating.

In detachment of thirty-second regiment of Illinois volunteers (company C) carried on board: Captain Phillips, gunshot wound of leg, flesh; Daniel Messick, orderly sergeant, killed.

Respectfully,

THOS. H. KEARNEY,
Assistant Surgeon, U. S. Gunboat Service.

Lieut. Commanding W. Gwin.

United States Gunboat Lexington,
Savannah, Tennessee, March 1, 1862.

Sir: In company with the gunboat Tyler, Lieutenant Commanding Gwin, I this day proceeded in this vessel up the river to a landing on the west side, called Pittsburg, distant about nine miles from this place.

When we had arrived within twelve or thirteen hundred yards of Pittsburg we were fired upon by a rebel battery, consisting, as well as I could judge, of six or eight field-pieces, one of which, at least, was rifled. We returned their fire with shell, which were exceedingly well directed, and continued until after their guns were silenced.

By order of Lieutenant Commanding Gwin, I despatched on shore two armed boats, in charge of Second Master Martin Dunn, containing, in addition to their own proper crews, a detachment of company K, thirty-second regiment Illinois volunteers, commanded by First Lieutenant John T. Rider, with orders to follow the motions of the Tyler's boats. While the boats were being landed we kept up a steady fire of grape and shell, raking the side of the hill.

The landing party having accomplished their object and being met by a much superior force, retired, receiving in their retreat a terrific fire of musketry. The enemy also fired several volleys of musketry at the gunboats, and then retired back from the brow of the hill. After the boats returned, we gave the rebels a few more shell, and, receiving no answer, we dropped down the river to this place.

My men report having seen several dead rebels upon the hill, and I myself saw a shell from this vessel, after the return of the boats, take effect upon a field officer, emptying his saddle, and dropping three foot soldiers.

I cannot speak in too high terms of the gallantry, good discipline, and patriotic spirit evinced by the officers and men whom I have the honor to command. For the efficient services of himself and his command I am greatly indebted to First Lieutenant John T. Rider, company K, 32d regiment Illinois volunteers.

I regret to have report the following casualties, viz: James Sullivan, seaman, killed; Patrick Sullivan and Thomas M. Borland, seamen, missing; John Hines, corporal, company K, 32d regiment Illinois volunteers, missing. James Sullivan was seen to fall upon the field shot through the breast.

During the action there were expended forty-five eight-inch shell, twenty-five six-inch shell, and sixteen stand of grape.

Two rifles and one musket are missing. They are those taken by the unfortunate men whom we have lost.

I have the honor to be, sir, your most obedient servant,

JAMES W. SHIRK,
Lieutenant Commanding.

Flag-Officer A. H. FOOTE,
Commanding U. S. Naval Forces, Cairo, Illinois.

Flag-Officer Foote reports the evacuation of Columbus, March 1, 1862.

CAIRO, *March* 1, 1862.

SIR: Lieutenant Commanding Phelps, sent with a flag of truce to-day to Columbus, has this moment returned, and reports that Columbus is being evacuated. He saw the rebels burning their winter quarters and removing their heavy guns on the bluffs, but the guns in the water batteries remain in tact. He also saw a large force of cavalry drawn up ostentatiously on the bluffs, but no infantry were to be seen as heretofore, and the encampment seen in our armed reconnoissance a few days since has been removed. Large fires were visible in the town of Columbus and upon the river banks below, indicating the destruction of the town, military stores, and equipments.

I shall consult General Cullum, and we shall probably proceed to Columbus, with the force we have ready, soon after daylight. General Polk informs us that he will send a flag of truce at meridian to-morrow to the point where the flags of truce met to-day, in reference to which we shall be governed according to circumstances. But as General Cullum has not been fully consulted, I can give no particular information of our movements to-morrow.

I have the honor to be, &c.,

A. H. FOOTE, *Flag-Officer.*

Hon. GIDEON WELLES,
Secretary of the Navy.

Flag-Officer Foote reports fall of Columbus, and his purpose to proceed to New Madrid.

UNITED STATES FLAG-STEAMER CINCINNATI,
Columbus, March 4, 1862.

SIR: I have the honor to forward a copy of the telegram sent to the department to-day announcing the fall of Columbus.

The fleet not being in a condition to proceed down to Island No. 10 and to New Madrid where the rebels are represented as fortifying, I leave for Cairo immediately to make the necessary preparation for going down the river with a suitable force of gunboats and mortar boats in a proper condition for effective service. I am fully impressed with the importance of proceeding to New Madrid as soon as possible, where General Pope has arrived with 10,000 men; but such is the condition of my command that I shall decline moving, as I informed Generals Sherman and Cullum, unless I am ordered to do so by the Secretary of the Navy, as I must be the judge of the condition of the fleet, and when it is prepared for the service required.

It is due to Commander Pennock, the fleet captain, and to Mr. Sanford, the ordnance officer of the flotilla, to say to the department that these efficient officers earnestly entreated me to permit them to go on this expedition, as well as up the Tennessee and Cumberland rivers; but their services in preparing the gun and mortar boats at Cairo being absolutely necessary, I reluctantly denied their application from a sense of duty to the government, yet their services should be regarded as equally important to the great object of the expedition as if they had participated personally in the different actions.

I have the honor to be, very respectfully, your obedient servant,

A. H. FOOTE,
Flag-Officer, Commanding Naval Forces, &c.

Hon. GIDEON WELLES,
Secretary of the Navy.

COLUMBUS, KENTUCKY, *March* 4, 1862.

SIR: Columbus is in our possession. My armed reconnoissance, on the 2d instant, caused a hasty evacuation, the rebels leaving quite a number of guns and carriages, ammunition, and a large quantity of shot and shell, a considerable number of anchors, and the remnant of the chain lately stretched across the river, with a large number of torpedoes. Most of the huts, tents, and quarters are destroyed.

The works are of very great strength, consisting of formidable tiers of batteries on the water side, and on the land side surrounded by a ditch and abatis.

General Sherman, with Lieutenant Commanding Phelps, not knowing that the works were last evening occupied by four hundred of the 2d Illinois cavalry, on a scouting party sent by General Sherman from Paducah, made a bold dash to the shore under the batteries, hoisting the American flag on the summit of the bluff, greeted by the hearty cheers of our brave tars and soldiers.

The force consisted of six gunboats, four mortar boats, and three transports, having on board two regiments and two battalions of infantry, under command of Colonel Buford—General Cullum and General Sherman being in command of the troops. The former leaving a sick bed to go ashore, discovered what was evidently a magazine on fire at both extremities, and immediately ordered the train to be cut, and thus saved the lives of the garrison.

While I cannot express too strongly my admiration of the gallantry and wise counsels of this distinguished aid and engineer of General Halleck, (General Cullum,) I must add that Commanders Dove, Walke, and Stembel, and Lieutenants Commanding Paulding, Thompson, Shirk, and Phelps, the latter being in command of the mortar division, assisted by Lieutenant Sanford, of the ordnance department of the United States army, nobly performed their duty.

I have my flag on board the Cincinnati, commanded by the gallant Commander Stembel. General Sherman remains temporarily in command at Columbus.

A. H. FOOTE, *Flag-Officer.*

Hon. GIDEON WELLES,
Secretary of the Navy.

Flag-Officer Foote forwards report of Lieutenant Commanding Gwin, of the gunboat Tyler, March 5, 1862, *communicating important information.*

CAIRO, *March* 6, 1862.

SIR: I have the honor to forward a report just received from Lieutenant Commanding Gwin, of the Tyler, communicating important information, which, with a telegram just received from General Grant, commanding at Fort Henry, stating that the rebels were fortifying Savannah, on the Tennessee river, and calling for an additional gunboat, has been communicated to General Halleck. I shall probably send an additional gunboat, making three boats on that river.

The Assistant Secretary of War is now in my office, and is informed of the state of things, and we shall be able to meet the demands, I trust, by having a force at hand sufficient to prevent any fortifications being erected on the Tennessee as far up as the stage of water will permit the gunboats to ascend the river.

I have the honor to be, very respectfully, &c.,

A. H. FOOTE, *Flag-Officer.*

Hon. GIDEON WELLES,
Secretary of the Navy.

UNITED STATES GUNBOAT TYLER,
Cairo, Illinois, March 5, 1862.

SIR: I have returned from up the Tennessee, having left Pittsburg (the place of our late engagement) last night. The enemy has not renewed his attempt to fortify. I watched the point closely, and yesterday landed under a flag of truce, which was allowed to go a mile from the river before being stopped by their pickets. No sign of a renewed attempt could be discovered.

In my report of the engagement I stated that I felt confident the enemy had suffered severely. I can now report that on the morning after the engagement (Sunday) nine dead bodies and one hundred wounded—many of them mortally—were counted in their camp, which had been removed the evening of the engagement, three miles back of the river. Some tents, where they were carrying badly wounded men, they would not allow any one to visit; they were still bringing in wounded.

There is no doubt of the correctness of the above. It was reported that they buried fifteen the evening of the engagement. I think I can safely put their loss down at twenty killed and one hundred wounded. Their force engaged on that day was 1,000 infantry (Louisiana) and 500 cavalry, Mississippi,) besides a battery of six pieces of field artillery. Two guns (32-pounders) were on the ground, but were not mounted.

I have reliable information that the enemy have now at Corinth, Mississippi, eighteen miles from the Tennessee river (Pittsburg) junction of Mobile and Ohio and Memphis and Charleston railroads, fifteen to twenty thousand troops. At Henderson station, eighteen miles from Coffee landing, Tennessee river, and thirty-five miles by railroad from Corinth, some ten or twelve thousand, and bodies of troops arriving every day, mostly from Columbus, and some from Louisiana. At Bear Creek bridge, seven miles back from Eastport, Mississippi, they have from eight to ten thousand, and are fortifying. At Chickasaw, Alabama, I understand they are erecting heavy batteries. This last is not very reliable.

Information received last night near Savannah, Tennessee, from a reliable source, indicates that General Johnson, with all his force, is falling back from Murfreesboro' to Decatur, Alabama, the place where the Memphis and Charleston railroad crosses the Tennessee river, and the junction of the railroad leading from Nashville to that place, showing that they are preparing to send large re-enforcements to Bear creek.

The result of the recent elections in Harden and McNairy counties, South Tennessee, will prove to you that the Union sentiment is very strong throughout that section of the State. The former gave five hundred majority for the Union candidate out of a poll of one thousand votes. The latter gave two hundred Union majority out of a poll of eighteen hundred votes. The constant cry from them to me is, "Send us arms and a sufficient force to protect us in organizing, and we will drive the secessionists out of Tennessee ourselves."

I have enlisted a few more men; Captain Phillips recruited several for his company. I have captured J. B. Kendrick, of Captain Fitzgerald's company of Tennessee volunteers, who represents himself as a colonel of militia of the State of Tennessee, and Clay Kendrick, private in Captain Fizgerald's company (Colonel Crew's regiment) Tennessee volunteers.

Very respectfully, &c.,

WILLIAM GWIN,
Lieutenant Commanding.

Flag-Officer A. H. Foote, U. S. N.,
Commanding Naval Forces, Western Waters.

[Telegram.]

Engagement with five rebel forts below Columbus, Kentucky.

Flag-Ship Benton, *March* 8, 1862.

We have this moment returned to our anchorage after five hours' fighting with five rebel forts, in which we have not suffered materially other than in the bursting of a rifled gun aboard the St. Louis, killing and wounding fourteen officers and men, and some injury sustained by the Cincinnati. This vessel was struck four times, two of the shots passing through upper decks. We damaged the nearest fort, and, had not darkness prevented, would have silenced it, as their men at one time were seen running from it. The place is stronger and more difficult to take than Columbus ever was, as a long line of forts on the river command one another. The mortar boats do well, and, had we a place to put them out of sight of the forts, we could soon shell out the rebels. They have done good execution as it is. I will write as soon as possible.

A. H. FOOTE, *Flag-Officer.*

Hon. GIDEON WELLES,
Secretary of the Navy.

Lieutenant Commanding Gwin's report of reconnoissance to Chickasaw, Alabama.

UNITED STATES GUNBOAT TYLER,
Pittsburg, March 16, 1862.

SIR: I have the honor to report that, in obedience to your orders, I reported to General Grant, at Fort Foote, on the 7th instant, and remained at Danville bridge, twenty-five miles above, awaiting the fleet of transports, until Monday morning, by direction of General Grant, when General Smith arriving with a large portion of his command, forty transports, I convoyed them to Savannah, arriving there without molestation on the 11th. The same evening, with General Smith and staff on board, made a reconnoissance of the river as high as Pittsburg. The rebels had not renewed their attempts to fortify at that point, owing to the vigilant watch that had been kept on them in my absence by Lieutenant Commanding Shirk.

The same evening, at 11.45, stood up the river with the Lexington, Lieutenant Commanding Shirk, for the purpose of reaching Eastport by daylight, it having been reported to me that the rebels had erected a battery at Chickasaw, Alabama, one and a half mile above that place. Arriving there at 7.30, this vessel and the Lexington opened fire on the point which had been indicated. The rebels immediately responded. After expending sixty-three shell, having accomplished my object, which was to ascertain the strength of their battery, both vessels retired without any damage having been done on our side. As well as I can judge, their battery consists of five pieces—three rifled, and, with the exception of one, I should think, not less than 32-pounders. Both vessels have since been actively employed in convoying transports to and covering the landing of troops at different points above Savannah in this river.

The river is again very high, and rising. The people have given substantial evidence of the strength of the Union sentiment so often expressed to me before in this vicinity, as very many have enlisted in the different regiments. The Tyler is lying at Pittsburg for the protection of General Sherman's division, which has occupied that point. The Lexington is lying at Crump's landing, protecting the division of General Wallace, which occupies that point. Everything is working favorably for the cause of the Union. Enclosed you will find Lieutenant Commanding Shirk's report.

I have the honor to be, &c.,

WILLIAM GWIN,
Lieutenant, Commanding Division of Gunboats, Tennessee River.

Flag-Officer A. H. FOOTE, U. S. N.,
Commanding Naval Forces, Western Waters.

Lieutenant Commanding Shirk's report of proceedings, March 15, 1862.

UNITED STATES GUNBOAT LEXINGTON,
Pittsburg, Tennessee, March 15, 1862.

SIR: I have the honor to make the following report of my proceedings since my last arrival in this river.

We reached Savannah on the 6th instant. The next morning I received on board this vessel twenty armed men, refugees from Wayne county, Tennessee, who asked my protection from the rebel marauding cavalry. Six of these men were from a rebel regiment which had been stationed at Clarksville, and had been told, upon the fall of Fort Donelson, to make the best of their way home. Their arms were those that had been issued at Clarksville. Some of these twenty men have shipped on board this vessel, and the remainder have enlisted in regiments in General Smith's command.

I then proceeded up the river to take a look at this place, and discovered several flags of truce on the hill. I sent a boat to communicate with a rebel officer at the landing, and received a letter from Lieutenant Commanding Gwin in relation to exchange of prisoners. No work had been done since the bombardment of the place on the 1st instant by the Tyler and this vessel. The nights of the 7th and 8th I lay at Craven's landing, protecting many Union men from Robinson's rebel cavalry. During the 8th and 9th I conveyed about one hundred and twenty refugees from Craven's and Chalk bluff to Savannah for safety. On the 9th I paid another visit to Pittsburg, having on board Colonel Worthington, of General Smith's advance. On the 10th I took on board some more arms at Chalk bluff. That night I lay opposite Savannah, the transport with the forty-sixth Ohio volunteers lying at the town.

On the 11th the United States gunboat Tyler arrived, followed by General Smith with his command, in sixty-three transport steamers. At midnight this vessel followed the Tyler up the river, to make a reconnoissance, and at 7.20 a. m. on the 12th instant reached Chickasaw, Alabama, where we discovered that the rebels had erected a battery, as had been reported. The two gunboats opened fire upon it at long range, which was returned by the enemy. This vessel expended twenty-five shell. There were no casualties. The battery consisted of at least five pieces, two or three of which were rifled. One of the latter was a 32-pounder, and had a very great range—great enough to prevent the landing of troops at Eastport. At 11.30 a. m. we reached Savannah again. That evening I convoyed a division of the army, under General Wallace, to Crump's landing, and lay there that night and the following day and night. This morning I convoyed another division, under General Hurlburt, to this place, and went on with the transport Crescent City to where General Sherman had his command, about ten miles below Eastport. I returned at 5 p. m., and will await here further orders.

There are no rebel troops near here at present; General Cheatham, who was at Shiloh (three miles back from here) day before yesterday, having gone with his command to Purdy. The river is rising very rapidly, and there is so much back water that General Sherman found it impossible to perform the duty upon which he was sent. General Wallace succeeded, night before last, in destroying about half a mile of the railroad, a few miles north of Purdy. Twelve new-made graves have been found upon the hill at this place. The small arms which I have taken from Craven's and Chalk bluff belong to Union men, and I have promised that they should eventually be returned to their owners.

I have the honor to be, &c.,

JAMES W. SHIRK, *Lieutenant Commanding.*

Flag-Officer A. H. FOOTE,
Commanding Naval Forces, &c.

Flag-Officer Foote's report of operations at, and capture of, Island No. 10, *and correspondence connected therewith.*

UNITED STATES FLAG-STEAMER BENTON,
Off Island No. 10, *March* 17, 1862.

SIR: Leaving Cairo on the 14th instant with seven iron-clad gunboats and ten mortar boats, and being joined at Columbus on the same day by Colonel Buford, in command of some twelve hundred troops, I reached Hickman that evening with the flotilla and transports, when the Louisville, Commander Dove, was found leaking in her boilers, and was sent back to Columbus for repairs.

On the 15th instant, at daylight, the flotilla and transports moved down the river, arriving in the vicinity of Island No. 10 at 9 a. m. The rain and dense fog prevented our getting the vessels in position, other than two mortar boats, for the purpose of ascertaining their range.

Early on the morning of the 16th instant I placed the mortars in as good position as the circumstances would admit, when they shelled several regiments out of their encampments, and, at extreme range, reached the batteries on No. 10, the floating battery, and the five batteries on the Tennessee shore. The mortar boats are in charge of Captain Maynadier, United States army, as ordnance officer, assisted by Acting Lieutenant Commanding J. P. Sandford, United States navy, who volunteered his services.

This morning, the 17th instant, soon after daylight, the mortar boats being in position, I had the Benton lashed between two other steamers, the Cincinnati and St. Louis, and with the remaining iron-clad steamers made an attack on the forts, at a distance of two thousand yards or more, on account of the rapid current, rendering the boats too unmanageable to come within a shorter range, without endangering their being carried under the enemy's guns; and as a nearer approach would expose the bow and quarter of the vessels, their most vulnerable points, to a fire of six other batteries, mounting forty-three guns. We opened fire on the upper fort on the Tennessee shore at meridian, and continued to give and receive quite a brisk fire from this and also four other batteries on the same shore until darkness obscured the forts from view. The ten mortars, in the mean time, shelled the troops out of range, excepting those manning the batteries.

The upper fort was badly cut up by the Benton and the other boats with her. We dismounted one of their guns, and the men, at times, ran from the batteries.

Colonel Buford has been busily, and, I trust, profitably, engaged in making reconnoissances, and is preparing to mount his siege guns.

In the attack of to-day this vessel received four shots; while a rifle gun burst aboard the St. Louis, killing and wounding fifteen, officers and men; I enclose a list of casualties. The Cincinnati has had her engines injured, which may render it necessary for me to send her to Cairo for repairs.

I hope to be able to silence the upper battery to-morrow; after which we can plant the mortars in a position where we expect to be able to shell the rebels out of their batteries. This place is even stronger and better adapted for defence than Columbus has ever been. Each fortification commands the one above it. We can count forty-nine guns in the different batteries, where there are probably double the number, with ten thousand troops.

From exhaustion, arising from continuous service and want of sleep, you will excuse this incoherent discursive report.

Our shells bursting prematurely we have to drown them before loading the guns. The fuzes, many of which, I am informed, were made before the Mexican war, ought to have been condemned.

I have the honor to be, very respectfully, your obedient servant,

A. H. FOOTE,
Flag-Officer, Comd'g Naval Forces, Western Waters.

Hon. GIDEON WELLES,
Secretary of the Navy.

List of killed and wounded on gunboat St. Louis, March 17, 1862.

Killed, by bursting of a rifle gun, Jas. Jackson, seaman, Chicago, Illinois; P. S. Goth, seaman, Maine.

Wounded, by bursting of rifle gun, S. H. McAdam, master's mate, Chicago, severely; John A. McDonald, gunner, Baltimore, slightly; H. T. Bly, seaman, New Bedford, severely; J. W. Sprowl, seaman, Bristol, Maine, severely; P. Mulhenin, seaman, Boston, Massachusetts, severely; Wm. Kelcher, seaman, Boston, Massachusetts, severely; Rich'd Gouger, seaman, severely; Frank Clemens, seaman, severely; Charles Wolf, seaman, severely; Charles Wilson, seaman, Philadelphia, severely; Henry Joy, seaman, Worcester county, Massachusetts, slightly; M. C. Donaghho, seaman, Fredericktown, Pennsylvania, slightly; Peroc Leon, seaman, Sardinia, slightly.

J. B. McDILL,
Assistant Surgeon, United States Gunboat St. Louis.

Respectfully submitted.

LEONARD PAULDING, *Lieutenant Commanding.*

FLAG-STEAMER BENTON,
Off Island No. 10, *March* 19, 1862.

SIR: On the 17th instant I communicated to the department an account of our leaving Cairo for the purpose of attacking Island No. 10, and expressing the hope that to-morrow (yesterday) we should be able to capture the upper fort at this point.

Yesterday we were firing on the upper fort at long range, reaching it occasionally, and dismounted another gun, while the mortars were playing on the lower fortifications, having driven the encampments down the river, just out of range of our shells. As the forts are distinct from each other, and occupy but little space, and have been mostly constructed for four or five months, it is impossible to use the mortars with as much effect as could have been done at Columbus, where the batteries were more compact and exposed, and the troops having less shelter than here. We are, however, keeping up an occasional fire day and night, to prevent the enemy from repairing his damages, gradually approaching his strongest holds, and I trust we will be able, in co-operation with General Pope's division of the army, soon to get possession of the place. This position was selected by the rebels on account of its being inaccessible by land, in a high stage of water, on the Missouri side, which side General Pope's army occupies, at New Madrid; and he has no transports of any kind with which to cross over to the Tennessee side and march in upon the rear of the rebels. I have this morning sent him two tugs, and hope to be able to get two gunboats also through the same bayou or slough to him. If we can do this, with the two gunboats coming up and attacking the forts from below with the land attack, I have no doubt but that we shall secure a complete victory. We must proceed here slowly and cautiously, which alone can prove effective, especially bearing in mind the rapid current and certainty of falling into the hands of the enemy in these slow boats if we run as close to the batteries as we might do were the rebels up stream. Colonel Buford, commanding the troops here, amounting to about 1,500, will be ready to perform all service required until the arrival of General Pope in force. We shall not be able to make the grand attack for several days. This will depend upon the arrival of General Pope.

Your obedient servant,

A. H. FOOTE, *Flag Officer.*

Hon. GIDEON WELLES, *Secretary of the Navy.*

FLAG-STEAMER BENTON,
Off Island No. 10, *March* 20, 1862.

SIR: Most of the iron-clad steamers, including this vessel, are still lying within long range of the rebel forts, and occasionally, with the mortar-boats, are throwing shells into the enemy's batteries, which have induced them to withdraw all their superfluous men not required for serving their guns. To-day the upper battery opened upon us, but was silenced in half an hour, this ship dismounting a gun. I send, to-night, a boat to sound in a narrow and shallow channel, in hopes the present rise of water in the river will enable me to despatch a small steamer with light draught to General Pope, near New Madrid, who, as I have already informed the department, has several times requested that I would send him two or three gunboats to enable him to cross over to the Tennessee side, with the view of attacking the rebels in the rear at this point, while we make the attack in front or on the river side. I am apprehensive, however, from our ill success thus far, that this project may not prove feasible. To-day, for the first time since I have been in command of the flotilla, I called a council of war, with the view of ascertaining the opinions of the officers with reference to sending, or attempting to send, aid to General Pope. The officers, with one exception, were decidedly opposed to running the blockade, believing it would result in the almost certain destruction of the boats which should attempt to pass the six forts, with fifty guns bearing upon the vessels. I have been seriously disposed to run the blockade myself with this vessel, which is better protected than the other boats, although she is slow and works sluggishly; but, upon reconsideration, as her loss would be so great if we failed, and my personal services here are considered so important with the fleet and transports, I have, for the present, abandoned the idea.

This place is admirably chosen for defence by the rebels, as its rear can only be approached, in this stage of water, from the river side opposite New Madrid, it being surrounded by bayous or sloughs, while its long line of six forts, commanding one another from the river front, render it almost impregnable to an attacking force. General Pope has no transports, and, without our reaching him by running the blockade, is unable to cross over to the Tennessee side from New Madrid, where he now is in force, and it is impossible for him, from the inundated state of the country, to send or march his troops to this point. Were we to attempt to attack these heavy batteries with the gunboats, or attempt to run the blockade and fail, as I have already stated in a former communication, the rivers above us—Mississippi, Ohio, and Cumberland—would be greatly exposed, not only frustrating the grand object of the expedition, but exposing our towns and cities bordering those rivers; especially so should General Pope be unable to hold his position at New Madrid. Under these circumstances, and our boats being so ill-adapted to fighting down the river, with two rifle guns having burst, and our shells imperfect, I am induced to act with great caution, and expose the flotilla less than under more favorable circumstances it would be my duty to do, for the great object for which the fleet was created. For the future, in the absence of instructions from higher authority, I shall be governed by circumstances as they may arise. When the object of running the blockade becomes adequate to the risk, I shall not hesitate to do it. The place may be occupied by us in a short time without an assault, as the rebels must be cut off from their necessary supplies. Still, if this does not soon take place, it may become necessary to force the blockade, or adopt some other measures which have not yet suggested themselves.

Your obedient servant,

A. H. FOOTE, *Flag-Officer.*

Hon. GIDEON WELLES,
Secretary of the Navy.

UNITED STATES FLAG-SHIP BENTON,
Island No. 10, *March* 26, 1862.

SIR: Since my communication of the 20th instant we have been lying off the forts at long range, occasionally giving a rifle shot, and more frequently throwing mortar shells upon the island and at the fortifications on the Tennessee shore. The rebels still hold the forts, but the encampments are moved beyond range, with a sufficient number of men to serve their heavy guns, which seem to be well protected from our shells by their breastworks. A communication from General Halleck (a copy of which is enclosed) leads me to hope that we may yet derive support from the army, irrespective of General Pope's force, which will cross over from New Madrid and attack the rebels in the rear, while we make the attack in front, in case we succeed in getting two steamers and several cutters, which are now working their way towards that point, through the bayous or sloughs. Should this effort be successful, I hope to hear that a land force of some 10,000 men will be in the rebels' rear in the course of five or six days. With the exception of a ridge, or higher land, on the river bank on the Tennessee side, from directly opposite New Madrid to nearly opposite Island No. 10, the whole country is inundated, or at least so much so as to prevent troops from other points reaching the rebels' rear, showing how admirably their position has been chosen for defence.

We now have here six iron-plated gunboats, one wooden gunboat, the Conestoga, and sixteen mortar-boats; one iron-clad gunboat being at Nashville, one guarding Columbus and Hickman, and two wooden boats up the Tennessee; while the Essex, Commander Porter, is repairing at St. Louis. We have all the mortar-boats that we can use to any advantage, and still want two tow-boats for these in greater force, as we have a strong current, requiring the greatest vigilance to prevent them and the gunboats from being carried down stream, from the want of steam-power of the latter. Colonel Buford, commanding the troops, has a force of between 1,900 and 2,000 men; but who, in fact, living as they necessarily do, aboard the transports—the banks being overflowed, and they surrounded by water—cannot accomplish anything of consequence. Thus we are waiting to open communication with General Pope, at New Madrid.

I forward herewith a copy of a letter sent to me by General Strong, commanding at Cairo, from which it will be seen that the rebels have thirteen gunboats, independent of the five below New Madrid, and the Manassas, or ram, at Memphis. I presume that these boats are not equal to ours; still, we have no means of ascertaining their character, especially those at New Orleans. I have ordered the rifle guns as they arrive at Cairo to be sent to us, as our rifles are unsafe, and must be condemned as soon as others can be supplied. The rifle shells, as well as those of the 8-inch guns and thirty-twos, also burst prematurely, and I have been obliged to drown all fuses at a distance exceeding one thousand yards.

I shall proceed with caution in our work here, being fully aware of our disadvantages. If, however, any disaster should occur, from circumstances beyond my control, I have ordered the two iron-clad gunboats Cairo and Louisville, with the wooden boats Tyler and Lexington, to meet at Cairo, or as far down as Columbus and even Hickman, to prevent the rebel gunboats from ascending the river beyond Cairo, which place is now so nearly overflowed as to render it necessary for us to remove all our ammunition.

I have the honor to be, &c.,

A. H. FOOTE, *Flag-Officer.*

Hon. GIDEON WELLES,
Secretary of the Navy.

P. S.—Were we able even to shell the forces out of their fortifications, they would reoccupy as we passed down the river, as we have less than 2,000 troops to take possession.

A. H. F.

Letter from General Halleck to Flag-Officer Foote.

HEADQUARTERS DEPARTMENT OF THE MISSISSIPPI,
St. Louis, March 21, 1862.

SIR: I have just received your report (without date) of your operations against the enemy's batteries in the vicinity of Island No. 10. While I am certain that you have done everything that could be done successfully to reduce these works, I am very glad that you have not unnecessarily exposed your gunboats. If they had been disabled it would have been a most serious loss to us in the future operations of the campaign; whereas the reduction of these batteries this week or next, is a matter of very little importance indeed. I think it will turn out in the end that it is much better for us that they are not reduced till we can fully cut off the retreat of their troops.

Everything is now progressing well on the Tennessee river toward opening your way down the Mississippi. The reduction of these works is only a question of time, and we are in no hurry on that point. Nothing is lost by a little delay *there.* I am directing all my attention now to another object, and when that is accomplished the enemy must evacuate or surrender.

Very respectfully, your obedient servant,

H. W. HALLECK,
Major General Commanding.

Flag-Officer A. H. FOOTE,
Commanding Naval Forces, &c.

Letter from General Strong to Flag-Officer Foote.

HEADQUARTERS UNITED STATES FORCES,
Cairo, Illinois, March 24, 1862.

MY DEAR COMMODORE: I enclose you a copy of a letter received this morning from Captain Dresser. It contains important information relating to movements of the enemy down the river. I have sent General Pope, also Colonel Buford, a copy of the same.

Very truly, yours,

W. K. STRONG,
Brigadier General Commanding.

Flag-Officer FOOTE,
On the Benton, near Island No 10.

CAIRO, *Illinois, March* 24, 1862.

GENERAL: I left Savannah, Tennessee, yesterday morning, and while at Perrysville, some forty miles this side of Savannah, we took on board a man by the name of M. A. Clark, formerly of Paducah, Kentucky, late of New Orleans. He left New Orleans a week ago last Thursday; I gained from him the following statement: Fort Pillow was being evacuated when he was at Memphis last Wednesday; confederates moving all their stores from Memphis to Corinth. The heavy guns of Fort Pillow were left under water; Beauregard was at Jackson on Thursday last; would leave with his troops on Friday for Corinth. Eleven engines and two hundred cars were taken from the Mississippi Central railroad to the Memphis and Charleston railroad, to move Johnson's forces from Decatur to Corinth. Confederates are building thirteen gunboats at New Orleans—twelve of them for river and one for sea service. One—Murray's boat—carries thirty guns; would be ready last week, and balance this week; were to come up the river as soon as finished; Bragg and Polk were at Corinth.

Very respectfully,

JASPAR M. DRESSER, *Captain.*

Brigadier General STRONG,
Commanding, Cairo.

Letter from Flag-Officer Foote to General Halleck.

BENTON, *off No.* 10, *March* 26, 1862.

GENERAL: In view of the rebels having, as is reported, thirteen gunboats at New Orleans, irrespective of four or five below New Madrid, with the Manassas, or ram, at Memphis, I respectfully suggest, in view of the contingency of their passing up the river, that it would be desirable to have a river battery placed at Columbus which would sweep the river below that point. Cairo, being now almost overflowed, presents a less defensible position than Columbus.

I am, sir, very respectfully, &c.,

A. H. FOOTE, *Flag-Officer.*

Major General H. W. HALLECK,
Commanding, St. Louis, Missouri.

FLAG-STEAMER BENTON,
Island No. 10, *March* 26, 1862.

SIR: You will inform the commander of the gunboats Cairo, Tyler, and Lexington, not to be caught up the rivers with too little water to return to Cairo. They, of course, before leaving, will consult the generals with whom they are co-operating. As it is reported, on the authority of different persons from New Orleans, that the rebels have thirteen gunboats finished and ready to move up the Mississippi, besides the four or five below New Madrid and the Manassas, or ram, at Memphis, the boats now up the rivers and at Columbus or Hickman should be ready to protect Cairo or Columbus, in case disaster overtakes us in our flotilla. * * * * *

Respectfully, &c.,

A. H. FOOTE, *Flag-Officer.*

Commander PENNOCK, *Cairo, Illinois.*

Letter from Flag-Officer Foote, enclosing report of Colonel Roberts.

UNITED STATES FLAG-STEAMER BENTON,
Off Island No. 10, *April* 2, 1862.

Last night an armed boat expedition was fitted out from the squadron and the land forces at this point, under command of Colonel Roberts, of the 42d Illinois regiment.

The five boats comprising the expedition were in charge of First Master J. V. Johnson, of the St. Louis, assisted by Fourth Master G. P. Lord, of the Benton; Fourth Master Pierce, of the Cincinnati; Fourth Master Norgan, of the Pittsburg, and Master's Mate Scoville, of the Mound City, each with a boat's crew of ten men from their respective vessels, carrying in all one hundred men, exclusive of officers, under command of Colonel Roberts.

At midnight the boats reached the upper or No. 1 fort, and, pulling directly in its face, carried it, receiving only the harmless fire of two sentinels, who ran on discharging their muskets, while the rebel troops in the vicinity rapidly retreated; whereupon Colonel Roberts spiked the six guns mounted in the fort and retired with the boats uninjured.

The commanding officer represents all under his command, from their coolness and determination, as being ready to perform more hazardous service had it been required to the fulfilment of the object of the expedition. Enclosed is the report of Colonel Roberts.

I have the honor to be, very respectfully, &c., your servant,

A. H. FOOTE, *Flag-Officer.*

Hon. GIDEON WELLES,
Secretary of the Navy.

ON BOARD STEAMER MEMPHIS, *April* 2, 1862.

In obedience to your orders, I have the honor to report that last evening, at half past five o'clock, I took command of an expedition designed against the rebel battery No. 1, on the Tennessee shore. My force consisted of five boats furnished by the gunboats Benton, St. Louis, Cincinnati, Pittsburg, and Mound City, manned by crews of these boats, respectively, and transporting a detachment of fifty men from company A, 42d regiment Illinois volunteers.

My first endeavor was to proceed through the overflowed woodland on the Kentucky shore, and thus escape observation; this proved to be impracticable, as well because of the fall of the river as of the large amount of drift accumulated among the trees. We then dropped down to the first mortar boat and lay by until 11 o'clock p. m, when all the boats were got under way and proceeded, one after the other, keeping close under the shadow of the shore. The Benton's boat led until the outlines of battery No. 1 wer well defined, when the order of attack, the suggestion of First Master J. V. Johnson, was taken up as follows: The boats of the St. Louis, Benton, and Pittsburg advanced in line, the Benton's boat in the centre; the remaining boats followed a few yards behind.

We approached the battery with muffled oars, in such silence that we were less than ten yards distant when the sentinels at the guns discovered us. They cried out in great surprise, fired twice on our boats, and ran away. We landed in good order and with great expedition, the rear boats falling to the right and left of the centre boat of the advanced line, and at once commenced spiking the guns. Lieutenant Church, with twenty men, advanced toward the supposed rebel camp to anticipate an attack, and, at the same time, protect the men engaged in spiking the guns. No such attack was made.

The work was done with perfect coolness on the part of our men, but as rapidly as possible, for the rebel gunboat Grampus had taken alarm at the sentinels' fire, and was standing toward us. I did not go on board to return until I had first personally inspected every gun. I report, sir, that every gun in the battery except one (dismounted and lying in the water) was spiked by our party. I believe the spiking will prove effectual. The object of the expedition being thus accomplished, we took to our boats and returned without any loss whatever.

To the naval officers in command of the boats great praise is due for the admirable manner in which our approach was conducted. The officers of the detachments were prompt and efficient, while the men of both land forces and marines, by their implicit obedience of orders, have proved themselves worthy of any service whatever. The kindness of Captain Phelps, of the Benton, in giving personal attention to the outfit of the expedition, is kindly remembered.

I am, sir, respectfully, your obedient servant,

GEO. W. ROBERTS,
Colonel Commanding 42d Regiment Illinois Volunteers.

Flag-Officer A. H. FOOTE.

CAIRO, *April* 4, 1862.

This morning the Benton, Cincinnati, and Pittsburg, with three mortar boats, opened, and continued for more than an hour a fire on the rebels' heavy floating battery at Island No. 10, when the latter, having received several shells from the rifles and mortars, cut loose from her moorings and drifted down the river two or three miles. The shells were thrown from the flotilla into different forts of the island and into the rebel batteries lining the Tennessee shore. The return fire produced no effect on the squadron. No more men than were actually necessary to man the batteries were visible.

A. H. FOOTE, *Flag-Officer, &c.*

Hon. GIDEON WELLES,
Secretary of the Navy.

FLAG-STEAMER BENTON,
Off Island No. 10, *April* 6, 1862.

SIR: I have the honor to inform the department that the gunboat Carondelet ran the blockade on the night of the 4th instant, under a heavy fire of forty-seven guns, and reached New Madrid safely, without even receiving a shot. Captain Walke, his officers and crew, merit the commendation of the government for their gallantry, coolness, and general conduct on this occasion. I would especially call the attention of the department to the acting first master, Mr. Hoel, of Cincinnati, who so creditably volunteered his services to go in the Carondelet, and did go in her, although he was attached to the gunboat Cincinnati.

I enclose a correspondence, or a copy of it, between Major General Pope, at New Madrid, and myself, in relation to another gunboat attempting to run the blockade for his relief or assistance.

The rebels are very strongly fortified here, and seem determined to do all in their power to maintain their position. I trust, however, when General Pope crosses with his army and moves upon their rear that we shall be able, by an attack in front, to carry the place.

I have the honor to be, very respectfully, your obedient servant,

A. H. FOOTE, *Flag-Officer.*

Hon. Gideon Welles,
Secretary of the Navy.

Instructions to Commander Walke.

United States Flag-Steamer Benton,
Off Island No. 10, *March* 30, 1862.

Sir: You will avail yourself of the first fog or rainy night, and drift your steamer down past the batteries on the Tennessee shore and Island No. 10, until you reach New Madrid.

I assign you this service, as it is vitally important to the capture of this place that a gunboat should soon be at New Madrid for the purpose of covering General Pope's army while he crosses at that point to the opposite or to the Tennessee side of the river, that he may move his army up to Island No. 10, and attack the rebels in rear while we attack them in front.

Should you succeed in reaching General Pope, you will freely confer with him, and adopt his suggestions, so far as your superior knowledge of what your boat will perform will enable you to do, for the purpose of protecting his force while crossing the river.

You will also, if you have coal, and the current of the river will permit, steam up the river when the army moves, for the purpose of attacking their fortifications. Still you will act cautiously here, as your own will be the only boat below.

You will capture or destroy the rebel steam gunboat Grampus, and the transports, if possible, between this place and No. 10, at such time as will not embarrass you in placing yourself in communication with General Pope at the earliest possible time after leaving this place.

On this delicate and somewhat hazardous service to which I assign you I must enjoin upon you the importance of keeping your lights secreted in the hold or put out, keeping your officers and men from speaking at all when passing the forts, above a whisper, and then only on duty, and of using every other precaution to prevent the rebels suspecting that you are dropping below their batteries.

If you successfully perform this duty assigned you, which you so willingly undertake, it will reflect the highest credit upon you and all belonging to your vessel, and I doubt not but that the government will fully appreciate and reward you for a service which, I trust, will enable the army to cross the river and make a successful attack in rear while we storm the batteries in front of this stronghold of the rebels.

Commending you and all who compose your command to the care and protection of God, who rules the world and directs all things, I am, respectfully, your obedient servant,

A. H. FOOTE, *Flag-Officer*.

Commander H. WALKE,
Commanding Carondelet.

P. S.—Should you meet with disaster, you will, as a last resort, destroy the steam machinery, and, if possible to escape, set fire to your gunboat, or sink her, and prevent her from falling into the hands of the rebels.

A. H. F.

UNITED STATES FLAG-STEAMER BENTON,
Off Island No. 10, *April* 4, 1862.

GENERAL: The gunboat Carondelet, Commander Walke, left her anchorage this evening, at 10 o'clock, in a heavy thunder-storm, for the purpose of running the fire of the batteries on Island No. 10 and those lining the Tennessee shore, to join your forces at New Madrid. By a previous concerted signal of three minute-guns, twice fired at intervals of five minutes, which have since been heard, as near as the heavy thunder would enable us to ascertain, leads me to hope that the blockade has been run successfully, although the batteries opened upon her with forty-seven guns while passing.

I am, therefore, so exceedingly anxious to hear the fate of the noble officers and men who so readily were disposed to attempt the hazardous service, that I beg you will immediately inform me by bearer if Commander Walke has arrived with his vessel, and the condition in which you find her and her officers and men.

I am, respectfully, your obedient servant,

A. H. FOOTE, *Flag-Officer*.

Major General JOHN POPE,
Commanding Army at New Madrid, Missouri.

Letter from General Pope to Flag-Officer Foote.

HEADQUARTERS DISTRICT OF THE MISSISSIPPI,
New Madrid, April 5, 1862.

SIR: Your note of yesterday has just been received. Captain Walke arrived safely with the Carondelet, not a shot having touched her. Officers and men are in good condition for service.

I requested Colonel Scott, Assistant Secretary of War, to write to you yesterday in relation to sending another one of the gunboats, and, with profound respect, I venture to urge you still further on the subject. I have not a doubt but that one of them could run the batteries without any serious injury. Notwithstanding their inferior character, the enemy's gunboats pass and repass our batteries in the night without injury.

My best artillerists—officers of the regular army, of many years' experience—state positively that it is impossible, in the night, to fire with any kind of certainty the large guns (32s) of our batteries, especially at a moving object. The shot fired at the Carondelet passed 200 feet above her.

I am thus urgent, sir, because the lives of thousands of men, and the success of our operations, hang upon your decision. With the two boats all is safe; with one it is uncertain. The lives of the men composing this army are in my keeping, and I do not feel justified in omitting any steps to fortify this movement against any accident which might occasion disaster not to be repaired.

Certainly the risk to a gunboat running down in the night is not nearly so great, and involves no such consequences, as the risk to ten thousand men crossing a great river in the face of the enemy.

You will excuse me, I am sure, if I seem urgent. A sense of duty impels me to present the facts as forcibly as possible.

I am, sir, very respectfully, your obedient servant,

JOHN POPE,
Maojr General Commanding.

Flag-Officer A. H. FOOTE,
Commanding Mississippi Flotilla.

Letter from Flag-Officer Foote to General Pope.

FLAG-STEAMER BENTON,
Off Island No. 10, *April* 6, 1862.

GENERAL: Your letter of this day's date, announcing the safe arrival of the Carondelet at New Madrid, was received at 8 o'clock this evening. The telegram of Assistant Secretary Scott reached me a few minutes later.

Colonel Bissel, who has charge of the steamers and barges now in the slough, *en route* to New Madrid, has requested that two tugs, even, might be sent to you, which would, with arrangements he could make, enable you to transport your forces to the opposite side of the river, in case it was deemed inexpedient to send a gunboat for that purpose. You, yourself, in a late letter, apply for a gunboat, our smallest gunboat, even, for that purpose. I could last night, had you made a point of having two gunboats, sent them with comparative safety, as the night was dark, while the vivid lightning enabled the pilots to keep the channel. Again, it is now too late to obtain the hay and other necessary articles for the protection of the gunboat to-night, to say nothing of the clear atmosphere, rendering a boat as visible, or as good an object to sight, as in the daytime. For these reasons I cannot, neither does a single navy officer, and, I presume, not a pilot, in the squadron, consider that a gunboat could run the blockade to-night without an almost certainty of its being sunk in the attempt, especially if the guns were served with any degree of skill or ability whatever.

I am sorry to find the expression in your letter, "The success of our operations hangs upon your (my) decision," especially referring to my directing a gunboat to attempt running the blockade in this clear night; for, in my judgment, and that of all the other officers, the boat might as well expect to run it in the daytime. I cannot consider the running of your blockade, where the river is nearly a mile wide, and only exposed to a few light guns, at all comparable to running it here, where a boat has not only to pass seven batteries, but has to be kept "head on" to a battery of eleven heavy guns at the head of Island No. 10, and to pass within 300 yards of this strong battery. If it did not sink the gunboat, we would, in the navy, consider the gunners totally unfit for employment in the service; and, therefore, my responsibility for the lives of the officers and men under my charge induces me to decline a request which would, especially without protection to the boat, were the rebels at all competent to perform their duty, result in the sacrifice of the boat, her officers, and men, which sacrifice I should not be justified in making—certainly not now, when, by your own admission, it will be easy for the new rebel steamers, reported to be on their way up the river, to pass your batteries in the night, and if they meet my squadron' reduced by loss, so as to be unable to cope with them, can continue up the Mississippi or Ohio to St. Louis or to Cincinnati.

In view, however, of rendering you all the aid you request, and no doubt require, while I regret that you had not earlier expressed the apprehension of the necessity of two gunboats, instead of the smaller gunboat, I will, to-morrow, endeavor to prepare another boat; and if the night is such as will render her running the blockade without serious disaster at all probable, I will make the attempt to send you the additional boat requested in your letter of this day's date.

I am, respectfully, your obedient servant,

A. H. FOOTE,
Flag-Officer Commanding Naval Forces, Western Waters.

Major General JOHN POPE,
Commanding Army at New Madrid.

UNITED STATES FLAG-STEAMER BENTON,
Off Island No. 10, *April* 5, 1862.

SIR: I have the honor to enclose several letters and papers referring to our action here within the last three or four days.

By spiking the rebel guns in one fort, and compelling the floating battery to cut adrift from her moorings on the following day from our effective fire upon her, these have enabled the Carondelet, Commander Walke, to run, as I hope, successfully the blockade, and join General Pope at New Madrid, who has been urging me to send him one or two gunboats to cover his troops while he lands in force to attack them in front. While the Carondelet was running the blockade last night in the midst of a heavy thunder-storm, the batteries opened upon her with forty-seven guns. Still, as the preconcerted signal with that vessel of firing minute guns was made as far as the heavy thunder would enable us to hear, I trust that she is now safely at New Madrid.

I have the honor to be your obedient servant,

A. H. FOOTE, *Flag-Officer.*

Hon. GIDEON WELLES,
Secretary of the Navy, Washington, D. C.

Passage of rebel batteries by the Carondelet.

UNITED STATES GUNBOAT CARONDELET,
New Madrid, April 5, 1862.

SIR: I have the honor to report my arrival here last night, about 1 o'clock, all well. On our way all of the rebel batteries and a large number of infantry opened fire upon us, which was continued until we were out of range. Providentially, no damage was done to the vessel or the officers and crew, who conducted themselves with admirable courage and fidelity. The terrible storm which prevailed at the time rendered it impossible to make any reliable observation.

Most respectfully, sir, your obedient servant,

H. WALKE,
Commander, U. S. Navy.

Flag-Officer A. H. FOOTE,
Commanding U. S. Naval Forces, Western Waters.

[Telegrams.]

STEAMER BENTON,
Off Island No. 10, *April* 7, 1862.

Two officers have this instant boarded us from Island No. 10, stating that, by order of their commanding officer, they are ordered to surrender Island No. 10 to the commodore commanding the gunboats. As these officers knew nothing of the batteries on the Tennessee shore, I have sent Captain Phelps to ascertain something definite on the subject. I will telegraph when further information is received.

With General Pope now advancing from New Madrid in strong force to attack in rear, I am, with the gun and mortar boats, ready to attack in front, while General Buford here is ready to co-operate with the land forces; but it seems as if the place is to be surrendered without further defence.

A. H. FOOTE,
Flag-Officer Commanding Naval Forces, Western Waters.

Hon. GIDEON WELLES,
Secretary of the Navy.

FLAG-STEAMER BENTON,
Off Island No. 10, *April* 8—1 *a. m.*

My telegram, three hours since, informed the department that Island No. 10 had surrendered to the gunboats. Captain Phelps has this instant returned, after having had an interview with the late commandant. I have requested General Buford, commanding the troops, to proceed immediately, in company with two of the gunboats, and take possession of the island. The batteries on the Tennessee shore have been hastily evacuated, where we shall find, no doubt, in the morning, large quantities of munitions of war.

I communicate with General Pope, who has, under cover of the two gunboats which gallantly ran the blockade in the thunder storm, crossed the river in force, and was ready, as well as the gun and mortar boats, with General Buford and his troops, to make a simultaneous attack upon the rebels, had they not so hastily evacuated the Tennessee shore and surrendered Island No. 10.

A full report will be made as soon as we can obtain possession of the land batteries and I am able to communicate with General Pope.

A. H. FOOTE, *Flag-Officer, &c.*

Hon. GIDEON WELLES,
Secretary of the Navy.

[Telegram, *via* Cairo.]

FLAG-STEAMER BENTON,
Off Island No. 10, *April* 8, 1862.

This morning at 2 o'clock, in a heavy thunder-storm, the gunboat Pittsburg, Lieutenant Commanding Thompson, ran the blockade, under fire of seventy-three guns, and has probably reached New Madrid, and is now with the Carondelet, Commodore Walke, as reports of heavy guns are heard opening upon the rebel batteries on the opposite shore, to destroy them, that General Pope, with his army, may land on the Tennessee side, preparatory to moving to attack the rear of the rebels at this place while we attack them in front.

A. H. FOOTE, *Flag-Officer, Commanding.*

Hon. GIDEON WELLES,
Secretary of the Navy, Washington, D. C.

FLAG-STEAMER BENTON,
Island No. 10, *April* 9, 1862.

SIR: I have the honor to enclose a copy of a telegram of my report to the department of the surrender of Island No. 10.

I also send a copy of the rebel navy signals. Commander Kilty, of the gunboat Mound City, captured the signal-book, signals, and telegraphic dictionary. As we shall probably meet the rebel gunboats, I retain the signal-book, which is almost a copy from ours. I will soon send the drawings and plans of the celebrated floating battery, which lies submerged between here and New Madrid.

General Pope is now with me, and reports that he has captured 6,000 prisoners, including three generals. He wishes to move an army of 25,000 men down the river; but as time is important, and I am ready to move with the flotilla, I have asked him to send some 3,000 or 5,000 with us, by which I hope to move on Fort Pillow by day after to-morrow. It is important that an early move should be made on our part on Fort Pillow, before the rebels recover from their panic, and then we are on to Memphis.

I write in the greatest haste, and trust that this incoherent report will be excused.

I have the honor to be, &c.,

A. H. FOOTE, *Flag-Officer.*

Hon. GIDEON WELLES,
Secretary of the Navy.

FLAG-SHIP BENTON,
Island No. 10, *April* 8, 1862, *(via Cairo.)*

I have the honor to inform the department that since I sent the telegram last night, announcing the surrender to me of Island No. 10, possession has been taken of both the island and the works upon the Tennessee shore by the gunboats and the troops under command of General Buford. Seventeen officers and three hundred and sixty-eight privates, besides one hundred of their sick and one hundred men employed on board the transports, are in our hands, unconditional prisoners of war.

I have caused a hasty examination to be made of the forts, batteries, and munitions of war captured. There are eleven earthworks, with seventy heavy cannon, varying in calibre from 32 to 100-pounders, rifled. The magazines are well supplied with powder, and there are large quantities of shot, shells, and other munitions of war, and also great quantities of provisions. Four steamers afloat have fallen into our hands, and two others, with the rebel gunboat Grampus, are sunk, but will be easily raised. The floating battery of sixteen heavy guns, turned adrift by the rebels, is said to be lying on the Missouri shore below New Madrid. Two wharf boats, loaded with provisions, are also in our possession.

The enemy upon the main land appears to have fled with great precipitation after dark last night, leaving, in many cases, half-prepared meals in their quarters; and there seems to have been no concert of action between the rebels upon the island and those occupying the shore, but the latter fled, leaving the former to their fate. These works, erected with the highest engineering skill, are of great strength, and, with their natural advantages, would have been impregnable if defended by men fighting in a better cause.

A combined attack of the naval and land forces would have taken place this afternoon or to-morrow morning had not the rebels abandoned this stronghold. To mature these plans of attack absolutely required the last twenty-three days of preparation. General Pope is momentarily expected to arrive with his army at this point, he having successfully crossed the river yesterday, under a heavy fire, which, no doubt, led to the hasty abandonment of the works last night. I am unofficially informed that the two gunboats which so gallantly ran the fire of the rebel batteries a few nights since yesterday attacked and reduced a fort of the enemy opposite, mounting eight heavy guns.

The following is a copy of the order of General Mackall on assuming command of the rebel forces on the 5th instant:

"HEADQUARTERS, MADRID BEND, *April* 5, 1862.

"SOLDIERS: We are strangers, commander and commanded, each to the other. Let me tell you who I am. I am a general made by Beauregard; a general selected by Beauregard and Bragg for this command when they knew it was in peril. They have known me for twenty years; together we have stood on the fields of Mexico. Give them your confidence now; give it to me when I have earned it.

"Soldiers, the Mississippi valley is intrusted to your courage, to your discipline, to your patience. Exhibit the vigilance and coolness of last night, and hold it.

"W. D. MACKALL,
"*Brigadier General Commanding.*"

I regret that the painful condition of my foot, still requiring me to use crutches, prevented me from making a personal examination of the works. I was therefore compelled to delegate that duty to Lieutenant Commanding S. L. Phelps, of the flag-ship Benton.

I am, sir, respectfully, &c.,

A. H. FOOTE,
Flag Officer, Commanding N. F, Western Waters.

Hon. GIDEON WELLES,
Secretary of the Navy.

Engagement of the Carondelet and Pittsburg with the enemy in the vicinity of New Madrid, April 6, 1862.

UNITED STATES STEAMER BENTON,
Island No. 10, *April* 11, 1862.

SIR: I have the honor to enclose a report from Commander Walke, of the gunboat Carondelet, detailing the services rendered by him and the Pittsburg, Lieutenant Commanding Thompson, in the vicinity of New Madrid, from which it will be seen that the boats opened upon and effectually silenced and captured several heavy batteries on the Tennessee side of the river, on the 6th and 7th instant, without which destruction it would have been impossible for General Pope to have crossed the river for the purpose of attacking the rebels in the rear at No. 10, while the gun and mortar boats would make the attack in front.

There has been an effective and harmonious co-operation between the land and naval forces, which has, under Providence, led to the glorious result of the fall of this stronghold, No. 10, with the garrison and munitions of war, and I regret to see in the despatches of Major General Halleck, from St. Louis, no reference is made to the capture of forts, and the continuous shelling of gun and mortar boats, and the navy's receiving the surrender of No. 10, when, in reality, it should be recorded as an historical fact that both services equally contributed to the victory—a bloodless victory—more creditable to humanity than if thousands had been slain.

I also enclose reports from Lieutenants Commanding Gwin and Shirk, of the gunboats Tyler and Lexington, in the Tennessee, giving a graphic account of that great battle, and the assistance rendered by these boats near Pittsburg; stating that "when the left wing of our army was being driven into the river, at short range, they opened fire upon them, silencing the enemy, and, as I hear from many army officers on the field, totally demoralizing his forces, and driving them from their position in a perfect rout, *in the space of ten minutes.*"

These officers and men, as well as those of Commander Walke, and the officers and men of the Carondelet and Pittsburg, behaved with a degree of gallantry highly creditable to themselves and the navy.

I proceeded to-day, with the entire flotilla, to New Madrid, and leave to-morrow for Fort Pillow, or the next point down the river which may attempt to resist the raising of the blockade.

I have the honor to be, very respectfully, your obedient servant,

A. H. FOOTE, *Flag-Officer.*

Hon. Gideon Welles,
Secretary of the Navy, Washington, D. C.

Report of Commander Walke.

United States Gunboat Carondelet,
Off Tiptonville, Tenn., April 8, 1862.

Sir: In accordance with the instructions of General Pope, I received on board General Grainger and staff on the morning of the 6th instant, and proceeded down the Mississippi river opposite this place, making an extensive reconnoissance.

On our way down we exchanged a few shots with some of the enemy's batteries on the Tennessee side, and on our way back we attacked one of two siege guns, 28-pounders, which had engaged us. We disabled and spiked these guns without receiving any injury. The remainder of the enemy's batteries fired upon us on our way to New Madrid, as long as we were within range.

After my return to New Madrid General Pope informed me of your intention to send another gunboat, and requested that I should go down the river and destroy the remaining rebel batteries above Point Pleasant.

At dawn the following morning, and after a given signal, he would land his army and attack that of the enemy at or near Island No. 10. The Pittsburg did not arrive until 5 o'clock in the morning; but, as the transports, (one at least,) without troops on board, were under way, going down, I got under way at 6.30, (having ordered Commander Thompson verbally, and by signal, to follow my motions,) and proceeded down to the enemy's lower and heaviest battery, consisting of one 64-pound gun and two 64-pound siege howitzers. We opened a constant, deliberate, and well-directed fire upon it for three quarters of an hour, feebly assisted by our batteries on shore, when the enemy slackened his fire. A shot passed through our fourth cutter and starboard quarter, cutting away the sheave of our wheel-rope, striking our stern-gun, and bounding over our stern. About this time the Pittsburg commenced firing at long range, as she came down. As soon as our steering gear was repaired, I gradually closed on the enemy, firing a shot now and then, (the Pittsburg, at a distance astern, throwing shell in a dangerous position across our bow,) until the fort was deserted by the enemy. I spiked and disabled the guns of this fort, and I then proceeded up 300 yards further, and found a 64-pounder siege howitzer dismounted; 300 yards further on I spiked another 64-pounder siege howitzer, and 480 yards further we found a fine 64-pound gun on a pivot, spiked, and being deserted by the enemy, who set fire to a private residence there, and upon whom we fired as they ran off. A large quantity of ammunition was left by them at each fort. I then made the required signal, crossed over to our army, received further instructions from General Pope, and covered their disembarkment on the Tennessee shore, at the captured fort, above Point Pleasant. At evening we steamed down to our camp opposite the enemy's fort at this place, and headed the gunboats for the enemy's battery until early this morning, when we got under way and crossed over to Tiptonville, the enemy having disappeared.

The officers and crew of this vessel, during the trials and dangers of their battles, conducted themselves with admirable coolness and ability; to do justice to many of whom will require a more special letter.

Most respectfully, your obedient servant,

H. WALKE,
Commander, U. S. N.

Flag-Officer A. H. Foote,
Commanding U. S. Naval Forces, Western Waters.

Report of Lieutenant Commander Gwin.

United States Gunboat Tyler,
Pittsburg, Tennessee, April 8, 1862.

Sir: I have the honor to inform you that the enemy attacked our lines on the left the morning of the 6th instant, at 6.30, and, by his overwhelming numbers, forced our men to fall back in some confusion. At 9.25, finding that the rebels were still driving our left wing back, I steamed up to a point one mile above Pittsburg, taking a good position to support our troops, should they be forced down to the banks of the river. At 10.15 the Lexington, Lieutenant Commanding Shirk, joined me, having come up from Crump's landing. After a short time she returned, for the purpose of supporting the command of General Wallace, which occupied that point.

Not having received any instructions from the commanding general in regard to the service to be rendered by the gunboats, I awaited them patiently, although, for an hour or more, shot and shell were falling all around us. Feeling that, could some system of communication be established, the Tyler might be of great advantage to our left wing, at 1.25 p. m. I sent an officer, requesting that I might be allowed to open on the woods in the direction of the batteries and advancing forces of the enemy. General Hurlburt, who commanded on our left, sent me word to do so, giving me directions how to fire that I might do it with no danger to our troops, and expressing himself grateful for this offer of support, saying that without re-enforcements he would not be able to maintain the position he then occupied for an hour. Therefore, at 2.50 I opened fire in the line directed, with good effect, silencing their battery on our left; at 3.50 ceased firing, and dropped down opposite the landing at Pittsburg.

Sent Mr. Peters, gunner, on shore, to communicate with General Grant for further instructions. His reponse was, to use my own judgment in the matter. At 4 p. m. the Lexington, Lieutenant Commanding Shirk, having arrived from Crump's landing, the Tyler, in company with the Lexington, took position three-quarters of a mile above Pittsburg, and opened a heavy fire in the direction of the rebel batteries on their right, the missiles from which were falling all around us. We silenced them in thirty minutes. At 5.30, the rebels having succeeded in gaining a position on our left, an eighth of a mile above the landing at Pittsburg and half a mile from the river, both vessels opened a heavy and well-directed fire on them, and in a short time, in conjunction with our artillery on shore, succeeded in silencing their artillery, driving them back in confusion.

At 6 p. m. the Tyler opened deliberate fire in the direction of the enemy's right wing, throwing 5″ and 10″ shell; at 6.25 ceased firing.

At 9 p. m. the Tyler again opened fire, by direction of General Nelson, (who greatly distinguished himself in yesterday's engagement,) throwing 5″, 10″, and 15″ shell and an occasional shrapnell from the howitzer, at intervals of ten minutes, in the direction of the enemy's right wing, until 1 a. m., when the Lexington relieved us, and continued the fire at intervals of fifteen minutes, till 5 a. m., when, our land forces having attacked the enemy, forcing them gradually back, it made it dangerous for the gunboats to fire.

At 7 I received a communication from General Grant—enclosed is a copy—which prevented the gunboats taking an active part throughout the rest of the day. Lieutenant Commanding Shirk deserves the highest praise for the efficient manner in which the battery of the Lexington was served. At 5.35 p. m. the enemy were forced to retreat in haste, having contested every inch of ground with great stubbornness during the entire day.

The officers and men of this vessel displayed their usual gallantry and enthusiasm during the entire day and night. Your "old wooden boats," I feel confident, rendered invaluable service, on the 6th instant, to the land forces. Gunner Herman Peters deserves great credit for the prompt and courageous manner in which he traversed our lines, conveying communications from this vessel to the commanding general.

The rebels had a force of 100,000 men; A. S. Johnson, (killed—body found on the field,) Beauregard, Hardee, Bragg, and Polk being their commanding generals. Governor Johnson, provisional governor of Kentucky, is a prisoner in our hands, mortally wounded. Loss severe on both sides; ours probably 10,000; the rebels suffered a much greater one. I think this has been a crushing blow to the rebellion.

I am happy to state that no casualties occurred on either of the gunboats.

The Tyler expended 188 shell, four solid shot, two stand of grape, and six shrapnell. Enclosed I send you Lieutenant Commanding Shirk's report.

Your obedient servant,

WM. GWIN,

Lieutenant Commanding Division of Gunboats on Tennessee River.

Flag-Officer A. H. FOOTE,

Commanding Naval Forces on Western Waters.

Report of Lieutenant Commander Shirk.

UNITED STATES GUNBOAT LEXINGTON,

Pittsburg, Tennessee, April 8, 1862.

SIR: On the morning of the 6th instant, while lying at Crump's landing, I heard severe cannonading in the direction of Pittsburg. I got under way, and stood up the river to communicate with Lieutenant Commanding Gwin, of the Tyler.

Upon my reaching this place I found that an attack had been made by the rebels in force. I returned to Crump's to support the division under command of General Lew. Wallace, when I found that his division had proceeded to join the main force, back of Pittsburg landing.

I then steamed back to this place, and no instructions reaching the gunboats from the commanding general on shore, we were forced to remain inactive hearers of the desperate fight, until the left wing of our forces having been forced back and completely turned, and the rebels getting so near the river that the missiles from their batteries fell thick and fast over and around us, enabled us to use our great guns with such effect that the fire of the enemy was silenced in thirty minutes.

This was between 4.10 and 4.40 p. m. Again, at 5.35, the enemy having gained a position on the left of our lines, within an eighth of a mile of the landing and of the transports, we again, with the Tyler, opened fire upon them, silencing the enemy, and, as I hear from many army officers on the field, totally demoralizing his forces, and driving them from their position, in a perfect rout, *in the space of ten minutes*.

The firing on the part of the land forces then ceased. At eight o'clock I went down to Crump's landing, and finding that everything was quiet there returned to this place.

At 1 a. m. on the 7th I relieved the Tyler, Lieutenant Commanding Gwin, in a position immediately above the landing, and fired, until daylight, a shell every fifteen minutes into the enemy's camp.

Yesterday, at daylight, the fight recommenced between the two parties on shore, and continued until 5 p. m., when the enemy made a hurried retreat.

The gunboats occupying a position on the left of our lines not being allowed to fire, I spent the morning and part of the afternoon in acts of mercy—picking up the wounded who had found their way to the river and conveying them to the hospital boats.

I must say that the gallantry and good conduct of the officers and men whom I have the honor to command, displayed upon this occasion, as often before, are beyond all praise.

I have the honor to be, sir, your most obedient servant,

JAMES W. SHIRK,
Lieutenant Commanding.

Flag-Officer A. H. FOOTE,
United States Navy, Commanding United States
Naval Forces on Western Waters, Cairo, Illinois.

Thanks of the department to certain officers.

NAVY DEPARTMENT, *April* 12, 1862.

SIR: The department desires you to convey to Commander Henry Walke and the officers and men of the Carondelet, also to Acting First Master Hoel, of the Cincinnati, who volunteered for the occasion, its thanks for the gallant and successful service rendered in running the Carondelet past the rebel batteries on the night of the 4th instant. It was a daring and heroic act, well executed, and deserving of special recognition.

Commendation is also to be extended to the officers and crew of the Pittsburg, who, in like manner, on the night of the 7th instant performed a similar service. These fearless acts dismayed the enemy, enabled the army under General Pope to cross the Mississippi and eventuated in the surrender to yourself of Island No. 10, and finally in the capture, by General

Pope, of the forts on the Tennessee shore, and the retreating rebels under General Mackall.

I would also, in this connexion, render the acknowledgments which are justly due the officers and crews of the several boats who, in conjunction with a detachment of the forty-second Illinois regiment, under Colonel Roberts, captured the first rebel battery and spiked the guns on Island No. 10 on the night of the 1st instant. Such services are duly appreciated by the department, which extends its thanks to all who participated in the achievement.

I am, respectfully, your obedient servant,

GIDEON WELLES.

Flag-Officer A. H. Foote,
Commanding Gunboat Flotilla, &c., Cairo, Illinois.

Destruction of trestle-work of the Memphis and Charleston railroad.

United States Gunboat Tyler,
Pittsburg, Tennessee, April 14, 1862.

I have the honor to inform you that the Tyler and Lexington convoyed two transports, containing two thousand troops, infantry and cavalry, under the command of General Sherman, to Chickasaw, Alabama, where they disembarked and proceeded rapidly to Bear Creek bridge, the crossing of the Memphis and Charleston railroad, for the purpose of destroying it and as much of the trestle-work as they could find.

I am happy to state that the expedition was entirely successful. The bridge, consisting of two spans, one hundred and ten feet each, was completely destroyed, (*i. e.*, the superstructure,) together with some five hundred feet of trestle-work and half a mile of telegraph line.

The rebels made a feeble resistance to our cavalry, one hundred and twenty in number, but soon made a hasty retreat, losing four killed; our loss, none.

I regret to state that, in firing a salute on the 12th, John D. Seymour, boatswain's mate, was so much injured by the premature discharge of a gun as to cause his death yesterday morning.

Allow me to congratulate you, and those under your command, on your great success at Island No. 10. Enclosed I send you Lieutenant Commanding Shirk's report.

Very respectfully, &c.,

WILLIAM GWIN,
Lieutenant, Commanding Division of Gunboats on Tennessee River.

Flag-Officer A. H. Foote,
Commanding Naval Forces, Western Waters.

Flag-Officer Foote reports having gone to New Madrid from Island No. 10.

Flag-Steamer Benton,
Off Fort Pillow, April 14, 1862.

Sir: I have the honor to report that on the 11th instant I proceeded with the flotilla from Island No. 10 to New Madrid, and left that place with all our force on the 12th instant, and anchored the same evening near and just below the Arkansas line, fifty miles distant from New Madrid.

Early in the morning General Pope, with transports conveying his army of twenty thousand men, arrived from New Madrid. At 8 o'clock five rebel gunboats rounded the point below us, when the gunboats, the Benton in advance, immediately got under way and proceeded in pursuit; and when within long range opened upon the rebels, followed by the Carondelet, and Cincinnati, and the other boats. After an exchange of some twenty shots, the rebel boats rapidly steamed down the river and kept beyond our range until they reached the batteries of Fort Pillow, a distance of more than thirty miles. We followed them to within a mile of Fort Pillow, within easy range of their batteries, for the purpose of making a good reconnoissance, at considerable expense, however; but it was not till we had rounded to and ran some distance up the stream when the enemy opened fire upon us, and then with no effect, their shot, most of them, going beyond us. Having accomplished our object, I tied the flotilla up to the banks on the Tennessee side, out of range of the forts, for the night.

General Pope, with Assistant Secretary Scott, came aboard at 3 p. m., when it was arranged that the mortar boats should be placed in the morning on the Arkansas shore, within range of the forts, to be protected by the gunboats, and General Pope, with most of his force, should land five miles above, with the view of getting his army, if possible, to the rear of the fortifications and make the attack in rear, while we should, with gun and mortar boats, attack them in front.

This place has a long line of fortifications, with guns of heavy calibre; their number and the number of their men I have not yet been able to ascertain. The secession feeling here, as I learn from several persons coming on board, is very strong, and they express the opinion that the resistance will be very determined.

Three p. m.—General Pope has returned with his transports, and informs me that he is unable to reach the rear of the rebels from any point of the river above, and proposes to cut a canal on the Arkansas side, which will enable us to get three or four of the gunboats below, and thus enable him to cross the river below the upper forts, and thus cut off the batteries. We shall thus have three iron-clad boats above and four below, which I presume will be all that will be required in case the six gunboats of the rebels make an attack upon either division, as three of our gunboats ought successfully to cope with six of theirs.

The mortars are now firing, and have driven the rebel gunboats out of range down the river.

I shall continue to keep the department advised of our movements.

The effects of my wound have quite a dispiriting effect upon me from the increased inflammation and swelling of my foot and leg, which have induced a febrile action, depriving me of a good deal of sleep and energy. I cannot give the wound that attention and rest it absolutely requires until this place is captured.

I have the honor to be, your obedient servant,

A. H. FOOTE, *Flag-Officer.*

Hon. GIDEON WELLES,
Secretary of the Navy.

Flag-Officer Foote's report of operations off Fort Pillow.

UNITED STATES FLAG-STEAMER BENTON,
Off Fort Pillow, April 17, 1862.

SIR: I have the honor to inform the department that yesterday, and the day preceding, I had, with General Pope, made such arrangements, by combining our own with the forces of the army, that our possession of this stronghold seemed to be inevitable in less than six days. I had even stronger hopes of this desirable result than I entertained even at No. 10, till the actual surrender was tendered. Our object, then, after leaving a force to garrison the place, was to proceed to Memphis immediately, where, I have good authority for stating, we would have been received without opposition. But the sudden withdrawal of the entire army of General Pope this morning, under orders to proceed directly up the Tennessee river to join General Halleck's command at Pittsburg, has frustrated the best matured and most hopeful plans and expectations thus far formed in this expedition. Two volunteer regiments, under command of Colonel Fitch, were left here by General Pope to co-operate with the flotilla. While I deeply regret the withdrawal of General Pope's command, I am not at all questioning the propriety, and even the necessity, of its presence at Pittsburg, and I shall use every exertion with the force remaining to accomplish good results.

It is a great object to obtain early possession of this place and Memphis, as ten of the rebel gunboats are now at Fort Pillow, and ten others are reported as *en route* to Memphis, and daily expected at that place. It is reported that Commodore Hollins left Fort Pillow on Sunday to bring up the heavy gunboat Louisiana, now about completed at New Orleans. With the exception of this vessel, however, we have little to apprehend from the other rebel gunboats, according to the representation of the four or six deserters lately coming to us from the gunboats at Fort Pillow. At all events, the department may rest assured of every exertion being made on our part to accomplish the great work intrusted to this expedition. * * *

I have the honor to be your obedient servant,

A. H. FOOTE, *Flag-Officer.*

Hon. Gideon Welles,
Secretary of the Navy, Washington, D. C.

United States Flag-Steamer Benton,
Off Fort Pillow, April 19, 1862.

Sir: I have the honor to inform the department that since my last communication of the 17th instant we have been occasionally throwing shells into the rebel fortifications from the mortar boats, which have been returned from their rifled guns, without producing any effect. Ours have compelled one encampment to remove its quarters, and from several deserters we learn have otherwise discomforted them.

One or two examinations made by Colonel Fitch, commanding the two regiments left to co-operate with the flotilla by General Pope on withdrawing his army, have been unsuccessful, thus far, in finding a bayou for our boats, and a position below Fort Pillow, where a battery can be placed to command the river below. I shall again render him assistance by sending over small boats, in hopes that at a distance further up the river we may be able to discover a bayou leading into a lake, in which water sufficient may be found for our gunboats, with a view of erecting a battery under their protection, which will blockade the river below and enable his force, although not exceeding fifteen hundred men, to come upon the rebels in rear, while, with the remaining gunboats here, we attack them in front.

I am greatly exercised about our position here, on account of the withdrawal of the army of 20,000 men, so important an element to the capture of the place. Fort Pillow has for its defence at least forty heavy guns in position and nine gunboats—six of them, however, being wooden boats, but armed with heavy guns—with a force of six thousand troops. Our force consists of seven iron-clad and one wooden gunboat, sixteen mortar boats, only available in throwing shells at a distance, and even worse than useless for defence, and a land force of two regiments, not exceeding 1,500 troops. Under these circumstances an attack on our part, unless we can at first establish a battery below the fort under the protection of the gunboats, and to co-operate with it after its completion, would be extremely hazardous, although its attempt might prove successful, and even be good policy under other circumstances; but it can hardly now be so regarded, as a disaster would place all that we have gained on this and other rivers at the mercy of the rebel fleet, unless the batteries designed to command the river from below are completed at No. 10, or at Columbus, which I very much doubt. I therefore hesitate about a direct attack upon this place now, more than I should were the river above properly protected, although by it and loss of time the rebels may succeed in getting up to Fort Pillow their entire fleet of gunboats. As I stated in my last communication, had not General Pope's army been withdrawn we have every reason for believing that a plan we had adopted would have insured the fall of Fort Pillow in four days, and enabled us to have moved on Memphis in two days afterwards. It has always been my expectation that a large army would co-operate with the gunboats, and now the fall of Corinth and movements of our troops on to Memphis seem to be essential to our holding this place and reaching Memphis with the flotilla. * * * * * * * *

I have the honor to be, very respectfully, your obedient servant,

A. H. FOOTE, *Flag-Officer.*

Hon. GIDEON WELLES,
Secretary of the Navy, Washington, D. C.

UNITED STATES FLAG-STEAMER BENTON,
Off Fort Pillow, April 23, 1862.

SIR: I have the honor to inform the department that since my last communication, with the exception of a day or two, when the heavy rains caused the mortars to recoil dangerously on the wet platform, we have been shelling the rebel batteries at Fort Pillow, and most of the time kept their gunboats beyond our range. Colonel Fitch, in command of the 1,200 infantry left here by General Pope, has been examining bayous and creeks, with a view of getting guns to blockade the river, and prevent the new gunboats from coming up from New Orleans and Memphis; but, as the rebels are in great force, and no tools or conveniences for cutting through the swamps were left by General Pope when his army, so unfortunately for us, was withdrawn, he has made as yet no satisfactory progress.

I am doing all in my power towards devising ways and means preparatory to a successful attack on the forts, and shall continue to do so; but, as the capture of this place was predicated upon a large land force co-operating with the flotilla, or its being turned by the army marching upon Memphis, and considering the difficulties of fighting the flotilla down stream with our slow boats compared with up-stream work, the department will not be surprised at our delay and having made no further progress towards the capture of this stronghold of the rebels. I shall, however, do all in my power to be successful here, and exert myself, even beyond my impaired health and strength, towards the accomplishment of this great object.

The rebels are strongly fortified on land, and have eleven gunboats lying near, or rather below their fortifications. A resident of the place informs me this morning that thirteen gunboats are now here, seven of which, however, are mere river steamers with boilers and machinery sunk into the hold, and otherwise protected; but they carry from four, six, to eight guns of heavy calibre, some of which are rifled. The other boats are iron-plated or filled in with cotton. The large steamer of sixteen or twenty guns being plated, and named the "Louisiana," has not arrived, but is daily expected from New Orleans.

I have thus given the department the best information I can obtain from the most reliable sources—from resident Union men, and the twelve deserters from the enemy, whose accounts, however, are conflicting, many of them giving fabulous numbers of men, guns, and gunboats. We have not force enough to hold the place if we take it.

I have the honor to be, very respectfully, your obedient servant,

A. H. FOOTE, *Flag-Officer.*

Hon. GIDEON WELLES,
Secretary of the Navy, Washington, D C.

P. S.—In a picket skirmish yesterday the rebels lost one killed and one or two wounded. No loss on our side.

A. H. F.

Report of action near Fort Pillow, Mississippi river.

[Telegram.]

FLAG-SHIP BENTON,
Above Fort Pillow, Mississippi River, May 10, 1862.

The naval engagement, for which the rebels have been preparing, took place this morning. The rebel fleet, consisting of eight iron-clad gunboats, four of which were fitted with rams, came up handsomely. The action lasted one hour. Two of the rebel gunboats were blown up, and one sunk, when the enemy retired precipitately under the guns of the fort. Only six vessels of my squadron were engaged. The Cincinnati sustained some injury from the rams, but will be in fighting condition to-morrow. Captain Stembel distinguished himself. He is seriously wounded. The Benton is uninjured. Mortar boat No. 16, in charge of Second Master Gregory, behaved with great spirit. The rebel squadron is supposed to be commanded by Commodore Hollins.

C. H. DAVIS,
Captain, Com'dg West. Flotilla, pro tem., Mississippi River.

Hon. GIDEON WELLES,
Secretary of the Navy.

Captain C. H. Davis's report of an engagement with rebel gunboats off Fort Pillow, May 10, 1862.

UNITED STATES FLAG-STEAMER BENTON,
Off Fort Pillow, May 11, 1862.

SIR: I have the honor to inform the department that yesterday morning a little after seven o'clock the rebel squadron, consisting of eight iron-clad steamers, four of them, I believe, fitted as rams, came around the point at the bend above Fort Pillow and steamed gallantly up the river, fully prepared for a regular engagement.

The vessels of this squadron were lying at the time tied up to the bank of the river, three on the eastern and four on the western side, and—as they were transferred to me by Flag-Officer Foote—ready for action. . Most of the vessels were prompt in obeying the signal to follow the motions of the commander-in-chief.

The leading vessels of the rebel squadron made directly for mortar-boat No. 16, which was for a moment unprotected. Acting Master Gregory, and his crew, behaved with great spirit. During the action he fired his mortar eleven times at the enemy, reducing his charge and diminishing the elevation.

Commander Stembel, in the gunboat Cincinnati, which was the leading vessel in the line on that side of the river, followed immediately by Commander Kilty, in the gunboat Mound City, hastened to the support of the mortar-boat, and were repeatedly struck by the enemy's rams at the same time that they disabled the enemy and drove him away.

The two leading vessels in the middle of the enemy's line were successfully encountered by this ship. The boilers or steam-chest of one of them was exploded by our shot, and both of them were disabled; they, as well as the first vessel encountered by the Cincinnati, drifted down the river.

Commander Walke informs me that he fired a fifty-pound rifle-shot through the boilers of the third of the enemy's gunboats of the western line, and rendered her for the time being helpless. All of these vessels might easily have been captured if we had possessed the means of towing them out of action; but the steam-power of our gunboats is so disproportionate to the bulk of the vessels that they can accomplish but little beyond overcoming the strength of the current even when unencumbered.

The action lasted during the better part of an hour, and took place at the closest quarters. The enemy finally retreated with haste below the guns of Fort Pillow.

I have to call the especial attention of the department to the gallantry and good conduct exhibited by Commanders Stembel and Kilty, and Lieutenant Commanding S. L. Phelps.

I regret to say that Commander Stembel, Fourth Master Reynolds, and one of the seamen of the Cincinnati, and one of the Mound City, were severely wounded; the other accidents of the day were slight.

The Cincinnati and Mound City are injured, and must sooner or later go up the river to be repaired.

I have the honor to be your most obedient servant,

C. H. DAVIS,
Captain, Commanding Mississippi Flotilla pro tem.

Hon. GIDEON WELLES,
Secretary of the Navy, Washington, D. C.

Flag-Officer Davis's report of the surrender of Memphis.

UNITED STATES FLAG-STEAMER BENTON,
Memphis, June 6, 1862.

SIR: In my despatch of yesterday, dated at Fort Pillow, I had the honor to inform the department that I was about moving to this place with the men-of-war and transports. I got under way from Fort Pillow at noon, leaving the Pittsburg, Lieutenant Commanding Egbert Thompson, to co-operate with a detachment of Colonel Fitch's command in holding possession of Fort Pillow and securing public property at that place, and also the Mound City, Commander A. H. Kilty, to convoy the transports containing the troops not then ready to move.

On the way down I came suddenly, at a bend of the river, upon the rebel transport steamer Sovereign, which turned immediately to escape from us. I sent forward Lieutenant Joshua Bishop, with a body of small-armed men, in a light tug, by whom she was captured. She is a valuable prize.

The gunboats anchored, at 8 o'clock p. m., at the lower end of Island No. 45, about a mile and a half above the city of Memphis. The mortar-boats, tow-boats, ordnance, commissary and other vessels of the fleet, tied up at Island No. 44 for the night.

At daylight this morning the enemy's fleet, consisting of the rebel rams and gunboat, now numbering eight vessels, were discovered lying at the levee. They dropped below Railroad Point, and, returning again, arranged themselves in front of the city.

At 4.20 the flotilla, consisting of the following five vessels—the flag-ship Benton, Lieutenant Commanding S. L. Phelps; the Louisville, Commander B. M. Dove; the Carondelet, Commander Henry Walke; the Cairo, Lieutenant Commanding N. C. Bryant; and the St. Louis, Lieutenant Commanding Wilson McGunnegle—got under way by signal, and dropped down the river.

The rebels, still lying in front of the town, opened fire, with the intention of exposing the city to injury from our shot. The fire was returned, on our part, with due care in this regard. While the engagement was going on in this manner two vessels of the ram fleet, under command of Colonel Ellet—the Queen of the West and Monarch—steamed rapidly by us and ran boldly into the enemy's line. Several conflicts had taken place between the rams before the flotilla, led by the Benton, moving at a slower rate, could arrive at the closest quarters. In the mean time, however, the firing from our gunboats was continuous, and exceedingly well directed.

The General Beauregard and the Little Rebel were struck in the boilers and blown up.

The ram Queen of the West, which Colonel Ellet commanded in person, encountered with full power the rebel steamer General Lovel, and sunk her, but in doing so sustained some serious damage.

Up to this time the rebel fleet had maintained its position, and used its guns with great spirit. These disasters, however, compelled the remaining vessels to resort to their superiority in speed as the only means of safety. A running fight took place, which lasted nearly an hour, and carried us ten miles below the city. It ended in the capture or destruction of four of the five remaining vessels of the enemy; one only, supposed to be the Van Dorn, having escaped. Two of the rams—the Monarch and Lancaster No. 3—pursued her, but without success. They brought back, however, another prize

The names and fate of the vessels composing the rebel fleet are as follows:

The General Lovel, sunk in the beginning of the action by the Queen of the West She went down in deep water, in the middle of the river, altogether out of sight. Some of her crew escaped by swimming; how many went down in her I have not been able to ascertain.

The General Beauregard, blown up by her boilers, and otherwise injured by shot, went down near shore.

The Little Rebel, injured in a similar manner, made for the Arkansas shore, where she was abandoned by her crew.

The Jeff Thompson, set on fire by our shells, was run on the river bank and abandoned by her crew. She burned to the water's edge, and blew up by her magazine.

The General Price was also run on the Arkansas shore. She had come in contact with one of the rams of her own party, and was otherwise injured by cannon balls. She also was abandoned by her crew.

The Sumter is somewhat cut up, but is still afloat.

The fine steamer General Bragg is also above water, though a good deal shattered in her works and hull.

The Van Dorn escaped.

Of the above-named vessels, the Sumter, General Bragg, and Little Rebel will admit of being repaired. I have not received the reports of the engineers and carpenters, and cannot yet determine whether it will be necessary to send them to Cairo, or whether they can be repaired here.

The pump of the Champion No. 3 will be applied to raise the General Price. No other vessels of the rebel flotilla will, I fear, be saved.

I have not received such information as will enable me to make an approximate statement of the number of killed, wounded, and prisoners on the part of the enemy.

One of the vessels going down in deep water, carried a part of her crew with her; another, the General Beauregard, having been blown up with steam, many of her crew were frightfully scalded. I doubt whether it will ever be in my power to furnish an accurate statement of these results of the engagement.

The attack made by the two rams under Colonel Ellet, which took place before the flotilla closed in with the enemy, was bold and successful.

Captain Maynadier, commanding the mortar fleet, accompanied the squadron in a tug, took possession of the Beauregard, and made her crew prisoners. He captured, also, other prisoners during the action, and received many persons of the rebel fleet who returned and delivered themselves up after their vessels had been deserted. It is with pleasure that I call the attention of the department to his personal zeal and activity, the more conspicuous because displayed while the mortar-boats under his command could take no part in the action.

The officers and men of the flotilla performed their duty. Three men only of the flotilla were wounded, and those slightly. But one ship was struck by shot.

I transmit herewith copies of my correspondence with the mayor of Memphis, leading to the surrender of the city.

At 11 o'clock a. m. Colonel Fitch, commanding the Indiana brigade, arrived and took military possession of the place.

There are several prizes here, among them four large river steamers, which will be brought at once into the service of the government.

I have the honor to be, very respectfully, your most obedient servant,

C. H. DAVIS, *Flag-Officer,*
Comd'g Western Flotilla, Mississippi river, pro tem.

Hon. GIDEON WELLES,
Secretary of the Navy, Washington, D. C.

UNITED STATES FLAG-STEAMER BENTON,
Off Memphis, June 6, 1862.

SIR: I have respectfully to request that you will surrender the city of Memphis to the authority of the United States, which I have the honor to represent.

I am, Mr. Mayor, with high respect, your most obedient servant,

C. H. DAVIS,
Flag-Officer, Commanding, &c., &c.

His Honor the MAYOR *of the city of Memphis, Tenn.*

MAYOR'S OFFICE, *Memphis, June* 6, 1862.

SIR: Your note of this day is received and contents noted.

In reply I have only to say that the civil authorities have no resources of defence, and, by the force of circumstances, the city is in your power.

Respectfully,

JOHN PARK, *Mayor.*

C. H. DAVIS, *Flag-Officer, Commanding, &c.*

UNITED STATES FLAG-STEAMER BENTON,
Off Memphis, June 6, 1862.

SIR: The undersigned, commanding the military and naval forces of the United States in front of Memphis, have the honor to say to the mayor of the city that Colonel Fitch, commanding the Indiana brigade, will take military possession of Memphis immediately.

Colonel Fitch will be happy to receive the co-operation of his honor the mayor and city authorities in maintaining peace and order; and to this end he will be pleased to confer with his honor at the military headquarters at 3 o'clock this afternoon.

The undersigned have the honor to be, with high respect, your most obedient servants,

C. H. DAVIS,
Flag-Officer, Commanding afloat.
G. N. FITCH,
Colonel, Commanding Indiana Brigade.

His Honor the MAYOR *of the city of Memphis, Tenn.*

MAYOR'S OFFICE, *Memphis, June* 6, 1862.

GENTLEMEN: Your communication is received, and I shall be happy to co-operate with the colonel commanding in providing measures for maintaining peace and order in the city.

Your most obedient servant,

JOHN PARK, *Mayor.*

Flag-Officer C. H. DAVIS and Colonel G. N. FITCH.

Flag-Officer Davis encloses report of action at St. Charles.

[Telegram.]

UNITED STATES FLAG-STEAMER BENTON,
Memphis, via Cairo, June 21, 1862.

The gunboat Conestoga, returning from White river, reports the capture of two batteries mounting seven guns, at St. Charles, 80 miles from the mouth. The attack was commenced by Captain Kilty, in the gunboats, who silenced the first battery. The second battery was gallantly carried by Colonel G. N. Fitch, at the head of the 46th Indiana volunteers. A shot caused the explosion of the steam-drum of the Mound City, by which the greater part of her officers and crew were killed and wounded. I write by to-day's mail.

CHAS. H. DAVIS, *Flag-Officer.*

Hon. GIDEON WELLES,
Secretary of the Navy.

Flag-officer Davis encloses report of action at St. Charles, Arkansas, June 17, 1862.

UNITED STATES FLAG-STEAMER BENTON,
Memphis, June 23, 1862.

SIR: I have the honor to acknowledge the receipt of your letter of the 17th instant, appointing me flag-officer in command of the United States naval forces employed in the Mississippi river and its tributaries.

I transmit by this envelope a detailed report of the action at St. Charles, from Lieutenant Commanding W. McGunnegle, the senior officer on duty after Commander Kilty was wounded.

* * * * * * * * *

I have the honor to be, very respectfully, your obedient servant,

C. H. DAVIS,
Flag-Officer, Commanding Mississippi Flotilla, Mississippi river.

Hon. GIDEON WELLES,
Secretary of the Navy, Washington, D. C.

UNITED STATES FLAG-STEAMER BENTON,
Memphis, June 19, 1862.

SIR: The Conestoga, Lieutenant Commanding G. W. Blodgett, arrived here to-day from White river. She brings information of the capture of two batteries at St. Charles, eighty miles from the mouth, the first of which mounted four Parrott guns, and the second three 42-pound rifled guns. These guns, it is understood, were taken from the gunboat Mariposa, which, after being dismantled, was sunk.

There is now but one gunboat remaining in White river, the Pontchartrain, mounting three or five guns, and having her machinery protected by iron and cotton.

The enemy has attempted to block up the river by driving piles and by sinking boats, but no serious obstructions have yet been encountered.

The Conestoga will return to White river to-night with re-enforcements, accompanied by an additional transport laden with commissary stores.

The victory at St. Charles, which has probably given us the command of White river, and secured our communication with General Curtis, would be unalloyed with regret but for the fatal accident to the steam-drum and heater of the Mound City, mentioned in my telegraphic despatch. Of the crew, consisting of 175 officers and men, 82 have already died, 43 were killed in the water or drowned, 25 are severely wounded, and are now on board the hospital boat; among the latter is Captain Kilty. They promise to do well. Three officers and twenty-two men escaped uninjured.

After the explosion took place the wounded men were shot by the enemy while in the water, and the boats of the Conestoga, Lexington, and St. Louis, which went to the assistance of the scalded and drowning men of the Mound City, were fired into both with great guns and muskets, and were disabled, and one of them forced on shore to prevent sinking. The forts were commanded by Lieutenant Joseph Fry, late of the United States navy, who is now a prisoner and wounded.

The department and the country will contrast these barbarities of a savage enemy with the humane efforts made by our own people to rescue the wounded and disabled, under similar circumstances, in the engagement of the 6th instant.

Several of the poor fellows who expired shortly after the engagement expressed their willingness to die when they were told that the victory was ours.

I have the honor to be, very respectfully, your most obedient servant,

C. H. DAVIS,

Flag-Officer, Commanding Western Flotilla, Mississippi river.

Hon. Gideon Welles,

Secretary of the Navy, Washington, D. C.

United States Gunboat St. Louis,

St. Charles, White River, Ark., June 18, 1862.

Sir: I have the honor to submit the following report:

On the morning of the 16th instant, the Conestoga and transports having reached us, we got under way from a point called "Arkansas Cut-off," and stood up the river to within about five miles of this place, when we anchored for the night. Captain Kilty sent off a reconnoitring party in the tug. At 6 o'clock the next morning we got under way, and proceeded up the river in the following order, viz: Mound City, St. Louis, Lexington, Conestoga, and transports. When within two miles of the fortifications we discovered the enemy's pickets; the Mound City and other gunboats immediately opened fire; at the same time Colonel Fitch landed his regiment, and, as we drove them in, they followed them up. We continued to stand on, firing on either side and ahead as we went. Soon we came to a bend in the river, which I conceive to be about a mile in length; almost at the upper end were sunken three boats across the river, (they afterwards proved to be the rebel gunboat Maurepas, and river boats Eliza G. and Mary Patterson,) and abreast of these obstructions on the port hand was a bluff on which we imagined the batteries would be situated, although we could not see a gun on account of the trees. Captain Kilty stood boldly on, closely followed by the other gunboats, firing as we went; soon the enemy responded. The moment we discovered the situation of the enemy's battery the cannonading from our side became terrific. In a few moments the Mound City had advanced to within about six hundred yards of their enemy, when a well-directed shot from a new battery, situated a little higher up the bluff, penetrated her port casement a little above and forward of the gunport, killing three men in its flight, and exploding her steam-drum. So soon as this sad accident occurred many of her crew leaped overboard; all boats were instantly sent to their relief. The position of the gunboats at this time was as follows: the Mound City, followed by the St. Louis and Lexington, the Conestoga being abreast of the latter vessel. The Mound City drifted down and across the stream. The Conestoga boldly came up and towed her out of action. The St. Louis and Lexington moved closer to the upper battery, (the lower one being by this time relieved,) and continued to pour in shot and shell, the enemy shooting the while at the St. Louis, and the wounded of the Mound City struggling in the water. Some two minutes after the explosion on board the Mound City, Colonel Fitch made signal for us to cease firing, which I did, and in five minutes after we ceased firing he gallantly charged their battery, and carried it without the loss of a single man. Eight of the enemy were left dead, twenty-nine were taken prisoners, including Captain Jos. Fry, commander of the post, late lieutenant United States navy, and all their guns and ammunition. Our victory was a complete one, but the loss of life on board the Mound City by the explosion of the steam-drum is frightful. Their batteries consisted of two 12-pounder brass pieces, two 9-pounder Parrott rifled, and two 42-pounder rifled sea-coast howitzers. So soon as I was sure we had gained the victory, I repaired to the Mound City, and to endeavor to describe the howling of the wounded and the moaning of the dying is far beyond the power of my feeble pen. Among the scalded and suffering was the brave Commander Kilty, who but a short time before I had seen proudly pacing his deck with the enemy's balls whizzing past him. He fought his ship most gallantly. All honor to his name! My first care, after assuming command of the gunboats, was to make the best possible provision for the wounded in this, as in the previous engagement with the enemy. Lieutenants Commanding Shirk and Blodgett rendered every assistance in the power of man. For their skill and bravery in action, and the energy displayed by them to assist the wounded, they are deserving of the highest honors; and in this connexion I will also mention that Dr. George W. Garver, of the Lexington, and Dr. William H. Wilson, of the Conestoga, were untiring in their attention to the wounded. The above four officers I think richly deserve to be especially mentioned. After consulting with the commanding officer, it was decided to send the wounded to Memphis on board the Conestoga and Musselman, (Colonel Fitch kindly loaning the latter named boat,) with all the surgeons, but what to do with the Mound City was a more perplexing question. I was told by the pilots that it would take several days to tow her out of the river, it being so narrow and crooked. The surgeons represented that the delay would prove fatal to many whose lives might be saved. From what I had seen and heard on this river I must push on with all haste lest the enemy would fortify. After mature deliberation I concluded to get as many men from Colonel Fitch as he could spare, and with First Master John H. Duble in charge, together with two other officers, and the men unhurt of her own crew, would leave her here and proceed up the river as far as I could prudently, with the river falling as rapidly as it is.

The only two officers that were not wounded or killed on board the Mound City were the first master, Mr. Dominy, and the gunner, Mr. McElroy. I deemed it best to send Mr. Dominy up to Memphis, not that he did not perform his duty well, for I am sure he did, as I saw him in the thickest of the fight moving about on the upper deck, but simply for a change; he having witnessed the horrible catastrophe, his mind appeard to be greatly exercised. Mr. McElroy is now on board the Mound City. We buried, last night, fifty-nine of her crew; there are now twenty-six on board unscathed. Many, very many, must have been killed by the enemy while they were struggling in the water. I was quite close to the spot, and distinctly saw and remarked on the cowardly act, at the moment they were perpetrating it. An accident also happened to the transport New National; one of the bow guns of the Mound City being loaded, cocked, and primed, the lock string lying on the deck, one of the wounded men rolled on it, which set it off. It was loaded with grape. One of the shot passed through the steam-pipe of the New National, fortunately injuring no one, but she will have to run on one wheel. I found your instructions to Captain Kilty to guide him in this expedition, and be assured I will exert myself in every endeavor to carry them out. In conclusion, let me inform you that the officers I command displayed gallant conduct during the action, and I am happy to say there were no casualties on board this gunboat.

I am, very respectfully, your obedient servant,

W. McGUNNEGLE,
Lieutenant Commanding.

Flag-Officer C. H. Davis,
Commanding Western Flotilla, Mississippi river, Memphis, Tenn.

UNITED STATES FLAG-STEAMER BENTON,
Memphis, June 20, 1862.

SIR: The number of wounded men on board the hospital-boat Red River is forty-one. The account given me yesterday was incorrect. I shall still wait for further knowledge before presenting a final report of the casualties attending the capture of the St. Charles forts. The department will be gratified to learn that the patients are, most of them, doing well. The surgeon assures me that Commander Kilty is out of danger; but he is severely crippled in his hands and feet, and suffers a great deal. He is a brave gentleman and a loyal officer. He has always been conspicuous in this squadron for acting his part in the best spirit of the profession. In the attack on the batteries at St. Charles he occupied the leading place, and received his wounds at the head of his line in the zealous performance of his whole duty. Although himself wounded and helpless, he attended to the wants and comforts of his injured officers and men.

I have gratefully to acknowledge our obligations to Major General Wallace and to Dr. Jessup, of the 24th Indiana, and to Dr. McClellan, of the 1st Nebraska regiment, for their valuable sympathy and assistance.

Sister Angela, the Superior of the Sisters of the Holy Cross, (some of whom are performing their offices of mercy at the Mount City hospital,) has kindly offered the services of the sisters for the hospital-boat of this squadron, when needed. I have written to Commander Pennock to make arrangements for their coming.

I have the honor to be, very respectfully, your obedient servant,

C. H. DAVIS, *Flag-Officer,*
Commanding Western Flotilla, Mississippi River, pro tem.

Hon. GIDEON WELLES,
Secretary of the Navy, Washington, D. C.

Flag-Officer Davis reports the arrival of the ram Arkansas under the guns of Vicksburg.

UNITED STATES FLAG-STEAMER BENTON,
Off Vicksburg, July 16, 1862.

SIR: In my despatch of July 14, I had the honor to inform the department that I was about sending an expedition up the Yazoo river.

The plan of this expedition, as finally agreed upon between Flag-Officer Farragut, Brigadier General Williams, and myself, was to despatch the gunboats Carondelet and Tyler, and the ram Queen of the West, strengthened by sharpshooters from the army, at four o'clock yesterday morning, to procure correct information concerning the obstructions and defences of the river.

Repeated examinations of the Yazoo had informed us that there was a raft obstructing the passage eighty miles from the mouth, with a battery near it below, and the new ram Arkansas above, a vessel represented to be well protected by iron, and very formidable in her battery.

Shortly after the expedition entered the river yesterday morning it encountered the Arkansas coming down.

After a severe fight with the Tyler and Carondelet, in which both vessels were partially disabled, she entered the Mississippi, and passing through the combined squadrons, took refuge under the batteries of Vicksburg.

Her appearance was so sudden and the steam of almost every vessel in the squadron so low, or, in other words, so entirely unprepared were we, that she had an opportunity to pass without positive obstruction, though she was severely injured by shot.

The Benton, Lieutenant Commanding S. L. Phelps, got under way and followed her down to the point, but at her usual snail's pace, which renders anything like pursuit ludicrous.

I engaged the upper batteries for half an hour; and in the course of the morning renewed the engagement, with Flag-Officer Farragut on board, for reconnoitring purposes.

At half past six o'clock in the evening an engagement again took place, which lasted for an hour, between this ship, the Louisville, Commander Dove, and the Cincinnati, Lieutenant Commanding B. Wilson, and the upper batteries, the object of which was to cover the passage of Flag-Officer Farragut's fleet. He had determined, during the day, to run below, for the double purpose of supporting the remainder of his squadron and of destroying the rebel ram in passing; to assist in which I had added the ram Sumter, Lieutenant Commanding Erben, to his force.

A note from him this morning informed me that the ram was so entirely concealed, by her situation, that the attack upon her did not prove to be as destructive as expected. The loss of life in his squadron, in its passage before these formidable batteries, is wonderfully small, and must be attributed to the rapid and well-directed fire from his ships, by which the guns of the enemy were silenced as soon as reached.

I shall give further particulars of this day's work by the next mail, and transmit the reports of Commander Walke, Lieutenant Commanding Phelps, and Lieutenant Commanding Gwin.

The loss of life in the squadron under my command has been thirteen killed, thirty-four wounded, and ten missing.

Among the killed and wounded are several of the sharpshooters supplied by General Williams, who performed their duty in the most faithful manner.

I have the honor to be, very respectfully, your most obedient servant,

C. H. DAVIS, *Flag-Officer,*
Commanding United States Naval Forces, Western Waters.

Hon. GIDEON WELLES,
Secretary of the Navy, Washington, D. C.

Attack on the upper batteries at Vicksburg and the ram Arkansas, July 22, 1862.

UNITED STATES FLAG-STEAMER BENTON,
Off Vicksburg, July 23, 1862.

SIR: In my communication of July 16, I mentioned the passage of Flag-Officer Farragut's fleet by the batteries at Vicksburg, with the double purpose of joining his fleet below and of destroying the rebel ram Arkansas in passing. The latter object was defeated by the darkness of the night. Yesterday morning, shortly after daylight, the Benton, Cincinnati, and Louisville attacked the upper batteries for the purpose of covering the Essex and the ram Queen of the West, both of which vessels went down and attacked the Arkansas in her place at the levee.

I transmit a copy of Commander W. D. Porter's report of the results of his engagement. The ram Queen of the West, commanded by Lieutenant Colonel Ellet, struck the Arkansas with sufficient force to do her some injury. Colonel Ellet behaved on this, as on previous occasions, with great gallantry. The shot from the Essex did serious injury to the casemates of the rebel ram and gunboat.

I have the honor to acknowledge the receipt of the communications of the department of the 14th and 15th instant. Our mail boats from Cairo have been fired into lately, and a small extra boat, put on for a special occasion, is reported to have been burned.

My force at this moment is very much reduced. It is reduced in the most formidable manner by sickness and death. Of the one hundred and thirty men of the mortar fleet, one hundred are sick and off duty. The crews of the gunboats are, many of them, reduced to one-half their number. I am in want of at least five hundred men to fill up vacancies and render the vessels under my command efficient.

My force is also reduced by the absence of eight gunboats, three of which are guarding important points of the river, and five of which are undergoing repairs. I have said that I am in want of five hundred men to insure the efficiency of the flotilla. In this calculation I make allowance for the return to duty of many of the sick; but six hundred men would not be too many to send to me. The most sickly part of the season is approaching, and the department would be surprised to see how the most healthy men wilt and break down under the ceaseless and exhausting heat of this pernicious climate. Men who are apparently in health at the close of the day's work sink away and die suddenly at night, under the combined effects of heat and malarial poison. The enemy, however, suffers a great deal more than we do. He counts seventeen or twenty thousand men on his rolls, but can hardly muster five thousand in his ranks. To sickness are added, in his case, the want of hospital accommodations, the want of medicines, and the want of suitable food. I learned that General Williams is about to move down the river. Should it prove so, it will be very unfortunate in its results. This is one of the points at which the co-operation of the army is most essential.

I have the honor to be, very respectfully, your most obedient servant,

C. H. DAVIS, *Flag-Officer,*
Commanding U. S. Naval Forces, Western Waters.

Hon. GIDEON WELLES,
Secretary of the Navy, Washington, D. C.

Report of Commander W. D. Porter.

ON BOARD GUNBOAT ESSEX,
Below Vicksburg, July 22, 1862.

SIR: I have the honor to inform you of the arrival of this ship below Vicksburg, Mississippi, and that we lost one man killed and two wounded.

I delivered several shot into the rebel ram Arkansas, as I believe, with effect. I endeavored to strike her, but as we approached they let go her bow line and the current drifted her stern on. The consequence was, this vessel only grazed her side, and ran, with great force, high on the bank, where she lay at least ten minutes, subject to a terrible fire from the shore battery.

The officers all did their duty, and with great coolness. Permit me to draw your attention to Master Willie Coates, of only 14 years of age. This young gentleman volunteered to act as my aid. His conduct was, throughout the action, marked by great coolness and bravery. He has no connexion whatever with the service; but I hope you will bring to the notice of the Navy Department the conduct of this little gentleman, as I think he has earned, by his loyalty, coolness, and bravery, an appointment at the Naval Academy.

I am, very respectfully, your obedient servant,

W. D. PORTER, *Commander.*

Flag-Officer C. H. DAVIS,
Commanding Flotilla, Western Waters.

Flag-Officer Davis reports having left Vicksburg for the mouth of the Yazoo river.

FLAG-STEAMER BENTON,
Helena, August 1, 1862.

SIR: In my last communication, dated July 25, and written from the anchorage above Vicksburg, I had the honor to inform the department that Flag-Officer Farragut and Brigadier General Williams had gone down the river; the forces of the latter being prostrated by sickness. The departure of General Williams rendered it necessary that I should abandon the position I then held, because it gave the enemy the possession of the point, from the canal down.

In making this canal General Williams used it as a means of defence, by constructing a continued breastwork and rifle-pit on the lower border, and an angle on the upper border to enfilade the canal where it was crossed by the levee. This levee, distinguished as the *new* levee, formed in itself a convenient breastwork. It was no longer safe for the hospital, commissary, ordnance boats, coal and ice barges, mail boats, &c., to lie at the bank; I therefore moved up, with my whole command, to the mouth of the Yazoo.

When I sent the Sumter and Essex below the batteries I was prepared for Flag-Officer Farragut's leaving; but I had no idea that General Williams intended to abandon his position. I expected to maintain uninterrupted communication with these vessels across the neck, and employ them in blockading the town from below. But now, the army having gone, these vessels must go to Baton Rouge or New Orleans for their supplies, and are permanently separated from my command.

In my despatch of the 23d ultimo I informed the department that several of our mail boats from Cairo had been fired into, and one sunk. It now appears that the communications in my rear are so seriously threatened that they could only be kept open by gunboats, and the three light and fleet gunboats are all undergoing repairs at Cairo. Information of a reliable and circumstantial character came to me that wagons, &c., had been called in to transport guns from the Yazoo to the vicinity of Islands Nos. 92 and 94. I learn from the captains of the mail boats that flying artillery had been taken from bank to bank, on the great bends of the river, and used twice on the same vessel. Light guns and muskets, in the hands of guerilla bands, had been fired into our unarmed vessels from several points between Carolina landing and Gaines's landing. The same thing is said to have occurred near Napoleon. Thus my supplies, as well as mails, were cut off, unless sent under convoy.

We have been repeatedly told that General Price was crossing from Mississippi into Arkansas to make a junction with General Hindman.

I have already spoken, in a previous despatch, of the alarming extent to which the efficiency of the few vessels remaining with me has been reduced by the endemic fever, and also transmitted a report of the surgeon on this subject.

Having maturely considered all the circumstances just recited, I determined to leave Vicksburg, where my own force, unaided and very much encumbered, could be of no further service; to close up my lines, now too extended; to open again the sources of communication and supply, and to resume my conjunction with the army. Accordingly, I have moved with all the fleet to this place, where I anchored last night at 9 o'clock.

But I wish the department to particularly understand that this movement does not involve any loss of control over the river below. Between this place and Vicksburg there are no bluffs—no high lands suited to fortifications. Guns can only be mounted on the level bank, where, to be sure, the levee often serves as a breastwork; but they will have no advantage of ground, and can be easily dislodged.

Your telegraphic despatch of the 25th ultimo was received on the 29th, at 4 a. m., when this ship was opposite Greenville. Flag-Officer Farragut left Vicksburg on the 24th.

I have the honor to be, very respectfully, your obedient servant,

C. H. DAVIS,

Flag-Officer, Com'dg U. S. Naval Forces, Western Waters.

Hon. GIDEON WELLES,

Secretary of the Navy, Washington, D. C.

Fleet Captain Pennock's report of expedition up the Ohio river to Evansville, Henderson, &c., in July, 1862.

UNITED STATES NAVAL DEPOT,

Cairo, August 6, 1862.

SIR: I have the honor to transmit to the department Fleet Captain Pennock's report of a joint naval and military expedition up the Ohio river to Evansville, Henderson, &c., undertaken in pursuance of a telegram from Governor Morton, and having for its object the pursuit and punishment of certain parties of guerillas which had threatened Henderson.

I invite the special attention of the department to the promptness with which Captain Pennock, who took a leading part in this service, organized his forces and proceeded to the scene of action.

The enclosed letter of General Love bears the most honorable testimony to Captain Pennock's conduct.

Very respectfully, your most obedient servant,

C. H. DAVIS, *Flag-Officer.*

Hon. GIDEON WELLES, *Secretary of the Navy.*

UNITED STATES NAVAL DEPOT,

Cairo, Ill., July 24, 1862.

SIR: I reported to you on Saturday, the 19th instant, that in consequence of a telegram received from Governor Morton, (a copy of which I forwarded you,) I would leave Cairo for Evansville with the United States receiving ship Clara Dolsen, armed with four 12-pounder rifled howitzers, J. M. Pritchett, lieutenant commanding, and tug Restless, armed with one 12-pounder howitzer, Master Ford commanding.

I was accompanied by Colonel Moro, with a battalion of 63d regiment Illinois volunteers, and Brigade Surgeon E. C. Franklin, who kindly volunteered his services for the occasion.

I arrived at Evansville on Monday at 6 a. m., and had an interview with Major General Love, who informed me of his plans to capture the guerillas who had control of Henderson, Kentucky, and his intention to occupy that place. My co-operation and that of the troops associated with me were desired in carrying out the plans of the enterprise.

The same afternoon Major Staning, chief of artillery of the district of Mississippi, arrived with the following force: Captain Robinson, company A, 20th battalion 16th regulars, 60 men; Captain Noyce, company H, 13th Wisconsin volunteers, 48 men; and Lieutenant Becker, with one section Stenbeck's battery, 2d Illinois artillery, 25 men, who reported to me for co-operation, by order of Brigadier General Strong, commanding district of Cairo. At the request of General Love, Major Staning, with his force, on board steamer Rob Roy, went in advance, for the purpose of occupying and picketing the city, the Clara Dolsen following with Major General Love and staff, with an addition of 500 men, consisting of infantry and a section of artillery. After landing the stores and troops, Colonel Moro was ordered by Major General Love to occupy and hold the city, while the Indiana troops and the section of Stenbeck's battery took up their line of March for the interior.

During the day several arrests were made, including two of the guerillas who were prominent in robbing the hospitals at that place and destroying government property, who were placed in irons on board the Clara Dolsen, and subsequently delivered up to the provost marshal.

General Love having received a despatch the following night that guerillas in force, were occupying Uniontown, with intent to cross the river to attack Mount Vernon, on the Indiana shore, Major Staning was despatched with a force to look after this matter, in the Rob Roy, accompanied by the armed tug Restless. Soon after I joined him at Uniontown, all being quiet at Mount Vernon.

During the afternoon several arrests were made of prominent secessionists and a number of boats destroyed, by order of Major General Love. Toward evening Surgeon Franklin and Lieutenant Commanding Pritchett, while reconnoitring the outskirts of the town, came upon a squad of guerillas and captured three, who were brought in and sent on board the Rob Roy under guard, to be sent to headquarters at Henderson.

Proceeding down the river, we arrived early in the evening at Shawneetown, where I received despatches from Captain Wise, announcing the presence of guerillas on the Kentucky shore opposite Cairo; and having no force there, naval or military, he advised that a portion of the force under my command should return with all possible despatch. Early this morning the Clara Dolsen and tug started for Cairo, and arrived here at 4 p. m., with two companies of Major Staning's command; he returning with the remainder of his force to Henderson in the Rob Roy, aboard of which I had placed a 12-pounder howitzer.

In conclusion, I regret to state that I found but little Union feeling on the Kentucky shore, and am of opinion that the interests of government and safety of steamers navigating the Ohio require that light-draught gunboats should be kept moving constantly up and down the river. Enclosed please find copy of letter received from Major General Love.

Acting Lieutenant Hoel, in conjunction with Mr. Sheeley, of the General Price, and Mr. Perkins, my assistant, consented to act as pilots for the expedition. This latter also assisted me in other duties.

Very respectfully, your obedient servant,

A. M. PENNOCK,
Commander and Fleet Captain.

HENDERSON, KENTUCKY, *July* 23, 1862.

CAPTAIN: I cannot permit you to leave me without expressing my sense of the gratitude with which the citizens of Indiana, and of this locality, will reward the prompt co-operation of yourself and your officers in this emergency, which threatened their security, and for the polite personal attention of yourself and Captain Pritchett to myself and staff.

I beg you to accept my sincere thanks and my best wishes for your safe return to Cairo.

I am, captain, with great respect, your obedient servant,

JOHN LOVE,
Major General, Indiana Legion.

A. M. PENNOCK,
Fleet Captain Gunboat Flotilla, on board Clara Dolsen.

Capture of rebel transport Fairplay, and large quantities of arms, ammunition, &c., in August, 1862.

CAIRO, ILLINOIS, *August* 26, 1862.

The combined naval and military operation, planned between General Curtis and myself before leaving Helena, has returned to the latter place, having accomplished its work with great success.

The rebel transport Fairplay has been captured, containing twelve hundred new Enfield rifles, four thousand new muskets, with accoutrements complete, a large quantity of fixed ammunition, four field guns, mounted howitzers, and small arms. Colonel Woods landed and captured the encampment of the 31st Louisiana regiment with arms, the enemy flying before him.

He captured another camp, with tents, baggage, and provisions, burning the depot and eight cars, and destroying the telegraph. The combined expedition proceeded up the Yazoo, where it captured a battery, consisting of sixty-four 42-pounder and 32-pounder guns, and 24 and 12-pounder field pieces, with seven thousand pounds of powder, one thousand shell, shot, and grape. Colonel Woods dispersed the rebel forces in several places. Will send further particulars by mail to-morrow.

C. H. DAVIS, *Commodore.*

Hon. GIDEON WELLES,
Secretary of the Navy.

Lieutenant Commanding S. L. Phelps reports a successful attack on the enemy at Bolivar, Mississippi, in August, 1862.

UNITED STATES FLAG-STEAMER BENTON,
Helena, August 27, 1862.

SIR: In my last report, sent by the Switzerland on the 23d instant, I informed you that we had found the enemy in some force at Greenville, Mississippi, and had dispersed him. I have now to report that as soon as Colonel Woods's force had returned from the pursuit, it was re-embarked, and we proceeded up the river, stopping to examine every point where a rebel force was likely to be posted; but we were unsuccessful in again finding an enemy till we reached Bolivar, Mississippi. Colonel Woods then landed his infantry and cavalry, and two mountain howitzers, and soon discovered the rebels to the number of about 3,000 posted on a plantation above the town. I moved up with the Benton to support our small force—not more than 500 men—in its gallant attack, and effectively used the battery in clearing the fields.

The enemy, after a brisk skirmish, fled, leaving seven prisoners and ten cavalry horses in our possession. Colonel Woods lost one man killed and two wounded. The loss of the enemy in killed is not known, but numbers of horses were running over the fields without riders, and the negroes reported his loss quite heavy.

From Bolivar to Helena, where we arrived this morning, we did not succeed in again encountering an enemy. The troops returned in good spirits and health, while the condition of the sick on board the gunboats was not injuriously affected by the eleven days' cruise below.

I am, respectfully, your obedient servant,

S. L. PHELPS,
Lieutenant Commander.

Flag-Officer CHARLES H. DAVIS,
Commanding Naval Forces, Western Rivers.

Loss of the gunboat Cairo.

UNITED STATES MISSISSIPPI SQUADRON,
United States Steamer Black Hawk, December 17, 1862.

SIR: I regret to inform you that the Cairo (iron-clad) has been blown up by a torpedo in the Yazoo river—nobody hurt. The vessel went down in twelve minutes. I gave Captain Walke orders to hold Yazoo river at all hazards, and it was while the vessels were employed in taking up the torpedoes (of which great numbers have been planted there) that the Cairo incautiously proceeded too far ahead, another steamer being in advance of her, when the torpedo exploded under her, knocking out her bottom. It was all done in the line of duty, and will not prevent me from carrying out my original intentions. We may lose three or four vessels, but will succeed in carrying out the plan for the capture of Vicksburg. The wires of the torpedoes are being cut, and the torpedoes removed, and we are now in command of the landings for the disembarcation of the army destined to march into the city.

Respectfully, your obedient servant,

DAVID D. PORTER,
Acting Rear-Admiral, Com'dg Mississippi Squadron.

Hon. GIDEON WELLES,
Secretary of the Navy.

Report of Captain Walke, commanding the Carondelet.

UNITED STATES GUNBOAT CARONDELET,
Mouth of the Yazoo River, December 13, 1862.

SIR: On the 11th instant I despatched the Marmora and Signal up the Yazoo river on a reconnoissance, and they returned in the afternoon, having ascended about twenty miles, where they were apprised of the presence of a number of torpedoes by the unaccountable number of small scows and stationary floats of various kinds along the channel of the river, and the explosion of one of them near the Signal. They immediately returned down the river, the Marmora exploding another by firing their muskets at the head of it, which was visible above the water.

Captains Getty, of the Marmora, and Scott, of the Signal, informed me that they could destroy all of these torpedoes with perfect safety if I would have them protected by one or two gunboats, as there was water enough to admit them, and the river is rising. I resolved, therefore, after consulting with Lieutenants Commanding Walker, Selfridge, and Hoel, of the Baron De Kalb, Cairo, and Pittsburg, to send Lieutenant Commanding Selfridge, at his own request, (the Cairo being the fastest and lightest draught gunboat, with the Pittsburg, Lieutenant Commanding Hoel, and with the ram Queen of the West, whose commander desired to accompany the expedition, to protect the Marmora and Signal while clearing the river of torpedoes.

I cautioned the commanding officers of all the boats of the expedition, (being present,) and Captain Selfridge in particular, to be very careful not to run their vessels in among the torpedoes, but to avoid the channel where they were set, to scour the shore with small boats, and haul the torpedoes on shore and destroy them before proceeding further up the river; that this duty would be performed by the Marmora and Signal, and the ram would follow astern of them, and the gunboats should be kept in the rear of all, so that they could shell the banks of the river above them if necessary. These instructions I repeated positively; and also that if there was any apparent danger in the execution of them, to relinquish the project and return, until better means could be obtained to scour the shore and drag out the torpedoes.

At half past seven o'clock yesterday morning the expedition proceeded up the Yazoo, according to my orders, and returned, minus the Cairo, about five o'clock in the afternoon of the same day. Lieutenant Commanding Selfridge came on board and reported the loss of the Cairo, by the explosion of a torpedo under his port bow, while urging the Marmora (having passed the other boats) through the midst of them, he being under the impression that they were harmless, or that there was no danger to be apprehended from them. After the explosion, which blew a very large hole up through the forecastle near the port bow gun, the Cairo was run on shore, and sunk in about ten minutes out of sight, except her light spars and smoke-stacks. After the accident to the Cairo ten torpedoes were destroyed by the expedition.

I have ordered the Marmora to proceed to Cairo with the officers and crew of the gunboat Cairo, and I have ordered Lieutenant Commanding Selfridge to report to you in person. Fortunately there were but a few persons injured on board the Cairo, and none of them very seriously.

I herewith enclose the reports of the several commanders of vessels on that sad occasion, which would have been avoided if my instructions had been followed.

I am, sir, very respectfully, your obedient servant,

H. WALKE,
Captain, United States Navy.

Acting Rear-Admiral D. D. PORTER,
Com'dg Mississippi Squadron, Cairo, Ill.

Report of Lieutenant Commander Thomas O. Selfridge.

UNITED STATES GUNBOAT SIGNAL,
Off Yazoo River, December 13, 1862.

SIR: It becomes my painful duty to announce to you the total loss of the gunboat Cairo, while under my command, from the explosion of two torpedoes under or near her, placed in the Yazoo river, some sixteen miles from its mouth.

I left our anchorage at about 8 o'clock a. m., December 12, in company with the gunboats Pittsburg, Marmora, Signal, and ram Queen of the West, under orders from Captain Walke to proceed carefully up the Yazoo to where torpedoes had been discovered the day before, and to effect the destruction of as many as possible. It was understood that the light gunboats were to go ahead, followed by myself and the Pittsburg, to protect them by shelling the woods on the river bank.

Arriving near the spot indicated, when the leading gunboat, the Marmora, was partially hidden by a bend in the river, a heavy fire of musketry opened; the steamer commenced backing at the same time, leading me to suppose she was attacked from the shore. I hastened up to her support, when I found the firing was from the Marmora at an object, a block of wood floating in the water.

I ordered her to cease firing and to lower a boat to examine. They either did not hear my order or were loth to obey it, and showing no signs of executing it, I lowered one of my own boats. They fished it up and found it to be a portion of a torpedo which had exploded the day before.

In the meanwhile, the head of the Cairo having got in towards the shore, I backed out to straighten up stream, and ordered the Marmora to go ahead slow. I had made but half a dozen revolutions of the wheel, and gone ahead perhaps half a length, the Marmora, a little ahead, leading, when two sudden explosions in quick succession occurred, one close to my port quarter, the other apparently under my port bow; the latter so severe as to raise the guns under it some distance from the deck. She commenced to fill so rapidly that in two or three minutes the water was over her forecastle. I shoved her immediately for the bank, but a few yards distant, got out a hawser to a tree, hoping to keep her from sliding of into deep water. The pumps, steam and hand, were immediately manned, and everything done that could be. Her whole frame was so completely shattered that I found immediately that nothing more could be effected than to move the sick and the arms. I ordered the Queen of the West alongside, and passed what articles I could get at into her, with a portion of the crew, the remainder taking to our boats. The Cairo sunk in about twelve minutes after the explosion, going totally out of sight, except the top of the chimneys, in six fathoms of water. I am happy to say that though some half a dozen men were injured, no lives were lost.

I cannot speak too highly of the officers' and men's behavior; there was perfect discipline and order to the last. The crew remained at the quarters until ordered away, and did what little could be done under the circumstances.

The most of the bags and hammocks were saved, as was everything that floated from the wreck. In the meanwhile I directed Captain Hoel, of the Pittsburg, to send boats up the shore, under cover of his guns, to destroy and discover the mode of firing these torpedoes. Several of them were destroyed, but I leave the particulars to his report.

Having accomplished all that was in our power, and destroyed what vestige of the unfortunate Cairo that remained above water, it was with deep regret and melancholy that I felt obliged to return down the river.

I have nothing to add in justification of myself that does not appear in this report.

Though I found we were in the vicinity of torpedoes, there were no signs to show at the time that any were in my immediate neighborhood, the Marmora having passed ahead of me.

Very respectfully, your obedient servant,

THOMAS O. SELFRIDGE,
Lieutenant Commander.

Captain HENRY WALKE, U. S. N.,
Commanding Naval Forces off Yazoo River.

Acting Rear-Admiral Porter's detailed report of the loss of the Cairo.

No. 251.] UNITED STATES MISSISSIPPI SQUADRON,
December 17, 1862.

SIR: When I sent you my despatch notifying you of the loss of the Cairo I had not examined carefully all the accompanying reports, being pressed for time, and I left it to the department to judge where the blame laid. My own opinion is that due caution was not observed, and that the vessels went ahead too fast. These torpedoes have proved so harmless heretofore (not one exploding out of the many hundreds that have been planted by the rebels) that officers have not felt that respect for them to which they are entitled. The torpedo which blew up the Cairo was evidently fired by a galvanic battery, as in some of them, which were afterwards taken up, the officers followed the wires over four hundred yards from the river bank, and would have followed them up but for fear of surprises. Lieutenant Commander Selfridge was proceeding with proper caution *before* the accident, and the Marmora was proceeding ahead of him some distance, while the boats were cutting the wires and dragging the torpedoes to the bank. Several had been safely disposed of when the Signal commenced firing musketry; and as the river bank was full of sharpshooters, Lieutenant Commander Selfridge went to assist her, supposing she was attacked. It appears she was firing at floating torpedoes. Not obeying the signal made to her to return, Lieutenant Commander Selfridge went up to hail her, and in doing so lost his vessel. The boats were doing their work very effectually, and had the orders of Captain Walke been carried out no accident could have occurred. The torpedoes were known to be there in numbers, and every precaution should have been observed. Lieutenant Commander Selfridge, however, did not go ahead with his vessel until his pilot assured him that everything was clear. In my orders to Captain Walke I directed him as follows: "Send on the Signal and Marmora, with some good marksmen, besides their crews; let them hold on to all they can until you can get your large vessels in. We must make a landing for the army at all hazards, and prevent the rebels from raising batteries," &c., &c. The first part of the order was executed, and the Signal and Marmora proceeded thirty miles up the river until stopped by the batteries. They were attacked by guerillas, whom they easily drove off, but they returned again to Captain Walke, and enabled the rebels to plant the torpedoes between that time and the return of the second expedition, when the Cairo was lost. What was the cause of the return of the light-draught vessels in the face of my order I have yet to learn. I do not see anything to reprehend in the course of Lieutenant Commander Selfridge, except being rather incautious. His vessel was a great loss to us; she was in splendid order, and had just been made shot-proof with railroad iron where she was before vulnerable. He is too good an officer to lose his services just now, and I have put him in command of the Conestoga, which was vacant, trusting that he may be more fortunate hereafter, this being the second time during the war his vessel has gone down under him. The conduct of the officers and crew was admirable; everything was conducted with perfect coolness, and not a man was lost, although so short a time elapsed between the explosion of the torpedo and the sinking of the vessel that nothing was saved except a few hammocks and bags, belonging to the men, which floated off. In a few minutes after the Cairo sunk nothing could be seen but the top of her pipes, which the ram Lioness hauled out and sunk to prevent the rebels from finding the spot. This affair will give me some extra trouble, but I hope to succeed, nevertheless, though this leaves me only six vessels which can go under a battery.

Very respectfully, your obedient servant,

DAVID D. PORTER,
Acting Rear-Admiral, Com'dg Mississippi Squadron.

Hon. GIDEON WELLES,
Secretary of the Navy, Washington, D. C.

Acting Rear-Admiral Porter's instructions to Captain Walke.

UNITED STATES MISSISSIPPI SQUADRON,
November 21, 1862.

SIR: On receipt of this communication you will take with you all the iron-clads, except the Benton and the General Bragg, and proceed down as near the mouth of the Yazoo as you can get, and, if possible, enter it. The object is to prevent the erection of batteries at the mouth of the Yazoo river, or as far as our guns will reach, and in case you see anything of the kind, your duty will be to destroy the batteries if you can. If the rebels have not covered them in, there will be no difficulty in driving them away and destroying the guns. The best time to do that kind of business is about daylight in the morning.

In case you cannot get into the Yazoo with the large vessels, you will send in the Signal and Marmora, with some good marksmen on board, besides their crews. Let them hold on to all they can until you are enabled to get large vessels up. We must make a landing for the army; at all events, we must prevent the rebels from raising forts right under our noses. You are directed to take with you (besides the iron-clads that can get to Helena) the Lexington and Tyler, which you will pick up as you go along; or, if they come to Helena, I will see that they are with you in time.

I have no means of ascertaining the height of water in the Yazoo, and think the only way to find out is to go, or send and see.

I shall feel better satisfied when I know we cannot get in, for then I shall know that the rebels cannot get out. In the matter of attacking batteries you must exercise some judgment, and no doubt, by a little consultation with those connected with you on this expedition, you will arrive at a just conclusion.

The object is to prevent the enemy from blocking up the approach to the river with batteries. General McClernand will move now in about two weeks, and we must have the places clear for him to land his troops. The object is to get possession of as much of the Yazoo as we can, and hold it until he comes.

I will be pushing down small and light-draught boats as fast as I get them finished and armed, and I hope to have about ten ready in the course of ten days.

Fill your vessels up with coal. Carry very low steam going down, to save your fuel, and, if necessary, detain the B. to tow down a couple of barges to enable you to keep up your steam. The B. will also act as a despatch boat, if necessary, to send me any communications.

If you find that you can enter the Yazoo, push on and go as far as you can; keep the communication open behind you. There are a number of fine large river boats up the Yazoo; try and secure them. Everything you fall in with will be a prize, and remember that there are no Union men who can lay claim to anything in that region.

In case you are successful, I beg leave to suggest that there is but one way of making war, and that is, by using the most stringent means, even to military executions, in order to preserve subordination among conquered people. Allow no parties to land near Vicksburg except on duty assigned by yourself. No intercourse of any kind to be kept up with the rebels; if any retreat to your vessels for protection, see that they do not go on shore again; at the same time get out of them all the information you can. Pick up all the good contrabands you can get, and something may be learnt from the most intelligent of them. After you have gained any information of any consequence, despatch it to me.

I am well informed that an active trade is carried on between the Yazoo and the Red rivers; the sooner we stop it the better.

Captain Selfridge will join you from Memphis. The Cincinnati, Lieutenant Bache, has left here on her way down; the Pittsburg has been ordered to join you; the Baron De Kalb will be off on Monday, and, with the Lexington, Tyler, Signal, and Marmora, you will likely do something. Keep me advised if anything should occur to render my presence necessary. And now, trusting to your good judgment, hoping that no opportunity to annoy the enemy may escape you,

I remain, very respectfully, &c.,

DAVID D. PORTER,
Acting Rear-Admiral, Com'dg Mississippi Squadron.

Captain H. WALKE,
Commanding Carondelet, Helena.

P. S.—I will have a couple of Ellet's rams to report to you when you will be ready for anything.

Engagement with the Yazoo batteries.—Co operation with General Sherman against Vicksburg.

UNITED STATES MISSISSIPPI SQUADRON,
Yazoo River, December 27, 1862.

SIR: This morning we commenced early the work of removing the torpedoes. The boats worked under a brisk fire from the concealed riflemen in pits, but the enemy gradually receded before our vessels, and by three o'clock in the evening we had worked up to within half or three quarters of a mile of the batteries, the strength of which it was desirable to feel. The army in the mean time advanced towards the heights. My object was to draw off a large portion of the troops from Vicksburg, to prevent our ascent of the Yazoo, by which we could throw troops on the Milldale road. At half past two the forts commenced firing briskly at our boats with eight heavy guns, without driving them in. The way being apparently clear of torpedoes, the channel having been thoroughly dragged with all sorts of contrivances, Lieutenant Commander Gwin, at three o'clock, advanced to the furthest point where the boats had finished their work, (which was about twelve hundred yards from the forts,) and opened his batteries. The other vessels were also ordered up, all of which were lying close behind. The river was, however, too narrow at that point to get even two vessels abreast, and the Benton bore the brunt of the fight. It lasted two hours, during which time the Benton was much cut up, but nothing happened to impair her efficiency; her armor was shot-proof when it was struck, except on deck, but still I regret to say there were some serious casualties. Lieutenant Commander Gwin was most seriously wounded by a rifle-shot striking him on the right breast, and carrying away the muscle of the right arm. He refused to enter the shot-proof pilot-house, saying that a captain's place was on the quarter deck. While there is life there is hope, and I trust the life of this gallant officer may be spared to us; the country can ill afford to lose his services. Mr. Lord, the executive officer of the vessel, was wounded severely in the foot, but fought the vessel gallantly after the captain had been carried below, and retired when the batteries were all unmasked, and when the object was accomplished for which the vessels went up. I had three of the iron-clads, and the Lexington, the Marmora, and the ram Queen of the West lying as a reserve, but none of them were struck, though in action, except the Cincinnati, Lieutenant Bache, by which no material damage occurred to the vessel.

The army advanced at the same time we were attacking the forts, making the enemy believe we were going to force the river forts. This induced them to draw off a large part of their forces from Vicksburg, and their cavalry were kept employed driving the men back to their guns.

I send you a sketch of the present position of affairs. The fighting is going on now, but with what success I know not. Our troops, though, are gaining at every step, and I am in hopes that by morning General Sherman will cut the communication between Vicksburg and Milldale, which should, by rights, end the affair.

The railroads have all been cut leading into Texas, and there will be no hope of supplies, even if Vicksburg can hold out for a short time.

The enemy cannot approach the left wing of our army until they reach the heights without coming in range of our gunboats. At that point the army will have all the fighting to do themselves.

The following is a list of the killed and wounded: Lieutenant Commander William Gwin, severely wounded on the right breast, lacerating the pectoral muscles extensively, also tearing away a portion of the muscles of the right forearm; George P. Lord, executive officer, severe contusion of the foot; Elias Reese, executive officer of the Marmora, slightly wounded; N. B. Willets, gunner, severely wounded; Robert Rhoyal, master-at-arms, killed; Thomas Smith, seaman, mortally wounded; Alexander W. Lynch, seaman, severe contusion of the head; Alexander Campbell, seaman, severely wounded; Stephen Moss, slightly wounded; George Collender, boy, slightly wounded.

I have the honor to be, very respectfully, your obedient servant,

DAVID D. PORTER,

Acting Rear-Admiral, Com'dg Mississippi Squadron.

Hon. GIDEON WELLES,

Secretary of the Navy, Washington, D. C.

Detailed report of the attack on the Yazoo batteries.

UNITED STATES MISSISSIPPI SQUADRON,

Yazoo River, December 31, 1862.

SIR: I have already written you a hurried report of the attack on the Yazoo batteries by the Benton, and have the honor to relate occurrences up to this date.

On the 27th instant Lieutenant Commander Walker, of the Baron De Kalb, had cleared the river Yazoo of torpedoes to the place nearly where the Cairo was sunk, and had obtained possession of two landings. The enemy, to the number of two thousand, were contesting every inch of ground from rifle-pits and from behind levees, where, from high overhanging banks, they could fire on our vessels almost with impunity. The light-draught iron-clads Signal, Juliet, and Romeo were very serviceable in performing this duty, being perfectly bullet-proof all over, except in their upper cabins, which were pretty badly cut up.

I did not deem the landings already secured sufficiently good, and on the 23d instant Lieutenant Commander Gwin, according to order, proceeded up the river in the Benton, accompanied by the Tyler, Lieutenant Commander Pritchett; Lexington, Lieutenant Commander Shirk; ram Queen of the West,

Captain E. W. Sutherland; ram Lioness, Master T. O. Reilly; Signal, Acting Master Scott; Romeo, Acting Ensign Smith; Juliet, Acting Volunteer Lieutenant Shaw. The 24th, 25th, and 26th were occupied in getting up the torpedoes, of which there were a great many; but, as the water had risen in the river, our vessels were enabled to keep off the sharpshooters, and the boats, being well covered, drove them back when they came in small numbers. Thus the work continued until the boats turned the bend in the river, where a series of forts, dotted all around the hills, and a heavy raft, covered with railroad iron, seemed to forbid all further progress. I directed the work to go on in the boats as near to the forts as possible, and they proceeded until the forts opened on them, at a distance of twelve hundred yards. Though much annoyed by the fire, on the 27th the boats continued their work, and the Benton closed up to cover them. It was blowing very hard at the time, and, the current being checked by the wind, the Benton, at all times an unmanageable ship, had a tendency to turn head or broadside to wind; in consequence of which she had to be tied to the bank. Then the enemy opened fire on her, almost every shot hitting her somewhere. Seven or eight heavy guns were firing from the different forts—50-pound rifles and 64-pounders solid. After she made fast to the bank she was hit thirty times. Whenever the shots hit the pilot-house or the defence on her sides they did but little harm, in some places scarcely leaving a mark; but whenever they struck her deck they went through everything, killing and wounding ten persons; among the latter Lieutenant Commander Gwin. The wind blew so hard that the other iron-clads were unmanageable, and, though they brought their batteries to bear (as did the Lexington and Tyler) as well as the very narrow stream would permit, they could not fire very effectually. Two of the guns in the forts were silenced, and, the boats being unable to work any longer, the vessels dropped back, around the point, out of fire. The object of the firing was only to cover the boats, as the forts can only be taken by a landing party, and a very strong one at that.

The Benton was not rendered inefficient in the least, though two of her guns were damaged so that they are no longer serviceable, having been hit with shot.

On the 28th General Sherman had advanced his forces within skirmishing distance of the enemy, and I sent up a strong force to make a feint on the forts, and to fire across on the Milldale road, to prevent re-enforcements from being sent that way from the Yazoo forts to Vicksburg. Owing to late heavy rains General Sherman found the ground almost impassable, and was headed off at every step by innumerable bayous. On the 29th the assault was to commence on the hills behind Vicksburg, provided the army could find an opening through the abattis, which was piled up before them in all directions, and thousands of sharpshooters, in rifle-pits, picking off the officers at every step. I brought up the only two mortars I had been able to get down here, and placed them in position (backed by the gunboats) to shell the woods on the right and left of our army, to prevent the enemy from doubling on either wing, also placing a portion of them at different points to protect the transports.

The battle commenced early in the day on the 29th, and our troops, with great heroism, went to the assault. One division succeeded in getting into the batteries on the hill, and drove the enemy out; but one of the two divisions that were to assault being behind time, the assault was unsuccessful; the men had to retire again, and lay on their arms that night in a cold, heavy rain, that must have decimated the army.

My opinion is that the present rain, which is heavy, will render any attempts of our army to enter Vicksburg in that way useless. They could scarcely move the artillery at first; it will be doubly troublesome now. In the mean time the rebels are receiving re-enforcements by every train, and are almost if not quite as numerous as our troops. Our army will have to intrench themselves until the ground will enable them to move. We have a good position, and the gunboats cover the army in a semicircle of eight miles.

Since I came below, the commanders of the different posts have all urgently demanded gunboats, many of them holding positions where they could drive off three or four times their number. At Island No. 10 I have been notified that the commander had been ordered to abandon that post and spike his guns. I have ordered the Pittsburg up there to hold it and to break up the guns, as they are old ones and fit for nothing; still the rebels might get them in some of these stampedes. The commanding officer at Columbus hears that forty thousand men are advancing on him, and wants a gunboat. I sent him the New Era, and ordered Commander Pennock to fit 32-pounders on the old mortar rafts, and plant them in front of Columbus and Hickman. General Curtis calls for a large force of gunboats, to meet General Gorman on the 5th of January, 1863. General Curtis has ordered movements from the east up the Arkansas on Little Rock. General Gorman wants two gunboats at Helena. He says he is utterly powerless with five thousand infantry and two thousand cavalry. I suppose I must raise them. The General Bragg is stationed at Memphis, to protect that place and repair her machinery. I have sent the Conestoga to the mouth of Arkansas river, to protect the troops about to be stationed there, and to prevent any intercourse up or down the Arkansas. As the light-draughts are finished they will be stationed at different points on the river.

What our future operations will be here I cannot yet tell. We expected that General Grant would have been in the rear of Vicksburg by this time, and that General Banks would have been at Port Hudson; both of which movements were, I believe, part of the plan of operations. We hear nothing of either of these generals.

The rebels are going to throw a powerful force into Vicksburg, to hold it at all hazards, and the heavy rains at this time will cause a change in the military operations. General Sherman is quite equal to the emergency, and nothing daunted by his want of success. Part of the programme of the rebels is to threaten our river ports, to make us draw off our troops from here, but with the position held by the commanders of these ports they can defy any force brought against them if they do their duty, and keep despatch boats ready to notify the gunboats that will soon be stationed on the river. If there is a delay, it will enable us to get down our iron-clads from above, of which I see no prospect at present.

Five light-draught steamers, under Lieutenant Commander Fitch, are up the Tennessee river, and will be able to operate there, now that the water is rising. We will soon have two others on the Ohio.

Everything in the squadron in the shape of a steamer has a gun of some kind mounted on her, and our vessels pass up and down without molestation.

The vessels now here are the Black Hawk, Benton, Baron De Kalb, Carondelet, Louisville, Cincinnati, Mound City, Lexington, Tyler, Signal, Romeo, Juliet, Forest Rose, Rattler, Marmora, rams Monarch, Queen of the West, Switzerland, Lioness, storeship Sovereign, ordnance vessels Judge Torrence and Great Western, floating smithery Sampson, tug-boat Champion, and six small tugs and two mortars, water-logged.

The health of the squadron is improving. The hospital ship is on her way down here.

I have the honor to be, very respectfully, your most obedient servant,

DAVID D. PORTER,

Acting Rear-Admiral, Com'dg Mississippi Squadron.

Hon. GIDEON WELLES,

Secretary of the Navy, Washington, D. C.

Report of Acting Rear-Admiral Porter relative to assault by General Sherman.

UNITED STATES MISSISSIPPI SQUADRON,
White River, January 18, 1863.

SIR: The army will move to-morrow on Vicksburg, with re-enforcements furnished by General Grant, who, I believe, will accompany the expedition as commander-in-chief. Had the combinations been carried out in our last expedition, General Grant advancing by Grenada, General Banks up river, and General Sherman down the river, the whole matter would have assumed a different aspect, but General Sherman was the only one on the ground. The army of General Grant had been cut off from its supplies. General Banks never came up the river, and General Sherman having attempted to take the enemy by surprise, lost about 700 wounded, 300 killed, and about 400 prisoners. All this was owing to Colonel De Courcy (who has since resigned) not following General Blair, who had no difficulty in getting into the works of the enemy. Had our troops been able to hold these works for three minutes, Vicksburg would have been ours; but that chance was lost, and will not offer again. The enemy crowded in 20,000 men from Grenada, and 10,000 from Jackson, and outnumbered us two to one. The rain forced General Sherman to embark, and we did so without the enemy being aware of it, until everything was on board. Not a thing of consequence was left behind. When the enemy did discover it, they sent down three regiments with field-pieces to attack the line of transports, which was covered at every point by the gunboats and light-draughts. The Lexington, Marmora, Queen of the West, and Monarch opened on the enemy with shrapnell, and cut them up very severely, causing them to fly in all directions, and not losing a man on our side. This is a short history of this affair. The operations to come will be of a different character. It will be a tedious siege—the first step, in my opinion, towards a successful attack on Vicksburg, which has been made very strong by land and water. I have always thought the late attempt was premature, but sometimes these dashes succeed, and certain it is that but for the want of nerve in the leader of a brigade the army would have succeeded.

The operations of the navy in the Yazoo are worthy to be ranked among the brightest events of the war. The officers in charge of getting up the torpedoes and clearing eight miles of the river distinguished themselves by their patient endurance and cool courage under a galling fire of musketry from well-protected and unseen riflemen, and the crews of the boats exhibited a courage and coolness seldom equalled. The navy will scarcely ever get credit for these events. They are not brilliant enough to satisfy our impatient people at the north, who know little of the difficulties attending an expedition like the one mentioned, or how much officers and men are exposing themselves, while they wonder why we do not demolish mountains of granite.

The department may rest assured that the navy here is never idle. The army depends on us to take entire charge of them on the water, and it employs every vessel I have. I have none too many. The light-draught vessels have only half crews. I am making up deficiencies with contrabands as fast as I can.

We expect to disembark the troops opposite Vicksburg in four or five days. In the mean time I want to gather up the fleet which are operating at different points with the army. My opinion is that Vicksburg is the main point; when that falls all subordinate posts will fall with it. Arkansas is or will be quiet for the present, and all smaller expeditions should be attached to the large one at Vicksburg. This will enable me to employ the gunboats to better advantage, which I cannot do now. The commander of every post requires a gunboat, but

I do not encourage them always in their expectations, as it makes them very careless about defending themselves.

Very respectfully, your obedient servant,

DAVID D. PORTER,
Acting Rear-Admiral, Com'dg Mississippi Squadron.

Hon. GIDEON WELLES,
Secretary of the Navy.

Position of affairs at Vicksburg.

UNITED STATES MISSISSIPPI SQUADRON,
Yazoo River, January 3, 1863.

SIR: The army has changed its position, which it was obliged to do owing to the heavy rains. The men have been without shelter for five days, the rain at times coming down in torrents. It was impossible for any army to work under the circumstances. They failed in the first assault only because the supporting division did not come up to its work, and the reserve fired (it is said) into our own men. Could the first division have held the batteries (which they took) for three minutes longer, our army could have commanded the hills back of Vicksburg. So desperate were the rebels that they fired grape and canister into and through their own retreating men, and mowed them down by the dozens.

The point of attack, at one time practicable, was no longer so after the assault of our army. It was rendered impassable by abattis and stockades. It was then determined by General Sherman and myself to attempt the forts on the Yazoo, at Drungel's bluff, by a night attack. Ten thousand men were to have been thrown right at the foot of the cliffs, risking the loss of the transports, while all the iron-clads were to open fire on the batteries and try and silence them temporarily. The ram Lioness, under Colonel Ellet, was fitted with an apparatus for breaking torpedo wires and was to go ahead and clear the way. Colonel Ellet was also provided with fifteen torpedoes to blow up the raft and enable the vessels to get by if possible. This desperate duty he took upon himself cheerfully, and no doubt would have performed it well had the opportunity occurred. The details of the expedition were left to me, and it was all ready to start at 3.30 a. m. A dense fog unfortunately set in at midnight and lasted until morning, when it was too late to start. It was so thick that vessels could not move; men could not see each other at ten paces. The river is too narrow for operations in clear weather, much less in a fog. After the fog, there was in the afternoon every indication of a long and heavy rain. The general very wisely embarked his whole army without being disturbed by the enemy, and is now lying five miles above Vicksburg, waiting for good weather and for McClernand to take command. The latter arrived before the army left its position, and approved the change. As we left the rain poured down in torrents, and will continue to do so or some time longer, rendering land operations perfectly impracticable. While the army leaders are deciding what to do, I have enough employment for the vessels here to patrol the river and occupy those posts which have been partially deserted, or where apprehension of invasion is felt.

I have the honor to be, very respectfully, your obedient servant,

DAVID D. PORTER,
Acting Rear-Admiral, Com'dg Mississippi Squadron.

Hon. GIDEON WELLES,
Secretary of the Navy, Washington, D. C.

Additional report of Acting Rear-Admiral Porter.

UNITED STATES MISSISSIPPI SQUADRON,
Mouth of Yazoo River, January 24, 1863.

SIR: I have the honor to report my arrival at this place.

The army are landing on the neck of land opposite Vicksburg. What they expect to do I don't know, but presume it is a temporary arrangement. I am covering their landing and guarding the Yazoo river.

The front of Vicksburg is heavily fortified, and unless we can get troops in the rear of the city I see no chance of taking it at present, though we cut off all their supplies from Texas and Louisiania.

A few days since I withdrew the gunboats from the mouth of the Yazoo, as they were entirely out of coal, and it was not proper to let them remain under the circumstances. The moment I could get coal I sent them down again, and they arrived just in time to block up eleven steamers in the Yazoo that had gone up for provisions and stores under the impression that we had left altogether. These vessels have been employed carrying supplies and arms from Vicksburg to Port Hudson. This will render the reduction of that place an easier task than it otherwise would have been, as there are no steamers on the river except two that will be kept at Vicksburg.

I have the honor to be, very respectfully, your obedient servant,

DAVID D. PORTER,
Acting Rear-Admiral, Com'dg Mississippi Squadron.

Hon. GIDEON WELLES,
Secretary of the Navy, Washington, D. C.

Services of the ram fleet, under the command of Lieutenant Colonel Ellet, on the Yazoo river.

UNITED STATES MISSISSIPPI SQUADRON,
Mississippi River, January 5, 1863.

SIR: In my different communications relating to the operations on the Yazoo river I omitted to mention the services of the ram fleet. I intended to have made a separate report, but have been unable to do so sooner.

From his first connexion with this squadron, Colonel Charles Rivers Ellet, the immediate commander of the ram fleet, has displayed great zeal in carrying out my orders, and when we have been threatened at different points, and having no vessel to send from Cairo, he has, on two occasions, furnished vessels at an hour's notice. When the expedition started down the river, the ram fleet was with us, and our main dependence in case we should encounter other rams.

We had none of the navy proper. Although, like ourselves, half manned, the ram fleet was ready to do anything required of it. In ascending the river, the Queen of the West, Captain E. K. Sutherland and Master J. O. Reilly, were very efficient in repelling the sharpshooters, their construction enabling them to fire over the banks, which our iron-clads could not do. Captain Sutherland kept unceasing watch in advance of the fleet while our boats were at work, and won golden opinions by his assiduity. On the night of the 31st of December, when it was intended to assault the batteries by land and water, Colonel Ellet took upon himself the perilous duty of running up in the Lioness, in face of the batteries, to clear out the torpedoes or break the wires, and to plant torpedoes on the raft which had a battery at each end of it. No doubt he would have performed it or lost his life and his vessel. I have great confidence in the commander of the rams and those under him, and take this opportunity to state to the department how highly I appreciate the commander and his associates.

I have the honor to be, very respectfully, your obedient servant,

DAVID D. PORTER,

Acting Rear-Admiral, Com'dg Mississippi Squadron.

Hon. GIDEON WELLES,

Secretary of the Navy, Washington, D. C.

Capture of Arkansas Post.

UNITED STATES MISSISSIPPI SQUADRON,

Arkansas Post, January 11, 1863.

SIR: The gunboats Louisville, De Kalb, Cincinnati, and Lexington attacked the heavy fort at Post of Arkansas last night, and silenced the batteries, killing many of the enemy. The gunboats attacked it again this morning and dismounted every gun, eleven in all. Colonel Dunnington, (late of the United States navy,) commandant of the fort, requested to surrender to the navy. I received his sword. The army co-operated on the land side. The forts were completely silenced, and the guns, eleven in number, were all dismounted in three hours. The action was at close quarters on the part of the three iron-clads, and the firing splendid. The list of killed and wounded is small. The Louisville lost twelve, De Kalb seventeen, Cincinnati none, Lexington none, Rattler two. The vessels, although much cut up, were ready for action in half an hour after the battle. The light-draught Rattler, Lieutenant Commander Watson Smith, and other light-draughts, joined in the action when it became general, as did the Black Hawk, Lieutenant Commander K. R. Breese, with her rifle guns. Particulars will be given hereafter.

Very respectfully, your obedient servant,

DAVID D. PORTER,

Acting Rear-Admiral, Com'dg Mississippi Squadron.

Hon. GIDEON WELLES,

Secretary of the Navy.

Detailed report of Acting Rear-Admiral D. D. Porter.

UNITED STATES MISSISSIPPI SQUADRON,

Arkansas Post, January 11, 1863.

SIR: I have the honor to inform you that on the 4th of January General McClernand concluded to move up river upon the Post of Arkansas, and requested my co-operation.

I detailed three iron-clads, the Louisville, Baron De Kalb, and Cincinnati, with all the light-draught gunboats, all of which had to be towed up the river. On the 9th we ascended the Arkansas river, as high as Arkansas Post, when the army landed within about four miles of the fort. The enemy had thrown up heavy earthworks and extensive rifle-pits all along the levee. While the army were making a detour to surround the fort, I sent up the iron-clads to try the range of their guns, and afterwards sent up the Rattler, Lieutenant Commander Watson Smith, to clear out the rifle-pits and the men behind an extensive breastwork in front of our troops. The Black Hawk also opened on them with her rifled guns, and, after a few fires, the enemy left the works, and our troops marched in. At 2 o'clock General McClernand told me the troops would be in position to assault the main fort, a very formidable work, and I held all the vessels in readiness to attack when the troops were in position. At 5.30 p. m. General McClernand sent me a message, stating that everything was ready, and the Louisville, Baron DeKalb, and Cincinnati advanced to within 400 yards of the fort, which then opened fire from three heavy guns, and eight rifled guns, and with musketry.

The superiority of our fire was soon manifest; the batteries were silenced, and we ceased firing, but no assault took place; and it being too dark to do anything, all the vessels dropped down, and tied up to the bank for the night.

The Baron DeKalb, Lieutenant Commander Walker; Louisville, Lieutenant Commander Owen; and the Cincinnati, Lieutenant Commanding Bache, led the attack, and when hotly engaged, I brought up the light-draught vessels, the Lexington and the Black Hawk, to throw in shrapnell and rifle shell. This fire was very destructive, killing nearly all the artillery horses in and about the fort.

When the battery was pretty well silenced, I ordered Lieutenant Commander Smith to pass the fort in the light-draught iron-clad Rattler and enfilade it, which he did in a very gallant and handsome manner, but suffered a good deal in his hull in doing so. All his cabin works were knocked to pieces, and a heavy shell raked him from stem to stern in the hull. Strange to say, two heavy shell struck his iron plating ($\frac{3}{4}$-inch) on the bow, and never injured it. He got past the fort, but became entangled among the snags placed in the river to impede our progress, and had to return.

In this evening attack the vessels of all the commanders were well handled, particularly the iron-clads. It was close quarters all the time, and not a gun was fired from our side until the gunboats were within 400 yards of the fort. The condition of the fort attests the accuracy of fire, and the persons inside give the Baron DeKalb, Lieutenant Commander Walker, the credit of doing the most execution.

I was informed again this morning, by General McClernand, that the army was "waiting for the navy to attack, when they would assault the works." I ordered up the iron-clads, with directions for the Lexington to join in when the former became hotly engaged, and for the frailer vessels to haul up in the smoke, and do the best they could. The Rattler, Lieutenant Commander Smith, and the Glide, Lieutenant Commander Woodworth, did good execution with their shrapnell, and when an opportunity occurred I made them push through by the fort again (also the ram Monarch, Colonel Charles Ellet,) and they proceeded rapidly up the river to cut off the enemy's retreat by the only way he had to get off. By this time all the guns in the fort were completely silenced by the Louisville, Lieutenant Commander E. K. Owen; Baron de Kalb, Lieutenant Commander J. G. Walker, and Cincinnati, Lieutenant Commanding G. M. Bache; and I ordered the Black Hawk up for the purpose of boarding it in front. Being unmanageable, she had to be kept up the narrow stream, and I took in a regiment from the opposite side to try and take it by assault. As I rounded to do so, and the gunboats commenced firing rapidly, knocking everything to pieces, the enemy held out a white flag, and I ordered the firing to cease. The army then entered and took possession. Colonel Dunnington, the commander of the fort, sent for me, and surrendered to me in person. General Churchill, of the rebel army, surrendered to the military commander. Our army had almost surrounded the fort, and were preparing to assault, and would no doubt have carried it with ease. They enfiladed it with rifle field-pieces, which did much damage to the houses and light work, leaving their marks in all directions.

I do not know yet what were the operations on the land side. I was too much interested in my own affairs, and in placing the vessels as circumstances required.

In all this affair there was the greatest zeal on the part of the officers commanding to carry out my orders, and not a mistake of any kind occurred. No fort ever received a worse battering, and the highest compliment I can pay those engaged is to repeat what the rebels said: "You can't expect men to stand up against the fire of those gunboats."

A large number of persons were captured in the fort—I don't know how many, and at sundown the army were hurrying in the cavalry and artillery.

I herewith enclose the report of the commanding officers, and a list of killed and wounded, and will take another occasion to mention to the department the names of those officers who have distinguished themselves particularly, though it is hard to discriminate when all did their duty so well.

I have the honor to be, very respectfully, your obedient servant,

DAVID D. PORTER,
Acting Rear-Admiral, Com'dg Mississippi Squadron.

Hon. GIDEON WELLES,
Secretary of the Navy, Washington, D. C.

Report of Lieutenant Commander E. K. Owen, commanding United States steamer Louisville.

UNITED STATES MISSISSIPPI SQUADRON,
U. S. S. Louisville, off Arkansas Post, Ark., January 11, 1863.

SIR: I have the honor to transmit the report of the killed and wounded on board this vessel, of the damages sustained from the enemy's guns, and the amount of ammunition expended during the engagements of yesterday and to-day with the enemy's batteries at Arkansas Post.

The damages sustained in the hull, as shown by the carpenter's report, though serious, have not in the least unfitted her for duty. I can only add that every officer and man did his duty.

Very respectfully, your obedient servant,

E. K. OWEN,
Lieutenant Commander, U. S. N.

Acting Rear-Admiral DAVID D. PORTER,
Commanding Mississippi Squadron.

Report of Acting Assistant Surgeon W. D. Hoffman of casualties on the Louisville.

UNITED STATES MISSISSIPPI SQUADRON,
Arkansas River, Ark., January 11, 1863.

SIR: The following is a list of the killed and wounded on board United States gunboat Louisville:

Frederick H. Gilhardy, seaman, wounded in head, mortally; Adam Bradshaw, seaman, wounded in thorax, mortally; James Mulherrin, seaman, wounded in thighs, severely; Jim Sullivan, seaman, contusion of thorax and abdomen; Thomas Spencer, seaman, wounded in elbow, slightly; Thomas Jackson, seaman, wounded in leg, slightly; Albert Mowry, seaman, wounded in knee, slightly; James Blaisdale, seaman, wounded in hand, slightly; George Holmes, seaman, contusion of shoulder, slightly; J. T. Blatchford, ensign, wounded in leg, severely; Walter Williams, seaman, killed.

WM. D. HOFFMAN,
Acting Assistant Surgeon.

Acting Rear-Admiral DAVID D. PORTER,
Commanding Mississippi Squadron.

Report of Lieutenant Commander J. W. Shirk, commanding United States steamer Lexington.

U. S. MISSISSIPPI SQUADRON, U. S. GUNBOAT LEXINGTON,
Off Post of Arkansas, Ark., January 11, 1863.

SIR: I have the honor to report that there were expended on board this ship, during the attack upon this fort by the forces under your command, on the night of the 10th instant, fourteen (14) Parrott shells and two (2) 8-inch shells; and during the final and victorious assault of to-day, forty-nine (49) 8-inch shells and forty (40) Parrott shells.

I am happy to report no casualties. The wood work of the ship and two of our boats are somewhat damaged.

I have the honor to be, sir, your most obedient servant,

JAMES W. SHIRK,
Lieutenant Commander.

Acting Rear-Admiral DAVID D. PORTER,
Commanding Mississippi Squadron.

Report of Lieutenant Commander John G. Walker, commanding the United States steamer Baron De Kalb.

U. S. MISSISSIPPI SQUADRON, U. S. GUNBOAT BARON DE KALB,
Arkansas Post, January 12, 1863.

SIR: I have the honor to report that in the attack on this place, on the evening of the 10th, this vessel was struck several times, but met with no serious injury to vessel or crew.

In the attack on the 11th, one of the 10-inch guns was struck in the muzzle, and both gun and carriage destroyed; one 32-pounder carriage struck and destroyed; one of the iron plates on forward casemate badly broken by shot; the wood work about two of the ports badly torn by shot, and one lower deck beam cut off by a plunging shot through the deck. The other injuries, although considerable, can be repaired on board in a few days. I lost two men killed and fifteen wounded; two probably mortally, and several seriously.

Before going into action, I covered the bow sides and pilot-house with slush, which, I think, was of much assistance in turning the shot, as the vessel was repeatedly struck by 8 and 9-inch shot, at very short range, and the iron was in no case penetrated. The loss was from shot and shell entering the ports.

My officers and men behaved with the greatest gallantry and coolness, and the practice with the guns was excellent. I expended forty-two 10-inch shells, nine 10-inch shrapnell, seventy 7-inch shells, and thirty-seven 32-pounder Parrott shells. Enclosed I send the surgeon's report of killed and wounded.

I am, sir, very respectfully, your obedient servant,

JOHN G. WALKER,
Lieutenant Commander, United States Navy.

Acting Rear-Admiral PORTER,
Commanding Mississippi Squadron.

Report of Acting Assistant Surgeon John Wise of casualties on the Baron De Kalb.

The surgeon's report of killed and wounded on board the United States gunboat Baron De Kalb in the attack on Arkansas Post, January 11, 1863, is as follows:

Killed.—John Ryan, landsman, and Theo. Bender, third-class boy.

Wounded.—Peter Colton, cockswain, penetrating wound in throat, also wounded in thigh and wrist, (probably fatal;) Alfred H. Boyle, yeoman, contusion of shoulder and back (not dangerous;) Seamen George Smith, fracture of skull, (probably fatal;) Joseph Eader, compound fracture of leg below knee, (may lose the leg;) John Farren, compound fracture of skull and extensive laceration of scalp; William Smith, penetrating wound through left shoulder blade; M. C. Donohs, severe injury of foot and ankle joints by penetration of shell, (very serious cases;) William Smiley, laceration of scalp and face; Joseph H. Mallow, laceration of scalp and face; Oscar Jordon, small piece of shell in poplical space of thigh; Antonio DeUoroa, contusion of left arm from splint; George Fales, penetrating wound of left leg from pieces of shell; William Kelly, contusion of back; Pierre Leon, splinters in face; John Glenn, contused wound in side, (none of which are dangerous.)

Respectfully, your obedient servant,

JOHN WISE,
Acting Assistant Surgeon.

JOHN G. WALKER,
Lieutenant Commanding.

Report of Lieutenant Commanding George M. Bache, commanding United States steamer Cincinnati.

UNITED STATES MISSISSIPPI SQUADRON,
U. S. Gunboat Cincinnati, off Arkansas Post, July 12, 1863.

SIR: I have the honor to report having sustained no serious damage in the attack on the 10th. One shell struck us at the water-line forward, and a second went through the upper works.

We were equally fortunate during the attack of yesterday, although struck nine times on the bow casemate, pilot-house, and upper works.

This vessel fired the first gun at 1.30 p. m., and in half or three-quarters of an hour the right casemate gun of the fort (the one assigned us) was silenced, when our fire was directed on the left casemate and barbette guns, and afterwards in shelling the interior of the fort. We engaged the fort at three hundred yards.

I have to mention Acting Ensign A. F. O'Neil, Acting Master's Mate Henry Broby, and Acting Gunner John F. Riblett, the officers commanding the bow guns, for coolness and skill in directing their fire.

Very respectfully, your obedient servant,

GEORGE M. BACHE,
Lieutenant Commanding.

Acting Rear-Admiral DAVID D. PORTER,
Commanding Mississippi Squadron.

List of officers captured at Arkansas Post.

No. 47.]

UNITED STATES MISSISSIPPI SQUADRON,
Arkansas River, January 12, 1863.

SIR: I enclose a list of officers belonging to the staff of Colonel Dunnington, late of the navy and commander of the post, who delivered their swords and surrendered to the navy. I have sent them to Captain Pennock, at Cairo, to be provided for, &c.

I advise that these officers be exchanged at Richmond; they will then not return to this river.

Very respectfully, your most obedient servant,

DAVID D. PORTER,
Acting Rear-Admiral, Com'dg Mississippi Squadron.

Hon. GIDEON WELLES,
Secretary of the Navy, Washington, D. C.

List of officers belonging to the Confederate States navy captured at Arkansas Post January 12, 1863.

John W. Dunnington, colonel commanding third brigade, and first lieutenant Confederate States navy, commanding naval forces; Joseph Preble, acting master Confederate States navy; Frank Ranger, acting master Confederate States navy; F. M. Roby, first lieutenant and brigade ordnance officer, and midshipman Confederate States navy; N. M. Read, assistant surgeon Confederate States navy; W. S. Campbell, major and quartermaster third brigade and captain's clerk Confederate States navy; Howell Quigley, second assistant engineer Confederate States navy; Samuel Suttioan, third assistant engineer Confederate States navy; Joseph Nutter, master's mate Confederate States navy; W. A. Lang, captain's steward Confederate States navy; George Elliot, boatswain's mate; John McDonald, boatswain's mate; W. C. Fisher, master-at-arms; Charles Lettig, quartermaster; John B. Hassett, quartermaster; Michael Kemmett, quartermaster; John Shephard, quartermaster; P. J. Fitzpatrick, purser's steward; James Hussey, surgeon's steward; Richard Scott, gunner's mate; Charles Loewenberg, ship's cook; T. J. Jackson, ward-room cook; Charles Crowley, seaman; Charles Williams, seaman; Patrick Kelly, ordinary seaman; Pliny Cox, ordinary seaman; John Lee, ordinary seaman; Henry Peters, landsman; Edward Walsh, first-class fireman; George Dehman, first-class fireman; John Fuller, coal-heaver; Aleck Martin, first-class boy; John Brown, first-class boy; Christopher Kain, second-class boy; Michael Knackley, second-class boy; Samuel H. Bink, captain, acting general; A. M. Williams, captain of engineers.

Report of Acting Rear-Admiral Porter, commendatory of the officers engaged in the action

UNITED STATES MISSISSIPPI SQUADRON,
Arkansas Post, January 13, 1863.

SIR: The general report of an action embraces all those engaged in it; and although on this occasion the conduct of all the officers met my approbation, I must give a little more credit to some than to others. Lieutenant Commander John G. Walker is a man of more than ordinary intelligence, with cool, calm judgment in time of action, and one on whom the government can rely to perform any duty. He managed and fought his vessel most beautifully, and I never had to correct a movement of his during the action. I look upon him as one of the most reliable officers in the service. The rebels admit that they never saw such firing in their lives as came from the 10-inch guns of the Baron De Kalb, and I know of no instance on record where every gun in a fort was dismounted or destroyed. Lieutenant Commander Watson Smith is well known to the department, and I believe they appreciate his gallantry as an officer. He performed on this occasion a daring act, passing a strong fort under a heavy fire of cannon and musketry; for the enemy, having no one at the time to contend with in the rear, directed the fire of six thousand muskets on our vessels.

Lieutenant Commanding George M. Bache is a very young officer, but displayed the coolness of a veteran. His vessel was not hurt, nor did he lose a man, because he silenced so soon the guns which I directed him to fire on.

Lieutenant Commander Elias K. Owen, of the Louisville, managed his vessel handsomely, and did his work as well as the others. He labored under the disadvantage of having two shell burst in his ports, killing and wounding eleven men, which for a moment only stopped his fire.

Lieutenant Commander James W. Shirk brought up the Lexington in good time, and opened his broadside on the fort. One of his first guns destroyed a rifled piece which was boring him pretty effectually.

Lieutenant Selim E. Woodworth, in the Glide, passed through with Lieutenant Commander Watson Smith, and helped to cut off the retreat of the rebels, thirty or forty only of whom escaped by a ferry, ten miles up the river. The ferry was destroyed by the two officers above mentioned, and the rebel army all fell into our hands.

Lieutenant Commander K. Randolph Breese, of the Black Hawk, brought up his ship sufficiently close into action to do much execution with his rifled 30-pounders, and headed the men in the two attempts we made to board the fort, which was only prevented by the parting of the wheel-ropes.

I have endeavored to do full justice to all the above-mentioned officers, and have not said a word too much in their praise.

I have the honor to be, very respectfully, your obedient servant,

DAVID D. PORTER,

Acting Rear-Admiral, Com'dg Mississippi Squadron.

Hon. GIDEON WELLES,

Secretary of the Navy, Washington, D. C.

Sketches of Fort Hindman and of the casemates destroyed.

UNITED STATES MISSISSIPPI SQUADRON,

January 17, 1863.

SIR: I have the honor to enclose a chart and sketches of Fort Hindman, Post of Arkansas, showing the position and destructive fire of the iron-clads Louisville, Baron De Kalb, and Cincinnati.

I have the honor to be, very respectfully, your obedient servant,

DAVID D. PORTER,

Acting-Rear Admiral, Com'dg Mississippi Squadron.

Hon. GIDEON WELLES,

Secretary of the Navy, Washington, D. C.

VIEW OF FORT HINDMAN, ARKANSAS POST.

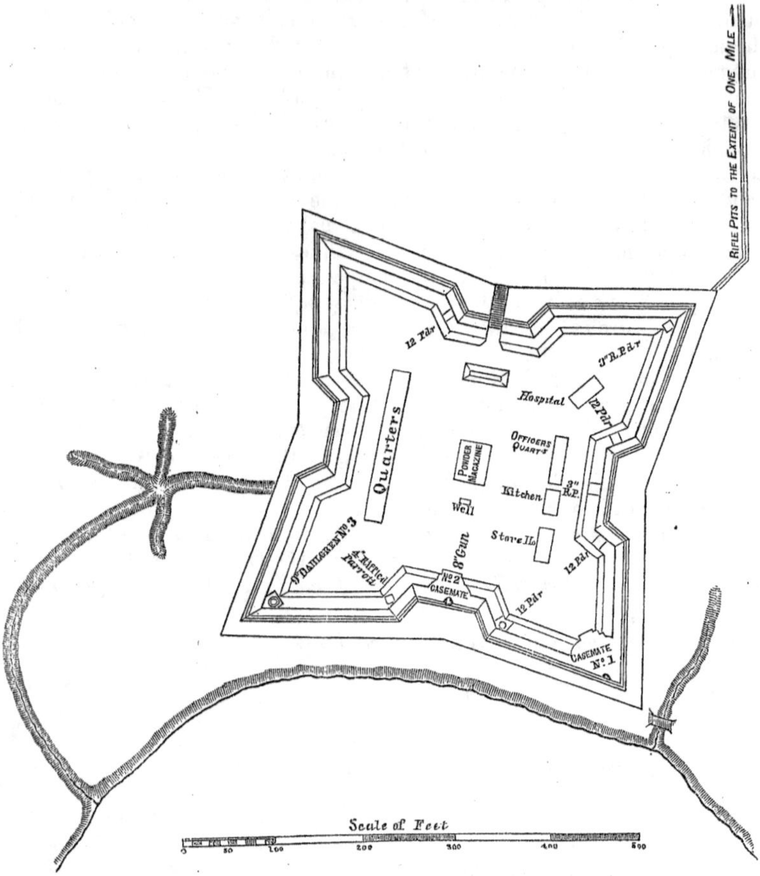

RIFLE PITS TO THE EXTENT OF ONE MILE
12 Pdr
3" R. Pdr
Hospital
12 Pdr
Quarters
POWDER MAGAZINE
OFFICERS QUART'S
Kitchen
3" R.P.
Well
Store H.
8" Gun
No 2 CASEMATE
9" DAHLGREN No 3
4" Rifled Parrott
12 Pdr
12 Pdr
CASEMATE No 1

Scale of Feet
0 50 100 200 300 400 500

APPEARANCE OF IX-INCH GUN SILENCED BY THE "CINCINNATI."

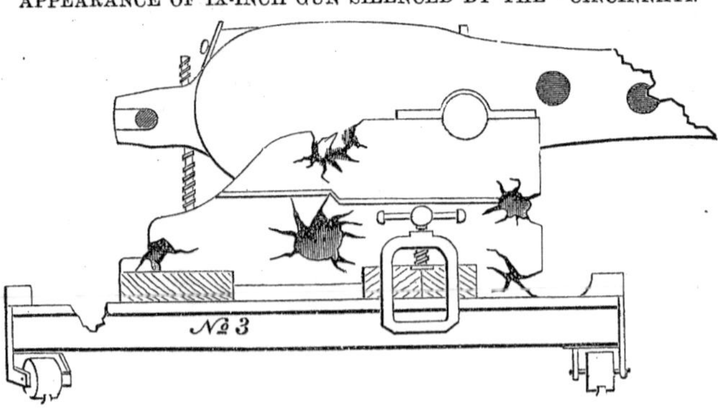

CASEMATE NO. 1, DESTROYED BY THE U. S. GUNBOAT "BARON DEKALB."

APPEARANCE OF CASEMATES BEFORE THE ATTACK.
(Covered with railroad iron.)

CASEMATE NO. 2, DESTROYED BY THE U. S. GUNBOAT "LOUISVILLE."

REAR VIEW OF CASEMATE NO. 2.

Acting Rear-Admiral Porter reports the evacuation of St. Charles, on the White river.

UNITED STATES MISSISSIPPI SQUADRON,
Arkansas River, January 16, 1863.

SIR: On the morning of the 12th instant, after taking Fort Hindman, I sent the gunboats Baron De Kalb and Cincinnati, under the command of Lieutenant Commander John G. Walker, to St. Charles, on the White river, to capture the fort and guns there, General Gorman moving up at the same time with transports and troops. They reached St. Charles on the 14th, and found the rebels had evacuated, leaving their defences unfinished. The enemy succeeded in carrying off two 8-inch guns in the Blue Wing, an army transport the guerillas captured a short time since.

I have sent two light-draught steamers to Lieutenant Commander Walker, with instructions to pursue the Blue Wing as long as he can hear of her, and get the guns if it is possible. This escape would not have taken place had an attack been made on both places at the same time, which should have been done. About such matters, however, I have no control at present, but hope to have hereafter.

I presume we will now move down the Mississippi to carry out what I conceive to have been the plans for which this army was organized, viz: the capture of Vicksburg.

It is rather a waste of time stopping here after the defences are destroyed.

We cannot go any higher (until April) up this river, nor can anything of any draught get down. The Pontchartrain, a rebel ram, is up at Little Rock, but preparations have been made to destroy her. I presume by this time she has shared the fate of other rebel rams. She draws eleven feet, and cannot possibly get down; besides, she has no guns, her battery having been destroyed at Fort Hindman.

I have the honor to be, very respectfully, your obedient servant,

DAVID D. PORTER,
Acting Rear-Admiral, Com'dg Mississippi Squadron.

Hon. GIDEON WELLES,
Secretary of the Navy, Washington, D. C.

Report of Lieutenant Commander John G. Walker.

UNITED STATES STEAMER BARON DE KALB,
St. Charles, Arkansas, January 14, 1863.

SIR: I have the honor to report that, in obedience to your order of the 12th, I left Arkansas Post on that day, with the Cincinnati and this vessel, and met General Gorman with his command the next morning at Prairie landing, on White river. Having a transport to tow each of the gunboats, I reached this point at 11 a. m. to-day, and found it evacuated. From information received here, it appears that the small body of troops stationed here left on the evening of the 12th on board the Blue Wing, taking two 8-inch guns and a field battery with them, and went up the river.

They left one casemate unfinished and an extensive range of rifle-pits.

General Gorman has asked that one of the vessels shall go up the river with a part of his force, and the other remain at this place.

I have ordered the Cincinnati to remain here, and shall go up the river myself this afternoon.

Very respectfully, your obedient servant,

JOHN G. WALKER,
Lieutenant Commander, United States Navy.

Acting Rear-Admiral D. D. PORTER,
Commanding Mississippi Squadron.

Burning of the steamers Jacob Mussbrain and Grampus.—Retaliatory measures.

UNITED STATES MISSISSIPPI SQUADRON,
January 18, 1863.

SIR: I have the honor to enclose a communication from Lieutenant Commander Joshua Bishop in relation to investigations made about the burning of the steamers Jacob Mussbrain and Grampus above Memphis.

I have the honor to be, very respectfully, your obedient servant,

DAVID D. PORTER,
Acting Rear-Admiral, Com'dg Mississippi Squadron.

Hon. GIDEON WELLES,
Secretary of the Navy, Washington, D. C.

Report of Lieutenant Commander Joshua Bishop, commanding United States steamer General Bragg.

UNITED STATES STEAMER GENERAL BRAGG,
Memphis, January 13, 1863.

SIR: I respectfully report that I went on board the light-draught gunboat Linden, on the afternoon of the 12th, to visit the place where the Jacob Mussbrain and Grampus were burned. The Linden had on board the part of the 89th regiment of Indiana volunteers under the command of Major Cabborly. Proceeded up the river, passing by way of Mound City, (where the steamer Grampus was burned;) anchored near Bradley's landing, (where the Jacob Mussbrain was burned.) About 10 p. m. a steamer passed down, and when a short distance below us a signal-light was shown on the bank; the steamer blew her whistle and made a landing. Perceiving that she was landing, I hailed her with the steam-whistle, which she did not notice. Got under way, and the vessel which had left the bank sounded the whistle and fired a gun. After chasing the vessel some distance, brought her to and boarded her—the steamer Chippeway Valley; finding nothing wrong, permitted her to proceed on down the river.

Steamed back to Bradley's landing and anchored. At 7 a. m. got under way and landed at Bradley's landing to communicate. Ascertained that there was quite a force of guerillas in the neighborhood; that they intended destroying steamers; that their rendezvous was at Mound City, Marion, and Hopefield; that a man named Cheek was instrumental in burning the steamers. At 9 a. m. left Bradley's landing and proceeded to Mound City—firing shells at intervals into the woods, as it was supposed there were guerillas thereabouts. At 10 a. m. landed at Mound City and disembarked the troops; the infantry made prisoners of several citizens who had been harboring guerillas; set fire to and burned several unoccupied houses belonging to Mr. Cheek and others, as there was evidence that they had been lately occupied.

The infantry proceeded by land to Hopefield, searching houses for arms. At

2 p. m. landed at Hopefield and embarked the troops. Steamed down to Fort Pickering and disembarked the troops.

The pickets exchanged shots with some mounted men, and a number of shotguns, rifles, and revolvers, &c., were captured.

I am, sir, very respectfully, your obedient servant,

JOSHUA BISHOP,
Lieutenant Commander.

Lieut. Com'dr THOMAS O. SELFRIDGE, U. S. N.,
Com'dg U. S. Steamer Conestoga, Senior Officer, Memphis, Tenn.

Acting Rear-Admiral Porter's report of expedition up the White river.

UNITED STATES MISSISSIPPI SQUADRON,
January 20, 1863.

SIR: I have the honor to inform you that the naval expedition up White river, under the command of Lieutenant Commander John G. Walker, was successful in accomplishing the duty on which it was sent. Lieutenant Commander Walker pushed on to Duvall's Bluff in the Baron de Kalb, and reached there just as the two 8-inch guns were being placed on the cars for Little Rock. He landed his men and took possession of all rebel property; the rebels fled. The capture of these guns makes it very difficult for the rebels to defend the approaches to Little Rock, and the State of Arkansas is completely in our power. When all the light-draught gunboats join me I will see that the river is kept under surveillance. * * * * * * *

I sent Lieutenant Commander Walker three swift, light-draught vessels as soon as I could, and with these and the Baron De Kalb he is pursuing the Blue Wing, and any other steamers that are there.

The Cincinnati remains at St. Charles to guard the river thereabouts. The Baron De Kalb has already ascended the White river over three hundred and fifty miles.

I enclose a copy of Lieutenant Commander Walker's report.

I beg leave to state that all the property that was on board the Blue Wing when she fell into the enemy's hands is in our possession, excepting the mails. It only remains to take her, or have them destroy her. I enclose a list of prisoners captured and paroled.

I have the honor to be, very respectfully, your obedient servant,

DAVID D. PORTER,
Acting Rear-Admiral, Com'dg Mississippi Squadron.

Hon. GIDEON WELLES,
Secretary of the Navy, Washington City, D. C.

Lieutenant Commander Walker's report.

UNITED STATES GUNBOAT BARON DE KALB,
Duvall's Bluff, White River, January 16, 1863.

SIR: I have the honor to report my arrival at this place. Leaving the transports at Arkapola, four miles below, I cleared for action and steamed up, arriving at about 3 p. m. Meeting with no resistance, I made fast to the bank, and landing a party took possession of all the public property.

I found two fine 8-inch guns and carriages, about two hundred stand of arms, with accoutrements, and three platform cars.

The guns were upon skids, and were being parbuckled upon the cars, when the rebels took the alarm and fled. The supper for the soldiers was cooking when I arrived, and they left blankets and traps of all kinds behind. I took seven prisoners, and from them and the negroes learned that the troops engaged in loading the cars ran about fifteen minutes before I arrived, and at the same time the steamer Blue Wing went up the river. The guns and carriages are in good order, and many of the small-arms are new Enfield rifles.

Upon the arrival of General Gorman's troops I drew off my men, and turned over to the army.

I am, sir, very respectfully, your obedient servant,

JOHN G. WALKER,
Lieutenant Commander.

Acting Rear-Admiral DAVID D. PORTER,
Com'dg United States Mississippi Squadron.

Results of the White River Expedition.

UNITED STATES MISSISSIPPI SQUADRON,
January 26, 1863.

SIR: I have the honor to enclose a report from Lieutenant Commander John G. Walker, in relation to the winding up of the White river expedition, which was as successful as could be desired, with the exception of the recapture of the Blue Wing. The troops will not move without a gunboat, and Lieutenant Commander Walker had to return with them, much to his and my disappointment. Every gun of any importance has now been captured or destroyed in Arkansas; thirteen (13) fort guns taken by the navy in the defences or in transit, and eighteen (18) field-pieces by the army, which cut the guns off at Fort Hindman, in all thirty-one (31) guns and a large amount of stores and ammunition. All our vessels were much broken in ascending and descending the narrow rivers, (Arkansas and White,) but all hands are at work repairing damages, and are now ready to go at anything when all the army arrives here, and pronounce themselves ready for action.

Lieutenant Commander Walker performed the duty I sent him on much to my satisfaction, and deserves all the credit for the capture of guns, other rebel property, and prisoners.

The army is still landing. I cannot see, though, what can possibly be done by the entire army landing on the neck of land opposite Vicksburg. They have no siege guns, except four, with which I supplied them; and a sudden rise of water, overflowing the levee, will drown them all out, and destroy much government property.

The naval vessels, however, are busily employed, doing all they can to cover the troops, convoy them up and down the river, and guard those points from which guerillas fire on the boats.

Very respectfully, your obedient servant,

DAVID D. PORTER,
Acting Rear-Admiral, Com'dg Mississippi Squadron.

Hon. GIDEON WELLES,
Secretary of the Navy, Washington, D. C.

Report of Lieutenant Commander John G. Walker.

UNITED STATES GUNBOAT BARON DE KALB,
Mississippi River, January 22, 1863.

SIR: On the 18th I received your letter, directing me, if General Gorman would furnish a detachment of troops, to push up White river, and endeavor to capture or destroy the Blue Wing and other steamers. General Gorman gave me the troops, and I was about starting, when orders from Generals Curtis and Grant obliged him to withdraw his troops from the river, and prevented the expedition. I therefore followed the transports down the river. Before leaving Duvall's Bluff the depot building and cars were set on fire by the troops. The wood of which the depot was built was green cypress, and covered with snow. Seeing that but little damage was likely to be done by the fire, I sent an officer and boat's crew, who cut away the upright timbers, and bending a line to the building, pulled it down and burned it. At the same time the chief engineer, with a party of men with sledges, broke the car wheels and journals to pieces, utterly ruining them. The cars were also burned.

On my way down I remained at Clarendon until the cavalry force there started for Helena. At St. Charles I assisted an officer of General Hovey's staff to blow up the magazine, using the powder I captured at Des Arc. The iron gun-slides I threw upon the burning timber of the casemates. I believe everything of use to the enemy at St. Charles that could be destroyed was destroyed by the army or ourselves.

Very respectfully, your obedient servant,

JOHN G. WALKER.
Lieutenant Commander, United States Navy.

Acting Rear-Admiral DAVID D. PORTER,
Commanding Mississippi Squadron.

Additional report of Acting Rear-Admiral Porter.

UNITED STATES MISSISSIPPI SQUADRON,
January 28, 1863.

SIR: I mentioned in one of my reports to you that the army had captured eighteen field-pieces at Arkansas Post on the field. Only seventeen guns were captured in all, six besides the guns in the fort, captured by the navy. I was misinformed.

I have the honor to be, very respectfully, your obedient servant,

DAVID D. PORTER,
Acting Rear-Admiral, Com'dg Mississippi Squadron.

Hon. GIDEON WELLES,
Secretary of the Navy, Washington, D. C.

Expedition up the Cumberland River.

OFFICE OF MISSISSIPPI SQUADRON,
Cairo, Illinois, January 31, 1863.

SIR: I have the honor to enclose herewith the report of Lieutenant Commander S. L. Phelps, whom I sent up the Cumberland river, in the United States gunboat Lexington, on special duty, to examine the condition of that river, and report its requirements to me.

The Lexington will be sent up the river again to-night, and will be placed under the command of Lieutenant Commander Le Roy Fitch temporarily. That vessel had been ordered by Acting Rear-Admiral D. D. Porter to return to the fleet in the Lower Mississippi as soon as she had conveyed the prisoners captured at the Post of Arkansas to this place, and had received some necessary repairs here; but deeming that the emergency of the case would excuse my action, and that the telegrams from the department and General Rosecrans would warrant it, and knowing that much time must elapse before I could communicate with the acting rear-admiral, and receive an answer, I sent her, together with the Silver Lake, up the Cumberland.

I shall endeavor, in every way in my power, to co-operate with the army, and I trust that I shall be able to carry out the directions of the department and acting rear-admiral in regard thereto in every respect.

I have the honor to be, very respectfully, your obedient servant,

A. M. PENNOCK,
Fleet-Captain and Commandant of Station.

Hon. GIDEON WELLES,
Secretary of the Navy, Washington, D. C.

Report of Lieutenant Commander Phelps.

OFFICE OF MISSISSIPPI SQUADRON,
Cairo, Illinois, January 30, 1863.

SIR: In obedience to your order, I proceeded up the Cumberland river with the gunboat Lexington to Nashville, Tennessee, and returned to this place last night. Meeting with a transport that had been fired upon by artillery, twenty miles above Clarksville, I at once went to that point, and landing, burned a storehouse used by the rebels as a resort and cover. On leaving there to descend to Clarksville, where I had passed a fleet of thirty-one steamers, with numerous barges in tow, convoyed by three light-draught gunboats, under Lieutenant Commander Fitch, the Lexington was fired upon by the enemy, who had two Parrott guns, and struck three times, but the rebels were quickly dislodged and dispersed.

I then returned to Clarksville, and, agreeable to the arrangement already made by Lieutenant Commander Fitch, left that place at midnight, with the whole fleet of boats, and reached Nashville the following night without so much as a musket-shot having been fired upon a single vessel of the fleet. Doubtless the lesson of the previous day had effected this result.

From the best information to be had it appears that the rebels had a number of guns, with a considerable covering force, extending along Harpeth shoals, a distance of some eight or ten miles. This force can readily operate upon both the Cumberland and Tennessee rivers. Besides these guns, the enemy also has several pieces about Savannah, on the Tennessee. No steamer should be permitted to run on either river, above Forts Henry and Donelson, without the convoy of a gunboat. Lieutenant Commander Fitch has not, at present, an adequate force to protect government transports upon the two streams, and I would suggest the propriety of sending him the Lexington. Her heavy guns have great effect with the rebels, and while they will fire upon vessels immediately under the howitzers of the light-draught gunboats, they will not show themselves where the heavier gunboats are. I have no doubt, with the aid of the Lexington, Captain Fitch will be able effectually to protect all the government vessels in those rivers.

I am, sir, respectfully, your obedient servant,

S. L. PHELPS,
Lieutenant Commander.

Captain A. M. PENNOCK, U. S. N.,
Fleet-Captain and Commandant of Station, Cairo, Ill.

Telegram from Lieutenant Commander Le Roy Fitch.

[By telegraph from Smithfield, Kentucky, 1863.]

UNITED STATES MILITARY TELEGRAPH,
Cairo, January 31, 1863.

The Robb joined me yesterday at this place. Nothing very serious up Tennessee river. Have sent the Robb and St. Clair to Paducah to bring up our coal barge.

The small-pox is in that place. Have another large convoy to take to Nashville, and one to bring down. No danger of either river being blockaded by the rebels.

LE ROY FITCH,
Lieutenant Commander.

Fleet-Captain A. M. PENNOCK,
Commandant of Naval Station.

Passage of the Vicksburg batteries by the Queen of the West.—Proceedings below Vicksburg.

YAZOO RIVER, *February* 2, 1863.

SIR: I have the honor to report that on the 1st February I gave the following order to Colonel Charles R. Ellet, of the ram fleet.

This order was carried out, excepting the destruction of the vessel, and we are now enabled to prevent supplies reaching the enemy at Vicksburg and Port Hudson by the Mississippi river.

The Queen of the West passed the batteries in broad daylight, instead of in the dark, as I intended, and received twelve shot and shell; but as I had ordered her covered with two thicknesses of cotton bales, no damage was done to the hull, though she was exposed to the fire of all the batteries for fifty (50) minutes. Some of the heaviest shot struck her. My orders were handsomely and gallantly carried out, and if the Vicksburg was not sunk, it was because of her wide guards and great strength. I have ordered the Queen of the West to proceed down as low as Red river, to capture and destroy all the rebel property she may meet with. The first favorable opportunity I will re-enforce her, and if we cannot take Vicksburg, the enemy will have to evacuate its other points on the river for want of supplies and transportation.

I send Colonel Charles R. Ellet's report. I cannot speak too highly of this gallant and daring officer. The only trouble I have is to hold him in and keep him out of danger; he will undertake anything I wish him to without asking questions, and these are the kind of men I like to command. The enemy fired over fifty (50) heavy guns and many field-pieces.

The calibre of shot that struck the Queen of the West was 100-pounder rifle, 64-pounder solid and shell, 50-pounder shell, 30-pounder shell, and 32-pounder smooth-bore. The Vicksburg is in a sinking condition, and has her steam-pump going all the time.

I have the honor to remain, very respectfully, your obedient servant,

DAVID D. PORTER,
Acting Rear-Admiral, Com'dg Mississippi Squadron.

Orders to Colonel Ellet.

YAZOO RIVER, *February* 1, 1863.

SIR: You will proceed with the Queen of the West to Vicksburg, and destroy the steamer Vicksburg, lying off that place; after which, you will proceed down the river as far as our batteries, below the canal, and report to me. In going down you will go along under low speed, having steerage-way enough, and keeping close to the right-hand shore going down. Before you start, it would be better to have a large bed of coal in, so that you will not have to put in fresh coal. The smoke might betray you. After you have destroyed the steamer, go down stream, and when clear of the city, show three vertical lights, that our batteries may not fire on you. If you get disabled, drift down until abreast of our batteries, and the small army steamer will go to your assistance. Have every light in your ship put out before you leave for Vicksburg, except the three lights to be shown to our batteries, which must be kept covered up. See that no lights show from the stern, as you pass the town, enabling them to rake you; and adopt every means of concealment. The best place to strike the steamer is twenty feet forward of her wheel. After disabling her there, so that she will sink, fire through her boilers and in among her machinery as she goes down.

It will not be part of your duty to save the lives of those on board. They must look out for themselves, and may think themselves lucky if they do not meet the same fate meted out to the Harriet Lane. Think of the fate of that vessel while performing your duty, and shout Harriet Lane into the ears of the rebels. If you can fire turpentine balls from your bow field-pieces into the light upper works, it will make a fine finish to the sinking part.

Further orders for duty to be performed below will be given after your report.

Respectfully, your obedient servant,

DAVID D. PORTER,
Acting Rear-Admiral, Com'dg Mississippi Squadron.

Colonel CHAS. R. ELLET,
Ram Queen of the West.

Report from Colonel Ellet.

UNITED STATES STEAM RAM QUEEN OF THE WEST,
Below Vicksburg, February 2, 1863.

ADMIRAL: In compliance with your instructions, I started on the Queen of the West, at half past four o'clock this morning, to pass the batteries at Vicksburg and sink the rebel steamer lying before that city.

I discovered immediately on starting that the change of the wheel from its former position to the narrow space behind the Queen's bulwark did not permit the boat to be handled with sufficient accuracy. An hour or more was spent in rearranging the apparatus, and when we finally rounded the point the sun had risen, and any advantage which would have resulted from the darkness was lost to us.

The rebels opened a heavy fire upon us as we neared the city, but we were only struck three times before reaching the steamer. She was lying in nearly the same position that the Arkansas occupied when General Ellet ran the Queen into her on a former occasion. The same causes which prevented the destruction of the Arkansas then, saved the City of Vicksburg this morning. Her position was such that if we had run obliquely into her as we came down, the bow of the Queen would inevitably have glanced. We were compelled to partially round to in order to strike. The consequence was, that at the very moment of collision, the current, very strong and rapid at this point, caught the stern of my boat, and, acting on her bow as a pivot, swung her round so rapidly that nearly all her momentum was lost. I had anticipated this result, and therefore caused the starboard bow gun to be shotted with three of the incendiary projectiles recommended in your orders. As we swung round, Sergeant J. H. Campbell, detailed for the purpose, fired this gun. A sixty-four pound shell crashed through the barricade just before he reached the spot, but he did not hesitate. The discharge took place at exactly the right moment, and set the rebel steamer in flames, which they subsequently succeeded in extinguishing.

At this moment one of the enemy's shells set the cotton near the starboard wheel on fire, while the discharge of our own gun ignited that portion which was on the bow. The flames spread rapidly, and the dense smoke rolling into the engine-room suffocated the engineers. I saw that if I attempted to run into the City of Vicksburg again, my boat would certainly be burnt. I ordered her to be headed down stream, and turned every man to extinguishing the flames. After much exertion we finally put the fire out by cutting the burning bales loose. The enemy of course were not idle. We were struck twelve times, but though the cabin was knocked to pieces, no material injury to the boat or to any of those on her was inflicted.

About two regiments of rebel sharpshooters, in rifle-pits, kept up a continual fire, but did no damage. The Queen was struck twice in the hull, but above the water-line. One of our guns was dismounted and ruined.

I can only speak in the highest terms of the conduct of every man on board. All behaved with cool, determined courage.

I remain, very respectfully,

CHARLES RIVERS ELLET,
Colonel, Commanding Ram Fleet.

David D. Porter,
Acting Rear-Admiral, Com'dg Mississippi Squadron.

United States Mississippi Squadron,
February 2, 1863.

The following is a list of the officers on board the ram Queen of the West while running the batteries at Vicksburg to-day:

Colonel Charles Rivers Ellet, Captain E. W. Sutherland, First Lieutenant J. E. Tuttle, Master Sims Edison, Master J. C. Duncan, Engineer Reuben Townsend.

Letter of Acting Rear-Admiral Porter.

United States Mississippi Squadron,
Mouth of the Yazoo, February 5, 1863.

Sir: After the ram Queen of the West had "reported progress" before Vicksburg, I ordered her down the river to sink and destroy all vessels she met with. Colonel Ellet returned this morning, passing the fort at Warrenton in broad daylight, and was hit several times. He destroyed below three large steamers loaded with pork, sugar, molasses, and army supplies. He captured five captains and two lieutenants. A number of rebel officers made their escape by jumping overboard. Colonel Ellet came within two hours of catching General Dick Taylor with a transport load of troops.

The Queen of the West went ten miles up the Red river, where there are many fine steamers that are supplying Port Hudson. They will likely not attempt to go out while the ram is about. She is now out of coal, and had to return on that account. I am going to supply her, either by drifting a barge around at night or by sending across the land.

Colonel Ellet learns from the prisoners that General Banks is seven miles from Port Hudson. They had a severe engagement a few days ago. The rebels withdrew and went back to the fort, and our troops went back to their camp; a "drawn battle," I presume.

The ram took all the vessels by surprise; the people did not dream of anything of the kind. If we cannot take just now the six miles of river in front of Vicksburg, we can take anything that steams upon that portion of the Mississippi between Vickskurg and Port Hudson.

Very respectfully,

DAVID D. PORTER,
Acting Rear-Admiral.

Hon. GIDEON WELLES,
Secretary of the Navy, Washington, D. C.

Further report of Acting Rear-Admiral Porter, relative to the Queen of the West.

UNITED STATES MISSISSIPPI SQUADRON,
February 8, 1863.

SIR: I am happy to inform you that the steamer Vicksburg was so badly injured by the ram Queen of the West that she has to be kept afloat with large coal barges fastened to her side. Her machinery has been taken out, and she will likely be destroyed. This is the fifth steamer we have deprived the rebels of. The Vicksburg was the largest and strongest steamer on this river, and I think they were preparing to use her against our transports, being very fleet. Her wheel and guards were all smashed in, and a large hole knocked in her side; so deserters report.

Last night I started a coal barge with twenty thousand bushels of coal in, from the anchorage up river, to "run the batteries at Vicksburg." It had ten miles to go to reach the Queen of the West, and arrived safely within ten minutes of the time calculated, not having been seen by the sentinels. This gives the ram nearly coal enough to last a month, in which time she can commit great havoc if no accident happens to her.

I have the honor to be, very respectfully, your obedient servant,

DAVID D. PORTER,
Acting Rear-Admiral, Com'dg Mississippi Squadron.

Hon. GIDEON WELLES,
Secretary of the Navy, Washington, D. C.

Instructions to Colonel Ellet.

UNITED STATES MISSISSIPPI SQUADRON,
February 8, 1863.

COLONEL: When you have taken in your coal you will proceed, at night, after dark, with the De Soto and the coal barge down the river, showing no lights. When you get near Red river, wait until daylight, above the mouth; from there you will be able to see the smoke of any steamer, over the trees, as she comes down Red river. When you capture them do not burn them until you have broken all the machinery; then let go the anchors, and let them burn under your own eyes at their anchors. There will be no danger then of any part of them floating down to the enemy.

There is one vessel, the Webb, that you must look out for. If you get the first crack at her you will sink her, and if she gets the first crack at you she will sink you. My advice is to put a few cotton bales over your bow about fifteen (15) feet abaft the stem, and if she strikes you there, there will be no harm done. It is likely that an attempt will be made to board you; if there is, do not open any doors or ports to board in return, but act on the defensive, giving the enemy steam and shell. Do not forget to wet your cotton before going into action. Do not lose sight of the De Soto, unless in chase, and under circumstances where it will be perfectly safe. When your coal is all out of the barge you can take the De Soto alongside. You can help each other along. Destroy her at once when there is the least chance of her falling into the hands of the enemy. She is now, though, a government vessel, and should be brought back if possible. Destroy all small boats you meet with on the river; also wharf-boats and barges. If you have a chance, and have plenty of coal, take a look at Port Hudson, and give them a few rifle shots, but do not pass by. Communicate with the squadron below by signal if possible. The great object is to destroy all you can of the enemy's stores and provisions, and get your vessel back safe. Pass all batteries at night. If the canal is opened I will keep you supplied with coal. Keep your pilot-house well supplied with hand grenades, &c., in case the enemy should get on your upper decks. Do not show your colors along the river, unless necessary in action.

Very respectfully,

DAVID D. PORTER,
Acting Rear-Admiral, Com'dg Mississippi Squadron.

Colonel CHARLES R. ELLET,
Commanding Mississippi Ram Fleet.

Reports of Colonel Ellet of his proceedings.

U. S. MISSISSIPPI SQUADRON,
February 6, 1863.

SIR: I have the honor to enclose herewith Colonel Ellet's reports of his proceedings down the river.

I hope to be able to get him off again as soon as I can get coal around to him.

I have the honor to be, very respectfully, your obedient servant,

DAVID D. PORTER,
Acting Rear-Admiral, Commandiag Mississippi Squadron.

Hon. GIDEON WELLES,
Secretary of the Navy, Washington, D. C.

MISS. RIVER RAM FLEET, U. S. STEAM RAM QUEEN OF THE WEST,
Below Vicksburg, February 5, 1863.

ADMIRAL: I have the honor to report to you that I left the landing, below the cut-off, about 1 o'clock p. m. on the 2d instant, and proceeded down the river. At Warrenton, a few miles below, the enemy had two batteries of four pieces each, of which four are twenty-pounder rifled guns. They opened upon us as we passed, but only struck us twice, doing no injury.

On reaching the Big Black river I attempted to ascend it, but found it impossible from the narrowness of the stream,

Passing it, we reached Natchez just at midnight. I landed at Vidalia, on the opposite shore, threw out some pickets, and went into the village in the hope of picking up some rebel officers. There can be no telegraphic line between Vicksburg and this point, for not a word of our coming had reached the place, and the people scarcely knew who we were. One rebel, Colonel York, was halted, but made so rapid a retreat that he escaped the shots fired after him.

Leaving this point, I kept on down the river. We passed Ellis's cliffs at 3 o'clock a. m. There are no fortifications at that or any other point between Warrenton and Port Hudson.

We had got about fifteen miles below the mouth of Red river, when we met a side-wheel steamer coming up. Her pilot blew the whistle for the Queen to take the starboard side, supposing her to be a southern boat. Receiving no answer, and not liking the Queen's looks, as she bore straight down upon him, he ran his boat ashore. As we neared her, numerous rebel officers sprang into the water and made their escape. She proved to be the A. W. Baker, had just discharged her cargo at Port Hudson, and was returning for another. We captured on her five captains, two lieutenants, and a number of civilians, among them seven or eight ladies.

I had just placed a guard on the boat, when another steamer was seen coming down the river. A shot across her bows brought her to. She proved to be the Moro, laden with one hundred and ten thousand pounds of pork, nearly five hundred hogs, and a large quantity of salt, destined for the rebel army at Port Hudson. I placed Captain Asgill Connor in command of the captured boats, and as the Queen's supply of coal was very limited, I thought it best to return. A short distance above our landing I destroyed twenty-five thousand pounds of meal, awaiting transportation to Port Hudson.

On reaching Red river I stopped at a plantation to put ashore the ladies, who did not wish to go any further; I also released the civilians. While doing so, another steamboat, the Berwick Bay, came out of Red river, and was immediately seized. She was laden with supplies for the rebel forces at Port Hudson, consisting of two hundred barrels of molasses, ten hogsheads of sugar, and thirty thousand pounds of flour. She had also on board forty bales of cotton.

I ascended Red river fifteen miles in the hope of getting some more boats, but found nothing. Night came on as we again started on our return. I found at once that the progress of the three prizes was so slow that our short supply of coal would not permit us to wait for them. I accordingly ordered them to be set on fire. We had not time to transfer their cargoes.

We met with no interruption on our return until we reached Warrenton. Before arriving at this point, I landed and sent my prisoners around by land, under a strong guard, to avoid exposing them to the enemy's fire.

On passing Warrenton we found that another battery had been erected there, and the three combined opened a very heavy fire upon us. They struck us several times, but did no damage worth mentioning.

Very respectfully, your obedient servant,

CHARLES RIVERS ELLET,
Colonel, Commanding Ram Fleet.

DAVID D. PORTER,
Acting Rear-Admiral, Com'dg Mississippi Squadron.

UNITED STATES RAM QUEEN OF THE WEST,
Below Vicksburg, February 8, 1863.

ADMIRAL: I have the honor to report to you that the coal barge reached me in good condition at half past eleven o'clock last night. I secured it without difficulty, and removed it this morning into the slough, where it is entirely out of danger from the enemy's shot. I shall coal immediately.

I have mounted one of the thirty-pounder Parrott guns on the De Soto.

I hope to be able to procure cotton enough down the river to thoroughly protect her.

Very respectfully, your obedient servant,

CHARLES RIVERS ELLET,
Colonel, Commanding Ram Fleet.

DAVID D. PORTER,
Acting Rear-Admiral, Com'dg Mississippi Squadron.

Approaches and defences of Vicksburg—proceedings and designs of Admiral Porter.

UNITED STATES MISSISSIPPI SQUADRON,
February 7, 1863.

SIR: I have the honor to forward you a chart of the approaches and defences of Vicksburg, as far as we can detect them; the number of guns has not yet been ascertained, though we know of over fifty of heavy calibre. This chart has been made by Messrs. Strauss and Fendall, of the Coast Survey, and is the best and most accurate one constructed.

The rebels at Vicksburg were very amicable in permitting the two above-mentioned gentlemen to prosecute their labors unmolested, having fired at them particularly only once, while they fired on the army surveyors constantly.

On one occasion an officer from the rebel side came over in a boat, and, without landing, inquired what our party were about with that table, (meaning the plane table.) He was told to come on shore and see, which he declined doing. Still the rebels did not molest us, though only 750 yards from us.

This enabled the party to get the heights of hills, prominent buildings, shape of forts, and, in fact, everything but the guns, which are so completely covered that it is impossible to make them out.

On the morning when the ram Queen of the West went by the batteries, I had officers stationed all along to note the places where guns were fired from, and they were quite surprised to find them firing from spots where there were no indications whatever of any guns before.

The shots came from banks, gulleys, from railroad depots, from clumps of bushes, and from hill-tops two hundred feet high. A better system of defence was never devised.

Vicksburg was by nature the strongest place on the river, but art has made it impregnable against floating batteries—not that the number of guns is formidable, but the rebels have placed them out of our reach, and can shift them from place to place, in case we should happen to annoy them (the most we can do) in their earthworks.

In a report I made to the department while attached to the mortar flotilla, I remarked "that the navy could silence the water batteries whenever it pleased, but that the taking of Vicksburg was an army affair altogether," and it would have to be taken by troops. At that time it mounted twenty guns, all told, scattered along as they are now, and ten thousand men could have marched right into it without opposition.

When Admiral Farragut's fleet first went there, Vicksburg had mounted five guns, and three thousand men might have taken it with ease. Even as late as six months back no extra defences were put on at Vicksburg, or on the Yazoo, and our gunboats went sixty miles up that river (which they should never have left) without molestation. The long-talked-of expedition for the capture of Vicksburg, and the various plans that were expressed by our treacherous press, gave the rebels warning, and before I came into these waters Vicksburg was inaccessible in front, and unapproachable by the Yazoo, on account of the strength and position of their batteries.

The people in Vicksburg are the only ones who have, as yet, hit upon the method of defending themselves against our gunboats, viz: not erecting water batteries, and placing the guns some distance back from the water, where they can throw a plunging shot which none of our iron-clads could stand.

I mention these facts to show the department that there is no possible hope of any success against Vicksburg by a gunboat attack, or without an investment in the rear of the city by a large army. We can, perhaps, destroy the city and public buildings, but that brings us no nearer the desired point (the opening of the Mississippi) than we are now, and would likely put out the little spark of Union feeling still existing in Vicksburg.

The attack of the army having failed at the enemy's weakest point, for want of nerve in the leader of a brigade, the next thing to be done is to attack them at some unsuspected point. The canal is a failure, and not even practicable, as yet, for taking through a coal barge, and the army (in daily danger of having it burst its frail embankments) have wisely retreated to higher ground, leaving the enemy still in wonder at their eccentric movements. In the mean time General Grant and myself have been studying maps, and consulting about what is the best course to pursue. I sent down the ram as a diversion, to cut off the enemy's supplies here, and at Port Hudson; the result has met my most sanguine expectations. Over two hundred thousand dollars' worth of property was captured and destroyed, amongst it many supplies for the rebel army at Port Hudson. At present we command the Mississippi, and the first step towards the evacuation of the stronghold has been adopted. After that, General Grant proposes to cut a canal into Lake Providence. This lake communicates with the Tensas river, a deep stream, and the Tensas runs into the Washita, which empties into the Red river, near the mouth of the latter. The canal is not yet finished, and what the result will be no one can foresee. Some think that the great rush of the Mississippi will clear away everything before it, and the Tensas river become a fine navigable stream for the largest steamers: it is now capable of passing medium-size steamers; at all events it will give us the command of Red river, and cut off all supplies from that quarter; the result no one can calculate.

While General Grant was cutting his canal at Lake Providence, I proposed cutting away the levee, at a place called Delta, near Helena, into Old Yazoo Pass; and General Grant sending a detachment of diggers, I sent the Forest Rose up to enter the channel, when it should be cut out; this used to be the main way to Yazoo city, and the rivers Tallahatchie and Yallabusha, before the southern railroad was built, and it was closed up to reclaim some millions of acres of land that laid useless. It leads into the Tallahatchie river, and through it we command the heart of the Mississippi, and all the resources of the enemy around Vicksburg.

The levee was cut, and the water rushed in with such force, sweeping everything before it, that it at once cut a channel eighty yards wide, and at last accounts the water was sweeping everything before it. It will take some days for the water to reach its level, having a fall of nine feet; and in the mean time I have fitted out a force of five light-draughts, and the iron-clad Chillicothe, to go through and take the enemy by surprise. The commander of the expedition,

Lieutenant Commander Watson Smith, has instructions to destroy all the means of transportation the enemy has, destroy all gunboats and rams, and break up the bridges over the Tallahatchie and Yallabusha.

If this expedition is successful in getting through, General Grant will follow with his army, and Vicksburg attacked in the rear, in a manner not likely dreamed of; the troops at Vicksburg will be obliged to evacuate, as they have heretofore done other strongholds; that accomplished, Port Hudson must fall, and if I have the gunboats I could keep the river open.

By looking over the map of Mississippi, you will perceive the importance of this move, if successful; if it is not, it will overflow a large tract of country from which the rebels draw their supplies.

I am trying to get coal to Colonel Ellet, that he may continue his attacks on the enemy below, and in the Red river, before they can wake up from their astonishment at his first appearance.

I have endeavored to give you, sir, a fair account of the situation here, that you may not expect too much from the present fleet. What it is possible to do, will be done. My main object is to meet with no defeats, and I shall undertake nothing where there is no chance of success.

A defeat of the navy on this river would be considered a calamity, but the world will not blame us for waiting until we are perfectly prepared.

So many of my men's time is out, and the vessels being less than half manned, I applied to General Grant for a regiment of soldiers, which he has promised me, to be detailed for detached service. This makes us comfortable again. I hope it meets with the approval of the department. It will take a couple of weeks to break them in.

I have the honor to be, sir, very respectfully, your obedient servant,

DAVID D. PORTER,
Acting Rear-Admiral, Com'dg Mississippi Squadron.

Hon. GIDEON WELLES,
Secretary of the Navy, Washington, D. C.

Attack on the rebels at Dover, Tennessee.

No. 14.]

OFFICE MISSISSIPPI SQUADRON,
Cairo, Illinois, February 9, 1863.

SIR: I have the honor to enclose herewith a copy of a report of Lieutenant Commander Le Roy Fitch, United States navy, giving his account of his attack on the rebels who had surrounded and were attacking the post at Dover, Tennessee. I had been informed that the enemy were attacking that post, but I felt no uneasiness in regard to the result, for I was sure that the gunboats were near Fort Donelson, and that Lieutenant Commander Fitch would hasten with them to the rescue of those who were so gallantly defending it against a very superior force.

I have the honor to be, very respectfully, your obedient servant,

A. M. PENNOCK,
Fleet Captain and Commandant of Station.

Hon. GIDEON WELLES,
Secretary of the Navy, Washington, D. C.

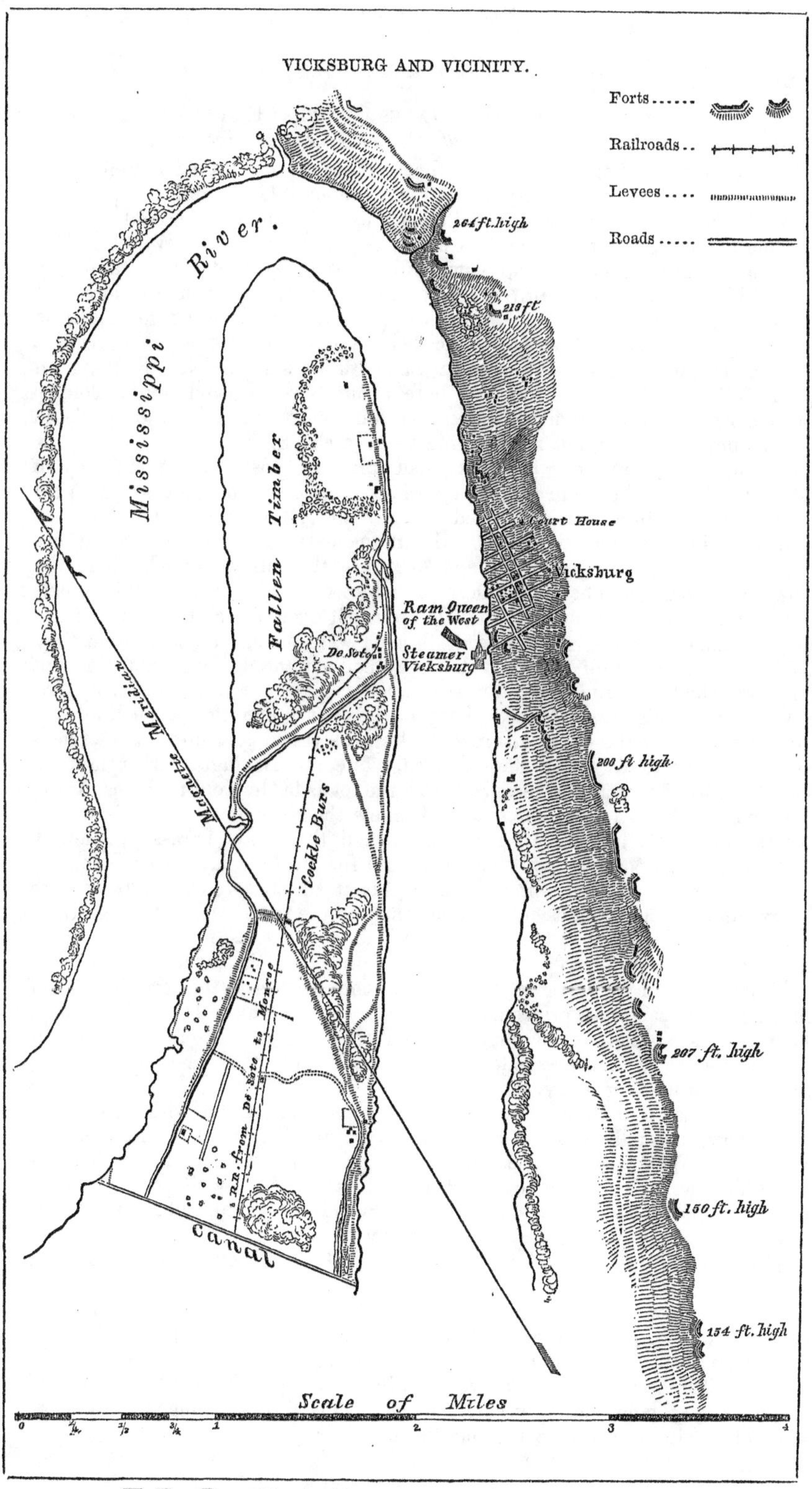
VICKSBURG AND VICINITY.
Forts
Railroads
Levees
Roads
264 ft. high
213 ft
Mississippi River.
Fallen Timber
Court House
Vicksburg
Ram Queen of the West
Steamer Vicksburg
De Soto
Magnetic Meridian
Cockle Burs
R.R. from De Soto to Monroe
200 ft high
207 ft. high
150 ft. high
154 ft. high
Canal
Scale of Miles
0
1/4
1/2
3/4
1
2
3
4

Report from Lieutenant Commander Le Roy Fitch.

UNITED STATES GUNBOAT FAIRPLAY,
Off Dover, Tennessee, February 4, 1863.

SIR: I have the honor to report, that on the 3d instant I left Smithland, Kentucky, with a fleet of transports and the gunboats Lexington, Fairplay, St. Clear, Brilliant, Robb, and Silver Lake, as convoy up the Cumberland river.

When about twenty-four miles below Dover I met the steamer Wild Cat with a message from Colonel Harding, commandant of the post at Dover, informing me that his pickets had been driven in, and that he was attacked in force. I immediately left the transports and made signals to the gunboats to follow on up as fast as possible. A short distance below the town I met another steamer, bringing the intelligence that the place was entirely surrounded. Pushing on up with all possible speed, I arrived here about 8 p. m., and found Colonel Harding's force out of ammunition and entirely surrounded by the rebels in overwhelming numbers, but still holding them in check.

The enemy not expecting gunboats, had unwisely posted the main body of his army in line of battle in the graveyard at the west end of the town, with his left wing resting in a ravine that led down to the river, giving us a chance to throw a raking fire along his lines. Simultaneously the gunboats opened fire up this ravine, into the graveyard, and over into the valley beyond, where the enemy had horses hitched, and, most probably, kept his reserve. The rebels were so much taken by surprise that they did not even fire a shot, but immediately commenced retreating. So well directed was our fire on them, that they could not even carry off a caisson that they had captured from our forces, but were compelled to abandon it, after two fruitless attempts to destroy it by fire.

After having dispersed the main body of the enemy, I stationed the Robb and Silver Lake below the town to throw shell up the ravine and prevent the rebels from returning to carry off the wounded, while the Lexington, Fairplay, St. Clair, and Brilliant went above, and shelled the roads leading out to the eastward.

Supposing the retreating forces would follow the river for a short distance, I sent the Lexington and St. Clair on up to shell the woods, harass and annoy them as much as possible, while this boat and the Brilliant lay opposite the upper ravine and threw shells up the road. About 10 p. m. we ceased firing, with the exception of now and then a random shell up the roads. At 11 p. m., learning from Colonel Harding that the enemy had entirely disappeared, we ceased firing and took position to guard the roads approaching the town.

Although much of our firing was at random, we have the gratification of knowing that scarcely a projectile went amiss, and that out of 140 buried to-day, the gunboats can claim their share. Even when the Lexington and St. Clair went above, many of their shells fell right in the midst of the retreating rebels, killing and wounding many.

It is reported that the attacking force numbered some 4,500, with eight pieces of artillery, under the command of Major General Wheeler, Brigadier Generals Forrest and Wharton. It is certainly very gratifying to us to know that this entire force was cut up, routed, and despoiled of its prey by the timely arrival of the gunboats, and that Colonel Harding and his gallant little band were spared to wear the honors they have so fairly won.

At first I regretted that I was not here with the gunboats sooner, but, upon reflection, I do not think I could better have arranged the time, had it been in my power. Had we been here before Wheeler he would not have made the attack, but, most probably, would have marched on Fort Henry. Had we arrived during the day he would have seen our strength, and would have retreated with but little loss. Arriving as we did, after dark, and when he least expected us, and was so sanguine of success, we caught his forces arranged in the most favorable position to receive a raking fire from our guns.

The officers and men were very glad to have a shot at these river infesters, and only regret that they did not remain within reach of our guns a little longer. As it is, they claim the honor of dispersing them and saving Fort Donelson.

Very respectfully, your obedient servant,

LE ROY FITCH, *Lieut. Commander.*

Fleet Captain A. M. PENNOCK, U. S. N.,
Commandant of Naval Station, Cairo, Illinois.

Passage of the Vicksburg batteries by the Indianola.

UNITED STATES MISSISSIPPI SQUADRON,
February 14, 1863.

SIR: I ordered the Indianola, Lieutenant Commander George Brown, down the river, and she ran the batteries last night under a heavy fire, without, I believe, receiving any damage. She carried with her two coal barges, enough to last two months. This gives us entire control of the Mississippi, except at Vicksburg and Port Hudson, and cuts off all the supplies and troops from Texas. We have below now two XI-inch guns, two IX-inch guns, two 30-pounder rifles, six 12-pounders, and three vessels. They have orders to burn, sink, and destroy.

I send you a copy of my instructions to Lieutenant Commander Brown, and have the honor to remain, very respectfully, your obedient servant,

DAVID D. PORTER,
Acting Rear-Admiral, Com'dg Mississippi Squadron.

Hon. GIDEON WELLES,
Secretary of the Navy, Washington, D. C.

[Strictly confidential.]

Instructions to Lieutenant Commander George Brown.

UNITED STATES MISSISSIPPI SQUADRON,
February 12, 1863.

SIR: You will take two coal barges alongside, that have been somewhat lightened of coal, and stand by to run past the batteries at Vicksburg, and join the vessels below. The object in sending you is to protect the ram Queen of the West and the De Soto against the Webb, the enemy's ram; she will not attack you both. I do not wish you to go below Red river, but to remain there while Colonel Ellet reconnoitres Port Hudson, and prevent his being taken by vessels from Red river. Keep your guns loaded with solid shot, or, if you are attacked by vessels protected with cotton bales, fire shrapnell, which are good incendiary shell. If you can capture a good steamer, I want you to keep her. Go to Jeff. Davis's plantation, and his brother Joe's, and load up said steamer with all the cotton you can find, and the best single male negroes. If you cannot get cotton enough to protect the steamer you capture, obtain it at Acklen's landing, and when you have filled the prize up with as much as she will carry and make good speed, send her up to run the batteries and join me here. To do this daub over her white paint with mud, so that she cannot be seen in the dark. Dispose the cotton bags so that everything is well protected, and no light can possibly show in any part of the boat. You must select dark and rainy nights for running the blockade, and don't show yourself below Warrenton as you come up. After you pass the batteries at Vicksburg show two red lights on your bow, that our people at the canal may know you. If you receive any damage from the batteries send me a short report from the other side, and go on with care until you are the other side (some distance) of Warrenton; lay by there until the moon is up and proceed to Red river. When the Queen of the West returns, Colonel Ellet and yourself will go up Red river (provided you can get good pilots) and destroy all you meet with in the shape of enemy's stores. This part must be left to your discretion; Ellet and yourself will consult together what is best to be done; and whatever you undertake, try and have no failure. When you have not means of certain success, undertake nothing; a failure is equal to a defeat. Never leave your coal barge unprotected by the De Soto, and never leave her between you and the enemy. Don't forget that I had your vessel strengthened to perform the part of a ram—don't hesitate to run anything down. When you have emptied the coal barges, either destroy them, so that the enemy cannot possibly use them, or fill them with cotton and bring them back. Make your calculations to get back here with plenty of coal on board. Tell Colonel Ellet when he gets to Port Hudson to send a communication in a barrel, (barrel to be marked "Essex,") and tell the commander, in said communication, that I direct him to pass Port Hudson in a dark night and join the vessels above. Have your casemates and sides well covered with tallow and slush before you start.

Very respectfully,

DAVID D. PORTER,
Acting Rear-Admiral, Com'dg Mississippi Squadron.

Lieutenant Commander GEORGE BROWN, U. S. N.,
Commanding Indianola, Mississippi Squadron.

Report of Lieutenant Commander George Brown.

UNITED STATES MISSISSIPPI SQUADRON,
Yazoo River, February 24, 1863.

SIR: I have the honor to enclose you a communication from Lieutenant Commander George Brown. We still hold the mouth of Red river.

Very respectfully, your obedient servant,

DAVID D. PORTER,
Commanding Mississippi Squadron.

Hon. GIDEON WELLES,
Secretary of the Navy, Washington, D. C.

UNITED STATES STEAMER INDIANOLA,
Mouth of Red River, February 18, 1863.

SIR: I have the honor to report that, in obedience to your written instructions, I left the anchorage in the Yazoo river at 10.15 p. m. on the 13th instant, having in tow two barges of coal containing about seven thousand bushels each. The weather was all I could desire. At 11.10 p. m. I was abreast of the upper batteries, which did not open fire; the rebel lookouts at those batteries could not have seen us. The first gun that was fired at us was at 11.22 p. m., from a battery abreast the point.

At this time we were running very slowly, but at once started at full speed; other guns opened on us in very quick succession, and rockets were sent up at the upper batteries. At 11.41 p. m. the last gun was fired. Eighteen guns were fired at us in the space of nineteen minutes, none of which struck us. They were generally good line shots, but all passed over us. Every shot came from abaft the beam. When abreast of the lower end of the canal I showed two red lights on the starboard side. At Warrenton two musket shots were fired at us. At 1 a. m. on the 14th instant we anchored about four miles below

Warrenton. At 5.20 a. m. we got under way and proceeded slowly down the river. Nothing of importance transpired until the morning of the 16th, being at anchor about eight (8) miles below Natchez, when a steamboat was heard approaching from below. I got under way at once and stood across the river, when the fog lifted, and I made the steamboat Era, No. 5; I hailed her and learned that she was in charge of Colonel Ellet, having on board the few officers and men who were saved from the Queen of the West. The particulars of her capture will be reported to you by Colonel Ellet.

I again anchored, and, after consulting with Colonel Ellet, concluded to proceed on down the river as soon as the Era could be put in running order. At 4.30 p. m. we started down, the Era ahead. At 5.10 a steamer was seen abreast of Ellis's Cliff, which I at once recognized as being the rebel gunboat Webb. At the same time the Era's whistle was blown, indicating that she saw danger ahead. I cleared for action, and was going ahead at full speed, when the Webb turned and started down. I fired two 11-inch shot at her, both of which were good line shots; one struck within at least fifty yards of her. Both guns had all the elevation that the port would admit of. The Webb at this time was making most excellent speed, and soon disappeared behind the point. As we rounded the point the fog set in so thick that not even her smoke could be seen. On account of the dense fog we anchored for the night under Glasscock's island. Thinking it probable the Webb might get ashore in the fog, and knowing that if she did we would drift by her without seeing her, I thought it best to remain at anchor until I could run with safety, and be certain of seeing everything on either side of the bank as we passed. At 1 p. m. on the 17th instant, the fog lighting up, we got under way and proceeded on down the river as far as the mouth of Red river, opposite which place we anchored at about 5 p. m. I sent on shore for Colonel Acklen, who informed me that three boats had accompanied the Webb in chase of Colonel Ellet, but that they had all turned back and gone up Red river. I was informed that Colonel Lovell, who commanded the Webb and the expedition, said that he would make a stand at Norman's landing, where he could have the assistance of the fort at that place. I was also informed that the Queen of the West has been hauled off and towed up to Norman's (sometimes called Gordon's) landing; that she was injured only in her steam and escape pipes, which could easily be repaired. That the rebels will make use of her to attack us I do not doubt, but I feel prepared to meet both the Queen and the Webb. A deserter from the Webb reports that she has no iron on her bow, but that the machinery below the spar deck is well protected by cotton. On account of her walking-beams, which are not at all protected, she will not come within close range of our guns.

Two boats are being fitted up with cotton at Port Hudson—for what particular service I am unable to learn.

My only trouble is to look out for the coal barges, which I can tow up stream at a slow rate, and I cannot run the risk of losing sight of them, unless in case of some pressing emergency. I keep the coal-bunkers full at all times, so that in the event of my losing the barges we will have plenty of coal to take us to Vicksburg. Colonel Ellet thinks that it is important that he should go up the river at once and communicate with you; I am convinced that I can remain alone in this vicinity for some time, but at the same time I consider it important that there should be at least one other serviceable vessel with me.

If the river rises one foot more, of which there is a strong probability, Port Hudson will be unapproachable by land; so you can readily understand the importance of the stoppage of all river communication.

I am, sir, very respectfully, your obedient servant,

GEORGE BROWN,

Lieutenant Commander, United States Navy.

Acting Rear-Admiral DAVID D. PORTER,

Commanding Mississippi Squadron, Yazoo River.

Loss of the United States steamer Glide.

UNITED STATES MISSISSIPPI SQUADRON,
February 15, 1863.

SIR: I enclose herewith reports of Captain A. M. Pennock and Acting Lieutenant Selim E. Woodworth, in relation to the burning of the Glide; and also enclose general orders, showing that I omitted no precaution against fire previous to my leaving Cairo.

I have ordered an investigation of the matter.

I have the honor to be, very respectfully, your obedient servant,

DAVID D. PORTER,
Acting Rear-Admiral, Commanding Mississippi Squadron.

Hon. GIDEON WELLES,
Secretary of the Navy, Washington, D. C.

Report of Fleet Captain Pennock.

OFFICE OF THE MISSISSIPPI SQUADRON,
Cairo, Illinois, February 7, 1863.

SIR: I have the honor to report to you that at about 5.20 o'clock this morning the gunboat Glide was reported to be on fire. On my arrival at the place where she was moored, (between the inspection boat and the General Price, at the stern of the wharf boat,) I found that she was on fire in the fore hold. Every exertion was made by her commander, officers, and crew, and those attached to the Eastport and to this station, to extinguish the fire; but finding that their efforts were of no avail, and that the fire was gaining, and fearing that it would be communicated to the Abraham and General Price, I directed that a bow-line be veered away until her bow was clear of the stern of the Price, and when it was cast off, a tug canted her and towed her out into the strength of the current. After burning some time, she grounded about two miles below, on the Kentucky shore. I think that her guns and machinery will be saved.

It is reported that two contrabands were lost.

The cause of the fire is not known; but I shall have the whole matter thoroughly investigated, the result of which will be reported to you.

I have the honor to be, very respectfully, your obedient servant,

A. M. PENNOCK,
Fleet Captain and Commander of Station.

Rear-Admiral D. D. PORTER,
Commanding Mississippi Squadron.

P. S.—Captain Woodworth's report will be forwarded to you as soon as possible. The officers and crew have lost everything they possessed.

Report of Acting Volunteer Lieutenant S. E. Woodworth.

CAIRO, ILLINOIS, *February* 7. 1863.

SIR: I have to report to you the loss of the United States steamer Glide by fire, late under my command.

Although having assumed charge of the General Price, I still retained my quarters on board the Glide, she lying alongside.

Mr. Dahlgren had taken charge of her outfits and equipments as executive officer in command.

About 5.15 this morning I was aroused by the ringing of the fire-bell on the naval depot wharf boat; but not seeing any light or smoke when I looked out, supposed the alarm proceeded from fire in town. I dressed myself with all haste, and proceeded to the forward part of the boat to call the officers and crew, when I discovered smoke proceeding from the fire-scuttle and forward hatches, they having been forced open by Mr. Dahlgren, who was already engaged, with the officers and crew of the Glide, in drawing and passing water, and making every exertion to extinguish the fire. I at once started with some contrabands to drown the magazines, but they were not fitted with bilge cocks, and we could only introduce water in them through the hatches with buckets.

Captain Pennock was on hand with a strong force of officers and laborers, and made every exertion, with such facilities as were at hand, to extinguish the fire; but, from the extreme cold weather, leaving everything frozen, but little was effected by the use of buckets.

The Glide was moored astern of and to the warf boat, outside of the boat Abraham, with the General Price outside of her. Having made every preparation to drop the Glide clear of the tier by running lines, &c., a tug was procured and made fast to the quarter of the steamer. Renewed exertions were now made to extinguish the fire by cutting through the deck with axes, but the light and inflammable materials about the boilers were soon in a living flame.

Upon consultation with Captain Pennock it was deemed impossible to save the Glide; and, at this time, the flames were endangering the inspection boat and the General Price, and leaving the wharf boat also in danger. Captain Pennock ordered cast off and drop out of the tier, but not until the whole forward part of the vessel was in flames. The tug having her in charge succeeded in reaching the middle of the river, out of reach of the naval station, where she was cast off. She drifted ashore at Fort Holt, and burned to the water's edge.

The magazines did not explode, but the fixed ammunition seemed to be fired slowly, as shell and shrapnell continued to burst in the air, from time to time, for an hour after she grounded.

To the efficient aid rendered by Captain Pennock, Captain Sanford, and Captain Phelps, and the officers and men under their command, may be attributed the safety of all the public property at the wharf boat.

Acting Ensign Wright and the engineer of the tug Dahlia are deserving of much credit in holding on to the Glide until she was so far removed as not to endanger the lives or property at Cairo by the explosion of her magazines. They did not leave her until her fasts were burned off, and the small arms being discharged in every direction.

The wreck of the Glide is now lying in five feet of water on the Kentucky shore. Her guns, engines and boilers can be readily recovered, also all the iron plates from her sides.

The officers and crew of the Glide have lost all but their clothes in which they dressed. The crew have been transferred to the Henry Millen, which vessel will be despatched as soon as ready.

I have the honor to be, very respectfully, your obedient servant,

SELIM E. WOODWORTH,

Acting Vol. Lieut. U. S. N., late Com'dg U. S. Steamer Glide.

Rear-Admiral D. D. Porter.

Capture of the Queen of the West.

United States Mississippi Squadron,

Yazoo River, February 22, 1863.

Sir: The best calculations are liable to be upset, and mine have been disarranged by the capture of the Queen of the West up Red river. That vessel grounded under the guns of a battery, which she foolishly engaged, and received a shot through her boilers and steam drum which drove most of her people overboard. Many escaped in a prize, the steamer New Era, No. 5, but most of the deck hands and contrabands fell into the power of the rebels. The officers and Colonel Ellet were then chased up the Mississippi river by the Webb and some two or three other vessels, until they met the Indianola, which vessel saved them and drove the rebels back. This is all I can learn of this affair.

The colonel arrived here safe with the New Era, No. 5, having ran the batteries all along the river, and had 120 shots fired at him without being hit, bringing up 170 bales of cotton. It is said that he left the Indianola and Webb engaged. I hope to get a report from him in a day or two; he is on the other side and sick, and the road is almost impassable. * * * * *

DAVID D. PORTER,
Acting Rear-Admiral, Com'dg Mississippi Squadron.

Hon. GIDEON WELLES,
Secretary of the Navy, Washington, D. C.

Additional report of Acting Rear-Admiral Porter.

UNITED STATES MISSISSIPPI SQUADRON,
Yazoo River, February 23, 1863.

SIR: Colonel Ellet has arrived on this side of the river. He informs me that his ram was not destroyed, but fell into the hands of the rebels. He could not destroy her without sacrificing his wounded.

She will not be worth anything for some time to the rebels, and is much used up; will not do to ram with any longer, being too weak and shattered. I am going to try it again with another one. The ram committed great havoc on Red river—destroyed many stores, also, along the river. She destroyed and captured altogether over one hundred thousand dollars of confederate property. He returned with cotton to the value of seventy thousand dollars, and a boat worth about eighteen thousand.

I enclose herewith Colonel Ellet's report.

I have the honor to remain, very respectfully, your obedient servant,

DAVID D. PORTER,
Acting Rear-Admiral, Com'dg Mississippi Squadron.

Hon. GIDEON WELLES,
Secretary of the Navy, Washington, D. C.

Report from Colonel Ellet.

UNITED STATES STEAMER ERA, No. 5,
Below Vicksburg, Mississippi, February 21, 1863.

ADMIRAL: I have the honor to report to you that I left the landing below Vicksburg, in obedience to your written instructions, on the night of the 10th instant, taking with me the De Soto and coal barge, and proceeded down the river. We passed Warrenton without interruption, and reached Red river on the following evening. I destroyed, as you directed, the skiffs and flatboats along either shore.

I ascended Red river on the morning of the 12th as far as the mouth of the Atchafalaya, leaving the De Soto and coal barge in a secure position. I proceeded down this stream. Six miles from its mouth I met a train of twelve army wagons returning from Simsport. I landed and destroyed them. On reaching Simsport I found that two rebel steamboats had just left, taking with them the troops and artillery stationed at this point. They had left on the bank seventy barrels of government beef, which I broke open and rolled into the river. I pursued another train of wagons for some distance, but they retreated into the swamps and escaped. One of their wagons, loaded with ammunition and stores, fell into our hands and was destroyed.

On her return at night a party of overseers and other civilians fired into the Queen from behind a levee, and immediately fled under cover of the darkness. First Master James D. Thompson, a gallant and efficient officer, was shot through the knee. Anchoring at the mouth of the Atchafalaya, I waited until morning, and then returned to the spot from which we had been attacked. All the buildings on three large adjoining plantations were burned by my order.

I started up Red river the same day, and reached Black river by night. On the morning of the 14th instant, when about fifteen miles above the mouth of Black river, a steamboat came suddenly around a sharp bend in the river, and was captured before she could escape. She proved to be the Era, No. 5, laden with forty-five hundred bushels of corn. She had on board two rebel lieutenants and fourteen privates; the latter I at once paroled and set ashore.

Hearing of three very large boats lying with steam down at Gordon's landing, thirty miles above, I decided on making an effort to capture them, intending to return if I should find the battery at that point too strong, and ascend the Washita. I left the Era and coal barge in charge of a guard. We reached the bend just below Gordon's landing before dark. The dense smoke of several boats, rapidly firing up, could be seen over the tops of the trees as we approached. I ordered the pilot to proceed very slowly, and merely show the bow of the Queen around the point. From the sharp bend which the river makes at this place, there was no apparent difficulty in withdrawing out of range of the enemy's guns whenever it might be desired. The rebels opened upon us with four 32-pounders the moment we came in sight. Their guns were in a fine position, and at the third shot I ordered Mr. Garocy, the pilot, to back the Queen out. Instead of doing so he ran her aground on the right-hand shore. The position at once became a very hot one. Sixty yards below we would have been in no danger; as it was, the enemy's shot struck us nearly every time. The chief engineer had hardly reported to me that the escape-pipe had been shot away, when an explosion below, and a rush of steam around the boat, told me that the steam-pipe had been shot in two. Nothing further, of course, could be done. I gave orders to lower the yawl at the stern of the Queen to carry off Captain Thompson, who lay wounded in my state-room. Some person had already taken the yawl, however, and it was gone. The other yawl was on the De Soto, a short distance below. Fortunately the cotton bales with which the Queen was protected afforded an avenue of escape, and the majority of the men and officers succeeded in reaching the De Soto. I ordered this boat to be brought up as far as it was practicable, without being struck, and sent her yawl to the Queen. Lieutenant Tuthill and Third Master Duncan bravely volunteered for this purpose. I remained with the De Soto over an hour, picking up men on cotton bales. Lieutenant Tuthill barely succeeded in escaping from the Queen, the rebels boarding her in skiffs as he escaped. Mr. Duncan staid too long, and was captured. The Queen could easily have been burned, but this could not be done while Captain Thompson was on board, and it was impossible to remove him; all the passages had been blocked up with cotton. The interior of the boat was intensely dark, full of steam, and strewed with shattered furniture. The display of a light enabled the batteries to strike her with unerring certainty. To have brought the De Soto alongside would have insured her destruction, as the light from the latter's furnaces rendered her a conspicuous mark.

A dense fog sprang up as we started down in the De Soto. and she lost her rudder by running into the bank. Drifting down fifteen miles, I took possession of the Era, and scuttled and burnt the De Soto and barge, knowing that the rebels would lose no time in pursuing. I pushed on down through the fog, throwing off the corn to lighten her. We reached the Mississippi at dawn, opposite Ellis's cliffs. Mr. Garocy ran the Era, a boat drawing less than ten feet of water, hard aground, actually permitting her wheels to make several evolutions after she had struck. It was with the utmost difficulty that she could be gotten off. The disloyal sentiments openly expressed by Mr. Garocy a few hours previous to this occurrence rendered it necessary for me to place him under arrest, and forced upon me the unwilling conviction that the loss of the Queen was due to the deliberate treachery of the pilot. It is to be regretted that the unfortunate illness of Mr. Scott Long, who piloted the Queen past Vicksburg, rendered it necessary for me to intrust the Queen to the management of Mr. Garocy.

The next morning, a short distance below Natchez, I met the Indianola. Captain Brown thought that he might be able to ascend the Red river and destroy the battery at Gordon's landing, and I accompanied him down in the Era, leading the way. I had not gone three miles when a break in the fog disclosed a steamer rapidly moving up stream, about a mile ahead. I at once rounded to, and caused the whistle to be blown to warn Captain Brown of her presence.

As soon as the rebel steamer, which was undoubtedly the Webb, perceived the Indianola, she turned and fled. The latter fired two shots at her, but without effect. I learned afterwards that three other armed boats had been sent in pursuit of the Era, and had been turned back by the Webb on her retreat. They all went back up Red river. On reaching this stream Captain Brown decided not to ascend it, and I thought it best to return at once.

Thinking we might be attacked on the way up, I seized a hundred and seventy bales of cotton, and protected the Era's machinery as far as practicable. At St. Joseph's I landed and seized the mails, and learned from them that Colonel Adams was waiting for us at Grand Gulf, with two pieces of artillery. Thirty-six shots were fired at the Era while passing this point, none of which took effect. On reaching Island No. 107, a body of riflemen opened a heavy fire upon the Era from the Mississippi shore. Suspecting it to be a ruse to drive us to the other side of the river, I decided in keeping to the right of the island. The furnaces of the Era became so clogged at this point that I found it necessary to stop and have them cleaned out, causing a delay of twenty minutes. The Era had scarcely passed the island, when a battery of three guns opened upon her from the Louisiana shore. Forty-six shots were fired, but did no injury.

At Warrenton the rebels opened fire upon the Era with two rifled 20-pounder guns. They fired twenty-four shots, but did not succeed in striking her.

Extraordinary as it may seem, there is every reason to believe that no one was killed on the Queen. It is probably attributable to the fact that those below got into the hold through the numerous hatches, and thus escaped the effects of the steam.

Mr. Taylor, one of the engineers, is reported to be badly scalded, by a deserter from the Webb. Twenty-four men were taken prisoners, ten of whom were civilians employed on the boat. Assistant Surgeon Booth was the only commissioned officer captured.

I am, very respectfully, your obedient servant,

CHARLES RIVERS ELLET,
Colonel, Commanding Ram Fleet.

DAVID D. PORTER,
Acting Rear-Admiral, Com'dg Mississippi Squadron.

List of prisoners captured on board the United States steam ram Queen of the West, in Red river, Louisiana, February 14, 1863.

Daniel S. Booth, assistant surgeon; C. S. Eddison, mate; H. S. Duncan, 2d mate; Edward Taylor, engineer; James W. Foster, carpenter; Richard Greve, blacksmith; G. W. Hill, steward; John Bates, 1st sergeant company I, 63d I. M.; Carrol Smith, private, company C, 63d I. M.; Charles D. Faulkner, private, company I, 63d I. M.; William Brown, private, company F, 63d I. M.; M. Cullan, private, company F, 63d I. M.; Leo. C. Tarbol, private, company K, 18th I. M.; John Foley, deck hand; John Williams, cabin boy; E. G. Holstein, private; T. F. Rice, private; Thomas L. Williams, private; Charles Lamner, private; George Watson, deck hand; George W. Bailey, private.—Total, 21.

Capture of the Indianola.

UNITED STATES MISSISSIPPI SQUADRON,
February 27, 1863.

SIR: I have just received information through one of the men who escaped from the Indianola that she had an encounter on Tuesday night with the two rams, Webb and Queen of the West, and that after being struck six times, and the report being made that she was sinking, she was surrendered to the enemy. The commander then ran her on shore, when the man who gives the information got on shore with some others, and he brought me the news. He could not see whether the vessel had sunk or not. From his account it appears that Lieutenant Commander Brown laid at the mouth of Red river three days, (just about time to allow the Queen of the West to repair damages,) and then, being apprehensive of attack, or reading over my instructions, and finding out that he was sent down *only to protect the Queen of the West,* and was ordered to *attempt nothing when he was not certain of success,* he started up the Mississippi river with the two coal barges in tow, giving the enemy all that advantage. I had cautioned Lieutenant Commander Brown so much, before he started, about the management of his ship, and told him particularly to use his butting powers, which would have defeated both his antagonists; but he was caught with the two barges alongside, and his vessel must have been unmanageable.

I had every reason on this expedition to demand the most perfect success. The rebels had but one old boat, (the Webb,) so weak that they had to take her iron off the bows, and, as one of her crew informs me, with planking too old to calk. She carried three thirty-two pounders. The vessels I sent down carried twelve heavy guns.

The importance of this move to our army here cannot be estimated. We had already broken the communications of the enemy in Texas with Vicksburg and Port Hudson.

We had cut off all supplies and means of transportation, having destroyed some of their best boats. In a week more the water would have surrounded Port Hudson, and there being no means of getting away, they would have been obliged to evacuate in time. We hoped in a short time to force this thing by getting one or two more gunboats below, and troops enough to land close to Port Hudson. That place evacuated, General Banks could have ascended the river. The department has a copy of my instructions to Colonel Charles R. Ellet and Lieutenant Commander George Brown, and they will, I am sure, do me the justice to say that my plans were well laid; the object contended for was a very important one, and that I was sufficiently cautious in sending down twelve guns to contend with three.

There is no use to conceal the fact, but this has, in my opinion, been the most humiliating affair that has occurred during this rebellion; and after taking so much trouble to make matters sure, it almost disheartens me and puts me out of the conceit of sending off any expedition, unless I can go with it. I certainly had a right to expect that two vessels, carrying twelve guns, that had passed all the batteries at Vicksburg, Warrenton, Carthage, and other places on the river, could manage, between them, to take one old steamer, or else have the wisdom and patriotism to destroy their vessels, even if they had to go with them.

A flag of truce is, I believe, coming up, and I shall know in a short time whether the Indianola sunk, or whether the enemy will be able to save her.

A terrific explosion occurred last night in the direction of the Indianola, and my only hope is that she has been blown up.

In conclusion, had the Indianola thrown off her coal barges and run up stream with the speed she is reported to have, she could have disabled both the rams with her two 11-inch guns in iron casemates before either of them could get alongside of her. They tracked her along from point to point, found out exactly how she was operating, and made their disposition accordingly.

I have the honor to be, very respectfully, your obedient servant,

DAVID D. PORTER,

Acting Rear-Admiral, Com'dg Mississippi Squadron.

Hon. GIDEON WELLES,

Secretary of the Navy, Washington, D. C.

Detailed report of Lieutenant Commander George Brown.

WASHINGTON, D. C., *May* 28, 1863.

SIR: At this, my earliest opportunity, I respectfully submit to the department a report of the operations of the United States steamer Indianola while below Vicksburg, Mississippi; also, the particulars of the engagement with the rebel armed rams Queen of the West and William H. Webb, and armed cotton-clad steamers Dr. Batey and Grand Era, in which the Indianola was sunk and her officers and crew made prisoners.

In obedience to an order from Acting Rear-Admiral Porter, commanding Mississippi squadron, I passed the batteries at Vicksburg and Warrenton on the night of the 13th of February last, having in tow two barges containing about seven thousand bushels of coal each, without being once struck, although eighteen shots were fired, all of which passed over us.

I kept on down the river, but, owing to dense fogs, made but slow progress, until the morning of the 16th, when, about ten miles below Natchez, I met the steamboat Era No. 5, having on board Colonel Ellet, of the ram fleet, and a portion of the officers and crew of the steamer Queen of the West. I then learned for the first time of the loss of that boat, and after consulting with Colonel Ellet I concluded to continue on down as far as the mouth of the Red river. On the afternoon of the same day I got under way, the Era No. 5 leading. On nearing Ellis's cliffs the Era made the pre-arranged signal of danger ahead, soon after which I made out the rebel steamer William H. Webb. Before I got within range of the Webb she had turned, and was standing down stream with great speed. I fired two shots from the eleven-inch guns, but both fell short of her. She soon ran out of sight, and in consequence of a thick fog setting in I could not continue the chase, but was obliged to anchor.

I reached the mouth of the Red river on the 17th of February, from which time until the 21st of same month I maintained a strict blockade at that point.

I could procure no Red river pilots, and therefore did not enter that river.

The Era No. 5 being unarmed, and having several prisoners on board, Colonel Ellet decided to go up the river and communicate with the squadron, and sailed at noon on the 18th of the same month for that purpose.

On learning that the Queen of the West had been repaired by the rebels and was nearly ready for service, also that the William H. Webb and four cotton-clad boats with boarding parties on board were fitting out to attack the Indianola, I left the Red river for the purpose of getting cotton to fill up the space between the casemate and wheel-houses, so as to be better able to repel the boarding parties.

By the afternoon of the 22d of same month I had procured as much cotton as I required, and concluded to keep on up the river, thinking that I would certainly meet another boat the morning following, but I was disappointed. I then concluded to communicate with the squadron as soon as possible, thinking that Colonel Ellet had not reached the squadron, or that Admiral Porter would expect me to return when I found that no other boat was sent below.

I kept the bunkers of the Indianola filled with coal, and would have sunk what remained in the barges; but knowing that if another boat was sent below Vicksburg I would be expected to supply her with coal, I concluded to hold on to the barges as long as possible. In consequence of having the barges alongside we could make but slow progress against the current; the result of which was, that I did not reach Grand Gulf until the morning of the 24th of the same month, at which point and at others above we were fired on by parties on shore. As I knew that it would be as much as I could do to get by the Warrenton batteries before daylight the next morning, I returned the fire of but one party.

At about half-past nine p. m. on the 24th of the same month, the night being very dark, four boats were discovered in chase of us. I immediately cleared for action, and as soon as all preparations were completed I turned and stood down the river to meet them. At this time the leading vessel was about three miles below, the others following in close order. As we neared them I made them out to be the rams Queen of the West and William H. Webb, and two other steamers, cotton-clad and filled with men.

The Queen of the West was the first to strike us, which she did after passing through the coal barge lashed to our port side, doing us no serious damage. Next came the Webb. I stood for her at full speed; both vessels came together bows on, with a tremendous crash, which knocked nearly every one down on board of both vessels, doing no damage to us, while the Webb's bow was cut in at least eight feet extending from about two feet above the water-line to the keelson.

At this time the engagement became general and at very close quarters. I devoted but little attention to the cotton-clad steamers, although they kept up a heavy fire with field-pieces and small-arms, as I knew that everything depended on my disabling the rams. The third blow crushed the starboard barge, leaving parts hanging by the lashings, which were speedily cut. The crew of the Indianola not numbering enough men to man both batteries, I kept the forward guns manned all the time, and fired them whenever I could get a shot at the rams. The night being very dark, our aim was very uncertain, and our fire proved less effective than I thought it at the time. The peep-holes in the pilot-house were so small that it would have been a difficult matter to have worked the vessel from that place in daylight, so that during the whole engagement the pilots were unable to aid me by their knowledge of the river, as they were unable to see anything. Consequently they could do no more than obey such orders as they received from me in regard to working the engines and the helm. No misunderstanding occurred in the performance of that duty, and I was enabled to receive the first five blows from the rams forward of the wheels, and at such angles that they did no more damage than to start the plating where they struck.

The sixth blow we received was from the Webb, which crushed in the starboard wheel, disabled the starboard rudder, and started a number of leaks abaft the shaft. Being unable to work the starboard engine, placed us in an almost powerless condition; but I continued the fight until after we received the seventh blow, which was given us by the Webb. She struck us fair in the stern, and started the timbers and starboard rudder box so that the water poured in in large volumes. At this time I knew that the Indianola could be of no more service to us, and my desire was to render her useless to the enemy, which I did by keeping her in deep water until there was two and a half feet of water over the floor, and the leaks were increasing rapidly as she settled, so as to bring the opening made by the Webb under water.

Knowing that if either of the rams struck us again in the stern, which they then had excellent opportunities of doing on account of our disabled condition, we would sink so suddenly that few if any lives would be saved, I succeeded in running her bows on shore by starting the screw-engines. As further resistance could only result in great loss of life on our part, without a corresponding result on the part of the enemy, I surrendered the Indianola, a partially sunken vessel, fast filling with water, to a force of four vessels, mounting ten guns, and manned by over one thousand men.

The engagement lasted one hour and twenty-seven minutes. I lost but one killed, one wounded, and seven missing; while the enemy lost two officers and thirty-three men killed, and many wounded. Before the enemy could make any preparations for endeavoring to save the Indianola, her stern was under water. Both rams were so very much crippled, that I doubt whether they would have tried to ram again had not their last blow proved so fatal to us. Both signal-books were thrown in the river by me a few minutes before the surrender.

In conclusion, I would state that the 9-inch guns of the Indianola were thrown overboard, and the 11-inch guns damaged by being loaded with heavy charges and solid shot, placed muzzle to muzzle, and fired by a slow match, so that they were rendered useless.

This was done in consequence of the sham Monitor, sent from above, having grounded about two miles above the wreck of the Indianola.

I have the honor to remain, very respectfully, your obedient servant,

GEORGE BROWN,
Lieutenant Commanding, U. S. Navy.

Hon. Gideon Welles,
Secretary of the Navy, Washington, D. C.

Expedition through Steele's Bayou and Deer Creek.

Mississippi Squadron,
Yazoo River, March 26, 1863.

Sir: Since my last communication with the department I have been absent on an expedition into the enemy's country, or that part which he professes to hold.

I have for some time past been under the impression that, by cutting our way through the woods, (which are all under water,) I could find an entrance into the river Yazoo, and thus get into the rear of Vicksburg without loss of life or vessels.

In consequence of this idea, and from information obtained from a negro, I made a reconnoissance with Lieutenant Commanding Murphy.

We started up Steele's bayou, which at low stages of water is nothing but a ditch, following it for about thirty miles. This part of the route was perfectly practicable, the creek, though very narrow, having five fathoms of water in it. Black bayou seemed to oppose our further progress; but, on a closer examination, we found that, by removing the trees, we could heave the vessels around the bends, which were very short, and left us not a foot to spare.

All we could hear of the route in advance was very favorable, having obtained as pilot a man well acquainted with the country. I determined to start immediately, having made arrangements with General Grant by which the army could co-operate with us.

On the 14th I started with the Louisville, Lieutenant Commander Owen, Cincinnati, Lieutenant Commanding Bache, Carondelet, Lieutenant Commanding Murphy, Mound City, Lieutenant Commanding Wilson, Pittsburg, Lieutenant Commanding Hoel, four mortars and four tugs.

The expedition went along finely until it reached Black bayou, a place about four miles long, leading into Deer creek. Here the crews of the vessels had to go to work to clear the way, pulling up trees by the roots or pushing them over with the iron-clads, and cutting away the branches above. It was terrible work, but in twenty-four hours we succeeded in getting through these four miles, and found ourselves in Deer creek, where we were told there would be no more difficulties.

General Sherman had arrived up with a small portion of his command; and as he had only twelve miles to march to Rolling Fork, (where we would meet with no further difficulties,) while I had to go thirty-two miles by water, I determined to push on. I found the channel much narrower than I expected, filled with small willows, through which we could scarce make our way, and the branches much overhanging. Still we made at first about a mile an hour, being assured by the pilot that we would find it better as we advanced. It certainly could not get worse.

We had succeeded in getting well into the heart of the country before we were discovered. No one would believe that anything in the shape of a vessel could get through Black bayou, or anywhere on the route. Still, however, as we molested no one, the inhabitants looked on in wonder and astonishment, and the negroes flocked in hundreds down to the banks of the creek to see the novel sight. Soon we were discovered by the government agent, who immediately began to apply the torch to the cotton, public and private. All along, as far as the eye could see, there was nothing but cotton fires burning up, and many dwellings consuming with it. The only persons who saved their cotton were those who would not obey the order to burn. They felt confident we were not going to molest their private property, and their confidence saved them their cotton, which is still in their possession.

It was melancholy to see such fanatical destruction; but as we abstained from anything of the kind ourselves, it placed the two parties in strong contrast before the people of the country, and there were many remarks made not at all complimentary to the confederate government.

Finding that our presence was discovered, I pushed on the vessels as fast as the obstacles would permit, not making more than half a mile an hour. We were passing through a beautiful country, filled with live stock of all kinds, and containing large granaries of corn belonging to the confederate government. The people were more than surprised at the presence of such an expedition, having supposed themselves far removed from the "horrors of war," and there was a good deal of change of opinion on the part of some who never supposed they would be under the protection of the American flag once more.

After very great labor we arrived within seven miles of the Rolling Fork, where everything would be plain sailing before us.

We were here informed that some confederate agents, and some of the citizens, were forcing the negroes to cut down trees in our path. I immediately pushed on the tug Thistle, which had a boat howitzer on her, and she succeeded in reaching the first tree before it was cut down. She proceeded on, under charge of Lieutenant Commanding Murphy, while I followed in the Carondelet, the leading ship. The enemy succeeded at last in getting a large tree down, which stopped the progress of the tug, and then the negroes, with muskets at their breasts, were made to ply their axes until the creek was supposed to be sealed against our further advance.

The labor of clearing out these obstructions was very great, but there is nothing that cannot be overcome by perseverance. The character of the American sailors for endurance was particularly manifested on this occasion, as they worked night and day, without eating or sleeping, until the labor was accomplished.

I hoped by this time to have seen something of our army coming on, but they had their difficulties to contend with, as well as ourselves, and did not reach us in time. The transportation could not be procured at a moment's notice, and we had gone on faster than they expected.

When within three miles of Rolling Fork we discovered smoke in the direction of Yazoo river, and I was informed that the enemy were already landing troops to dispute our passage. I did not mind the troops so much as the timber they would cut in Rolling Fork. I immediately sent on Lieutenant Commanding Murphy, with two boat howitzers and 300 men, to hold Rolling Fork until we could cover it with our guns; which he did, occupying also an Indian mound some sixty feet high, which commanded the whole country.

After working all night and clearing out the obstructions, which were terrible, we succeeded in getting within 800 yards of the end of this troublesome creek; had only two or three large trees to remove, and one apparently short and easy lane of willows to work through. The men being much worn out, we rested at sunset.

In the morning we commenced with renewed vigor to work ahead through the willows, but our progress was very slow; the lithe trees defied our utmost efforts to get by them, and we had to go to work and pull them up separately, or cut them off under water, which was a most tedious job. In the mean time the enemy had collected and landed about 800 men and seven pieces of artillery, (from 20 to 30-pounders,) which were firing on our field-pieces from time to time, the latter not having range enough to reach them.

I was also informed that the enemy were cutting down trees in our rear to prevent communication by water, and also to prevent our escape; this looked unpleasant. I knew that 5,000 men had embarked at Haines's Bluff for this place immediately they heard that we were attempting to go through that way, and, as our troops had not come up, I considered it unwise to risk the least thing; at all events, never to let my communication be closed behind me. I was somewhat strengthened in my determination to advance no further until re-enforced by land forces, when the enemy at sunset opened on us a cross fire with six or seven rifled guns, planted somewhere off in the woods, where we could see nothing but the smoke. It did not take us long to dislodge them, though a large part of the crew being on shore at the time, we could not fire over them or until they got on board.

I saw at once the difficulties we had to encounter with a constant fire on our working parties, and no prospect at present of the troops getting along. I had received a letter from General Sherman informing me of the difficulties in getting forward his men, he doing his utmost, I know, to expedite matters.

The news of the falling trees in our rear was brought in frequently by negroes who were pressed into the service for cutting them, and I hesitated no longer about what to do. We dropped down again, unshipped our rudder, and let the vessels rebound from tree to tree.

As we left, the enemy took possession of the Indian mound, and in the morning opened fire on the Carondelet, Lieutenant Murphy, and Cincinnati, Lieutenant Bache; these two ships soon silenced the batteries, and we were no longer annoyed.

The sharpshooters hung about us, firing from behind trees and rifle-pits; but with due precaution we had very few hurt—only five wounded by rifle balls, and they were hurt by being imprudent.

On the 21st we fell in with Colonel Smith, commanding 8th Missouri and other parts of regiments; we were quite pleased to see him, as I never knew before how much the comfort and safety of iron-clads, situated as we were, depended on the soldiers. I had already sent out behind a force of 300 men to stop the felling of trees in our rear, which Colonel Smith now took charge of. The enemy had already felled over forty heavy trees, which Lieutenant Commander Owen, in the Louisville, working night and day, cleared away almost fast enough to permit us to meet with no delay.

Colonel Smith's force was not enough to justify my making another effort to get through; he had no artillery, and would frequently have to leave the vessels in following the roads.

On the 22d we came to a bend in the river, where the enemy supposed they had blockaded us completely, having cut a number of trees altogether, and so intertwined that it seemed impossible to move them. The Louisville was at work at them, pulling them up, when we discovered about three thousand rebels attempting to pass the edge of the woods to our rear, while the negroes reported artillery coming up on our quarter.

We were all ready for them, and when the artillery opened on us we opened such a fire on them that they scarcely waited to hitch up their horses. At the same time the rebel soldiers fell in with Colonel Smith's troops, and after a sharp skirmish fled before the fire of our soldiers. After this we were troubled no more, and dropped down quietly until we fell in with General Sherman, who, hearing the firing, was hurrying to our support. I do not know when I felt more pleased to see that gallant officer, for without the assistance of the troops we could not without great loss have performed the arduous work of clearing out the obstructions. We might now have retraced our steps, but we were all worn out. The officers and men had for six days and nights been constantly at work, or sleeping at the guns. We had lost our coal barge, and the provision vessel could not get through, being too high for such purposes.

Taking everything into consideration, I thought it best to undertake nothing further, without being better prepared, and we finally, on the 24th, arrived at Hill's plantation, the place we started from on the 16th.

Altogether this has been a most novel expedition. Never did those people expect to see iron-clads floating where the keel of a flatboat never passed. Though nothing has resulted from it more than annoying the enemy and causing him to expend his resources, it has been of great service to the crews, and given me an insight into the character of the commanders and officers of the expedition. I must say that they deserve my warmest commendation for the perseverance and coolness they exhibited during the arduous undertaking. As to the iron-clads themselves, I beg leave to withdraw everything I may have said to their disparagement, for I never yet saw vessels so well adapted to knocking down trees, hauling them up by the roots, or demolishing bridges; we necessarily destroyed all that came in our way, and it has cut off for the present all the means of transporting provisions to Vicksburg.

We destroyed a large amount of confederate corn, captured a large number of mules, horses, and cattle. The rebels themselves burnt over twenty thousand bales of cotton, and we burnt all that we found marked C. S. A.; have taken on our decks, and on the mortar boats, enough to pay for the building of a good gunboat.

The soldiers enjoyed the excursion amazingly, the fine country through which we travelled being quite different from the swamp where they have spent the winter. Had we succeeded entirely, it would have been a severe blow to this part of the country; but it was not to be, and we must console ourselves with the damage we did the enemy and the moral effect of penetrating into a country deemed inaccessible. There will be no more planting in those regions for a long time to come. The able-bodied negroes left with our army, carrying with them all the stores laid up by their masters (for whom they showed little affection) for harder times. I regret to say that we lost one officer, Henry Sullivan, acting third assistant engineer of the tug Dahlia, who was struck by a rifle shot and died of his wounds. Only two were severely wounded. The boats of some of the vessels were badly damaged (which was about the only serious injuries) in crashing through the trees.

We performed a distance of seventy miles each way, making one hundred and forty miles of the most severe labor officers and men ever went through. We found our new mortar boats (though badly built) well adapted for this kind of business, and very useful in clearing the woods of sharpshooters.

I have the honor to be, very respectfully, your obedient servant,

DAVID D. PORTER,

Acting Rear-Admiral, Com'dg Mississippi Squadron.

Hon. GIDEON WELLES,

Secretary of the Navy, Washington, D. C.

Additional.

I look upon it as a great misfortune that this expedition did not get through, for it would have been a most perfect surprise; would have thrown into our hands every vessel in the Yazoo, and every granary from which the rebels could draw a supply.

The great difficulty seems to have been for want of more promptness in moving the troops, or rather I should say, want of means for the moving of troops, for there were never yet any two men who would labor harder than Generals Grant and Sherman to forward an expedition for the overthrow of Vicksburg.

At one time I felt most uncomfortable, finding the enemy increasing in strength in front of me, cutting down trees behind me, and in front a chance of blocking up the feeders of the canal and letting the water out, and not a soldier of ours in sight, or (by the answers I received to my communication) any prospect of any coming in time to prevent a landing of the enemy. I never knew how helpless a thing an iron-clad could be when unsupported by troops; our guns were three feet below the levee; the woods stood just far enough back to enable the sharpshooters to pick off our men, without our being able to bother them, except with the mortars, which kept them off.

When the army did come up it was without provisions; we had to subsist them partly. They left their artillery at Hill's landing, to protect that place, and I felt uneasy about them whenever they would get away from the guns of the iron-clads. Under the circumstances I could not afford to risk a single vessel, and therefore abandoned the expedition. I knew the difficulties to be overcome ahead after we were once discovered, and the impossibility of doing anything with the want of preparation on the part of the army to follow this matter up. The army officers worked like horses to enable them to accomplish what was desired, but they were behind time, and that ended the matter. No other general could have done better, or as well, as Sherman, but he had not the means for this peculiar kind of transportation.

With the end of this expedition end all my hopes of getting into Vicksburg in this direction; had we been successful, we could have made a sure thing of it, provided the army had been pushed on in sufficient numbers. It is not likely that they would have been, want of a certain kind of transportation being felt.

All we can do here now is to harass the enemy by keeping his troops moving to and fro; they will never again be caught by surprise, for after this attempt they will guard every ditch leading into the Yazoo.

As to any harm that gunboats can do Vicksburg, it is not to be taken into consideration at all; the batteries at that place could destroy four times the number we have here, and not receive any damage in return.

There is but one thing now to be done, and that is to start an army of 150,000 men from Memphis *via* Granada, and let them go supplied with everything required to take Vicksburg; let all minor considerations give way to this, and Vicksburg will be ours. Had General Grant not turned back when on the way to Granada, he would have been in Vicksburg before this.

Admiral Farragut's vessels can cut off the supplies at Port Hudson and Red river if he confines them solely to that business—it is the only way in the world of their getting supplies; but if he risks his vessels by trying to capture the Queen of the West or the Webb, he might as well not attempt the blockade.

The Yazoo Pass expedition at first bid fair to do well, but I am afraid it won't amount to much—merely a kind of duel between batteries and iron-clads, in which shell and powder are expended without any use.

Though I feel relieved to get back safe with all the vessels, yet, sir, I see the misfortune of not having succeeded. It would have been a splendid performance.

Now we must console ourselves with the damage we did the enemy, in having his cotton burned and his corn and live stock destroyed. The demoralization of the negroes was complete, and I much fear that terrible scenes will be enacted in the district through which we went. The slave there has been told that he is free, and more than any place that I have seen do the slaves seem determined to maintain what to them seems a most precious boon. I do not blame them, for slavery exists in its worst form in the valley of the Mississippi.

Excuse me, sir, for sending you so long a communication.

Very respectfully, your obedient servant,

DAVID D. PORTER,
Acting Rear-Admiral, Com'dg Mississippi Squadron.

Hon. GIDEON WELLES,
Secretary of the Navy, Washington, D. C.

YAZOO PASS EXPEDITION, U. S. MISSISSIPPI SQUADRON,
Flag-Ship Black Hawk, March 26, 1863.

SIR: I have the honor to enclose a report from Lieutenant Commander Foster, of the Chillicothe, and one from Lieutenant Commander Smith. The Yazoo Pass expedition does not seem to be doing much beyond exchanging shots with the batteries. The Chillicothe, from all accounts, has proved herself unfit to engage a battery, the bolts confining the iron to the ship having been found very destructive to those on board. The Chillicothe has suffered a good deal in killed and wounded, as will appear by the report of her commander.

* * * * * * *

Lieutenant Commander Smith, who commanded the Yazoo Pass expedition, was taken sick soon after entering the Tallahatchie and after operations commenced, and was sent back in, I fear, a dying condition. I depended a good deal on his energy in carrying out my orders, for the success of the expedition. Unless the fort is taken before this, General Grant has ordered the troops to return. They have only retarded our movements so far, there being no chance of landing them at the place where the rebels have blockaded the river.

I have the honor to be, very respectfully, your obedient servant,

DAVID D. PORTER,
Acting Rear-Admiral, Com'dg Mississippi Squadron.

Hon. GIDEON WELLES,
Secretary of the Navy, Washington, D. C.

Report of Lieutenant Commander Watson Smith.

UNITED STATES SHIP RATTLER,
Tallahatchie River, March 11, 1863.

SIR: Stood on this morning to within a mile of the battery, and went ahead with General Rush, in the Chillicothe, to observe. A turn brought us within view of the enemy's works; almost immediately they opened fire from five guns. One shell struck the Chillicothe on the starboard side of the starboard forward port, damaging the plate, and breaking and starting several bolts; another struck on the port side, ahead, six inches above water—a conical rifle shot, making as great an indentation as possible without breaking through; another glanced from the deck. Captain Foster, in reply, threw three shells from his 11-inch guns. With this knowledge of their strength and position, we then turned the point until covered by the trees, and arranged to advance as soon as the army should report ready, which would not be until morning. In the afternoon the rebels appeared to be shipping cattle and goods from the battery, which we believed to be indications that they were preparing to leave.

Advanced the Chillicothe, the De Kalb following, the Lioness in readiness, and was about to bring up the Rattler, but going on board the Chillicothe, found her already much injured by the shot of the enemy, one of which struck between the slide-covers of the port forward port, which was at the time sufficiently ajar to allow the rammer handle to pass out. The men were in the act of sending the shell down, when this shell striking the Chillicothe's shell, both exploded, (fragments of each being found,) killing two men, and wounding eleven others, three of them perhaps mortally. The 11-inch was struck on the muzzle, damaging, but not disabling it; the slide-covers of this port were blown off, one going overboard. Other shots struck, killing one man. The Chillicothe and De Kalb were strengthening themselves with cotton when advanced, and I now withdrew them for the purpose of completing that defence. The short distance, and the stream being narrow, prevents the easy use of two vessels upon the fort. I have, therefore, landed the 30-pounder Parrott gun from the broadside of this vessel; and, with the assistance of the troops, expect to have it in position to annoy the rebels' best gun, at about six hundred yards, by morning, and well protected by cotton and earth. Of the seven shells fired by the Chillicothe, two appeared to burst well, and two to strike a steamboat lying just beyond the fort below Greenwood. There is a steamer sunk there by the rebels, not quite in position desired by them.

A rebel called over this afternoon, stating that they had a vessel ready for the Chillicothe. She will be guarded, and, if boarded, will, if possible, be swept by our own vessels, her crew going below. This is different from engaging with head up stream. The Chillicothe works well, but the De Kalb and other stern-wheels are very awkward. The base of a rifle shell, measuring $6\frac{1}{2}$ inches, shows the size of one of their guns; another seems like a sixty-eight; another a $4\frac{1}{2}$-inch rifle.

Mr. Morton, the pilot, was badly blown by the explosion of the shells on board the Chillicothe; he is not seriously injured, and will soon be on duty.

I shall use all the means we have of silencing this battery—the mortar, with the others, when it arrives. The Chillicothe's turret is not well backed; neither she nor the De Kalb can stand those rifled shot.

I have not ascertained sufficiently about the raft to speak of it with certainty.

My letter of yesterday acquaints you with our situation as regards provisions and fuel. Those of us that are but partly manned feel the want of men; the soldiers serve the guns well, but the others are needed. It is with difficulty that the small boats can be manned.

The small army steamer has arrived, not having been interfered with by guerillas.

Midnight.—The rebels are busy at something; don't think they are leaving. The Yallabusha is probably fortified at each bluff, as they feared for Granada. I am obliged to keep steam now at night, which is exhausting to the coal.

Respectfully yours,

WATSON SMITH,
Lieutenant Commander.

Acting Rear-Admiral D. D. PORTER,
Commanding Mississippi Squadron.

Report of Lieutenant Commander James P. Foster.

UNITED STATES GUNBOAT CHILLICOTHE,
Tallahatchie River, Mississippi, March 22, 1863.

SIR: When I last wrote you, a retrograde movement was unanimously agreed upon, it being hazardous to remain longer. This movement was postponed, but, on the morning of the 19th instant, was reagreed upon, and we started for Helena in the perfect belief that there was no hope of reducing Fort Greenwood (or Pemberton) without a strong re-enforcement of heavy iron-clads.

Since our departure (to-day) we have met on the Tallahatchie river General Quimby and his command *en route* for Fort Greenwood. General Quimby states to me that other large land forces were on their way also to join in the attack on Fort Greenwood, and that his forces and armament would be such, that with the gunboats of the Mississippi squadron, composing the Yazoo Pass expedition, failure is impossible, in his opinion. I send you a copy of his letter of request, and while I feel the responsibility, without consulting you of it, being impossible, I still feel and hope that, in complying with General Quimby's request, I shall meet your hearty approval, notwitstanding the disabled condition of the Chillicothe, and the shortness of ammunition and provisions; the latter, General Quimby promises to furnish for the present. It is proper for me to say that General Ross, with whom the gunboats have heretofore been co-operating, and who, during the whole expedition, has been indefatigable in his exertions to render it successful, had it been possible with the forces before engaged, remains quiet, but thinks we can take the fort if re-enforced by gunboats.

From my knowledge of General Ross, I have to say that I believe him to be as sincere as I know him to be magnanimous and brave. Colonel Wilson joins in the renewal of the Yazoo Pass expedition, and from his known engineering abilities, and his well-established patriotism, I can but accord to his opinion great weight.

I hope that the expedition will redound to our cause, and I fervently hope to despatch to you that the gunboats of the Yazoo Pass expedition, in conjunction with the army, have added other laurels to our flag.

After we pass Fort Greenwood, if not before, I think it will be absolutely necessary to our perfect success to have at least two more heavy iron-clads. Two months' provisions are required now for what gunboats are here of all classes.

I regret to say that I have just heard pretty reliably that the Rattler, *en route* for Helena, and in command of Acting Master Fentress, late executive officer of the Rattler, was attacked in the Tallahatchie river, and during the action lost two men killed and several wounded. I also regret to say that Lieutenant Commander Smith was said to be dying.

The wounded of the Chillicothe, in the actions of the 11th, 13th, and 16th, that have been retained here, are doing well. I, however, sent the worst cases to the fleet surgeon, except the wounded soldiers doing duty as marines. These latter I sent to the army hospital boat. I will remain off Fort Greenwood ten days, and await your answer to former despatches.

I am, very respectfully, your obedient servant,

JAS. P. FOSTER,
Lieutenant Commander.

Acting Rear-Admiral D. D. PORTER,
Commanding Mississippi Squadron.

List of killed and wounded on board the Chillicothe

UNITED STATES MISSISSIPPI SQUADRON,
United States Gunboat Chillicothe, March 11, 1863.

The following is a list of the killed and wounded during the action of to-day: J. F. Morton, pilot, wounded; Thos. Greenslade, quarter-gunner, killed; Jerry Norton, marine, killed; Jno. G. Singleton, marine, killed; Jno. Henderson, marine, killed; Henry B. Levague, boatswain's mate, wounded; Newton Porter, marine, wounded; Jas. M. Young, marine, wounded; Jas. F. Holladay, marine, wounded; Patrick Conner, marine, wounded; Robt. Brown, marine, wounded; J. A. Briton, marine, wounded; C. C. Huff, marine, wounded; Stephen N. Cornell, seaman, wounded.

W. C. FOSTER,
Acting Assistant Surgeon.

List of the wounded on board the United States gunboat Chillicothe, in the action before Fort Greenwood, on March 13, 1863.

Francis O'Neil, landsman, wounded badly in arm; Leopold Trost, marine, wounded in the face; Roney Hupple, seaman, contusion of the hand; John Mitchell, seaman, violent contusion of brain; D. Miller, marine, wounded in the hand; Harrison Gill, landsman, wound of the hand.

W. C. FOSTER,
Acting Assistant Surgeon, Chillicothe.

List of killed and wounded on board the United States gunboat Chillicothe, during the action at Fort Greenwood, March 16, 1863.

John Young, seaman, wounded in right side; Christopher Talbot, cabin boy, wounded, by falling overboard, as we were going into action.

W. C. FOSTER,
Acting Assistant Surgeon, United States Navy.

Report of killed and wounded on the Rattler.

UNITED STATES MISSISSIPPI SQUADRON,
Yazoo River, April 7, 1863.

SIR: I have the honor to enclose a list of the killed and wounded on board the United States steamer Rattler, on her passage out of the Tallahatchie river, March 19, 1863.

Very respectfully, your obedient servant,

D. D. PORTER,
Acting Rear-Admiral, Com'dg Mississippi Squadron.

Hon. GIDEON WELLES,
Secretary of the Navy, Washington, D. C.

UNITED STATES STEAMER RATTLER,
Tallahatchie River, March 19, 1863.

SIR: I have the honor to report the following killed and wounded aboard this vessel:

Killed.—Jeremiah Harrington, seaman; ball passing through external carotid artery.

Wounded.—George S. West, acting ensign; ball entered left side, between ninth and tenth ribs, passing round anterior to the bowels, lodging below right nipple. The patient will recover.

Respectfully, your obedient servant,

W. H. WILSON,
Acting Assistant Surgeon, Steamer Rattler.

WALTER E. H. FENTRESS,
Acting Master, Com'dg U. S. Steamer Rattler.

Extract from report of Rear-Admiral Porter.

YAZOO RIVER, *April* 11, 1863.

* * * * * * * * * *

The Yazoo Pass expedition has done harm to the enemy, though not as successful as I intended it to be. It caused the enemy to sink the Star of the West, Magnolia, and Natchez—three of their best vessels. The squadron chased the steamer Thirty-fifth Parallel on shore, where she was burnt, with three thousand bales of cotton. One steamer transport was sunk by our shells, and one other, I believe, destroyed to avoid falling into our hands.

The fort (Pemberton) was silenced at one time by our gunboats, and remained so for a day. The army did not think themselves strong enough to attempt the assault; waited for re-enforcements and lost their chance.

I remain, sir, very respectfully, your obedient servant,

DAVID D. PORTER,
Acting Rear-Admiral, Com'dg Mississippi Squadron.

Hon. GIDEON WELLES,
Secretary of the Navy, Washington, D. C.

Further report of Acting Rear-Admiral Porter.

MISSISSIPPI SQUADRON,
Yazoo River, April 13, 1863.

SIR: I have the honor to enclose you a report of the Yazoo Pass expedition, from Lieutenant Commander Foster, who took command after Lieutenant Commander Watson Smith was obliged to give up from extreme illness.

The department will observe that the Chillicothe has proved herself entirely unfit for a fighting vessel, as she now is; her backing of fine wood, twelve inches thick, being found inadequate to stand shot.

The Baron De Kalb, supposed to be an inferior vessel, received no damage of any consequence.

The department can form their opinion of the importance of the expedition from the report of Lieutenant Commander Foster. Fort Pemberton was fairly whipped and silenced by the De Kalb and Chillicothe. No attempt was made by the troops to assault or take possession. At one time the enemy had not a charge of powder in the fort; and the shells of our vessels were passing through seven bales of cotton, which must have made the place untenable.

There were difficulties in the way of an assault, but whether they were sufficient to stop the troops, when the fort was silenced, I am unable to say.

I remain, sir, very respectfully, your obedient servant,

DAVID D. PORTER,
Acting Rear-Admiral, Com'dg Mississippi Squadron.

Hon. GIDEON WELLES,
Secretary of the Navy, Washington, D. C.

Additional report of Lieutenant Commander Foster.

UNITED STATES STEAMER CHILLICOTHE,
April 13, 1863.

SIR: On the 18th March, in consequence of the ill health of Lieutenant Commander Watson Smith, I fell into the command of the Yazoo Pass expedition, and have to make the following report:

The orders which were turned over to me by Lieutenant Commander Smith were positive, and urged the necessity of pushing on, urging him by no means to delay, as the success of the expedition depended entirely upon the rapidity of the movement. Had these instructions been carried out, I have no doubt that the expedition would have been successful, and that we would have reached Yazoo City in half the time that we were in making Fort Pemberton; and as there was no opposition at that time of sufficient force to check us, we would have had complete control of the river, with all their steamers at our mercy.

Success here, and the controlling power of the Cold Water, Tallahatchie, Yalabusha, and Yazoo rivers, would, in my opinion, have opened a sure road to Vicksburg, as it is by these rivers that they receive most of their supplies.

The first attack made on Fort Pemberton was on the 11th of March, on a reconnoissance, about 11 a. m., when five or six shots where exchanged, doing little or no damage. On the afternoon of the same day the Chillicothe again went down and opened fire on the fort. During the action the Chillicothe had four men killed and fifteen wounded; after having a whole gun's crew disabled the Chillicothe withdrew.

The Chillicothe is a perfect failure, as a fighting vessel, and will have to be repaired before going into action again.

On the 13th the Chillicothe and Baron De Kalb got under way at 11.30 a. m., and commenced the attack on Fort Pemberton, at seven hundred and eighty yards. The Chillicothe remained in action one hour and thirty-eight minutes. During this action she received forty-four shots; and after expending nearly all her ammunition of five-inch and ten-inch shells, retired by order of the commanding officer. On the retiring of the Chillicothe the fort ceased firing, although the De Kalb remained, and kept firing slowly during the remainder of the day.

Deserters and prisoners captured reported that their guns were silenced, and that the fort would have been taken had our forces advanced, as they were entirely without ammunition.

On the 18th we retired, believing the fort too strong for the forces there engaged, and being short of ammunition.

The day after leaving Fort Pemberton the Chillicothe, De Kalb, light-draughts, &c., arrived before the fort again; and at the suggestion of General Quimby the Chillicothe took her old position before the fort, firing three shots for the purpose of drawing the enemy's fire; failing in this, she withdrew. We, along with those on shore, were under the impression that the enemy blew up a torpedo, just forward the Chillicothe's bow.

We remained twelve days waiting for the army to do something; and when General Quimby was ordered to withdraw his forces, we brought up the rear.

We captured five prisoners, three of whom I have paroled at Helena; the remaining two I shall send to you.

On our return to the fort we remained twelve days, and during the whole of that time nothing was done by General Quimby towards the reduction of the fort. On meeting General Quimby, I told him that it was impossible to take the fort without heavy siege guns; he said that he had a number of heavy 24-pounders, and would procure others without delay, and expressed his entire confidence as to the capture of Fort Pemberton. I then, at his earnest and written request, (a copy of which I have sent you,) returned with him, and remained until the army was ordered to withdraw. The cotton captured and destroyed is about 4,000 to 5,000 bales.

The Yazoo Pass, Cold Water, and Tallahatchie, at the present, are in good condition, and no difficulty is experienced in their navigation.

The enemy burnt two large steamers, the 35th Parallel (supposed to have on board 2,500 bales of cotton) and the Magnolia; cargo reported to be cotton. In addition to these, they sunk the Star of the West near the fort. The enemy lost, by his own acknowledgment, 12 men in killed and wounded.

The gunboats, had they pushed on even after the delay at Helena, would have reached Fort Pemberton before a spade was put in the ground for its erection.

In conclusion, let me again say, had the expedition been carried out as it was originally planned, and had not the army detained us by the slowness of their movements, the expedition would have been a complete success.

I am, sir, very respectfully, your obedient servant,

JAS. P. FOSTER,
Lieutenant Commander.

Acting Rear-Admiral DAVID D. PORTER,
Commanding Mississippi Squadron.

MAP OF OPERATIONS OF THE YAZOO PASS EXPEDITION, UNDER COMMAND OF LT. COM. WATSON SMITH, U. S. N., 1863.

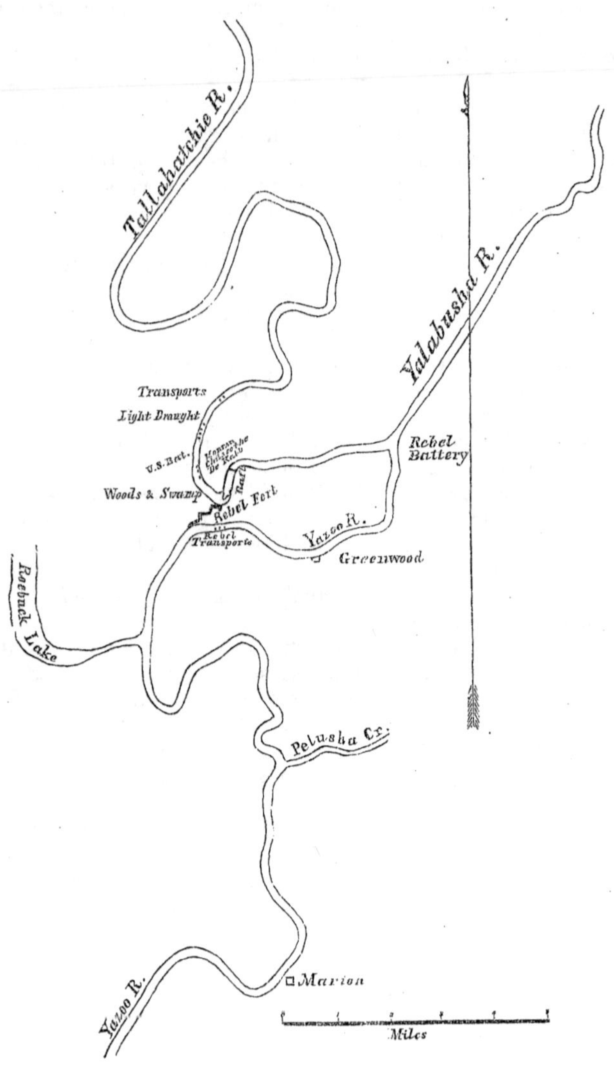

MAP SHOWING THE ROUTE OF THE LATE EXPEDITION, COMMANDED BY REAR-ADMIRAL PORTER, U. S. N., IN ATTEMPTING TO GET INTO THE YAZOO RIVER BY THE WAY OF STEEL'S BLUFF AND DEER CREEK.

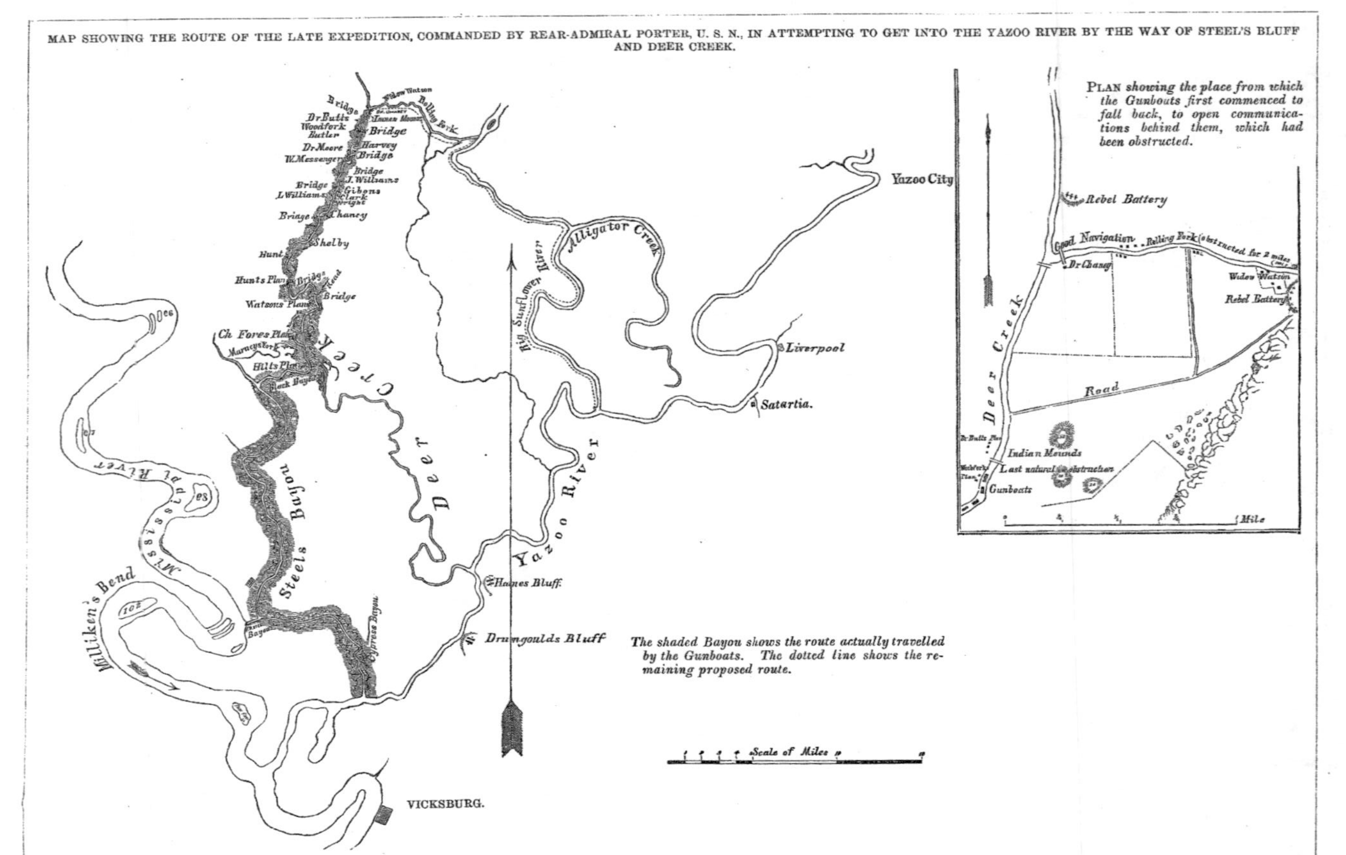

The shaded Bayou shows the route actually travelled by the Gunboats. The dotted line shows the remaining proposed route.

Report of Lieutenant Commander John G. Walker.

UNITED STATES GUNBOAT BARON DE KALB,
Mouth of Yazoo, April 13, 1863.

SIR: I have the honor to submit the following report of the operations of this vessel before Fort Pemberton, Tallahatchie river:

We arrived before the fort on the 11th of March, and after examining the work prepared for action, but, owing to the temporary disabling of the Chillicothe by a shot from the enemy, were ordered to withdraw. On the 13th went into action at 10.45 p. m., in company with the Chillicothe and mortar boat, engaging the fort at about eight hundred yards. The engagement was severe until about 2 p. m., when the Chillicothe was forced to retire for the want of ammunition. This vessel remained in her position until dark, firing upon the enemy at intervals of fifteen minutes, the enemy having ceased firing. After dark, by order of Lieutenant Commander Smith, she was backed up to her old position.

The enemy fired but few shots after 2 p. m. On the 15th, landed an 8-inch gun, with a supply of ammunition, and placed it in battery on shore, with a crew to work it. At 12.30 p. m., on the 16th, we again moved into action, but the Chillicothe, being disabled in a few minutes after getting under fire, withdrew by order. On the 19th took on board the 8-inch gun from the shore battery.

In the engagement of the 13th the loss on board this vessel was:

John O'Neil, quartermaster, killed; Robert Murphy, ordinary seaman, killed; F. E. Davis, master's mate, mortally wounded, since dead; G. W. Male, seaman, lost a leg; John McGovern, seaman, slightly wounded; Frank McGuire, seaman, slightly wounded.

This vessel was considerably cut up, losing ten gun-deck beams, having the wheel-house and steerage badly knocked to pieces, and various other damages to the wooden parts of the vessel, but nothing to render her unserviceable.

I am, sir, very respectfully,

JOHN G. WALKER,
Lieutenant Commander.

Rear-Admiral D. D. PORTER,
Commanding Mississippi Squadron.

Sinking of the Lancaster and Switzerland (rams) in passing the Vicksburg batteries.

MISSISSIPPI SQUADRON,
Yazoo River, March 26, 1863.

SIR: During my absence on an expedition into the enemy's country General Ellet, at the request of Admiral Farragut, sent the rams Switzerland and Lancaster to run the batteries at Vicksburg.

The Lancaster was sunk and the Switzerland disabled. These vessels were not at all prepared for so hazardous an adventure, nor at all suited for any service that will take them any distance from a machine shop.

I send you a letter from General Ellet on the subject, in answer to one from me.

I have the honor to be, very respectfully,

DAVID D. PORTER,
Acting Rear-Admiral, Com'dg Mississippi Squadron.

Hon. GIDEON WELLES;
Secretary of the Navy, Washington.

Letter of Acting Rear-Admiral Porter to General A. W. Ellet.

UNITED STATES MISSISSIPPI SQUADRON,
Yazoo River, March 26, 1863.

GENERAL: Will you please inform me by what authority you sent the rams Lancaster and Switzerland past the batteries at Vicksburg in open day, and without taking any precaution to guard their hulls. One of these vessels has, in consequence, been sunk, and the other damaged extensively, which might very well have been expected under the circumstances.

You will also inform me who were the commanders of those vessels, and all of the circumstances attending this unfortunate affair.

Very respectfully, &c.,

DAVID D. PORTER,
Acting Rear-Admiral, Com'dg Mississippi Squadron.

Brigadier General A. W. ELLET,
Com'dg Marine Brigade, Mississippi Squadron.

Report of General A. W. Ellet.

HEADQUARTERS MISSISSIPPI MARINE BRIGADE,
Flag-Ship Autocrat, above Vicksburg, March 25, 1863.

ADMIRAL: In compliance with your instructions, I would respectfully report that the Switzerland and Lancaster were sent past the batteries at Vicksburg by my order this morning, in consequence of receiving an urgent request from Admiral Farragut for their assistance to aid him in keeping the river open from Vicksburg to Port Hudson, and in destroying the enemy's communication from Red river, and also for the purpose of passing troops over the river to Warrenton to aid in the destruction of the formidable batteries now being constructed at that point.

The boats started before daylight. You have been misinformed of the passage being made in open day. It is true that in consequence of the injury that the boats sustained they did not get past before the sun had risen; yet, if they had not been injured and obliged to float, they would have made the passage before it was fully light.

The Lancaster, I regret to say, is a total loss. Her boilers were exploded, and being a very rotten boat she went to pieces and sunk immediately. She was commanded by Lieutenant Colonel John A. Ellet.

The Switzerland was commanded by Colonel Charles R. Ellet in person, who also commanded the expedition. She received a number of shots, but being a stronger boat was not much injured. Her boiler was exploded by a plunging shot. In other respects the damage was not material. She will be repaired in a few days, and is in a position where I trust she may be able to redeem whatever of mishap has attended the passage of the Vicksburg batteries.

I have the honor to be, very respectfully,

ALFRED W. ELLET,
Brigadier General, Com'dg Miss. Marine Brigade.

Acting Rear-Admiral D. D. PORTER,
Commanding Mississippi Squadron.

Letters from Rear-Admiral Farragut to Acting Rear-Admiral Porter.

UNITED STATES FLAG-SHIP HARTFORD,
Below Vicksburg, March 25, 1863.

DEAR ADMIRAL: I find myself in a most awkward predicament, being here with only my ship and the little Albatross as a tender, perfectly unable to do anything but go up and down the river, or, what is of much more importance, blockade the mouth of Red river for a limited period. I have expressed the desire to you to have an iron-clad, one at least, and two rams, to assist me in this matter; and I now repeat it, so that, when it becomes absolutely necessary for me to go down the river to replenish my provisions and resume my duties in command of the blockading squadron, I may be able to do so without reopening the Red river trade. There is nothing below, or in Red river, that could successfully compete with an iron-clad and two rams. General Ellet called on me to know if I desired two of his rams; I replied to him that I needed such vessels and would be very much gratified to have them, but I would not interfere with Admiral Porter—that I understood his boats to be a component part of your fleet. He said all he desired was to know if I considered it a benefit to the country and the cause to have them below Vicksburg; to which I replied "certainly;" and he said that was all he wanted to know, and that he should run two down in the night. I told him although I was very anxious for the force I had asked of you, and was ignorant of your relative positions, I feared he was wrong in doing so, although it might be done with safety during the darkness of the night, which he said he would avail himself of. I had made an arrangement with General Grant, and more particularly with Colonel Wood, of the 76th Ohio volunteers, to convoy a party to Warrenton and cover their attack on that place for the purpose of breaking up a casemated battery the enemy had built there, which General Ellet proposed his two rams could carry over, while we attacked the battery when they should arrive below. All these arrangements were made; the troops ready for embarcation; the night serene and beautiful, so much so that I sincerely hoped the general would not think of sending his vessels down; and, just as I had come to that conclusion, between half past 5 o'clock and 6 in the morning, I heard the batteries open. I felt that all was lost unless by the merest accident. My fears were realized. The Lancaster was totally destroyed; the Switzerland had two shots in her boilers, otherwise not materially injured. My engineer says her boilers can be repaired in a week; not a man killed; two or three unfortunate negroes were badly scalded, some of whom may die. It was a wonderful escape for the crew.

I write this letter for two purposes; first, to exonerate myself from any charge of a disposition to interfere with your command; and, secondly, with a hope to excuse General Ellet from any feeling to do that which he thought would be disagreeable to you; but, on the contrary, all who surrounded him at the time thought, and so expressed themselves, that it would be in accordance with your wishes if you were present. In conclusion, I beg leave to state that I shall now return to the mouth of Red river, which I consider the limit of my jurisdiction under my old orders, but which will be curtailed to below Port Hudson, when once I pass that place, until it is captured by our forces. On my arrival below I shall endeavor to communicate with General Banks, across the isthmus opposite Port Hudson, when he will have a full understanding of General Grant's views as to an attack on that place above and below.

Very respectfully, your obedient servant,

D. G. FARRAGUT,
Rear-Admiral.

Acting Rear-Admiral D. D. PORTER,
Commanding Western Flotilla.

UNITED STATES FLAG-SHIP HARTFORD,
Below Vicksburg, March 25, 1863.

DEAR ADMIRAL: Since my last letter I have received your last letter by my secretary, Mr. Gabaudon, and am delighted to find that our ideas agree so well on the subject of the blockade of Red river, but you say nothing of the iron-clads and rams to assist me in that operation, when I shall be compelled to leave them and make my way down to New Orleans. I was in hope that you would have been here in time and sent me an iron-clad down to assist me in demolishing the casemated battery at Warrenton, unless a force is landed and captures it—a thing I think easily accomplished at present, as the town is surrounded by water, and assistance, except by infantry, is not easily obtained. My isolated position requires that I should be more careful of my ship than I would likely be if I had any fleet with me, as I cannot get to a machine shop to obtain the most ordinary appliances for repairs without fighting my way to them. I deeply regret the rashness of General Ellet in sending his boats past the batteries in broad daylight, as it afforded the enemy nothing but a target practice. You say truly when you say that I have had some disasters in my own fleet similar to those of the Indianola. I consider the Galveston affair the greatest blow that the navy has sustained during the war. It has emboldened our enemies, and, in many cases, demoralized our own people. We are pretty well prepared for their boarding. Wishing you every success in your undertaking,

Your friend and obedient servant,

D. G. FARRAGUT,
Rear-Admiral.

Admiral D. D. PORTER,
Commanding Western Flotilla.

Extract from despatch of Rear-Admiral Porter.

MISSISSIPPI SQUADRON,
Yazoo River, April 11, 1863.

SIR: I have the honor to acknowledge the receipt of your communication of the 3d instant. I have already informed you of the cause of the disaster to the ram Lancaster, in relation to which I had nothing to do, being absent at the moment, and being unwilling at any time to send down that class of vessels unless at night and properly prepared.

Selfridge's "Cut-off."

No. 195.]

MISSISSIPPI SQUADRON,
Yazoo River, April 16, 1863.

SIR: I have the honor to enclose a letter from Lieutenant Commander Thomas O. Selfridge, which is interesting from the fact that it shows how easily cut-offs are made in the Mississippi, when conducted with ordinary intelligence. I send a diagram which will explain the operation. We have been threatened for some time past with an attack from the Arkansas rebels in steamers. Every provision was made to meet it. Lieutenant Commander Selfridge saw the difficulty in defending the mouths of White and Arkansas rivers while kept so far apart by a useless neck of land, and proposed to me to cut it. I ordered him to do so, and he passed through with his vessel twenty-four hours after he cut the bend, thus saving a distance of over ten miles. The mouths of Arkansas and White rivers are now brought close together, and a small force can defend both.

One of the worst points for guerillas is also cut off, as those pests of the human race could, from the isthmus, attack a vessel on one side and be ready to meet her on the other as she came round, the distance being ten miles around and half a mile across.

Captain Selfridge deserves credit for cutting this new river route, Had the Vicksburg canal (which was first proposed by Captain Alden, United States navy, and myself to General Butler) been cut originally in the right place, we would have had a good ship channel, well clear of Vicksburg; as it is, it amounted to nothing. By looking at the map you will perceive that the two necks are very similar in conformation.

I have force enough at Arkansas and White rivers to prevent any attack.

I remain, sir, very respectfully, your obedient servant,

DAVID D. PORTER,
Acting Rear-Admiral, Com'dg Mississippi Squadron.

Hon. GIDEON WELLES,
Secretary of the Navy, Washington, D. C.

Report of Lieutenant Commanding Thos. O. Selfridge.

UNITED STATES STEAMER CONESTOGA,
Off Arkansas River, April 14, 1863.

SIR: I have the honor to report the arrival of the Curlew, Cricket, Rattler, and Prairie Bird, also the ram; permit me to thank you for the strong re-enforcements you have sent.

If you are willing, I should prefer to meet an attack in the Mississippi, rather than the Arkansas, as the latter river is falling fast, and it gives me so much more room to ram the steamers.

The cut-off, above Alexander's, made on Saturday last, I passed through on Sunday—the first steamer through. It shortens the distance between the two rivers at least ten miles, and enables me to concentrate our strength very completely. I enclose diagram of the different stations.

Though my information of an intended attack was entirely through the negroes, it came in so many different ways that I think confidence could be placed in their statements. Since, though, I have learned through a prisoner, and also some women that came last Saturday from Pine Bluff, that the Arkansas river is too low for steamers to get out. I do not think, therefore, that an attack can be made until a rise of the river, or will be made with the present imposing force. Should they attempt it, there will be none go back. I have moved the coal barges to a point about a mile below White river, a more secure position, more easily defended.

The force I now have I consider more than sufficient for this point. If you wish any of the light-draughts sent elsewhere, I shall give them all an inspection and report the result.

Learning that there were U. S. arms at McGhee's place, Carson's landing, I sent the Juliet up, which captured two men, Alexander Smith and J. N. Crow. These men have been employed hunting runaway negroes, and acknowledge to have shot some who attempted to escape; they are notorious rascals, and Smith was concerned in the burning of the Lake City. I found at McGhee's a United States Belgian rifle, sword bayonet with complete equipments, marked U. S., and a hunting rifle. Smith's story is that he purchased them from two of our deserters; the negroes say he robbed them of them.

I have these two in double irons on the Bragg. My intention was, if it met your approval, to punish them for their villany, and send them beyond the lines.

I was up through the cut-off into the Arkansas yesterday, on a reconnoissance. I captured a prisoner, Cornelius Jones, private of twenty-first Texas. He was employed as a mail or despatch carrier. He had on at the time a federal uniform, and attempted to pass himself off as a citizen. He says that all the pickets on the river had been drawn in. His regiment had gone to Batesville, Arkansas. From all I can learn there is some secret move on hand amongst their forces. What disposition shall I make of him?

I have sent the Signal to Memphis for provisions, and for some little repairs, that can be made during the short time she is there.

I have sent word to the Chillicothe to remain at Helena until she receives your orders.

Very respectfully, your obedient servant,

THOS. O. SELFRIDGE,
Lieutenant Commanding.

Acting Rear-Admiral DAVID D. PORTER,
Commanding Mississippi Squadron.

General Prentiss, at Helena, wishes all the negroes he can get, as he is forming them into regiments. Am I authorized to send up such as present themselves?

Passage of the Vicksburg batteries by Acting Rear-Admiral Porter with his fleet.

MISSISSIPPI SQUADRON,
Yazoo River, April 7, 1863.

SIR: There is nothing new at this point, with the exception that General Steele's division has been sent up to take possession of the country through which we lately took the gunboats. When that is secured we can reach the Yazoo when we please, provided the water keeps up.

I am preparing to pass the batteries of Vicksburg with most of the fleet. General Grant is marching his army below, and we are going to endeavor to turn Vicksburg and get to Jackson by a very practicable route. If General Grant can raise 60,000 men, which he says he can do, he cannot fail.

The enemy, owing to our late raids on them, have much reduced their force at Vicksburg. They are cut off from all supplies from below; so is Port Hudson.

I remain, sir, very respectfully, your obedient servant,

DAVID D. PORTER,
Acting Rear-Admiral, Com'dg Mississippi Squadron.

Hon. GIDEON WELLES,
Secretary of the Navy, Washington, D. C.

MISSISSIPPI SQUADRON,
New Carthage, Mississippi River, April 17, 1863.

SIR: I have the honor to inform you that I passed the batteries at Vicksburg, on the night of the 16th of April, with a large force for operations below. Three army transports were prepared to resist shot, and accompanied the squadron. I led in the Benton, and having drifted down on the batteries, got up with the first one without being discovered. At 11.16 p. m. the batteries opened on us; we immediately responding with a rapid fire, the vessels of the squadron all in line following our example.

MAP SHOWING THE NEW CUT-OFF MADE BY LT. COM. T. O. SELFRIDGE, U. S. N., 1863.
0 ½ 1 2 3 4 5
Scale of Miles
MONTGOMERY'S PT
White River
VICTORIA
Rose Branch
Selfridge's Cut-off.
Arkansas River
Mississippi
Very bad Guerilla Station Destroyed
NAPOLEON
Island No 74
Island No 75
River.

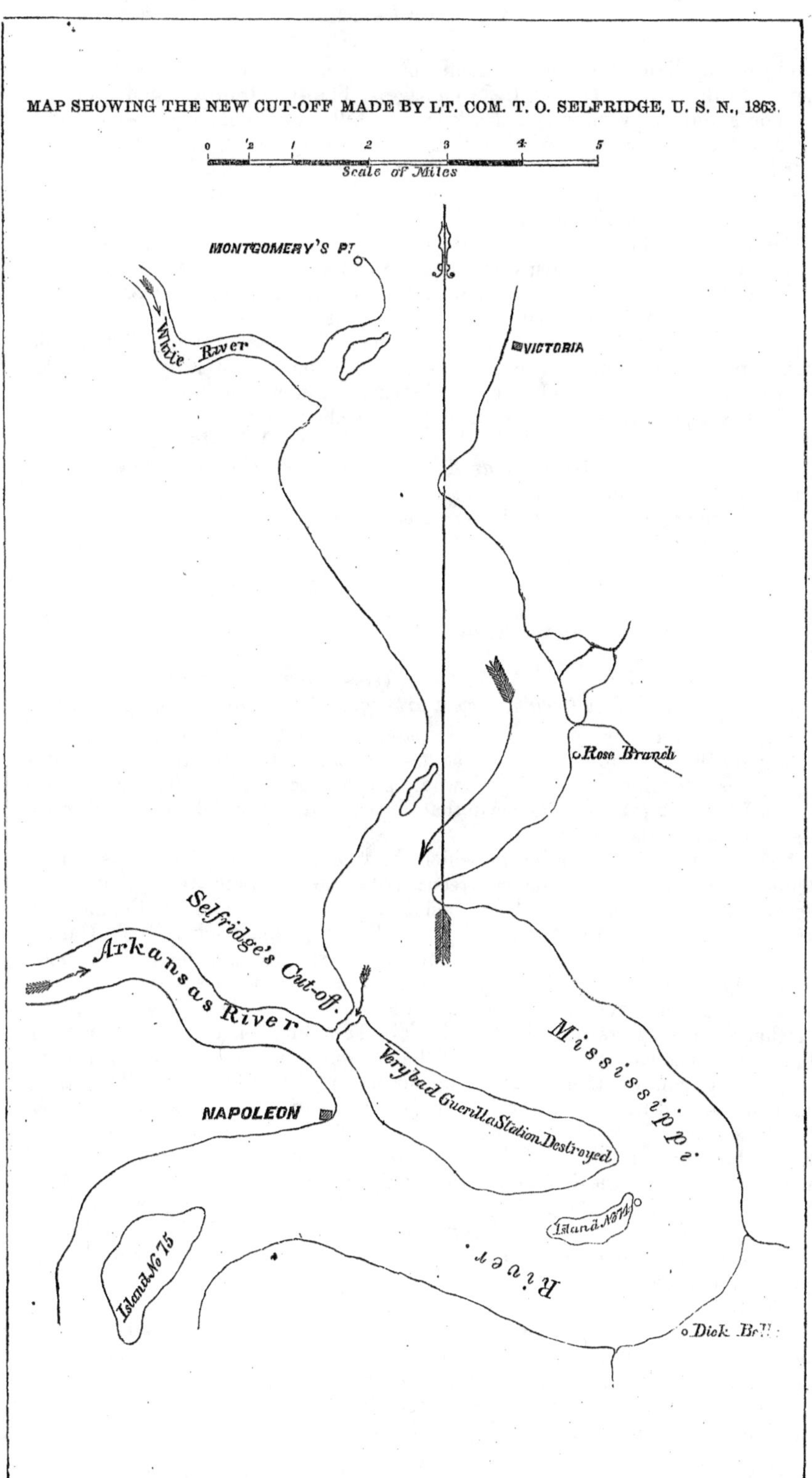

H. Ex. Doc. 69——31

The enemy lighted up the river on both sides, and we were fair targets for them. Still, we received but little damage. The squadron was under fire for two hours and thirty minutes. No one was killed, and only eight wounded—the greatest number on board this ship, which, being ahead, received a concentrated fire. An army transport, the Henry Clay, was sunk by a heavy shot. The Forest Queen, transport, became temporarily disabled, and was turned into safe quarters by the Tuscumbia.

The fire from the forts was heavy and rapid, but was replied to with such spirit that the aim of the enemy was not as good as usual.

The conduct of all the commanders met my entire approbation. All the vessels were ready for service half an hour after passing the batteries.

I had the Indianola examined to-day. She is much shattered. The rebels got her two 9-inch guns. One 11-inch gun was burst, and is lying on deck; the other fell overboard, and now lies alongside, in nine feet water.

I remain, sir, very respectfully, your obedient servant,

DAVID D. PORTER,

Acting Rear-Admiral, Com'dg Mississippi Squadron.

Hon. GIDEON WELLES,

Secretary of the Navy, Washington, D. C.

Detailed report of Acting Rear-Admiral Porter.

MISSISSIPPI SQUADRON,

Flag-Ship Benton, New Carthage, Mississippi, April 19, 1863.

SIR: Being anxious to send back despatches by General Grant, I wrote you a short report. I omitted to state the number and names of the vessels composing this expedition, as my letter would go through the Memphis post office; and as I have no great confidence in that department, I omitted names and numbers from prudential motives.

The following is the order in which the vessels started, fifty yards apart: Benton, Lieutenant Commander Green; Lafayette, Captain Walke, with the General Price lashed on starboard side; Louisville, Lieutenant Commander Owen; Mound City, Lieutenant Wilson; Pittsburg, Lieutenant Hoel; Carondelet, Lieutenant Murphy; and Tuscumbia, Lieutenant Commander Shirk; also the tug Ivy, lashed to the Benton. The three army transports were in the rear of the above-mentioned vessels, and the Tuscumbia was placed astern of all, to see that the transports did not turn back. This duty Lieutenant Commander Shirk performed handsomely. Two of the transports, when firing became heavy, attempted to run up stream, but Lieutenant Commander Shirk drove them back, and staid behind them until the Forest Queen was disabled. He then took her in tow and placed her out of reach of the enemy's shot. All the vessels, except the Benton, took in tow coal barges, containing each ten thousand bushels of coal, and all except the Lafayette brought them safely past the batteries. Having the General Price alongside, the Lafayette did not manage very well, and the coal barge got adrift, but was afterwards picked up at Carthage. The Louisville, Lieutenant Commander Owen, lost hers in the "melée," but picked it up again while under fire.

The Benton was beautifully handled by her pilot, Mr. Williams, who was also in the Essex when she ran the batteries. He kept the vessel's guns bearing on the town and water batteries all the time while drifting down. The guns of the Benton fired over eighty shell, well directed to the town and batteries.

The Pittsburg, Lieutenant Hoel; Tuscumbia, Lieutenant Commander Shirk; and Mound City, Lieutenant Wilson, were more fortunate than the others in not turning round as they came by, although no ill results happened to those vessels that did turn.

The pilots were deceived by a large fire started on the side opposite to Vicksburg by the rebels for the purpose of showing the vessels more plainly—fires being started on both sides of the river at once.

Altogether, we were very fortunate. The vessels had some narrow escapes, but were saved, in most instances, by the precautions taken to protect them. They were covered with heavy logs and bales of wet hay, which were found to be an excellent defence.

I cannot speak in too high terms of the conduct of all the commanders. They carried out my orders to the best of their ability, having great difficulties to contend with—strong currents and dangerous eddies, glaring fires in every direction that bothered the pilots, smoke almost enveloping the squadron, and a very heavy fire on vessels that were fair targets for the enemy. I have no cause to be dissatisfied with the result. No one was killed; only one or two badly wounded, and only twelve casualties in all. Most of the wounded are walking about.

The shot the enemy fired were of the heaviest calibre, and some of excellent pattern. They came on board, but did no material damage beyond smashing the bulwarks.

I am in hopes soon to have some of our Monitors down here, and if they are properly built we can silence some of the batteries at Vicksburg.

I am happy to inform you that no lives were lost on the transport Henry Clay, which was burned and sunk passing the batteries. We picked most of the crew up, and others got away in the yawl.

I enclose reports of the commanders of the different vessels, and also copy of general order issued in reference to the running of the batteries.

I have the honor to remain, very respectfully, your obedient servant,

DAVID D. PORTER.

Hon. GIDEON WELLES,
Secretary of the Navy, Washington, D. C.

Instructions to commanders of vessels relative to passing the Vicksburg batteries.

UNITED STATES MISSISSIPPI SQUADRON,
Flag-Ship Black Hawk, April 10, 1863.

SIR: You will prepare your vessels for passing the batteries at Vicksburg, taking every precaution possible to protect the hull and machinery against any accidental shot.

When the vessels do move, it will be at night, and in the following order: Benton, Lafayette, Price, Louisville, Mound City, Pittsburg, Carondelet, other vessels that may arrive hereafter, and army transports, passing as fast as they can. Every vessel will take in tow a coal barge, to be carried on the starboard side. No lights will be shown on any part of the ship. All ports will be covered up until such time as the vessels open fire, which they will do when their broadsides bear upon the town, or when it can be safely done without interfering with the pilot or endangering the other vessels. Before starting the hour of departure will be given, and every vessel will have her fires well ignited, so that they will show as little smoke as possible.

On approaching the batteries every vessel will exhaust in the wheel, so as to make but little noise.

If any vessel should receive such damage as to cause her to be in a sinking condition, the best plan will be to land her on the island below the canal. The vessels must not crowd each other, nor fire their bow guns when abreast of the town or batteries. Fifty yards is the closest they should be to each other. After rounding the point below, and being clear of the shoal water, hug the shore enough (or the side opposite Vicksburg) to get into the shade of the trees, and hide the hulls of the vessels. The crew must work the guns without light on the deck, and all the guns must be set for about nine hundred yards, which will reach light field-pieces and infantry. Fire shell, and sometimes grape. Don't fire after passing the town and main batteries—the lower batteries are not worth noticing. When arrived below Warrenton, the flag-ship Benton will burn a Coston signal, when each vessel will hoist a red light, that I may know who is missing.

The sterns of the vessels must be protected securely against raking shot.

The coal barges must be so arranged that they can be easily cut adrift.

No vessel must run directly astern of the other, so that in case of the headmost vessel stopping, the sternmost one will not run into her.

In case any vessel should ground under the enemy's batteries at Vicksburg with no prospect of getting off, she must be set fire to thoroughly, and completely destroyed.

Avoid running on the sunken levees opposite Vicksburg.

Very respectfully,

DAVID D. PORTER,
Acting Rear-Admiral, Com'dg Mississippi Squadron.

COMMANDERS of Benton, Lafayette, Price, Louisiana, Mound City, Pittsburg, Carondelet, and Tuscumbia.

Report from Captain Walke.

UNITED STATES GUNBOAT LAFAYETTE,
Diamond Island Bend, below Vicksburg, April 17, 1863.

SIR: I have most respectfully to report that, in obedience to your orders of the 10th instant, the gunboat Lafayette, now under my command, passed the batteries at Vicksburg last night, accompanying you with the following portions of your fleet, viz: Benton, (flag,) Lafayette, (towing a coal barge and the General Price,) Louisville, Mound City, Pittsburg, Carondelet, and three transports, namely: Forest Queen, Henry Clay, and Silver Wave, all of which passed safely down to this point with but trifling injury, except the transport Henry Clay, which caught fire and was burned, and the Forest Queen, which received a shot between wind and water, and was obliged to come to below Vicksburg.

The Lafayette received nine effective round and rifle cannon shots through her casemates while closely engaged with the rebel batteries. She was struck first in the port waist with a 100-pounder rifle shot, which passed through obliquely from forward aft to the starboard casemate. The second, a 32-pounder, struck upon the same plate at right angles, passing through and breaking upon the iron work and our stern capstan over the boilers. The third, a 100-pounder rifle, through the port wheel-house, port pitman, and through the cylinder timbers and starboard side. Fourth, a 100-pounder rifle, through the lower edge of the iron plating forward of the port wheel-house amidships into the sponsel, a few feet short of the port cylinder, in a direct line. Fifth, a 32-pounder, on port side, abaft the wheel-house, through plating. Sixth, a 32-pounder, on the port bow, through plating, broken. Seventh, a glance shot on the starboard bow port. Eighth, a glance shot on hog chain, bending in and through the upper pilot-house. Ninth, grape-shot through smoke-pipe; barge and mainmast slightly injured by shell. In consequence of the difficulty in seeing our position while passing in the smoke, fire, and noise, with the coal barge and Price alongside, she being reported on fire twice, the Lafayette came near running into the bank under the batteries at Vicksburg, which enabled the enemy to take unerring aim for the short time we were there. We returned the fire at the same time, but the fighting bolts of our 24-pounder broke adrift.

The safety of the vessel being paramount to all other advantages that could be derived from random shot, with the Louisville afoul of us, and the other gunboats passing us, I discontinued our firing after one or two rounds. The coal barge was sunk by a shot in her bow. The Price cast off after we passed the batteries, and we arrived safely at this place without the loss of a man killed or wounded. We left the Yazoo river at 9.30 p. m., and arrived here at 1.30 a. m., being under fire one hour and twenty minutes.

I am, sir, most respectfully, your obedient servant,

H. WALKE,
Captain United States Navy.

Acting Rear-Admiral D. D. PORTER, U. S. N.,
Commanding Mississippi Squadron.

Report from Acting Lieutenant S. E. Woodworth.

NEW CARTHAGE, *April* 17, 1863.

SIR: I have the honor to report my safe arrival at this place with the United States steamer General Price, having passed the batteries at Vicksburg without the loss of a man, and but three slightly wounded. The Price is badly cut up in her upper works, particularly the ward-room and steerage, two 7½-inch rifle shell having exploded inside, destroying the officers' quarters and setting the vessel on fire twice. We were struck by thirteen different shot and shell and many musket balls.

While drifting down river, to enable the Lafayette to fire her guns, the Louisville ran into my quarter and stove one of my boats, at the same time obliged me to cast off from the Lafayette and make the rest of the trip alone, the coal barge between us being stove by a shell bursting in it.

I have the honor to be, very respectfully, your obedient servant,

SELIM E. WOODWORTH,
Commanding United States Steamer Price.

Admiral D. D. PORTER,
Commanding U. S. Mississippi Squadron.

Report from Lieutenant Commander James A. Greer.

UNITED STATES STEAMER BENTON,
New Carthage, Louisiana, April 17, 1863.

SIR: I respectfully submit the following: This vessel, bearing your flag, got under way from our anchorage, near the mouth of the Yazoo, yesterday evening at 9.15, and slowly steamed down towards Vicksburg. At 11.10 the enemy opened fire upon us with musketry from the upper batteries. At 11.16 the batteries opened upon us, firing slowly at first, but continuing to fire more rapidly as we passed by. At 11.23 we opened upon the batteries and town with the forward and port batteries. We passed within forty yards of the town, and could hear the rattling of falling walls after our fires. At 11.52 the enemy ceased firing upon us. At 1.15 a. m. we passed Warrenton, not a shot being fired at us. At 2.10 came to anchor twelve miles above New Carthage.

We expended the following projectiles: Eighteen 9-inch 5″ shells; three 9-inch shrapnell; sixteen 5″ 42-pounder rifle shell; two 32-pounder 5″ shell; twenty-three stands 32-pounder grape; a total of eighty-one shots.

The damages sustained were as follows: One 32-pounder round shot passed through the corner of the broadside and after casemate, grazed the coamings of the pitman hole and struck the "cylinder timber," and entered about four inches, glanced back and into a state-room.

A large rifle shot struck the port casemate about six inches above the upper after corner of No. 8 port, passing through the two and a half inch iron, splintering the wood all the way through, and knocking off the planking on the inside six feet in length and six feet wide.

Another shot struck the forward side of No. 7 port, shattering the casemate, and then glanced up and tore away the hammock nettings about the gangway.

A 10-inch solid round shot struck the port casemate about four feet from the spar deck, and about six inches from the angle of the forward casemate, passing through the light iron and shattering the casemate from top to bottom, and six feet fore and aft.

Another struck a chain cable which was suspended over the casemate, cutting the chain. All the damages were on the port side.

The casualties were one officer, Acting Ensign E. C. Brennen, and four men wounded.

Enclosed I send the assistant surgeon's report. I desire to call your attention to the good conduct of Mr. Brennen until he fell at his post.

I am, very respectfully, your obedient servant,

JAMES A. GREER,
Lieutenant Commander.

DAVID D. PORTER,
Acting Rear-Admiral, Com'dg Mississippi Squadron.

List of casualties on the Benton.

UNITED STATES GUNBOAT BENTON,
Mississippi Squadron, April 17, 1863.

SIR: I have the honor to report the following casualties on board this vessel while passing the batteries in front of Vicksburg, April 17, 1863:

Edward C. Brennen, acting ensign, flesh wound in right thigh; Charles Duss, seaman, left leg shot away, amputation performed below knee joint; William N. Taylor, landsman, wound from musket ball in left groin, severe, but not considered dangerous; Charles Hillyer, private, company F, 58th Ohio volunteers, contused wound from splinter, slight. The above are the only accidents which incapacitated any of the crew for duty.

I am, very respectfully, your obedient servant,

NEWTON L. BATES,
Assistant Surgeon, United States Navy.

Lieut. Com'dr JAMES A. GREER, U. S. N.,
Commanding United States Gunboat Benton.

Report of Lieutenant Commander E. K. Owen

UNITED STATES STEAMER LOUISVILLE,
Off New Carthage, Louisiana, April 17, 1863.

SIR: I have the honor to report the safe arrival of this vessel below the Vicksburg and Warrenton batteries. We were struck but four times, no shot doing any damage whatever.

In consequence of being misled by the bright light on the right-hand shore, I was compelled to make two full turns in the river abreast the light, and could fire but six shots.

I enclose reports of the gunner and carpenter.

I am, sir, very respectfully, your most obedient servant,

E. K. OWEN,
Lieutenant Commander.

Acting Rear-Admiral DAVID D. PORTER, U. S. N.,
Commanding Mississippi Squadron.

Report of Lieutenant Commander James W. Shirk.

UNITED STATES SHIP TUSCUMBIA,
Carthage, Louisiana, April 17, 1863.

SIR: I have the honor to make the following report: In obedience to your orders I got under way on the evening of the 16th instant, in the United States steamer Tuscumbia, under my command, and took my position in the line of vessels which were to pass the batteries of Vicksburg. We were to bring up the rear.

At 10.3 p. m. the three transports, Silver Wave, Forest Queen and Henry Clay, having taken their position ahead of us, we started down the river, going very slow until we reached the head of the "canal," opposite Vicksburg. Here we overtook the leading vessels. From this place we drifted down the river until we reached the head of the "point." The enemy opened fire about ten minutes before this, and caused a large fire to be kindled on the point, thus bringing the fleet into full relief between the shore batteries and the light, causing everything to be seen as plainly as in the open day.

Here I saw that two of the transports had their bows up stream, and were going ahead. Although your written order said that I was to "pass as fast" as I could, you had verbally informed me that I was to be the "whipper in" to the fleet. I knew that the passage of the batteries by the transports was essential to the complete success of your plans. Under these circumstances I deemed it my duty to remain astern of them, and if I saw any hesitation to pass, or inclination to go back, on their part, to force them to obey their orders. I therefore stopped, under the very heavy fire of the enemy, until the transport Henry Clay was set on fire, and the Forest Queen had turned around.

As we rounded the lower end of the "point," and were drifting, in order to keep our place in line, we struck the Louisiana bank of the river. We soon got off without any damage. As we were backing to get our bow down stream, we got foul of the transport Forest Queen, and the two vessels remained close together for some five or six minutes. This collision caused the rebels great rejoicing, as was made evident to us by their loud cheering, apparently right over our heads. For a few minutes the fire from shore seemed to be concentrated upon the Tuscumbia and Forest Queen, but providentially none of the shots did much damage. We were struck here on our port bow, below the water-line, starting seven planks and causing the vessel to leak freely. I started the forward force and syphon pumps, and soon had it under control.

After getting clear, we continued drifting down (as I did not want to pass the Forest Queen, and she was disabled by her steam-pipe being cut) until we were out of their fire. We passed the transport just below the mouth of the canal. I then turned around and went back, and took the Forest Queen in tow, and landed her on the Louisiana shore. She had fourteen inches of water in her, and her machinery was disabled.

Passing Warrenton I threw into the town an XI-inch shrapnell, which was quickly replied to by six discharges from not more than four light guns. I then gave them another shrapnell, and passed on until I reached the fleet, where I anchored near the United States steamer Benton, your flag-ship.

In addition to the shot under the bow already mentioned, a six-inch shot struck the iron "chock," or "lug," that supports the rail upon which the starboard port of the after casemate travels, making an indentation of an inch.

To the officers and men whom I have the honor to command great praise is due for their spirit and bravery exhibited upon this occasion. Most of them had never been under fire before, but I have no fault to find with any of them. When all did their duty so well, it would be invidious to make distinction. I must, however, bring to your notice the good services rendered me by Acting Master A. F. Tayon, the executive officer of this ship; Acting Ensign Thomas M. Farrell, who commanded the port XI-inch gun, (the only one engaged;) Assistant Paymaster George A. Lyon, United States navy, who acted as my aid on this occasion, and Pilots Joseph McCammant and Isaac N. Ashton.

I am happy to say there were no casualties on board of this ship.

I have the honor to be, sir, your most obedient servant,

JAMES W. SHIRK,
Lieutenant Commander.

Rear-Admiral DAVID D. PORTER, U. S. N.,
Com'dg U. S. Mississippi Squadron, Flag-Ship Benton.

Report from Lieutenant Commander Byron Wilson.

UNITED STATES GUNBOAT MOUND CITY,
New Carthage, Mississippi, April 17, 1863.

SIR: I have the honor to report that this vessel got under way about nine o'clock last evening, and took her position in line for passing and fighting the Vicksburg batteries.

After passing the upper end of the canal, we merely drifted down the river, and at 11 p.m. turned the right-hand point just above Vicksburg, which brought us in full view of the batteries.

We continued drifting down, never turning a wheel, and when nearly abreast of the heaviest battery in the heart of the city, a huge bonfire was kindled on the opposite point, making it almost as light as day. At this time I was obliged to pass the Lafayette, Price, and Louisville, in order to keep from turning round or becoming unmanageable, as they appeared to be.

While we were in the vicinity of this light we were made a splendid target for the enemy, who availed himself of the opportunity by sending a 10-inch shot through both casemates, passing out through the iron on the starboard side, wounding four (4) men. Besides this, we were struck four times while abreast these batteries, but sustained no injury from them.

As soon as we were able to bring our port broadside guns to bear, we put five second shot into their batteries, and when nearest the city gave them grape, and all, I think, with good effect, for we passed so slowly and leisurely that we could not help getting good aim.

At 12.50 we were struck on the port quarter by a random shot from the Warrenton batteries, which did no harm. We did not throw away any ammunition on this place, as it was too small an affair. The officers and men behaved splendidly. I herewith enclose the surgeon's report.

I am, very respectfully, your obedient servant,

BRYON WILSON,
Lieutenant Commanding.

Rear-Admiral DAVID D. PORTER,
Commanding Mississippi Squadron.

List of casualties on the Mound City.

UNITED STATES STEAMER MOUND CITY,
Mississippi River, April 17, 1863.

SIR: The following casualties occurred on board this vessel while passing the batteries of Vicksburg:

John Kelly, ship's painter, wounded; James Denty, cockswain first cutter, wounded; Swain Anderson, seaman, slightly wounded; Adam Isenberger, private, company B, 58th regiment Ohio volunteers, slightly wounded.

Very respectfully,

THOMAS RICE,
Acting Assistant Surgeon, United States Navy.

Lieutenant BYRON WILSON,
Com'dg United States Steamer Mound City.

Report from Acting Volunteer Lieutenant W. R. Hoel.

UNITED STATES STEAMER PITTSBURG,
James's Plantation, Mississippi River, April 17, 1863.

SIR: In running past the batteries at Vicksburg and Warrenton last night, I have the gratification to report no casualties occurred on board this vessel, neither did she receive any serious damage from the enemy's fire. She was struck but seven times; five of the shot passing through her upper works, the other two struck in the logs which I had triced up (by your order) on the port quarter for the protection of the magazine. One of the shots struck immediately at the water-line, and had it not been for the logs, would, undoubtedly, have passed into the magazine. On the passage past the batteries I fired forty-three rounds of 5″ and 10″ shells and one stand of grape.

I have the satisfaction to report that both officers and men behaved gallantly, and that I feel proud to have the honor of commanding them.

Most respectfully, your obedient servant,

W. R. HOEL,
Acting Vol. Lieut. Com'dg.

DAVID D. PORTER,
Acting Rear-Admiral, Com'dg Miss. Squadron.

Report from Acting Lieutenant J. McLeod Murphy.

UNITED STATES GUNBOAT CARONDELET,
Abreast of Ion Plantation, Mississippi River, April 17, 1863.

ADMIRAL: I have the honor to report the successful passage of this vessel by the Vicksburg and Warrenton batteries last night, in compliance with your written instructions of the 10th instant, and to enclose herewith copies of the statements of the several subordinate officers, from which you will be enabled to gather, in detail, the slight disasters and casualties of the occasion.

Opposite to the burning house on the right bank we were compelled to make a turn in the river, and although we were exposed to a heavy, concentrated fire for nearly an hour, I attribute to this fortunate *pirouette* the destruction of the enemy's ranges at us. Abreast of the Warrenton battery we responded to three shots. During the engagement the two 8-inch gun and the rifled 42-pounder of the port battery were the only ones used; these were in charge of Acting Ensign Charles H. Amerman, and were well served.

The coal barge which was assigned to our care was towed safely, and is now moored to the bank without leak or damage.

I am, admiral, very respectfully, your obedient servant,

J. McLEOD MURPHY,
Acting Lieut. U. S. N., Com'dg.

Acting Rear-Admiral DAVID D. PORTER,
Com'dg U. S. Miss. Squadron.

List of casualties.

UNITED STATES MISSISSIPPI SQUADRON,
Mississippi River, New Carthage, April 17, 1863.

SIR: The following is a list of the men wounded in the Mississippi squadron while passing by the batteries at Vicksburg last night:

On the United States steamer Benton, Assistant Surgeon N. L. Bates: Ed. C. Brennan, acting engineer, flesh wound in thigh, severe; Charles Doss, seaman, left leg shot away, amputation below knee; Wm. N. Taylor, landsman, wound from musket ball in left groin, severe but not dangerous; Charles Hillyer, private, Co. F, 58th Ohio volunteers, splinter wound, not severe.

On the United States steamer Carondelet, Assistant Surgeon D. R. Bannan: John Dorman, seaman, shell wound in face, slight; John Fallan, seaman, contusion from splinter in groin, not serious; Ray Cutler, seaman, splinter wound in neck; Geo. Fisher, seaman, splinter wound in face.

On the United States steamer Mound City, Acting Assistant Surgeon Thomas Rice: John Kelly, carpenter, splinter wound of leg, severe; James Deuty, cockswain, contusion of shoulder, severe; S. Anderson, seaman, splinter wound in abdomen; Idam Isenheizer, private, Co. B, 58th Ohio, contusion of face, slight.

The gunboats Lafayette, Pittsburg, General Price, and Louisville had none of their crews injured.

Very respectfully, your obedient servant,

J. C. BERTOLETTE,
Surgeon U. S. Navy.

Acting Rear-Admiral DAVID R. PORTER,
Com'dg Mississippi Squadron.

Running the batteries at Vicksburg.

U. S. MISSISSIPPI SQUADRON, U. S. STEAMER BLACK HAWK,
Yazoo River, April 17, 1863.

SIR: By direction of Admiral Porter, I have to inform you that he left this river last night at 10 p. m., in the Benton, accompanied by the Lafayette, General Price, Louisville, Mound City, Pittsburg, Carondelet, Tuscumbia, and three transports, and also that they arrived safely below the batteries at Vicksburg, with the exception of the transport Henry Clay, destroyed by fire.

The vessels suffered very little on the passage in killed and wounded—averaging, probably, one to each of the former and two to the latter.

The vessels themselves sustained no damage of any account. The firing was very heavy on both sides, but I think perceptibly slackened on the rebels' part as our fleet got their guns to bear.

Very respectfully, your obedient servant,

K. R. BREESE,
Lieutenant Commander.

Hon. GIDEON WELLES,
Secretary of the Navy, Washington, D. C.

Operations at Grand Gulf.

MISSISSIPPI SQUADRON, FLAG-SHIP BENTON,
Off New Carthage, April 24, 1863.

SIR: The rest of the squadron is now at Grand Gulf, waiting for the army to make a move. The enemy have heavily fortified Grand Gulf since the passage down of the Hartford, and are still working night and day to make the place impregnable, if they have time.

I went close to the upper battery on the 22d, in the Lafayette, and drove the men out of the works, and the vessels are now so arranged that they command the upper battery, mounting four heavy guns, and the mouth of Black river, through which ammunition and supplies are brought down, and by which the rebels have hitherto obtained supplies from Red river.

General Grant comes over here to-night, and I may know something more of his plans.

I did not wish to leave here to communicate with Admiral Farragut until I have landed the army safely on the other side of the river. When that is done, I shall feel at liberty to go below with all but two vessels, and take charge of the river from Red river up.

The rebels have fortified Grand Gulf so strongly that I do not deem it prudent to let one or two vessels go by, for I cannot get them up again against the current. When we do move it must be a combined attack, and one that cannot fail. The enemy have already 12,000 men at Grand Gulf, and are throwing in more with all the rapidity they can.

Until our communication is fairly opened with the other side by water the army can move but slowly; they have now to depend on us for coal barges to get them over the bayous and other streams, and all the provisions they have is what we brought down in the transports, seven of which have run the blockade. They were mostly damaged in machinery, but the engineers of the squadron have repaired them so that they can run. I have six weeks' provisions and coal, and have made arrangements to have supplies sent through by some means.

We will have to build a railroad, which will much facilitate matters. No one could imagine, unless they saw it, the difficulties of transportation; still I hope we will overcome it all, and though, at present, I see no certainty of a successful landing of our army on the Mississippi side, yet nothing will be left undone by me to facilitate it.

The portion of the squadron now here cannot even return *above* Vicksburg until that place is taken. It can, however, be maintained below, with great labor, and kept in active service on the river, provided that no damage is received in the machinery.

I shall endeavor to get our floating machine shop through, when we can repair almost any injury.

I remain, sir, very respectfully, your obedient servant,

DAVID D. PORTER,
Acting Rear-Admiral, Com'dg Mississippi Squadron.

Hon. GIDEON WELLES,
Secretary of the Navy, Washington, D. C.

Capture of the batteries at Grand Gulf, Mississippi.

MISSISSIPPI SQUADRON, FLAG-SHIP BENTON,
Below Grand Gulf, April 29, 1863.

SIR: I had the honor of sending you a telegram announcing that we had fought the batteries at Grand Gulf for five hours and thirty-five minutes with partial success.

Grand Gulf has been very strongly fortified since Admiral Farragut went down, to prevent his coming up again; and four batteries (some of very heavy guns) are placed at the distance of a quarter of a mile apart, on high points, and completely command the river. I ordered the Louisville, Carondelet, Mound City, and Pittsburg to lead the way and attack the lower batteries, while the Tuscumbia, Benton, and Lafayette attacked the upper ones—the Lafayette lying in an eddy and fighting stern down stream. The vessels below silenced the lower batteries, and then closed up on the upper one, which had been hotly engaged by the Benton and Tuscumbia, both ships suffering severely in killed and wounded. The Pittsburg came up just at the moment when a large shell passed through the Benton's pilot-house, wounding the pilot, Mr. Williams, and disabling the wheel. This made the vessel unmanageable for a short time, and she drifted down to the lower batteries, which she opened upon while repairing damages.

The Pittsburg, Acting Volunteer Lieutenant Hoel, for a short time bore the brunt of the fire, and lost eight killed and sixteen wounded. The Tuscumbia was cut up a great deal, (and proved herself a poor ship in a hot engagement.) As the fire of the upper battery slackened, (I presume from want of ammunition,) I passed up a short distance above the fort to communicate with General Grant, to see whether he thought proper to send the troops in the transports by the battery, under what was rather a feeble return to our fire. He concluded to land the troops, and march them across by a road two miles long, coming out below the batteries. As there was a prospect of expending a good deal of ammunition on the upper battery without being able to occupy it if it was silenced, the vessels moved up stream again by signal without being much fired at, or receiving any damage, while the enemy had a raking fire on them.

I then sent down Captain Walke, in the Lafayette, to prevent them from repairing damages, which they were doing with great diligence. He opened on them, to which they responded a few times, and finally left the fort, when he fired at intervals of five minutes until dark.

At 6 o'clock p. m. I again got under way (with the transports following us) and attacked the batteries again, the transports all passing safely down under cover of our fire. We are now in a position to make a landing when the general pleases. I should have preferred this latter course in the first instance; it would have saved many lives and many hard knocks. The Benton received forty-seven shots in her hull alone, not counting the damage done above her rail, but she was just as good for a fight when she got through as when she commenced.

All the vessels did well, though it was the most difficult portion of the river in which to manage an iron-clad—strong currents (running six knots) and strong eddies turning them round and round, making them fair targets, and the Benton's heavy plates did not stand the heavy shot, which, in many instances, bored her through.

The Tuscumbia showed great weakness as a fighting ship, though her commander did his best to keep her in a position where she did excellent service. The current turned her round and round, exposing her at every turn. It was a hard fight, and a long one, on both sides. The enemy fought his upper battery with a desperation I have never yet witnessed; for though we engaged him at a distance of fifty yards, we never fairly succeeded in stopping his fire but for a short time. It was remarkable we did not disable his guns; but though we knocked the parapets pretty much to pieces, the guns were apparently uninjured.

The conduct of the officers and men met with my warmest admiration. I will leave to the commanders of the vessels the pleasure of mentioning those under them who merited it.

I beg leave to mention favorably my secretary, Mr. Guild, who took the minutes of the action; my signal officer, Ensign Hunt; my aid, Ensign Brown, who was wounded; and Surgeon Bertolette, of the Black Hawk, who devoted himself to the wounded. It will not, I am sure, be an invidious distinction if I mention the handsome manner in which Acting Volunteer Lieutenant W. R. Hoel handled and fought the Pittsburg. I was much indebted to him for so promptly taking the place of the Benton when the loss of our wheel made us turn down stream.

All the commanders fought their ships gallantly, and, I think, effectively. The gentleman mentioned had the advantage of being one of the best pilots on the river, and knew exactly where to place his ship. I only hope I may always go into a fight with as good officers to back me.

The following is a list of the vessels engaged, and their commanders: Benton, Lieutenant Commander James A. Greer; Lafayette, Captain Henry Walke; Louisville, Lieutenant Commander E. K. Owen; Tuscumbia, Lieutenant Commander James W. Shirk; Mound City, Lieutenant Commander Byron Wilson; Carondelet, Acting Lieutenant J. McLeod Murphy; Pittsburg, Acting Volunteer Lieutenant W. R. Hoel. The General Price, Commander Selim E. Woodworth, was engaged in carrying troops and towing transports past the batteries.

The squadron has been six hours and a half to-day under a hot and well-directed fire, and is ready to commence at daylight in the morning. I will send a list of killed and wounded the first opportunity. No naval officers were killed or severely wounded. In our attack to-night only one man killed. He was on the Mound City.

I remain, sir, very respectfully,

DAVID D. PORTER,

Acting Rear-Admiral, Com'dg Mississippi Squadron.

Hon. GIDEON WELLES,

Secretary of the Navy, Washington, D. C.

Report of Captain Henry Walke.

MISSISSIPPI SQUADRON,

U. S. Gunboat Lafayette, off Grand Gulf, May 1, 1863.

SIR: I have the honor to report the particulars of the attack made by the Mississippi squadron on the morning of the 29th ultimo, in obedience to your general order of the 27th ultimo, so far as it came under my observation.

About 7 o'clock a. m. of the 29th ultimo the fleet got under way, in answer to your signals, and proceeded down to the rebel batteries of Grand Gulf in the following order: The Pittsburg led the attack with this vessel, which rounded to above the upper batteries, and opened a brisk fire upon the enemy with her 100-pounder rifle guns until the remainder of the fleet had passed down and taken their position, viz: Pittsburg, Louisville, Mound City, and Carondelet, attacking the lower batteries, while the Benton, (flag.) Lafayette, and Tuscumbia engaged the upper batteries. Each vessel rounded to against the enemy's batteries in order, and kept up a heavy firing with their broadside and bow guns as they were brought to bear upon the enemy. The Lafayette, after firing 35 rounds of 100-pounder rifle shell and shot, turned her broadside and 11-inch bow guns upon them, firing with good effect, apparently, until about 10 o'clock a. m. The admiral hoisted the guard flag (a preconcerted signal) for the Lafayette to change her position from before the upper batteries to the lower batteries, where she proceeded, and continued firing her 11-inch bow guns and her 9-inch 100-pounder rifle guns, and 24-pounder howitzer from the starboard broadside, thus continuing a vigorous and effective firing upon all the batteries, which, while we passed up with the rest of the fleet, were silenced. All the fleet passed above, except the Tuscumbia, landing at Ruth's plantation, in obedience to your signal. The Lafayette was struck by cannon shot about forty times during the day, five of which only did any serious damage.

I enclose our carpenter's, gunner's, and engineer's reports. Expended 160 11-inch shell and shrapnell, 28 9-inch, 50 rifle, and 10 24-pounder howitzer.

The officers and crew of the vessel deserve my highest praise for their coolness, courage, active and excellent conduct during the five hours and five minutes' fighting, none of whom, thank God, were hurt, but Lieutenant William T. Suttrell, slightly wounded.

At 3 p. m. we observed the enemy repairing their shattered batteries, and, by your order, the Lafayette ran down, and with a few rounds from her bow guns silenced the upper battery and dispersed the rebels, after which we turned her 100-pounder rifle guns upon them, firing at five-minute intervals until 8 o'clock p. m., when we anchored and piped to supper.

At 9 p. m. the fleet, with some transports, were observed coming down the river slowly, weighed anchor, beat to quarters, and, for a diversion, opened a brisk fire upon the upper battery with our 100-pounder rifles. While passing they fired into all the batteries, and the Lafayette followed in the rear, and came to at this plantation, without any serious casualty except several shot through our iron and into our casemating.

Most respectfully, sir, your obedient servant,

H. WALKE,
Captain United States Navy.

Acting Rear-Admiral D. D. PORTER,
Commanding Mississippi Squadron.

Reports of Lieutenant Commander James A. Greer.

UNITED STATES FLAG-SHIP BENTON,
Brainsburg, Mississippi, April 30, 1863.

SIR: I respectfully submit the following: At 7.45 yesterday evening this vessel, bearing your flag, got under way and stood out into the stream. At 8.28 stood down towards Grand Gulf, followed by the gunboats and transports. As we approached the bluffs, at 8.48, the enemy opened fire upon us, to which we responded with our bow guns; we then rounded to and engaged the batteries, using bow and starboard guns when they would bear. At 9.43, the transports all having passed, dropped slowly down the river and tied up to the Louisiana shore, about four miles below Grand Gulf.

We were struck six times; lost a boat that was astern, and had no one injured. The following ammunition was expended: Fourteen 5-second 9-inch shells; five 10-second 9-inch shells; one 5-second 42-pounder rifle shell; three 10-second 42-pounder rifle shells; eight 10-second 32-pounder shells—a total of thirty-one fires.

I am, very respectfully, your obedient servant,

JAS A. GREER,
Lieutenant Commanding.

Acting Rear-Admiral DAVID D. PORTER,
Commanding Mississippi Squadron.

UNITED STATES FLAG-SHIP BENTON,
Brainsburg, April 30, 1863.

SIR: I respectfully submit the following: This vessel, bearing your flag, got under way yesterday morning at 6.40 and headed up stream. After getting the fleet in line, we, at 7.30, slowly steamed down towards the batteries at Grand Gulf. At 7.55 the enemy opened fire on the leading vessel. At 8.13 we opened fire from the forward battery upon the guns on the bluff; rounded to with head up stream, and kept firing whenever a gun would bear, the enemy responding. While near the shore the enemy fired upon us with musketry. At 9 a shell penetrated the thin iron on our starboard quarter, and exploded in a state-room, setting it on fire; it was speedily extinguished. At 9.05 a shell from No. 5 gun carried away the enemy's flag-staff; it was soon replaced. At 10.10, having gotten into an eddy, were obliged to round out; did so, and fired with our port and stern guns when they would bear. We, in turning round, dropped down stream fifteen hundred yards, and ran into the bank to aid us in turning round. We then steamed up to the batteries on the bluff again, and continued the engagement. At 12.25 rounded out and stood up stream to communicate with General Grant, who was on a tug. While going up used our stern guns. At 12.50 the enemy ceased firing at us, this vessel having been under fire four hours and eleven minutes. At 1.57 tied up to the bank at Hard Times landing; the other vessels, except the Tuscumbia, following our motions. The following ammunition was expended: seventy 9-inch 5-second shells; forty 9-inch 5-second shrapnell; twenty-nine 9-inch grape; seven 9-inch canister; forty-five 5-second 42-pounder rifle shells; one 10-second 42-pounder rifle shell; sixty-nine 5-second 32-pounder canister; thirty 10-second 32-pounder shells; five 32-pounder solid shot; eleven 32-pounder canister; twenty-three 32-pounder grape; nine 50-pounder rifle shells; eight 50-pounder solid shot—a total of three hundred and forty-seven fires. We were struck forty-seven times—once in the hull, twenty-two times on casemates, and twenty-four times in upper works. The $\frac{5}{8}$-inch iron was penetrated twelve times; the $2\frac{1}{2}$ inch iron four times, three of which came entirely through the casemate. One shot went through the $1\frac{1}{2}$-inch iron on after part of pilot-house and lodged inside, wounding a pilot and shattering the wheel.

The casualties were seven men killed and nineteen persons wounded, four of whom were officers. Accompanying I enclose surgeon's report.

All the officers and men behaved well, and it would be difficult to particularize, yet I cannot pass without calling your attention to the good conduct of Acting Ensign J. F. Reed, who shot down the rebel flagstaff, and was wounded while serving his gun.

Acting Master and Executive Officer Charles A. Wright is deserving of much credit for the able manner in which he worked the batteries and fought a gun. Gunner N. B. Willetts served a 9-inch gun with great efficiency.

The pilots, Messrs. B. S. Williams and W. F. Tuley, are deserving of great credit for the coolness and efficiency they displayed in the working of the vessel. Mr. Williams was wounded in the early part of the action. Mr. Tuley then took charge, and with a shattered wheel managed the vessel very handsomely.

Very respectfully, your obedient servant,

JAS. A. GREER,
Lieutenant Commanding

Acting Rear-Admiral DAVID D. PORTER,
Commanding Mississippi Squadron.

Casualties on the Benton.

UNITED STATES GUNBOAT BENTON,
Mississippi Squadron, April 30, 1863.

SIR: The casualties in the engagement at Grand Gulf, Mississippi, yesterday are as follows:

Killed.—William H. Kinney, captain of hold; James Floyd, seaman; Michael Mahony, ordinary seaman; Henry Bostun, sergeant, Co. F, 58th Ohio volunteers; Jacob Wooley, sergeant, Co. F, 58th Ohio volunteers; Riley Suttles, private, Co. F, 58th Ohio volunteers; George D. Saas, private, Co. G, 58th Ohio volunteers.

Wounded.—Jacob Herring, first lieutenant, Co. G, 58th Ohio volunteers, wound of left knee, compound fracture of left forearm, amputation of thigh; Beverly S. Williams, pilot, wound of left foot, severe; J. Frank Reed, acting ensign, scalp wound and contusions; George M. Brown, ensign, flesh wound, slight; Henry Harming, Co. F, 58th Ohio volunteers, wound of head, serious; Francis G. Holmes, seaman, fracture of fibula and dislocation of ankle joint; Charles P. Simpson, captain after guard, flesh wound, slight; William Wilson, seaman, contusion, slight; George H. Brown, seaman, scalp wound, slight; Robert Germain, seaman, scalp wound, slight; Henry Smith, seaman, flesh wound, slight; Patrick Hurley, seaman, flesh wound, slight; Archibald Taylor, corporal, Co. F, 58th Ohio volunteers, contusion, slight; Geo. W. Sherlock, corporal, Co. F, 58th Ohio volunteers, contusion, slight; Solomon Lance, private, Co. F, 58th Ohio volunteers, scalp wound; Michael Engle, private, Co. G, 58th Ohio volunteers, scalp wound; S. J. Rhoades, private, Co. G, 58th Ohio volunteers, flesh wound, abdomen; Martin Bellers, private, Co. F, 58th Ohio volunteers, flesh wound and contusion, severe; John Brown, private, Co. F, 58th Ohio volunteers, severe contusion and flesh wound.

Total: killed, seven; wounded, nineteen.

I am, very respectfully, your obedient servant,

NEWTON L. BATES,
Assistant Surgeon United States Navy.

Lieut. Com'dr JAS. A. GREER,
Com'dg United States Gunboat Benton.

Report of Lieutenant Commander E. K. Owen.

UNITED STATES STEAMER LOUISVILLE,
Off Bayou Pierre, Louisiana, April 30, 1863.

SIR: I have the honor to make the following report of the part taken by this vessel in the two actions of yesterday: At 7.15 a. m., in obedience to the general signal, I got under way and took position in line of battle behind the Pittsburg, and proceeded down towards the batteries at Grand Gulf. At 8.15 the enemy opened fire from the Point of Rocks battery, which was replied to by this with bow and port broadside guns. Rounded to and opened fire on the second battery, mounting three heavy pieces of ordnance and two field-pieces. In conjunction with the other attacking vessels, this fort was silenced about 11 o'clock. At 11.30, in obedience to orders, moved up and attacked the Point of Rocks battery, at distances varying from three hundred to twelve hundred yards. At 1.15 p. m. followed the motions of the flag-ship in obedience to signal, and made fast to the bank at 2.30 p. m. The enemy had in their scattered batteries thirteen pieces of ordnance of different calibre, seven being heavy, the other field artillery. At 8.30 p. m. got under way and took position three hundred yards astern of the Benton. At 9.05 the enemy opened fire from the Point of Rocks battery, and the lower batteries opened fire with bow and broadside guns as they would bear upon the enemy's batteries. At 9.50 p. m. ceased firing, and followed the flag-ship Benton down the river. At 11 made fast to the Louisiana bank, at the Disharoon plantation.

I am happy to say no casualties occurred on board this vessel, and to express my great satisfaction at the conduct of the officers and men. We received but seven shots, four in the hull and three in the light works of the ship. We fired four hundred and forty-four shots during the two engagements—four hundred and eighteen in the first, and twenty-six in the last. I send the report of the gunner and carpenter.

I am, sir, very respectfully, your obedient servant,

E. K. OWEN.

Rear-Admiral D. D. PORTER,
Commanding Mississippi Squadron.

Report of Lieutenant Commander J. W. Shirk.

UNITED STATES SHIP TUSCUMBIA,
Mississippi River, below Grand Gulf, April 30, 1863.

SIR: I have the honor to make the following report of the part taken by this ship in yesterday's action between the squadron under your command and the rebel batteries at Grand Gulf.

In obedience to your order we got under way at 7 a. m. and followed the United States gunboat Mound City down the river. At 8.25 we engaged the upper and heaviest fort, the leading vessels having gone down to attack the lower batteries. This ship devoted the whole of her time to the upper fort, from positions above, below, and abreast of it, as the current and eddy made it necessary for us to take, until, at 25 minutes p. m., the port engine was disabled, when we endeavored to pass above by using the propellers, but were unable to stem the current. I therefore was compelled to drop down out of action to find an anchorage.

During the early part of the fight a rifle shell struck the outer edge of the port shutter of the midship port, opened it, and entering the turret exploded inside, killing four men and wounding several others. Another shell struck both shutters of the same port, jamming them so that they could not be used. This deprived me of the use of the midship gun for the remainder of the action. We used the starboard stern gun upon the lower battery, until a shell entered the after turret and exploded, disabling every man at the gun but one.

The shell that exploded in the forward turret threw sparks of fire into the shell-room and magazine passages. I most earnestly request that when an opportunity offers a different arrangement of these passages may be made.

We were struck very often upon the forward turret, but sustained no material damage, except the losing one plate of the armor overboard and the starting of several more. The plates were never put on in a proper manner, and wherever a shot struck the armor the bolts were started. The light wood-work on deck is completely riddled.

Great praise is due the officers and men of this ship for their gallantry and spirit displayed throughout the fight. My thanks are due to the executive officer, Acting Master A. F. Tayon, who ably seconded me during the battle; also to Acting Ensigns Marshall, Farrell, Edson, and Dunlap, who had charge of the guns. Assistant Paymaster George A. Lyon acted as my aid, taking notes, until with my approbation he volunteered to assist the medical officer in taking care of the wounded.

The engines were ably managed by Acting Chief Engineer J. W. Hartupes and his assistants. Pilot Joseph McCammant did his duty faithfully at the wheel until he was wounded and fainted from loss of blood. Pilot Isaac Ashton performed his duty bravely and well during the whole of the fight. Assistant Surgeon F. E. Potter was assiduous in his attention to the wounded.

In conclusion, I have to report that the ship will need very extensive repairs before she will again be able to run.

I am sorry to report a large number of casualties. Among the dead is First Lieutenant Samuel Bagsley, of the 29th regiment Illinois volunteers, who commanded a detachment of his company (company D) at present on duty on board this ship. He was a brave and gallant soldier.

The ship was struck eighty-one (81) times by shot and shell. Grape and shrapnell were also used upon us.

I enclose herewith reports from Assistant Surgeon Fred. E. Potter, United States navy, the medical officer of the ship; Acting Carpenter John Cronan, and Acting Gunner Reuben Applegate.

I have the honor to be, sir, your most obedient servant,

JAMES W. SHIRK,
Lieutenant Commander.

Rear-Admiral DAVID D. PORTER, U. S. N.,
Com'dg U. S. Mississippi Squadron, Flag-Ship Benton.

Casualties on the Tuscumbia.

UNITED STATES STEAMER TUSCUMBIA,
April 30, 1863.

SIR: I have to report the following casualties as having occurred on board this vessel in the action of yesterday:

Killed.—Samuel Bagsley, first lieutenant, company D, 29th regiment Illinois volunteers; Henri Loquet, ordinary seaman; John Manly, officers' cook; Wm. H. Wright, landsman; Francis Adams, ordinary seaman.

Wounded.—James Marshall, acting ensign, contusion of left forearm; A. H. Edson, acting ensign, contusion of forearm and elbow; Joseph McCammant, pilot, flesh wound left leg; Ernest Clark, acting master's mate, contusion of neck and right thigh; Reinhardt Underberg, seaman, compound commuted fracture frontal bone with hernia cerebri, wounds of right forearm, wrist, and left eye; Michael Dinan, quartermaster, compound commuted fracture of left parietal bone, with hernia cerebri; John Campbell, ordinary seaman, compound commuted fracture of right temporal bone, with hernia cerebri; Michael Kearns, seaman, wound of right dorsal region; Gustavus Hastings, private, company D, twenty-ninth regiment Illinois volunteers, wound of left thigh; William Flinn, landsman, right eye and root of neck; Thomas Mears, landsman, left side of abdomen and left forearm; Edward Brown, private, company D, twenty-ninth regiment Illinois volunteers, wound of superciliam, and left forearm; Robert Storey, seaman, wound of right forearm and hand; Vergerian Simonson, landsman, centurim of right thigh; Robert Walker, ordinary seaman, slight wound of face and right hand; John Groves, captain of forecastle, wound of left hand and fingers; Stephen Lockwood, seaman, left wrist; Henry Housington, landsman, wound of chest, slight; Charles Smith, seaman, contusion of left elbow; William Brown, quarter gunner, wound of face and neck; Rudolph Reinhardt, seaman, left side of abdomen and face; George Buhlage, seaman, wound of scalp; Michael Shea, coxswain, wound of left eyelid; Robert McFarland, seaman, wound of scalp.

I am, very respectfully, your obedient servant,

FRED. E. POTTER,
Assistant Surgeon, U. S. N.

Lieut. Com'dr JAMES W. SHIRK, U. S. N.,
United States Steamer Tuscumbia.

Report of Lieutenant Commander Byron Wilson.

UNITED STATES GUNBOAT MOUND CITY,
Below Grand Gulf, April 30, 1863.

SIR: I have the honor to report that, in obedience to your orders, I got under way yesterday morning, and took my position in line of battle astern of the Carondelet, and moved down the river, opening fire on the upper of the Grand Gulf batteries at 7.50 a. m., delivering first the bow and then the starboard broadside guns.

Steaming on down, I rounded to below the lower batteries and commenced firing at one thousand yards, using 5″ shell and occasionally shrapnell. These lower batteries were silenced after a heavy shelling of nearly four hours. In obedience to signal, and following our leader, we moved up to the upper battery, and steamed around in a circle several times, immediately in front of it, and passing within three hundred yards, using all of our guns in succession. We were unable, however, to hit the guns of the enemy, owing to the skilful and scientific arrangement of the embrasures. At 12.45, after five hours' hard fighting, and in obedience to signal, I steamed up the river out of range. During the action I am happy to say that no one was injured. The light work was considerably cut up, but no serious damage done to the hull.

In the evening, at 7.40, I got under way and took my position in line of battle for the purpose of engaging the Grand Gulf batteries while the army transports passed them. We gained our object, keeping the batteries so well employed that probably not a transport was even fired at. We used our bow and starboard broadside guns, firing with the greatest deliberation. The transports having passed, I dropped down and tied up to the bank. During this action the vessel was struck several times—a very heavy one, which struck on the starboard side, killed First Sergeant Fritz Vermold, company A, fifty-eighth Ohio volunteers, instantly. The worst injury the hull of this vessel received was from the Louisville running into the port side, she heading down the river while I was heading up. In both the above actions the officers and men were distinguished for their bravery and coolness, the officers of the gun divisions especially. We expended two hundred and sixty-one projectiles.

I am, very respectfully, your obedient servant,

BYRON WILSON,
Lieutenant Commanding.

Rear-Admiral DAVID D. PORTER,
Commanding Mississippi Squadron.

Report of Acting Lieutenant J. McLeod Murphy.

UNITED STATES STEAMER CARONDELET,
Mississippi River, three miles below Grand Gulf, May 2, 1863.

SIR: I have the honor to submit the following report of the part taken by this vessel in the action of the 29th ultimo.

In obedience to the signal, I took my position in the line of battle astern of the Louisville, and approached the upper battery at the Point of Rocks, Grand Gulf, within about fifteen hundred yards distance, at 8 a. m., and opened fire on it with the three 9-inch guns comprising the bow battery; then steamed slowly down, passed all the batteries, discharging our bow and port side guns (one 42-pounder rifle and two 8-inch guns) as occasion offered. I then rounded to under the bar, steamed up stream, preserving the line of order, and manœuvred the vessel so as to bring our guns to bear most efficiently. The bow and starboard guns were actively engaged. Obeying the signal, I ordered the firing to cease, and steamed up the river, arriving at Hard Times landing at 2 p. m. The action continued almost incessantly about five hours.

At about 8 p. m. we again steamed down the river with the squadron, firing at the batteries as we passed, and rounded to abreast of the lower battery, which was silenced. The army transports having passed, we steamed down and made a landing at this point. In the two attacks the vessel was struck five times, occasioning not very serious damages; and in the engineer department our loss was two wheel arms, two circle segments, and two wheel braces cut off.

No casualties, fortunately, occurred among the officers and crew, who conducted themselves throughout with great coolness, courage, and efficiency.

I enclose the gunner's report of ammunition expended.

I am, respectfully, your obedient servant,

J. McLEOD MURPHY,
Acting Lieutenant Commanding.

Admiral D. D. PORTER, U. S. N.,
Commanding Mississippi Squadron.

Report of Acting Volunteer Lieutenant W. R. Hoel.

UNITED STATES STEAMER PITTSBURG,
Mississippi River, May 1, 1863.

SIR: I have the honor to report that on April 29, in accordance with instructions from you, I proceeded with this vessel to engage the enemy's batteries at Grand Gulf at 8.10 a. m. Although struck by the enemy's shot thirty-five times during the engagement, and severely cut up by them, she is in no way disabled. While engaging the enemy, four hundred and twenty-nine rounds were fired, principally from her bow and starboard broadside batteries, consisting of shot, shell, shrapnell, grape, and canister.

At 1.30 p. m., in obedience to orders, (by signal from the Louisville,) I withdrew my vessel from the engagement.

I regret to have to report the following casualties: Killed six, wounded thirteen.

While passing below, and engaging the batteries the same night, I fired twenty-one rounds. The vessel received but two shots, neither doing serious damage; casualties none. The conduct of both officers and crew during both actions was that of *men who had the cause of their country at heart.*

I enclose reports of surgeon, gunner, engineer, and carpenter.

I am, most respectfully, your obedient servant,

W. R. HOEL,
Acting Volunteer Lieutenant Commanding.

Acting Rear-Admiral DAVID D. PORTER,
Commanding Mississippi Squadron.

Casualties on the Pittsburg.

UNITED STATES STEAMER PITTSBURG,
April 30, 1863.

SIR: I have the honor to report the following list of casualties occurring on board this vessel during the engagement at Grand Gulf, April 29, 1863:

Killed.—John Carroll, captain forecastle; Richard Gray, landsman; William Springer, Gottlieb Stinger, Absalom E. Leffler, marines; James Haywood, contraband.

Wounded.—James Ovatt, master's mate, slightly; James Kelroe, Austin Fowler, John Scott, seamen, severely; Alexander Smith, Charles Strand, Robert Hartly, Frederick Kruse, seamen, slightly; J. Fartiz, marine, amputated leg; A. Westenberger, marine, severely; D. Hufford, Addison Deets, marines, slightly.

Respectfully,

F. M. FOLLETT,
Acting Assistant Surgeon.

Acting Volunteer Lieut. WILLIAM R. HOEL,
Commanding U. S. Steamer Pittsburg.

Additional report of Acting Rear-Admiral Porter.—Description of Grand Gulf and the batteries.

MISSISSIPPI SQUADRON, FLAG-SHIP BENTON,
Grand Gulf, Mississippi, May 3, 1863.

SIR: I have the honor to report that I got under way this morning, with the Lafayette, Carondelet, Mound City, and Pittsburg, and proceeded up to the forts at Grand Gulf for the purpose of attacking them, if they had not retreated. The enemy had left before we got up, blowing up their ammunition, spiking the large guns, and burying or taking away the lighter ones. The forts consisted of thirteen guns in all; the works are of the most extensive kind, and would seem to defy the efforts of a much heavier fleet than the one which silenced them. The forts were literally torn to pieces by the accuracy of our fire. Colonel Wade, the commandant of the batteries, was killed, also his chief of staff. Eleven men were killed that we know of, and many wounded—so our informant says; he also says no one was permitted to go into the forts after the action except those belonging there. We had a hard fight with these forts, and it is with great pleasure I report that the navy holds the door to Vicksburg.

Grand Gulf is the strongest place on the Mississippi; had the enemy succeeded in finishing the fortifications, no fleet could have taken them. I have been all over the works, and found them as follows: One fort on Point of Rocks, seventy-five feet high, calculated for six or seven guns, mounting two 7-inch rifles and one 8-inch, and one Parrott gun on wheels (carried off.) On the left of this work is a triangular work, calculated to mount one heavy gun; these works are connected with another fort by a covered way and double rifle-pits, extending three-quarters of a mile, constructed with much labor, and showing great skill on the part of the constructor. The third fort commands the river in all directions; it mounted one splendid Blakely 100-pounder and one 8-inch; two 32-pounders were lying bursted and broken on the ground. The gunboats had so covered up everything with earth that it was impossible to see at a glance what was there. With the exception of the guns that were dismounted or broken, every gun that fell into our hands was in good condition, with a large quantity of ammunition.

This is by far the most extensive built work, with the exception of those at Vicksburg, I have yet seen; and am happy to say we hold it. I am dismounting the guns, and getting on board the ammunition; and, as I leave in an hour for Red river, Lieutenant Commander Owen will carry out my instructions.

I hear nothing of our army as yet. Was expecting to hear their guns as we advanced on the forts.

Since making the above examination, two new forts have been found, nearly finished; they have no guns, but were complete of the kind as regards position, and had heavy field-pieces in them.

I am, sir, very respectfully, your obedient servant,

DAVID D. PORTER,
Acting Rear-Admiral, Com'dg Miss. Squadron.

Hon. GIDEON WELLES,
Secretary of the Navy, Washington, D. C.

U. S. MISSISSIPPI SQUADRON, FLAG-SHIP BLACK HAWK,
Near Vicksburg, June 5, 1863.

SIR: I have the honor to send you a chart and plan of Grand Gulf, captured by the Mississippi squadron May 3, 1863.

Very respectfully, your obedient servant,

DAVID D. PORTER,
Acting Rear-Admiral, Com'dg Miss. Squadron.

Hon. GIDEON WELLES,
Secretary of the Navy, Washington, D. C.

These batteries mounted one 100-pounder, two 64-pounders, two 7-inch rifle cannon, one 30-pounder Parrott shifting gun, two 30-pounder Parrotts in battery, two 20-pounder Parrott near main magazine in covered way, three 10-pounder Parrotts on the hills. Batteries engaged by the gunboats for five hours and thirty-five minutes; the lower battery silenced and covered up in three hours; the upper batteries silenced, with the exception of one gun, which could not train on any vessel, being clogged with earth. The Layfayette laid opposite this battery, and kept the people from working until dark, when it was partially repaired. The defences were all earthworks.

In addition to the above, four or five small field-pieces were used by the rebels, and shifted about from place to place.

(Copied from a survey made by T. M. Farrell, United States navy, May, 1863, by Alexander Strauz, United States coast survey.)

Capture of Forts De Russy, Red river, and Alexandria, Louisiana.

MISSISSIPPI SQUADRON, FLAG-SHIP BENTON,
Alexandria, Louisiana, May 7, 1863.

SIR: I left Grand Gulf at noon on the 3d instant, and arrived that night at the mouth of Red river.

After communicating with Admiral Farragut, and being kindly supplied by Commodore Palmer with men and ammunition to supply deficiencies, I proceeded up Red river on the 4th with the Benton, Lafayette, Pittsburg, Price, ram Switzerland, and tug Ivy. Meeting two of Admiral Farragut's vessels, the Arizona and Estrella, coming down, I detained them, and took them back

BATTERIES AT GRAND GULF CAPTURED BY THE UNITED STATES MISSISSIPPI SQUADRON, MAY 3, 1863.

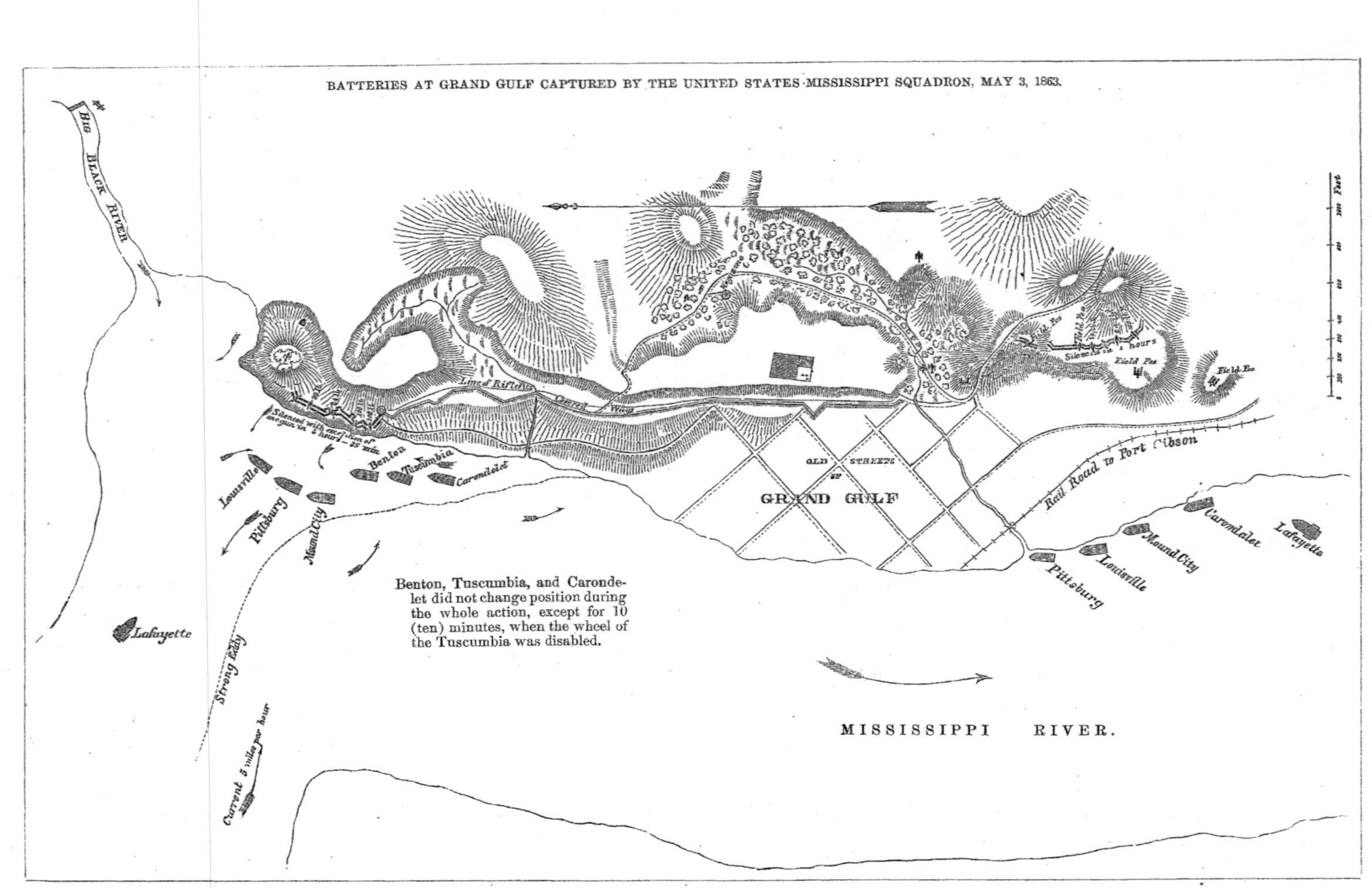

Benton, Tuscumbia, and Carondelet did not change position during the whole action, except for 10 (ten) minutes, when the wheel of the Tuscumbia was disabled.

with me. We arrived next evening at Fort De Russy, a powerful casemated work, (three casemates,) and a flanking battery nearly at right angles with it, calculated to mount seven guns. The enemy had, however, evacuated the works, taking away all but one gun, a 64-pounder, and only the day before had managed to get away the XI-inch and the IX-inch guns captured from the Indianola; they had, however, destroyed the carriages and equipments.

The enemy had at this point a heavy raft that cost $70,000 to build; it was landed on either bank of the river, and fastened with chains. The Price, however, soon opened it by running against the end, and made a passage for the rest of the steamers.

I laid by the fort that night, and, upon close examination, finding that it would take too much time to destroy it effectually, pushed on to Alexandria, where we arrived this morning early.

I sent the Arizona ahead last night to surprise any steamer that might be at the town, and this morning took formal possession without any resistance; indeed, there seemed to be great cordiality shown us all along this river.

In the town there was great rejoicing among the Union men at our arrival, and no indisposition on the part of any one to meet us in a friendly spirit. I have seized all the rebel property here, but they removed only as late as last night some of the most valuable. What steamers they had here had been lightened and taken above Shreveport, (which is 350 miles by river from here,) and are out of our reach for the present. I send the gunboats to-morrow up Black river, where there are twenty transports, some of which we may capture.

This evening General Banks came into Alexandria, having made a rapid march from Opelousas, and reached here one day sooner than I expected him. I turned over the city to him, and shall return in a few days to Grand Gulf. The water is too low for us to ascend higher up Red river and return with safety. As we ascended, the rebels fled before us, abandoning also some works they were erecting seven miles below Alexandria.

I am, sir, very respectfully, your obedient servant,

DAVID D. PORTER,

Acting Rear-Admiral, Com'dg Mississippi Squadron.

Hon. GIDEON WELLES,

Secretary of the Navy, Washington, D. C.

Destruction of Fort De Russy and reconnoissance on Black river.

MISSISSIPPI SQUADRON, FLAG-SHIP GENERAL PRICE,
Grand Gulf, Mississippi, May 13, 1863.

SIR: I had the honor to inform you from Alexandria of the capture of that place and the forts defending the approaches to the city by the naval forces under my command. Twenty-four hours after we arrived the advance guard of United States troops came into the city, and General Banks arriving soon after, I turned the place over to his keeping. The water beginning to fall, I deemed it prudent to return with the largest vessels to the mouth of Red river. I dropped down to the forts De Russy in the Benton and undertook to destroy those works. I only succeeded, however, in effectually destroying the three heavy casemates commanding the channel, and a small water battery for two guns, about 600 yards below it. I also destroyed (by bursting) one heavy 33-pounder and some gun-carriages left in their hurry by the enemy. The main fort on a hill some 900 yards from the water I was unable to attend to. It is quite an extensive work, quite new and incomplete, but built with much labor and pains; it will take two or three weeks to pull it to pieces. I had not the powder to spare to blow it up; the vessels will be ordered to work on it occasionally, and it will soon be destroyed.

Plan showing the defences of the fort on Red River, built by Gen. De Russy, rebel army, destroyed May 9, 1863, by the Flag-ship Benton.

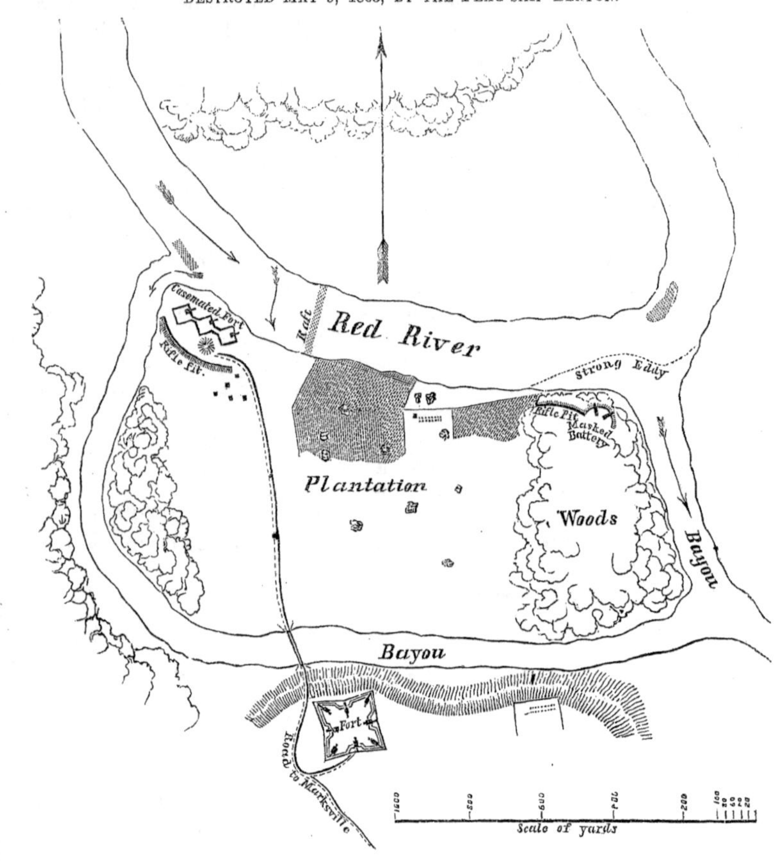

In this last-mentioned fort was mounted the XI-inch gun which I am led to believe lies in the middle of the river near the fort, the rebels throwing it overboard in their panic at the approach of the gunboats.

The raft which closed the entrance I have blown up, sawed in two, and presented it to the poor of the neighborhood.

I sent Commander Woodworth, in the Price, with the Switzerland, Pittsburg, and Arizona, up Black river to make a reconnoissance. They found heavy batteries at Harrisonburg, and as the rebels refused to surrender, the boats shelled them, but without much effect. Our force being small, and the forts on high hills, Commander Woodworth sent back to report to me; but as I had no time to attend to the Harrisonburg forts at the moment, I ordered the return of the expedition. Commander Woodworth destroyed a large amount of rebel stores, (valued at three hundred thousand dollars,) consisting of salt, sugar, rum, molasses, tobacco, and bacon.

I left the place blockaded, and returned to Grand Gulf to look after other portions of the squadron.

I left Captain Walke, in the Lafayette, at Alexandria for the present, also the Switzerland, Arizona, and Estrella, to co-operate with General Banks in case he should require the services of the navy.

I am, sir, very respectfully, your obedient servant,

DAVID D. PORTER,
Acting Rear-Admiral, Com'dg Mississippi Squadron.

Hon. GIDEON WELLES,
Secretary of the Navy, Washington, D. C.

Sketch of Fort De Russy.

MISSISSIPPI SQUADRON, FLAG-SHIP BLACK HAWK,
Yazoo River, May 16, 1863.

SIR: I have the honor to enclose herewith a sketch of Fort De Russy, on Red river, captured by a portion of this squadron on the 9th of May.

I am, sir, very respectfully, your obedient servant,

DAVID D. PORTER,
Acting Rear-Admiral, Com'dg Mississippi Squadron.

Hon. GIDEON WELLES,
Secretary of the Navy, Washington.

Feigned attack on Haines's Bluff.

MISSISSIPPI SQUADRON, FLAG-SHIP BENTON,
Mouth of Red River, May 12, 1863.

SIR: I have the honor to enclose herewith the reports of Lieutenant Commander K. R. Breese and others, in relation to a feigned attack on Haines's Bluff, to prevent the enemy from sending re-enforcements to Grand Gulf.

The plan succeeded admirably, though the vessels were more exposed than the occasion called for; still, as they met no casualties, with the exception of hits in the hulls, it mattered but little.

I am, &c., very respectfully,

DAVID D. PORTER,
Acting Rear-Admiral, Com'dg Mississippi Squadron.

Hon. GIDEON WELLES,
Secretary of the Navy, Washington, D. C.

Report of Lieutenant Commander K. R. Breese.

UNITED STATES STEAMER BLACK HAWK,
Yazoo River, May 2, 1863.

SIR: Enclosed I send a copy of a letter from General Grant to General Sherman.

I co-operated with him in a feigned attack upon Haines's Bluff, its object being to prevent heavy re-enforcements sent to repel the land attack at Grand Gulf.

At 1 p. m. of the 29th of April this portion of the squadron, consisting of the Tyler, Choctaw, De Kalb, Signal, Romeo, Linden, Petrel, and Black Hawk, with three 13-inch mortars, in tow of tugs, proceeded up the river, followed by ten large transports carrying Major General Blair's division to Chickasaw bayou, all under command of Major General W. T. Sherman, where we remained for the night. A regiment was sent out near the old battle-ground without any important discovery. At 9 on the morning of the 30th the whole force, except the Petrel, stationed at Old river, proceeded up the river in the above order, and took position as in the accompanying sketch.

The Choctaw and De Kalb opened fire upon the main works at Droomgould's Bluff, and the Tyler and this ship, with 30-pounder rifles, upon the field-works and batteries. I refer you to enclosed reports of commanders for particulars.

The De Kalb was handled with the skill always exhibited by Lieutenant Commander Walker; and the management and whole conduct of the Choctaw, Lieutenant Commander Ramsay, was worthy of the best of your tried commanders.

From the high stage of the water the Choctaw and De Kalb could not be brought head on to the batteries without too great exposure, which neither the force nor circumstances would permit; and although they were fought nearly at a broadside, I am happy to state that no casualties occurred, nor did any in the whole expedition while in action. I soon saw the disadvantageous way the Choctaw was compelled to fight, and the De Kalb necessarily, from her vulnerable sides, could share little of the exposure of the heavy fire concentrated upon her; but as the demonstration was considered so important by General Sherman, I felt compelled to make it appear as much of a real attack as possible without too great risk; accordingly the vessels were allowed to remain under fire upwards of three hours and a half, when I made the signal to retire.

Lieutenant Commander Ramsay remained upon deck during the whole engagement, and you will judge from his report the heavy fire he was under. Scarce a moment but a jet of water was thrown up near her, or a shot struck her. The Tyler was obliged to retire early, from receiving a Whitworth shot at the water's edge, causing her to leak badly, but was soon ready for action again. The position of this ship was changed several times, as the enemy nearly got our range.

At 6 p. m. the troops were landed, and marched up towards Haines's Bluff on the only roadway—the levee, making quite a display, and a threatening one also. As the pickets and skirmishers approached the road leading to the bluffs a very heavy battery was opened, sweeping the narrow causeway, upon which not more than two men could walk abreast. Videttes, &c., were thrown out, and at dark the troops were quietly embarked, leaving our pickets, &c. The next day a regiment was landed on the opposite side, and marched up in the direction of the bluffs, but before reaching the river were met by an impassable bayou and the heavy fire of the forts on the bluffs.

It was observed in the morning that new works had been thrown up during the night, some of the old ones extended, and several new and apparently heavy guns placed in position. At 3 p. m., by previous arrangement, the De Kalb, Choctaw, Tyler, and this ship, opened upon these works, and drew the fire from a 32-pounder rifle gun and a Whitworth gun. They were silenced, having fired not more than four rounds each. Our practice was excellent, and it would be difficult to determine to which ship belonged the credit of silencing these guns.

Observing heavy ox teams, apparently drawing heavy guns, our fire was turned toward them, and to the valleys adjacent, in which troops were supposed to be concealed, with what damage is not known. Our firing gradually slackened, until at dark it ceased altogether; and at 8 p. m., General Sherman having received orders to take his corps to the other side, the vessels all returned to their old anchorage, in the mouth of the Yazoo, without accident. The rebel lieutenant captured by Captain Walker being wounded, I turned over to General Sherman, who, having a hospital boat with him, could properly attend to his case.

This prisoner states that a major and three privates of his party were killed; that they have eleven heavy guns in their batteries, from 10-inch smooth bore to the heaviest rifled, and two brigades to guard it, its only approach being that over the narrow causeway before mentioned, which were entirely commanded by guns sweeping in all directions; also that the raft had broken adrift, proof of which was evident enough as we advanced. He also stated that it was reported that Port Hudson had been evacuated.

During the ten days' operations this ship fired 227 30-pounder shells. I regret that I can make nothing of the paper case time fuze furnished us. In all our experiments and in actual service they could not be relied upon, scarcely ever bursting.

Ensigns Bridgman and Miller had each charge of a gun, and the accuracy of their fire elicited much applause, and must have discomfited the enemy much. We were firing at about 3,000 yards.

Respectfully, your obedient servant,

K. R. BREESE,
Lieutenant Commander.

Acting Rear-Admiral DAVID D. PORTER,
Commanding Mississippi Squadron.

Report of Lieutenant Commander John G. Walker.

UNITED STATES GUNBOAT BARON DE KALB,
Mouth of Yazoo, May 2, 1863.

SIR: I have the honor to forward the following report of the part taken by this vessel in the feigned attack upon Droomgould's Bluff on April 30 and May 1:

Upon the first day I moved into position and opened fire at 10.50 a. m., and continued firing heavily until about 2 p. m., when I retired by signal. As the attack was but a feint, and being ordered not to risk my vessel, I covered her with the river bank, avoiding the enemy's fire as much as possible.

At 2 p. m., while dropping out of action, the others having retired, was fired upon by musketry from some buildings on the east bank of the river at a distance of about fifty yards. I immediately ran into the bank and landed Acting Master C. S. Kendrick, with about twenty-five men, who dislodged the enemy from the buildings and chased them five or six hundred yards into the swamp, killing one officer and three privates, and taking a second lieutenant, of the third Louisiana infantry, prisoner. Mr. Kendrick behaved very gallantly, capturing the prisoner in a hand to hand fight by knocking him down with his pistol. The prisoner reports the officer killed to have been a major. E. N. House quartermaster, was shot through the right arm by a rifle ball, but not seriously injured. At 6 p. m. I again moved up near my former position to cover a movement of troops, and remained until the following day.

The enemy fired sharply until sunset, but fortunately without effect. On the second day, at 3.10 p. m., got under way and dropped down to the squadron, firing upon the enemy as my guns bore, and continued firing until dark. The enemy failed to reply after the first half hour, although the whole squadron was within easy range. During the two days I expended two hundred rounds of ammunition.

Very respectfully, your obedient servant,

JOHN G. WALKER,
Lieutenant Commander.

Lieut. Comd'r K. R. BREESE,
Senior Officer present.

Report of Lieutenant Commander F. M. Ramsay.

UNITED STATES STEAMER CHOCTAW,
Yazoo River, May 3, 1863.

SIR: I have the honor to report that on the 20th ultimo, in company with the squadron, I engaged the enemy's batteries on Droomgould's Bluff from 10 a. m. to 1.40 p. m., when, in obedience to signal from flag-ship, I dropped down a short distance and tied to the right bank of the river.

The enemy's shot struck this vessel forty-six times, besides cutting away six smoke-stack guys. The turret was struck six times, a 10-inch solid shot penetrating the crown and a 6-inch pointed shot burying itself. Two shot struck below water-line on starboard side forward of turret; one carried away starboard forward warping chock; eleven struck the smoke-stacks; one the starboard forward ventilator; one carried away first cutter's after davit and store gig; one struck casemate below pilot-house and glanced; one penetrated iron on starboard side, forward of wheel-house curve, and glanced; five struck curve forward of starboard wheel; two penetrating iron and wood; one penetrating wood casemate inside of starboard wheel; four struck starboard wheel-house, carrying away one outside circle and three arms of starboard wheel; six struck port wheel-house, carrying away one outside circle and ten arms of port wheel; one struck ward-room skylight; one through storage-room; one cut away pendant staff, one the ensign staff, and one the forward wheel beam hog chain. A shot is supposed to have struck under water on starboard side abreast of boilers. Two men were slightly bruised on the wrist by splinters. In the evening the enemy's batteries again opened fire. I moved to the left bank of the river and returned it for a short time. On the 1st instant, at 3 p. m., I opened again on the batteries and fired slowly until 7 p. m.

During the two days sixty-nine shells and three solid shot were fired from the 100-pounder Parrott gun, and forty-five shells and five solid shot from the 9-inch gun. The 100-pounder gun was commanded by Acting Ensign W. C. Bennet, and the 9-inch by Acting Master's Mate C. C. Johnson, under the superintendence of Acting Ensign and Executive Officer W. A. Abbott.

The officers and men under my command deserve great credit for the manner in which they performed their duty. The greater portion of the crew had been only eight days on board when the engagement took place, and owing to the unfinished state of the vessel, had had only three days' exercise at the guns.

The 10-second fuzes for the Parrott shells did not burn properly, the shells having them in exploded much too soon, and one of them so close to the muzzle of the gun that the pieces struck the forecastle deck in three places and set fire to the vessel.

Very respectfully, your obedient servant,

FRANK M. RAMSAY,
Lieutenant Commanding.

Lieut. Com'dr K. R. BREESE,
Senior Naval Officer, mouth of Yazoo River.

Report of Lieutenant Commander Jas. M. Pritchett.

UNITED STATES GUNBOAT TYLER,
Yazoo River, May 2, 1863.

SIR: I have the honor to submit the following report of the part taken by this vessel in the demonstration upon Droomgould's Bluff, April 30 and May 1: On the morning of the 30th got under way at 9.16, and took my position astern of the Baron de Kalb. At 10.15 came within range of the lower batteries, which I opened on with my 30-pounder rifles. At 10.30 made fast to the left bank of the river, and kept up the fire on these batteries. At 11 a. m. was struck between wind and water on starboard side, and was obliged to drop out of the fire and keel the vessel over to stop the hole. After repairing, the order was given to retire. At 2.30 p. m. received orders to drop down about two miles below the transports to prevent the rebels from planting a field battery. Laid there until 9.30 next morning, when I got under way and stood up the river, and made fast to the right bank and astern of the Choctaw, and within range of two small batteries, which the enemy had erected during the night. At 3 p. m. opened a steady and well-directed fire on these batteries until 7 p. m. This vessel was struck once in the wheel-house by a large fragment of shell.

At 9.30 p. m. got under way and returned to my anchorage at the mouth of Yazoo river.

During the two days fired eighty-one Parrott shells and thirty VIII-inch.

Very respectfully,

JAS. M. PRITCHETT,
Lieutenant Commander.

Lieut. Com'dr K. R. BREESE,
Senior Officer present.

Report of Lieutenant Commander Le Roy Fitch of his operations on the Tennessee and Cumberland rivers.

MISSISSIPPI SQUADRON, FLAG-SHIP BENTON,
Mouth of Red River, May 12, 1863.

SIR: I have the honor to enclose herewith a report from Lieutenant Commander Le Roy Fitch, in relation to operations in the Tennessee and Cumberland rivers.

I am, sir, very respectfully, your obedient servant,

DAVID D. PORTER,
Acting Rear-Admiral, Com'dg Mississippi Squadron.

Hon. GIDEON WELLES,
Secretary of the Navy, Washington, D. C.

Reports of Lieutenant Commander Fitch.

UNITED STATES GUNBOAT LEXINGTON,
Paducah, Kentucky, April 2, 1863.

SIR: I have the honor to report operations on the upper Tennessee river during the last few days.

Acting Volunteer Lieutenant Jason Gowdy was patrolling the river with the gunboats Robert and Silver Lake.

Enclosed I forward his report of operations up to the time I joined him at Fort Hindman, on the 27th of March. I took from the fort one hundred and fifty soldiers under command of Colonel Graig, and after distributing them on the three boats proceeded on up the river. I made several landings along on the route, reported to be infested by guerillas, but found none till we reached the neighborhood of Savannah, being informed that back of Boyd's landing, about four miles, was a cotton factory owned by, and doing work for, the rebels. I had determined to destroy it. I therefore landed at Boyd's, and sent out an expedition, numbering about two hundred soldiers and sailors. Colonel Graig took charge of the force. The executive officer of this steamer, Acting Volunteer Lieutenant Dunn, took charge of the sailors. The expedition moved out to the factory with caution, as Colonel Cox's cavalry regiment was stationed but two or three miles beyond. Arriving at the mill, breastworks of cord-wood were thrown across the road, and inquiries made regarding the operations of the factory.

From what could be learned, the mill was run on shares with the country people; the material went in an indirect way to the rebel soldiers, through their friends at home. The books were all clean, and contained nothing to condemn the factory; but knowing that the mill did aid in an indirect manner the rebels, it was thought proper not to burn it, but to effectually prevent its doing more work, which was done by removing the running gear, pistons, cylinder heads, brasses, and all like portable portions, and placing it on board this vessel. Two mules and a wagon, which were pressed to haul the machinery down to the boat, were retained as lawful prizes, as it was ascertained they belonged to Colonel Cox's rebel cavalry. Two horses also were captured by Mr. Dunn, belonging to guerillas.

A short distance above this landing, and about three miles from the river, was reported a plantation owned by a noted rebel—Smith. The boats were landed, and an expedition sent out to the place. This plantation was occupied by a man by the name of Dillihunty, and is known to be a rendezvous for guerillas. Yet this Dillihunty claims to be loyal, has *taken the oath,* and says he bought the farm of Smith. This may be true, but he had no papers to prove it, has never been molested by the guerillas; and in fact, as I have since learned, was at the time raising a guerilla company, as several men were at the time on his premises, one of which I took prisoner, he having been engaged in the guerilla service; and as our men were fired at by a guerilla near his place, the indications were such as to render his position very doubtful.

I therefore took from the farm twenty-five bales of cotton (to be held till he proves his loyalty) and some cavalry horses.

After leaving this landing, I proceeded on up to Chickasaw, at the foot of Colvert shoals; there was scant five feet on the shoals, so I sent the Robert and Silver Lake above with orders to make thorough reconnoissance and return the same night, as the river was falling too fast to risk them above longer. Acting Volunteer Lieutenant Gowdy reports the enemy in force on both sides of the river at Florence. He shelled and drove them out of their camp on the left bank, but was not able to tell their number nor to ascertain the calibre of their heavy guns, as the wind was blowing a gale right across the river, and he was fearful of getting caught above the shoals by falling water. Before reaching Florence he surprised a picket guard, captured five horses, some carbines, and one prisoner. He joined me at Chickasaw just at dark.

Returning down the river, I stopped at a farm belonging to a notorious rebel by the names of Hays, who had been very zealous in enforcing the conscript law and feeding the guerillas—sent a detachment back three miles, to his house, and brought away about one thousand pounds of bacon, and all the corn we could carry, also three mules and a wagon belonging to him. Colonel Graig took charge of the bacon, as the army at Fort Hindman were short of supplies.

The result of the several small expeditions is as follows: eight guns, (cavalry carbines,) 25 bales of cotton, 15 horses, (three broke loose and escaped at Fort Hindman,) twelve mules, (one shot through the thigh, and left at Fort Hindman,) and two wagons; also eight prisoners.

I would state that all men along the river above Fort Henry must be either disloyal in sentiments or actually engaged in the rebel cause; from what the numerous refugees tell me, none expressing sentiments the least loyal are permitted to remain at home and cultivate their farms.

Since so many of these guerillas have been found dead on the battle-field with the oath of allegiance in their pockets, I am forced to believe no man living with these guerillas, though he had taken the oath forty times.

I have given transportation to over sixty refugee families since I have been on these waters; but applications for conveyance out of the river have become so very numerous from young men fleeing from the conscript, that I have been induced to give the captains of boats instructions to render all the aid in their power to families, but under no circumstances to bring or pass out able-bodied young men. We are in want of men for the gunboats, and if they love the Union better than rebellion, now is the proper time to show it; they must take sides either one way or the other. This has already had the effect of sending some thirty or forty into General Dodge's cavalry, and has given the gunboats some eight or ten recruits. I deem it high time that some of these loyal refugees were showing some proof of their loyalty.

I hope, as soon as there is another slight rise in the Tennessee, to be able, with General Dodge's cavalry co-operating, to capture all the force on the Tuscumbia side at Florence.

My plan will be this: to watch the river closely; as soon as there is the least indication of a rise, get forces from General Dodge, take the infantry over Culvert shoals, land them at Tuscumbia landing, let the cavalry come in on the Tuscumbia road, and while the forces are getting in the enemy's rear I will push on up with four or five of the lightest-draught boats, and engage them in front.

I have written to General Dodge to this effect, and rely upon his hearty co-operation to complete the programme. With his co-operation I am confident of success.

Very respectfully, your obedient servant,

LE ROY FITCH,
Lieutenant Commander.

Acting Rear-Admiral DAVID D. PORTER,
Commanding Mississippi Squadron.

UNITED STATES GUNBOAT LEXINGTON,
Smithland, Kentucky, April 6, 1863.

SIR: I have the honor to report, that on the third instant, while coaling at this place preparatory to again ascending the Tennessee, I received a telegram from Acting Volunteer Lieutenant J. S. Hand, commanding gunboat St. Clair, that the fleet under his convoy had been attacked at Palmyra, and that the St. Clair was disabled.

I got under way immediately, and started up the river with the Lexington, Brilliant, Robert, Silver Lake, and Springfield, having been informed that the enemy were in strong force, and had heavy field batteries.

Below Donelson I met the St. Clair, being towed down and followed by her consort, the Fairplay. I turned the Fairplay back to follow me and proceeded on up. Arriving at Palmyra, I found the enemy had retreated towards Harpeth shoals. I landed opposite the town and sent a detachment on shore under command of Acting Master Fitzpatrick, of this vessel, with instructions to burn every house in the place, and to allow no one under his command to pillage or remove the smallest article. Just after the boat landed, several stragglers from the guerillas broke from their concealment and ran; our men fired on them, killing one and wounding another.

The town was burned; not one house left. I had for some time been suspicious of this place; one or two loyal men did live here, but were driven out by the rebels.

The town was one of the worst secession places on the river, and as unarmed transports were fired on from the dwellings, I gave them the full benefit of your order, which I trust will be a lesson to them in the future. Enclosed I send a letter from Port Hudson, which may perhaps be of some little interest.

I left the same evening with the transports and gunboats for Harpeth shoals. At Clarksville I landed and made arrangements with the commandant of the post for infantry and cavalry to accompany me, with a hope of being able to get in the rear of and capture the enemy's artillery. Pushing on up, I landed the soldiers a few miles below Harpeth in the forenoon of the 5th, and moved on up with the boats to draw attention, but, much to my regret, the enemy had intimation of our approach, and had again retreated this time back from the river towards Charlotte. The cavalry followed them six miles back, but not being able to come up with them, returned, as it was not prudent to venture further with so small a force.

As the river was falling too fast for me to risk this boat over the shoals, I sent the transports on to Nashville under convoy of three light-draughts, and returned to this place with a view of carrying out my plans up the Tennessee.

It has always been my aim to have the means of communication and times of meeting between the boats on this and the Tennessee river so perfect that at a moment's warning I can, in case of necessity, concentrate the entire force at any one point.

I am happy to state that thus far I have been able to accomplish this, and hope to be in future equally successful.

Very respectfully, your obedient servant,

LE ROY FITCH,
Lieutenant Commander.

Acting Rear-Admiral DAVID D. PORTER,
Commanding Mississippi Squadron.

UNITED STATES STEAMBOAT LEXINGTON,
Hamburg Landing, April 28, 1863.

SIR: I have the honor to report that on the 24th instant, while cruising down the river ahead of General Ellet's fleet, I met the steamer Emma Duncan, Acting Master Griswold, commanding, coming up to report his vessel for duty. Learning that he had been attacked by a field battery at Green Bottom bar, and had three men badly wounded, I proceeded on down the river, giving him orders to follow me, in hopes of catching the rebels at or near the same place. Enclosed I send his report; also the surgeon's.

I passed the bar about dusk in the evening, but the enemy was nowhere to be seen. Being short of coal, I proceeded on down to Fort Henry, where I procured some from one of General Ellet's barges and started back up the river the evening of the 25th instant.

Arriving at the foot of Green Bottom bar about midnight, I anchored till morning. Still seeing nothing of the enemy, I proceeded on up the river to meet and communicate with General Ellet. The Emma Duncan remaining nearly a mile in my rear, caught a ferry flat coming out of a creek after I had passed; the guerillas in the flat jumped out and made their escape in the woods; the flat, however, was destroyed and set adrift. I cruised on up leisurely, keeping a good lookout for the enemy along the right bank, but saw no sign of them till I arrived at Duck River shoals, where I heard musketry and artillery a short distance (not a mile) ahead. I pushed on over the bar and met General Ellet's fleet just at the head of the shoals, engaging the rebel battery. I was then in good range, and at once opened fire on the enemy. There was not room for his boats to round to or to back out of the channel; he was therefore compelled to push on over the bar before he could effect a landing. I took the battery side and moved on up to cover his boats as much as possible, at the same time raking the bank with our heavy guns. The ram Monarch by this time came in range and opened fire also. As soon as I rounded the point the enemy fired a farewell shot at one of the brigade boats, limbered up, and were off; some few sharpshooters remaining behind fired a few shots at a transport having on board sick and wounded.

I followed on up the bank, throwing shell after them till I thought them out of range, and ceased firing; by this time General Ellet had landed and was pursuing them.

Several of the enemy were found dead on the bank, and many more were dragged off in the woods. I should suppose that their loss in killed and wounded is about twenty-five or thirty.

I believe General Ellet lost two killed and one wounded on his boats; also some horses killed.

About 11 p. m. I left General Ellet at the foot of the bar and proceeded on up the river with this boat and the Emma Duncan to communicate with the fleet above. I arrived at Eastport on the afternoon of the 27th instant, receiving a communication from General Dodge at Tuscumbia. Enclosed I send a copy of it.

I send the transports below Big Bend shoals, and remained at Eastport landing myself with the gunboats Emma Duncan and Queen City till morning, the 28th instant, in hopes of again being able to communicate with General Dodge before moving the transports out of the river. I then returned to Hamburg, and finding no means of communication there, sent the Covington and Emma Duncan back to Chickasaw to wait till the morning of the 29th instant, and then, if no messengers arrived from General Dodge, to report back to me at this place.

I will move down from here with the transports to-morrow.

Very respectfully, your obedient servant,

LE ROY FITCH,
Lieutenant Commander.

Acting Rear-Admiral DAVID D. PORTER,
Commanding Mississippi Squadron.

Destruction of a water battery at Warrenton by the Mound City, Lieutenant Commander Byron Wilson.

UNITED STATES MISSISSIPPI SQUADRON,
Flag-Ship Black Hawk, Yazoo River, May 15, 1863.

SIR: I have the honor to report my return to this place for a few days to look after provisions, and make some arrangements with regard to the upper portion of the squadron.

A few days since the Mound City, Lieutenant Commander Byron Wilson, came up as far as Warrenton to reconnoitre, and see what guns were there likely to annoy our transports.

The rebels have been engaged for some months in building a strong casemated water battery, intending to mount 8 ten-inch guns on it. This work was built with cotton bales, covered with logs, the logs covered with railroad iron, and the whole covered with earth. On approaching the forts Lieutenant Commander Wilson sent a party on shore to reconnoitre; on climbing up the casemate to look in, the party discovered that a company of artillerists had taken refuge there, supposing themselves perfectly secure. Our men fired their revolvers into the crowd, and warned the vessel that rebels were about. Lieutenant Commanding Wilson then commenced shelling the fort, and in a short time it was all in a blaze; after burning strongly for some time, the whole work was destroyed. Thus ended a fort, in the space of an hour, which had taken the rebels five months to build, working mostly day and night. I proceeded to Warrenton this morning to be certain that the work was thoroughly destroyed; it required nothing more done to it—the Mound City had finished it. The rebels set all their houses containing their stores on fire as the gunboats approached, and what they left I ordered to be destroyed. Warrenton has been a troublesome place, and merits its fate.

I am, sir, very respectfully, your obedient servant,

DAVID D. PORTER,
Acting Rear-Admiral, Com'dg Mississippi Squadron.

Hon. GIDEON WELLES,
Secretary of the Navy, Washington, D. C.

Destruction of the fortifications at Haines's Bluff.

FLAG-SHIP BLACK HAWK,
Haines's Bluff, Yazoo River, May 20.

On the morning of the 15th I came over to Yazoo river to be ready to co-operate with General Grant, leaving two of the iron-clads at Red river, one at Grand Gulf, one at Carthage, three at Warrenton, and two in the Yazoo. This left me a small force to operate with; still I disposed of them to the best advantage.

On the 18th, at meridian, firing was heard in the rear of Vicksburg, which assured me that General Grant was approaching the city. The cannonading was kept up furiously for some time, when, by the aid of glasses, I discovered a company of our artillery advancing, taking position, and driving the rebels before them.

I immediately saw that General Sherman's division had come in to the left of Snyder's Bluff, and that the rebels at that place had been cut off from joining the forces in the city. I despatched the De Kalb, Lieutenant Com-

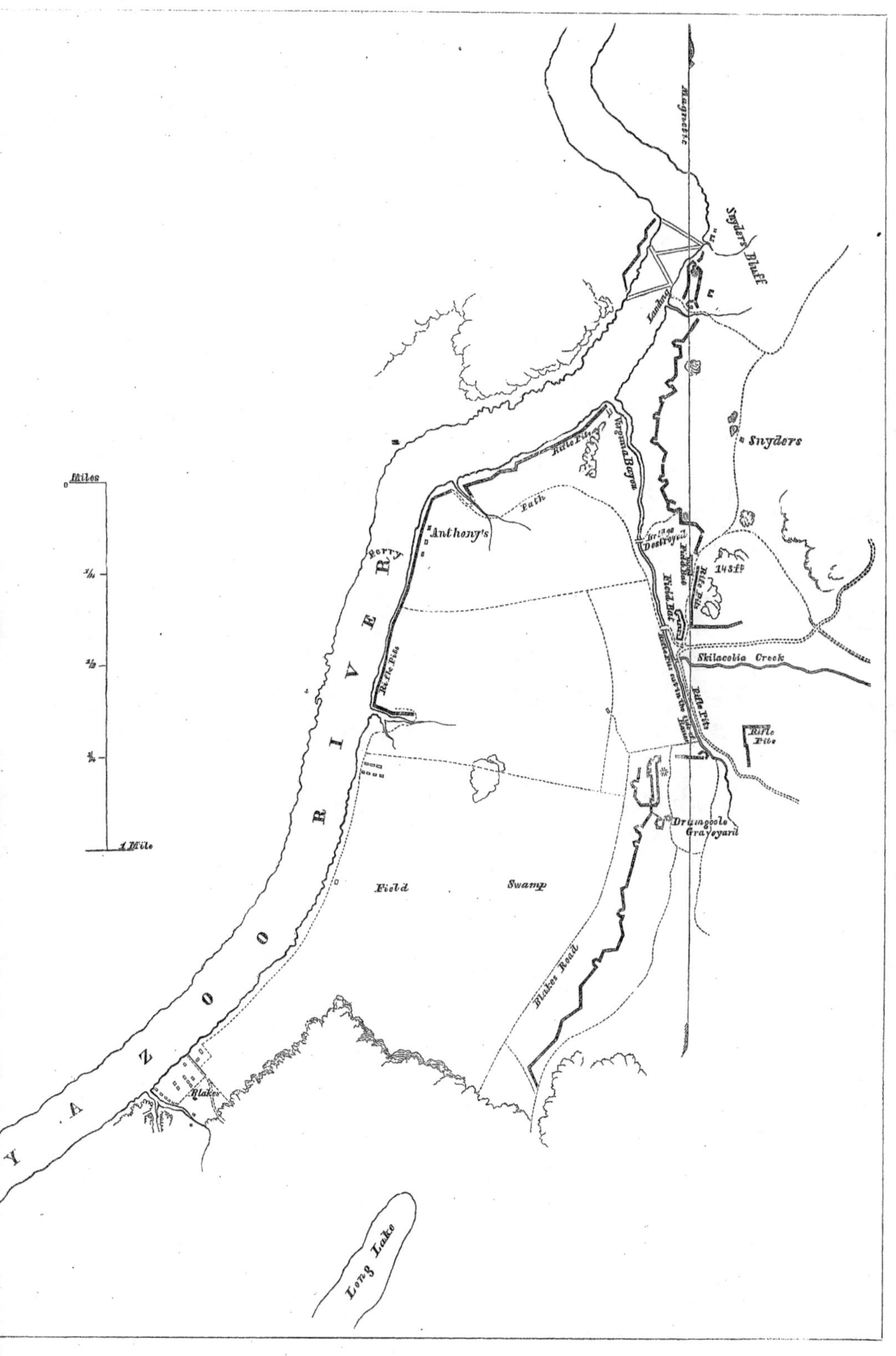

Magnetic
Snyders Bluff
Landing
Snyders
Virginia Bayou
Rifle Pits
Path
Anthony's
Ferry
Bridge Destroyed
Field Bat
Rifle Pits
143 ft
Skilacolia Creek
Rifle Pits
Drumgoole Graveyard
Field
Swamp
Blakes Road
Blakes
YAZOO RIVER
Long Lake
Miles
0
1/4
1/2
3/4
1 Mile

mander Walker, Choctaw, Lieutenant Commander Ramsey, the Linden, Romeo, Petrel, and Forest Rose, all under command of Lieutenant Commander Breese, up the Yazoo, to open communication in that way with Generals Grant and Sherman.

This I succeeded in doing, and in three hours received letters from Generals Grant, Sherman, and Steele, informing me of their vast successes, and asking me to send up provisions, which was at once done.

In the mean time Lieutenant Commander Walker, in the De Kalb, pushed on to Haines's Bluff, which the enemy had commenced evacuating the day before, and a party remained behind in the hope of destroying or taking away a large amount of ammunition on hand. When they saw the gunboats they ran out, and left everything in good order, guns, fort, tents, and equipage of all kinds, which fell into our hands.

As soon as the capture of Haines's Bluff and fourteen forts was reported to me, I shoved up the gunboats from below Vicksburg to fire at the hill batteries, which fire was kept up for two or three hours. At midnight they moved up to the town and opened on it for about an hour, and continued at intervals during the night to annoy the garrison. On the 19th I placed six mortars in position, with orders to fire night and day as rapidly as they could.

The works at Haines's Bluff are very formidable. There are fourteen of the heaviest kind of mounted 8-inch and 10-inch, and 7½-inch rifled guns, with ammunition enough to last a long siege. As the gun-carriages might again fall into the hands of the enemy, I had them burned, blew up the magazines, and destroyed the works generally. I also burned the encampments, which were permanently and remarkably well constructed, looking as if the rebels intended to stay for some time.

These works and encampments covered many acres of ground, and the fortifications and the rifle-pits proper of Haines's Bluff extend about a mile and a quarter. Such a network of defences I never saw. The rebels were a year constructing them, and all were rendered useless in an hour.

As soon as I got through with the destruction of the magazines and other works, I started Lieutenant Commander Walker up the Yazoo river with sufficient force to destroy all the enemy's property in that direction, with orders to return with all despatch, and only to proceed as far as Yazoo City, where the rebels have a navy yard and storehouses. In the meanwhile General Grant has closely invested Vicksburg, and has possession of the most commanding points.

In a very short time a general assault will take place, when I hope to announce that Vicksburg has fallen, after a series of the most brilliant successes that ever attended an army.

There has never been a case during the war where the rebels have been so successfully beaten at all points, and the patience and endurance shown by our army and navy for so many months is about to be rewarded.

It is a mere question of a few hours, and then, with the exception of Port Hudson, which will follow Vicksburg, the Mississippi will be open its entire length.

DAVID D. PORTER,
Acting Rear-Admiral, Com'dg Mississippi Squadron.

Hon. GIDEON WELLES,
Secretary of the Navy.

Attack on the Vicksburg batteries 22d and 27th of May, 1863.

MISSISSIPPI SQUADRON,
Flag-Ship Black Hawk, May 23, 1863.

SIR: On the evening of the 21st I received a communication from General Grant, informing me that he intended to attack the whole of the rebel works at 10 a. m. the next day, and asking me to shell the batteries from 9.30 until 10.30 a. m. to annoy the garrison. I kept six mortars playing rapidly on the works and town all night; sent the Benton, Mound City, and Carondelet up to shell the water batteries and other places where troops might be rested during the night.

At 7 o'clock in the morning the Mound City proceeded across the river, and made an attack on the hill batteries opposite the canal. At 8 o'clock I joined her with the Benton, Tuscumbia, and Carondelet; all these vessels opened on the hill batteries, and finally silenced them, though the main work (on the battery containing the heavy rifled gun) was done by the Mound City, Lieutenant Commanding Byron Wilson. I then pushed the Benton, Mound City, and Carondelet up to the water batteries, leaving the Tuscumbia (which vessel is still out of repair) to keep the hill batteries from firing on our vessels after they had passed by. The three gunboats passed up slowly, owing to the strong current; the Mound City leading, Benton following, and Carondelet astern.

The water batteries opened furiously, supported by a hill battery on the starboard beam of the vessels. The vessels advanced to within 440 yards, (by our marks,) and returned the fire for two hours without cessation, the enemy's fire being very accurate and incessant. Finding that the hill batteries behind me were silenced, I ordered up the Tuscumbia to within 800 yards of the batteries, but her turret was soon made untenable, not standing the enemy's shots, and I made her drop down.

I had been engaged with the forts an hour longer than General Grant asked; the vessels had all received severe shots under water, which we could not stop up while in motion, and not knowing what might have delayed the movement of the army, I ordered the vessels to drop out of fire, which they did in a cool, handsome manner.

This was the hottest fire the gunboats have ever been under; but, owing to the water batteries being more on a level with them than usual, the gunboats threw in their shell so fast that the aim of the enemy was not very good.

The enemy hit the vessels a number of times, but, fighting bow on, the shot did but little damage; not a man was killed, and only a few wounded. I had only ammunition enough for a few moments longer, and set all hands to work to fill up from our depot below. After dropping back, I found that the enemy had taken possession again of one of the lower hill batteries, and was endeavoring to remove his guns, and had mounted a 12-pound field-piece to fire at General McArthur's troops, which had landed a short time before at Warrenton. I sent the Mound City and Carondelet to drive him off, which they did in a few moments.

The officers and men of all the vessels behaved with their usual gallantry; they had none of them been to rest for three days and nights, most of them having been engaged in firing on the batteries and town, and I allowed them to devote the afternoon to the necessary repose.

I beg leave to enclose a letter from General McArthur, explaining why he did not (to use his own expression) "take advantage of the results gained by the gunboats." I have since learned from General Grant that the army did assault at the right time vigorously; in the noise and smoke we could not see or hear it; the gunboats, therefore, were still fighting when the assault had proved unsuccessful.

The army had terrible work before them, and are fighting as well as soldiers ever fought before, but the works are stronger than any of us dreamed of.

General Grant and his soldiers are confident, and I am confident, that the brave and energetic generals in this army will soon overcome all obstacles and carry the works.

I am, sir, your obedient servant,

DAVID D. PORTER,
Acting Rear-Admiral, Com'dg Mississippi Squadron.

Hon. GIDEON WELLES,
Secretary of the Navy, Washington, D. C.

Letter of Brigadier General J. McArthur to Acting Rear-Admiral Porter.

HEADQUARTERS 6TH DIVISION 17TH ARMY CORPS,
In field, near Vicksburg, Mississippi, May 23, 1863.

ADMIRAL: I received your communication regarding the silencing of the two batteries below Vicksburg, and, in reply, would say that I witnessed with intense satisfaction the firing on that day, being the finest I have yet seen. I would have taken advantage of the results then gained by your vessels, and had given the necessary orders to do so, when I received peremptory orders from Major General McClernand to move my command around to the right of my position, to support a portion of his troops who had gained a lodgment in the enemy's works. I arrived, however, too late, and have now been ordered back to my former position, and to follow up any advantage your vessels may gain. I have made a request to have some rifled guns sent me, which I require, and on receipt of which I expect to be able to enfilade Whistling Dick's position—at any rate I will try.

I am informed to-night that there is a levee running from the spur of the hill opposite my camp to the river, which I intend to have explored to-morrow, when I expect to communicate more fully with your vessels.

I will watch their action and co-operate.

I am, your obedient servant,

J. McARTHUR,
Brigadier General, Com'dg 6th Div. 17th A. Corps.

Admiral D. D. PORTER,
Commanding United States Mississippi Squadron.

Letter of Acting Rear-Admiral Porter, transmitting reports of commanders of the iron-clads.

UNITED STATES MISSISSIPPI SQUADRON,
Near Vicksburg, May 27, 1863.

SIR: I have the honor to forward the reports of the commanders of the iron-clads engaged in the actions of the 22d of May and the 27th of May.

Very respectfully, your obedient servant,

DAVID D. PORTER,
Acting Rear-Admiral, Com'dg Mississippi Squadron.

Hon. GIDEON WELLES,
Secretary of the Navy, Washington, D. C.

Report of Lieutenant Commander James A. Greer, commanding the Benton.

UNITED STATES GUNBOAT BENTON,
Below Vicksburg, May 24, 1863.

SIR: I respectfully submit the following report of the movements of this vessel:

On May 19th got under way from Naval landing, and stood up towards rebel batteries, the Tuscumbia and Carondelet in company. At 12.30 p. m. the lower hill batteries opened fire on us, which we returned at long range; fired seven shots, the other vessels also firing, and then went to the bank and tied up on Louisiana side. At 4.30 p. m. the three vessels again got under way, and when within range opened on the batteries.

This vessel fired fifty-five times. Towards dark dropped down and tied up to the bank. The rebels fired slowly and deliberately at us, but fortunately none of the vessels were struck. At 11 p. m. this vessel and the Carondelet stood up above the canal, on the Louisiana shore, and opened on the town at long range, the enemy firing but a few shots in return. This vessel fired forty-three times; then dropped down out of range.

At 2 a. m., May 20, got under way, and stood up within range of rebel batteries, and fired forty-one times upon them and the town. At 2.30 dropped down out of range. The Carondelet then passed up to shell the town. At 9.10 p. m. got under way, accompanied by the Carondelet and Mound City, and proceeded slowly up towards Vicksburg, crossed over to the Mississippi shore, and approached the Hospital battery. At 11.28 opened fire, and engaged this battery thirty-three minutes; then dropped down, the Mound City and Carondelet coming up in turns. We fired forty-two times. The enemy responded, but not rapidly. We were struck twice in the upper works; no one was injured.

At 12.30, May 21, tied up to Louisiana shore. At 2.45 this vessel got under way again; was detained some time by tiller-chain parting; then stood up on Louisiana side, and fired eleven times upon batteries at long range; then dropped down. The Mound City occupied lower batteries from 8 a. m. till noon; the Carondelet from 1 till 5.

At 5.28 we stood up and opened fire on rebel batteries; fired twenty-six times. The vessels went up in turns during the night and shelled Hospital battery and town. At 1 a. m., May 22, this vessel went up and fired twenty-four times, with but one or two shots in return from the rebels.

At 7.30 a. m. this vessel, with the whole squadron, stood up towards Vicksburg, fighting and passing the lower batteries. This vessel advanced well up to the Hospital battery, firing whenever a gun would bear, the enemy firing upon us very rapidly, and from nearly all his batteries. We opened fire at 8.23; at 10.40 the signal to discontinue action was made. We then dropped down, and after communicating with you, went into the Mississippi shore and tied up.

In this short action we fired two hundred and eighty-three times. We were struck thirteen times, four times at the water-line, once on each bow, and twice on starboard side.

At first the vessel leaked some, but we have it now completely under control. Fortunately no one was hurt.

Very respectfully, your obedient servant,

JAMES A. GREER,
Lieutenant Commanding.

Acting Rear-Admiral D. D. PORTER,
Commanding Mississippi Squadron.

Report of Lieutenant Commander Byron Wilson, commanding the Mound City.

UNITED STATES GUNBOAT MOUND CITY,
Below Vicksburg, May 22, 1863.

SIR: I have the honor to enclose the executive officer's report of the damage sustained by this vessel during the fight to-day; also the surgeon's report of the wounded. One hundred and seventy (170) projectiles were expended.

The officers of the gun divisions deserve great credit for their skilful handling of the guns under a most galling fire.

I am, very respectfully, your obedient servant,

BYRON WILSON,
Lieutenant Commanding.

Rear-Admiral DAVID D. PORTER,
Commanding Mississippi Squadron.

Report of Acting Ensign Coleman of damages to the Mound City.

UNITED STATES GUNBOAT MOUND CITY,
Below Vicksburg, May 25, 1863.

SIR: I beg leave respectfully to report the damages received by this vessel in the engagement with the Vicksburg batteries, May 22, 1863.

1. A shot struck and lodged in starboard bow, near the stem, and five feet under water, not doing much damage, the timbers being four or five feet thick.

2. A shot went through the forecastle on port side, into the coal locker, and lodged in the coal, cutting the deck plank only.

3. A shot on starboard side went through the hammock netting and starboard chimney at the lower band, tearing the chimney half off, then through the galley and overboard.

4. A shot in front passed through two plates of heavy boiler iron, the iron of the pilot-house, near deck, and through the deck, cutting away carlin, and lodged in a mess chest.

5. A shot on starboard side cut through half of the hog-chain stanchion, passed through wheel-house, cutting away iron wheel and brace; then through steerage, tearing up about eight feet of the plank and breaking carlin and wood-work in wardroom.

6. A shell burst close to No. 6 Dahlgren gun, starboard side, knocking off a small piece of the muzzle.

7. A shot on the starboard side struck the iron near the top, cutting half through and bending one of the plates, knocking out a stanchion and starting the bolts on the inside.

8. A shot on starboard side struck the muzzle of No. 7 gun, 32-pounder, cracking the gun about five inches; then glanced, and went through the hammock netting and four or five clothes bags, and dropped over alongside pitman.

9. A shot struck iron on starboard side, over shell-room hatch, knocking off the plate, and driving a piece of it, about the size of the ball, through the casemate.

10. A shot on starboard quarter cut away an awning stanchion and passed through cabin skylight close to the deck, tearing up the plank.

11. A shot struck port chimney twenty feet from the deck.

12. A shot through brace of forward stanchion's skylight.

13. A shot on starboard side struck iron plating between guns Nos. 4 and 5, three feet above the water, and glanced off, bending the plates and starting bolts.

14. A shot on the starboard side, at shell-room, two feet under water-line, glanced without doing any damage.

15. A shot struck knuckle on port quarter and glanced, knocking a hole in the casemate.

16. The lower block of one of the boat tackles was shot away and the davit badly bent.

Respectfully, your obedient servant,

J. T. COLEMAN,
Acting Ensign and Executive Officer.

Lieutenant Commanding BYRON WILSON, U. S. N.,
Commanding United States Steamer Mound City.

Report of Acting Assistant Surgeon Thomas Rice of casualties on the Mound City.

UNITED STATES STEAMER MOUND CITY,
Mississippi River, below Vicksburg, May 22, 1863.

SIR: The following casualties occurred on board this vessel to-day during the engagement with the Vicksburg batteries, viz: Theodore Scheid, lieutenant of infantry, contused wounds of left eye and right side; Christopher Luft, private, company A, 58th Ohio volunteers, contused wounds of right forearm, slight; Frank Holly, master-at-arms, contused wound of back, slight; Charles Gunnerson, fireman, contused wound of left side and punctured wound of shoulder.

Very respectfully,

THOMAS RICE,
Acting Assistant Surgeon, United States Navy.

BYRON WILSON, Esq.,
Commanding United States Steamer Mound City.

Report of Commander S. E. Woodworth, commanding the General Price.

U. S. STEAMER GENERAL STERLING PRICE,
Below Vicksburg, May 27, 1863.

SIR: I have the honor to acknowledge the receipt of your communication, (at 6 a. m. this day,) dated May 26, in which I am directed, with all the gunboats, to engage, at 8 o'clock, the hill batteries.

At the appointed hour got under way and proceeded up to the point designated, opposite the canal, and immediately engaged the hill batteries. Discovering a number of men occupying the extreme lower hill battery, our vessels opened on them with shell and shrapnell. After a space of about half an hour discovered them to be our troops, they hoisting an American flag. I immediately made signals for the vessels to desist their fire on this battery.

We continued to engage the other hill batteries until the Cincinnati was seen to return up river, when, after a period of thirty minutes to make certain of the withdrawal of the Cincinnati, we retired from action. We were engaged one hour and fifteen minutes with the hill batteries, but were not able to silence them. They replied to our fire, however, but slowly.

The Tuscumbia was not able to go up, owing to her being without a pound of coal. I left directions for her to take on coal sufficient to last about three hours, should it arrive, and come up; but it did not reach her until our return.

Enclosed I forward you the report of Captains Greer, Murphy, and Wilson; also the report of the gunner, as to the amount of ammunition expended on this vessel.

I am happy to state that no one was injured during the action, although the enemy's shot fell thick around us.

Very respectfully, your obedient servant,

SELIM E. WOODWORTH,
Commander, Commanding Price.

Acting Rear-Admiral DAVID D. PORTER,
Commanding Mississippi Squadron.

Report of Lieutenant Commander Greer of engagement of May 27.

UNITED STATES STEAMER BENTON,
Below Vicksburg, May 27, 1863.

SIR: I have respectfully to report that this morning this vessel, with the other vessels of the squadron under your command, stood up, and at 8.20 opened fire on the lower hill battery. We worked in quite close to the Mississippi shore, and fired very deliberately, and only when we could plainly see the enemy's guns. The enemy responded as rapidly as his large gun would allow him to work it, a number of his shot falling quite close to us; fortunately we were not struck. We fired fourteen 9-inch 10-second shell; seven 42-pounder rifle 10-second shell, and three 32-pounder 10-second shell: a total of twenty-four fired. Owing to the action of the current and the height of the battery above us, I was at times obliged to be silent for several minutes while working out to get the range.

Very respectfully, your obedient servant,

JAMES A. GREER,
Lieutenant Commanding.

Commander S. E. WOODWORTH,
Com'dg U. S. Steamer General Price, Senior Officer present.

Report of Lieutenant Commander Byron Wilson of engagement of May 27.

UNITED STATES GUNBOAT MOUND CITY,
Below Vicksburg, May 27, 1863.

SIR: I have the honor to report that this morning, about 8 o'clock, in obedience to signal, I got under way, and took my station astern of the Benton, for the purpose of engaging the battery on the hill below Vicksburg.

I did not get a good position for firing, as I had to keep below the Benton, and the trees hid the guns almost entirely from my sight. No one was injured on board. Enclosed is a list of the ammunition expended.

I am, very respectfully, your obedient servant,

BYRON WILSON,
Lieutenant Commanding.

Commander S. WOODWORTH, U. S. N.,
United States Steamer General Price.

Report of Acting Lieutenant J. McLeod Murphy, commanding the Carondelet.

UNITED STATES STEAMER CARONDELET,
Off Vicksburg, May 27, 1863.

SIR: I have the honor to report as follows, in reference to the engagement of to-day:

In accordance with a signal from the United States steamer Sterling Price, this vessel engaged the lower batteries at about 8.15 a. m., and withdrew to the Louisiana shore at about 9.55 a. m. The bow battery and the battery on the starboard side, respectively in charge of Acting Ensigns Benjamin and Amerman, were engaged. The range of shot was in the direction of the bluffs, and as near the locality of the batteries as could be determined from our position and the random fire of the enemy. The elevation varied from four to seven degrees. Enclosed is the gunner's report of expenditure of ammunition.

I am glad to report the good behavior of officers and men, and the absence of accident or casualties. It becomes my duty, however, to recall the attention of Admiral Porter to the leaky condition of the ship, and the precarious state of the boilers.

I have the honor to be, very respectfully, your obedient servant,
J. McLEOD MURPHY,
Acting Lieutenant Commanding.

Com'dr SELIM E. WOODWORTH, U. S. N.,
Senior Officer in charge.

Report relative to the Tuscumbia.

U. S. MISSISSIPPI SQUADRON, FLAG-SHIP BLACK HAWK,
Young's Point, Louisiana, May 26, 1863.

SIR: I have the honor to acknowledge the receipt of a communication from you in relation to the Tuscumbia.

The persons who report that her difficulties originated from overloading are mistaken. We had not weight enough in her, and I partly remedied the difficulty by filling her up under the boilers with bomb-shells.

The Tuscumbia looks as if she could stand anything. The material used in her construction is of the best kind. The only difficulty is in the manner in which the iron is put on, and the want of sufficient backing of wood under the iron. I have a good deal of confidence in Mr. Brown, the constructor of this vessel, having found him very zealous, and doing the work for the government well and cheaply. But whoever he appointed to superintend this vessel neglected their duty, and injured her efficiency in the most important point.

The arrangement of the magazine is due to the ordnance officer who had charge. It would have been much better on deck, exposed, than the way it is now.

The vessel depends too much on hog chains, the cutting of one of which brings all the weight on her ends. All her hog chains and most of the stanchions were cut away. She is capable yet of being made a strong vessel, but with many alterations.

I found fault with Mr. Brown for some of her arrangements, but he was not permitted to carry out his plans. He had three vessels building at different places, which is a bad plan. A builder cannot do justice to the government in that way, especially as some of his work is let out by contracts, and he has to depend upon superintendents.

I send you Lieutenant Commander Shirk's report of the Tuscumbia in the last attack on Vicksburg.

If there are any more vessels building with plate iron, I think it would be well to have the bolts go all the way through and be riveted with a washer on the other side. This method will stand, provided the wood backing is not less than thirty-six inches of oak.

Very respectfully, your obedient servant,

DAVID D. PORTER,
Acting Rear-Admiral, Commanding Mississippi Squadron.

Hon. GIDEON WELLES,
Secretary of the Navy, Washington, D. C.

UNITED STATES STEAMER TUSCUMBIA,
Below Vicksburg, May 22, 1863.

SIR: During to-day's action with the enemy's batteries at Vicksburg this ship was struck three times, once upon the hull, doing no damage, once through the wood work, injuring the upper deck slightly, and once upon the iron plating of the fighting pilot-house. This shot was broken into small fragments, but the effect upon the pilot-house was to start every bolt, throw out of place every iron plate, and start every timber in the forward part of the pilot-house.

I again most respectfully call your attention to the outrageous manner in which this ship has been put together. The bolts that held the iron on the front of the pilot-house were not more than five inches long. They could be drawn out, after the house was struck, by one's fingers. I enclose two drawings, one a fore-and-aft midship section of the turret and fighting pilot-house.

By this you will see that from *x* to *y* there is no protection to the wheel from a shot or shell entering the forward midship port, and also that *z*, the hatchway of the magazine passage, is very much exposed. During the engagement at Grand Gulf sparks of fire did enter it.

U v is the iron armor intended to protect the upper part of the pilot-house, laid on as in the drawing.

O is the look-out hole. There are two of these on the forward part of the house; the shot above mentioned struck the port one.

The second drawing represents the present appearance of the upper part of the pilot-house.

I have the honor to be, sir, your most obedient servant,

JAMES W. SHIRK,
Lieutenant Commander.

Rear-Admiral DAVID D. PORTER, U. S. N.,
Com'dg U. S. Mississippi Squadron, Flag-Ship Black Hawk.

Expedition up the Yazoo.—Destruction of rebel steamers.

MISSISSIPPI SQUADRON, FLAG-SHIP BLACK HAWK,
Near Vicksburg, May 24, 1863.

SIR: I have the honor to inform you that the expedition I sent up Yazoo river, the day after I took possession of the forts on Synder's Bluff, has returned, having met with perfect success.

As the steamers approached Yazoo City, the rebel property was fired by Lieutenant Brown, (of the ram Arkansas;) and what he had begun, our forces finished. Three powerful rams were burnt: the Mobile, a screw vessel, ready for her plating; the Republic, being fitted for a ram with railroad-iron plating; and a vessel on the stocks, (a "monster,") three hundred and ten feet long, and seventy feet beam. This vessel was to have been covered with 4½-inch iron plating—was to have had six engines, four side-wheels, and two propellers. She would have given us much trouble.

The rebels had under construction a fine navy yard, containing fine sawing and planing machines, an extensive machine shop, carpenter and blacksmith shops, and all the necessary appliances for a large building and repairing yard. Lieutenant Commander Walker burned all these, with a large quantity of valuable building lumber; he also burned a large saw-mill that had been used in constructing the monster ram. The material destroyed, at a moderate estimate, cost more than two millions of dollars.

We had one man killed and seven wounded, by field-pieces, from the enemy's batteries, going up the river, but the wounded are doing well. I enclose you Lieutenant Commander Walker's report in relation to this affair. He deserves much credit for the handsome manner in which he performed the duty assigned him. If he could have obtained pilots, he would have succeeded in getting possession of all the rebel rams, instead of having them burnt.

I am, very respectfully, your obedient servant,

DAVID D. PORTER,

Acting Rear-Admiral, Com'dg Mississippi Squadron.

Hon. Gideon Welles,

Secretary of the Navy, Washington, D. C.

Report of Lieutenant Commander John G. Walker.

United States Steamer Baron De Kalb,

Mouth Yazoo River, May 23, 1863.

Sir: I have the honor to report that, in obedience to your order, I started from Snyder's Bluff on the 20th instant with the De Kalb, Choctaw, Forest Rose, Linden, and Petrel, on an expedition to Yazoo City.

Arriving at Haines's Bluff, I landed a force and spiked an 8-inch gun in the works there, and burned the carriage. I also burned some forty tents left standing, and a steam saw-mill. Arriving at Yazoo City at 1 p. m. on the 21st instant, I was met by a committee of citizens, who informed me that the place had been evacuated by the military authorities, and asking protection. Enclosed I send copies of the communications received, and my reply. The navy yard and vessels had been fired by the enemy, and I sent a working party to insure the destruction of everything valuable to the rebels. The vessels burned were the Mobile, a screw steamer ready for her plating, the Republic, which I understand was being fitted for a ram, and the vessel on the stocks, a monster, 310 feet long and 70 feet beam.

The navy yard contained five saw and planing mills, an extensive machine shop, carpenter and blacksmith shops, and all the necessary fixtures for a large building and repairing yard, which, with a very large quantity of lumber, was burned. I also burned a large saw-mill a little above the town. Most of the public stores had been removed; such as I found in town were taken on board the vessels or destroyed. Enclosed I send the lists of articles removed or destroyed by Acting Volunteer Lieutenant Brown, the officer detailed for that purpose. In the hospitals I found and paroled 115 soldiers, a list of whom I enclose. Returning, I left Yazoo City this morning, arriving here at 4 p. m.

At Liverpool landing, in a sharp bend of the river, we were attacked by a force of three field-guns and about 200 riflemen concealed in the bushes, and for a few minutes the firing was very sharp. The enemy retreated as soon as the vessels got into position to use their guns with effect. The Petrel, Linden, and Choctaw were struck by shot, but with no particular injury to either.

Sergeant Stockinger, of this vessel, was killed by a rifle shot. The Linden had five wounded, the Petrel two, and the Choctaw one. Most of the wounds, I am happy to say, are slight.

Very respectfully, your obedient servant,

JOHN G. WALKER,
Lieutenant Commanding.

Acting Rear-Admiral DAVID D. PORTER,
Commanding Mississippi Squadron.

Operations of fleet on Tennessee river under Lieutenant Commander S. L. Phelps.

UNITED STATES STEAMER BLACK HAWK,
Mississippi Squadron, near Vicksburg, May 25, 1863.

SIR: I have the honor to forward the following extract from a report made by Lieutenant Commander Phelps, commanding fleet on Tennessee river, giving an account of his operations on said river:

"UNITED STATES GUNBOAT CHAMPION,
"*Tennessee River, May* 14, 1863.

"SIR: On the 5th instant I left Paducah with the Covington, Queen City, Argosy, Silver Cloud, and this vessel, and proceeded up this river, destroying on the way every kind of boat that could serve the rebels to cross the river. On the 11th we were at Cerro Gordo, and I then sent the Covington, Argosy, and Silver Cloud to Eastport, the highest navigable point at this stage of water, and myself dropped down a few miles to communicate, by previous appointment, with Lieutenant Colonel W. R. M. Breckenridge. Along the river I heard of detachments of cavalry at various points, whose occupation chiefly consisted in plundering, in carrying off Union men, and in taking conscripts. At Linden, in Perry county, Tennessee, there was a rebel force of this kind posted. I arranged with Colonel Breckenridge to cross a small force and cover different points with the gunboats, places to which he could retreat, if need be, while he should attempt to surprise Linden. The boats above rejoined me on the 12th, having found all quiet above, and at night I dropped down the river to the landing for Decaturville, where I found the colonel with but fifty-five men of his regiment, all he had with him. Some from a Michigan regiment that were to join had failed to come in. We at once took the cavalry on board, crossed it over with little noise, and the boats took their position at intervals along the river some miles above and below. Colonel Breckenridge's movements were timed so that his arrival at Linden (twelve miles from the river) should be just at daybreak, and he completely surprised the place. The rebel pickets fired upon him and dispersed. Only some twenty of the 118 rebels at muster the evening before had time to reach the rendezvous at the court-house before it was surrounded. The little party returned with Lieutenant Colonel Frierson, one captain, four lieutenants, one surgeon, thirty regular rebel soldiers, ten conscripts, fifty horses, two transportation wagons, arms, &c., &c. With the court-house were burned a lot of arms and supplies. Three of the enemy were killed. Our loss, none; only one horse killed."

Very respectfully, your obedient servant,

DAVID D. PORTER,
Acting Rear-Admiral, Com'dg Mississippi Squadron.

Hon. Gideon Welles,
Secretary of the Navy, Washington, D. C.

Loss of the United States steamer Cincinnati.—Engagement with the Vicksburg batteries.

United States Mississippi Squadron,
Near Vicksburg, May 28, 1863.

Sir: I have the honor to inform you that, in accordance with Generals Grant and Sherman's urgent request, and being led to believe that the enemy had moved his guns to the land side, I fitted the Cincinnati for the occasion by packing her with logs and hay, and sent her down to enfilade some rifle-pits which barred the progress of our army. I had my doubts about the strength of the position, and took every precaution I could think of.

The Cincinnati started from the anchorage at 9 a. m., and, thinking it was only an attack on rifle-pits, I went down after her in a tug to direct the operations, if necessary. As I approached her I saw that she was coming up stream at a great rate under a heavy fire from all the enemy's guns in that vicinity; they had moved none, and were pouring the shot and shell into her very rapidly; still I could see none strike her, and went across the river to direct the firing of the mortar boats. She disappeared in a bayou, and I supposed she was taking a short cut through Old river to avoid the enemy's fire. In an hour after two of her seamen came to the bank, and I sent a boat for them. I was then informed that she had sunk. I enclose the captain's report and the telegraphic messages that passed between General Sherman and myself on the occasion. The general had good reason for supposing the guns had been removed, as it had been done at most of the other hill batteries. The Cincinnati went down with her colors flying, and kept them up after she was sunk, the rebels still firing on her. She can be raised when the water falls a little. Officers and men lost all their effects, only the public money being saved. As near as we can learn, twenty-five men were killed and wounded, and about fifteen missing—supposed to be drowned. The pilot was killed as she rounded to abreast of the batteries. Lieutenant Commanding Bache steered her out of the action himself.

Very respectfully, your obedient servant,

DAVID D. PORTER,
Acting Rear-Admiral, Com'dg Mississippi Squadron.

Hon. Gideon Welles,
Secretary of the Navy, Washington, D. C.

Letter of Major General Sherman.

Headquarters 15th Army Corps,
Walnut Hills, May 19, 1863.

Dear Admiral: My right is on the Mississippi. We have possession of the bluff down a mile or more below the mouth of the bayou. Can't you send immediately a couple of gunboats down? They can easily see and distinguish our men, and can silence a water battery—that is, the extremity of their flank on the river—and enfilade the left flank of their works.

I think nearly all the guns of their upper batteries are moved inside of Vicksburg, and are now on the land front.

You will have no trouble in distinguishing our flank; it is about $\frac{1}{4}$ mile below a cattle pen on the immediate shore of the Mississippi.

I would get General Grant to make this request, but he is far on the left flank, and it would take hours to find him.

Truly yours,

W. T. SHERMAN, *Major General.*

Admiral PORTER,
Or SENIOR OFFICER at mouth of Yazoo.

Report of Lieutenant Commander George M. Bache.

MISSISSIPPI SQUADRON,
Flag-Ship Black Hawk, above Vicksburg, May 27, 1863.

SIR: In obedience to your order, the Cincinnati got under way this morning at seven o'clock and steamed slowly down until a little abreast of where the mortars lay, when we rounded to. The enemy fired several shots from a gun called "Whistling Dick," but soon gave up.

At half past eight, with a full head of steam, we stood for the position assigned us.

The enemy fired rapidly and from all their batteries. When abreast of our position and rounding to a ball entered the magazine, and she commenced filling rapidly. Shortly after the starboard tiller was carried away. Before and after this time the enemy fired with great accuracy, hitting us almost every time. We were especially annoyed by plunging shots from the hills, an eight-inch rifle and a ten-inch smooth bore doing us much damage. The shots went entirely through our protection—hay, wood, and iron.

Finding that the vessel would sink, I ran her up stream, and as near the right-hand shore as our damaged steering apparatus would permit. About ten minutes before she sank we ran close in, got out a plank and put the wounded ashore. We also got a hawser out to make fast to a tree to hold her until she sank. Unfortunately, the men ashore at the hawser left it without making fast, the enemy still firing. The boat commenced drifting out, and I sang out to the men to swim ashore, thinking we were in deeper water (as was reported) than we really were. I suppose about fifteen were drowned and about twenty-five killed and wounded, and one probably taken prisoner, will sum up the whole loss.

The boat sank in about three fathoms of water, lies level, and can easily be raised. She lies within range of the enemy's batteries.

The vessel went down with her colors nailed to the mast, or rather the stump of one, all three having been shot away. Our fire, until the magazine was drowned, was good, and I am satisfied did damage.

We only fired at a two-gun water battery.

Very respectfully, your obedient servant,

GEORGE M. BACHE,
Lieutenant Commanding.

Acting Rear-Admiral D. D. PORTER,
Commanding Mississippi Squadron.

Additional despatch from Rear-Admiral Porter.

UNITED STATES MISSISSIPPI SQUADRON,
Flag-Ship Black Hawk, near Vicksburg, May 30, 1863.

SIR: I have the honor to enclose a communication from Lieutenant Commanding Bache, containing further particulars concerning the Cincinnati, with a list of killed, wounded, and drowned.

Also a letter from General Sherman, who witnessed the affair. From all accounts, the officers and crew of the Cincinnati behaved in the most handsome manner.

Very respectfully, your obedient servant,

D. D. PORTER,
Acting Rear-Admiral Com'dg Mississippi Squadron.

Hon. GIDEON WELLES,
Secretary of the Navy, Washington, D. C.

Additional report of Lieutenant Commander Bache, with list of casualties on the Cincinnati.

UNITED STATES STEAMER BLACK HAWK,
May 29, 1863.

SIR: I have to make the following additional report of the affair between the Cincinnati and the Vicksburg batteries. The only shot which did not penetrate us struck the bow casemate, which was well greased. Two shots entered the shell-room—one coming through the fantail and ricocheting up through the recess of the wheel, below the water-line; the other passing through the side, capsizing nearly all the boxes on the port side of the alley. It was immediately filled with water. A third shot entered the magazine, flooded it almost instantly, thereby preventing us from returning (any more) the enemy's fire. I believe she was hulled twice after this, as she was felt to lift bodily without other apparent cause. A heavy rifle shot penetrated through the pilot-house; the starboard tiller was shot away. All of her staffs were shot away, rendering it necessary to nail the flag to the stump of the fore staff. Several plunging shots went through the deck. One IX-inch, an VIII-inch, a rifle 30-pounder, a 32-pounder, and a 12-pounder howitzer were disabled. Two shots were fired after the vessel sank, one of them throwing up a shower of mud and water, drowning several men swimming.

I cannot notice one of my officers without the rest, all behaved so remarkably well.

I have to recommend for medals the following-named men, viz:

Thomas Hamilton, quartermaster, severely wounded at the wheel, afterwards returned to lend a hand, and had to be sent below; Frank Bois, quartermaster, coolness in making signals, also nailing the flag to the stump of fore staff when I called for *some one* to do so; Thomas Jenkins, seaman, Martin McHugh, seaman, F. E. Corcoran, landsman, and, from the Choctaw, Andrew Dow, (boatswain's mate,) were conspicuous for their bravery and coolness. There were no ordinary cases of performance of duty, for we were suffering terribly from a severely-accurate fire.

The casualties were as follows, viz: Killed—Henry Altonborough, pilot; Tobias Cody, carpenter's mate; James Thompson, landsman, Choctaw. Wounded—Daniel Hand, landsman, Choctaw, mortally, (since dead;) Peter Dalton, landsman, Choctaw, mortally; Gilbert J. Coleman, ensign, contusion; Simeon Shultice, first assistant engineer, slightly; Henry Boobey, ensign, slightly; G. H. Stevens, acting carpenter, contusion, severe; Charles Bratton, seaman, Choctaw, fracture of right forearm; William Woodruff, contraband, second-class fireman, fracture of forearm; Cloves O. Smith, landsman, splinter wound in right arm; Thomas W. Hamilton, quartermaster, contusion; Solomon Guess, master-at-arms, contusion; Patrick Rocket, first cabin boy, scalp wound; Geo. Washington, contraband, contusion; William H. Cohen, paymaster's steward, contusion; Isaac Foreman, contraband, captain's steward, contusion; Fred. Young, private, company C, 58th Ohio volunteers. Missing (drowned)—James Cooper, captain after guard; Patrick Burns, captain after guard; Henry Thornbury, seaman; Cornelius O'Neal, seaman; Leopold Snyder, landsman; James Pettingill, landsman; James Wilson, contraband, first cabin boy; Henry Truman, contraband, first cabin boy; Albert Williams, contraband, first cabin boy; Richard Howard, contraband, first cabin boy; William Redhom, corporal, company C, 58th Ohio volunteers; Martin Campbell, private, company C, 58th Ohio volunteers; George Just, private, company C, 58th Ohio volunteers. Thomas Smith, landsman, taken prisoner and paroled.

Respectfully, &c.,

GEORGE M. BACHE,
Lieutenant, Commanding.

P. S.—*June* 1, 1863.—John McMorrow, seaman, drowned.

Letter from Major General Sherman.

HEADQUARTERS FIFTEENTH ARMY CORPS,
Walnut Hills, May 28, 1863.

DEAR ADMIRAL: I was on the hill to our extreme right yesterday, ready to take advantage of any success to be gained by the gunboat attack on the enemy's left flank. At nine a. m. I saw four gunboats advance from below and engage the enemy's lower batteries, and soon the Cincinnati came down from above, steering directly for the upper water batteries.

From our position we could only see the hill which shielded them from the rear. As the gunboat approached she was fired upon from three points. We directed 38-pounder Parrotts, some 6-pounder guns, and our musketry opened on all points within reach, but these batteries were covered by the shape of ground. As the Cincinnati neared she fired several of her bow guns; but as the current would have carried her below, she rounded to, firing from her broadside guns, but soon presented her stern. The enemy's shot at first went wild, but soon got her range and struck her several times, and twice right under her stern. She ran slowly up stream, keeping mid-channel, and when about one and a half mile up, steered directly to the shore in the bend. I saw that her larboard quarter-boat was shot away, and her flagstaff, but otherwise she appeared uninjured. She ran to the shore and soon sank; her bow appeared down and her stern up, her upper decks out of water. The moment I saw her sink I sent a company of the 76th Ohio to her relief. I could see by a glass she was near shore, and her people on the bank.

Waiting a couple of hours to hear more definite news from her, I came to the centre of my line and despatched one of my aids, Lieutenant Hill, to see that all possible assistance should be afforded the crew, and received a message that a boat had been sent to you, and that, as soon as dark would make it safe, you would send a boat down with all the assistance required. I received the following official report. Inasmuch as you must know all, I have no occasion to report more than that the style in which the Cincinnati engaged the batteries elicited universal praise, and I deplore the sad result as much as any one could.

The importance of the object aimed to be accomplished, in my judgment, fully warranted the attempt. It has proved successful, and will stimulate us to further efforts to break the line which terminates on the Mississippi in such formidable batteries.

I am, with great respect, your obedient servant,

W. T. SHERMAN, *Maj. Gen.*

Admiral D. D. PORTER,
Commanding Mississippi Squadron.

Letter of thanks from Secretary of the Navy to Lieutenant Commander Bache.

NAVY DEPARTMENT, *June* 12, 1863.

SIR: Acting Rear-Admiral Porter has forwarded to the department copies of your reports of the 27th and 29th ultimo, detailing the circumstances of the loss of the United States steamer Cincinnati, under your command, in an attack upon the Vicksburg batteries.

Whilst regretting the loss of a ship that has so often successfully engaged the enemy, the sad casualties attending it, and the sorrows that have been brought to the hearts of the families of those who gave up their lives in the service of their country, it is gratifying to feel that the officers and crew of the Cincinnati performed their duty nobly and faithfully. All reports yet received testify to this fact; and General Sherman, with whom you were directed especially to co-operate, and who was an eye-witness, says, "the style in which the Cincinnati engaged the battery elicited universal praise."

Amidst an incessant fire of shot and shell, even when the fate of the vessel had been sealed, and destruction both from the elements and the enemy was threatened, the officers and men appear to have stood bravely at their posts, and it is a proud record of the Cincinnati that when her last moments came "she went down with her colors nailed to the mast."

It is with no ordinary pleasure that I express to you, and to the surviving officers and crew of the Cincinnati, the department's appreciation of your brave conduct.

Very respectfully, &c.,

GIDEON WELLES,
Secretary of the Navy.

Lieutenant GEORGE M. BACHE,
Late in command of U. S. Steamer Cincinnati, Miss. Squadron.

Expedition up the Yazoo river, and destruction of rebel transports.

MISSISSIPPI SQUADRON,
Near Vicksburg, June 1, 1863.

SIR: After the return of the expedition under Lieutenant Commander Walker up the Yazoo, and the destruction of the rams and navy yard, I despatched the same officer up again, with instructions to capture transports. The enclosed is his report. Besides those steamers mentioned as burnt, the rebels burnt the Acadia and Magenta, also two of their best transports. My object was to break up the transportation on the Yazoo, and, with the exception of a few steamers beyond Fort Pemberton, the rebels can transport nothing by water on that river. Steamers to the amount of seven hundred thousand dollars were destroyed by the late expedition; nine in all.

The Star of the West has sunk, completely blockading the Yallabusha river, and the gunboat Ivy was found sunk near Liverpool landing.

I am, sir, very respectfully, your obedient servant,

DAVID D. PORTER,
Acting Rear-Admiral, Commanding Mississippi Squadron.

Hon. GIDEON WELLES,
Secretary of the Navy, Washington, D. C.

Report of Lieutenant Commander John G. Walker.

UNITED STATES STEAMER BARON DEKALB,
Mouth of Yazoo River, June 1, 1863.

SIR: I have to report that I left this place on the morning of the 24th May with the DeKalb, Forest Rose, Linden, Signal, and Petrel. I pushed up the Yazoo as speedily as possible for the purpose of capturing or destroying the enemy's transports in that river. The Signal knocked down her smoke-stacks and returned the same night. Leaving the DeKalb with orders to come on as fast as possible, I pushed on, with the Forest Rose, Linden and Petrel, to within fifteen miles of Fort Pemberton, when I found the steamers John Walsh, R. J. Lockland, Golden Age, and Scotland sunk on a bar, completely blockading it up.

Failing in my efforts to make a passage through the blockade, I fired them, destroying all but such parts of the hulls as were under water. These steamers were fine boats, in good order, and if I had had the means, could have been raised and saved. I remained at that point during the night, and next morning at daylight was attacked by a force of the enemy, but after a sharp fire of a few minutes they beat a hasty retreat. Our only loss was two men belonging to the Petrel, wounded.

Returning down the Yazoo, I burned a large saw-mill twenty-five miles above Yazoo City.

At Yazoo City I landed and brought away a large quantity of bar, round, and flat iron from the navy yard.

Arriving at the mouth of Big Sunflower, I proceeded up that river about one hundred and eighty miles, until stopped by shoal water. At Indian Shoot I sent Volunteer Lieutenant Brown, of the Forest Rose, with boats through to Rolling Fork. He found a quantity of corn belonging to the rebels, which he burned. At the mouth of Bayou Quirer, hearing of steamers, I sent Lieutenant Brown, with the boats of the Forest Rose and Linden, up after them. After ascending ten miles he burned the Dew Drop and Emma Bett. The Linden burnt the Argo in a small bayou about seventy-five miles up Sunflower.

I also found the Cotton Plant sunk in Lake George, with nothing out of water but the tops of her smoke-stacks.

At Gawin's landing, on the Sunflower, I found and brought away a cutter which was lost on the Deer creek expedition. Returning, I arrived here last evening.

I have been much indebted to Lieutenants Brown, of the Forest Rose, and Smith, of the Linden, for their zeal and efficiency during the expedition.

I have as prisoners two engineers and a pilot in the service of the rebels, and several deserters and refugees.

I am, very respectfully, your obedient servant,

JOHN G. WALKER,
Lieutenant Commander, United States Navy.

Acting Rear-Admiral DAVID D. PORTER,
Commanding Mississippi Squadron.

Reports of Acting Rear-Admiral Porter of the siege of Vicksburg, and co-operation of the navy with the army.

UNITED STATES MISSISSIPPI SQUADRON,
Flag-Ship Black Hawk, near Vicksburg, June 9, 1863.

SIR: I have nothing particular to communicate with regard to the position of affairs here.

The army is still advancing close to the works. General Sherman is so close that he cannot get nearer without going in.

When the other generals are up with him, I presume that an assault will be made. Three batteries have been erected of naval guns, one consisting of two 8-inch guns, in General Steele's front, under command of Lieutenant Commander Selfridge.

This battery opened fire day before yesterday, and cleared everything before it. One battery of two 9-inch guns is being erected in General McPherson's front, and two 8-inch guns in front of General McClernand. These latter did not require naval assistance, only the guns; and have not made as much progress, the guns not being yet mounted. They will be in position very soon.

The mortars keep constantly playing on the city and works, and the gunboats throw in their shells whenever they see any work going on at the batteries, or new batteries being put up.

Not a soul is to be seen moving in the city; the soldiers lying in their trenches or pits, and the inhabitants being stowed in caves or holes dug out in the cliffs. If the city is not relieved by a much superior force from the outside, Vicksburg must fall without anything more being done to it. I only wonder it has held out so long.

If the city is relieved, and our army have to retire, we will lose everything we have—all of which could be prevented by an addition of thirty thousand men, which men can be spared from Missouri alone. If we do not get Vicksburg now, we never will.

The rebel steamer Lady Walton came down from Little Rock, Arkansas, a few days since, and gave herself up to the commanding officer at White river. I sent her to Cairo to the judge of the district.

Very respectfully, your obedient servant,

DAVID D. PORTER,
Acting Rear-Admiral, Com'dg Mississippi Squadron.

HON. GIDEON WELLES,
Secretary of the Navy, Washington, D. C.

UNITED STATES MISSISSIPPI SQUADRON,
Flag-Ship Black Hawk, near Vicksburg, June 20, 1863.

SIR: I have the honor to inform you that I received a notification from General Grant, last night at 12 o'clock, that he intended to open a general bombardment on the city at 4 a. m., and continue it until 10 o'clock.

I sent word to Commander Woodworth, at the lower fleet, to move up with all the vessels below and attack at the time specified.

Giving Lieutenant Commander Ramsay charge of a 100-pounder rifle, a 10-inch and a 9-inch gun, fitted on scows, I placed them after midnight close to the point opposite Vicksburg, protected by the bank.

At the time specified all our shore batteries opened, also the guns on the scows, and the mortars. A little later the gunboats also opened and kept up a heavy fire, advancing all the time, and throwing shells into all the batteries along the hills and near the city.

There was no response whatever; the batteries were all deserted. At 10 o'clock the vessels ceased firing, as did the scows and mortars also. The only demonstration made by the rebels from the water front was a brisk fire of heavy guns from the upper batteries on two 12-pounder rifled howitzers that were planted on the Louisiana side by General Ellet's marine brigade, which has much annoyed the enemy for two or three days, and prevented them from getting water.

I enclose you the reports of the commanders.

Very respectfully, your obedient servant,

DAVID D. PORTER,
Acting Rear-Admiral, Com'dg Mississippi Squadron.

Hon. GIDEON WELLES,
Secretary of the Navy, Washington, D. C.

Report of Commander S. E. Woodworth, commanding the General Price.

UNITED STATES STEAMER STERLING PRICE,
Below Vicksburg, June 20, 1863.

SIR: Agreeable to your instructions contained in your order of this morning, I proceeded with the Mound City to the point designated, but was unable to open fire on account of the hazy atmosphere which hung over the Vicksburg shore, completely hiding it from view.

After 7 o'clock was able to distinguish somewhat the location of the batteries. Opened fire on Whistling Dick battery, which was soon silenced; it fired twice, but not in our direction.

We also bombarded the other hill batteries as far up as the Hospital battery, driving every one from them, so much that not a single gun was fired after the silencing of Whistling Dick.

We also shelled the lower line of works of the enemy, running from the water to the crest of the hill, until there was no longer any appearance of an enemy to fire at.

Our army batteries ceased firing about 10 a. m. We continued to fire at intervals until 11 a. m. whenever the sign of an enemy would make its appearance within our range.

About the time we were retiring from action a rifle gun from the other side of Young's Point commenced firing at a battery occupied by General Herron's command, from which was flying an American flag. Sent a courier across the point to notify them of the fact.

Having been engaged for three and a half hours, and General Grant's lines being perfectly silent, we retired from action, leaving the Benton in her old position at the head of the towhead, and will send the Mound City back to Warrenton as soon as I obtain Captain Wilson's report. Enclosed I forward the reports of Captains Greer and Wilson, containing expenditure of ammunition. * * * * * * * * *

Very respectfully, your obedient servant,

SELIM E. WOODWORTH,
Commanding Price.

Acting Rear-Admiral D. D. PORTER,
Commanding Mississippi Squadron.

Report of Lieutenant Commander James A. Greer, commanding the Benton.

UNITED STATES STEAMER BENTON,
Below Vicksburg, June 20, 1863.

SIR: I have respectfully to report that, in obedience to your order of this date, this vessel got under way at 5.40 a. m. and stood up the canal. It was so thick and hazy that I could not see the batteries or any landmarks. I threw a few shells into the woods to the northward of Whistling Dick. At 8.30 it cleared away a little, and I fired at Whistling Dick, and a little northward of it; also at some cattle which I saw on the lowlands. Whilst lying above the canal a rifle gun from over the point fired, its shell bursting in the neighborhood of the position held by our troops. Seeing a soldier on horseback on the bank, I ran in and sent him over to the officer commanding the rifle to state where the shells were falling. We were not fired on, although in good range of Whistling Dick for a long time. We fired five 9-inch 15-second shells, and seventeen 10-second 9-inch shells. At 10.55 stood down the river to our old anchorage. I have also to report that last night I received a letter from Major General Herron asking for some more ammunition for the 32-pounder which he has belonging to this vessel. I supplied him with all I could spare.

Very respectfully, your obedient servant,

JAMES A. GREER,
Lieutenant Commander.

Commander S. E. WOODWORTH,
Senior Officer, below Vicksburg.

Report of Lieutenant Commander Byon Wilson, commanding the Mound City.

UNITED STATES GUNBOAT MOUND CITY,
Below Vicksburg, June 20, 1863.

SIR: In obedience to your orders of this date, I got under way at Warrenton at 5 a. m. and proceeded up the river with all despatch to join in the attack on the hill batteries.

About 7 a. m. I joined the Benton at the mouth of the canal. We were obliged to lie there some time, owing to the intense fog which hung over the hills, and it was not till 7.35 that we were enabled to throw a shell with any certainty.

I continued to fire as the batteries came in sight, till 10 a. m., when the signal to cease firing was made.

We continued up the river about half a mile above the canal, and at 11 o'clock returned down to our anchorage.

Strange to say, during all this time we received no response.

We expended (35) thirty-five 15-second 9-inch shells, (5) five 15-second 80-pounder rifle shells, and (4) four percussion Dahlgren shells.

I am, very respectfully, your obedient servant,

BYRON WILSON,
Lieutenant Commander.

Commander SELIM WOODWORTH.
Senior Naval Officer present.

Report of Rear-Admiral Porter.

UNITED STATES FLAG-SHIP BLACK HAWK,
Mississippi Squadron, near Vicksburg, June 26, 1863.

SIR: I was in hopes, ere this, to have announced the fall of Vicksburg, but the rebels hold out persistently, and will, no doubt, do so while there is a thing left to eat.

In the mean time they are hoping for relief from General Johnson. A vain hope; for even if he succeeded in getting the better of General Sherman, (one of the best soldiers in our army,) his forces would be so cut up that he could take no advantage of any victory that he might gain. General Sherman has only to fall back to our intrenchments at Vicksburg, and he could defy twice his own force.

The rebels have been making every effort to bring relief to Vicksburg through Louisiana, but without avail; with the few men we have at Young's Point, and the gunboats, we keep them in check, and a few days since, (as I reported to you,) the marine brigade, General Ellet, with General Mower's brigade, chased them away from this part of the country.

They have lined the river bank, and are annoying the transports a little, but the gunboats are so vigilant, and give them so little rest, that they have done no damage worth mentioning.

I have lined the river from Cairo to Vicksburg with a good force; the upper part under command of Lieutenant Commander Phelps, whom I have withdrawn, with those of his vessels which draw too much water, from the Tennessee. He has the Eastport, which he says is much improved in every way, and is a much superior vessel to what she was. I have had the Indianola's leaks stopped, machinery cleaned off, and hope to float her off the first rise in the river. I am having the Cincinnati's guns removed, and Colonel Wood, of the army, is erecting a battery on shore with them. I had now ten (10) heavy naval guns landed from the gunboats in the rear of Vicksburg, some of them manned by sailors. They have kept up a heavy fire for some days, doing great execution.

The enemy very seldom fire now, and *never* from the land side.

The mortars at this moment are throwing shells into the enemy's main water battery, which is quite silent and deserted. Deserters say they have six days' provisions, and will not yield until that is gone.

General McPherson blew up the main fort yesterday, and took possession of it; will mount our two 9-inch guns on it to-night, and some 30-pounder Parrotts. This fort commands all Vicksburg.

I am sorry to say that the health of the squadron is not good. We have many sick officers and men; the duty has been incessant, and most laborious working in a very hot sun.

Still the officers and men never murmur, and stand at their posts until they can stand no longer.

Very respectfully, your obedient servant,

DAVID D PORTER,
Acting Rear-Admiral, Com'dg Mississippi Squadron.

Hon. GIDEON WELLES,
Secretary of the Navy, Washington, D. C.

Surrender of Vicksburg.

UNITED STATES MISSISSIPPI SQUADRON,
Flag-Ship Black Hawk, Vicksburg, July 4, 1863.

SIR: I have the honor to inform you that Vicksburg has surrendered at last to the United States forces, after a desperate but vain resistance. That she has not done so sooner has not been for the want of ability on the part of our military commanders, but from the magnitude of the defences, which were intended to repulse any force the government could possibly send there.

What bearing this will have on the rebellion remains yet to be seen; but the magnitude of the success must go far towards crushing out this revolution, and establishing once more the commerce of the States bordering on this river.

History has seldom had an opportunity of recording so desperate a defence on one side, with so much courage, ability, perseverance, and endurance on the other; and if ever an army was entitled to the gratitude of a nation, it is the army of the Tennessee and its gallant leaders.

The navy has necessarily performed a less conspicuous part in the capture of Vicksburg than the army; still it has been employed in a manner highly creditable to all concerned.

The gunboats have been constantly employed below Vicksburg in shelling the works, and with success, co-operating heartily with the left wing of the army.

The mortar boats have been at work for forty-two days, without intermission, throwing shells into all parts of the city, even reaching the works in the rear of Vicksburg and in front of our troops, a distance of three miles. Three heavy guns, placed on scows—a 9-inch, 10-inch, and a 100-pound rifle—were placed in position a mile from the town, and commanded all the important water batteries. They have kept up an accurate and incessant fire for fourteen days, doing all the damage that could be done by guns under such circumstances. Five 8-inch, two 9-inch, two 42-pounder rifles, and four 32-pounder shell guns have been landed, at the request of the different generals commanding corps, from the gunboats, and mounted in the rear of Vicksburg, and whenever I could spare the officers and men from our small complement, they were sent to manage the guns—with what ability I leave to the general commanding the forces to say.

In the mean time I stationed the smaller class of gunboats to keep the banks of the Mississippi clear of guerillas, who were assembling in force, and with a large number of cannon, to block up the river and cut off the transports bringing down supplies, re-enforcements, and ammunition for the army. Though the rebels, on several occasions, built batteries, and with a large force attempted to sink or capture the transports, they never succeeded, but were defeated by the gunboats with severe loss on all occasions.

Without a watchful care over the Mississippi the operations of the army would have been much interfered with; and I can say honestly that officers never did their duty better than those who have patrolled the river from Cairo to Vicksburg. One steamer only was badly disabled since our operations commenced, and six or seven men killed and wounded. While the army have had a troublesome enemy in front and behind them, the gunboats, marine brigade under General Ellet, and a small force of troops under Generals Dennis and Mower, have kept at bay a large force of rebels, over 12,000 strong, accompanied by a large quantity of artillery. Though offered battle several times and engaged, they invariably fled, and satisfied themselves by assaulting half-disciplined and unarmed blacks.

The capture of Vicksburg leaves us a large army and naval force free to act all along the river, and I hope soon to add to my department the vessels which have been temporarily lost to the service, viz: the Indianola and Cincinnati.

The effect of this blow will be felt far up the tributaries of the Mississippi; the timid and doubtful will take heart, and the wicked will, I hope, cease to trouble us for fear of the punishment which will sooner or later overtake them.

There has been a large expenditure of ammunition during the siege. The mortars have fired 7,000 mortar-shells, and the gunboats 4,500; 4,500 have been fired from the naval guns on shore, and we have supplied over 6,000 to the different army corps.

I have the honor to remain, very respectfully, your obedient servant,

DAVID D. PORTER,
Acting Rear-Admiral, Com'dg Mississippi Squadron.

Hon. GIDEON WELLES,
Secretary of the Navy, Washington, D. C.

Detailed report of Acting Rear-Admiral Porter.

UNITED STATES MISSISSIPPI SQUADRON,
Flag-Ship Black Hawk, off Vicksburg, July 13, 1863.

SIR: I have made reports to the department of the different actions that have occurred on this river since the investment of Vicksburg; and it now remains for me to give credit to the different officers who have participated in the events transpiring here.

When I took command of this squadron this river was virtually closed against our steamers from Helena to Vicksburg. It was only necessary to impress the officers and men with the importance of opening communication with New Orleans, and every one, with few exceptions, have embarked in the enterprise with a zeal that is highly creditable to them, and with a determination that the river should be opened if their aid could effect it.

With such officers and the able general who commanded the army I have not feared for the result, though it has been postponed longer than I thought it would be.

First and foremost allow me to speak of Captain Pennock, fleet-captain, and commandant of station at Cairo. To him I am much indebted for the promptness with which he has kept the squadron supplied with all that was required or could be procured. His duty has been no sinecure, and he has performed it with an ability that could not have been surpassed by any officer of the navy. He has materially assisted me in the management of the Tennessee and Cumberland squadrons, keeping me promptly informed of all the movements of the enemy, and enabling me to make the proper dispositions to check him, exercising a most discreet judgment in moving the vessels to meet the rebels when there was no time to hear from me.

The war on the banks of the Tennessee and Cumberland has been carried on most actively. There has been incessant skirmishing between the guerillas and gunboats, in which the rebels have been defeated in every instance. So constant are these attacks that we cease to think of them as of any importance, though there has been much gallantry displayed on many occasions.

Lieutenant Commanders Phelps and Fitch have each had command of these rivers, and have shown themselves to be most able officers. I feel no apprehension at any time with regard to the movements in that quarter. Had it not been for the activity and energy displayed by Lieutenant Commander Fitch, Captain Pennock, and Lieutenant Commander Phelps, General Rosecrans would have been left without provisions.

To Captain Walke, Commander Woodworth, Lieutenant Commanders Breese, Greer, Shirk, Owen, Wilson, Walker, Bache, Murphy, Selfridge, Pritchett, Ramsey, and Acting Volunteer Lieutenant Hoel, I feel much indebted for their active and energetic attention to all my orders, and their ready co-operation with the army corps commanders at all times, which enabled them to carry out their plans successfully.

The Benton, Lieutenant Commander Greer, Mound City, Lieutenant Commander Byron Wilson, Tuscumbia, Lieutenant Commander Shirk, Carondelet, Acting Lieutenant Murphy, and the Sterling Price, Commander Woodworth, have been almost constantly under fire of the batteries at Vicksburg since the forty-five days' siege commenced.

The attack of the 22d of May, by the Benton, Mound City, Carondelet, and Tuscumbia, on all the water batteries, in which three were silenced and four guns injured or dismounted, was one of the best contested engagements of the kind during the war.

On the next attack of the same gunboats, when General Grant opened all his batteries for six hours, the river batteries were all deserted, and the gunboats moved up and down without having a shot fired at them, showing the moral effect the first attack had.

The attack of the Cincinnati, Lieutenant Commander Bache, on the water battery, will long be ranked among the most gallant events of the war; and, though Lieutenant Bache had the misfortune to have his vessel sunk under him, he well deserves the handsome commendations bestowed upon him by the department.

To Lieutenant Commander Ramsey, of the Choctaw, was assigned the management of three heavy guns placed on scows and anchored in a position to command the town and water batteries. Every gun the enemy could bring to bear on these boats was fired incessantly at them, but without one moment's cessation of fire on the part of our seamen, though the enemy's shot and shell fell like hail among them. This battery completely enfiladed the batteries and rifle-pits in front of General Sherman, and made them untenable.

The mortar boats were under charge of Gunner Eugene Mack, who for thirty days stood at his post, the fire continuing night and day. He performed his duty well, and merits approval. The labor was extremely hard, and every man at the mortars was laid up with sickness, owing to excessive labor. After Mr. Mack was taken ill, Ensign Miller took charge and conducted the firing with marked ability. We know that nothing conduced more to the end of the siege than the mortar firing, which demoralized the rebels, killed and wounded a number of persons, killed the cattle, destroyed property of all kinds, and set the city on fire. On the last two days we were enabled to reach the outer works of the enemy by firing heavy charges of twenty-six pounds of powder; the distance was three miles, and the falling of shells was very annoying to the rebels; to use the words of a rebel officer, "our shells intruded everywhere."

Lieutenant Commander Breese has been very efficient in relieving me of a vast amount of duty, superintending personally all the requirements made on the navy, and facilitating the operations of the army in every way that laid in his power. In every instance where it was at all possible to bring the Black Hawk into action against the enemy's batteries, he has not hesitated to do so, though she is not fortified exactly for such a purpose. His long-range guns have done most excellent service at different times.

I beg leave to mention the different commanders of the light-draughts, who have carried out my orders promptly, aided in keeping guerillas from the river, convoyed transports safely, and kept their vessels in good condition for service, viz: Acting Volunteer Lieutenant George W. Brown, commanding Forest Rose; Acting Volunteer Lieutenant C. Dominey, commanding Signal; Acting Volunteer Lieutenant J. S. Hurd, commanding Covington; Ensign Wm. C. Handford, commanding Robb; Acting Master J. C. Bunner, commanding New Era; Acting Volunteer Lieutenant J. V. Johnstone, commanding Romeo; Acting Volunteer Lieutenant John Pierce, commanding Petrel; Acting Master W. E. Fentress, commanding Rattler; Acting Volunteer Lieutenant T. E. Smith, commanding Linden; Acting

Volunteer Lieutenant E. C. Brennand, commanding Prairie Bird; Acting Volunteer Lieutenant J. Gandy, commanding Queen City. There are others who deserve commendation, but these seem to me the most prominent.

The action of the 4th of July, at Helena, wherein the Tyler participated so largely, has already been reported to the department. There is no doubt left on the minds of any but that the Tyler saved Helena, for, though General Prentiss fought with a skill and daring not excelled in this war, his little force of thirty-five hundred men were fast being overpowered by the enemy with eighteen thousand men, when the Tyler took a position and changed the fortunes of the day.

I must not omit to mention Acting Volunteer Lieutenants Hamilton and Richardson, of the powder vessels Great Western and Judge Torrence. They were unremitting in their attention to their duties during the siege, supplying without delay every requisition made on them by army and navy, and volunteering for any service.

When the army called on the navy for siege guns, I detailed what officers and men I could spare to man and work the batteries. Lieutenant Commander Selfridge had command of the naval battery on the right wing, General Sherman's corps. This battery was worked with marked ability, and elicited the warmest praises from the commanding general. One thousand shells were fired into the enemy's works from Lieutenant Commander Selfridge's guns. His services being required up the river, I relieved him a few days before the surrender, and Lieutenant Commander Walker supplied his place and conducted the firing with the same ability.

Acting Master Charles B. Dahlgren was ordered to report to General McPherson for duty, and was assigned the management of two nine-inch guns, which were admirably served.

Acting Master Reed, of the Benton, had charge of the batteries at Fort Benton—so named by General Herron, in honor of the occasion. General Herron generously acknowledged the services of those I sent him, which communication I enclose with this report.

I have endeavored to do justice to all who were immediately engaged in the struggle for the mastery of the Mississippi. To the army do we owe immediate thanks for the capture of Vicksburg; but the army was much facilitated by the navy, which was ready at all times to co-operate. This has been no small undertaking. The late investment and capture of Vicksburg will be characterized as one of the greatest military achievements ever known. The conception of the idea originated solely with General Grant, who adopted a course in which great labor was performed, great battles were fought, and great risks were run. A single mistake would have involved us in difficulty; but so well were all the plans matured, so well were all the movements timed, and so rapid were the evolutions performed, that not a mistake has occurred from the passage of the fleet by Vicksburg, and the passage of the army across the river, up to the present time. So confident was I of the ability of General Grant to carry out his plans when he explained them to me, that I never hesitated to change my position from above to below Vicksburg. The work was hard, the fighting severe, but the blows struck were constant.

In forty-five days after our army was landed, a rebel army of 60,000 men had been captured, killed, and wounded, or scattered to their homes, perfectly demoralized, while our loss has been only about 5,000 killed, wounded, and prisoners, and the temporary loss of one gunboat.

The fortifications and defences of the city exceed anything that has been built in modern times, and are doubly unassailable from their immense height above the bed of the river.

The fall of Vicksburg insured the fall of Port Hudson and the opening of the Mississippi river, which, I am happy to say, can be traversed from its source to its mouth without apparent impediment, the first time during the war.

I take this opportunity to give to Mr. Fendal and Mr. Strausz, assistants in the Coast Survey, the full credit they deserve for their indefatigable industry. Since they have been attached to the squadron they have been connected with almost every expedition that has been undertaken; they have kept both army and navy supplied with charts, when they could not otherwise be obtained; they were found ready at all times to go anywhere or do anything required of them, whether it was on a gunboat expedition or in the trenches before Vicksburg, engineering, when the general commanding called for volunteers from the navy. They have added to our collection of maps many geographical corrections which are valuable, and they have proved to me that no squadron can operate effectively without a good corps of surveyors.

I have the honor to be, very respectfully, your obedient servant,

DAVID D. PORTER,
Acting Rear-Admiral, Com'dg Mississippi Squadron.

Hon. GIDEON WELLES,
Secretary of the Navy, Washington.

Letter from Major General Herron to Admiral Porter.

HEADQUARTERS LEFT DIVISION INVESTING FORCES,
Vicksburg, July 5, 1863.

ADMIRAL: While congratulating you on the success of the army and navy in reducing the Sebastopol of rebeldom, I must at the same time thank you for the aid my division has had from yourself and your ships.

The guns received from the Benton, under charge of Acting Master Reed, a gallant and efficient officer, have formed the most effective battery I had, and I am glad to say that the officer in charge has well sustained the reputation of your squadron. For the efforts you have made to co-operate with me in my position on the left I am under many obligations.

Very respectfully, your obedient servant,

F. J. HERRON,
Major General.

Admiral D. D. PORTER,
Commanding Mississippi Squadron.

Letter from Major General Herron to Lieutenant Commander Greer.

HEADQUARTERS LEFT DIVISION INVESTING FORCES,
Vicksburg, July 5, 1863.

CAPTAIN: Having had from your ship, since the first of our siege operations on the left of the investing line, four of your heavy guns, under charge of Acting Master J. Frank Reed, I must, before their return to the ship, express to you my thanks for the good service they have rendered, and the admirable and officer-like manner in which they were handled by Acting Master Reed. His battery (which I have named, after your ship, battery Benton) has been our main support in advancing, and I learn has been a terror to the rebels in our immediate front.

The management and conduct of Acting Master Reed and his subordinates, William Moore and W. P. Brownell, cannot be too highly spoken of, and I can assure you they have nobly sustained the reputation of your ship and the Mississippi squadron.

Acting Master Reed is well worthy of promotion.

Congratulating you, captain, on the combined successes of the army and navy in reducing this Sebastopol of the rebels, I remain, very truly, yours,

F. J. HERRON,
Major General.

Captain J. H. GREER,
Commanding Benton.

Report of Lieutenant Commander Selfridge, commanding naval battery.

UNITED STATES STEAMER CONESTOGA,
Mississippi River, July 8, 1863.

SIR: I have the honor to present the following report of the naval battery, consisting of two 8-inch columbiads, whilst under my command.

Acting under your orders of June 1st, I reported to General Sherman, who located the battery nearly on the extreme right, not far from the river. After many delays I succeeded in getting one gun in position the night of June 4th. Fire was opened from it the next morning, and the next night the other was got in position. Opposed to us was an 8-inch columbiad, six hundred yards distant, and a 32-pounder, one thousand yards distant.

The columbiad was disabled by our fire the second day, and no further use made of it; the 32-pounder was also effectually silenced. There was nothing left at which to direct our fire but rifle-pits. Upon these I kept a slow and steady fire at different intervals during the day. Operating upon earthworks, it was impossible to know the damage inflicted. Deserters report, however, that our fire was so accurate as to cause the battery to be greatly feared, and that it had done them much harm. On June 25, agreeably to your orders, I turned my command over to Captain Walker.

It gives me pleasure to bear testimony to the good conduct of my officers and men. The labor imposed upon them was very arduous—working their guns under a hot sun, and frequently employed half the night repairing the damage inflicted during the day.

Very respectfully, your obedient servant,

THOMAS O. SELFRIDGE,
Lieutenant Commander.

Acting Rear-Admiral DAVID D. PORTER,
Commanding Mississippi Squadron.

Letter from Major General Sherman to Admiral Porter.

HEADQUARTERS EXPEDITIONARY ARMY,
Black River, July 4, 1863.

DEAR ADMIRAL: No event in my life could have given me more personal pride or pleasure than to have met you to-day on the wharf at Vicksburg—a Fourth of July so eloquent in events as to need no words or stimulants to elevate its importance.

I can appreciate the intense satisfaction you must feel at lying before the very monster which has defied us with such deep and malignant hate, and seeing your once disunited fleet again a unit, and, better still, the chain that made an enclosed sea of a link in the great river broken forever. In so magnificent a result I stop not to count who did it. It is done, and the day of our nation's birth is consecrated and baptised anew in a victory won by the united navy and army of our country. God grant that the harmony and mutual respect that exist between our respective commanders, and shared by all the true men of the joint service, may continue forever, and serve to elevate our national character, threatened with shipwreck. Thus I muse as I sit in my solitary camp out in the wood, far from the point for which we have jointly striven so long and so well, and, though personal curiosity would tempt me to go and see the frowning batteries and sunken pits that have defied us so long, and sent to their silent graves so many of early comrades in the enterprise, I feel that other tasks lie before me, and time must not be lost. Without casting anchor, and despite the heat, and the dust, and the drought, I must again into the bowels of the land, to make the conquest of Vicksburg fulfil all the conditions it should in the progress of this war. Whether success attend my efforts or not, I know that Admiral Porter will ever accord to me the exhibition of a pure and unselfish zeal in the service of our country.

It does seem to me that Port Hudson, without facilities for supplies or interior communication, must soon follow the fate of Vicksburg and leave the river free, and to you the task of preventing any more Vicksburgs or Port Hudsons on the bank of the great inland sea.

Though further apart, the navy and army will still act in concert, and I assure you I shall never reach the banks of the river or see a gunboat but I will think of Admiral Porter, Captain Breese, and the many elegant and accomplished gentlemen it has been my good fortune to meet on armed or unarmed decks of the Mississippi squadron. Congratulating you and the officers and men of your command at the great result in which you have borne so conspicuous a part,

I remain, as ever, your friend and servant,

W. T. SHERMAN,
Major General.

Admiral D. D. PORTER,
Commanding Fleet.

Congratulatory letter to Rear-Admiral Porter on the surrender of Vicksburg.

NAVY DEPARTMENT, *July* 13, 1863.

SIR: Your despatch of the 4th instant, announcing the surrender of Vicksburg on the anniversary of the great historic day in our national annals, has been received. The fall of that place insures a severance of the rebel territory, and must give to the country the speedy uninterrupted navigation of the rivers which water and furnish the ocean outlet to the great central valley of the Union. For the past year the key to the Mississippi has been Vicksburg, and so satisfied of this was the rebel chief who pioneered the rebellion and first gave the order to open the fires of civil strife, that he staked his cause upon its retention. By the herculean efforts of the army under the admirable leadership of General Grant, and the persistent and powerful co-operation of the navy, commanded by yourself, this great result under the providence of Almighty God has been achieved. A slave empire, divided by this river into equal parts, with liberty in possession of its banks, and freedom upon its waters, cannot exist. The work of rescuing and setting free this noble artery, whose unrestricted vital current is essential to our nationality, commenced with such ability by the veteran Farragut and the lamented Foote, and continued by Davis, is near its consummation. You have only to proceed onward and meet that veteran chief whose first act was to dash through the gates by which the rebels assumed to bar the entrance to the Mississippi, whose free communication to and above New Orleans he has ever since proudly maintained.

When the squadrons of the upper and lower Mississippi shall combine, and the noble river be again free to a united people, the nation will feel its integrity restored and the names of the heroic champions who signalized themselves in this invaluable service will be cherished and honored. Present and future millions on the shores of those magnificent rivers which patriotism and valor shall have emancipated, will remember with unceasing gratitude the naval heroes who so well performed their part in these eventful times.

To yourself, your officers, and the brave and gallant sailors, who have been so fertile in resources, so persistent and enduring through many months of trial and hardship, and so daring under all circumstances, I tender, in the name of the President, the thanks and congratulations of the whole country on the fall of Vicksburg.

Very respectfully, &c.,

GIDEON WELLES,
Secretary of the Navy.

Rear-Admiral DAVID D. PORTER,
Commanding Mississippi Squadron, Vicksburg, Miss.

Engagement at Milliken's Bend.

MISSISSIPPI SQUADRON,
Flag-Ship Black Hawk, near Vicksburg, June 9, 1863.

SIR: I have the honor to inform you that on the 7th instant, owing to a report that the rebels (in force about 4,000) were threatening Milliken's Bend, where a quantity of army stores were kept, (guarded by the two black regiments and part of the 29th Iowa,) I despatched the gunboats Choctaw and Lexington to that place to protect them.

Our troops had thrown up some extra intrenchments near the levee, and prepared to receive the rebels, with some doubts as to the issue. The enemy made his attack before daylight, and many of our men had not arrived at that point. The blacks, however, met the onset manfully, and a company of the Iowa regiment stood at their posts until they were slaughtered to a man, killing an equal number of rebels. The fight was desperate, and our men, overpowered, had to retreat behind the bank, near the water's edge, followed closely by the rebels. Then the gunboats opened on the rebels with shell, grape and canister, and they fled in wild confusion, not knowing the gunboats were there, or expecting such a reception.

They retreated rapidly to the woods and soon disappeared. Eighty dead rebels were left on the ground, and our trenches were packed with the dead bodies of the blacks, who stood at their posts like men. When last heard from the enemy was bound in the direction of Lake Providence. I despatched gunboats to meet him.

I am, sir, very respectfully,

DAVID D. PORTER,
Acting Rear-Admiral, Com'dg Mississippi Squadron.

Hon. GIDEON WELLES,
Secretary of the Navy.

Report of Lieutenant Commander F. M. Ramsay, commanding the Choctaw.

UNITED STATES MISSISSIPPI SQUADRON,
Flag-Ship Black Hawk, near Vicksburg, June 11, 1863.

SIR: I beg leave to enclose you the report of Lieutenant Commander Frank M. Ramsay, commanding United States steamer Choctaw, in relation to the part taken by the gunboats in the action at Milliken's Bend on the 7th instant.

Very respectfully, your obedient servant,

DAVID D. PORTER,
Acting Rear-Admiral, Com'dg Mississippi Squadron.

Hon. GIDEON WELLES,
Secretary of the Navy, Washington, D. C.

UNITED STATES STEAMER CHOCTAW,
Near Vicksburg, June 10, 1863.

SIR: In obedience to your order, I proceeded to Milliken's Bend on the 6th instant. At 3.15 a. m. on the 7th an army officer hailed the vessel and stated that our pickets had been attacked by the enemy. At 3.35, seeing sharp firing close into the camp of our troops, I opened fire with the 100-pounder rifle and 9-inch gun. Our troops, with the exception of the 23d Iowa, broke immediately and got under the bank of the river.

It was impossible for me to see the enemy on account of the high bank, and I could learn their position only by hailing our troops. About 8.30 the enemy commenced to retreat. At 9 the Lexington came up and threw a few shells into the woods.

Had not a gunboat been present the enemy would have captured everything. I fired forty-six percussion shells, (captured from the enemy at Haines's Bluff,) seventeen shrapnell, and five 5″ shells from the 100-pounder rifle, and thirty-four 5″ shells from the 9-inch gun.

The percussion shells captured at Haines's Bluff are superior to all the shells that have been furnished this vessel for the 100-pounder.

They are eleven and a quarter inches in length and weigh sixty pounds. Not one of them turned over; and only one or two failed to explode. Every one of our 5″ shells commenced turning over as soon as it left the gun. The shells from the 9-inch gun exploded at the proper time. I sent boats and brought on board twenty wounded officers and men, who received every care and attention from Acting Assistant Surgeon E. P. Robbins. Two of the officers died. The others were transferred to army transports to be carried to hospitals.

Very respectfully, your obedient servant,

FRANK M. RAMSAY,
Lieutenant Commander.

Acting Rear-Admiral DAVID D. PORTER,
Commanding Mississippi Squadron.

Movements of the gunboat fleet on the Tennessee river.

UNITED STATES MISSISSIPPI SQUADRON,
Flag-Ship Black Hawk, June 14, 1863.

SIR: I have the honor to forward a report of Captain S. L. Phelps, reporting the late movements of the gunboat fleet on the Tennessee river.

Very respectfully, your obedient servant,

DAVID D. PORTER,
Acting Rear-Admiral, Com'dg Mississippi Squadron.

Hon. GIDEON WELLES,
Secretary of the Navy.

Report of Lieutenant Commander S. L. Phelps.

UNITED STATES GUNBOAT COVINGTON,
Fort Henry, June 3, 1863.

SIR: Beginning with the date of the last report I had the honor to forward, I have now to inform you that the three gunboats left to co-operate in a movement across the Tennessee at Hamburg effected that purpose. On the 24th the Covington, at Savannah, crossed and covered a small force, which proceeded a few miles back and destroyed a cotton and woolen factory and a mill used by the rebels.

On the evening of the 26th fifteen hundred cavalry, with four howitzers, under Colonel Cornyn, 10th Missouri cavalry, arrived at Hamburg from Corinth, and the gunboats safely crossed the force over the river.

Colonel Cornyn made a forced march to Florence, Alabama, which place he captured after a sharp fight. He destroyed an immense amount of property of various kinds belonging to the enemy and in use by him, among which were three large cotton mills, and also large deposits of corn. The colonel estimates the value of the property destroyed at $2,000,000. He returned to Hamburg on the 30th, with sixty prisoners of war.

Meanwhile one hundred and fifty cavalry had landed at Savannah, under cover of the guns of the Covington, intended to operate in that neighborhood, and keep open communication between Colonel Cornyn and the gunboats.

The Fanny Barker and Robb covered the landing opposite Hamburg. The force at Savannah had captured some stock and brought it in, but on the 30th, while returning from an expedition with considerable stock, the commander found himself pressed by a rebel force, and was obliged to abandon his stock, and he barely succeeded in getting into Savannah, where I found him on the river bank protected by the Covington. Colonel Biffle, the rebel commander, had invested the town, demanding a surrender of our forces, and giving an hour for the removal of women and children if this demand was not complied with.

He received for answer, from both our commanding officers, a short and more expressive than civil reply, "to come and take them." Not wishing to interfere with Colonel Biffle's projects for getting his command badly cut up, it turned out as I expected, mere gasconade. I went on to Hamburg, where Colonel Cornyn had arrived, and I crossed his command over that night, with some one thousand additional animals captured.

It appears the enemy had pushed considerable force from Spring Hill and Columbia, General Bragg's left wing, towards Hamburg, in the hope of cutting off Colonel Cornyn's force, but had come up too late.

There was brisk skirmishing during the time we were crossing our people. In the morning the enemy was discovered in the woods near where the crossing was effected, and we shelled him out.

Numerous Union families from Harden county, Tennessee, became alarmed at the rebel threats of vengeance, and begged me to bring them down the river, and I have done so, having a large load of household effects they have been able to save.

Descending the river to as far as Perryville on the 21st, I there crossed a small force under Lieutenant Colonel Breckenridge, for the purpose of securing a quantity of leather at different tanneries. The rebels are seizing it wherever found, to carry off for army purposes. Eight hundred of them are reported encamped twenty miles distant, with the object of covering their part of this leather-seizing operation. I have on board a considerable quantity of hides, to be turned over at Paducah.

* * * * * * * * *

I am, respectfully, your obedient servant,

S. L. PHELPS, *Lieutenant Commander.*

I have ommitted to mention, there seemed to be reliable evidence that large detachments from Bragg's army are moving in a southerly direction. I ordered Lieutenant Goudy to look after one of these, said to be 10,000 strong, but probably much less, moving towards Clifton, on this river.

There is no doubt but that Bragg's army has been drawn on for re-enforcements for Vicksburg. Not one word in regard to General Rosecrans or his movements ever reaches this command. I left three gunboats with Lieutenant Goudy, the senior officer, to operate till my return, with coal and supplies.

S. L. PHELPS.

Engagement at Richmond, Louisiana, between the marine brigade, General Ellet, and the rebels.

UNITED STATES MISSISSIPPI SQUADRON,
Flag-Ship Black Hawk, near Vicksburg, June 18, 1863.

SIR: I have the honor to inform you that, hearing the enemy had collected a force of 12,000 men at Richmond, in Louisiana, nine miles from Milliken's Bend, I sent General Ellet to General Mowry, at Young's Point, to act in conjunction to break them up.

General Mowry promptly acceded to the request, and with about twelve hundred men, in company with the marine brigade, Brigadier General A. W. Ellet, commanding, proceeded to Richmond, where they completely routed the advance guard of the rebels, consisting of four thousand men and six pieces of artillery, captured a lot of stores, and the town was completely destroyed in the melée.

This duty was handsomely performed by the different parties concerned in it. I enclose Brigadier General Ellet's report.

I am, very respectfully, your obedient servant,

DAVID D. PORTER,
Acting Rear-Admiral, Com'dg Mississippi Squadron.

Hon. GIDEON WELLES,
Secretary of the Navy, Washington, D. C.

Report of Brigadier General A. W. Ellet.

HEADQUARTERS MISSISSIPPI MARINE BRIGADE,
Flag-Ship Autocrat, above Vicksburg, June 17, 1863.

ADMIRAL: I have the honor to inform you that, in accordance with your consent, I landed my forces at Milliken's Bend on the morning of the 15th instant, and proceeded toward Richmond, Louisiana.

At the forks of the road, within three miles of Richmond, I met General Mowry's command, and we proceeded forward together, my forces being in the advance. We met the enemy about a mile from town, who opened upon our advance line of skirmishers from behind hedges and trees and gullies, but they fled before our advance and took shelter behind the levee on the opposite side of the bayou, near the town.

The position was a good one, and very defensible. I deemed it imprudent to advance our line across the open field without any cover for my men against an enemy superior in number and well intrenched. I therefore ordered the artillery to the front and opened upon their position, and after a vigorous cannonade of near an hour, with all our guns, advanced our infantry through the woods on the right, with the intention of turning the enemy's left wing. They returned the fire of our artillery very vigorously for a time. Soon it slackened, and finally ceased altogether. When I arrived at the left of their position I found it abandoned and the enemy fled. He had destroyed the bridge over the bayou to prevent our following. We found three of the enemy dead upon the field, two mortally wounded, and captured eleven prisoners and about sixty stand of small-arms.

The enemy was commanded by Major General Walker, was a part of Kirby Smith's command, and consisted of two brigades, containing seven regiments, four thousand strong, with six pieces of artillery.

They retreated towards Delhi, where General McCulloch is said to be posted with a command about equal in strength to the one we encountered.

This was the same force that attacked the negro regiment at Milliken's Bend, a week before, and was repulsed.

Our entire loss was three men wounded—one, only, dangerously.

General Mowry's command participated throughout the fight most vigorously, and I feel indebted to the general for his prompt co-operation and advice, and his skilful manner of handling his forces. I returned the same day to my boats.

Very respectfully, your obedient servant,

ALFRED W. ELLET,
Brigadier General, Com'dg Mississippi Marine Brigade.

Admiral D. D. PORTER,
Commanding Mississippi Squadron.

Movements of the marine brigade from April 5 to May 29, 1863.

UNITED STATES MISSISSIPPI SQUADRON,
Flag-Ship Black Hawk, near Vicksburg, June 18, 1863

SIR: I have the honor to enclose Brigadier General A. W. Ellet's report of the movements of the marine brigade from April 5 to May 29, inclusive.

I am, very respectfully, your obedient servant,

DAVID D. PORTER,
Acting Rear-Admiral, Com'dg Mississippi Squadron.

Hon. GIDEON WELLES,
Secretary of the Navy, Washington, D. C.

Report of Brigadier General Ellet.

HEADQUARTERS MISSISSIPPI MARINE BRIGADE,
Flag-Ship Autocrat.

ADMIRAL: I have the honor to report that, agreeable to your order received at Greenville, Mississippi, on the 5th of April, I immediately got under way and proceeded as rapidly as possible to the Tennessee. The difficulty of obtaining coal caused me several days' detention at Cairo, Illinois. I left Cairo the morning of the 14th; reached Fort Henry on the following day. There I met Colonel Straight and his command, which, after one day's delay, was ready to accompany me. I found at Waverly landing a gunboat waiting for us, which continued to accompany us until we arrived at Eastport, without any enemy being visible.

From Eastport opened a communication with General Dodge, who requested I should drop my fleet down to Savannah, and make a demonstration from that place, to attract the enemy's attention while he advanced against Tuscumbia. At Savannah I disembarked my cavalry under the command of Major Hubbard, with orders to proceed eastward to Craven's mill, a point eighteen miles from Savannah, where the rebel Colonel Cox, with his regiment, made their headquarters, and to burn the mill and stores, &c., at that point. The march was effected in the night—the orders executed to the letter.

A large amount of flour, meal, and bacon was destroyed, several of Colonel Cox's pickets captured, and the major returned without any loss.

From Savannah to Clifton we burned several mills and a large amount of lumber. I stopped repeatedly and pushed my command back in the interior from various points. Finally, the water becoming so low as to create apprehensions for the safety of my boats, I determined to drop below Duck River shoals for their security.

On the morning of the 26th of April, some three miles below the mouth of Duck river, we were attacked by a regiment of Colonel Woodward's command, seven hundred strong, with two pieces of artillery. The attack was very fierce, but lasted only a few moments. The enemy had evidently mistaken us for unarmed boats, and were unprepared for the resistance they met with. We repulsed them with severe loss. We effected a landing as quickly as possible, (the nature of the banks causing considerable detention,) and pursued their retreat some twelve miles. We found the commanding officer, Major White, of the 6th Texan rangers, lying mortally wounded in a house four miles from the battle-ground, left by his men in their precipitate retreat. The enemy abandoned their dead, eight in number, and we buried them. Their wounded they succeeded in carrying off with them, owing to the necessary delay occasioned in landing my troops, from the unfavorable condition of the river banks, and the narrowness of the river at the spot.

Our loss was two killed and several wounded—only one seriously. We remained until the next day at this place, then proceeded to Fort Henry. We remained at Fort Henry three days for the purpose of mustering the command, and to coal the boats, and then proceeded again up the river. We found the water too low to ascend above Reynoldsburg, and were obliged to return.

On the 7th of May we left the river. We destroyed a great many flats and ferry-boats, and brought out a great many Union refugees, flying from the effects of the rebellion.

I arrived at Cairo on the 8th of May, and immediately proceeded to repair the damage my boats had sustained in the tortuous navigation of the Tennessee river.

Being unable to obtain any instructions from you, I telegraphed to the department at Washington, and was ordered to proceed down the Mississippi river, as the Tennessee was too low for my boats to act longer there.

On the 16th of May I left Cairo, stopping frequently to exercise my horses and drill my men. On the 22d of May I left Memphis. About thirty-five miles above Helena my commissary and quartermaster boat was fired into from the Mississippi side, about six miles above Austin. She was at the time some distance in the rear of the fleet. I received the report late at night, after the fleet had come to anchor, and made immediate arrangements to return in the morning and punish the perpetrators of the outrage. I landed at Austin before sunrise; could learn nothing from the inhabitants of the existence of any enemy near there. I discovered the wreck of a small trading boat that had recently been burned, and finally learned from an old negro that some rebels had just left the place upon our approach; that they had burned the boat the night before, captured the crew, and carried off the freight in wagons.

I immediately ordered the cavalry in pursuit, the infantry to follow as rapidly as possible. Major Hubbard came upon the enemy about eight miles out, near one thousand strong, with two pieces of artillery. He was surrounded, and his retreat cut off, but he was able to find a position where, by dismounting his men, he repelled the enemy's repeated charges upon his little band of less than two hundred men, and maintained his position until relieved by the arrival of the infantry. Our loss was two killed and nineteen wounded, mostly very slight wounds. We found five of the enemy dead on the field, obtained twenty-two stand of arms, captured one wagon and team, and three prisoners, besides several horses and mules.

I burned the town of Austin. By searching the houses we found that a lively trade of smuggling goods was carried on at this place. Whiskey, salt, molasses, fish, dry-goods, and medicines, in large quantities and unbroken packages, were discovered. As the fire progressed the discharge of fire-arms from the houses was constant and rapid, notwithstanding we had searched them all. Two heavy explosions of powder also occurred. We returned to Helena the same evening. On the following day I received a request from General Prentiss that I should remain with my command before Helena, as the place was threatened with an attack, until he could find something of the enemy's purpose.

On the 26th of May we left Helena, and, hearing of no enemy, proceeded slowly down the river, and arrived above Vicksburg on the morning of the 29th of May.

Very respectfully, your obedient servant,

ALFRED W. ELLET.

Acting Rear-Admiral D. D. PORTER.

Report of Acting Ensign W. C. Hanford, commanding gunboat Robb, of action at Cerro Gorda.

UNITED STATES GUNBOAT ROBB,
Fort Hindman, Kentucky, June 24, 1863.

SIR: I send you a report of the action that took place, on the morning of the 19th instant, at Cerro Gorda, resulting in the loss of one of my men, and two severely wounded.

On the afternoon of the 18th I suggested to Captain Hurd the possibility of catching some of Colonel Biffle's men, if I placed a couple of pieces of artillery at Cerro Gorda, opposite to where they came and fired across the river during the departure of gunboats from that place. It met Captain Hurd's approval.

In the evening I got a horse and rode down to Cerro Gorda, in order to pick out a good situation for the battery. Having found one to suit me, I returned and got my guns mounted on field carriages, and at 10 p. m. started down and had everything fixed ready, taking particular care to double picket all the roads to guard against surprise. I sent to man the battery sixteen of my best men. It was my instruction in the morning to run down to Saltillo, five miles, in order to give the "rebs" a good chance to come in.

On the morning of the 19th, about 4.30, I heard my guns firing. The Silver Cloud and myself started down, where we found that Biffle had made a charge on the battery with four hundred men; but my men were prepared for them, and opened their ranks well. I have learned since (but it is only a picked-up report) that Biffle lost fifty killed and wounded. I believe their loss was about that as they charged four abreast, (dismounted,) and came to within twenty yards of the cannon's mouth, while canister was being fired into them like rain. I lost, killed, Crawford J. Hill, fireman, and buried him at Craven's landing; Madison M. Hill, quarter gunner, and John N. Matthews, quartermaster, severely wounded. These I have sent to Smith's and to their homes.

Too much credit cannot be awarded to the men who manned the battery. They did their duty faithfully.

I am, sir, very respectfully, your obedient servant,

W. C. HANFORD,
Commanding Robb.

Acting Rear-Admiral DAVID D. PORTER,
Commanding Mississippi Squadron.

Respectfully forwarded. Mr. Hanford has proved himself to be a most faithful officer on all occasions.

DAVID D. PORTER,
Acting Rear-Admiral.

Attack on black troops at Goodrich's Landing, &c.

UNITED STATES MISSISSIPPI SQUADRON,
Flag-Ship Black Hawk, July 2, 1863.

SIR: On the 29th of June I received a communication from General Dennis, commanding the post at Young's Point, informing me that our black troops at Goodrich's landing had been attacked, and the rebels were getting the upper hand of them. I had already despatched a gunboat to that point, but sent off another without delay. I also directed General Ellet to proceed with the marine brigade to the scene of action, and remain there until everything was quiet.

The headmost vessel of the brigade (John Rains's) arrived there as the rebels were setting fire to the so-called government plantation, and, supposing her to be an ordinary transport, they opened fire on her with field-pieces, but were much surprised to have the fire returned with shrapnell, which fell in among them, killing and wounding a number. The result was a retreat on the part of the rebels, and the escape of a number of negroes whom they had imprisoned.

The gunboat Romeo also came from up the river about this time, and hearing the firing, hurried to the scene of action. The commander soon discovered the rebels setting fire to the plantation, and commenced shelling them. This he kept up for a distance of fifteen miles, chasing them along the river banks, the rebels setting fire to everything as they went along. The result was an almost total destruction of houses and property along the river front in that vicinity. The rebels carried off about 1,200 negroes who were employed working on the so-called government plantation.

* * * * * * * *

General Ellet landed his forces, and, in company with a black brigade, proceeded to chase the rebels, who were making a hasty retreat when they found there was a force after them. It was no part of their system to fight; they only came to plunder and carry off the negroes. General Ellet found the road strewn with broken carts and furniture, which the rebels left in their haste to get away from our forces. He pursued them as far as Tensas river, where they had crossed, burnt the bridges, and intrenched themselves for a battle. This was soon offered them, and our artillery opened on them and soon put them to flight, notwithstanding it was reported that they had twenty field-pieces.

General Ellet, not knowing the country very well, and having only a small force with him, deemed it proper not to pursue the rebels much further. He sent two hundred infantry across the bayou, and found that the rebels were retreating to Delhi, leaving all their plunder—splendid furniture, pianos, pictures, &c.—strewn along the road.

The unexpected re-enforcement of the brigade, and the gunboats, saved the whole of the black troops.

It is only a temporary peace, though, for as long as the blacks remain in such small force, so long will they be an object of attack.

The party who made this attack on the so-called government plantations are the same that attacked Milliken's Bend some short time since; they are a half-starved, half-naked set, and are in hopes of capturing some of the transports with clothing and provisions. They have not done so yet, and I think the precautions I have taken will prevent their doing so at any time.

* * * * * * * *

The siege of Vicksburg progresses as usual, the weather being so hot that little can be done between 9 a. m. and 4 p. m. The mortars are kept going constantly night and day, and the gunboats below the city co-operate with the army on shore, (General Herron's division,) and generally succeed in silencing the batteries. I am also placing nine, ten, and 100-pounder guns on scows, and have stationed them at the point nearest Vicksburg. They obliged the rebels to withdraw some troublesome guns from the fort which sunk the Cincinnati, and commanded every point in and about the city.

We have to be sparing with our ammunition, as the army depend upon us entirely for supplies for the heavy siege guns. I have landed from the gunboats, for the use of the army in the rear of Vicksburg, five 8-inch guns, two 9-inch guns, two 42-pounder rifles, four 32-pounder smooth-bores, besides the Cincinnati's guns, which are being mounted on shore by Colonel Woods, of General Sherman's division.

Whenever I could do so without impairing the efficiency of the vessels, I sent officers and crews with the guns. I have also supplied the carriages and ammunition wanted for the heavy guns captured from the enemy at Haines's Bluff, which place the army have strongly fortified inland.

Very respectfully, your obedient servant,

DAVID D. PORTER,
Acting Rear-Admiral, Com'dg Mississippi Squadron.

Hon. GIDEON WELLES,
Secretary of the Navy, Washington, D. C.

Letter of Rear-Admiral Porter enclosing Brigadier General Ellet's report.

UNITED STATES MISSISSIPPI SQUADRON,
Flag-Ship Black Hawk, off Vicksburg, July 8, 1863.

SIR: I have the honor to enclose Brigadier General Ellet's report of the operations of the marine brigade at Goodrich's landing and vicinity on the 30th ultimo.

I have the honor to remain your obedient servant,

DAVID D. PORTER,
Acting Rear-Admiral, Com'dg Mississippi Squadron.

Hon. GIDEON WELLES,
Secretary of the Navy, Washington, D. C.

Report of Brigadier General A. W. Ellet, commanding marine brigade.

HEADQUARTERS MISSISSIPPI MARINE BRIGADE,
Flag-Ship Autocrat, above Vicksburg, July 3, 1863.

ADMIRAL: I have the honor to report that, in accordance with your instructions, I proceeded without delay, on the evening of the 29th June, to Goodrich's landing with my whole available command. I found the troops at that point all under arms, and could plainly see the evidence of the ememy's operations in the burning mansions, cotton gins, and negro quarters, as far as the eye could reach. It was 2 o'clock on the morning of the 30th June when I reached the scene of operations. I at once ordered the entire force to disembark, infantry, artillery, and cavalry, and at daylight started in search of the enemy, Colonel Wood, commanding the negro troops, accompanying me with his whole force. About five miles out we reached Colonel Wood's outposts, where the night before two companies of negro troops with their officers had been surrounded and captured after a spirited resistance and considerable loss to the enemy. From this point I started the cavalry in advance to push the retreating enemy, and, if possible, hold them until the main body could be brought up forward. They overtook the enemy resting on the opposite side of the Bayou Tensas, and immediately engaged him, and held him in check till I arrived with the main body. The enemy had shown a large force of cavalry and several pieces of artillery. He endeavored to cross the bayou with one regiment of cavalry and turn my right flank, which movement was promptly met by our advance line of skirmishers, who repulsed the enemy handsomely. At the same time my artillery opened upon him with effect, and he retreated precipitately, having piled all the bridge flooring together and burned it to prevent our crossing. I crossed three companies on the sleepers, who followed the line of retreat for near two miles. They found the road strewn with abandoned booty stolen from the houses they had burned; among other articles, a very fine piano.

Three of the enemy's dead were found on the field, and some thirty stand of small-arms picked up. The enemy was undoubtedly, from information subsequently obtained, more than double our strength, and were provided with artillery and cavalry, but they were evidently not inclined to make a standing fight, their main object being to secure the negroes taken from the plantations along the river, some hundreds of whom they had captured. In passing by the negro quarters, on three of the burning plantations, we were shocked by the sight of the charred remains of human beings who had been burned in the general conflagration. No doubt they were the sick negroes whom the unscrupulous enemy were too indifferent to remove.

I witnessed five such spectacles myself in passing the remains of those plantations that lay in our line of march, and do not doubt there were many others on the twenty or more plantations that I did not visit, which were burned in like manner.

Our loss in the engagement was, Captain Wright, Co. D, cavalry, mortally wounded, (since dead,) and two negroes of Colonel Wood's, slightly wounded.

The day was intensely hot. I returned to the boat by slow marches, having marched the entire command nearly twenty-five miles without food, and almost without water.

Of course, the increase of sickness has been very great; over one hundred cases had to be removed to the hospital the following day, and many more are still suffering from the effects of such severe labor.

The steamer Raino, of my brigade, under command of Major Hubbard, arrived at Goodrich's landing a few hours in advance of us. As she passed a point two miles below Lake Providence, the enemy drew up in line of battle and fired a couple of shots from their howitzers at her. The Raino immediately replied from her two twelve-pounder brass guns, and the enemy fled in great haste.

Major Hubbard immediately landed in pursuit. He found three dead rebels, killed by his shells, gathered up twenty-six stand of small-arms, and rescued some hundreds of captured negroes.

Very respectfully, your obedient servant,

ALFRED W. ELLET,
Commanding Mississippi Marine Brigade.

Acting Rear-Admiral D. D. PORTER,
Commanding Mississippi Squadron.

Rebel attack on Helena, Arkansas.—Co-operation of the gunboats.

UNITED STATES MISSISSIPPI SQUADRON,
Flag-Ship Black Hawk, off Vicksburg, July 9, 1863.

SIR: On the 21st of June I received intimation from various sources, spies, deserters, &c., that the rebel General Price was moving from Arkansas towards the Mississippi river, with a large force in three columns, and a quantity of heavy artillery, for the purpose of seizing on some point on the river, cut off our transports, and relieve Vicksburg. I immediately made the proper dispositions to meet the rebels at such points as I knew to be assailable, and Helena being a desirable point for the rebels to get possession of, I sent what I considered a sufficient force to that vicinity. The Bragg, Tyler, and Hastings were the vessels detailed. General Prentiss had, however, no apprehension of an attack.

The Bragg remained there, while the other two cruised in the vicinity. On the 1st or 2d of July Lieutenant Commander Phelps, whom I had put in charge of the upper river, sent the Tyler back to Helena, anticipating an attack there. When Lieutenant Commander Pritchett arrived, General Prentiss had received notice of the advance of General Price on Helena, with 15,000 men. Having only 3,500 men, he made the best disposition for the attack that he could make under the circumstances. The rebels attacked the outworks of our troops on July 4 with their whole force, and as the works were slight, succeeded in driving in the small force opposed to them, getting possession of a small fort and four light guns. Proceeding on and overpowering our weak outposts, the rebels succeeded in reaching the crest of the hill which commanded the town of Helena, and would likely have obtained possession of it, but the gunboat Tyler opened on them with her heavy battery of shell guns at easy range, and cut them up very badly, while two thirty-pounders on the hill, manned by the troops, also opened a cross-fire on them, and between the gunboat and small fort the enemy were cut to pieces. Many of them threw down their arms and fled in a panic. The troops under General Prentiss behaved bravely and fought most gallantly. They charged the discomfitted mass of the rebels with the bayonet while the Tyler was mowing down the retreating mob with shrapnell and shell, and the victory was ours. The garrison pursued and captured over nine hundred men as prisoners, and I am informed that quite one thousand five hundred were killed and wounded—nearly as many as composed our garrison at Helena.

This has been one of the most signal defeats the enemy have met with for some time. Lieutenant Commander Pritchett deserves great credit for the share he took in the fight; the effective manner in which he delivered his fire, and the position he took, enabled him to check the enemy when they were very certain in their own mind of getting possession of Helena.

This affair will likely break up Price's army, and he is now retreating towards Alexandria. In the morning I shall send a strong force of gunboats up the Red river to ascend the Tensas and Washita, in hopes of intercepting him and his command. He has eleven transports up the Tensas, which I am pretty sure of disabling.

I have the honor to remain, very respectfully, your obedient servant,

DAVID D. PORTER,
Acting Rear-Admiral, Com'dg Mississippi Squadron.

Hon. GIDEON WELLES,
Secretary of the Navy, Washington, D. C.

Report of Lieutenant Commander J. M. Pritchett.

UNITED STATES GUNBOAT TYLER,
Helena, Arkansas, July 6, 1863.

SIR: I have the honor to report that General Holmes attacked this place on the morning of the 4th instant, with about 18,000 men, between the hours of 4 and 5 a. m., and after eight hours' hard fighting we repulsed the enemy with a loss of nearly three thousand men killed and wounded, and prisoners; we have already shipped to Memphis, Tennessee, between eight hundred and nine hundred prisoners.

General Prentiss has now between four hundred and five hundred of the enemy's wounded, found on the field, and they are still coming in.

I am informed by the officers of the army that, had it not been for the assistance rendered by this vessel, the town would have been captured.

It affords me great pleasure to state that my officers and crew conducted themselves in the most creditable manner.

Very respectfully, your obedient servant,

JAS. M. PRITCHETT,
Lieutenant Commander.

Rear-Admiral D. D. PORTER,
Commanding Mississippi Squadron.

Additional particulars of the attack on Helena.

UNITED STATES MISSISSIPPI SQUADRON,
Flag-Ship Black Hawk, off Vicksburg, July 11, 1863.

SIR: I have the honor to enclose you a full report of the late affair at Helena, where the gunboat Tyler saved the day, and enabled our little band of soldiers to capture a number of the enemy.

I remain, very respectfully, your obedient servant,

DAVID D. PORTER,
Acting Rear-Admiral, Com'dg Mississippi Squadron.

Hon. GIDEON WELLES,
Secretary of the Navy, Washington, D. C.

Report of Lieutenant Commander S. S. Phelps.

UNITED STATES IRON-CLAD RAM EASTPORT,
Helena, Arkansas, July 8, 1863.

SIR: General Holmes, with a reported force of eighteen thousand rebels, attacked this place at daylight on the morning of the 4th instant, and was repulsed after a hard-contested fight of several hours' duration.

The enemy attacked the centre of the defences and carried the rifle-pits and a battery upon the crest of the hills in the rear, which commanded not only Helena itself, but also all the other defensive works, including Fort Curtis. After possessing himself of that position, he pushed large forces down the slope of the ridge into the gorges, and his sharpshooters began the work of driving the artillerists from the guns in the main fort. Rebel guns, both above and below the town, had been planted upon commanding positions, and opened fire upon the line of defensive works across the river bottom, about one thousand yards in width, and his troops were in force near them to secure the advantages the capture of the works upon the hills would offer for closing upon the town from both directions along the river bottom. The Tyler had been covering the approach by the old town road; but Captain Pritchett discovered the enemy pressing down the hill-side after the capture of the battery in the centre, and took up such a position that, while his broadside guns poured a destructive fire upon the slopes and enfiladed the ravines, his stern guns effectually silenced the rebel battery below, and his bow guns played simultaneously upon the upper one. The slaughter of the enemy at this time was terrible, and all unite in describing the horrors of that hill-side and the ravines after the battle as baffling description, the killed being literally torn to pieces by shell, and the avenging fire of the gunboat pursued the enemy two or three miles to his reserve forces, creating a panic there which added not a little to the end of victory.

The enemy's loss is very heavy. Our forces have buried three hundred and eighty of his killed, and many places have been found where he had himself buried his dead. His wounded number eleven hundred, and the prisoners are also eleven hundred. Our cavalry forces are hourly discovering dead and wounded in the surrounding country, and are bringing in stragglers and deserters. Boats passing up the river for two days after the battle were continually hailed by deserters from the rebel ranks wishing to get on board to escape.

An examination of the field and the reports I hear convince me that the Tyler contributed greatly to the defeat of the enemy, and the terrible slaughter in his ranks is largely hers. It is due to Captain Pritchett to add that he took up an admirable position, and used his battery in a manner alike creditable to himself and to his officers and men.

First at Belmont, then at Pittsburg landing, and now here, the Tyler has been of inestimable value, and has saved the fortunes of the day. The garrison, numbering but three thousand three hundred men, with lines entirely too extensive for such a force, evidently fought with a courage and determination without superior example in this war.

Our loss in killed and wounded is about one hundred and eighty.

I am, respectfully, your obedient servant,

S. L. PHELPS, *Lieut. Com'dr,*
Commanding Second Division Mississippi Squadron.

Acting Rear-Admiral DAVID D. PORTER,
Commanding Mississippi Squadron.

Letter from Major General Prentiss, complimenting Lieut. Com'dr Pritchett.

HEADQUARTERS DISTRICT OF EASTERN ARKANSAS,
Helena, Arkansas, July 9, 1863.

ADMIRAL: I take pleasure in transmitting to you my testimony concerning the valuable assistance rendered me during the battle at this place on the 4th instant by Lieutenant Commander James M. Pritchett, of the gunboat Tyler. I assure you, sir, that he not only acquitted himself with honor and distinction during the engagement proper, but with a zeal and patience as rare as they are commendable. When informed of the probabilities of an attack on this place he lost no time and spared no labor to make himself thoroughly acquainted with the topography of the surrounding country; and I attribute not a little of our success in the late battle to his full knowledge of the situation, and his skill in adapting the means within his command to the end to be obtained. Nor can I refrain from mentioning that after the engagement, and while we were expecting a renewal of the attack, Commander Pritchett, commanding a division of your fleet, was unusually efficient in procuring timely re-enforcements.

Permit me to add, sir, that I can conceive of no case wherein promotion would be more worthily bestowed than in the case of Commander Pritchett, and it will afford me much pleasure to learn that his services have received a proper reward. I write this communication, sir, quite unsolicited, and without the knowledge of Commander Pritchett.

I have the honor to be, sir, with much respect, your obedient servant,

B. M. PRENTISS, *Major General.*

DAVID D. PORTER,
Rear-Admiral, Commanding Mississippi Squadron.

Congratulatory letter to Lieutenant Commander James M. Pritchett.

NAVY DEPARTMENT, *July* 27, 1863.

SIR: I have received from Rear-Admiral Porter the reports of your successful co-operation with the army in repelling an attack of a much superior rebel force upon the troops of General Prentiss at Helena, Arkansas, on the 4th instant.

Your prompt action on the occasion deserves and receives the unqualified approbation of the department. Rear-Admiral Porter and General Prentiss compliment you in terms of great praise for your skill and the effective management of the guns of the Tyler, which were served with such disastrous and signal effect upon the ranks of the enemy.

It is no reflection upon the troops of General Prentiss, who are represented to have fought with determined gallantry and bravery against overwhelming numbers, to say that they were saved, in all probability, from serious disaster by the valuable assistance rendered by the Tyler, under your command.

Accept the department's congratulations for yourself and the officers and men under your command for your glorious achievement, which adds another to the host of brilliant successes of our navy and army on the anniversary of our national independence.

Very respectfully, &c.,

GIDEON WELLES,
Secretary of the Navy.

Lieut. Com'dr JAMES M. PRITCHETT, U. S. N.,
Com'dg U. S. Gunboat Tyler, Mississippi Squadron.

Naval and military expedition to Yazoo City.—Engagement with batteries.

UNITED STATES MISSISSIPPI SQUADRON,
Flag-Ship Black Hawk, off Vicksburg, July 14, 1863.

SIR: Hearing that General Johnson was fortifying Yazoo City with heavy guns, and gathering troops there for the purpose of obtaining supplies for his army from the Yazoo country, also that the remainder of the enemy's best transports were there, showing a possibility of his attempt to escape, Major General Grant and myself determined to send a naval and military expedition up there to capture them. The Baron De Kalb, New National, Kenwood, and Signal were despatched, under command of Lieutenant Commander John G. Walker, with a force of troops, numbering five thousand, under Major General Frank J. Herron.

Pushing up to the city, the Baron De Kalb engaged the batteries, which were all prepared to receive her, and after finding out their strength, dropped back to notify General Herron, who immediately landed his men, and the army and navy made a combined attack on the enemy's works. The rebels soon fled, leaving everything in our possession, and set fire to four of their finest steamers that ran on the Mississippi river in times past.

The army pursued the enemy, and captured their rear guard of 260 men, and at last accounts were taking more prisoners. Six (6) heavy guns and one vessel, formerly a gunboat, fell into our hands, and all the munitions of war. Unfortunately, while the Baron De Kalb was moving slowly along she run foul of a torpedo, which exploded and sunk her. There was no sign of anything of the kind to be seen. While she was going down another exploded under her stern. The water is rising fast in the Yazoo, and we can do nothing more than get the guns out of her and then get her into deep water, where she will be undisturbed until we are able to raise her.

But for the blowing up of the Baron De Kalb it would have been a good move. We have generally obtained information of torpedoes from negroes and deserters, but heard nothing of this. Many of the crew were bruised by the concussion, which was severe, but no lives were lost. The officers and men lost everything. She went down in fifteen minutes. We must have her up again as soon as possible. We have much to contend with in these narrow rivers, and cannot guard against these hidden dangers while an enemy's flag floats. The usual lookout was kept for torpedoes, but this is some new invention of the enemy, which we will guard against hereafter. An attempt was made by the perpetrator, late Lieutenant Isaac N. Brown, to plant torpedoes once before, but the people of Yazoo City threatened to hang him if he did so. We felt sure they would not permit it on this occasion.

While a rebel flag floats anywhere, the gunboats must follow it up. The officers and men risk their lives fearlessly on these occasions, and I hope the department will not take too seriously the accidents which happen to the vessels, when it is impossible to avoid them.

I have the honor to be, very respectfully, your obedient servant,

DAVID D. PORTER,

Acting Rear-Admiral, Com'dg Mississippi Squadron.

Hon. GIDEON WELLES,

Secretary of the Navy, Washington, D. C.

Expedition into Red river region.—Capture of steamers.

UNITED STATES MISSISSIPPI SQUADRON,

Flag-Ship Black Hawk, off Vicksburg, July 18, 1863.

SIR: I have the honor to inform you that the expedition I sent into the Red river region proved very successful. Ascending the Black and Tensas rivers, (running parallel with the Mississippi,) Lieutenant Commanding Selfridge made the head of navigation—Tensas lake and Bayou Macon, thirty miles above Vicksburg, and within five or six miles of the Mississippi river.

The enemy were taken completely by surprise, not expecting such a force in such a quarter. The rebels that have ascended to that region will be obliged to move further back from the river, if not to go away altogether. Lieutenant Commanding Selfridge divided his forces on finding that the transports which had been carrying stores to Walker's army had escaped up some of the narrow streams. He sent the Manitou and Rattler up the Little Red river, (a small tributary of the Black,) and the Forest Rose and Petrel up the Tensas. The night was dark, and it was raining very hard, and the Manitou and Rattler succeeded in capturing the rebel steamer Louisville, one of the largest and perhaps the best steamers now in the western waters. Up the Tensas, or one of its tributaries, the Forest Rose and Petrel captured the steamer Elmira, loaded with stores, sugar, and rum for the rebel army.

Finding that the steamers which had conveyed General Walker's army had returned up the Washita, the expedition started up that river, and came suddenly upon two rebel steamers; but the rebels set them on fire, and they were consumed so rapidly that their names could not be ascertained. One steamer loaded with ammunition escaped above the fort at Harrisonburg, which is a very strong work, and unassailable with wooden gunboats. It is on an elevation over one hundred feet high, which elevation covers what water batteries of heavy guns there are.

Lieutenant Commander Selfridge was fortunate enough, however, to hear of a large quantity of ammunition that had lately been hauled from Natchez and deposited near Trinity, (nearly due west of Natchez,) and from whence stores, provisions, cattle, guns, and ammunition are transported. He captured fifteen thousand rounds of smooth-bore ammunition, one thousand rounds of Enfield rifle and two hundred and twenty-four rounds of fixed ammunition for guns, a rifle thirty-pounder Parrott gun-carriage, fifty-two hogsheads of sugar, ten puncheons of rum, nine barrels flour, fifty barrels salt, all belonging to the confederate government.

At the same time he heard of a large amount of ammunition that had started from Natches for Trinity, and was lying in wagons on the road half way across. He despatched a boat around to inform me of it, but General Ransom, who had landed a few days before at Natchez, hearing of it, also sent a detachment of cavalry and captured the whole. Thus Walker's army is left almost without ammunition.

The officers and men have shown great energy on this expedition, and have met with no mishaps. They procured a good deal of information by which future movements will be regulated.

The people in the whole of that section are very hostile to the government—rank rebels.

I have the honor to be, &c.,

DAVID D. PORTER,
Rear-Admiral, Com'dg Mississippi Squadron.

Hon. GIDEON WELLES,
Secretary of the Navy.

Destruction of steam foundry in Vicksburg.

UNITED STATES MISSISSIPPI SQUADRON,
Flag-Ship Black Hawk, off Vicksburg, July 20, 1863.

SIR: I forwarded by last mail, which should have been accompanied with this letter, a report of General Ellet in relation to a battery of small guns placed opposite Vicksburg, which is said to have annoyed the enemy very much. I think I can approve all that General Ellet has said in relation to the officer in charge of it. It certainly stopped the work in the foundry and prevented the rebels from casting cannon balls, at which they were busily engaged.

Very respectfully, your obedient servant,

DAVID D. PORTER,
Acting Rear-Admiral, Com'dg Mississippi Squadron.

Hon. GIDEON WELLES,
Secretary of the Navy, Washington, D. C.

Report of Brigadier General Ellet.

HEADQUARTERS MISSISSIPPI MARINE BRIGADE,
Flag-Ship Autocrat, Young's Point, July 9, 1863.

ADMIRAL: I have the honor to enclose a report from Captain Groshon respecting the operations of the 20-pounder Parrott gun placed on a point opposite Vicksburg by my order, and worked by himself, for the purpose of destroying the steam foundry operating in that city.

I am glad to be able to inform you that the gun accomplished all for which it was intended. The work at the foundry was stopped, the boiler having been exploded by a shot, and considerable damage was done to that and other buildings.

I cannot refrain, in this connexion, from calling your attention to the merit of this undertaking. To erect a battery in the very face of such frowning forts as protected the river front of Vicksburg; to fire it continually for a space of ten days, in open view, in defiance of the concentrated discharge of all the enemy's guns, and this without the slightest injury to a single person engaged, and with the most complete results as to the object for which it was intended, render those worthy of special mention who so faithfully discharged that duty. The fort was erected and the gun put in position by Lieutenant Colonel George E. Currie, aided by First Master Samuel Herricks, with the soldiers from the Lieutenant Adams, of this command. The gun was commanded and sighted by Captain Groshon in person.

Very respectfully, your obedient servant,

ALFRED W. ELLET,
Brigadier General, Com'dg Mississippi Marine Brigade.

Admiral D. D. PORTER,
Commanding Mississippi Squadron.

Report of Captain Thomas C. Groshon, of the Marine Brigade.

HEADQUARTERS FORT ADAMS, *July* 5, 1863.

SIR: In compliance with your request, I submit the following report:

Your order to Lieutenant Colonel George E. Currie to plant the 20-pounder Parrott gun (belonging to United States steamer B. J. Adams) on the point opposite the foundry in Vicksburg, to reduce said foundry, was commenced on the night of the 19th of June. As soon as it was sufficiently dark Lieutenant Colonel Currie, in company with Captain O. F. Brown, 1st battalion cavalry, Mississippi marine brigade; Captain Hews, company C; Captain Fishers, company E; companies F and K, 1st infantry, Mississippi marine brigade, repaired to the place selected by him to plant the gun. After four days' and nights' hard work, with the assistance of Masters Hendricks and Malbon, of the Autocrat and Adams, we succeeded in building a casemated fort within a mile of the city of Vicksburg, on the opposite side of the river, covering it with one thickness of railroad iron, deeming it sufficient protection for both men and gun.

On the morning of the 23d of June, at 9 o'clock, I opened fire on the city—fired five rounds. The enemy responded promptly 77 rounds, from five different guns—32, 64, and 128-pounders. Although there was no damage done to the fort, it was thought best to strengthen the work by adding one more thickness of railroad iron, which made it sufficiently strong to withstand the heaviest imaginable fire.

On the 24th I fired seven rounds; the enemy returned seventy-eight rounds. The fort was struck once, but the majority of the shots were too high. These shots came principally from the 128-pounders; no damage done yet. I fired twenty rounds on the 25th, all of which were directed at the foundry and machine shop, the effects of which accomplished the desired object. The enemy returned but six rounds, doing no damage whatever. On the 26th I fired eight rounds at different buildings in the city. The enemy returned thirteen rounds; no damage done. On the 27th I fired twenty-eight rounds. This day I suppose the shots had but little or no effect, or else the enemy thought it impossible to silence the gun, as they did not return the fire at all. On the 28th I fired seven rounds, the enemy returning sixty-four rounds. They had by this time got perfect range of the fort, and struck it three times during the day's firing. The damage done was but slight, and easily repaired. I fired but two rounds on the 29th, the enemy returning fifteen rounds. They still kept the range, and seemed to strike the fort at their pleasure. Four shots struck the fort, doing no damage to it, but the shot cut in pieces railroad iron and ties that were lying in front and on the top of the fort; also tearing up the ground in every direction, rendering it unsafe for the men to venture outside of the fort, as it appeared the enemy could see all our movements, and would fire the moment a man exposed himself outside. No material damage was sustained. I did no firing on the 30th of June and 1st of July, as the fleet moved up the river to Goodrich's landing, and took part in an engagement near that place. On the 2d I fired seven rounds. The enemy made no reply. The 3d and last day I fired fourteen rounds, six of which I directed at sky-parlor, (which was used by the enemy for a lookout.) They did not seem to like it, and tried their best to silence the gun by firing ninety shots at the fort, six of which struck it, knocking off railroad ties and tearing up the ground on top of and around the fort. No damage done to the fort whatever. At 6 o'clock p. m. orders came to cease firing, as the city was about to be surrendered.

Before concluding this report, I would say great credit is due to both officers and men of the companies herein mentioned for the work done, and the spirit manifested in the building of the fort. Since the surrender of the city I have learned from the foreman of the foundry that fourteen shots struck the foundry and machine shop, two of which penetrated the boilers, rendering them useless for further operation. The machine shop was also badly damaged by the shots. The six shots thrown at the sky-parlor had good effect, killing two men, and doing considerable damage otherwise.

I am, sir, very respectfully, your most obedient servant,

THOMAS C. GROSHON,

Captain Co. F, 1st Infantry, M. M. B., Com'dg Fort Adams.

Brigadier General A. W. ELLET,

Commanding Mississippi Marine Brigade.

Loss of the United States steamer Baron De Kalb.

U. S. MISSISSIPPI SQUADRON, FLAG-SHIP BLACK HAWK,

Off Vicksburg, July 22, 1863.

SIR: I had the honor to inform you of the blowing up of the Baron De Kalb by a hidden torpedo, seventeen having been planted in the river, without wires attached to them. The water having risen two or three feet during the night, enabled all the vessels but the De Kalb to pass over them.

I am not sure that we shall be able to raise the De Kalb, as she sunk in twenty (20) feet of water, and we cannot yet ascertain the injuries, but every effort will be made. I ordered her guns, and every article that could be got, to be removed, and this duty was performed under the most difficult circumstances; every gun and carriage was saved undamaged; also everything else of value.

Officers and men vied with each other in endeavoring to save the guns and stores; the work had all to be performed in fifteen to twenty feet of water, and the officers set the example in diving down to make fast the gun-carriages; all the small-arms were saved in the same way; also the paymaster's books and government funds.

We are somewhat compensated for the loss of the De Kalb by the handsome results of this expedition. Five of the largest and best boats that ever run on this river were destroyed by the rebels to prevent their falling into our hands; they were burnt entirely up, and one smaller one was captured. The rebels sustained a great loss in these boats; any one of them could have been converted into a powerful ram or gunboat, and the loss of them breaks up their chances of transporting troops.

Besides the destruction above mentioned, the combined forces captured five (5) heavy guns, and a lighter one, and all the ammunition and stores of the enemy. The rebels cannot afford to lose all this material of war; it frees the Yazoo river of rebel troops.

As the people of Yazoo City did not take the trouble to warn us of the existence of torpedoes after the enemy fled, which they had an opportunity of doing, three thousand bales of cotton were seized by General Herron, to pay for the gunboat that was lost through their treachery. The loss to the enemy in this expedition has been all the guns left on Yazoo river, eight hundred thousand dollars' worth of steamers, five hundred and fifty thousand dollars' worth of cotton, and as much more in other stores necessary for the maintenance of an army. The officers and men composing the naval part of this expedition have lost no reputation on account of the sinking of the De Kalb, but have exhibited a perseverance and attention to duty worthy of the highest praise; their labors in recovering their guns and stores will not be surpassed by any one on any other occasion.

I have the honor to remain, very respectfully, your obedient servant,

DAVID D. PORTER,
Acting Rear-Admiral, Com'dg Miss. Squadron.

Hon. GIDEON WELLES,
Secretary of the Navy.

Expedition to recover the Baron de Kalb.

MISSISSIPPI SQUADRON, FLAG-SHIP BLACK HAWK,
Cairo, August 23, 1863.

SIR: In the last expedition I sent up the Yazoo to recover the Baron de Kalb, it was ascertained that she was too much damaged to save her hull, two torpedoes having exploded under her, tearing her bow and stern all to pieces.

Her guns and stores were saved, (with the exception of her provisions,) and part of her machinery taken off. The water was falling so rapidly that the gunboats were obliged to return precipitately from the river, to escape being kept up there the rest of the season.

The iron and all other portions of the hull were removed, to prevent it being of use to the enemy, in case he should return to those parts, which is not likely. I find that our visits to the Yazoo river cost the rebels more than I at first supposed.

Captain Walker received information to be relied on, that, besides the five large steamers destroyed at or near the city of Yazoo, Isaac N. Brown, late lieutenant in the United States navy, in a panic, and for fear they would fall into our hands, set fire to and sunk fourteen others, among them nine large ones, the machinery of which was intended to be sent to Selma, for the gunboats building at that place. This makes fourteen steamers lost to the enemy on the last visit, and eight on the second. Confirmatory of this, I enclose an extract from a rebel paper.

There are no more steamers on the Yazoo; the large fleet that sought refuge there, as the safest place in rebeldom, have all been destroyed.

I hear to-day that Lieutenant Commander Bache has captured two rebel steamers in White river, loaded with stores—all the steamers that were up there. I have received no official report of the transaction as yet.

I am, sir, very respectfully,

DAVID D. PORTER,
Rear-Admiral.

Hon. GIDEON WELLES,
Secretary of the Navy, Washington, D. C.

Engagement at Providence.

UNITED STATES GUNBOAT MOUND CITY,
Lake Providence, August 9, 1863.

SIR: The last of General Read's brigade left this place on the 7th instant. Yesterday morning the notorious John McNail, captain C. S. A., and commanding some seventy men, made a raid into Providence for the purpose of stealing mules and negroes, a large number of the latter having congregated there during its occupation by the army. As soon as he made his appearance on the levee I opened on him with the port battery, when he fled to the woods in great confusion, leaving seven dead on the fields back of Providence, and I doubt not many more wounded. I do not think that he will again trouble the banks near here.

I am, very respectfully, your obedient servant,

BYRON WILSON,
Lieutenant Commander.

Rear-Admiral DAVID D. PORTER,
Commanding Mississippi Squadron.

Raising of the Cincinnati.

MISSISSIPPI SQUADRON, FLAG-SHIP BLACK HAWK,
Cairo, August 16, 1863.

SIR: I had the pleasure of seeing the Cincinnati afloat before I left Vicksburg. We raised her with the means we had at hand without any expense. I gave Acting Volunteer Lieutenant James F. Richardson charge of the duty. He worked night and day for a week, and was rewarded for his labor by his success. He fairly dug her out of the mud, for she was full inside from her keel to her upper deck. She was much cut up, the shot going through and through her, but we will soon have her ready for service again. May I venture to ask that the department will notice Volunteer Lieutenant Richardson's zeal? Every article in the Cincinnati was saved.

I am visiting the different stations on the river as far as this place, and shall return as soon as possible below, where arrangements are being made to drive the rebels away from Louisiana

I am, sir, very respectfully,

DAVID D. PORTER,
Rear-Admiral, Com'dg Mississippi Sqnadron.

Hon. GIDEON WELLES,
Secretary of the Navy, Washington, D. C.

Morgan's raid into Indiana—services of the gunboats under Lieutenant Commander Le Roy Fitch.

MISSISSIPPI SQUADRON, FLAG-SHIP BLACK HAWK,
Cairo, August 18, 1863.

SIR: I have the honor to enclose herewith report of Lieutenant Commander Le Roy Fitch in regard to the late Morgan raid in Indiana.

I am, sir, very respectfully,

DAVID D. PORTER,
Rear-Admiral, Com'dg Mississippi Squadron.

Hon. GIDEON WELLES,
Secretary of the Navy, Washington, D. C.

Report of Lieutenant Commander Le Roy Fitch.

UNITED STATES STEAMER MOOSE,
Buffington Island, July 19, 1863.

SIR: I have the honor to state that, since my last reports regarding Morgan, I have followed on up the river, keeping on his right. In some instances I was compelled to get out warps to get over the falls, shoals, and swift water, but I had determined to cut him off at all hazards.

This morning I had the good fortune to intercept him just above this island, making for the river and attempting to ford. I at once engaged him, drove him from the banks, and captured two pieces of his artillery, a portion of his baggage train, horses, small-arms, &c. During this time General Judah was pressing on his rear.

He did not engage us over an hour, when his forces broke in the utmost confusion, throwing away their arms and clothing and taking to the hills; a portion, however, moved up along the bank in hasty retreat, but I followed them so closely that they soon broke and disappeared up the ravines and over the hills. In this column moving up along the bank were several buggies and carriages, which were abandoned to us. One of the carriages, in which Morgan was said to be riding, was upset by one of our shells and both horses disabled. The road along the bank was literally strewn with his plunder, such as cloth, boots, shoes, small-arms, and the like, but I had not time to land and take possession of these things, as I wished to keep on up the river with the remnant of his scattered band, knowing that General Judah would look out for those left in the rear. About fifteen miles above this point I again fell in with another portion of his forces fording. The current was so very swift and the channel so narrow that it was some time before I could get within range of them. As soon as possible I opened fire on them, killing two and causing many of the horses to leave their riders in the water. Some had already got across, but many put back and again took up the river.

It was reported afterwards that some twenty-five or thirty were drowned. I left standing on both banks some fifteen or twenty horses without riders, but had not time to stop for them. Pushing on up the river, I again saw another squad of some twenty-five or thirty crossing, but could not, in consequence of very shoal and swift water, get within range of them till they had crossed.

Having reached as high as it was safe for me to venture at this stage of water, and the river still falling, I dropped down below Buffington island, where I will remain till morning, and then proceed below Leertast Falls.

Although I could get but two vessels (the Moose and Alleghany Belle) in the engagement to-day, owing to the numerous shoals and shape of the river, yet I can testify to the energetic, prompt, and efficient part the officers and crews of the steamers Reindeer, Naumkey, Victory, and Springfield took in the chase.

The officers and crew of this vessel and the Alleghany Belle acted in the most commendable manner, and although many of them had never before been under fire, they did their duty well.

I know not the number of killed, wounded, and prisoners, but am told the enemy suffered severely, and that nearly the entire force was captured.

Very respectfully, your obedient servant,

LE ROY FITCH, *Lieut. Com'dr.*

Acting Rear-Admiral DAVID D. PORTER,
Commanding Mississippi Squadron.

Complimentary letters from Generals Burnside and Cox.

MISSISSIPPI SQUADRON, FLAG-SHIP BLACK HAWK,
August 10, 1863.

SIR: I have the honor to enclose herewith copies of telegrams received from Generals Burnside and Cox, in relation to the operations of the gunboats under command of Lieutenant Commander Le Roy Fitch.

I remain, sir, very respectfully, your obedient servant,

DAVID D. PORTER,
Rear-Admiral, Com'dg Mississippi Squadron.

Hon. GIDEON WELLES,
Secretary of the Navy, Washington, D. C.

CINCINNATI, *July* 31, 1863.

SIR: It affords me great pleasure to bear testimony to the efficient services performed by the gunboats of the Upper Ohio squadron, under the command of Lieutenant Commander Le Roy Fitch, in the pursuit of the rebels under John H. Morgan. Too much praise cannot be awarded the naval department at this place for the promptness and energy manifested in this movement. I would also gladly bear testimony to the faultless and efficient services of Acting Master A. H. Bowen, whose hearty and energetic co-operation in this pursuit, and, in fact, every movement of his connected with the navy since I first assumed command of this department, has been attended with most beneficial results. The brilliant success which has attended the joint operations of the army and navy in this movement, gives abundant evidence of the good feeling between these two efficient arms of the service, and promises much for the future success of all such operations.

I am, very respectfully, your obedient servant,

A. E. BURNSIDE, *Major General.*

Rear-Admiral PORTER,
Commanding Mississippi Fleet.

CINCINNATI, *Ohio, July* 31, 1863.

SIR: I take pleasure in stating officially the high appreciation I have of the services of the gunboats of the Upper Ohio squadron, commanded by Lieutenant Le Roy Fitch, during the late operations against the force of the rebel General Morgan. The activity and energy with which the squadron was used to prevent the enemy recrossing the Ohio, and to assist in his capture, were worthy of the highest praise. I also am glad to have the opportunity of acknowledging the valuable services rendered by Acting Master A. H. Bowen, in charge of the naval rendezvous here, whose zeal in every work which could make the navy efficient in its co-operation with our troops has been most beneficial to the united services. The mutual good understanding thus shown promises much for the success of all future joint operations.

Very respectfully, your obedient servant,

J. D. COX, *Brigadier General.*

Rear-Admiral PORTER,
Commanding Mississippi Squadron.

Congratulatory letter to Lieutenant Commander Le Roy Fitch.

NAVY DEPARTMENT, *July* 27, 1863.

SIR: Since your attachment to the Mississippi squadron, it has been gratifying to the department to observe the commendable zeal, as shown by reports to it, displayed by you in the execution of the duties with which you were intrusted.

In affording convoy on the Tennessee and Cumberland rivers, in punishing and dispersing the guerilla bands which infested the banks of those streams, and in your timely and important assistance to the garrison of Fort Donelson, when attacked on the 3d of February last, by the rebels under General Wheeler and others, you have acted with promptness and reflected credit on the naval service.

Your recent pursuit of the flying guerilla Morgan—following him upwards of five hundred miles, intercepting him and frustrating him in his attempt to recross the Ohio, capturing his train, a portion of his guns, and routing his band, all of which materially crippled his strength, and led to his final capture, gives additional evidence of your zeal and ability, and reflects additional credit on the service and yourself.

The department takes pleasure in expressing its appreciation of your meritorious services, and thanks you and those under your command for your many blows to the rebellion and active measures for the perpetuation of the Union.

Very respectfully, &c.,

GIDEON WELLES,
Secretary of the Navy.

Lieut. Com'dr LE ROY FITCH, U. S. N.,
Com'dg U. S. Steamer Moose, Mississippi Squadron.

Expedition up White river, under Lieutenant Commander G. M. Bache.

MISSISSIPPI SQUADRON,
Flag-Ship Black Hawk, Cairo, August 24, 1863.

SIR: I have the honor to enclose a report of Lieutenant Bache in relation to the White river expedition. The report is interesting, showing the condition of affairs in that region of country, where the rebels must have been much surprised to see our gunboats. Lieutenant Bache also sends notice that Lieutenant Dunnington (captured in command of Arkansas Post) is fitting out, at Little Rock, the Pontchartrain, the last ram the rebels have in these waters. I shall be glad to see her this side of the shoals that have prevented us from reaching her heretofore.

Very respectfully, your obedient servant,

DAVID D. PORTER,
Rear-Admiral, Com'dg Mississippi Squadron.

Hon. GIDEON WELLES,
Secretary of the Navy.

Report of Lieutenant Commander G. M. Bache.

UNITED STATES STEAMER LEXINGTON,
Clarendon, August 16, 1863.

SIR: I have the honor to report my arrival at this point yesterday, after an entirely successful expedition of three days with this boat, the Cricket, and Marmora.

At Des Arc, our first stopping place, we burnt a large warehouse filled with confederate corn, meal, &c., destroyed the telegraph for nearly half a mile, and obtained some information that we wanted from the citizens, three of whom I seized and brought down to General Davidson.

The second morning, having arrived off the mouth of Little Red river, a narrow and tortuous tributary of the White, I sent the Cricket up after the steamers Tom Gregg [Suggs] and Kaskaskia, (which I had reason to believe were hid up there,) while with the Marmora and this vessel proceeded on to Augusta, thirty miles further, and seventy-five miles from Jacksonport.

Here my information as to the rebel army was confirmed, and one object of the expedition accomplished. The grand southern army was concentrating at Brownsville, intending to make their line of defence on Bayou mountains. Price was there, and Kirby Smith in Little Rock; Marmaduke had recrossed the White some days before, and was then crossing Little Red. Having received this information, I pushed down stream again, and leaving the Marmora off the mouth, went up the Little Red with the Lexington. When about twenty-five miles up, and nearly as high as we could go, we met the Cricket with her two prizes, which she had captured at Scurcy, fifteen miles further on. She also destroyed there Marmaduke's pontoon bridge, leaving a portion of his brigade on the other side of the stream. When a few miles above us the Cricket had been fired into by a portion of Marmaduke's men, when several soldiers (of whom we carried up about one hundred and fifty) and Mr. Morehead, of the Cricket, were wounded. After meeting her, about dusk, we were all again attacked by sharpshooters, without any damage, however. Captain Langthorne I cannot thank too much for his zeal, efficiency, and judgment, not only on this occasion, but ever since under my command.

With the prizes were captured the enclosed list of prisoners, fourteen bales of cotton, three horses, and a few arms.

The Tom Gregg is a fine little side-wheel boat, and I think would make an excellent light-draught gunboat for these rivers.

The Kaskaskia, also a side-wheel, though a somewhat older boat, has still a good hull. For the present, having officered and manned them, and put a howitzer on each, I shall retain them to co-operate with the army, who are much in need of transports all along the banks of the rivers White and Little Red as far as we went. Two hundred and fifty miles on the one, and forty on the other, we found the isolated farmers glad to see us, and many Union demonstrations were made. I am satisfied the people here would be glad to see us in possession.

The capture of the two boats, the only means of transportation the rebels had on this river, is a severe blow to them; and, at this time, the boats can be made of great service to us.

Going up the river we were not at all molested; but coming down were fired on with small arms from almost every available spot, though by no very large number of men.

The river is still high, though falling at the rate of twenty-four inches in forty-eight hours.

I shall send the Lexington down to-morrow. The Marmora, Cricket, and Romeo are all leaking severely, and otherwise out of repair.

The advance division of General Steele's command arrived yesterday. I have no doubt our army will be able to drive the enemy from their line of defence on Bayou mountains into Texas.

Enclosed I hand the report of Captain Langthorne, of the Cricket.

I have the honor to be, very respectfully, your obedient servant,

GEORGE M. BACHE,

Lieutenant, Comd'g White River Expedition.

Rear-Admiral D. D. PORTER,

Commanding Mississippi Squadron.

Report of Acting Vo unteer Lieutenant A. R Langthorne.

UNITED STATES STEAMER CRICKET,

August 15, 1863.

SIR: In obedience to your order, I proceeded up Little Red river at 9 o'clock a. m. About ten miles up I hailed some men on the bank, inquiring of them if the steamers Suggs and Kaskaskia were up the river. They said one of them had passed a short time before. I continued on up, saw some rebel pickets at West Point, and made further inquiries about the steamboats, which satisfied me they were up the river. We arrived at Scurcy's landing at 2 o'clock p. m., and the two steamers, the Thomas Suggs and Kaskaskia. I landed the infantry, and put officers on board the steamers; had them fired up ready to start. The rebels had a fine pontoon bridge built across the river, which I effectually destroyed. We then left for down river. At 3 o'clock took on fourteen bales of cotton on our way. As we arrived near West Point we were fired upon by the rebel sharpshooters; the engagement lasted about an hour, wounding nine of our men, one mortally, (since died.) Mr. Morehead was piloting the Kaskaskia; he stood at the wheel nobly until disabled; he received two shots, and fell. Mr. Lightner was pilot of the Suggs. During the engagement he stood at his post without flinching. Mr. Claycomb, pilot of the Cricket, also showed great bravery and coolness. Surgeon Bodman, although sick, attended to the wounded with much credit. Every officer and man deserves great praise for the manner in which they discharged their duties.

Very respectfully, your obedient servant,

A. R. LANGTHORNE,

Acting Vol. Lieut. U. S. Navy, Com'dg U. S. S. Cricket.

GEORGE W. BACHE,

Lieutenant, Commanding White River Squadron.

Affairs on Red river.—Capture of rebel paymasters and currency.

MISSISSIPPI SQUADRON,
Flag-Ship General Lyons, off Cairo, September 15, 1863.

SIR: I have just returned from the mouth of Red river, where I went to see what could be done to co-operate with General Banks. As I knew beforehand, the river was quite dry in places, and a dry bar formed across the head of Old river. All I could do was to plant three guns on scows—a 100-pounder rifle, a X-inch, and a IX-inch—close to the bar to command the entrance to the Atchafalaya. This will prevent steamers passing to and fro. If the military officers would confer with me a little more freely, I could give them hydrographic information which they cannot get elsewhere, and enable them to time their expeditions so that they may have naval co-operation.

The vessels at the mouth of Red river were unable to enter and co-operate with the army at the attack on Harrisonburg. The rebels blew up the works as our troops advanced, and set fire to the casemates; they also destroyed all their ammunition, which ends the stronghold on the Washita. I am sorry to say that the guns were not brought away, except two field-pieces, or destroyed.

The river below seems quiet. There has been but one attempt made to obstruct commerce or transportation. A body of guerillas, five hundred strong, on the 30th August, attacked the gunboat Champion from behind the levee, while she was convoying a body of troops below. The troops passed on safely, and the Champion stopped and fought the rebels until she made them retire, losing some of their men, report says fifty-seven. They have not been heard of since, excepting that they were falling back on Alexandria, General Herron having given chase to them with his division. The only way to keep guerillas down is to chase them up with troops. Gunboats can only drive them away temporarily.

As I came up I overtook a part of the marine brigade, under Colonel Curry. He reported to me that he had just captured at Bolivar three rebel paymasters with two million two hundred thousand dollars in confederate money to pay off the soldiers at Little Rock. He also captured the escort, consisting of thirty-five men.

This will not improve the dissatisfaction now existing in Price's army; and the next news we hear will be that General Steele has possession of Little Rock. The gunboats pick up deserters every day, who say that the rebels don't intend to fight in Arkansas; and that with proper steps Arkansas will be in the Union again in forty days.

Lieutenant Bache captured a Colonel Matock, who was on a conscription expedition, and it gave universal satisfaction to all the people.

* * * * * * * * * * *

I am, sir, very respectfully, your obedient servant,

DAVID D. PORTER,
Rear-Admiral.

Hon. GIDEON WELLES,
Secretary of the Navy, Washington, D. C.

Expedition to Red river.—Destruction of rebel steamers.

MISSISSIPPI SQUADRON,
Flag-Ship Black Hawk, Cairo, October 17, 1863.

SIR: I have the honor to report that on the 7th of October Acting Volunteer Lieutenant James B. Couthouy, having received information that a rebel steamer was tied up to the bank on Red river, fitted out an expedition under charge of Acting Chief Engineer Thomas Doughty, with twenty men, and Mr. Hobbs, who crossed over from the Mississippi to Red river, and after great labor in getting through the entanglements of the bushes and other undergrowth, Mr. Doughty's party got a sight of the steamer lying at the bank.

He managed to get up to her and capture her. A few moments afterwards he was enabled to capture another one, and found himself in possession of two steamers and nine prisoners, one of the prisoners an aid to the rebel General Taylor. The rebel officer had been sent up expressly for the last steamer, the Fulton, (a very fine boat,) to ferry some troops across the Atchafalaya, and the other was one of the few boats the rebels could get provisions by from the seaboard.

Mr. Doughty, finding he could not get the steamers over the bar and out of Red river, set fire to them, and burnt them up.

This is a great loss to the rebels at this moment, as it cuts off their means of operating across that part of Atchafalaya where they lately came over to attack Morganzia. This capture will deter others from coming down Red river. The affair was well managed, and the officers and men composing the expedition deserve great credit for the share they took in it.

I enclose Acting Chief Engineer Doughty's report.

I am, sir, very respectfully, your obedient servant,

DAVID D. PORTER, *Rear-Admiral.*

Hon. GIDEON WELLES,
Secretary of the Navy, Washington.

Report of Acting Chief Engineer Thomas Doughty.

UNITED STATES STEAMER OSAGE,
Off Mrs. Jontee's, October 7, 1863.

SIR: In obedience to your order, I, with a party of twenty men, with the assistance of Mr. Hobbs, started for Red river this morning. Arriving at Red river, I could see no signs of a steamboat. I divided the party, sending eight men down the river to look into the bend below, and with twelve started up the river. When we had travelled about half a mile I saw the chimneys of a steamer. The woods were found so dense that we could not penetrate them, and the only alternative was to advance in sight. The steamer was on the opposite side of the river, and I feared those on board might see us in time to escape before we were near enough to use our rifles. No one saw us, and we chose a spit opposite her, where we could see any one who attempted to escape. I hailed her; two men were seen to run forward and disappear. I directed three files on the right to fire. The fire brought the men out, and at my command they brought to my side of the river two skiffs which belonged to the boat. I was about to embark a party to burn her, when I heard a steamboat descending the river. I ordered the men out of sight, behind a large log and some bushes, and in two minutes I saw a steamer round the point above. I waited until she was within 400 yards, and showed myself, and ordered her to stop. She did so, and I found myself in possession of nine prisoners and two steamboats. I knew I could not get them out of the river, and I ordered the destruction of the first one captured, named the Argus, and embarked on board the second, the Robert Fulton, and steamed down to the landing where I first struck the river, where I ordered her to be set on fire, and in a few minutes she was one mass of flame. She was the better vessel of the two, and was valued by her owner at $75,000. Neither of them had any cargo on board. I captured all the officers of the boats, and one first lieutenant in the confederate army, and three negroes.

Names of officers of the Argus.—Captain George Fraser, Chief Engineer James Goodwin.

Names of the officers of the Robert Fulton.—Captain J. F. Saunders, Chief Engineer A. S. Auld, Mate William Kelly, Pilot William C. Smith, First Assistant Engineer G. W. Chapman, Carpenter J. Chataigner.

Name of army officer.—First Lieutenant J. M. Avery.

Arms taken.—1 Enfield rifle, 2 double-barrelled shot-guns, 2 revolvers.

All of which is respectfully submitted.

THOMAS DOUGHTY,
Acting Chief Engineer.

Acting Volunteer Lieut. J. P. COUTHOUY, U. S. N.,
Commanding United States Steamer Osage.

Jontee's, or Gentry's, is about three miles below Union Point.

J. P. COUTHOUY, *Commanding.*

Attack upon General Dana at Morganzia.—Co-operation of the navy.

MISSISSIPPI SQUADRON,
Flag-Ship Black Hawk, Cairo, October 18, 1863.

SIR: I have the honor to enclose herewith a copy of a report from Lieutenant Commander James P. Foster, commanding second district of this squadron, in relation to operations in his district.

I am, sir, very respectfully, your obedient servant,

DAVID D. PORTER.

Hon. GIDEON WELLES,
Secretary of the Navy, Washington, D. C.

Report of Lieutenant Commander James P. Foster.

UNITED STATES STEAMER LAFAYETTE,
Morganzia, September 30, 1863.

SIR: Yesterday the advanced guard of General Dana was attacked by General Green some five or six miles from Morganzia, and we lost about four hundred and fifty (450) men in prisoners, killed, and wounded.

I immediately went up to Morganzia with the Kenwood, to co-operate with General Dana, and the arrival of the gunboats was hailed by their forces with perfect delight.

On the following day I moved up the Lafayette, and have no doubt by this means the enemy were deterred from attacking General Dana in his position at Morganzia, as they had about four brigades to do it with, while our forces did not amount to more than fifteen hundred. I shall return to-morrow with the Lafayette to Bayou Sara, leaving the Signal and Neosha at Morganzia.

We have captured here and in Morganzia about eight or ten prisoners, one major, one captain, and one lieutenant, which I have turned over to the general commanding at Morganzia. Everything below Bayou Sara is quiet. Scott, the guerilla, is still outside of Bayou Sara, doing pretty much as he pleases, but gives the Lafayette a wide berth. It is his men that I have been capturing.

I am, very respectfully, your obedient servant,

JAMES P. FOSTER,
Lieutenant Commander, Com'dg Second District.

Rear-Admiral DAVID D. PORTER,
Commanding Mississippi Squadron.

MISCELLANEOUS REPORTS.

Rear-Admiral Goldsborough's opinion of iron-clads.

WASHINGTON CITY, *February* 26, 1864.

SIR: In obedience to your instructions, I beg to submit the following remarks on the subject of iron-clads:

The problem is yet, so to speak, but inchoate. In truth, the still continued and startling developments in ordnance are alone enough to keep it in abeyance. They, in short, together with the general use of steam and the substitution of iron for wood, have completely ignored and consigned to history numerous ideas formerly regarded as fundamental, and thus imposed a new necessity for others in their stead, many of which, to say the least, are extremely perplexing. Hence the remarkable state of transition which now pervades the naval world.

Notwithstanding all that has been done, and the enormous expenditures incurred, to secure an invulnerable hull *throughout*, and to guard, at the same time, against too great a sacrifice of sea qualities and other essential attributes, but, at least, an indifferent success has been reached in any quarter, and this condition of things, coupled with an appreciation of the inherent difficulties involved, has already induced some respectable minds abroad, if not among ourselves, to despair of accomplishing much more. The efficiency or intrinsic worth of an iron-clad, intended for the ocean or for coast purposes, is to be estimated according to her strength throughout *every part* of the hull, her sea qualities, the disposition and character of her battery, and the ability of its use in all cases of fighting weather; the efficiency of height of her deck above the water to resist the vaulting efforts of a spoon-bowed opponent; the substantive protection afforded by her plating; her capacity to move rapidly and turn quickly; her space for requisite accommodations; and (pardon the word) her habitability.

These are the essential properties that constitute the offensive and defensive powers of the vessel, and all of them bear so intimately upon efficiency that no one of them can be disregarded or neglected with impunity. To unite them all in one hull, with sufficient harmony, is the problem in view, and, I repeat, it is one yet to be solved.

The Warrior, the *chef d'œuvre* of iron-clads, in the minds of some, has been produced, but it is vain to claim for her the renown of embodying its solution, when we are told, unquestionably, that she rolls in a sea-way 38 degrees, and when we know that the ditto of her sides has been both penetrated and smashed readily; that her extremities are unguarded, and that her capacity to turn quickly depends upon the efforts of a solitary screw acting upon her great length.

Apart from the consideration of the effect of plating upon sea qualities, strain of bottom, &c., costly and carefully conducted experiments afford us no hope that a sea-going vessel-of-war can be covered with iron *throughout* her vulnerable parts, so as to render her proof against the penetration of rifle projectiles at even a tolerably near fighting distance, or against the still more destructive effects of large round shot, impinging with high velocity.

It is very clear that no vessel confined to rational dimensions can support, throughout her exposed parts, more than a very limited thickness of iron plating; and, already, a greater thickness perhaps than she can thus support, and still remain fit for the ocean, has been penetrated even by shells, under certain favorable conditions. They, at any rate, when of great size and with large bursting charges, have been made to penetrate a thickness of at least five and a half inches, and to do destructive smashing work besides. But it should be borne in mind that penetration is not indispensable to the destruction of either plates or vessel. Any iron plate that can be applied to a vessel—indeed, I might perhaps say any that can be forged—can be smashed to pieces by the round shot, if not shells, of a powerful gun; and, again, any iron vessel certainly can be sunk by such projectiles in the absence of entire penetration on the part of any of them. The blows received must necessarily be expended upon her—must be taken up by her—and, ultimately, their effect in the way of vibration would be to break her fastenings of rivets, and thus produce, beyond question, I think, a destructive leak, more especially if delivered from a concentrated broadside of such guns against a vessel with a thin or weak bottom, in comparison with her upper works. The strength of bottom, compared with that of upper works, of an ordinary wooden vessel, is much greater than it is or can be in any iron-clad; yet, it is obvious that no vessel requires such absolute strength, in this particular, as the latter. It is a feature of vital importance, and one, therefore, deserving the most serious attention.

The destruction of plates by the process of smashing would undoubtedly result far more disastrously to the vessel than though they were simply penetrated by non-explosive projectiles, or rifle bolts, elsewhere than below the water-line.

Iron conveys vibration with wonderful facility, and is therefore regarded as a perfect conductor in this respect; and, hence, a leak in the bottom of an iron-clad once produced, as mentioned, could scarcely fail to spread itself rapidly, and thus, in all probability, consign her to the bottom either during a contest or no great while afterwards.

The Weehawken had been struck one hundred and thirty-seven times by the projectiles of the enemy up to the time of her sinking in the harbor of Charleston, a few weeks after her last engagement, and it would be well, I think, to ascertain, on her recovery, the real cause of the disaster. It may have proceeded from vibration produced by shot.

If any solid benefit is to be derived from iron plating applied to a sea-going vessel—any benefit commensurate with its cost and probable efficacy—it is quite apparent to my mind that it is only to be done by limiting its use to her most vitally exposed parts, and having it of such practicable thickness as to secure immunity in those places against the explosive effect of shells generally, and against the damaging effect of other projectiles striking obliquely, or otherwise unfavorably to the material injury of iron; and the vessel so provided, when required to perform fighting service in harbors or rivers, might have chain cables faked over the unplated parts of her hull as a temporary expedient. In connexion with this way of using plates, effective water-tight bulkheads are indispensable. A hull arranged after this fashion, with turrets for the battery, is, I conceive, about all that can be done in the way of plating with iron, consistently with all the considerations involved; and even this would be of but poor account unless the other elements of efficiency mentioned above were duly secured.

Among those elements is that of celerity in turning, and as it is a point to which sufficient attention has not been given hitherto, I wish to impress my convictions in regard to it.

Every iron-clad, as a matter of course, should be an unexceptionable ram; or, in other words, susceptible herself of being used as a projectile. This, however, cannot be the case unless she can be directed with a great degree of promptness to any desired quarter, or turned with every degree of quickness necessary. But celerity in turning is not to be estimated only by the advantage it gives in offensive movements, for it is also of the greatest consequence in defensive operations, and, as an instance, it confers the power to parry, generally, the intended blow of an antagonist ram, if not to avoid it altogether frequently. The offensive and defensive qualities of a vessel-of-war are so inseparably connected that each, generally, if not always, constitutes an essential part of the other. They, in fact, occupy a Siamese relation.

In regarding the value of celerity in turning, it may be well to consider the fact that it is utterly idle to attempt the construction of a sea vessel with the hope of rendering her able to resist the blow of a formidable ram. No combination of any materials known can possibly accomplish this end. Even the Warrior, although a vessel of vast size and enormous strength, could be crushed by a ramming blow from the Dictator, as though she were nothing more than an immense egg. Indeed, she could be crushed to destruction by a blow of the sort from a vessel greatly inferior to the Dictator in momentum. To appreciate these assertions fully, scarcely more is necessary than to compute the momentum of the Dictator arising from her weight of 4,500 tons, when, at her normal draught of twenty feet, impelled with a velocity of fifteen knots per hour, or twenty-five feet per second. It sums up to two hundred and fifty-two millions of pounds, and is, therefore, equal, in point of shock, to that of a ball weighing two hundred and fifty-two thousand pounds (more than a quarter of a million) striking with a velocity of one thousand feet per second; or, to that of an iron ball, ten feet two and three-quarter inches in diameter, striking with that velocity.

This comparison, it will be perceived, concerns only the force of the blow. As to whether the vessel or ball would produce the greater destructive effect, the very wedge-shaped and cutting bow of the former, contrasted with the bluff front the latter would necessarily have to present, is, I suppose, enough to settle the question.

To my apprehension the Dictator, with a velocity of fifteen knots, on striking favorably for the purpose any sea vessel whatever that either now exists or ever will exist, would infallibly cause her to separate almost immediately into two parts. Even an oblique blow from her might work terrific results, and it is by no means certain that a direct one would not be sufficient to split an iceberg of formidable dimensions. Nor, judging from what is known of kindred collisions, would the probability of escaping disastrous injury on delivering the blow against even a vessel of the Warrior's stamp be unfavorable to the Dictator, if only her bottom were much better calculated than it is to withstand violent vibration, and as strong as it seems to me it ought to have been made to be in keeping with her massive and ponderous upper works and the kind of service she is liable to be called upon to render?

But, to return to the point of celerity in turning, no practical means, in my judgment, should be neglected, more particularly in the construction of an iron-clad, to secure this cardinal quality; and, drawing my conclusions from experiments that have been made, and discussions that have followed them, I am induced to think that the system of turn-screws and independent engines affords the very best means extant of accomplishing the purpose.

With the same application of power, it is said to afford not only a higher velocity than the single screw, but a vastly superior facility in turning. The simple fact that backing on one side, and going ahead on the other, can take place simultaneously, is enough to settle the point. And there is also claimed for it another great advantage, the facility of steering independently of the rudder, or of guiding effectually when the rudder can no longer be used, by merely varying the force of either screw according to circumstances. These are but the more prominent advantages of the system. There are others of an incidental character which are regarded as of consequence, but it is, perhaps, unnecessary for me to dwell upon them on this occasion. I will remark, however, that this system of propulsion is extending itself in England, if not elsewhere.

Velocity, involving as it does the capacity of prompt presentation wherever required—of making, in effect, the vessel herself a terrific projectile; of turning rapidly, and of avoiding hostile demonstrations whenever necessary—is of such primary importance that an insufficiency is to be regarded as fatal to efficiency. With regard to the interesting and mooted question of guns best suited for an ron-clad, which must of necessity be comparatively few, owing to the large proportion of floating power absorbed in giving requisite strength, and by the application of plates, I am decidedly of the impression that, as a very general rule, those adapted to round shot are greatly to be preferred, provided they be of the largest calibre that can be used with facility and safety, and at the same time calculated to throw their shot with a high initial velocity; and I say this because I attach a much higher consequence, on the score of general destructive effect, to the smashing influence of solid round shot than to the boring results of rifle projectiles, not that I am disposed, however, by any means, to ignore rifled guns, but that I am inclined to a restriction of their use, and to make them the exception and never the rule either for iron-clads or any other class of war vessel. In truth, the work to be done should be the criterion of choice between the two, or with regard to their association. If, for instance, the object to be accomplished were one on shore, within the effective reach of the rifle, but beyond that of the smooth-bore, it is clear that the latter would be quite useless for the occasion; but, on the other hand, if it were assailable effectually by the latter, the preference, to my view, as a very general thing, should be given to it, using the other, however, in a complementary way, or to the extent that it would probably facilitate smashing by boring. Considering, though, the general purposes an iron-clad is intended to subserve, and to answer the question as to the kind of armament she should have in general terms, I say, unhesitatingly, give her all smooth-bores of the sort mentioned above; more especially when the necessity of the case imposes the condition of a very limited number of guns. An effective Parrott rifle, associated with smooth-bores in cases where the latter are not really few in number, as a permanent arrangement, would no doubt prove advantageous in the general course of service; and I beg to state that I distinguish this rifle purposely above all others, because I believe it to be by far the best for naval purposes that has been produced by any of our projectors, and fully equal, if not superior, to any that has been produced elsewhere of which I have any information. It is, perhaps, not as generally known as it should be, that this gun admits, without the slightest detriment, the free use of round shot, an advantage of much moment at times; but this is only one among the number of merits which constitute its intrinsic and distinctive worth.

A difference of opinion also exists among naval minds, both at home and abroad, as to whether the better expedient is to use the guns of an iron-clad *turretwise*, or in broadside ports under a covering plated deck. For my own part, I have little doubt upon the subject, particularly if the vessel herself be confined, as in my judgment she ought to be, to moderate dimensions—to such, in effect, as, with a high velocity, will offer sufficient momentum, used as a ram, to crush effectually any antagonist whatever, capable of sea-service; and more than this, to my apprehension, is obviously worse than superfluous.

The turret I regard as decidedly preferable, and mainly for these reasons: It renders one gun of a class equivalent to at least two of the same disposed in opposite broadside ports, and this with a great reduction of crew. It admits the use of much heavier guns. It does not necessarily involve a breadth of beam antagonistic to velocity. It affords a better protection to guns and men, and, withal, it secures the fighting of guns longer in a sea-way.

But, to derive all the benefits from a turret of which it is susceptible, I am quite persuaded that no fastenings of rivets should be used in its construction. The device of a jacket, or interior lining, to prevent broken fastenings from flying inwards injuriously, is, at best, but an incomplete alternative; for although it may, and does undoubtedly, answer that end, yet at the same time it conceals from detection the great number of those fastenings that are broken by vibration, and do not fly from their places, or scarcely start at all; and it is very evident that it exerts no influence to check disintegration of the turret itself, occasioned by the effect of vibration in sundering rivets.

It is no sufficient answer to these remarks to urge the difficulty of constructing a competent turret without the use of rivets. I am aware of it, but still I am satisfied that it can be overcome; and furthermore, that it may be at an early period, if our artisans are challenged and encouraged to the task. When it is, a very superior order of turret will result.

According to my impressions, a gun of 12,000 pounds is about the heaviest that can be used to advantage in the *broadside ports* of any vessel whatever; and I would respectfully urge that one of this weight, cast upon Rodman's method, shaped essentially according to the form determined by Bomford, bored as a IX-inch in every particular, and intended for a normal charge of powder of twenty pounds, be prepared forthwith, and submitted to searching experiment; for whether iron-clads are or are not to have broadside guns to throw the heaviest round shot with the highest velocity that circumstances will permit, other vessels will certainly require them; and as no gun of this character now exists in our navy, I take the liberty of suggesting the one in view as an attempt to fill the void.

Could the Cumberland have thrown her solid IX-inch shot with a charge of twenty pounds of powder, and kept recoil under control, the Merrimack, in my belief, would have fared very differently. It is true she might still have rammed the former as she did; but in lying near at hand afterwards, if not in passing by at a close range previously, with the view of turning for the purpose, her protective plating would, I think, have been damaged sorely, and to an extent forbidding further efforts, perhaps compromitting safety, and thus, probably, the Congress and many lives, at least, might have been saved, and much subsequent annoyance avoided. I am not sure that the Cumberland did use in her nine-inch guns, generally, a charge of powder of more than ten pounds, but I am quite confident that she could not have used in them, at any time during the action, one of more than thirteen pounds—the maximum prescribed. Even with the charges she did use, the Merrimack's plating was sensibly injured, and all that was wanting to bring about the results of which I speak was, a material increase of projectile velocity, such (I repeat my belief) as charges of twenty pounds of powder applied to similar though considerably heavier guns would have conferred. I am told, upon authority, that the present IX-inch guns are capable, in strength, of throwing their solid shot with a charge of twenty pounds of powder. That they may be; but no one of any experience, I take it, will venture to advocate the use, with solid shot, of a higher charge to those guns than the one now allotted as the maximum; no one, I am sure, who has witnessed on board ship the effect of the recoil of those guns when fired for awhile with solid shot and with this maximum charge. Nor, to speak frankly, have I much faith in the sufficiency of the gun itself to withstand a higher charge with solid shot.

I only ask that a fair and thorough trial of the gun I propose—a trial to determine its relative merits, in every respect, as a broadside gun to throw the heaviest solid round shot with the highest velocity that circumstances will permit—may be made.

I am fully aware that the New Ironsides has now on board still heavier guns, and of larger calibre, carried broadside-wise—guns of 16,000 pounds in weight and eleven inches in calibre—but I am not aware that either they, or their carriages, which occupy unavoidably so much space, have been subjected continuously, in action or at sea, to the effect of the use of solid shot, with charges of powder approaching one-fourth the weight of the projectiles. The test no doubt *would prove palpably* excessive in many respects. In all the actions of this vessel off Charleston, the rule with her, as I understand, was loaded shells with corresponding charges; and if she ever has resorted to solid shot, with a large increase of charge, I am uninformed of the fact.

As already intimated, a marked pause must occur in the progress of ordnance before a fixed or definite conclusion can be reached as to the relative immunity obtainable by iron plates, even when of the best quality, and when applied in the most feasible manner. Absolute immunity is out of the question.

That progress has already produced the effect of restricting their application, in the case of sea-going vessels, to the more vitally exposed parts; and it is quite possible that it may yet do considerably more; that it may go on in the way of narrowing those limits, and bring them down first to *some* only of those parts, and finally to establish the conviction that such plating, for such vessels, viewing impartially the *pros* and *cons*, is really of no marked consequence. This is no groundless speculation, however it may present itself at the first blush; for facts and deductions from experiments distinctly point to the conclusion. In the mean time the tendency of its effects must be to impress the value of rams, and thus of reviving a mode of naval warfare which, on a miniature scale comparatively, existed long before the invention of gunpowder.

The value of rams, at this very moment, cannot be overestimated. With a few of them in each of our prominent commercial ports, none scarcely of more than half the displacement or weight of the Dictator, no enemy, I care not how powerful, could blockade those ports successfully; for possessing the great advantage of biding and selecting their own time, they could so manage the delivery of their blows as to annihilate his vessels. Nor could those ports, in my judgment, be assailed successfully. The protection of harbors, now-a-days, does not lie in ports. They, for this particular purpose, are immeasurably effete, or, at most, but of subsidiary importance. It lies essentially in powerful steam rams, aided, when necessary, by obstructions in passage-ways. Is it the forts of Charleston, I would ask, that now secure the place from capture? Certainly not. They alone, or any other forts alone, (by which I mean in the absence of rams and obstructions,) can be passed by fast and powerful vessels with impunity, assuming, of course, that there is water enough to float them.

Rams, intended purely for harbor defence, would be better without than with guns. They themselves are to be the projectiles; or, if you please, they are to be the shot, and the steam is to be the powder; and the effect of both, properly combined, would be absolutely irresistible. Guns, I repeat, would be detrimental to unity of purpose, and also in other respects; or, in short, be of more harm than good in the long run. Besides, to fit the rams for them would be to swell the item of cost largely, and thus abridge their multiplication; and the distinctive plating which their protection would involve could be used to more advantage elsewhere about the hull. The essential points to be secured in these rams, each to a degree as consistently with all the rest as practicable, are great strength throughout every part of the hull, not overlooking the bottom by any manner of means; every protection that supportable plating can afford; a high velocity; an ample security of machinery; the utmost rapidity in turning; and a suitable bow.

I have met with no ideas with regard to sea-going iron-clads that have impressed me so forcibly as those of Captain Coles, of the British navy; and I think his system, in the main, is about the best that can be adopted at present. In my humble opinion, he meets the difficulties of the case better than they have yet been met in any other quarter; and he displays throughout his exposition a fertility of resource, a fund of ingenuity, common sense, and professional experience, that confers upon him distinguished credit.

But to come more immediately to the requirements of your communication, it strikes me that it is inexpedient to construct iron-clads to perform only a particular service, except mere rams, unprovided with guns, for harbor defence, and also vessels for interior river operations, in a country like this, in case of intestine difficulty. They should, I think, be made to answer as many naval purposes as possible, and their cost alone, independently of other considerations, is enough to determine this question. All, therefore, barring the exceptions just mentioned, should, it seems to me, possess the attribute of seaworthiness; by which I mean the capacity of being sailed or steamed anywhere over the ocean, and of keeping the sea as long as a vessel of the class would probably be called upon to do so. Without this attribute their sphere of usefulness must inevitably be but local and contracted.

Putting the Galena aside as a sad mistake, and as unworthy of naval criticism, the Monitors we have already constructed and used in service I am impelled to regard as open to the serious objections of a marked deficiency in ability for general naval purposes, and in strength of bottom, seaworthiness, speed, turning qualities, height of deck above the water, and habitability; yet, for mere smooth-water harbor operations—the object, I suppose, for which they were intended—they undoubtedly do possess formidable offensive and defensive properties, viewed in a relative sense.

Their absolute worth, however, in these particulars, I cannot regard as entitled to the extravagant merit claimed for it, induced, I apprehend, in a great measure by conclusions drawn from the encounters of the first Monitor and Weehawken with the Merrimack and Atlanta, without a sufficient knowledge of the facts attending them, and without any (or more than an unwilling) reference to the cases of opposite results, as, for instance, the Ogeechee, and the repeated displays before Charleston. That the charm of novelty in construction, or quaintness in appearance, had anything to do with the matter, I will not undertake to assert, although I may, perhaps, be allowed to indulge suspicion as to probable effect. Popular opinion is not always right on such subjects, nor do I know that it is apt to be when it runs counter to popular naval opinion. At any rate, I do know that the latter is not likely to be very wrong in relation to professional matters of the kind.

Their offensive and defensive power, even for the kind of service they are alone expected to perform, is most materially marred or restrained, I conceive, by their disproportionate and inadequate strength of bottom, their exposed and ill-protected deck, and their want of speed, height of deck, and habitability.

If there be those who think that a bottom composed essentially of nothing more than ½-inch iron plates, secured to frames of angle iron 4 by 4 by ½, spaced 18 inches from centre to centre, and sustaining a stupendous, ponderous, and overhanging superstructure, is enough, or anything like enough, to endure the vibration to which an iron-clad is exposed under a severe fire from heavy guns, much less the terrific vibration when used as a ram, or, I might almost say, to endure the strain of that superstructure itself under all circumstances of exposure to weather to which the vessel is unavoidably liable in going only from harbor to harbor, I confess, frankly, that I am not one of the number. Two of the iron-clads in view—the Monitor and Weehawken—have already gone to the bottom, and neither was under fire at the time, nor had either been so very recently. The sinking of the Monitor was occasioned by an actual (though partial in extent) separation between the top and bottom upper works; but how much of this may have been due, if any at all, to the shock of all kinds she experienced in her struggle with the Merrimack, it is of course impossible to determine. But whether any part of this fatal disaster is or is not to be so ascribed, the fact of the separation itself is conclusive to my mind as to the insufficiency of relative strength between her top and bottom works; nor am I aware that this feature has been changed at all materially for the better in the construction of the other Monitors; nor, indeed, that it is susceptible of ample modification in the premises. As to the case of the Weehawken, I prefer suspending an expression of opinion until more is positively known in relation to it. She certainly went down in a most mysterious and startling way, yet under circumstances that *do* furnish grounds for conjecture. Besides the number of times she had been struck by the enemy's projectiles, and fired her own 15-inch and 11-inch guns, she had previously gone through quite a severe gale of wind at sea.

The deck of the Monitors has been penetrated at a distance judged to be 1,200 yards, and, therefore, it is a plain inference, considering its attitude, that at quarters close enough to render firing upon it at all plunging, the vessel herself could be readily sunk. To render this defect less glaring, additional plating, I believe, was to have been applied, and a quantity of it was sent to Port Royal for the purpose; but, on further reflection, the scheme, I am told, was generally abandoned as impracticable.

Their speed, after being in the water some little time, as I am informed by credible authority, is but, on the average, about 4½ knots, rather less than more. To trace this sad defect more at large than I have already done is a needless task. It proclaims its own consequences.

Their height of deck above the water, being, as I am also credibly informed, only some 12 or 15 inches, and their remaining floating power scarcely exceeding 200 tons, a strong temptation is presented to a light and active antagonist, with a curved or spoon-shaped bow, to bide his time and throw himself astride of it; nor have I the slightest doubt, particularly with their sluggishness of motion, that the attempt might be successful, and if so, that the result would be destruction.

And as to the remaining point to be remarked upon—the want of habitability—it is, in a warm climate or season, obnoxious to grave objections. The physical prostration it produces is inordinate, and hence a more frequent change of officers and others than is compatible with order or convenience is rendered a necessity.

The New Ironsides I regard as a much more efficient type of iron-clad than the Monitors just discussed, because of her possessing decided advantages over them in the particulars of fitness for general purposes, seaworthiness, relative strength of bottom, or absolute capacity to endure vibration thereat, security against an antagonist vessel getting astride of her, speed, and habitability. Had she been planned for turrets, instead of to use guns at broadside ports, she would have been, I think, still more formidable; nor is she unexceptionable in other respects, and among them speed and turning qualities. It is necessary to try her more at sea, and more at closer quarters with an enemy, than she has yet been tried, in order to determine positively her relative merits in some highly important particulars.

The Roanoke, although presenting a powerful and well-protected battery, cannot, if I am correctly informed, be used at sea owing to her excessive rolling motion; and her great draught of water is a serious obstacle to her worth even for harbor purposes. She, also, is deficient in speed and turning qualities, and, indeed, in other respects. She is but a converted vessel, however, (to use a technical term,) gotten up under a pressing demand; and her plating, turrets, &c., can be transferred hereafter to a more suitable hull. I know too little of the iron-clads on our western waters to venture an opinion as to their merits; and as to those in the course of construction, or not yet commissioned, on our Atlantic seaboard, I would remark that their probable fitness to answer ends is to be measured by the prospect they present of combining the properties I have mentioned in an early part of this letter as essential to efficiency.

Considering the pressing and peculiar circumstances under which our iron-clads were produced—the newness of the problem itself, and its inherent difficulties—it is not in the slightest degree surprising that we have not achieved more satisfactory results. No desire to do the best that could be accomplished, and certainly no elevation of purpose nor energy, has been wanting in the proper quarter. The efforts we have made are so many lessons upon the subject, and they afford us the advantage of profiting by wholesome teachings. Experience is a great source of wisdom, and to be enabled to recede from error is a means of advancing in truth.

I have thus, sir, given you, somewhat at large, the views I entertain on the subject of iron-clads, and of those we have constructed, called for, most unexpectedly to myself, by your communication of the 3d instant. In arriving at the conclusions I express I have indulged no other disposition than to probe the subject itself, and to consult the good of our navy, well knowing from the character and position you sustain that any course of less candor on my part would have been as repugnant to your wishes as to my own inclination.

Very respectfully, your obedient servant,

L. M. GOLDSBOROUGH,
Rear-Admiral, United States Navy.

Hon. GIDEON WELLES,
Secretary of the Navy, Washington City.

Rear-Admiral Dahlgren's opinion of the Monitors.

FLAG-STEAMER PHILADELPHIA,
Off Morris Island, January 28, 1864.

SIR: Conformably to the wishes of the department, I submit the following review of the services of the Monitors while under my command; and as some knowledge of the circumstances under which they have been tested may afford a better appreciation of their qualities, I shall briefly narrate some of the leading events in which they have participated during the operations at this place.

On the 6th July Rear-Admiral DuPont delivered to me the command of the naval forces occupying the coast of South Carolina, Georgia, and part of Florida; they embraced seventy (70) vessels of all classes, and were distributed at various points along an extent of more than three hundred miles. There was no concentration, the purpose being rather to distribute the vessels in order to enforce an efficient blockade.

Of the iron-clads, the Ironsides was off Charleston bar, two Monitors were at Edisto, one at Stono, three at Port Royal, and one at Ossabaw.

The orders of the department (June 24, 1863) only directed me to assume the command; they went no further, nor was there need that they should. There was an enemy in front, and it was my duty to compel him to obedience, so far as my means permitted.

On the day that I arrived, an interview occurred with General Gillmore, in which the details for a descent on Morris island were arranged to commence on the Wednesday following, but which were postponed first to Thursday and then to Friday, in order to allow General Gillmore to perfect his arrangements.

In the absence of specific instructions, I was obliged to assume the responsibility of action, which the department was advised of.

The naval part of the operations consisted of—

1. In assembling the iron-clads at the Charleston bar, so as to cross at early daylight on the day named, to cover the attack of the troops, to prevent the arrival of re-enforcements during that attack, and to engage the rebel batteries, particularly Fort Wagner.

2. To furnish a convoy for the column that was to ascend to Stono, cover its landing, and shell James's island.

3. To guard the depots of the army at Hilton Head and at Seabrook during the withdrawal of the troops concentrated on Folly island.

I should here state that Mr. Ericsson had decided to increase the thicknesses of the pilot-houses of all the Monitors and add heavy circles of metal to the bases of the turrets and pilot-houses.

The three at Port Royal were already in hand for this purpose, and some progress had been made. A part of my preparation consisted in putting a stop to the work, and having the vessels fitted temporarily for service.

This was effected in season, and before daylight of the 9th of July the Monitors were off the bar, ready to pass in at the first sign of movement by the United States batteries on Folly island.

The plan was to open from the masked batteries on the north end of Folly island, cross the bar with the Monitors, and enfilade the rebel position on the eminences of Morris island, while the troops were to cross the narrow inlet which divides Morris island from Folly island when the proper moment arrived.

The obscurity of the night still rested on land and sea when I went on board the Catskill, (July 10,) and not a symptom of preparation on shore was visible to us.

It was important that the Monitors should not by their appearance give any intimation of what was meditated by being seen on the bar, until the details ashore were completed; so I waited the first fire of the batteries. This was not long coming, and I led with my flag in the Catskill, followed by Captains Fairfax, Downes, and Colhoun, in the Montauk, Nahant, and Weehawken. Steering for the wreck of the Keokuk, and passing it, the Monitors were laid in line about parallel to the land, opposite the southern eminences of Morris island, and poured in a steady fire among the rebel garrison, who were there posted, making a feeble and ineffectual return to the storm of shot and shell that came upon their front and flank. I could see plainly the great confusion into which they were thrown by this sudden and overwhelming onslaught. It was a complete surprise, both as to time and to power developed.

The Monitors were run in as close as the shoal waters permitted, so that the shells from our own batteries on Folly island passed close ahead of and at times over some of them.

About 8 o'clock a body of men were seen coming over the low sand beach of Morris island, and while hesitating whether to treat them to some volleys of grape, the sight of the Union flag* told who they were. They composed the brigade which had been brought from the Folly river by the boats of the squadron under Lieutenant Commander Bunce and Lieutenant Mackenzie.

I paused for a moment to observe the gradual accumulation of our men in masses, and their advancing movement; then pushed forward to accelerate with our enfilading fire the retreat of the rebels.

The sight was now of great interest. Our own troops could be seen taking possession of the sand hills where the enemy had rested the sole defence of this end of the island, while some battalions were moving along the beach. The defeated rebels were hurriedly making way along the low flat land north of their position, and some two or three detached dwellings were in flames, while the Monitors skirting the shore maintained a steady fire on the retreat. Presently they reached Fort Wagner, and here we were advised that our advance was checked, at least for the day, though it was but 9 o'clock. The discomfited rebels were safe in the work, and our own men halted at a reasonable distance from it.

The Monitor with my flag was now anchored as near the beach as the depth of water permitted, (twelve hundred yards,) and the other Monitors in line to the southward. A steady fire was begun about 9.30—the fort replying

* The first planted on Morris island by Lieutenant Robeson.

briskly—and maintained through the day, except the dinner hour, until six in the evening; then I retired and anchored lower down.

Next morning before six o'clock the flag-lieutenant reported to me that an assault had been made at daybreak by our troops and failed, and about nine o'clock I had a note in pencil from the general, saying: "We attempted to carry Fort Wagner by assault this morning and reached the parapet, but the men recoiled and fell back with slight loss."

It is known *now* that re-enforcements had been hurried to the island by the rebels, and had entered the work about midnight.

I had no notice whatever of the general's intent, and could, therefore, render no aid in time.

Here ended the first part of the enterprise against Morris island. It had been in all respects a surprise, and so complete that the rebels do not seem to have had any idea of it until the day before; and it is not certain they were then aware of the scale on which it was to be conducted.

Had a work like Wagner crowned the sand hills of the south end, we could not have established our position on the island—even a surprise would probably have been out of the question. But there were to be no more surprises—the undertaking was to be completed only by hard work patiently endured in the trenches, and by batteries ashore and afloat.

The general now decided to make a second assault in force, and to cover it by some light batteries established at distances varying from one thousand to seventeen hundred yards.

While the preparations for this design were going on the Monitors were daily at work to occupy the attention of Wagner, and keep down its fire—the gunboats assisting at long range.

On the 18th July, all being ready, about noon I led up in the Montauk, followed by four Monitors and the Ironsides, anchored at twelve hundred yards, as near as the state of the tide would permit, and opened fire—the gunboats firing at a greater distance, and the shore batteries also in action.

As the tide rose the Montauk gradually closed in, until at seven o'clock she was about three hundred yards from Wagner, when I ordered grape to be used. Unable to endure the fire of the vessels the guns of the fort were now silent, and not a man was to be seen.

About sunset a note in pencil from General Gillmore announced his intention to assault, but it was quite dark before the column reached the work. The fire of the vessels was continued so long as it was safe for our own men ashore, but ceased when the darkness made it impossible to distinguish friend from foe. The rattle of musketry soon made known the commencement of the assault, and continued with little intermission until 9.30, when it ceased, and then came the painful tidings of our defeat.

This was the end of the second part of the operation, and proved that the work was too strong and too pertinaciously defended to be taken by any off-hand blow. The slow and laborious operation by trench and cannon only were capable of reducing it.

And here I may remark, that in this necessity is to be found a principal cause for the delay in reaching Charleston that subsequently ensued. It was no doubt unavoidable, for it is to be presumed that no more troops could *then* be spared from the main armies. If there had been sufficient to make such an assault as would have overpowered all opposition, Wagner might have been carried at the first assault, Gregg would have yielded immediately, Sumter would soon have followed as a matter of course, and the iron-clads, untouched by severe and continued battering, would have been in condition to come quickly in contact with the then imperfect interior defences.

The rebel movements clearly indicate that they admitted the impracticability of defending Morris island, and consequently Sumter, after our position on it was fully established and covered by the iron-clads. They only sought to hold the island long enough to replace Sumter by an interior position; hence, every day of defence by Wagner was vital to that of Charleston.

This policy was successful for two months, (10th July to 7th September,) and gave time to convert Fort Johnson from a forlorn old fort into a powerful earthwork—improved by the experiences of Wagner. Moultrie received similar advantages, and most of the cannon of Sumter were divided between Johnson and Moultrie. Batteries were established along the south shore of the channel from Johnson towards the city; and thus an interior defence was completed which, though it separated more widely the salient and principal works of the defence, by substituting Johnson for Sumter, yet rendered access to the upper harbor far more difficult, because a more powerful fire was concentrated from additional batteries upon vessels attempting to enter.

And thus it was that, even after Morris island was evacuated and Sumter dismantled, the fleet must still pass the fire of Moultrie and Bee to find itself in presence of a formidable earthwork, supported by continuous batteries, and commanding obstructions more difficult than any between Sumter and Moultrie.

The real nature of these obstructions was not suspected until the winter freshets had broken away and floated into our hands a fair specimen of them, which were certainly far more formidable than had been anticipated.

So well do the rebels keep their counsel that the best informed refugees, who had been constantly engaged about the harbor, appeared to know as little about them as we did.

During the progress of the engineers towards Wagner the iron-clads played an important part, using their guns whenever an opportunity, offered as shown in the instances quoted on page 583. It may be readily conceived, that, all things being equal, it was just as easy for the rebels to have worked towards our position as it was for our troops to work towards theirs. But there was a serious difference in the fact that the cannon of the iron-clads, and also of the gunboats, completely enfiladed the entire width of the narrow island, and absolutely interdicted any operation of the kind on the part of the rebels. In addition, whenever their fire was bearing severely on our own workmen, a request from the general always drew the fire of the vessels; and I do not know that it failed to be effective in any instance.

As a consequence the rebels were restricted to Wagner, and were powerless to hinder the progress of the trenches that were at last carried into the very ditch of the work, and decided its evacuation without assault.

The day before the contemplated assault, I led in the iron-clads in force, as agreed on, and battered the fort all day, tearing it into a sand heap.

The next morning it was to have been stormed, but the enemy had fled: they foresaw the inevitable result.

The vessels thus shared fully with the army in the operation that led to the abandonment of the works on Morris island, and besides what is already mentioned, prevented the access of re-enforcements or their accumulation between Wagner and Gregg.

The boats of the squadron were also engaged on picket duty by night along the sea-shore of Morris island, and the little stream on its inner border.

A detachment of seamen and marines, under Captain Parker, participated in the practice of the batteries at Fort Sumter, by working four navy rifle cannons, landed for the purpose.

The duties of the iron-clads were not performed under idle batteries. The guns of Wagner never failed to open on them, and fired until their crews were driven, by those of our iron-clads, to take shelter in the bomb-proofs. One of these cannon, a 10-inch, left deep dents on every turret, that will not easily be effaced.

The operations of the iron-clads against Morris island were appropriately closed by a severe contest with Fort Moultrie, Batteries Bee, Beauregard, &c.,

to relieve the Weehawken, which had grounded under their fire, and was finally got off with some severe injuries, owing to the falling tide having exposed the hull under the overhang.

There were other occasions when severe conflicts occurred with the rebel works on Sullivan's island.

And besides the principal attacks in force, there were few days from the first attack on Morris island (July 10) to its evacuation (September 7) that some iron-clads or gunboats were not engaged in firing at the enemy's works, so as to facilitate the labor of our troops ashore, as will be perceived by the following sample from the record:

Date.	Object.	Vessels engaged.
1863.		
July 18	Assault on Wagner	Montauk, (flag,) Ironsides, Catskill, Nantucket, Weehawken, Patapsco; gunboats Paul Jones, Ottawa, Seneca, Chippewa, Wissahickon.
July 22	Wagner	Nantucket, Ottawa, (gunboat.)
July 24	Wagner, to cover advance	Weehawken, (flag,) Ironsides, Catskill, Montauk, Patapsco, Nantucket; gunboats Paul Jones, Seneca, Ottawa, Dai Ching.
July 25	Wagner	Gunboats Ottawa, Dai Ching, Paul Jones.
July 28	Wagner	Weehawken, Catskill, Ottawa, (gunboat.)
July 29	Wagner	Ironsides, Patapsco.
July 30	Wagner	Ironsides, Catskill, Patapsco, Ottawa, (gunboat.)
July 31	Rebel batteries on Morris island	Ottawa, (gunboat.)
Aug. 1	Wagner	Montauk, Patapsco, Catskill, Weehawken, Passaic, Nahant, Marblehead, (gunboat.)
Aug. 2	Wagner	Ottawa, Marblehead, (gunboats.)
Aug. 4	Wagner	Montauk, Marblehead, (gunboat.)
Aug. 6	Wagner	Marblehead, (gunboat.)
Aug. 8	Wagner	Ottawa, Marblehead, Mahaska, (gunboats.)
Aug. 11	Wagner and vicinity	Patapsco, Catskill.
Aug. 13	Rebel batteries on Morris island	Gunboats Dai Ching, Ottawa, Mahaska, Wissahickon, Racer.
Aug. 14	Rebel batteries on Morris island	Gunboats Wissahickon, Mahaska, Ottawa, Dai Ching, Racer, Dan. Smith.
Aug. 15	Wagner	Mortar-boats Racer, Dan. Smith.
Aug. 17	Rebel batteries on Morris island, to direct fire from our batteries which opened on Sumter.	Weehawken, Ironsides, Montauk, Nahant, Catskill, Passaic, Patapsco; gunboats Canandaigua, Mahaska, Ottawa, Cimarron, Wissahickon, Dai Ching, Lodona.
Aug. 18	Wagner, to prevent assault	Ironsides, Passaic, Weehawken; gunboats Wissahickon, Mahaska, Dai Ching, Ottawa, Lodona.
Aug. 19	Wagner	Ironsides.
Aug. 20	Rebel batteries on Morris island	Ironsides; gunboats Mahaska, Ottawa, Dai Ching, Lodona.
Aug. 21	Sumter and Wagner	Ironsides, Patapsco; gunboats Mahaska, Dai Ching.
Aug. 22	Wagner	Weehawken, Ironsides, gunboat Montauk.
Aug. 23	Sumter	Weehawken, Montauk, Passaic, Patapsco, Nahant.
Sept. 1	Sumter and obstructions	Weehawken, Montauk, Passaic, Patapsco, Nahant, Lehigh.
Sept. 5	Between Sumter and Gregg	Lehigh, Nahant.
Sept. 6	Wagner and Gregg	Ironsides, Weehawken, Montauk, Passaic, Patapsco, Nahant, Lehigh.
Sept. 7	Batteries on Sullivan's island	Ironsides, Patapsco, Lehigh, Nahant, Montauk, Weehawken, (ashore.)
Sept. 8	Batteries on Sullivan's island	Ironsides, Patapsco, Lehigh, Nahant, Montauk, Weehawken, (ashore.)

I shall now briefly comment on the various qualities of the Monitors.

1st. Capacity for resistance.
2d. Power of ordnance.
3d. Draught of water.
4th. Speed.
5th. Number of crew.

1st. *Endurance.*—During the operations against Morris island the nine iron-clads fired eight thousand projectiles, and received eight hundred and eighty-two (882) hits. Including the service at Sumter in April and the Ogechee, the total number was eleven hundred and ninety-four (1,194,) distributed as follows:

Service of iron-clads. South Atlantic blockading squadron. Shots fired and hits received by them during operations against Morris island.

Vessels.	No. of shots fired.		Hits.	Hits April 7, 1863.	Hits at Ogechee.	Total hits.
	15-in.	11-in.				
Catskill	138	425	86	20	....	106
Montauk	301	478	154	14	46	214
Lehigh	41	28	36	....	....	36
Passaic	119	107	90	35	9	134
Nahant	170	276	69	36	....	105
Patapsco	178	230	96	47	1	144
Weehawken	264	633	134	53	....	187
Nantucket	44	155	53	51	....	104
Ironsides	....	4,439	164	....	....	164
Total	1,255	6,771	882	256	56	1,194

	No. of shots fired.	Weight of proj. fired, in tons.
By Ironsides	4,439	288½
11-inch, by Monitors	2,332	151½
15-inch by Monitors	1,255	213½
Total	8,026	653½

Of the eight Monitors, one was always absent at Wassaw (Nahant or Nantucket) to blockade the rebel ram. The Lehigh did not arrive until August 30, therefore was only able to participate in the operations of the remaining seven days, but did good work.

For some time only five Monitors were available for general attack, and then six, which was the greatest number disposable at any one time.

The consequences of the protracted firing and hard usage to which the Monitors were exposed during these two months of incessant service, were unavoidably very considerable in the aggregate; and the greater, also, that all repair which could possibly be dispensed with was postponed to the conclusion. It was therefore necessarily extensive when entered upon. The battering received was without precedent. The Montauk had been struck two hundred and fourteen (214) times; the Weehawken one hundred and eighty-seven (187) times, and almost entirely by 10-inch shot. What vessels have ever been subjected to such a test?

It is not surprising that they should need considerable repair after sustaining such severe pounding for so long a time, but only that they could be restored at all to serviceable condition. The force of the 10-inch shot must be experienced to be appreciated. Any one in contact with the part of the turret struck falls senseless, and I have been nearly shaken off my feet in the pilot-house when engaging Moultrie.

All the little defects of detail were marked by such a searching process. Decks were cut through; cannon were worn out; side armor shaken; tops of pilot-houses crushed, &c. But all these were reparable, and no vital principle was seriously touched.

With such workshops and means as a northern navy yard includes, the repair of all Monitors would have been speedily executed; but when machinery, tools, labor, and material have all to be obtained, as they were here, from a great distance, there was of necessity considerable delay; and, moreover, it was not admissible to withdraw but a portion of the Monitors at a time from the blockade.

The additions that were deemed advisable for strengthening the pilot-houses and turrets were also put on at this time, and the bottoms cleaned, for they had now become so foul with oysters and grass that the speed was reduced to three or three and a half knots, and, with the strong tide of this harbor, added considerably to the difficulties of working the vessels properly under fire.

On one night I was caught by heavy weather from the southeast while close up to Sumter, when I had gone to attack it, and it was well that the darkness of the night prevented the slowness of our motion from being perceived while extricating the Monitors from their position.

Power of ordnance.—Each turret contains two guns, and from the peculiar facility which it has for giving direction to the heaviest ordnance, no doubt, arises the desire to make these of the heaviest description. How far other considerations should control the character of the ordnance is necessarily an unsettled question.

To strike an armored ship it may be best to use a gun capable of the greatest power; but whether this shall be derived from a projectile of great weight, driven by low velocity, or of less weight, and high velocity; whether it shall be a fifteen-inch gun, fired with thirty-five or forty pounds, or a thirteen-inch, fired with fifty pounds of powder, is not here material; the weight of the gun for either purpose will not vary to any important degree. But in operations against earthworks, whose material cannot be damaged permanently, but only disturbed, and which are only to be dealt with by keeping down their fire, a much lighter projectile would be preferable, in order that the practice may be as rapid as possible. Hence a piece of 16,000 pounds for ten-inch or eleven-inch shot and shell.

When a number of Monitors are brought together it would be better also to have guns of like kind in each turret, and bring into action whichever might be preferable. Each of the Monitors of this squadron had a fifteen-inch and a smaller gun, (eleven-inch or eight-inch rifle,) and hence the rapidity of fire, which was most desirable, was not attained. That this was due to the calibre of the gun, and not to its being located in a turret, may be shown by one notable instance.

November 9, 1863, the Montauk, Captain Davis, was engaged in battering Sumter. In so doing the eleven-inch gun fired twenty-five shells successively in one hour, of which twenty-one hit the wall of the fort aimed at—distance sixteen hundred yards. This is at the rate of one shell in 2.4 minutes, which is not only rapid but also exceedingly accurate practice. There is no reason why another eleven-inch, if placed in the adjoining carriage, (instead of the fifteen-inch,) could not have been fired in the same time, at which rate that Monitor would have delivered an eleven-inch shell every 1.2 minute.

The rates of fire reported for the Ironsides, by Captain Rowan, are—

	Time. h. m.	No. fired.	Time for each fire. m.
Most rapid	0.50	25	1.74
Continuous	2.55	490	2.86
Assumed	1.00	360	1.33
Montauk	1.00	25	2.40

It will be perceived that for a short space of time the frigate delivered a shell from each gun in 1.74 minute, for three hours in 2.86 minutes, and it is believed that a fire could be sustained at the rate of 1.33 minute. The last rate is therefore possible, but I am sure it would be difficult to sustain it long with much regard to good aim and considerable distances; and I believe, on the whole, that for every practical purpose there would be all desirable rapidity of fire from the eleven-inch in turret. Thus it is to be presumed that there will be equality of ordnance power in the same number of eleven-inch guns as to rapidity of fire, whether in a turret or broadside.

Draught of water.—The Monitors of the Passaic class draw about eleven and a half (11½) feet of water when properly trimmed. On this coast ten and eleven feet is the most convenient draught of water for penetrating all the principal sounds and rivers and navigating them to any extent. A greater draught restricts a vessel in movement, and in many instances excludes her from several ports, except under very favorable circumstances.

Speed.—The speed of the Monitors is not great, (seven knots,) but it is quite respectable with a clean bottom, and is fully equal to that of the Ironsides. Their steerage is peculiar, but, when understood and rightly managed, not difficult of control. They pivot with celerity and in less space than almost any other class of vessel.

Number of men.—The number of men required to work them and the guns is only eighty, which is very moderate.

In common with all iron-clads, the scope of vision is much restricted, for the plain reason that in such vessels apertures of any size must be avoided. There are some other defects, but they are not inherent, and it is believed are susceptible of being remedied wholly or in part. So much for the Monitors.

The Ironsides is a fine, powerful ship. Her armor has stood heavy battering very well, and her broadside of seven eleven-inch guns and one eight-inch rifle has always told with signal effect when opened on the enemy. Draught of water about 15½ to 16 feet. Speed six to seven knots, and crew about four hundred and forty men.

The defects of the vessel are the unplated ends, which are consequently easily damaged by a raking fire, and involve the rudder and screw more or less, while she can return no fire in either direction. This was particularly and frequently inconvenient in attacking the works on Morris island, for at certain stages of the tide vessels tail nearly across the channel, and present bow and stern to the beach of Morris island, so that sometimes it was necessary to delay placing the vessel in position, and at others she would swing around very awkwardly when engaged.

The Monitors, on the other hand, were almost equally well defended on all sides, and could fire in any direction. The Ironsides was also open to descending shot, and her scope of fire too much restricted by badly placed ports.

The desire for comparison which rages just now can easily be satisfied by bringing the above data in juxtaposition.

Just as they are, the Ironsides is capable of a more rapid and concentrated fire, which, under the circumstances, made her guns more effective than the fifteen-inch of the Monitors. On the other hand, she was restricted by draught to the mid-channel, was very vulnerable to a raking fire, and the direction of her own guns was very limited laterally.

The Monitors could operate in most of the channels—could direct their fire around the whole circle—and were almost equally well defended on all sides.

The defects in both classes of vessels are susceptible of being remedied partially or entirely. The defence of the Ironsides could be made complete, and that of the Monitors equally so. The armament of the Monitors could be perfected so as to give all desirable rapidity of fire, but by no contrivance could the Ironsides be enabled to use much heavier guns than those mounted. Yet when such changes were made as experience has suggested, there still would remain to the Monitors the lighter draught, choice of guns from the heaviest to the lightest, defensibility, and direction of fire around the whole circle; consequently the ability to carry a heavy battery into the least depth of water, with equal power of offence and defence in any direction, and that with half the number of guns carried in broadside by another vessel.

The comparison now made is to be understood as having relation to existing circumstances, and not at all intended as conclusive in regard to the general merits of iron-clads.

It is in this sense that the action of the Navy Department is to be considered with reference to the selection of one class of vessels over another.

It is evident that it was not designed to adopt any one style exclusively, for of the three vessels first ordered two were of the ordinary broadside class—the Ironsides and the Galena. The latter was quickly proved to be absolutely inefficient, and so must any armored steamer of that size. It is universally admitted that plates of less than four and a half (4½) inches cannot stand the shock of heavy projectiles, and vessels so armored must be of considerable tonnage.

I presume the department only intended to build such vessels as were best adapted to the service at the scene of war.

Keeping in view the peculiar exigencies of the case, which required light draught and great ordnance power, it appears that the selection of the department could not have been more judicious in preferring a number of Monitors to operate from a heavy frigate as a base; and if the intent of the department could have been carried out in regard to numbers, we should now have been in entire possession of the coast from the capes of Virginia to New Orleans, including Wilmington, Charleston, Mobile, &c.

Many defects of both classes are easily remediable, but some of those in the Monitors could only be determined by the test of battle; before that, approximation only was possible.

What other style of vessel could the department have chosen? Certainly none that has been built by English or French naval authorities. The Warrior and her class are exceedingly powerful, but could not get within gunshot here.*

On the other hand, there is very little navigable water on this coast which is not accessible to the Monitors. They command supremely all that is near the shore, and cannot themselves be reached by vessels of heavier draught. So that when there was some reason to apprehend the appearance of certain rams in this quarter, I assured the department that the iron-clads could maintain position so long as coal and provisions lasted.

It may appear that I speak too positively on the subject, but some experience with them certainly gives a right to do so. With a single exception I have been on board a Monitor in all the principal actions, and the recurrence of

* According to Rear-Admiral Paris, the French Gloria draws 28 feet; the British Warrior 26 feet; the Black Prince 23½ feet; even those of inferior class, Defence and Resistance, draw 24 feet. Not one of these vessels could cross the Charleston bar, and would be perfectly impotent to render the least service in any of the operations now being carried on.

casualties to the fleet captains* near me shows that I was in a situation to judge. I was once in the Ironsides in an attack on Moultrie and Sumter. I have also watched the behavior of the Monitors at anchor through all the phases of winter weather in this exposed situation.

The completeness with which four little Monitors, supported by an iron-clad frigate, have closed this port, is well worth noting.

Very soon after entering the roads I advanced one Monitor well up towards the inner debouches of the northern channels, supported by another. On the night of the 19th of July an English steamer attempted to run in, and having eluded the hot pursuit of the outside blockade, no doubt indulged in the belief that all danger was past. But the gallant Captain Rodgers was in advance that night with the Catskill, and a shell sent suddenly by him ahead of the culprit steamer signified no escape. In despair or alarm the latter grounded on a shoal, and her wreck has since served as a warning to like evil-doers. Two or three steamers that were in managed to get out immediately after, and one or two may have gotten in, for the crews of the Monitors were often too fatigued then with a day's battle to keep watch at night; but there ended the business as such, and for several months not a vessel has passed in or out.

These four Monitors, who thus keep watch and ward, muster eight (8) guns and three hundred and twenty (320) men, which is almost insignificant in contrast with the work done.

I have thus put on paper the general impressions now uppermost, but very hastily and under great pressure of business, which will, I hope, excuse such imperfections as may have inadvertently occurred.

With more leisure I could do full justice to this interesting subject.

I have the honor to be, very respectfully, your obedient servant,

JNO. A. DAHLGREN,
Rear-Admiral, Commanding S. A. B. Squadron.

Hon. GIDEON WELLES,
Secretary of the Navy, Washington, D. C.

Rear-Admiral Porter's views upon iron-clads.

No. 40.] MISSISSIPPI SQUADRON, FLAG-SHIP BLACK HAWK,
Cairo, February 16, 1864.

SIR: I have the honor to report that I have made a visit to Cincinnati to examine the iron-clads there, and see what prospect there was of getting some of these vessels into immediate service. * * * * * *

It is much to be regretted that the boats at Cincinnati are not finished, as I am certain they would accomplish all that can be done by Monitors. No complaint, however, can be justly made against the contractors for want of activity in the performance of the work on these boats.

When I visited Cincinnati a little over a year ago no preparations were then made to commence these vessels. Now they are in a fair way of being completed, and I think can all be put in the water and ready to operate against an enemy by the first of June.

When the government do get these boats, they may rest assured of receiving as good Monitor-built vessels as have yet been contracted for, for though I have not seen many to which I can compare them, I am glad to say that in workmanship, model, and probably in speed, these vessels will be equal, if not superior, to any Monitors yet built, at least of those that I have seen. I can only draw comparison between these and the first Ericsson Monitor, which I was sent by order of the department to examine. I remember pronouncing

---

* Captain George Rodgers was next ahead when killed off Wagner, and his successor, Captain Badger, had his leg broken by an iron splinter in the attack on Sumter.

that vessel "a perfect success," "and capable of defeating anything that then floated." I was looked upon at that time as something of an enthusiast, as my opinions were widely at variance with those of some scientific gentlemen. The results have justified me in forming a high estimate of the Monitor principle, and I was pleased to see that on our western waters we can build them as well, if not better, than in the workshops of the north. No better proof is wanted of the ability of the west to supply all demands of the government for iron-clad vessels than is given in those building at Cincinnati. The work is perfect in every respect, and put together so well that it may be compared to joiner's work. The hulls are as strong as can possibly be desired, the speed will be good, and the only fault in the vessels, if they have any, is the "overhang" aft, which is of no consequence in a smooth sea, but must be injurious when the Monitors have to go from port to port.

The nearest to completion of these Monitors is one of those in the Greenwood building; she can be launched in a month, and I am of opinion, when finished, could commence at Cairo, and going down the river, could destroy every vessel we have on these waters, unless they took advantage of their greater speed and ran away. The heaviest and best vessel we have, the Benton, would stand a poor chance against the Monitor alluded to. If she failed to sink the Benton with shot, she could surely do it with her beak or ram, which is not the least formidable thing about her; this is saying a great deal, for the Benton is a very formidable vessel, and since she has been under my command has been struck 130 times in the hull without any apparent damage. Three of the Monitors at Cincinnati are on the improved Ericsson plan, while the two light-draughts building at the Hamilton Works are to be submerged when going into action. I do not like that as well as the Ericsson model, as there is more machinery about them than is desirable; simplicity of arrangement being the object to be aimed at in vessels-of-war. The plan of these latter mentioned vessels is a good one, provided their armor and backing is strong enough to stand heavy shot, which I think will be the case if they only encounter the ordinary rifle projectile.

From the information received from the different officers I have sent on duty at various times to the points where these iron vessels are building, the same favorable report is made of their efficiency, and the good work that is being put on them; and in six months we will have a fleet of vessels that will keep this river against the fleets of the world, and be enabled to carry the war into the enemy's quarters where there is anything like an equality in guns. I think too much has been expected of Monitors heretofore, and the fact that two or three of them were not able to overcome obstacles formidable enough to keep out a large fleet of three-deckers has, in a measure, weakened the confidence of the public (who generally know little or nothing about such matters) in them.

But the Monitors, for harbor defence, are just as valuable as they were on the day when the first one drove the leviathan "Merrimack" back to her hole, and saved the honor of the nation. I am sure that Monitors would have done much better on this river than the old Pook gunboats did, which were built for temporary purposes only, or until Monitors could take their places. Earthworks on elevated positions are difficult to silence, it is true, except by a concentrated fire of many guns, and Monitors are not well provided in numbers. No vessels have been more successful than the Mississippi gunboats whenever they have been called on to attack such works. Still they were very deficient in one respect, as they were very vulnerable, suffered a good deal, and proved that in the end the Monitor principle, from its invulnerability, was the only thing that could be safely depended on. For this reason I often wished that I had been provided with *one* good Monitor, with which, at certain times, I could have accomplished more than with a fleet of such boats as we have here.

A new boat, the Ozark, has just arrived here. As far as her turret is concerned she is all right, but her hull is too high out of water, and she lacks speed; she can only be considered one of the temporary vessels, and will be valuable only under an ordinary fort.

The two light-draught Monitors, Osage and Neosho, do very well for light work, but are not at all suitable for rough weather or heavy service; and I would not recommend the building of any more vessels of this kind. A more uncomfortable class of vessels it is not possible to think of; they are perfectly killing to officers and men. The work on them is not as good as that done at Cincinnati and Pittsburg, but it is quite creditable for first attempts.

If it is the intention of the government to build any more Monitors, or, indeed, iron-vessels of peculiar construction, I would beg leave to recommend that a fair portion of patronage be given to the western foundries. I believe the work will be done cheaper and better than it can be done elsewhere. Vessels of any size can be built in any part of these rivers. The senseless cry about the want of water, here or there, should not be taken into consideration for a moment, for at low water the whole Mississippi is a chain of sand bars, and no place then possesses any advantage over another. There is less water below Cairo than there is at Cairo and neighborhood, and at dead low water a boat drawing six feet cannot get above Helena, while, for eight months in the year, a vessel drawing ten feet could traverse nearly the whole length of the river. It matters little, then, what point on the river is occupied as a building point; proper encouragement on the part of the government would cause workshops to spring up in all directions, and government would have vessels built by private enterprise cheaper than could be built at government works out here, which in this region would cost large outlays before they would be ready to build a steamer.

It is astonishing how little these western manufacturers require to commence operations with; and while the government officials would be laying out the yard to work in, they would have the vessel built.

I do not know that any useful information can be gained by a history of the iron-clads used on this river, for I presume and hope that there is no intention of building any more vessels of that class; they were temporary expedients, and they have done their work well. I do not think it desirable, however, that any more should be built. No vessels have done harder fighting anywhere; they have averaged twenty-one hours each under fire since they were first built and put in commission. Some of them have been sunk and others badly cut up, but they have seldom failed to achieve their object, and have opened, or helped to open, over 3,600 miles of river once in the hands of the enemy. Had they been Monitors, they would have accomplished their work in much less time, as there was never sufficient confidence in their ability to stand shot, except when opposed to a fort bow on, in which case I know of no failure on their part to silence a battery, though they could not always take possession. Had they been Monitors, many things would have been undertaken that were deemed too hazardous in semi-wooden vessels, and many forts would have been captured or attacked successfully that were deemed impregnable against anything but Monitors. I can say, however, that no backwardness was ever shown by the commanders of the temporary gunboats in attacking any fort that was erected on the river with more or less success; and the reason why more casualties did not occur on board the vessels was owing to their fighting bow on, and presenting their strongest part. These vessels have a wood backing on their bow of twenty-four inches of oak, which is covered with three inches of iron. I know of no instance where the iron on the bow was perforated. Some of the plates were cracked and badly indented, but were always serviceable afterwards, and it was seldom thought necessary to repair them.

In connexion with this matter, I beg leave to say that from my observation the resistance of iron depends more on the wooden backing than on the thickness of the iron—that is, two inches of iron on thirty-six inches of oak will resist more than three inches of iron on fifteen inches of oak. I have, moreover, noticed that where there is a backing of wood covered with three-inch iron, and *that* iron with wood again, the resistance of the latter will prevent balls of heavy size from entering the iron. In fact, it is hardly indented. This was particularly demonstrated in the passage of the fleet past Vicksburg, when it was necessary to take every precaution to insure success and prevent injury to the steamers. Heavy logs, twenty inches in diameter, were hung perpendicularly on the sides of the vessel close together, and so secured that no shot could strike the side without passing through the logs. Bales of hay were also packed over the decks and sterns in sufficient thickness (it was supposed) to prevent the passage of any shot. Suffice it to say, the pressed hay was no protection whatever against shot or shell. They passed through four or five bales, and very much endangered the vessels by setting the hay on fire. Wherever the projectiles of the enemy struck the logs, they did no further damage; they would pass through the logs, strike the iron without leaving more than an indentation, and glance off. Many instances of narrow escapes could be mentioned where the vessels were saved by the intervention of the wood, and in no instance were the vessels damaged where the logs were properly placed. The incidents of that night—the passage of the Vicksburg batteries—suggested to me the idea of first having a heavy backing of wood, then a layer of iron, and then a covering of wood over the iron, which will, I am convinced, make a vessel perfectly shot-proof. I notice that the idea is not an original one, but has been discovered and recommended by several persons. There are two vessels in this squadron, the Lafayette and Choctaw, which give proof of the value of heavy backing to iron. These vessels were built with heavy frames, covered on the outside with gutta-percha, and then with a light thickness of iron. Whenever these vessels have been struck on the iron where the wood backing was heavy, they resisted the shot of heaviest calibre, but where the backing was light shot went in at one side and out at the other. The defence of gutta-percha was not of the slightest use; on the contrary, it was a detriment, and aided very much in destroying the vessels by rot. It is so much extra weight that the vessels have to carry, without deriving the slightest benefit from it. The money that built the Lafayette and Choctaw would have built three Monitors of such a model; that one Monitor would have destroyed both of the first. I would here state that these two vessels will only be serviceable for a short time, as they are already showing signs of weakness. They are not very serviceable, have not speed enough, and are too unwieldy for rams, and in some parts are very vulnerable. They have, however, fine machinery, and when they wear out it can be fitted to better hulls. I consider these vessels only as temporary expedients, to give way to the Monitor class when there is a sufficient number built.

Another class of vessels in this squadron deserves mention, as showing the different expedients resorted to to open and defend the Mississippi river. I allude to the Tuscumbia, Chillicothe, and Indianola. Two of these have been tried under batteries, and the Indianola in battle against vessels, and have shown that the Monitor principle only was the right one. Their turrets were in no instance found impenetrable to the heavy rifled shot, and besides they were soon damaged in their wheels, which afforded fine targets for the enemy to fire at. Still, two of these vessels remained under fire as long as any Monitors have been known to remain at one time, and if they did not come up to the Monitors in invulnerability, they accomplished all that was required at the time, viz: the capture of the enemy's stronghold. The builders never claimed that they should be considered more than *temporary* expedients with which to harass the enemy; and taken in that sense, they certainly may be considered very good vessels, and have fairly repaid all the money spent on them, taking into consideration the work they have done.

As to approving of any of the above-mentioned styles of gunboat as part of a permanent system of national defence to be adopted in this country, that I cannot do. Any professional man who will lay aside his prejudices caused by the discomforts incident to the Monitors, must admit that as a harbor defence they are the best and only vessels to be built; and I hope we shall see every harbor in the United States where there is a chance of an enemy penetrating, supplied with two or three of these floating batteries. If they have not been able to penetrate the harbor of Charleston, where fifty guns to one was opposed to them, and where they had to contend with obstructions placed in their way impossible to be removed, it in no way detracts from their well-earned reputation for efficiency. They have done at Charleston what no other vessels ever built *could possibly have accomplished;* and though the army, as usual when combined operations are carried on, has monopolized all the honors, it is a very certain fact that the Monitors held their own as no other vessels could have done, and under their shelter the army was enabled to perform their work successfully.

I hope, sir, you will excuse the unreasonable length of this communication on the subject of the Monitors; but I know their value when properly used, have felt the want of them so much at times that I would have exchanged several even of the best of my vessels for one of them properly fitted. I have seen a whole army kept at bay for the want of one of these little "shot-proofs," and have, now and then, been tempted to do foolish things in hopes of accomplishing what I deemed impracticable. The Cincinnati was sunk when my own judgment told me it was wrong to place her where I was called upon to order her to. With a single Monitor results would have been very different; and on that day, instead of having a vessel sunk, the right wing of our army would have gained a position commanding the most important works in and about Vicksburg. Vulnerable as this vessel was, it would not have done for the navy to hesitate, when the *army thought there was a prospect of success.*

In conclusion, sir, permit me to express the hope that the west may be converted into a large workshop for the building of future Monitors of all sizes. I know of no part of the Union where the work can be done better or quicker.

I have the honor to be, sir, very respectfully, your obedient servant,

DAVID D. PORTER,
Rear-Admiral.

Hon. GIDEON WELLES,
Secretary of the Navy, Washington, D. C.

Commodore John Rodgers's opinion of iron-clads.

WASHINGTON, D. C., *April* 7, 1864.

SIR: I have the honor to reply to your letter in regard to armored vessels. There are two classes of iron-clad vessels-of-war in use, in which two different principles are involved; these classes have each their peculiar defects and advantages. I refer to the Ironsides class and to the Monitor class.

In the Ironsides class the hull of a wooden man-of-war, as constructed for general purposes, is clad with iron. It is true some modification of shape and increase of size is required to meet the additional weight which she has to carry, but still, in essentials, she is a vessel of the ordinary model; she has the advantages of ample quarters for her crew, with free access to her decks in storms, with natural ventilation, with abundance of light, with numerous guns, giving her a rapidity of fire unattainable in a Monitor, and essential in battering forts; and she is as able to carry canvas as other men-of-war.

The Monitor class, as far as I know, is new. If I understand the idea, it is to cut off all the surface above water, except that which may be necessary to flotation, and to carry the guns in a revolving turret, or turrets, near the centre of motion, and supported upon the keel and kelsons.

The plans upon which Mr. Ericsson has worked out this idea of his may be modified by further experience, but the idea itself will be employed while iron-clad vessels are used in warfare.

It has these advantages: The Monitor has the least possible surface to be plated, and, therefore, takes the least possible tonnage to float armor of a given thickness, or with a given tonnage allows the greatest possible thickness of armor, and consequently the greatest possible impenetrability. The ability to carry armor is proportionate to the tonnage; but the Monitors of 844 tons have actually thicker plating than the Ironsides of 3,480 tons, and than the Warrior of 6,000 tons, and yet the Ironsides and Warrior have only the middle portion of their hulls plated, their ends being merely of wood without armor.

The guns of the Monitors, near the centre of motion, are supported upon the keel and kelsons, upborne by the depth of water under them, and carried by the whole strength of the hull. In Monitors heavier guns are therefore practicable than can ever be carried in broadside out upon the ribs of a ship.

In Monitors, concentration of guns and armor is the object sought. In them the plating is compressed into inches of elevation, while in the Ironsides class it is extended over feet, and the comparatively numerous guns distributed over the decks of the Ironsides class are moulded into a few larger ones in the turrets of the Monitors.

When power is required in the individual guns, enough to crush and pierce the side of the adversary at a single blow, the most formidable artillery must be employed, and fifteen-inch guns are the most formidable which, so far, we have tried; but no vessel of the Ironsides class can carry these guns, and the Monitors actually do carry them.

If target experiments are reliable, a shot from the fifteen-inch gun will crush in the sides of any vessel of the Ironsides class in Europe or America. A single well-planted blow would sink either the Warrior, Glorie, Magenta, Minotaur, or Bellerophon.

The Dictator, of 3,000 tons, has armor thick enough, I believe, to withstand fifteen-inch guns.

The objections to the Monitor class, such as I have seen in use, are from fewness of guns; the lack of rapidity of fire in battering forts or wooden vessels; the loss of accommodation from dispensing with the upper deck or decks; the greater unhealthiness from dampness and from confinement below, in even a moderate sea; from the loss of light; and from depending upon blowers driven by steam for ventilation.

The Monitors are slower than their steam power would seem to promise. In all of them the slip of their screws is excessive. This I attribute to the overhang, which, if a source of strength in action from its use as a ram, and from its protecting the propeller and rudder, is a source of weakness and strain at sea. The overhang has the advantage of keeping the vessel very steady. She cannot roll with these wing-like projections holding up her sides, nor pitch, nor send with the immense flat surface of the overhang to resist those motions; but as the Monitor is slower than other vessels of like tonnage and power, it must be presumed that the difference of shape makes the difference of speed; and the overhang constitutes the sole difference of shape.

If ordinary vessels can endure the pitching and rending motions, it may be inferred that the Monitors can endure them. If ordinary vessels can have their rams below water, so may the Monitors; nor is it necessary to equality that the rudder and propeller of the Monitor should be better protected than those of her competitors.

The Monitor model rolls very little, and is extremely easy in a sea-way. In a gale of wind it was found on board the Monitor Weehawken that while her companion, the wooden corvette Iroquois, (deemed a very perfect model,) had an excessively violent motion, so violent indeed that no one could stand upon her decks without the assistance of life-lines, the Weehawken had so little motion that a bottle of claret stood for an hour upon its narrow base on the dinner-table in the cabin, when it was put away.

I do not consider the lowness of the Monitors in the water a source of unsafeness. They start to sea with sufficient buoyancy, and, by the consumption of coal and provisions, they hourly grow lighter. Anything lighter than water will float upon it, and however deeply buried, while lighter than water, it must come to the surface; but effectual means must be used to keep the vessel tight, for any considerable accumulation of water in the hull will sink her, which is true also of ships generally.

The casemated vessels, such as the Ironsides, if not safer than Monitors, are more comfortable, and, therefore, probably more healthy, with greater facilities for carrying canvas than the Monitor class seems to admit of.

To sum up my conclusions, I think that the Monitor class and the Ironsides class are different weapons, each having its peculiar advantages; both needed to an iron-clad navy, both needed in war; but that when the Monitor class measures its strength against the Ironsides class, then, with vessels of equal size, the Monitor class will overpower the Ironsides class, and, indeed, a single Monitor will capture many casemated vessels of no greater individual size or speed; and as vessels find their natural antagonists in vessels, and only their exceptional antagonists in forts, it must be considered that, upon the whole, the Monitor principle contains the most successful elements for plating vessels for war purposes.

I have the honor to be, very respectfully, your obedient servant,

JOHN RODGERS,
Commodore United States Navy.

Hon. GIDEON WELLES,
Secretary of the Navy.

Brigadier General Barnard's opinion of turreted vessels.

HEADQUARTERS CHIEF ENGINEER OF DEFENCES,
Washington, February 4, 1864.

SIR: In reply to your letter of the 3d, I have to say that, having occasion in October last to visit New York on business connected with my former duties there, and having been for several months serving as a member of the "permanent commission," constituted by the Navy Department for examining the numerous projects and inventions pressed upon it, I felt it desirable to have a little more practical acquaintance with the construction of our iron-clads than I had, and desired from the Secretary of War an order.

The object of getting the order was to cover my expenses while doing a public duty, and to avoid being rated as on "leave of absence," while really engaged in public duties.

The order I took with me was prepared on a memorandum written by the Secretary himself, and simply directed me to proceed to New York and inspect the iron-clads. Subsequently a more formal order was made out to inspect all the iron-clads, and to report to the War Department. The order thus modified was never seen by me until my return. Believing it to have arisen from a mere misapprehension of the original intent, I did not think it worth while to say why I had not executed it. Nevertheless, had I been able, I should have returned and completed the inspection. As it was, I was met here by important duties. Then by an order placing me on a board for altering the armament for the defences of Washington; then by an order to examine the shore of Lake Erie, &c., &c.; so that it has been entirely incompatible with my duties to make such an inspection and study of our iron-clads as would justify an official report to the War Department.

The information I got was for my own use, as a member of your commission, and as an engineer officer. I formed a high opinion of armored and turreted vessels built after Mr. Ericsson's designs, particularly as harbor-defence vessels—in fact, coming to the conclusion that his plans furnish the best solution of the problem of constructing vessels for this purpose. I also believed that in the Dictator and Puritan we should have vessels capable of encountering the heaviest seas, if not of keeping the sea a long time, and making trans-Atlantic voyages, and that, from their armament and slight exposure to an enemy's shot, they would contend successfully with anything afloat.

I am, very respectfully, your most obedient,

J. G. BARNARD,
Brigadier General.

G. V. Fox, Esq.,
Assistant Secretary of the Navy.

Letter of Governor Morgan to the President asking that an iron-clad be stationed in New York harbor.

STATE OF NEW YORK,
Executive Department, Albany, October 31, 1862.

DEAR SIR: I enclose a copy of a letter received from the Hon. Gideon Welles, Secretary of the Navy, dated 17th September last, being a reply to a telegraphic despatch to him, sent by me on the 16th of the same month, asking for an iron-clad government steamer to be placed in New York harbor for its defence.

The startling events which have since occurred upon the ocean, and information through the newspapers and private sources as to the designs of the rebels in building and purchasing iron-clad vessels in Europe, freely show the necessity for the means of defence asked for.

The subject is of the greatest importance, and I therefore feel it to be my duty to renew my request, and to make it directly to you, not because the Navy Department has shown an indisposition to act, but because of the importance of the measure to the interests of the city and State of New York and the country, that if the abilities of the Navy Department will not permit a compliance, your excellency will direct that provision be otherwise made to meet this imperative necessity.

What I desire is that an armed iron-clad steamer be sent to New York to defend its harbor, and that the necessary order to that end be immediately given by you. The people of New York are alarmed already, but they would be much more so if the defenceless condition of that city was more fully known to them.

I am, with great respect, your obedient servant,

E. D. MORGAN.

His Excellency ABRAHAM LINCOLN, *President.*

NAVY DEPARTMENT, *September* 17, 1862.

SIR: I have the honor to acknowledge the receipt of your telegraphic despatch, dated Albany, September 16, 5.30 p. m., suggesting "that the new iron-clad government steamer can be put to no use more important for all interested than by placing her at once in New York harbor."

The steamer referred to is probably the New Ironsides, now at Philadelphia, where her presence is most earnestly requested by Governor Curtin. The Galena and Monitor are guarding the entrance of the James river in anticipation of the Merrimac No. 2. Under these circumstances it would seem to be impossible to comply with your request. In this connexion, I desire to present for your consideration a letter addressed by this department to the chairman of the House Naval Committee, dated March 25, 1862; also, as bearing on the same subject, the letter of General Totten, dated May 10, 1862, addressed to the Secretary of War, and communicated to the House.

I am, respectfully, your obedient servant,

GIDEON WELLES,
Secretary of the Navy.

His Excellency E. D. MORGAN,
Governor of the State of New York, Albany.

Memorial from the Committee of Boston Board of Trade, asking that the Nahant may remain at Boston.

OFFICE OF THE BOARD OF TRADE,
Boston, November 12, 1862.

SIR: The undersigned, a committee of this board on the subject of "defence of the harbor," appointed soon after the beginning of the present war, have already more than once asked the attention of the government to the comparatively defenceless state of the harbor of Boston, and have also to-day addressed the honorable Secretary of War on this subject. In view of the recent reckless depredations of the piratical steamer Alabama, and her reported near proximity to our bay, and also the apparently well authenticated fact recently made public that powerful rams are now partially constructed in England to be used by the rebels in an attack on our principal cities on the northern coast, added to an apprehension (by no means unfounded) that our country may suddenly be involved in a foreign war, it cannot be regarded strange that this community should be pervaded by deep solicitude as to the absence of immediate means to make any adequate defence against an attack from either of the sources referred to. A public meeting on the Exchange, on this subject, has been proposed, but discountenanced by more reflecting minds as calculated to do much harm by advertising to the world the weakness of our means of defence, and it is probable that from similar considerations so little has been published in the papers of the day. Under these circumstances it is hoped that you will appreciate the motives which lead the undersigned, respectfully but earnestly, to urge on your immediate consideration the importance of your co-operation with the War Department in causing this harbor to be completely fortified with the least possible delay. The three forts, Warren, Independence, and Winthrop, which are designed to mount 554 guns, are now ready to receive 475 guns. Only 153 guns are now actually mounted, and none of these can be said to be of sufficiently large calibre to make a successful defence against an armor-plated steamship, especially if she should attempt to enter the harbor through "Broad Sound." The works to receive nearly all the guns—say about 475—are now complete, so far as it depends on the engineer's department. It only remains for the requisite ordnance to be supplied. Until this is done, and even afterwards, this harbor cannot be said to be in a proper state of defence without a floating battery. We are not unaware of the embarrassment which the government has suffered from the limited means of supplying ordnance in its great emergency, nor would we make the claims of Boston harbor for protection unduly prominent, but you will pardon us if we suggest that, after a war of twenty months, the harbor of the third commercial city in the Union ought no longer to be allowed by its very weakness to invite the aggression of a desperate enemy. It is believed by practical men that through "Broad Sound," (one of the two principal entrances to this harbor,) a reckless and daring piratical iron-clad steamer might enter without serious injury and lay our city under contribution. Apart from all other considerations, we need only allude to the moral effect of such an act on our cause at home and abroad. It is believed that our statement as to the present actual condition of the forts will be found substantiated by recent official reports.

In view of the foregoing facts, we beg respectfully to suggest that the new iron-clad steamer Nahant, (of the Monitor class,) now nearly completed by Mr. Loring, be allowed to remain in this harbor for its defence, at least until the necessary guns are placed in the several fortifications of the harbor and the pirate Alabama has been either captured or destroyed, provided that such disposal of the Nahant be, in any reasonable degree, compatible with the immediate or more important requirements of some other branch of the public service.

At this point we need not say that we do not presume to dictate, although we should be derelict in our duty if we omitted to present to your mind the great importance of at once placing this harbor in a state of defence, and the deep solicitude of this board and of the community generally in reference to this matter. May we not hope that this subject will receive the prompt action that its importance demands.

We remain, respectfully, your most obedient servants,

EDWARD S. TOBEY,
F. W. LINCOLN, Jr.,
W. T. GLIDEN,
C. O. WHITMORE,
THOMAS ASPINWALL,
WILLIAM E. COFFIN,
JOSEPH S. FAY,
Committee.

Hon. Gideon Welles,
Secretary of the Navy, Washington.

Letter of Governor Morgan relative to defence of New York harbor.

State of New York,
Executive Department, Albany, November 17, 1862.

Sir: On my return from Washington I find your letter of the 11th instant, enclosing a copy of a communication to Rear-Admiral Paulding, in reference to the anchorage of the school-ship Savannah.

I take this occasion to refer to the subject of our interview with you in reference to the defences of New York harbor, and to express my gratification at its result. I had then just been informed that Rear-Admiral Paulding was satisfied that the Savannah was unsuitable for the service specified. Accordingly you wisely determined that the Roanoke should be placed at the disposal of the rear-admiral immediately on her completion as an iron-clad. In the mean time you directed that one of the present iron-clads be left in the harbor until the Roanoke is completed.

The great importance of this decision is shown by the proposed action of the municipal authorities of New York, who have already taken some measures for raising a fund to protect the harbor by private subscription.

I am, with much respect, your obedient servant,

E. D. MORGAN.

Hon. Gideon Welles,
Secretary of the Navy.

Memorial from Committee of Boston Marine Society, calling attention to the defenceless condition of Boston harbor.

BOSTON, *November* 18, 1862.

SIR: The undersigned, a committee of the Boston Marine Society, have been instructed to call to your notice the defenceless condition of the harbor of Boston, and to respectfully solicit that official action which shall place it secure against the attack of an enemy.

Our citizens are deeply concerned on the subject, and look to the government, who are possessed with all the powers which are required to make such arrangements as will afford that protection which shall allay their fears and anxieties.

There are obvious reasons in the history and condition of the city of Boston which might tempt an audacious and ambitious foe to lay it under contribution, or to waste and destroy the property of its people. The navy yard, the marine and navy hospitals, and other public institutions, are so situated that they almost invite the assault of a rigorous foe. The applause with which such an act would be hailed by the enemies of the Union in the southern States would nerve the invader to run the risk, while the moral effect abroad, should it be unfortunately successful, might be disastrous to the cause in which our country is engaged.

A recent memorial to your department from the Board of Trade of this city has so fully set forth the facts in the case, that it precludes the necessity of a more elaborate detail. We heartily indorse the appeal for a larger and more efficient armament for the forts, as well as the suggestion that the Nahant may remain in this harbor; or if that is not possible, that some other iron-clad vessel may be permanently stationed in its waters.

We would also, in addition, respectfully suggest the expediency of having at the navy yard, fully armed and equipped, a vessel of war, which should be ready at a moment's notice to proceed to sea and meet the foe at the entrance of the harbor, should pilots or homeward-bound vessels give notice of their approach.

Having thus, in obedience to the instructions of the Marine Society, laid the subject before you,

We have the honor to remain, very truly, yours,

OSBORN HOWES
THOMAS LAMB.
F. W. LINCOLN, JR.
CALEB CURTIS.
WILLIAM BRUMHALL.
ROBERT B——.
THOMAS C. SMITH.

Hon. GIDEON WELLES,
Secretary of the Navy.

[Telegram.]

Telegram from Governor Morgan and Collector Barney.

NEW YORK, *November* 20, 1862.

We respectfully request that the Passaic remain for the defence of this harbor until the Montauk is ready for that service.

E. D. MORGAN.
HIRAM BARNEY.

Hon. GIDEON WELLES,
Secretary of the Navy.

Mr. Ericsson on improvements in the Monitors.

NEW YORK, *January* 14, 1863.

MY DEAR SIR: As Mr. Stimers has the entire charge of carrying out the fast Monitors, I do not see how I can prepare the "memorandum of the changes that have been or are to be made" which you desire. Mr. Stimers will himself, in a few days, be able to state distinctly the nature of the changes, so that you can give the needed orders to the contractors.

Your important suggestions regarding the construction of our iron-clads have been anticipated, all but the *width* of the side-armor projection. The overhang at the bow in the swift Monitors and the big ships has been done away with. The stern overhang has been reduced to such a degree in the ships, as well as in the Monitors alluded to, that it barely affords the intended protection to rudder and propeller. The side armor I am not willing to reduce at all, as thereon depends our impregnability. A sponsing, running out *half* the width of the armor shelf, I am not, however, prepared to resist, although I fear it will permit the big ships to roll, owing to their semi-cylindrical midship bodies. To meet your wishes I will, however, greatly reduce the projection of the armor timbers at the bow—in other words, the length of the ram. I have been able to do this without sacrificing impregnability, by an expedient which I will explain, by drawing, very soon. As to strength to meet the upward strain under the ram and under the stern overhang, I beg of you to have no fears. The "warning" came just in time—to a day, almost. The manner in which the said overhang of the Dictator is now being secured is such, that the entire weight of the ship would not have power enough to endanger the security of the junction.

The Sangamon, Lehigh, and Catskill are now being made strong enough to stand any weather.

I forwarded to you by express, some days ago, one of the sub-marine percussion locks, but no wafers, as Mr. Stimers said he would set out for Washington almost immediately and show you the affair in operation. A trial the day before yesterday proved the detonating power of the wafer too great. * *

I have omitted to say that Lieutenant Greene, who stood for two hours on the gunwale of the Monitor holding on to the rope, assured me that there was no strain or vibration produced by the action of the sea under this side armor, and that the vibration experienced was confined to the overhangs at the bow and stern. Lieutenant Greene does not think that the armor was one foot out of water at any time. In proof of this, he states the rolling to have been so inconsiderable that at 10 o'clock p. m., during the height of the gale, his wine bottle, half full, standing on his desk without support, had not been displaced. Lieutenant Greene authorizes me to make these statements.

Yours truly,

J. ERICSSON.

Hon. G. V. FOX,
Assistant Secretary of the Navy, Washington.

Rear-Admiral Gregory relative to gutta-percha life rafts.

No. 12.] NEW YORK, *February* 2, 1863.

SIR: I have the honor to state that one of the gutta-percha life rafts, ordered by authority of the department for the Monitors, was experimented upon at the navy yard yesterday—very much to the satisfaction of all present. The four sections composing it were inflated in about twelve minutes, when about twenty got on and rowed about the stream with as much facility as any boat could have done; afterwards, a crowd of persons got on, to the number of seventy-five, without half immersing it, and it was apparent that it would sustain any number of men that could get upon it; its flexibility is such that no injury can take place from collisions, as would be the case with any kind of boats, and I consider it a most perfect thing for the purpose required, and am of opinion that all Monitors should have one.

The one made is twenty-four feet in length—four feet longer than the plan submitted—which the maker estimated to cost about two hundred dollars a section; from the enlargement of the size (which was necessary) and great advance in the price of all the materials, he charges for the one made $250 a section, or one thousand dollars. I have inquired very minutely into the cost of materials, and find they are very costly. The canvas has to be made of a greater width than usually manufactured, and covers nearly half the charge; the other principal material—gutta-percha—is also at a very high price. The expense of making is considerable, having to be put in ovens under intense heat, and though the charge may appear large, I do not consider it unreasonably so. When regarding the consequences in case of disaster to one of the Monitors, involving the lives of the crew, any expense insuring safety would be insignificant, and should not be regarded.

The one made has been despatched to the Patapsco; the other vessels can be furnished immediately, should it be your pleasure so to direct, of which early notice is desirable, in order that no time be lost.

I have the honor to be, very respectfully, your most obedient servant,

F .H. GREGORY,
Rear-Admiral, Superintendent.

Hon. GIDEON WELLES,
Secretary of the Navy, Washington, D. C.

Mr. Ericsson in reference to construction of the Monitors.

NEW YORK, *February* 8, 1863.

SIR: I have examined with much attention the reports of the commanders of the Passaic, Montauk, and Weehawken, which you have done me the honor to transmit.

A very careful analysis of the *facts* reported shows that, thus far, not the slightest weakness, yielding, or rupture has been discovered in the hulls or overhangs of the three vessels which have now been tried in actual service.

Captain Drayton's several reports show how necessary it is to receive with caution the statements made and inferences drawn even by experienced and impartial seamen in relation to our new system. Captain Drayton reported to you, January 1, that "the sea was gradually making large openings through the forward armor projection, through which the water poured in a large stream." He added, confidently, "that a few hours of heavy sea would go far to tear the whole thing off." Without having, during the interval, lifted a hammer or driven a rivet, the same officer reported, January 22, that although two days and one night it "blew so very hard that the Passaic could not make the light vessel," yet "there was no difficulty in keeping her free with the bilge pump (only five inches in diameter) and *one* donkey pump working two hours out of every four."

Comment on the discrepancy of Captain Drayton's reports of the 1st and 22d of January is unnecessary. It is important, however, to notice the reported expedient of removing the ballast, which he says "had most inconsiderately been placed inside the false bow." Captain Drayton means the ballast placed on the forward overhang. In a former report Captain Drayton described the fearful action of the sea *under* this overhang, which tended to "tear it up." The weight which I had directed to be stowed in the overhang, to counteract this upward force and prevent the projecting bow from being lifted up, the report of January 22 informs you, was, as a necessary measure of "precaution," removed. In order that the great stress laid on the "choking of the limbers" may not lead to the inference that I had committed an error of construction by making the keel channel too small, a full-sized drawing of this channel is enclosed, to which I beg to call your special attention. It will be found not only ample, but probably the largest keel channel of any iron ship afloat. I refrain from detaining you by noticing the numerous minor difficulties with the Passaic, since, fortunately, they have not been discovered in the sister vessels.

Without intending any disrespect to the commander of the Passaic, I cannot abstain from calling your attention to his singular custom of drawing on the imagination in order to show what *might* have happened under certain contingencies, and what dire consequences would have resulted from occurrences which happily did not take place.

The result of the observations made by Captains Rodgers and Worden are stated with much precision, but the opinion expressed by these officers that their vessels are subjected to severe strain, is unsupported by practical evidence. So far, not a rivet has started nor a seam opened; no working has been observed at any point within the vessel. The absence of buoyancy in heavy sea, supposed by Captain Worden to be a defect, is in reality a favorable feature. It is in heavy weather that ordinary ships suffer most from the excessive and violent movements caused by the sudden rise and fall with the sea. Under similar circumstances the Monitor craft becomes partially immersed by the waves which *pass over its decks*, instead of violently tossing it up and down during their oscillations. Without disparaging the judgment of the two commanders last alluded to, I would suggest that their impression regarding great strain on the vessel has been produced by the strong sound which accompanies the lashing of the sea against an iron hull. An observer, accustomed only to the light, dull sound of a wooden vessel, is startled by the sharp, harsh ring of the metallic hull, and imagines a severe strain where, in fact, nothing but a very natural and harmless sound occurs.

Further trial and observations may possibly develop new features, but, so far, fact and actual experience do not point to the necessity of an organic change in the construction of the Monitor vessels. There is one blemish, however, which all reports clearly establish, viz., the want of tightness about the deck openings. The omission of calking between the deck plank and the anchor and propeller wells has caused much trouble by admitting large quantities of water to the overhangs both fore and aft. The water thus admitted, in running over the corner of the overhang into the body of the vessel, no doubt gave rise to the supposition that the junction had started. The extraordinary number of deck lights introduced by the government inspector, in opposition to my views, is a fruitful source of leakage. The great leaks complained of in the several deck hatches have been the result of a direct violation of my instructions. These hatches are all composed of wrought-iron frames accurately faced, having iron hatch covers planed perfectly true. The joint between the cover and frame may be made as perfectly tight as that of the cylinder cover of an engine. Disregard of my instructions, and the adoption of the sailor expedient, in this case improper, of calking from without, have thus occasioned the annoying hatch leaks. Proper attention in laying and calking the decks, and a good code of instructions, rigidly enforced, directing how to make the joints of the deck openings, permit me to assure you, will infallibly obviate the difficulties hitherto experienced in keeping the Monitors free from water.

I am, sir, respectfully, your obedient servant,

J. ERICSSON.

Hon. GIDEON WELLES,
Secretary of the Navy, Washington.

Trial of the Nantucket.

NEW YORK, *March* 4, 1863.

SIR: I have the honor to state that the Nantucket arrived here this morning, and to forward a letter from Commander Fairfax, enclosing one from his engineer. I have (with the engineer) visited and inspected the vessel, and measures have already been taken to remedy the defects reported; they do not seem to be of such magnitude as to occasion any great delay—probably but a few days.

I have also been on board the Keokuk this morning; the work engaged upon has been completed, and steam was being raised to ascertain the results.

It has been reported to me, informally, that the first assistant engineer is too ill to attend duty, and it may be well for the department to make some provision for his relief, should it be necessary.

I have the honor to be, very respectfully, your most obedient servant,

F. H. GREGORY,
Rear-Admiral, Superintendent.

Hon. GIDEON WELLES,
Secretary of the Navy, Washington.

—

UNITED STATES IRON-CLAD NANTUCKET,
Navy Yard, New York, March 4, 1863.

SIR: I have the honor to report the arrival of the Nantucket last night from Provincetown, where a southeast blow detained her over twenty-four hours. My telegraph dated 1st instant would advise you of our putting in there. Off Cape Cod found a heavy swell and some sea, sufficient to prove the tightness of the hull, but deck leaks badly over cabin and state-rooms, around deck plates; the accompanying report of the engineer will inform you how satisfactory the machinery worked. Off New London broke the steering-gear, and bad weather apparently coming on, determined to keep the tug-boat that I might reach them without delay.

Very respectfully, your obedient servant,

D. M. FAIRFAX,
Commander U. S. N.

Hon. GIDEON WELLES,
Secretary of the Navy.

Forwarded.

F. H. GREGORY,
Rear-Admiral.

—

UNITED STATES IRON-CLAD STEAMER NANTUCKET,
Navy Yard, New York, March 4, 1863.

SIR: I would most respectfully report that the working of the machinery of this vessel during her trip from Boston to this place has been most satisfactory. The engines and boilers have performed their various duties without causing any extra trouble or anxiety. The greatest number of revolutions made was 54 per minute, which was maintained but for a short time on account of the boilers foaming badly. The vessel, so far as I have been able to examine her, is as tight as when she started. The blowing engines and blowers have been running steadily, and the ventilation is as perfect as could be expected.

I am, very respectfully, your obedient servant,

GEO. H. WHITE,
2d Assistant Engineer U. S. N., Senior Engineer.

Commander D. McN. FAIRFAX,
Commanding U. S. Iron-clad Steamer Nantucket.

Captain Ericsson upon speed and seaworthiness of the Monitors.

NEW YORK, *June* 15, 1863.

SIR: I had the honor to address you on the 5th instant in relation to the report of the commanders of the Monitor gunboats, dated North Edisto, May 25, 1863. I now propose to submit a few observations with reference to speed and seaworthiness of those vessels, and to notice briefly the grounds on which they have been reported to be unfit for sea-service.

The assumed "liability to spring leak" rests on mere assertions. The Passaic, now on the marine railway at Hunter's Point, so far from exhibiting signs of strain or leak at the junction of the hull and overhang, the supposed weak point of a Monitor craft, affords positive practical evidence to the contrary. Not a single rivet has been started, nor a single joint opened at any point where the side-armor shelf or end projections join the hull. All is firm and solid. It seldom happens that erroneous statements promulgated officially receive such positive contradiction as the actual state of the Passaic gives to Captain Drayton's report, dated January 1, 1863. "I found," said the commander of the Passaic, "that the armor projection thumping into the sea was gradually making large openings there, through which the water poured in a large stream, and I am seriously of opinion that a few hours of heavy sea, end on, would go far to rip the whole thing entirely off the main body." The absurdity of this opinion is rendered manifest by the perfect condition of the Passaic's hull. I have shown, in a former communication, that the ability of the Monitor vessels to resist the strain to which they are subjected in a sea-way is by no means a subject beyond computation, and that, owing to their almost entire submersion, the strain, even during a gale, is quite moderate. The perfect state of the Passaic's hull, before adverted to, furnishes the best evidence in support of my theory.

It may be added, that the most experienced builders of iron vessels all pronounce the hulls of the Passaic class of gunboats to be very strong. In view of these facts, the remark contained in the report that the Monitors "have been exaggerated into vessels capable of keeping the seas" is, to say the least, uncalled for.

The opinion so emphatically expressed by the commanders of the Monitor fleet, at North Edisto, that their vessels are incapable of making headway in a heavy gale, even in tow of a powerful steamer, will surprise all naval engineers who are aware of the engine power applied; nautical science teaches the fact that submerged bodies are but little affected by the violence of a gale. The frail raft drifts unharmed with the sea, while the top-hamper, the iron-bound masts of a first-class ship are torn to splinters. The nautical student knows that the actual progress, the onward movement, of the sea during a gale is but moderate, and he knows also that at a small depth below the surface the water is stationary, and that still lower down its motion is retrograde to the direction of the wind.

* * * * * * * * * *

I am, sir, respectfully, your obedient servant,

J. ERICSSON.

Hon. GIDEON WELLES,
Secretary of the Navy, Washington.

Major General Wool anxious that the Roanoke should remain in New York harbor.

[Telegram.]

NEW YORK, *June* 27, 1863.

SIR: The iron-clad steamer Roanoke ought not to be taken from this great emporium from which you are supplied with money and almost everything to carry on the war against the rebels. The militia, as well as all the troops, except about seven hundred, are ordered elsewhere. To take the Roanoke from this city, at the present moment, will produce a very great excitement among all classes—friends as well as foes.

JOHN E. WOOL,
Major General.

Hon. GIDEON WELLES,
Secretary of the Navy.

Mayor Opdyke desires the Roanoke to remain at New York.

[Telegram.]

NEW YORK, *June* 27, 1863.

SIR: I learn from General Wool that so large a share of the troops garrisoning the fortifications of this harbor have been forwarded to the seat of war, that they cannot be relied on to prevent the approach of armed vessels. I must therefore ask that the Roanoke be left in our harbor until the city can devise other means of securing its safety from a naval attack which its importance to the nation imperiously demands. Please so instruct Admiral Paulding.

GEORGE OPDYKE, *Mayor.*

Hon. GIDEON WELLES.

Governor Morgan earnestly requests sailing orders of the Roanoke to be countermanded.

[Telegram]

NEW YORK, *June* 27, 1863.

Hon. GIDEON WELLES: Your communication of the 26th received. I earnestly request that the order for the Roanoke to leave this port be countermanded.

E. D. MORGAN.

General Wool urges the retention of the Roanoke.

NEW YORK, *June* 28, 1863.

SIR: I telegraphed you last night in relation to the retention in this port of the iron-clad steamer Roanoke. In reply, you say that your orders in relation to her future disposition cannot b revoked. I regret to learn this, for since then I have examined the navy yard. There is, save the Roanoke, no vessel that will be fit for service under some ten days. I again repeat that this great emporium, from which both army and navy receive their supplies as well as pay, ought not to be left without means of defence. The volunteers and militia of this city are being sent to Pennsylvania to aid in the defence of that State. We shall be at the mercy of any privateer that may think proper to assail this city. The temptation is indeed great, for the want of men to man the guns in the forts of the harbor.

I have the honor to be, very respectfully, your obedient servant,

JOHN E. WOOL,
Major General.

Hon. GIDEON WELLES,
Secretary of the Navy, Washington.

P. S.—I was accompanied in my visit to the navy yard by ex-Governor Morgan, now United States senator.

JOHN E. WOOL,
Major General.

Leak in the Sangamon.

NEW YORK, *December* 13, 1863.

SIR: Having been furnished with the enclosed copy of a report made by Local Inspector Thomas with reference to the Sangamon, I have respectfully to protest against his proposed application of turn-buckles for securing the plank-shear. It would be very objectionable to make an attachment between the bilge of the vessel and the wood work, under all circumstances. In the present instance no necessity exists for such an expedient. Bolts passed through the plank-shear and screwed up by means of nuts under lugs attached to the frames, as shown at C on the enclosed drawing, will effectually remedy the difficulty with the Sangamon's plank-shear.

Assuming that you may see fit to order my suggestions to be carried out, I have furnished Mr. Betts with plans, and instructed him to proceed to Philadelphia to communicate my views to Inspector Thomas.

I cannot omit, on this occasion, to impress the department with the necessity of ordering the commanders of the Monitor class not to load their vessels so deep as to bring the top angle iron of the hull under the water-line. The wood work above this angle iron, varying from 7 to 9 inches in the several classes, can never be made so tight as to keep the water out under the *constant* pressure caused by overloading. The alternating pressure resulting from the action in a sea-way, on the other hand, is of no moment. The ballast at the bow originally put into the Sangamon has been removed, in consequence of which the stern is so deep with full complement of coal in, as to bring the top angle iron of the hull under water.

The enclosed drawing shows the manner of holding down the plank-shear of the large ships and the Tecumseh class, by means of bolts bassing through plank-shear and top angle iron of the hull. This expedient will effectually prevent the difficulty now complained of in the Sangamon.

I am, sir, respectfully, your obedient servant,

J. ERICSSON.

Hon. GIDEON WELLES,
Secretary of the Navy, Washington.

PHILADELPHIA, *December* 12, 1863.

SIR: Agreeably to your order, I have, in concert with Mr. Betts, examined into the cause of the leak in the United States iron-clad steamer Sangamon, and find that amidships or abreast the coal-bunkers the gunwale of the vessel and the plank-shear have separated, thus allowing the water to flow into the vessel. Mr. Betts and myself have decided, as the best plan for remedying this, to put 1½-inch bolts, running from the top of the deck plating through the plank-shear and provided turn-buckles, for the purpose of drawing the separated parts to; the lower ends of the bolts to be fastened to a gusset-piece riveted to the frames at the bilge with a piece of angle iron, the same size as the frame angle iron on the opposite side of the gusset-pieces; after the bolts are in place and screwed up the seams between the gunwale and plank-shear may be calked with oakum. It will be necessary to remove the coal from the bunkers.

I am, respectfully,

W. K. THOMAS,
Local Inspector of Iron-clad Steamers.

C. K. STUBBING, U. S. N.
Commandant Philadelphia Navy Yard, Philadelphia, Pa.

[Indorsed.]

I fully concur with the within report.

CHARLES T. BETTS,
Superintendent Ship Puritan.

WASHINGTON, D. C., *May* 1, 1861.

MY DEAR SIR: I sincerely regret that the failure of the late attempt to provision Fort Sumter should be the source of any annoyance to you. The practicability of your plan was not, in fact, brought to test. By reason of a gale, well known in advance to be possible and not improbable, the tugs, an essential part of the plan, never reached the ground, while by an accident, for which you were in no wise responsible, and possibly *I* to some extent was, you were deprived of a war vessel with her men, which you deemed of great importance to the enterprise.

I most cheerfully and truly declare that the failure of the undertaking has not lowered you a particle, while the qualities you developed in the effort have greatly heightened you in my estimation. For a daring and dangerous enterprise of a similar character you would, to-day, be the man, of all my acquaintances, whom I would select. You and I both anticipated that the cause of the country would be advanced by making the attempt to provision Fort Sumter even if it should fail, and it is no small consolation now to feel that our anticipation is justified by the result.

Very truly your friend,

A. LINCOLN.

Captain G. V. FOX.

NAVY DEPARTMENT,
December 7, 1863.

SIR: My letter to you under date of the 4th ultimo was accompanied with the copy of a letter addressed to the department by the Assistant Secretary of the Navy, containing, amongst other papers, copies of orders under which he acted in reference to a proposition he made to provision Fort Sumter.

The enclosed copy of a letter of the President of the United States forms an important connexion with those papers, and is therefore furnished to you.

Very respectfully,

GIDEON WELLES,
Secretary of the Navy

Rear-Admiral S. F. DUPONT,
Wilmington, Delaware.